THE OXFORD HANDBOOK OF

CORPORATE GOVERNANCE

THE OXFORD HANDBOOK OF

CORPORATE GOVERNANCE

Edited by
MIKE WRIGHT, DONALD S. SIEGEL,
KEVIN KEASEY,
and
IGOR FILATOTCHEV

OXFORD
UNIVERSITY PRESS

OXFORD
UNIVERSITY PRESS

Great Clarendon Street, Oxford, OX2 6DP,
United Kingdom

Oxford University Press is a department of the University of Oxford.
It furthers the University's objective of excellence in research, scholarship,
and education by publishing worldwide. Oxford is a registered trade mark of
Oxford University Press in the UK and in certain other countries

© Oxford University Press 2013

The moral rights of the authors have been asserted

First published 2013
First published in paperback 2014

Impression: 1

All rights reserved. No part of this publication may be reproduced, stored in
a retrieval system, or transmitted, in any form or by any means, without the
prior permission in writing of Oxford University Press, or as expressly permitted
by law, by licence or under terms agreed with the appropriate reprographics
rights organization. Enquiries concerning reproduction outside the scope of the
above should be sent to the Rights Department, Oxford University Press, at the
address above

You must not circulate this work in any other form
and you must impose this same condition on any acquirer

Published in the United States of America by Oxford University Press
198 Madison Avenue, New York, NY 10016, United States of America

British Library Cataloguing in Publication Data

Data available

ISBN 978–0–19–964200–7 (Hbk.)
ISBN 978–0–19–870881–0 (Pbk.)

Links to third party websites are provided by Oxford in good faith and
for information only. Oxford disclaims any responsibility for the materials
contained in any third party website referenced in this work.

Contents

List of Figures	ix
List of Tables	xi
Abbreviations	xii
Contributors	xvi

1. Introduction — 1
   MIKE WRIGHT, DONALD S. SIEGEL, KEVIN KEASEY, AND
   IGOR FILATOTCHEV

PART I REGULATION AND HISTORY

2. Regulation and Comparative Corporate Governance — 23
   RUTH V. AGUILERA, MICHEL GOYER, AND LUIZ RICARDO
   KABBACH DE CASTRO

3. The History of Corporate Governance — 46
   BRIAN R. CHEFFINS

4. Capital Markets and Financial Politics:
   Preferences and Institutions — 65
   MARK J. ROE

5. An International Corporate Governance Index — 97
   MARINA MARTYNOVA AND LUC RENNEBOOG

PART II CORPORATE GOVERNANCE MECHANISMS AND PROCESSES

6. Boards and Governance: 25 Years of Qualitative
   Research with Directors of FTSE Companies — 135
   ANNIE PYE

7. Process Matters: Understanding Board Behavior
   and Effectiveness — 163
   TERRY MCNULTY

8. Board Committees 177
PHILIP STILES

9. The Governance of Director Networks 200
LUC RENNEBOOG AND YANG ZHAO

10. Executive Compensation and Corporate Governance: What Do We "Know" and Where Are We Going? 222
PAMELA BRANDES AND PALASH DEB

11. Corporate Governance: Ownership Interests, Incentives, and Conflicts 246
DAVID S. BOSS, BRIAN L. CONNELLY, ROBERT E. HOSKISSON, AND LASZLO TIHANYI

12. Financial Leverage and Corporate Governance 269
ROBERT WATSON

13. Financial Reporting, Disclosure, and Corporate Governance 290
CHRISTOF BEUSELINCK, MARC DELOOF, AND SOPHIE MANIGART

14. Auditing and Corporate Governance 308
ANDREA MENNICKEN AND MICHAEL POWER

15. The Market for Corporate Control 328
CHARLIE WEIR

PART III THE CORPORATE GOVERNANCE LIFE CYCLE

16. The Life Cycle of Corporate Governance 349
STEVE TOMS

17. Corporate Governance in High-Tech Firms 365
FABIO BERTONI, MASSIMO G. COLOMBO, AND ANNALISA CROCE

18. Family Business and Corporate Governance 389
LORRAINE M. UHLANER

19. Corporate Governance in IPOs 421
IGOR FILATOTCHEV AND DEBORAH ALLCOCK

20. Corporate Governance, Multinational Firms, and Internationalization 449
    NAI H. WU AND LASZLO TIHANYI

21. Corporate Governance in Business Groups 465
    DAPHNE W. YIU, XING CHEN, AND YUEHUA XU

22. Governance in Financial Distress and Bankruptcy 489
    KENNETH M. AYOTTE, EDITH S. HOTCHKISS, AND KARIN S. THORBURN

PART IV TYPES OF INVESTORS

23. Venture Capital and Corporate Governance 515
    DOUGLAS CUMMING AND SOFIA JOHAN

24. Private Equity, Leveraged Buyouts, and Corporate Governance 539
    MIKE WRIGHT, DONALD S. SIEGEL, MIGUEL MEULEMAN, AND KEVIN AMESS

25. Hedge Fund Activism and Corporate Governance 564
    NA DAI

26. The Financial Role of Sovereign Wealth Funds 581
    VELJKO FOTAK, JIE GAO, AND WILLIAM L. MEGGINSON

PART V CORPORATE GOVERNANCE, STRATEGY, AND STAKEHOLDERS

27. Corporate Governance and Nonprofits: Facing up to Hybridization and Homogenization 607
    JENNY HARROW AND SUSAN D. PHILLIPS

28. Corporate Governance and Labor 634
    ANDREW PENDLETON AND HOWARD GOSPEL

29. Corporate Governance and Principal–Principal Conflicts 658
    MIKE W. PENG AND STEVE SAUERWALD

30. Multiple Agency Theory: An Emerging Perspective on Corporate Governance 673
    ROBERT E. HOSKISSON, JONATHAN D. ARTHURS, ROBERT E. WHITE, AND CHELSEA WYATT

31. An Age of Corporate Governance Failure?
    Financialization and its Limits　　　　　　　　　　　　　　　703
    GEOFFREY WOOD AND MIKE WRIGHT

32. Corporate Governance and Corporate Social Responsibility　　719
    STEPHEN J. BRAMMER AND STEPHEN PAVELIN

Index　　　　　　　　　　　　　　　　　　　　　　　　　　745

List of Figures

4.1	Correlation of Labor's power and large firm ownership separation in post-war wealthy west	70
4.2	Shifting political center of gravity	89
5.1	Percentage of listed companies under majority control	115
5.2	Percentage of listed companies with a blocking minority of at least 25 percent	115
5.3	Anti-director index based on LLSV: total index	116
5.4	Shareholder rights protection index methodology: total index	117
5.5	Shareholder rights protection index by legal origin: appointment rights sub-index	118
5.6	Shareholder rights protection index by legal origin: decision rights sub-index	119
5.7	Shareholder rights protection index by legal origin: trusteeship sub-index	120
5.8	Shareholder rights protection index by legal origin: transparency sub-index	121
5.9	Minority shareholder rights protection index by legal origin: total index	122
5.10	Minority shareholder rights protection index by legal origin: appointment rights sub-index	123
5.11	Minority shareholder rights protection index by legal origin: decision rights sub-index	124
5.12	Minority shareholder rights protection index by legal origin: trusteeship sub-index	125
5.13	Minority shareholder rights protection index by legal origin: affiliation rights sub-index	126
5.14	Creditor rights protection index by legal origin: total index	127
6.1	FTSE 100 share index, 1998–2010	140
6.2	Disciplinary cross-fertilizations in corporate governance	143
6.3	Average remuneration—FTSE 100 directors, 1999–2008	150
9.1	Example of a CEO's professional network	210
9.2	A director network graph	211

10.1	Determinants and consequences of executive compensation	224
16.1	Product, entrepreneurial, and financial life cycles	352
16.2	An integrated life-cycle model	355
18.1	Overall research framework for family business and corporate governance	394
21.1	The contingent effects of governance mechanisms in business groups	475
23.1	Canadian venture capital securities, all types of venture capital funds and entrepreneurial firms, 1991(Q1)–2003(Q3)	527
23.2	Canadian venture capital securities, private independent limited partner venture capitalists and start-up entrepreneurial firms only, 1991(Q1)–2003(Q3)	528
29.1	Causes and consequences of principal–principal conflicts	659
30.1	Layered relationships and embedded agency in the modern organization	674

List of Tables

5.1	Methodology employed to construct corporate governance regulation indices	105
9.1	An example of a director network	212
10.1	Premier publications explored for this review	225
10.2	Examples of theoretical frameworks used in representative studies	226
11.1	Ownership interests and incentives	249
11.2	Ownership impact on management and strategy	251
11.3	Possible conflicts between owners	256
19.1	Content and findings of key papers focused on corporate governance in IPO firms	424
21.1	Governance structures and governance outcomes of different types of business groups	481
23.1	Specific terms used in VC contracts	524
26.1	Global sovereign wealth funds, 2010	585
26.2	Characteristics of the sample of SWF investments in publicly traded firms	588
26.3	Companies held by Central Huijin Investment Ltd. as of Dec. 31, 2011	597
26.4	Investments by international strategic investors	598
27.1	Explanatory theoretical lenses for nonprofit governance, following Kreutzer (2009)	610
27.2	Ownership issues in nonprofit governance, selected literatures	615
27.3	Nonprofit, governance models, reflecting contrasting environmental features, drawn from Bradshaw (2007: 9–13)	618
32.1	Recent evidence relating to board characteristics and CSR	727
32.2	Recent evidence relating to firm ownership characteristics and CSR	732

Abbreviations

ABC	Agriculture Bank of China
ABF	Associated British Foods
ADBC	Agricultural Development Bank of China
ADIA	Abu Dhabi Investment Authority
AICPA	American Institute of Certified Public Accountants
AIF	Alternative Investment Fund
AIFM	Alternative Investment Fund Management
AIMR	Association for Investment Management and Research
AIU	Audit Inspection Unit
ALI	American Law Institute
APB	Auditing Practices Board
APR	absolute priority rule
BCCI	Bank of Credit and Commerce International
BOC	Bank of China
BOFI	banks and other financial institutions
BRIC	Brazil, Russia, India, and China
Calpers	California Public Employees Retirement System
CBC	Construction Bank of China
CCB	China Construction Bank
CDB	China Development Bank
CE	corporate entrepreneurship
CEO	chief executive officer
CFP	corporate financial performance
CG	corporate governance
	Chexim Export–Import Bank of China
CIC	China Investment Corporation
CIC	community interest company
CII	Council of Institutional Investors
Co Sec	Company Secretary

CSID	Canadian Social Investment Database
CSR	corporate social responsibility
DBIS	Department of Business, Innovation and Skills
D/E	debt-to-equity ratio
DIP	debtor-in-possession
EBIT	earnings before interest and tax
EC	European Commission
ED	executive director
EIRIS	Ethical Investment Research Service
ENA	*Ecole Nationale d'Administration*
EPA	Environmental Protection Agency
EPS	earnings per share
ESMA	European Securities and Markets Authority
(ESO)	executive share option
EU	European Union
FASB	Financial Accounting Standards Board
FC	fixed costs
FCF	free cash flow
FD	finance director
FDI	foreign direct investment
FDIC	Federal Deposit Insurance Corporation
FEEM	Fondazione Eni Enrico Mattei
FRC	Financial Reporting Council
FSA	Financial Services Authority
GAAP	Generally Accepted Accounting Principles
GDP	gross domestic product
GPFG	Government Pension Fund-Global (Norway)
GRI	Global Reporting Initiative
HLT	highly leveraged transaction
HPWP	high-performance work practices
HRM	human resource management
HTP	Human Toxicity Potential
IAS	international accounting standards
IASB	International Accounting Standards Board
IBO	investor-led buyout

ICAEW	Institute of Chartered Accountants of England and Wales
ICBC	Industrial and Commercial Bank of China
IFAC	International Federation of Accountants
IFRS	International Financial Reporting Standards
IPO	initial public offering
IPR	intellectual property rights
IRRC	Investor Responsibility Research Center
IRS	Internal Revue Service
ISA	International Standards on Auditing
ISC	International Schareholder Committee
ISS	Institutional Shareholder Services
KEJI	Korea Economic Justice Institute
KERP	key employee retention plan
KIA	Kuwait Investment Authority
KLD	Kinder, Lydenberg, and Domini
LBO	leveraged buyout
LLSV	La Porta, Lopez-de-Silanes, Shleifer, and Vishny
LTIP	long-term incentive plan
M&A	merger and acquisition
MBI	management buy-in
MBO	management buyout
MIB	Milano Italia Borsa
MNC	multinational corporation
MNE	multinational enterprise
NASD	National Association of Securities Dealers
NED	non-executive director
NPL	nonperforming loan
NPV	net present value
NYSE	New York Stock Exchange
OECD	Organisation for Economic Co-operation and Development
OFT	Office of Fair Trading
OL	operational leverage
OLS	ordinary least squares
OTC	over the counter
PA	principal–agent

PAGVS	Panel on Accountability and Governance
PBOC	People's Bank of China
PCAOB	Public Company Accounting Oversight Board
PE	private equity
PE-LBO	Private equity or leveraged buyout
P/E	price to earnings
PIPE	private investment in public equity
POB	Professional Oversight Board
PP	principal–principal
PTP	public to private
QIA	Qatar Investment Authority
R&D	research and development
Reg FD	Regulation Fair Disclosure
REIT	real estate investment trusts
Rem Co	remuneration committee
ROA	return on assets
ROE	return on equity
SDNY	Southern District of New York
SERPs	Senior Executive Retirement Programs
S&P	Standard and Poor's
SE	European Company
SEC	Securities and Exchange Commission
SID	senior independent director
SFAS	Statement of Financial Accounting Standards
SIRI	Sustainable Investment Research International Company
SME	small and medium-sized enterprise
SOE	state-owned enterprise
SOX	Sarbanes-Oxley Act
SWF	sovereign wealth fund
SWX	Swiss Stock Exchange
TMT	top management team
UAE	United Arab Emirates
VC	variable costs
VC	venture capital
VC	venture capitalist
VOC	varieties of capitalism

Contributors

Ruth V. Aguilera, Department of Business Administration and a fellow at the Center for Professional Responsibility of Business and Society at the University of Illinois at Urbana-Champaign

Deborah Allcock, Bradford University School of Management

Kevin Amess, Nottingham University Business School, University of Nottingham

Jonathan D. Arthurs, Department of Management, Information Systems, and Entrepreneurship, Washington State University

Kenneth M. Ayotte, Northwestern University School of Law, Chicago

Fabio Bertoni, Department of Management, Economics and Industrial Engineering, Politecnico di Milano

Christof Beuselinck, Tilburg School of Economics and Management, Tilburg University

David S. Boss, Mays Business School, Texas A&M University

Stephen J. Brammer, Warwick Business School, University of Warwick

Pamela Brandes, Whitman School of Management, Syracuse University

Brian R. Cheffins, Faculty of Law, Cambridge University

Xing Chen, Department of Management, Chinese University of Hong Kong

Massimo G. Colombo, Department of Management, Economics and Industrial Engineering, Politecnico di Milano

Brian L. Connelly, College of Business, Auburn University

Annalisa Croce, Department of Management, Economics and Industrial Engineering, Politecnico di Milano

Douglas Cumming, Schulich School of Business, York University

Na Dai, University at Albany—SUNY

Palash Deb, Management and Marketing Department, California State University San Marcos

Marc Deloof, Antwerp Management School, University of Antwerp

Igor Filatotchev, Cass Business School, City University London

Veljko Fotak, Price College of Business, University of Oklahoma

Jie Gao, University of International Business and Economics (Beijing), Fulbright Fellow, University of Oklahoma

Howard Gospel, Management Department, King's College London, and Said Business School, University of Oxford

Michel Goyer, Warwick Business School, University of Warwick

Jenny Harrow, Cass Business School, City University London

Robert E. Hoskisson, Jesse H. Jones Graduate School of Business, Rice University

Edith S. Hotchkiss, Carroll School of Management, Boston College

Sofia Johan, Schulich School of Business, York University

Luiz Ricardo Kabbach de Castro, Universitat Autònoma de Barcelona

Kevin Keasey, Leeds University Business School, University of Leeds

Sophie Manigart, Vlerick Leuven Gent Management School, University of Ghent

Marina Martynova, Management School, University of Sheffield

Terry McNulty, Management School, University of Liverpool

William L. Megginson, University of Oklahoma

Andrea Mennicken, Department of Accounting, London School of Economics

Miguel Meuleman, Vlerick Leuven Gent Management School, University of Ghent

Stephen Pavelin, School of Management, University of Bath

Andrew Pendleton, York Management School, University of York

Mike W. Peng, Jindal School of Management, University of Texas at Dallas

Susan D. Phillips, School of Public Policy and Administration, Carleton University

Michael Power, Centre for the Analysis of Risk and Regulation, London School of Economics

Annie Pye, Centre for Leadership Studies, University of Exeter

Luc Renneboog, Department of Finance and CentER, Tilburg University

Mark J. Roe, Harvard Law School, Harvard University

Steve Sauerwald, Jindal School of Management, University of Texas at Dallas

Donald S. Siegel, School of Business, University Albany—SUNY

Philip Stiles, Centre for International Human Resource Management, Judge Business School, University of Cambridge

Karin S. Thorburn, Department of Finance and Management Science, Norwegian School of Economics

Laszlo Tihanyi, Mays Business School, Texas A&M University

Steve Toms, Leeds University Business School, University of Leeds

Lorraine M. Uhlaner, Center for Entrepreneurship, Nyenrode Business Universiteit

Robert Watson, IE Business School, Madrid

Charlie Weir, Institute for Management Governance and Society, Robert Gordon University

Robert E. White, College of Business, Iowa State University

Geoffrey Wood, Warwick Business School, University of Warwick

Mike Wright, Imperial College Business School, Imperial College

Nai H. Wu, Mays Business School, Texas A&M University

Chelsea Wyatt, Jones Graduate School of Business, Rice University

Yuehua Xu, Department of Management, Chinese University of Hong Kong

Daphne W. Yiu, Department of Management, Chinese University of Hong Kong

Yang Zhao, Cardiff Business School, Cardiff University

CHAPTER 1

INTRODUCTION

MIKE WRIGHT, DONALD S. SIEGEL, KEVIN KEASEY, AND IGOR FILATOTCHEV

In recent decades, there has been a substantial increase in interest among policymakers and academics in corporate governance. Since the publication of the Cadbury Report in the UK in 1992, we have witnessed the international diffusion of corporate governance codes and regulations by both individual countries and intergovernmental agencies. Recent legislation, such as the Sarbanes-Oxley Act of 2002 and the Dodd-Frank Act of 2010, and institutional changes, such as the New York Stock Exchange listing rules of 2003, were designed to improve corporate governance practices. A review of corporate governance practices by Walker (2009) reports that the global financial crisis has reduced confidence in the quality of corporate governance. The author even asserts that poor governance systems may have been a root cause of the economic crisis.

As a result, there is also a burgeoning, scholarly literature on corporate governance, as reflected in the numerous conferences and special issues of academic journals on this topic and the development of specialized journals in this area (e.g. *Corporate Governance: An International Review* and the *Journal of Management and Governance*). Recent spirited debates in the academic literature regarding executive compensation and the relationship between corporate and environmental social responsibility and corporate governance (e.g. exchanges in *Academy of Management Perspectives* between Jim Walsh of the University of Michigan and Steve Kaplan of the University of Chicago on CEO Pay (Kaplan, 2008; Walsh, 2009), and Don Siegel of the University at Albany—SUNY and Alfie Marcus of the University of Minnesota on whether top-level managers should engage in "green management" practices (Marcus and Fremeth, 2009; Siegel, 2009)) have stimulated new interest in examining the antecedents and consequences of corporate governance practices. A concomitant trend is the growing number of graduate courses and programs relating to corporate governance in business and law schools. Until now, there has not been a definitive source that integrates and synthesizes academic studies of corporate governance. That is the purpose of our *Handbook*.

The volume integrates and synthesizes academic studies of corporate governance from a wide range of perspectives, notably, economics, strategy, international business, organizational behavior, entrepreneurship, business ethics, accounting, finance, and law. We also go beyond traditional principal–agent theory to incorporate different theoretical perspectives relating to the numerous stakeholders in the firm.

We consider corporate governance issues at several levels of analysis: the individual manager, firms, institutions, industry, and nation. Critiques of traditional governance research based on agency theory have noted its "under-contextualized" nature and its inability to accurately compare and explain the diversity of corporate governance arrangements across different institutional contexts. This *Handbook* aims at closing these theoretical and empirical gaps. Thus, in analyzing the effects of corporate governance on performance, we consider a variety of indicators, such as accounting profit, economic profit, productivity growth, market share, proxies for environmental and social performance, such as diversity and other aspects of corporate social responsibility, and, of course, share price effects.

Another unique aspect of the *Handbook* is that we devote considerable attention to corporate governance practices and issues in emerging industries and nations. It is important to note that much of the extant research on this topic has focused on large companies in the US and Europe that operate in mature industries. Since corporate governance is a global phenomenon, we present a substantial amount of international evidence and our contributing authors have been selected on the basis of their ability to reflect a wide variety of national perspectives on this topic. Finally, besides providing a high-level review and analysis of the existing literature, each chapter develops an agenda for further research on a specific aspect of corporate governance.

Part I: Regulation and History

The purpose of this part is to provide an overview of the history of corporate governance and the development of specific codes and other forms of regulation. It also considers issues relating to the self-regulation, compliance versus legal regulation debate.

In Chapter 2 on the evolution of corporate governance regulation, Aguilera, Goyer, and Kabbach discuss how regulation affects corporate governance. They adopt a comparative perspective and a broad view of corporate governance. The authors consider the classic tension in regulation theory between the interests of policymakers and regulators in influencing governance, and discuss some of the key limitations of this approach. The chapter examines the two main perspectives in studying regulation in corporate governance, namely law and economics and politics. Finally, the chapter explores how regulation has different impacts on corporate governance practices across national contexts. It concludes with a discussion of hard and soft law and the consequences of such for effectiveness in corporate governance around the world.

In Chapter 3, Cheffins provides an historical perspective on corporate governance, taking as his starting point its coming into vogue in the 1970s in the United States. Within 25 years corporate governance had become the subject of debate worldwide by academics, regulators, executives and investors. This chapter traces developments occurring between the mid-1970s and the end of the 1990s, by which point "corporate governance" was well-entrenched as academic and regulatory shorthand. The chapter concludes by surveying briefly recent developments and by maintaining that analysis of the interrelationship between directors, executives, and shareholders of publicly traded companies is likely to be conducted through the conceptual prism of corporate governance for the foreseeable future.

A political institutional perspective is provided in Chapter 4 where Roe argues that for capital markets to function effectively, political institutions must support capitalism and, especially, the capitalism of financial markets. Roe notes that capital markets' shape, support, and extent are often contested in the polity. Powerful elements—from politicians to mass popular movements—have reason to change, co-opt, and remove value from capital markets. And players in capital markets have reason to seek rules that favor their own capital channels over those of others. How these contests are settled deeply affects the form, the extent, and the effectiveness of capital markets. Investigation of the primary political economy forces shaping capital markets can point us to a more general understanding of economic, political, and legal institutions. A considerable amount of important research has been conducted in recent decades on the vitality of institutions. Less well emphasized thus far is that widely shared, deeply held preferences, often arising from current interests and opinions, can at times sweep away prior institutions or, less dramatically but more often, sharply alter or replace them. When they do so, old institutions can be replaced by new ones, or strongly modified. Preferences can at crucial times trump institutions, and how the two interact is well-illustrated by the political economy of capital markets.

Building on these earlier chapters, Chapter 5, by Martynova and Renneboog provides a comprehensive comparative analysis of corporate governance regulatory systems and their evolution since 1990 in 30 European countries and the US. The authors propose a methodology to create detailed corporate governance indices which capture the major features of capital market laws in the analyzed countries. These indices indicate how the law in each country addresses various potential agency conflicts between corporate constituencies: namely, between shareholder and managers, between majority and minority shareholders, and between shareholders and bondholders. The authors' analysis of regulatory provisions within the suggested framework enables a better understanding of how corporate law works in a particular country and which strategies regulators adopt to achieve their goals. The 15-year time series of constructed indices and large country-coverage also allows us to draw conclusions about the convergence of corporate governance regimes across countries.

PART II: CORPORATE GOVERNANCE MECHANISMS AND PROCESSES

This part considers mechanisms and processes of corporate governance. The chapters in this part include approaches that review the quantitative empirical literature as well as those that examine the processes of corporate governance, especially the operation of boards. Authors have incorporated evidence from different institutional contexts. The chapters focus first on the role of boards and board processes.

The first chapter in this section (Chapter 6), by Pye, presents insights from the evolution of board processes in large companies over the past quarter of a century. It reflects on a series of three ESRC-funded studies into the people side of corporate governance. Adopting a process-oriented, sensemaking (Weick, 1995) approach to understanding corporate directing across time and context, this longitudinal qualitative research (1987–2011) effectively creates a unique dataset of FTSE 100 directors across a particularly vibrant period of economic history. In order to pay attention to changing context, interviews have also been conducted with selected investors, auditors, regulators, and others who have influence on the process and practice of corporate directing. Based on findings from these studies across time and context, the author highlights key changes in roles and relationships which affect how companies have been and are currently run. The chapter also highlights some paradoxes identified during this series of studies and which underpin corporate directing.

The following chapter, by McNulty, extends our understanding of board behavior and processes. McNulty summarizes qualitative studies on the exercise of board power, influence, and accountability. The chapter discusses studies which model boards as strategic decision-making groups and tests the relationship between board processes and performance. These distinct strands and styles of research provide evidence that the key to understanding the work and effects of boards lies in attention to behavioral processes. McNulty notes that now law and governance codes have substantial influence over matters of board composition and structures. Thus it is ever more important for the theory and practice of corporate governance to get beyond the form and appearance of boards to the substance of board effectiveness.

In Chapter 8, Stiles provides additional insights into the workings of boards. Most significant board decisions are made not within the whole board setting, but within the context of specific committees, yet our understanding of how board committees work remains limited. Stiles examines the three primary board committees—audit, remuneration, and nomination. Research on key aspects of their composition is assessed—chiefly independence and expertise, and also work on the processes by which committees operate. Overall, there is a positive relationship between the independence and expertise of board committees with key effectiveness measures, but process research indicates the tensions committees face in their work. In addition to their role in the inside working of boards, directors can contribute through the networks they bring to the corporation.

In Chapter 9, Renneboog and Zhao point out that director networks have attracted growing attention from finance, management, and sociology. They argue that these networks play an intriguing role in corporate governance. On one hand, networks provide a company with improved information access. On the other hand, networks can be misused by top managers to gain excess power over the board. This chapter first reviews the regulation of director networks in major developed countries. Second, it summarizes the main results from the academic literature on director networks from different disciplines. By means of examples, the chapter demonstrates how director networks can be empirically captured and network information quantified.

In Chapter 10, Brandes and Deb focus on the contentious issue of executive remuneration, which has attracted renewed policy and media interest in the aftermath of the global financial crisis of 2008. Reviewing the now extensive literature on executive remuneration, they develop a framework that integrates the main themes. Their framework highlights how internal governance mechanisms (board power and ownership), institutional governance (regulatory, normative, and mimetic), and market governance factors (labor markets, analysts, product markets, and the market for corporate control) interact with CEO characteristics and firm factors (strategy and reporting choices) to influence the level and structure of executive compensation and the way in which performance measures are defined as the basis for setting compensation. The authors go on to examine the intended and unintended consequences of these interrelationships. They note that, while intended consequences can be positive, negative unintended consequences can involve senior managers' reluctance to invest in their firms, re-pricing and re-dating option grants, fraudulent reporting in the presence of duality and other governance shortcomings, as well as earnings manipulation where options are out of the money. Concerted actions by groups of concentrated institutional investors can exert pressure on executive remuneration decision-makers but there may also be a need for greater attention to the recruitment of remuneration committee board members with the real expertise to monitor senior managers and set compensation.

The nature and distribution of ownership in a firm is an important dimension of corporate governance. In Chapter 11, Boss, Connelly, Hoskisson, and Tihanyi extend research that tends to focus on the influence of a single form of ownership or type of owner. The authors examine ownership at a broader level, comparing different types of owners and demonstrating how they act both independently and together to influence firm outcomes. They show that, while these different types share some similarities, various forms of internal and external owners differ from each other in terms of preferences, incentives, and motivations. As a result, conflicts may arise among them, leaving top-level managers with competing pressures and difficult choices to make about their firm's strategic direction. The authors draw attention to these conflicts and suggest future research in areas where scholars might explore how to better understand the influence of a portfolio of owners on firm-level actions and outcomes.

Shareholders are not the only investors playing a role in corporate governance. Debt providers are also important. Further, there are interrelationships between different governance mechanisms that may have consequences for corporations. In Chapter 12, Watson examines the interrelationships among corporate performance, business risk, financial leverage, and their impact upon managerial incentives, financial reporting behavior, and the likelihood of costly and unanticipated corporate governance failure. It is argued that the latter will become much more probable because of a systematic board loyalty bias that has resulted in executives being awarded generous and highly leveraged compensation packages that motivate the pursuit of high business risk and high financial risk strategies that are not consistent with shareholder interests. In essence, managers are being unduly rewarded for taking hidden financial risks, i.e. both shareholder and debt holder risk exposures will be underestimated and hence underpriced, and this dynamic transfers wealth from financial stakeholders to managers.

Information, of course, plays a crucial role in the governance process. While firms worldwide are subjected to disclosure regulations, many public and private firms voluntarily disclose more information than required. In Chapter 13, Beuselinck, Deloof, and Manigart discuss the benefits and costs of such voluntary disclosure at the firm and societal levels. They review the empirical literature on the association between a firm's corporate governance and its disclosure policies. They report mixed evidence, concluding that contingencies, e.g. the institutional environment or the type of dominant shareholder, may be important. Besides public corporations, this chapter further explores disclosure by private firms, which has received limited attention so far.

Pursuing the accounting information theme, Mennicken and Power, in Chapter 14, discuss the role of auditors in corporate governance systems, drawing on international comparisons: they emphasize the changing regulatory, institutional, and methodological dimensions of auditing, both internal and external. First, they position auditing within a fluid and evolving corporate governance space as the provision of assurance regarding financial statement and internal control quality. Second, the chapter focuses on auditing knowledge and standards, and related pressures to govern the quality of the market for auditing. Third, auditing is analyzed as a powerful model of governance in its own right and a number of regulatory and research challenges are evaluated.

While the previous chapters in this section focus on internal governance structures and processes, external governance mechanisms may also be important and interact with internal dimensions. The market for corporate control plays a primary external governance role and is discussed in Chapter 15, the final chapter in this section, by Weir. Manne (1965) argues that the market for corporate control can be seen as a response to the managerial discretion afforded in the managerial models that show the consequences of the separation of ownership and control (Berle and Means, 1932). Manne's central argument is that managers are constrained by shareholders, who can sell their shares if they believe that incumbent management is not acting in their best interests. Weir considers the relationship between the market for corporate control and hostile takeovers. He also examines the contribution of the market for corporate control to innovations within the takeover market, for example public to private transactions and leveraged buyouts (considered in more detail in Chapter 24). There may, however, be obstacles to the operation of the market for corporate control, including the free-rider problem, management resistance to bids, and anti-takeover defenses. These impediments to the functioning of the market are analyzed.

Part III: The Corporate Governance Life Cycle

In the corporate governance literature, there has been considerable attention devoted to mature firms. More attention needs to be paid to corporate governance mechanisms and processes involving firms in earlier stages of the life cycle (Filatotchev and Wright, 2005).

This part considers the different life-cycle stages and examines different forms of governance at each phase and the problems involved in transitioning from one phase to the next.

To begin, Toms explains the concept of the corporate governance life cycle in Chapter 16. The chapter adopts a framework that shows how the firm's resource base evolves through each stage of the life cycle and how the functions of corporate governance evolve in tandem. At key points in its evolution, the firm is shown to cross a series of thresholds implying fundamental changes in governance arrangements. As the resource base and governance arrangements change, so too do the functions of corporate entrepreneurship and the financial structure of the firm. To explain these dynamic interactions, the chapter presents a four-stage analytical model of the life cycle. Each stage, and each transition between stages, is illustrated with examples from the research literature. Subsequent chapters consider governance in firms which are at different stages.

In Chapter 17 Bertoni, Colombo, and Croce provide a survey of the literature on the role of corporate governance on the innovative activity of high-tech firms. The authors argue that a value protection perspective only allows a partial understanding of the scope of corporate governance in high-tech companies, and that a value creation perspective should instead be used. Following this broader perspective, Bertoni et al. analyze three dimensions of corporate governance: ownership structure, internal governance mechanisms, and external governance mechanisms. They show that the value protection dimension of corporate governance is often curtailed in high-tech companies. In contrast, in high-tech companies corporate governance has a very substantial value creation potential.

The intersection of family and business objectives and values within family businesses give rise to particular corporate governance challenges. In Chapter 18, Uhlaner provides an overview of research on family business and corporate governance—spanning both publicly and privately held companies. An initial overview of the field of family business identifies its prevalence and economic importance globally, as well as key terms (i.e. family business, corporate governance). The chapter is organized according to a framework, represented by nine research questions, which analyzes key findings from the extant literature according to a range of antecedents (but especially family ownership) and consequences of governance (financial performance as well as intermediate outcomes).

While high-tech and family firms are largely privately owned, at least initially, stock market entry through an initial public offering (IPO) represents a subsequent stage in a firm's life cycle. In Chapter 19, Filatotchev and Allcock discuss the context and provide an evaluation of governance issues at an IPO. The chapter provides vital keys to specific governance influences that affect firms at this particular point in their life cycle. Areas of challenge at this time for the firm are changes in the board of directors, the role of the entrepreneurial founder, developing new remuneration schemes, and external governance influences by early stage investors such as venture capital companies. The authors' analysis indicates that the IPO market is rapidly changing, as are the challenges for companies to develop robust governance mechanisms. As a result, a number of policy issues specific to this stage of a firm's development are raised.

As corporations mature, they may become large multinational firms. Although there is an extensive literature on the internal organization and governance of multinationals, relatively little is known about corporate governance relating to these organizations (Filatotchev and Wright, 2011). As Wu and Tihanyi discuss in Chapter 20, multinational firms are complex organizations, as are their corporate governance mechanisms. The authors begin with a review of the literature on the governance of multinational firms and identify three research streams: coordination and control of foreign subsidiaries, headquarter governance, and knowledge flow within multinational firms. Second, the chapter reviews the literature on the influence of governance on the internationalization process and discusses the governance problems presented by the classic models of international business, including internationalization strategy, mode of entry, and the managerial perception of the internationalization process.

Large business groups, whether multinationals or not, need to develop distinctive governance mechanisms to govern their group affiliates. These issues are addressed in Chapter 21 by Yiu, Chen, and Xu, who identify vertical governance mechanisms (including concentrated ownership, pyramidal ownership, and strategic control) and horizontal mechanisms (including cross-shareholdings, interlocking directorates, and relational governance) that are commonly found in business groups. The authors also point out, however, that business groups also face salient governance problems such as tunneling and propping, cross-subsidization, and mutual entrenchment. Given that business groups vary in ownership structures, they also examine how governance structures and related governance outcomes differ among family-controlled, state-owned, and widely held business groups.

In Chapter 22, Ayotte, Hotchkiss, and Thorburn examine the interplay of formal and informal corporate governance mechanisms relating to firms in distress. First, they outline the framework that determines when and how control rights are exercised. The authors also present extensive empirical evidence, which provides important insights on the evolution of governance involving distressed firms. Their principal focus is on the US, where the key provisions of Chapter 11 of the US Bankruptcy Code influence the behavior of firms even prior to a default.

A central feature of Chapter 11 is that it enables the debtor to remain in possession, thus enabling continuity and removing a disincentive to delay filing. They examine in turn the role of each of the firm's main constituencies who influence a potential restructuring. These constituencies involve shareholders, managers, and boards, on one hand, and senior and junior creditors on the other. Further, the authors also discuss the role of law, courts, and judges. Based on their review of the evidence, the authors conclude that it remains somewhat debatable whether management engages in riskier investment on behalf of equity holders, or whether they act more conservatively as the firm becomes distressed. They also note evidence for shareholder bargaining power in the prevalence of deviations from absolute creditor priority toward equity, although this problem appears to have declined in recent years. The authors also conclude that the idea that bankruptcy provides a safe haven for management is refuted by empirical research, which shows that managers frequently lose their jobs in financial distress. Recent evidence is cited of an ex ante expected median personal bankruptcy cost of $2.7 million (in constant 2009 dollars), or three times the typical annual compensation. They suggest that this high cost will likely have a strong impact on managers' behavior prior to distress, providing incentives to choose lower leverage or less risky investments. However, given the complicated interplay of formal and informal control rights in bankruptcy, Ayotte et al. suggest that it remains an open empirical question as to whose interests management actually represents when a firm is distressed. The evidence does, however, indicate that senior creditors play an active role in corporate governance and the restructuring of distressed firms outside of bankruptcy.

Of particular relevance to the current financial crisis, recent evidence also indicates that banks are being driven by financial regulations and regulatory policy to push their bankrupt borrowers to sell assets rather than reorganize under Chapter 11. To the extent the assets are sold at fire-sales prices, the suggestion is that this could lead to a suboptimal allocation of corporate assets. Improvement in post-restructuring operating performance of distressed firms is greater when vulture investors (including hedge funds) gain control of the restructured firm or sit on the board, suggesting that these investors bring valuable governance to the target. Labor unions are also found to maintain substantial bargaining power in Chapter 11 and influence the restructuring outcome in terms of the number of lay-offs.

PART IV: TYPES OF INVESTORS

While the previous part considered the type of firm, this part considers the array of different investors that may be involved in corporate governance. These range from venture capital firms that may be involved in newer firms, to the heterogeneity of traditional institutional investors in mature firms that may have short-term versus long-term objectives. The part also considers newer investors that may play an important role in stimulating the restructuring of mature firms, such as private equity (PE) firms and hedge funds.

As Cumming shows in Chapter 23, corporate governance in the venture capital arena is largely influenced by contractual relationships. Venture capitalists are intermediaries between institutional investors and entrepreneurial firms. As such, there are two main types of contracts: limited partnership contracts (with institutional investors) and term sheets (with entrepreneurial firms). Cummings explains how these contracts are structured, reviews international evidence on the factors that shape the contracts in practice, and discusses the implications of the use of different contractual terms for the governance and success of the venture capital investment process. It is also recognized that contracts are invariably incomplete, so that non-contractual corporate governance plays a vital role in venture capital.

Closely linked to venture capital firms are private equity firms. The terms are sometimes used interchangeably, but private equity has come to refer primarily to the funding of leveraged buyouts (LBOs) of established firms. As Wright, Siegel, Meuleman, and

Amess show in Chapter 24, private equity became the subject of considerable controversy and public scrutiny after a flurry of activity between 2005 and 2007. In the light of this attention, this chapter seeks to enhance understanding of LBOs and private equity by providing a review of theory relating to private equity and of the evidence on its impact. The review encompasses a wide range of articles in finance, economics, entrepreneurship, strategy, and human resource management. First the authors outline theoretical perspectives relating to why private equity governance may be expected to have positive or negative effects on financial, economic, and social performance. Second, the authors review the relevant empirical evidence. The evidence from what is now a large number of studies covering both the first wave of the 1980s and the second wave shows that the gains are not limited to cost cutting, but also include benefits from entrepreneurial growth strategies. Active monitoring by PE firms, especially by more experienced firms, contributes to these gains. Nevertheless, questions remain as to whether gains in second-wave PE buyouts will be as great as for those in the first wave.

Hedge funds have emerged as a related but distinct form of active investor and have attracted similar controversy to private equity firms. As Dai shows in Chapter 25, hedge funds have become critical players in the financial market, constituting over $2 trillion in market value at the end of 2011. Dai discusses the development of hedge fund activism and its implications for corporate governance by reviewing the recent key works in this area. Specifically, the chapter describes the nature of hedge fund activism, how and why it differs from activism by traditional institutional investors, as well as by private equity funds and venture capital funds, the tactics commonly applied by hedge fund activists when targeting underperforming firms and distressed firms, respectively; and the short-term and long-term effects of hedge fund activism on corporate governance, firm performance, and value.

Sovereign wealth funds represent another form of investor with novel corporate governance implications. In Chapter 26, Fotak, Gao, and Megginson examine the role sovereign wealth funds (SWFs) play in the global financial system. They argue that SWFs are the result of a process of evolution of state ownership and that their function is to mitigate the governance problems associated with government control of productive assets. The chapter first defines sovereign wealth funds, describes their historical evolution, and details their investment patterns. Next, the chapter describes a model of the role SWFs can and do play in corporate governance in the companies in which they invest. Finally, the model is used to analyze the case of the success that China's SWF has been able to achieve in restructuring the domestic banking system.

Part V: Corporate Governance, Strategy, and Stakeholders

In this final part we examine how corporate governance approaches adapt to the varying objectives and stakeholders in the firm.

In Chapter 27 Harrow and Phillips examine the context of nonprofit organizations. Nonprofit organizations are under pressure to show that they act for the public benefit in transparent ways with demonstrated impact. Consequently, questions of accountability and ownership have infused nonprofit corporate governance. The effect is not necessarily to be more "business-like," but to address stakeholder relationships and corporate governance systems more effectively when such matters are too easily obfuscated by the wide range of "owners" and players involved. Harrow and Phillips argue that the theories of nonprofit governance represent a kaleidoscope of lenses that can support the environmental contingencies and increased hybridization of corporate forms and business models in the nonprofit sector, whilst still promoting accountability. Accommodation to such innovation has to be squared with the drive for greater homogeneity created by more expansive state and self-regulation and by a consulting industry promoting "best practices." The second part of the chapter addresses whether increased societal and state regulation will conjoin to enhance corporate governance practices or simply create a muddle which enables governance mediocrity.

The overriding argument of Pendleton and Gospel in Chapter 28 is that there are three main actors in corporate governance: owners, managers, and labor. The chapter focuses especially on the role of labor in corporate governance and the effects of governance regimes and practices on labor. Initially the chapter examines the role of labor in the main corporate governance perspectives and in various strands of political thought. It then turns to perspectives on corporate governance regimes, drawing attention to those in which labor plays an important and direct role and those in which it does not. Various ways are identified in which labor may be involved in governance: representation on company boards and pension funds, ownership of company shares, information provision, and relationships with owners and investors. The chapter concludes by presenting a model of the impacts of corporate governance on labor, and by showing how governance can affect employment, rewards, skills development and work organization, and industrial relations.

The following two chapters address developments in corporate governance that extend the traditional principal–agent approach that is typically applied to listed corporations in developed Anglo-American countries. There is increasing recognition that the principal–agent framework is too simplistic, as it envisions a homogeneous set of shareholder and manager relationships. Peng and Sauerwald in Chapter 29 examine the problem of principal–principal (PP) conflicts between controlling shareholders and minority shareholders, which give rise to major governance problem in many parts of the world. They address the antecedents of PP conflicts and discuss potential remedies in the form of internal and external governance mechanisms. They highlight important organizational consequences of PP conflicts in four key areas: managerial talent, mergers and acquisitions, executive compensation, and tunneling/self-dealing. They suggest that to enhance corporate governance in the context of PP conflicts there is a need for further understanding of informal institutions, transition from family management to professional management, and collaboration among shareholders.

In contrast, Hoskisson, Arthurs, White, and Wyatt address the problem of multiple agent conflicts in Chapter 30. They assert that a majority of ownership is derived from institutional investors who are themselves agents to ultimate principals (those investing funds with the institutional investors). Many of these institutional investors, or "agent-owners," have dual identities, transcending outside relationships, and investment time horizon differences that lead to new and sometimes unexpected agency problems. The authors expand agency theory by analyzing the potential conflicts and ramifications caused by agent-owners and other important governance actors in several contexts, including initial public offerings, mergers and acquisitions, alliances and joint ventures, leveraged buyouts, and firm bankruptcy.

The 2008 financial crisis has raised fundamental questions regarding the extent to which large-scale corporate governance failures have undermined the basis of the global economy. The literature on financialization suggests that the decline of the managerial revolution and its replacement by a supposedly shareholder dominant paradigm has been little of the sort; rather, both ordinary investors and traditional managers have been emasculated through the rise of financial intermediaries. In Chapter 31, Wood and Wright critique the financialization perspective on corporate governance. They argue that the process of financialization is not a coherent phenomenon, and does not constitute a new epoch. Rather, it suggests that socio-economic change is a process of continual evolution (with uncertainty regarding ultimate direction), and one that embodies continuities going back to preceding eras. Institutions are not likely to be perfectly aligned with and follow what is done at firm level. At the same time, this diversity may make for different strengths and weaknesses than those encountered in Chandlerian managerial capitalism. Hence, much of the literature on financialization seems to be at some variance with the evidence.

The final chapter, by Brammer and Pavelin, examines the nexus between corporate governance and corporate social responsibility. Although there is growing interest in both issues, the academic literatures on these topics are somewhat disjointed. The authors review recent theoretical and empirical studies on the relationship between these two phenomena. They conclude that there is no consensus, either theoretically or empirically, on the nature of this relationship. They also lament the fact that there is little yet in the academic literature of major practical significance to managers or policymakers. To aid in this effort, the authors provide some guidance for additional research on this topic.

Conclusions: Corporate Governance in the New Financial Landscape

This *Handbook* covers numerous governance topics and provides considerable international evidence, based on quantitative and qualitative methods. The continuing financial crisis and disasters, such as BP's oil spill in the Gulf of Mexico, have focused greater attention on corporate governance, which has been stretched to the limit and found to be wanting on a number of occasions. Some of the symptoms of the stress within the current regimes of corporate governance are:

- It would seem that the pressures on businesses to perform in the short term are such that risks are taken that are detrimental to the long term.
- Directors (especially non-executive directors (NEDs)) now face almost unlimited responsibilities, but very limited time and resources to meet those responsibilities.
- The financial crisis has cast a long, dark cloud over the efficacy of the external audit.

While poor corporate governance is not the sole cause of the current crisis, it has been a contributing factor. Furthermore, the balance between risk taking and risk avoidance, which is key to sustainable innovation and performance, has gone out of kilter. One aspect of this imbalance is the risk and reward culture which developed into "extreme asymmetric forms" over the past decade.

Executive Remuneration and Bonuses—Compensation Remains a Contentious Issue

The recent Wall Street bailout raised concerns and anger regarding executive pay. This anger reached its peak in March 2009 when the public learned that many AIG (a bailed-out insurance company) employees would receive multi-million dollar bonuses. At the time, legislation was proposed that would have taxed bonuses at a rate of 90 percent for all financial managers. Although this legislation was never enacted, executive compensation continues to be subject to greater scrutiny.

A comprehensive review of the literature in this volume indicates that Congress was wise not to intervene. However, some actions are required to address some of the systematic abuses. These include aggressive actions by institutional investors and a much greater focus on choosing the best remuneration committee board members. These board members should have the appropriate expertise to design the appropriate compensation structure and monitor the performance of senior managers.

Overarching Regulatory Framework—Especially for Financial Firms

After the heightened policy and media debate in 2006–8, especially about the alleged impact of private equity and hedge funds on asset stripping and short-termism, and that the financial and economic returns achieved were down to adverse implications for R&D, investment, managerial practices, and employment, a number of attempts are being made to change the regulation of these firms. Although private equity firm activity has declined sharply since this peak period, the area remains one where controversy is not far below the surface. In the US, the role of private equity and its managerial implications assumes particular importance in an election year. Recent research has pointed to differences in private equity activity in Republican and Democrat states (Gottschalg and Pe'er, 2011). The Republican presidential candidate, Mitt Romney, had a career background in private equity that was the subject of scrutiny (<http://nymag.com/news/politics/mitt-romney-2011-10/>).

In the UK, self-regulation was introduced in 2007 in the form of The Walker Guidelines, which brought greater transparency to the private equity industry's largest investments and investors. These guidelines require that private companies report the same kind of information to the public that would be provided if the companies were publicly traded, covering ownership, board composition and key executives, and a business review of the same type as publicly traded companies. Compliance with the guidelines is monitored by the Guidelines Monitoring Group, consisting of a chairman, two independent representatives from industry and/or the trade unions, and two representatives from the private equity industry. The guidelines reinforce existing practice in reporting to investors and reiterate that valuations should follow existing international guidelines. This reflects the argument that current communication practices have generally been seen to be satisfactory by both limited partners and general partners. The new element is the requirement to communicate more broadly with any and all interested parties. The information required is included in an annual review published on the private equity fund's website. Compliance has been increasing, with the third report published in 2010 noting a higher standard of compliance than in previous years and that reporting was in line with, and in some cases better than, FTSE350 companies. The Monitoring Group issued a guide providing practical assistance to companies to help improve levels of transparency and disclosure, and which included examples of portfolio company reporting reviewed by the Group over the last two years.

Perhaps reflecting the more heated debate in Europe, The Alternative Investment Fund Management (AIFM) Directive was passed by the European Parliament in November 2010. The Directive applies to relatively few Alternative Investment Fund (AIF) managers who are based in the European Union (EU) or market funds, or invest in the EU, with total funds under management above €500 million. Funds falling under the directive are restricted in the people to whom they may market their funds. Initial proposals designed to stop asset stripping would have prevented leveraged buyouts where the loan was secured on the assets of the target company, which would effectively have removed the business model used in leveraged buyouts. The measures included in the Directive have been significantly diluted from these original proposals.

The Directive contains provisions to limit the levels of leverage that can be used by AIFs within funds. However, leverage at the portfolio or holding company level used by private equity firms is not included in the definition of leverage in the Directive. This recognizes that loans secured on the assets of the portfolio company do not create a systematic risk. There are requirements for AIFMs to have minimum capital related to the size of the underlying funds. Arguably these are misguided where the funds are inherently illiquid, as in most private equity funds. The Directive requires AIFMs to introduce a remuneration policy, including carried interest, consistent with, and which promotes, sound and effective risk management. An AIFM must prepare an annual report which must be provided to the relevant EU competent authorities, as well as to investors on request. An AIFM must notify its voting rights to its relevant regulator when it acquires voting rights of 10/20/30/50/75 percent of a non-listed company, with additional disclosures being required at ownership levels above 50 percent. The PE firm needs to disclose to regulators the chain of decision-making regarding the voting rights of investors in the company; and practices to be put in place to communicate to employees. In changes to the original draft, there is no longer a need to disclose detailed information on the PE firm's strategic plans for the company. Overall the directive represents a significant increase in regulatory disclosures and regulatory burden, but does not materially impede any private equity fund manager from continuing their business.

Governance and Risk Management

It is clear that boards have a role to play in ensuring better governance and risk management practices. Below we consider a number of arguments regarding risk management which revolve around a greater commitment of the board to engendering a culture of better practice. This, however, raises the issue of what needs to be done at board level to lead such improvements. In addition to ensuring that directors are selected with the appropriate skills and experience, the following aspects need to be considered if boards are to be kept up to date, offer a range of challenging perspectives, and be independent in their judgment: namely, the rotation of committee members, board diversity, independent chairmanship, lead independent director, and auditor rotation.

The turbulence in the financial markets and the recent BP oil spill disaster in the Gulf of Mexico have raised many questions over the governance of organizations and more importantly how risk management aligns with broader governance principles.

In terms of the financial crisis, many papers have outlined the basic causes, including innovation, complexity of structured products, the originate and distribute model, an inability to measure tail risk, the role of the credit rating agencies, and the role of fair value accounting. Against this set of causes, there is also a need to consider how more mundane matters had a role to play—i.e. risk concentrations, maturity mismatches, high levels of gearing, inadequate and opaque risk management processes and procedures. Keeping a focus on the financial crisis for the moment, who owns the risk and how risk is measured are two issues of risk management that need further consideration.

Risk management and governance have tended to be seen as separate entities/activities within organizations with their own individual committees and processes. The problem with this approach is that it can give rise to box ticking, instead of an integrated embedding. The BP oil spill disaster has clearly shown that the board has to own both the general governance of the organization and its many and varied risk activities—it is not good enough to assume that risk management is being tackled within parts of the organization and there is no need for board ownership and oversight of the issue. As is the case with governance, while a separate committee might give profile to the topic, it also runs the danger of directors assuming that the matter is being handled elsewhere and is not a key part of their duties. While specialist committees and processes are laudable, the topics of governance and risk management are so important that they have to be embedded in the organization so that they are the responsibility of every stakeholder.

An integrated and embedded approach to risk management and governance will depend on at least the following aspects being balanced: the balance between the need to conduct business and achieve/meet performance expectations and the appetite for/acceptance of risk; how far senior management see themselves as being responsible for the identification and understanding of material risks and the mitigation thereof; how much effort senior management put into the flow of information within and across the business; and the extent to which open discussion of risk matters is encouraged across the business.

The segregation of risk and governance within the firm creates at least two major issues. First, there can be no appreciation of the overall risk of the organization and, second, there can be no cross-learning of risk understanding, risk mitigation, and how these two should be integrated into broader governance structures. An obvious point for consideration is how managers and owners can be better aligned in terms of risk activities, performance, and executive remuneration. This is clearly a topic that is receiving substantial media attention (see above), especially in the bailed-out banks/insurers which continue to make losses and pay large bonuses to the management.

In terms of the measurement and disclosure of risk, the Senior Supervisors Group (2011) report offers a number of insights into the measurement and disclosure of risk. First, better performing firms had greater management involvement in stress testing and had a greater selection of tools. There was a greater sharing of qualitative and quantitative data across the firm. Second, some firms were able to use the integrated data to give them an earlier warning of significant risk. Third, firms which suffered from risk problems seem to depend on a small number of risk measures and were unable to give them sufficient critical evaluation and challenge. Finally, the risk-prone firms were unable to get management to give sufficient time and attention to future-looking risk scenarios.

Essentially, good risk management should avoid an overreliance on single risk measures and specific models; instead having an open mind and a broad range of methodologies is essential. Encouraging challenge and avoiding silos of thinking/approach are key to good risk management; and it goes without saying that these are essential qualities of a healthy governance environment.

In summary, existing risk management practices, in general, are insufficient to deal with the risks and turbulence many companies are encountering in the current economic environment. Most of the guidance is too high level, wedded to too few methodologies, and not sufficiently grounded in the business. Risk management has to be a culture deeply embedded in the actions of the business and not overly process driven. Management needs to encourage a broad-based risk management culture that traverses traditional organizational boundaries. This would be a culture where the board stresses the benefits of good governance, strong ethical principles, and ongoing monitoring, management, and mitigation of risk. Boards need to be encouraged to take a broad-based view of their responsibilities, which includes a detailed understanding of the risk management of the business; in essence, they have to understand the totality of their roles.

Corporate Governance and National Institutions

Despite the enormous influence of agency theory, extending this approach to cross-nationally comparative work on corporate governance remains problematic. Although the pioneering efforts of agency theorists contributed to understanding goal incongruence among principals (shareholders) and agents (managers) as a function of contractual relationships set up within the firm, the subsequent empirical corporate governance research has failed to fully contextualize how different sets of institutions modify this basic relationship by creating different sets of incentives or resources for monitoring. The problem setting for the vast majority of studies reflects a basic separation of ownership and control, as well as emphasis on individual incentives and active external markets for capital and labor that characterize the corporate economy in the US. But one cannot assume that theories and empirical evidence developed in the US apply to other institutional settings in a universal fashion. These conditions of the "Anglo-Saxon model" constitute the exception rather than the rule when looking at corporate governance in Continental Europe, East Asia, India, and emerging economies in other regions. In most countries, ownership is substantially more concentrated. Legal institutions also differ widely, as do managerial career patterns and the salience of social norms around shareholder value.

Given the "under-contextualized" nature of most theories of corporate governance, a challenge remains to more explicitly understand and compare how corporate governance operates effectively in different organizational environments and institutional contexts. The literature in organizational sociology has argued that different corporate governance practices may be more or less effective depending upon the contexts of different organizational environments and is related to the institutionalization of different legitimate values across societies and over time (see Aguilera et al., 2008). This literature stresses a shift away from the focus on principals and agents as a universal phenomenon and looks more at the patterned variation of organizational forms under different settings. Rather than economic efficiency, these theories seek to understand external factors that shape the effectiveness and legitimacy of corporate governance practices.

While institutional approaches are well-established within the social sciences, institutional theory has had an important but limited influence on agency theory. More generally, one major strand of the literature examines the role of legal origins (La Porta et al., 2000). This literature argues that, in common law societies, investors are willing to take more risks and use "arm's-length" control mechanisms, since they have legal remedies such as the ability to sue in the courts if board members and managers do not act in their best interests and maximize firm profitability. In civil law countries, weaker legal protection for investors has led to the persistence of more concentrated forms of ownership, albeit with different roles for families, governments, banks, or other types of blockholders across countries. Thus, the role of various types of investors may be different in civil law environments, where fewer legal remedies are available compared with common law countries. While this approach acknowledges the role of institutions, the perspective is also limited by seeing institutions in relation to a single universal principal–agent problem. Furthermore, the less contextualized categorization of common law versus civil law systems in examining the role of legal origins has been questioned, and a better comparative understanding of corporate governance around the world requires a more developed institutional view of corporate governance that goes beyond the agency theory paradigm. In essence, corporate governance research needs to pay closer attention to how the effectiveness of well-known corporate governance practices differ across institutional environments due to broader sets of complementarities within the social and political environment.

REFERENCES

AGUILERA, R. V., FILATOTCHEV, I., GOSPEL, H., and JACKSON, G. (2008). "An Organizational Approach to Comparative Corporate Governance: Costs, Contingencies and Complementarities," *Organization Science*, 19: 475–92.

BERLE, A., and MEANS, G. (1932). *The Modern Corporation and Private Property*. New York: Commerce Clearing House.

FILATOTCHEV, I., and WRIGHT, M. (2005). *The Life-Cycle of Corporate Governance*. Cheltenham: Edward Elgar.

——(2011). "Agency Perspectives on Corporate Governance of Multinational Enterprises," *Journal of Management Studies*, 48(2): 471–86.

GOTTSCHALG, O., and PE'ER, A. (2011). "Red and Blue: The Relationship between the Institutional Context and the Performance of Leveraged Buyout Investments," *Strategic Management Journal*, 32(12): 1356–67.

KAPLAN, S. N. (2008). "Are U.S. CEOs Overpaid?" *Academy of Management Perspectives*, 22(2): 5–20.

LA PORTA, R., LOPEZ-DE-SILANES, F., SHLEIFER, A., and VISHNY, R. (2000). "Investor Protection and Corporate Governance," *Journal of Financial Economics*, 58: 3–27.

MANNE, H. (1965). "Mergers and the Market for Corporate Control," *Journal of Political Economy*, 73: 110–20.

MARCUS, A. A., and FREMETH, A. R. (2009). "Green Management Matters Regardless," *Academy of Management Perspectives*, 23(3): 17–26.

Senior Supervisors Group (2011). *Observations on Developments in Risk Appetite Frameworks and IT Infrastructure*. New York: Financial Stability Board.

SIEGEL, D. S. (2009). "Green Management Matters Only If it Yields More Green: An Economic/Strategic Perspective," *Academy of Management Perspectives*, 23(3): 5–16.

WALKER, D. (2009). *Walker Review of Corporate Governance of UK Banking Industry*. London: Financial Reporting Council.

WALSH, J. P. (2009). "Are U.S. CEOs Overpaid? A Partial Response to Kaplan," *Academy of Management Perspectives*, 23: 73–5.

WEICK, K. (1995). *Sensemaking in Organizations*. Thousand Oaks, CA: Sage.

PART I
REGULATION AND HISTORY

CHAPTER 2

REGULATION AND COMPARATIVE CORPORATE GOVERNANCE

RUTH V. AGUILERA, MICHEL GOYER, AND
LUIZ RICARDO KABBACH DE CASTRO

Introduction

This chapter analyzes the relationship between regulation and corporate governance. Regulation, the issue and implementation of administrative directives and rules by legally mandated agencies, constitutes a major aspect of the governance of social and economic life (Majone, 1994 and 1997; Carrigan and Coglianese, 2011). The advent and spread of important economic transformations such as privatization and deregulation occur through the creation of new regulatory institutions (Levi-Faur, 2005). Policy-making in an increasingly liberalized environment is characterized by a paradigm shift in the role of the state from interventionist to regulatory (Vogel, 1996). The liberalization of economic sectors across economies does not imply the withdrawal of the state, but a redefinition of its role. Most notably, but not exclusively, this shift occurs through important political choices regarding the degree of independence, scope, and granted power of regulatory agencies. Corporate governance, on the other hand, refers to the structure of rights and responsibilities of the different stakeholders and its consequences for the process by which companies are controlled and operated (Aoki, 2001; Gourevitch and Shinn, 2005). Effective corporate governance entails mechanisms to ensure executives respect the rights and interests of company stakeholders, as well as guaranteeing that stakeholders act responsibly with regard to the generation, protection, and distribution of wealth invested in the firm.

Two theoretical perspectives are prominent in the study of regulation: principal–agent and governance. First, the study of regulation has traditionally focused on the principal–agent problem, i.e. the interactions between policymakers and regulators

(Laffont and Tirole, 1991). The analytical starting point is the divergence of interests between these two actors since the actions of (unelected) regulators might differ from the preferences of elected officials (Breyer, 1982). In particular, regulatory agencies can be subject to regulatory capture, i.e. aligning themselves with those they are supposed to regulate (Stigler, 1971). Theories of regulation based on regulatory capture highlight how regulators are more prone to adhere to the demands of organized groups rather than meeting the preferences of dispersed groups even if their mission is to protect the latter (Peltzman, 1976; Stigler, 1983). The process of regulatory capture emphasizes collective action and the intensity of preferences of the negatively affected parties to lobby for protection (Wilson, 1980 and 1989; see also Olson, 1965).

Building on the prominence of the principal–agent problem, regulation theorists have focused on how the electorally accountable principals seek to control the activities of regulatory agencies (Weingast and Moran, 1983; Moe, 1987). A critical dimension associated with attempts to control the behavior of regulatory authorities is that the independence of regulatory authorities is often seen as a key factor in limiting the potentially biased influence of elected officials (Thatcher and Stone Sweet, 2002). Two main mechanisms have been identified in this tightrope walk, namely the simultaneous delegation of independence and control over the activities of regulators (McCubbins and Schwartz, 1984). The first one, a police-control mechanism, is characterized by the direct and centralized interventions of elected officials, aimed at detecting deviations in the assigned missions of regulatory agencies. The emphasis is placed on formal institutional design, aimed at structuring the process of appointment/dismissal of regulators and the determination of budgets (Kiewet and McCubbins, 1991). The second mechanism, a fire-alarm oversight, is characterized by the presence of a system of rules and procedures that enable organized groups and citizens to detect such deviations and alert government officials. The emphasis is placed on the design of mechanisms that heighten the provision of external information flows, thereby enabling the principal to develop monitoring capabilities that could be used as a counterweight to the expertise of regulatory agencies. These two mechanisms share a command-and-control regulatory approach, namely the design of institutional regulatory features that would best serve to lessen agency costs.

Even though the principal–agent focus has been influential in the study of regulation, the need for the incorporation of the insights of complementary perspectives has been noted. For instance, the ability of organized interest groups to capture regulatory authorities fluctuates both over time and across institutional contexts (Wilson, 1980; Culpepper, 2011). This variation strongly suggests the importance of both the institutional context in which actors are embedded (Aguilera and Jackson, 2003; Gourevitch and Shinn, 2005) and the extent to which an issue is politically salient to the electorate (Culpepper, 2011). Part of the reason accounting for the low political salience of regulation is its complexity as it is not often easily translatable into issues that can be grasped by the electorate. Moreover, the ability of policymakers to shape and influence regulators' behavior is contingent not only on the presence of institutional control mechanisms, but also on the use of these mechanisms (Moe, 1985). The circumstances and issue areas where elected officials choose to exercise their legally based authority over the actions of regulators exhibit significant variations (Thatcher, 2002).

Second, the study of regulation has also been characterized by the importance of the governance approach (Kagan, 1994). The process of regulation is not simply a confrontation between the diverging interests of elected officials and regulatory authorities; it is also characterized by an interaction based on cooperation (Scholz, 1984). The assumption of the governance approach is that the failure of regulators to meet the preferences of policymakers does not reflect the presence of diverging interests, but that of the complexities of policy contexts; and that effective regulation requires coordination between the legislative authority of the principal and the activities of agents (Dorf and Sabel, 1998). Institutional mechanisms of authority delegation involve the setting of performance standards by the principal, but with the granting of substantial flexibility on the design of the most efficient and cost-effective procedure to meet these standards (Viscusi, 1983). Some monitoring mechanisms in this perspective are disclosure requirements, self-regulation initiatives, and legal requirements imposed on regulated authorities to gather information about their activities. An explicit assumption behind the cooperation and coordination nature of the interaction between elected officials and regulatory authorities is that regulators can often take a long-term view on problems given the absence of direct electoral pressures. Regulatory authorities can seek to protect their independence and enhance their reputation by rising above self-interested policy-making pressures (Carpenter, 2001).

The field of corporate governance possesses close affinities with the study of regulation. First, the literature in comparative corporate governance has emphasized the importance of the principal–agent problem in different forms. Early studies of corporate governance focused on the divergence of interests between principals and agents (Berle and Means, 1932; Jensen and Meckling, 1976). The key idea is that unmonitored managers will pursue goals that are not in the interests of shareholders—ranging from actions that allow them to profit personally (embezzlement, misappropriations) to empire building (hubris). These studies were organized around the following puzzle: why would minority investors provide funding to companies run by unaccountable, dominant managers? These early law and economics analyses of corporate governance, however, are plagued by a fundamental shortcoming despite their influence over the intellectual development of the discipline. The main point of contention is that ownership dispersion is only characteristic of a few countries, essentially Anglo-Saxon economies. Moreover, the analytical foundations of these early studies of corporate governance lacked a comparative focus. A second wave of studies based on the principal–agent problem emerged in the early 1990s with the aim of accounting for diversity in ownership structures across national systems of corporate governance. The extent to which minority investors are protected by law from expropriation by managers or controlling shareholders is the key argument accounting for differences in ownership structures (La Porta et al., 2000). The theoretical implication flowing from the presence of different ownership structures is that the nature of agency costs differs across national systems of corporate governance. There are many varieties of agency costs—which all contribute to destroy shareholder value—but for which different institutional solutions should prevail (Coffee, 2005; see Roe, 2002, for a critical analytical overview). A first type of agency costs is diversion by managers—stealing, embezzling, and shirking. A second variety of agency costs comes in the form of managerial mistakes—executives not being up to running the firm, plausibly because of changed circumstances. Institutions that work well in solving the first type of agency costs might not be as effective in dealing with the second variety.

Second, the area of corporate governance is also well suited to the study of regulation given the presence of different mechanisms of regulatory activities. Attempts to control the behavior of agents are also found alongside mechanisms of corporation. Some important monitoring mechanisms of corporate governance are found in the domain of corporate law and emphasize the importance of mandatory rules (Coffee, 1989; Gordon, 1989). However, regulation in the field of corporate governance is increasingly characterized by soft law where actors self-regulate themselves without possessing full legislative authority (Hopt, 2011). Soft law is characterized by the prominence of standardized reporting based on the comply-or-explain principle. Regulatory outputs based on hard versus soft law entail a tradeoff between flexibility and enforceability, with optimal governance being based on the importance of the local context (Aguilera et al., 2008). Hard law, such as the Sarbanes-Oxley Act, provides regulatory outputs that cover all companies operating in a jurisdiction, thereby ensuring the implementation of high minimum standards, but at the cost of the lack of flexibility regarding the characteristics of companies—blue chip versus start-up; family-owned versus ownership diffused; unmonitored insiders versus legally constrained blockholders. Soft law, such as the Cadbury recommendations of good governance in the United Kingdom, enables listed companies to mix different practices of corporate governance in diverse organizational environments, but could result in weaker degrees of enforcement.

Third, the growing importance of regulation in corporate governance connects to important debates that deal with the uneven impact of globalization on the evolution of national business systems. The advent of multiple market reforms—deregulation, privatization, liberalization, trade agreements, and the removal of controls on inward/outward movements of capital—is triggering change across national systems of corporate governance, yet without leading to full convergence of systems (Whitley, 1999; Hall and Soskice, 2001; Vogel, 2001). In a similar vein, the rise of the regulatory state across economies (such as the European Union) has been prominent, but has taken different forms across different varieties of capitalist economies (Vogel, 1996; Fioretos, 2011). In particular, the concept of regulation highlights the persistence of different types of state intervention in the wake of privatization and liberalization via the spread of national regulatory authorities (Vogel, 1996; Thatcher, 2002). The privatization and liberalization process should not be equated with deregulatory laissez-faire, but with the implementation of new settings of regulation (Jordana and Levi-Faur, 2004). The process of regulation highlights the importance of institutional redeployment in policy-making, i.e. state intervention taking place with the use of new policy instruments and redeployed on behalf of new objectives (Levy, 2006; Schmidt, 2009).

The rest of the chapter is organized as follow. In the next section, we discuss the two main theoretical perspectives on the origins of regulation: law and politics. We then highlight the contextually bounded consequences associated with regulation for the evolution of national systems of corporate governance. The issue of hard versus soft law is further examined in the concluding section of the chapter.

The Origins of Regulation: Theoretical Perspectives

The introduction and spread of regulatory agencies across national systems of corporate governance has been impressive (Majone, 1994; Jordana et al., 2011). The range of economic sectors that have experienced the double movement of the decline of the interventionist state and the rise of the regulatory state is extensive (Levi-Faur, 2006). Nonetheless, the rise of the regulatory state has not resulted in convergence across national systems of corporate governance (Gourevitch and Shinn, 2005; Lütz, 2004). Important differences remain in the degree of independence of regulatory authorities, and the relationship of regulators with the business regulated (Thatcher, 2002). Economies, and national systems of corporate governance, exhibit significant variations with regard to the party politicization of appointments to posts at national regulatory agencies, legal impediments for the removal of regulatory officials, financial and staffing of regulatory agencies, and the use of legally entitled powers to overturn decisions made by regulators (Enriques, 2002; Etzion and Davis, 2008; Fioretos, 2010). Variations on these features result in differences in the degree of independence of regulators from elected officials. Moreover, the impressive spread of regulatory authorities across national systems of corporate governance is associated with an extensive range of outcomes regarding the extent to which appointed regulators have escaped the preponderant influence of corporate interests (Johnson and Kwak, 2010; Roubini and Mihm, 2010). The extent to which regulators moved back and forth between governmental positions and the (regulated) private sector exhibits substantial variations between national systems of corporate governance in the context of the widespread diffusion of regulatory agencies. Therefore, an important question concerns the factors that best account for the origins of these differences. The issue is not about the increasing importance of regulatory agencies, but of the presence of differences in the degree of independence of regulatory authorities, and the relationship of regulators with the business regulated. We provide an analytical overview of the contribution of two major theoretical perspectives on the origins of regulation in corporate governance: law and economics, and politics.

First, the law and economics perspective on corporate governance emphasizes the importance of institutional-legal arrangements in protecting the rights of minority investors given the extensively documented differences in ownership structures across countries (La Porta et al., 2000). Dispersed shareholders need some form of assurance that they will get a return on their investment before departing with their financial assets since a combination of standard tort law and private bonding is not sufficient to grant adequate guarantees to outsiders (Shleifer and Vishny, 1997; Glaeser et al., 2001). Specific institutions—rules and enforcement—in the areas of stock exchange regulations, accounting standards and financial transparency, corporate law, and takeover regulation protect minority investors better than some other institutions (La Porta et al., 2000; Coffee, 2006).

The development of regulation, and the presence of institutional differences between regulatory states, is at the core of the law and economics perspective on corporate governance, namely the closer affinities between independent regulatory authorities and institutional arrangements of legal protection found in common law systems. Legal rules in systems of common law are made by judges, based on jurisprudence, and inspired by general principles such as fiduciary duty (Coffee, 1999; Johnson et al., 2000). These general principles are applicable in new situations even when specific conduct that would violate the rights of minority shareholders has not yet been prohibited by statutes. Judges in common law systems have exercised greater discretion in evaluating whether even unprecedented conduct by the insiders is unfair to outside investors.

The development of regulation in some national systems of corporate governance is characterized by the high degree of independence, and authority, of regulatory authorities from elected officials (McCubbins and Schwartz, 1984; Thatcher, 2002). For the law and economics perspective, the development of regulation in corporate governance constitutes a largely technocratic endeavour where the main task of policymakers is to implement institutional features that better protect the rights of minority investors (La Porta et al., 2000 and 2006). Regulatory institutions characterized by understaffing and underdeveloped budgets will fare poorly in law enforcement, a phenomenon interpreted as a regulatory failure (Enriques, 2002; Jackson, 2007).

The law and economics perspective is highly influential in the area of regulation of corporate governance. It is intuitively correct in that why would outside investors provide funding if their legal rights were not well protected? Nonetheless, the perspective has been criticized on several grounds. First, the construction of institutional arrangements that protect minority shareholders is not "rocket science"—the reason why non-common law advanced capitalist economies have refrained for a long time from building them is better accounted for by their reluctance to embrace principles of shareholder value that are more likely to be associated with independent regulatory authorities (Roe, 2003). Second, the law and economics approach conceptualizes regulatory arrangements that protect minority investors as fixed endowments that are both necessary for economic activities to occur and that, once in place, are themselves immune to change. By contrast, Milhaupt and Pistor (2008) highlight the continuous interactive process between legal arrangements and markets that results from three features: the extent to which legal systems are centralized/decentralized in relation to law-making and enforcement processes; the presence of multiple functions performed by the legal system in supporting economic activities beside that of shareholder protection, and the contested nature of legal institutions that follows from their asymmetric distribution of gains for political and social actors. Third, the legal perspective on corporate governance is unable to account for the variation and similarities in the character of regulation. In the first instance, the United Kingdom and the United States—two common law legal systems—

have often implemented different types of regulation: the former has relied on voluntary approaches to regulation, while the latter, especially in recent years, has enacted mandatory features (Sarbanes-Oxley Act 2002; Dodd-Frank Act 2010). Moreover, differences between civil and common law legal systems have experienced erosion in recent years since both systems continue to regulate and codify; and recent legislation has generated opposite results than would have been predicted by the law and economics perspective. An example is the quite directive Sarbanes-Oxley Act in the United States in contract to the market-preferring, transparency-enhancing Kontrag Law in Germany (Roe, 2006: 468–82).

The second theoretical approach to regulation and corporate governance is the political perspective (Roe, 2003; Gourevtich and Shinn, 2005). The above discussion of regulation in corporate governance highlights the importance of politics. The point is not that institutional differences between legal families do not matter, but that current differences between national systems of corporate governance are probably better accounted for by more recent political decisions that lead some countries to embrace/denigrate principles of shareholder value than institutional-legal variables introduced some centuries ago (Roe, 2007).

The central feature of the political perspective on regulation in corporate governance is that differences in regulatory institutions of corporate governance reflect the extent to which the political climate of a country is conducive to the pursuit of market-oriented and shareholder value-driven policies (Roe, 2003). The diversity of regulatory institutional features represents the different outcomes of political, economic, and social struggles across national systems of corporate governance (Roe and Gilson, 1999). In European social democracies and in Japan, policymakers have traditionally emphasized distributional considerations that privileged employees over shareholders.

The political perspective on regulation in corporate governance highlights two elements of the relationship between regulatory institutions and outcomes. First, regulatory institutions are secondary to politics. The absence of institutional arrangements that would protect the rights and promote the interests of minority shareholders in advanced capitalist economies cannot be attributed to technological shortcomings or financial issues (Roe, 2002). For instance, the understaffing of stock market regulatory agencies in continental Europe and Japan is not a problem of expertise or budgetary constraints, but rather a politically conscious decision not to empower an institution whose goal would be diverging from political norms of legitimate market operations. Conversely, the presence of regulatory institutions that promote shareholder value in dispersed ownership economies reflects the prior acceptance of market principles that privileges, or does not discriminate against, the preferences of minority shareholders (Roe, 2002). Second, the existence of institutional variation within families of corporate governance, namely social democracies versus those where principles of unfettered markets are legitimate, is not central to the argument (Roe, 2003: 27–46). Regulatory institutional features designed to dampen the ability of management to implement strategies of shareholder value have been achieved in different ways in economies that were/are characterized by ownership concentration: legal rights of codetermination in

Germany, state activism in France, and social norms and informal arrangements in Japan.

The political perspective on regulation and corporate governance is highly insightful and has contributed to our understanding of the diversity of national systems. The design and implementation of regulatory institutions entail important distributional consequences (Hancké et al., 2007). The differences in the degree of authority and independence of regulatory authorities do matter for the allocation of resources in the economy via, most notably but not exclusively, their effects on the distribution of authority inside companies. Politics is highly important for regulatory governance. Nonetheless, the political perspective on corporate governance and regulation needs to be complemented by the notion of coalition formation (Aguilera and Jackson, 2003; Gourevitch and Shinn, 2005) and the extent of institutional complementarities leading to distinct varieties of capitalism (Hall and Soskice, 2001; Hall and Gingerich, 2009). In the first place, coalition formation inside a national system of corporate governance is not limited to a class conflict pitting employees against managers/shareholders as presented by Roe. Sectoral (shareholders against employees/managers) and transparency coalitions (managers against employees/shareholders) are also important across issues and between national systems of corporate governance. In the second place, national systems of corporate governance are embedded in specific varieties of capitalism characterized by significant differences regarding the extent and strength of institutional complementarities at the national level. Institutional complementarities are important in liberal market economies (e.g. United Kingdom and United States) and coordinated market economies (e.g., Germany and Japan). The insider model of corporate governance in liberal market economies fits well with external flexibility in industrial relations and general/transferable skills in education. The outsider model of corporate governance in liberal market economies fits well with the rigidity of employment relations and the firm-specific skills of employees. By contrast, institutionally hybrid market economies (e.g. France and Spain) are characterized by the absence of complementarities between the different spheres of the economy, most notably, although not exclusively, reflecting the presence of general/transferable skills and rigid labor markets (Maurice et al., 1986; Hall and Gingerich, 2009, Goyer, 2011).

The insight from the coalition model formation and the concept of institutional complementarities is that institutional regulatory features exhibit important variations within families of corporate governance. The low prominence of shareholder value in European social democracies can be achieved by either a class conflict or sectoral coalition type (Aguilera and Jackson, 2003; Gourevitch and Shinn, 2005). Moreover, the presence of labor market rigidities (difficult to fire employees) in European social democracies (OECD, 1999) constitutes a source of constraints on managerial autonomy in settings characterized by the importance of general/transferable skills, while representing an enabling feature that incentivizes insiders to build on the long-term skill of employees in settings dominated by the presence of firm-specific skills (see e.g. Goyer, 2011). Thus, corporate governance in European social democracies is compatible with important variations in the size of the private benefits of control (high in Italy; low in

Germany) and with employee participation (Germany) or exclusion (France) in the strategic direction of companies.

The Impact of Regulation on Corporate Governance: A Contextualized Approach

An important debate for both policymakers and scholars is the extent and the form by which regulation shapes corporate governance outcomes within and across countries. How does regulation matter? For the specific case of corporate governance, the last two decades have witnessed the "globalization" of regulatory reforms across economies with the aim of increasing the rights of minority investors (Deminor Rating, 2005; Goergen et al., 2005; Cioffi and Hoepner, 2006; Burkart and Lee, 2008). The rise of the regulatory state in corporate governance reflects in great part the strategy of international diversification of institutional investors from liberal market economies (Goyer, 2006; Clark and Wojcik, 2007). The preferences of shareholder value-oriented funds stand at odds with the mode of governance of firms in non-liberal market economies characterized by the lower prominence of the rights of minority shareholders (Roe, 2000). The strategy of international diversification of UK/US institutional investors has generated an industry of best corporate governance practices characterized by the publication of guidelines lists of what are considered fundamental strategies to unlock shareholder value most notably, but not exclusively, in the form of codes of good governance (Davis et al., 2006; Aguilera and Cuervo-Cazurra, 2009). Among these best practices are the rules governing the market for corporate control (mandatory bid rule, ownership disclosure, principle of equal treatment), the independence of directors, voting rights characterized by the one share-one vote principle, and the expansion of issues for which shareholder approval is needed (Goergen et al., 2005; Dalton et al., 2007; Adams and Ferreira, 2008; Burkart and Lee, 2008).

Nonetheless, the impact of regulatory reforms designed to enhance minority shareholders' rights should not be interpreted in a cumulative manner, namely the more the better. A cumulative assumption on regulation neglects the importance of contexts (Goertz, 1994; Hall, 2010; Goyer, 2011). Even assuming the best-case scenario for regulation theorists, a high degree of independence of regulators from both elected officials and from regulated corporations, national systems of corporate governance remain different from each other. The consequences associated with the enactment of regulatory reforms are mediated by the characteristics of the institutional environment of the system of corporate governance in which they are embedded. In other words, the impact of any regulatory reform on corporate governance is dependent on the structure of existing institutional arrangements (Hall, 2007; Hall and Thelen, 2009). Even when dealing with identical regulatory reforms, the presence of interaction between institutions insures that the impact of such reforms will vary significantly across national systems of corporate governance (Hall and Soskice, 2001; Aguilera et al., 2008; Hall and Gingerich, 2009). Four examples illustrate well the contextually bounded consequences of regulatory reforms: boards of directors in Germany, private benefits of control, takeover regulatory reforms in the European Union, and the abolition of deviations from the one share-one vote standard in Germany. We discuss each of them in turn.

First, Roe (1999) provides an insightful treatment of context in his analysis of codetermined boards in Germany. The boards of directors (i.e. supervisory boards) of German companies have largely failed to act as a mechanism to defend the interests of minority shareholders since employee representatives occupy half of the seats. The other half is composed of directors elected by shareholders. These directors have not been independent for the most part. The size of supervisory boards in Germany is also large and reflects the introduction of codetermination. Nonetheless, Roe cautions about regulatory reforms that would increase the independence of directors elected by shareholders—and who would be serving alongside employee representatives. The key contextual issue in this instance is the empowerment of the boards of directors. Empowering the shareholder-elected part of the board in the form of director independence might produce unintended consequences from a shareholder value perspective. Empowering supervisory boards would also empower their employee half against atomistic, and independent, directors comprising the other half. Thus, substandard board governance is likely to be less problematic for minority shareholders than a fully empowered board where employee-elected directors could coordinate their activities. Legal reforms designed to promote shareholder value in Germany via greater board independence is likely to produce unintended consequences given the institutional arrangement of board codetermination.

Second, the extent to which private benefits of control, and regulatory reforms designed to eliminate them, are damaging for shareholder value remains an unresolved issue. The notion of the private benefits of control refers to the aggregate value a controlling owner can extract from her ability to determine corporate policies at the expense of minority shareholders (Johnson et al., 2000; Nenova, 2003; Dyck and Zingales, 2004). Control over the corporate strategy of the firm is valuable since large shareholders receive private benefits that are not shared with minority investors. Examples of private benefits of control are the ability of the controlling shareholder to transfer assets at below market prices between different companies in which he possesses a dominant position, increases in equity stakes through dilutive share issues and minority freeze-outs, and synergy benefits from the use of information in the operations of a firm that would be exploited by other companies also controlled by the large owner (Zingales, 1998; Johnson et al., 2000). The gains associated with these strategic options are not shared by minority investors. Nonetheless, regulatory reforms designed to reduce the ability of the controlling shareholder to extract private benefits of control entail ambiguous consequences for shareholder value. Gilson (2006) highlights the presence of a tradeoff associated with the presence of a controlling shareholder: monitoring of managers versus the extraction of private benefits of control (see also Mayer, 2001). Agency costs come in the form of managerial entrenchment (ownership diffusion) and extraction of private benefits of control (ownership concentration)

(Roe, 2001; Coffee, 2005). Moreover, empirical data reveals the presence of large disparities in the amount of private benefits of control in systems of corporate governance dominated by ownership concentration (Nenova, 2003; Dyck and Zingales, 2004). In other words, controlling shareholders could be associated with low or high private benefits of control. Thus, the impact on shareholder value associated with regulatory reforms to reduce the extraction of the private benefits of control is contingent upon the specific context of national systems of corporate governance. Several contextual variables have been highlighted: social norms about corruption and personal enrichment (Coffee, 2001), presence of non-pecuniary benefits of control (Gilson, 2006), strength of firm-level employees that act as monitors on insiders (Gourevitch and Shinn, 2005: 59–67; Fauver and Fuerst, 2006), and the presence of institutional arrangements that constrain large shareholders in related-party transactions for both actions that result/do not result in bankruptcy (Conac et al., 2007).

Third, the introduction of an impressive array of regulatory reforms aimed at providing greater protection to minority shareholders in the European Union has been largely inconsequential for the development of a level playing field in the area of the market for corporate control. Regulatory reforms of takeovers in the European Union have been important in several areas: increased ownership disclosure requirements, mandatory bid rule, and adoption of the principle of equal treatment for all categories of shareholders (Goergen et al., 2005). These reforms have decreased the ability of bidders to proceed to the acquisition of controlling stakes without being detected as well as preventing side deals that would result in no/low takeover premiums for minority shareholders. Nonetheless, markets for corporate control still exhibit important differences in the European Union in regard to the overall importance of takeover activities, the identity of acquiring and target companies, the methods of payment, the friendly versus hostile character of the transaction, the characteristics of the post-acquisition reorganization process, and the rules governing the bidding process (Rossi and Volpin, 2004; Capron and Guillén, 2009; Culpepper, 2011). The key contextual factor is that managerial protection against takeovers reflects the importance of functional equivalency, namely the presence of alternative mechanisms of protection against unwanted takeover bids. In particular, institutional arrangements of ownership structure and deviations from the one share-one vote standard have not converged in the European Union, with the implication that some firms are better protected than others against unsolicited takeover bids (Valdivieso del Real, 2009). The consequences associated with the introduction of many pro-minority shareholder measures in the European Union reflect the interaction between the new institutions and those that were already in place.

Fourth, regulatory reforms aimed at eliminating deviations from the one share-one vote principle will produce different consequences according to the prevailing ownership structures of listed companies and the types of deviations previously used by firms (Adams and Ferreira, 2008; Burkart and Lee, 2008). The regulatory reforms of German corporate law (Kontrag law) illustrate this point in two ways. In the first instance, the power of banks in German corporate governance has been sharply reduced with regulatory reforms of proxy voting (Deeg, 1999; Hoepner and Krempel, 2004). Prior to the

1998 Kontrag law, financial institutions in Germany were able to exercise significant voting power in companies through their role as custodian of shares since minority shareholders did not generally provide banks with specific voting instructions (Edwards and Fischer, 1994). With the introduction of the Kontrag law, however, German banks are unable to use voting power associated with custodian shares unless they have been authorized to do so. Regulatory reforms of proxy voting in Germany are potentially conducive to shareholder value but only in a specific context. The Kontrag law has undoubtedly reduced the power of banks—a specific category of shareholders who were almost always allied with management (Deeg, 1999; Fiss and Zajac, 2004; Gourevitch and Shinn, 2005: 164–7). On the other hand, however, large-controlling owners are unaffected by the Kontrag regulatory reforms since they never faced coordination problems, as compared with small-dispersed shareholders, to vote their equity stakes themselves. Large owners in Germany did not rely on the proxy voting of banks to protect themselves against takeovers, but on ownership concentration (Culpepper, 2011; see also Kogut and Walker, 2001).

In the second instance, the regulatory reforms of the Kontrag law have not necessarily promoted the interests of minority shareholders since they have in fact encouraged further ownership concentration in some German companies by eliminating all forms of deviations from the one share-one vote standard. The importance of institutional arrangements of voting rights in corporate governance reflects the process by which shareholders translate their equity stake into voting power (Yermack, 2010). There are three main forms of deviation from the one share-one vote principle: voting rights ceiling which caps the amount of votes any shareholder may cast regardless of the total number of stocks held; unequal voting rights which award multiple voting rights to specific categories of (usually long-term) shareholders; and non-voting shares which (usually) provide fixed dividends payments at the expense of participation in the affairs of the company (Goergen et al., 2005; Burkart and Lee, 2008). All forms of deviations from the one share-one vote standard have been eliminated with the passage of the Kontrag law in Germany.

The presence of deviations from the one share-one vote standard has been interpreted as strategic choices to deter takeovers and, thus, contrary to the interests of minority shareholders (Zingales, 1995; Nenova, 2003). However, the introduction of regulatory reforms designed to eliminate deviations from the one share-one vote standard should not be interpreted as a straightforward improvement of the rights of minority shareholders. The dominant ownership structure specific to a national system of systems of corporate governance shaped the dynamics of the consequences of regulatory reforms (Cools, 2004; Enriques and Volpin, 2007). The use of voting ceiling caps is best suited to settings characterized by ownership diffusion (Goergen et al., 2005: 252–3). Voting ceiling caps reflect managerial attempts at entrenchment in the context of ownership diffusion, thereby highlighting the divergence of interests between dispersed shareholders and managers (Morck et al., 1988; Davis, 1991). Unequal voting rights and non-voting shares, in contrast, constitute mechanisms by which large blockholders seek to create a gap between their ownership stake and their voting power (Zingales, 1995). Controlling shareholders can maintain their control over the strategic direction of companies at lower costs by raising additional equity funding from the greater public through unequal voting rights and non-voting shares. However, the effective use of unequal voting rights and non-voting shares presupposes the prior existence of some form of ownership concentration. The implication of the above discussion is that while the elimination of unequal voting rights in Germany has made it harder for large owners to control companies without committing funding, the abolition of voting ceilings caps has provided strong incentives for bidders to acquire large stakes in companies without fearing that their new position as controlling owner would not be diluted by limited voting power. The impact of the elimination of deviations from the one share-one vote standard is inconclusive (Burkart and Lee, 2008).

Similarly, and more broadly, Enriques and Volpin (2007) cast a critical eye on newly implemented regulatory reforms designed to improve the legal rights of minority shareholders in France, Germany, and Italy. Their skepticism reflects the presence of two types of agency costs faced by minority shareholders: separation of ownership from control and the incentives of controlling shareholders to capture private benefits of control (Roe, 2002). These two types of agency costs contribute to the destruction of shareholder value, but their containment is shaped by different legal-institutional arrangements (Coffee, 2005). The issue is that regulatory reforms in these three continental European economies have primarily aimed at controlling the behavior of opportunistic managers, not at curtailing the expropriation incentives of controlling shareholders (Conac et al., 2007). Legal empowerment of shareholders is more likely to translate into shareholder value in the presence of ownership diffusion, thereby highlighting how the same regulatory reform may engender different consequences based on the importance of ownership structure as a contextual variable.

Hard and Soft Law in Corporate Governance

Corporate governance regulation is embedded in the legal apparatus of corporate law which primarily deals with five common characteristics of business associations, which are: legal personality, limited liability, transferable shares, delegated management under a board structure, and the ownership structure (Hansmann and Kraakman, 2004). One corporation can have, at once, all these characteristics, i.e. a large-scale publicly held firm. Others might have some deviations from one or more of the five characteristics to adjust the contingencies of the business, such as a small or closely held (i.e. private) firms, and cooperatives. Yet, despite differences in the forms of business organization, the baseline regulatory paradigm provides legal mechanisms to control these five core attributes of firms and to constrain corporate actors by requiring them not to take particular actions, or engage in transactions, that could harm the interests of other stakeholders (i.e. shareholders, and other corporate constituents such as management, employees, and creditors).

There are two broad regulatory mechanisms in corporate governance (Aguilera and Cuervo-Cazurra, 2009; Hopt, 2011). Regulation can take the form of statutory rules (i.e. hard law) which relate to prohibiting some kind of behavior and are characterized by the use of a "one size fits all" approach designed to address common governance problems; regulation can also constitute standards of best practice, leaving the compliance determination to firms, i.e. they are not legally binding by nature, and are characterized by the "comply-or-explain" approach that allows firms to carry out the governance mechanism that best fits their particular contingencies (Kraakman et al., 2004).

The importance of the soft law approach in corporate governance can be traced to the launch of the Cadbury Committee Report (FRC, 1992) by the Financial Reporting Council in the United Kingdom and of the Principles of Corporate Governance (ALI, 1992) by the American Law Institute in the United States. Aguilera and Cuervo-Cazurra (2004) highlight how corporate governance codes are designed to address deficiencies in corporate governance systems by recommending comprehensive sets of norms on good practices to firms in different regulatory environments. The content of many of these codes stipulates guiding principles on board composition, ownership structure, shareholder activism, and executive compensation schemes (see also Aguilera and Cuervo-Cazurra, 2009). Indeed, most advanced and emerging economies have relied on codes of good governance based on the "comply-or-explain" principle as an expediting mechanism to update their corporate governance regulation. For example, according to the European Corporate Governance Institute, 88 industrialized and developing countries had issued 310 corporate governance codes and/or principles by 2011. The spread of corporate governance codes was particularly encouraged by the European Union (EU) Directive 2006/46/EC, which promotes their application by requiring that listed companies refer in their corporate governance statement to a code and that they report on their application of that code on a "comply-or-explain" basis.

It is important to inquire why soft law prevails on the international corporate agenda when national regulators and stock exchange commissions have the power to enact hard laws that legally bind governance practices. According to Ogus (1995: 97), the materialization of self-regulation is justified in terms of public interest where three conditions are satisfied. First, that the activities of the firm are affected by some form of market failure, in particular negative externalities and information asymmetries. Second, that private law is inadequate or too costly to correct under failure. Third, that self-regulation is a better method to solve problems instead of using public regulation. Hart (1995: 688) advances the case for the government to impose statutory rules on corporate governance on the grounds that "the world has changed" is not strong, as it does not allow firms to adapt governance mechanisms to their contingencies in an efficient manner. Indeed, the UK Corporate Governance Code, when defining the "comply-or-explain" approach seeks to recognize that "... an alternative to following a provision may be justified in particular circumstances if good governance can be achieved by other means. A condition of doing so is that the reasons for it should be explained clearly and carefully to shareholders, who may wish to discuss the position with the company and whose voting intentions may be influenced as a result" (FCR, 2006).

In an opposite direction and despite its new voluntary code of good governance (i.e. "Principles of Corporate Governance," NYSE, 2010), the federal government in the United States has developed and implemented substantial regulation to set stringent requirements to achieve extensive oversight of corporate management by the board and audit committee (i.e. Sarbanes-Oxley Act 2002), to limit executive pay and the firm's control of the proxy process (i.e. Dodd-Frank Act 2010), and to ban specific corporate governance provisions (e.g. staggered boards and CEO duality) (Shareholder Bill of Rights Act and Shareholder Empowerment Act 2009) (Larcker et al., 2011).

Therefore, a relevant question is what factors may account for country's choice of approach to regulation. Two broad perspectives have been identified. First, the choice of regulation reflects the ability of regulated interest groups to capture the state (Djankov et al., 2002). Regulation is conceptualized as a less efficient mechanism where interest groups (regulated firms) may extract considerable private benefits if they can formulate and themselves enforce the relevant legislation. The incentives of regulated groups, as well as their ability to capture the state, entail a path-dependent evolution in the introduction and implementation of new regulatory mechanism (see e.g. Bebchuk and Roe, 1999).

Second, various institutional factors may affect a country's choice of approach to regulation. For example, in the UK there is a long tradition of self-regulation (Cheffins, 1997). In addition to the existence of powerful professional and shareholders associations, such as the National Association of Pension Funds (NAPF), the Association of British Insurers (ABI) has been granted important powers of self-regulation. Although their influence on corporate governance matters is open to debate (Becht et al., 2009), their presence, together with other institutional features of the UK economy such as strong networks within the City of London,[1] and the path-dependence character of the self-regulation mechanism, provide the foundations for the UK governance regulation emphasized by the "comply-or-explain" principle.

Another important institutional factor that might explain the distinction between the regulatory arrangements is the characteristics of institutional investors. Aguilera and Williams (2006) argue that the attitude and behavior of shareholder value-oriented institutional investors constitute the missing link to understand the dissimilarities between UK and US corporate governance. In the British case, pension funds and insurance companies, which are long term oriented, are the dominant categories of investors. On the other hand, mutual funds, which have a shorter-term outlook, are dominant in the American capital markets. In the former, corporate governance codes are suited to long-term orientation of pension funds. In the United States, in contrast, listed companies increasingly have found themselves confronted by shareholders who want to influence corporate management both directly through activism, and indirectly, provoking further arguments for government regulation (Copland, 2011).

Another important question is whether hard and soft law is effective in triggering good corporate governance practices and in solving corporate governance problems. Corporate governance scandals and empirical studies show that compliance with rules (i.e. hard law) and standards (i.e. soft law) has not always translated into effective governance (Larcker and Tayan, 2011). Regarding hard law, an interesting example is the case of Enron (Coffee, 2002), which was compliant with NYSE requirements at the time of the corporate governance scandal in 2001. In the case of soft law, a recent study (RiskMetrics, 2009) concludes that the "comply-or-explain" approach formally adopted by the European Commission in 2006, while receiving strong acceptance from the corporate and the institutional investor community, suffers from implementation deficiencies, particularly concerning the level and quality of information on deviations by companies and a low level of shareholder monitoring.

Additionally, the corporate governance and financial literatures are not conclusive on whether these governance mechanisms, hard or soft law, have an effect on firm performance. On the one hand, Alves and Mendez (2004) find that the Portuguese code of corporate governance does not have a systematic effect on firm returns; yet, compliance with the structure and functioning of the board of directors is positive correlated with abnormal returns. DeJong et al. (2005) report that the Netherlands' self-regulation initiative had no effect on corporate governance practices nor on their relationship with value. On the other hand, Fernández-Rodríguez et al. (2004) suggest that the market reacts positively to announcements of compliance with the code of corporate governance in Spain. In the UK, Dedman (2000 and 2002) provides consistent evidence that, after the implementation of the recommendations of the Cadbury Committee, firms' governance practices reduced the agency cost of managerial entrenchment and enhanced board oversight with respect to the manipulation of accounting numbers and the discipline of the top executive. Additionally, Goncharov et al. (2006) show that firms with higher compliance are generally priced at a premium in Germany. These mixed and inclusive findings suggest the importance of the context in which firms are embedded (Aguilera et al., 2008). The same regulatory variables can result in different outcomes across contexts that are characterized by interacting institutions (Goyer, 2011; see also Goertz, 1994).

Thus, we have described two mechanisms of corporate governance regulation, namely the "one size fits all" approach from hard law and the "comply-or-explain" approach of soft law. In addition to these two "ideal" cases, there are also interesting hybrid forms of hard and soft-law. For example, in 2000, the Brazilian Stock Exchange (i.e. BMF & Bovespa), aiming to solve legal deficiencies in investment protection and to foster the capital market, designed a dual regulatory regime where firms can choose among four levels of listing requirements, offering progressively higher levels of minority shareholder protection (Gilson et al., 2011). The innovative dimension of the Brazilian market regulation is that it recognizes that some existing listed firms would find it difficult to adopt the new rules since they are quite demanding from a legal perspective compared to the traditional market rules. The BMF & Bovespa proposed two differentiated levels of corporate governance practices, level 1 and level 2 (Carvalho and Pennacchi, 2012). This innovative regulatory duality provides protection to entrenched owners (who would otherwise be opposed to the reforms), while advancing a new governance regulation in order to attract new sources of capital.

Conclusion

In this chapter, we have presented an analytical survey of the main forces shaping regulation and how in turn regulation becomes an important contextual factor for corporate governance practices. However, we caution against becoming overly structuralist for two reasons. First, as we have shown in the last section on soft versus hard law, there are plenty of unwritten regulations, such as implicit codes of conduct, that mandate how economic exchanges take place. These soft norms fill in voids for formal hard law and often become an important mechanism for innovation in the regulatory sphere. Second, firms and actors within firms have the ability to make choices within institutional constraints and more precisely within regulatory choices (see e.g. Whittington, 1988). Regulation has become increasingly important for issues of corporate governance, but its impact remains contextually bounded. We are referring not just to the radical choice of complying or not with regulation, but also to the degree to which firms internalize the regulations into their organizational and strategic firm choices. Hence, future research should pay attention to these complementary and substitutive relationships as well as to the levels of regulation internalization.

There are two interesting areas of research on regulation and corporate governance that need further attention. The first concerns the regulatory existence of the multinational firm, and related multinational enterprise ventures, and how they structure their governance, not only around foreign subsidiaries in different regulatory regimes but also in relation to other international governance forms such as strategic alliances and equity joint ventures. Second, in the currently shifting world of nations where emerging market firms from state capitalism systems are becoming established in the traditionally industrialized world, and also turning into world leaders in many different industrial sectors, we need to better understand how their often hybrid forms of public-private ownership, professional-political managers, and overall different rules of operating within the governance realm might affect not only their competitiveness but also those of non-emerging market firms (*The Economist*, 2012).

Note

1. We thank Igor Filatotchev for highlighting this point.

References

Adams, R., and Ferreira, D. (2008). "One Share-One Vote: The Empirical Evidence," *Review of Finance*, 12(1): 51–91.

Aguilera, R. V. (2009). "Codes of Good Governance," *Corporate Governance: An International Review*, 17(3): 376–87.

AGUILERA, R. V., and CUERVO-CAZURRA, A. (2004). "Codes of Good Governance Worldwide: What is the Trigger?" *Organization Studies*, 25: 417–46.

—— and JACKSON, G. (2003). "The Cross-National Diversity of Corporate Governance: Dimensions and Determinants," *Academy of Management Review*, 28(3): 447–65.

—— and WILLIAMS, C. (2006). "Corporate Governance and Social Responsibility: A Comparative Analysis of the U.K. and the U.S.," *Corporate Governance: An International Review*, 14(3): 147–57.

—— FILATOTCHEV, I., GOSPEL, H., and JACKSON, G. (2008). "An Organizational Approach to Comparative Corporate Governance: Costs, Contingencies, and Complementarities," *Organization Science*, 19(3): 475–92.

ALI (1992). *Principles of Corporate Governance: Analysis and Recommendations*. Philadelphia, PA: American Law Institute Publishers.

ALVES, C., and MENDES, V. (2004). "Corporate Governance Policy and Company Performance: The Portuguese Case," *Corporate Governance: An International Review*, 12: 290–301.

AOKI, M. (2001). *Toward a Comparative Institutional Analysis*. Cambridge, MA: MIT Press.

BEBCHUK, L., and ROE, M. (1999). "A Theory of Path Dependence in Corporate Ownership and Governance," *Stanford Law Review*, 52(1): 127–70.

BECHT, M., FRANKS, J., MAYER, C., and ROSSI, S. (2009). "Returns to Shareholder Activism: Evidence from a Clinical Study of the Hermes UK Focus Fund," *The Review of Financial Studies*, 22(8): 3093–129.

BERLE, A. A., and MEANS, G. C. (1932). *The Modern Corporation and Private Property*. New York: Commerce Clearing House.

BREYER, S. G. (1982). *Regulation and its Reform*. Cambridge, MA: Harvard University Press.

BURKART, M., and LEE, S. (2008). "One Share-One Vote: The Theory," *Review of Finance*, 12: 1–49.

CAPRON, L., and GUILLÉN, M. (2009). "National Corporate Governance Institutions and Post-Acquisition Target Reorganization," *Strategic Management Journal*, 30(8): 803–33.

CARPENTER, D. P. (2001). *The Forging of Bureaucratic Autonomy: Reputations, Networks, and Policy Innovation in Executive Agencies 1862–1928*. Princeton: Princeton University Press.

CARRIGAN, C., and COGLIANESE, C. (2011). "The Politics of Regulation: From New Institutionalism to New Governance," *Annual Review of Political Science*, 14: 107–29.

CARVALHO, A. G., and PENNACCHI, G. G. (2012). "Can a Stock Exchange Improve Corporate Behavior? Evidence from Firms," *Journal of Corporate Finance*, 18(4): 883–903.

CHEFFINS, B. R. (1997). *Company Law: Theory, Structure, and Operation*. Oxford: Clarendon Press.

CIOFFI, J., and HOEPNER, M. (2006). "The Political Paradox of Finance Capitalism: Interests, Preferences, and Center-Left Party Politics in Corporate Governance Reform," *Politics and Society*, 34: 463–502.

CLARK, G. L., and WOJCIK, D. (2007). *The Geography of Finance: Corporate Governance in the Global Marketplace*. Oxford: Oxford University Press.

COFFEE, J. (1989). "The Mandatory/Enabling Balance in Corporate Law: An Essay on the Judicial Role," *Columbia Law Review*, 89: 1618–91.

—— (1999). "Privatization and Corporate Governance: The Lessons from Securities Market Failure," *The Journal of Corporation Law*, 25: 1–39.

—— (2001). "Do Norms Matter? A Cross-Country Evaluation," *University of Pennsylvania Law Review*, 149(6): 2151–77.

—— (2002). "Understanding Enron: It's about the Gatekeepers, Stupid," *Business Lawyer*, 57: 1403–20.

—— (2005). "A Theory of Corporate Scandals: Why the USA and Europe Differ," *Oxford Review of Economic Policy*, 21: 198–211.

—— (2006). *Gatekeepers: The Professions and Corporate Governance*. New York: Oxford University Press.
CONAC, P., ENRIQUES, L., and GELTER, M. (2007). "Constraining Dominant Shareholders' Self-Dealing: The Legal Framework in France, Germany, and Italy," *European Company and Financial Law Review*, 4: 491–528.
COOLS, S. (2004). "The Real Difference in Corporate Law between the United States and Continental Europe: Distribution of Powers," Discussion Paper no. 490, Olin Center for Law, Business, and Economics, Harvard Law School.
COPLAND, J. R. (2011). *Proxy Monitor 2011: A Report on Corporate Governance and Shareholder Activism*. New York: Center for Legal Policy at the Manhattan Institute.
CULPEPPER, P. (2011). *Quiet Politics and Business Power: Corporate Control in Europe and Japan*. New York: Cambridge University Press.
DALTON, D. R., HITT, M. A., CERTO, S. T., and DALTON, C. M. (2007). "The Fundamental Agency Problem and its Mitigation: Independence, Equity, and the Market for Corporate Control," *Academy of Management Annals*, 1: 1–64.
DAVIS, G. (1991). "Agents without Principles? The Spread of the Poison Pill through the Intercorporate Networks," *Administrative Science Quarterly*, 36: 583–613.
DAVIS, S. M., LUKOMNIK, J., and PITT-WATSON, D. (2006). *The New Capitalists: How Citizen Investors are Reshaping the Corporate Agenda*. Boston: Harvard Business School Press.
DEDMAN, E. (2000). "An Investigation into the Determinants of UK Board Structure before and after Cadbury," *Corporate Governance: An International Review*, 8: 133–53.
—— (2002). "The Cadbury Committee Recommendations on Corporate Governance: A Review of Compliance and Performance Impacts," *International Journal of Management Reviews*, 4: 335–52.
DEEG, R. (1999). *Finance Capitalism Unveiled: Banks and the German Political Economy*. Ann Arbor: University of Michigan Press.
DEJONG, A., DEJONG, D. V., MERTERS, G., and WASLEY, C. E. (2005). "The Role of Self-Regulation in Corporation Governance: Evidence and Implications from The Netherlands," *Journal of Corporate Finance*, 11: 473–503.
Deminor Rating (2005). "Application of the One Share-One Vote Principle in Europe," Report Commissioned by the Association of British Insurers, Brussels.
DJANKOV, S., LA PORTA, R., LOPEZ-DE-SILANES, F., and SHLEIFER, A. (2002). "The Regulation of Entry," *The Quarterly Journal of Economics*, 117(1): 1–37.
DORF, M. C., and SABEL, C. F. (1998). "A Constitution of Democratic Experimentalism," *Columbia Law Review*, 98(2): 267–473.
DYCK, A., and ZINGALES, L. (2004). "Private Benefits of Control: An International Comparison," *Journal of Finance*, 59(2): 537–600.
Economist, The (2012). "Special Report on the Rise of State Capitalism," January 21–27.
EDWARDS, J., and FISCHER, K. (1994). *Banks, Finance and Investment in Germany*. New York: Cambridge University Press.
ENRIQUES, L. (2002). "Do Corporate Law Judges Matter? Some Evidence from Milan," *European Business Organization Law Review*, 3(4): 765–821.
—— and VOLPIN, P. (2007). "Corporate Governance Reforms in Continental Europe," *Journal of Economic Perspectives*, 21(1): 117–40.
ETZION, D., and DAVIS, G. (2008). "Revolving Doors: A Network Analysis of Corporate Officers and US Government Officials," *Journal of Management Inquiry*, 17(3): 157–61.

FAUVER, L., and FUERST, M. (2006). "Does Good Corporate Governance Include Employee Representation? Evidence from German Corporate Boards?" *Journal of Financial Economics*, 82(3): 673–710.

FERNÁNDEZ-RODRÍGUEZ, E., GÓMEZ-ANSÓN, S., and CUERVO-GARCÍA, A. (2004). "The Stock Market Reaction to the Introduction of Best Practices Codes by Spanish Firms," *Corporate Governance: An International Review*, 12(1): 29–46.

FIORETOS, O. (2010). "Capitalist Diversity and the International Regulation of Hedge Funds," *Review of International Political Economy*, 17(4): 696–723.

—— (2011). *Creative Reconstructions: Multilateralism and European Varieties of Capitalism after 1950*. Ithaca, NY: Cornell University Press.

FISS, P., and ZAJAC, E. (2004). "The Diffusion of Ideas over Contested Terrain: The (Non) Adoption of a Shareholder Value Orientation among German Firms," *Administrative Sciences Quarterly*, 49: 501–34.

FRC (1992). *Report of the Committee on the Financial Aspects of Corporate Governance*. London: Burgess Science Press.

GILSON, R. (2006). "Controlling Shareholders and Corporate Governance: Complicating the Comparative Taxonomy," *Harvard Law Review*, 119: 1641–79.

—— HANSMANN, H., and PARGENDLER, M. (2011). "Regulatory Dualism as a Development Strategy: Corporate Reform in Brazil, the United States, and the European Union," *Stanford Law Review*, 63: 475–536.

GLAESER, E. L., JOHNSON, S., and SHLEIFER, A. (2001). "Coase versus the Coasians." *Quarterly Journal of Economics*, 113(3): 853–99.

GOERGEN, M., MARTYNOVA, M., and RENNEBOOG, L. (2005). "Corporate Governance Convergence: Evidence from Takeover Regulation Reforms in Europe," *Oxford Review of Economic Policy*, 21: 243–68.

GOERTZ, GARY (1994). *Contexts of International Politics*. New York: Cambridge University Press.

GONCHAROV, I., WERNER, J. R., and ZIMMERMANN, J. (2006). "Does Compliance with the German Corporate Governance Code Have an Impact on Stock Valuation? An Empirical Analysis," *Corporate Governance: An International Review*, 14(5): 432–45.

GORDON, J. N. (1989). "The Mandatory Structure of Corporate Law," *Columbia Law Review*, 89: 1549–98.

GOUREVITCH, P. A., and SHINN, J. (2005). *Political Power and Corporate Control: The New Global Politics of Corporate Governance*. Princeton: Princeton University Press.

GOYER, M. (2006). "Varieties of Institutional Investors and National Models of Capitalism: The Transformation of Corporate Governance in France and Germany," *Politics and Society*, 34(3): 399–430.

—— (2011). *Contingent Capital: Short-Term Investors and the Evolution of Corporate Governance in France and Germany*. Oxford: Oxford University Press.

HALL, P. (2007). "The Evolution of Varieties of Capitalism in Europe," in B. Hancké, M. Rhodes, and M. Thatcher (eds.), *Beyond Varieties of Capitalism: Conflict, Contradictions, and Complementarities in the European Economy*. Oxford: Oxford University Press.

—— (2010). "Politics as a Process Structured in Space and Time." Paper presented at the 2010 Annual Meeting of the American Political Science Association, Washington, DC.

—— and GINGERICH, D. (2009). "Varieties of Capitalism and Institutional Complementarities in the Political Economy: An Empirical Analysis," *British Journal of Political Science*, 39(3): 449–82.

—— and Soskice, D. (eds.) (2001). *Varieties of Capitalism: The Institutional Foundations of Comparative Advantage*. Oxford: Oxford University Press.

—— and Thelen, K. (2009). "Institutional Change in Varieties of Capitalism." *Socio-Economic Review*, 7: 7–34.

Hansmann, H., and Kraakman, R. (2004). "Agency Problem and Legal Strategies," in R. Kraakman, P. Davies, H. Hansmann, G. Hertig, K. Hopt, H. Kanda, and E. Rock (eds.), *The Anatomy of Corporate Law: A Comparative and Functional Approach*. Oxford: Oxford University Press.

Hart, O. (1995). "Corporate Governance: Some Theory and Implications," *The Economic Journal*, 105(430): 678–89.

Hancké, B., Rhodes, M. and Thatcher, M. (2007). "Introduction: Beyond Varieties of Capitalism," in B. Hancké, M. Rhodes, and M. Thatcher (eds.), *Beyond Varieties of Capitalism: Conflict, Contradictions, and Complementarities in the European Economy*. Oxford: Oxford University Press.

Hoepner, M., and Krempel, L. (2004). "The Politics of the German Company Network." *Competition and Change*, 8(4): 339–56.

Hopt, K. (2011). "Comparative Corporate Governance: The State of the Art and International Regulation," *The American Journal of Comparative Law*, 59(1): 1–73.

Jackson, H. (2007). "Variation in the Intensity of Financial Regulation," *Yale Journal of Regulation*, 24(2): 253–90.

Jensen, M. C., and Meckling, W. (1976). "Theory of the Firm: Managerial Behavior, Agency Costs and Ownership Structure," *Journal of Financial Economics*, 3: 305–60.

Johnson, S., , and Kwak, J. (2010). *13 Bankers: The Wall Street Takeover and the Next Financial Meltdown*. New York: Pantheon Books.

—— LaPorta, R., López-de-Silanes, F., and Shleifer, A. (2000). "Tunneling," *American Economic Review*, 90: 22–7.

Jordana, J., and Levi-Faur, D. (eds.) (2004). *The Politics of Regulation: Institutions and Regulatory Reforms for Age of Governance*. Northampton, MA: Edward Elgar.

—— —— and Fernandez Marin, X. (2011). "The Global Diffusion of Regulatory Agencies: Channels of Transfer and Stages of Diffusion," *Comparative Political Studies*, 44(10): 1343–69.

Kagan, R. (1994). "Regulatory Enforcement," in D. Rosenbloom and R. Schwartz (eds.), *Handbook of Regulation and Administrative Law*. New York: Marcel Dekker.

Kogut, B., and Walker, G. (2001). "The Small World of Germany and the Durability of National Networks," *American Sociological Review*, 66: 317–35.

Kraakman, R., Davies, P., Hansmann, H., Hertig, G., Hopt, K., Kanda, H., and Rock, E. (eds.), (2004). *The Anatomy of Corporate Law: A Comparative and Functional Approach*. Oxford: Oxford University Press.

Laffont, J., and Tirole, J. (1991). "The Politics of Government Decision-Making: A Theory of Regulatory Capture," *The Quarterly Journal of Economics*, 106(4): 1089–127.

La Porta, R., López-de-Silanes, F., and Shleifer, A. (2006). "What Works in Securities Laws?" *Journal of Finance*, 61: 1–32.

—— —— —— and Vishny, R. (2000). "Investor Protection and Corporate Governance," *Journal of Financial Economics*, 58: 3–27.

Larcker, D. F., Ormazabal, G., and Taylor, D. J. (2011). "The Market Reaction to Corporate Governance Regulation," *Journal of Financial Economics*, 101(2): 431–48.

—— and Tayan, B. (2011). "Seven Myths of Corporate Governance," Rock Center for Corporate Governance at Stanford University Closer Look Series: Topics, Issues and

Controversies in Corporate Governance No. CGRP-16. Available at SSRN: <http://ssrn.com/abstract=1856869>.

Levi-Faur, D. (2005). "The Global Diffusion of Regulatory Capitalism," *The Annals of the American Academy of Political and Social Science*, 598(1): 12–32.

Levi-Faur, D. (2006). "Regulatory Capitalism: The Dynamics of Change beyond Telecoms and Electricity," *Governance*, 19(3): 497–525.

Levy, J. D. (2006). *The State after Statism: New State Activities in the Age of Liberalization*. Cambridge, MA: Harvard University Press.

Lütz, S. (2004). "Convergence within National Diversity: The Regulatory State in Finance," *Journal of Public Policy*, 24(2): 169–97.

Majone, G. (1994). "The Rise of the Regulatory State in Europe," *West European Politics*, 17(3): 77–101.

—— (1997). "From the Positive to the Regulatory State: Causes and Consequences of Changes in the Mode of Governance," *Journal of Public Policy*, 17(2): 139–67.

Maurice, M., Sellier, F., and Silvestre, J. J. (1986). *The Social Foundations of Industrial Power: A Comparison of France and Germany*. Cambridge, MA: MIT Press.

Mayer, C. (2001). "Firm Control," in J. Schwalbach (ed.), *Corporate Governance: Essays in Honor of Horst Albach*. Berlin: Springer-Verlag.

McCubbins, M., and Schwartz, T. (1984). "Congressional Oversight Overlooked: Police Patrols versus Fire Alarms," *American Journal of Political Science*, 28: 165–79.

Milhaupt, C., and Pistor, K. (2008). *Law and Capitalism: What Corporate Crises Reveal about Legal Systems and Economic Development around the World*. Chicago: Chicago University Press.

Moe, T. (1985). "Control and Feedback in Economic Regulation," *American Political Science Review*, 26(2): 197–224.

—— (1987). "An Assessment of the Positive Theory of Congressional Dominance," *Legislative Studies Quarterly*, 12(3): 475–520.

Morck, R., Shleifer, A. and Vishny, R.W. (1988). "Management Ownership and Market Valuation: An Empirical Analysis," *Journal of Financial Economics*, 20: 293–315.

Nenova, T. (2003). "The Value of Corporate Voting Rights and Control: A Cross-Country Analysis," *Journal of Financial Economics*, 68: 325–51.

NYSE (2010). "Report of the New York Stock Exchange Commission on Corporate Governance." Available at <http://www.nyse.com/pdfs/CCGReport.pdf>, September 23.

OECD (1999). *OECD Employment Outlook*. Paris: OECD.

Ogus, A. (1995). "Rethinking Self-Regulation," *Oxford Journal of Legal Studies*, 15(1): 97–108.

Olson, M. (1965). *The Logic of Collective Action*. Cambridge, MA: Harvard University Press.

Peltzman, S. (1976). "Toward a More General Theory of Regulation," *Journal of Law and Economics*, 19: 211–40.

RiskMetrics (2009). "Study on Monitoring and Enforcement Practices in Corporate Governance in the Member States." Available at <http://ec.europa.eu/internal_market/company/docs/ecgforum/studies/comply-or-explain-090923_en.pdf>.

Roe, M. (1999). "Codetermination and German Securities Markets," in M. Blair and M. Roe (eds.), *Employees and Corporate Governance*. Washington, DC: Brookings Institution Press.

—— (2000). "Political Preconditions to Separating Ownership from Corporate Control," *Stanford Law Review*, 53: 539–606.

—— (2001). "Rents and their Corporate Consequences," *Stanford Law Review*, 53: 1463–94.

—— (2002). "Corporate Law's Limits," *Journal of Legal Studies*, 31: 233–71.

—— (2003). *Political Determinants of Corporate Governance: Political Context, Corporate Impact*. New York: Oxford University Press.

—— (2006). "Legal Origins, Politics, and Stock Markets," *Harvard Law Review*, 120: 462–527.
—— (2007). "Juries and the Political Economy of Legal Origins," *Journal of Comparative Economics*, 35: 294–308.
—— and GILSON, R. (1999). "Lifetime Employment: Labor Peace and the Evolution of Japanese Corporate Governance," *Columbia Law Review*, 99: 508–40.
ROSSI, S., and VOLPIN, P. (2004). "Cross-Country Determinants of Mergers and Acquisitions," *Journal of Financial Economics*, 74(2): 277–304.
ROUBINI, N., and MIHM, S. (2010). *Crisis Economics: A Crash Course in the Future of Finance*. New York: Penguin Press.
SCHMIDT, V. A. (2009). "Putting the Political Back into the Political Economy by Bringing the State Back Yet Again," *World Politics*, 61(3): 516–48.
SCHOLZ, J. (1984). "Cooperation, Deterrence, and the Ecology of Regulatory Enforcement," *Law and Society Review*, 18: 179–224.
SHLEIFER, A., and VISHNY, R. W. (1997). "A Survey of Corporate Governance," *The Journal of Finance*, 52(2): 737–83.
STIGLER, G. J. (1971). "The Theory of Economic Regulation," *The Bell Journal of Economics and Management Science*, 2(1): 3–21.
—— (1983). "Nobel Lecture: The Process and Progress of Economics," *Journal of Political Economy*, 91(4): 529–54.
THATCHER, M. (2002). "Regulation after Delegation: Independent Regulatory Agencies in Europe," *Journal of European Public Policy*, 9(6): 954–72.
—— and STONE SWEET, A. (2002). "Delegation to Independent Regulatory Agencies: Pressures, Functions and Contextual Mediation," *West European Politics*, 25(1): 125–47.
VALDIVIESO DEL REAL, R. (2009). "The Evolution of the Spanish and British Electricity Sectors: An Analysis of the Market for Corporate Control and Human Resource Management Practices in a Liberalized Environment," Ph.D., Department of Management, Birkbeck College, University of London, London.
VISCUSI, W. K. (1983). *Risk by Choice: Regulating Health and Safety in the Workplace*. Cambridge, MA: Harvard University Press.
VOGEL, S. (1996). *Free Markets, More Rules: Regulatory Reform in Advanced Industrial Countries*. Ithaca, NY: Cornell University Press.
—— (2001). "The Crisis of German and Japanese Capitalism: Stalled on the Road to the Liberal Model?" *Comparative Political Studies*, 34(10): 1103–33.
WEINGAST, B., and MORAN, M. (1983). "Bureaucratic Discretion or Congressional Control: Regulatory Policymaking by the FTC," *Journal of Political Economy*, 91: 765–800.
—— (1989). *Bureaucracy: What Government Agencies Do and Why They Do It*. New York: Basic Books.
WHITLEY, R. (1999). *Divergent Capitalisms: The Social Structuring and Change of Business Systems*. Oxford: Oxford University Press.
WHITTINGTON, R. (1988). "Environmental Structure and Theories of Strategic Choice," *Journal of Management Studies*, 25(6): 521–36.
WILSON, J. Q. (1980). *The Politics of Regulation*. New York: Basic Books.
YERMACK, D. (2010). "Shareholder Voting and Corporate Governance," *Annual Review of Financial Economics*, 2: 103–25.
ZINGALES, L. (1995). "What Determines the Value of Corporate Votes?" *Quarterly Journal of Economics*, 110(4): 1047–73.
—— (1998). "Why it's Worth Being in Control," in G. Bickerstaffe (ed.), *Mastering Finance*. London: Pearson Education.

CHAPTER 3

THE HISTORY OF CORPORATE GOVERNANCE

BRIAN R. CHEFFINS

THERE is no definitive historical treatment of corporate governance and there may never be one, given the vastness of the subject. Corporate governance has been with us since the use of the corporate form created the possibility of conflict between investors and managers (Wells, 2010: 1251). The history of corporate governance correspondingly extends back at least to the formation of the East India Company, the Hudson's Bay Company, the Levant Company, and the other major chartered companies launched in the 16th and 17th centuries. Addressing all relevant aspects of this history in a systematic way would be a daunting challenge. *A History of Corporate Governance Around the World* (Morck, 2005) illustrates the point. Despite being 687 pages in length, the volume only deals with 11 countries and only addresses one corporate governance issue in detail, this being share ownership patterns.

This chapter, rather than surveying the history of corporate governance in a general way, focuses on the process through which debates about managerial accountability, board structure, and shareholder rights became channeled through the term "corporate governance." In so doing, it describes how a phrase that only came into vogue in the 1970s in a single country—the United States—became within 25 years the subject of debate worldwide by academics, regulators, executives, and investors. The chapter traces developments occurring between the mid-1970s and the end of the 1990s, by which point "corporate governance" was well-entrenched as academic and regulatory shorthand. The analysis is necessarily American in orientation, given that corporate governance only acquired a strong international dimension in the 1990s. The chapter concludes by bringing matters up to date and by commenting briefly on corporate governance's future.

Corporate Governance Comes on to the Agenda

In the decades immediately following World War II, the US experienced a prolonged economic boom and its leading corporations grew rapidly. Amidst the widespread corporate prosperity, the internal governance of companies was not a high priority (Cheffins, 2009: 6) and the phrase "corporate governance" was not in use (Greenough and Clapman, 1980: 917). With the "managed corporations" that were in the US economic vanguard during this era "managers led, and directors and shareholders followed (Pound 1995: 91)." Boards, absent an outright corporate crisis, were expected to be collegial and supportive of management, a reasonable presupposition given that top executives strongly influenced the selection of directors (Seligman, 1987: 330–2). As for stockholders, the retail investors who dominated share registers were "known for their indifference to everything about the companies they own except dividends and the approximate price of the stock" (Livingston, 1958: 81).

The federal Securities and Exchange Commission (SEC) brought corporate governance on to the official reform agenda in the mid-1970s. By 1976, the year the term "corporate governance" first appeared in the Federal Register (Ocasio and Joseph, 2005: 167), the official journal of the federal government, the SEC was beginning to treat managerial accountability issues as part of its regulatory remit. In 1974, the SEC brought proceedings against three outside directors of Penn Central—a railway which had diversified into pipelines, hotels, industrial parks, and commercial real estate—alleging that they had misrepresented the company's financial condition under federal securities law by failing to discover a wide range of misconduct perpetrated by Penn Central executives (Schwartz, 1976: 399–401). Penn Central had gone bankrupt in 1970, with many criticizing the company's board for its passivity (Seligman, 1982: 536–7).

The discovery in the mid-1970s of widespread illicit payments by US corporations to foreign officials drew the SEC further into the corporate governance realm. Few, if any, of the outside directors of the numerous companies involved knew that the firms they were ostensibly directing were paying bribes, owing in part to falsification of corporate records of which senior executives were quite often aware (Seligman, 1982: 537). The widespread corporate bribery represented, according to a 1976 SEC report, "frustration of our system of corporate accountability" (Seligman, 1982: 542). The federal agency resolved numerous cases it brought with settlements where the companies involved undertook to make board-level changes, such as the appointment of additional outside directors and the creation of an audit committee (Sommer, 1977: 130–1). Also, in 1976 the SEC prevailed upon the New York Stock Exchange (NYSE) to amend its listing requirements to require each listed company to maintain an audit committee composed of independent directors and the NYSE complied.

The chairman of the New York Stock Exchange said in 1977 the greatest challenge facing US business and private enterprise generally might be "The prospect of pervasive government supervision and control over corporate governance and management" (*Chicago Tribune*, 1977). Indeed, the SEC held that year six weeks' worth of hearings into "shareholder participation in the corporate electoral process and corporate governance generally," receiving in the process information from over 300 corporations, individuals, public interest groups, and law firms (Securities and Exchange Commission, 1980: A-1–A-2). Ultimately, though, the SEC refrained from orchestrating major changes, with key reforms being restricted to requiring publicly traded firms to disclose information on the independence of their directors and the use of audit, nomination, and compensation committees (Seligman, 1982: 534, 550).

Harold Williams, who was appointed SEC chairman in 1977 by Democratic President Jimmy Carter, made numerous references in speeches to corporate governance and maintained that an "ideal" board would have only one managerial appointee (the chief executive officer) and would establish an audit committee, a nomination committee, and a compensation committee. He was reluctant, however, to force his views on the corporate world and instead advocated voluntary reform by corporations (Kripke, 1981: 178; Seligman, 1982: 548–50). Similarly, when in 1980 SEC staff issued a report on the SEC's 1977 corporate governance hearings (Securities and Exchange Commission, 1980), the report generally refrained from recommending regulatory measures concerning board structure or related governance issues. Corporate governance-oriented law reform was, however, on the agenda elsewhere.

In 1978, Senator Howard Metzenbaum, chairman of the Judiciary Committee's Subcommittee on Citizens and Shareholder Rights and Remedies, appointed a "blue-ribbon" advisory committee on corporate governance composed of representatives of industry, consumers, shareholders, and labor. The advisory committee agreed that improvements in corporate governance were vital to the future of the economic system but failed to achieve a compromise on legislation to propose (Metzenbaum, 1981). Nevertheless, Caspar Weinberger, who served in the Nixon, Ford, and Reagan administrations, argued in 1979 that corporate governance had moved from a "fuzzy notion" to a candidate for a major Congressional battle (*Chicago Tribune*, 1979). Metzenbaum indeed introduced to Congress the Protection of Shareholders' Rights Act of 1980, a bill that prescribed minimum federal standards of corporate law for large public companies and contained provisions mandating an independent director majority on boards, requiring the establishment of audit and nomination committees composed solely of independent directors, and giving shareholders the right to nominate candidates for election to the board of directors (Metzenbaum, 1981: 932–3).

Debates in the US about corporate governance were not restricted to the corridors of power in Washington, DC. Ralph Nader, Mark Green, and Joel Seligman's (1976) *Taming the Giant Corporation*, a book that likely provided the earliest available theorization of the term "corporate governance" (Ocasio and Joseph, 2005: 167), spelled out a legal image of corporate governance, with shareholders electing directors who were authorized to manage the corporation, who in turn would delegate as appropriate to executives serving as corporate officers. Nader et al. (1976) argued the legal model bore little relation to the practical reality of a dysfunctional "corporate autocracy" oriented around executives where "checks upon management have all but disappeared," resulting in "irrational decisions, hurried decisions, decisions based upon inadequate factual analysis or executive self-favoritism" (Nader et al., 1976: 77). They maintained that corporate governance should be reformed through the enactment of federal laws returning the board to its historical role as internal auditor of the corporation responsible for constraining management from violations of law and breaches of trust (Nader et al., 1976: 119). Their prescription for change resembled that offered by Melvin Eisenberg in an influential 1976 book on corporate law where he advocated, without specifically invoking the cause of corporate governance, replacing the received legal model of the board with a "monitoring" model where a majority of directors would be independent of management and the primary task of boards would be to foster managerial accountability (Eisenberg, 1976: 164–5, 174–7).

An American Bar Association corporate law subcommittee, animated by "current concerns in areas of public policy and emerging trends of corporate governance," issued in 1976 a *Corporate Director's Guidebook* that recommended that there be substantial outside director representation on boards and that executive directors be excluded from audit, compensation, and nominating committees boards established (Subcommittee on the Functions and Responsibilities of Directors, 1976: 11; Small, 2011: 133). The following year the American Assembly, a Columbia University think tank, issued a report characterized by the *New York Times* as "the first draft of a new constitution for corporations" (*New York Times*, 1977) that provided the departure point for a 1978 symposium on "Corporate Governance in America." In 1978, the Business Roundtable, a group established in 1974 to represent the views of 180 chief executive officers of major corporations, issued a statement on "The Role and Composition of Directors of the Large Publicly Owned Corporation" that discussed the place of the board in "the corporate governance triad of shareowners/directors/operating management" and acknowledged that boards of public companies should typically be composed of a majority of non-management directors and should establish audit, compensation, and nomination committees dominated by outside directors (Business Roundtable, 1978: 2089, 2108).

The American Law Institute (ALI), a private organization composed of practicing lawyers, academics, and judges that produces scholarly work to clarify and modernize the law, committed itself in principle in 1978 to undertake a project on corporate governance (Seligman, 1987: 342–3; Small, 2011: 135) and followed up by organizing in 1980 a conference co-sponsored with the American Bar Association and the New York Stock Exchange that senior corporate executives, academics, lawyers, and government officials attended. There was at the conference a consensus in favor of the ALI's efforts, with business community support arising in part from a belief the ALI could provide, at least in comparison with legislative proposals Congress might come to consider, a restrained response to the events of the 1970s. As one chief executive said, "We're in a period of transition and instability in corporate governance. We might as well have it happen in the way that will remake the corporation in a way we'd like" (*New York Times*, 1980). A political earthquake would soon mean the business community would be less conciliatory to the ALI project.

Corporate Governance Reform: A 1980s Counter-Reaction

In 1980, William Greenough, trustee of a major pension fund and a director of the New York Stock Exchange, said he believed "the battle over governance is as fundamental as anything that has happened on the corporate scene in decades" (Greenough, 1980: 74). A political shift to the right, exemplified by Ronald Reagan's election to the presidency that year, would rapidly change the parameters of debate and effectively ended the 1970s movement for corporate governance reform. The Protection of Shareholders' Rights Act of 1980 stalled in Congress, and, as Senator Metzenbaum acknowledged in 1981, with Congress having become more conservative, it was unlikely to pass legislation of a similar sort for the foreseeable future (*Los Angeles Times*, 1981). Likewise, the SEC seemed unlikely to pursue corporate governance reform with great vigor, with John Shad, Reagan's choice as chairman, saying in 1981 that his predecessor Harold Williams "was identified very much with corporate governance, and I hope to be identified with capital formation" (*Wall Street Journal*, 1981). In the early 1980s debates about corporate governance reform correspondingly focused largely on the ALI's corporate governance project (Weiss, 1984: 1). The deregulatory impulse was in evidence here as well.

The ALI's corporate governance "reporters"—academic members of the ALI drafting on its behalf—released their first public output, Tentative Draft No. 1, in 1982. The corporate world reacted with horror. While the New York Stock Exchange had co-sponsored the 1980 national conference that set the stage for the ALI project, its board of directors declared its unanimous opposition to Tentative Draft No. 1 being placed on the agenda at the ALI's next annual meeting for ALI members to endorse (Andrews, 1982: 35). The Business Roundtable likewise urged its members to oppose ALI adoption of the draft and issued a paper strongly criticizing the document (Seligman, 1987: 345).

One explanation for the strong counter-reaction was that, with the threat of federal corporate governance reform having abruptly abated, various business leaders felt they could abandon backing restrained ALI-led change and oppose regulatory reform outright (Seligman, 1987: 345, 359–60). Corporate executives, however, were also alarmed at the content of Tentative Draft No. 1 and feared that ALI policy missteps could be implemented as formal legal doctrine by the courts and by legislators (Bainbridge, 1993: 1049). In particular, concerns were expressed that Tentative Draft No. 1's treatment of directors' duties and litigation procedure would expand markedly the liability risk directors faced (Seligman, 1987: 363–4, 377–8). Also, critics from the business community said that Tentative Draft No. 1, which proposed mandatory rules requiring boards to have a majority of independent directors, to establish audit and nomination committees, and to refrain from doing more on the managerial front than overseeing senior executives, failed to make due allowance for beneficial governance innovations already occurring voluntarily in US public companies and for wide variations that could appropriately exist regarding the functioning of boards (Mofsky and Rubin, 1983: 174–6).

ALI critics from the business community had vocal academic allies who were analyzing corporate law from a new, market-oriented "law and economics" perspective (Macey, 1993: 1213). While the reporters on the ALI corporate governance project avoided spelling out explicitly their own normative model of corporate governance (West, 1984: 638–41), Adolf Berle and Gardiner Means' (1932) classic *The Modern Corporation and Private Property* was, consistent with mainstream academic thought in the corporate law area, the intellectual departure point (Mofsky and Rubin, 1983: 180). Berle and Means' contention that ownership had typically separated from managerial control in large US public companies dominated the research agenda of American corporate law scholars for 50 years following its publication, with the inference typically being drawn that without robust regulation shareholders would be short-changed by powerful executives (Cheffins, 2004: 40–4).

The corporate law academics who initially embraced economic analysis rejected the Berle and Means' (1932) inspired pro-regulation orthodoxy that underpinned the ALI corporate governance project at its inception. As Jonathan Macey, a leading law and economics scholar, said, "the law and economics movement was replacing the traditional view that shareholders were helpless pawns ruthlessly exploited by management" (Macey, 1993: 1225). Agency cost theory was highly influential in this context, with economically inclined corporate law professors (e.g. Fischel, 1982: 1261–4) taking their cue from papers by Jensen and Meckling (1976) and Fama (1980) that offered intellectually elegant accounts of various market-oriented limitations on the exercise of managerial discretion. Law and economics scholars correspondingly criticized the initial ALI corporate governance proposals on the basis that the ALI reporters had ignored the pressures market forces exert on those running public companies to establish governance structures that shareholders value (Easterbrook, 1984: 542, 555–7). Law and economics scholars also chastised the ALI for proposing board reform without taking into account empirical evidence on point and for failing to make the case in an explicit or convincing way that fostering litigation would improve on the decisions made by corporate executives or serve shareholders' interests generally (Wolfson, 1984: 632–3, 636–7).

Senior figures at the ALI were initially taken aback by the firestorm Tentative Draft No. 1 elicited (Manning, 1993: 1325), but the ALI ultimately sought to mollify critics of its corporate governance project. It replaced the chief reporter responsible (Elson and Shakman, 1994: 1763) and added Ronald Gilson, a prominent law and economics scholar, as a reporter (Bainbridge, 1993: 1048), while the ALI corporate governance reporters recast the proposed mandatory guidance on board structure as mere recommendations (Karmel, 1984: 548–9). What E. Norman Veasey, Chief Justice of the Delaware Supreme Court from 1992 to 2004, characterized as a "very responsible process of dialogue and negotiation ensued" (Veasey, 1993: 1267), with management's views being channeled into the deliberative process by CORPRO, a panel of lawyers with close professional connections to the business community (Elson and Shakman, 1994: 1764–8).

Ultimately, the version of the ALI's *Principles of Corporate Governance: Analysis and Recommendations* approved in 1992 and published in 1994 was modified to the point where the contents closely resembled the existing law, meaning even formerly vociferous critics had relatively few complaints (Macey, 1993: 1224, 1232). By this time, however, the deliberations of the ALI had largely receded from wider view, with one law professor observing in 1989 that in relation to problems of corporate governance the "current debate over the ALI project offers no solution because it has bogged down over trivia" (Dent, 1989: 902). Other factors, however, were sustaining and accelerating corporate governance's rise to prominence.

Institutional Shareholders "Find" Corporate Governance

The law and economics scholars of the early 1980s who critiqued the Berle and Means-inspired pro-regulatory orthodoxy maintained that the widely acknowledged tendency of shareholders to eschew active involvement in corporate governance posed few dangers for investors because the market for corporate control combined with other market mechanisms to align substantially the interests of managers and shareholders (Fischel, 1982: 1264, 1267–8, 1276–80; Easterbrook, 1984). This stance was understandable, given the context. The 1980s, sometimes referred to as "the Deal Decade," was exemplified by bidders relying on aggressive, innovative financial and legal techniques to engineer takeover bids offering generous premiums to shareholders of target companies to secure voting control. Also, as the decade got under way it was widely acknowledged that shareholders were poorly positioned to play a pivotal role in overseeing potentially wayward executives (Kripke, 1981: 177, 193; Hessen, 1983: 288). Even a "shareholder democracy" advocate such as law professor Donald Schwartz conceded in a 1983 paper that "most sophisticated observers" assumed "that shareholder participation is not capable of working well because of its impracticability and because of the rational indifference of shareholders to participation in corporate affairs" (1983: 55, 65).

Shareholders, or more accurately institutional shareholders, would in fact become during the 1980s increasingly logical contenders to play a major corporate governance role. Enhanced voting power was one reason—the proportion of shares in US public companies institutional investors owned rose from 16 percent in 1965 to 47 percent in 1987 and again to 57 percent in 1994 (Useem, 1996: 25–6). The growth in stakes held by institutional investors also meant it was becoming more common for them to have shareholdings in particular companies that were large enough to preclude them from relying readily on the traditional "Wall Street Rule" and selling out when a company was poorly run (Black, 1990: 572–3; Useem, 1996: 6, 30). Institutional investors correspondingly began to develop a corporate governance agenda during the Deal Decade, with the market for corporate control being the initial setting (Wilcox, 1997: 46–7).

1980s executives, faced with the prospect of unwelcome takeover bids, often reacted defensively (Kahan and Rock, 2002: 74–5). In various instances, companies made "greenmail" payments to buy out putative bidders who had obtained a sizeable "toehold" stake. Companies also commonly introduced management entrenchment devices such as the poison pill to deter hostile takeover offers from being launched. A shareholder-oriented counter-reaction ensued. In 1984, Jesse Unruh, state treasurer of California, was outraged when Texaco, in which the California Public Employees Retirement System (Calpers) held a 1 percent stake, paid the Bass brothers, a potentially hostile suitor, a 12 percent premium over the market price for the Basses' 10 percent Texaco stake without offering the same opportunity to Calpers or other shareholders (Rosenberg, 1999: 99; Fox, 2009: 271–2). More generally, institutional investors often disposed of sizeable blocks of shares in takeovers and they wanted to protect the option to sell their stock in response to a premium-priced bid (*Wall Street Journal*, 1989).

Stifling the managerial counter-reaction to takeovers proved to be an uphill struggle. Only rarely were anti-takeover schemes that required a shareholder vote for adoption rejected outright (Black, 1990: 571). More generally, an economic downturn combined with a debt market chill to bring the merger wave of the 1980s to a halt and the deployment of takeover defenses, backed by anti-takeover statutes in many states, meant hostile bids were particularly hard hit (Kahan and Rock, 2002: 879–80). When shareholders used litigation to attack the adoption of defensive tactics in the courts, the judiciary generally upheld steps taken if outside directors exercising independent judgment endorsed what was done. This judicial stance helped to entrench the outside director as a key corporate governance player (Gordon, 2007: 1522–5).

Though shareholder efforts on the takeover front ultimately foundered, a shareholder-oriented corporate governance infrastructure nevertheless emerged. In 1985 Unruh and Calpers launched the Council of Institutional Investors (CII), an association of public pension funds, to act as a lobbying group for shareholder rights (Fox, 2009: 272). They did so with the encouragement of Robert A. G. Monks, who had just kicked off within the Department of Labor a controversial policy initiative that would ultimately result in pension fund trustees being under a legal onus to vote shares held (Rosenberg, 1999: 91–3, 99–100, 112–14). Monks, who fancied himself as "an entrepreneur of the idea of corporate governance," left the Department of Labor in 1985 and established Institutional Shareholder Services as a voting services company that would provide disinterested advice to institutional investors lacking the expertise to vote their shares in an informed manner (Rosenberg, 1999: 118–25). One fund manager had correctly anticipated the career change, telling Monks, "Guys like you, you go into government and start a forest fire and then you come and try to sell us all fire extinguishers" (Rosenberg, 1999: 117).

As the 1990s dawned, institutional investors broadened their corporate governance agenda in various ways. One change was the development and publication of policy statements for use as benchmarks to evaluate directors and boards (Wilcox, 1997: 49). Calpers and other major public pension funds also began urging boards to remove underperforming chief executives, and between 1991 and 1993 boards of prominent companies such as Westinghouse, American Express, IBM, Kodak, and General Motors complied (Pound, 1993: 1006, 1059).

During the early 1990s institutional investors additionally began to pressure companies to overhaul existing executive pay arrangements to replace a traditional bias toward "pay-for-size" in favor of pay-for-performance (Dobbin and Zorn, 2005: 189). The message got through, as a dramatic increase in equity-based compensation—most prominently the awarding of stock options—would increase markedly CEO pay-to-performance sensitivity (Holmstrom and Kaplan, 2001: 133; Gordon, 2007: 1530–1). Moreover, Calpers and other public pension funds, with the backing of various academics, lobbied for the relaxation of rules that reputedly created obstacles to shareholder intervention in corporate affairs (Zalecki, 1993: 840–1). In 1992, following three years' worth of debate, the SEC amended its regulations governing the solicitation of proxies to ensure institutional shareholders discussing privately particular investee companies would not have to comply with requirements imposed on parties seeking change through the proxy process, such as a potentially onerous obligation to file relevant documentation with the SEC to obtain advance clearance (Wilcox, 1997: 47).

The Economist said in a 1993 article entitled "Shareholders Call the Plays," "These are heady days for America's corporate governance enthusiasts" (*The Economist*, 1993). The potential for a rebalanced relationship between shareholders and executives, however, ultimately went unfulfilled in large measure. Public pension funds, which were by some distance the most vocal advocates of corporate governance intervention, constituted only a minority of institutional investors. Other US institutional shareholders—most prominently mutual funds and private pension funds—shied away from taking a "hands on" corporate governance role (Coffee, 1991: 1292–3; Useem, 1996: 54–61).

Overall, during the 1990s institutional shareholders typically spent only trivial amounts on their governance efforts, rarely acted in tandem when they interacted with companies, routinely disclaimed having the ability to resolve beneficially company-specific policy debates and did not seek representation on corporate boards (Black, 1998). Institutional shareholder activism was correspondingly restricted to participating episodically in behind-the-scenes discussions with executives, demanding periodically shareholder votes on contentious corporate governance practices and voting against policies management supported when a shareholder advisory service recommended doing so (Kahan and Rock, 2007: 1042–5, 1056–7). Regardless, the rise of institutional shareholders in the 1980s and early 1990s sharpened the focus on basic questions concerning the allocation of power within corporations and caused a shift in the vocabulary of corporate governance debate toward shareholders and shareholder returns (Ocasio and Joseph, 2005: 170–1).

AND ECONOMISTS TOO

A 2001 *Review of Financial Economics* survey of 25 years' worth of corporate governance literature observed the "sheer volume of papers that have been written on the subject makes the prospect of surveying corporate governance a daunting task" (Denis, 2001: 191). Nevertheless, economists were somewhat late joining the corporate governance bandwagon. A 1981 review of the published proceedings of the American Assembly's

1978 symposium on "Corporate Governance in America" observed "the focus of the book is so alien to the concerns of the academic economist that one's first reaction is to dismiss this book as another example of the mushiness we so often attribute to our colleagues in management" (Carroll, 1981: 1168). In a 1988 corporate governance literature review providing an annotated bibliography of 110 publications on point, not one was a paper from a major economics or finance journal (Cochran and Wartick, 1988: 36–63).

The fact that economists were relative latecomers to analysis of corporate governance seems odd given that Jensen and Meckling's 1976 paper on agency cost theory is the most widely cited in corporate governance research and Fama's 1980 paper on agency problems is also among the most frequently cited papers in the field (Durisin and Puzone, 2009: 270–2, 281–2). However, these papers did not mention "corporate governance" explicitly and distinguished economist Oliver Williamson remarked in a 1984 article that up to that point in time there had been a "failure to address the economics of corporate governance in microanalytic terms" (Williamson, 1984: 1197). Changing perceptions of the efficacy of the publicly traded company as an organizational form would soon help, however, to marry up economists and corporate governance.

A key theme in the pioneering work on agency costs was to explain how the widely held company thrived in spite of the apparent handicap of a separation of ownership and control, with emphasis being placed on how successfully boards, the market for managerial talent, and the market for corporate control addressed the potential divergence of interest between managers and shareholders (Jensen, 1983: 328–9, 331; Easterbrook, 1984: 543–6). The implicit message, then, was that there was no corporate governance problem to solve, which was why early law and economics scholars drew on agency theory scholarship to critique the ALI's reform efforts.

A 1992 presidential address by Jensen to the American Finance Association signaled that perceptions were shifting markedly among economists. (Jensen, 1993: 850, 852, 871) said "[s]ubstantial data support the proposition that the internal control systems of publicly held corporations have generally failed to cause managers to maximize efficiency and value" and observed that "[c]onflicts between managers and the firm's financial claimants were brought to center stage by the market for corporate control in the last two decades," while bemoaning "the shutdown of the capital markets as an effective mechanism for motivating change, renewal, and exit". Jensen (1993: 873) also argued "For those with a normative bent, making the internal control systems of corporations work is the major challenge facing economists and management scholars in the 1990s".

Growing awareness in the economics fraternity that there was something amiss with publicly traded companies that merited analysis did not guarantee that economists would adopt corporate governance nomenclature as they pursued their research. When the phrase first achieved prominence, it connoted a political structure to be governed and political characterizations of the firm were incongruent with mainstream economic theory (Ocasio and Joseph, 2005: 174). By the late 1980s, however, "governance" was becoming part of economists' lexicon, a trend reflected by Jensen and Jerold Warner using the term multiple times in a *Journal of Financial Economics* paper that served as the introduction for published proceedings from a 1987 conference entitled "The

Distribution of Power among Corporate Managers and Directors" (Jensen and Warner, 1988). By the early 1990s corporate governance was even being characterized as a "rapidly evolving social science" (*Wall Street Journal*, 1993).

The growing shareholder orientation of corporate governance helps to explain the transition. With institutional investor concerns about takeover defenses, board structure, and executive pay being cast in corporate governance terms, beginning in the mid-1980s the phrase "corporate governance" became increasingly associated with the preservation and promotion of shareholder value (Ocasio and Joseph, 2005: 174). This resonated with the concerns of economists, who ultimately tended to equate corporate governance with mechanisms designed to ensure suppliers of finance received a satisfactory risk-adjusted return on their investments (Shleifer and Vishny, 1997: 737–8). With the term "corporate governance" also offering the advantage of linguistic accessibility, its prominence within economic discourse was duly assured (Ocasio and Joseph, 2005: 174).

CORPORATE GOVERNANCE GOES INTERNATIONAL

During the 1970s and 1980s analysis of corporate governance focused pretty much exclusively on US corporations (Denis and McConnell, 2003: 1). By the early 1990s, the situation was changing and by 2003 there had been "an explosion of research on corporate governance around the world" (Denis and McConnell, 2003: 2). The reorientation of corporate governance analysis along international lines began in the US but quickly gained momentum elsewhere.

Following World War II it was implicitly assumed in the US that the managerial corporation, characterized by executive dominance in a context of dispersed share ownership, was the pinnacle in the evolution of organizational forms (Gilson and Roe, 1993: 873). The dominance of the managerial model, seemingly exemplified by US global corporate success, meant corporate governance arrangements in other countries that differed were largely ignored. As law professors Ronald Gilson and Mark Roe (1993: 873) put it, "Neither laggards nor dead-ends made compelling objects of study".

Matters changed as the 1990s began. With faith in the US economy taking a hit amidst recessionary conditions, the competitive threat posed by German and Japanese companies alarmed many and generated a substantial literature exploring the causes of, and proposed solutions to, the ostensible economic decline of the US. Corporate governance featured prominently in the discussion, as there was a growing sense that competition existed between governance systems as well as products, with the US often coming out second best (Gilson and Roe, 1993: 873). A key theme was that US corporate executives, compelled by takeovers and related financial market pressures to focus on the next quarter's earnings at the expense of performance over the long haul, were handicapped by "time horizon" problems that did not arise in Germany and Japan due to their having corporate governance regimes focused on long-term relational investment (Porter, 1992;

Blair, 1995: 6–7). Boards of US public companies also stood accused of having become counterproductively complacent and detached due to the unusual stability and prosperity America enjoyed following World War II (Johnson, 1990).

Corporate governance would soon come on to the agenda elsewhere. Britain led the way. Corporate governance generally attracted little attention in the UK prior to the 1990s, with the term "corporate governance" only being mentioned once in the *Times* newspaper up to 1985 (*The Times*, 1978) and with *The Economist* refraining from using the phrase until 1990 (*The Economist*, 1990). The pattern began to change when the accountancy profession, the London Stock Exchange, and the Financial Reporting Council, which regulates accounting standards in the UK, established in 1991 the Committee on the Financial Aspects of Corporate Governance.

As the Committee's chairman, Sir Adrian Cadbury, acknowledged in his forward to the Committee's 1992 report, the Committee's launch did not catch the headlines but its proceedings would become the focus of unanticipated attention (Committee on the Financial Aspects of Corporate Governance, 1992: 9). One reason was that, soon after the Cadbury Committee was established, a number of prominent British public companies collapsed in circumstances suggesting that a lack of accountability on the part of top executives had contributed to the problems which had arisen. Also, Britain was in the midst of a recession that fostered concern about the country's relative decline in terms of competitiveness, with managerial shortcomings left unaddressed by inattentive boards reputedly causing Britain's economic standing to suffer (Cheffins, 1997: 72).

A *Financial Times* columnist observed in 1999 that "The 1990s have been the decade of corporate governance" (*The Financial Times*, 1999). The momentum was sustained in the UK with a 1995 report on executive pay by a blue-ribbon committee chaired by Sir Richard Greenbury (1995) and a 1998 report by a committee chaired by Sir Ronald Hampel that reviewed the work done by the Cadbury and Greenbury committees (Committee on Corporate Governance, 1998). The 1992 Cadbury Report also achieved notoriety internationally. The Cadbury Committee encapsulated its recommendations in a Code of Best Practice and arranged for enforcement by persuading the London Stock Exchange to add the Code as an appendix to the London Stock Exchange's listing rules, with listed companies becoming obliged either to comply with the provisions of the Code or explain why they had failed to do so (Cheffins, 1997: 76–7). The Cadbury Code would soon serve as a model for the development of corporate governance codes in various countries around the world (Cheffins, 2000: 12–13). As the Hampel Report said, Cadbury had "struck a chord in many overseas countries; it has provided a yardstick against which standards of corporate governance in other markets are being measured" (Committee on Corporate Governance, 1998: para. 1.5).

Interest in the Cadbury Code coincided with a change in tone in debates concerning comparative corporate governance. While the topic first came to prominence when the US was suffering a crisis of confidence, by the mid-1990s the US economy had rebounded smartly. With the US reputedly reaping the dividends of a "golden age of entrepreneurial management" (*The Economist*, 1995: 2), Japan being in the midst of a prolonged and pronounced recession following a frenzied boom in the 1980s and Germany struggling to cope with costly post-unification economic adjustments, the US corporate governance model was suddenly being hailed as the one to follow (Becht et al., 2003: 42).

At the same time as the US approach to corporate governance was finding favor the corporate governance "movement" that had begun in the US and had become established in the UK put down roots in continental Europe and Japan (*The Financial Times*, 1993). Corporate governance controversies occurring in the mid-1990s at companies such as German shipbuilder Bremer Vulkan, German metals and mining group Metallgesellschaft, the Spanish bank Banesto, French conglomerates Navigation Mixte and Suez, and the Italian conglomerate Ferruzzi prompted calls for reform (Berglöf, 1997: 93). Liberalization of capital markets also helped to put corporate governance on the agenda. European firms that were seeking capital to restructure in response to challenges posed by growing cross-border competition turned increasingly to equity markets as a source of funding, meaning they were under an onus to be responsive to the concerns of shareholders (*The Financial Times*, 1996). Institutional investors aiming to diversify their holdings beyond their domestic markets were among the most receptive when European companies tapped equity markets, but there was a quid pro quo. American public pension funds, having already emerged as the most vocal shareholder proponents of better corporate governance in the US, took their campaign to Europe and Japan in the mid-1990s, seeking allies from pension funds based elsewhere in so doing (Kissane, 1997).

The process would soon repeat itself elsewhere. Weaknesses in corporate governance arising from family control of major publicly traded companies were cited as a cause of the Asian stock market crash of 1997, prompting calls for legal reforms designed to protect minority shareholders (*Asian Wall Street Journal*, 2000). Asia's tycoons also found themselves under pressure to adopt a more shareholder-friendly "western" style of business as their reliance on Anglo-American equity capital grew (*The Economist*, 2000). A 1998 report by an Organisation for Economic Co-operation and Development (OECD) advisory group that provided the departure point for the OECD's issuance of corporate governance principles in 1999 confirmed that companies that strengthened their corporate governance arrangements should be advantageously positioned when it came to attracting capital to finance growth (Business Sector Advisory Group on Corporate Governance, 1998: 7, 14). A widely publicized 2000 report by management consultancy McKinsey & Co. did likewise, as it indicated institutional investors would pay a premium of nearly 30 percent for shares in well-governed companies operating in countries believed to have weak shareholder rights (*The Financial Times*, 2000).

Epilogue

As the 20th century drew to a close, corporate governance had clearly "arrived." In the space of 25 years, a term that US regulators and academic lawyers were just beginning to deploy had become, to quote the 1998 report by the OECD's corporate governance advisory group, a topic "of great international interest and concern" (Business Sector Advisory Group on Corporate Governance, 1998: 7, 14). The tenor of debate admittedly would soon change markedly. As the 2000s began, the US was riding high. Its corporate governance system seemed to be functioning well and there were various predictions of global convergence along American lines (Cheffins, 2009: 9). Calpers was in the vanguard, using its platform as the most important institutional investor activist in the US to promote better corporate governance by issuing a set of global proxy voting principles (Hawley and Williams, 2005: 1998).

Perceptions changed promptly and dramatically as the 2000s got under way. A sharp stock market decline precipitated by the demise of a "dot.com"-driven bull market in shares and scandals that rocked major US public companies such as Enron and WorldCom discredited the US model of corporate governance domestically and made it much more difficult to sell abroad (*Los Angeles Times*, 2002). Regardless, corporate governance was well-entrenched as an intellectual construct, both in the United States and elsewhere. A "corporate governance complex," composed of a dense array of public institutions, private firms, and academic centers, had emerged that was dedicated to the pursuit of "better" corporate governance (Stevens and Rudnick, 2010). Accordingly, during the financial crisis of 2008 and in its immediate aftermath "corporate governance" would be the term that academics, policymakers, investors and corporate executives around the world would typically deploy when analyzing issues of managerial accountability, board structure, and shareholder involvement in publicly traded companies.

Will corporate governance's analytical grip prove to be durable going forward? In 2010, a corporate social responsibility consultant proclaimed corporate governance was "dead. Gone. Pfffft" (Richardson, 2010). This bold claim raises a valid point, which is that it is unclear whether there are major new corporate governance frontiers that remain to be explored. Instead, corporate governance's "core" themes have been well-defined for some time. As we have seen, board structure has been debated in the corporate governance context since the 1970s. Likewise, since the 1990s shareholder activism has been high on the corporate governance agenda, as has executive pay (Murphy, 2002: 856–7), and corporate governance has had a strong international dimension.

While it may be the case that from an analytical perspective the basic terrain of corporate governance is now well known, a declaration of death is premature. The possibility of conflict between investors and managers has been with us for centuries and will continue to be a matter for concern so long as business activity is conducted through the corporate form. Corporate governance now provides a tested and familiar nomenclature for addressing the issues involved, and a substitute analytical paradigm has yet to emerge. Moreover, corporate governance is unlikely to become moribund from a policy or intellectual perspective. Future economic shocks and corporate scandals will no doubt raise afresh concerns about managerial and corporate accountability. Empirical analysis should also provide fresh insights concerning familiar research questions. For the foreseeable future, then, debates concerning the interrelationship between directors, executives, and shareholders of publicly traded companies seem destined to be conducted through the conceptual prism of corporate governance.

References

ANDREWS, K. R. (1982), "Rigid Rules Will Not Make Good Boards," *Harvard Business Review*, 60: 34–46.
Asian Wall Street Journal (2000). "Bombard the Boardroom," *Asian Wall Street Journal*, September 27: 10.
BAINBRIDGE, S. M. (1993). "Independent Directors and the ALI Corporate Governance Project," *George Washington Law Review*, 61: 1034–83.
BECHT, M., BOLTON, P., and RÖELL, A. (2003). "Corporate Governance and Control," in G. M. Constantinides, M. Harris, and R. M. Stultz (eds.), *Handbook of the Economics of Finance*, vol. 1A. Amsterdam: Elsevier, 1–109.
BERGLÖF, E. (1997). "Reforming Corporate Governance: Redirecting the European Agenda," *Economic Policy*, 12: 93–123.
BERLE, A. A., and MEANS, G. C. (1932). *The Modern Corporation and Private Property*. New York: Harcourt, Brace and World.
BLACK, B. S. (1990). "Shareholder Passivity Revisited," *Michigan Law Review*, 89: 520–608.
—— (1998). "Shareholder Activism and Corporate Governance in the United States," in Peter Newman (ed.), *The New Palgrave Dictionary of Law and Economics*, vol. 1. Basingstoke, UK: Macmillan, 459–65.
BLAIR, M. M. (1995). *Ownership and Control: Rethinking Corporate Governance for the Twenty-First Century*. Washington, DC: Brookings Institution.
Business Roundtable (1978). "The Role and Composition of Directors of the Large Publicly Owned Corporation," *Business Lawyer*, 33: 2083–113.
Business Sector Advisory Group on Corporate Governance (1998). *Corporate Governance: Improving Competitiveness and Access to Capital in Global Markets*. Paris: OECD.
CARROLL, T. M. (1981). "Review: Running the American Corporation," *Southern Economic Journal*, 47: 1168–70.
CHEFFINS, B. R. (1997). "Corporate Governance in the United Kingdom: Lessons for Canada," *Canadian Business Law Journal*, 28: 69–106.
—— (2000). "Corporate Governance Reform: Britain as an Exporter," *Hume Papers on Public Policy*, 8(1): 10–28.
—— (2004). *The Trajectory of (Corporate Law) Scholarship*. Cambridge: Cambridge University Press.
—— (2009). "Did Corporate Governance 'Fail' During the 2008 Stock Market Meltdown? The Case of the S&P 500," *Business Lawyer*, 65: 1–65.
Chicago Tribune (1977). "NYSE Chairman Sees Bigger Government Role," *Chicago Tribune*, August 10: E9.
—— (1979). "How to Put Feds in Control of Everything: A Case Study," *Chicago Tribune*, January 28: A6.
COCHRAN, P. L., and WARTICK, S. L. (1988). *Corporate Governance: A Review of the Literature*. Morristown, NJ: Financial Executives Research Foundation.

COFFEE, J. C. (1991). "Liquidity versus Control: The Institutional Investor as Corporate Monitor," *Columbia Law Review*, 91: 1277–368.
Committee on Corporate Governance (Sir Ronald Hampel, chair) (1998). *Report*. London: Gee.
Committee on the Financial Aspects of Corporate Governance (Sir Adrian Cadbury, chair) (1992). *Report*. London: Gee.
DENIS, D. K. (2001). "Twenty-Five Years of Corporate Governance Research...and Counting," *Review of Financial Economics*, 10: 191–212.
—— and MCCONNELL, J. J. (2003). "International Corporate Governance," *Journal of Financial and Quantitative Analysis*, 38: 1–36.
DENT, G. W. (1989). "Toward Unifying Ownership and Control in the Public Corporation," *Wisconsin Law Review*, 881–924.
DOBBIN, F., and ZORN, D. (2005). "Corporate Malfeasance and the Myth of Shareholder Value," *Political Power & Social Theory*, 17: 179–98.
DURISIN, B., and PUZONE, F. (2009). "Maturation of Corporate Governance Research, 1993–2007: An Assessment," *Corporate Governance: An International Review*, 17: 266–91.
EASTERBROOK, F. H. (1984). "Managers' Discretion and Investors' Welfare: Theories and Evidence," *Delaware Journal of Corporate Law*, 9: 540–71.
Economist, The (1990). "Bored Directors," January 27.
—— (1993). "Shareholders Call the Plays," April 24.
—— (1995). "Back on Top? A Survey of American Business," September 16.
—— (2000). "The End of Tycoons," April 29.
EISENBERG, M. (1976). *The Structure of the Corporation: A Legal Analysis*. (Boston: Little, Brown.
ELSON, A., and SHAKMAN, M. L. (1994). "The ALI Principles of Corporate Governance: A Tainted Process and a Flawed Product," *Business Lawyer*, 49: 1761–92.
FAMA, E. F. (1980). "Agency Problems and the Theory of the Firm," *Journal of Political Economy*, 88: 288–307.
Financial Times, The (1993). "Governance Goes Global," September 13.
—— (1996). "Crumbs from the Table," September 25.
—— (1999). "Moves to Halt Another Decade of Excess," August 5: 10.
—— (2000). "Investors Pay Premiums for Well-Governed Companies," June 20,
FISCHEL, D. R. (1982). "The Corporate Governance Movement," *Vanderbilt Law Review*, 35: 1259–92.
FOX, J. (2009). *The Myth of the Rational Market: A History of Risk, Reward, and Delusion on Wall Street*. New York: HarperCollins.
GILSON, R. J., and ROE, M. J. (1993). "Understanding the Japanese Keiretsu: Overlaps between Corporate Governance and Industrial Organization," *Yale Law Journal*, 102: 871–906.
GORDON, J. N. (2007). "The Rise of Independent Directors in the United States, 1950–2005: Of Shareholder Value and Stock Market Prices," *Stanford Law Review*, 59: 1465–568.
GREENBURY, R. (1995). *Directors' Remuneration: Report of a Study Group* (chaired by Sir Richard Greenbury). London: Gee.
GREENOUGH, W. C. (1980). "Keeping Corporate Governance in the Private Sector," *Business Horizons*, 58: 71–4.
—— and CLAPMAN, P. C. (1980). "The Role of Independent Directors in Corporate Governance," *Notre Dame Law Review*, 56: 916–25.
HAWLEY J. P., and WILLIAMS, A. T. (2005). "Shifting Ground: Emerging Global Corporate-Governance Standards and the Rise of Fiduciary Capitalism," *Environment and Planning*, 37: 1995–2013.

HESSEN, R. (1983). "The Modern Corporation and Private Property: A Reappraisal," *Journal of Law & Economics*, 26: 273–89.

HOLMSTROM, B., and KAPLAN, S. N. (2001). "Corporate Governance and Merger Activity in the United States: Making Sense of the 1980s and 1990s," *Journal of Economic Perspectives*, 15: 121–44.

JENSEN, M. C. (1983). "Organization Theory and Methodology," *Accounting Review*, 58: 319–39.

—— (1993). "The Modern Industrial Revolution, Exit, and the Failure of Internal Control Systems," *Journal of Finance*, 48: 831–80.

—— and MECKLING, W. H. (1976). "Theory of the Firm: Managerial Behavior, Agency Costs and Ownership Structure," *Journal of Financial Economics*, 3: 305–60.

—— and WARNER, J. B. (1988). "The Distribution of Power among Corporate Managers, Shareholders and Directors," *Journal of Financial Economics*, 20: 3–24.

JOHNSON, E. W. (1990). "An Insider's Call for Outside Direction," *Harvard Business Review*, 68: 46–55.

—— and ROCK, E. B. (2002). "How I Learned to Stop Worrying and Love the Pill: Adaptive Responses to Takeover Law," *University of Chicago Law Review*, 69: 871–915.

KAHAN, M. (2007). "Hedge Funds in Corporate Governance and Corporate Control," *University of Pennsylvania Law Review*, 155: 1021–93.

KARMEL, R. S. (1984). "The Independent Corporate Board: A Means to What End?" *George Washington Law Review*, 52: 534–56.

KISSANE, M. E. (1997). "Global Gadflies: Applications and Implementations of U.S.-Style Corporate Governance Abroad," *New York Law School Journal of International and Comparative Law*, 17: 621–75.

KRIPKE, H. (1981). "The SEC, Corporate Governance, and the Real Issues," *Business Lawyer*, 36: 173–206.

LIVINGSTON, J. A. (1958). *The American Stockholder*. Philadelphia: J. B. Lippincott Company.

Los Angeles Times (1981). "Activists, Executives Clash on How Firms Should be Run," January 12: E1.

—— (2002). "U.S. Business Model a Tough Sell Overseas," *Los Angeles Times*, July 7: A1.

MACEY, J. R. (1993). "The Transformation of the American Law Institute," *George Washington Law Review*, 61: 1212–32.

MANNING, B. (1993). "Principles of Corporate Governance: One Viewer's Perspective on the ALI Project," *Business Lawyer*, 48: 1319–32.

METZENBAUM, H. M. (1981). "Legislative Approaches to Corporate Governance," *Notre Dame Law Review*, 56: 926–35.

MOFSKY, J. S., and RUBIN, R. D. (1983). "Introduction: A Symposium on the ALI Corporate Governance Project," *University of Miami Law Review*, 37: 169–85.

MORCK, R. (ed.) (2005). *A History of Corporate Governance around the World*. Chicago: NBER.

MURPHY, K. J. (2002). "Explaining Executive Compensation: Managerial Power versus the Perceived Cost of Stock Options," *University of Chicago Law Review*, 69: 847–69.

NADER, R., GREEN, M., and SELIGMAN, J. (1976). *Taming the Giant Corporation*. New York: W. W. Norton.

New York Times (1977). "Management: The First Draft of a New Corporate Constitution," April 22: 91.

—— (1980). "Board 'Outsiders' Win Favor," March 31: D1.

Ocasio, W., and Joseph, J. (2005). "Cultural Adaptation and Institutional Change: The Evolution of Vocabularies of Corporate Governance, 1972–2003," *Poetics*, 33: 163–78.

Porter, M. E. (1992). "Capital Choices: Changing the Way America Invests in Industry," *Journal of Applied Corporate Finance*, 5: 4–16.

Pound, J. (1993). "The Rise of the Political Model of Corporate Governance and Corporate Control," *New York University Law Review*, 68: 1003–71.

—— (1995), "The Promise of the Governed Corporation," *Harvard Business Review*, 73: 89–98.

Richardson, J. (2010). "Corporate Governance is Dead," *Global Investment Watch*, December 28, 2010, available online at <http://globalinvestmentwatch.com/corporate-governance-is-dead/> (last visited November 19, 2012).

Rosenberg, H. (1999). *A Traitor to His Class: Robert A.G. Monks and the Battle to Change Corporate America*. New York: John Wiley.

Schwartz, D. J. (1976). "Penn Central: A Case Study of Outside Director Responsibility under Federal Securities Law," *UMKC Law Review*, 45: 394–421.

Schwartz, D. E. (1983). "Shareholder Democracy: A Reality or a Chimera?" *California Management Review*, 25: 53–67.

Securities and Exchange Commission (1980). *Staff Report on Corporate Accountability*. Washington: US Government Printing Office.

Seligman J. (1982). *The Transformation of Wall Street: A History of the Securities and Exchange Commission and Modern Corporate Finance*. Boston: Houghton, Mifflin.

—— (1987). "A Sheep in Wolf's Clothing: The American Law Institute Principles of Corporate Governance Project," *George Washington Law Review*, 55: 325–81.

Shleifer, A., and Vishny, R. W. (1997). "A Survey of Corporate Governance," *Journal of Finance*, 52: 737–83.

Small, M. L. (2011). "The 1970s: The Committee on Corporate Laws Joins the Corporate Governance Debate," *Law & Contemporary Problems*, 74: 129–36.

Sommer, A. A. (1977). "The Impact of the SEC on Corporate Governance," *Law and Contemporary Problems*, 41: 115–45.

Stevens, S., and Rudnick, M. (2010). "What Berle and Means have Wrought," *The Deal Magazine*, May 14. Available at <http://www.thedeal.com/magazine/ID/034421/special-reports-1/corporate-governance/what-berle-and-means-have-wrought.php> (last visited November 19, 2012).

Subcommittee on the Functions and Responsibilities of Directors, Committee on Corporate Laws, Section of Corporation, Banking and Business Law (1976). "Corporate Directors' Guidebook," *Business Lawyer*, 32: 5–52.

Times, The (1978). "A Second Opinion?" November 6: 21.

Useem, M. (1996). *Investor Capitalism: How Money Managers are Changing the Face of Corporate America*. New York: Basic Books.

Veasey, E. N. (1993). "The Emergence of Corporate Governance as a New Legal Discipline," *Business Lawyer*, 48: 1267–70.

Wall Street Journal (1981). "SEC's Shad Shows Pro-business Tilt but Says He Won't be a Pushover," September 16: 29.

—— (1989). "Pension Funds Plot against Takeover Law," *Wall Street Journal*, April 5: C1.

—— (1993). "Shareholders at the Gate," *Wall Street Journal*, February 2: A15.

Weiss, E. J. (1984). "Economic Analysis, Corporate Law, and the ALI Corporate Governance Project," *Cornell Law Review*, 70: 1–37.

WELLS, H. (2010). "The Birth of Corporate Governance," *Seattle University Law Review*, 33: 1247–92.

WEST, R. R. (1984). "An Economist Looks at the ALI Proposals," *Delaware Journal of Corporation Law*, 9: 638–44.

WILCOX, J. C. (1997). "A 10-Year Quest for Director Accountability," *Directors & Boards*, 22: 46–50.

WILLIAMSON, O. (1984). "Corporate Governance," *Yale Law Journal*, 93: 1197–231.

WOLFSON, N. (1984). "A Critique of the American Law Institute Draft Proposals," *Delaware Journal of Corporate Law*, 9: 629–37.

ZALECKI, P. H. (1993). "The Corporate Governance Roles of the Inside and Outside Directors," *University of Toledo Law Review*, 24: 831–58.

CHAPTER 4

CAPITAL MARKETS AND FINANCIAL POLITICS

Preferences and Institutions

MARK J. ROE

Introduction

For capital markets to function, political institutions must support capitalism in general and the capitalism of financial markets in particular. Yet it's not so obvious how and why political institutions come to support a deep, wide, well-functioning capital market, because many interests have reason to undermine the capital market and because the immediate beneficiary of a strong capital market is a minority of wealthy capital owners. The polity in a functioning democracy must come to see capital markets as benefiting the majority, despite the fact that the benefit is indirect and not always vivid.

Here I outline the main weaknesses in the interaction between political institutions and capitalism, indicate the most common resolution of these weaknesses, and show how the interaction between capital markets and politics has been seen in the academic literature. I focus not on the standard and important channel of how institutions affect preferences and outcomes, but on how and when immediate preferences can trump, restructure, and even displace established institutions.

Two core categories of problems afflict the interaction between politics and financial markets, both emanating from the fact that capitalism can generate large pools of financial assets whose disposition and use the polity can contest. The first is that the have-nots, eyeing those assets, may use the political arena to obtain a slice of those assets that they cannot obtain in the economic arena, thereby creating a pernicious contest between the haves and the have-nots, one that burns resources and that must be settled or accommodated. How that contest is resolved deeply affects both the shape and extent of the capital market.

The second recurring problem is that the haves—typically the capital owners themselves, but not always, since managers without capital often have considerable political influence due to the control over assets that they do not themselves formally own—may fight among themselves, both privately and in the political arena, for rights to those assets.

While it is tempting to explain the survival of longstanding financial and corporate structures as resulting from rational optimization of private goals, these surviving structures are often just as much a consequence of reactions to conflicts among capital owners, or mandates from the winners. I will give some examples in the United States of how conflicts among capitalists and their managers largely explain core features of the capital market for the large American public firm. Other examples can be had from Western Europe. Private optimization explanations alone cannot fully explain these fundamental events that construct capital markets institutions.

Many of the real world's interactions between politics and capitalism are permutations of these two fundamental contests, between have and have-nots, and among the haves themselves. And a considerable portion of the academic world's analysis of modern political economy involves variations of these two fundamental problems.

When we see weak capital markets in a nation, or when we ask why a nation's capital market takes on a particular configuration, we tend to look to efficiency and institutional explanations for the result: the country doesn't need securities markets for this or that reason; banks fit best with the production technology then prevailing in that economy; or the country never developed the institutions of investor protection. These are surely relevant to a full explanation. Less well-highlighted, even today, are that political economy explanations are also core to any full explanation. Look to the dominant political interests and decision-makers in the society—if we do not see strong capital markets, it's often because it's not in the politically decisive players' interest to allow them to be strong. If their interests change (or if their power declines), the capital markets' character can also change.

This political explanation is especially likely to be in play in nations that have had little difficulty in building other resilient institutions: particularly for such nations, political support for capital markets is more likely to be a policy choice rather than an issue of institutional capabilities.

Complications abound. Causation is bidirectional; several economic, institutional, and political features are determined simultaneously. Few political features are fully discrete. Most key features interact, with coalitions and multiple political forces in play. I sketch here the simple stories first, then show several of the interactions, complications, and causation reversals.

Financial markets can be seen as primarily a function of a nation's governing institutions. Considerable progress has been made in economics since North (1990) demonstrated institutions' importance. But institutions interact with preferences and, indeed, widespread deeply held preferences (presumably emanating from immediate interests and, at times, overall ideologies) can bend, destroy, and build institutions. Here I give more emphasis than is typical to the role of preferences in constructing the institutions of financial markets.

I divide the inquiry along two major dimensions. First, what is the political economy of capitalist finance for the nation's haves versus the have-nots, focusing on how preferences and institutions interact? And second, what is the political economy of capitalist finance that divides the nation's haves? Subsidiary to each dimension, I ask how these questions play out in the world's richer nations and how they play out in the world's developing nations. Are there enough commonalities across nations, so that patterns can be discerned?

I also show how this inquiry highlights the importance of attending to the interaction between institutions and immediate preferences. The former have been central in scholarship of the past few decades. Institutions are indeed important—but so are preferences and interests, and these preferences and interests are not always shaped by their institutional environment, but can arise from immediate conditions that might not last, but can then become embedded in new institutions. That is, what seems sometimes obscured in the literature is that preferences, when sufficiently powerful, can wash institutions away as easily as shacks collapse in a hurricane. That does not happen often outside of severe crisis, but it does often happen then. And preferences can then build the institutions that can withstand (some of) the future's fickleness. Today's institutions developed out of the preferences that dominated in the past. And tomorrow's institutions may well be as much a function of today's preferences as they are of today's institutions.

Concept

Capital Markets' Dependence on Political Institutions

If a nation's polity does not support a capital market, that nation will not have one. Examine whether strong capital markets are in the interest of the decisive political actors—or what shape of capital markets best implements their interests—and one is likely to have a primary explanation for the shape and extent of the nation's capital market. The concept is simple, but powerful.

The Interests that Support, or Denigrate, Capital Markets

Capital owners typically have an interest in promoting capital markets and their supporting institutions, but other interests may not. Local interests may oppose centralized financial institutions that move capital. Those with strong human capital could fear that strong capital markets would erode that human capital's value, by forcing more market-oriented change more quickly. Those without financial capital today and with poor prospects of acquiring capital in the future could prefer that the polity take capital from those who have it and use it to benefit those who do not.

Capital is often unevenly distributed in a nation, facilitating conflict between haves and have-nots. Even when income and property are more evenly distributed, economic rationality demands aggregation institutions, like banks and securities markets, to achieve operational economies of scale. These aggregations can become vivid in the polity and attract negative attention.

Capital markets are not generic. Banks have an interest in preserving bank financing channels and in weakening securities market channels. Securities dealers and investment bankers have an interest in preserving and expanding securities markets. Dominant owners, such as families traditionally or private equity firms more recently, have an interest in preserving their privileges. Owners of existing firms want access to cheap capital, but prefer that their competitors should not have the same easy access.

Government bureaucracies can be wary of rival power centers in capital markets or, sometimes, wish to promote them as counterweights to other power centers in their society.

These, then, are the relevant concepts. The next sections illustrate them.

Capital Markets and Financial Politics in the Developed World

Two basic political splits organize the inquiry here for developed nations: one, the contest between those who control capital and those who do not, and, two, contests among those who control capital.

Haves vs Have-Nots

Governmental power vs private power The most basic political economy have versus have-not conflict is between governmental authorities and private sector players who command capital. While not usually seen as a conflict between haves and have-nots, it is indeed such a conflict—as government often seeks to obtain for itself capital that it lacks or to command its private sector use. In extreme form, a non-democratic, dictatorial government could prefer to directly allocate capital itself, stifling the development of a private sector in general, and capital markets in particular, since such markets can become rival power centers in the nation.

Governmental authorities can build, shape, or destroy capital markets, for their own reasons and not as tools of other interests or ideologies. The governmental authorities may wish to denigrate a rival power center, one that could seek to control the government. Governmental authorities could be susceptible to ideologies and beliefs that capital markets will not produce social welfare and that government needs to direct and control capital flows to better produce wealth or justice. Finally, governmental authorities may see government action as the vanguard of economic and social development; in pursuing policies to implement their goals, they can crowd out private capital markets and thereby prevent them from developing nicely.

More standard accounts, which I shall address below, examine how interests can capture government decision-making and use captured governmental institutions for the interests' own ends. But the concept differs in this section. Government authorities are themselves an interest, with their own interests and ideology separate from those in the civil, nongovernmental society. Their own direct interests and beliefs can motivate their actions vis-à-vis capital markets. See Douglas (1940: 11, 14) (statement from the chair of the Securities and Exchange Commission (SEC): people who dominate financial markets have "tremendous power.... Such [people] become virtual governments in the power at their disposal. [Sometimes it is] the dut[y] of government to police them, at times to break them up...."); see also Skocpol (1979).

Populism vs power Populism can affect financial markets and institutions, often in reaction to financial crises and poor economic results. Popular opinion may seek as much to punish financiers and their institutions as to improve the financial system's functioning, as the two—punishment and improvement—could be conflated in the popular mind. When this feature is powerful in politics, it can induce an institutionalization of anti-capital rules and reaction. Then, once institutionalized, interests arise with reason to perpetuate the newly made, underlying rules and the resultant arrangements. Thus, even when the popular animus against finance dissipates in more normal political times, the created interests can stymie a return to the previous arrangements.

Business elites vs masses Workers could dislike capital and capital markets. Farmers may blame financial markets for their misfortunes as much as bad weather. Each group may have simple redistributional goals, or their thinking and voting may be influenced by envy.

Social democracy vs capital markets Social democracy played a central role in how capital markets developed in post-World War II Western Europe. By social democracy I mean a nation committed to private property, but where distributional considerations are vital, where labor is typically powerful, and where government action to foster economic equality is central on the political agenda.

For diffuse stock markets to persist, the diffuse capital owners must see their firms as managed by agents who are sufficiently loyal to shareholders to provide shareholder value. For dominant shareholders to turn their firm over to ownership in liquid stock markets and, hence, to managerial control, they must expect that the net value of the turnover is beneficial to themselves. If the benefits to stockholders of liquidity and professional management are offset by managerial disloyalty, fewer dominant stockholders will turn their firms over to managers than otherwise. For shareholders to count on this managerial loyalty, they need institutions and norms that induce that kind of loyalty. But if a polity will not provide those institutions, or if it denigrates such norms, dominant stockholders can obtain more shareholder value by keeping control of the firm. Managerial control will not ordinarily appear and will be unstable if it does. Stock markets will not be strong in such nations, because managerial agency costs will be too high and it will be too hard to lower them to levels that stockholders would find acceptable.

Figure 4.1 illustrates the relationship between labor power (quantified by union and job security rules) and the degree to which large firms have large blockholders. Greater labor power is associated with greater ownership concentration; weaker labor power is

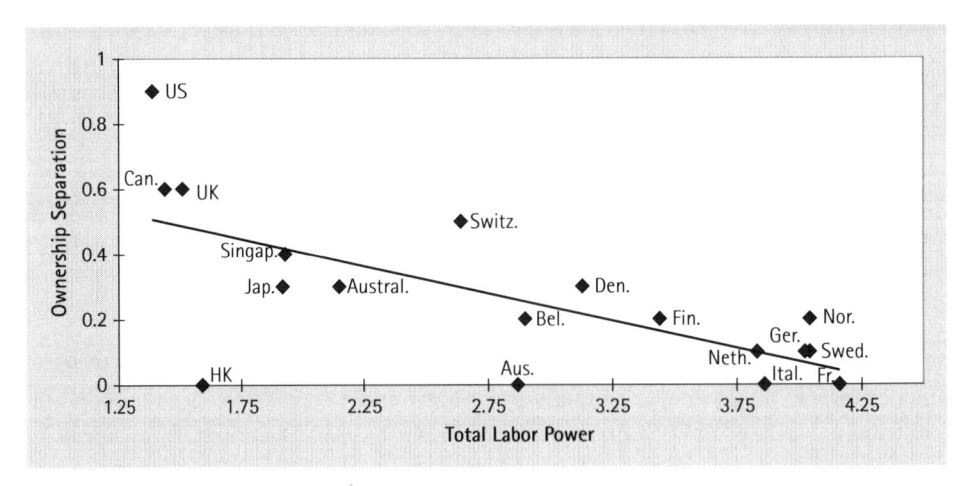

FIGURE 4.1. Correlation of labor's power and large firm ownership separation in post-war wealthy west

associated with more diffuse ownership. Details, sources, and background to the figure can be found in Roe (2000, 2003).

Visible incentive compensation that ties managers to owners may be denigrated in a social democracy more than it is in a more conservative polity. Any resulting wealth disparity could especially demoralize lower-level employees and lead them to demand further compensation for themselves. And, as noted above, governmental players can be less willing to provide capital-market-supporting institutions, such as disclosure rules and enforcement, insider trading sanctions, and commercial courts, as the authorities may see these difficulties as disputes among the well-to-do—disputes that the public authorities need not attend to. These barriers to controlling managerial agency costs can be particularly severe in social democratic polities.

A considerable literature has developed on the primacy of institutions in property rights protection, which has obvious relevance to protection of capital market investors. While institutions are surely important, the possibility exists that the academic literature is over-sold on institutions now, while underestimating simple, basic political power. Politicians can mold institutions. Even in the United States, where property rights institutions are typically seen as being as strong as they can be, a Congress that wanted to attack capital markets could do so and do so effectively.

What may well count as much as institutions for the United States is that there is no political will for a frontal assault on American capital markets. And, indeed, recent worldwide evidence indicates that right-leaning governments are perceived by property owners to protect their property better than left-leaning ones and that this partisanship dimension dominates institutional characteristics in explaining the degree of perceived property protection.[1]

Those then are the major have versus have-not breaks affecting capital markets in developed nations.

Haves vs Haves

Vertical conflict—between the capital markets' haves and the have-nots—is not the only political economy array here. There's a horizontal dimension as well, of conflict among the haves, one that comes in three major varieties: conflicts between capital owners, conflicts between large firm managers and capital markets, and conflicts between controlling shareholders and capital markets.

Capital markets' internal fissures—especially that of banks vs stock market capitalism

If securities markets are weak, more capital will flow through the banking system. This flow will of course benefit bankers. Deposit banks have an interest in keeping securities markets weak, unless they can control securities flows themselves. The interests seek to protect themselves using the political realm. Macey and Miller (1991) showed that in the United States deposit banks often lobbied for blue sky laws that raised the costs of stock sales.

Small banks have an interest in stifling competition from big banks. In the United States, this historically took the primary form of small banks inducing political decision-makers to bar the large, money-center banks from entering the small banks' local market. The result was that the small banks had local monopolies or oligopolies, while large banks lacked a nationwide deposit base. Roe (1994) emphasizes this feature of 19th century (and most of the 20th century) American financial history, particularly when the power of local bankers combined with populist opinion that militated against large, centralized financial institutions. With even the largest banks relatively small in relation to the economy, banks could not readily provide the financing for continent-spanning industries at the end of the 19th century. The consequence was that the demand and need for securities markets was enhanced.

Intra-capital-market tactical conflict can have unexpected, but profound, outcomes, as Langevoort (1987) shows. During the 1933 banking crisis, larger money-center banks sought to dissuade Congress from enacting deposit insurance, because they thought they would end up paying disproportionately for the insurance and, if no banks were insured, deposits would run off from smaller, country banks to the larger, more stable money-center banks. (Yes, there was a time when such large, money-center banks were seen as the most stable in the American economy.) Because they knew that Congress would insist on doing something, they suggested and supported splitting investment from commercial banking (as they were not making much money in the securities business anyway). By so suggesting, they hoped to dissuade Congress from mandating deposit insurance. Congress did sever investment from commercial banking via the famous Glass-Steagall Act of 1933, as the large banks suggested. But Congress also decided nevertheless to insure banks deposits, which the large money-center banks had opposed.

Managers vs capital markets

Managers of large diffusely owned firms have reason to disrupt their shareholders' capacity to aggregate their stock ownership. Although they do not necessarily own much of the firm's capital themselves, they control the firm and they seek to maintain their control. They seek laws that impede or bar hostile takeovers. They seek rules that make it costly for shareholders to take large, active positions. They seek shareholder voting rules that make it hard for shareholders to elect directors other than those that incumbent managers support. (Corporate election contests are costly. Stockholder votes need to be solicited, corporate election contest rules have to be complied with, and publicity needs to be sought. The firm pays the election costs for the incumbents' nominees, but insurgents generally pay their own costs, although any gains they bring about accrue to all shareholders. Free-rider problems abound, deterring otherwise valuable contests.) These conflicts could be characterized alternatively as politically powerful haves (the managers) strengthening their grip on the firm and keeping control away from the less politically powerful, but economically well-to-do, haves—namely, the firm's capital owners.

These managerial efforts have been significant in the United States historically and continue today. Managers have successfully opposed the strongest proposals in this past decade to allow shareholders easy access to the firm's proxy statement, which would allow dissidents to more easily elect directors. Prior outbreaks of the shareholder voting reform efforts in the United States, starting in the 1940s, also died after managers successfully opposed the proposals. There's a considerable literature on managerial-shareholder conflict in the United States.[2] The literature on the spillover of managerial preferences and authority into the political sphere is thinner, although efforts can be found in Grundfest (1990), Roe (1990, 1993), and Bebchuk and Neeman (2010).

Managers of fully stockholder-controlled firms could not readily seek such rules initially, as their controlling shareholders would have been unhappy with such managerial lobbying. But once ownership became diffuse, perhaps because of the combined impact of American populism and the interests of small-town bankers in the 19th century, managers could more readily engage in such political action, free from a dominant shareholder's veto.

Controlling shareholders vs capital markets

Controlling shareholders have reason to maintain rules that allow them to shift value to themselves. Corporate rules affect the private benefits of control—such as the ease with which small shareholders can reverse related-party transactions between the firm and the controlling insiders, and the ease with which controlling shareholders can squeeze out minority stockholders at an unfair price. Once a player controls a public firm, it has an interest in maintaining (or expanding) its capacity to shift value to itself.[3] This feature seems to have been important in recent decades in several Western European nations.[4]

Capital Markets and Financial Politics in the Developing World

Rudiments without Government Institutions

Development authorities often focus on bolstering institutions that promote financial markets, in the belief that better financial markets will lead to economic development. They seek to develop superior corporate laws, better securities laws, and better courts and other institutions to enforce financial and other contracts. These efforts are appropriate, but the initial conditions needed historically for financial markets have been simple, with political economy conditions central. If the developing nation is sufficiently stable politically and socially, the first steps for financial markets institutions can be taken, and often have been taken, with limited targeted government action. Thereafter, as the financial markets develop, there will be interests that seek to institutionalize that development and push it to the next level—and who have the know-how to do so.

This sequence—first social and political stability, then financial market development, and then legal consolidation later—is illustrated in studies of the initial development of the planet's strongest securities markets. They all show a rather weak corporate institutional environment initially, but one embedded in a sufficiently stable environment so that reputational forces could propel initial, extra-legal financial market development. Related concepts of repeated games are relevant here, with economic actors' expectations of long time lines for the repetition, generating mild but real institutional self-enforcement.[5]

Consider Bradford DeLong's (1991) famous piece on Morgan's directors. In an environment of weak corporate law in end-of-the-19th-century America (see Rock, 2001), the Morgan firm put their partners on firms' boards, in order to offer their own reputation to protect shareholders from scurrilous or incompetent management. (And, it must be added, perhaps facilitating cartelization, through the Morgan partners sitting on boards of competitors.) Pernicious insider dealings, or undiscovered managerial incompetence, would cost the Morgan firm dearly, so they warranted (albeit weakly) that such nefarious or incompetent results would be unlikely to occur in the firms on whose boards they sat. Outside investors might mistrust the firm, but they had more reason to trust the Morgan directors. Other investment banking firms presumably acted similarly.

Miwa and Ramseyer (2002) find an analogous reputational market at work in the nascent Japanese stock market of post-Meiji Restoration, late 19th century Japan. Firms sought directors with sterling reputations, to warrant to smaller stockholders that the firm had, and would continue to have, adequately fair and satisfactorily competent management. The reputational directors had a lot to lose socially and perhaps psychologically, so they cared what happened inside the firm. Franks, Mayer, and Rossi (2009) and Mayer (2008) demonstrate a similar process at work in Britain at the end of the 19th and early 20th centuries. Reputations and repeat dealings supported a nascent stock market. Hard-edged, government-facilitated legal institutions came later.

The point here is not that reputational structures are a panacea, obviating the need to build supportive institutions. Rather, the point is twofold: a financial market can start developing without preexisting strong institutional support, but it needs a stable political and social environment that makes the reputational markets valuable (and possible) to build. Once a rudimentary capital market is in place, a constituency in the nation that would support more rigorous institutions to regulate and promote capital markets begins developing.

The steps toward more rigorous institutions do not need to lead immediately to "hard" law. Stock markets' enforcement, for example, can initially be built, again albeit weakly, by the financial players. They can punish miscreants by exclusion (such as by de-listing in stock market terms or breaking the miscreant's trading bench at medieval trading fairs; points made, respectively, by North and Weingast (1989) and Mahoney (1997)).

These private, exclusionary mechanisms were important in the development of American stock markets.[6] But such private ordering is imperfect, as the punishments the private players can invoke—typically exclusion or a besmirched reputation—cannot reach the severity that public punishments can, via criminal penalties and fines. Still, the point persists that some sanctions can start before the public authorities act, as long as the political and social setting is sufficiently stable.

Presumably such private ordering mechanisms could come forth and be effective in other nations, including developing nations today. But for many nations without sufficient political stability, such reputational and private ordering institutions are difficult or impossible to start up. Hence, those seeking to promote capital markets should have reason to inquire into the sources of political stability, a subject I examine below.

Elites' Interests

Some nations' elites may have little interest in promoting financial markets. Two self-interested reasons could be in play. First, the elites may have satisfactory access to capital through, say, family banks or informal channels. Their grip on the polity may also allow them to stifle entry into banking, thereby keeping capital in the channels they already control. But a widespread, deep capital market could also challenge the elite's monopoly status by facilitating upstart competitors' access to capital and, hence, increasing the upstarts' capacity to compete with the elites.

Rajan and Zingales (2003a) analyze this channel in several contexts, of both developing and developed nations, and show how trade openness affects a nation's elites' calculations. If the nation is open to trade, then the elites' underlying businesses must compete, simultaneously making efficient allocation of capital vitally important to them and making any suppression of competition with local upstarts less valuable (because international, cross-border competition will be intense anyway). Thus, Rajan and Zingales (2003b) conclude, in open-trade countries, elites would be less likely to oppose capital market development. Elites in closed countries would have greater incentives to suppress capital market development.

For developing nations, Engerman, Haber, and Sokoloff (2000), and Acemoglu, Johnson, and Robinson (2001), Engerman and Sokoloff (2002, 2005) each indicate how land and agricultural conditions, settlement conditions, and factor endowments could affect early colonial structures so as to strengthen (or weaken) elites with repressive interests and capacities. Particularly where settlement conditions were difficult due to terrain or climate, or where plantation-style agriculture was most efficient, colonial conditions induced powerful, concentrated elites who had little need for either broad-based property rights or open opportunity societies. Those original conditions persist or they induced equality-impeding institutions that continue today. In other colonial settings, particularly where land, climate, and agriculture made European settlement easy and favored smaller, more widely distributed and often individually owned farms, colonization induced broad-based property rights, with weaker elites. These contrasting original settlement conditions then set the stage for equality-enhancing or equality-impeding institutions, which in turn affected property rights and financial markets over the long run. Analyses of the same general genre can be found in Rodrik (1999) and Boix (2003: 45–4, 93), see also Olson (1984).

For Russia, Sonin (2003) and Hoff and Stiglitz (2008) evaluate the political economy of the elites—there, the "oligarchs"—analogously. Property protection can be provided privately or publicly. The oligarchs were well-positioned to protect their property from other less powerful private players. Yet, they judged that publicly provided property protection would facilitate competition from the less powerful, because the already powerful can protect themselves adequately anyway, so they opposed stronger property rights. Hence, financial markets did not develop. (The oligarchs' opposition to stronger property rights, and the concomitant financial market development, may have been short-sighted: the private, elite oligarchs were advantaged in property protection vis-à-vis less well-placed private actors, but they did less well when pitted against emboldened public players when Putin came to power. Had stronger property protection and financial market depth been in place when the stronger state emerged, the government might have had more difficulty in suppressing the oligarchs in as many dimensions as it did.)

This elite suppression of competition explanation is important, although incomplete, because the elites that can shut down local financial markets can presumably *also* shut down open border trading markets. The explanation works well when trade barriers decline for an exogenous reason, such as European political goals of fostering a continent-wide economy in recent decades, in ways that overrode local interests. But these trade-based explanations work less well in other nations at other times, where exogenous shocks do not reduce trade barriers.

Moreover, in a democracy, one must explain why the democratic polity accedes to the elites' interests. A plausible starting point is that the elites' interests coincide with those of others, making a politically dominant coalition possible. A common example is that labor in the elites' industries also has reason to stifle product competition. The two may ally, with labor providing the democratic voting muscle, as Roe (2001, 2003) indicates. Consideration of more complex coalitions comes below. Here let us observe that movement to democracy, all else equal, should foster deeper capital markets, as elites have less weight in the nation's decision-making and, hence, their goal of suppressing competitive upstarts will be harder to attain. However, all else will not be equal when an oligarchy becomes a democracy, as the elites would be pressed then to form coalitions with broader voting groups, like labor. Corporatism and varieties of capitalism concepts may have contained this kind of coalition of elites with similarly interested non-elites embedded in the conceptualization.

Non-Elites' Interests

Non-elites in developing nations can affect property protection and capital markets. If they are living a subsistence life, then appropriating capital can make their lives much better in the short run. If they have weak prospects or are currently calorie-deprived, their immediate survival considerations should trump long-run development goals. Their long run may be capital markets' short run.

And the converse problem of the haves seeking to suppress the rise of new competitors can occur. The have-nots can see property rights, such as investor protection, as protecting the haves. They could conclude that weaker investor protection would enable them to become the equivalent of squatters on the elites' financial assets.

These two dimensions could lead to complex calculations of self-interest: elites may want the government to protect them against financial squatters, but their offsetting desire to suppress new competition may weaken their interest in greater property protection. The have-nots may want to protect their meager property, and a few of the upwardly mobile may think they could enter the elite. But most conclude that investor protection protects the elites' capital from the have-nots' incursions. So they oppose strong property rights for capital. Capital markets and their supporting institutions then do not easily develop.

Political Stability

Roe and Siegel (2011) advance a complementary idea—that financial markets cannot develop easily in severely unstable political environments. As Huntington (1968: 8) observes, "[a]uthority has to exist before it can be limited, and it is authority that is in scarce supply in those modernizing countries where government is at the mercy of alienated intellectuals [and] rambunctious colonels...." Roe and Siegel find that political instability robustly explains differing levels of financial development, even after controlling for trade openness and the level of economic development—and does so in both country-fixed-effects and instrumental variable regressions, and across multiple measures of instability and financial development. In an unstable society, investors' basic property rights cannot be secure, because they cannot be sure what the polity will look like over the life of their investments.

Moreover, a political economy literature plants instability's roots in inequality-perpetuating institutions and ethnic fractionalization.[7] The first factor, economic inequality, fits tightly with explaining why investor protection doesn't develop in unstable environments: For the unstable polity to protect investors, it would have to protect the most favored elements in that polity. Yet that unstable polity is riven by contention over the division of wealth and income—i.e., whether the favored can keep their wealth. They use proxies for inequality-perpetuating institutions and social fractionalization of the type that Engerman and Sokoloff (2002) brought forward and that Easterly (2007) validated, as further evidence for the old idea that inequality induces instability. A developing nation needs to break the negative causal chain of inequality-to-instability-to-weak-financial-development in order to position itself to develop its capital market.

Inequality

It bears separate emphasis that inequality is at the base of several of these theories. Severe inequality undermines political stability, but that political stability is foundational for financial market development privately and then publicly. Yet it may not be easy to reduce that inequality, not just for the obvious reason that those who lose from reducing inequality do not always support its reduction. Inequality may be due to the production technologies available in the economy; it may be endogenous to the polity itself.

Yet several of the world's most developed financial markets are in nations, like the United States, that have quite high Gini coefficients for the distribution of wealth and property. This characteristic deserves further inquiry.

Original conditions

Path dependence could explain this outcome. The nation's income and wealth distribution may have been substantially equal when financial markets first developed and then the nation accepted the inequality later. For the United States, this path dependence result is plausible, as American income and property distribution until the end of the 19th century was relatively flat.[8] Financial markets started to develop during that era and, without a major political break, persisted. Preferences were not always pro-capital market, but they sought to channel that market, not destroy it. Conversely, in countries that suffered a major political break, the distribution of income and wealth during the period in which the capital market was reconstructed could have profoundly influenced its subsequent shape.

A similar sequential process holds true for England. England was the locus of the first industrial revolution. Its severe labor shortage at the time and its energy abundance have been noted as foundations for the technological developments of the first industrial revolution.[9] Less well-noted is that the higher wage rate that accompanies scarce labor would also mitigate inequality, thereby reducing potential political instability and, hence, giving capital market development an opening.

Engerman and Sokoloff (2002: 44–6, 63–83), as noted previously, offer a general structure of the political economy of property rights in the developing world, in which we can place rights in the capital market as a subset. If a colonizing power came to land areas best used for plantation-style crops or, say, mining activities using much unskilled labor, then the original political institutions would reflect the underlying land use characteristics. The colonists from the colonizing country had little reason to foster broad-based property rights, as they could protect themselves well enough. They had little reason to foster developing broad-based education and skills for their plantation workers, since the elites only needed unskilled labor.[10] The consequence is that the nation early on, while still a colony, lacked widely distributed property and had weak property protection institutions. Oppressive institutions persisted and capital markets had little role in future development.[11]

Conceptualizing economic inequality

A second characteristic is related but not identical. Politically destabilizing inequality may not be a function of the raw ratio of wealth and income of the richest to that of the poorest. Rather it might be based on something more complex, which we can call a severity ratio. That is, we look at how close the poorest are to being unable to obtain (say) their 2000 calories per day. That is the denominator. The numerator is the excess (above 2000 calories per day) of the richest in that nation.[12]

In these terms, unlike in the conventional Gini concept, the United States is not all that severely unequal—even the bottom fifth can usually get their 2000 calories per day, unlike in other nations with sharp income inequality. In another polity, where the bottom fifth struggles to obtain only 1800 calories per day, the reconceptualized severity ratio could be quite high, even though the usual Gini calculation would consider the nation to be more equal than the United States.

Mapping inequality and equality onto race

Race, ethnicity, and religion can be central in a polity, particularly when wealth and income disparities cleave along racial or ethnic lines. If race and class map onto one another, that can make it easier for groups to demonize and dehumanize opposing groups and make a stable polity harder to achieve. Several studies have found such ethnic conflicts to be central to political instability.[13]

Race and ethnicity can have other effects, a result that makes analysis of their impact difficult. They can make it easier for capital markets to flourish by diverting conflict from economic to non-economic issues, thereby pushing conflict between haves and have-nots lower on the political agenda. If the polity cleaves along cultural or multiple identity lines that do not map onto distributional differences, those distributional differences can recede in political contentiousness. Sombart (1906), Schattschneider (1960), Benson (1961), and Dahl (1971) speak to this kind of issue in varying ways.

If class and property-owning fault lines are also race and ethnicity lines, capital-market-debilitating conflict would seem likely to be enhanced. If they are not, then the polity may turn away from the economic and social conflict that could damage financial markets, making stability and financial market development more likely.

Contemporary and Historical Examples

In this section, I expand upon several of these classifications, with an eye on political economy configurations around the developed world in recent decades. Several examples evince something other than systemic optimization inside a set of standing institutions as primarily explaining how and why capital markets develop or do not develop. Instead, powerful even if ephemeral preferences and interests seem to explain outcomes as well as, or better than, the economy's preexisting institutions.

Contemporary

Labor in Europe   After World War II, labor was particularly powerful in Europe, in ways that profoundly affected capital markets development. Capital markets institutions were poorly supported in terms of budgets and personnel for the capital markets' regulatory apparatus, even decades after the war.[14] With labor able to make strong claims on firms' cash flows, owners had more reason to stay in place and run the firm, or keep a close watch on the managers, to have more of that cash directed to owners than to workers than weakly monitored managers in capital markets would tend to direct. In the weakened international trading markets after the war, labor and owners had reason to unite to preserve their market position, keep out competition, and divide the spoils.[15]

Managers in the United States   Managers in the United States—the major American corporate "haves"—are a powerful interest group in making the rules governing corporate finance and capital markets. In the 1980s, for example, capital markets created the hostile takeover, which aggregated enough stock such that an outside firm or entrepreneur could acquire an established firm that had a diffusely owned stock structure, facilitating capital markets' capacity to control managers and boards. (As is well-known, American diffuse ownership facilitated the growth of managerial agency costs, because managers lacked a day-to-day boss and often drifted away from shareholders' interests, with high executive compensation, unnecessary expansion, and mistaken operating policies.)

In reaction to this agency-cost structure, outside firms and entrepreneurs would offer to buy up a target firm's stock, with a view to changing management policy or changing management itself. Yet managers and directors were able to disrupt those hostile takeovers transactionally and politically. Transactionally, firms developed poison pills and staggered boards that made it costly for the outsider to buy up the target company's stock. Politically, managers, through their lobbying organizations such as Chambers of Commerce, the Business Roundtable, and, yes, the American Bar Association, obtained favorable laws through the political process—laws that validated and often added to these disruptions of the hostile takeover.

Historical

American populism   The populism of the have-nots can affect financial markets and institutions. Andrew Jackson's destruction in the 1830s of the Second Bank of the United States is the most famous example in American history. It was a seminal event in American financial political history, leaving the United States without a truly national banking system until the latter part of the 20th century. The effect was to make securities markets more vital for the United States and to deny the United States even the rudiments of a central bank until the beginning of the 20th century (or perhaps not until the expansion of the Federal Reserve's authority in 1935). American capital markets could not develop via a nationwide banking system in the 19th and most of the 20th centuries. Roe (1994) attributes a significant fraction of American differences from the rest of the world to the aftermath of Jackson's veto and the institutions that developed to accommodate and perpetuate the resulting weak national banking system.

It could have gone the other way, as two early American Congresses and two American presidents chartered the first and second banks, making the decision to have a quasi-central bank a closer one than basic history books usually have it. Happenstance of political maneuvering was relevant, as an ambitious Henry Clay thought that early passage of a re-chartering would put Jackson on the defensive, forcing him to approve it, while at the same time the incumbent head of the Second Bank of the United States, Nicholas Biddle, proved to be politically clumsy. Yet Clay underestimated both Jackson's resolve and the influence of smaller, weaker banks that preferred not to be challenged by the Second Bank's regulatory impulses. Jackson's veto and destruction of the Second Bank left the United States without a strong, national banking system. And it created the interests—small banks, scattered throughout the country—that deeply influenced financial market development in the country for the next century and a half.

Political economy and populist political impulses persisted, and institutions created by earlier preferences had staying power. After Jackson's 1830s destruction of the Bank, there were multiple efforts to facilitate a truly national banking system. However, these failed on the twin shoals of smaller banks' influence in Congress and populist opinion that did not want a truly national banking system.

During the Civil War, for example, the United States built institutions that were called national banks and that substantively received their charter from Washington. But these banks were not national in their operation, as the National Bank Act long restricted their operations to a single physical location. This limit was challenged in the 1890s, as the Treasury proposed to allow nationwide branching, but the challenge failed in Congress. It was challenged again in the 1920s and 1930s, but it was only mildly tweaked: branching of banks was still limited to a single state at most and, for many states, a smaller geographic profile.

Popular animus played a role in major banking and insurance legislation historically. Glass-Steagall's separation of investment and commercial banking, the Bank Holding Company Act of 1956's limits on bank activities (recall, for those familiar with the politicians of the time, Wright Patman's influence), and the major life insurance companies' lack of power to own common stock (due to the Armstrong investigation of 1906) all can be traced in major part to this popular animus. This left the United States with severe limits on national financial operations: a lack of a national banking system, banks without power to engage in commerce, and insurance companies without authority to own common stock. Although other nations have had some of these limits, few have had them all. Britain, for example, has had powerful insurers. Germany has had universal banks with substantial stock ownership and even more powerful control of their customers' votes. Japan has had nation-spanning banks with significant stock ownership.

German codetermination   German codetermination is a formal institution reflecting a shareholder–labor balance of power, vividly illustrating the political economy effects on core corporate institutions. To settle raw political conflict at several moments in the 20th century, German social democracy led to laws mandating that labor be represented in firms' boardrooms, culminating in approximately parity representation for labor in 1976 for the nation's largest firms. Since unconstrained managers' agendas for continuance, size, and risk avoidance (see Jensen, 1986) maps onto employees' own agendas for the same, an implicit, albeit rough, coalition can easily form between managers and employees. Shareholders will want to have a cohesive counter-coalition in the boardroom. Concentrated ownership is a primary way to concretize that counter-coalition.

Preference Aggregation and Combinatorics

Thus far I have here generally examined discrete interests and their preferences for and against various capital markets forms. But, as the German codetermination experience shows, discrete interests can overlap and coalitions can arise. In this section, I examine, first, examples of how coalitions can form, persist, and morph. Second, I examine the political institutions of preference aggregation and how they affect the political economy outcomes that in turn affect capital market results.

Shifting Coalitions

No one group may dominate the polity's capital market decisions. Coalitions may affect who wins and who loses, and capital markets' configuration.

Banks and labor in Europe One of the more interesting instances of a capital-market-affecting coalition can be seen in post-World War II Western Europe. Perotti and von Thadden (2006) provide compelling argumentation and significant data to support the idea that Western European polities in the post-World War II era had the equivalent of a banker-labor coalition that impeded capital market development.

The argument begins with the median voter theorem: in post-World War II Western Europe, they posit that the median voter had strong human capital but little financial capital. As such, the median voter had little interest in promoting financial markets, fearing that powerful financial markets could and would readily erode their human capital. Stronger capital markets punish slow-moving firms. Capital markets that demand that firms more quickly adopt profitable new technologies could readily erode the value of human capital skills tied to the old technologies. If the median voter's human capital was that which capital markets would erode, the median voter preferred not to have strong capital markets.

At the same time, banks—to the extent their creditors' interest dominated their other financial interests—were moderately, like that median voter, risk averse (because the downside disproportionately affected their loans, while the upside benefited stockholders). Accordingly, banks that became primary corporate governance players had a risk-averse profile that fit well with the median voter's preferences. Labor with limited capital preferred banks to stock markets—and that is what they sought from the polity and, powerful as they were at the time, that is what they got. The median voter voted for bank-oriented capitalism.[16]

Moreover, if a decisive, median-voter middle class had seen its savings and wealth destroyed by the interwar inflation, it would plausibly put a premium on pension obligations guaranteed by the government over private savings. Because the government became the principal provider of pension and retirement funding, private pension funds were not very important. These public pension funds are, in contrast, a major conduit for capital in the United States.[17]

Managers and populism American managers indirectly benefited from American populism. A plausible view of the sequential development of American capital markets history is the following. In the 1890s, national enterprises became viable: railroads spanned the American continent, making the nation into a single market, and engineering economies of scale made large-scale production especially valuable, inducing local firms to merge to form nation-spanning enterprises in industry after industry. With American populism having facilitated a weak national banking system in the 1830s and thereafter, mergers in the 1890s needed stock market financing. With stock market financing in place, ownership started separating from control and managers increasingly gained control over the firm. Stockholder-owners became geographically distant, poorly informed about the firm's operations, and not motivated to influence the firm's day-to-day operations. Once ownership separated from control, managers could become political actors in their own right, via their lobbying organizations such as the Business Roundtable, the National Association of Manufacturers, and Chambers of Commerce. Their interest was to preserve and enhance managerial authority, which they have accomplished.

Managers and labor in the United States   Another American coalition could be found in the 1980s. Hostile takeovers made managers' lives considerably more difficult during that decade, as is well known. But they also disrupted workers' expectations in their firm's future, by putting their jobs at risk. Even if a takeover would not leave the target firm's workers unemployed, they would find themselves in a disrupted work environment. Thus they, like managers, opposed hostile takeovers.

This kind of of managerial–labor coalition was often decisive in making for state anti-takeover law. When a Pennsylvania corporation was targeted for a hostile takeover, it sought strong anti-takeover law from the state's legislature. For many Pennsylvania legislators, voting for the legislation was easy, as both the Chamber of Commerce and the AFL-CIO supported the legislation. Roe (1993: 339), quotes a contemporary comment:

> [The] lobbying effort is the product of teamwork between...Pennsylvania labor unions and a coalition of over two dozen corporations working for the passage of the bill under the well-organized direction of the Pennsylvania Chamber of Business and Industry.

Constituency statutes, which allow boards to consider labor interests when deciding whether to support or oppose a takeover, are a manifestation of this coalition.

Dominant stockholders and labor   Dominant stockholders could ally with labor. As we've seen, business elites often have an interest in suppressing financial markets, as upstarts need access to capital to compete with incumbent elites, which they cannot get without strong financial markets. But this then begs the question of why, in a democracy, the polity would accede to the elites' interests.

Mistake is one possibility. Ideology is another. A coalition is a third: labor at the incumbent firms may get a slice of the incumbent firm's revenues, motivating labor at the business elites' firms to support the elites' interests in suppressing new competitors, because the elites' interests here coincide with their own. If labor obtains such a rent, it wants to suppress product market competition with their employer, suppress upstarts' access to new finance, and suppress open trade with foreign competitors—trade that would erode both labor's rents and those of the elite.

A sophisticated rendition of the multiple possible coalitions can be found in Gourevitch and Shinn (2005), who show how there are almost as many permutations in play between and among labor, owners, and managers as there are rich nations to study. Labor power can dominate owners and managers (Sweden). Or owners and managers can coalesce to dominate workers (Korea). (Or owners can dominate both, as in oligarchic nations. Or workers and owners can coalesce to dominate managers. Or workers and managers can dominate owners, as in corporatist states (Germany, Japan, and the Netherlands).

Western European nations have been analyzed as corporatist systems for some time, with analysts viewing the economy as largely governed by tripartite decision-makers: the government, peak labor associations, and employer representatives. The varieties of capitalism literature (Hall and Soskice, 2001) integrated this thinking of the commonality of interests between employers and employees in some economies with specific production characteristics. That literature argues that economies that depend on skilled labor tend not to have liquid stock markets, which would disrupt labor skills. Conversely, economies that depend less on labor with firm-specific skills could handle capital markets' disruptions. These analyses look at the informal institutions of coalition formation. Business leaders would want to be represented at the centralized decision-making institutions, thereby putting a thumb on the scale for close ownership and, hence, weaker capital markets as well.

Political Institutions and Preference Aggregation

Here I shift focus from how raw preferences and interests can shape institutions and financial markets to how the political economy of institutions shapes financial outcomes. Conceptually more traditional than the former, the political economy of institutional structure deserves to be applied to capital markets formation and merits summary and development here.

Particularly since Arrow's impossibility theorem, political scientists have examined mechanisms of preference aggregation in a polity, as these profoundly affect policy outcomes. As is well known, the impossibility theorem's conceptual power comes from voters having differently ordered preferences. When a choice between two of three viable options is presented, with the winner facing off against the third choice, the winner may differ from that which would result if the ordering of the choices had been otherwise.

Parliamentary vs presidential systems: proportional representation and party-lists   Pagano and Volpin (2005) adapt Persson and Tabellini's (2000, 2005) general inquiry into parliamentary systems, proportional representation, and presidential systems to corporate and capital markets. Party-list, proportional representation enables a coalition among business owners and labor to enact rules that poorly protect capital providers (so that incumbent business owners benefit at the expense of outside investors) and that protect incumbent labor well. Decisions are not driven by the median voter, but by the way a dominant coalition forms. Iversen and Soskice (2006) argue that proportional representation structures facilitate center-left redistributive coalitions, while majoritarian, presidential, first-past-the-post systems facilitate center-right, low redistribution outcomes. In majoritarian systems, they indicate, the decisive middle class vote will side with the well-to-do for fear of being taxed by the poor; but in proportional representation systems, the middle class can ally with the poor to redistribute from the well-to-do while still maintaining enough influence in the middle-poor coalition to ensure that the middle class are not themselves the target for redistribution.

Mueller (2006) shows further how first-past-the-post electoral systems, such as those in the United States, can affect corporate governance outcomes. In such political systems, a national interest group, such as labor, needs to persistently recapture a working majority in the legislature, working district by district, legislator by legislator. This process is costly for interest groups. But in a party-list system, the identity of the particular legislator is not vital to the interest group getting that legislator's vote: the legislator follows party discipline, thereby facilitating national deal-making in which national labor institutions can be quite influential. In systems with first-past-the-post territorial elections, such as the United States, such national coalitions (and their concomitant influence) are harder to create and maintain. It's thus no accident that Tip O'Neill's famous aphorism—that all politics is local—came from an American national politician, the locally elected leader of the House of Representatives, a legislative body that is a collection of locally elected representatives who make national policy.

Mechanisms for preference aggregation can have a profound impact on the ability of players to form coalitions and, consequently, on the influence they can exert on the development of capital markets.

American federalism: I   The organization of the American Congress is relevant here in another dimension. If all politics (in the United States) is local, local interests can determine national outcomes. One reason why all politics is local is that the House of Representatives is organized by, and elected by, local, geographically discrete districts. With representatives dependent on local interests for their election, the House was responsive historically to local bankers who wished to be shielded from out-of-district competition. When technology was such that only localized bricks-and-mortar banking was possible (i.e., before the era of automated teller machines, online banking, and modern inexpensive telecommunications), bankers had the means and the motivation to influence their local representatives' voting on whether to facilitate nationwide bank branching, a result that we've seen deeply affected American capital markets. The state-by-state organization of the Senate presumably had a similar, albeit weaker, impact.

Hence, one can see a structure-driven process: American political structure promoted local interests. When local banking was technologically possible, this local power *overly* emphasized local banking, making national banking markets impossible during the formative years of national industry. This meant that large industrial firms had to raise their capital from disparate sources that could not readily concentrate their stockholdings, facilitating a shift in authority inside the firm from financiers and owners to managers.

American federalism: II, Delaware   American corporate and capital markets law is made in two principal jurisdictions: Delaware (via the law of corporate organization) and Washington (via the law covering securities regulation). Unlike other polities, the

United States has long allowed the corporation to choose its own state of incorporation, regardless of where it does business in the nation; the corporation thus chooses its own governing law. Most major American public firms choose to incorporate in Delaware.

The federal organization of American corporate lawmaking has long been a focus of US corporate law academics, who have seen competition among states for corporate charters (and their resulting revenues) as a core driver in making corporate law, thereby applying Tiebout's (1956) insights on political jurisdictional mobility to the specifics of corporate lawmaking. Some thought the competition was "to the top" in making corporate law more efficient,[18] while others saw the competition as one to the bottom, by favoring the corporate players most central to the incorporation decision—managers, controlling shareholders, and their lawyers.[19]

Federal organization of the polity can affect capital markets, as interests dominant at the state level can pass rules that a busy Congress might not pass. During the hostile takeover era, many states passed strong anti-takeover laws, making it transactionally more expensive for an outsider to buy up stock of a public firm. In the political balance were managerial, labor, and capital interests: local managers did not want the hostile takeover to proceed. Local labor employed by the target company did not want the offer to proceed. While shareholders in the capital market presumably wanted the takeover to proceed, many of them were not local, because capital markets were national, or international. Hence, the balance favored in-state managerial and labor interests over capital market interests.[20] Again, politics is (often enough) local.

American federalism: III, Delaware and Washington   The parallel state-federal structure of American corporate lawmaking can affect capital markets in another dimension. The interests that dominate in Delaware are not the same as those making corporate and securities law in Washington. Particularly during times of financial crisis or scandal, the populist input to weaken shareholder and financial strength in the corporation, or to punish managers who are seen as overly compensated, is strong in Washington and weaker in Delaware, where the interests of managers and shareholders dominate, nearly to the exclusion of other interests and forces.

In areas that are of overlapping concern to national and Delaware lawmakers, the national and local polities interact in two major ways. First, Delaware may preemptively pass financial and corporate law that it might not have passed otherwise, to reduce the chances of federal intervention. It may do so out of self-preservation: if Delaware is way out of line with national sentiment, corporate law could move to Washington, which could replace Delaware lawmaking with national lawmaking, turning corporate law, like securities law, into national, congressionally made law. Second, it may do so to protect its local interests: with first-mover advantages, Delaware may pass rules that go some but not all of the way to satisfying the national appetite. Doing so would allow it to preserve as much autonomy for managers (or value for shareholders) as possible, by persuading the national player that enough had been done, so that the national players need not act. This is analogous to the process Spiller and Gely (2008) posited for the Supreme Court, by which the Court often decides in ways to diminish the chance of congressional action (by coming closer to congressional preferences than it would have otherwise), a process that Roe (2005, 2012) analyzed for Delaware–Washington interaction.

Corporatism and varieties of capitalism   Western European nations have been analyzed as corporatist systems for some time, with analysts viewing the economy as being largely governed by a tripartite of decision-makers: the government, peak labor associations, and employer representatives. The varieties of capitalism literature[21] integrated this thinking into production characteristics. That literature argues that economies that depend on skilled labor tend not to have liquid stock markets, which would disrupt labor skills. Conversely, economies that depend less on labor with firm-specific skills could handle capital markets' disruptions. While not exactly formal preference aggregation, these analyses do look at the informal institutions of coalition formation. Business leaders would want to be represented at the centralized decision-making institutions, thereby putting a thumb on the scale for close ownership and weaker capital markets as well.

Weak capital after World War II   Earlier in the chapter, I indicated that a defining feature of the political economy of American capital markets can be found in the destruction of the Second Bank of the United States, which left the United States without a nationwide banking system during the 19th century, when a continent-wide, nationwide industrial economy arose. The interests, ideologies, and institutions that resulted tended to reinforce themselves during times of crisis, and no crisis was so severe as to leave the economy flat, destroyed, and needing a fully new set of institutions. Even the 1930s New Deal tended to strengthen preexisting interests, not destroy them.

Could there be a similar foundational political economy event for Western European and East Asian capital markets? I think there is, but as of now that possibility must be seen as a hypothesis, needing further theoretical and factual development.

The concept would be that after World War II political and economic institutions had been sufficiently destroyed in Europe that a substantial new construction of those institutions took place. In those years, capital owners and labor interests sought to establish the rules of the game that would thereafter govern markets and finance from that time onward.

The twist arises from the following difficulty: we know that the rules of the game on the European continent had a pro-labor and not a pro-capital tilt in the subsequent decades. But with capital scarce after World War II—the continent's physical capital was, after all, largely destroyed—and with labor, especially skilled labor, relatively more abundant, the bargaining process in the economic arena should have *favored* the scarce resource's preferences.

Yet, at least as far as the rules were concerned, the results went the other way. Labor markets, including wage rates and other benefits, were favored in the post-World War II decades.

The hypothesis I advance here and that should be developed elsewhere is a political economy one: when the bargaining began for a new post-war understanding as to how to organize capital and labor markets, the pro-capital markets players were relatively weak in the political arena—weak relative both to labor at the time and to their own more usual strength in influencing results. Their physical capital had largely been destroyed during the war; they had limited capacity to affect the politics of the time with campaign contributions, with lobbying, or otherwise when the foundational deals were made. Only later could they afford the time, money, and personnel for such efforts; then they made sure that they were represented at the peak bargaining of the corporatist model. By that later time, however, labor had acquired its post-war favored status. For now, the original conditions idea—that the preferences and weak institutional structure in continental Europe right after World War II set the institutional framework for subsequent, relatively weak capital market development—is a hypothesis for further development. During the immediate post-war period, strongly held popular preferences and politically weak ownership interests could well have established the new institutional arrangements that would endure, affecting capital markets' structure for decades.

Geopolitics

Geography and international politics can influence democratic political preferences and a nation's internal political economy. Geographic features of the last half of the 20th century are relevant and can be quickly sketched out. Geographic features over time are more subtle, but can also be seen.

Countering the Soviet Union

The central geopolitical fact in continental Europe in the second half of the 20th century was the looming presence of the Soviet Union. In the initial post-war elections, the communist party did quite well in France and Italy, making it important for centrist and conservative parties to co-opt the communist program, which they did. The result was policy that favored incumbent labor and that disfavored capital markets.

One can think of the geopolitics as lying along a continuum: in Eastern Europe, communists gained power and capital markets ended. In Western Europe, to stave off communist power, the political center had to adopt some of the left's program. For Japan, South Korea, and Taiwan, the relationship with China in the immediate post-war decades could well have brought similar domestic sensibilities into play.

European geography over the centuries

The state has been seen as stronger in Europe than in the United States. This view maps onto the view of state actors as their own interest group that seeks to diminish the power of private capital markets, as outlined in the initial section of this chapter. The strength of the European state could have first originated in European geography: the open east-west plains of Europe meant that local security from invasion was always at issue and that vulnerability induced national militaries and strong states (Roe, 2007). Post-war geopolitics reproduced the incentives for a strong state.

This geographic history would then contrast with that of the United States and Britain historically, and with that of Europe today. The United States and Britain were both separated from invaders by bodies of water—narrow but real in Britain's case and wide for the United States. That geographic separation meant that centralized, standing armies were not needed for national security, and the state could be weaker than otherwise, thereby leaving space for private capital markets to develop. And, today, after the fall of the Berlin Wall and a safer European geopolitical reality, one including European economic integration, the geopolitics of a centralized state for smaller European nations is historical, not current.

Political Change: Rightward and Leftward Shifts over Time

The left-right split's impact on financial markets (see Roe, 2003; Perotti and von Thadden, 2006) can be tested over time, but tests done thus far are not dispositive. That is, financial markets in the developed nations strengthened in the 1990s, even in nations with locally left-of-center governments (Botero et al., 2004; Culpepper, 2011).

This is an understandable misconception.[22] The problem and its misconception can easily be conceptualized (and diagrammed; see Figure 4.2). Over time, the center of gravity in a polity can change, sometimes sharply. As an example, Tony Blair's election as prime minister in 1997 marked not the ascendancy of the hard left that long dominated the Labour Party, but rather the ascendancy of the *moderating* of the left as it tacked toward the center. Yet it would be coded as the ascent of a left-of-center government in the usual academic studies thus far. But capital markets may draw comfort from a tame left and flourish not because the left was in power but because the left had moved rightward. Brazil's experience with a market-friendly former union leader in the recent decade also illustrates the phenomenon and potential for a left-right attribution error.

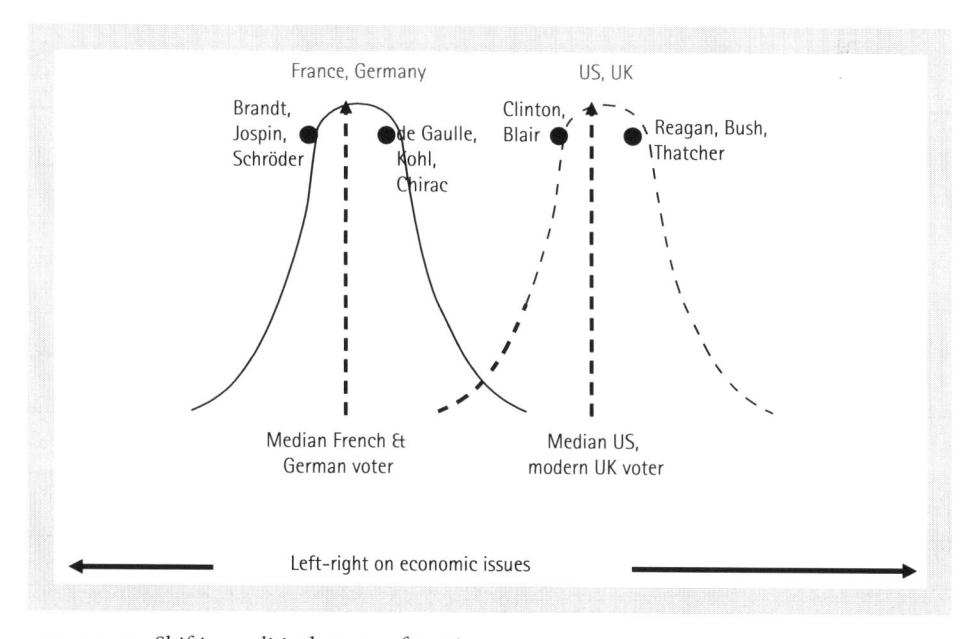

FIGURE 4.2. Shifting political center of gravity

Similarly, the Clinton presidency represented the shifting of the American left-of-center to a particularly market-friendly status. That administration—left-of-center in American terms—was as market-oriented as a right-tilting government in Western Europe in many eras.

Indeed, in a pure median voter theory, the *identity* of the party in power makes no difference for the nation's policy output: it's the *left-right location* of the median voter that determines the polity's policies. Since some of the most substantial empirical work done thus far on left-right influence on capital markets suffers from this misconception, more work needs to be done here.

In particular, Eichengreen (2007: 333) explains one reason why a left-of-center government can enact reforms that, in a prior decade, only a right-of-center government would have considered: "The German chancellor Gerhard Schröder's Agenda 2010 of labor-market reforms was motivated, in part, by the specter of German manufacturing moving east if steps were not taken to reduce labor costs."

And, here again, preferences seem as important as ongoing institutions in explaining capital markets outcomes.[23] The institutions may persist, but changing preferences over time induce differing outcomes.

Indeterminacy, Overgeneralization, and Local Variation

Two characteristics can undermine the influence of the political economy academic agenda in understanding capital markets. First, although politics may well be decisive in determining capital markets' shape and extent, too many political explanations are local: a particular coalition in this nation, the happenstance of deal-making in that nation. A narrative of national financial legislation may reveal its own particular political economy story, but the explanation may not test well, because a testable characteristic may not repeat in a sufficient number of nations to run the required regressions. Consequently, only the most general of political economy theories may be susceptible to strong empirical analysis. National case studies via econometrically weak investigatory modes could be how we see what explains capital markets' depth, or lack of it. Armour and Lele (2009: 492–3), for example, study Indian financial markets and investment protection in this manner, concluding with the primacy of political considerations: "In industries that were subject to planning, the dominant interest groups lobby for redistributive rules to maintain their protected status. By contrast, in sectors that were never subject to central planning, the dominant interest groups seek rules that allow markets to function more effectively. In short, the quality of investor protection and sectoral development have co-evolved on paths that have been to a large degree determined by past political choices."

A second problem afflicts a political economy approach. Often underlying our analysis is the goal of finding out what works for policy and recommending that policy's adoption.

If we can recommend a new rule or two that helps capital markets, or can find an existing one that hinders them without ancillary benefit, then we can recommend which rules to adopt and which to repeal. But a political economy analysis does not yield us such strong, precise normative outputs. National politics is hard enough to understand, much less to influence with academic work.

But understanding the political economy inputs is still vital to normative analysis. If there's a menu of improvements for financial markets, but some will run into political economy problems, while others will not, then policymakers can choose accordingly. International aid agencies may be particularly susceptible to ignoring political economy influences because they see it as illegitimate for them to seek political influence. But if the earlier focus on the centrality of political instability is correct, they can better choose how to allocate their aid and advice. Highly unstable polities are unlikely to benefit from even good rules; attempts to graft institutions for finance into such polities will be unlikely to "take." Hence, the development agencies can channel their efforts into nations that already have sufficient stability for success to be possible. They can also choose among capital markets development policies, emphasizing those that are more likely to stabilize than to destabilize the polity.

Conclusion

Two fundamental fractures can lead to crippling instabilities in the politics of capitalism. One is the contest between the haves and the have-nots. Have-nots can conclude that they gain too little from capital markets, so they may expropriate capital from the haves. Capitalism may persist in form, but its productivity would be demolished, as savers will not save—i.e., will not create capital—because, in such polities, owners of physical and financial capital do not see their capital as safe. Instead, they will consume it, for if they do not, the have-nots will take it. Alternatively, the haves may capture political institutions themselves and seek to put in place institutions that redistribute value to themselves. In the tension, capitalist institutions such as financial markets may not survive or, if they do survive, would fail to provide prosperity.

The second problem cuts the polity along another dimension: the capitalist haves may split and contest the polity among themselves. Those haves who have captured political institutions may seek to redistribute value away from other haves. The winners obtain rules that further their own type of capital markets. And with their wealth, they have both the strength and the motivation to preserve their position and to suppress competitive upstarts. If the institutions are roughly democratic, they will find it valuable to form alliances with voting masses, presumably starting with labor from their own industry.

The political problem of capitalism is to find institutions and preference distributions that keep the depth and costs of such fissures low. No country succeeds in making them approach zero. Much that seems superficially inefficient to an economics-oriented analyst is a polity's effort to keep these fissures from rupturing the terrain.

These two problems arise in multiple dimensions in the economy, affecting welfare and social payments, antitrust policy, taxation, corporate law, income distribution, and financial markets. Many seemingly small problems in implementation of rules and laws are local manifestations of one of these two problems. I have for the most part analyzed these two basic problems in the politics of capitalism in terms of how they specifically affect financial markets and corporate structures. The issues may be more general.

We have made much headway in the past few decades, since North's (1990) essay, in understanding how institutions persist through time. Institutions, though, are created at some point in time. And institutions can also be torn down and replaced. People and polities with preferences and interests create them, change them, and at times destroy them. Sometimes previously created institutions can withstand a tidal wave from current preferences, sometimes they cannot. Sometimes preferences create new institutions that endure. Sometimes today's result can be predicted from the preexisting institutional framework; sometimes currently created preferences that emerge from an economic or political crisis determine today's result and tomorrow's institutions. The political economy of capital markets well illustrates this interaction between preferences and institutions. Only when we understand how preferences for and against capital markets interact with institutions in the political economy will we understand the shape and extent of the capital market. Preferences can at times overwhelm existing institutions and establish new ones that support, channel, and determine the strength, nature, and quality of capital markets. Today's preferences when effective and dominant in the political arena become tomorrow's governing institutions.

Notes

1. Weymouth and Broz (2008).
2. E.g. Berle and Means (1933); Jensen and Meckling (1976).
3. Bebchuk and Roe (1999).
4. Morck (2000) (concentrated ownership).
5. Greif (2006: ch. 3 and 441–3); cf. Scott (1987).
6. Mahoney (1997); Coffee (2001); Roe (2001).
7. E.g. Alesina and Perotti (1996); cf. Ayyagari et al. (2008).
8. Lindert (2006: 2–624).
9. Allen (2009).
10. Cf. Bobonis (2008).
11. See also Engerman et al. (2000) and Acemoglu et al. (2001). Cf. Glaeser (2006).
12. Williamson (2009).
13. See Easterly and Levine (1997); Alesina et al. (2003).
14. Jackson and Roe (2009).
15. Roe (2000, 2001, 2003).
16. Or, analogously, their political parties made appropriate deals to support bank-oriented capitalism (Pagano and Volpin, 2005).
17. See Perotti and Schwienbacher (2009 Alesina et al. (2003)).

    It's possible to recast the argument I offer in this chapter in property-owning terms. The relevant question would be whether the median voter owns property, not simply whether

he or she owns financial property. If the median voter owns significant property—a house, a car—then he or she may support property rights generally, which include rights to financial property.
18. Winter (1977); Romano (1993).
19. Bebchuk (1992); Cary (1974) Kahan and Kamar (2002) question how intense that state competition really is.
20. E.g. Romano (1988); Roe (1993); Miller (1998).
21. Hall and Soskice (2001).
22. See Pinto et al. (2010); Culpepper (2011).
23. The rents-oriented version of the social democratic theory helps to explain Eichengreen's observation. Let's posit, again, that rents to labor and owners in key industries help to fuel the social democratic conventions demeaning capital markets, whose corrosive effects would erode rents to elites (see Rajan and Zingales, 2003a) and to the favored labor sectors that induce social democratic governments to oppose capital market development (see Roe, 2001, 2003). As the rents erode, labor and its allies have fewer reasons to be wary of capital market development. Hence, their preferred policies would change.

Preferences and institutions interact. For example, many British corporate institutions developed early in the 20th century (Franks et al., 2009), when Britain was a conservative polity. These institutions could have persisted, even when the polity moved leftward. The polity might not have allowed those institutions to arise in that era, but the extant interests (and institutions) could have been strong enough to resist severe destruction.

References

ACEMOGLU, D., and PEROTTI, R. (1996). "Income Distribution, Political Instability, and Investment," *European Economic Review*, 40: 1203–28.

——— JOHNSON, S., and ROBINSON, J. A. (2001). "The Colonial Origins of Comparative Development: An Empirical Investigation," *American Economic Review*, 91: 1369–401.

ALESINA, A., DEVLEESCHAUWER, A., EASTERLY, W., KURLAT, S., and WACZIARG, R. (2003). "Fractionalization," *Journal of Economic Growth*, 8: 155–94.

ALLEN, R. (2009). *The British Industrial Revolution in Global Perspective*. Cambridge: Cambridge University Press.

ARMOUR, J., and LELE, P. (2009). "Law, Finance, and Politics: The Case of India," *Law & Society Review*, 43: 491–526.

AYYAGARI, M., DEMIRGÜÇ-KUNT, A., and MAKSIMOVIC, V. (2008). "How Well Do Institutional Theories Explain Firm's Perceptions of Property Rights?" *Review of Financial Studies*, 21: 1833–71.

BEBCHUK, L. (1992). "Federalism and the Corporation: The Desirable Limits on State Competition in Corporate Law," *Harvard Law Review*, 105: 1435–510.

——— and NEEMAN, Z. (2010). "Investor Protection and Interest Group Politics," *Review of Financial Studies*, 23: 939–61.

——— and ROE, M. (1999). "A Theory of Path Dependence in Corporate Ownership and Governance," *Stanford Law Review*, 52: 127–70.

BENSON, L. (1961). *The Concept of Jacksonian Democracy: New York as a Test Case*. Princeton: Princeton University Press.

BERLE, A., and MEANS, G. (1933). *The Modern Corporation and Private Property*. New York: Macmillan.
BOBONIS, G. J. (2008). "Political Institutions, Labor Coercion, and Emergence of Public Schooling: Evidence from the 19th Century Coffee Boom," Working Paper, University of Toronto.
BOIX, C. (2003). *Democracy and Redistribution*. New York: Cambridge University Press.
BOTERO, J., DJANKOV, R., LA PORTA, R., LOPEZ-DE-SILANES, F., and SHLEIFER, A. (2004). "The Regulation of Labor," *Quarterly Journal of Economics*, 119: 1339–82.
CARY, W. L. (1974). "Federalism and Corporate Law: Reflections upon Delaware," *Yale Law Journal*, 83: 663–705.
COFFEE, J. C. (2001). "The Rise of Dispersed Ownership," *Yale Law Journal*, 111: 1–82.
CULPEPPER, P. (2011). *Quiet Politics and Business Power: Corporate Control in Europe and Japan*. New York: Cambridge University Press.
DAHL, R. (1971). *Polyarchy: Participation and Opposition*. New Haven: Yale University Press.
DELONG, J. B. (1991). "Did J. P. Morgan's Men Add Value," in P. Temin, (ed.), *Inside the Business Enterprise*. Chicago: University of Chicago Press.
DOUGLAS, W. O. (1940). *Democracy and Finance*. New Haven: Yale University Press.
EASTERLY, W. (2007). "Inequality does Cause Underdevelopment: Insights from a New Instrument," *Journal of Development Economics*, 84: 755–76.
—— and LEVINE, R. (1997). "Africa's Growth Tragedy: Policies and Ethnic Divisions," *Quarterly Journal of Economics*, 62: 1203–50.
EICHENGREEN, BARRY. (2007). *The European Economy Since 1945: Coordinated Capitalism and Beyond*. Princeton: Princeton University Press.
ENGERMAN, S. L., and SOKOLOFF, K. L. (2002). "Factor Endowments, Inequality, and Paths of Development among New World Economies," *Economia*, 3: 41–109.
—— —— (2005). "Institutional and Non-institutional Explanations of Economic Differences," in C. Ménard and M. M. Shirley (eds.), *Handbook of New Institutional Economics*. New York: Springer, 639–65.
—— HABER, S. H., and SOKOLOFF, K. L. (2000). "Inequality, Institutions and Differential Paths of Growth Among New World Economies," in C. Ménard (ed.), *Institutions, Contracts and Organizations: Perspectives from New Institutional Economics*. Northampton, MA: Edward Elgar, 108–34.
FRANKS, J., MAYER, C., and ROSSI, S. (2009). "Ownership: Evolution and Regulation," *Journal of Financial Studies*, 22: 4009–56.
GLAESER, E. (2006). "Inequality," in B. Weingast and D. Wittman (eds.), *Oxford Handbook of Political Economy*. New York: Oxford University Press, 624–41.
GOUREVITCH, P., and SHINN, J. (2005). *Political Power and Corporate Control: The New Global Politics of Corporate Governance*. Princeton: Princeton University Press.
GREIF, A. (2006). *Institutions and the Path to the Modern Economy: Lessons from Medieval Trade*. New York: Cambridge University Press.
GRUNDFEST, J. (1990). "Subordination of American Capital," *Journal of Financial Economics*, 27: 89–114.
HALL, P. A., and SOSKICE, D. (eds.) (2001). *Varieties of Capitalism: The Institutional Foundations of Comparative Advantage*. New York: Oxford University Press.
HOFF, K., and STIGLITZ, J. E. (2008). "Exiting a Lawless State," *Economic Journal*, 118: 1474–97.
HUNTINGTON, S. P. (1968). *Political Order in Changing Societies*. New Haven: Yale University Press.

IVERSEN, T., and SOSKICE, D. (2006). "Electoral Institutions, Parties and the Politics of Coalitions: Why Some Democracies Redistribute More than Others," *American Political Science Review*, 100: 165–81.

JACKSON, H. E., and ROE, M. J. (2009). "Public and Private Enforcement of Securities Laws: Resource-Based Evidence," *Journal of Financial Economics*, 93: 207–38.

JENSEN, M. (1986). "Agency Costs of Free Cash Flow, Corporate Finance, and Takeovers," *American Economic Review*, 76: 323–9.

—— and MECKLING, W. (1976). "Theory of the Firm: Managerial Behavior, Agency Costs and Ownership Structure," *Journal of Financial Economics*, 3: 305–60.

KAHAN, M., and KAMAR, E. (2002). "The Myth of State Competition in Corporate Law," *Stanford Law Review*, 55: 679–749.

LANGEVOORT, D. (1987). "Statutory Obsolescence and the Judicial Process: The Revisionist Role of the Courts in Federal Banking Regulation," *Michigan Law Review*, 85: 672–733.

LINDERT, P. (2006). "Economic Inequality and Poverty," in S. B. Carter et al. (eds.), *Historical Statistics of the United States*. Cambridge: Cambridge University Press.

MACEY, J., and MILLER, G. (1991). "Origin of the Blue Sky Laws," *Texas Law Review*, 70: 347–97.

MAHONEY, P. (1997). "The Exchange as Regulator," *Virginia Law Review*, 83: 1453–500.

MAYER, C. (2008). "Trust in Financial Markets," *European Financial Management*, 14: 617–32.

MILLER, G. (1998). "Political Structure and Corporate Governance: Some Points of Contrast between the United States and England," *Columbia Business Law Review*, 51–78.

MIWA, Y., and RAMSEYER, M. (2002). "The Value of Prominent Directors: Corporate Governance and Bank Access in Transitional Japan," *Journal of Legal Studies*, 31: 273–301.

MORCK, R. (ed.) (2000). *Concentrated Corporate Ownership*. Chicago: University of Chicago Press.

MUELLER, D. (2006). "The Economics and Politics of Corporate Governance," in G. Ferrarini and E. Wymeersch (eds.), *Investor Protection in Europe: Corporate Law Making, the MiFID and Beyond*. Oxford: Oxford University Press, 3–30.

NORTH, D. (1990). *Institutions, Institutional Change, and Economic Performance*. Cambridge: Cambridge University Press.

—— and WEINGAST, B. (1989). "Constitutions and Commitment: The Evolution of Institutions Governing Public Choice in Seventeenth-Century England," *Journal of Economic History*, 4: 803–32.

OLSON, M. (1984). *The Rise and Decline of Nations: Economic Growth, Stagflation, and Social Rigidities*. New Haven: Yale University Press.

PAGANO, M., and VOLPIN, P. (2005). "The Political Economy of Corporate Governance," *American Economic Review*, 95: 1005–30.

PEROTTI, E. C., and SCHWIENBACHER, A. (2009). "The Political Origin of Pension Funding," *Journal of Financial Intermediation*, 18: 384–404.

—— and VON THADDEN, E.-L. (2006). "The Political Economy of Corporate Control and Labor Rents," *Journal of Political Economy*, 114: 145–74.

PERSSON, T., and TABELLINI, G. (2000). *Political Economics*. Cambridge, MA: MIT Press.

—— —— (2005). *The Economic Effect of Constitutions*. Cambridge, MA: MIT Press.

PINTO, P., WEYMOUTH, S., and GOUREVITCH, P. (2010). "The Politics of Stock Market Development," *Review of International Political Economy*, 17: 378–409.

RAJAN, R., and ZINGALES, L. (2003a). "The Great Reversals: The Politics of Financial Development in the Twentieth Century," *Journal of Financial Economics*, 69: 5–50.

Rajan, R., and Zingales, L. (2003b). *Saving Capitalism from the Capitalists*. New York: Crown.
Rock, E. (2001). "Encountering the Scarlet Woman of Wall Street," *Theoretical Inquiries in Law*, 2: 237–64.
Rodrik, D. (1999). "Where Did All the Growth Go?—External Shocks, Social Conflict, and Growth Collapses," *Journal of Economic Growth*, 4: 385–412.
Roe, M. J. (1990). "Political and Legal Restraints on Corporate Control," *Journal of Financial Economics*, 27: 7–41.
—— (1993). "Takeover Politics," in M. Blair (ed.), *The Deal Decade*. Washington, DC: Brookings, 321–52.
—— (1994). *Strong Managers, Weak Owners: The Political Roots of American Corporate Finance*. Princeton: Princeton University Press.
—— (2000). "Political Preconditions to Separating Ownership from Corporate Control," *Stanford Law Review*, 53: 539–606.
—— (2001). "Rents and their Corporate Consequences," *Stanford Law Review*, 53: 1463–94.
—— (2003). *Political Determinants of Corporate Governance*. Oxford: Oxford University Press.
—— (2005). "Delaware's Politics," *Harvard Law Review*, 118: 2491–543.
—— (2007). "Juries and the Political Economy of Legal Origin," *Journal of Comparative Economics*, 35: 294–308.
—— (2012). "The Corporate Shareholder's Vote and Its Political Economy, in Delaware and in Washington," *Harvard Business Law Review*, 2: 1–xx.
—— and Siegel, J. (2011). "Political Instability: Effects on Financial Development, Roots in the Severity of Economic Inequality," *Journal of Comparative Economics*, 37: 279–309.
Romano, R. (1988). "The Future of Hostile Takeovers: Legislation and Public Opinion," *University of Cincinnati Law Review*, 57: 457–506.
—— (1993). *The Genius of American Corporate Law*. Washington, DC: AEI Press.
Schattsneider, E. E. (1960). *The Semi Sovereign People: A Realist's View of Democracy in America*. New York: Holt, Rinehart and Winston.
Scott, R. E. (1987). "Conflict and Cooperation in Long-Term Contracts," *California Law Review*, 75: 2005–54.
Skocpol, T. (1979). *States and Social Revolutions: A Comparative Analysis of France, Russia and China*. New York: Cambridge University Press.
Sombart, W. (1906). *Why Is there No Socialism in the United States?* trans. P. Hocking and C. T. Husbands. New York: International Arts and Sciences Press, 1976.
Sonin, K. (2003). "Why the Rich May Favor Poor Protection of Property Rights," *Journal of Comparative Economics*, 31: 715–31.
Spiller, P., and Gely, R. (2008). "Strategic Judicial Decision-Making," in K. Whittington, D. Kelemen, and G. Caldeira (eds.), *The Oxford Handbook of Law and Politics*. New York: Oxford University Press, 34–45.
Tiebout, C. (1956). "A Pure Theory of Local Expenditures," *Journal of Political Economy*, 64: 416–24.
Weymouth, S., and Broz, J. L. (2008). "Partisanship versus Institutions as Determinants of Property Rights: Firm-Level Evidence," available at <http://ssrn.com/abstract=1080259>.
Williamson, J. (2009). "History without Evidence: Latin American Inequality since 1491," NBER Working Paper 14766, available at <http://www.nber.org/papers/w14766>.
Winter, R. (1977). "State Law, Shareholder Protection, and the Theory of the Corporation," *Journal of Legal Studies*, 6: 251–92.

CHAPTER 5

AN INTERNATIONAL CORPORATE GOVERNANCE INDEX

MARINA MARTYNOVA AND LUC RENNEBOOG[1]

INTRODUCTION

TRIGGERED by the seminal work of La Porta, Lopez-de-Silanes, Shleifer, and Vishny (1997, 1998; hereafter LLSV), the economic effects of corporate governance regulation have received notable academic attention over the past decade. The new stream of literature on law and finance provides a comparative analysis of institutional frameworks around the world and their impact on economic behavior and on the governance of firms. Although the importance of regulation on economic activities has been stressed since the late 1930s (e.g. Coase, 1937), LLSV have moved this topic to the top of the research agenda by documenting empirically the relationship between the law and economic growth, the development of markets, and the governance of firms. Importantly, LLSV developed the tools that enable researchers to compare institutional environments across countries and to study empirically the effects of corporate regulation. These tools comprise, amongst others, a country classification by legal origin and indices that characterizes the quality of regulatory provisions covering the protection of corporate shareholders and creditors, as well as law enforcement. However, the LLSV indices have some limitations. First, some of these indices are static. In the late 1990s and early 2000s, many countries have undergone substantial reforms of their corporate legislations. There is little evidence regarding the scope of these reforms and their impact on the protection of the rights of corporate investors and the corporate governance system overall. The LLSV indices have been updated in Djankov et al. (2008). A second limitation of the LLSV corporate governance indices is that the authors use a comparative approach to construct them. LLSV opt for the US corporate law as the reference legal system and identify the key legal provisions in the governance of US companies. It is therefore not surprising that countries with legal systems most closely resembling that of the US receive the highest score on the LLSV rating. This approach, however, typically ignores the regulatory principles that prevail in other countries but not in the US. Spamann (2006, 2010) recognizes this problem, identifies measurement errors in the LLSV indices and their successors,[2] and reconstructs those indices.

In this chapter we first develop three corporate governance indices that reflect the quality of national laws aimed at protecting (i) corporate shareholders from being expropriated by the firm's management; (ii) minority shareholders from being expropriated by the large blockholder; and (iii) creditors from being expropriated by the firm's shareholders. When constructing the indices, we do not use the comparative approach employed by LLSV but use a functional approach instead. This way we try to avoid the usual criticism on quantifying corporate governance regulation that "one size does not fit all" (Rose, 2007; Baghat et al., 2008; Goergen and Renneboog, 2008; Bebchuk and Cohen, 2009; Spamann, 2010). That is, we identify all major provisions of corporate laws by country and classify them according to the degree of protection they offer to the above-mentioned principals. Subsequently, we quantify the regulatory provisions using three indices that characterize the effectiveness of the legal system in reducing the three basic agency problems: those arising between the management and the shareholders, between majority and minority shareholders, and between creditors and shareholders. The advantage of the functional approach is that it covers all regulatory provisions in existence in all European countries and the US and allows us to construct indices that capture both the weak and strong aspects of the various corporate governance regimes. Second, we empirically document the evolution of corporate governance regulations for all (30) European countries and the US. We analyze whether regulatory convergence has been started, and, if so, detect the main patterns of the convergence process.

The analysis in this chapter is based on a unique corporate governance database that comprises the main changes in corporate governance regulations in the US and all European countries in the period 1990–2005. The database on corporate legislations/ governance regulation is based on a questionnaire which was sent to leading corporate governance specialists and on subsequent direct interviews with these legal specialists. The questionnaire contains 50 questions that cover the most important provisions of company law, stock exchange rules, and bankruptcy and reorganization law at both the national and supranational level. In particular, the questions cover the following: (i) shareholder and creditor protection regulation; (ii) accounting standards; (iii) disclosure rules; (iv) takeover regulation (mandatory bid, squeeze-out rule; takeover defense measures, etc.); (v) insider trading regulation; (vi) regulation regarding the structure of the board of directors and voting power distribution; and (vii) adoption of codes of good practice.

The Role of Corporate Governance Regulation

Agency Problems between Corporate Constituents

A typical public corporation represents a legal entity with limited liability, transferable shares, delegated management under a board structure, and investor ownership (Hansmann and Kraakman, 2004). Together, these characteristics make a corporation the most attractive form of business organization. However, they also generate the potential for agency problems.

The conflict of interest between management and shareholders frequently arises in companies with a dispersed ownership structure. In these firms, small shareholders cannot effectively manage the firm due to coordination problems and hence have to delegate control over the firm to professional managers. However, the separation of ownership and control leads to a divergence of interests between managers and shareholders (Berle and Means, 1932). The managers may forgo the shareholders' wealth maximization objective and undertake actions which maximize their personal interests instead of the value of the company. Research on corporate governance shows that shareholders may prevent the misuse of corporate assets by managers either by aligning the managerial interests with their own through executive compensation contracts (Goergen and Renneboog, 2011; Kulich et al., 2011) or by effectively monitoring managerial actions (see e.g. Grossman and Hart, 1980; Shleifer and Vishny, 1986; Becht et al., 2003; Goergen, Reeneboog, et al., 2008; Crespi and Renneboog, 2010). Since the coordination problem among small shareholders prevents them from effectively monitoring the management themselves, they have to rely on external monitoring via the market for corporate control (Fama and Jensen, 1983; Jensen, 1988).

The conflict of interest between management and shareholders is less severe in companies with concentrated ownership structure. In these firms, the controlling shareholders have strong incentives to monitor management and replace it if their firm performs poorly (Franks et al., 2001). However, the presence of a controlling shareholder may induce another agency problem: the potential opportunistic behavior of the large blockholder toward minority shareholders (see e.g. Faccio and Stolin, 2006). The activities aimed at expropriating minority shareholders are reduced when the management is held accountable to the interests of all shareholders, including minority shareholders (Calcagno and Renneboog, 2007).

The legal entity of public corporations and limited liability of their shareholders may engender another potential conflict of interest, namely that between creditors and shareholders. The equity of a leveraged firm can be viewed as a call option on the firm's assets whose value increases with the volatility of future cash flows. This means that the management can maximize shareholder wealth by increasing the risk of the projects it invests in, and hence redistribute wealth from creditors to its shareholders.

Why Do We Need Corporate Governance Regulation?

The theoretical literature gives us a number of reasons. First, regulatory intervention helps markets to achieve the maximization of social welfare rather than the welfare of individual investors (e.g. Pigou, 1938). To illustrate this in the context of corporate governance regulation, consider an example of the disclosure requirements related to corporate activities. In the absence of the disclosure requirements, managers may be tempted to conceal some details of the projects in which their company is involved for perfectly legitimate reasons, e.g. to keep their competitors uninformed and gain a competitive advantage in the future. However, more detailed information about corporate projects allows investors to assess the corporate growth potential better and to invest their money in companies that can generate the highest returns for a specific level of risk. Therefore, if all companies were to conceal information about their activities, a more inefficient allocation of capital would arise, leading to lower economic growth. Hence, a redistribution of wealth between competing companies caused by a higher level of disclosure seems less harmful for the economy than the misallocation of capital caused by lack of transparency. As such, mandatory rules that impose more disclosure enable economies to achieve a more optimal outcome.

The second reason for adopting a specific corporate governance regulation is that it forces companies to commit credibly to a higher quality of governance (Becht et al., 2003). Even if companies initially design efficient governance rules, they may break or alter them at a later stage. Investors anticipate this and are willing to provide firms with funds at lower costs only when companies find ways to commit credibly to good governance.

The importance of corporate governance regulation for corporate activities and economic growth has been further emphasized in a growing number of empirical studies. These papers show that a corporate governance regime has a significant impact on the availability and cost of capital, corporate performance, and the distribution of corporate value between the firm's stakeholders: shareholders, creditors, employees, consumers, and suppliers. Weak legal environment combined with weak enforcement of the law distorts an efficient allocation of resources, undermines the ability of companies to compete internationally, and hinders investment and economic development (see e.g. Levine, 1998, 1999; La Porta et al., 2002; Djankov et al., 2008).

Evolution of Legal Systems and Corporate Governance Regimes

Given the beneficial impact of corporate governance regulation on economic growth, the development of markets, and the governance of firms, a natural question to ask is whether or not a particular national legal system has a competitive advantage over other legal systems and, if so, whether the alternative regimes ought to converge toward it.

So far, based on an extensive body of research, no consensus has arisen as to what is the best system of corporate law (for an overview of this literature see Goergen et al., 2005). Some law and economics academics have proclaimed the superiority of the UK and US legal systems, characterized by a focus on shareholder value and good shareholder protection. There are also supporters of the alternative legal systems characterized by a focus on the welfare of employees, creditors, and other types of stakeholders and weak shareholder protection. They claim that the long-term interests of shareholders and stakeholders are not necessarily at odds, such that the different types of governance regimes may produce similar outcomes in terms of long-term economic growth. However, the lack of consensus regarding the optimal system of corporate regulation has implications for law reforms. It raises the question as to the direction that the reformers of national systems should adopt.

Bebchuk and Roe (2000) argue that the direction of legal reforms is typically predetermined by the initial institutional structures in a country. In particular, ownership and control concentration is an important factor that affects the role and function of corporate legislation and hence the direction of its reforms. This is because the degree of ownership and control concentration plays a key role in the relationships between the different corporate stakeholders. In countries where widely held companies prevail, the main function of corporate governance regulation is to protect shareholders from being expropriated by the management. In countries where a vast majority of companies have a concentrated ownership and control structure, the function of corporate governance regulation is to minimize the extent of agency problems between majority and minority shareholders and that between shareholders and creditors.

Bebchuk and Cohen (1999) show that, in the presence of large private benefits of control, better protection of shareholders is unlikely to affect the degree of ownership concentration. Even if better protection from expropriation by the management were introduced, an incumbent blockholder is unlikely to sell his stake because a third party acquiring a controlling block is unable to compensate him for his private benefits of control. Thus, where private benefits of control are high, regulatory reforms aimed at improving investor protection are likely to reinforce the existing ownership and control structures.

Roe (2002) proposes an alternative scenario. In his view, if the costs of monitoring management are high relative to the private benefits of control a blockholder enjoys, better legal protection from expropriation by the management may lead to a shift from concentrated to dispersed ownership. This shift may be further enhanced by some other drawbacks of concentrated control, such as the costs of low liquidity and undiversified risk. We conclude that corporate law reforms that improve investor protection are likely to lead toward more dispersed ownership provided that private benefits of control are relatively low. An overview of the conjectures relating corporate governance regulation and ownership concentration is given in Martynova and Renneboog (2011).

In sum, the adoption of a unified corporate governance regulation by countries with different initial institutional structures (in terms of voting structure, ownership and control, capital market development, etc.) may not necessarily lead to the convergence of their legal corporate governance regimes. However, the adoption of country-specific corporate legislations may induce the convergence of wider corporate governance systems (Goergen, Manjon et al. 2008).

Corporate Governance Database

We explore a unique corporate governance database that comprises the main features of corporate governance regulation in the US and all European countries (including countries from Central and Eastern Europe) since 1990. The database is based on the study of various corporate governance regulations, on the results from a detailed questionnaire sent to more than 150 legal experts, and on direct interviews with some of these experts.

Our approach can be summarized as follows: based on corporate legislation, corporate governance codes, and the scientific literature, we have drafted a detailed set of questions about the main aspects of corporate governance regulation that apply to listed companies. A final set of 50 questions was put to leading corporate governance experts (mostly academic lawyers but also some practitioners from law firms). As we focus on listed companies, we have asked the contributors to this project to consider regulation (including soft law), comprising: (i) (hard) corporate law; (ii) stock exchange regulations (listing requirements); (iii) codes of good practice, provided there is a legal basis for these codes (the law refers to a code of good practice which is itself not incorporated in the law); and (iv) corporate practice.

Corporate Governance Indices

As discussed, corporate law plays an important role in mitigating the three central conflicts of interest between the main corporate constituencies: the agency problems which arise between the management and the shareholders, between majority and minority shareholders, and between creditors and shareholders. In this section, we provide a concise overview of the existing corporate governance regulations in Europe and the US. We classify the main provisions of the existing regulations according to their efficiency in mitigating the conflicts of interest within a corporation. Based on this classification, we quantify the regulatory provisions for each country and combine them into three indices that characterize how well national legislations minimize the extent of the agency issues.

The economic literature suggests two main approaches to resolve principal–agent problems: (i) create incentives such that agents act in the interest of their principals; and (ii) enhance the disciplining power of principals (see e.g. Becht et al., 2003). To implement these approaches, the law can deploy a number of governance strategies. Hansmann and Kraakman (2004) suggest the following classification of such strategies: (i) strengthening the appointment rights of principals; (ii) reinforcing the decision rights of principals; (iii) augmenting the trusteeship; (iv) enhancing corporate transparency; and (v) adopting an affiliation strategy. The appointment rights strategy regulates shareholders' power to select or remove directors. The decision rights strategy grants shareholders the power to intervene and initiate or ratify managerial decisions. The trusteeship strategy allows shareholders to appoint an independent body (a trustee) that will represent their interests in the firm and monitor managers. The transparency strategy seeks to eliminate conflicts of interest by enforcing strict disclosure requirements on corporate policies and contracts directly related to managers. Finally, an affiliation strategy sets the terms on which shareholders affiliate with managers. These typically involve shareholder rights to enter and exit their ownership in the firm on fair terms. The strategies are not limited to reducing the agency problem between shareholders and managers, but can also be deployed to address other agency problems (e.g. between minority and majority shareholders or between shareholders and creditors).

The analysis of regulatory provisions within the framework of the above governance strategies enables us to understand better how corporate law works in a particular country and which strategies regulators adopt to achieve their goals. Hence, we classify the regulatory provisions (i) by type of agency problems and (ii) by governance strategies within each type of agency problem. We model our corporate governance indices as a sum of sub-indices that indicate the scope of legal protection through different strategies.

Regulatory Provisions Addressing Management-Shareholder Relations

When shareholders have limited power, agency problems may be substantial: management may then pursue their own interests (among others: corporate growth at the expense of value creation, excessive remuneration, value-reducing mergers and acquisitions (M&As) or a so-called "empire building" strategy). These managerial objectives may be detrimental to shareholders' interests (which is corporate value or getting a fair return on their investment). To assess the relative shareholder power granted by law, we study the regulatory provisions that aim at mitigating managerial opportunistic behavior.

The appointment rights strategy

Appointment and replacement rights enable shareholders to shape the basic structure, power, and the composition of a firm's internal governance structure. Voting rules and requirements on the board's composition are the main components of these shareholder rights.

Among voting rules, we distinguish between requirements for nomination to the board by shareholders, voting procedures (whether or not proxy voting by mail is allowed, whether or not shareholders are required to register and deposit shares prior to the general meeting), and restrictions imposed on the length of directors' contracts.

With their right to elect directors, shareholders can affect the composition of the board. This power should ensure the board's responsiveness to shareholder interests. Some jurisdictions like the Netherlands restrict shareholders' election power in order to ensure the representation of labor interests in the boardroom. However, labor representation may erode shareholder power. A similar problem arises when a jurisdiction mandates employee representation on the board (as is the case in Germany, Luxembourg, and Norway). The presence of employee representatives ("codetermination") on the board reduces the power of directors elected by shareholders which may make it more difficult for them to implement corporate strategies in the best interest of shareholders.

Whereas codetermination redistributes the power from shareholders to employees, cross-shareholdings between two firms increase the relative power of management. Company's shares held by its subsidiary (or a firm in which the company has a controlling stake) are typically more under the discretion of the company's management. The management may use these shares to affect corporate decisions that are to be approved by the shareholder assembly (board members' election, in particular) to its own benefit. This makes the agency problems between management and shareholders more severe. Regulatory restrictions on cross-shareholdings are seen as an instrument mitigating these potential distortions. We expect shareholder interests to be better protected in countries where cross-shareholdings are addressed at the regulatory level and limits are imposed on share stakes held by subsidiaries in their parent firms.

When shareholders cannot vote by mail and are required to register and/or deposit shares prior to the meeting, their participation in the election of board directors may be substandard and may augment inside managers' power to appoint their own candidates. The requirement to register and block shares several days prior to a general meeting is seen as a barrier for many shareholders to participate in the meeting, and decreases shareholders' participation in corporate decision-making. Therefore, we consider the election rules that enable shareholders to send their votes by mail and prohibit companies from requiring share deposits prior to the meeting as instruments that ensure better representation of the shareholder interests in the boardroom.

Restrictions on the length of managerial contracts encourage shareholders to assess managerial performance on a regular basis and replace board members when they do not satisfy shareholder requirements. Long-term contracts with board members are seen as a barrier to replace inefficient directors. The shorter the contractual tenure, the more incentives directors have to act in the interest of shareholders in order to be re-elected for another term. In countries where the mandatory frequency of director rotation is high, the management–shareholder conflict of interest is likely to be less pronounced.

We consider the regulatory provisions mentioned above to be important legal mechanisms that grant shareholders appointment and replacements rights. We therefore quantify these provisions into an index capturing the efficiency of appointment and replacement rules that align the interests of management and shareholders. The components of the index and their coding are given in Table 5.1. A higher index score indicates higher likelihood that management acts in the interest of shareholders.

Table 5.1. Methodology employed to construct corporate governance regulation indices

1. The *shareholder rights protection index (Max = 32)* reflects the shareholders' ability to mitigate managerial opportunistic behavior. The index is constructed by combining the following 4 sub-indices:

1.1 The appointment rights index (Max = 12) is based on the rules to appoint and replace executive and non-executive directors. It measures the degree of alignment of the interests of management and shareholders. The regulatory provisions are quantified as follows:

- Employee representation: 0 if required, 2 if not
- Nomination to the board by shareholders: 2 if required, 0 if not
- Tenure on the board: 0 if more than 4 years, 1 if 4 years, 2 if less then 4 years
- Cross-shareholdings:
  o Cross-shareholdings between 2 independent companies: 1 if regulated, 0 if not
  o Maximum shareholding of a subsidiary in its parent company: 1 if regulated, 0 if not
- Election rules:
  o Proxy voting by mail: 2 if allowed, 0 if not
  o Requirement to Deposit/Register shares prior to a general meeting:
    ⇒ Bearer shares: 0 if deposit is required, 1 if only registration of shares is required, 2 if none is required
    ⇒ Nominal shares: 0 if deposit is required, 2 if deposit requirement is forbidden

1.2 The decision rights index (Max = 8) captures the shareholders' ability to mitigate managerial discretion. The decision rights index cover regulatory provisions that mandate direct shareholder decision-making. The regulatory provisions are quantified as follows:

- Shareholders' approval of anti-takeover defense measures: 2 if required, 0 if not
- Shareholders' approval of preemption rights: 2 if required, 0 if not
- Percentage needed to call for extraordinary meeting: 0 if no rule or more than 20%, 1 if 20% or less but more than 5%, 2 if 5% or less
- Voting caps: 0 if allowed, 2 if not

1.3 The trusteeship index (Max = 5) measures the efficiency of the board of directors in monitoring the actions of CEOs. The following regulatory provisions are quantified as follows:

- Board independence:
  o 2 if CEO cannot be the chairman of the board of directors (in 1-tier board structure), 0 otherwise
  o 2 if the overlap between management and supervisory board is forbidden (in 2-tier board structure), 0 otherwise

(continued)

Table 5.1. Continued

- Employee representation: 0 if required, 2 if not
- Separate board of auditors: 1 if required, 0 otherwise

1.4 The transparency index (Max = 7) is based on the quality of information about company, its ownership structure, and management available to investors

- Requirement to disclose managerial compensation: 0 if not required, 1 if required on aggregate basis, 2 if required on individual basis
- Requirement to disclose any transactions between management and company: 2 if required, 0 if not
- Frequency of financial reports: 0 if once per year, 1 if twice per year, 2 if more than twice per year
- Comply or explain rule: 1 if the requirement is present, 0 otherwise

The higher each index, the better is the protection of the shareholders.

2. *The minority shareholders protection index (Max = 27)* is based on the regulatory provisions aimed at increasing the relative power of the minority shareholders in a context of strong majority shareholders. The index is constructed by combining the following 4 sub-indices:

4.1 Minority shareholders appointment rights index (Max = 5) is based on the appointment rights that can be used to protect minority shareholders. These include rights to reserve seats on the board of directors for minority shareholders or to limit voting power of large shareholders. The regulatory provisions are quantified as follows:

- Minority representation on the board: 2 if required, 0 otherwise
- Voting caps limiting power of large shareholders: 1 if voting caps are allowed, 0 if no.
- One-share-one-vote rule: 0 if both multiple voting rights and non-voting shares are allowed; 1 if one of the two is allowed; 2 if none is allowed

4.2 Minority shareholders decision rights index (Max = 4) captures the ability of minority shareholders to affect fundamental corporate transactions that require a shareholder vote. The regulatory provisions are quantified as follows:

- Supermajority requirement for approval of major company's decisions: 0 if 50% or less; 1 if more then 50% but less then 75%; 2 if 75% or more
- Percentage needed to call for extraordinary meeting: 0 if the rule is not present or required percentage is 20% or more; 1 if the required percentage is between 20 and 5%; 2 if the percentage is 5% or less

4.3 The minority shareholders trusteeship rights index (Max = 4) indicates the extent to which the board of directors serves as a trustee for minority shareholder, i.e. the directors are independent from the firm's controlling shareholders. The regulatory provisions are quantified as follows:

- Nomination to the board by shareholders: 2 if shareholders voting to elect non-executive directors is not required (2-tier boards); 0 if required or 1-tier board
- Board independence: 2 if CEO cannot be the chairman of the board of directors (in 1-tier board structure) or if the overlap between management and supervisory board is forbidden (in 2-tier board structure), 0 otherwise

4.4 The minority shareholders affiliation rights index (Max = 14) groups the remaining regulatory provisions aimed at protecting minority shareholders: the principle of equal treatment (or shared returns) and rights for entry and exit on fair terms. The regulatory provisions are quantified as follows:

- Equal treatment rule: 2 if required, 0 if not
- Mandatory disclosure of large ownership stakes: 0 if disclosure is not required or the minimum percent is 25% or more; 1 if 10% or more (less then 25%); 2 if 5% or more (less then 10%); 3 if less then 5%
- Mandatory bid rule: 0 if not required; 1 if 50% or control; 2 if between 50 and 30%; 3 if 30% or less
- Sell-out rule: The squeeze-out rule is used as a proxy for the sell-out rule (assumption: sell-out is always in place if squeeze-out is adopted, with the same terms as squeeze-out): 0 if no squeeze-out; 1 if squeeze-out at 95% or more; 2 if squeeze-out at 90% or less
- Minority claim: 0 if no; 1 if 10% or more; 2 if 5% or more; 3 if less then 5%
- Breakthrough rule: 1 if required; 0 if not

The higher each index, the better is the protection of the minority shareholders

3. The creditor rights protection index (Max = 5) is based on regulatory provisions that allow creditors to force repayment more easily, take possession of collateral, or gain control over firm in financial distress. The regulatory provisions are quantified as follows:

- Debtor-oriented versus creditor-oriented code: 1 if no reorganization option (liquidation only); 0 if reorganization + liquidation option
- Automatic stay on the assets: 1 if no automatic stay is obliged in reorganization (if debt-orient code) or liquidation procedure (if liquidation code); 0 otherwise
- Secured creditors are ranked first: 1 if secured creditors are ranked first in the liquidation procedure; 0 if government and employees are ranked first
- Creditor approval of bankruptcy: 1 if creditor approval is required to initiate reorganization procedure (if debtor-oriented code) or liquidation procedure (if liquidation code); 0 otherwise ootherotherwise;
- Appointment of official to manage reorganization/liquidation procedure: 1 if it is required by law in a reorganization procedure (if debtor-oriented code) or a liquidation procedure (if liquidation code); 0 otherwise

The higher each index, the better is the protection of the creditors

The decision rights strategy

The right to participate in corporate decisions enables shareholders to effectively monitor the management and prevent the misuse of corporate assets. However, due to coordination problems, (atomistic) shareholders are unable to participate in daily decision-making but can only be expected to weigh on major corporate decisions (e.g. the use of takeover defense measures, new equity issues, and mergers and acquisitions). Shareholders have the power to affect these activities if corporate legislation grants them pre-emption rights, rights to approve the adoption of anti-takeover measures, and rights to call for an extraordinary general meeting.

Hostile takeovers constitute a real threat of losing their jobs for corporate managers. Therefore, managers may be unduly tempted to implement takeover-defense measures that discourage potential buyers from taking over the company, even if this violates shareholders' interests. The shareholders' right to approve anti-takeover measures is a mechanism that mitigates managerial discretion over the firm's cash flows. Pre-emption rights can also be considered as an anti-takeover mechanism; therefore a shareholders' vote on their approval is required to lessen managerial discretion.

Shareholders disagreeing with certain managerial decision should have the right to call an extraordinary general meeting. The lower the minimum percentage needed to call such a meeting, the easier shareholders can intervene in critical situations and present their concerns about any mismanagement of the company.

A major shareholder in a firm typically has a decisive power and strong incentives to monitor management and replace it in poorly performing companies (Franks et al., 2001). Bolton and von Thadden (1998) argue that the advantage of monitoring by blockholders is that it takes place on an ongoing basis. In contrast, disciplining by atomistic shareholders only occurs in crisis situations. If the interests of the major shareholder coincide with those of minority shareholders, managerial–shareholder conflicts of interest are likely to be mitigated by blockholder monitoring. However, an introduction of voting caps may reduce major shareholders' power to affect corporate decisions and may hence weaken the monitoring of management. Therefore, a regulation prohibiting voting caps can be considered as an additional mechanism to reduce managerial opportunism.

Using the regulatory provisions discussed, we construct a decision rights index that captures the legal power of shareholders to participate in corporate decision-making. A higher index score (Table 5.1) indicates that managers have less discretion.

The trusteeship strategy

Another way for shareholders to monitor corporate managers (indirectly) is through the appointment of directors on the board. The board's independence from the management is essential. In practice, two board models are used: one-tier and two-tier board structures. Under the two-tier board, the governance functions are granted to a supervisory board (a board consisting of non-executive directors) which monitors top management assembled in the management board. In a unitary board system, both top management and non-executive directors make up the board. In order to guarantee board independence, overlap between the management and supervisory boards in two-tier systems is restricted. In a one-tier system, the CEO is usually forbidden to hold the position of chairman simultaneously. Separating the executives' and non-executives' roles on the board enhances the monitoring of management.

In virtually all countries, part of the (supervisory) board comprises the audit committee. The audit committee should be chaired by a non-executive director and is the ultimate anti-fraud committee in a firm. It has authority over the non-executive directors, can ask for all internal information, and employees suspecting fraud can contact them. All listed companies are also required to have their books audited by an external audit firm. In addition, some countries also require companies to establish a separate board of auditors (e.g. Italy). The main purpose of the board of auditors, which consists of people who do not serve as non-executive directors, is to ensure that the management provides sufficient and truthful information about all corporate activities to regulatory authorities and shareholders. As such, it facilitates monitoring by the market and thereby contributes to improvements in the management–shareholder relationship. In contrast, employee representation on the board is likely to have a negative effect on the management–shareholder relation. Labor interests are often in conflict with those of company's shareholders. Lack of consensus on corporate strategy, caused by a conflict of interest between directors representing employees and shareholders, increases the discretion of the management to implement corporate policies to their own benefit. Therefore, employee representation on the board is considered to be harmful to shareholders.

Transparency

Transparency regulation aims to improve the quality of information about the company and the management. It should be noted that the intention of this legal strategy is not to improve the quality of the accounting procedures as these are usually not incorporated in corporate law but are set by accounting standards boards. More disclosure increases the informativeness of the market on e.g. corporate policies and contracts directly related to the management. More specifically, corporate legislation regulates the extent to which information is released on the managerial compensation package (on an aggregate or individual basis) and the requirement to disclose any transactions between management and company (e.g. consulting contracts, interest-free loans) (Goergen and Renneboog, 2011). Most listed companies have introduced remuneration committees— forced by law or a code of good governance. These committees should advise the board on compensation packages offered to executive directors. It goes without saying that conflicts of interest should be avoided by not including executive directors on the committee (Renneboog and Zhao, 2011). The quality of transparency is more reliable when the law or the stock exchange regulations include a comply-or-explain principle. It is important that codes of best practice—which exist in almost every country—are legally enshrined.

Therefore, we collect information on the following transparency provisions: (i) requirement to disclose managerial compensation on an aggregate or individual basis; (ii) requirement to disclose any transactions between management and the company; (iii) frequency of financial reporting (annually, semi-annually, quarterly); and (iv) the presence of comply-or-explain rules. We quantify these provisions into the transparency index. A higher index score (Table 5.1) reflects more transparency about corporate and managerial activities and profits.

Regulatory Provisions Addressing Majority-Minority Shareholders' Relationship

We also study the relative power of the minority shareholders, which is particularly important when strong majority shareholders are present. This aspect of corporate governance is particularly important in Continental Europe where most of the listed firms are closely held, with one shareholder (group) often controlling a majority of the voting rights. In a firm with concentrated ownership, it is possible that the dominant shareholder influences managerial decisions to his own benefit and at the expense of minority shareholders. The minority shareholder legal protection rests on the regulatory provisions that increase the relative power of the minority shareholders and reduce the private benefits of control that the controlling blockholder can exploit to the detriment of these shareholders. In this respect, the vital rules are the direct minority shareholder rights (board representation, minority claims, extraordinary general meetings, blocking minorities), the one-share-one-vote principle (dual class shares, voting caps, breakthrough rule, and equal treatment principle), ownership transparency, and relative power in case of a takeover threat.

Appointment Rights Strategy

The appointment rights strategy aims at protecting minority shareholders as it gives minority shareholders a say in the appointment of the management and the internal governance system (the body of non-executive directors). The most straightforward legal approach is to grant minority shareholders a right to nominate their representative to the board. This director is independent of large blockholders and monitors the management in order to prevent it from acting to the benefit of large shareholders only.

Additional legal solutions aimed at increasing the power of minority shareholders when a strong blockholder is present include the use of voting caps and adherence to the one-share-one-vote principle. Voting caps curb the voting power of the large shareholder and hence reduce his influence on managerial actions, leaving more scope for minority shareholders to participate in corporate governance. The one-share-one vote principle aligns the blockholders' cash flow and voting rights. Issuing dual class shares or non-voting shares allows some shareholders to accumulate control while limiting their cash investment. A ban on deviating from the one-share-one-vote principle should discourage the accumulation of controlling blockholdings, as this makes them relatively more expensive than when deviation from the principle is allowed (Goergen et al., 2005). Less power concentration in the hands of large blockholders improves the status of minority shareholders in the firm and their role in the firm's corporate governance.

Overall, we expect the following regulatory provisions of an appointment rights strategy to contribute to minority shareholder protection: (i) mandatory minority shareholder representation on the board; (ii) rules that allow voting caps to be applied; and (iii) a ban on dual class shares (non-voting and multiple-votes shares). We quantified the use of these regulations in our minority shareholders appointment rights index. A higher index score (Table 5.1) reflects that the law upholds the rights of minority shareholders.

The Decision Rights Strategy

The most powerful regulatory strategy to enable minority shareholders to participate in the governance of their firm is to grant them strong decision rights. This is achieved either by introducing the need for supermajority approval of major corporate decisions such that minorities who own a combined blocking minority are able to block corporate policies that may harm their interests. Therefore, the higher is the majority percentage the law requires for a corporate decision to be approved by shareholders, the more powerful are the minority shareholders. Regulations that grant shareholders the right to call for an extraordinary meeting may also strengthen minority shareholders' incentives to monitor management. The level of protection depends on the minimum percentage of share capital ownership required to call for an extraordinary shareholders' meeting. The lower the percentage, the more easily minority shareholders can express their concerns to the company's management. We quantify the two types of legal provisions discussed above into the minority shareholders decision rights index. A higher index score (Table 5.1) reflects more power for minority shareholders to affect corporate decisions.

The Trusteeship Strategy: Independence of Directors from Controlling Shareholders

The right to elect directors to the board gives large shareholders the opportunity to affect board composition as well as the board's decisions. This may harm the interests of minority shareholders. Some jurisdictions, like the Netherlands, restrict the election power of shareholders such that large shareholders' influence on the board's decision-making process is limited. Consequently, potential opportunistic behavior by the large blockholder is strongly reduced, thereby increasing the protection of small shareholders.

We quantify the provisions open to the trusteeship strategy into the minority shareholders trusteeship rights index. A higher index score reflects that the board of directors acts more independently of the controlling shareholder and hence is more accountable to minority shareholders (Table 5.1).

The Affiliation Rights Strategy

Our final, but probably most powerful strategy of corporate law to enhance the power of minority shareholders is to provide them with entry and exit rights on fair terms. Most of the regulatory provisions of this category are part of the takeover regulation. The relevant clauses include the mandatory bid, the principle of equal treatment of shareholders, the sell-out rule, and the breakthrough rule. The mandatory bid rule requires the acquirer to make a tender offer to all the shareholders once she has accumulated a certain percentage of the shares. The mandatory bid requirement is justified on the grounds that an investor who obtains control may be tempted to exploit private benefits of control at the expense of minority shareholders. As such, the role of the mandatory bid rule is to protect minority shareholders by providing them with an opportunity to exit at a fair price. The principle of equal treatment complements the mandatory bid rule by requiring controlling shareholders, the management, and other constituencies to treat all shareholders within each individual class of shares equally. Although the principle of equal treatment constitutes an important principle of corporate governance regulation with respect to any type of corporate activities, it is particularly important in takeovers where the possibilities of violations of the rights of minority shareholders are far-reaching. The equal treatment principle mandates an acquirer to offer minority shareholders an opportunity to exit on terms that are no less favorable than those offered to shareholders who have sold a controlling block. Both the mandatory bid rule and the equal treatment principle have received wide recognition at the regulatory level in European countries. An article on the breakthrough rule was included in the European directive on mergers and acquisitions, but virtually all European countries have opted out of this article (see Goergen et al., 2005).

A minority claim is another legal device that grants shareholders the right to exit a company on fair terms when they fear that their rights are expropriated. Some regulations stipulate a minimum (combined) percentage which enables shareholders to launch a minority claim. The lower the percentage of ownership required, the easier it is for shareholders to use minority claim rights to challenge important managerial decisions.

A fundamental element of corporate governance that provides minority shareholders with the entry right consists of the disclosure of voting and cash flow rights. Information about major share blocks allows the regulator, minority shareholders, and the market to monitor large blockholders in order to avoid the latter extracting private benefits of control at the expense of other stakeholders. In other words, transparency minimizes potential agency problems ex ante. Moreover, transparency allows the regulator to investigate, for instance, insider trading or self-dealing by large blockholders.

The legal devices that provide minority shareholders with the right to entry and exit on fair terms are quantified into a minority shareholders affiliation rights index. A higher index score reflects the fact that the expropriation of minority shareholders by the controlling blockholder is less likely (Table 5.1).

Regulatory Provisions Aimed at Creditor Rights Protection

Creditor protection hinges on the regulatory provisions that allow creditors to force repayment more easily, take possession of the collateral, or even gain control over a firm. We closely follow the LLSV approach to assess the efficiency of national bankruptcy and reorganization laws in terms of protecting the interests of creditors from being dismissed by managers acting in the interest of shareholders. LLSV argue that creditors are less vulnerable to the opportunism and negligence of managers (shareholders) when the law empowers them with the right to pull collateral from a firm without waiting for the completion of the reorganization procedure; when they are ranked first in the distribution of the proceeds that result from the disposition of the assets of a bankrupt firm; and when they have the decision power to approve or veto the reorganization (liquidation) procedure initiated by management (shareholders). The protection of creditor rights also increases when the law requires the court or the creditors to appoint an independent official responsible for the operation of the business during the reorganization (or liquidation) procedure.

We complement the LLSV set of regulatory provisions on creditor rights protection by emphasizing the difference between creditor-oriented and debtor-oriented insolvency codes. A creditor-oriented code is a pure liquidation bankruptcy code according to which an insolvent company (or its creditors) has to initiate a liquidation procedure and all of the company's (bankrupt) property is claimed in the interest of the creditors. The key point of a pure liquidation bankruptcy code is that it does not provide for the possibility of a reorganization procedure, such that the insolvent company has to be declared bankrupt and its assets sold on behalf of the creditors. In contrast, a debtor-oriented code incorporates a reorganization option which may enable the company to continue its operations after restructuring. The purpose of the reorganization is to enable companies in financial distress, but with prospects of continued profitable activity, to restructure without resorting to bankruptcy. Asset restructuring usually also involves financial restructuring, whereby creditors write down their claims. Examples of debtor-oriented codes are the Chapter 11 procedure in the US and the administration procedure in the UK. As insolvency codes that facilitate corporate reorganization focus on corporate survival which leads to substantial write-downs of creditor claims, the (more senior) creditors may lose more in debtor-oriented codes than in creditor-oriented ones. A higher index score (Table 5.1) signifies stronger creditor rights.

Evolution of Corporate Governance Regulations around the World

It is important to realize that good governance regulations are not sufficient by themselves. The enforceability of regulation and effectiveness of the courts are crucial and should be taken on board when evaluating corporate governance regulation, as we have argued. Moreover, the effectiveness and relevance of regulation also depends on the control structures of firms, as proxied by the voting power derived from stock ownership. Heterogeneity in corporate governance regulation is hence not necessarily bad since the effectiveness of rules depends on the institutional context (McCahery and Renneboog, 2002; Burton et al., 2010). We amalgamate the information presented so far and show how the protection of shareholders, minority shareholders, and creditors has evolved over time, but we first sketch in the next subsection the context of corporate governance regulation by showing how ownership concentration differs across countries.

Ownership Structure around the World

The need to reform corporate governance regulation may be different in each country because of the differences in control structures. The stakeholder-based regime prevails in most of Continental Europe and is characterized by majority or near-majority holdings of stock held by one shareholder or a small group of investors. In contrast, the shareholder-based system of the US, UK, and the Republic of Ireland is characterized by a dispersed equity structure. Although the difference in ownership between Continental Europe, on the one hand, and the UK, US, and Ireland, on the other, is remarkable, there is still variation in the percentage of companies under majority or blocking minority control across Continental European countries (see Figure 5.1). Figure 5.2 reports that the percentage of Continental European companies controlled by investors owning a blocking minority of at least 25 percent is very high.

The Protection of Shareholder Rights

We develop two indices capturing the protection of shareholder rights: an "anti-directors" right index employing the LLSV methodology and a broader index. While the former captures a limited set of criteria, the broader shareholder rights index also measures the shareholders' power to appoint directors, shareholder decision power, the board structure, and the information available to shareholders. Figure 5.3 shows the updated "anti-directors" right index of LLSV. We classify all countries into six groups according to their legal origin and economic development. Countries from the former communist block are classified according to their (staged) accession to the European Union, as this event has had an important impact on their legislative reforms prior to the accession.

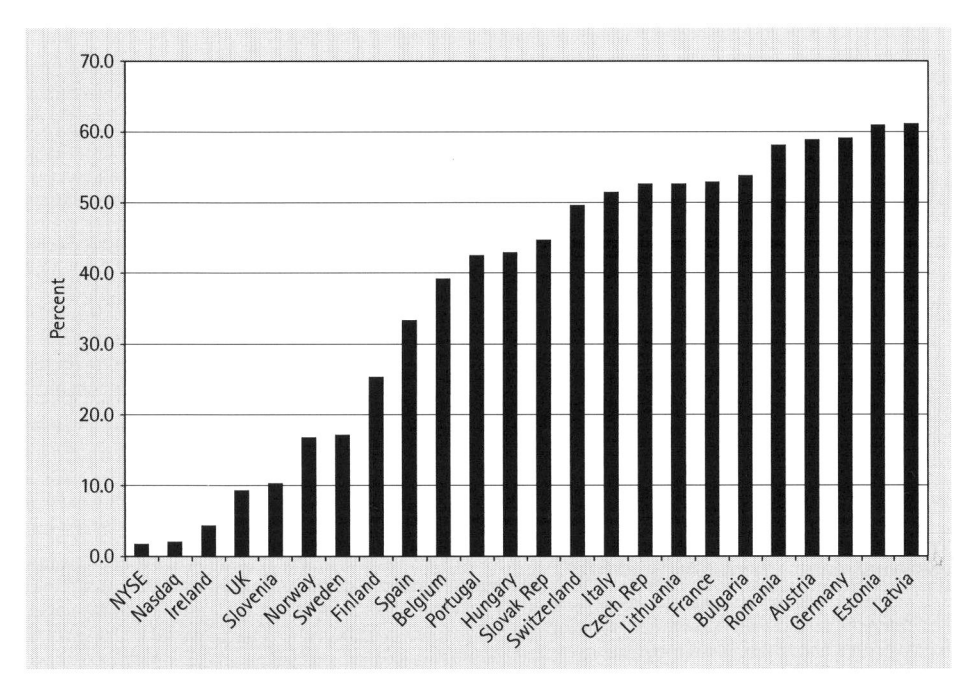

FIGURE 5.1. Percentage of listed companies under majority control

Source: Faccio and Lang (2002) for European countries with law of English, German, French, and Scandinavian origin; Barca and Becht (2001) for the US; and the ECGI project "Corporate Governance & Disclosure in the Accession Process" (2001) for the EU accession countries.

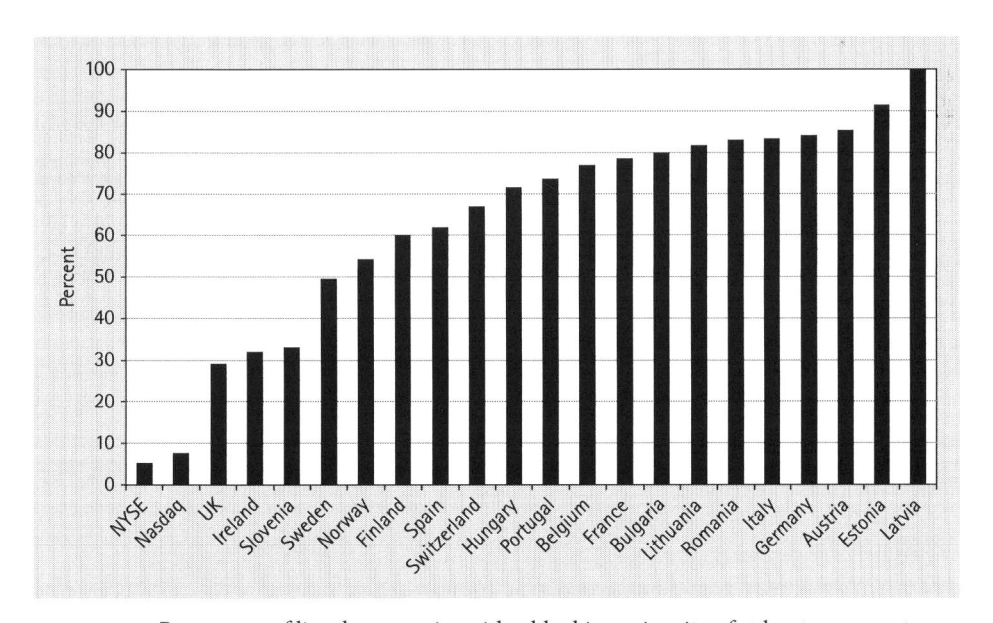

FIGURE 5.2. Percentage of listed companies with a blocking minority of at least 25 percent

Data source: Faccio and Lang (2002) for European countries with law of English, German, French, and Scandinavian origin; Barca and Becht (2001) for the US; and the ECGI project "Corporate Governance & Disclosure in the Accession Process" (2001) for the EU accession countries.

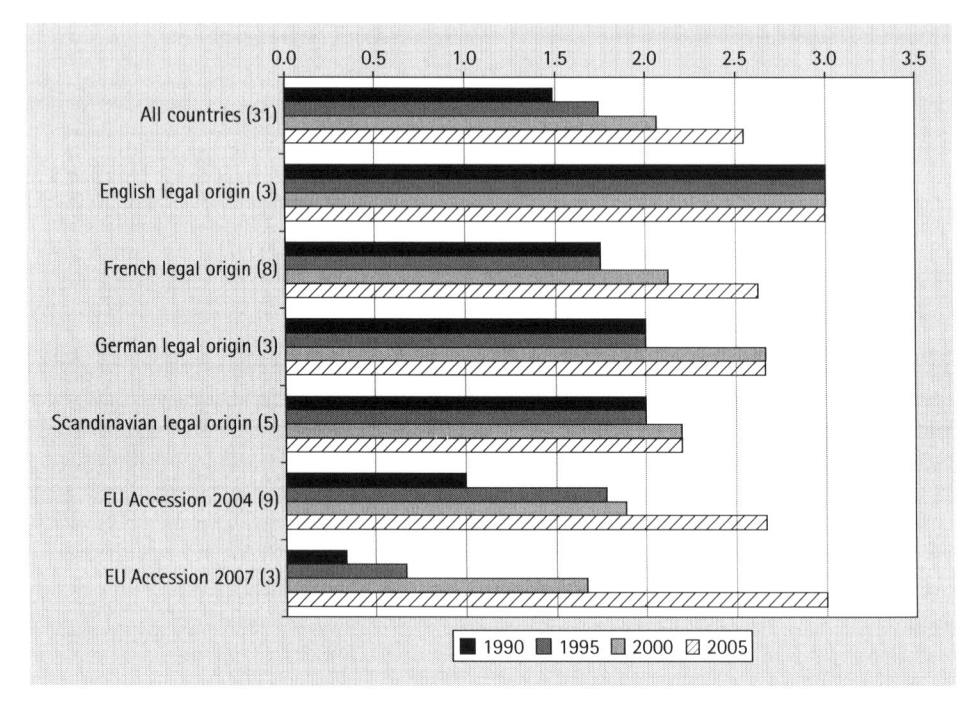

FIGURE 5.3. Anti-director index based on LLSV: total index

Notes: The countries are categorized based on their legal origin and based on the EU enlargement process. The countries belong to these types: *English legal origin* (Republic of Ireland, UK, and US); *German legal origin* (Austria, Germany, Switzerland); *French legal origin* (Belgium, France, Greece, Italy, Luxembourg, Netherlands, Portugal, and Spain), *Scandinavian legal origin* (Denmark, Finland, Iceland, Norway, and Sweden), *2004 EU Accession* (Czech Republic, Cyprus, Estonia, Hungary, Latvia, Lithuania, Poland, Slovenia, and Slovak Republic), *2007–9 likely EU Accession* (Bulgaria, Croatia, and Romania).
The x-axis shows the mean value of each index.

Source: Martynova and Renneboog (2011).

Figure 5.4 shows the dynamics in the protection of shareholder rights captured by our shareholder rights protection index and reveals that in virtually every European country significant changes in corporate law have been implemented since 1990. Nonetheless, the countries of English legal origin remain the leaders in terms of the quality of shareholder protection. However, in the meantime, the French legal origin countries have evolved and reach a level close to the English origin standard. The lowest level of investor protection is nowadays observed in countries of German and Scandinavian legal origins, as well as in the countries which joined the EU in 2004.

The countries achieving the strongest improvement in their legal environment over the period 1990 to 2005 are the former communist-bloc countries that have recently joined the EU, whereas the least improvement is observed in Scandinavian countries (where shareholder protection has even decreased somewhat). The EU accession process has had an important impact on legislative reforms in Bulgaria, Croatia, and Romania. However, as discussed, one needs to put the shareholder protection index in perspective; an improvement in shareholder protection may not be meaningful if the enforcement of these rights in courts is difficult. This may be particularly difficult in Italy, and in Central and Eastern Europe.

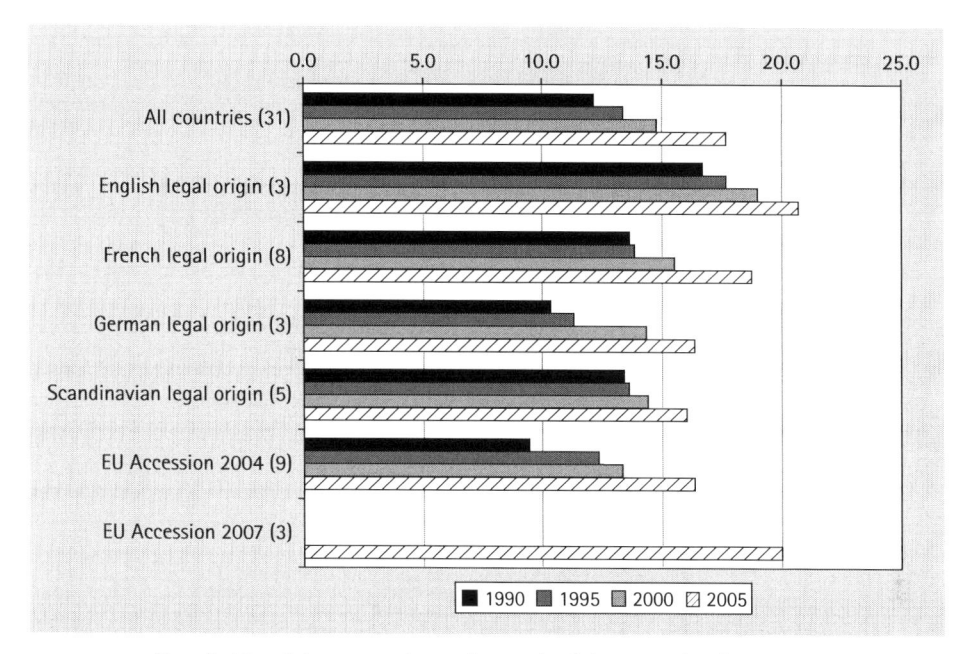

FIGURE 5.4. Shareholder rights protection index methodology: total index

Notes: The countries are categorized based on their legal origin and based on the EU enlargement process. The countries belong to these types: *English legal origin* (Republic of Ireland, UK, and US); *German legal origin* (Austria, Germany, Switzerland); *French legal origin* (Belgium, France, Greece, Italy, Luxembourg, Netherlands, Portugal, and Spain); *Scandinavian legal origin* (Denmark, Finland, Iceland, Norway, and Sweden); *2004 EU Accession* (Czech Republic, Cyprus, Estonia, Hungary, Latvia, Lithuania, Poland, Slovenia, and Slovak Republic), *2007–9 likely EU Accession* (Bulgaria, Croatia, and Romania). The x-axis shows the mean value of each index.

Source: Martynova and Renneboog (2011).

Figures 5.5 through 5.8 dissect the shareholder protection index of Figure 5.4 into appointment rights, decision rights, trusteeship, and transparency sub-indices. For each of these constituting elements, there are striking differences across legal origins. Whereas the German origin countries and the EU 2004 accession countries focus on reforms that provide shareholders with more decision rights in the firm (see Figure 5.6), countries of English legal origin and those countries of the 2007 EU accession direct their reforms to the establishment of a trusteeship relation (a board of directors representing the interest of shareholders; see Figure 5.7). A strategy that all countries deploy to improve shareholder protection is to provide investors with more transparency. Figure 5.8 shows dramatic changes in overall transparency standards. Introducing (more strict) disclosure regulation is likely to affect the broader corporate governance system because it reduces the private benefits of control to major blockholders and also helps investors to monitor the management better. This may induce further convergence toward a shareholder-based corporate governance regime with dispersed ownership and control structures and strong shareholder protection.

118 REGULATION AND HISTORY

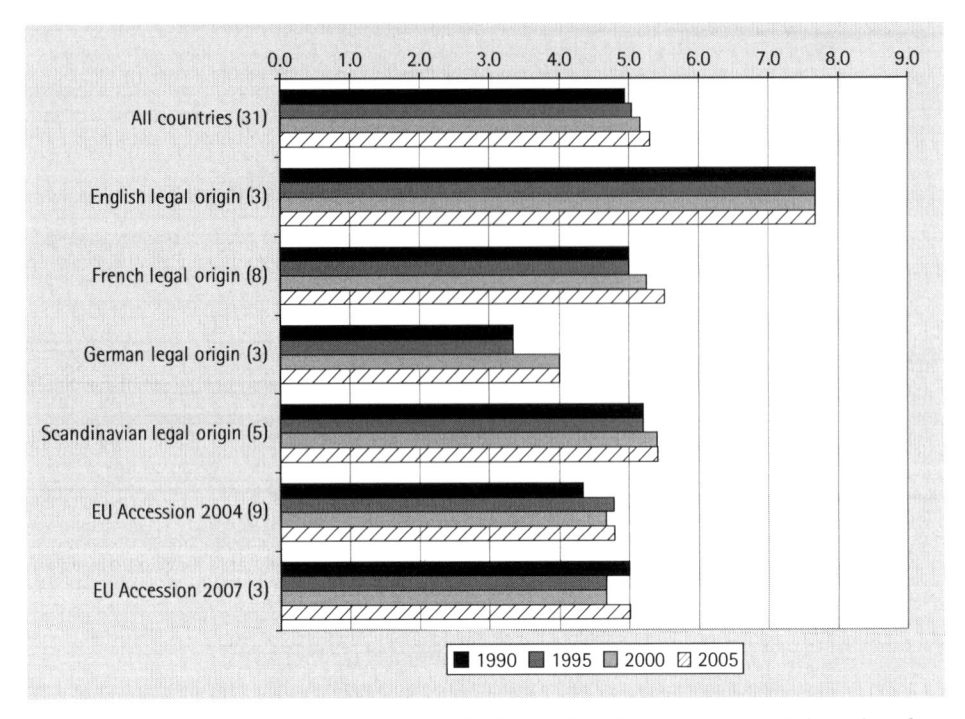

FIGURE 5.5. Shareholder rights protection index by legal origin: appointment rights sub-index

Note: For the classification of legal origins, see notes to Figures 5.3 and 5.4. The x-axis shows the mean value of the index.

Source: Martynova and Renneboog (2011).

The Protection of Minority Shareholder Rights

Fewer regulatory changes have taken place in the protection of minority shareholders since 1990. Figure 5.9 exhibits the changes in the minority shareholder rights protection index by legal origin. The problem of the misalignment of interests between minority and majority shareholders has been addressed at a regulatory level in almost all countries with the exception of the US, the Netherlands, and Spain. Countries of French and German legal origin and former communist countries are the leaders among the reformers, whereas English and Scandinavian legal origin countries are much less involved in the reforms (Figure 5.9). Until the late 1990s, the highest level of minority protection was observed in countries of English legal origin, but nowadays the level of minority rights protection is relatively similar across all countries, with only the Scandinavian countries lagging somewhat behind.

We also dissect the minority shareholders protection index into three parts: an appointment rights, decision rights, trusteeship, and affiliation sub-index. As in the case of the shareholder rights protection index, countries are able to achieve an increase in

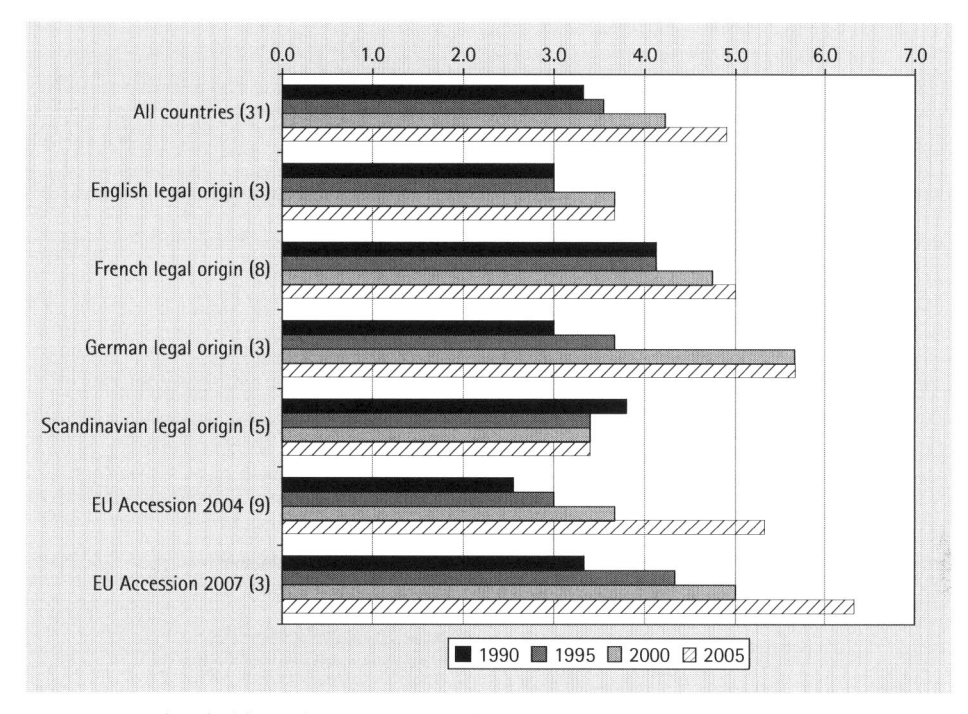

FIGURE 5.6. Shareholder rights protection index by legal origin: decision rights sub-index

Note: For the classification of legal origins see notes to Figures 5.3 and 5.4. The x-axis shows the mean value of the index.

Source: Martynova and Renneboog (2011).

minority shareholder protection using different strategies (see Figures 5.10 to 5.13). The appointment rights, decision rights, and trusteeship strategies are mainly employed by the EU 2004 and EU 2007 accession countries and by only a few countries of French and Scandinavian legal origins (Italy, Finland, and Iceland). In these countries, the relative power of minority shareholders vis-à-vis a strong blockholder has been increased by stronger board representation, blocking minorities, minority claims, and voting caps.

The affiliation strategy is pursued in virtually all countries to improve minority protection (see Figure 5.13). It is associated with granting minority shareholders the right to entry into and exit from the company on fair terms. The entry right is strengthened by the introduction of (more strict) disclosure requirements regarding corporate control structures and managerial activities. This should make investors aware of the firm's governance structure and potential agency problems before they decide to buy a firm's shares. Reforms of takeover regulation, introduction of the principle of the equal treatment of shareholders, mandatory bid, and sell-out rules in particular enable minority shareholders to exit without being expropriated.

An increase in the power of minority shareholders when a large blockholder is present in the firm reduces the private benefits of control of this blockholder, which may lead to

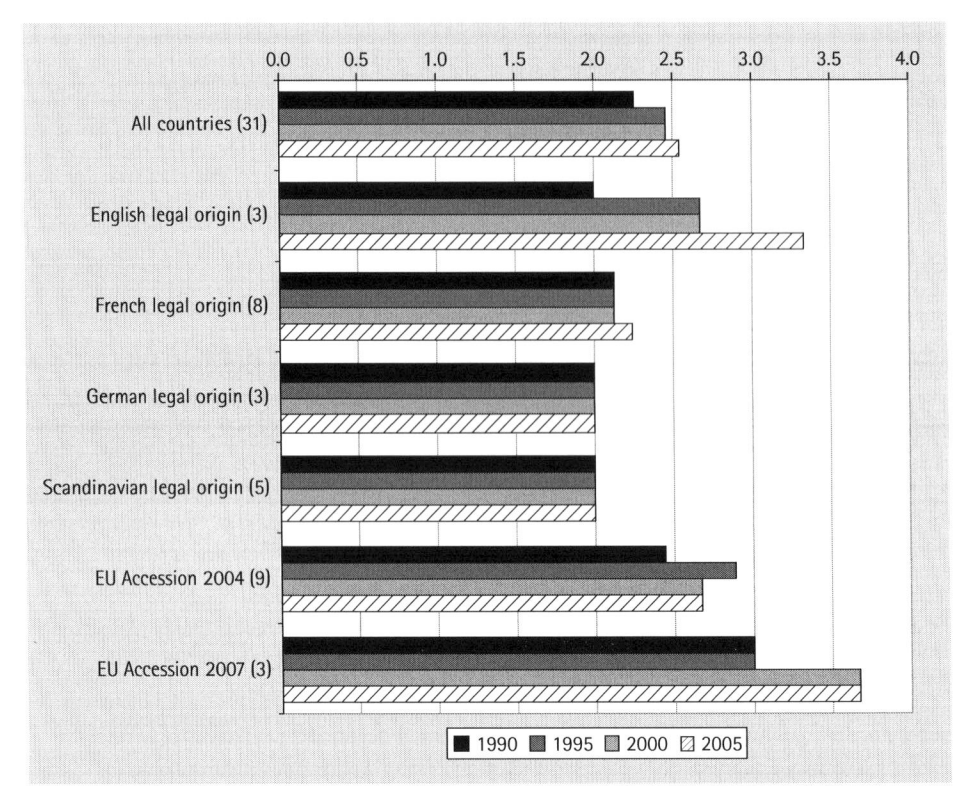

FIGURE 5.7. Shareholder rights protection index by legal origin: trusteeship sub-index

Note: For the classification of legal origins, see notes to Figures 5.3 and 5.4. The x-axis shows the mean value of the index.

Source: Martynova and Renneboog (2011).

more ownership dispersion. Therefore, one could expect a shift toward more dispersed ownership in the leading reformers in the area of minority shareholder protection, namely: the French and German legal origin countries and the former communist countries. To conclude, on this aspect of corporate governance too, we observe more convergence toward a shareholder-based system with lower ownership concentration.

The Protection of Creditor Rights

Figure 5.14 reports the evolution of the legal environment with respect to creditor rights protection. Strikingly, we find that countries have very different perspectives on the protection of creditor rights. There are three different scenarios: first, in countries of French, German, and Scandinavian legal origin creditor protection has weakened significantly. Second, former communist countries have in contrast moved toward more creditor pro-

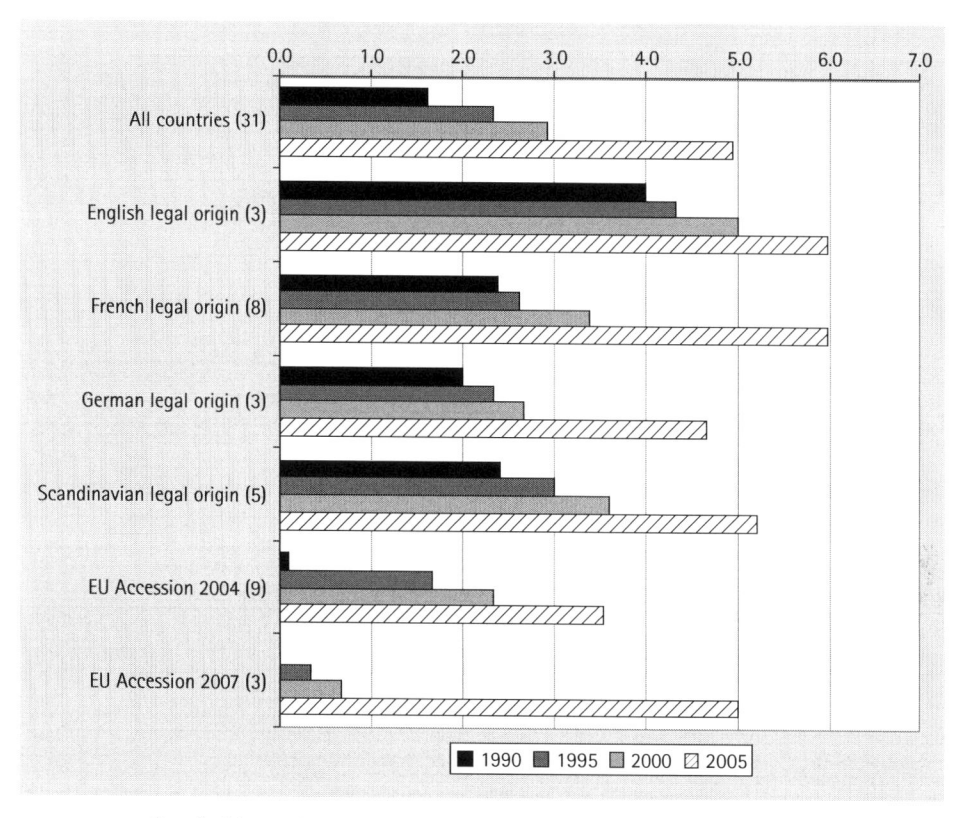

FIGURE 5.8. Shareholder rights protection index by legal origin: transparency sub-index

Note: For the classification of legal origins, see notes to Figures 5.3 and 5.4. The x-axis shows the mean value of the index.

Source: Martynova and Renneboog (2011).

tection. Finally, English legal origin countries have abstained from reforming their bankruptcy and reorganization legislation and currently have a system which is least protective for creditors.

Most of the French, German, and Scandinavian legal origin countries have reorganized their bankruptcy legislation by introducing a reorganization procedure that enables companies to restructure their debts and escape liquidation. By the late 1990s, a large majority of Continental European countries (with the exception of the former communist bloc) have a debtor-oriented corporate insolvency code that includes two tracks: a reorganization part (e.g. administration in the UK) and a pure liquidation code (e.g. receivership in the UK). It is not in fact surprising that in a number of countries creditor protection has diminished, since one can observe an increase in shareholder protection in these countries. We believe that the lack of a well-developed equity market is one of the main reasons for regulators of EU accession countries to increase creditor protection. Better protection of creditors reduces the costs of debt financing,

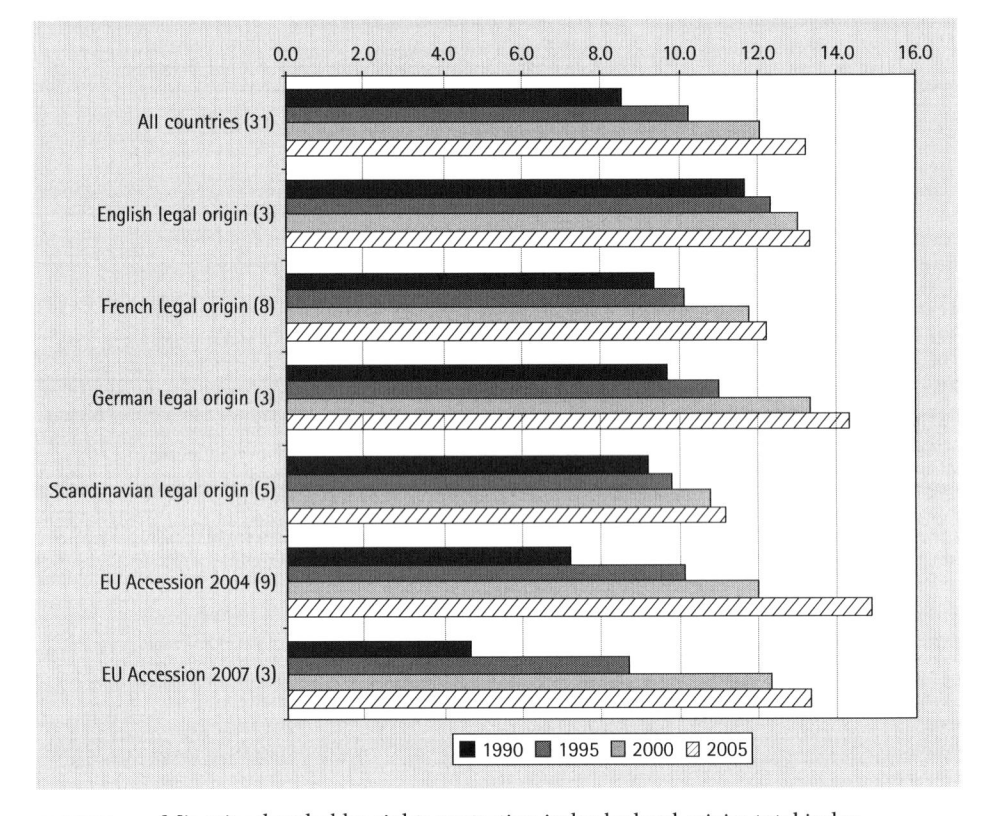

FIGURE 5.9. Minority shareholder rights protection index by legal origin: total index
Note: The x-axis shows the mean value of the index.
Source: Martynova and Renneboog (2011).

which is essential for companies in such countries. Further equity market development in these countries may lead to a new wave of bankruptcy law reforms, which will reduce creditor rights.

Conclusion

This chapter performs a comparative analysis of the corporate governance legal regimes and their evolution in 30 European countries and the US. The analysis is based on a unique corporate governance database that comprises the main changes in corporate governance regulations over the period 1990 to 2005. We develop three new corporate governance indices that reflect the quality of national laws aimed at protecting (i) corporate shareholders from being expropriated by management; (ii) minority shareholders from being expropriated by large blockholders; and (iii) creditors from being expropri-

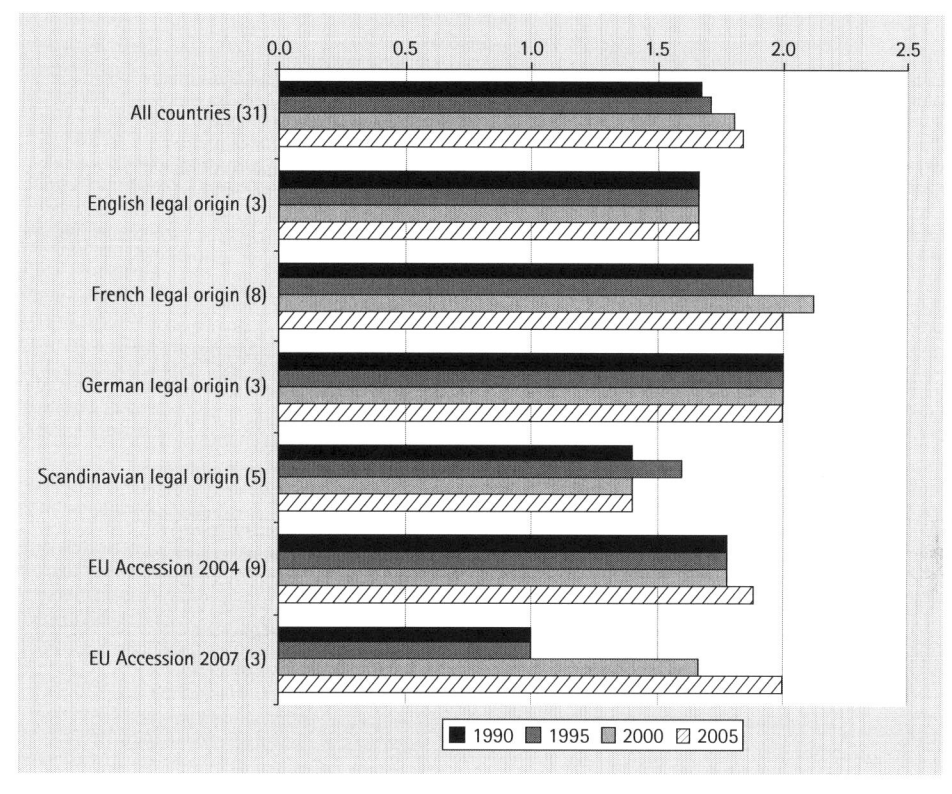

FIGURE 5.10. Minority shareholder rights protection index by legal origin: appointment rights sub-index

Note: The x-axis shows the mean value of the index.

Source: Martynova and Renneboog (2011).

ated by shareholders. We further dissect these indices along various dimensions of regulator strategies (as captured by e.g. the sub-indices expressing relative decision power, appointment rights, trusteeship, and corporate transparency). We find that, in contrast to the LLSV ranking system, our new governance indices capture a broader scope of corporate governance regulation reforms and their dynamics.

Time-series analysis of the newly constructed indices reveals that virtually every country from our sample has been involved in substantial changes in their corporate legislations since 1990. The changes relate to all three major types of agency problems. The improvement of corporate transparency has been a dominant legal strategy across countries to address both the protection of shareholders from the misuse of corporate assets by managers, and the protection of minority shareholders from expropriation by a strong blockholder. A large majority of Continental European countries also strengthened protection of minority shareholders in their takeover regulations.

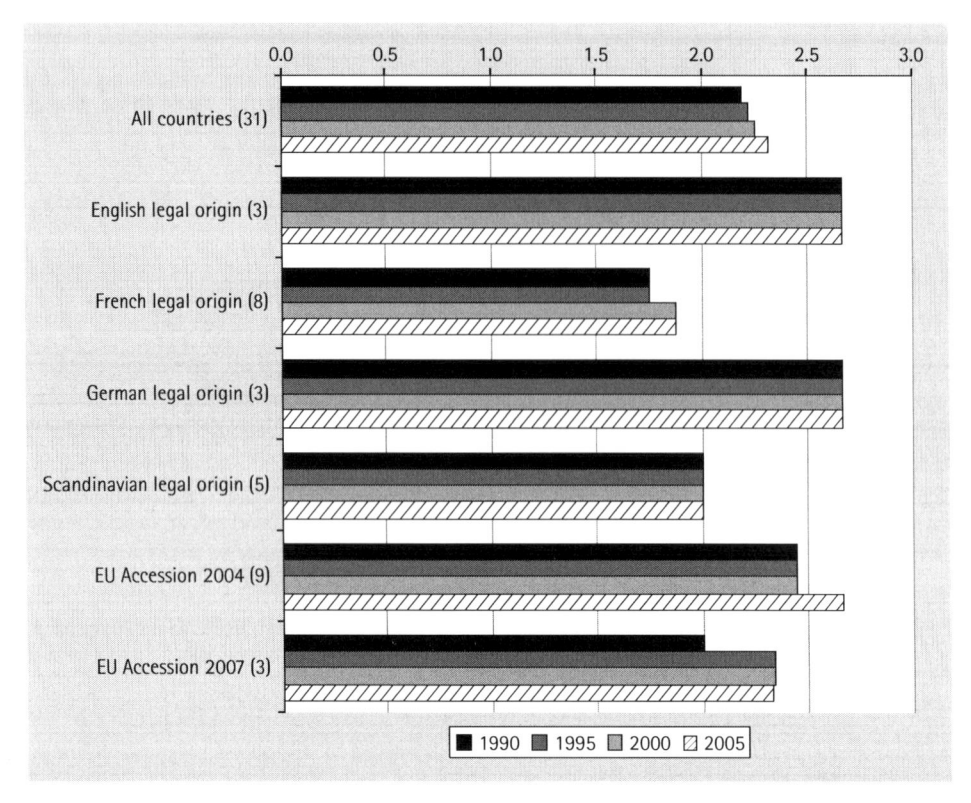

FIGURE 5.11. Minority shareholder rights protection index by legal origin: decision rights sub-index

Note: For the classification of legal origins, see notes to Figures 5.3 and 5.4. The x-axis shows the mean value of the index.

Source: Martynova and Renneboog (2011).

We also detect some differences in the patterns of legal reforms across countries. For instance, in their attempts to improve shareholder protection, German legal origin and EU 2004 accession countries focus on reforms that provide shareholders with more decision rights in the firm, while countries of English legal origin (and those of the EU 2007 accession) direct their reforms to representation of investors on the board of directors (trusteeship) and effective monitoring by boards. Furthermore, countries have very different perspectives on how to deal with financial distress and bankruptcy. Whereas French, German, and Scandinavian legal origin countries put less emphasis on creditor protection, former communist countries move in the opposite direction and strengthen creditor protection. Countries of English legal origin have not modified their bankruptcy and reorganization codes.

While the varying degrees of creditor protection that were recently introduced in national bankruptcy laws show that the global convergence of legal systems toward a single system of corporate regulation is unlikely, there are still signs of increasing con-

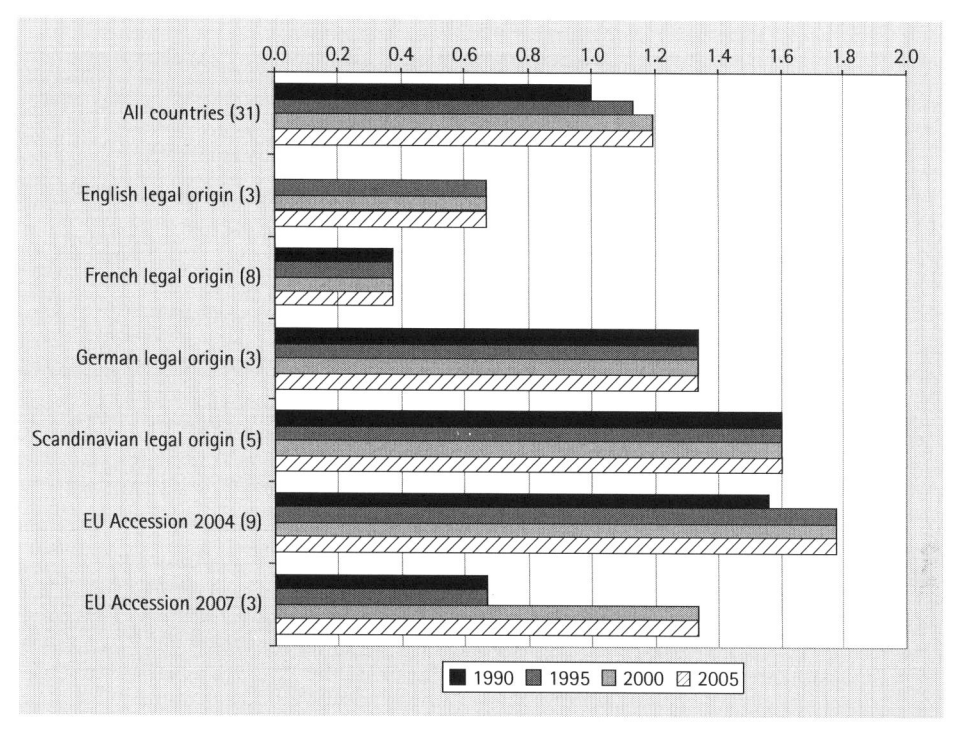

FIGURE 5.12. Minority shareholder rights protection index by legal origin: trusteeship sub-index

Note: For the classification of legal origins, see notes to Figures 5.3 and 5.4. The x-axis shows the mean value of the index.

Source: Martynova and Renneboog (2011).

vergence by national corporate governance regulations toward a shareholder-based regime when the protection of (minority) shareholders is considered. The recent legislative changes in countries of French and German legal origin may bring about more ownership dispersion in time. A stakeholder-based system is likely to be maintained in Scandinavian and former communist countries. Over the past 15 years, Scandinavian countries have substantially lagged behind other West European countries in terms of increasing the level of (minority) shareholder rights protection, such that their legal reforms may be insufficient to induce changes in corporate control. In contrast to Scandinavian countries, the former communist countries have undertaken dramatic revisions of their national corporate legislation in order to guarantee (theoretically) more (minority) shareholder protection. However, the ownership structure is unlikely to evolve toward more dispersion because their reforms also augment creditor rights in case of financial distress. This regulatory choice may discourage the development of efficient equity markets and hence changes in corporate control.

Countries of English legal origin still provide the highest quality of shareholder protection. In the meantime, many Continental European countries have improved their

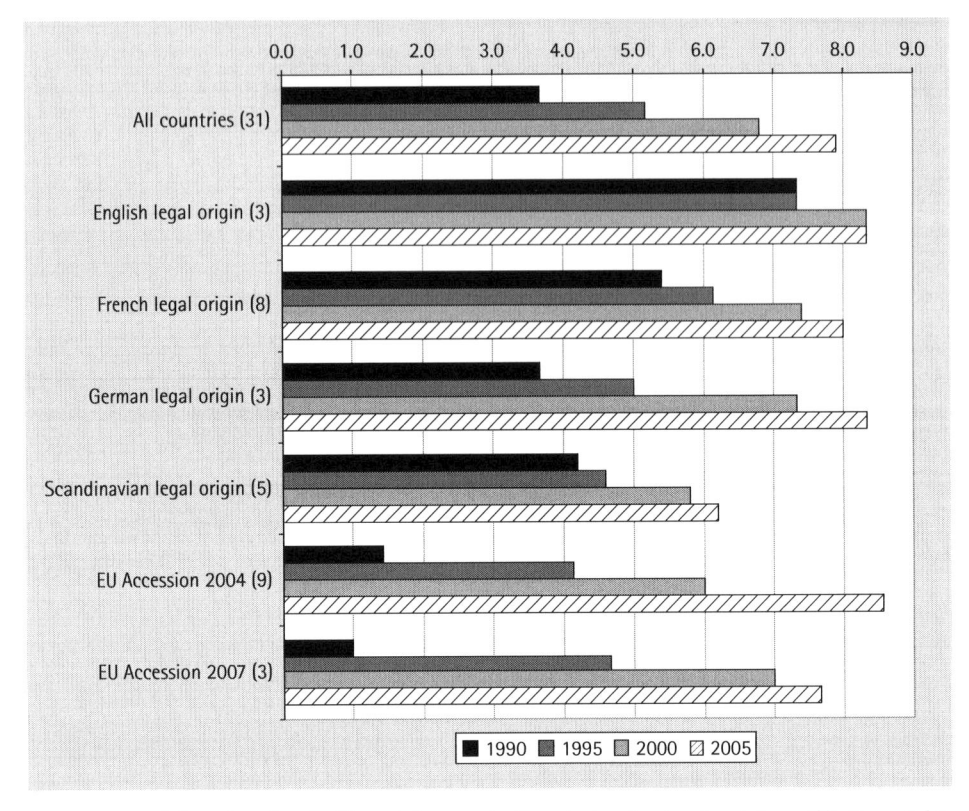

FIGURE 5.13. Minority shareholder rights protection index by legal origin: affiliation rights sub-index

Note: For the classification of legal origins, see notes to Figures 5.3 and 5.4. The x-axis shows the mean value of the index.

Source: Martynova and Renneboog (2011).

legal system up to the standard set by the English legal system. Whether and to what extent these reforms will lead to changes in the degree of ownership and control concentration remains an attractive topic for future research.

This leaves us with the question of whether corporate governance standards will have real economic consequences. Let us analyze two examples where this is the case in the context of takeovers. We ask the question whether differences in regulation influence cross-border acquisitions and whether the costs of financing are affected by differences in corporate governance across countries. First, Martynova and Renneboog (2008) show that differences between the bidder and target corporate governance standards have an important impact on returns from cross-border mergers and acquisitions. In a full takeover, the corporate governance standards of the bidder may be imposed on the target. When the bidder is from a country with stronger shareholder orientation, part of the total synergy value of the takeover may result from the fact that the stronger shareholder focus of the acquirer may generate additional returns due to better management

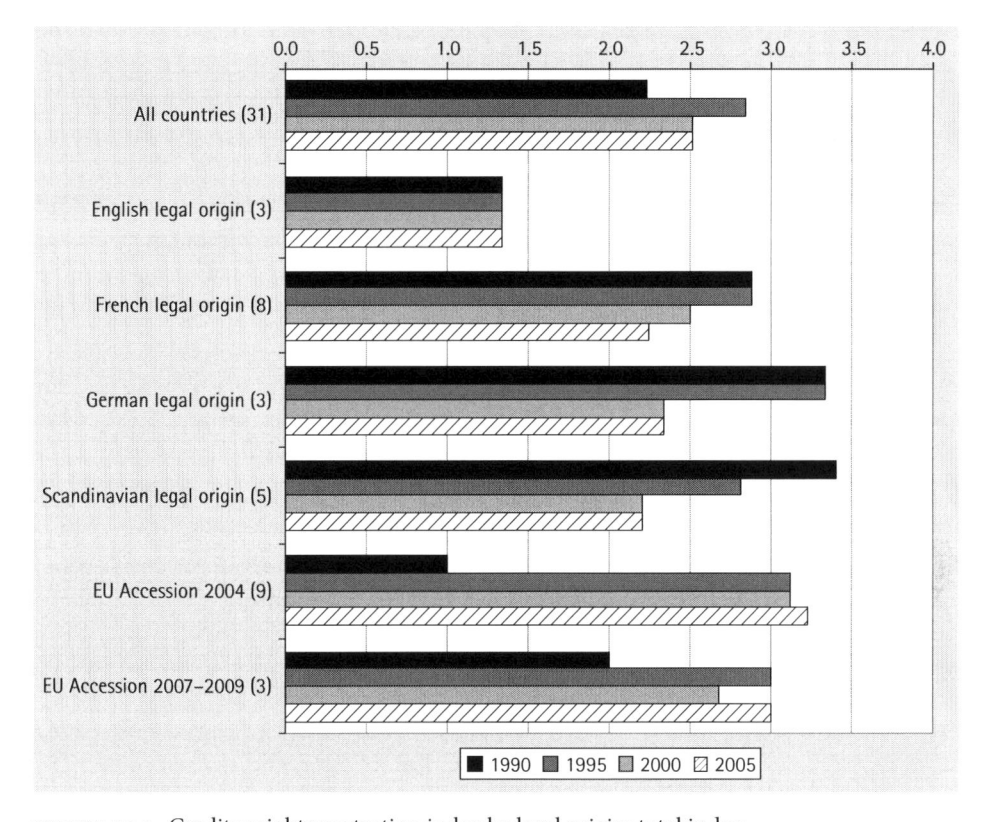

FIGURE 5.14. Creditor rights protection index by legal origin: total index

Note: For the classification of legal origins, see notes to Figures 5.3 and 5.4. The x-axis shows the mean value of the index.

Source: Martynova and Renneboog (2011).

of the target assets. They label this the *positive spillover by law hypothesis*. Given that this future value creation can be anticipated at the time of the takeover announcement, the abnormal returns will reflect this potential. The authors expect both the bidder and target firms to share the returns from better corporate governance (stronger shareholder rights protection) and that their relative bargaining power will determine how these returns are shared. Their empirical analysis corroborates the *positive spillover by law hypothesis*: the better the bidder corporate governance standards, the higher are the bidder and target takeover announcement returns. While the *positive spillover by law effect* applies to full takeovers, they define the *spillover by control hypothesis* for partial takeovers (whereby a bidder acquires majority control but buys less than 100 percent of the voting rights). In partial takeovers, the bidder may impose its governance standards, which may yield positive returns if it is from a country that protects shareholder rights better than the target. The bidder may voluntary opt to apply such standards or may be pressurized by the minority shareholders of the target firm. Their results confirm the *spillover by control hypothesis*: both the bidder and target returns are higher in a partial acquisition if the bidder is subject to stronger shareholder rights protection than the target. In full takeovers where the bidder is from a country that protects shareholders less well than the target country, the *negative spillover by law hypothesis* states that the target and bidder anticipated gains will be lower given that the poorer corporate governance regime will be imposed on the target. The alternative *bootstrapping hypothesis* is that poor-governance bidders voluntarily bootstrap to the better-governance regime of the target, which yields a share price increase. The evidence of Martynova and Renneboog (2008) supports the *bootstrapping hypothesis*: the bidder abnormal returns are higher when a bidder with weaker shareholder orientation acquires a target with better standards. Importantly, the effect is only valid for partial acquisitions or, in other words, for deals which still involve some of the target shareholders (who did not sell out) and for which the target firm remains listed on the stock exchange in the country of the target. Overall, the results suggest that cross-border takeovers between bidders and targets with dissimilar corporate governance standards can generate synergies which are partially related to corporate governance improvements (especially those consisting of increases in shareholder rights).

The second example is on the impact of corporate governance standards on the financing costs of acquisitions. Martynova and Renneboog (2009) study the bidder's choice of the sources of financing in European corporate takeovers. Their findings are consistent with the view that the financing decision is influenced by the bidder's concerns about the cost of capital, which is influenced by corporate governance legislation. Bidders operating in a better corporate governance environment benefit from lower costs of external capital: debt financing is more likely when creditor rights are well protected by law and the courts, and the use of equity financing increases when shareholder rights protection is high.

Note

1. We would like to thank all the corporate governance regulation experts and lawyers who contributed to this chapter by providing input on the corporate governance regulations of their own country: Susanne Kalls, Christian Nowotny, Stefan Fida, Eddy Wymeersch, Christoph Van der Elst, D. Plamen, Tania Bouzeva, Ivaylo Nikolov, Domagoj Racic, Josip Stajfer, Andrej Galogaža, Drago Čengić, Edita Culinovic-Herc, Marios Clerides, Christiana Vovidou, Lubos Tichy, Martin Abraham, Rostislav Pekar, Petr Kotáb, Milan Bakes, Stanislav Myslil, Jan Bárta, Jesper Lau Hansen, Ulrik Rammeskow, Bang-Pedersen, Andres Vutt, Toomas Luhaaar, Peeter Lepik, Katri Paas, Matti J. Sillanpää, Ingalill Aspholm, Ari-Pekka Saanio, Johan Aalto, Alain Couret, Simon Benoit Le Bars, Alain Pietrancosta, Viviane de Beaufort, Gerard Charreaux, Peter Muelbert, Klaus Hopt, Alexander Hellgardt, Theodor Baums, Tobias Pohl, Loukas Spanos, Harilaos Mertzanis, Georgios Sotiropoulos, Tamás Sándor, Andras Szecskay, Orsolya Görgényi, Adam Boóc, Anna Halustyik, Gunnar Sturluson, Olafur Arinbjorn Sigurdsson, Aðalsteinn E. Jónasson, David Thorssteinsson, Blanaid Clarke, Kelley Smith, Guido Ferrarini, Andrea Zanoni, Magda Bianco, Alessio Pacces, Luca Enriques, Kalvis Torgans, Pauls Karnups, Uldis Cerps, Virgilijus Poderys,

Egle Surpliene, Rolandas Valiūnas, Jaunius Gumbis, Dovilė Burgienė, Paulius Cerka, Tomas Bagdanskis, Jacques Loesch, Daniel Dax, Jaap Winter, Marcel van de Vorst, Gijs van Leeuwen, Johan Kleyn, Barbara Bier, Pieter Ariens Kappers, Kristin Normann, Aarum Tore Brathen, Jan Andersson, Stanisław Sołtysiński, Andrzej W. Kawecki, Igor Bakowski, Piotr Tamowicz, Maciej Dzierżanowski, Michał Przybyłowski. Anna Miernika-Szulc, Victor Mendes, Carlos Ferreira Alves, Manuel Pereira Barrocas, Jorge de Brito Pereira, Manuel Costa Salema, Carlos Aguiar, Pedro Pinto Antonio, Alfaia de Carvalho, Gelu Goran, Sorin David, Adriana Gaspar, Catalin Baiculescu, Horatiu Dumitru, Catalina Grigorescu, Jozef Makuch, Stanislav Škurla, Frantisek Okruhlica, Janez Prasnikar, Aleksandra Gregoric, Miha Juhart, Klemen Podobnik, Ana Vlahek, Candido Paz-Ares, Marisa Aparicio, Guillermo Guerra, Per Samuelsson, Gerard Muller, Rolf Dotevall, Catarina Sandeberg, Annina Persson, Björn Kristiansson, Urs P. Gnos, Gerard Hertig, Michel Haymann, Wolfgang Drobetz, Karl Hofstetter, Peter Nobel, Marcel Würmli, Antony Dnes, Dan Prentice, Jenny Payne, Brian Cheffins, Richard Charles Nolan, John Armour, Paul Davies, Gerard N. Cranley, Holly Gregory, Ira Millstein, Eva Lomnicka, Mark Roe, Edward Rock, William Bratton, and Roberta Romano. The authors gratefully acknowledge support from the European Commission via the New Modes of Governance project (NEWGOV) led by the European University Institute in Florence. Luc Renneboog is also grateful to the Netherlands Organization for Scientific Research for a replacement subsidy of the program "Shifts in Governance."

2. Djankov, La Porta, Lopez-de-Silanes, and Shleifer (2006); Djankov, McLiesh, and A. Shleifer (2007); Djankov, Hart, McLiesh, and Shleifer (2008). Djankov, La Porta, Lopez-de-Silanes and A. Shleifer (2008). This chapter is based on Martynova and Renneboog (2011).

References

Baghat, S., Bolton, B., and Romano, R. (2008). "The Promise and Perils of Corporate Governance Indices," *Columbia Law Review*, 108: 1803–82.

Barca, F., and Becht, M. (2001). *The Control of Corporate Europe*. Oxford: Oxford University Press.

Bebchuk, L., and Cohen A. (2009). "What Matters in Corporate Governance?" *Review of Financial Studies*, 22(2): 783–827.

—— and Roe, M. (2000). "A Theory of Path Dependence of Corporate Ownership and Governance," *Stanford Law Review*, 52: 775–808.

Becht, M., Bolton, P., and Röell, A. (2003). "Corporate Governance and Control," in G. Constantinides, M. Harris, and R. Stulz (eds.), *The Handbook of the Economics of Finance*, Amsterdam: Elsevier.

Berle, A., and Means, G. (1932). *The Modern Corporation and Private Property*. New York: Macmillan.

Bolton, P., and von Thadden, E. (1998). "Blocks, Liquidity and Corporate Control," *Journal of Finance*, 53: 1–25.

Calcagno, R., and Renneboog, L. (2007). "The Incentive to Give Incentives: On the Relative Seniority of Debt Claims and Managerial Compensation," *Journal of Banking and Finance*, 31(6): 1795–815.

Coase, R. (1937). "The Nature of the Firm," *Economica*, 4: 386–405.

CRESPI, R., and RENNEBOOG, L. (2010). "Is (Institutional) Shareholder Activism New? Evidence from UK Shareholder Coalitions in the Pre-Cadbury Era," *Corporate Governance International Review*, 18: 274–95.

DJANKOV, S., LA PORTA, R., LOPEZ-DE-SILANES, F., and SHLEIFER, A. (2006). "The Law and Economics of Self-Dealing," Working Paper, Harvard University, April.

—— MCLIESH, C., and SHLEIFER, A. (2007). "Private Credit in 129 Countries," *Journal of Financial Economics*, 84: 299–329.

—— LA PORTA, R., LOPEZ-DE-SILANES, F., and SHLEIFER, A. (2008). "The Law and Economics of Self-Dealing," *Journal of Financial Economics*, 88: 430–65.

FACCIO, M., and LANG, L. (2002). "The Ultimative Ownership of Western European Companies," *Journal of Financial Economics*, 65(3): 365–95.

—— and STOLIN, D. (2006). "Expropriation vs. Proportional Sharing in Corporate Acquisitions," *Journal of Business*, 79(3): 1413–44.

FAMA, E., and JENSEN, M. (1983). "Separation of Ownership and Control," *Journal of Law and Economics*, 26: 301–25.

FRANKS, J., MAYER, C., and RENNEBOOG, L. (2001). "Who Disciplines Management of Poorly Performing Companies?" *Journal of Financial Intermediation*, 10: 209–48.

GOERGEN, M., and RENNEBOOG, L. (2008). "Contractual Corporate Governance," *Journal of Corporate Finance*, 14: 166–82.

—— —— (2011). "Managerial Remuneration," *Journal of Corporate Finance*, 17(4): 1068–77.

—— —— and ZHANG, C. (2008). "Do UK Institutional Investors Monitor their Investee Firms?" *Journal of Corporate Law Studies*, 8: 39–56.

—— MARTYNOVA, M., and RENNEBOOG, L. (2005). "Corporate Governance Convergence: Evidence from Takeover Regulation Reforms in Europe," *Oxford Review of Economic Policies*, 21(2): 243–68.

—— MANJON, M., and RENNEBOOG, L. (2008). "Is the German System of Corporate Governance Converging towards the Anglo-American Model?" *Journal of Management and Governance*, 12: 37–71.

GROSSMAN, S. J., and HART, O. (1980). "Takeover Bids, the Free-Rider Problem, and the Theory of the Corporation," *Bell Journal of Economics*, 11(1): 42–64.

HANSMANN, H., and KRAAKMAN, R. (2004). "The Basic Governance Structure," in R. Kraakman, P. Davies, H. Hansmann, G. Hertig, K. Hopt, H. Kanda, and E. Rock (eds.), *The Anatomy of Corporate Law*. New York: Oxford University Press, 33–70.

JENSEN, M. (1988). "Takeovers: Their Causes and Consequences," *Journal of Economic Perspectives*, 2: 21–48.

KULICH, C., HASLAM, S. A., RENNEBOOG, L., RYAN, M., and TROJANOWSKI, G. (2011). "Who Gets the Carrot and Who Gets the Stick? Evidence of Gender Disparities in Executive Remuneration," *Strategic Management Journal*, 32: 301–21.

LA PORTA, R., LOPEZ-DE-SILANES, F., SHLEIFER, A., and VISHNY, R. (1997). "Legal Determinants of External Finance," *Journal of Finance*, 52: 1131–50.

—— —— —— —— (1998). "Law and Finance," *Journal of Political Economy*, 106: 1113–55.

—— —— —— —— (2002). "Investor Protection and Corporate Valuation," *Journal of Finance*, 57: 1147–70.

LEVINE, R. (1998). "The Legal Environment, Banks, and Long-run Economic Growth," *Journal of Money, Credit, and Banking*, 30: 688–726.

—— (1999). "Law, Finance, and Economic Growth," *Journal of Financial Intermediation*, 8: 36–67.

MARTYNOVA, M., and RENNEBOOG, L. (2008). "Spillover of Corporate Governance Standards in Cross-Border Mergers and Acquisitions," *Journal of Corporate Finance*, 14: 200–23.

—— —— (2009). "What Determines the Financing Decision in Corporate Takeovers: Cost of Capital, Agency Problems, or the Means of Payment?" *Journal of Corporate Finance*, 15(3): 290–315.

—— —— (2011). "Evidence on the International Evolution and Convergence of Corporate Governance Regulations," *Journal of Corporate Finance*, 17(5): 1531–57.

MCCAHERY, J., and RENNEBOOG, L. (2002). "Recent Developments in Corporate Governance," in McCahery et al. (eds.), *Convergence and Diversity of Corporate Governance Regimes and Capital Markets*. Oxford: Oxford University Press, 1–22.

PIGOU, A. (1938). *The Economics of Social Welfare*. London: Macmillan.

RENNEBOOG, L., and ZHAO, Y. (2011). "Us Knows Us in the UK: On Director Networks and Managerial Compensation," *Journal of Corporate Finance*, 17(4): 1132–57.

ROE, M. (2002). *Political Determinants of Corporate Governance*. Oxford: Oxford University Press.

ROSE, P. (2007), "The Corporate Governance Industry," *Journal of Corporation Law*, 32: 101–32.

SHLEIFER, A., and VISHNY, R. (1986). "Large Shareholder and Corporate Control," *Journal of Political Economy*, 94: 461–88.

SPAMANN, H. (2006). "On the Insignificance and/or Endogeneity of La Porta et al.'s 'Anti-Director Rights Index' under Consistent Coding," Harvard John M. Olin Center for Law, Economics, and Business Fellows' Discussion Paper 7, Harvard Law School; ECGI Law Working Paper 67, ECGI.

—— (2010). "The 'Anti-Director Rights' Index Revisited," *Review of Financial Studies*, 23(2): 467–86.

PART II

CORPORATE GOVERNANCE MECHANISMS AND PROCESSES

CHAPTER 6

BOARDS AND GOVERNANCE

25 Years of Qualitative Research with Directors of FTSE Companies

ANNIE PYE

THE majority of research in the field of corporate governance is based on the assumptions of agency theory, is quantitative in approach, and analyzes US corporate databases or large US companies. As Wright et al. (Chapter 1 in this volume) have noted, a common critique of agency theory is of "its 'under-contextualized' nature." Attention to context also means the time of conduct and research is particularly relevant: for example, corporate governance practice has changed notably following the recent banking crisis (2007–8). In addressing these challenges, this chapter reflects on a series of three qualitative, contextualized, ESRC-funded studies[1] of UK directors, top management teams (TMTs), and key investors which began in 1987–9, was repeated in 1998–2000 and again in 2009–11. This unique longitudinal research into the people side of corporate governance effectively takes up Daily, Dalton, and Cannella's (2003) call to "dismantle the fortress of agency theory" by adopting a process-oriented "sensemaking" (Weick, 1995) approach to understanding corporate directing across time and context.

Both theory and practice in this field have changed considerably in the last 25 years. The first study in 1987 built on Hambrick and Mason's (1984) study of the extent to which the values and personalities of executives influenced upper echelons' behavior. By 1998–2000, this field of interest was more regularly seen in terms of corporate governance, although the core research question in each of these three studies has remained the same: how does a small group of people run a large company? This redefinition alone raises some interesting questions about the extent to which behavior has been redefined and the implications which such re-framing has for how action is interpreted and shaped anew. It also emphasizes the need to pay attention to time and "context," which provides the setting in which behavior is interpreted. There have been frequent calls throughout this time to develop behavioral analyses of board behavior (e.g. Pettigrew, 1992; Zajac and Westphal, 1998; Pye, 2000; Leblanc and Gillies, 2005; Pye and Pettigrew, 2005; Huse, 2007). This chapter will address these issues by first, sketching out the changing context of this inquiry and highlighting the conceptual challenge of the notion of context. It will then go on to draw attention to some of the changes in academic theorizing during this period, with regard to what happens at this level of organization. Third, it will reflect on findings from these studies across time and context to highlight key changes in roles and relationships which affect how companies are currently run. The final section will draw conclusions and highlight some paradoxes from this series of studies.

The Changing Context of Inquiry

The timing of these studies has fortuitously spanned what may be considered one of the most interesting periods in recent business history, comprising not just dramatic economic change, but also significant political, social,[2] technological, and regulatory change (see also Appendix 6.2). This has meant that the context in which directors now work is fundamentally different from that of 1987. Importantly, this has also had a major impact on *how* they work and *what is expected of them*, not just by those closest to them in the company but also by shareholders, regulators, "the media," employees, customers, suppliers, and many other stakeholders. By focusing on people and their behavior, it is important to note how such changes also appear to have impacted on *what they expect of themselves and others* with whom they work in the corporate upper echelons.

The features of "context" in this section have largely been drawn from the comments of research participants about important features of the context in which they work. Thus they tend to relate more specifically to the corporate/economic rather than social environment, and also include reference to significant global change which has impacted on their business and conduct, such as: the Berlin Wall coming down in 1989, which led to redrawing state boundaries across Eastern Europe; and the Twin Towers in New York, which were demolished by a suicide bomber attack in 2001, killing over 2,000 people, most of them working in financial services and with a significant and enduring effect on global travel, organizational security, and risk evaluation. These help introduce some of the wider, global changes which have significantly impacted on what FTSE 100 directors do and how they do it, and provide a backdrop to those identified in the following sections.

Economic and Political Change Impacting on FTSE Boards and Governance

In terms of economic change, this research began at a time which followed on from, the then Prime Minister, Margaret Thatcher's deregulation of the financial markets in 1984.

This had had a significant effect on the City of London, drawing businesses in from other global financial centers as well as providing a vibrant platform for developing new markets. Although inflation had been problematic through the 1980s, the economy was now buoyant, with substantial growth in corporate wealth, relatively easy access to capital, and with high property values and mortgage interest rates that reached 15 percent.

This was then followed by a period of downturn, during which the UK housing market collapsed and the economy suffered further through an array of corporate failures. These included the Barings Bank disaster (Brown, 2005) as well as the Asil Nadir/Polly Peck International and the Maxwell/Mirror Group pensions scandals in the early 1990s. Around that time, Sir Adrian Cadbury took on the role of chairing a panel of experts put together by the Financial Reporting Council (FRC), the London Stock Exchange, and the Institute of Chartered Accountants of England and Wales (ICAEW) to examine the auditing of UK companies. In the face of what was happening in the economic and corporate world, his brief steadily widened to become a review of UK corporate governance practices. This was followed by a series of review panels, further refining the focus and analysis of different aspects of UK corporate governance and was ultimately implemented as the first Combined Code of Corporate Practice (1998). This marked a turning point in corporate practice and laid the foundations for the plethora of corporate regulation and guidance which has followed.

Following the 1998–2000 study, there was another period of economic downturn, led by the crash in dot.com stocks which were found to have been overvalued. There was also a string of other corporate disasters during the early 2000s such as those concerning the Long-Term Capital Management hedge fund, Equitable Life, and the Marconi collapse. Key scandals at this time in the US included WorldCom and Enron, which also brought down Andersen (the long-established audit firm), and led to the Sarbanes-Oxley Act (2002) which had a major impact on financial reporting in global companies.

Regulatory Change Impacting on FTSE Boards and Governance

The recessionary period which followed the collapse of the dot.com boom was keenly felt and, in the UK, led to the Smith Review (2003) of audit practice and the Higgs Review (2003) of the role and effectiveness of non-executive directors. Authors such as Norburn (2011) have compiled extensive analyses of these different regulations. However, there has been further regulation since then which has significant implications for boards, TMTs, and governance—including revising and renaming the Combined Code (2008) as the UK Corporate Governance Code (2010), updating the Higgs Review of the Role of Non-Executive Directors (2003) as what is now the FRC (2011) Guidance on Board Effectiveness. The FRC has also implemented The Stewardship Code (2010) which relates to investor behavior. Similarly, the Financial Services Authority (FSA) has undertaken many reviews and issued guidance statements, not least of which comprises the

FSA (2009) Remuneration Code which applies to larger banks and broker dealers. These codes now provide a very weighty collection of guidance documents with which companies are expected to comply (see Appendix 6.2) and the review process continues unabated as FRC and FSA responsibilities are taken up by the Financial Stability Board and the Bank of England, with investigations into banking, audit practice, board diversity, corporate reporting, and remuneration.

UK regulation continues to be based on the "comply-or-explain" basis which underpinned Cadbury's (1992) recommendations of best practice, requiring companies either to comply with the code or give reasons for any non-compliance. Regrettably, this has led to a "tick-box" approach to compliance as can be seen in the governance sections of many companies' Annual Report and Accounts. Perhaps not surprisingly, in the preface to the Corporate Governance Code (2010: 2), Sir Christopher Hogg (FRC Chairman) noted "more attention needs to be paid to following the spirit of the Code as well as its letter" of compliance.

During this time, and after conducting extensive and lengthy rounds of consultation, the UK government passed a new Companies Act (2006), which is over 700 pages long, is structured into 47 parts which together comprise 1,300 propositions, each of which has several subclauses. For any positivist scholar of corporate law or governance, each proposition provides the basis for a hypothesis to test, potentially furnishing an entire academic lifetime of research. For practitioners, it is an extremely long and complex piece of legislation which, for the first time in UK legal history, defines seven principles of director behavior. In lay terms, the seven principles are that a director must: act in the interests of the company; act within the company's powers; promote the success of the company; exercise independent judgment; has a duty of skill, care, and diligence; must avoid conflicts of interest; and must not accept benefits from third parties. As with its predecessor, it assumes there is only one category of director, even though the Corporate Governance (2010) Code differentiates between executive and non-executive roles.

"Ownership" Changes Impacting on FTSE Boards and Governance

Another factor which is often overlooked during the course of this period in corporate practice is the extent to which institutional investment behavior in the City of London has changed, which has also had implications for understanding the notion of corporate ownership. Investors are not a homogeneous group but have different goals, time scales, and evaluation criteria as well as styles and patterns of engagement (Hendry et al., 2006). The context in which they operate has also been characterized by dramatic highs and lows as well as by notable changes in market competition. Thus their view of the Stewardship Code also varies such that as one investor in the 2009–11 study asked, "how realistic is it to expect the shareholding community to play the role of guardians of the whole corporate system?" Gaved (1997) noted that, during the early 1990s, institutional investment in London had become so concentrated that 20 institutions held approx 67 percent of UK equity. These figures have changed considerably since then, not least with increases in private equity and hedge fund holdings in the mid-2000s and, with approximately 40 percent of UK equity now being held by overseas investors. By 2009–11, we had been through one of the biggest global economic downturns since the 1930s, largely triggered by the collapse of Northern Rock plc in 2007 and Lehman Brothers investment bank in 2008. This has had dramatic consequences which continue to be felt globally, and are also reflected in tightening FSA regulation of UK banks through the Walker Review of Banks and Other Financial Service Interests (Walker Review, 2009).

Board–investor relationships remain important to practice (Westphal and Zajac, 1998). However, with around 80–90 percent of publicly quoted UK shareholdings now controlled by financial institutions (including 40 percent overseas) and roughly 32 percent of daily trades conducted by high frequency trading (Haldane, 2010), the nature of share ownership and how these relationships are conducted has also changed significantly with new technologies.[3] Yet, as many a CEO who has seen their share price go down while announcing improved corporate results will attest, interpreting corporate performance still depends on human judgment of (an)other human beings in which the way they appear to interrelate can have a strong effect (Pye, 2001).

Corporate Changes Impacting on FTSE Boards and Governance

The FTSE has also changed significantly across this time, not just in terms of share price performance (see Figure 6.1) but also composition. In 1999, the top ten FTSE 100 largest market capitalizations comprised three pharmaceuticals, two banks, two telecoms, two oil companies, and an IT company. By 2009, this balance had shifted such that of the top ten largest constituents as measured by market capitalization, four were oil and gas, two were mining, two were pharmaceutical companies, one was a tobacco company, and the other was a bank. In effect, the balance has shifted away from service companies in 1999 to mining and drilling in 2009. In turn, this has implications for the skills and abilities required not only of employees but also of the managers and directors who seek to lead them.[4]

From a boards and governance point of view, it is also important to note how the scale of FTSE 100 companies has changed since 1987, with noteworthy implications for both executive and non-executive directors of these enterprises. For example, in comparison with 20 years ago, these companies are now substantially international in terms of sales and assets such that, in some cases, UK operations contribute a relatively small, if not the smallest, part of the balance sheet. In addition, three of the current FTSE 100 have their head office in an overseas location (Chile, Florida, and Mumbai). Hence, not only has the nature of the director job changed for executive directors (EDs) and non-executive directors (NEDs) (see section on changes in director roles), but, with that, it is

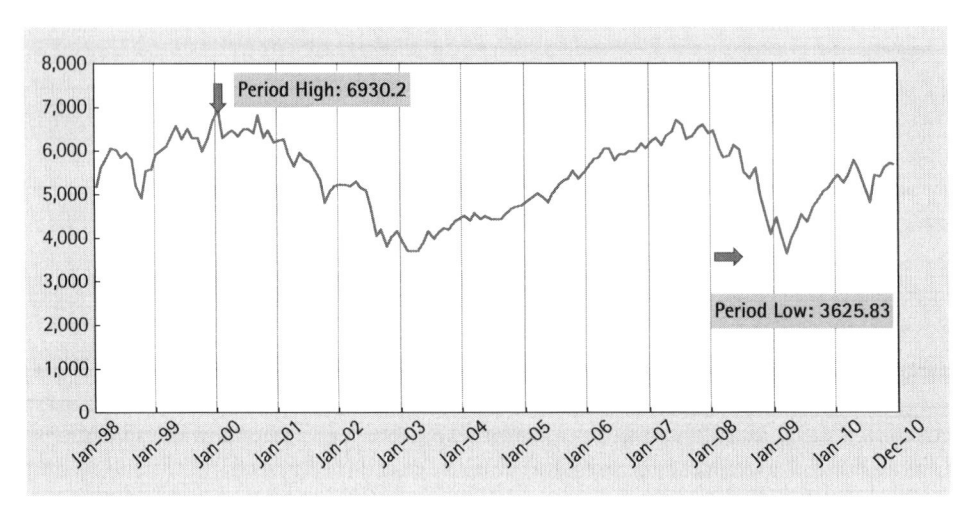

FIGURE 6.1. FTSE 100 share index, 1998–2010

also likely that the skills and competencies required to be effective in these roles will also have changed.

Technological Changes Impacting on FTSE Boards and Governance

This entire period of corporate history has been underpinned by significant changes in technology. In the 1987–9 study, many companies still used electric typewriters, fax machines were considered to be advanced forms of business technology, and computers still often only existed as substantial mainframes, requiring large separate offices of their own. Photocopiers formed the daily staple diet of office information exchange and BlackBerry pinging, Google, instant messaging, and high-frequency share trading had yet to be invented. The current business environment depends entirely on electronic equipment, such that many directors now use secure intranet sites to access relevant corporate documents and also have iPads to have instant and paperless access for reading board papers. This offers a marked contrast to the often dreaded "Friday night paper drop" (in 1998–2000), when the courier service delivered a substantial mountain of papers to be read in time for a board meeting the following week.

While my focus has been predominantly on the people running companies, the need to contextualize behavior in order to make sense of it requires attention to key features in this changing landscape which have a significant effect on director conduct. These technological changes have had a particularly significant effect, not least in terms of the ease of information availability and exchange and also the way in which people communicate with and respond to each other. Technology and database manipulation has also given rise to a relatively new industry called analytics, which provides service to large companies as well as investor rating agencies and risk assessment organizations. The change facilitated by technological innovation in the nature of share ownership across the last 20 years has also had a notable impact on the concept of ownership. The classically time-consuming and expensive process of buying share certificates from a stockbroker is now overtaken by nanosecond "shareholding" of high frequency share traders, whose purchase is generated by computer software.[5]

Reflecting on Conceptualizing Context

It is important to contextualize studies of organizations and their governance in particular (Pye and Pettigrew, 2005). However, the nature of context is open to a variety of definitions according to different interpretations and conceptualizations (Johns, 2006; Fairhurst, 2009; Liden and Antonakis, 2009), and remains personal to the individual enactor (Weick, 1979). The contextual features identified in the preceding subsections might be considered "external" to directors, as these have largely taken place "outside" their companies, although they clearly impact on what happens "inside." However, as Pye and Pettigrew (2005: S31) noted on the distinction between inner and outer context: "This is a handy simplification, although it may not be so easy to identify in practice, as these boundaries are sometimes permeable," as drawing boundaries between each inevitably depends on the position from which one is starting.

Reflecting on these contextual changes across the last 25 years, a pattern of behavior becomes apparent, reflecting a period of "high performance followed by disaster followed by review, followed by regulation" which runs repeatedly across time and appears to become amplified with each cycle. With hindsight, the corporate disasters of the early 1990s appear to look relatively minor in comparison with the dot.com disasters, which themselves now look relatively small in comparison with the banking collapse of 2008 and subsequent Eurozone crisis. However, the effects of that crash have gone much further and deeper into the fabric of daily life than any of their predecessors, and the increase in UK regulation since 2008 has been considerable. The EU Corporate Governance Code is in a period of consultation at the time of writing, although it appears on reflection across this period of corporate history as if global regulation might be more appropriate. That is, given the global nature of corporate practice and financial markets together with current concern about sovereign debt and potential unraveling of the global financial system, change in any one part of this "entanglement" will undoubtedly have effects elsewhere. In conclusion, while recognizing that both "context" and "history" remain open to interpretation, this section has endeavored to exemplify and emphasize why the notion of context is essential to understanding behavior. In so doing, it also draws attention to the need for qualitative research which focuses on behavior, to recognize the important influence which contextual changes may have on behavior.

Changing Academic Theorizing

There are several extensive summaries of corporate governance and upper echelons research which provide a useful starting point for this section (e.g. Daily et al., 2003; Hambrick, 2007; Hambrick et al., 2008; Durisin and Puzone, 2009; Brown et al., 2011). As Daily, Dalton, and Cannella (2003: 371) pointed out: "The overwhelming emphasis in governance research has been on the efficacy of the various mechanisms available to protect shareholders from the self-interested whims of executives." They went on to note that "it has not always been clear, however, whether practice follows theory, or vice versa," such that there is an element of "the blind leading the blind in this field of research" (Daily et al., 2003: 371). They went on to encourage research from perspectives other than the agency assumptions which have predominantly underpinned studies in this area.

Inevitably, corporate governance is a contested concept, and there is no commonly agreed definition of the term. There is little value in listing different definitions here, other than to note that amongst the classics which endure are: Cadbury's (1992, para. 2.5) statement that it is "the system by which companies are directed and controlled"; and Tricker's (1994: xi) summation of it as "the issues facing boards of directors, such as the interaction with top management, and relationships with the owners and others interested in the affairs of the company, including creditors, debt financiers, analysts, auditors and corporate regulators."

It has become such a popular area of research that in their electronic screening of Google Scholar using the term "corporate governance," Brown, Beekes, and Verhoeven (2011) generated 50,000 + hits. However, when they further refined this sample, it showed only 0.3 percent which addressed corporate governance + TMTs. As Ahrens, Filatotchev, and Thomsen (2011: 312) also observed, "...despite this enormous volume of research, we still know very little about corporate governance." It is also very rare to find longitudinal qualitative research in this field such that the research reported in this chapter is unique. In contrast to those reviewing breadth of literature, some review articles focus instead on smaller samples of core conceptual contributions. In so doing, Hambrick, Werder, and Zajac (2008) draw together different disciplinary perspectives into a framework, reflecting internal and external organizational-focused research, across three different governance research foci (see Figure 6.2).

This helpfully clusters an array of approaches around six core dimensions which engage with organizational research interests. While this may also speak to some qualitative studies of director behavior with regard to power (e.g. Pettigrew and McNulty, 1995, 1998; McNulty and Pettigrew, 1999; Maclean et al., 2010) or behavioral process (McNulty et al., 2005), there are several perspectives that fall outside this framework, such as stewardship, stakeholder, and political (Blair, 1994; Turnbull, 1997; Clarke, 2005). It also overlooks: the language of accounting and finance which does much to frame and focus behavior at this level; the burgeoning process research interest in organization

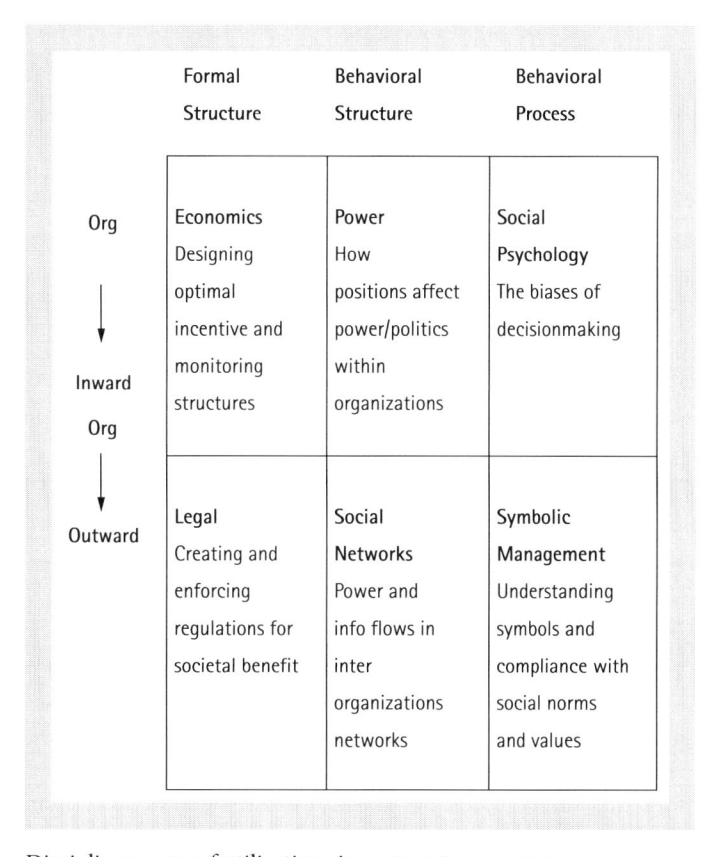

	Formal Structure	Behavioral Structure	Behavioral Process
Org ↓ Inward	Economics Designing optimal incentive and monitoring structures	Power How positions affect power/politics within organizations	Social Psychology The biases of decisionmaking
Org ↓ Outward	Legal Creating and enforcing regulations for societal benefit	Social Networks Power and info flows in inter organizations networks	Symbolic Management Understanding symbols and compliance with social norms and values

FIGURE 6.2. Disciplinary cross-fertilizations in corporate governance

Source: Hambrick et al. (2008).

studies which may also potentially address the lack of longitudinal research; and it does not refer to context, which is a core defining feature of behavior at this level. For example, what might be considered reckless risk-taking from one perspective may be seen as innovatory problem resolution from another (Tett, 2009).

The series of studies reported in this chapter develops a distinctively different perspective. Underpinned by a sensemaking approach (Weick, 1979, 1995) to understanding what goes on in these upper echelon settings, this research takes account of context and dynamic processes over time in this entangled web of threads comprising FTSE 100 boards' environment and practice. This is not constrained by disciplinary boundaries such that all of the disciplinary interests identified in Hambrick et al.'s (2008) model are reflected to the extent that they may influence the sense which people make. This contributes much-needed empirical material, as called for in Weick, Sutcliffe, and Obstfeld's (2005: 417) comprehensive analysis of sensemaking research and helps to provide a dynamic reflection of corporate directing.

The notion of corporate directing is an integrative summation of behavior relating to governing, strategizing, and leading/organizing in the context of large FTSE companies

(Pye, 2002). Part of this modeling endeavored to speak to different literatures relating to process dynamics at this level of organization, and was based on the assumption that behavior took place and was defined by others in context: a process which was ongoing over time. In this way, history can become rewritten as stories about the past become embellished or re-described, contemporary contexts reflect group influence processes to some degree, and the nature of future developments hinges on many elements including the dynamics of power embedded in "constitutively entangled" (Orlikowski, 2007) systems of relationships which may facilitate more or less opportunity in future.

The 12 sample companies in 1987–9 were each selected because they were reputed by analysts and commentators at that time to have "interesting managements and boards doing interesting things" (with the exception of Avon Rubber, a local SME (small and medium-sized enterprise) where we pilot-tested our method). UK listing has remained a selection criterion and, as far as possible, I have also sought to insure representation from different sectors across the FTSE 100 in each project. Each subsequent sample has comprised at least ten core companies in which semi-structured interviews have been conducted with three to seven directors, including at minimum the chief executive, chairman, and finance director. In addition, in the second and third projects, interviews were conducted with all directors from the previous sample who continued to have board positions, usually non-executive. The second study also included a small sample of active directors and the latest study has included interviews with selected investors, auditors, regulators, remuneration and executive search consultants. Secondary data have also been collected from multiple sources, including annual reports and accounts, company documentation, BoardEx, the ThomsonReuters database, corporate websites, and media coverage. All except three interviews have been conducted face to face, almost all have been one hour or more in length, and all have been transcribed.

In each project, qualitative data have been analyzed using a classic coding approach (Miles and Huberman, 1994) and also considered comparatively with the preceding project(s), in answer to the research question asked of core sample company directors, which is "how does a small group of people run a company?" Interviews with others, such as investors, have gathered their views on how they perceive such directors' conduct and their own part in influencing this. This process has not only necessitated strategies for data reduction but also required attention to many of the challenges of process data analysis described by Langley (1999), including complexity, multiplicity, and ambiguity, as well as variable time and space, precision, duration, and relevance.

In sum, in developing a path through this maze of work, this series of research studies has sought to bring together a contextualized understanding of people *and* processes which comprise the running of large, complex, UK-listed companies. This will be reflected in the next section, which explores empirical findings about changing roles and responsibilities which steer how contemporary FTSE 100 boards and directors work.

Changes in Director Roles, Relationships, and Conduct

Given the changes in context, content, and regulations outlined above, it is not surprising that director roles and conduct have also changed. Of particular interest with regard to the people side of governing is the extent to which this may have affected what characterizes skillful and effective directorship. However, as Barnard (1938: 235) pointed out, this is more easily recognized than described. Mangham and Pye (1991) concluded that effective directors were highly skilled in "reading, wrighting[6] and relating" and spent much of their time, in effect, explaining their organizing. These skills remain pertinent today. However, the nature of their reading, wrighting, and relating has changed, such that there is a different quality to the critical incidents to which they attend and the way in which they account for them, not least in terms of different key roles and responsibilities. In short, a director needs to exhibit skilled behavior, but the nature of what is considered skilled has changed over time.

Key Board Roles and Conduct

Two relationships stand out as critical in providing the axis to board and TMT performance. One is the relationship between CEO and chairman which impacts significantly on board practice and process and is also notably influential in terms of TMT expectations and conduct. The other is the relationship between CEO and finance director (FD), who together, both literally and metaphorically, account for their organizing. In the late 1980s, many CEOs were also chairmen and, where the chair and CEO roles were separated, the chairman tended to play the role of "back-stop" to the CEO and often remained out of public view. By 1998–2000, the chair-CEO roles were rarely combined and the chairman role had become more one of monitor and advisor to the CEO, and they were beginning to have more public presence in media coverage. By 2009–11, the role was often described in terms of CEO and chairman being in a partnership, in which they talked with each other frequently, and where both are now more likely to be in the public spotlight. Although previous studies found reference to the importance of knowing where the boundary lines between them lie, this emphasis has been particularly noticeable in the latest study. Interviews with CEOs and chairmen in 2009–11 all show that each of these individuals holds the other in high regard and has great respect for and trust in each other. While this has similarly been the case in previous rounds of the study, there have also been a few occasions where this has not been demonstrated through their conduct. Hence it seems as if, in the contemporary context, it is untenable for there to be any perceived weakness in this relationship. The quality of their relationship clearly has influence both in terms of TMT and board process and performance. In terms of TMTs, it appears in some cases as if they reflect similar conduct and process to that found in the

CEO-chairman relationship – for example, based on clear lines of communication, expectations of each other, and boundary lines, as well as respect, trust, and due regard. In one case in particular, the TMT dynamic appeared to be more based on principles of federation (i.e. a relationship in which the parts effectively convey power to the center underpinned by a tight set of principles), which clearly reflects a different cultural dynamic to that of partnership.

With regard to NEDs in general, there were relatively few NED s on most boards in 1987 and their role was described as akin to "baubles on a Christmas tree...they look nice but add little value" (Keenan, 2004: 172). We were told of one NED in our sample of that time who routinely unsealed the brown envelope of board papers as he walked into a board meeting and then put them back into the envelope and gave them to the secretary as he left the room and headed off for his board lunch. Perhaps not surprisingly, NEDs were rarely mentioned in interviews we conducted at that time and the board role was often seen as "rubber stamping" executive proposals.

Following regulatory change in 1998, FTSE boards were then required to separate chairman and CEO roles, ensure NED independence, and be composed of more NEDs than EDs. In the 1998–2000 study, some NEDS reported that they sometimes felt overwhelmed with information, although this was often perceived as data dumping in order to obscure more significant details. In comparison, contemporary NEDs may well have their board papers delivered via iPad, although there remains a fine line between valuable information and overload. For example, some but not all boards circulate all board members with the minutes of each executive board meeting. Sometimes this is accompanied by a one page CEO summary and, in at least one case in my recent study, the CEO routinely provides a one-page business update fortnightly for NEDs between board meetings, which NEDS reported to provide valuable additional information. These different practices create a different sense of engagement between EDs and NEDs in each board situation, not least in terms of their ability to use board meeting time more effectively, but also in the relationship between them with important implications for how they work together.

During the course of the 2009–11 study, FRC introduced Guidelines for Board Effectiveness (2011: 3) which emphasized that a board "should not necessarily be a comfortable place. Challenge, as well as teamwork, is an essential feature," so challenge is to be expected although often not welcomed in these classically consensual settings. As one NED apparently said, following a disagreement with the CEO in a board meeting which had clearly upset the CEO, "wouldn't you (the CEO) prefer me to make life uncomfortable in this board room rather than someone else do it in public?" However, as noted by other interviewees, over time executives get to know whose NED contribution they value more than others, and the same is true of NEDs, as each side weighs up the other to adjudge "do I have respect for this person and their judgement?" and "can I trust him/her?" Thus not only is it important to be able to attend to board task purpose, it is also essential to have good board process awareness and skills to facilitate skillful group intervention if/as appropriate to ensure dysfunctional group dynamics do not become embedded.

The number and length of meetings has undoubtedly increased since 1987. The pattern in 1987 was commonly a three-hour board meeting, four to six times per year, followed by an haute cuisine board lunch. Contemporary boards hold between eight and ten full board meetings per year which usually take at least half a day, if not a whole day and are usually preceded by and/or followed by subcommittee meetings, often involving an evening meal as well as an overnight stay. They are also now more likely to vary the venue of at least one board meeting per year, often visiting an overseas subsidiary. In addition to this, most boards continue to have at least one if not two annual "awaydays" to discuss strategy, and have regular strategic updates on board meeting agendas. With the common use of BlackBerrys, email, conference calls, and virtual meeting arrangements, there appears to be little time away from business information exchange in between meetings. This raises interesting questions about the changing nature of conduct, form, and response of/to such exchanges which are significantly different from more traditional exchanges in 1987 (Pye and Colville, 2010), as well as their implications for subsequent decision-making. There also remains an asymmetry in this process such that NEDs continue to depend on executives to provide relevant and useful information for their consideration, and must feel able to trust their executive colleagues in order to feel confident in their own ability to perform their role.

Some Significant Role Changes

With recent regulation, the roles of the chairman and also NEDs have become further clarified and the importance of their role has grown in terms of board conduct and performance. The Corporate Governance Code (2010) now has an entire section entitled Leadership, which includes 15 bullet points which identify what a chairman should do. Chairmen are responsible for ensuring that board effectiveness is reviewed annually, for conducting annual performance reviews, and giving personal development feedback to directors. One experienced chairman/NED recently described these meetings as "an embarrassed formality," conducted in order to comply with regulation. Otherwise, most of the skills and abilities which characterize effective behaviors in this context are felt to have been learnt and demonstrated through the course of one's career, en route to a senior executive role and then to a board directorship.

Another role which has become more significant in supporting the chairman, although remaining largely unrecognized in academic literature, is that of the company secretary. With increasing regulation and clear guidance as to the leadership role of chairman and requirements for board effectiveness reviews etc., the company secretary role has quietly become ever more influential. An important variation is where the function of company secretary is also combined with the role of the general counsel, which potentially gives rise to conflicting interests between whom is one advising, on what basis, and in what capacity. This also leads to more practical difference in terms of the scale of function being overseen by the company secretary, ranging from perhaps a group of ten to more than 100 employees, where this also involves the legal department.

As part of their role in organizing the board's work, i.e. distributing information packs for NEDs, organizing meetings, etc., company secretaries have considerable influence as gate keepers, in terms of bringing forward issues for an agenda as well as shaping how those are represented and informed. Some company secretaries seem to have a deeply embedded part in shaping agendas and writing minutes for an array of senior executive meetings, which has the benefit of ensuring they are well informed and knowledgeable about key issues before they reach board level, and hence are able to keep the chairman and NEDs well briefed. However, this also means their role is particularly powerful and influential in terms of board process and effectiveness. As one company secretary summarized it: "...I think the company secretary role is probably under-rated. People on the outside tend to regard it as a purely technical function...you're the one person in the company whom they can actually talk to in a rather more open way and where it works well is that the company secretary has to be completely discrete but there is that sort of relationship which chairmen, particularly if they are coming in completely new..., is really helpful to them and helpful to the company as a result."

In 1987, some boards had a deputy chairman whose role was to step in to the chair role, should anything untoward happen to him. However, the 1998 Combined Code began to formalize a role called the senior independent director (SID) role, for which the Higgs Review (2003) developed further guidance. This role is becoming increasingly significant in board conduct, not least as a sounding board for the chairman and also for conducting the chairman's annual performance review, but also as the person who takes responsibility for appointing a new chairman. In practice, SIDs also provide a bridge between chair and other board members or groupings, such as EDs and/or NEDs, as well as being available to investors should this be necessary. Rather like the company secretary role, successful SID performance requires great political sensitivity, skill, and the trust of others as they tread a fine line between EDs, NEDs, and the chairman. It also requires independence of mind and strength of character to know how and when to take the initiative, for example in replacing the chairman, and the will, skill, dexterity, and courage to persist in doing so.

While there remain regulatory differences between what is expected of EDs and NEDs in their conduct of directing, it is interesting to note that legally there is only one category of director, although clearly there is a significant difference between a full-time executive appointment (i.e. with operational responsibility and authority) and a part-time non-executive one. Garratt (2005) proposed that in order to professionalize the conduct of directors, it might be better for EDs to have two contracts such that, as they entered the board room, they could leave their operational executive responsibilities at the door. This is not something which has happened. However, the proportion of executive to non-executive roles has decreased, in part in line with regulation, in part through the influence of key investors, and in some cases in large part reflecting board and/or CEO preference. The worrying implication in this shift away from executive representation on boards is that NEDs have to rely more heavily on the CEO and FD for insight into operational issues. In my 2009–11 study, one FTSE 100 CEO pointed out that, in his view, it also helps NEDs realize that they are not running the business. However, another director noted: "we have two-tier boards in this country now, don't let anybody fool you. The number of executive directors on main plc boards has plummeted." This does not necessarily imply a return to the 1987–9 days of managerial hegemony and "rubber stamping" board, but now reflects a characteristic of boards enacting their responsibilities and accountabilities in current times. It is undoubtedly the case too that boards now make more substantial use of subcommittees to enable them to perform their role more effectively and efficiently.

Subcommittee Chairmen

With increasing reliance upon board subcommittees, the role of subcommittee chairs has become more important, and in particular, the chair of audit and chair of remuneration committees (Rem Cos), as well as how and where responsibility lies for risk management. There have been influential regulatory reviews of the audit role (Turnbull, 1999; Smith, 2003) and once again, following crisis, another is currently being conducted by FRC. Hence the chair of audit committee continues to hold a significant role in overseeing the audit function and efficacy. In addition, the chair of Rem Co appears to be a particularly challenging role. This is in part because investors pay close attention to executive remuneration levels as a basis on which to judge performance effectiveness and make their decision about whether or not to intervene. Although remuneration setting appears to be characterized by herd-like behavior, Rem Co chairs seek to avoid being "red-topped" (i.e. publicly challenged by investors, forewarning of a vote against remuneration proposals), yet the level of voting against remuneration proposals has recently increased. This has certainly not stopped levels of executive remuneration from continuing to rise significantly (see Figure 6.3) and the extent to which investors fully understand the increasing complexity of contemporary remuneration packages remains questionable. From a board research point of view, it sometimes appears as if remuneration gets "too much attention" to the detriment of other important performance factors, although this shows little sign of changing at least in the short term. Endeavoring to find an appropriate balance between rewarding and incentivizing executive behavior, one board advisor recently described this process as being one of "painting-by-numbers": that is, the strength and depth of color in the picture may change, but the different component parts of it do not. It also graphically depicts the challenge faced by Rem Co chairs in making good sense of what is almost becoming a science in itself.

During the course of this research, there has been frequent government and media attention, seeking to encourage constraint with regard to ever-increasing executive remuneration. The conclusion drawn through this study raises the question: in whose interest is it to change these awards? Boards and investors claim that they do not want to lose key EDs and, indeed, want to reward and encourage good performance, and EDs do not want to see or feel themselves being undervalued. Hence, it appears likely that the remuneration bubble will continue to grow unless there is some external, policy intervention.

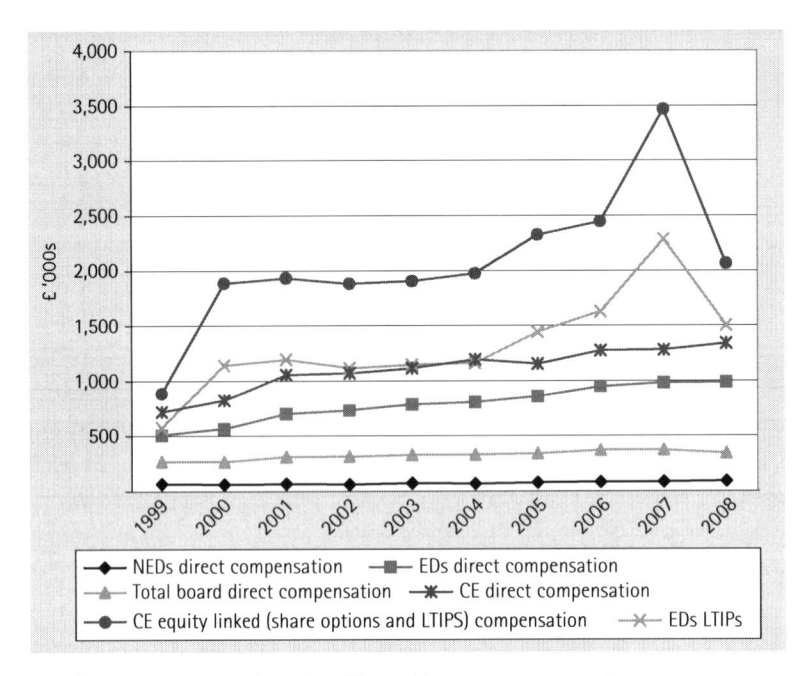

FIGURE 6.3. Average remuneration—FTSE 100 directors, 1999–2008

Source: Drawn from an unpublished report prepared by Pye, Kaczmarck, and Kimino for interviewees in the 2009–11 study.

Risk is undoubtedly a key issue with which contemporary boards must deal. For some directors, risk and strategy are merely two sides of the same coin. The UK Code of Corporate Governance (2010: 7) also notes: "The board is responsible for determining the nature and extent of the significant risks it is willing to take in achieving its strategic objectives. The board should maintain sound risk management and internal control systems." All the FTSE 100 companies in my recent research exhibit high-level risk evaluation processes, which at the very least reflect adherence to regulation. Technology has certainly helped in developing traffic light systems for representing risk, although, as became apparent in the recent financial crisis, highlighted in the Walker Review (2009), such analyses often fail to recognize systemic risk. While the latest software enables risk to be represented in a risk "heat map," in which individual risks identified and the backdrop is color coded to represent the systemic implications should the event happen, all such representations still depend on interpretation. How people perceive, interpret, and "deal" with risk reflects personal attitudes and individual predilections and is also shaped and influenced by social influences (March and Shapira, 1987).

With such increasing differentiation of roles and responsibilities, it remains curious that there is still little formal/legal or overt difference in terms of criteria against which NED performance is generally evaluated. Furthermore, dependent on the size, nature, maturity, and life cycle of the company as well as of the board, director roles and effective performance will vary, such that performance management of NED contribution remains elusive (Pye and Camm, 2003). They are not a homogeneous group and one size does not fit all. Hence, regulation is necessary but not sufficient to ensure high performance amongst these upper echelons groups.

Concluding Remarks

As noted at the outset, Daily, Dalton, and Cannella (2003) encouraged researchers to "dismantle the fortress" of agency theory. In this chapter, I have sought to offer insight into the people side of corporate governance which may help in developing a new line of theorizing which more adequately reflects a contextualized understanding of director conduct at particular times. It has been a qualitative, interpretive, series of studies, grounded in interview data collected from participants across time. Hence Frost and Stablein's (1992: 291) question, effectively asking how one does grounded theory when the ground is moving, remains a persistent methodological challenge. This has involved first exploring the notion of context, which has a powerful effect on shaping how directors see and take action, and which also further refines what they subsequently give attention to and the sense they make of this (Weick, 1979, 1995).

Contextualizing and comparing such longitudinal data serves to highlight what has changed and what remains the same. In conclusion, there appear to be several paradoxical challenges which characterize corporate directing, with relevance for both theory and practice as well as offering opportunities for future research. For example, while the FRC advises challenge as well as teamwork, how does a NED do this without undermining ED/NED relationships which are essential to effective conduct? To this end, it is important to leave egos outside the room, in order to keep attention on the issue not the person, facilitating partnership amongst critical friends. This alone is a major personal challenge for the kinds of people often appointed to such positions. It is also essential that they stay alert to group process dynamics to avoid slipping into complacency or "groupthink" (Janis, 1972). Perhaps not surprisingly, achieving the principles of partnership in this setting remains challenging.

The relationship between chairman and CEO stands out as critical to effective board conduct and company leadership, although the quality of this has changed with each decade, and purposeful partnership seems to characterize the best. An important test of this board leadership capability remains in the ways and extent to which this is reflected not just in board culture but throughout the value system underpinning the organization. Thus social dynamics and quality of embeddedness play a crucial role in shaping boardroom culture, process, and dialogue, evidenced in all three research projects in this series. To this end, effective director skills remain best summed up as the three Rs of directing: reading (situations), wrighting (as in shaping something new from "a tradition"), and relating (Mangham and Pye, 1991). Clearly the nature of their reading of situations, the materials with and means by which they wright, and the influence of key relationships have changed and will continue to do so, depending on context and judgment.

The same can also be seen in relationships between EDs and NEDs. While they meet each other in the same, often collegial or consensual, unitary board setting, they have different interests and personalities, work from different agendas, and are guided by their personal experience to help them judge the efficacy, reliability, and significance of statements made by the other party. In so doing, they engage in group performance, which may be considered as teamwork. However, paradoxically, the board of directors appears to work most like a team when tackling some serious challenge which, had they previously been performing effectively as a team, might well have been averted.

Relationships between executives, NEDs, and investors lie at the heart of board performance, and this is deeply embedded in a complex web of accountabilities in which their interactions and interpretations matter for corporate action and outcomes. So who is accountable to whom, for what, and how, in terms of context, content, and process, is accountability enacted? Regardless of statutory and regulatory change in the UK, such enduring questions about accountability persist, not least because of the classic paradox of group behavior which holds individuals responsible for action which is understood (i.e. gains meaning) at a particular time and in a particular (group/social) context. In this setting, this paradox is further compounded by the fact that the individual contribution to and accomplishment of collective responsibility and effective accountability ultimately hinges on the leadership dynamic between chairman and CEO.

There is a limit to which regulation can determine or prescribe behavior, as the human factor in corporate governance is and will remain crucial. Here Tetlock's (2005) observations about expert political judgment resonate well by addressing (i) the limits of knowledge; (ii) the limits of open-mindedness; and (iii) the limits to objectivity and accountability which lie at the heart of the core problem of (iv) seeking to qualify the unquantifiable in an endeavor to evaluate judgment. All these factors are reflected in the nature of corporate directing as evidenced by the data throughout these studies, and is highlighted most particularly in the recent project.

Corporate governance regulation during the 1990s aimed to facilitate openness and transparency, yet appeared to have a counter-effect of pushing more behavior backstage, rendering it potentially more opaque (Pye, 2001). From my contemporary research findings, this paradox seems to persist. Increasing regulation merely indicates increasing one's trust in a system of regulation, rather than increasing trust in the behavior or people being regulated.

Several other paradoxes appear to persist in these board processes. For example, given the nature of their roles, there will always be an information asymmetry to the roles of part-time NEDs and full-time EDs. This can only be overcome by developing trust and confidence in the other party to the relationship, which may potentially and paradoxically undermine the NED requirement to be independent, if ED and NED become too closely entrusting.

Paradoxically, the NED role effectively requires them to play the role of both coach and referee to EDs. The monitoring and policing side of their role is fundamental to their place on the board. However, they are also expected to contribute to strategy development and to give EDs the benefit of their experience and advice to help facilitate high performance. In this regard, they are effectively also in the role of coach: often not the best-placed person to judge performance.

While academics see such issues as paradoxical, it is often the case that practitioners adopt a view more akin to pragmatist philosophy (Rorty, 1982) and see them as a fact of daily life which one has to and is usually able to deal with (Mangham and Pye, 1991). Underpinning this is their moral compass guidance system, which shapes their purpose, values, and judgment and effectively motivates their conduct. From this series of three studies, it seems that to deal with these paradoxes and deliver effectively on their responsibilities, effective NEDs need to develop something akin to Socratic abilities to work systematically through different levels of questioning: first, to clarify thinking; then challenging the assumptions, evidence, and alternatives; and ultimately, questioning the question. Underpinning this, however, is also a sense of purpose and integrity, demonstrating constructive partnership, as this remains key to their direction as well as to sustaining their appetite and enjoyment.

As Tetlock (2005) would concur, such notions are crucial to expert political judgment, yet remain hard to capture. Boards are the group setting at the apex of organizations, where the chairman and chief executive play the lead roles in leading their enterprise, yet must rely on a crew to keep the boat ship-shape and on course. This presumes that action is being taken to achieve a course, rather than being blown to wherever the winds might take you. With this comes an array of hard work which requires skill and experience, as well as partnership, anticipation, and collaboration to achieve a successful outcome. While each director is an individual, none can perform alone and it is important to remember that organizing, leading, corporate directing, and governing are all things which people do together. The notion of individual director may provide the legal basis for director accountability, while experience also alerts astute directors to be mindful of the social settings, sensibilities, and sensitivities within which they work as one size most definitely does not fit all.

My aim in this chapter was to highlight some of the issues and uncertainties which people deal with in FTSE corporate directing, reflecting on changes in board practice and corporate governance over time. In so doing, I encourage future research in this field to pay more attention to the context in which behavior takes place and sense is made. There is also need for more research into understanding the nature of different director roles as well as the skill and efficacy of director performance in different group contexts. This is particularly relevant in the light of recent regulation which has given particular guidance on effective director conduct—for example, chairmen, senior independent directors, and company secretaries. There is also need and opportunity for research into the role and influence of (now more diverse) investors and board advisory consultants who all have influence, albeit it predominantly backstage rather than in the boardroom. Given change in the global economic climate since 2008 and its impact on corporate capability and conduct, it would be particularly valuable to consider such findings in terms of what may be needed to help develop the next generation of directors. Each of these areas for future research also has the potential to provide insight into what may be required for developing skillful future directors, which would be a worthy and relevant outcome for educators in this field of interest.

Acknowledgements

In addition to my thanks to ESRC for their consistent funding of this research, I am particularly grateful to the 200 plus senior figures from business, investment, regulation, auditing and remuneration consultancy who have contributed to each project: contributors to the 2009–11 research are listed in Appendix 6.1. I am also very grateful to Dr Ian Colville for his support and advice throughout the history of this research, and acknowledge Dr Szymon Kaczmarek and Dr Satomi Kimono, who were employed in the latest study to build and analyze quantitative datasets.

Appendix 6.1. Interviewees in the 2009–11 study

	First Name	Surname	Position at Time of Interview	Company Name
	Geoff	Armstrong	Former Director General	CIPD
	Kent	Atkinson	NED	Northern Rock Asset Management
Sir	John	Banham	Chairman	Johnson Matthey plc
	Barry	Bateman	President	Fidelity
	Brian	Beazer	Chairman	Beazer Homes
	Keith	Bedell-Pearce	SID	F&C Asset Mgt
	David	Bell	Director of People	Pearson plc
Sir	Winfried	Bischoff	Chairman	Lloyds Banking Group plc
Sir	Victor	Blank	Formerly Chairman	Lloyds Banking Group plc
	Jonathan	Bloomer	CEO	Cerebus European Capital
	Charles	Blundell	Director of Public Affairs	Rolls Royce plc
	Peter	Boreham	UK Head of Executive Remuneration	Hay Group
	Kate	Bostock	Executive Director	Marks & Spencer plc
	Craig	Boundy	CEO (UK)	Logica
	Julia	Budd	Founding Partner	Zygos
	Mark	Burgess	Head of Active Equities	Legal & General Investment
	Terry	Burns	NED	Pearson plc
	Peter	Butler	Founder Partner and CEO	Governance for Owners
Sir	Bryan	Carsberg	Chairman	Inmarsat plc
	Christopher	Collins	Chairman	Old Mutual
Sir	Michael	Colman	Chairman & CEO	Colman Peppermint Tea Farm
	Frank	Curtiss	Head of Corporate Governance	Railpen

BOARDS AND GOVERNANCE

	First name	Surname	Role	Organisation
	J. Eric	Daniels	CEO	Lloyds Banking Group plc
	Richard	Davey	Senior Independent NED	Severn Trent plc
	Gareth	Davis	CEO	Imperial Tobacco plc
Sir	Peter	Davis	Chair of Marie Curie Cancer	VP Bangor University
	Will	Dawkins	Managing Partner	Spencer Stuart
	Bob	Dyrbus	Finance Director	Imperial Tobacco plc
	Ian	Dyson	Group Finance and Operations Director	Marks & Spencer plc
Sir	Peter	Ellwood	Chairman	Rexam
	Mike	Fairey	Chairman	Horizon Acquisition plc
	Rona	Fairhead	Chairman and Chief Executive	FT Group Pearson plc
	Mike	Farley	Group CEO	Persimmon plc
	Robin	Freestone	CFO	Pearson plc
	Stephen	Green	CEO	HSBC
Sir	Richard	Greenbury	NED	Philips
	John	Griffith-Jones	Joint Chairman and Senior Partner	KPMG
	Mike	Hartley	NED	ITE Group
	Jeff	Hewitt	NED	Cookson Group
	Chris	Hodge	Secretary to Corporate Governance Committee	FRC
Sir	Christopher	Hogg	Chair	FRC
	Steve	Holliday	CEO	National Grid plc
	Alison	Horrocks	Company Secretary	Inmarsat plc
	Ken	Hydon	Chair of Audit Committee	Pearson plc
	Daniel	Jarman	Head of Governance Research	RiskMetrics
	Martyn	Jones	Senior Technical Partner	Deloitte
	Alison	Kennedy	Head of Governance Engagement	Standard Life
	Mike	Killoran	Group Finance Director	Persimmon plc
	Ian	King	CEO	BAE Systems plc
	Justin	King	CEO	Sainsburys plc
	Triphonas	Kyriakis	Vice President	MSCI
	Paul	Lee	Director	Hermes EOS
Dr	Tracy	Long	Founder	Boardroom Review
	Simon	Lowe	Managing Partner	Grant Thornton
	Gary	Luck	Director, Consulting Services	Towers Watson
	Ewen	Macpherson	NED	New Energy Technology
	Helen	Mahy	Company Secretary	National Grid plc
	David	Mayhew	Chairman	J.P. Morgan Cazenove
	Don	McCrickard	Director	Epic Investment Partners
	Harvey	McGrath	Chairman	Prudential plc
	William	McGrath	CEO	AgaFoodServices plc
	Michael	McLintock	CEO M&G Group	Prudential plc
	Colin Skene	Melvin	CEO	Hermes EOS
Sir	David	Michels	Deputy Chairman	Marks & Spencer plc
	Tony	Mitchard	Retired NED	
	Peter	Montagnon	Senior Investment Advisor	FRC

(continued)

Appendix 6.1. Continued

	First Name	Surname	Position at Time of Interview	Company Name
	Glen	Moreno	Chairman	Pearson plc
Sir	Paul	Myners	Former Labour Govt. Treasury Lord	Treasury
	Jonathan	Nicholls	NED	SIG plc
	Dick	Olver	Chairman	BAE Systems plc
	Simon	Osborne	Joint Head of ICSA Board Evaluation	ICSA
Sir	John	Parker	Chairman	National Grid plc
	David	Paterson	Head of Corporate Governance	NAPF
Lady	Louise	Patten	NED	Marks & Spencer plc
	William	Pattisson	CEO	Ardevora Asset Management
	Jenny	Peters	Head of Corporate Communications	Premier Farnell
	David	Peters	Partner	Heidrick & Struggles
Sir	Brian	Pitman (Deceased)	Senior advisor	Morgan Stanley
	David	Prince	NED	Adecco
Sir	Simon	Robertson	Non-executive Chairman	Rolls Royce plc
Sir	Stuart	Rose	Chief Executive and Chairman	Marks & Spencer plc
Sir	John	Rose	CEO	Rolls Royce plc
	Peter	Salsbury	Chairman	TR Property Investment Trust
	Vernon	Sankey	NED	Allied Zurich
Dame	Marjorie	Scardino	Chief Executive	Pearson plc
	Anne	Simpson	Executive Director	ICGN
	Anita	Skipper	Corporate Governance Director	Aviva Investors
	Andy	Smith	Director of Water Services	Severn Trent plc
	Brian	Smith	Retired	
	David	Smith	CEO	Westbury Homes
	Terry	Smith	CEO	Tullett Prebon
	Steve	Stone	Councillor	SW Science & Industry Council
	Murray	Stuart	NED	Veolia
	Andrew	Sukawaty	CEO and Chairman	Inmarsat plc
	Daniel	Summerfield	Co-head of Responsible Investment	USS
	Jim	Sutcliffe	Chairman	Old Mutual
	Tidjane	Thiam	Group Chief Executive	Prudential plc
	Mark	Tucker	CEO	Prudential plc
Sir	David	Walker	Senior Advisor	Morgan Stanley
	John	White	Non-executive Chairman	Persimmon plc
	Sarah	Wilson	Chief Executive	Manifest
	Richard	Wilson	Senior Partner	Ernst & Young
	Tony	Wray	CEO	Severn Trent plc
	Philip	Wright	Chairman, NED program	PriceWaterhouseCoopers

Appendix 6.2. Synopsis of recent corporate governance regulation in the UK

Report Title	Main Theme
1. Cadbury Review (1992)	"Report of the Committee on the Financial Aspects of Corporate Governance." A milestone marking the beginning of the development of corporate governance regulations.
2. Greenbury Report (1995)	"Directors' Remuneration." The study group on executive compensation.
3. Hampel Report (1998)	"Committee on Corporate Governance: Final Report." A review of the implementation of the findings of Cadbury and Greenbury committees.
4. Combined Code of Corporate Practice (1998), with subsequent editions in 2003, 2006, and 2008	The first corporate governance code in the UK (principle-based approach), bringing together recommendations from the Cadbury Report (1992), Greenbury Report (1995), and Hampel Report (1998). Subsequent editions in 2003, 2006, and 2008 were based on further rounds of review of corporate governance practice, coordinated and published by the Financial Reporting Council (FRC). Importantly, this was established on the principle of "comply or explain."
5. Turnbull Review (1999)	"Internal Control: Guidance for Directors on the Combined Code." Best practice in terms of internal control with significant impact on internal audit.
6. Myners Report (2001)	"Institutional Investment in the United Kingdom: A review." A review of types and process of UK institutional investment, e.g. pension funds, actuaries, pooled investment vehicles, investment decision-making by trustees.
8. Smith Review (2003)	"Audit committees: Combined Code guidance." A report and proposed guidance by an FRC-appointed group providing best practice insights into the role of audit firms and audit committees.
9. Higgs Review (2003)	"A review of the role and effectiveness of non-executive directors." The purpose of the review was to shed some light on the role of the non-executive director in the boardroom and to make recommendations to enhance their effectiveness.
10. Tyson Report (2003)	"The Tyson Report on the Recruitment and Development of Non-executive Directors." A report commissioned by the Department of Trade and Industry following the publication of the Higgs Review of the Role and Effectiveness of Non-executive Directors in January 2003.
11. Companies Act (2006)	After almost ten years in consultation, this Act forms the primary source of UK company law. It is one of the longest acts in British Parliamentary history: 1,300 sections, covering nearly 700 pages, and containing no fewer than 15 schedules. It superseded the Companies Act 1985 and for the first time, included seven principle duties for company directors and was brought into force in stages, with the final provision being implemented on October 1, 2009.
12. FSA Walker Review (2009)	"A review of Corporate Governance in UK Banks and Other Financial Industry Entities." This report was commissioned (February 2009) by the Prime Minister to review corporate governance in UK banks in the light of critical loss and failure throughout the banking system, following collapse of Northern Rock, Lehman Brothers, and other BOFIs.

(continued)

Appendix 6.2. Continued

Report Title	Main Theme
13. FRCUK Corporate Governance Code (2010)	This corporate governance code supersedes the Combined Code (2008) and maintains the UK's principle-based approach to governance through "comply or explain." It was informed through consultation by the FRC and the Walker Review, undertaken during the 2008 financial crisis. Similar to its predecessors, the Code is based on the underlying principles of: accountability, transparency, and probity, and focuses on the sustainable success of an entity over the longer term. Published by the FRC, the new Code applies to accounting periods beginning on or after June 29, 2010, and, as a result of the new Listing Regime (in April 2010), applies to all companies with a Premium Listing of equity shares regardless of whether they are incorporated in the UK or elsewhere.
14. FRCUK Stewardship Code (2010)	The Code sets out good practice on engagement with investee companies, to create a stronger link between governance and the investment process, and lend greater substance to the concept of "comply or explain" as applied by listed companies. The FRC therefore sees it as complementary to the UK Corporate Governance Code (2010) for listed companies.
15. FRC Guidance on Board Effectiveness (2011)	This updates the Higgs Guidance on "improving board effectiveness" and includes greater detail on the role of chairman, as well as advice for conducting board effectiveness reviews.

Source: Copies of these UK regulatory review reports can be downloaded from: <http://www.icaew.com/en/library/subject-gateways/corporate-governance/codes-and-reports/>.

NOTES

1. I am grateful to the ESRC for their continued funding of this work; registered under grant numbers WF 2925 0020 (1987–9), R 000236868 (1998–2000) and RES-062-23-0782 (2009–11).
2. The social changes across the last two decades are practically impossible to capture succinctly in relation to the contextual change relevant to this inquiry. For example, unemployment in the UK is currently running at 2.5 million (the highest it has been in the last decade), and is particularly acute amongst under 25-year-olds; the retired population is increasing; education standards and levels of achievement amongst school leavers have also changed notably; the nature of the media has changed; there is more global travel; and levels of internet access and use are increasing, particularly amongst under 25-year-olds, and social networking is a commonplace worldwide form of interaction.
3. Share-trading has changed across the last decade with an increasing role for private equity, sovereign wealth funds, and new forms of exchange and inter-broker trading as well as concerns about "dark pools" and unlit markets which effectively comprise influential shadow arenas which lie well beyond the realms of this study.

4. In 1989, primary attention was given to the FTSE 30 rather than the FTSE 100 and, given changes in protocols of listing (e.g. with regard to insurers), it is difficult to compare with contemporary data. With regard to core sample companies in this study, it is interesting to note that in 1989, the top ten companies with regard to FTSE market valuation included at least two conglomerates which, primarily due to investor pressure, no longer existed in this form by 1998.
5. This practice is of concern to both the European Securities and Markets Authority (January 2011) and the UK Department of Business, Innovation and Skills (DBIS) (November 2010), who are now conducting formal investigations into high-frequency trading. There is also concern about the apparent growth of "dark markets"—off-exchange or over-the-counter (OTC) markets—where share trades are done privately between parties and made public only after trades are done. These appear to be growing, such that the relevance of "lit markets" may be diminishing.
6. We used this term "…in the sense that a playwright 'wrights'…," i.e. "…inherits and is shaped by a tradition…yet remains capable of going beyond and shaping it.… whose work is never finished, always evolving" (Mangham and Pye, 1991: 26).

REFERENCES

AHRENS, T., FILATOTCHEV, I., and THOMSEN, S. (2011). "The Research Frontier in Corporate Governance," *Journal of Management and Governance*, 15(3): 311–25.

BARNARD, C. (1938). *The Functions of the Executive*. Cambridge, MA: Harvard University Press.

BLAIR, M. M. (1994). *Ownership and Control: Who's at Stake in the Corporate Governance Debates?* Washington, DC: Brookings Institution.

BROWN, A. D. (2005). "Making Sense of the Collapse of Barings Bank," *Human Relations*, 58(8): 1579–604.

BROWN, P., BEEKES, W., and VERHOEVEN, P. (2011). "Corporate Governance, Accounting and Finance: A Review," *Accounting and Finance*, 51: 96–172.

Cadbury Review (1992). *Report of the Committee on the Financial Aspects of Corporate Governance*. London: Gee.

CLARKE, T. (2005). *Theories of Corporate Governance: The Theoretical Foundations*. London: Routledge.

The Combined Code on Corporate Governance (2008). London: Gee.

Companies Act (2006). Available at <http://www.legislation.gov.uk/ukpga/2006/46/contents>.

DAILY, D. M., DALTON, C. R., and CANNELLA, A. A. (2003). "Corporate Governance: Decades of Dialogue and Data," *Academy of Management Review*, 28(3): 371–83.

DURISIN, B., and PUZONE, F. (2009). "Maturation of Corporate Governance Research, 1993–2007: An Assessment," *Corporate Governance: An International Review*, 17(3): 266–91.

FAIRHURST, G. T. (2009). "Considering Context in Discursive Leadership Research," *Human Relations*, 62(11): 1607–33.

Financial Reporting Council (2010a). *The UK Corporate Governance Code*. London: FRC.

—— (2010b). *The UK Stewardship Code*. London: FRC.

—— (2011). *Guidance on Board Effectiveness*. London: FRC.

Financial Services Authority (2009). *Remuneration Code for Banks and Other Financial Institutions*. London: FSA.

FROST, P., and STABLEIN, R. (eds.) (1992). *Doing Exemplary Research*. London: Sage.

GARRATT, B. (2005). "A Portrait of Professional Directors: UK Corporate Governance in 2015," *Corporate Governance: An International Review*, 13(2): 122–26.

GAVED, M. (1997). *Closing the Communications Gap: Disclosure and Institutional Shareholders*. London: Institute of Chartered Accountants of England and Wales.

HALDANE, A. G. (2010). "Patience and Finance," London: Bank of England. Available at <http://www.bankofengland.co.uk/publications/speeches/2010/speech445.pdf>.

HAMBRICK, D. C. (2007). "Upper Echelons Theory: An Update," *Academy of Management Review*, 32(2): 334–43.

—— and MASON, P. A. (1984). "Upper Echelons: The Organization as a Reflection of its Top Managers," *Academy of Management Review*, 9(2): 193–206.

—— WERDER, A. V., and ZAJAC, E. J. (2008). "New Directions in Corporate Governance Research," *Organization Science*, 19: 381–5.

HENDRY, J., SANDERSON, P., BARKER, R., and ROBERTS, J. (2006). "Owners or Traders? Conceptualizations of Institutional Investors and their Relationships with Corporate Managers," *Human Relations*, 59(8): 1101–32.

Higgs Review (2003). "The Role and Effectiveness of Non-Executive Directors." London: FRC.

HUSE, M. (2007). *Boards, Governance and Value Creation: The Human Side of Corporate Governance*. Cambridge, UK: Cambridge University Press.

JANIS, I. L. (1972). *Victims of Groupthink: A Psychological Study of Foreign-Policy Decisions and Fiascoes*. Oxford: Houghton Mifflin.

JOHNS, G. (2006). "The Essential Impact of Context on Organizational Behavior," *Academy of Management Review*, 31(2): 386–408.

KEENAN, J. (2004). "Corporate Governance in UK/US Boardrooms," *Corporate Governance: An International Review*, 12(2): 172–6.

LANGLEY, A. (1999). "Strategies for Theorizing from Process Data," *Academy of Management Review*, 24(4): 691–710.

LEBLANC, R., and GILLIES, J. (2005). *Inside the Boardroom: What Directors, Investors, Managers and Regulators Must Know about Boards*. Chichester: J. Wiley.

LIDEN, ROBERT C., and ANTONAKIS, J. (2009). "Considering Context in Psychological Leadership Research," *Human Relations*, 62(11): 1587–605.

MACLEAN, M., HARVEY, C., and CHIA, R. (2010). "Dominant Corporate Agents and the Power Elite in France and Britain," *Organization Studies*, 31(3): 327–48.

MANGHAM, I. L., and PYE, A. J. (1991). *The Doing of Managing: A Study in Executive Process*. Oxford: Blackwell.

MARCH, J., and SHAPIRA, Z. (1987). "Managerial Perspectives on Risk and Risk Taking," *Management Science*, 33(11): 1404–18.

MCNULTY, T., and PETTIGREW, A. (1999). "Strategists on the Board," *Organization Studies*, 20(1): 47–74.

—— STILES, P., and ROBERTS, J. (2005). "Beyond Agency Conceptions of the Work of the Non-Executive Director: Creating Accountability in the Boardroom," *British Journal of Management Special Issue*, 16: SI1–22.

MILES, M., and HUBERMAN, M. (1994). *Qualitative Data Analysis: An Expanded Sourcebook*. London: Sage.

NORDBERG, D. (2011). *Corporate Governance: Principles and Issues*. London: Sage Publications.
ORLIKOWSKI, W. J. (2007). "Sociomaterial Practices: Exploring Technology at Work," *Organization Studies*, 28: 1435–48.
PETTIGREW, A. M. (1992). "On Studying Managerial Elites," *Strategic Management Journal*, 13: 163–82.
—— and MCNULTY, T. (1995). "Power and Influence in and around the Board-room," *Human Relations*, 48(8): 845–73.
—— —— (1998). "Sources and Uses of Power in and around the Boardroom," *European Journal f Work and Organizational Psychology*, 7(2): 197–214.
PYE, A. (2000). "Changing Scenes in, from and outside the Board Room: UK Corporate Governance in Practice from 1989 to 1999," *Corporate Governance: An International Review*, 8(3): 335–46.
—— (2001). "Corporate Boards, Investors and their Relationships: Accounts of Accountability and Corporate Governing in Action," *Corporate Governance: An International Review*, 9(3): 186–95.
—— (2002). "Corporate Directing: Governing, Strategizing and Leading in Action," *Corporate Governance: An International Review*, 10(3): 153–63.
—— and CAMM, G. (2003) "Moving beyond the One-Size-Fits-All View," *Journal of General Management*, 28(2): 43–61.
—— and COLVILLE, I. D. (2010). "Talk, Text and Tools: Materiality Really Matters," Paper presented to the Strategy-as-Practice Workshop at GEPS, HEC, Montreal, Canada, August.
—— and PETTIGREW, A. M. (2005). "Studying Board Context, Process and Dynamics: Some Challenges for the Future," *British Journal of Management*, 16(s1): S27–35.
RORTY, R. (1982). *Consequences of Pragmatism*. Minneapolis: University of Minnesota Press.
Smith Review (2003). "Audit Committees: Combined Code Guidance." London: Financial Reporting Council.
TETLOCK, P. E. (2005). *Expert Political Judgment: How Good is it? How Can we Know?* Princeton: Princeton University Press.
TETT, G. (2009). *Fool's Gold: How Unrestrained Greed Corrupted a Dream, Shattered Global Markets and Unleashed a Catastrophe*. London: Little, Brown.
TRICKER, B. (1994). *International Corporate Governance*. Englewood Cliffs, NJ: Prentice Hall.
Turnbull Review (1999). *Corporate Guidance for Internal Control*. London: Gee.
TURNBULL, S. (1997). "Corporate Governance: Its Scope, Concerns and Theories," *Corporate Governance: An International Review*, 54(4): 180–205.
Walker Review (2009). *Review of Corporate Governance of the UK Banking Industry*. London: FRC.
WEICK, K. E. (1979). *The Social Psychology of Organizing*. New York: McGraw-Hill.
—— (1995). *Sensemaking in Organizations*. London: Sage.
—— SUTCLIFFE, K. M., and OBSTFELD, D. (2005). "Organizing and the Process of Sensemaking," *Organization Science*, 16(4), 409–21.
WESTPHAL, J. D., and ZAJAC, E. J. (1998). "The Symbolic Management of Stockholders: Corporate Governance Reforms and Shareholder Reactions," *Administrative Science Quarterly*, 43(1): 127–53.

ZAJAC, E. J., and WESTPHAL, J. D. (1998). "Toward a Behavioral Theory of the CEO/Board Relationship: How Research Can Enhance Our Understanding of Corporate Governance Practices," in D. C. Hambrick, D. A. Nadler, and M. L. Tushman (eds.), *Navigating Change: How CEOs, Top Management Teams and Boards of Directors Steer Transformation.* Cambridge, MA: Harvard University Press.

CHAPTER 7

PROCESS MATTERS

Understanding Board Behavior and Effectiveness

TERRY MCNULTY

INTRODUCTION

Over the last three decades boards and corporate governance have been implicated in corporate failure and collapse. Reform on an international scale, using legislation and voluntary codes, has focused on improving the way boards work and enhancing the confidence of interested others, such as investors, in what happens on boards (Aguilera and Cuervo-Cazurra, 2009). In parallel a large research literature about corporate governance has developed that seeks to establish links between board structures, board outcomes, and firm performance (Hermalin and Weisbach 2003; Dalton and Dalton, 2011). However, a focus on the attributes and effects of boards has yielded an inconclusive body of knowledge and limited evidence to support agency theory, the dominant theory of the field and its particular view on board functions and effectiveness. Finkelstein and Mooney (2003) were moved to remark that the key to making boards work better rests in attention to "board process," that is: matters such as engaging in constructive conflict and avoiding destructive conflict; working together; being involved in strategy; and addressing decisions in a comprehensive fashion. A similar proposition is that while structure, composition, and independence condition board effectiveness, it is the actual conduct of the non-executive vis-à-vis the executive that determines board effectiveness (Roberts et al., 2005). Within the literature on boards the impetus is now in favor of studying behavioral processes (Hambrick et al., 2008) to explain governance at firm level.

This chapter discusses research that attends to board behavior and process in order to understand board and governance effectiveness. The discussion is oriented to unitary boards of publicly listed companies as these tend to dominate the literature. Studies of boards of non-profit organizations (Nicholson and Kiel, 2007; Parker, 2007), small firms (Machold et al., 2011), family business (Van den Heuval et al., 2006), and unlisted companies (Kula, 2005) offer much by way of coverage of governance in other types of organizations. Also the chapter draws on a particular subset of a much larger literature on boards, as it seeks to complement rather than replicate existing meta-analysis and reviews, as well as chapters in this volume by Pye and Stiles. For fuller reviews of the wider literature about boards and governance see: Durisin and Puzone's (2009) meta-analysis of corporate governance research between 1993–2007; Pugliese et al.'s (2009) review of the literature about board of directors' contribution to strategy; Ahrens, Filatochev, and Thomsen's (2011) discussion of research frontiers in corporate governance; Deutsch's (2005) review of the impact of board composition on firms' critical decisions; Boyd et al.'s (2011) review of CEO–board relations; and Ryan et al.'s (2010) review of research at the intersection of business ethics and corporate governance.

"Process" has a variety of meanings and usages in the organizational and governance literature (Van de Ven, 1992; Pye and Pettigrew, 2005). This chapter takes a broad and inclusive approach by focusing on studies of behavioral processes that enhance understanding of boards and governance at firm level. Initially, the chapter identifies qualitative research studies that have engaged with debates of board power, influence, and accountability through accessing boards and directors and generating data about board behavior. In the second half, it identifies studies which model boards as strategic decision-making groups and test the relationship between board processes and performance. The chapter concludes by suggesting that momentum for understanding board process remains crucial to analyzing the appearance and substance of corporate governance.

Board Behavior: Processes of Power, Influence, and Accountability

Viewed as a key mechanism of corporate governance, boards of directors are charged with carrying out a mix of control/monitoring, resource, service, and strategy tasks (Daily et al., 2003). A large literature has developed, focusing on aspects of these tasks and drawing on (often) competing theoretical perspectives (Golden and Zajac, 2001; Hillman and Dalziel, 2003; Hillman et al., 2008; Boyd et al., 2011), but researchers are equivocal, even skeptical about the effects of boards. Meta-analyses that sought to establish a link between structural and compositional characteristics of boards, for example, board size, duality of CEO and chairman role, ratio of outside/inside directors and firm financial performance (Johnson et al., 1996; Dalton et al., 1999; Hermalin and Weisbach, 2003; Dalton and Dalton, 2011), are inconclusive and inform calls for studies of intervening variables and processes that may explain board performance and effects at firm level (Daily et al., 2003; Finkelstein et al., 2009; Pugliese et al., 2009).

Zahra and Pearce (1989) did much to set the tone and direction for studying board process and dynamics. Focusing on the relationship between boards and company financial performance, they synthesized existing work, noted contradictory findings, and called for a different approach to research in order to better understand how boards operate as instruments of corporate governance. To stimulate a research agenda they proposed an integrative model containing four board attributes (composition, characteristics, structure, and process) and three critical board roles (service, strategy, and control). Specifically, they noted the low number of empirical investigations into board processes, identifying it as one of the most challenging areas for future research on the contribution of boards. Using process to refer to decision-making activities, they identified effective board process as essential for the performance of the board's service, strategy, and control roles. Their particular proposition was that board characteristics, structure, and process exert a significantly stronger influence on board roles and company performance than board composition.

Following on their model, Pearce and Zahra (1991) examined the relationship of board power to organizational effectiveness using a survey of CEOs of the largest Fortune 1000 industrial and service firms. After measuring CEO power, board power, and board process, the study showed significant differences among four board types concerning their characteristics, process, and effectiveness. Boards that had power equal to or greater than the CEO (e.g. proactive and participative boards) were described by the CEO as being more efficient, better informed, more careful, yet quicker in making decisions than weaker boards (caretaker and statutory). These powerful board types were also viewed by CEOs as more progressive and supportive of CEO efforts. Participative boards were associated with the highest level of company financial performance. This study opened up research to CEO-board power as an important contingency to consider when studying the relationship between boards and company performance. Rather than seeking universal associations, multiple indicators of board and CEO relative powers could be used to classify board types and study their distinguishing qualities and processes.

As well as proposing their own model, Zahra and Pearce (1989) called for field studies of board behavior which would shed light on the nature of board processes and how boards impact on corporate governance and performance. Pettigrew (1992) developed this point, also describing the field of research on boards as at an early stage of development and requiring of more behavioral studies. Concerned about tenuous links between dependent and independent variables, he called for research studies that are closer to the actors and settings of governance and generate more insight about behavior and relationships in and around the boardroom. Lorsch and MacIver (1989) was cited as a rare example of research that was able to get closer to the actual operation of the strategic apex of the enterprise, resulting in the important finding that real power lies with the governed and that boards have a problem translating their legal mandate into effective power over the top managers. For Pettigrew, another feature of the Lorsch and MacIver study was that it added to knowledge about how norms of conduct on boards influence power relationships between outside and inside directors and the CEO. Consequently, his subsequent approach to fieldwork was less inclined to test theories of board power, such as managerial hegemony or agency theory, and more concerned to contribute to these debates by further identifying conditions, behavior, and relationships that inform the exercise of power and influence by boards.

Using interview data from company chairs, chief executives, executive and non-executive directors in UK plcs, Pettigrew and McNulty (1998, 1995) explore the dynamics of board behavior with respect to the contribution, power, and influence of part-time board members (non-executive directors and chairs who are not CEO). Power was defined as the ability to create intended effects in line with one's perceived interests. Power was conceptualized as a structural and relational phenomenon that is generated, maintained, and lost in the context of relationships with others. Quests for power and influence were seen as situational, that is, shaped by features of the content, context, and politics of issues, as well as dynamic and inherently unstable. Using data about behavior, the study presents boardroom power and influence as related to macro and micro features of structure and context. For example, features of company history and board culture; norms of conduct in and around the boardroom; patterns of role selection and socialization; chief executive and chairman attitudes and behavior were all identified as determining and reinforcing the rules of the game within which boards and non-executive directors operate. Alongside these issues, power sources, such as relevant expertise and experience, as well as director will and skill, were found to be critical to the process by which power is mobilized into influence in and around boards. At board level, where personalities may be large and individuals can be selected for personal qualities, the willingness of directors to intervene and their skill in matching behavior to the requirements of the situation were viewed as integral to their influence and impact. To further emphasize how and why a variety of interrelated features of structure and context shape the possibilities of non-executive power and influence, the study utilized a distinction between "minimalist" and "maximalist" board cultures. Minimalist boards are those in which a set of conditions severely limit the involvement and influence of the board and its incumbent non-executive directors on the affairs of the firm. By contrast, a maximalist boards is one where the board and non-executives actively contribute to dialogue within the board and build their organizational awareness and influence through contacts with executive directors, managers, and other non-executives beyond the boardroom. Variation in the processes and effects of boards was further examined by McNulty and Pettigrew (1999) through their differentiation of three modes of behavior on boards in respect of strategy: "taking strategic decisions," "shaping strategic decisions," and "shaping the content, context and conduct of strategy." By virtue of these different levels of involvement in strategy, the study identifies differences in boards' ability to influence processes of strategic choice, change, and control. Subsequently, Stiles (2001) reported the review of strategic initiatives to be a central feature of board contribution that helps to "raise the bar" in terms of the quality of executive strategic proposals and the effectiveness of decision-making. Ongoing attention to board involvement in strategy is contributing to the development of a behavioral perspective within governance research (Pugliese et al., 2009).

Around the same time a number of other "field studies" gained access to directors to shine light on board behavior. Demb and Neubauer (1992: 82) identified challenges that non-executive directors face in becoming involved in decision-making processes. Hill's (1995) study of UK boards found non-executives working with managers reviewing and refining the strategic decisions of their organizations. Pye (2002), discussed in more detail elsewhere in the *Handbook*, identifies the task of "corporate directing," involving strategizing, governing, and leading. Westphal (1999) reported that social ties between a CEO and the board provide strong benefits, including the enhancement of mutual trust, space for advice-seeking on the part of the executives, a reduction in defensive and political behavior within the board, and an opportunity for enhanced learning. Roberts and Stiles (1999) found chair and chief executive relationships to fall into two types—competitive and complementary—each with very different consequences for board effectiveness. As a result of these studies, the field began to generate a greater sense of the cumulative behaviors that contribute to unfolding dynamics of relationships on boards that in turn serve to either undermine or promote board influence and effectiveness.

Subsequently, Roberts, McNulty, and Stiles (2005) drew on this earlier work and fused it with arguments about accountability (Roberts, 2001) to develop a notion of board effectiveness defined as "creating accountability." Theoretically, this study cautions against taking a polarized view of the non-executive role as either "control" or "service," engendered by theoretical divisions between agency and stewardship theory, and also control versus collaboration models of the board process (Sundaramurthy and Lewis, 2003). Using interview-based research among directors of UK FTSE 350 companies, the study identified conditions that allow non-executives to create accountability, and some of the key attitudes and skills that this involves. It found the work of the non-executive director to be vital both in enhancing the actual effectiveness of boards, and as a source of confidence for distant investors as to the effectiveness of what goes on in boards. It identified that non-executives can both support the executives in their leadership of the business and monitor and control executive conduct. Rather than discovering an inherent tension in these two aspects of the role, the study suggests that the key to board effectiveness lies in the degree to which non-executives, acting individually and collectively, are able to create accountability within the board in relation to *both* strategy *and* performance. Accountability is in practice achieved through a wide variety of behaviors—challenging, questioning, probing, discussing, testing, informing, debating, exploring, encouraging—that are at the very heart of how non-executives seek to be effective. In particular, the study identifies three linked sets of behaviors that suggest the non-executive should be "engaged but non-executive," "challenging but supportive," and "independent but involved." All in all, Roberts et al. (2005) seek to identify the potential, within the unitary board, for a positive dynamic of relationships between executives and non-executives based on executive perceptions of the relevance and value of non-executive contributions. However, they also identify why boards may experience negative dynamics that spiral downwards into factionalized and mistrustful relations.

Stimulated by Zahra and Pearce (1989) and Pettigrew (1992), field studies have come to recognize boards as fragile human systems, the strength or fragility of which lies in the quality of the interactions of the parties involved. Through being able to study and describe behavior, we have come to generate ideas about the antecedents and conditions which inform effective boards. Echoing a proposition to come out of the study by Roberts et al. (2005), we are now in a better position to articulate that board structure and composition may condition the way boards operate, but actual board effectiveness depends on the behavioral dynamics of the board, including the conduct and relationships of non-executives vis-à-vis the executives (Roberts et al., 2005). In the next part of the chapter, we proceed to a different but complementary stream of research which has developed in the last decade and is now subjecting board processes, as suggested by Zahra and Pearce (1989), to formal modeling and testing. The next part of the chapter focuses on studies that are investigating the relationship between social-psychological processes and boards, board performance, and company outcomes.

BOARD PROCESS AND PERFORMANCE: BOARDS AS STRATEGIC DECISION-MAKING GROUPS

An important development in the governance literature is the identification of social and psychological processes that impact on board decision-making. Westphal and colleagues have contributed to this stream of work by revealing social control processes which can render boards as passive and reduce board control over management. Westphal and Khanna (2003) identify a phenomenon called "social distancing," a form of sanction that applies to directors as members of a corporate elite. The sanction results from involvement in the exercise of control over management and negatively affects both future opportunities and their willingness to engage in board governance. Another social and psychological phenomenon is "pluralistic ignorance," a characteristic of board dynamics and decision-making, whereby members fail to express concerns and opinions (Westphal and Bednar, 2005). By contrast with "group-think," a group decision-making failure rooted in highly cohesive groups (Janis, 1983), pluralistic ignorance rests in a misperception by directors about the extent to which others share their views and concerns. The perception prevents directors voicing concerns about strategic matters for fear of marginalization. Pluralistic ignorance is put forward as an alternative explanation to a lack of director independence for the frequent failure of boards to exert influence over corporate strategy under conditions of poor firm performance. Westphal and Bednar (2005) also suggest that pluralistic ignorance may shed light on recent corporate scandals by explaining why directors who suspected wrongdoing failed to speak out. An implication of this phenomenon for board effectiveness is that more emphasis needs to be placed on measures that improve the process of board decision-making by enabling directors to share concerns and voice dissenting opinions. A third social process with implications for board control and access to board positions is that of ingratiation. Westphal and Stern (2006) identify that ingratiation may smooth the pathway to board positions, albeit with implications for embedding board deference to management and the diminution of board control.

Another stream of work about social and psychological processes flows from a model of boards as strategic decision-making groups (Forbes and Milliken, 1999). Underlying the model is a view that boards are relatively large, elite workgroups of seasoned, high-level executives who meet episodically through an informal, egalitarian leadership structure, have little interaction with each other, and minimal involvement with the organization for which they have considerable legal, ethical, and fiduciary responsibilities. By way of outcomes, boards are expected to make significant, interdependent strategic decisions by consensus, taking into account the collective wisdom, skills, and experience of the entire group. However, the effectiveness of boards as strategic decision-making entities is vulnerable to "process losses" which can impact on board task performance. While most of the governance literature takes the (financial) performance of the firm to be the key dependent variable when considering the functioning of the board, Forbes and Milliken suggest measuring board task performance directly, namely over those tasks related to a board's control and service functions. All in all, Forbes and Milliken define an effective board as one that can perform distinctive service and control activities successfully (task effectiveness) and yet continue working together (cohesiveness). Furthermore, they propose that effective boards will be characterized by high levels of interpersonal attraction (cohesiveness) and task-oriented disagreement (cognitive conflict). Under the variable "board processes," three particular constructs are identified as important to board task performance: "effort norms," "cognitive conflict," and the "use of knowledge and skills." Effort norms refers to the extent to which directors are prepared, participate in the board's work, and the level of attention given to board tasks. Cognitive conflict refers to the level of "issue-related" disagreement amongst group members. The presence of, and use of directors' knowledge and skills refers to the way in which relevant expertise is coordinated and ultimately used by the board.

The work of Forbes and Milliken is proving to be an important contribution to the literature as evidenced by subsequent empirical studies that utilize and build on the model to reveal significant relationships between board process, board performance, and firm effects. A study of publicly listed companies in Singapore by Wan and Ong (2005) reports a significant relationship between board process and board performance, with effort norms, cognitive conflict, and knowledge and skills all positively related to board roles. A study of 300 large manufacturing firms in Italy by Zona and Zattoni (2007) concludes that process variables, and to a lesser extent, demographic variables significantly influence board task performance. In particular, efforts norms and use of knowledge and skills are positively associated with the board monitoring and service roles. Van Ees et al.'s (2008) study of the chairs and chief executives of Dutch firms concurs that the use of knowledge and skills is related to board performance. Minichilli et al. (2009) also identify board members' commitment as more important than board demographics for predicting board task performance. Commitment is defined as the time and preparation devoted by directors before meetings and involvement in board discussion with critical questions and observations. By comparing Italian data with data from Norwegian companies, Minichilli et al. (2010) show that effort norms have a positive effect on both control and advisory task performance. With reference to previous qualitative studies, they suggest that these findings resonate with arguments about the benefits of engaged, empowered boards that avoiding minimalistic behavior such as "rubber-stamping" of executive proposals (Mace, 1971; Lorsch and MacIver, 1989; McNulty and Pettigrew, 1999; Stiles, 2001). They also suggest that effort and the use of knowledge and skills counteract habits of "pluralistic ignorance" (Westphal and Bednar, 2005). Most recently, McNulty et al. (forthcoming) found financial risk-taking to be lower where non-executive directors had high effort norms (as evidenced by the conduct of board meetings, preparation for board meetings, and the frequency of dialogue between executives and non-executives) and where board decision processes were characterized by cognitive conflict.

In addition to the work of Westphal and colleagues, and studies that draw on Forbes and Milliken (1999), some other studies also reveal a relationship between board process and performance. Using transcripts of board meetings, Tuggle, Sirmon, et al. (2010) examine the time given by boards to monitoring. The study finds that selective attention limits boards' information-processing and calculation capabilities, hence impacting on monitoring behavior. Such "selective attention allocation" by boards and directors results from contextual and structural factors, with "prior performance" and "duality" being especially relevant to explanations of the monitoring behavior of boards. These researchers conclude that monitoring is about "engagement" of board members, but that such engagement may be lessened in times of positive performance and heightened in times of negative performance. These findings shed light on why boards may have their attention diverted, fail to employ due scrutiny, and be surprised by crises and negative performance. They also suggest a link between board structure and process by concluding that CEO duality reduces attention to monitoring. By way of a contrasting focus, another study by Tuggle, Schnatterly, et al. (2010) examines boards' attention to enterprise. It also uses the approach of analyzing board minutes, focusing on the time spent in board meetings discussing new product or market issues. However, in probing the "black box" relationship between board diversity and performance, the study draws on upper echelons theory to analyze how heterogeneous and homogeneous characteristics of directors affect how boards work together and the attention that is given to entrepreneurial opportunities. Also using "fault-line theory" to identify dividing lines that may split a group into subgroups, the proposition is that boards with weak fault-lines will allow more discussion than boards with strong fault-lines. The study concludes that the amount of time a board spends discussing entrepreneurial issues is positively and significantly correlated with heterogeneity, weak fault-lines, and board informality, amongst other factors.

Finally, using survey and archival data from a sample of Fortune 1000 companies, Payne et al. (2009) modeled board effectiveness by identifying attributes of high-performing groups. The attributes are: knowledge, information, power, incentives, and sufficient opportunity and time to prepare for and complete tasks. Four of the five variables: knowledge, information, power, opportunity/time were found to be significantly related to board effectiveness and, in turn, effective boards were seen to contribute to the positive financial performance of their respective organizations. The overall conclusion is that board effectiveness is a significant predictor of company financial performance.

By way of reflecting on the studies described above, they all share an interest in the social and psychological dynamics of boards as decision-making groups. Whilst empirical findings are by no means entirely consistent there is enough to encourage further research into a set of process constructs that relate to board effectiveness. Findings about effort norms, commitment, selective attention, critical debate and knowledge, pluralistic ignorance, and social distancing all reveal possibilities and limitations to human rationality that may impact on the work and effects of boards and directors. Notions of pluralistic ignorance and selective attention explain why boards can be passive, inactive, ineffectual entities. On the other hand, findings about board effort norms, cognitive conflict, and knowledge shed light on why some boards can develop as powerful active groups capable of exercising control and other important effects. Furthermore, these internal processes may result from social processes and contextual circumstances outside of the board and host company.

Conclusion

The last three decades have witnessed corporate events that have brought corporate governance into the full glare of public scrutiny and attention. From the corruption and failure of Maxwell Communications in the UK in the 1980s to the Asian economic crisis of the 1990s, and Enron debacle early in this millennium, few parts of the globe have been immune from corporate governance failure. The worldwide diffusion of codes of governance (Aguilera and Cuervo-Cazurra, 2009) has signified boards being subject to both blame and reform. Codes are directed at reforming the composition and structure of boards through promoting a balance of executive and independent, non-executive directors, a clear division of responsibilities between the chairman and the chief executive officer, and procedures for the appointment of new directors, financial reporting, and internal control (Zattoni and Cuomo, 2008; Aguilera and Cuervo-Cazurra, 2009). However, problems remain in spite of codes and the financial crisis, the latest development in the recurrent crisis of corporate governance (MacAvoy and Millstein, 2003), has renewed attention to the efficacy of corporate governance mechanisms, in particular boards of directors.

Within academic research on boards progress has been made in shedding light on the ongoing problems of boards and potential solutions. Board research has now taught us to be skeptical about the direct effects of board of board structure and composition on board and company performance (Hermalin and Weisbach, 2003; Dalton and Dalton, 2011). Especially now that law and governance codes have such influence over matters of board composition and structures, it is ever more important to get beyond appearances to the substance of board effectiveness. One of the frustrations about recent events involving companies is that boards with apparently perfect governance arrangements and credentials were implicated in major cases of governance failure. Clearly, appearances as represented by matters of board form and structure can triumph over substance (Roberts et al., 2005; Westphal and Graebner, 2010).

In seeking to identify the substance of board effectiveness, this chapter has revealed literature that provides better understanding of board behavior and effectiveness. Though displaying distinct strands and styles of research the literature reveals some convergence of interest in respect of access boards and directors and a focus on board practice and behavior. There is much that is positive in the present attempts to model and research board processes in the context of decision-making models: not least, growing evidence that it is board process rather than board structure or composition that best predict board performance and effects. In this respect, these models and related empirical studies are now testing relationships and lending credence to earlier qualitative accounts that have described how certain behavior and relationships serve to create influence, promote accountability, and enhance board effectiveness. For instance, contrary to agency theory assumptions, there is growing theoretical and empirical support that boards are well served by a behavioral dynamic that involves open and trusting relationships between executives and non-executives rooted in perceptions of the relevance and value of each other's respective contributions. This dynamic encourages executives into a greater openness and trust that in turn builds non-executive knowledge and confidence. By contrast, a negative dynamic is possible in which executives come to resent or be frustrated by non-executive contributions that they perceive to be either ill-informed or inappropriate. This in turn can contribute to a downward spiral of deteriorating board relationships characterized by withholding of information and mistrust (Roberts et al., 2005).

To view the development of the field of research in a positive light is not to overlook further research that is needed in respect of board behavior and process. Whilst we find positive relationships between board process and performance, there is some inconsistency about which processes matter most to task performance. Also, the theorized distinction between service, control, and strategy should be further scrutinized. Are these roles so distinct in practice, or are they so inextricably related as to suggest that by being active in one task you will be active in another? Finally, the more one attends to boards as decision-making entities reliant on their internal processes, the more one needs to consider processes of board leadership. Qualitative studies such as those discussed above suggest that board leadership by chairs is critical to board effectiveness (Pettigrew and McNulty, 1995; Roberts and Stiles, 1999). However it is timely to further address this important issue (Roberts, 2002; Gabrielsson et al., 2007; Machold et al., 2011; McNulty et al., 2011). Board leadership has been largely studied through attention to one element of board composition, namely when the chief executive officer (CEO) also chairs the board of directors, or as it is commonly termed, CEO duality (Boyd et al., 2011). This focus should be extended to address the specific function of board chairs, especially given that contemporary developments in corporate governance reform are directed at board design, which increasingly includes a separation of the roles of chair and CEO. The body of research that seeks to link features of composition to effects suggests that structural independence, as pursued by a separation of the role of chair and chief executive, may not be reliable as a single proxy for understanding how boards actually function in terms of behavioral processes and effects. Rather, it is necessary to probe more deeply the behavior and effects associated with the structure and influence of board leadership. The question of whether the position of board chair actually translates into substantive influence over the conduct of the board, key decision processes, and board effectiveness is of growing theoretical and empirical significance.

References

AHRENS, T., FILATOCHEV, I., and THOMSEN, S. (2010). "The Research Frontier in Corporate Governance," *Journal of Management and Governance*, 14: 1–31.

AGUILERA, R. V., and CUERVO-CAZURRA, A. (2009). "Codes of Good Governance," *Corporate Governance: An International Review*, 17(3): 376–87.

BOYD, B., HAYNES, T. K., and ZONA, F. (2011). "Dimensions of CEO-Board Relations," *Journal of Management Studies*, 48(8): 1892–923.

DAILY, C. M., DALTON, D. R., and CANNELLA JR., A. A. (2003). "Corporate Governance: Decades of Dialogue and Data," *Academy of Management Review*, 28: 371–82.

DALTON, D. R., and DALTON, C. M. (2011). "Integration of Micro and Macro Studies in Governance Research: CEO Duality, Board Composition and Financial Performance," *Journal of Management*, 37(2): 404–11.

—— DAILY, C. M., JOHNSON, J. L., and ELLSTRAND, A. E. (1999). "Number of Directors and Financial Performance: A Meta-Analysis," *Academy of Management Journal*, 42: 674–86.

DEMB, A., and NEUBAUER. F. F. (1992). *The Corporate Board*. New York: Oxford University Press.

DEUTSCH, Y. (2005). "The Impact of Board Composition on Firm's Critical Decisions: A Meta-Analytical Review," *Journal of Management*, 31(3): 424–44.

DURISIN, B., and PUZONE, F. (2009). "Maturation of Corporate Governance Research, 1993–2007: An Assessment," *Corporate Governance: An International Review*, 17(3): 2666–291.

FINKELSTEIN, S., and MOONEY, A. C. (2003). "Not the Usual Suspects: How to Use Board Process to Make Boards Better," *Academy of Management Executive*, 17(2): 101–13.

—— HAMBRICK, D. C., and CANNELLA JR., A. A. (2009). *Strategic Leadership: Theory and Research on Executives, Top Management Teams, and Boards*. New York: Oxford University Press.

FORBES, D. P., and MILLIKEN, F. J. (1999). "Cognition and Corporate Governance: Understanding Boards of Directors as Strategic Decision-Making Groups," *Academy of Management Review*, 24(3): 489–505.

GABRIELSSON, J., HUSE, M., and MINICHILLI, A. (2007). "Understanding the Leadership Role of the Board Chairperson through a Team Production Approach," *International Journal of Leadership Studies*, 3(1): 21–39.

GOLDEN, B. R., and ZAJAC, E. (2001): "When Will Boards Influence Strategy? Inclination X Power = Strategic Change," *Strategic Management Journal*, 22(12): 1087–111.

HAMBRICK, D. C., WERDER, A.V., and ZAJAC, E. J. (2008). "New Directions in Corporate Governance Research," *Organization Science*, 19: 381–5.

HERMALIN, B. E., and WEISBACH, M. S. (2003). "Boards of Directors as an Endogenously Determined Institution: A Survey of the Economic Literature," *Economic Policy Review—Federal Reserve Bank of New York*, 9(1): 7–26.

HILL, S. (1995). "The Social Organisation of Boards of Directors," *British Journal of Sociology*, 46: 245–78.

HILLMAN, A. J., and DALZIEL, T. (2003). "Boards of Directors and Firm Performance: Integrating Agency and Resource Dependence Perspectives," *Academy of Management Review*, 28(3): 383–96.

—— NICHOLSON, G., and SHROPSHIRE, C. (2008). "Directors' Multiple Identities, Identification and Board Monitoring and Resource Provision," *Organization Science*, 19(3): 441–56.

JANIS, I. (1983). *Groupthink: Psychological Studies of Policy Decisions and Fiascos*, 2nd ed. Boston: Houghton Mifflin.

JOHNSON, J. L., DAILY, C. M., and ELLSTRAND, A. E. (1996). "Boards of Directors: A Review and Research Agenda," *Journal of Management*, 22: 409–38.

KULA, V. (2005). "The Impact of the Roles, Structures and Process of Boards on Firm Performance: Evidence from Turkey," *Corporate Governance: An International Review*, 13(2): 265–76.

LORSCH, J. W., and MACIVER, E. (1989). *Pawns or Potentates: The Reality of America's Corporate Boards*. Boston: Harvard Business School Press.

MACAVOY, P. W., and MILLSTEIN, I. M. (2003). *The Recurrent Crisis in Corporate Governance*. New York: Palgrave.

MACE, M. L. (1971). *Directors: Myth and Reality*. Boston: Harvard University Press.

MACHOLD, S., HUSE, M., MINICHILLI, A., and NORDQVIST, M. (2011). "Board Leadership and Strategy Involvement in Small Firms: A Team Production Approach," *Corporate Governance: An International Review*, 19(4): 368–83.

MCNULTY, T., and PETTIGREW, A. (1999). "Strategists on the Board," *Organization Studies*, 20: 47–74.

—— PETTIGREW, A., JOBOME, G., and MORRIS, C. (2011). "The Role, Power and Influence of Company Chairs," *Journal of Management and Governance*, 15: 91–121.

—— FLORACKIS, C., and ORMROD, P. (forthcoming). "Boards of Directors and Financial Risk During the Credit Crisis," *Corporate Governance: An International Review*.

MINCHILLI, A., ZATTONI, A and ZONA, F. (2009). "Making Boards Effective: An Empirical Examination of Board Task Performance," *British Journal of Management*, 20(1): 55–74.

—— —— NIELSEN, S., and HUSE, M. (2010). "Board Task Performance: An Exploration of Macro and Micro Level Determinants of Board Effectiveness," *Journal of Organizational Behaviour*. Available at <http://wileyonlinelibrary.com>. DOI: 10.1002/job.743.

NICHOLSON, G. J., and KIEL, G. C. (2007). "Can Directors Impact Performance? A Case Based Test of Three Theories of Corporate Governance," *Corporate Governance: An International Review*, 15(4): 585–607.

PARKER, D. L. (2007). "Internal Governance in the Non-profit Boardroom: A Participant Observer Study," *Corporate Governance: An International Review*, 15(5): 923–34.

PAYNE, G. T., BENSON, G. S., and FINEGOLD, D. (2009). "Corporate Board Attributes, Team Effectiveness and Financial Performance," *Journal of Management Studies*, 46(4): 704–31.

PEARCE, J. A., and ZAHRA, S. A. (1991). "The Relative Power of CEOs and Boards of Directors: Associations with Corporate Performance," *Strategic Management Journal*, 12(2): 135–53.

PETTIGREW, A. M. (1992). "On Studying Managerial Elites," *Strategic Management Journal*, 13: 163–82.

—— and McNulty, T. (1995). "Power and Influence in and around the Boardroom," *Human Relations*, 48: 845–73.
—— —— (1998). "Sources and Uses of Power in and around the Boardroom," *European Journal of Work and Organizational Psychology*, 7(2):197–214.
Pugliese, A., Bezemer, P.-J., Zattoni, A., Huse, M., Van den Bosch, F., and Volberda, H. (2009). "Boards of Directors' Contribution to Strategy: A Literature Review and Research Agenda," *Corporate Governance: An International Review*, 17(3): 292–306.
Pye, A. (2002). "The Changing Power of 'Explanations': Directors, Academics and Their Sensemaking from 1989 to 2000," Journal of Management Studies, 39(7): 907–25.
—— and Pettigrew, P. (2005). "Studying Board Context, Processes and Dynamics," *British Journal of Management*, 16(s1): S27–38.
Roberts, J. (2001). "Trust and Control in Anglo-American Systems of Corporate Governance: The Individualising and Socialising Effects of Processes of Accountability," *Human Relations*, 54(12): 1547–72.
—— (2002). "Building the Complementary Board: The Work of the Plc Chairman." *Long Range Planning*, 35: 493–520.
—— and Stiles, P. (1999). "The Relationship between Chairmen and Chief Executives: Competitive or Complementary Roles?" *Long Range Planning*, 32(1): 36–48.
—— McNulty, T., and Stiles, P. (2005). "Beyond Agency Conceptions of the Work of the Non-Executive Director: Creating Accountability in the Boardroom," *British Journal of Management*, 16: S1–S22.
Ryan, L. V., Buchholtz, A. K., and Kolb, R. W. (2010). "New Directions in Corporate Governance and Finance: Implications for Business Ethics Research," *Business Ethics Quarterly*, 20(4): 673–94.
Stiles, P. (2001). "The Impact of Boards on Strategy: An Empirical Examination," *Journal of Management Studies*, 38(5): 27–50.
Sundaramurthy, C., and Lewis, M. (2003). "Control and Collaboration: Paradoxes of Governance," *Academy of Management Review*, 28(3): 397–415.
Tuggle, C. S., Schnatterly, K., and Johnson, R. A. (2010). "Attention Patterns in the Boardroom: How Board Composition and Processes Affect Discussion of Entrepreneurial Issues," *Academy of Management Journal*, 53(3): 550–71.
—— Sirmon, D. G, Reutzel, C. R., and Bierman, L. (2010). "Commanding Board of Director Attention: Investigating How Organizational Performance and CEO Duality Affect Board Members Attention to Monitoring," *Strategic Management Journal*, 31(9): 946–68.
Van den Heuval, J., Van Gils, A., and Voordeckers, W. (2006). "Board Roles in Small and Medium Sized Family Businesses: Performance and Importance," *Corporate Governance: An International Review*, 14(5): 467–85.
Van de Ven, A. H. (1992). "Suggestions for Studying Strategy Process: A Research Note," *Strategic Management Journal*, 13(summer): 169–91.
Van Ees, H., Van der Laan, G., and Postma, T. J. B. M. (2008). "Effective Board Behaviour in the Netherlands," *European Management Journal*, 26: 84–93.
Westphal, J. D. (1999). "Collaboration in the Boardroom: Behavioural and Performance Consequences of CEO-Board Social Ties," *Academy of Management Journal*, 42: 7–24.
—— and Bednar, M. K. (2005). "Pluralistic Ignorance in Corporate Boards and Firms' Strategic Persistence in Response to Low Firm Performance," *Administrative Science Quarterly*, 50: 262–98.

WESTPHAL, J. D. and GRAEBNER, M. E. (2010). "A Matter of Appearances: How Corporate Leaders Manage the Impressions of Financial Analysts about the Conduct of their Boards," *Academy of Management Journal*, 53(1): 15–43.

——— and KHANNA, P. (2003). "Keeping Directors in Line: Social Distancing as a Control Mechanism in the Social Elite," *Administrative Science Quarterly*, 48: 361–98.

——— and STERN I. (2006). "The Other Pathway to the Boardroom: Interpersonal influence Behaviour as a Substitute for Elite Credentials and Majority Status in Obtaining Board Appointments," *Administrative Science Quarterly*, 51: 169–204.

WAN, D., and ONG, C. H. (2005). "Board Structure, Process and Performance: Evidence from Public Listed Companies in Singapore," *Corporate Governance: An International Review*, 13(2): 277–90.

ZAHRA, S. A., and PEARCE, J. A. (1989). "Boards of Directors and Corporate Financial Performance: A Review and Integrative Model," *Journal of Management*, 15(2): 291–334.

ZATTONI, A., and CUOMO, F. (2008). "Why Adopt Codes of Good Governance: A Comparison of Institutional and Efficiency Perspectives," *Corporate Governance: An International Review*, 16(1): 1–15.

ZONA, F., and ZATTONI, A. (2007). "Beyond the Black Box of Demography: Board Processes and Task Effectiveness in Italian Firms," *Corporate Governance: An International Review*, 15(5): 852–64.

CHAPTER 8

BOARD COMMITTEES[1]

PHILIP STILES

How a company chooses its directors, rewards them, and also holds them to account in terms of the financial probity of the organization are three of the most contentious issues in corporate governance. Yet the governance mechanisms designed to provide oversight and reassurance on these matters—the nomination, remuneration, and audit committees—have received comparatively little research attention. Since many significant board decisions are made not within the whole board setting, but within the context of specific committees (Harrison, 1987; Bilimoria and Piderit, 1994; Securities and Exchange Commission, 2003; Bédard and Gendron, 2010), there is a strong mandate for focusing on board committees and analyzing how they work and to what extent they are effective (Kesner, 1988; Carson, 2003).

The role of board committees in enhancing corporate governance lies primarily in their potential for independent monitoring role. Board committees are part of a series of structural mechanisms which emerged, chiefly through the formalization of codes, which highlighted the importance of subcommittees in bringing greater specialization and objectivity by members, as well as greater attention to discrete issues (Cadbury, 1992; Turnbull, 1999; Smith, 2003).

Explicit in this approach is the theoretical underpinning of the firm as a nexus of contracts (e.g. Jensen and Meckling, 1976; Fama and Jensen, 1983). This approach has placed the principal–agency problem at the heart of corporate governance research. The role of board committees in reducing agency costs through enhancing the monitoring of executives has been the primary rationale for their role (Cotter and Silvester, 2003).

Despite their potential as oversight mechanisms, boards and board committees have come under critical scrutiny (Agrawal and Chadha. 2005; Carcello, Hermanson, et al., 2011). The incidence of high profile corporate fraud and failure, involving failures of internal and external controls, continuing concerns about excessive executive remuneration, and allegations of cronyism in terms of director selection have called into question the adequacy of board committees (Vicknair et al., 1993; DeZoort et al., 2002). This has led to the belief on the part of many scholars that the adoption of board committees may be primarily symbolic and that the benefits associated with them are more rhetorical than substantive (Kalbers and Fogarty, 1998; Beasley et al., 2009: Bédard and Gendron, 2010).

Such variation has emerged as a central concern of institutional theory (e.g. Scott, 1987; Lawrence and Suddaby, 2006; Lounsbury, 2007). Institutional theory views some governance activities and structures as driven by the need to produce legitimacy. Through regulation and best-practice prescriptions, organizations conform to certain norms and these become signs of legitimacy and accountability. However, this may entail that the activities and structures are primarily ceremonial or ritualistic. Practices may become decoupled from or "loosely coupled" to organizational goals (Fiss, 2008) with the effect that a structure is only minimally tied to the technical work it is tasked to achieve (Meyer and Rowan, 1977).

With regard to work on board committees, Spira's (1999) study with participants in audit committees concludes that the ceremonial function is important primarily through validating organizational legitimacy, which in turn enables access to valued resources. Similarly, other studies that provide self-report data on board committee activity claim that directors continually balance monitoring with promoting legitimacy (e.g. Beasley et al., 2009). For example, Main et al.'s (2008) qualitative work on committee process argues explicitly for a legitimacy aim for remuneration committees.

This tension between independent monitoring and symbolic functions of board committees is reflected in calls for greater understanding of the relational dynamics in and around the committee (e.g. Turley and Zaman, 2004; Main et al., 2008). This chapter responds to such calls, and seeks to address not just general governance characteristics of board committees such as independence and expertise, but also governance processes—what board committees actually do and how they do it (e.g. Schneider et al., 2009; Bédard and Gendron, 2010). We examine the three major board committees, audit, remuneration, and nomination, and explore the issues involved with board committee membership, process, and outcomes. We argue that paying attention to the institutional and the relational aspects of the works of the board committee provides a richer picture of board committee work and the expectations companies may have of them.

The chapter is organized as follows. First, we take each of the major board committees and examine the research in terms of their composition, effectiveness, and process. We then argue for a widening of theoretical scope for work on board committees and, in conclusion, we set out academic and practical implications.

BOARD COMMITTEE COMMONALITIES: INDEPENDENCE AND EXPERTISE

In public corporations, the standard practice is that, in addition to meeting as a full board, directors are assigned to board committees that monitor different aspects of the corporation's business and finance matters. A certain number of board committees are required by law or regulation (e.g. by stock exchange rule) and, in this chapter, we focus on these solely: audit, remuneration, and nomination. Corporate law empowers boards to delegate certain matters to these committees, and the assignment of particular board members to committees is a matter to be decided by the entire board (Fanto, 2005). Best-practices guidelines provide that membership on a particular committee should depend upon both the independence and the expertise of a director.

Regarding independence, a common feature of stock exchange or regulatory prescription is that board committees should be composed solely or primarily of independent directors. Though definitions of independence vary according to code and jurisdiction, a common element is that for a director to be considered independent, he or she should have no "material relationship" with the organization. This definition is intended to be broadly construed. For example, according to the Higgs report (2003), "material relationship" could "include commercial, industrial, banking, consulting, legal, accounting, charitable and familial relationships (among others)." A controversial area in defining independence concerns the ownership of stock. On an agency theory account, share ownership on the part of audit committee members would increase the incentive to monitor management and their financial reporting (see e.g. Klein, 2002; Carcello and Neal, 2003; Abbott et al., 2004; Bédard et al., 2004; Lee et al., 2004).

However, an alternative argument is that board members who hold a significant share stake might seek to exert more influence on management and may even collude with them to protect their investments, at the expense of other shareholders' interests. For example, Mangena and Pike's (2005) study of UK listed companies found a significant negative association between shareholding of audit committee members and interim disclosure.

Carcello and Neal (2003) show that firms in which audit committee members' share ownership was high were more likely to dismiss an external auditor after issuing a going concern report. Their explanation is that the impact of such a report on their share stake would make it more likely they would disagree with the external auditor.

A significant further issue concerning independence is whether the requirements of independence may be too restrictive in terms of director selection, and whether this has led to the shrinking of the available talent pool for non-executive directors (Bronson et al., 2009).

Regarding expertise, the rise of board committees has emphasized the idea of the professionalization and specialization of directors (Fanto, 2005). On audit committees, for example, a number of codes now mandate that at least one member of the committee should have significant financial expertise (US House of Representatives, 2002: s. 407; Higgs, 2003; Smith, 2003). This expertise may be demonstrated by previous or current employment in finance or accounting and/or membership of a professional financial or accounting body (see, for example, Smith, 2003: para. 3.16). In remuneration committees, the increasing complexity of executive compensation also places high demands on the independent director. In most cases, the remuneration committee relies on advisors and consultants, both external and internal (Conyon et al., 2009), but the professionalism of the remuneration committee lies in its ability to consider the views of consultants and of the executives, while coming to its own opinion. Similarly with the nominations committee; the chief activity of members is the identification and screening of persons thought appropriate to come to the board. Here too there are professionals who assist the committee in this task, notably search firms, but again the committee members' task is to take sufficient expertise whilst retaining the capability to make a sound independent judgment on nominations matters.

With large diverse organizations, the complexity of some financial transactions in terms of their accounting, actuarial, legal, insurance, risk management, and other aspects presents significant demands on the expertise of board committees, particularly those dealing with audit and remuneration. Discerning the implications of certain decisions or approvals within these committees for the organization may be very difficult. Board committee members, and reward and audit professionals, like all individuals, operate under conditions of bounded rationality and so errors which arise from committee decisions may be the result of lack of competence rather than being due to opportunistic self-seeking behavior suggested by classic agency theory (Hendry, 2002).

The notions of independence and expertise for board committee members are usually linked to discussions about the *critical mass* of directors. For board committees, a number of reports suggest that a minimum level of membership for corporations is three independent directors (Cadbury, 1992; BRC, 1999; Smith, 2003). The increasing complexity of board matters in the committee domain is producing pressure on director resources, particularly on expertise and time. This may entail that larger committees may be more effective, given that they will have more directors dedicated to the issues and who can distribute the load and the time more effectively. Bédard et al. (2004) argue that a larger audit committee is more likely to uncover and resolve potential problems in the financial reporting process due to increased strength and diversity of expertise to provide more effective oversight. However, Bédard et al. (2004) report no significant relationship between audit committee size and earnings management; similarly with Abbott et al. (2004).

In addition to how many independent directors comprise each board committee is the issue of who else is allowed to be present at committee deliberations. For audit committees "no one other than the audit committee's chairman and members is entitled to be present at a meeting of the audit committee" (Smith, 2003: para. 3.6), but the audit committee can decide if non-members should attend for particular purposes. For example "It is to be expected that the external audit lead partner will be invited regularly to attend meetings as well as the finance director" (Smith, 2003: para. 3.6).

Gendron et al. (2004) found that, in addition to audit committee members, others in attendance at the audit committee meeting were the internal and external auditors, the CEO, CFO, and corporate secretary. Such attendance will place a premium on the independence and expertise of the independent audit committee members.

For the remuneration committee and nominations committee, there is a similar formulation in terms of membership—only members of the committee have the right to attend committee meetings, but others, such as the CEO, the director of human resources, and external advisors may be invited to attend (ICSA, 2008). Main et al. (2008) found that, in a UK listed company sample, most remuneration committees were attended by the chairman and the CEO, except at times when their own remuneration was under discussion: "it is generally accepted that to set appropriate incentives it is necessary to have a sense for what will work, and in this respect the view of the CEO was essential in determining whether a particular design was one which promoted the desired behaviour by the executives" (Main et al., 2008: 229). Pivotal in this process is the role of the remuneration committee chair, who establishes key relationships with relevant stakeholders and ensures challenge and negotiation with advisors and executives.

Although much of the research on board committees focuses on the aspects of independence and expertise, there is also a small but growing literature on *processes* within board committees. A number of scholars have called for more fine-grained work on how board committees actually operate (e.g. Spira, 2002; Turley and Zaman, 2004; Main et al., 2008; Beasley et al., 2009: Bédard and Gendron, 2010). The small but growing literature in this area has added considerably to our knowledge of the workings of the board committee and, taken together with research on structural aspects of committees, a picture emerges of board committee activity that supports a number of theoretical approaches—chiefly, agency, institutional theory, and resource dependence—but also points to several large gaps in our knowledge of board committee work. In the next section, we examine the work of the audit committee, focusing first on its roles and second on process. Following this, the remuneration committee and nomination committee will be explored.

Audit Committees

The primary role of audit committees is to ensure the integrity of financial reporting and the audit process. The audit committee has responsibility for ensuring the company has sound internal financial control systems and systems for the control of non-financial risks (Turnbull, 1999). This includes ensuring the external auditor is independent and objective. The audit committee should comprise members who are knowledgeable about the business environment, and of whom one has accounting or financial management expertise (BRC, 1999; Smith, 2003). Without such knowledge, the oversight role of the committee will be reduced in credibility in the judgment of management and auditors (Knapp, 1987). The audit committee in large companies should meet no fewer than three times a year (FRC, 2008), with some meeting considerably more often—between six and ten times per year (KPMG, 2006). In research on audit committees, there is a variable picture in terms of the effectiveness in each role. In the next section we shall review this literature. We shall then go on to discuss the small but important literature on audit committee process.

OVERSIGHT OF FINANCIAL REPORTING QUALITY

A number of studies examine the quality of financial reporting, primarily in terms of the incidence of negative outcomes, notably fraud and such irregularities as earnings misstatements and abnormal accruals.

Two attributes of audit committees outlined earlier—those of independence and financial expertise—are chiefly used to assess effects on financial reporting quality. The general finding is that audit committees play an important role in improving the quality of financial reporting (Krishnamoorthy et al., 2003; Chen et al., 2007). In research on US corporations, for example, SEC allegations of fraudulent financial reporting (found in Accounting and Auditing Enforcement Releases) are negatively related to board committee and audit committee independence (Beasley et al., 2000, 2010). In particular, companies with financial reporting problems are less likely to have audit committees composed solely of outside directors (McMullen and Raghunandan, 1996).

A common measure of poor financial reporting is earnings misstatements. In this stream of research, companies with audit committees are found to be less likely to produce such reports than companies without audit committees. Audit committee independence and financial expertise are negatively related to restatements (DeFond and Jiamhalvo, 1991; Dechow et al., 1996; Abbott et al., 2004; Agrawal and Chadha 2005). Cohen et al. (2010) found that restatements are negatively related to audit committee industry expertise. Abbott et al. (2004) indicate a negative relationship between financial expertise and financial statements fraud.

However, where the independence of the audit committee member is compromised, for example, by the CEO being involved in the director selection process, the strength of an audit committee is significantly reduced (Carcello, Neal, et al., 2011).

A second area of study is the effect of audit committees on earnings management, which is the practice of manipulating the financial performance of the firm to misrepresent the results to stakeholders. Here, too, audit committee independence is significantly associated with a lower likelihood of earnings management (Davidson et al., 2005). Financial expertise on the audit committee is also positively related to the prevention of earnings management (Klein, 2002; Xie et al., 2003; Naiker and Sharma, 2009). For example, Dhaliwal et al. (2010) find that accruals quality is positively related to accounting expertise on the audit committee, especially when accounting expertise and finance expertise are both present. Firms that change their boards and/or audit committees from majority independent to minority independent have significantly larger increases in abnormal accruals relative to their counterparts (Klein, 2002).

Investor perceptions regarding audit committees show that stock price reactions are positively related to the appointment of audit committee members with financial expertise (Davidson et al., 2004; DeFond et al., 2005).

Oversight of External Audit

The audit committee's role with respect to the external audit is to ensure that the external auditor is fully independent, and to discuss critical accounting policies and their treatment within the organization. The issue of independence is highlighted in a number of studies. For example, Lennox and Park (2007) find that more independent audit committees appear to promote auditor independence. The presence of audit committees has been found to create a perception of enhanced auditor independence among consumers of financial statements (Gwilliam and Kilcommins, 1998). The relationship with the external auditor can also be measured by the likelihood of external auditor resignation. A number of studies show a negative relationship between financial expertise and auditor dismissal or resignation in cases of auditor–management disagreements (DeZoort and Salterio, 2001; Carcello and Neal, 2003; Lee et al., 2004; Bronson et al., 2009).

In terms of the relationship between auditors and management, Beattie et al. (2000) found that audit committees reduced the confrontational intensity of interactions between auditors and management by increasing the level of discussion and reducing the level of negotiation. In disputes between the auditor and external management, the audit committees which are composed of independent directors tend to side with the auditor (Knapp, 1987; DeZoort and Salterio, 2001).

Internal Control

The audit committee reviews with internal auditors any identified problems revealed by their audit and their solutions or recommendations, and the department's budget and needs (Smith, 2003). The audit committee is also responsible for the supervision and hiring of senior internal audit personnel. The committee also reviews the relationship between internal and external audit processes.

The aims of the internal audit function are therefore strongly aligned with the oversight mandate of the audit committee (Scarbrough et al., 1998; Goodwin and Yeo, 2001; Goodwin, 2003). Greater independence of the audit committee from executive management promotes a more active role on the part of audit committees in internal audit (Turley and Zaman, 2004). In an examination of whether experience affects audit committee members' oversight judgments, it was found that audit committee members with financial experience made internal control judgments more like auditors than did members without experience (DeZoort, 1997, 1998). The influence of the audit committee on internal control activities was examined by Abbott et al. (2010), who found that the relative focus on the part of the internal audit team on internal control increased with audit committee oversight of internal audit.

Process

Though the major focus on audit committees has been through the examination of the independence and financial expertise of the members, a key element in the effectiveness of audit committees lies in the process of the committee. In the few process studies on audit committees, evidence for a largely ceremonial role is pronounced. Spira (1998, 1999, 2002), using participants' accounts of audit committee activity, suggests that audit committees provide a comforting display of concern for corporate governance standards, validate company legitimacy, and enable access to resources for survival and growth. Similarly, a study of auditors' experiences of audit committees revealed that audit committees were perceived by auditors to be ineffective in controlling the financial reporting process (Cohen et al., 2004). A follow-up study post-Sarbanes-Oxley (SOX) found an improved situation, with audit committees more active, diligent, knowledgeable, and powerful. But there was still strong evidence to show that management were responsible for auditor appointments and terminations, contra SOX prescriptions (Cohen et al., 2004).

Beasley et al. (2009) looked at a number of process areas within audit committees in post-SOX US firms and found practices which supported both substantive and ceremonial interpretations of audit committee activity. Gendron et al. (2004) conducted a field study in the audit committees of three Canadian public corporations and highlighted key matters that audit committee members emphasize during meetings, including the accuracy of financial statements; appropriateness of the wording used in financial reports; effectiveness of internal controls; and the quality of the work performed by auditors. A key aspect of the work carried out by audit committee members consisted of asking challenging questions and assessing responses provided by managers and auditors. In a subsequent study, Gendron and Bédard (2006) conducted a second round of interviews with audit committee chairs and found that, when considering the effectiveness of the audit committee, members attended to both substantive issues—independence and expertise of the members—and ceremonial features of audit committee meetings.

From the point of view of the auditor, some work points to the passivity of the audit committee. The study by Cohen et al. (2002) of 36 auditors showed that the interviewees characterized their meetings with audit committees as a one-way process, with the audit reporting major elements, rather than a dialogue occurring. In the same study, practicing auditors stated that their discussions with audit committees never affect the type of audit report issued. However, in a subsequent study (Cohen et al., 2007) of 38 auditors, perceptions of auditors regarding the audit committee showed increased diligence and expertise following SOX introduction.

The importance of informal processes relating to audit committees is highlighted by Turley and Zaman's (2007) study. Focusing on a UK company, and using interviews with the audit committee chair, external auditors, internal auditors, and senior management, the study found that informal networks between audit committee participants condition the impact of the audit committee and that the committee meeting was not the place to challenge issues—that activity was reserved for informal meetings.

In summary, the prior literature focusing on audit committee characteristics shows that audit committee effectiveness depends on independence and expertise. However, in the literature on audit committee process, there is strong evidence that both substantive and ceremonial functions are in play. For audit committee effectiveness therefore, the independence and expertise of members has to be augmented by an emphasis on relational issues, such as the voicing of challenging opinions and the demand for complete transparency.

Remuneration Committees

The role of the remuneration committee is to determine and agree with the board the framework for the remuneration of the chief executive, the chairman, and other members of the executive management where appropriate (Smith, 2003). Remuneration committees should meet at least twice per year, once close to the year end to review the directors' remuneration report, which, for quoted companies, is submitted to shareholders for approval at the AGM (ICSA, 2008). The appropriate design of reward structures for management is a central plank in the alignment of managerial and shareholder interests (Main and Johnston, 1993; Conyon and Leech, 1994; Conyon et al., 1995; Ezzamel and Watson, 1997).

Research on the effectiveness of remuneration committees however has been mixed. In an explicit test of agency theory, Conyon and He (2004), using data on 455 US firms that went public in 1999, found that the presence of significant shareholders on the compensation committee (defined as those with share stakes in excess of 5 percent) is associated with lower CEO pay and higher CEO equity incentives. Firms with higher paid compensation committee members are associated with greater CEO compensation and lower incentives. Their conclusion was that there was little evidence to support the idea of managerial capture of the compensation committee. According to Conyon (2006), "the balance of evidence suggests that the composition of the (compensation) committee does not lead to severe agency problems" (2006: 38). In this stream of work, the presence of affiliated (non-independent) directors does not lead to greater executive pay awards (Newman and Mozes, 1999; Vafeas, 2003). For example, Conyon and Peck (1998), using panel data on large, publicly traded UK companies gathered between 1991 and 1994, examined the role of board control and remuneration committees in determining management compensation. Board monitoring, measured in terms of the proportion of non-executive directors on a board and the presence of remuneration committees and CEO duality, had only a limited effect on the level of top management pay. Daily et al. (1998) examined the relationship between the composition of a firm's compensation committee and CEO compensation. They found no evidence that "captured" directors led to greater levels of, or changes in, CEO compensation.

However, in looking at the impact of executive compensation consultants on pay, using a cross-sectional design on UK and US firms, Conyon et al. (2009) found CEO pay is generally greater in firms that use compensation consultants, and a greater amount of equity, such as stock options, is associated with use of consultants. Given consultants' use of comparison data in their deliberations, this may suggest a "bidding up" process in remuneration.

A number of studies have argued for such a ratcheting effect with remuneration committees. For example, Ezzamel and Watson (1997) have suggested that "a 'cosy collusion' exists between executive and non-executive directors, who sit on each other's remuneration committees and thereby bid up executive earnings" (1997: 73). Similarly, Main and Johnston (1993) found evidence that management pay was significantly higher in companies that adopted remuneration committees. However, one problem with this strand of work lies in its cross-sectional nature, which leaves open the possibility of reverse causation for explanation (in other words, better companies tend to pay more and, at the time of the study, be likely to adopt remuneration committees (Conyon, 2006)). Taking a longitudinal design, Benito and Conyon (1999) showed that there was a negative relationship between remuneration committee adoption and the emoluments of the highest paid directors. However, in a panel study of CEO pay in water companies from 1992–2001, Ogden and Watson (2004) found that remuneration committees did not attempt to fully adjust CEO remuneration in line with higher pay levels of other benchmark private sector UK businesses, despite their companies performing well in terms of conventional financial performance criteria.

Process

A number of studies focusing on process have highlighted the conformity of remuneration committees to institutional pressures. Main et al. (2008) interviewed 22 members of UK remuneration committees and found that remuneration committee members felt constrained in their choice by the coercive effect of institutional norms, and "they commonly fail to allocate the time or resource to calibrate or confirm the effective operation of the chosen remuneration plan; and many of their actions are dominated by a perceived need to be able to justify any high pay outcomes in communications with shareholders and institutional investors" (2008: 230).

Similarly, Perkins and Hendry (2005) found non-executive members of remuneration committees perceiving themselves as being "outmaneuvered" by management on reward issues, through factors such as role ambiguities and power asymmetries between the major actors. Though this study found that a high degree of discretion was given to the remuneration committee; "what matters is how rewards appear, not whether performance is being objectively over-valued" (2005: 1464). This decoupling of remuneration activity from alignment of pay with the strategic aims of the firm to reflect rather the external perception of the reward process is supported by Spira and Bender (2004). This work affirmed the desire of remuneration committees to be able to demonstrate ex post that pay is in alignment with governance codes, rather than in terms of the alignment between pay and the strategic profile of the company.

This drive to demonstrate legitimacy gains further backing from the work of Ogden and Watson (2008), which, drawing on five UK privatized water companies, showed that the remuneration committees, concerned about potential stakeholder criticism, devoted considerable time and resources to ensure that their choice of long-term incentive plan comparators and performance metrics would be regarded as legitimate. Further, "the indeterminacy and incoherence of normative guidelines for implementing good governance in areas of executive remuneration made for difficult contexts for remuneration committees" (2008: 45).

In summary, there is a contrasting picture of remuneration committee effectiveness. The effects of the remuneration committee on CEO earnings show mixed results, using measures of the presence of the committee as well as its independence. In process studies, too, the pressures on remuneration committee members by management are considerable and concern to provide legitimate outcomes to investors may be at the expense of substantive contributions.

Nomination Committees

The role of the nomination committee is to lead the process for board appointments and make recommendations to the board (Smith, 2003). In particular the committee is responsible for identifying, and nominating for the approval of the board, candidates to fill board vacancies as and when they arise. This task requires that the committee establish a process whereby it identifies qualified individuals for board membership and decides upon the re-nomination of existing directors. Best-practice guidelines suggest nominations committees should meet at least twice a year, once close to the year end, in particular to consider whether directors retiring by rotation should be put forward for re-appointment at the annual general meeting (ICSA, 2009).

For many jurisdictions, this committee is a "best-practice" guideline, and, in companies where there is not a formal nominations committee, directors are expected to show that the nominations process has upheld strong independent principles. In some jurisdictions, the nomination committee is mandatory for public companies. For example, in the US, following a number of corporate scandals in which there was perceived to be too close a relationship between the board and management, the New York Stock Exchange (NYSE) proposed to make the nomination committee mandatory in 2003, which was sanctioned by the SEC. In addition, the committee would also have further governance duties which are:

> (1) conducting the board's annual governance review; (2) monitoring compliance with the NYSE's corporate governance guidelines; (3) establishing and implementing a process for the board's self-assessments (including board and committee self-assessments and director assessments); and (4) recommending director compensation. (SEC, 2003)

These duties would fall under the title of "governance committee" and would take up duties that had previously been handled by the full board or perhaps not fulfilled at all (Mahoney and Shuman, 2003). For the main part of the nomination committee role, the process is the identification and screening of persons eligible to be directors (Vafeas, 1999). Lee et al. (1992: 58) state that "although the board is legally authorized to ratify and monitor managerial decisions, critics have argued strongly that management generally dominates the board by its influence over the selection of outside directors, and by its control over the agenda of board meetings and the information provided to outside board members." The introduction of a nomination committee delegates the director selection process to an independent group which can make independent recommendations (Ruigrok et al., 2006). This is crucial, for if a board is to effectively provide oversight of the company's management, they cannot be handpicked by the management, since they may feel a loyalty to them which may inhibit voice or challenge of decisions or strategies (Westphal, 1999).

However, in practical terms, it is usually the CEO or other executives who are best able to identify candidates who might be suited to the company and to the board. The role of the nomination committee is therefore not to allow the recommendations of the CEO or executives to overly influence the director selection process. The dangers of not doing this are highlighted by Shivdasani and Yermack (1999) who report that when the CEO serves on the nominating committee or no nominating committee exists, firms appoint fewer independent outside directors and more grey outsiders with conflicts of interest. Stock price reactions to independent director appointments are significantly lower when the CEO is involved in director selection.

By contrast, the effect of nomination committees on new CEO dismissal has been examined. In a study of 204 newly appointed CEOs, if, at the time of succession, the firm's board has a nominating committee that is independent and/or on which outside directors have few external directorships, the likelihood of dismissal is lower (Zhang, 2008).

A major element for consideration at nomination committees is the selection of directors under the criterion of diversity. Diversity is argued to have strong benefits, through a broadened range of task-relevant resources (such as knowledge, skills, and perspectives) that are both cognitive and demographic (Williams and O'Reilly, 1998). This variety may enable a cross-fertilization of ideas and a synergistic combination of resources that may ultimately enhance performance. Nomination committees try to ensure that the composition of the board is optimal in terms of functional and professional capability. Increasingly, however, diversity is becoming of high importance for board members.

In a survey of the top 200 companies in the S&P 500 index, Spencer Stuart (2010) found that 16 percent of board members were women. In the Fortune 500, the figure was 15.7 percent. In the UK, 17.5 percent of independent directors in the FTSE are women, but only 5 percent of executive directors. The Davies Report in the UK proposes that, by 2015, 25 percent of board roles within listed companies should be held by women. Other quota approaches are being used by Spain (40% women by 2015); Norway (40% women, already exceeded); Netherlands (30% by 2016); Italy (30% by 2015); and France (20% by 2014, 40% by 2017).

Work by Ruigrok et al. (2006) assesses the corporate governance-related antecedents of nomination committee adoption, and the impact of nomination committees' existence and their composition on board independence and board demographic diversity. Using a longitudinal study of board composition amongst 210 Swiss public companies from January 2001 through December 2003, a period during which the Swiss (Stock) Exchange (SWX) introduced new corporate governance-related disclosure guidelines, they found firms with nomination committees are more likely to have a higher number of independent and foreign directors, but not more likely to have a higher number of female board members. Further, the existence of nomination committees is associated with a higher degree of nationality diversity, but is not related to board educational diversity.

On the governance aspects of the committee, the role is to assess the performance of the CEO, the board, and individual board members in relation to the goals and performance criteria established by the committee and the board (as set forth in the firm's corporate governance guidelines). Evaluation also includes the committee's evaluation of its own performance. Boards of directors of companies traded on the NYSE are required to conduct a board performance self-evaluation at least annually. So too for Combined Code requirements (2006). While there has been a good deal of work on prescriptive advice about how such reviews should take place, the role of the nomination/governance committee in this process has yet to be explored fully.

Process

Studies on nomination committees are in their infancy (Carson, 2003). The director selection process has long been subject to criticism as powerful CEOs, rather than shareholders, often select directors (Pfeffer, 1972; Westphal and Zajac, 1994; Van Ees and Postma, 2004). For example, Lorsch and MacIver (1989) reported that boards often have only limited influence over the new director nomination process. However, there have been few studies to assess how nomination committees make judgments, set policy, and interact with the board overall and with head-hunters and the HR department.

In summary, the small number of studies on the nomination committee show positive effects regarding some aspects of diversity and indicate support for the implementation of board reviews. However, the nomination committee highlights the problem of committee member independence. In work on the nomination *process*, CEOs and executives will often have a strong preference for a particular candidate and, while this suggestion should be entertained by the committee, it cannot determine its choice. This difficult balancing act provides support to the view that non-executive roles in general, and board committee members in particular, have to simultaneously combine information and advice from the executives but not be captured by their views (Roberts et al., 2005).

Interactions between Committees

The three oversight committees and their effects tend to be treated in isolation; little is known about the interactions and effects of the board committees. One research tradition is concerned with director overlap—the extent to which directors sit on a number of board committees within the same organization. Because the audit and compensation and nomination committees are subgroups of the board of directors, some of the same directors may sit on both committees. The benefit of director overlap resides in the potential for knowledge transfer across committees, which can lead to increased awareness and diligence among committee members. A panel study by Zheng and Cullinan (2010) of S&P 500 firms found that the overlapping of the compensation committee and the audit committee may bring benefits in terms of the design of compensation schemes because of the knowledge spillover between the two committees. However, a major policy initiative (Higgs, 2003) suggests that the same outside director should not serve on the audit, compensation, and nominating committee, in order that there not be too much influence focused on one individual (Higgs, 2003: 13.2).

Theoretical Pluralism

The three committees we have discussed in this chapter—audit, remuneration, and nomination—are traditionally given the overarching name "committees of oversight." This points to their role as monitors of major aspects of corporate activity and chimes well with their connection with agentic models which highlight that governance has to be achieved often by overcoming self-serving or manipulative behavior. However, reflecting process work on boards of directors (Pettigrew and McNulty, 1995; Stiles and Taylor, 2001), it is clear there is variation in the enactment of board committee duties. A common theme emerging from the process studies on board committees is that, while the diffusion of board committee structures and principles are widespread, their enactment takes a variety of forms.

This chapter underlines how agency and institutional accounts of board committee work are not mutually exclusive. Further, the aims of effective oversight and in securing legitimacy are to promote the assurance of probity and conformity to high standards of governance. These aims have important consequences for the level of resources that may be secured by organizations. Resource dependence theory, which states that the board's main role is to assist management in securing key organizational resources (Cohen et al., 2007; Nicholson and Kiel, 2007), has resonance for board committees as well as for the board as a whole (Pfeffer and Salancik, 1978; Hillman and Dalziel, 2003). Cohen et al. (2007) find that auditors consider both traditional agency variables and resource dependence variables when evaluating corporate governance for the purpose of audit planning. But more studies examining the processes by which board committees secure valued resources for the organization would be valuable.

Board structure, composition, and independence all help to create the conditions within which non-executives can be effective, but they do not by themselves ensure effectiveness. Two issues are particularly relevant here: first, the social psychological forces acting against independence and the objective use of expertise and, second, the need to attend to board committee process.

First, an issue affecting the independence of board committee members is the demographic similarity of independent directors (Main et al., 2008). The small talent pool for independent directors and the need to widen the market for them has been identified (see e.g. Higgs, 2003). If directors are of a similar social demographic background, this encourages a mutual reinforcement or "consensual validation" of each individual's beliefs (Byrne et al., 1966: 223), enhancing interpersonal attraction and producing bias in director selection (Westphal, 1999). The similarity of background and view may have advantages in terms of expertise, but may limit independence of mind (Roberts et al., 2005). In addition, there are norms of reciprocity among directors who also serve as independent directors on other boards which may hinder the performance of independent oversight (Westphal and Zajac, 1994).

Second, focusing on board behavior and relationships offers a different, and in our view, more subtle understanding of the real drivers of board effectiveness. Board committee effectiveness depends upon the behavioral dynamics of the committee, and how the web of interpersonal and group relationships between executive and non-executive directors, and between committee members and key external constituencies, is developed in particular company contexts. It is clear that board committee effectiveness is a function of committee composition, authority, resources, and diligence (DeZoort et al., 2002). Independence and expertise are crucial elements in the composition of the committee, while the need for committees to insist on the highest standards from internal and external sources (for example, from the internal and external auditor, or on the HR function for the performance of executives) makes authority a key asset. Having the resources to carry out the roles (for example, being given enough information from the company to make accurate judgments, and having access to key sources of professional guidance) is highly important, and showing diligence in terms of the motivation and thoroughness to review committee material ensures the right attention to committee matters.

Much of the difference between a substantive versus ceremonial role for board committees stems from the attitude of management toward governance mechanisms. Creating and sustaining accountability within the boardroom is heavily dependent on the attitudes and actions of executive directors regarding their non-executive colleagues, the work of the chairman in creating the conditions for non-executive effectiveness, the experience, skill, and judgment of non-executives, and the manner in which they bring these to bear on the conduct of a company. The scope, depth, and effectiveness of these relationships in turn depend upon executive and non-executive director conduct. This conduct is the absolute basis of the effectiveness of the non-executives within board committees.

Future Research

When considering the effectiveness of board committees, attempts to infer from characteristics such as independence and expertise to organizational outcomes are difficult, since the benefits to performance may be gained from other features of corporate governance. Further, the use of certain proxies to measure different governance possibilities is not consistently applied and the research base as a result is non-additive. For greater understanding of the contribution of board committees, more attention needs to be paid to the processes by which board committees carry out their functions and also how they interact with other committees and also the board overall.

As well as greater in-depth understanding of the relational dynamics within the board committee and with their key constituencies, work focusing on an individual level of analysis, exploring the cognitive and motivational aspects of board committee members, would be welcome. As Spira (1999) argues, a key feature of board committee activity lies in the asking of questions, but to what extent directors speak up and when they remain silent (Morrison and Milliken, 2000), and just how the questioning process links to the achievement of governance benefits remains unclear.

The importance of informal interactions and communications in accomplishing a board committee's objectives would also be an important research avenue (Spira, 2002; Gendron and Bédard, 2006; Turley and Zaman, 2007). Further research on the relation between board committees and key stakeholders through informal means such as influencing and political behavior (Ferris et al., 2007) would make an important contribution to governance research.

This chapter highlights that there is only limited and mixed evidence of effects to support claims and perceptions about the value of board committees. Most of the existing research has focused on factors associated with issues of structural and background variables such as independence, and the expertise of board committee members, but there is little evidence on the processes associated with how board committees operate. Since it is clear that board committees are increasingly widely accepted in the world, within both unitary and two-tier governance systems (Collier and Zaman, 2005), and given the fact that key governance deliberations actually happen within board committees, rather than at the level of the board as a whole, increasing our understanding of the practices within and between committees becomes a pressing research and practical need.

Acknowledgement

I am grateful to the editors of this volume and to Don MacKinlay for very helpful comments of this chapter.

References

ABBOTT, L. J., PARKER, S., and PETERS, G. F. (2004). "Audit Committee Characteristics and Restatements," *Auditing: A Journal of Practice & Theory*, 23(1): 69–87.
—— —— —— (2010). "Serving Two Masters: The Association between Audit Committee Internal Audit Oversight and Internal Audit Activities," *Accounting Horizons*, 24(1): 1–24.
AGRAWAL, A., and CHADHA, S. (2005). "Corporate Governance and Accounting Scandals," *Journal of Law and Economics*, 48(2): 371–406.
BEASLEY, M. S., CARCELLO, J. V., HERMANSON, D. R., and LAPIDES, P. D. (2000). "Fraudulent Financial Reporting: Consideration of Industry Traits and Corporate Governance Mechanisms," *Accounting Horizons*, 14(4): 441–54.
—— —— —— and NEAL, T. L. (2009). "The Audit Committee Oversight Process," *Contemporary Accounting Research*, 26(1): 65–122.
—— —— —— —— (2010). "Fraudulent Financial Reporting 1998–2007: An Analysis of U.S. Public Companies," Durham, NC: Committee of Sponsoring Organizations of the Treadway Commission (COSO). Available at: <http://www.coso.org/documents/COSOFRAUDSTUDY2010_001.pdf>.
BEATTIE, V., FEARNLEY, S., and BRANDT, R. (2000). "Behind the Audit Report: A Descriptive Study of Discussions and Negotiations Between Auditors and Directors," *International Journal of Auditing*, 4: 177–202.
BÉDARD, J., and GENDRON, Y. (2010). "Strengthening the Financial Reporting System: Can Audit Committees Deliver?" *International Journal of Auditing*, 14(2): 174–210.
—— CHTOUROU, S. M., and COURTEAU, L. (2004). "The Effect of Audit Committee Expertise, Independence, and Activity on Aggressive Earnings Management", *Auditing: A Journal of Practice & Theory*, 23(2): 13–35.
BENITO, M., and CONYON, M. (1999). "The Governance of Directors' Pay: Evidence from UK Companies," *Journal of Management and Governance*, 3: 117–36.
BILIMORIA, D., and PIDERIT, S. (1994). "Board Committee Membership: Effects of Sex-Based Bias," *Academy of Management Journal*, 37(6): 1453–77.
Blue Ribbon Committee (BRC) (1999). "Report and Recommendations of the Blue Ribbon Committee on Improving the Effectiveness of Corporate Audit Committees," New York:

BRC. Copies of the entire report can be obtained from the public affairs offices of the NYSE and the NASD, or online from <http://www.nyse.com> and <http://www.nasd.com>.

BRONSON, S. N., CARCELLO, J. V., HOLLINGSWORTH, C. W., and NEAL, T. L. (2009). "Are Fully Independent Audit Committees Really Necessary?" *Journal of Accounting and Public Policy*, 28(4): 265–80.

BYRNE, D., CLORE, G. L. J., and WORCHEL, P. (1966). "Effect of Economic Similarity-Dissimilarity on Interpersonal Attraction," *Journal of Personality and Social Psychology*, 4(2): 220–24.

Cadbury Committee (1992). *Report of the Committee on the Financial Aspects of Corporate Governance*. London: Gee.

CARCELLO, J. V., and NEAL, T. L. (2003). "Audit Committee Characteristics and Auditor Dismissals Following 'New' Going-Concern Reports," *The Accounting Review*, 78(1): 95–117.

——HERMANSON, D. R., and ZHONGXIA, Y. (2011). "Corporate Governance Research in Accounting and Auditing: Insights, Practice Implications, and Future Research Directions," *Auditing: A Journal of Practice & Theory*, 30(3): 1–31.

————PALMROSE, Z. V., and SCHOLZ, S. (2011). "CEO Involvement in Selecting Board Members, Audit Committee Effectiveness, and Restatements," *Contemporary Accounting Research*, 28(2): 396–430.

CARPENTER, V. L., and FEROZ, E. H. (2001). "Institutional Theory and Accounting Rule Choice: An Analysis of Four US State Governments' Decisions to Adopt Generally Accepted Accounting Principles," *Accounting, Organizations and Society*, 26(7–8): 565–96.

CARSON, E. (2003). "Factors Associated with the Development of Board Sub-Committees," *Corporate Governance: An International Review*, 10(1): 4–18.

CHEN, L., CARSON, E., and SIMNETT, R. (2007). "Impact of Stakeholder Characteristics on Voluntary Dissemination of Interim Information and Communication of its Level of Assurance," *Accounting & Finance*, 47(4): 667–91.

COHEN, J., KRISHNAMOORTHY, G., and WRIGHT, A. (2002). "Corporate Governance and the Audit Process", *Contemporary Accounting Research*, 19(4): 573–94.

————(2004). "The Corporate Governance Mosaic and Financial Reporting Quality", *Journal of Accounting Literature*, 23: 87–152.

————(2007). "The Impact of Roles of the Board on Auditors' Risk Assessments and Program Planning Decisions," *Auditing: A Journal of Practice & Theory*, 26(1): 91–112.

——GAYNOR, L. M., KRISHNAMOORTHY, G., and WRIGHT, A. M. (2007). "Auditor Communications with the Audit Committee and the Board of Directors: Policy Recommendations and Opportunities for Future Research," *Accounting Horizons*, 21(2): 165–87.

——KRISHNAMOORTHY, G., and WRIGHT, A. (2010). "Corporate Governance in the Post Sarbanes-Oxley Era: Auditors' Experiences," *Contemporary Accounting Research*, 27(3): 751–86.

COLLIER, P., and ZAMAN, M. (2005). "Convergence in European Corporate Governance: The Audit Committee Concept," *Corporate Governance: An International Review*, 13: 753–68.

CONYON, M. J. (2006). "Executive Compensation and Incentives," *Academy of Management Perspectives*, 20(1): 25–44.

——and HE, L. (2004). "Compensation Committees and CEO Compensation Incentives in U.S. Entrepreneurial Firms," *Journal of Management Accounting Research*, 16: 35–56.

——and LEECH, D. (1994). "Top Pay, Company Performance and Corporate Governance," *Oxford Bulletin of Economics and Statistics*, 56(3): 229–47.

—— and Peck, S. I. (1998). "Board Control, Remuneration Committees, and Top Management Compensation," *Academy of Management Journal*, 41(2): 146–57.

—— —— and Sadler, G. V. (2009). "Compensation Consultant and Executive Pay: Evidence from the United States and the United Kingdom," *Academy of Management Perspectives*, 23(1): 43–55.

—— Gregg, P., and Machin, S. (1995). "Taking Care of Business: Executive Compensation in the UK," *Economic Journal*, 105: 704–15.

Cotter, J., and Silvester, M. (2003). "Board and Monitoring Committee Independence," *Abacus*, 39(2): 211–32.

Daily, C. M., Johnson, J. L., Ellstrand, A. E., and Dalton, D. R. (1998). "Compensation Committee Composition as a Determinant of CEO Compensation," *Academy of Management Journal*, 41(2): 209–20.

Davidson, W. N., Xie, B., and Xu, W. (2004). "Market Reaction to Voluntary Announcements of Audit Committee Appointments: The Effect of Financial Expertise," *Journal of Accounting and Public Policy*, 23(4): 279–93.

Davidson, R., Goodwin-Stewart, J., and Kent, P. (2005). "Internal Governance Structures and Earnings Management," *Accounting & Finance*, 45(2): 241–67.

Dechow, P., Gloan, R., and Sweeney, A. (1996). "Causes and Consequences of Earnings Manipulation: An Analysis of Firms Subject to Enforcement Actions by the SEC," *Contemporary Accounting Research*, 13(1): 1–36.

DeFond, M. L., Hann, R. N., and Hu, X. (2005). "Does the Market Value Financial Expertise on Audit Committees of Boards of Directors?" *Journal of Accounting Research*, 43(2): 153–93.

—— and Jiamhalvo, J. (1991). "Incidence and Circumstances of Accounting Errors," *The Accounting Review*, 66(3): 643–55.

DeZoort, F. (1997). "An Investigation of Audit Committees," Oversight Responsibilities, *Abacus*, 33(2): 208–27.

—— (1998). "An Analysis of Experience Effects on Audit Committee Members' Oversight Judgments," *Accounting, Organizations and Society*, 23(1): 1–21.

—— and Salterio, S. (2001). "The Effects of Corporate Governance Experience and Audit Knowledge on Audit Committee Members' Judgments," *Auditing: A Journal of Practice & Theory*, 20(2): 31–47.

—— Hermanson, D., Archambeault, D., and Reed, S. (2002). "Audit Committee Effectiveness: A Synthesis of the Empirical Audit Committee Literature," *Journal of Accounting Literature*, 21: 38–75.

Dhaliwal, D. S., Naiker, V., and Navissi, F. (2010). "The Association between Accruals Quality and the Characteristics of Accounting Experts and Mix of Expertise on Audit Committees," *Contemporary Accounting Research*, 27(3): 787–827.

Ezzamel, M., and Watson, R. (1997). "Wearing Two Hats: The Conflicting Control and Management Roles of Non-Executive Directors," in K. Keasey, S. Thompson, and M. Wright (eds.), *Corporate Governance: Economic, Management and Financial Issues*. Oxford: Oxford University Press.

Fama, E., and Jensen, M. (1983). "Separation of Ownership and Control," *Journal of Law and Economics*, 26(2): 301–25.

Fanto, J. A. (2005). "Board Committees," in Fanto, J. A. (eds.), *Directors' and Officers' Liability* (2nd ed.). New York: Practising Law Institute, 3(1): 3–132.

Ferris, G. R., Treadway, D. C., Perrewe, P. L., Brouer, R. L, Douglas, C., and Lux, S. (2007). "Political Skill in Organizations," *Journal of Management*, 33(3): 290–320.

Financial Reporting Council (FRC) (2008). *Guidance on Audit Committees.* London: Financial Reporting Council.

FISS, P. C. (2008). "Institutions and Corporate Governance," in R. Greenwood, C. Oliver, R. Suddaby, and K. Sahlin-Andersson (eds.), *The Sage Handbook of Organizational Institutionalism.* London: Sage, 390–410.

GENDRON, Y., and BÉDARD, J. (2006). "On the Constitution of Audit Committee Effectiveness," *Accounting, Organizations and Society,* 31(3): 211–39.

GENDRON, Y., and BÉDARD, J., and GOSSELIN, M. (2004). "Getting Inside the Black Box: A Field Study of Practices in 'Effective' Audit Committees," *Auditing: A Journal of Practice & Theory,* 23(1): 153–71.

GOODWIN, J. (2003), "The Relationship between the Audit Committee and the Internal Audit Function: Evidence from Australia and New Zealand," *International Journal of Auditing,* 7: 263–76.

—— and YEO, T. Y. (2001). "Two Factors Affecting Internal Audit Independence and Objectivity: Evidence from Singapore," *International Journal of Auditing,* 5: 107–25.

GWILLIAM, D., and KILCOMMINS, M. (1998). "The Impact of Audit Firm Size and Audit Committee on Perceptions of Auditor Independence and Financial Statement Reliability in Ireland," *Irish Accounting Review,* 5(1): 23–56.

HARRISON, J. R. (1987). "The Strategic Use of Corporate Board Committees," *California Management Review,* 30(1): 109–25.

HENDRY, J. (2002). "The Principal's Other Problems: Honest Incompetence and the Specification of Objectives," *Academy of Management Review,* 27(1): 98–113.

Higgs Report (2003). "Review of the Role and Effectiveness of Non-Executive Directors." London: Department of Trade and Industry.

HILLMAN, A. J., and DALZIEL, T. (2003). "Boards of Directors and Firm Performance: Integrating Agency and Resource Dependence Perspectives," *Academy of Management Review,* 28(3): 383–96.

ICSA (2008). "Guidance on Terms of Reference—Remuneration Committee." London: Institute of Company Secretaries and Administrators.

—— (2009). "Guidance on Terms of Reference—Nominations Committee." London Institute of Company Secretaries and Administrators.

JENSEN, M. C, and MECKLING, W. H. (1976). "Theory of the Firm: Managerial Behavior, Agency Costs, and Ownership Structure," *Journal of Financial Economics,* 3(4): 305–60.

KALBERS, L. and FOGARTY, T. J. (1998). "Organizational and Economic Explanations of Audit Committee," *Journal of Managerial Issues,* 10(2): 129–51.

KESNER, I. (1988). "Directors' Characteristics and Committee Membership: An Investigation of Type Occupation, Tenure and Gender," *Academy of Management Journal,* 31(1): 66–84.

KLEIN, A. (2002). "Audit Committee, Board of Director Characteristics, and Earnings Management," *Journal of Accounting and Economics,* 33(3): 375–400.

KNAPP, M. C. (1987). "An Empirical Study of Audit Committee Support for Auditors Involved in Technical Disputes with Client Management," *The Accounting Review,* 62(3): 578–88.

KPMG Audit Committee Institute (2006). *Audit Committee Agenda Setting.* Montvale, NJ: KPMGACI.

KRISHNAMOORTHY, G., WRIGHT, A., and COHEN, J. (2003). "Audit Committee Effectiveness and Financial Reporting Quality: Implications for Auditor Independence," *Australian Accounting Review,* 13(29): 3–13.

Lawrence, T. B., and Suddaby, R. (2006). "Institutions and Institutional Work," in S. R. Clegg, C. Hardy, T. B. Lawrence, and W. R. Nord (eds.), *Handbook of Organization Studies*, 2nd edition. London: Sage, 215-54.

Lee, C. L., Rosenstein, S., Rangan, N., and Davidson, W. N. (1992). "Board Composition and Shareholder Wealth: The Case of Management Buyouts," *Financial Management*, 21(1): 58-72.

Lee, H. Y., Mande, V., and Ortman, R. (2004). "The Effect of Audit Committee and Board of Director Independence on Auditor Resignation," *Auditing: A Journal of Practice & Theory*, 23(2): 131-46.

Lennox, C. S., and Park, C. W. (2007). "Audit Firm Appointments, Audit Firm Alumni, and Audit Committee Independence," *Contemporary Accounting Research*, 24(1): 235-58.

Lorsch, J. W., and MacLver, E. (1989). *Pawns or Potentates: The Reality of America's Corporate Boards*. Boston: Harvard Business School Press.

Lounsbury, M. (2007). "A Tale of Two Cities: Competing Logics and Practice Variation in the Professionalization of Mutual Funds," *Academy of Management Journal*, 50: 289-307.

Mahoney, D. M., and Shuman, S. (2003). "The Corporate Governance Committee," *Corporate Governance Advisor*, 11(5): 32-6.

Main, B. G. M., Jackson, C., Pymm, J., and Wright, V. (2008). "The Remuneration Committee and Strategic Human Resource Management," *Corporate Governance: An International Review*, 16(3): 225-38.

—— and Johnston, J. (1993). "Remuneration Committees and Corporate Governance," *Accounting and Business Research*, 23: 351-62.

Mangena, M., and Pike, R. (2005). "The Effect of Audit Committee Shareholding, Financial Expertise and Size on Interim Financial Disclosures," *Accounting and Business Research*, 35(4): 327-49.

McMullen, D. A., and Raghunandan, K. (1996). "Enhancing Audit Committee Effectiveness," *Journal of Accountancy*, 182(2): 79-81.

Meyer, J. W., and Rowan, B. (1977). "Institutionalized Organizations: Formal Structure as Myth and Ceremony," *American Journal of Sociology*, 83: 340-63.

Morrison, E. W., and Milliken, F. J. (2000). "Organisational Silence: A Barrier to Change and Development in a Pluralistic World," *Academy of Management Review*, 25(4): 708-25.

Naiker, V., and Sharma, D. S. (2009). "Former Audit Partners on the Audit Committee and Internal Control Deficiencies," *Accounting Review*, 84(2): 559-87.

Newman, H. A., and Mozes, H. A. (1999). "Does the Composition of the Compensation Committee Influence CEO Compensation Practices?" *Financial Management*, 28(3): 41-53.

Nicholson, G. J., and Kiel, G. C. (2007). "Can Directors Impact Performance? A Case-Based Test of Three Theories of Corporate Governance," *Corporate Governance: An International Review*, 15(4): 585-608.

Ogden, S., and Watson, R. (2004). "Remuneration Committees and CEO Pay in the UK Privatized Water Industry," *Socio-Economic Review*, 2: 33-63.

—— —— (2008). "Executive Pay and the Search for Legitimacy: An Investigation into how UK Remuneration Committees Use Corporate Performance Comparisons in Long-Term Incentive Pay Decisions," *Human Relations*, 61(5): 711-39.

Perkins, S., and Hendry, C. (2005). "Ordering Top Pay: Interpreting the Signals," *Journal of Management Studies*, 42(7): 1443-68.

Pettigrew, A., and McNulty, T. M. (1995). "Power and Influence in and around the Boardroom," *Human Relations*, 48(8): 845-73.

PFEFFER, J. (1972). "Size and Composition of Corporate Boards of Directors: The Organization and its Environment," *Administrative Science Quarterly*, 17: 218–28.
—— and SALANCIK, G. R. (1978). *External Control of Organizations: A Resource Dependence Perspective*. New York: Harper & Row.
ROBERTS, J., MCNULTY, T. M., and STILES, P. (2005). "Beyond Agency Conceptions of the Work of the Non-Executive Director: Creating Accountability in the Boardroom," *British Journal of Management*, 16: S5–26.
RUIGROK, W., PECK, S., TACHEVA, S., GREVE, P., and HU, Y. (2006). "The Determinants and Effects of Board Nomination Committees," *Journal of Management and Governance*, 10(2): 119–48.
SCARBROUGH, D. P., RAMA, D. V., and RAGHUNANDAN, K. (1998). "Audit Committee Composition and Interaction with Internal Auditing: Canadian Evidence," *Accounting Horizons*, 12: 51–62.
SCHNEIDER, A. A., GRAMLING, D., HERMANSON, R., and YE, Z. (2009). "A Review of Academic Literature on Internal Control Reporting under SOX," *Journal of Accounting Literature*, 28: 1–46.
SCOTT, W. R. (1987). "The Adolescence of Institutional Theory," *Administrative Science Quarterly*, 32(4): 493–511.
Securities AND Exchange Commission (SEC). (2003). "Final Rule: Standards Relating to Listed Company Audit Committees." Release 33–8220.
SHIVDASANI, A., and YERMACK, D. (1999). "CEO Involvement in the Selection of New Board Members: An Empirical Analysis," *Journal of Finance*, 54(5): 1829–53.
Smith Committee (2003). "Audit Committees—Combined Code Guidance." London: Financial Reporting Council.
SPENCER STUART (2010). *Spencer Stuart Board Index 2010*. New York: Spencer Stuart.
SPIRA, L. (1998). "An Evolutionary Perspective on Audit Committee Effectiveness," *Corporate Governance: An International Review*, 6: 29–38.
—— (1999). "Ceremonies of Governance: Perspectives on the Role of the Audit Committee," *Journal of Management and Governance*, 3: 231–60.
—— (2002). *The Audit Committee: Performing Corporate Governance*. Dordrecht: Kluwer.
—— and BENDER, R. (2004). "Compare and Contrast: Perspectives on Board Committees," *Corporate Governance: An International Review*, 12: 489–99.
STILES, P., and TAYLOR, B. (2001). *Boards at Work: How Directors View their Roles and Responsibilities*. Oxford: Oxford University Press.
TURLEY, S., and ZAMAN, M. (2004). "The Corporate Governance Effects of Audit Committees," *Journal of Management and Governance*, 8(3): 305–32.
—— —— (2007). "Audit Committee Effectiveness: Informal Processes and Behavioural Effects," *Accounting, Auditing and Accountability Journal*, 20(5): 765–88.
TURNBULL REPORT (1999). *Internal Control: Guidelines for Directors on the Combined Code*. London: Institute of Chartered Accountants in England and Wales.
US House OF Representatives (2002). *Sarbanes-Oxley Act of 2002. Public Law No. 107–204*. Washington, DC: Government Printing Office.
VAFEAS, N. (1999). "The Nature of Board Nominating Committees and their Role in Corporate Governance," *Journal of Business Finance & Accounting*, 26(1): 199–225.
—— (2003). "Further Evidence on Compensation Committee Composition as a Determinant of CEO Compensation," *Financial Management*, 32(2): 53–72.

VAN EES, H., and POSTMA, T. (2004). "A Comparative Institutional Analysis of Board Roles and Member (S)Election Procedures," *International Studies of Management and Organization*, 34(2): 90–112.

VICKNAIR, D., HICKMAN, K., and CARNES, K. C. (1993). "A Note on Audit Committee Independence: Evidence from The NYSE on 'Grey' Area Directors," *Accounting Horizons*, 7(1): 53–57.

WESTPHAL, J. D. (1999). "Collaboration in the Boardroom: Behavioural and Performance Consequences of CEO-Board Social Ties," *Academy of Management Journal*, 42(1): 7–24.

—— and ZAJAC, E. J. (1994). "Substance and Symbolism in CEO's Long-Term Incentive Plans," *Administrative Science Quarterly*, 39: 367–90.

WILLIAMS, K. Y., and O'REILLY, C. A. (1998). "Demography and Diversity in Organizations: A Review of 40 Years of Research," in B. M. Staw and L. L. Cummings (eds.), *Research in Organizational Behaviour*, Greenwich: JAI Press, 77–140.

XIE, B., DAVIDSON, W., and DADALT, P. (2003). "Earnings Management and Corporate Governance: The Role of the Board and the Audit Committee," *Journal of Corporate Finance*, 9: 295–316.

ZHANG, Y. (2008). "Information Asymmetry and the Dismissal of Newly Appointed CEOs: An Empirical Investigation," *Strategic Management Journal*, 29(8): 859–72.

ZHENG, X., and CULLINAN, C. P. (2010). "Compensation/Audit Committee Overlap and the Design of Compensation Systems," *International Journal of Disclosure and Governance*, 7(2): 136–52.

CHAPTER 9

THE GOVERNANCE OF DIRECTOR NETWORKS

LUC RENNEBOOG AND YANG ZHAO

INTRODUCTION

SOCIAL and professional networks govern our lives; they are established through common education, sports interests, club memberships, as well as connections resulting from professional lives. The economics and finance literature has begun to give more attention to the influence of managers' and non-executive directors' connections on corporate decision-making and corporate monitoring. Indeed, it may be that professional networks have a bigger impact on corporate policy than we anticipate, and even influence the effectiveness of institutionalized governance structures (such as boards of directors) or the role of governance regulation.

Director networks, also known as director interlocks, are networks formed by executive and non-executive directors sitting on corporate boards. Links within director networks are established when two directors are sitting on the same board. Research on director networks emerged at the beginning of the 20th century, when director networks were considered a tool to foster corporate collusion. The following quote was from Louis Brandeis as the associate justice of the US Supreme Court. He made this statement before the passing of the Clayton Act (1913: 51), which prohibited extensive director networks as these could lead to collusion in concentrated industries. The quote appeared in the US House of Representatives Staff Report to the Antitrust Committee (1965: 3).

> The practice of interlocking directorates is the root of many evils. It offends laws human and divine... Applied to corporations which deal with each other it tends to disloyalty and to violation of the fundamental law that no man can serve two masters. In either event it tends to inefficiency; for it removes incentive and destroys soundness of judgment. It is undemocratic for it rejects the platform: "A fair field and no favors." (Brandeis, 1913)

In recent years, the number of directorships held by one individual has been capped in some countries.[1] However, within these legal boundaries, the power of director networks can still be significant. In the developed countries, director networks are important among large corporations: one-fifth of the 1,000 largest companies in the US share at least one board member with another of the top 1,000. More than 1,000 board members sit on four or more corporate boards, and 235 sit on more than six (Krantz, 2002). The four largest oil companies have interlocking directorates with the international megabanks. Exxon Mobil shares board members with JP Morgan Chase, Citigroup, Deutsche Bank, Royal Bank of Canada, and Prudential. Chevron Texaco has interlocks with Bank of America and JP Morgan Chase. BP Amoco shares directors with JP Morgan Chase. RD/Shell has ties with Citigroup, JP Morgan Chase, N. M. Rothschild & Sons, and the Bank of England (Henderson, 2010). As regulations on director networks differ across countries, these cross-border director networks between powerful international corporations are not tightly regulated. Lastly, besides the professional connections, directors may also be connected by education, membership of social clubs, etc. Such informal director networks seem to gain in importance.

In this chapter, we review the history and current status and regulation of director networks in some major western countries in the next section. The academic literature on director networks is then summarized. Different approaches to analyzing director networks are discussed and compared in the following section. The final section concludes.

Director Networks in History and Today

Networks in the US

The earliest director network documented can be found in the incorporation documents of New England textile mills in the US in 1790. A small group of wealthy businessmen became owners of each other's companies and could thus be called an ownership network. In 1845 a larger group of 80 people, known as the "Boston Associates," controlled 20 percent of the textile industry. Seventeen of these men served as directors in Boston banks, 20 were directors in six insurance companies, and 11 were directors of five railroad companies (Dalzell, 1987). During the mid and late 19th century, director networks, usually led by families and large owners, became widespread in the major industries in the US. Banks and other financial institutes were at the center of this powerful director network. This situation finally led to the adoption of the Clayton Act in 1914.

Section 8 of the Clayton Act is specifically designed to restrict director interlocks. At the beginning, director interlocks were defined as two competing corporations sharing one or more common directors. In the meantime, the act has been amended six times since its enactment. Today, Section 8 prohibits, with certain exceptions, any person from serving as a director or officer in two competing corporations. In Section 8, competitor corporations are defined as firms with capital, surplus, and undivided profits aggregating to more than $10,000,000, with the exception that no corporation is covered if the competitive sales of either corporation are less than $1,000,000. Section 8 does not affect companies in the banking sector. Interlocking in the banking sector is governed by Federal Deposit Insurance Corporation (FDIC), under "Part 348, Management official interlocks," which has even more stringent rules regarding director interlocks.

With Section 8 of the Clayton Act outlawing a large part of director connections, director networks became much weaker in competitive firms and the banking sector. As a consequence of the separation of ownership and control, the networks between companies in the early 1900s had become less dominated by families and bankers. Instead, professional managers became gradually more interlocked, a trend which continued until the late 1900s. The majority of networked directors are professional, white, male managers. Only recently, since the end of the 20th century, the diversification of director networks has increased, with more women and people of color joining corporate boards. Although more restrictions have been put on boards, many firms still have large networks. For instance, in 2005, Citigroup had 25 links to other companies through shared directors. Most of these firms were the biggest in their sectors, such as AT&T, Ford Motors, PepsiCo, Time Warner, and Xerox (Domhoff, 2006). It is not surprising to hear the claim that the American economy is controlled by a small group of corporate elites from these large and connected companies.

Since the financial crisis of 2007–8, the Securities and Exchange Commission (SEC) is planning to enforce a new code on good corporate governance to further discourage multiple directorships, because serving on too many boards decreases the time and energy one can invest in any individual company.

Networks in the UK

The situation in the UK bears many similarities as financial companies are also the most connected companies in the economy. But due to differences in regulation and culture, the development and structure of director networks differs from the American situation.

The first research documenting the UK director networks is Beesley (1951). He traced down the director networks existing between all companies in British Midland metal industries. He found that in 1948 connections had been forged between the largest companies, which employed one-third of the industry's workers. Beesley considered this director network a protective device to ensure that individual investment decisions would not be harmful to other group members. The coordination mechanism was, according to Beesley, harmful since it delayed investment in research and development. In recent years, director networks in the UK have been more "concise" compared to the US case. Directors usually do not have more than two connections with other boards. The connections between companies are often maintained by one common director (Santella et al., 2008). Nevertheless, Renneboog and Zhao (2011) still find some network superstars in their UK sample: Andy Hornby was sitting on four boards, while being the CEO in one of these firms in 2006. Peter Cawdron was a non-executive director or chairman in nine companies. Another feature of the British director networks is that there are connections between financial institutions through common directors, since this is not prohibited by the UK regulation.

The UK Corporate Governance Code (known as the Combined Code up to 2010) is a set of rules provided by the Financial Reporting Council (FRC) as a guide to good board practice (Higgs Report, 2003). Section A proposes guidelines for the appointment of independent directors. In order to judge whether a non-executive director is independent, several criteria are provided. A director is not independent if he "holds cross-directorships or has significant links with other directors through involvement in other companies or bodies" (A.3.1). As for executive directors, A.4.5 states: "The board should not agree to a full time executive director taking on more than one non-executive directorship in a FTSE 100 company nor the chairmanship of such a company" (Higgs Report, 2003). A.3.1 and A.4.5 strongly discourage multiple directorships but are not binding: should the company insist on allowing multiple directorships, a clear explanation is to be given to the regulation authority as well as the investors.

From these elements of the regulation and codes of best practices in the US and the UK, it is clear that the regulatory authorities consider director networks potentially harmful to corporate competition, to the independence of non-executive directors, and the efficiency and responsibility of executive directors.

Networks in Other Developed Countries

Besides the US and the UK, director networks are popular in other countries too. Since the 1970s, director networks in Germany have come under pressure from the financial press. According to Prinz (2006), an overwhelming majority of the listed companies are connected by directors and/or financial ties. He claims that influential director networks diminish the motivation to compete and restructure. Similar to the US and the UK, the German regulator also imposes limitations on director networks. German business legislation (100, 105 AktG, since 1965) limits the number of supervisory board mandates to a maximum of ten seats per person, whereas a position as president of the supervisory board is given double weight. Moreover, mutual exchange-directorships are forbidden. These rules effectively limit the growth of director networks in Germany. Nonetheless, Heinze (2002) shows that, although over time there has been a quantitative reduction in director networks, the qualitative structure remained stable over the period of 1989 to 2001.

Director networks in France are different from most other countries as they are determined by the educational and political backgrounds of the directors. First, directors are drawn from a limited set of *Grandes Ecoles*, which have powerful alumni networks. Second, a large proportion of the business elites are former civil servants, who have built connections through political relations. These two networks are of overwhelming importance in the French business world. ENA (*Ecole Nationale d'Administration*) and graduates of the *Ecoles Polytechniques* run more than 20 percent of the listed firms, which accounts for around 70 percent of all assets traded on the Paris Stock Exchange. Twenty percent of the firms are run by former high-ranking bureaucrats (Kramarz and Thesmar, 2006). To sum up, director networks in France are based on education and past civil service, rather than mere professional ties.

Director networks in Italy and Spain are strong too. Compared to the US, the UK, and Germany, director networks in the southern European countries show a high network density. In an Italian sample of 40 blue-chips in the S&P-MIB (Standard & Poor's/Milano Italia Borsa) 40 index, 31 companies are connected and one out of ten directors is sitting on two or more boards (Santella et al., 2008). The ratio is similar for Spain (Crespi and Pascual-Fuster, 2008). On average, a Spanish director serves on 1.22 boards; some directors even sit on five boards simultaneously.

To conclude, director networks have a long history and remain influential in most developed countries today. The potential harm of director networks is recognized by the regulatory authorities. Several restrictions have been imposed to deter excess director networks. However, over time director networks evolve and adapt to the new regulatory environment and retain their influence in the corporate world. In the next section, we review the academic literature on director networks in order to obtain more insights about the motivation, mechanism, and impact of director networks.

Research on Director Networks

Director Networks and Collusion

Concerns about director networks have attracted public and academic attention in Germany (Jeidels, 1905) and the US since the early 1900s. Toward the end of 19th century, the growth and concentration of some industries, for instance iron and steel production and railroads, induced stronger corporate connections through interlocking directorates. In the US the debate even triggered a government investigation and led to the Clayton Act in 1914, which eventually prohibited interlocking directorates in the railroad industry, competing firms, and banks. Research on this period usually concentrates on the interlocks of a few large companies in the economy, ignoring the networks between other companies (see e.g. Dooley, 1969). As it is often argued that interlocks are a product of the development of monopolistic structures, studies on interlocks are embedded in antitrust research. In the mid-20th century, antitrust research also included investigations of the types of interlocked directors, company types, and whether interlocks are related to geography and industry factors (Mizruchi, 1982). The pioneering studies in Germany and the US were soon mimicked for the UK (Aaronovitch, 1961) and the Netherlands (Baruch, 1962). Aaronovitch (1961) describes the networks among British companies as an instrument used by capitalists to control the industry. Baruch (1962) documents that director networks in the four large Dutch banks also played a crucial role in fortifying control over a large range of related companies. Although the intensity of interlocking was lower in these countries in the early 20th century, they share many features with the German and American markets, such as the high interlocking level in the finance industry. In a comparative study covering the first half of the 20th century, Fennema and Schijf (1978) report that the number of interlocks declined in the US but increased in most other countries. The most plausible explanation for this is the introduction of legal restrictions in the US.

Although regulation has tried to reduce the potential collusion of director networks, research has shown that director networks may also yield political influence. A pioneering study on director networks and firms' political action by Koenig (1979) found that connected companies contribute more to election campaigns. Studies by Mizruchi and Koenig (1986) confirm this finding, but also report that interlocks via financial institutions can be used to predict the political positions of companies. They argue that companies interlocked through indirect ties can better coordinate with each other and are hence more likely to express similar positions in congressional hearings. This is contradicted by Burris (1987). Since companies can likely benefit from director networks involving politicians, Agrawal and Knoeber (2001) document that politically experienced directors are more prevalent in companies where the costs of environmental regulation, sales to government, and exports are greater, and lobbying is more important.

Motivations to Create Director Networks

Mizruchi (1996) presents a comprehensive review of the director network studies from the 1970s to the 1990s. In his paper, four motivations for the establishment of networks are developed: (i) collusion; (ii) monitoring; (iii) legitimacy; and (iv) career advancement. While the collusion argument has been discussed above, the monitoring argument is that interlocks are created to better monitor the management. Westphal and Zajac (1996) state that (the lack of) interlocks result(s) from the power struggle between the CEO and the board. They find that powerful CEOs select and retain passive board members in order to maintain control. In contrast powerful boards prefer new board candidates with monitoring experience. Furthermore, better monitoring is supposed to lead to better corporate performance. Burt (1983) confirms this expected positive relation between profitability and interlocks, but Dooley (1969) and Lang and Lockhart (1990) draw opposite conclusions. In addition to the ambiguous results on the relation between interlocks and performance, another unresolved issue in these papers is causality. In other words, is it profitability that triggers interlocks, or the other way around? Richardson's (1987) research provides some answers to the causality question: his interviews with bankers confirm that bankers often join boards of companies in financial difficulties. The legitimacy argument is that recruiting reputable directors onto the board earns the trust of investors and financial institutions (Scott, 1992). Most studies prior to the late 1990s have overlooked directors' individual incentives to initiate connections. Career advancement is one of the most prominent of individual motivations to participate in director networks. On this topic, the pioneering studies by Stokman et al. (1988) and Zajac (1988) show that directors join other boards for reasons of prestige and extra compensation. A recent empirical test by Kirchmaier and Kollo (2007) confirms the role of several individual factors, such as prestige, title, and education, which contribute to the expansion of director networks.

A motivation for the creation of director networks is their information value. More explicitly, director networks can transfer valuable information, knowledge, skills, and experience between companies. Davis et al. (2003) study the composition of the small world of American corporate elite for the period 1982–2001 and find that board members who have been involved in crucial board decisions, for example mergers and acquisitions (M&As) and business alliances, are more likely to be invited by other companies to serve as non-executive board members. This implies that director networks function as channels for gathering information for corporate decision-making. Myint et al. (2005) present a case from the Cambridge hi-tech cluster and show that valuable multiple directorships create new business opportunities and transfer management expertise. Another case study, conducted by Shaw and Alexander (2006), documents the knowledge transfer of supermarket retail techniques from North America to Britain. During the 1950s British supermarket retailers faced difficulties in adopting American methods of self-service selling. Some of the British supermarket retailers (e.g. Tesco and Sainsbury) solved this problem by direct observation of the US market, but others (such as Melias) transferred the knowledge via shared directors after having gained control of an American supermarket retailer. These cases provide textbook examples of how director networks can acquire knowledge and management experience to aid companies entering a new business (model).

Director Networks and Corporate Governance

We can categorize the literature on this topic into several strands: (i) M&A strategies; (ii) financing opportunities; (iii) managerial compensation; (iv) managerial succession; and (v) corporate performance.

The first strand of the literature is on interlocks and M&A strategies. Interlocked firms are more likely to adopt similar strategies, such as takeover defenses (Davis 1991) and friendly acquisitions (Palmer et al., 1995). D'Aveni and Kesner (1993) find that takeover resistance is more likely to be weaker if top managers from the bidder and target are connected. Haunschild (1993) studies 327 US firms in four industries and shows that firms are more likely to engage in acquisitions if they are connected with other firms that have recently made acquisitions. Lastly, on the issue of the probability of being the target in a takeover, Davis and Stout (1992) believe there is no association between the presence of a banker on the board and the likelihood of the firm being a target, whereas Fligstein and Markowitz (1993) find a positive correlation. The latter study also shows that bankers are often appointed to boards of firms experiencing financial difficulties, which are likely to become takeover targets.

The second strand comprises financing opportunities for which interlocks between firms and banks are of importance. Ratcliff (1980) finds that the interlocks of a bank are positively associated with corporate lending, but negatively associated with mortgage lending. Stearns and Mizruchi (1993a, 1993b) document a positive association between the presence of a banker on a firm's board and the additional financing this firm attracts from that specific bank. Still, the study also suffers from the typical causality problem. On the one hand, a banker's presence in a firm may facilitate borrowing, but on the other hand, a firm with high leverage may invite a banker to its board.

In line with agency or tournament theories, director networks can be regarded as a tool for top managers to extend their power over the board in order to extract private benefits. Interlocks can also be indicators of busy boards (lacking time to monitor the firm) and hence ineffective corporate governance. In the remainder of this section, we review the director network studies on managerial compensation, managerial turnover, and firm performance.

Cochran et al. (1985) find that the proportion of outside directors is positively associated with the top manager's chance of receiving excessive severance pay, which is confirmed by Singh and Harianto (1989), Wade et al. (1990), and Davis (1994). A likely explanation for this seemingly paradoxical finding is that the CEO appoints friends as outside directors in order to have little resistance to (controversial) corporate policies. Several studies following the seminal paper by Hallock (1997) find a positive correlation between board interlocks and CEO compensation. Recent papers based on better measurement of director networks confirm that a CEO's compensation increases with his centrality level in his network (Barnea and Guedj, 2009). The explanation is that the CEO's personal influence can be enhanced by the power derived from the network. Furthermore, non-executive directors serving on a board with a powerful CEO may be more lenient in the CEO's remuneration contract design. Moreover, if a company has too many non-executive directors with outside directorships, this busy board may not be able to spend sufficient time on the firm's policies (including the remuneration policy). Both effects can result in a suboptimal remuneration scheme that overpays the CEO or does not link pay to performance. Such a relationship between directors' level of connectedness and their payment is also found by Devos et al. (2006) and Kuhnen (2006). An alternative explanation for the relation between CEO connectedness and pay is offered by Engelberg et al. (2009), who argue that companies pay their CEO for the connections. By counting the past connections, and the educational and social connections of the CEO, Engelberg et al. (2009) find that one additional connection to the CEO increases his total pay by up to 10 percent.

Concerning the issue of managerial turnover and succession, Fich and Shivdasani (2006) and Barnea and Guedj (2009) have analyzed the turnover decision of the CEO: better connected CEOs are less likely to be dismissed when performance of the company goes down. Not surprisingly, the turnover-performance sensitivity declines when the board is occupied by directors with many outside directorships. Moreover, evidence of the importance of weak ties (Granovetter, 1973) is also found in the top managerial labor market. Liu (2008) demonstrates that better connected candidates are more likely to be chosen as the new CEO (especially when they are external candidates).

How do director networks affect corporate performance? Early studies, conducted by Carrington (1981), Meeusen and Cuyvers (1985), and Baysinger and Butler (1985), claim that there is either no correlation between interlocks and profitability or a negative one. In the recent literature, Carpenter and Westphal (2001) find that strategically related interlocks improve board involvement when firms are in a stable business environment. When this environment is unstable, strategically heterogeneous links are proven to be more effective. Ong et al. (2003), Myint et al. (2005), Hochberg et al. (2007), and Gutierrez and Pombo (2010) show that multiple directorships improve the performance of the company. Meanwhile Kiel and Nicholson (2006) find no evidence of a relationship between financial performance and director connections. Recently, more studies show evidence of an adverse impact of director networks on performance, for example Core et al. (1999), Fich and White (2003), Larcker et al. (2006), Kuhnen (2006), Kirchmaier and Stathopoulos (2008), Subrahmanyam (2008), Santos et al. (2009). Other researchers point to the relation between interlocks and poor corporate governance. For instance, poor investor protection and lack of transparency contribute to synchronicity in returns data. In academic research, stock price synchronicity is often used as a measure of corporate governance efficiency. Khanna and Thomas (2009) find a significantly positive relation between the degree of firm interlocks and stock price synchronicity, which suggests that director networks between firms may harm corporate governance.

In general, there is much more past and current evidence on the detrimental effects of director networks on performance. However, one needs to be aware of the common drawbacks in this literature. First, the causality and endogeneity issues mentioned above remain an issue even in many recent studies. For instance, in studies on the relation between performance and director networks, it is important to realize that the positive correlation between connections and performance may not result from interlocks improving performance but from connections being a proxy for past good performance. Second, selection biases are prominent in director network research. Some studies focus on the largest companies only or on an industry, which may reduce the integrity of the key network measures used. Third, many (especially early) studies do not appropriately control for factors (such as CEO, board, firm, and industry characteristics) that may influence the dependent variable, hampering the accuracy and generalizability of the results.

ANALYZING DIRECTOR NETWORKS

Network Measures

Director networks can be measured or proxied in the following ways:

- The existence of (external) connections

The basic method to quantify director networks consists of the use of dummy variables that identify whether directors are sitting on more than one board (they are then tagged as "connected"). The limitations of the dummy variable approach are obvious. A director with multiple connections (sitting on more than two boards) is treated in the same way as a director with only one connection. Hence, the dummy variable approach fails to capture the impact of directors with large networks. Nor does it capture the location of a director in the overall network, which is important for network functions such as information gathering.

- The basic centrality measure: degree or the number of connections

Degree stands for the number of directors connected to a specific director. By counting the number of connections, the level of connectedness of directors with multiple board positions can be compared. Variations on this theme consist of using the number of external board positions (external director connections). This simple approach has been widely used in academic research as an indicator of a manager's network influence. However, it does not capture the positional advantage in the director networks, which makes the number of connections an inferior measure for studying the information collection efficiency.

- Other centrality measures

Developed within graph theory, centrality measures consist of the numbers and ratios that reflect the network properties of a vertex in a graph. Centrality measures have been widely used in computer science, biology, and sociology studies, where network properties can affect individuals' behavior. Centrality measures such as betweenness and closeness show how central a director is within the whole network, which makes them excellent measures of information collection efficiency. An example of how to calculate centrality measures can be found in the following sections.

Graph Theory in Practice

Figure 9.1 depicts the director network surrounding Andy Hornby, the CEO of HBOS plc, a banking and insurance company. In 2006, Andy Hornby was also a non-executive director in the life assurance and unit trust company St. James's Place plc, and in the retail companies GUS plc and Home Retail Group plc. This example is a fragment of a complete director network where a director is denoted by a *vertex* (or node). A connection between two vertices is called a *link* (or edge, tie). The system of these vertices and links is a *graph* (or map). As links between two vertices are established when two directors are sitting on the same board, Andy Hornby's four directorships create connections with 38 directors. Besides Andy Hornby, HBOS and St. James's Place shared another two directors: Jo Dawson and James Crosby. Jo Dawson was an executive director in HBOS and a non-executive director in St. James's Place. James Crosby was the CEO of HBOS before Andy Hornby. Similarly, GUS and Home Retail Group shared three directors,

Oliver Stocken, John Coombe, and Terry Duddy. Oliver Stocken was a non-executive director in GUS and chairman of the board in Home Retail Group. John Coombe was a non-executive director of GUS and a senior non-executive director of Home Retail Group. Terry was an executive director of GUS and the CEO in Home Retail Group.

A sequence between two vertices, visiting no vertices more than once, is called a path. In Figure 9.1, there exist multiple paths between John Peace and Richard Ashton. For example: Peace—Duddy—Ashton, Peace—Stocken—Ashton, Peace—Coombe—Hughes—Ashton—etc. The length of a path is the number of links it comprises and a *geodesic path* is the shortest path between two vertices (which is not necessarily unique). In the above example, both Peace—Duddy—Ashton and Peace—Stocken—Ashton are both geodesic paths between Peace and Ashton.

A CEO's network grows stronger when he accepts more external directorships. Reciprocal interlocks (the mutual exchange of directors) also occur more frequently. Such a network can be used to extend CEO power which could enable the CEO to influence board decision-making (possibly to his own benefit). The connections built for the purpose of accumulating managerial influence are referred to as *managerial influ-*

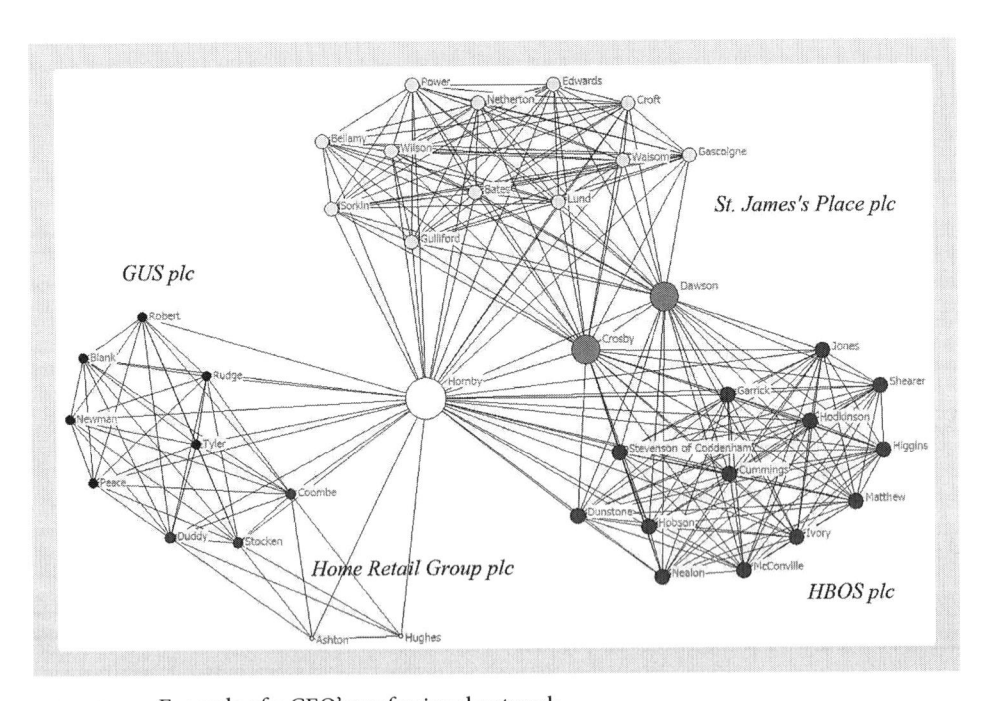

FIGURE 9.1. Example of a CEO's professional network

Notes: This figure depicts the director networks surrounding Andy Hornby (white circle in the middle of the graph), who serves in four companies, including St. James's Place (upper), HBOS (right), Home Retail Group (bottom), and GUS (left). Directors in these four companies are represented as circles (vertices) around Andy Hornby. Directors in the same company are clustered together. Directors sitting on the same board established links between them. In this figure, the lines between circles represent the links between directors. The size of a circle is proportional to the number of links it has.

Source: Renneboog and Zhao (2011).

ence-oriented connections. Networks not only increase a director's influence but also bring additional skills, knowledge, and information to the company, which may lead to corporate governance and performance improvements. Connections maintained for the sake of information collection are referred to as *information value*-oriented connections. Centrality measures that capture the level of connectedness in the local region based on adjacent connections are called the *direct centrality measures* (degree, eigenvector centrality). They are used to measure managerial influence-oriented connections. Centrality measures that analyze the position of a director in the entire network based on distances between target director and other directors are called *indirect centrality measures* (e.g. closeness and betweenness). They are used to evaluate information value-oriented networks. In order to explain various centrality measures, we construct a hypothetical network (Figure 9.2) with six companies and ten directors. In Table 9.1, the numbers refer to firms and letters stand for directors (Table 9.1, Panel A).

The *degree* centrality of a vertex is calculated as the number of links held by that vertex. In the above example, the number of links for director *a* is 6, so director *a* has degree centrality of 6. This can also be seen from Panel A of Table 9.1, director *a* is connected to two directors in company 3 and four directors in company 5. Note that the degree counts the vertex affected by factors influencing board size.

The *closeness* of a vertex is defined as the sum of geodesic distances between this vertex and all other vertices that can be reached. Higher closeness value in fact suggests the vertex is further from other vertices. Thus this definition of closeness is also referred to as "farness" by some scholars. Another way to define closeness, which is more commonly used in the research, is to calculate the inverse of the sum of all geodesic paths from the focal vertex to any other vertex. Compared to the previous definition, the high closeness value here means a shorter distance to all other vertices, which suggests the target vertex is more central in the network.

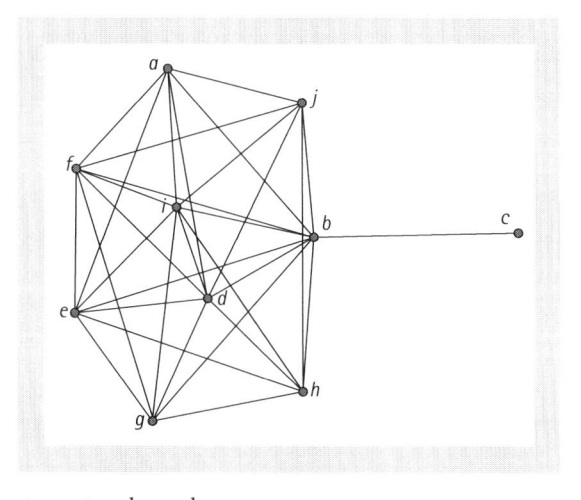

FIGURE 9.2. A director network graph

Note: This figure is a hypothetical director network graph used for centrality illustration.

Table 9.1. An example of a director network

Panel A: Example of a network

Company	Director	Company	Director
1	a	5	a
		5	b
2	b	5	j
2	c	5	f
		5	d
3	a		
3	e	6	b
3	f	6	g
		6	d
4	h	6	e
4	d	6	h
4	i	6	i
4	j		

Panel B: Centrality measures

	Degree	Closeness	Eigenvector	Betweenness
a	6	12	0.299	0.167
b	9	9	0.379	8.933
c	1	17	0.054	0.000
d	8	10	0.372	0.933
e	7	11	0.336	0.567
f	7	11	0.336	0.567
g	6	12	0.299	0.167
h	6	12	0.293	0.367
i	8	10	0.372	0.933
j	6	12	0.293	0.367

Notes: The panels explain how director networks are mathematically recorded and calculated. Panel A is an overview of the example network. Panel B shows the basic centrality measures calculated for this example network.

Source: Renneboog and Zhao (2011).

The *eigenvector centrality* of a vertex equals the sum of all adjacent vertices' eigenvector centrality scores. This calculation process begins with assigning a random score to all the vertices. At each iteration, the score of vertex v is calculated as the sum of all adjacent vertices' scores received in the previous iteration multiplied by a constant. This process is repeated for a sufficient number of times until the eigenvector centrality for each vertex is stable. The advantage of eigenvector centrality over other centrality measures is that it does not only capture how many vertices are linked to the target vertex (as degree centrality does), but also includes the centrality of those adjacent vertices (the degree of these linked vertices). Hence, a vertex will have a higher eigenvector centrality score if it is connected to more vertices with higher centrality scores.

The *betweenness* of a vertex is defined as the sum of its betweenness ratios. The betweenness ratio is the number of geodesic paths from any other two vertices (say s and t) passing through the focal vertex, divided by the number of all geodesic paths between s and t. In the above example, no geodesic path needs to pass director c, therefore his betweenness score is zero. Director b has a high betweenness score, because b is the only director connected to c. Thus, geodesic paths between director c and all the other directors need to pass director b, which leads to the high betweenness score of director b.

The resulting centrality measures for all directors in the above example can be seen in Panel B above.

Degree and eigenvector centrality measures focus on direct connections to adjacent vertices only. Closeness and betweenness analyze the distance between the target vertex and all other vertices (closeness) or the position of the target vertex on other geodesic paths (betweenness). Therefore, we categorize degree and eigenvector centrality measures as direct measures. Closeness and betweenness are regarded as indirect measures. Networks designed to accumulate managerial influence and information collection ability can be measured by different types of centrality measures. A CEO with many external directorships which contribute to his reputation and fame among the connected companies may be more influential. Such influence is captured by the direct measures. Valuable information can spread through the connections in the network and reach directors depending on network structure. A higher closeness score implies a shorter distance to other vertices, in which case the CEO is able to acquire the information earlier. A CEO's high betweenness score implies that he may be standing on the "brokerage position" between some otherwise separated groups. Such a position enhances the probability that a CEO receives new information earlier. Hence, centrality measures capturing indirect links (closeness and betweenness) are used to measure the access to information through networks. One may argue that direct connections bring in information as well. This is true, but direct centrality measures are inferior to indirect ones in terms of quantifying information collection efficiency. For instance, directors with numerous direct connections in an isolated corner of the whole network can hardly receive information as quickly as directors in the center of the network (even with fewer direct connections). Moreover, as suggested by Granovetter (1973), information from direct connections is likely to be of lower quality than that from distant connections, because directly connected individuals tend to have redundant (similar) information sources. Therefore, the indirect centrality measures are better proxies of the information collection efficiency of the CEO's director network.

Renneboog and Zhao (2011) examine the relation between directors' networks, CEO compensation, and pay-for-performance. They distinguish between two functions of networks: the accumulation of managerial influence and the collection of valuable information and resources. The former implies that powerful CEOs may take advantage of their position to extract high benefits such as compensation at a cost to the shareholders. The latter function is beneficial to the company (and the director). The existing literature does not allow for this difference, but they make this distinction by employing network centrality measures at the direct and indirect levels. Strong direct networks (measured by degree and eigenvector centrality) proxy for managerial influence, whereas strong indirect networks (measured by closeness and betweenness) proxy for the information-collection value. Renneboog and Zhao (2011) find that both strong direct and indirect networks are rewarded by higher compensation (fixed salary, bonus, and equity-based compensation) and that pay-for-performance sensitivity decreases in the direct centrality measure. The combination of high CEO compensation and low pay-for-performance corroborates the managerial influence hypothesis. While the information value of indirect networks is reflected in higher CEO compensation, this function of networks does not influence the pay-for-performance relation.

Director Networks from Non-professional Origins

Directors do not only have networks through their executive and non-executive positions on corporate boards (*professional networks*), but also develop networks that originate from shared high school, college, or university education, elite or sports club memberships, or other social occasions (*social networks*). Kirchmaier and Kollo (2007) and Hwang and Kim (2009) demonstrate that the larger a director's social network, the higher is his compensation. Brown et al. (2009) and Engelberg et al. (2009) discover that past connections are also important components in the CEO networks and also have a positive impact on the size of executive compensation. Furthermore, the authors discuss the social connections' negative impact on pay-for-performance sensitivity and turnover-for-performance sensitivity. Lastly, Kirchmaier and Stathopoulos (2008) find that a CEO's social networks hamper firm performance.

In most of the existing literature on networks, only one type of network is analyzed, (professional, usually), which jeopardizes the integrity of the measurement of director networks and affects the accuracy of centrality measures. To solve this problem, one needs to consider director networks from different origins simultaneously. The current professional connections form the *primary network*. Connections from all other origins (including past professional networks) form *secondary networks*. The aggregation of all such types of networks is referred to as the *hybrid network* of a director. Secondary networks can enhance or supplement the primary one. For example, managers with the same education background (a degree from the same school) may be more closely related than otherwise. Secondary networks can also establish links between people not connected through primary networks. For example, directors working for different companies can still be friends with each other thanks to their common club membership.

Renneboog and Zhao (2010b) study the hybrid director network and its impact on CEO compensation. They suggest that the directors' primary networks (current professional connections) are "enhanced" by secondary networks based on past director, educational, and nationality-related connections. Their results confirm that director networks enhanced by means of past, educational, and nationality relations are positively correlated with a CEO's total remuneration while controlling for many other explanations, including corporate performance and ownership concentration.

Corporate Networks and Other Corporate Governance Issues

Besides CEO compensation and turnover, other corporate governance issues may be related to director networks. Renneboog and Zhao (2010a) study the CEO labor market and director networks. Their results show that a CEO's direct networks (capturing managerial power) shield him from dismissal when performance drops; CEOs' information collection networks improve their chances of departing from their current position.

M&As may be based on decisions influenced by networks as connections facilitate strategic information transmission between companies. When an executive director holds a non-executive position in another firm, more information about the latter company (e.g. its suitability as a takeover target) may flow to the former firm. Ishii and Xuan (2010) find evidence that connected CEOs have a larger chance of being rewarded with a larger bonus for completing an M&A transaction. They also demonstrate that abnormal stock returns are lower and that more target firm directors are retained in the combined company if the target and the acquirer were connected through their directors prior to the M&A.

CEO and director insider trading may result from lack of monitoring and/or leakage of price-sensitive information. Both factors may be induced by director networks. Networks may yield directors better information access, which enables them to spot insider trading opportunities in the connected companies. Therefore, we expect that well-connected directors are more likely to trade on insider information.

Recently, the network of remuneration consultants has been studied. An interesting finding is that CEO compensation increases with the number of these consultants hired by the company, ceteris paribus (Conyon et al., 2009, and Kabir and Minhat, 2010). When two companies are hiring the same remuneration consultant, they can be considered connected through the remuneration consultant's networks. Renneboog and Zhao (2011) find that companies are more generous with CEO compensation when the remuneration consultant networks they belong to are larger.

Conclusion and Future Research Agenda

In this chapter, we have shown the influence of director networks on corporate governance in the past and today. We have reviewed the development of director networks since the early 20th century and summarized the main regulatory changes. In order to get a better understanding of director networks, we have presented a survey of director network research and illustrated the most common and latest research on network measurement. Several studies point out that director networks have a significant impact on remuneration, turnover, and some other corporate governance issues. In remuneration-related studies, most researchers conclude that excessive director networks contribute to large and inefficient CEO compensation. Analysis with advanced network measures further reveals that CEOs use director networks to accumulate managerial power and acquire larger compensation without achieving better performance. In research on director networks and the managerial labor market, the results suggest that the managerial labor market is influenced by networks: directors with larger networks are more likely to find new positions. Lastly, the debate on whether director networks affect firm performance is still unclear. On one hand, director networks can be abused and can shift the balance of power in the boardroom to the CEO. On the other hand, director networks bring information and expertise into the company, which is particularly valuable when the firm is entering a new business or considering takeovers. To sum up, director networks research—a new research area in financial economics with continuously advancing techniques—has already generated many interesting results. This interdisciplinary research still has significant academic potential. We summarize a few topics for the future research agenda.

Methodology

The endogeneity problem in director network studies has not been solved. For instance, in the relationship between performance and networks the causality problem still remains: do networks lead to better performance or do networks merely reflect past corporate performance (as reflected in the number of outside directorships a director subsequently accumulates)? More advanced econometric techniques and carefully chosen instrumental variables may contribute to the resolution of this problem.

Scope of Networks

Currently, in most studies only directors' professional connections are used to map networks. Yet professional connections are only one part of the true network. A more comprehensive network should also contain past (professional) connections as well as links based on common educational background, membership of social, elite, or sports clubs, nationality etc. Although the private nature of non-professional connections makes data collection on social networks difficult, some early attempts on social connections show promising results.

Network effects on corporate governance

The role of networks could still be studied further for some more aspects of corporate decision-making. For instance, M&A activity may be influenced by director networks. Also, cross-country studies on director network effects should also become more prominent because director networks are shaped by local regulation and local culture. Thus director networks are likely to differ in their structures and impacts across countries.

Notes

1. For instance, in the US, the Council of Institutional Investors proposes that full-time directors should have no more than two other directorships. In the UK, full-time executive directors should not have directorships in other FTSE 100 companies.

References

Aaronovitch, S. (1961). *The Ruling Class: A Study of British Finance Capital.* London: Lawrence and Wishart.
Agrawal, A., and Knoeber, C. (2001). "Do Some Outside Directors Play a Political Role?" *Journal of Law and Economics*, 44(1): 179–98.
Barnea, A., and Guedj, I. (2009). "Director Networks, EFA 2007," Ljubljana Meetings Paper, University of Texas at Austin.
Baruch, F. (1962). *Grote Macht in een Klein Land. Een Beeld van het Monopoliekapitaalen zijn Invloed in Nederland.* Amsterdam: Pegasus.
Baysinger, B., and Butler, H. (1985). "Corporate Governance and the Board of Directors: Performance Effects of Changes in Board Composition," *Journal of Law and Economics and Organization*, 1: 101–24.
Beesley, M. (1951). "Concentration in Midland Metal Industries," Ph.D. thesis, Birmingham University.
Brandeis, L. D. (1913). *Other People's Money and How the Bankers Use It.* New York: Frederick A. Stokes.
Brown, R., Lee, N., Gao, E., and Stathopoulos, K. (2009). "What Are Friends For?" CEO Networks, Pay and Corporate Governance, Working Paper, The University of Melbourne.
Burris, V. (1987). "The Political Partisanship of American Business: A Study of Political Action Committees," *American Sociology Review*, 52: 732–44.

Burt, R. (1983). *Corporate Profits and Cooptation: Networks of Market Constraints and Directorate Ties in the American Economy.* New York: Academic Press.

Carpenter, M. A., and Westphal, J. D. (2001). "The Strategic Context of External Network Ties: Examining the Impact of Director Appointments on Board Involvement in Strategic Decision Making," *Academy of Management Journal,* 44(4): 639–60.

Carrington, P. (1981). "Horizontal Co-optation through Corporate Interlocks," Ph.D. thesis, Department of Sociology, University of Toronto.

Cochran, P., Wood R., and Jones, T. (1985). "The Composition of Boards of Directors and Incidence of Golden Parachutes," *Academy of Management Journal,* 28: 664–71.

Conyon, M., Peck, S., and Sadler, G. (2009). "Compensation Consultants and Executive Pay: Evidence from the United States and the United Kingdom," *The Academy of Management Perspectives,* 23: 34–55.

Core, J., Holthausen, R., and Larcker, D. (1999). "Corporate Governance, Chief Executive Officer Compensation and Firm Performance," *Journal of Financial Economics,* 51: 371–406.

Crespi-Cladera, R., and Pascual-Fuster, B. (2008). "Executive Directors' Pay and Networks in Spanish Listed Companies," Working Paper, Universitat Illes Balears.

Dalzell, R. (1987). *Enterprising Elite: The Boston Associates and the World they Made.* Cambridge, MA: Harvard University Press.

D'Aveni, R., and Kesner, I. (1993). "Top Managerial Prestige, Power, and Tender Offer Response: A Study of Elite Social Networks and Target Firm Cooperation during Takeovers," *Organization Science,* 4(2): 123–51.

Davis, G. (1991). "Agents without Principles? The Spread of the Poison Pill through the Intercorporate Network," *Administrative Science Quarterly,* 36: 583–613.

—— (1994). "The Interlock Network as a Self-reproducing Social Structure," Unpublished manuscript, Kellogg Graduate School, Northwestern University.

—— and Stout, S. (1992). "Organization Theory and the Market for Corporate Control, 1980–1990," *Administrative Science Quarterly,* 37: 605–33.

—— Yoo, M., and Baker, W. (2003). "The Small World of the American Corporate Elite, 1982–2001," *Strategic Organization,* 1: 301–26.

Devos, E., Prevost, A., and Puthenpurackal, J. (2006). "Are Interlocked Directors Effective Monitors?" Working Paper, University of Texas at El Paso.

Domhoff, G. (2006). *Who Rules America? Power, Politics, and Social Change,* 5th edition. New York: McGraw-Hill.

Dooley, P. (1969). "The Interlocking Directorate," *The American Economic Review,* 59: 314–23.

Engelberg, J., Gao, P., and Parsons, C. (2009). "The Value of a Rolodex: CEO Pay and Personal Networks," Working Paper, University of North Carolina.

Fennema, M., and Schijf, H. (1978). "Analyzing Interlocking Directorates: Theory and Methods," *Social Networks,* l: 297–332.

Fich, E., and Shivdasani, A. (2006). "Are Busy Boards Effective Monitors?" *The Journal of Finance,* 61: 689–724.

—— and White, L. J. (2003). "CEO Compensation and Turnover: The Effect of Mutually Interlocked Boards," *Wake Forest Law Review,* 38: 935–59.

Fligstein, N., and Markowitz, L. (1993). "Financial Reorganization of American Corporations in the 1980s," in W. J. Wilson (ed.), *Sociology and the Public Agenda.* Beverly Hills, CA: Sage, 185–206.

GRANOVETTER, M. (1973). "The Strength of Weak Ties," *American Journal of Sociology*, 78(6): 1360–80.

GUTIERREZ, L., and POMBO, C. (2010). "Outside Directors, Board Interlocks and Firm Performance: Empirical Evidence from Colombian Business Groups," Working Paper, Universidad del Rosario.

HALLOCK, K. (1997). "Reciprocal Interlocking Boards of Directors and Executive Compensation," *Journal of Financial and Quantitative Analysis*, 32: 331–44.

HAUNSCHILD, P. (1993). "Interorganizational Imitation: the Impact of Interlocks on Corporate Acquisition Activity," *Administrative Science Quarterly*, 38: 564–92.

HEINZE, T. (2002). "Die Struktur der Personalverflechtung Großer Deutscher Aktiengesellschaften Zwischen 1989 und 2001," *Zeitschrift für Soziologie*, 31(5): 391–410.

HENDERSON, D. (2010). *Big Oil and their Bankers in the Persian Gulf: Four Horsemen, Eight Families and their Global Intelligence, Narcotics and Terror Network*. CreateSpace.

HIGGS, D. (2003). *Review of the Role and Effectiveness of Non-Executive Directors*. London: Department of Trade and Industry/HMSO.

HOCHBERG, Y., LJUNGQVIST, A., and LU, Y. (2007). "Whom You Know Matters: Venture Capital Networks and Investment Performance," *The Journal of Finance*, 62: 251–301.

HWANG, B., and KIM, S. (2009). "It Pays to Have Friends," *Journal of Financial Economics*, 93: 138–58.

ISHII, J., and XUAN, Y. (2010). "Acquirer-Target Social Ties and Merger Outcomes," Working Paper, Stanford Graduate School of Business.

JEIDELS, O. (1905). *Grossbanken zur Industrie mit besonderer Berücksichtigung der Eisenindustrie*. Liepzig: Duncker & Humblot.

KABIR, R., and MINHAT, M. (2010). "Multiple Compensation Consultants and CEO Pay," Working Paper, University of Twente.

KHANNA, T., and THOMAS, C. (2009). "Synchronicity and Firm Interlocks in an Emerging Market," *Journal of Financial Economics*, 92(2): 182–204.

KIEL, G. C., and NICHOLSON, G. J. (2006). "Multiple Directorships and Corporate Performance in Australian Listed Companies," *Corporate Governance: An International Review*, 14(6): 530–46.

KIRCHMAIER, T., and KOLLO, M. (2007). "The Role of Prestige and Networks in Outside Director Appointments," Working Paper, University of Manchester.

—— and STATHOPOULOS, K. (2008). "From Fiction to Fact: The Impact of CEO Social Networks," FMG Discussion Papers, Financial Markets Group.

KOENIG, T. (1979). "Interlocking Directorates among the Largest American Corporations and their Significance for Corporate Political Activity," Ph.D. thesis, University of California.

KRAMARZ, F., and THESMAR, D. (2006). "Social Networks in the Boardroom," IZA Discussion Paper No. 1940.

KRANTZ, M. (2002). "Web of Board Members Ties Together Corporate America," *USA Today*.

KUHNEN, C. (2006). "Business Networks, Corporate Governance and Contracting in the Mutual Fund Industry," *Journal of Finance*, 64(5): 2185–220.

LANG, J., and LOCKHART, D. (1990). "Increased Environmental Uncertainty and Changes in Board of Director Linkage Patterns: The U.S. Trunk Airlines during Deregulation," *Academy of Management Journal*, 33: 106–28.

LARCKER, D., RICHARDSON, S., SEARY, A., and TUNA, I. (2006). "Back Door between Directors and Executive Compensation," Working Paper, The Wharton School, University of Pennsylvania.

LIU, Y. (2008). "CEO Network and CEO Turnover," Working Paper, University of Maryland.

MEEUSEN, W., and CUYVERS, L. (1985). "The Interaction between Interlocking Directorships and the Economic Behaviour of Companies," in F. N. Stokman, R. Ziegler, and J. Scott (eds.), *Networks of Corporate Power: A Comparative Analysis of Ten Countries*. Oxford: Polity Press.

MIZRUCHI, M. (1982). *The American Corporate Network 1904–1974*. Beverly Hills, CA: Sage.

—— (1996). "What Do Interlocks Do? An Analysis, Critique, and Assessment of Research on Interlocking Directorates," *Annual Review of Sociology*, 22: 271–98.

—— and KOENIG, T. (1986). "Economic Sources of Corporate Political Consensus: An Examination of Inter-industry Relations," *American Sociology Review*, 5: 482–91.

MYINT, Y., VYAKARNAM, S., and NEW, M. (2005). "The Effect of Social Capital in New Venture Creation: the Cambridge High-Technology Cluster," *Strategic Change*, 14: 165–77.

ONG, C., WAN, D., and ONG, K. (2003). "An Exploratory Study on Interlocking Directorates in Listed Firms in Singapore," *Corporate Governance: An International Review*, 11(4): 322–34.

PALMER, D., BARBER, B., ZHOU, X., and SOYAL, Y. (1995). "The Friendly and Predatory Acquisition of Large U.S. Corporations in the 1960s: The Other Contested Terrain," *American Sociology Review*, 60: 469–99.

PRINZ, E. (2006). "Corporate Governance and the Uncertain Role of Interlocking Directorates: Director Networks in Germany and their Impact on Financial Performance," Working Paper 1061001, Université de Bourgogne–LEG/Fargo (Research Center in Finance, Organizational Architecture and Governance).

RATCLIFF, R. (1980). "Banks and Corporate Lending: An Analysis of the Impact of the Internal Structure of the Capitalist Class on the Lending Behavior of Banks," *American Sociological Review*, 45: 553–70.

RENNEBOOG, L., and ZHAO, Y. (2010a). "CEO Turnover, Succession and Director Networks," Working Paper, Tilburg University.

—— —— (2010b). "The Role of Directors' Professional and Social Networks," Working Paper, Tilburg University.

—— —— (2011). "Us Knows Us in the UK: On Director Networks and CEO Compensation," *Journal of Corporate Finance*, 17(4): 1132–57.

RICHARDSON, R. (1987). "Directorship Interlocks and Corporate Profitability," *Administrative Science Quarterly*, 32: 367–86.

SANTELLA, P., DRAGO, C., POLO, A., and GAGLIARDI, E. (2008). "A Comparison of the Director Networks of the Main Listed Companies in France, Germany, Italy, the United Kingdom, and the United States," Working Paper, Bank of Italy.

SANTOS, R., DA SILVEIRA, A., and BARROS, L. (2009). "Board Interlocking in Brazil: Directors' Participation in Multiple Companies and its Effect on Firm Value," Working Paper, University of São Paulo.

SCOTT, W. (1992). *Organizations: Rational, Natural, and Open Systems*. Englewood Cliff, NY: Prentice-Hall.

SHAW, G., and ALEXANDER, A. (2006). "Interlocking Directorates and the Knowledge Transfer of Supermarket Retail Techniques from North America to Britain," *The International Review of Retail, Distribution and Consumer Research*, 16: 375–94.

SINGH, H., and HARIANTO, I. (1989). "Management-Board Relationships, Takeover Risk, and the Adoption of Golden Parachutes," *Academy of Management Journal*, 32(1): 327–24.

STEARNS, L., and MIZRUCHI, M. (1993a). "Corporate Financing: Economic and Social Aspects," in R. Swedberg (ed.), *Explorations in Economic Sociology*. New York: Russell Sage, 279–307.

—— —— (1993b). "Board Composition & Corporate Financing: The Impact of Financial Institution Representation on Borrowing," *Academy of Management Journal*, 36: 603–18.

STOKMAN, F., VAN DER KNOOP, J., and WASSEUR, F. (1988). "Interlocks in the Netherlands: Stability and Careers in the Period 1960–1980," *Social Networks*, 10: 183–208.

SUBRAHMANYAM, A. (2008). "Social Networks and Corporate Governance," *European Financial Management*, 14(4): 633–62.

US House of Representatives (1965). "Report on Interlocks in Corporate Management," Staff of the Antitrust Subcommittee of the House of Commerce on the Judiciary, 89th Congress.

WADE, J., O'REILLY, C. A. III, and CHANDRATAT, I. (1990). "Golden Parachutes: CEOs and the Exercise of Social Influence," *Administrative Science Quarterly*, 35: 587–603.

WESTPHAL, J. D., and ZAJAC, E. (1996). "Director Reputation, CEO/Board Power, and the Dynamics of Board Interlocks," *Administrative Science Quarterly*, 41(3): 507–29.

ZAJAC, E. (1988). "Interlocking Directorates as an Inter-organizational Strategy," *Academy of Management Journal*, 31: 428–38.

CHAPTER 10

EXECUTIVE COMPENSATION AND CORPORATE GOVERNANCE

What Do We "Know" and Where Are We Going?

PAMELA BRANDES AND PALASH DEB

INTRODUCTION

"WHAT do you do for a living?" the conversation begins.

"I'm a university professor in a business school," I (the first author) reply.

"So, what do you study?" says the stranger.

"Executive compensation and corporate governance," I reply.

Even after writing in this area for more than a decade, the reaction of my new acquaintance is nearly always the same.

"Ohhh. That is a hot area right now!" The topic rarely fails to engender an animated discussion, whether in the (Wall Street) journal, the classroom, or even over dinner. A frequent follow-up question is, "What's new in executive compensation?"

In this chapter, we provide some insight into this question by introducing a framework that integrates corporate governance research related to executive compensation published in premier journals within management, accounting, finance, and economics since the Financial Accounting Standards Board (FASB) introduced FAS 123 in the US (i.e. changing the accounting for stock option compensation). These papers represent an exclusive cohort from which we expect modern classics to emerge. Although the discipline of law is a significant contributor to the domain of corporate governance and compensation, little of that work is empirical, and hence represents an unfortunate, but necessary, omission.

Although several reviews of executive compensation have been written (e.g. Bebchuk and Fried 2004; Finkelstein et al., 2008), we perceived a need for an integrative review across disciplines. We categorize the factors "leading" to compensation into internal, institutional, and market forms of governance, and summarize how these factors affect executive pay outcomes including pay levels, structure, and performance metrics. We also investigate how characteristics of both the firm and its CEO are related to pay. Figure 10.1 demonstrates our attempt to deduce themes across these domains into a larger conceptual framework. Finally, we look at some of the consequences of pay—some more desirable, some less desirable. Table 10.2 demonstrates the variety of theoretical frameworks used within the articles surveyed for this chapter.

INTERNAL GOVERNANCE

Board Power

Independence

Board independence continues to be a popular scapegoat for excesses in compensation. Much of this work has focused on the ability of boards to monitor management, and on how such monitoring may help rein in compensation. For example, Collins, Gong, and Li (2009) measured independence with structural measures related to the board, including proportion of insiders, "gray" outsiders, outsiders appointed by sitting executives, and tenure. Similarly, Pollock, Fischer, and Wade (2002) find that structural power (namely, duality) significantly increased the likelihood of repricing stock options, although other structural indicators (e.g. board appointments post-CEO entry, staggered boards) did not have the anticipated effects.

When the New York Stock Exchange (NYSE) required compensation, audit, and nominating committees to have independent directors in the early 2000s, boards lacking this requirement got the message, such that subsequent CEO compensation was associated with decreases in non-equity compensation (Chhaochharia and Grinstein, 2009), particularly in firms where there were no outside blockholders on the board of directors. However, Ittner, Larcker, and Rajan (1997) found no evidence that CEOs with more power over boards were able to sway the importance of financial metrics toward more non-financial performance metrics—incentives which have been cited as easier ways to increase CEO pay. From yet another perspective, Laux (2008) suggests that completely independent boards actually push CEOs to demand more compensation in the forms of larger severance arrangements and more stock options, as CEOs know that termination may be more likely. Similarly, Westphal (1998) finds that increases in structural board independence actually generate larger increases in subsequent CEO compensation due to higher levels of CEO interpersonal influence behaviors such as ingratiation and persuasion. Nonetheless, the general idea that board independence promotes increased monitoring and better governance has caught on, as evidenced not only from the increases in board independence to levels near 80 percent in recent years,

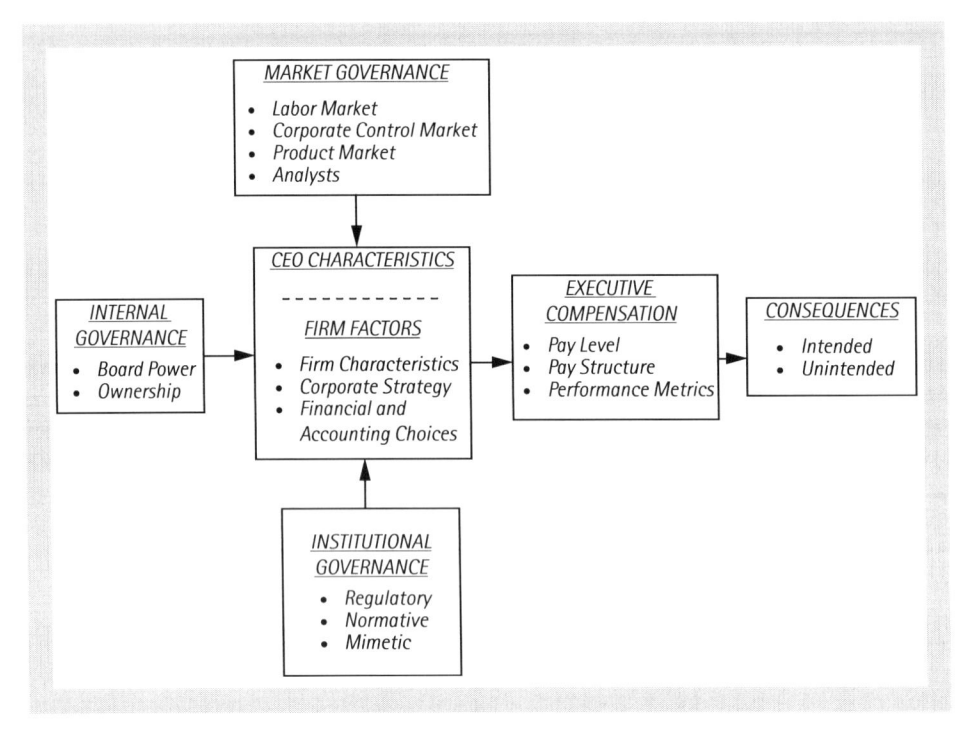

FIGURE 10.1. Determinants and consequences of executive compensation

but also by both exchange listing requirements and legislation, which will be discussed further later.

Boards and their Committees

Daily et al. (1998) suggested that perhaps it is not the full board, but the characteristics of the board's compensation committee that predict executive compensation. However, they found no evidence that a greater percentage of beholden directors is associated with greater compensation. This is in contrast to more recent work by Chhaochharia and Grinstein (2009) who suggest that "board level attributes are more important than committee-level attributes, consistent with the notion that the [full] board has [ultimate] power over the compensation committee…" (p. 244). Recent work also suggests the importance of board diligence in monitoring as a way to improve compensation practices. For example, consistent with a structural perspective, Laksmana (2008) finds that compensation committees with more members, and that meet more often, have better compensation disclosure practices. In addition, board diligence can also take the form of aligning incentives with strategic decisions. Harford and Li (2007) find that "strong" boards link pay and performance more directly, after mergers and acquisitions (M&As), whereas "weak" boards seemingly tolerate greater delinking of pay and performance post-acquisition.

Table 10.1. Premier publications explored for this review*

Accounting	The Accounting Review
	Contemporary Accounting Research
	Journal of Accounting and Economics
	Journal of Accounting Research
	Review of Accounting Studies
Economics	American Economic Review
	International Economic Review
	Journal of Economic Theory
	Journal of Political Economy
	Quarterly Journal of Economics
Finance	Journal of Finance
	Journal of Financial and Quantitative Analysis
	Review of Financial Studies
	Review of Economics and Statistics
Management	**Academy of Management Journal**
	Academy of Management Review
	Administrative Science Quarterly
	Organization Science
	Strategic Management Journal

Note: * Journals in bold are cited within this review.

Ownership

Institutional

Over the last 15 years, institutional ownership (which had reached a level of about 70 percent of total ownership for S&P 1500 firms in 2009) has received increasing attention in CEO compensation studies. Cadman, Klasa, and Matsunaga (2010) suggest that ExecuComp firms have lower institutional ownership concentration but higher pay-for-performance sensitivity compared to their non-ExecuComp counterparts. Chhaochharia and Grinstein (2009) suggest that institutional ownership can serve as a substitute for board monitoring, such that firms with greater institutional ownership concentration can lower total CEO compensation. Compensation may also result from the extent to which (institutional) owners are beholden to the firm in a way that may compromise monitoring. For example, David, Kochhar, and Levitas (1998) find that pressure-sensitive investors (i.e. those dependent on the firm for business) are unable to influence compensation in a manner consistent with shareholder interests, whereas investors that are pressure insensitive (i.e. those lacking such biases) are associated with lower total compensation and with greater proportions of long-term incentives within the pay mix.

Hartzell and Starks (2003) suggest that greater institutional ownership concentration is associated with better pay-for-performance sensitivity and may curb executive

Table 10.2. Examples of theoretical frameworks used in representative studies

Topical Area From Figure 10.1	Author(s)	Year	Journal	Theoretical Framework
Internal Governance	Wasserman, N.	2006	Academy of Management Journal	Agency and Stewardship Theories
	Hartzell, J. C., & Starks, L. T.	2003	Journal of Finance	Agency Theory (e.g. institutional monitoring)*
	Pollock, T. G., Fischer, H. M., & Wade, J. B.	2002	Academy of Management Journal	CEO Power
Market Governance	Murphy, K. J. & Zábojník, J.	2004	American Economic Review	Human Capital Theory
	Aggarwal, R. K. & Samwick, A. A.	1999	Journal of Finance	Bertrand and Cournot Models of Product Market Competition
	Davila, A., & Penalva, F.	2006	Review of Accounting Studies	Agency Theory (e.g. bargaining power argument)*
CEO Characteristics & Firm Factors	Dencker, J. C.	2009	Administrative Science Quarterly	Relative Bargaining Power Theory
	Ortiz-Molina, H.	2007	Journal of Accounting & Economics	Agency Cost of Debt and Agency Cost of Equity Hypotheses
	Boyd, B. K. & Salamin, A.	2001	Strategic Management Journal	Strategic Reward Systems
	Sanders, W. G. & Tuschke, A.	2007	Academy of Management Journal	Institutional Theory (e.g. diffusion, legitimization, isomorphism etc.)
Institutional Governance	Berrone, P. & Gomez-Mejia, L. R.	2009	Academy of Management Journal	Institutional and Agency Theories
	Carter, M. E., Lynch, L. J., & Tuna, I.	2007	The Accounting Review	Institutional Theory*
	Conyon, M. J., Peck, S. I., & Sadler, G. V.	2001	Strategic Management Journal	Tournament Theory
Executive Compensation	Bertrand, M. & Mullainathan, S.	2001	Quarterly Journal of Economics	Agency Theory (skimming versus contracting)
	Gabaix, X. & Landier, A.	2008	Quarterly Journal of Economics	Extreme Value Theory

Note: * Paper does not explicitly identify theoretical framework used, though it is apparent from reading the paper.

compensation levels. However, others suggest that it is not just the percentage of holdings an institutional owner has at a specific firm, but also how "busy" that investor might be in terms of the investor's other portfolio holdings. For example, Dharwadkar, Goranova, Brandes, and Khan (2008) suggest that the positive effects of concentration at the firm level are compromised by simultaneous large holdings in other firms. Transience of institutional ownership may also affect monitoring ability (e.g. Dharwadkar et al., 2008) and be associated with specific compensation designs. Dikoli, Kulp, and Sedatole (2009) suggest that institutional owners with high turnover focus more on annual returns than on earnings in setting bonuses, and are not only more likely to provide equity in executive rewards, but also to award larger amounts.

CEO Ownership

Generally, the management literature suggests that CEO ownership is useful for creating alignment with shareholder interests. Using a stewardship approach, Wasserman (2006) found that CEOs in founder-owner controlled firms received less (cash) compensation, and that the percentage of executive ownership was inversely related to (cash) compensation. In contrast, significant management ownership is associated with higher CEO compensation within acquiring firms (Kroll et al., 1997). Others suggest that CEO ownership may align interests but only under certain conditions. Stoughton and Talmor (1999) suggest that, when shareholders have bargaining power in the design of compensation contracts, providing additional executive ownership may be superfluous. However, Ofek and Yermack (2000) note that while compensation-setters utilize equity in hopes of incentivizing managers to take appropriate risks, executives typically just sell their shares upon exercise to avoid compensation risk. Others have also studied the effects of "too much" executive ownership. Collins et al. (2009) find that larger CEO ownership was associated with more backdating of options "consistent with the notion that higher ownership increases CEOs' entrenchment and ability to influence their own pay" (p. 422). Although ownership is often touted as essential to incentive alignment, executive ownership as a percentage of the firm's total ownership has decreased in recent years.

FUTURE CONSIDERATIONS: INTERNAL GOVERNANCE

According to the New York Stock Exchange CG Rules S 303A.04(a), -.05(a), -.06, -.07(b) (NYSE Listed Company Manual, 2009), boards must not only have key committees (namely, nominating, audit, and compensation committees), but also ensure that the committee members are independent (as is also required in the UK). Consequently, board independence is currently more the norm than the exception. With median board independence amounting to 80 percent of board memberships among firms, only one or two board members are typically insiders. In summary, while board independence is likely to appear in future studies, it may be relegated to a control variable compared to other variables discussed in this review.

Currently, the literature is amazingly silent on issues of board member expertise. Under the Sarbanes-Oxley Act of 2002 (popularly known as SOX, 15 USC 7265 Section 407 Disclosure of Audit Committee Financial Expert, e.g. Banks and Banks, 2010), at least one member of the audit committee must be a "financial management expert." This person "has, through education and experience as a public accountant or auditor or a principal financial officer, comptroller, or principal accounting officer of an issuer, or from a position involving the performance of similar functions—(1) an understanding of generally accepted accounting principles and financial statements; (2) experience in—(A) the preparation or auditing of financial statements of generally comparable issuers; and (B) the application of such principles in connection with the accounting for estimates, accruals, and reserves; (3) experience with internal accounting controls; and (4) an understanding of audit committee functions."

In contrast, while compensation committee members must be "independent," they do not have to be "literate" (?!). While some might suggest that directors already would have to know quite a bit about compensation to serve on compensation committees effectively, formalizing the requirements regarding board choices and potential consequences of various compensation structures should improve incentive alignment. Imagine if a credential had to be earned regarding executive compensation whereby directors on the compensation committee (or, at the very least, a "compensation expert" on the compensation committee) had to pass (and maintain) credentials related to his/her executive compensation knowledge. Such directors would be sought out, and possibly paid even more, for their expertise. Currently, the National Association of Corporate Directors offers a "Certificate of Director Education," whereby a member must attend 12 hours of class time, but he/she does not take any examination to verify his/her comprehension.

Institutional ownership and investor activism continue to gain momentum. Using recent reports by Georgeson (2010: 18) we found that over the years 2007–10 an average of 37 percent of shareholder resolutions involved executive compensation. As a percentage of all votes cast, shareholders voted: 62 percent against, 35 percent for, and 3 percent abstained, on these resolutions in the 2010 Proxy Season (Georgeson, 2010: 24). Common entities raising executive compensation resolutions included pension funds and individuals (some of which have been referred to as corporate "gadflies" in the business press). It will be interesting to watch the emerging role of other large investors in compensation, particularly as their ownership stakes approach blockholder status, including the state (e.g. previous US bailout of GM), foreign owners (e.g. sovereign funds), as well as hedge funds (e.g. Warren Buffet and shareholders at Monsanto).

As of 2011, shareholders of firms with $75 million or more in public shares are entitled to vote on pay (Lucchetti, 2011). Since the Dodd-Frank Wall Street Reform and Consumer Protection Act went into effect, proxy solicitors contacted for their opinions regarding pay-for-performance resolutions (i.e. Institutional Shareholder Services) have made "no" recommendations on 12 percent of those they reviewed (Syre, 2011). As a specific example, 54 percent of voting shareholders recently rejected pay plans at Jacobs

Engineering (Orol, 2011). Such shareholder votes are only advisory, but directors that overrule shareholder desires might not be re-elected to boards; according to Georgeson (2010), "at least six of the 41 directors that received majority withhold/against votes were targeted...for poor compensation practices" (p. 5). Shareholder angst will likely continue in the future (particularly during difficult economic times), but hopefully boards listen to the most appropriate shareholders' interests and not just those of the "squeaky wheels." There have already been several legal challenges to the Dodd-Frank Bill, including a federal ruling stopping proxy access in 2012 whereby shareholders could have more easily nominated directors (Pearl Meyer and Partners, 2011).

Market Governance

Labor Market

Scholars vary in their prediction of a CEO's worth. From an economic perspective, Murphy and Zábojník (2004) suggest that much of the escalation in executive salaries is because CEO jobs are increasingly focused on portable rather than firm-specific skills, as reflected in the premium paid for outside hires. Others (e.g. Finkelstein and Boyd, 1998: 182) cite many industry-related factors that implicitly affect the labor market for CEOs, suggesting market growth, demand instability, industry concentration, and regulation as significant constraints on CEO marginal productivity, and therefore CEO compensation. Similarly, Kaplan (2008) in partial answer to the question "Are U.S. CEOs Overpaid?" suggests that general macroeconomic and market indicators explain more of executive compensation than factors such as failures in board monitoring. Specifically, he cites long-term data that suggest that while CEO pay may have reached high levels, so has firm performance; that average CEO tenure is down (implying an increased willingness by boards to remove underperformers); and that other highly compensated individuals (e.g. lawyers, hedge fund managers, professional athletes) have also fared well without engendering the same levels of outcry aimed at CEOs.

Others suggest that CEO productivity differences are due to information-processing capabilities, and that such capabilities vary. Henderson and Fredrickson (1996) suggest that firms present CEOs with unique information-processing demands as a function of the firm's approach to diversification, as well as its capital and R&D expenses. They find that the increased complexity of these strategic decisions is generally associated with more cash compensation, more long-term compensation, and, consequently, more total compensation. Similarly, Sanders and Carpenter (1998) suggest that the internationalization strategy of the firm increases informational complexity both for the CEOs and the boards that monitor them, which is then associated with greater percentages of compensation paid in the form of long-term incentives, and greater overall compensation.

In contrast, others suggest that the celebrity status of CEOs is a great contributor to executive compensation. Wade et al. (2006) find that market "kudos" in the form of recognition as a top CEO is associated with greater short-term abnormal returns which disappear over time, evidence which Wade et al. (2006: 656) suggest is the "burden of celebrity"—having to beat one's own excellent previous performance. Malmendier and Tate (2009) suggest these subsequent performance reversals partially result from the trappings of outside activities resulting from "superstar" status (i.e. writing books, additional directorships). Being a non-CEO top manager under such CEOs is positively associated with one's own compensation, although these award-winning CEOs benefit more (Graffin et al., 2008; Malmendier and Tate, 2009).

Corporate Control Market

Davila and Penalva (2006) found that CEOs sheltered by anti-takeover measures ensure more consistent compensation by having their compensation weighted more toward accounting-based measures than toward market-based ones. Similarly, Cheng and Indjejikian (2009) studied the effects of anti-takeover provisions introduced in the 1980s. They suggest that, afterwards, CEO pay increased and became more sensitive to luck components of performance rather than to those attributable to skill.

Compensation is also related to "discrete" governance events such as mergers and acquisitions. For example, Cai and Vijh (2007) propose that CEOs have unstudied reasons for supporting M&As. They suggest that options and other rewards are subject to restrictions which are suddenly lifted under changes in control that make their pay more liquid. Such immediate vesting of stock awards and activation of severance benefits can create unexpected wealth, thereby biasing managers to undertake mergers. We further surmise that CEOs are typically paid bonuses for *signing* M&A deals versus being paid for the long-term successful *execution* of such deals, thereby providing additional incentives to undertake such deals.

Product Markets

Finally, product development and life cycles create compensation variability. Using proprietary data from a compensation consultant, Bushman, Indjejikian, and Smith (1996: 163) suggest that individual performance evaluation—the "weight, out of a total of 100%, placed on individual performance"—is positively related to the length of time associated with developing products and the length of time associated with the life of the product. They argue that such measures are used as part of incentive schemes giving additional non-market-based information regarding performance. Aggarwal and Samwick (1999a) suggest that the competitive environment within a firm's industry shapes executive compensation decisions such that firms within industries with more intense rivalries use less compensation indexing (i.e. relative performance evaluation). Similarly, Finkelstein and Boyd (1998) suggest that greater CEO latent discretion (specifically, choices regarding R&D, capital, and advertising expenditures) is associated with greater compensation.

Analysts

Wright, Kroll, and Elenkov (2002) find that changes in executive compensation following corporate acquisitions were associated with increased monitoring (e.g. more analyst coverage), whereas compensation changes in acquirers with less vigilant monitoring was better predicted by changes in firm size. Cadman et al. (2010) suggest that ExecuComp firms have more analysts following them than non-ExecuComp firms, implying additional external oversight not already afforded by internal governance. However, external governance by analysts may not be a complete check on management behavior. According to Bartov and Mohanram (2004), analysts were unable to predict large exercises of CEO options, suggesting analysts have no superior trading information regarding the value of the firm compared to that of CEOs. Instead, these scholars suggest that abnormally large CEO exercises were timed in order to take advantage of strong earnings in the short term that were reversed in the long term.

Future Considerations: Market Governance

Previous research in compensation often focuses on the value of discrete events. Although such events can significantly affect the value of the firm, they occur only a few times a year (in the case of earnings announcements) or could not even happen at all (in the case of M&As). Only recently has compensation research begun to consider the more continuous effects of market monitoring in the form of stock liquidity. For example, Cadman et al. (2010) suggest that greater stock liquidity among ExecuComp firms is associated with a more intense focus on stock price and earnings in compensation compared to non-ExecuComp firms whose stocks are comparatively illiquid.

CEO Characteristics

Managerial skills and abilities have also driven much of the debate regarding executive compensation, reminiscent of another question often asked of scholars in compensation: "is [insert any CEO's name here] really worth it?" Some suggest that CEO pay is a function of talent and labor markets. Harris and Helfat (1997) find that external successors "on average received 13% more in initial salary and bonus than did internal successors" (p. 915). They further noted that industry-relevant experience is priced differently for external successors such that outsiders with fewer industry-specific skills earn more compared with external successors who do have inside industry expertise.

Few have investigated the effects of age and tenure, and the supposed risk aversion they may induce among CEOs. One notable exception is Cheng (2004) who suggests that CEOs facing R&D investments encounter the "horizon" problem as they approach retirement (i.e. aged 63 or older), and must receive additional incentives to take on additional risk. Implicitly, boards acknowledge this dilemma such that firms in their study associated "a $1000 increase in R&D spending...with a $2.48 increase in the value of CEO annual option grants" (Cheng, 2004: 306). Similarly, when CEO retirement income from Senior Executive Retirement Programs (SERPs) is determined in part by the firm's earnings, there is more evidence of earnings management by CEOs in their years before retirement (Kalyta, 2009).

Firm Factors

Firm Characteristics

Firm size has often been cited as an important (if not the greatest) predictor of CEO compensation in research published in premier publications over the last 15 years. For example, Wright et al. (2002) found that post-acquisition CEO compensation was better predicted by firm size when the firm received less analyst coverage, implying that compensation is more aligned with shareholder interests after M&As when there is more analyst monitoring. Similarly, Wasserman (2006) also found that firm size (number of employees) was positively related to cash compensation. Using an economic perspective, Gabaix and Landier (2008) suggest that executives' compensation increases have largely been due to enormous increases in the size of companies from 1980–2003.

Recent work in accounting by Nwaeze, Yang, and Yin (2006) implicitly questions why there is so much research relating earnings to cash compensation, yet comparatively less work relating cash flow measures to compensation. Similar to Natarajan (1996), Nwaeze and colleagues (2006) suggest that cash flow from operations is less malleable, and therefore may provide unique information for inferring CEO performance over and above earnings-based measures. They find that both earnings and cash flows, particularly in firm contexts where internally generated cash is more important for business growth, explain CEO cash compensation.

Corporate Strategy

Several aspects of a firm's corporate strategy have been related to CEO compensation, including M&As, research and development (R&D), and diversification. Datta, Iskandar-Datta, and Raman (2001) suggest that CEOs of firms pursuing acquisitions receive more equity-based compensation both before and after purchase. Furthermore, they find that CEOs with more equity incentives took on more aggressive deals (e.g. paid less for targets, acquired targets with more risk but also more growth prospects) that were also associated with better performance. Kroll et al. (1997) suggest that acquisitions in manager-controlled firms were associated with negative abnormal returns, and that the subsequently increased firm size was associated with more cash rewards. Dow and Raposo (2005) reveal a recent bias toward what they call "dramatics" in corporate strategy (e.g. excessive mergers and/or downsizings, colossal change efforts) which can be linked to extremes in executive compensation that may run counter to shareholder interests.

R&D investments can be costly and may take time to yield significant results. Consequently, Duru, Iyengar, and Thevaranjan, (2002) suggest that pressures to protect accounting earnings can lead CEOs to avoid R&D investments. Xue (2007) suggests that the costs of "buy" decisions are more easily absorbed by the firm, and therefore CEOs will undertake different strategic decisions as a function of their pay formulas. Similarly, Duru et al. (2002) suggest that compensation committees bend GAAP principles in order to preserve CEO compensation. Similarly, boards also apparently adjust executive pay to implicitly avoid CEO underinvestment in R&D as CEOs near retirement (Cheng, 2004). Finally, Gomez-Mejia, Larraza-Kintana, and Makri (2003) find that increased R&D intensity is associated with less total compensation but also a greater proportion of long-term pay among family CEOs (compared to non-family CEOs).

Increased diversification causes additional informational processing demands that are positively related to compensation (Henderson and Fredrickson, 1996). Aggarwal and Samwick (2003) find that corporate leaders at divisional levels have less pay-for-performance sensitivity than their CEO bosses. This finding is fairly intuitive, as CEO pay is based in large part on stock prices, in comparison with other corporate leaders whose divisional-level outcomes are difficult to assess by markets. Boyd and Salamin (2001) confirmed that both business unit strategy and position within the organizational hierarchy affect levels of salary, bonus, and leverage in employee compensation. Within organizations, interdependence of business units causes a greater reliance on non-financial metrics to evaluate managers, whereas accounting returns are best employed when business leaders have a more measurable effect on returns (Bouwens and Van Lent, 2007).

Financial and Accounting Choices

Berger, Ofek, and Yermack (1997) find that CEOs who lack monitoring employ lower debt, whereas CEOs who face sudden changes to their job security increase debt within the firm's capital structure. Specifically, they find that unsuccessful tender offers (i.e. an entrenchment "shock") are associated with the largest increases in debt, a fact the authors suggest demonstrates CEOs' desire to implement their own change efforts rather than those of a potential buyer. Sundaram and Yermack (2007) cite Jensen and Meckling (1976), suggesting that much of the pensions and deferred compensation paid to executives are a form of "inside debt" which could have a significant impact on CEO decisions regarding financing and other strategic options. They suggest that CEOs with greater inside debt manage their firms more conservatively. The role of debt in compensation has been studied by other scholars in corporate governance. Ortiz-Molina (2007) offers a test of the agency costs of debt, specifically, that firm choices regarding the forms of debt are associated with differences in links between pay and performance.

On the equity side, Babenko (2009) finds that "a one-standard deviation increase in the fraction of repurchased equity is associated with a 30% increase in (management) stock option exercises," particularly among executives in "firms with highly volatile stock returns" (p. 118). In addition, she finds that executives are more likely to undertake such actions when employees have numerous restricted options. Finally, firms also make choices about financial reporting. Craighead, Magnan, and Thorne (2004) found that, prior to 1993 (when Canadian securities regulations began requiring more compensation disclosure), firms with dispersed ownership structures (i.e. those lacking a blockholder of 20 percent or more) had less contingent-based cash compensation for CEOs, but then moved quickly toward more contingent-based compensation post-regulation.

INSTITUTIONAL GOVERNANCE

Regulatory

Of all the topics within this review, we note that the impact of institutional governance on executive compensation is probably the least studied in the US. When such factors are addressed, it is commonly in the form of regulatory aspects. According to the United States Government Accountability Office (2006), institutional governance occurs through two mechanisms: the public sector (e.g. the Securities and Exchange Commission, State Boards of Accountancy), or through the private sector (e.g. Public Company Accounting Oversight Board, the exchanges). An article by Dechow, Hutton, and Sloan (1996) is a rare exception to the top journals' neglect of institutional factors, suggesting that firms were not merely passive recipients of regulatory action and actually lobbied rule makers in order to avoid fuller disclosure of their compensation (specifically, the expensing of stock option compensation).

Normative

Although normative associations do not enforce laws, they do affect the lawmaking process through private standard-setting organizations (e.g. the National Association of Securities Dealers (NASD), FASB) (as suggested by the United States Government Accountability Office, 2006). Carter, Lynch, and Tuna (2007) found that changes in FASB standards regarding the accounting of stock options did not change executives' total compensation, but was associated with a move from stock options to restricted stock. Over the last decade or so, stock option compensation within S&P 1500 firms has gone down from about 40 percent of total compensation to figures nearing 25 percent. Even among firms that voluntarily expensed options before it was formally required by FASB, Johnston

(2006) found evidence of generous assumptions regarding stock volatility among these firms which effectively lowered the expenses associated with stock options.

Mimetic

The desire to conform to industry pressures affects pay. Pressures related to pollution prevention and outputs have been seen as potential determinants of executive compensation (Berrone and Gomez-Mejia, 2009). Industry-wide practices can diffuse through regulation and professional standards setters, and through comparisons within industries or interlocked entities. For example, although Ezzamel and Watson (1998) do not mention the word "peer" to define benchmarks for CEO compensation, they show how compensation committees used CEO labor markets to encourage a "bidding up" (their term) of compensation in the UK. Adoption of compensation innovations is facilitated by legitimacy-enhancing interlocks (Sanders and Tuschke, 2007). Firms do value social capital resulting from CEO interlocks; Geletkancyz, Boyd, and Finkelstein (2001) suggest interlocked CEOs receive more total cash and options, especially when the firm is diversified. However, not all compensation practices diffusing through corporate networks add value for shareholders. Collins et al. (2009) found that firms backdating CEO stock options were more likely to be interlocked with other backdating firms.

Consultants can also be a conduit for diffusion of practices as well as copying among firms. While SOX stipulated the need for increased independence of external auditors, no such stipulations were made for compensation consultants. Although some compensation firms offer their clients no other services, seemingly improper conflicts of interest can come from simultaneously setting compensation and providing other human resources services (e.g. benefits, selection, recruitment, training, human resource information systems, actuarial, and/or other human capital related services). Murphy and Sandino (2010) find that the presence of compensation consultants providing additional services to the firm beyond CEO compensation (e.g. actuarial services) is linked with greater CEO compensation in both the US and Canada. However, this is in contrast to Cadman, Carter, and Hillegeist (2010), who found no hints that CEO pay was higher, or that pay-performance sensitivities were lower, for firms that utilize compensation consultants that simultaneously provide other non-compensation-related services.

EXECUTIVE COMPENSATION

Pay Level

These balking at excesses in executive compensation are most frequently objecting to CEOs' overall pay. Pay levels have been attributed to several factors within premier-level publications. Broader cycles have been suggested to be a major determinant; for example,

Matolcsy (2000) finds that CEO cash compensation (in Australia) is reasonably steady due to changes in performance during economic downturns, but changes more dramatically during economic expansion. In contrast, using economic modeling, Gabaix and Landier (2008: 50) suggest that "the sixfold increase of US CEO pay between 1980 and 2003 can be fully attributable to the sixfold increase in market capitalization of large companies during that period." They suggest that talent among CEOs varies only at the margin: "If we rank CEOs by talent and replace the CEO number 250 by the number one CEO, the value of his firm will increase by only 0.016%" (p. 50), seemingly in direct contrast to much of our discussion earlier on the marginal product of CEOs. They instead suggest that CEO pay is more a function of "both the size of his firm and the size of the average firm in the economy" (p. 50). Similarly, industry effects explain much of the variation in CEO pay levels and serve as key sources for benchmarking (Miller, 1995; Bertrand and Mullainathan, 2001). Interestingly, while existing CEO wealth was related to the power of ownership incentives, it was not related to absolute pay in Sweden (Becker, 2006); we would hope boards would consider that greater absolute CEO wealth might incite CEO risk aversion.

Pay Structure

Many studies have also investigated the mix of incentives, including relative tradeoffs between short and long-term compensation. Writing from the perspective of finance, Dittmann and Maug (2007) suggest that current (e.g. distributional) assumptions governing models of executive compensation create suboptimal contracts, and that better contracts would include smaller amounts of options, less cash (salary), and many more grants of restricted stock. Similarly, Narayanan (1996) finds that pay mixes vary such that CEOs receive more cash in rough years, and more equity incentives in good years. Cash paid to CEOs is sensitive to defined benefit pension accounting, and may be aided by compensation committees and/or by (overly) optimistic pension return assumptions by management (Comprix and Muller, 2006). Another common aspect of executive pay is separation pay. Severance arrangements also continue to receive scholarly attention. Almazan and Suarez (2003) revisit conventional assumptions regarding executive exit packages. Interestingly, they suggest that severance pay under comparatively weak boards may actually be better for shareholders, particularly under conditions where there is sufficient talent in the CEO labor market.

Fixed vs Variable Components

Craighead et al. (2004) found that dispersed ownership structures promoted lesser performance-based cash compensation than concentrated ownership. Tosi and Greckhamer (2004) suggest that cultural differences in power distance and individualism explain differences in the proportion of variable pay to total, as well as in the ratios of CEO pay to that of lower-level employees. Cadman et al. (2010) find that CEO bonus and salary are more influenced by earnings in ExecuComp firms, while other non-financial criteria are emphasized in non-ExecuComp firms. The mix of compensation may also be a function of one's employment prospects; managers with low bargaining powers relative to the firm are usually incentivized using a compensation structure that focuses more on bonus than on promotions or on adjustments to base salary (Dencker, 2009).

Performance Metrics

Many clamor for better pay-for-performance. But how should we measure performance? Research has investigated the use of non-financial measures in performance assessment. For example, Ittner et al. (1997) found no evidence that CEOs with more power over boards were able to influence the relative weight of financial vs non-financial performance metrics. However, they observed greater use of non-financial metrics (e.g. employee safety, customer satisfaction) among firms pursuing "innovation" and "quality" strategies—strategies whose financial impact may be hard to ascertain in the short run. They also found an increased use of non-financial measures in regulated industries. This is consistent with Davila and Venkatachalam (2004), who documented that non-financial metrics in the airline industry predicted CEO cash compensation beyond the contributions of financial and accounting measures of performance. Although many papers suggest executives are potent leaders who are worth their pay, other scholars (see e.g. Bertrand and Mullainathan, 2001; "skimming" notions) suggest that things outside CEO control like "luck" (i.e. largely industry-related factors) also influence pay, particularly in the presence of weak boards.

Related to "how" we measure performance is the issue of "performance relative to whom?" (Miller, 1995). Scholars have explored the extent to which executive pay should be/is benchmarked to the performance of others. Rajgopal, Shevlin, and Zamora (2006) suggest that indexing compensation to the overall market is unnecessary when a CEO's alternative job prospects are good. While disclosure of one's compensation peers is now commonplace, Byrd, Johnson, and Porter (1998) suggest that voluntary disclosure of compensation peers was due in large part to stakeholder desires (e.g. having a history of shareholder proposals on compensation) rather than to compensation reasonableness (i.e. high pay for high performance). Finally, benchmarks for compensation can also come from within the organization. Using a tournament model, Conyon, Peck, and Sadler (2001) suggest that the difference in pay between the CEO and the next reporting level (i.e. the tournament prize) increases with the number of executives on the top team, but that this gap is seemingly unrelated to differences in organizational performance.

Consequences

Intended

Compensation "done right" can have good outcomes. Cheng and Farber (2008) suggest that CEO compensation, specifically executives' pay mix, is typically revised for the two years following corporate earnings restatements in a direction away from stock options. The authors suggest these revisions are made in hopes of discouraging inappropriate risk taking, and are associated with improved operational performance. Early work by Gomez-Mejia (1992) suggested that a match between compensation strategy and diversification strategy resulted in higher firm performance. Similarly, Hall and Liebman (1998) find a "strong" relation between CEO compensation and firm performance, suggesting that stock options have made CEO pay more contingent on performance. Aggarwal and Samwick (1999b) find firms with less volatile stocks have greater pay-for-performance sensitivity. Datta et al. (2001) argue that CEOs are more likely to undertake acquisitions when their compensation includes more equity ownership, thereby providing some evidence that equity incentives can spur executive risk taking.

Unintended

However, compensation "done wrong" can hurt shareholder interests. Compensation schemes can affect managers' willingness to invest in their firms. Exceptionally big CEO stock option exercises can predict the future's poor earnings news (Bartov and Mohanram, 2004). In a related vein, repricing of stock options can result in increased short-term abnormal returns (Grein et al., 2005). However, from a non-employee shareholder's perspective, option repricing seems unfair, particularly as these owners do not get a "do-over" when stock prices decline. Chen (2004) suggests that firms that permit repricing do have better executive retention after stock price declines. In fact, he suggests that firms using obstructive "no repricing—ever!" policies often end up offering more options grants in hopes of avoiding executive exits. Shareholders must then decide if the threat of executive exit due in part to low stock prices is a good thing (e.g. indirectly force a poorly performing CEO to leave), or should the shareholders stay the course with their investments and ride out the bad times?

Early work suggested that managers made accounting choices in a bid to maximize the value of their bonuses (Healy, 1985). More recent work looks at how managers could increase their option payouts (by about 8%!) by carefully manipulating the date associated with their stock option grants (Narayanan and Seyhun, 2008). There can also be other unintended consequences associated with equity compensation. For example, Devers et al. (2008) suggest that the relationship between equity compensation and CEO risk taking is complicated, and must also account for non-equity (cash) compensation, as well as volatility. Executive ethics have also been tied to the use of CEO stock options. Fraud among firms with CEOs that received stock options was partially a function of CEO duality and director ownership incentives (O'Connor et al., 2006).

Zhang et al. (2008) found evidence of more earnings management when the CEO had more out-of-the money options, owned fewer shares, and the firm was not performing well. Similarly, Cheng and Warfield (2005) suggest the firms that give more equity compensation to CEOs are more likely to match or slightly exceed earnings forecasts, thereby implying the use of earnings management. Still others (e.g. Yermack, 1997) find that the timing of stock option awards can also drive the compensation a CEO receives, in ways counter to shareholder interests; for example, large, positive earnings surprises (measured by Yermack as "more than two standard deviations away from the mean analyst forecast," p. 464) most often occurred soon after grants of options.

The Future

Our goal was to review work done within premier publications in accounting, economics, finance, and management related to executive compensation. While other modern classics may materialize outside this list, we thought it informative to get a sense of just what the top quality publications across these fields considered important in executive compensation research. Future studies on the links between internal governance and executive compensation will likely increase their focus on ownership. Specifically, we visualize more investigations of institutional and other owners' activism. While owners disgruntled with executive compensation can always "vote with their feet," groups of similarly disgruntled investors may begin to share their concerns more with each other, perhaps even band together to advocate specific aspects or structures of compensation, or become more activist in their orientation (Brandes et al., 2005). This activism may become less the purview of corporate gadflies, and more the domain of large, concentrated owners, or even groups of owners, that may increasingly be able to gain the ear of compensation decision-makers. We also suggest that the true abilities of board members to objectively monitor and compensate executives should be given more research attention. These abilities may be cultivated through structural options (e.g. increased independence) but also through increasingly higher standards and additional proficiency requirements regarding compensation knowledge.

One thing is for sure—executive compensation will continue to garner the attention of both Wall Street and Main Street. For example, recent updates issued by Institutional Shareholder Services (ISS), arguably one of the most followed proxy advisory firms in the US, include several aspects related to compensation—no doubt triggered in part by the recent financial crisis and recession (Mueller et al., 2011). Just what and who defines a "peer company (compensation) comparison," although not frequently cited within the academic literature, will continue to remain a major focus for the ISS. In addition, Mueller et al. (2011) suggest that board compensation committee receptiveness to say-on-pay votes, and board rationales regarding how often such votes should be taken, will also capture ISS's attention this proxy season. In fact, board members that go against shareholder preferences on say-on-pay related votes may find themselves increasingly less electable the next time board elections take place (Mueller et al., 2011).

The shareholder response could be swift and steady as boards continue to declassify (i.e. directors are more often subject to annual vs triennial elections). All of the above are consistent with increasing investor demands for more relevant peer comparisons, increased transparency, and more voice in how CEOs are paid, making for more interesting proxy seasons both now and in the future.

References

Aggarwal, R. K., and Samwick, A. A. (1999a). "Executive Compensation, Strategic Competition, and Relative Performance Evaluation: Theory and Evidence," *Journal of Finance*, 54(6): 1999–2043.

—— (1999b). "The Other Side of the Trade-off: The Impact of Risk on Executive Compensation," *Journal of Political Economy*, 107(1): 65–105.

—— (2003). "Performance Incentives within Firms: The Effect of Managerial Responsibility," *Journal of Finance*, 58(4): 1613–50.

Almazan, A., and Suarez, J. (2003). "Entrenchment and Severance Pay in Optimal Governance Structures," *Journal of Finance*, 58(2): 519–48.

Babenko, I. (2009). "Share Repurchases and Pay-Performance Sensitivity of Employee Compensation Contracts," *Journal of Finance*, 64(1): 117–50.

Banks, T. L., and Banks, F. Z. (2010). *Corporate Legal Compliance Handbook*, 2nd edition. New York: Aspen Publishers.

Bartov, E., and Mohanram, P. (2004). "Private Information, Earnings Manipulations, and Executive Stock-Option Exercises," *Accounting Review*, 79(4): 889–920.

Bebchuk, L. A., and Fried, J. M. (2004). "Pay without Performance: Overview of the Issues," *Journal of Applied Corporate Finance*, 17: 8–23.

Becker, B. O. (2006). "Wealth and Executive Compensation," *Journal of Finance*, 61(1): 379–97.

Berger, P. G., Ofek, E., and Yermack, D. (1997). "Managerial Entrenchment and Capital Structure Decisions," *Journal of Finance*, 52(4): 1411–38.

Berrone, P., and Gomez-Mejia, L. R. (2009). "Environmental Performance and Executive Compensation: An Integrated Agency-Institutional Perspective," *Academy of Management Journal*, 52(1): 103–26.

Bertrand, M., and Mullainathan, S. (2001). "Are CEOs Rewarded for Luck? The Ones without Principals Are," *Quarterly Journal of Economics*, 116(3): 901–32.

Bouwens, J. A. N., and Van Lent, L. (2007). "Assessing the Performance of Business Unit Managers," *Journal of Accounting Research*, 45(4): 667–97.

Boyd, B. K., and Salamin, A. (2001). "Strategic Reward Systems: A Contingency Model of Pay System Design," *Strategic Management Journal*, 22: 777–92.

Brandes, P., Dharwadkar, R., and Das, D. (2005). "Understanding the Rise and Fall of Stock Options Compensation: Taking Principal-Agent Conflicts to the Institutional (Battle) field," *Human Resource Management Review*, 15(2): 97–118.

Bushman, R. M., Indjejikian, R. J., and Smith, A. (1996). "CEO Compensation: The Role of Individual Performance Evaluation," *Journal of Accounting and Economics*, 21(2): 161–93.

Byrd, J. W., Johnson, M. F., and Porter, S. L. (1998). "Discretion in Financial Reporting: The Voluntary Disclosure of Compensation Peer Groups in Proxy Statement Performance Graphs," *Contemporary Accounting Research*, 15(1): 25–52.

CADMAN, B., CARTER, M. E., and HILLEGEIST, S. (2010). "The Incentives of Compensation Consultants and CEO Pay," *Journal of Accounting and Economics*, 49: 263–80.

—— KLASA, S., and MATSUNAGA, S. (2010). "Determinants of CEO Pay: A Comparison of Execucomp and Non-Execucomp Firms," *Accounting Review*, 85(5): 1511–43.

CAI, J. I. E., and VIJH, A. M. (2007). "Incentive Effects of Stock and Option Holdings of Target and Acquirer CEOs," *Journal of Finance*, 62(4): 1891–933.

CARTER, M. E., LYNCH, L. J., and TUNA, I. (2007). "The Role of Accounting in the Design of CEO Equity Compensation," *Accounting Review*, 82(2): 327–57.

CHEN, M. A. (2004). "Executive Option Repricing, Incentives, and Retention," *Journal of Finance*, 59(3): 1167–99.

CHENG, S. (2004). "R&D Expenditures and CEO Compensation," *The Accounting Review*, 79(2): 305–28.

—— and INDJEJIKIAN, R. J. (2009). "The Market for Corporate Control and CEO Compensation: Complements or Substitutes?" *Contemporary Accounting Research*, 26(3): 701–28.

CHENG, Q., and FARBER, D. B. (2008). "Earnings Restatements, Changes in CEO Compensation, and Firm Performance," *The Accounting Review*, 83(5): 1217–50.

—— and WARFIELD, T. D. (2005). "Equity Incentives and Earnings Management," *Accounting Review*, 80(2): 441–76.

CHHAOCHHARIA, V., and GRINSTEIN, Y. (2009). "CEO Compensation and Board Structure," *Journal of Finance*, 64(1): 231–61.

COLLINS, D. W., GONG, G., and LI, H. (2009). "Corporate Governance and Backdating of Executive Stock Options," *Contemporary Accounting Research*, 26(2): 403–45.

COMPRIX, J., and MULLER, K. A. (2006). "Asymmetric Treatment of Reported Pension Expense and Income Amounts in CEO Cash Compensation Calculations," *Journal of Accounting and Economics*, 42(3): 385–416.

CONYON, M. J., PECK, S. I., and SADLER, G. V. (2001). "Corporate Tournaments and Executive Compensation: Evidence from the U.K," *Strategic Management Journal*, 22(8): 805–15.

CRAIGHEAD, J. A., MAGNAN, M. L., and THORNE, L. (2004). "The Impact of Mandated Disclosure on Performance-Based CEO Compensation," *Contemporary Accounting Research*, 21(2): 369–98.

DAILY, C. M., JOHNSON, J. L., ELLSTRAND, A. E., and DALTON, D. R. (1998). "Compensation Committee Composition as a Determinant of CEO Compensation," *Academy of Management Journal*, 41(2): 209–20.

DATTA, S., ISKANDAR-DATTA, M., and RAMAN, K. (2001). "Executive Compensation and Corporate Acquisition Decisions," *Journal of Finance*, 56(6): 2299–336.

DAVID, P., KOCHHAR, R., and LEVITAS, E. (1998). "Research Notes: The Effect of Institutional Investors on the Level and Mix of CEO Compensation," *Academy of Management Journal*, 41(2): 200–8.

DAVILA, F., and PENALVA, A. (2006). "Governance Structure and the Weighting of Performance Measures in CEO Compensation," *Review of Accounting Studies*, 11(4): 463–93.

DAVILA, A., and VENKATACHALAM, M. (2004). "The Relevance of Non-Financial Performance Measures for CEO Compensation: Evidence from the Airline Industry," *Review of Accounting Studies*, 9(4): 443–64.

DECHOW, P., HUTTON, A., and SLOAN, R. (1996). "Economic Consequences of Accounting for Stock Option Compensation," *Journal of Accounting Research*, 34(3): 1–20.

DENCKER, J. C. (2009). "Relative Bargaining Power, Corporate Restructuirng, and Managerial Incentives," *Administrative Science Quarterly*, 54(3): 453–85.

Devers, C. E., McNamara, G., Wiseman, R. M., and Arrfelt, M. (2008). "Moving Closer to the Action: Examining Compensation Design Effects on Firm Risk," *Organization Science*, 19(4): 548–66.

Dharwadkar, R., Goranova, M., Brandes, P., and Khan, R. (2008). "Institutional Ownership and Monitoring Effectiveness: It's Not Just How Much But What Else You Own," *Organization Science*, 19(3): 419–40.

Dikolli, S. S., Kulp, S. L. and Sedatole, K. L. (2009). "Transient Institutional Ownership and CEO Contracting," *Accounting Review*, 84(3): 737–70.

Dittmann, I., and Maug, E. (2007). "Lower Salaries and No Options? On the Optimal Structure of Executive Pay," *Journal of Finance*, 62(1) 303–43.

Dow, J., and Raposo, C. C. (2005). "CEO Compensation, Change, and Corporate Strategy," *Journal of Finance*, 60(6): 2701–27.

Duru, A., Iyengar, R. J., and Thevaranjan, A. (2002). "The Shielding of CEO Compensation from the Effects of Strategic Expenditures," *Contemporary Accounting Research*, 19(2): 175–93.

Ezzamel, M., and Watson, R. (1998). "Market Comparison Earnings and the Bidding-up of Executive Cash Compensation: Evidence from the United Kingdom," *Academy of Management Journal*, 41(2): 221–31.

Finkelstein, S., and Boyd, B. K. (1998). "How Much Does the CEO Matter? The Role of Managerial Discretion in the Setting of CEO Compensation," *Academy of Management Journal*, 41(2): 179–99.

—— Hambrick, D. C., and Cannella, B. (2008). *Strategic Leadership: Theory and Research on Executives, Top Management Teams, and Boards*. NewYork: Oxford University Press.

Gabaix, X., and Landier, A. (2008). "Why Has CEO Pay Increased So Much?" *Quarterly Journal of Economics*, 123(1): 49–100.

Geletkanycz, M. A., Boyd, B. K., and Finkelstein, S. (2001). "The Strategic Value of CEO External Directorate Networks: Implications for CEO Compensation," *Strategic Management Journal*, 22(9): 889–98.

Georgeson Annual Corporate Governance Review (2010). <http://www.georgeson.com/usa/acgr.php>. Accessed August 21, 2011.

Graffin, S. D., Wade, J. B., Porac, J. F., and McNamee, R. C. (2008). "The Impact of CEO Status Diffusion on the Economic Outcomes of Other Senior Managers," *Organization Science*, 19(3): 457–74.

Gomez-Mejia, L. R. (1992). "Structure and Process of Diversification, Compensation Strategy, and Firm Performance," *Strategic Management Journal*, 13: 381–97.

—— Larraza-Kintana, M., and Makri, M. (2003). "The Determinants of Executive Compensation in Family-Controlled Public Corporations," *Academy of Management Journal*, 46(2): 226–37.

Grein, B., Hand, J., and Klassen, K. (2005). "Stock Price Reactions to the Repricing of Employee Stock Options," *Contemporary Accounting Research*, 22(4): 791–828.

Hall, B. J., and Liebman, J. B. (1998). "Are CEOs Really Paid Like Bureaucrats?" *Quarterly Journal of Economics*, 113(3): 653–91.

Harford, J., and Li, K. A. I. (2007). "Decoupling CEO Wealth and Firm Performance: The Case of Acquiring CEOs," *Journal of Finance*, 62(2): 917–49.

Harris, D., and Helfat, C. (1997). "Specificity of CEO Human Capital and Compensation," *Strategic Management Journal*, 18(11): 895–920.

Hartzell, J. C., and Starks, L. T. (2003). "Institutional Investors and Executive Compensation," *Journal of Finance*, 58(6): 2351–74.

HEALY, P. (1985), "The Effect of Bonus Schemes on Accounting Decisions," *Journal of Accounting and Economics*, 7: 85–107.

HENDERSON, A. D., and. FREDRICKSON, J. W. (1996). "Information-Processing Demands as a Determinant of CEO Compensation," *Academy of Management Journal*, 39(3): 575–606.

ITTNER, C. D., LARCKER, D. F., and RAJAN, M. V. (1997). "The Choice of Performance Measures in Annual Bonus Contracts," *Accounting Review*, 72(2): 231–55.

JENSEN, M. C., and MECKLING, W. H. (1976). "Theory of the Firm: Managerial Behavior, Agency Costs and Ownership Structure," *Journal of Financial Economics*, 3(4): 305–60.

JOHNSTON, D. (2006). "Managing Stock Option Expense: The Manipulation of Option-Pricing Model Assumptions," *Contemporary Accounting Research*, 23(2): 395–425.

KALYTA, P. (2009). "Accounting Discretion, Horizon Problem, and CEO Retirement Benefits," *Accounting Review*, 84(5): 1553–73.

KAPLAN, S. (2008). "Are U.S. CEOs Overpaid?" *Academy of Management Perspectives*, 22(2): 5–20.

KROLL, M., WRIGHT, P., TOOMBS, L., and LEAVELL, H. (1997). "Form of Control: A Critical Determinant of Acquisition Performance and CEO Rewards," *Strategic Management Journal*, 18(2): 85–96.

LAKSMANA, I. (2008). "Corporate Board Governance and Voluntary Disclosure of Executive Compensation Practices," *Contemporary Accounting Research*, 25(4): 1147–82.

LAUX, V. (2008). "Board Independence and CEO Turnover," *Journal of Accounting Research*, 46(1): 137–71.

LUCCHETTI, A. (2011). "As Pay Votes Loom, Some Set Sights on Adviser Firms," *The Wall Street Journal*, February 7: C.1.

MALMENDIER, U., and TATE, G. (2009). "Superstar CEOs," *Quarterly Journal of Economics*, 124(4): 1593–638.

MATOLCSY, Z. P. (2000). "Executive Cash Compensation and Corporate Performance during Different Economic Cycles," *Contemporary Accounting Research*, 17(4): 671–92.

MILLER, D. J. (1995). "CEO Salary Increases may be Rational after All: Referents and Contracts in CEO Pay," *Academy of Management Journal*, 38(5): 1361–85.

MUELLER, R. O., ISING, E., BRIGGS, A., and LEVIT, K. V. (2011). "ISS Policy Updates for the 2012 Proxy Season," *Insights; The Corporate and Securities Law Advisor*, 25(12): 13–18.

MURPHY, K. J., and SANDINO, T. (2010). "Executive Pay and 'Independent' Compensation Consultants," *Journal of Accounting and Economics*, 49(3): 247–62.

—— and ZÁBOJNÍK, J. (2004). "CEO Pay and Appointments: A Market-Based Explanation for Recent Trends," *American Economic Review*, 94(2): 192–6.

NARAYANAN, M. P. (1996). "Form of Compensation and Managerial Decision Horizon," *Journal of Financial and Quantitative Analysis*, 31(4): 467–91.

—— and SEYHUN, H. N. (2008). "The Dating Game: Do Managers Designate Option Grant Dates to Increase their Compensation?" *The Review of Financial Studies*, 21(5): 1907–45.

NATARAJAN, R. (1996). "Stewardship Value of Earnings Components: Additional Evidence on the Determinants of Executive Compensation," *Accounting Review*, 71(1): 1–22.

NWAEZE, E. T., YANG, S. S. M., and YIN, J. Q. (2006). "Accounting Information and CEO Compensation: The Role of Cash Flow from Operations in the Presence of Earnings," *Contemporary Accounting Research*, 23(1): 227–65.

NYSE Listed Company Manual (2009). <http://nysemanual.nyse.com/lcm>. Accessed August 21, 2011.

O'CONNOR, J. J. P., PRIEM, R. L., COOMBS, J. E., and GILLEY, K. M. (2006). "Do CEO Stock Options Prevent or Promote Fraudulent Financial Reporting?" *Academy of Management Journal*, 49(3): 483–500.

OFEK, E., and YERMACK, D. (2000). "Taking Stock: Equity-Based Compensation and the Evolution of Managerial Ownership," *Journal of Finance*, 55(3): 1367–84.

OROL, R. D. (2011). "Say-on-Pay Vote Gives CEOs Early Trouble in 2011: Investors Reject CEO Pay at Jacobs Engineering, Send Message to Monsanto," MarketWatch, February 3. <http://www.marketwatch.com/story/say-on-pay-vote-gives-ceos-early-trouble-in-2011-2011-02-03>. Accessed March 30, 2012.

ORTIZ-MOLINA, H. (2007). "Executive Compensation and Capital Structure: The Effects of Convertible Debt and Straight Debt on CEO Pay," *Journal of Accounting and Economics*, 43(1): 69–93.

Pearl Meyer and Partners (2011). <http://www.pearlmeyer.com/Pearl/media/PearlMeyer/PDF/PMP-CA-ProxyAccessStruckDown-8-4.11.pdf>. Accessed September 27, 2011.

POLLOCK, T. G., FISCHER, H. M., and WADE, J. B. (2002). "The Role of Power and Politics in the Repricing of Executive Options," *Academy of Management Journal*, 45(6): 1172–82.

RAJGOPAL, S., SHEVLIN, T., and ZAMORA, V. (2006). "CEOs' Outside Employment Opportunities and the Lack of Relative Performance Evaluation in Compensation Contracts," *Journal of Finance*, 61(4): 1813–44.

SANDERS, W. G., and CARPENTER, M. A. (1998). "Internationalization and Firm Governance: The Roles of CEO Compensation, Top Team Composition, and Board Structure," *Academy of Management Journal*, 41(2): 158–78.

—— and TUSCHKE, A. (2007). "The Adoption of institutionally Contested Organizational Practices: The Emergence of Stock Option Pay in Germany," *Academy of Management Journal*, 50(1): 33–56.

STOUGHTON, N. M., and TALMOR, E. (1999). "Managerial Bargaining Power in the Determination of Compensation Contracts and Corporate Investment," *International Economic Review*, 40(1): 69–93.

SUNDARAM, R. K., and YERMACK, D. L. (2007). "Pay Me Later: Inside Debt and its Role in Managerial Compensation," *Journal of Finance*, 62(4): 1551–88.

SYRE, S. (2011). "Shareholders Get Their Say," *Boston Capital*, May 13. <http://www.boston.com/business/articles/2011/05/13/shareholders_get_their_say/>. Accessed on March 30, 2012.

TOSI, H. L., and GRECKHAMER, T. (2004). "Culture and CEO Compensation," *Organization Science*, 15(6): 657–70.

United States Government Accountability Office (2006). "Financial Restatements: Updates of Public Company Trends, Market Impacts, and Regulatory Enforcement Activities." <http://www.gao.gov/new.items/d06678.pdf>. Accessed September 27, 2011.

WADE, J. B., PORAC, J. F., POLLOCK, T. G., and GRAFFIN, S. D. (2006). "The Burden of Celebrity: The Impact of CEO Certification Contests on CEO Pay and Performance," *Academy of Management Journal*, 49(4): 643–60.

WASSERMAN, N. (2006). "Stewards, Agents, and the Founder Discount: Executive Compensation in New Ventures," *Academy of Management Journal*, 49(5): 960–76.

WESTPHAL, J. D. (1998). "Board Games: How CEOs Adapt to Increases in Structural Board Independence from Management," *Administrative Science Quarterly*, 43(3): 511–37.

WRIGHT, P., KROLL, M., and ELENKOV, D. (2002). "Acquisition Returns, Increase in Firm Size, and Chief Executive Officer Compensation: The Moderating Role of Monitoring," *Academy of Management Journal*, 45(3): 599–608.

XUE, Y. (2007). "Make or Buy New Technology: The Role of CEO Compensation Contract in a Firm's Route to Innovation," *Review of Accounting Studies*, 12: 659–90.

YERMACK, D. (1997). "Good Timing: CEO Stock Option Awards and Company News Announcements," *Journal of Finance*, 52(2): 449–76.

ZHANG, X., BARTOL, K. M., SMITH, K. G., PFARRER, M. D., and KHANIN, D. M. (2008). "CEOs on the Edge: Earnings Manipulation and Stock-Based Incentive Misalignment," *Academy of Management Journal*, 51(2): 241–58.

CHAPTER 11

CORPORATE GOVERNANCE

Ownership Interests, Incentives, and Conflicts

DAVID S. BOSS, BRIAN L. CONNELLY,
ROBERT E. HOSKISSON, AND
LASZLO TIHANYI

Introduction

In recent years theory and application in management have dedicated considerable attention to the topic of corporate governance. With the combination of high-profile debacles a decade ago, such as the implosion of Enron and firm behavior that precipitated or contributed to the ongoing financial crisis, the popular press has found renewed interest in understanding and solidifying corporate governance practices. The Sarbanes-Oxley Act in 2002 was the United States government's attempt to restore public trust in the corporate governance process and, since that time, a great deal has changed in how firms are governed. At the forefront of these developments is firm ownership, which has emerged as one of the most compelling forms of corporate governance (Connelly, Ireland, et al., 2011). As a result, scholars in disciplines such as finance (Demsetz and Villalonga, 2001), accounting (Bushee, 1998), economics (Gompers and Metrick, 2001), law (Bainbridge, 2003), and management (Hoskisson et al., 2002), have sought to contribute to our understanding of when, why, and how firm owners influence firm-level outcomes.

Firm owners often differ in their motivations, risk propensities, and time horizons. These differences create added complexity for managers. Specifically, the rise of institutional investors has changed the manager-owner relationship landscape for firm processes. Once a small percentage of owners (5% of NYSE holdings in 1950), institutional investors have grown to become some of the most substantial and active owners in corporate history, now comprising as much as 70 percent of all corporate stocks (Gillan and Starks, 2007; Westphal and Bednar, 2008). As a result, the collective goals of these owners often supersede those of other shareholders. Executives are likely to make sure that institutional investors' desires take high priority when making strategic decisions. Scholars have found, for example, that institutional investors may pressure managers to make changes in R&D (David et al., 2001), competitive strategies (Connelly et al., 2010), executive compensation practices (Werner et al., 2005), and investments and divestments (Bergh et al., 2007), as well as other business decisions. Nevertheless, institutional investors are just one group of owners, and changes in firm ownership structures occur at a rapid pace. As such, scholarly examination must keep pace in order to understand emerging developments and to develop theory as a means of understanding these behaviors. This study synthesizes information about firm ownership in the field of corporate governance and examines key differences between owners. We focus on articulating divergent, and potentially conflicting, interests and incentives and explicating how these might affect firm strategies. We conclude with suggestions for potential theoretical advancements to help facilitate understanding of these issues.

Ownership Structure

As noted above, scholars in many disciplines have found that various forms of ownership affect managerial decision-making and corporate strategy. However, since many different types of owners exist, it is important to understand their unique interests and incentives. According to agency theory, equity owned by insiders represents an "alignment" approach to corporate governance, where self-interest by management can be mitigated by allowing the agents to be principals so that by working toward their own interests they are also meeting the interests of other shareholders (Dalton et al., 2003). In contrast, equity owned by outsiders represents a "control" approach to governance. The control approach emphasizes outside owners' motivation to check up on managers to ensure that stakeholder interests are consistently being met and that equity owners receive the highest possible profits (Dalton et al., 2003). We consider these two broad forms of ownership in the following sections.

Inside Owners

Agency theory suggests that when insiders own equity in the company, the interests of managers and shareholders are more likely to be aligned (Fama and Jensen, 1983; Jensen and Murphy, 1990; Wright et al., 1996). Since insiders act as agents to carry out the expectations of owners, granting those agents shares and making them part owners of the company should incentivize them to put aside personal initiatives. Therefore, the use of bonding mechanisms (e.g. golden hellos, golden parachutes, bonuses, stock options) should align inside owners' self-interests with those of the owners they serve. There are three main bodies of insiders that could own shares of the firm: executives, board members, and employees. Each category differs with respect to their interests and incentives. Tables 11.1 and 11.2 highlight some of these key differences.

Executives Executives consist of the top management team (e.g. typically C-level executives or vice presidents), who often maintain some level of ownership in the company. For example, when consulting firms promote managers to partners, these individuals buy into their position. This requirement is intended to bond the executives to the firm, aligning personal and corporate goals (Connelly, Ireland, et al., 2011). Executive interest alignment through ownership has been studied by scholars in finance (Agrawal and Knoeber, 1996), law (Perry and Zenner, 2000), economics (Himmelberg et al., 1999), and strategy (Dalton et al., 2003) in an effort to understand the extent to which insider equity is effective as a mechanism of corporate governance. On the whole, results generally suggest that as executives gain greater ownership in the firm, they are more likely to employ firm resources toward long-term profitability and less likely to shirk.

Nonetheless, not all empirical evidence is in agreement on the issue. For instance, some research has shown that the higher the level of ownership, the more entrenched the executive becomes within the firm (Morck et al., 1988), which subsequently can lead to self-interested behavior by maintaining the firm's risk profile. As a result, managers may not make decisions intended to exploit opportunities and create growth, which could result in lower profits and possible decline (Lang et al., 1995). Therefore, if firms desire to grow, which most do, an entrenched manager protecting the firm's risk profile may still require monitoring by other owners.

Board members Ownership alignment is also applicable to board members, who may be insiders or outsiders (Hermalin and Weisbach, 2003). However, Fiss (2006) found that the vigilance of the board largely depends on the compensation of its members and the participation of major shareholders. This issue has become particularly germane in recent years as director pay has been ratcheted up to over $200,000 for directors of Fortune 500 firms, with commensurate increases in stock-option retainers. One reason for this increase could be due to the fact that board members with limited ownership may strive to act against shareholder interest (and subsequently behave like managers) by expanding the firm to feather their own nest, allowing inefficient acquisitions. One way to fix the problem is to give board members more ownership positions and options as the trend suggests.

As a consequence of acting with self-interest by initiating plans and processes that are contrary to the requests of shareholders (*The Economist*, 2006), board members risk losing the support of shareholders when the time comes for board elections and/or re-elections (Brandes et al., 2008). In addition, board members may face problems with publicity that plays out at shareholder meetings and in the business press. Such publicity can threaten board members' reputations and tenure (Neubaum and Zahra, 2006). In sum, board candidates must have a sincere commitment to alignment of focal issues vocalized by shareholders or face difficult ramifications with board elections and/or negative publicity (Brandes et al., 2008).

Table 11.1. Ownership interests and incentives

	Alignment or Control (Bonding/Monitoring/Incentives/Sanctions)	Decision-making (executive/firm level)	Structure of the owner	Shareholder behavior
Executives	Alignment: Bonding	Executive: Direct responsibility Firm: Assist the BOD for strategic implementation	Single CEO, vice presidents and directors	The greater the ownership of the firm, the more alignment of interests
Board Members	Alignment: Bonding and Monitoring	Executive: Assist CEO Firm: Direct responsibility	Firm and independent board members; CEO is often the chair; LID can monitor chair behavior	Board ownership and alignment are affected by voting shareholders and business press
Employees	Alignment: Bonding	Executive: Provide information for executive decisions Firm: Act collectively to drive strategy	Non-executive employees	Psychological commitment to firm with stock options
Blockholders	Control: Monitoring and Bonding	Depending on percentage ownership, influence varies for executive and firm decision-making Family: More influence Corporation: Less influence Government: Less influence	Individual, family, corporations, government	Large ownership constitutes voting rights for monitoring decision-making
Institutional	Control: Monitoring	Collective voting rights drive both executive and firm decision making incentives	Pension Funds, Investment Funds, endowments	Increasingly large ownership demands firm attention and priority; high monitoring activity

(continued)

Table 11.1. Continued

	Alignment or Control (Bonding/Monitoring/Incentives/Sanctions)	Decision-making (executive/firm level)	Structure of the owner	Shareholder behavior
Private equity	Control: Monitoring, Bonding, and Incentives	Angel and venture capital investors' large percentage of ownership set executive- and firm-level decisions. Private equity also controls these decisions to a degree	Angel Investors (individuals), Venture capitalist funds (organized early stage), private equity funds (organized late stage)	High control due to majority ownership
Hedge funds	Control: Monitoring, Sanctions	Executive: Broad activism may threaten executive decisions Firm: Decisions will be focused on short-run profits	Conglomerate of managers	Tactical, planned, and controversial

Table 11.2. Ownership impact on management and strategy

	Influence on Managers	Strategy Implications
Executives	Creating collective alignment for corporate mission	Strategies will be aligned with long-term initiatives
Board Members	Monitors self-interested behavior; aligns interests of shareholders with managers	Strategies will be aligned with what the board feels are stakeholder interests
Employees	Collective satisfaction/dissatisfaction encourages change	Strategies based on employee productivity
Blockholders	Family: high monitoring and high use of voice	Family: conservative strategies
	Government: low monitoring	Corporations: increased resources, less innovation
		Government: less motivation for strategy
Institutional	Pension funds: high monitoring and high use of voice	Pension Funds: strategies will be long-term focused with accounting stability as a central tenet
	Investment funds: Low monitoring and low use of voice	Investment funds: strategies will be short-term focused with market fluctuations as central tenet
	Endowments: Low monitoring and low use of voice	Endowments: little effect on strategy
Private equity	Angel: dominant, often becoming the managers	Angel and VC: strategies will focus on high growth to create return on investment
	VC: dominant, facilitating decision-making behavior	PE: Focus will be on turning the firm around, so differentiation and innovation will receive less attention than financial stability
	PE: depends on percentage ownership; high ownership will cause high influence	
Hedge funds	Confusion based on self-interest for profit on the part of hedge funds	General firm overhauls are possible; financially, hard to judge since losses *and* gains are appreciated

Employees Most firms offer employees an opportunity to own some stock (Blasi et al., 2003) and creating alignment is central to these incentives (Welbourne and Gomez-Mejia, 1995). Doing so forms a psychological bond with the company and with its objectives (Pierce, Rubenfeld, and Morgan, 1991). When employees have personal ownership in the company, job motivation improves, turnover decreases, and burnout is minimized (Jones and Kato, 1995). Some scholars maintain that this tactic works because employees appreciate the opportunity to participate and thereby foster increased share price (Pierce et al., 1991). Others explain that an internal feeling of influence and control is more central (Connelly, Ireland, et al., 2011). Either way, the major objective created by allowing stock incentives is to connect personal effort to corporate performance.

Outside Ownership

As noted earlier, with increases in institutional investments and blockholders in the marketplace, outside equity investors own an increasing percentage of corporate stocks, which emphasizes more collective control. Some of these outside investors are in a position to implement monitoring tactics to ensure that their own goals and objectives are met. In this section, we discuss the interests and incentives of four types of outside owners, and we summarize this discussion in Tables 11.1 and 11.2.

Blockholders According to the Securities and Exchange Commission (SEC), an owner must hold over 5 percent of firm equity to be classified as a blockholder. Blockholders can be either individual people or single corporations. In both cases, these individual blockholders differ from institutional investors because they do not act on behalf of different clients. Large block ownership by outside investors is motivated by two major factors. First, blockholders enjoy concentrated control of decision rights, which provides more monitoring influence (Demsetz, 1983). Second, they gain private benefits that other shareholders do not have, including trades priced at a premium over subsequent trades of other shareholders (Barclay and Holderness, 1989). Three types of blockholders are particularly common: family, corporations, and government ownership.

A firm has been represented in research to be family-owned when family members of the founder own over 5 percent of the company (Miller et al., 2007). Family organizations account for approximately 65 to 90 percent of all business establishments worldwide (Arregle et al., 2007). When a family owns a minor percentage of the organization (e.g. 5 to 10 percent), other owners may take a bonding approach to make sure these owners are paid a sufficient amount not to cause wealth appropriation through "tunneling." Tunneling refers to "transferring resources from firms in which a controlling family holds relatively small cash flow rights to a business group subsidiary in which the family owns substantial cash flow rights" (Bergstrom and Rydqvist, 1990). On the other hand, when family owners hold a high percentage of the firm, other non-member owners of the firm would have to align with the family interest.

Family firm research continues to receive increasing attention in the literature (Gomez-Mejia et al., 2011), particularly as it relates to socio-emotional wealth (Gomez-Mejia et al., 2007). For instance, family-owned firms are more likely to bow to institutional pressures to conform because their socio-emotional wealth success is tied up in the decision-making process (Gomez-Mejia et al., 2007). In essence, they behave, not due to economic interests, but to socio-emotional family rewards. In addition, family firms diversify less, and when they do, they prefer domestic regions that are "culturally close" (Gomez-Mejia et al., 2009). These findings suggest that the family could drive firm strategy to be more conservative, which may significantly affect their influence on managerial decision-making.

Corporations can be another type of blockholder when they acquire a minority share of another firm. Corporations often become blockholders before engaging in a takeover or complete sale of stock. Focal firms facing these actions from a corporation most likely see additional amounts of capital utilized to facilitate growth. However, the increased capital will potentially be coupled with increased control by the acquiring firm, affecting the structuring of resources (Connelly, Ireland, et al., 2011). Indeed, studies have found that when goods and services are transferred with prices favorable to the blockholder, the performance for the target firm is negatively affected (Mikkelson and Ruback, 1985; Rosenstein and Rush, 1990; Bogert, 1996).

The government is often referred to as either state ownership or sovereign wealth funds (SWF). State ownership means that the government entity owns the firm whereas SWFs are investment vehicles owned and managed by the government (Connelly, Ireland, et al., 2011; see Chapter 26). Unlike family firms, government ownership may be categorized as predictable within the marketplace, in that scholars can predict where the government will have more influence. Research suggests that government ownership tends to be higher in two areas: emerging economies (La Porta et al., 2002), and market failures, such as in the cases of natural monopolies (Connelly, Ireland, et al., 2011).

Research has shown that, in most cases, government ownership has a negative effect on the performance of focal firms. In emerging economies, government involvement tends to be large and pervasive, have underdeveloped financial systems, employ interventionist and inefficient governance mechanisms, and lack protection of property rights (La Porta et al., 2002). Other studies have found that the increase in state ownership in developed countries can create "soft" budget constraints, lack of innovation in the firm, poor financial performance, and increased corruption (Shleifer, 1998; D'Souza and Megginson, 1999; Megginson and Netter, 2001; Djankov and Murrell, 2002; Tihanyi and Hegarty, 2007). In addition, monitoring intensity tends to be lower, resulting in diversification patterns that are less related and more random (Hoskisson et al., 2005). Finally, government owners have been found to be as interested in political interests as in strategic gains (Jen, 2007). This has occurred in Chinese business groups with significant government ownership that are mainly interested in employing as many people as possible, not for economic gain or firm competitive advantage but to improve social welfare (White et al., 2008).

Institutional investors This is a label that applies to a number of different types of funds that may act very differently from one another. Pension funds, professional investment management funds (investment funds), and university endowment funds are all classified as institutional owners. Brickley, Lease, and Smith (1988) distinguish between pressure-sensitive institutions (e.g. insurance companies, banks, and non-bank trusts), pressure-resistant institutions (e.g. public pension funds, mutual funds or professional investment funds, endowments, and foundations) and pressure-indeterminate institutions (e.g. corporate pension funds, brokerage houses, investment counsel firms). Pension funds and professional investment funds are two dominant forms of pressure-resistant institutional investors that differ in their interests and incentives. Pension fund owners tend to own the stocks of fewer companies, but a higher percentage of the companies that they own. They also tend to hold their stocks for longer periods of time because of their interest in long-term gains. In addition, pension funds show more interest in corporate decision-making and are more likely to voice their opinions and concerns. Pension fund managers are often compensated based on salary instead of market performance (Scharfstein and Stein, 1990), suggesting they may be a better match as owners when managers make decisions that favor long-term outcomes, even if it entails short-term losses. For example, they may favor firms that engage in internal innovation rather than external innovation (e.g. buying new products) through acquisitions (Hoskisson et al., 2002). On the other hand, mutual fund managers are often compensated based on market performance (Scharfstein and Stein, 1990). As such, they tend to hold portfolios that are more diversified than pension fund managers. This "broad but shallow" approach emphasizes quick decision-making in an effort to exploit the arbitrage opportunities that exist on a daily basis in the market. They may, therefore, emphasize financial controls over strategic controls. Bushee (1998) characterized many of these types of investors as "transient" because their annual turnover ratio is high. They express their voice for short-run arbitrage decisions, but have little impact on pressuring for a change in overall strategy or managerial decision-making (Yan and Zhang, 2009). Other types of institutional investors include university endowment funds, foundations, and religious institutions, most of which follow a quasi-indexer approach to investing (Useem, 1996).

Venture capital/Private equity Almost all firms begin the entrepreneurial process as a private organization needing funding to grow. Angel investors are wealthy individuals or partnerships that hold informal ties to new companies and help them when they are too small to attract more formal venture capitalist or private equity firms (Prowse, 1998). Typically, angel investors are chosen by the founders because of their high net worth, ability to contribute knowledge or expertise, and established social networks. As a result, angel investors tend to exercise high levels of monitoring, and they may dominate decision-making with respect to the strategic direction of the firm.

Venture capitalist firms are a more organized mechanism of obtaining early funding, and are a form of private equity (Wright and Robbie, 1998). Once a small cottage industry, venture capital firms have expanded considerably since the 1980s. The process of gathering funds from a venture capitalist firm tends to raise the percentage owned by the investing firm, which creates more power for the venture capitalist over business decisions (Gompers and Lerner, 1995). Venture capitalists are distinguished in the literature as "inactive," "active advice giving," and "hands on," depending on their investment style (Elango et al., 1995). Hands-on venture capitalists, for example, identify and evaluate business opportunities, negotiate and close investments, and seek to attract additional capital with a view toward driving the company forward as fast as possible.

Private equity firms often obtain majority control of mature firms and serve an important purpose when mature organizations are struggling in the market and need extra funding to survive (Kaplan and Stromberg, 2009; see Chapters 24, 26). Leveraged buyouts (LBOs) are one way private equity funds can acquire a struggling organization (Jensen, 1989). When this occurs, the private equity firm's majority ownership gives them the power to manage change, to improve operations, facilitate better control, and implement new corporate governance structures (Wright et al., 2000). Even though innovation may be reduced in the buyout process of mature firms, financial stability tends to improve in LBOs, often providing better stockholder returns (Cumming et al., 2007).

Hedge Funds   Hedge fund owners are a type of institutional owner that has become a critical player in the corporate landscape but as yet has received little academic attention. They are private investment funds, but they employ a wider variety of tactics and instruments to make gains on the companies that they own and are subject to fewer restrictions (see Chapter 27). Portfolios are presumably "hedged," or protected, from declines in market valuation while maximized for greatest gain during market growth. Hedge fund activism differs from other institutional investors insofar as they often seek deep and lasting changes in the organization. As a result, hedge fund interests can sometimes diverge from other shareholders and their activism puts stress on firm regulatory systems, or systems designed to monitor firms to bring them into conformity with rules designed for fair practice (Kahan and Rock, 2009). Managers are still learning how to respond to hedge fund owners. On the one hand, these owners may be very skilled at recognizing opportunities that will maximize shareholder value. However, their search for quick profits could jeopardize the long-term health of firms and, more broadly, the economy (Kahan and Rock, 2009).

Conflict among Owners

Potential conflicts may occur between internal and external owners. In this section, we discuss some, but not all conflicts found in Table 11.3. Agency theory illuminates one possible tension that could arise. Inside owners have incentives that align their interests with those of shareholders, whereas outside owners strive to control management so that their interests are held as a high priority (Dalton et al., 2003). The former is an *a priori* mechanism that attempts to establish structures that will ensure the desired behavior, while the latter is an *ex post* mechanism that monitors behaviors after they occur with a

Table 11.3. Possible conflicts between owners

	Executives	Board Members	Employees	Blockholders	Institutional	Private equity	Hedge funds
Board Members	The BOD may have higher risk preferences than the CEO; CEO may also be board chair, limiting monitoring ease	—					
Employees	Employees differ from executives in their high financial goal focus	Board members are more focused on the overall firm strategy	—				
Blockholders	Family owners may disagree with CEOs' tactics for achieving goals	Board members may be large blockholders, creating a conflict of interest	Family owners may favor personal wealth more than employment	—			
Institutional	Mutual fund owners care less about long-term strategies	Pension fund owners may pressure the board to engage in activities contrary to firm vision	Collective institutional client preferences may overturn collective employee rights	Sovereign wealth funds monitor firms much less than pension funds	—		

(continued)

	Private equity	Hedge funds
Private equity	Venture capitalists and angel investors may become too engrossed with management responsibilities	Board may disagree with private equity position for corporate improvement
Hedge funds	CEO may not favor the hedge funds tactics for "shorting" firm stock	Broad restructuring tactics may not sit well with established board members
Private equity funds value bottom-line financial success more than employee stability	Losses for employees mean potential termination	
Family firms differ from venture capitalists in time and risk preference	Losses for sovereign wealth funds mean less employment, affecting political stability	
Angel investors are more individualistic than institutional investors	Hedge funds differ from institutional investors in terms of tolerance of loss	
—	Venture capitalists want the firm to succeed and may not feel the same motivation from hedge fund owners	

view toward retribution for wrong behavior. A general conflict occurs when the *a priori* alignment mechanisms do not match with the *ex post* control mechanisms due to asymmetric information. Managers need to have their interests aligned with those of shareholders, but shareholders also must recognize that they do not have all information. For example, while inside owners may be striving for long-term goals, outside owners may be striving for short-term incentives. Thus, the interests of shareholders may not always yield the optimum long-term outcome for the firm, and outside owners may face motivations of opportunism, instead of acting to the benefit of the organization (Shleifer and Summers, 1988). Indeed, Perrow (1986) identified the lack of consideration of owner opportunism as a significant weakness of agency theory.

Different preferences may also yield potential friction. Time horizons and risk propensities for strategic initiatives may differ between inside and outside owners. For example, since family firms are known to be more conservative, aggressive tactics by venture capitalists to expand quickly with high investment costs could disrupt family firm timetables and goals. In addition, hedge fund owners have a much higher tolerance for loss than investment fund owners, and corporate raiders may not share the same values as the board of directors. Owners' geographic preferences for marketing, property, plant, and equipment may differ, as well as their penchant toward different industry and political preferences. For instance, the largest SWFs representing the specific interests of governments, such as those of the United Arab Emirates (UAE), Russia, and China, have several hundred billion dollars to invest. Through such investments, SWFs can gain substantive control of large portions of major corporations. When these investors take appreciable ownership in a firm, they are likely to influence disposition toward expansion to a particular geographic region, such as the UAE SWF pushing to have investment in the UAE in particular and the Middle East more generally. Conflict may arise when SWFs from nations with poor social relations begin to share ownership in a common firm. The increase of heterogeneity brings new opportunities to study different preferences, and future research initiatives might focus on how to corroborate the outcomes of these differing control attempts.

In addition, owner differences in levels of activism may cause conflict. On the one hand, an owner that engages in a great deal of activism will naturally get more attention than an owner that does not. This leads to the question: does the "squeaky" ownership wheel get the "commitment" grease from managers? On the other hand, when multiple owners have high levels of activism, their differing agendas may create high friction. Consider, for instance, the April 2011 ouster of Parco CEO Hidekazu Hirano in Japan, which came at the hands of two powerful investors, Aeon Co and Mori Trust. These owners joined hands to apply pressure, but none of their shareholders was on board and some other owners felt the move was ill-timed as the firm was still recovering from the effects of the tsunami (Kachi and Sanchanta, 2011).

Both pension and hedge funds have been defined as active investors (Kahan and Rock, 2009). Investor activism levels are strong indicators of the probability that investor presence will be strong enough to impact performance (Ryan and Schneider, 2002). Yet, pension and hedge funds often approach profits and losses differently: while pension funds actively campaign for long-term goals (Smith, 1996), hedge funds strive for short-term initiatives (Kahan and Rock, 2009). This disconnect can potentially cause conflict among shareholder interests. Events in the biotechnology industry serve as an example. Several large owners of Actelion Ltd, including financier Rudolph Maag and Swiss investment company BB Biotech AG, are backing Actelion's strategy, management, and board (Mijuk, 2011)—supporting a long-term perspective. However, other key investors, following the advice of Institutional Shareholder Services (ISS), have expressed considerable reservation about the firm's strategy and have called for a management reshuffling and reduced emphasis on expansion of the firm's medical franchise—supporting a short-term perspective. The resulting tension between shareholders has played out in the boardroom and in the firm, occupying the time and attention of managers, creating uncertainty for employees, and making it difficult for the firm to implement a cohesive strategy.

In addition, some owners may prefer to be active regarding employee rights (Martin and Freeman, 2003), others may have environmental concerns (Waddock et al., 2002; Neubaum and Zahra, 2006), and others may be hands-off investors that do not advertise their preferences (Hoskisson et al., 2002). For instance, some institutional investors are very concerned about issues of sustainability and environmental protection. This is not limited to the socially responsible investors that emerged in the 1990s, but is far more prolific now as many funds market to their customers, at least to some extent, the importance of environmental concerns for firms in which they invest. While such matters may be at the forefront for a large number of investors, others may not share those values and could be discontent with investor pressure toward environmental or socially responsible ends. Once different levels of activism are properly gauged and measured, research efforts can focus on which types of owners, in the mix of ownership heterogeneity, receive more attention than others.

Owner level of understanding could also be an issue for discord. The board of directors understands the firm from a strategic perspective, while other stakeholders view it from a financial perspective. While both perspectives may be valid, they may yield different conclusions, resulting in misalignment and miscommunication of preferences (Baysinger and Hoskisson, 1990).

Finally, the level of third-party pressure among firm ownership heterogeneity may also cause conflict. Angel investors and some types of blockholders are small individual entities that act, monitor, and incentivize based on a single perspective. Institutional owners, on the other hand, represent many clients with many and varied demands. Since those clients give up their voting rights to the institution, there must be a collective approach to ownership interests and decisions. This introduces complexity about which monitoring, bonding, incentive, or sanctions receive highest priority (see Table 11.3 for conflicts among owners). Although institutional investors already unify a group of individual investors, they themselves are also unified by third-party organizations. The two largest of these, ISS and Glass-Lewis, are particularly influential. These advisory bodies provide corporate governance solutions to institutional investors by uncovering and assessing business, legal, governance, and accounting risks of invested firms. They strive to enable and empower shareholders with information needed to vote their proxies in the interest of long-term, sustainable value. As a result, managers may become concerned with how these advisory bodies rank their firms, and both ISS and Glass-Lewis have been highly successful at implementing a wide range of governance reforms, board shake-ups, and organizational realignments.

Future Research Directions

Because of increased diversity among owners, more research is needed to examine the consequences of heterogeneity. In this section we raise a number of issues worth exploring and describe a range of theoretical paradigms that could be utilized to help facilitate our understanding of the complexities that arise.

Handling Conflicts

When principals most interested in the firm's success do not agree on the firm's strategic direction, management can be forced to choose sides. Indeed, the rise of institutional ownership has complicated decision-making priorities—pressuring managers to choose a set of strategic implementations that conform to the owner with the greatest, or at least loudest, influence. One potential way of handling these conflicts is by utilizing impression management.

A growing number of scholars are focusing on the socio-political perspective of corporate governance, which emphasizes a manager's ability to ingratiate, persuade, and enact certain policies and procedures to convince and appease shareholders. We learn from Westphal and Zajac (1994, 1998) and Zajac and Westphal (1995) that CEOs may use impression management to actively associate themselves with practices displaying concern for shareholders' interests in order to enhance legitimacy with stockholders and other stakeholders. In addition, CEOs use ingratiation tactics to achieve board membership (Westphal and Stern, 2006), deter institutional owners from using power to make changes at the expense of top management (Westphal and Bednar, 2008), and improve shareholder appraisals by appearing to increase board independence (Westphal and Graebner, 2010). As managers encounter conflicts, such tactics may be necessary to appease the diverse number and types of shareholders.

For instance, Bushee (1998) found that firms tend to pursue the incentives of particular types of investors, finding that, in firms with a high degree of transient investors, managers tend to make short-term decisions to avoid an earnings drop, which would likely precipitate the exit of many of those investors. In these cases, an awareness and focus on impression management may lend valuable insight as managers strive to avoid the systemic managerial myopia that occurs when firms are overly concerned with short-term gains to the detriment of long-term outcomes. Such actions could subdue the concern that firms are set up for failure as managers pay heed to their most powerful investors, since the most active owners have frequently devised ways of eliminating managers and board members who do not comply.

As institutional investors continue to become more prevalent, and more concentrated, impression management may be necessary for owners to persuade managers to enact formidable policies and procedures. The Euro 100, a list of Europe's largest money managers, has increased its total holdings substantially over the past decade. This would suggest that firm ownership structures could actually be moving toward a *less* heterogeneous model. Therefore, as pension, mutual, and other institutional owners saturate the corporate governance landscape, managers may find themselves in a situation where they need to focus on fewer, but more powerful, owners. Perhaps this trend will encourage scholars to consider more carefully owners' ingratiating tactics in owner-manager relations. To date, little research has explored how owners go about the process of applying pressure on managers, beyond the obvious public expressions of media exposure and proxy battles. More qualitative studies and surveys of investment managers could help uncover the processes by which an increasingly powerful set of owners exerts their influence upon managers and how managers respond to these pressures.

Other blockholder preferences are difficult to ignore, despite their minority shares. For example, family firm ownership, consisting of the founder, multiple generations of the family, or both, holds tight control of decision-making preferences. Even if the institutional ownership percentage is greater than that of family ownership, the family strength may win competing preference battles. For example, members of the Weston family own, in large part, the UK's largest family firm, Associated British Foods (ABF). However, the firm has also attracted the attention of a large number of institutional investors via its listing on the London Stock Exchange. As ABF continues to grow and expand geographically throughout the EU and beyond, we could see family preferences overshadowing those of institutional investors. Scholars may want to investigate certain instances when firms do not follow institutional preferences. We could find, in some cases, that the collective opinions of the many do not always trump the power of the few.

Attracting the "Right" Investors

A great deal of research has focused on how investors seek firms. However, researchers have devoted less attention to how firms and their managers seek investors. Scholars are beginning to acknowledge that firms' pursuit of investors may be deliberate, and organizations may seek specific types of owners. Managers may seek certain types of investors that have goals that align with their own. For example, Bushee (1998) described how some firms may be primarily oriented toward short-term gains and could, therefore, be perfectly content with a slate of transient owners. However, firms that adopt a more long-term strategic focus could be more inclined to entice pension fund ownership and larger, more established blockholders. For example, one action managers may take to intentionally manipulate which investor types they attract would be to control the level of information asymmetry between them and the market. As less information becomes publicly and readily available, only higher quality (e.g. dedicated) investors would have enough in-depth knowledge of the industry and the firm to be willing to take a chance on investing. Consider, for instance, the following quote from Larry Page, CEO of Google: "As a public company, we will of course provide you with all information required by law, and we will also do our best to explain our actions. But we will not unnecessarily disclose all of our strengths, strategies, and intentions." Page may be positioning the firm to garner the attention of investors that are willing to stick with Google over the long haul.

On the contrary, some of the actions that attract owners may not be deliberate. Signaling theory may be informative in this regard (Connelly, Ketchen, et al., 2011). Managers may take a range of actions designed to signal to investors the underlying quality of their firm and their desire for shareholders who will stay the course. However, they could also inadvertently send "negative signals" that attract investors they did not intend to attract. Even worse, this inadvertent signaling of firm strategies or intentions could invite short-selling, where owners are actually betting on the firm's short-term decline (see Chapter 25 on hedge funds for further discussion). In addition, some corporate strategy positions may incentivize firms to pursue certain types of investors. For example, family firms may prefer investors that prefer debt financing in lieu of equity financing; unrelated diversified firms may aim to attract mutual funds with preferences for short-term restructuring actions; and related firms may prefer long-term institutional investors (pension funds). Securities analysts may also influence ownership of one kind or another, depending on the future outlook for the firm (Benner, 2010). Future research could focus on investor-seeking preferences of firms and the incentives that drive those firms to attract particular investor types.

Ownership Management

Ownership management focused on targeted as well as overall strategies firms have for managing owner relationships has received meager research in the management literature. As stakeholders and shareholders increase and become more diverse, appeasement approaches (e.g. Westphal and Bednar, 2008) may not be sufficient. For instance, in response to a possible takeover attempt, shareholders may take action in either a friendly or unfriendly manner. An example of a friendly shareholder action is that of a "white knight," where a shareholder enters the auction for the company and circumvents the takeover (Banerjee and Owers, 1996). An example of unfriendly shareholder action is greenmail, or the purchase of enough company stock by minority shareholders to risk a takeover of its own (Kosnik, 1987). In both cases, the board of directors' effectiveness is on the line for how they manage the acute situation (Kosnik, 1987). Under these circumstances, boards must handle the long-term goals of the firm, while still representing the needs of shareholders. The situation requires more than mere appeasement (e.g. Westphal and Bednar, 2008), but aggressive intervention.

Lions Gate Entertainment faced such a dilemma when the company's second largest shareholder, Carl Icahn, announced he would be buying off much of the company's debt, adding as many as four of his allies as board members, and potentially owning more than 20 percent of the company. In this precarious position, Lions Gate sought the help of its largest shareholder, MHR Fund Manager, and MHR's majority owner, Dr Mark Rachesky, to aid in blocking Icahn's advances (Grover, 2009). Further, Lions Gate was willing to incentivize Icahn to reconsider his advances through monetary means. Indeed, management was in a position where a crucial stockholder threatened their business strategy, their effectiveness depended on owner management, and their investor relations department was responsible for that owner management.

Investor relations departments represent an area of owner management with a rich opportunity for future research. These departments provide much more than information: they provide the expertise and experience necessary for handling difficult situations when the interests of shareholders collide. Although constrained by their context, managers can act to reduce environmental uncertainty and dependence (Hillman et al., 2009), which would explain the dilemma that firms face with competing owners. Specifically, investor relations departments might develop a marketing-oriented strategy to actively attract the right investors. This approach might spread to other stakeholders besides shareholders as well. Often, through strategic alliances, ownership arrangements exist with buyers and suppliers as well as other competitors (De Man and Roijakkers, 2009). These strategies often result in shared ownership arrangements, common control over vital resources, and shared power (Hillman et al., 2009).

Investor relations departments have the responsibility for communicating with shareholders (e.g. selling the company) and for regulating legal issues (e.g. financial disclosure rules) (Laskin, 2010). Yet, little research exists on how these departments manage conflict and align incentives, especially given the recent scholarly development regarding the pacification of institutional investors (Westphal and Bednar, 2008). As firms seek to gain control of more resources through shareholders and stakeholders, investor relations departments may be involved in recruiting suitable owners. Certainly, the examples of greenmail (Kosnik, 1987), white knights (Banerjee and Owers, 1996), and Lions Gate Entertainment (Grover, 2009) shed light on activity within these departments, and investigation of them represents an important research opportunity.

Other under-examined research areas that relate to investor relations department decisions and are worthy of mention include shared ownership among business groups (cross-ownership and pyramid ownership arrangements) and government ownership. Joint ownership strategies arising from pursuit of joint ventures or strategic alliances is another area where ownership conflict and control issues are likely to be of strategic importance (Kumar and Seth, 1998). Strategies pertaining to these subjects require more ownership management acumen and are deserving of further research, though space precludes delving into further detail here.

Conclusion

In sum, we have discussed the literature relating to several different forms of ownership that could contribute to corporate governance. By describing some of the different interests and incentives of various owners, we draw attention to the different ways in which they might influence managers. We highlight potential conflicts between different owners and areas where scholars can continue to expand our understanding of the changing ownership landscape. Doing so might help us to elucidate a more general theory of ownership as a form of governance—one that expands on our existing reliance on agency relationships. Keeping pace with changing business practices can be difficult for academics. We hope this chapter facilitates a search for new knowledge about evolving ownership structures.

References

Agrawal, A., and Knoeber, C. R. (1996). "Firm Performance and Mechanisms to Control Agency Problems between Managers and Shareholders," *Journal of Financial and Quantitative Analysis*, 31(3): 377–97.

Arregle, J. L., Hitt, M. A., Sirmon, D. G., and Véry, P. (2007). "The Development of Organizational Social Capital: Attributes of Family Firms" *Journal of Management Studies*, 44(1): 73–95.

Bainbridge, S. M. (2003). "Response to Increasing Shareholder Power," *Northwestern University Law Review*, 97: 547–606.

Banerjee, A., and Owers, J. E. (1996). "The Impact of the Nature and Sequence of Multiple Bids in Corporate Control Contests," *Journal of Corporate Finance*, 3(1): 23–43.

Barclay, M. J., and Holderness, C. G. (1989). "Private Benefits from Control of Corporations," *Journal of Financial Economics*, 25: 371–95.

Baysinger, B. D., and Hoskisson, R. E. (1990). "The Composition of Boards of Directors and Strategic Control: Effects on Corporate Strategy," *Academy of Management Review*, 15: 72–87.

Benner, M. J. (2010). "Securities Analysts and Incumbent Response to Radical Technological Change: Evidence from Digital Photography and Internet Telephony," *Organization Science*, 21: 42–62.

Bergh, D. D., Johnson, R. A., and DeWitt, R. L. (2007). "Restructuring through Spin-Off or Sell-Off: Transforming Information Asymmetries into Financial Gain," *Strategic Management Journal*, 29(2): 133–48.

Bergstrom, C., and Rydqvist, K. (1990). "The Determinants of Corporate Ownership: An Empirical Study on Swedish Data," *Journal of Banking and Finance*, 14(2–3): 237–53.

Blasi, J., Kruse, D., and Bernstein, A. (2003). *In the Company of Owners: The Truth about Stock Options and Why Every Employee Should Have Them*. New York: Basic Books.

Bogert, J. D. (1996). "Explaining Variance in the Performance of Long-Term Corporate Blockholders," *Strategic Management Journal*, 17(3): 243–49.

Brandes, P., Goranova, M., and Hall, S. (2008). "Navigating Shareholder Influence: Compensation Plans and the Shareholder Approval Process," *Academy of Management Perspectives*, 22(1): 41–57.

Brickley, J. A., Lease, R. C., and Smith, C. W. (1988). "Ownership Structure and Voting on Antitakeover Amendments," *Journal of Financial Economics*, 20(1–2): 267–91.

Bushee, B. J. (1998). "The Influence of Institutional Investors on Myopic R&D Investment Behavior," *Accounting Review*, 73(3): 305–33.

Connelly, B. L., Tihanyi, L., Certo, S. T., and Hitt, M. A. (2010). "Marching to the Beat of Different Drummers: The Influence of Institutional Owners on Competitive Actions," *Academy of Management Journal*, 53(4): 723–42.

—— Certo, S. T., Ireland, R. D. and Reutzel, C. R. (2011). "Signalling Theory: A Review and Assessment." *Journal of Management*, 37(1): 39–67.

—— Ketchen, D. J., and Slater, S. F. (2011). "Toward a 'Theoretical Toolbox' for Sustainability Research in Marketing," *Journal of the Academy of Marketing Science*, 39(1): 86–100.

Cumming, D., Siegel, D. S., and Wright, M. (2007). "Private Equity, Leveraged Buyouts and Governance," *Journal of Corporate Finance*, 13(4): 439–60.

Dalton, D. R., Daily, C. M., Certo, S. T., and Roengpitya, R. (2003). "Meta-Analyses of Financial Performance and Equity: Fusion or Confusion?" *Academy of Management Journal*, 46(1): 13–26.

David, P., Hitt, M. A., and Gimeno, J. (2001). "The Influence of Activism by Institutional Investors on R&D," *Academy of Management Journal*, 44(1): 144–57.

De Man, A. P., and Roijakkers, N. (2009). "Alliance Governance: Balancing Control and Trust in Dealing with Risk," *Long Range Planning*, 42: 75–95.

Demsetz, H. (1983). "The Structure of Ownership and the Theory of the Firm," *Journal of Law and Economics*, 26: 375–90.

—— and Villalonga, B. (2001). "Ownership Structure and Corporate Performance," *Journal of Corporate Finance*, 7(3): 209–33.

Djankov, S., and Murrell, P. (2002). "Enterprise Restructuring in Transition: A Quantitative Survey," *Journal of Economic Literature*, 40: 739–92.

D'Souza, J., and Megginson, W. L. (1999). "The Financial and Operating Performance of Privatized Firms during the 1990s," *Journal of Finance*, 54(4): 1397–438.

Economist The, (2006). "Battling for Corporate America," *The Economist*, March 11, 69–71.

Elango, B., Fried, V. H., Hisrich, R. D., and Polonchek, A. (1995). "How Venture Capital Firms Differ," *Journal of Business Venturing*, 10(2): 157–79.

Fama, E. F., and Jensen, M. C. (1983). "Agency Problems and Residual Claims," *Journal of Law and Economics*, 26(2): 327–49.

Fiss, P. C. (2006). "Social Influence Effects and Managerial Compensation Evidence from Germany," *Strategic Management Journal*, 27(11): 1013–31.

Gillan, S. L., and Starks, L. T. (2007). "The Evolution of Shareholder Activism in the United States," *Journal of Applied Corporate Finance*, 19(1): 55–73.

Gomez-Mejia, L. R., Haynes, K. T., Nunez-Nickel, M., Jacobson, K. J., and Moyano-Fuentes, J. (2007). "Socioemotional Wealth and Business Risks in Family-Controlled Firms: Evidence from Spanish Olive Oil Mills," *Administrative Science Quarterly*, 52: 106–37.

—— Makri, M., and Kintana, M. L. (2009). "Diversification Decisions in Family-Controlled Firms," *Journal of Management Studies*, 47(2): 223–52.

—— Cruz, C., Berrone, P., and Castro, J. D. (2011). "The Bind that Ties: Socioemotional Wealth Preservation in Family Firms," *Academy of Management Annals* 5(1): 653–707.

GOMPERS, P. A., and LERNER, J. (1995). "An Analysis of Compensation in the United-States Venture Partnership," *Journal of Finance*, 50(3): 971–2.

—— and METRICK, A. (2001). "Institutional Investors and Equity Prices," *Quarterly Journal of Economics*, 116(1): 229–59.

GROVER, R. (2009). "Lions Gate: An Alliance against Icahn?" *Businessweek Online*, 26, March 19.

HERMALIN, B. E., and WEISBACH, M. S. (2003). "Boards of Directors as an Endogenously Determined Institution: A Survey of the Economic Literature," *Economic Policy Review*, 9: 7–26.

HILLMAN, A. J., WITHERS, M. C., and COLLINS, B. J. (2009). "Resource Dependence Theory: A Review," *Journal of Management*, 35(6): 1404–27.

HIMMELBERG, C. P., HUBBARD, R. G., and PALIA, D. (1999). "Understanding the Determinants of Managerial Ownership and the Link between Ownership and Performance," *Journal of Financial Economics*, 53(3): 353–84.

HOSKISSON, R. E., HITT, M. A., JOHNSON, R. A., and GROSSMAN, W. (2002). "Conflicting Voices: The Effects of Institutional Ownership Heterogeneity and Internal Governance on Corporate Innovation Strategies," *Academy of Management Journal*, 45(4): 697–716.

—— —— TIHANYI, L., and WHITE, R. E. (2005). "Diversified Business Groups and Corporate Refocusing in Emerging Economies," *Journal of Management*, 31(6): 941–65.

JEN, S. (2007). "Sovereign Wealth Funds: What They Are and What's Happening," *World Economics*, 8: 1–7.

JENSEN, M. C. (1989). "Eclipse of the Public Corporation," *Harvard Business Review*, 67: 61–74.

—— and MURPHY, K. J. (1990). "Performance Pay and Top-Management Incentives," *Journal of Political Economy*, 98(2): 225–64.

JONES, D. C., and KATO, T. (1995). "The Productivity Effects of Employee Stock-Ownership Plans and Bonuses: Evidence from Japanese Panel-Data," *American Economic Review*, 85(3): 391–414.

KACHI, H. and SANCHANTA, M. (2011). "Update: Japan's Parco Bows to Shareholder Pressure, to Oust President," *Wall Street Journal*, <http://www.wsj.com>, April 20.

KAHAN, M., and ROCK, E. (2009). "Hedge Fund Activism in the Enforcement of Bondholder Rights," *Northwestern University Law Review*, 103(1): 281–321.

KAPLAN, S. N., and STROMBERG, P. (2009). "Leveraged Buyouts and Private Equity," *Journal of Economic Perspectives*, 23(1): 121–46.

KOSNIK, R. D. (1987). "A Study of Board Performance in Corporate Governance," *Administrative Science Quarterly*, 32(2): 163–85.

KUMAR, S., and SETH, A. (1998). "The Design of Coordination and Control Mechanisms for Managing Joint Venture-Parent Relationships," *Strategic Management Journal*, 19(6): 579–99.

LANG, L., POULSEN, A., and STULZ, R. (1995). "Asset Sales, Firm Performance, and the Agency Costs of Managerial Discretion," *Journal of Financial Economics*, 37: 3–37.

LA PORTA, R., LOPEZ-DE-SILANES, F., and SHLEIFER, A. (2002). "Government Ownership of Banks," *Journal of Finance*, 57(1): 265–301.

LASKIN, A. (2010). *Managing Investor Relations: Strategies for Effective Communication*. New York: Business Expert Press.

MARTIN, K. and FREEMAN, R. E. (2003). "Some Problems with Employee Monitoring," *Journal of Business Ethics*, 43: 353–61.

MEGGINSON, W. L., and NETTER, J. M. (2001). "From State to Market: A Survey of Empirical Studies on Privatization," *Journal of Economic Literature*, 39: 321–89.

MIJUK, G. (2011). "Actelion Wins Support in Fight against Elliott," *Wall Street Journal*, April 21.

MIKKELSON, W. H., and RUBACK, R. S. (1985). "An Empirical Analysis of the Interfirm Equity Investment Process," *Journal of Financial Economics*, 14(4): 523–53.

MILLER, D., BRETON-MILLER, I. L., LESTER, R. H., and CANNELLA JR., A. A. (2007). "Are Family Firms Really Superior Performers?" *Journal of Corporate Finance*, 13(5): 829–58.

MORCK, R., SHLEIFER, A., and VISHNY, R. W. (1988). "Management Ownership and Market Valuation: An Empirical Analysis," *Journal of Financial Economics*, 20(1–2): 293–315.

NEUBAUM, D. O., and ZAHRA, S. A. (2006). "Institutional Ownership and Corporate Social Performance: The Moderating Effects of Investment Horizon, Activism, and Coordination," *Journal of Management*, 32(1): 108–31.

PERROW, C. (1986). *Complex Organizations: A Critical Essay*. New York: Random House.

PERRY, T., and ZENNER, M. (2000). "CEO Compensation in the 1990s: Shareholder Alignment or Shareholder Expropriation?" *Wake Forest Law Review*, 35: 123–52.

PIERCE, J. L., RUBENFELD, S. A., and MORGAN, S. (1991). "Employee Ownership: A Conceptual Model of Process and Effects," *Academy of Management Review*, 16(1): 121–44.

PROWSE, S. (1998). "Angel Investors and the Market for Angel Investments," *Journal of Banking and Finance*, 22: 785–92.

ROSENSTEIN, S., and RUSH, D. F. (1990). "The Stock Return Performance of Corporations that are Partially Owned by Other Corporations," *Journal of Financial Research*, 13(1): 39–51.

RYAN, L. V., and SCHNEIDER, M. (2002). "The Antecedents of Institutional Investor Activism," *Academy of Management Review*, 27(4): 554–73.

SCHARFSTEIN, D. S., and STEIN, J. C. (1990). "Herd Behavior and Investment," *American Economic Review*, 80(3): 465–79.

SHLEIFER, A. (1998). "State versus Private Ownership," *Journal of Economic Perspectives*, 12(4): 133–50.

—— and SUMMERS, L. H. (1988). "Breach of Trust in Hostile Takeovers," in A. J. Auerbach (ed.), *Corporate Takeovers: Causes And Consequence*. Chicago: University of Chicago Press, 65–88.

SMITH, M. P. (1996). "Shareholder Activism by Institutional Investors: Evidence from CalPERS," *Journal of Finance*, 51: 227–52.

TIHANYI, L., and HEGARTY, W. H. (2007). "Political Interests and the Emergence of Commercial Banking in Transition Economies," *Journal of Management Studies*, 44: 788–813.

USEEM, M. (1996). *Investor Capitalism: How Money Managers are Changing the Face of Corporate America*. New York: Basic Books/HarperCollins.

WADDOCK, S. A., BODWELL, C., and GRAVES, S. B. (2002). "Responsibility: The New Business Imperative," *Academy of Management Executive*, 16(2): 132–48.

WELBOURNE, T. M., and GOMEZ-MEJIA, L. (1995). "Gainsharing: A Critical Review and a Future Research Agenda," *Journal of Management*, 21(3): 559–609.

WERNER, S., TOSI, H. L., and GOMEZ-MEJIA, L. (2005). "Organizational Governance and Employee Pay: How Ownership Structure Affects the Firm's Compensation Strategy," *Strategic Management Journal*, 26(4): 377–84.

WESTPHAL, J. D., and BEDNAR, M. K. (2008). "The Pacification of Institutional Investors," *Administrative Science Quarterly*, 53(1): 29–72.

Westphal, J. D., and Graebner, M. E. (2010). "A Matter of Appearances: How Corporate Leaders Manage the Impressions of Financial Analysts about the Conduct of their Boards," *Academy of Management Journal*, 53(1): 15–44.

—— and Stern, I. (2006). "The Other Pathway to the Boardroom: Interpersonal Influence Behavior as a Substitute for Elite Credentials and Majority Status in Obtaining Board Appointments," *Administrative Science Quarterly*, 51(2): 169–204.

—— and Zajac, E. J. (1994). "Substance and Symbolism in CEOs' Long-Term Incentive Plans," *Administrative Science Quarterly*, 39(3): 367–90.

—— —— (1998). "The Symbolic Management of Stockholders: Corporate Governance Reforms and Shareholder Reactions," *Administrative Science Quarterly*, 43(1): 127–53.

White, R. E., Hoskisson, R. E., Yiu, D. W., and Bruton, G. D. (2008). "Employment and Market Innovation in Chinese Business Group Affiliated Firms: The Role of Group Control Systems," *Management and Organization Review*, 4(2): 225–56.

Wright, M. and Robbie, K. (1998). "Venture Capital and Private Equity: A Review and Synthesis," *Journal of Business Finance and Accounting*, 25: 521–70.

—— Hoskisson, R. E., Busenitz, L. W., and Dial, J. (2000). "Entrepreneurial Growth through Privatization: The Upside of Management Buyouts," *Academy of Management Review*, 25: 591–601.

Wright, P., Ferris, S. P., Sarin, A., and Awasthi, V. (1996). "Impact of Corporate Insider, Blockholder, and Institutional Equity Ownership on Firm Risk Taking," *Academy of Management Journal*, 39(2): 441–63.

Yan, X., and Zhang, Z. (2009). "Institutional Investors and Equity Returns: Are Short-Term Institutions Better Informed?" *Review of Financial Studies*, 22: 893–924.

Zajac, E. J., and Westphal, J. D. (1995). "Accounting for the Explanations of CEO Compensation: Substance and Symbolism," *Administrative Science Quarterly*, 40(2): 283–308.

CHAPTER 12

FINANCIAL LEVERAGE AND CORPORATE GOVERNANCE

ROBERT WATSON

Debt is the prolific mother of folly and of crime; it taints the course of life in all its dreams. Hence so many unhappy marriages, so many prostituted pens, and venal politicians!

(Benjamin Disraeli, *Henrietta Temple: A Love Story*, 1837)

Introduction

The focus of this chapter is corporate debt, its relationships to corporate risk and performance, and some of the behavioral and governance implications that may arise from an overreliance upon debt for corporate investment initiatives. As the Disraeli quotation above[1] indicates, even for individuals who do not typically enjoy any limited liability in regard to their debts (short of bankruptcy), it has long been appreciated that the leverage opportunities of debt have often proved to be irresistible and by no means restricted only to sound (or legal) ventures. Consequently there are inevitably always individuals that become over-indebted due to poor investment choices (or simply bad luck) and who invariably face significantly impaired future financial and life prospects as a result.

There is also a systematic,[2] social, component to much indebtedness. The history of investment fads and busts provides an unambiguous demonstration that economic circumstances and expectations can have a significant impact on an individual's willingness and ability to get into debt even when, say during a boom period, these expectations have become detached from reality (i.e. are overly optimistic). Despite its potential dangers, in these circumstances debt may be especially difficult for even normally financially conservative individuals and/or management teams and boards of directors to resist. This is because, once an investment boom has begun, a variety of positive feedback mechanisms also typically come into play which appear to confirm and thereby to sustain investor optimism. Early investors will be seen to be doing well and this tends to encourage "herding" behavior and the adoption of "imitative" strategies involving the launch of similar ventures and financing arrangements, most of which will also tend initially to be profitable, at least for their promoters. However, these positive feedback mechanisms also tend to feed the subsequent downward spiral in expectations once debtors begin to experience difficulties and/or creditors begin to realize that their previous lending assumptions have been falsified by subsequent events and conditions.[3]

In this chapter it is argued that the corporate form of organization, rather than providing a restraint upon unrealistic expectations or otherwise mitigating the incentives and attractiveness of debt, encourages debt-financed risk taking. Limited liability generates moral hazard in the presence of high corporate debt due to the potentially highly leveraged and asymmetric (limited downside) payoffs that accrue to shareholders when the firm undertakes risky business investments with debt financing. However, the separation of ownership from control creates additional moral hazards, as management are provided with opportunities to make decisions that benefit primarily themselves rather than their shareholders. The likelihood that managers may exploit their control over corporate resources to make decisions that are inconsistent with the interests of their shareholders is, of course, the primary motivation for current corporate governance arrangements such as independent boards and financial information disclosure and audit rules. Of course, not all governance arrangements operate as intended. For example, the widespread practice of paying senior managers on the basis of earnings-based metrics is typically justified in terms of allegedly better aligning managerial and shareholder interests. In this chapter it is argued, however, that such pay schemes are more likely to generate a misalignment of interests since they greatly increase the incentives for managers to undertake debt-financed low value-high risk investments. Furthermore, it is argued that it would be a mistake to assume that current governance arrangements are likely to provide an effective safeguard against excessive, debt-financed, risk taking. Indeed, the large size and, largely management-induced, complexity of many public corporations and overconfidence in the ability of boards to control management appear to provide an organizational setting and mind-set especially conducive to the generation of overly optimistic expectations and a managerial bias toward egregious risk taking with borrowed funds. This is because effective governance requires too much of boards as currently constituted.

To be effective, the part-time, independent board members have to be knowledgeable about the relationships between financial risks and the specific business risks associated with the firms' current strategies and policies, the impact these have on corporate performance measures, and to have an acute awareness of managerial incentives to deliberately create complexity and to misreport accounting statements. Effective governance and the fulfillment of their fiduciary duties toward shareholders, however, also requires the independent directors to actively monitor managerial initiatives and to be prepared to be critical of their managerial board colleagues whenever the latter appear to be making decisions that deviate from shareholder interests.

Determining whether or not an action is in shareholders' interests can, of course, often be less than straightforward as the same incentives that motivate managers to take on excessive debt can also be expected to motivate the use of deceptive financial reporting practices to hide indebtedness and/or to flatter performance, particularly when managerial compensation is linked to earnings-based performance measures. Hence, diligent monitoring will inevitably be time-consuming as well as being likely to generate unwelcome conflict with management. The individual psychology and group decision literatures suggest that conflicting demands are typically resolved by choosing to concentrate on the least costly to fulfill demands and the downplaying of the importance or attention given to difficult and/or risk-prone responsibilities. It is argued that boards of directors tend to have insufficiently strong incentives to confront and prevent self-serving managerial initiatives. That is, independent directors resolve their governance dilemma by adopting an automatic and uncritical trust (a loyalty bias) in the competence of their incumbent managerial team and, as a consequence, they will tend to overwhelmingly downplay their responsibilities to shareholders.

This lack of monitoring and the combination of covertly risky investment, financing, reporting, and managerial remuneration policies have the effect of rendering firms far more vulnerable to "normal business hazards" than they appear on the basis of their published financial statements and accounting-based performance metrics. In essence, managers will be unduly rewarded for taking hidden financial risks and both shareholder and debt holder risk exposures will be underestimated and hence underpriced, i.e. this dynamic will transfer wealth from financial stakeholders to managers.[4] Generous managerial pay schemes that encourage moral hazard—that is, they further incentivize managers to adopt unwise operational and financial leverage strategies and to use deceptive financial reporting methods that hide debt and/or flatter corporate and managerial performance—are indicative of a systematic board governance failure. The chapter argues that acquiescent boards are generated from normal organizational and group dynamics premised on an unduly trusting and hence unrealistic and self-serving conceptualization of the executive–board relationship.[5] Significant structural and procedural reforms that provide greater incentives to independent directors to actively monitor management are likely to be required to improve governance in this area.

The remainder of the chapter is structured as follows. In the next section, a discussion of the corporate form of organization and its unique governance issues are undertaken. This is followed by a section that models the relationships between managerial investment and financing strategies, corporate wealth creation, and the earnings-based performance measures used to motivate managerial effort. An assessment of the incentives and behavior of boards in regard to monitoring, evaluating, and rewarding their executive colleagues is then undertaken. This includes a review of the operation of current institutional arrangements by which executive pay is determined—a board subcommittee made up of independent directors. The chapter concludes with a discussion of some possible reforms aimed at strengthening the willingness of boards to become more diligent and critical monitors of corporate management.

The Corporation and its Governance

In this section, we examine two distinctive characteristics of the corporate form, namely, the limited liability of its owners for the debts of the corporation and the agency problems stemming from the separation of ownership from control. The primary governance arrangements designed to mitigate debt financing risks to creditors are also discussed.

The separate legal identity of the corporation allows its owners to benefit from limited liability, i.e. the shareholders are not responsible for any unrecoverable debts of the corporation beyond the price they paid for their shares. With limited liability, the respective payoff functions to shareholders and debt holders are Max(0, V − D) and Min(D, V), where V = the value of the firms' assets and D = the firms' total debt obligations.

An implication of this truncated downside risk profile to equity holders of firms with high debt levels is that, if the firm defaults, some or all of these downside losses will be borne by the debt holders, whilst all the financially leveraged upside post-tax gains will accrue to the shareholders. It is clear from these payoffs that managers are exposed to extreme moral hazard at low values of V relative to D.[6] With little or no equity at risk, owner-managers have strong incentives to mislead outside investors regarding actual business risks, whilst also having the ability to alter the composition of the firm's assets and/or the riskiness of its business model.

An important corollary of limiting the liability of owners for the debts of the business is that creditors require additional protection to discourage owner-managers from taking excessive risks with their borrowed funds. It is worth emphasizing, however, that an inescapable aspect of any business venture is that it has to undertake risky projects in order to prosper. Trade creditors and financial institutions that provide financing to any business enterprise know that this exposes them to some risk of default because, by definition, not all risky projects are likely to be successful.[7] Nevertheless, the corporate form has required creditors to develop lending and trade credit policies that minimize their exposure to uncompensated business and financial risks.

In most jurisdictions the primary solution to this problem has consisted of developing an institutional infrastructure that includes:

- accessible and independent civil law courts to enforce contractual agreements,
- the overturning of the protection of limited liability when fraudulent intent has been established,
- greater disclosure and audit of financial information to outside creditors, credit rating agencies,
- debt covenant restrictions on the firms' behavior and, in the event of default,
- corporate bankruptcy laws that give creditors the right to take over the business and sell its assets to satisfy their outstanding financial claims (Roe, 1994; Rajan and Zingales, 2003; Watson and Ezzamel, 2005).

Though this is a potentially serious problem, it should also be apparent that owner-manager incentives to engage in opportunistic behavior at the expense of their creditors only occur when corporate equity (V − D) is insufficient to absorb business and financial risks, i.e. a situation that is relatively uncommon (but, as the occasional spectacular failure such as Enron suggests, not unknown) amongst the largest publicly listed corporations.

The limitation of liability also created a legal framework for the development of the widely held, publicly listed corporation. The ability to obtain equity finance from the general public via a public stock market listing has undoubtedly facilitated firm growth since publicly listed corporations dominate most sectors and tend to be far larger than their private competitors. Increasing firm size brings economies of scale and the separation of ownership from control, where the latter requires the employment of specialized managerial employees to run the firm on behalf of its many shareholders. Though public corporations clearly derive huge benefits from being managed by professional managerial employees, this does give rise to potentially serious incentive alignment problems, particularly as corporate managers have many opportunities to use their decision discretion to act in ways that further their own interests at the expense of their shareholders. Indeed, the history of corporate scandals and the large body of "agency theory" inspired studies documenting managerial excess strongly suggest that it would be very unwise for shareholders to simply trust that professional managers will always take business decisions that necessarily further their interests (Jensen and Meckling, 1976). The plethora of financial reporting and auditing regulations, the establishment of independent boards to oversee managerial actions, and the corporate governance code compliance requirements that we see across many jurisdictions today are largely institutional attempts to discourage and/or mitigate the potential negative wealth consequences associated with this central agency problem.

The major structural constraint that shareholders face in managing this "agency conflict" concerns the "public good" characteristics of monitoring and control. In essence this results in individual minority (non-managerial) shareholders rationally choosing to free-ride on the analysis of information intermediaries and/or the monitoring and control activities of any large ("block") shareholders. Mitigating the worst consequences of this less-than-optimal, degree of monitoring and control of managerial discretion is the province of governance codes and regulatory features, such as requiring independent boards, financial reporting, and other disclosure rules. The legal responsibilities of boards of directors in most jurisdictions is to collectively manage the business in accordance with its constitution for the benefit of its shareholders and to comply with the financial reporting and other disclosure requirements stipulated by Company Law and securities legislation. Thus, the board of directors is the primary institutional mechanism by which the shareholders render the executives appointed to manage the assets on their behalf accountable for their stewardship.

These governance arrangements effectively transfer the monitoring and control functions to the board of directors and, to a lesser extent, the capital markets, auditors, and other regulatory agencies (Fama and Jensen, 1983). In this chapter it is argued that it is somewhat unrealistic to expect independent directors, who are in practice no more involved in managing the business than are shareholders and no less dependent than shareholders upon the information provided by senior managers regarding their strategies and financial results (Turnbull, 2010), to be effective monitors. As discussed in the following section, managers are exposed to highly leveraged financial incentives to take excessive debt-financed investment risks and it is therefore far from obvious that part-time independent directors will have the skills, motivation, and resources by which to critically evaluate managerial business, financial or financial reporting strategies and choices.

Analysis of the Interrelationships between Performance, Leverage, and Earnings Based Executive Compensation

In this section, the relationships between corporate strategy, business risks, financial leverage, performance, and managerial incentives are analyzed. The most appropriate measure for evaluating the performance of the firm and/or the performance and rewarding of its managerial team ought to be a metric that reliably reflects their unique contribution. In this section we focus on the two most commonly used accounting performance measures, return on assets (ROA) and return on equity (ROE),[8] their relationship to each other, to business risk (the variance in performance attributable to external uncertainties, managerial strategies, and the management of operations) and to financial risk (leverage from using debt finance).

The definitions of ROA and ROE adopted—because there is an economically justifiable relationship between the numerators and denominators—are the following:

$$ROA = EBIT/(D + E); \qquad (1)$$

$$ROE = [(EBIT - kD)(1 - T)]/E, \qquad (2)$$

where EBIT = earnings before interest and tax, k = the interest rate on debt, D = the amount of debt finance, T = the corporate tax rate, and E = the equity finance of the firm.

Note, however, that for an all-equity firm (where D = 0), the after-tax ROA(1 – T) will be identical to ROE.

If we initially assume that the financial reporting system produces reasonable approximations to economic performance and the available resources used to generate income, then the ROA is a ratio that measures EBIT, the total income generated irrespective of how the firm has been financed, in relation to the total resources available (total assets, again, irrespective of how these assets have been financed). ROE however measures the after-tax income (i.e. the income belonging to the shareholders after the finance suppliers and the tax authorities have taken their respective cuts) as a proportion of the equity finance (share capital plus reserves, primarily retained earnings). This latter measure may appear to be the most appropriate measure for shareholders to judge the performance of their investment and the firms' management. However, because of the relationship with financial leverage this is not necessarily so.

Another relevant feature of the ROA metric in regard to assessing corporate and managerial performance is that it can be decomposed to reveal how the ROA was achieved. The most commonly used decomposition of ROA is the product of the profit margin on sales (EBIT/Sales) and the asset-turnover ratio (Sales/(E + D)). These ratios make it possible to infer the underlying business strategy (managerial contribution) that was responsible for the ROA achieved:

$$ROA = EBIT/Sales + Sales/(E + D). \tag{3}$$

These ratios reflect corporate pricing strategies and its investment and operating policies. For example, a generic drug company can be expected to face strong price competition since its products are not unique and it has no power to exclude competitors (e.g. patent protection). Hence, the typical strategy adopted by generic drug companies is to maximize sales revenue via low prices and to minimize operating costs, that is, such firms will tend to operate with a low profit margin (price competition) and a high asset-turnover ratio (reflecting a combination of high sales and an efficient use of assets). This strategy contrasts with a high R&D pharmaceutical company that has patent-protected drugs and which can charge a high mark-up on costs, but which is likely to have a lower asset turnover ratio as this strategy requires greater resources (e.g. laboratories, and significant testing and marketing-related assets). Such a strategy will therefore be reflected in a high profit margin and a relatively low asset turnover ratio.

Knowing what corporate strategy is, assessing whether it is likely to be sustainable and how the strategy is likely to be reflected in corporate performance metrics provides the initial indicator of the managerial contribution. However, the average ROA achieved is only the first moment of the ROA distribution; risk-averse shareholders will also be interested in the tradeoff between a high average ROA and business risk (the variance in ROA). Thus, if a high ROA involves exposure to high business risk, then it is not certain that risk-averse shareholders would necessarily approve of the strategy. In essence, business risk is a multiplicative function of two main factors: the variability in demand (g = percentage growth in sales revenues) and the firm's investment strategy (i.e. its cost structure or "operational leverage"):

$$Var(ROA) = Var(g)(OL). \tag{4}$$

Demand uncertainty ($Var(g)$) arises from changes in aggregate demand, the prices of substitute products, competition, and the ability of a firm's management to retain or increase their existing market share. Operational leverage (OL) involves the firm operating with high fixed-cost technologies/contracts. Such cost structures generate additional variance in ROA, i.e. they create operational leverage due to the high proportion of total costs that are fixed costs (FC), which, unlike variable costs (VC), do not vary with changes in output:

$$\text{Operational leverage (OL)} = (\text{Contribution}/\text{EBIT}) = (\text{Sales} - \text{VC})/(\text{Sales} - \text{VC} - \text{FC}). \quad (5)$$

Clearly from (5) above, firms with no fixed costs have OL of unity and all firms with FC > 0 will have OL > 1.

Uncertainty in respect of demand, that is the variance in the percentage growth in sales revenue (g), multiplied by operational leverage, gives the variance in ROA. Alternatively, the anticipated change in ROA, given sales growth g and operational leverage OL, will be equal to:

$$\text{ROA}_{t+1} = \text{ROA}_t (g)(\text{OL}). \quad (6)$$

Thus, evaluating a firm's business strategy involves a consideration of both current and anticipated profits (ROA) and the business risk (Var(ROA) = Var(g)(OL)) this strategy exposes the firm to. Note, however, that because business risk is a multiplicative function of revenue uncertainty and operational leverage, if a firm has low Var(g), then even large values of OL may not result in excessive business risk. For example, a utility firm with stable revenue flows (due to being a monopoly supplier with regulated prices) could probably operate comfortably with very high operational leverage, whereas even quite low levels of operational leverage may imply excessive business risk in the case of firms subject to high revenue uncertainty.

Several other important points to note in this zero debt case are as follows. First, at current sales levels, investments involving an increase in fixed costs may not reduce average costs or alter the firm's ability to increase revenues, that is, average ROA may be unaltered. The profitability of such high fixed cost strategies relies upon increasing demand (g > 0) to reduce average costs and thereby to increase future average ROA. Thus, high operational leverage investment strategies are largely a call option bet on continued future growth, since in the absence of g > 0 the fixed cost investment will be a negative net present value (NPV) proposition for risk-averse investors as the investment will have simply raised the variance of performance (by the factor OL) but not its mean. Nevertheless, the high fixed cost investment may still be preferred by managers if they are confident in achieving g > 0 over even quite small (relative to the investment cycle) timescales, say because favorable macroeconomic conditions are expected to sustain positive growth over the next two or three-year period. If managers also receive a fixed salary plus a bonus linked to reported corporate profits, then the attractiveness of the high OL strategy will increase. Thus, with executive pay linked to corporate profits, not only do shareholders now face higher business risk but also their expected returns will be reduced by the additional pay now awarded to executives, which, even for risk-neutral shareholders, would mean that the fixed-cost investment would be a negative NPV proposition. The ignoring of business risk and the option for management to exploit a trend and claim superior performance are inevitable consequences of basing pay on only the first moment of a performance metric's distribution.

Second, to determine with some certainty whether an investment is in reality a positive NPV project, i.e. that managers did indeed create value, the results over the whole investment cycle are required. Many such capacity-increasing (and with g > 0, average cost-reducing) investments take place during periods of optimism and rising demand and hence they appear to pay off in the early periods. However, similar investments by other firms and a subsequent economic downturn tend to create overcapacity and a collapse in corporate profitability. Thus, evaluating either the success of the investment or the quality of management on the basis of only the reported ROA achieved during the first few periods involves relying upon a necessarily very noisy signal. Furthermore, the empirical findings on reported accounting disclosures indicate that management are generally adept at exploiting accounting rules in regard to depreciation policies, the classification of lease contracts,[9] asset and goodwill write-offs, and allowances in order to "smooth" or otherwise flatter reported corporate performance.[10] The incentives for management to take investment and accounting decisions that disguise the riskiness of their business strategies and/or which flatter performance are greatly increased when a significant element of their total compensation is linked to a performance metric that the managers largely control.

Third, if reported corporate performance and the pay of managers are both seen to have benefited from undertaking capacity-increasing fixed-cost investments, then the managers of other firms are likely to be induced to imitate their competitors' investment strategies. For overinvestment not to eventually occur, the sector's revenue growth rate would need to increase at a faster rate than the increases in capacity; otherwise the average ROA of the sector will tend to decline, whilst at the same time the average pay of managers and the variance in firm performance will both increase due to the increased operational leverage.

Fourth, due to the lack of any debt finance, apart from tax, there is no difference in the ROA and ROE measures. In this no-debt situation it is therefore largely immaterial as to which performance metric should be used to evaluate and reward managers.

Once the all-equity financing assumption is dropped, the choice of performance metric takes on some importance because ROE then becomes a financially leveraged function of the after-tax ROA(1 – T):

$$ROE = ROA(1 - T) \times \text{financial leverage (FL)}, \qquad (7)$$

where financial leverage = $(1- (k_D/EBIT)) ((D + E)/E)$.[11]

That is, financial leverage is the product of the proportionate impact of debt on the numerator (the income measure) and denominator (the resource measure) of the ROA(1 – T).

This increase in the percentage ROE from using cheaper debt finance is, however, achieved only by increasing the financial risks shareholders and debtholders are exposed to. Though neither the mean nor variability of ROA is affected by financial leverage, both the mean and variability of ROE are increased by the factor FL relative to the no-debt case.

In summary, the size and variability of a firm's ROA results from business risk and will reflect the success or otherwise of the firm's business strategy and the efficiency of its operations, i.e. the impact of management. Financial risk (arising from the use of debt) does not create value (apart from the interest expense tax subsidy); the success or otherwise of the firm's risky investment strategies is what creates value and this will be reflected in an increased ROA. The increase in reported ROE arises solely from the return spread between a firm's return on assets (ROA) and its debt interest expense (k(D)). In essence, with any positive return spread (i.e. ROA > k(D)), the greater the proportion of debt finance used, the higher will be the reported return on shareholder's equity (ROE) relative to its ROA. Debt finance simply turns ROE into a leveraged (multiplicative) function of the firm's ROA.

A corollary, however, is that the variability in ROE also becomes a leveraged function of the variability in the ROA, i.e. the total risks that investors are exposed to will also have increased by the same financial leverage factor:

$$Var(ROE) = Var(ROA)(FL). \qquad (8)$$

ROE is therefore an extremely noisy signal of business and/or managerial performance even in the absence of financial reporting misstatements. Differences in ROE may arise due to differences in financial risk rather than differences in corporate/managerial performance. For example, an all-equity firm may have a lower ROE but a higher ROA than a more financially leveraged firm. An implication of evaluating firms/rewarding managers on the basis of ROE is that shareholders are willing to pay for financial leverage, i.e. to reward managers for taking financial risks that these investors are in principle perfectly capable of taking themselves if that is what they desire, without having to pay managers a premium to do it for them (e.g. shareholders could buy the firm's shares using borrowed money). Shareholders, it should be remembered, employ managers solely because of their superior business skills and knowledge relative to the shareholders. Therefore, if managers are to be rewarded for performance, then it makes most sense for shareholders to judge and reward managers in terms of their relative success in generating a high and sustainable (i.e. risk-adjusted) ROA, which arguably reflects to some degree the value of their specialist managerial inputs.

In summary, earnings (or net income) based corporate/managerial performance measures, e.g. earnings per share (EPS) or ROE, are an open invitation for managers to ignore risk. At high debt levels these earnings metrics become an increasingly poor measure of corporate or managerial performance due to the fact that ROE is a multiplicative function of the firm's after-tax return on assets (ROA) and financial leverage, i.e. ROE = ROA(1 – T) x financial leverage. Moreover, the incentives for managers to engage in egregious financial risk taking and to engage in deceitful financial reporting to hide the firm's true level of indebtedness and exposure to financial risk are both greatly increased by this linking of highly leveraged rewards to a performance metric that is itself the product of financial leverage rather than being closely or meaningfully related to managerial value creation.

It is argued in the following section that these pay practices are indicative of serious inadequacies in current board governance arising from the lack of incentives for independent directors to fulfill their primary corporate governance duties to monitor and control managerial decisions.

Board Effectiveness and Loyalty Biases

In this section, it is argued that the hierarchical management structures apparently needed to handle large organizational size and complexity create a dependency of the board upon senior executives that manifests itself as uncritical board loyalty (Morck, 2008). In the first subsection, the psychological and group decision processes that limit independent directors' effectiveness are discussed and in the second subsection the empirical evidence relating to remuneration (compensation) committee decision-making is reviewed.

Board Decision Processes

As they are almost totally reliant upon the CEO for their financial and other information regarding the performance of the firm, independent board members are particularly prone to "groupthink" (Evans and Krueger, 2009), a phenomenon whereby participants overly identify with and trust other group members and therefore often fail to see the risks and failings associated with their perspective on the world or the ethical implications of their current policies and behaviors.[12] As board loyalty develops, the tendency of boards to screen out negative information inconsistent with the board's current strategies and beliefs, "ethical fading," results in board members becoming incapable of seeing the situation as being in any way inconsistent with their primary fiduciary duties toward shareholders.

The problem is that large organizational size and complexity, a product of managerial initiatives, plus competitive pressures and other environmental uncertainties, generate a desperate demand from boards for a reassuringly decisive and self-confident hierarchical corporate leadership (Kets de Vries, 1991; Barnard, 2009). As only the most overconfident, energetic, and self-promoting individuals ever put themselves forward for such senior posts, this necessarily involves trusting some of the most narcissistic and self-serving representatives of the human race (Roberts 2001; Padilla, et al., 2007; Amernic and Craig, 2010) with considerable discretion (power) in regard to the use of corporate resources, information disclosures, and over other employees. Unfortunately, though boards appear to be no more expert in choosing successful leaders than any other group of humans (Kahneman et al., 1982; Kets de Vries, 1991), independent directors have few incentives to critically analyze an incumbent's performance, since the process of removing underperforming management and finding suitable replacements is inevitably personally stressful, time-consuming, and fraught with reputational dangers should mistakes be made.

In such an organizational setting of unequal power relations, normal, everyday, human cognition and decision processes, which involve "rationalization" (that is, the ability to fool ourselves that personally rewarding behaviors are also ethical and legitimate) and "trust,"[13] are all that are required to generate the "ethical fading" (Bazerman and Tenbrunsel, 2011) that leads to boards adopting a default attitude of uncritical trust in current management. With board loyalty secured and highly leveraged remuneration schemes that encourage risk taking, managerial discretion is frequently used to waste corporate resources on personally satisfying and/or remunerative projects that have a negative impact on shareholder wealth. The empirical corporate finance literature for example documents the prevalence of (and therefore board acquiescence to) self-serving, but value-destroying, executive decisions in areas as diverse as takeovers (Shleifer and Summers, 1988; Franks and Mayer, 1996; Goergen and Renneboog, 2004; Hodgkinson, and Partington, 2008), growth strategies, the manipulation of financial reporting (Agrawal and Chadha, 2005; Duchon and Drake, 2009), and the adoption of excessively risky and deceptive financial strategies (Keasey and Watson, 1991; Berenson, 2004).

This empirical evidence strongly suggests that an uncritical loyalty bias toward management is probably fairly widespread across the corporate sector, and that whatever the reputational fears/incentives of independent directors (Westphal, 1999; Yermack, 2004), these latter factors are, in practice, frequently insufficient to prevent independent directors from acquiescing to these value-destroying managerial initiatives. Independent directors also have to trade off competing interests because, whilst corporate governance codes impose special responsibilities upon independent board members to monitor and discipline executives, in law no such legal distinction exists and all board members are deemed to be equally responsible for the good management and governance of the corporation. This situation, whereby part-time independent directors are both part of the top management team whilst also being expected to act as the monitors and disciplining mechanism in regard to other board members, creates a dilemma that independent directors tend to psychologically reconcile by developing an unquestioning loyalty bias toward their current management teams (Ezzamel and Watson, 1997).

In summary, an adequate understanding as to why independent directors tend to develop a strong loyalty bias toward their executive board colleagues—a loyalty which conflicts with their legal duties to shareholders—will necessarily involve some analysis of "macro" or "structural" factors, such as the economic and organizational context/pressures and the interpersonal dynamics of group decision-making (Ashforth et al., 2008).

Psychological factors also greatly facilitate this attitudinal slide into uncritical loyalty given that these directors "bask in the reflected light of a successful CEO...directors become highly invested...they want their CEO to do well. Psychologically, they believe he or she will do well. And oftentimes they cannot bear for the CEO to fail. Failure impairs their own reputational capital. It also undermines their strongly held sense of competence and control" (Barnard, 2009: 427). Langevoort (2004) describes the organizational and psychological dynamics that generate board loyalty and an unconscious neglect of the boards' oversight responsibilities as follows:

> A streak of good fortune for the firm—which may be managerial skill, but may be just as much the state of the economy—creates a psychological dynamic that works to the CEO's favor. First, the CEO has ample opportunity and resources to expand the board's external influence, thereby making ingratiation tactics more effective. The social ties grow, which makes the inclination to monitor diminish. Not far under the surface here are cognitive dissonance and a related set of commitment biases: the longer the streak of positive information flows, the more board members attribute that success to the person they've put in place and hence develop mental schemata that credit the CEO with skill. Once these schemata are fixed, they become increasingly hard to disconfirm. Any negative information that subsequently appears tends to be dismissed until the threat is undeniable, partly because of simple cognitive conservatism, partly because the board—having committed itself to the CEO by virtue of both selection and generous compensation—is averse to acknowledging that it may have made an error. (2004: 310)

Milgram's (1974) experimental results on conformity suggest that unconscious loyalty biases toward individuals occupying positions of "authority" are also ubiquitous and deeply ingrained in human psychology. For example, Milgram's experiments clearly indicated that most people—irrespective of class, education, age, gender, or nationality—seemed prepared to obey orders from authority figures that were clearly in conflict with their professed moral codes and legal responsibilities. As Morck (2008) explains, even individuals such as independent directors, who neither gain from a CEO's wrongdoing nor fear reprisals for criticizing CEO behavior, appear no more immune to this desire to trust and obey those upon whom they have bestowed leadership status:

> Misplaced loyalty lies at the heart of virtually every recent scandal in corporate governance. Corporate officers and directors, who should have known better, put loyalty to a dynamic Chief Executive Officer above duty to shareholders and obedience to the law. The officers and directors of Enron, WorldCom, Hollinger, and almost every other allegedly misgoverned firm could have asked questions, demanded answers, and blown whistles, but did not. Ultimately they sacrificed their whole careers and reputations on the pyres of their CEOs. (Morck, 2008: 180)

Furthermore, in a competitive environment, this potentially toxic constellation of corporate policies is likely to prove to be highly contagious; that is, "herding in bad behavior" is likely to result as competition with these apparently high-performing firms induces the adoption of similar financing, financial reporting, and managerial compensation policies by other firms in the sector. Such "Gresham's Law" type processes, whereby bad but apparently more profitable policies drive out existing good but less profitable practices, can be expected to be particularly virulent when the behavior appears to be "legitimated" by appeal to commonly held and institutionally sanctioned notions of what constitutes "good governance" (Meyer and Rowan, 1977; Elsbach and Sutton, 1992; Suchman, 1995; Tenbrunsel and Messick, 2004). In the following subsection, the ideas and practices relating to executive pay are reviewed to illustrate how easily bad practices can become accepted and widespread when they serve powerful interests.

Executive Pay Practices

This subsection focuses on the UK experience regarding the determination of executive pay over the past 20 or so years because the UK is not untypical of what has occurred elsewhere in the English-speaking economies. Compensation (Remuneration) committees, consisting of part-time, non-executive directors, have been the institutional mechanism for determining senior executive pay awards in the US since the late 1980s. This system was introduced to the UK in 1993 after the publication of the Cadbury Report (1992) and then shortly after in most other English-speaking economies. In the UK, as has happened elsewhere, since the introduction of this board subcommittee system executive pay levels have continued to increase at a much faster rate than those of other professional groups. The complexity of executive pay packages has also greatly increased as the typical CEO pay package now includes in addition to a fixed salary a range of "incentive" and reward components such as an annual bonus, a long-term incentive plan, share award schemes, and executive option grants. What is particularly relevant here is that, despite the fact that all these additional incentive elements to executive pay packages are meant to better align manager and shareholder interests, virtually all executives appear to receive these generous awards most years (KPMG, 2009) irrespective of their firm's performance and, hence in practice, many empirical studies are unable to uncover a statistically reliable or economically meaningful relationship between pay awards and performance (Ogden and Watson, 2008).

Every UK corporate governance code from Cadbury (1992) to the Combined Code (2002) has recommended that remuneration committees take account of supposed labor market pressures by basing pay awards primarily upon what "comparable" companies were paying their executives and, for incentive alignment purposes, to make pay more closely related to improvements in firm performance.[14] This explicit encouragement of remuneration committees to focus on pay comparisons and earnings-related pay has resulted in increasing CEO pay levels primarily because risk-averse and resource-constrained remuneration committees have sought to minimize the possibility of boardroom conflict, avoid possible recruitment and retention problems, or inadvertently signal low managerial quality to outsiders, simply by paying their CEO somewhat more than the apparent market rate (Ezzamel and Watson, 1998, 2002). Though, from the perspective of each individual remuneration committee, being relatively generous to the CEO appears to be a reasonable strategy (not least because the additional costs are borne entirely by shareholders), the statistical impossibility for all CEOs to be paid more than average implies that their average pay levels will necessarily be "bid up" over time.[15]

This apparent "bidding-up" of executive pay has long been recognized as a problem by several interested parties. For example, the Institute of Directors (1995: 4) felt obliged to advise its members that remuneration committees "should avoid setting packages which are generous in relation to market levels and beware of pressure always to be in the 'upper quartile.'" In a similar fashion, the Combined Code has also highlighted this same problem:

> B.1.2 Remuneration committees should judge where to position their company relative to other companies. They should be aware what comparable companies are paying and should take account of relative performance. But they should use such comparisons with caution, in view of the risk that they can result in an upward ratchet of remuneration levels with no corresponding improvement in performance...

It will be noted that though they were both able to recognize the tendency for remuneration committee processes to raise pay levels, neither the Institute of Directors nor the drafters of the Combined Code have, to date, felt able to offer any suggestions as to how to reduce this problem.

Concluding Remarks

Not all governance reforms intended to provide agency cost-reducing outcomes necessarily succeed in achieving their prime objective, i.e. there are unanticipated, typically negative, consequences that tend to increase rather than decrease agency costs. The analysis of the interrelationships between firm performance, the different sources of risk and leverage, and earnings-based executive pay schemes suggests that managers will have strong incentives to act in ways that are contrary to shareholder interests. Furthermore, analysis of the overly loyal board and the operation of their remuneration committees indicates that the relatively recent development of ensuring that, for ostensibly incentive-alignment reasons, the pay of senior executives is related to shareholder performance metrics is likely to have further exacerbated, rather than reduced, the incentives for managers to engage in excessive, largely debt-financed, risk taking. This because paying executives significant amounts in cash bonuses, shares, and/or share options for exceeding[16] some earnings-related benchmark is effectively requiring shareholders to pay for financial leverage. Given the fact that capital structure decisions can have a major impact on earnings-related performance metrics and that this exposes shareholders to additional financial risk, it is far from obvious why shareholders should necessarily be willing to pay managers a significant premium for exposing them to such financial risks. If shareholders wish to be exposed to this type of risk, shareholders can perfectly adequately do so for themselves, say by borrowing to finance all or part of their equity investments.

As the analysis indicated, though the use of debt finance by corporations to fund a significant proportion their business operations typically results in a higher return on equity, this is not necessarily indicative of superior business or managerial performance. Indeed, apart from the corporate interest tax shield and the possible underpricing of risk by the suppliers of finance (both of which are really manifestations of moral hazard, i.e. wealth transfers to corporations from respectively taxpayers and debtholders), it is clear that debt finance does not actually create shareholder value once the additional financial risk that debt brings is incorporated into the analysis. Moreover, it is unclear that managers have any comparative advantage over shareholders in respect of assessing financial (rather than business) risks or that managers necessarily possess superior knowledge in regard to shareholder financial risk preferences. What is fairly obvious, however, is that the linking of managerial rewards to financially leveraged metrics greatly increases the incentives for managers to take on excessive amounts of debt and to engage in financial statement manipulations that flatter their apparent performance—particularly via the use of various forms of "off-balance sheet financing," such as leasing arrangements that are designed to hide debt and thereby mislead investors as to the true financial risk exposure of the business.

How might it be possible to reduce the incentives for managers to take excessive and often hidden risks? Retaining the notion that in order to get executives to act in shareholders' interests, some form of performance-related pay scheme is a necessity, then ROA-related performance metrics adjusted for excess operational risk ought to be preferred as the basis for determining additional pay awards, since these measures will be the ones most clearly related to why shareholders employ managers. As operational leverage increases the variability of ROA-type metrics, using operational leverage as the risk adjustment factor in determining any bonus paid would reduce the incentives to exploit short-term operational leverage effects.

More fundamentally, of course, the real underlying governance problem is the phenomenon of the loyalty bias displayed by boards and the (on average) overly generous "market comparisons" remuneration committees appear to use when framing their executive pay awards. Despite the fact that the very notion of a "managerial labor market" is highly problematic and has resulted in a ratcheting up of executive pay, whilst also giving executives highly leveraged incentives to take on excessive debt and to subvert their firms' financial statements to hide much of this debt, such notions remain central to, and are actively encouraged by, the UK's Corporate Governance Code.

Thus, getting boards to first recognize and then abandon their instinctive loyalty biases toward incumbent management is likely to involve several longer-term changes in values and the structure and powers of other institutions as much as any specific corporate governance reforms. For example, the Stewardship Code recently issued by the UK's Financial Reporting Council (FRC, 2010) represents an attempt to alter the relationship between shareholders and management. The Code is meant to encourage greater engagement by institutional investors as active investors by requiring them to disclose their voting records and to develop and publish protocols for constructively engaging with poorly performing management teams. Even so, the new Stewardship Code does not address the implications of the longstanding structural problems associated with the public good characteristics of managerial monitoring, in other words, the problem of free-riders and the inevitable delays, risks, and high costs of intervention relative to exit (Forbes and Watson, 1993).

In the absence of increasing market incentives to become more active owners, or significantly lowering intervention costs, simply requiring institutional investors to provide more information regarding their investment, monitoring, and intervention policies is unlikely to change either institutional shareholder behavior or board member's loyalty biases.

For these latter changes to occur would probably require a complete rethink regarding shareholder rights and how these rights can be effectively exercised, and the continued usefulness of the unitary board model, which creates a (largely unconscious) conflict of interests for independent board members. On the one hand, all board members have exactly the same legal responsibilities for the management and good governance of the company, whilst on the other hand corporate governance codes also require that independent board members monitor and, when necessary, discipline the senior managers, i.e. their board-room colleagues with whom they will have collaborated in agreeing the firms' current business strategy (Ezzamel and Watson, 1997). Relatively simple governance changes, such as independent director only meetings and restricting the job of independent board members to ratification, monitoring, and disciplinary roles, would perhaps make it clear that independent directors' first and only legitimate concern is the furtherance of shareholder interests.

Notes

1. Disraeli certainly had personal experience of indebtedness. Prior to his political career, which included holding the office of UK Prime Minister twice, Disraeli was a well-established and popular writer of novels, an occupation that he only took up as a way of paying off his business debts from earlier failed business ventures.
2. A systematic outcome refers to an outcome that is largely a function of collective processes, pressures, and institutional structures, and hence differences in individual ethical or personal motives are unlikely to provide a major explanation of, or a solution to (replacing individuals), the problem under discussion.
3. Note, however, that in order for a systematic over-indebtedness problem to subsequently arise, both borrowers and lenders have to have been infected by irrational optimism.
4. It is important to stress that individual wrongdoing is not the primary driver here; rather the situation provides an excellent example of what organizational theorists call "routine nonconformity" (Vaughan, 1999), which refers to the systematic and largely unanticipated negative organizational outcomes (e.g. financial losses, unethical behavior, the creation negative externalities, etc.) that arise simply from organizational participants following routine and apparently non-controversial organizational rules and practices.
5. Nevertheless, the "logic of the situation," i.e. the complex combination of external and internal pressures, human cognition limitations, and the incentives of managers and directors, will tend to generate negative wealth outcomes that, from the viewpoint of both shareholders and debtholders, may be difficult to distinguish from "looting" (Akerlof and Romer, 1993).

6. The respective payoffs for shareholders and debtholders are analogous to that of a "call option" holder and the writer of a "put option" on the underlying value of the firm and with strike prices equivalent to the value of the outstanding debt obligations.
7. Which suggests that the majority of business failures will tend to be the result of misconceived business strategies and poorer than expected outcomes (i.e. entrepreneurial "overconfidence") rather than representing any attempt by the owners to defraud creditors (Keasey and Watson, 1994).
8. In practice, it seems that most executive bonus, share, and option schemes are specified in terms of earnings per share (EPS) (KPMG, 2009). In the numerical analysis, EPS produces identical results to ROE simply by assuming that the equity of the firm consists solely of issued shares with a nominal value of $1. If this assumption is relaxed by assuming that firms have some retained earnings, then the EPS metric becomes a leveraged version of the ROE measure.
9. In 2009 the International Accounting Standards Board (IASB, the primarily non-US financial reporting system mandated within the EU and elsewhere) and the Financial Accounting Standards Board (FASB, the US accounting standards setter) jointly agreed new proposals that would essentially outlaw most uses of operating lease accounting precisely for the reasons discussed in this chapter. An article in *AccountancyAge* (2010), reporting on a survey of UK firms involved in leasing, unsurprisingly indicated strong opposition to these proposals, though their reasoning for taking this position essentially confirmed why the proposals needed to be implemented; namely, because capital lease accounting would on average double the reported debt to total assets ratios of firms that currently used operating lease accounting, which might then make obtaining further debt financing more difficult and expensive for them!
10. As most forms of accounting manipulation involve a choice regarding whether to recognize anticipated profits and losses early or later (when the assets are sold at a loss), these naturally tend to have a reverse impact upon reported profits later in the investment cycle.
11. Alternatively, rearranging the ROE expression (2) slightly (replacing EBIT with ROA x (D + E)) gives:

$$ROE = [(1 - T)ROA \times (D + E) - kD(1 - T)]/E,$$

which can be rearranged as:

$$ROE = (1 - T)ROA + [(1 - T)ROA - k(1 - T)] \times D/E.$$

The final expression is the more usual form of the relationship between ROE and the after-tax ROA (assuming an all-equity firm), i.e. ROA(1 − T) plus financial leverage, the latter being a premium (or discount) equal to the after-tax return spread between ROA and the after-tax cost of debt (k(1 − T)) multiplied by the debt-to-equity ratio (D/E).
12. In addition, those board members responsible for the appointment of the CEO may be especially enthusiastic toward escalating their commitment and placing excessive trust in their incumbent CEO (Kahneman and Lovallo, 1993).
13. As the extensive literature examining the psychology and economic bases of trust and its importance in lubricating economic and social interactions makes clear, trust is essential; indeed, it typically constitutes the default mode, primarily because it involves the least

cognitive effort. Moreover trust levels tend to increase when the two parties appear to share some common characteristic, e.g. similar ethnic or social background, or have similar interests and/or enjoy satisfactory working relations (Evans and Krueger, 2009).

14. It is worth stressing that none of the UK corporate governance reports (i.e. Cadbury, 1992; Greenbury, 1995; Hampel, 1998; Higgs, 2002) has suggested that remuneration committees ought to control or attempt to hold down executive pay.

15. Even prior to their widespread introduction in 1993, it was apparent that firms with remuneration committees tended to award relatively generous pay increases to their CEOs and were largely reliant upon the information and recommendations supplied by outside "pay consultants" regarding "comparable" market pay rates and the complexities of performance-related pay schemes (see Main and Johnston, 1993, and Forbes and Watson, 1993, for reviews of the evidence).

16. Since the majority of senior executives still receive additional non-salary awards each year, it is clear that in many cases the market benchmark need not even be met.

REFERENCES

Accountancy Age (2010). "New Leasing Rules Could Hit Bank Lending," August 19.
AGRAWAL, A., and CHADHA, S. (2005). "Corporate Governance and Accounting Scandals," *Journal of Law and Economics*, 48: 371–406.
AKERLOF, G., and ROMER, P. (1993). "Looting: The Economic Underworld of Bankruptcy for Profit," *Brookings Papers on Economic Activity*, 2.
AMERNIC, J. H. and CRAIG, R. J. (2010). "Accounting as a Facilitator of Extreme Narcissism," *Journal of Business Ethics*, 96(1): 79–93.
ASHFORTH, B. E., GIOIA, D. A., ROBINSON, S. L., and TREVINO, L. K. (2008). "Re-viewing Organizational Corruption," *Academy of Management Review*, 33(3): 670–84.
BARNARD, J. W. (2009). "Narcissism, Over-optimism, Fear, Anger and Depression: The Interior Lives of Corporate Leaders," *University of Cincinnati Law Review*, 77: 405–30.
BAZERMAN, M. H., and TENBRUNSEL, A. E. (2011). *Blind Spots: Why We Fail to Do What's Right and What to Do about It*. Princeton, NJ: Princeton University Press.
BERENSON, A. (2004). *The Number: How the Drive for Quarterly Earnings Corrupted Wall Street and Corporate America*. New York: Random House.
Cadbury Report (1992). "Report of the Committee on the Financial Aspects of Corporate Governance." London: Financial Reporting Council.
Combined Code (2002). "The Combined Code on Corporate Governance." London Stock Exchange. London: Gee & Co.
DUCHON, D., and DRAKE, B. (2009). "Organizational Narcissism and Virtuous Behavior," *Journal of Business Ethics*, 85: 301–8.
ELSBACH, K. D., and SUTTON, R. I. (1992). "Acquiring Organizational Legitimacy through Illegitimate Actions: A Marriage of Institutional and Impression Management Theories," *Academy of Management Journal*, 35: 699–738.
EVANS, A., and KRUEGER, J. (2009). "The Psychology (and Economics) of Trust," *Social and Personality Psychology Compass*, 3(6): 1003–17.
EZZAMEL, M., and WATSON, R. (1997). "Wearing Two Hats: An Analysis of the Monitoring and Control Functions of Non-Executive Directors," in K. Keasey, S. Thompson, and

M. Wright (eds.), *Corporate Governance: Economic, Management and Financial Issues*. Oxford: Oxford University Press, 54–79.

EZZAMEL, M., and WATSON, R. (1998). "Market Comparison Earnings and the Bidding-up of Executive Cash Compensation: Evidence from the UK," *Academy of Management Journal*, 41: 221–31.

—— —— (2002). "Pay Comparability Across and Within UK Boards: An Empirical Analysis of the Cash Pay Awards to CEO and Other Board Members," *Journal of Management Studies*, 39: 207–32.

FAMA, E., and JENSEN, M. C. (1983). "Agency Problems and Residual Claims," *Journal of Law and Economics*, 26: 325–44.

Financial Reporting Council (FRC) (2010). Stewardship Code for Institutional Investors, July 2. <http://www.frc.org.uk/getattachment/3006d141-4704-4712-9f13-771cf93897b8/The-UK-Stewardship-Code.aspx>.

FORBES, W., and WATSON, R. (1993). "Corporate Governance and Managerial Remuneration: A Review of the Issues," Evidence and Cadbury Committee's Proposals, *Accounting and Business Research*, Corporate Governance: Special Issue, 23(91A): 331–8.

FRANKS, J., and MEYER, C. (1996). "Hostile Takeovers and the Correction of Managerial Failure," *Journal of Financial Economics*, 40: 163–81.

GILSON, R., and GORDON, J. (2003). "Doctrines and Markets: Controlling Controlling Shareholders," *University of Pennsylvania Law Review*, 152: 785–813.

GOERGEN, M., and RENNEBOOG, L. (2004). "Shareholder Wealth Effects of European Domestic and Cross-Border Takeover Bids," *European Financial Management*, 10(1): 9–45.

Greenbury Report (1995). "Directors' Remuneration—Report of a Study Group," chaired by Sir Richard Greenbury. London: Gee & Co.

Hampel Report (1998). "The Committee on Corporate Governance—Final Report of the Study Group," chaired by Sir Ronald Hampel. London: Gee & Co.

HIGGS, D. (2002). "Review of the Role and Effectiveness of Non-Executive Directors," Consultation Paper, June 7.

HODGKINSON, L., and PARTINGTON, G. (2008). "The Motives for Takeovers in the UK," *Journal of Business Finance and Accounting*, 35: 102–26.

Institute of Directors (1995). "The Remuneration of Directors: A Framework for Remuneration Committees." London: Institute of Directors.

JENSEN, M. C., and MECKLING, W. H. (1976). "Theory of the Firm: Managerial Behavior, Agency Costs and Ownership Structure," *Journal of Financial Economics*, 3: 305–60.

KAHNEMAN, D., and LOVALLO, D. (1993). "Timid Choices and Bold Forecasts: A Cognitive Perspective on Risk Taking," *Management Science*, 39(1): 17–31.

—— SLOVIC, P., and TVERSKY, A. (eds.) (1982). *Judgement under Uncertainty: Heuristics and Biases*. Cambridge: Cambridge University Press.

KEASEY, K., and WATSON, R. (1991). "Financial Distress Prediction Models: A Review of their Usefulness," *British Journal of Management*, 2(2): 89–102.

—— —— (1994). "The 1986 Insolvency and Company Directors Disqualification Acts: An Evaluation of their Impact upon Small Firm Financing Decisions," *Small Business Economics*, 6(4): 257–66.

KETS DE VRIES, M. (1991). "On Becoming a CEO: The Transference and Addictiveness of Power," in Kets de Vries (ed.), *Organizations on the Couch*. San Francisco: Jossey Bass, 120–39.

KPMG (2009). *KPMG's Survey of Directors' Compensation 2009*. London: KPMG LLP (UK).

LANGEVOORT, D. C. (2004). "Resetting the Corporate Thermostat: Lessons from the Recent Financial Scandals about Self-Deception, Deceiving Others and the Design of Internal Controls," *Georgetown Law Journal*, 93: 285–307.

MAIN, B. G. M., and JOHNSTON, J. (1993). 'Remuneration Committees and Corporate Governance', *Accounting and Business Research*, 23(91A): 351–62.

MEYER, J. W., and ROWAN, B. (1977). "Institutionalised Organizations: Formal Structure as Myth and Ceremony," *American Journal of Sociology*, 83: 340–63.

MILGRAM, S. (1974). *Obedience to Authority*. New York: Harper & Row.

MORCK, R. (2008). "Behavioral Finance in Corporate Governance: Economics and the Devil's Advocate," *Journal of Management and Governance*, 12: 79–200.

OGDEN, S., and WATSON, R. (2008). "Executive Pay and the Search for Legitimacy," *Human Relations*, 61(5): 711–39.

PADILLA, A., HOGAN, R., and KAISER, R. (2007). "The Toxic Triangle: Destructive Leaders, Susceptible Followers and Conducive Environments," *The Leadership Quarterly*, 18: 176–94.

RAJAN, R., and ZINGALES, L. (2003). "The Great Reversals: The Politics of Financial Development in the Twentieth Century," *Journal of Financial Economics*, 69: 5–50.

ROBERTS, J. (2001). "Corporate Governance and the Ethics of the Narcissus," *Business Ethics Quarerly*, 11(1): 109–27.

ROE, M. (1994). *Strong Managers, Weak Owners: The Political Roots of American Corporate Finance Princeton*. New Jersey: Princeton University Press.

SHLEIFER, A., and SUMMERS, L. (1988). "Breach of Trust in Hostile Takeovers," in A. Auerbach (ed.), *Corporate Takeovers: Causes and Consequences*. Chicago: University of Chicago Press.

SUCHMAN, M. C. (1995). "Managing Legitimacy: Strategic and Institutional Approaches," *Academy of Management Review*, 20(3): 571–610.

TENBRUNSEL, A. E., and MESSICK, D. M. (2004). "Ethical Fading: The Role of Self-Deception in Unethical Behavior," *Social Justice Research*, 17(2): 223–36.

TURNBULL, S. (2010). "Why Anglo Corporations Should Not Be Trusted," *Corporate Board*, 1: 10–17.

VAUGHAN, D. (1999). "The Dark Side of Organizations," *Annual Review of Sociology*, 25: 271–305.

WATSON, R., and EZZAMEL, M. (2005). "Financial Structure and Corporate Governance," in K. Keasey, S. Thompson, and M. Wright (eds.), *Corporate Governance: Accountability, Enterprise and International Comparisons*. Chichester: John Wiley, 45–59.

WESTPHAL, J. D. (1999). "Collaboration in the Boardroom: Behavioral and Performance Consequences of CEO-Board Social Ties," *Academy of Management Journal*, 42: 7–24.

YERMACK, D. (2004). "Remuneration, Retention and Reputation Incentives for Outside Directors," *Journal of Finance*, 59: 2281–308.

CHAPTER 13

....

FINANCIAL REPORTING, DISCLOSURE, AND CORPORATE GOVERNANCE

....

CHRISTOF BEUSELINCK, MARC DELOOF, AND SOPHIE MANIGART

SUNLIGHT is the best disinfectant
    (Louis D. Brandeis in the Supreme Court's 1933 Securities Act)

INTRODUCTION

....

In a theoretical world where economies do not suffer from market frictions, all economic agents are equally well informed about a firm's past, current, and future performance. In reality, however, information asymmetries do exist. In public firms without inside shareholders, information asymmetries mainly occur between firm managers (insiders) and shareholders (outsiders). In public firms with controlling shareholders or large blockholders, such as family firms or firms embedded in pyramidal shareholder structures, a second type of information asymmetry arises between majority shareholders (insiders) and minority shareholders (outsiders). As information asymmetries increase agency costs, less-informed parties demand corporate disclosures about the underlying firm performance. Disclosure allows for the reduction of information asymmetries among investors and the disciplining of management (Bushman and Smith, 2003), since it enables evaluation of prior investment decisions as well as monitoring of the investment process of committed capital (Beyer et al., 2010). Disclosure may be done through regulated financial reports (financial statements and footnotes) required by national or international accounting regulatory bodies and stock exchanges. In addition, firms may engage in voluntary disclosures, such as management forecasts, analysts' presentations and conference calls, press releases, internet sites, and other corporate reports (Healy and Palepu, 2001).[1]

Despite the strong regulation of information provision, information problems do occur and are especially prominent in public companies. This is highlighted by the notorious examples of fraudulent corporate reporting in companies like Enron and Parmalat at the turn of the 21st century. In these companies, corporate insiders were caught cooking the books to beat analyst consensus forecasts, and providing untruthful information to outsiders. Therefore, it is not surprising that both the regulators' attention and the academic disclosure literature heavily focus on public companies. Disclosure demands, however, are not limited to public companies: they arise in all situations where different types of shareholders or stakeholders have different demands for and access to different levels of information on a firm's performance. As a consequence, research on disclosure in private corporations has emerged recently.

Producing transparent and truthful information on corporate functioning is not only important for individual stakeholders, but also for the proper functioning of worldwide capital markets, as witnessed once again by the financial crisis of 2008–9. A lack of transparency on the intrinsic risk characteristics of financial instruments triggered less informed investors to pull their capital out of financial markets when market prices plummeted in the second half of 2008, leading to a negative price spiral in financial markets. In order to enhance corporate transparency, national disclosure regulations and standardized financial reporting obligations have been strengthened. For example, the 1992 Cadbury Report in the UK and the 2002 Sarbanes-Oxley Act in the USA have been initiated to counter corporate governance and information problems.[2] As financial markets are more globalized than ever, financial regulators increasingly focus on enhancing the worldwide comparability of corporate information. For example, financial regulators such as the US Securities and Exchange Commission (SEC) or the European Securities and Markets Authority (ESMA) have joined forces with standard setters like the US Financial Accounting Standards Board (FASB) and the International Accounting Standards Board (IASB). Their overarching goal is to develop more transparent and perceptive financial disclosures, largely aimed at enhancing the quality of the information that public companies have to provide.

Corporate financial reporting and disclosure practices hence develop endogenously with the capital markets' information demands, but a firm's information environment is also shaped by its micro-level (i.e. firm/manager) incentives and corporate governance practices (Beyer et al., 2010). The goal of this chapter is to tie the academic literature connecting corporate disclosure and financial reporting at the firm level to corporate governance practices. The chapter starts with a discussion of the benefits and costs of disclosure. We then expand the discussion beyond the firm level to briefly discuss the debate on the need for disclosure regulation. There follows an exploration of the intertwined concepts of disclosure and corporate governance. We then provide an overview of the role of disclosure in private firms. We conclude by focusing on avenues for future research.

BENEFITS OF DISCLOSURE

Disclosure of information can take various meanings but generally refers to the revelation of inside information to the public, in order to reduce information asymmetries. National and transnational regulatory bodies set a minimum (*mandatory*) level of disclosure that firms need to obey.[3] Firms providing information over and above the mandatory minimum are *voluntary* disclosers, thereby trying to signal above average quality to outsiders.

As it is observed that many firms disclose more information than required, understanding the benefits associated with higher disclosure levels is important. In his seminal paper, Verrecchia (1983) argued that undisclosed proprietary information may bring costs to a firm. Proprietary information introduces uncertainty because investors cannot distinguish the bad news in the non-disclosed information set. This, in turn, induces investors to discount the value of the non-disclosing firm to the point that managers are better off disclosing what they know (Verrecchia, 1983).

In this line of reasoning, disclosure increases firm value by reducing the cost of capital or by increasing the expected cash flows to investors. First, disclosure can *directly* reduce the cost of capital, mainly by decreasing estimation risk and information risk. *Estimation risk* exists when investors are uncertain about the payoff distribution of the securities or investment projects (e.g. Brown, 1979; Barry and Brown, 1985). Even disregarding potential agency conflicts between managers and shareholders, improved disclosure enables investors to identify value-creating opportunities with less error, hence allowing more accurate and efficient allocation of capital and human resources (Bushman and Smith, 2003). *Information risk* arises when uninformed investors have less information about a firm than informed investors (Easley and O'Hara, 2004). More disclosure mitigates the information risk by making it more difficult and more costly for traders to become privately informed, thereby reducing the likelihood that uninformed investors are trading with a better informed counterparty.

Higher estimation risk and information risk increase the cost of capital when investors require a risk premium to hold shares of a firm in which they have an informational disadvantage. The negative impact of estimation and information risk on the cost of capital depends on the assumption that these risk factors are not diversifiable. This risk will hence only be priced if investor portfolios contain a significant proportion of low information securities (Clarkson et al., 1996) or if the economy is not large enough (Hughes et al., 2007). Bushee and Noe (2000) find that firms with higher disclosure rankings have greater institutional ownership and that improvements in disclosure scores result in even higher institutional holdings. However, they also show that increases in ownership following yearly improvements in disclosure rankings are primarily driven by "transient" institutions, characterized by aggressive trading strategies that make a firm's stock price more volatile. The net effect of higher disclosure on a firm's cost of capital through institutional ownership is therefore unclear (Bushee and Noe, 2000).

Disclosure can also directly influence the cost of capital in two additional ways. First, disclosure can lower systematic risk by reducing investors' assessments of the covariance of the firm's future cash flow with the cash flow of other firms in the economy (Lambert et al., 2007). Furthermore, if investors require a risk premium for taking a position in "neglected" stocks, disclosure can also increase investor recognition and hence reduce the cost of capital by increasing risk sharing (Merton, 1987).

Disclosure affects the cost of capital not only directly, but also *indirectly* by increasing stock liquidity. More disclosure is associated with a broader investor base and a reduction of the adverse selection component of transaction costs. Privately informed traders impose adverse selection costs on market makers, because they know something that market makers do not. The market makers must recoup the losses suffered in trades with well-informed traders by gains in trades with liquidity traders. They will compensate for losses with informed traders by widening the bid-ask spread, thereby increasing transaction costs for investors (Glosten and Milgrom, 1985). A reduction of the likelihood of privately informed trades via increased disclosure will therefore result in lower transaction costs and will increase the probability and amount of trading. If investors ask a lower risk premium for holding shares with lower transaction costs and higher liquidity, the cost of capital is reduced (e.g. Amihud and Mendelson, 1986).

A second major benefit of disclosure, next to decreasing the cost of capital, is that it increases the cash flows that outside investors can expect (e.g. Lambert et al., 2007; La Porta et al., 2000). It is indeed well documented that controlling shareholders and corporate insiders may extract private benefits of control. More disclosure limits the ability of insiders to extract private benefits, thereby increasing the residual cash flows to outsiders. However, it has to be taken into account that the extraction of private benefits does not necessarily constitute a cost to outside investors. Jensen and Meckling (1976) point out that investors may anticipate expropriation; if so, they incorporate it in the price they are willing to pay for the firms' securities. As a result, the insiders ultimately bear the costs of extracting private benefits of control. Furthermore, it could be argued that private benefits of insiders do not decrease the overall firm value. As long as insiders value the private benefits they expropriate at least as much as outside investors, private benefits merely constitute a transfer of wealth from outside investors to insiders without reducing total firm value (e.g. Beyer et al., 2010). In spite of these arguments, firm value may nevertheless be reduced as a result of expropriation of private benefits by insiders. For example, firm insiders may forego profitable investment opportunities for the sake of private benefits. This is especially apparent in cases of separation of the firm's ownership and control rights via pyramidal structures or of shares with differential voting rights (e.g. Bebchuk et al., 2000). Hence, information disclosure limiting the ability of insiders to extract private benefits is generally seen as beneficial for firm value and for outside shareholders.

The benefits of disclosure are conditional on the relevance and reliability of the disclosed information, such as its type, frequency, timeliness, and quality. While research suggests that voluntary disclosure is generally able to convey credible information to the market (Healy and Palepu, 2001), voluntary disclosure is not always valuable to outsiders, as controlling shareholders and managers might have incentives to mislead investors by manipulating the disclosed information. It is well documented that managers try to influence investor sentiment and to increase their firm's share price around equity offerings through increased disclosure (e.g. Lang and Lundholm, 2000). This raises questions about the perceived credibility of voluntary disclosure, especially if it is aimed at influencing investors' reactions (Jennings, 1987).[4] Hence, the decision whether or not to manipulate voluntarily disclosed information will depend on the tradeoff of the benefits of biased disclosure and the costs of possible penalties thereof, including reputation loss, litigation, and managerial dismissal. Frankel et al. (1995) show that such penalties can be sufficient to deter managers from making biased disclosures. We discuss the costs of disclosure in the next section.

Costs of Disclosure

Disclosure may also bring costs to firms. First, the direct costs of preparation, certification, and dissemination of accounting reports may be significant. Second, indirect costs may be even more important than direct costs, as the disclosed information can be used by third parties such as competitors in product markets, labor unions, customers, suppliers, regulators, and tax authorities. Wagenhofer (1990) demonstrates that firms have an incentive not to disclose information that will reduce their competitive position, even if non-disclosure makes it more costly to raise additional equity. Competitive costs of disclosure are especially relevant for firms operating in highly competitive environments, such as biotechnology firms. Guo et al. (2004), for instance, identify proprietary costs as important determinants for non-disclosure by biotech firms before an initial public offering (IPO). They show that pre-IPO biotechnology firms disclose more information when they have (a) patent(s) or when product development is at a later stage. Further, these firms also disclose more information if venture capital investors are shareholders, acting as a deterrent to competition entering the particular market segment (Guo et al., 2004). In all these situations, biotech firms are more strongly protected from product-market competition than their peers, leading to lower intrinsic disclosure costs and higher disclosure levels.

More publicly disclosed information may also hurt existing long-term relationships with banks, as these relationships are often strongly dependent on private information flows between the firm and the bank (e.g. Leuz and Wysocki, 2008). Long-term banking relationships are characterized by the exchange of more fine-grained and soft information between bank and borrower, which leads to more flexible contracting, intertemporal smoothing of contract terms, and better monitoring of activities and outcomes by the bank (e.g. Boot, 2000). When firms publicly disclose more information, the value of private information flows between bank and borrower decreases, and this will negatively affect the value of the long-term banking relationship. Although indirect in nature, this may therefore also constitute a significant cost to the firm.

The Need for Disclosure Regulation

As disclosure brings benefits as well as costs to firms, investors, and financial markets, defining the optimal level of mandatory corporate disclosure is not easy. Financial regulators have been discussing disclosure rules for almost a century, with ever stricter reporting and corporate governance rules being imposed mainly as a response to major financial and economic crises. Spurred by the 1929 stock market crash and the subsequent depression, the US Federal Government involved itself in regulating securities markets and demanded disclosures by corporations whose shares were traded on public markets (Benston et al., 2006). It was President T. Roosevelt himself who articulated the philosophy of one of the landmarks in disclosure regulation, the 1933 Securities Act, in a message to the US Congress:

> There is...an obligation upon us to insist that every issue of new securities sold in interstate commerce shall be accompanied by full publicity and information, and that no essentially important element attending the issue shall be concealed from the buying public...It should give impetus to honest dealing in securities and thereby bring back public confidence.

Corporate governance has also become more prominent on the agenda since the 1990s, following the example set by the Cadbury Committee in the UK, whose 1992 "Code of Best Practices" aimed at raising the standards of corporate governance and the level of confidence in financial reporting and auditing after a series of major corporate scandals. In the US, after the outbreak of a new wave of corporate scandals in the early 2000s, US federal authorities felt the need to intervene in the financial disclosure process and enacted the Sarbanes-Oxley (SOX) Act in 2002. In addition to a multitude of specifications and requirements on the financial system design and disclosure requirements, SOX also established the Public Company Accounting Oversight Board (PCAOB). This board regularly inspects accounting of public firms and conducts investigations and disciplinary proceedings. It reports outcomes directly to the SEC and hence serves as an extra layer in the financial inspection process. Its establishment was especially necessary to restore public confidence in the role of external certification by audit firms after the fraudulent involvement of Enron's auditor, Arthur Andersen.

The more stringent financial regulation in the US is not isolated and many countries and financial markets worldwide have followed similar, although often less far-reaching, standard-setting procedures. One recent example comes from Europe where policymakers attempted to improve integration of country-level markets by harmonizing existing disclosure regulations and improving enforcements. This led to the EU Transparency Directive, enacted in March 2007. The Transparency Directive requires issuers of traded securities to ensure appropriate transparency for investors by disclosing and disseminating periodic and ongoing regulated information. Christensen et al. (2010) document positive market liquidity and cost of capital effects shortly after EU countries tightened transparency rules. European regulation is not only concerned with disclosure of publicly traded securities, as the European Commission is currently debating mandatory information disclosure of alternative investment fund managers. The adoption of the AIFM Directive would impose more elaborate mandatory information disclosure on, for example, private equity, venture capital, real estate, and hedge funds and their managers.

A related example applies to Japan. The Japanese economy stagnated in the 1990s after a bubble economy in the 1980s and government felt the need to drastically change the economic environment, including the disclosure regulation, to restore international investor confidence. Japanese corporate reporting during this period was opaque and management was often "window-dressing" to portray its results in a way that was consistent with management's view (Benston et al., 2006). In 1996, Japanese policymakers therefore decided to install an independent regulator, the Japanese Financial Services Agency (JFSA), with strong powers to ensure transparency and disclosure in the market.

Despite worldwide movements toward more and more regulated corporate reporting, there is still an ongoing debate in academia and among standard setters as to what extent financial reporting should be regulated at all. A libertarian alternative to the current situation of high regulation would be zero regulation. If there were no financial reporting rules, firms would be compelled to figure out on their own what the markets want and what their idiosyncratic optimal level of disclosure is. Even in the absence of financial reporting regulation, firms have incentives to voluntarily disclose financial information if expected benefits exceed the costs. Historical studies on disclosure practices in the early 20th century in the US and Europe, when financial reporting was still largely unregulated, are consistent with this argument: financial reporting policies of firms listed on the New York Stock Exchange (NYSE) in 1929 or on the Brussels Stock Exchange in the early 20th century reflected managers' incentives to supply higher quality financial information demanded by investors (Barton and Waymire, 2004; Van Overfelt et al., 2010). For example, firms issuing new equity and young firms in technology-based industries on the NYSE had a higher reporting quality, while firms for which alternative information was available (for example because they operated in regulated product markets or because they provided valuable signals through their dividend policy) exhibited a lower reporting quality (Barton and Waymire, 2004). As a consequence, some may question the appropriateness of intervention in the regulation of financial information disclosure.

However, a problem with the argument for zero regulation is that the optimal level of disclosure for controlling insiders does not necessarily correspond to a socially desirable level of disclosure, for several reasons. First, as already mentioned, disclosure of information may allow for better screening of self-serving insiders and may reduce the opportunities for expropriation by insiders. This facilitates the operations of financial markets and, as a result, an efficient allocation of scarce financial and human capital to value-creating investment opportunities (Bushman and Smith, 2003). Second, mandatory disclosure may serve an impairment role as a *commitment* device. The commitment creates consistency in reporting absent the type of information in the news (good versus bad), which in turn directly mitigates information asymmetries and uncertainty (Bushee and Leuz, 2005). Third, disclosure creates positive externalities. A firm's disclosure may not only be informative to investors about its own financial position, but also about that of other firms. The disclosure decisions of firms may also affect other firms' real decisions, for example about entering or exiting product markets (e.g. Beyer et al., 2010). Since individual firms are unlikely to take these externalities into account in deciding upon their level of disclosure, the obligation to disclose information may improve social welfare.

While the above arguments suggest that the imposition of mandatory disclosure by regulators has a number of benefits, mandating disclosure also brings about some costs (e.g. Leuz and Wysocki, 2008), since mandatory disclosure is not only costly for firms to implement, but also costly for the state to enforce. Despite the costs of enforcing disclosure standards, several examples illustrate positive effects of mandatory disclosure rules. One example can be found in the US Regulation Fair Disclosure (Reg FD), which was adopted in 2000. Before 2000, it was common practice for quoted companies to reveal price-relevant information to specific investors (often large institutional investors and financial analysts) before spreading it to smaller, individual investors. This selective disclosure led to an informational advantage from which parties receiving the information early could profit at the expense of investors who were informed later, and the SEC was concerned that this practice might undermine investor confidence in the integrity of the capital markets. Hence, Reg FD now requires all price-sensitive information to be disclosed to all parties at the same time. In analyzing the effectiveness of Reg FD, Heflin et al. (2003) demonstrate a substantial increase in public availability of voluntary, forward-looking, and earnings-related financial disclosures. Further, the absolute price impact of information disseminated by financial analysts decreased by 28 percent in the post-Regulation FD period (Gintschel and Markov, 2004). This suggests that Reg FD is effective and financial markets benefit from not differentiating between investors in timing information disclosure.

Even though one might be convinced that mandatory disclosure is beneficial for proper market functioning, one should not be blind to possible pitfalls in regulating disclosure. This is because the efficiency of a mandated disclosure practice hinges upon the leniency it gives to management. The following example on segment disclosure requirements can illustrate this point. Under current accounting practices, both in US Generally Accepted Accounting Principles (GAAP) (Statement of Financial Accounting Standards (SFAS) 131) and International Financial Reporting Standards (IFRS 8), multinational firms' segment information should be reported consistently with the way management organizes the firm internally for making operating decisions and assessing performance (e.g. products and services, geographic area, legal entity, or customer segmentation). This method of segment reporting is referred to as the "management approach" (FASB, 1997: paragraph 4). This accounting standard is particularly innovative in that it is inspired by the motivation to allow investors and other financial statement users to see the company "through the eyes of management" (Herrmann and Thomas, 2000). Because of its management focus, disclosure requirements and specification are much less standardized and firms are less committed to reporting consistent numbers over time. As a consequence, opponents argue that this type of high-discretion disclosure standard may even be undesirable as it could create deceitful expectations that all firms in an economy are living up to a specific disclosure "minimum."

Segment disclosures play an important stewardship role, in that they may reveal unresolved agency problems and ultimately can lead to heightened external monitoring of geographical or product segments (Berger and Hahn, 2007). Consistent with the arguments above, research by Hope and Thomas (2008) shows that US multinationals which discontinue disclosure of geographic earnings in the post-SFAS 131 period experience greater expansion of foreign sales, yet produce lower foreign profit margins and have lower firm value compared to peers that continue foreign profitability information.

Disclosure and Corporate Governance

While the bulk of the accounting and finance literature assumes that proprietary costs are the prime reason why managers may be inclined to withhold information, some researchers point to other non-disclosure incentives. Most of the alternative explanations are grounded in the work by Williamson (1981) on the attributes of modern corporations where disclosure and corporate governance interact. Nagar et al. (2003), for instance, hypothesize that managers are generally only motivated to publicly disseminate private information when appropriate incentives to disclose are installed. Managers have a natural preference to limit the ability to be monitored by outsiders as this maximizes their private control benefits. Lower disclosure makes monitoring more difficult, since less information is available in capital and labor markets, hence benefiting managers (Shleifer and Vishny, 1989). Consistent with their conjecture, Nagar et al. (2003) find for a sample of US firms that management earnings' forecast frequency and Association for Investment Management and Research (AIMR) analyst ratings are both positively related to the proportion of CEO compensation tied to the firm's share price.

Related work by Eng and Mak (2003) examines the association between managerial ownership, blockholder ownership, and disclosure. The underlying idea is that firms with low managerial ownership or with widely diffused ownership suffer more from agency problems, calling for more voluntary disclosures. Empirical evidence is mixed, however, as Eng and Mak (2003) and Baek et al. (2009) find that lower managerial ownership is indeed associated with increased disclosure, but Huafang and Jianguo (2007) find no impact of managerial ownership. Further, Huafang and Jianguo (2007) report a positive association between increased blockholder ownership and firm disclosure, while Eng and Mak (2003) find no association.

The type of dominant shareholder may further influence firm disclosure policies as different types of shareholders may have different preferences for disclosure (Chen et al., 2008). For example, for firms listed on Asian stock exchanges, increased voluntary disclosure is found in firms with more foreign ownership, but the impact of government ownership is mixed (Eng and Mak, 2003; Huafang and Jianguo, 2007; Wang et al., 2008). Literature on disclosure in family firms is growing. It could be argued that family owners will prefer less public voluntary disclosure than non-family shareholders, because family owners are more likely to be actively involved in the firm's management and the interests of managers and shareholders hence converge (Chau and Gray, 2010). This not only results in lower information asymmetry between family members and managers, but monitoring by family owners may also reduce the need for public disclosure for non-family shareholders. Furthermore, since family owners tend to have longer investment horizons than other shareholders, the benefits of timely information such as trading profits may be lower for family owners, while the potential costs such as managerial short-termism may be more important to them (Chen et al., 2008).

On the other hand, litigation and reputation cost concerns may matter more to undiversified family owners than to other shareholders, which may result in a greater demand for voluntary disclosure by family owners as compared to other shareholders. Consistent with the alignment of interest argument, Chen et al. (2008) find that family firms are generally less likely to provide earnings forecasts. However, family firms provide more quarterly forecasts than non-family firms when firm performance is poor, which is consistent with family owners' greater litigation and reputation cost concerns (Ali et al., 2007; Chen et al., 2008). Further, the extent of voluntary disclosure is relatively low in Hong Kong-listed family firms with low levels of shareholding, consistent with a convergence of interests, but disclosure is higher at greater levels of family shareholding (Chau and Gray, 2010).

Next to ownership structure, a firm's corporate governance structure may also influence its disclosure policies. Bushman and Smith (2003: 65) define as a primary goal of a well-functioning corporate governance structure "to ensure that minority shareholders receive reliable information about the value of firms." While it is generally assumed that board independence is associated with higher disclosure levels, empirical evidence on the role of outside directors on disclosure is mixed. An increase in the proportion of outside directors increases corporate disclosure for firms listed on the Hong Kong, Madrid, and Milan stock exchanges and of S&P 500 firms (Chen and Jaggi, 2000; Babío Arcay and Muiño Vázquez, 2005; Patelli and Prencipe, 2007; Baek et al., 2009), but reduces it for firms listed on the Singapore Stock Exchange (Eng and Mak, 2003; Cheng and Courtenay, 2006). No association between the proportion of outside directors and firms listed on the Malaysian stock exchange is found (Haniffa and Cooke, 2002).

In general, empirical evidence on the association between corporate governance and firm disclosure is mixed, which suggests that contingencies might be important. For example, in a recent meta-analysis, García-Meca and Sánchez-Ballesta (2010) suggest that the positive association between board independence and voluntary disclosure only occurs in countries with high investor protection rights. Further, other country-level characteristics, such as political structures or legal regimes, or firm-level characteristics, such as ownership origin and structure or more refined indicators of board independence, might be important (Bushman and Smith, 2003; Babío Arcay and Muiño Vázquez, 2005; Cheng and Courtenay, 2006;Chau and Gray, 2010).

While the combined international evidence is generally in line with internal corporate governance and disclosure being endogenous mechanisms able to reduce the agency costs arising from the separation between ownership and control, Barth (2003) unravels some potential weaknesses in studies of this kind. An important critique relates to the assumption that information disclosures would only be able to solve information asymmetries if investors see the disclosed information as being credible. Managers may provide "cheap talk" and investors would consequently update their expectations of managers' behavior in light of the incentives that managers face. This is consistent with the above-discussed view that positive effects of voluntary disclosure policies only arise if firms credibly commit to a higher disclosure policy (Leuz and Verrecchia, 2000).

Disclosure and Closely Held Companies

Despite the predominance of private firms in the economy, the vast majority of research on disclosure relates to public companies. This is natural, as the demand for information by outside shareholders is critical and hence is the focus of most attention by regulators. In closely held firms, by contrast, shareholders are insiders and have access to most, if not all, private information, leading to lower demands for public information (Burgstahler et al., 2006). Some authors even claim that the ability of private firms to disclose information selectively is a major reason why private firms stay private, since this would yield higher benefits compared to the higher cost of capital associated with private firms (Farre-Mensa, 2010). This does not mean that private firms should not disclose information, but the goal of disclosure is somewhat different in the context of private firms. While the most important recipients of information in public companies are outside shareholders, private companies have different stakeholders, such as banks, customers, suppliers, or employees, for whom accounting information production is also important (Ball and Shivakumar, 2005). Finally, tax authorities primarily rely on accounting information, especially in high tax alignment countries (Van Tendeloo and Vanstraelen, 2008).

As a consequence, disclosure of accounting information helps to reduce information asymmetries with external parties and is expected to facilitate contracting in private firms as well (Francis et al., 2008). Specific stakeholders may however require inside information from the private companies with whom they interact, making the usefulness of and demand for public information lower (Ball and Shivakumar, 2005). For example, private equity funds regularly disclose information on asset valuations to their investors, but refrain from making this information public (Cumming and Walz, 2010). Public information nevertheless remains important when dealing with stakeholders. For example, private firms publishing more (or higher quality) information are associated with higher leverage levels, suggesting that public information does convey a valuable signal to creditors and banks above the information they may privately acquire (Van Caneghem and Van Campenhout, 2012).

Few studies to date address disclosure questions in private companies. Some studies specifically investigate the role of venture capital investors in the disclosure policies of their portfolio companies. Davila and Foster (2007) have shown that venture capital investors are typically strongly involved in implementing management control systems in the private companies in which they invest, allowing more relevant information to be produced by venture capital-backed companies. Private firms with venture capital or private equity investors voluntarily disclose more information, driven by stronger monitoring and reputation concerns of these investors (Beuselinck et al., 2008) and by stronger protection from competition (Guo et al., 2004).

Given the limited insight into the public disclosure policies of private firms, we proceed to review the literature on the quality of this information, suggesting that corporate governance has an important impact on the quality of publicly disclosed information in private companies. Ball and Shivakumar (2005) were among the first to study the quality of publicly available financial information on private firms. Based upon a large sample of public and private UK companies, they show that the quality of the information (in particular: the timely recognition of economic losses) provided by private firms is lower than that of comparable public firms. In a similar vein, Nichols et al. (2009) show that public banks report more conservatively than private banks. They explain this by the fact that shareholders of public banks face higher potential agency problems compared to shareholders of private banks, hence requiring more conservative accounting information (Nichols et al., 2009). In contrast, private equity firms provide lower quality *private* information on the valuation of their assets to their investors when investors face higher potential agency problems (Cumming and Walz, 2010). The fact that reporting quality in private firms is, overall, lower than that in public firms does not necessarily imply that private firms report suboptimally: it may be an optimal outcome in the market for financial reporting, not a failure in the supply of information (Ball and Shivakumar, 2005).

Accounting quality in private firms is affected by the environment in which the firm operates. For example, the voluntary adoption of international accounting standards (IAS) by private firms is strongly dependent on the economic development of a country (Francis et al., 2008). Further, auditors have stronger incentives to supply high audit quality in private firms in countries with high tax alignment, where financial statements are more strongly scrutinized by tax authorities, leading to higher quality of financial accounts of private firms in these countries (Van Tendeloo and Vanstraelen, 2008). Peek et al. (2010) further show that public versus private firms' difference in asymmetric timeliness is positively associated with a country's degree of creditor protection, suggesting that financial statements are responsive to creditors' reporting demands, in contrast with the idea that private creditors would use special purpose reports.

Recently, some research has also emerged that relates the reporting quality of private firms to their ownership. Private firms with private equity or venture capital investors as shareholders have higher quality financial statements than comparable private companies without private equity or venture capital investors (Beuselinck et al., 2009; Katz,

2009; Givoly et al., 2010), suggesting that the monitoring and reputation concerns of outside equity investors drive the information quality of their portfolio companies. The reporting quality is also found to be lower in firms where private equity investors have higher ownership stakes than in companies where they have a lower equity stake, as private equity investors have greater access to inside information in the former (Beuselinck and Manigart, 2007). While these attempts provide important new insights into the information environment for private firms, many questions still remain unresolved. In the concluding section, we therefore summarize some important questions that future research may wish to address.

Concluding Remarks and Suggestions for Future Research

In this study, we have reviewed the academic literature connecting corporate disclosure and financial reporting at the firm level and tied this literature to corporate governance. The abundant literature suggests that disclosure develops endogenously with the demand for information in capital markets. Important questions for future research may relate to how the firm-specific corporate governance context impacts voluntary disclosure decisions, contingent on firm-level and country-level characteristics. For example, how does corporate disclosure change over the life cycle of (private) firms and what drives such changes? How does ownership matter for a firm's disclosure policy? With respect to family ownership, do family-owned firms have a different disclosure policy compared to non-family firms, and does it matter whether the CEO and/or board chairperson belongs to the family (Prencipe et al., 2011)? Furthermore, does it matter whether different types of shareholders, such as foreign investors, institutional investors or governments, but also business angels, venture capital or private equity investors in private companies, participate in the company? To what extent does the quality or the reputation of external investors impact firms' disclosure policies? Recent research suggests that foreign institutional investors operating from strong investor protection countries reduce earnings from management activities (Beuselinck et al., 2011) and improve the corporate governance systems that are in place (Aggarwal et al., 2011). This raises the question whether investor-origin impacts disclosure styles as well.

Not only shareholder characteristics but also corporate governance mechanisms are associated with firm disclosure policies. The existing evidence on this association is mixed, however, and important questions remain. For example, what is the impact on voluntary disclosure policies of how the board is composed, whether the CEO and chairperson are the same person, or how the CEO is compensated? Further, most existing research focuses on public firms. It is only recently that modest attempts have been made to gain insights into disclosure in private companies. We therefore call for more studies on disclosure in private firms.

In addition to studies on voluntary disclosure of financial and/or accounting information, studies of corporate social responsibility (CSR) reporting may provide additional insights into how firms may benefit from reducing information asymmetries through disclosing a specific type of non-financial information to stakeholders. Dhaliwal et al. (2012) document that the issuance of standalone CSR reports, alongside the traditional mandatory annual reports, is associated with lower analyst forecast error. Moreover, this relationship seems most pronounced in countries that are more stakeholder-oriented. Other questions relating to CSR disclosure are the importance of external assurance of CSR reports and how CSR disclosures help to attract potential investors (Blair et al., 2010; GRI, 2011).

Finally, an innovative set of questions could relate to how firms can reduce investors' information acquisition costs by using new (real-time) information technology such as Twitter, Facebook, or other social media. In a recent working paper, Blankespoor et al. (2011) show for a sample of technology firms that managerial dissemination of firm-initiated news via Twitter is associated with lower bid-ask spreads, especially for less visible firms. While the aforementioned list is non-exhaustive, we believe that these and comparable questions are important to gain additional insights into the interaction between corporate governance and a firm's information environment.

Notes

1. Voluntary information disclosure is often qualitative in nature and is therefore difficult to quantify empirically. However, academics have been inventive in establishing disclosure proxies. These include self-constructed checklists of information components from the annual report (e.g. Botosan, 1997; Hail, 2002; Haniffa and Cooke, 2002); issuance and timing of management forecasts (Nagar et al., 2003; Ali et al., 2007); selective disclosure of non-financial information like the issuance of standalone corporate social responsibility (CSR) reports (Dhaliwal et al., 2012); and even the usefulness of firms' disclosures as perceived by expert users like financial analysts (Lang and Lundholm, 1996; Nagar et al., 2003).
2. The Cadbury Report, issued in December 1992 in the UK, suggested improvements to restore investor confidence in the corporate system after a series of corporate scandals at that time, thereby especially focusing on improving the British corporate governance system. The Sarbanes-Oxley Act, adopted by the US Congress on 24 July 2002, made important changes to US corporate law in response to widespread corporate fraud in the US just after the turn of the century. The Act brings about the biggest changes to US securities law since the 1933 Securities Exchange Act and addresses public disclosure, trading by directors, the role of audit committees, the independence of auditors, the regulation of accounting and the accounting profession in general.
3. Examples are the International Accounting Standards Board (IASB), a transnational standard-setting body and the Financial Accounting Standards Board (FASB), a US standard-setting body, both aimed at the development of accounting standards. Further, stock exchanges such as the New York Stock Exchange, Euronext, and others impose additional disclosure requirements for publicly listed firms.

4. The credibility issue regarding disclosure is also directly related to the cost of capital effect. Bushee and Noe (2000), for instance, argue that disclosures may indeed reduce a firm's cost of capital, but only if they are credible and not self-serving.

References

Aggarwal, R., Erel, I., Ferreira, M., and Matos P. (2011). "Does Governance Travel around The World? *Journal of Financial Economics*, 100(1): 154–81.

Ali, A., Chen, T., and Radhakrishnan, S. (2007). "Corporate Disclosures by Family Firms," *Journal of Accounting and Economics*, 44: 238–86.

Amihud, Y., and Mendelson, H. (1986). "Asset Pricing and the Bid-Ask Spread," *Journal of Financial Economics*, 17: 223–49.

Babío Arcay, M. A., and Muiño Vázquez, M. F. (2005). "Corporate Characteristics, Governance Rules and the Extent of Voluntary Disclosure in Spain," *Advances in Accounting*, 21: 299–331.

Baek, H. Y., Johnson, D. R., and Kim, J. W. (2009). "Managerial Ownership, Corporate Governance, and Voluntary Disclosure," *Journal of Business and Economic Studies*, 15(2): 44–61.

Ball, R., and Shivakumar, L. (2005). "Earnings Quality in UK Private Firms," *Journal of Accounting and Economics*, 38: 83–128.

Barry, C. B., and Brown, S. J. (1985). "Differential Information and Security Market Equilibrium," *Journal of Financial and Quantitative Analysis*, 20: 407–22.

Barth, M. (2003). "Discussion of 'Compensation Policy and Discretionary Disclosure,'" *Journal of Accounting and Economics*, 34: 311–18.

Barton, J., and Waymire, G. (2004). "Investor Protection under Unregulated Financial Reporting," *Journal of Accounting and Economics*, 38: 65–116.

Bebchuk, L., Kraakman, R., and Triantis, G. (2000). "Stock Pyramids, Cross-Ownership, and Dual Class Equity," in R. Morck (ed.), *Concentrated Corporate Ownership*. Chicago: University of Chicago Press, 445–60.

Benston, G., Bromwich, M., Litan, R., and Wagenhofer, A. (2006). *Worldwide Financial Reporting*. Oxford: Oxford University Press.

Berger, P. G., and Hann, R. (2007). "Segment Profitability and the Proprietary and Agency Costs of Disclosure," *The Accounting Review*, 82(4): 869–906.

Beuselink, C., and Manigart, S. (2007). "Financial Reporting Quality in Private Equity Backed Companies," *Small Business Economics*, 29: 261–74.

—— Deloof, M., and Manigart, S. (2008). "Private Equity Investments and Disclosure Policy," *European Accounting Review*, 17: 607–39.

—— —— —— (2009). "Private Equity Involvement and Earnings Quality," *Journal of Business Finance and Accounting*, 36: 587–615.

—— Blanco, B., and Garcia-Lara, J. M. (2012). "Herding PIGS? The Role of Foreign Shareholders in disciplining financial reporting," INTACCT Working Paper.

Beyer, A., Cohen, D. A., Lys, T. Z., and Walther, B. R. (2010). "The Financial Reporting Environment," *Journal of Accounting and Economics*, 50: 296–343.

Blair, N., Jagolinzer, A., and Rogers, G. (2010). "Disclosure Dilemma," Stanford GSB Case Study, Case A-200.

Blankespoor, E., Miller, G., and White, H. (2011). "Firm Dissemination, Direct-Access Information Technology and Information Asymmetry," version: May 17, 2011. University of Michigan Working Paper, Available at SSRN: <http://ssrn.com/abstract=1657169>.

Boot, A. (2000). "Relationship Banking" *Journal of Financial Intermediation*, 9: 7–25.
Botosan, Christine A. (1997). "Disclosure Level and the Cost of Equity Capital," *The Accounting Review*, 72: 323–49.
Brown, S. (1979). "The Effect of Estimation Risk on Capital Market Equilibrium," *Journal of Financial and Quantitative Analysis*, 14: 215–20.
Burgstahler, D., Hail, L., and Leuz C. (2006). "The Importance of Reporting Incentives," *The Accounting Review*, 81(5): 983–1016.
Bushee, B. J., and Leuz, C. (2005). "Economic Consequences of SEC Disclosure Regulation," *Journal of Accounting and Economics*, 39: 233–64.
—— and Noe, C. F. (2000). "Corporate Disclosure Practices, Institutional Investors, and Stock Return Volatility," *Journal of Accounting Research* (Supplement: Studies on Accounting Information and the Economics of the Firm), 38: 171–202.
Bushman, R. M., and Smith, A. J. (2003). "Transparency, Financial Accounting Information, and Corporate Governance," *FRBNY Economic Policy Review*, 9(1): 65–87.
Chau, G., and Gray, S. J. (2010). "Family Ownership, Board Independence and Voluntary Disclosure," *Journal of International Accounting, Auditing and Taxation*, 19(2): 93–109.
Chen, C. J. P., and Jaggi, B. (2000). "Association between Independent Non-Executive Directors, Family Control and Financial Disclosures in Hong Kong," *Journal of Accounting and Public Policy*, 19(4–5): 285–310.
Chen, S., Chen, X., and Cheng, Q. (2008). "Do Family Firms Provide More or Less Voluntary Disclosure?" *Journal of Accounting Research*, 46(3): 499–536.
Cheng, E. C. M., and Courtenay, S. M. (2006). "Board Composition, Regulatory Regime and Voluntary Disclosure," *The International Journal of Accounting*, 41(3): 262–89.
Christensen, H., Hail, L., and Leuz, C. (2010). "Capital Market Effects of Securities Regulation," Working Paper, University of Chicago-Booth School of Business.
Clarkson, P., Guedes, J., and Thompson, R. (1996). "On the Diversification, Observability, and Measurement of Estimation Risk," *Journal of Financial and Quantitative Analysis*, 31: 69–84.
Cumming, D., and Walz, U. (2011). "Private Equity Returns and Disclosure around the World," *Journal of International Business Studies*, 41: 727–54.
Davila, A., and Foster, G. (2007). "Management Control Systems in Early-Stage Startup Companies," *The Accounting Review*, 82: 907–37.
Dhaliwal, D., Radhakrishnan, S., Tsang, A., and Yang, G. (2012). "Nonfinancial Disclosure and Analyst Forecast Accuracy," *The Accounting Review*, 87(3): 723–60.
Easley, D., and O'Hara, M. (2004). "Information and the Cost of Capital," *Journal of Finance*, 59: 1553–83.
Eng, L. L., and Mak, Y. T. (2003). "Corporate Governance and Voluntary Disclosure," *Journal of Accounting and Public Policy*, 22: 325–45.
Farre-Mensa, J. (2010). "Why are Most Firms Privately-Held?" Working Paper, New York University.
FASB (1997). "Statement of Financial Accounting Standards No. 131," Financial Accounting Standards Board (FASB) of the Financial Accounting Foundation.
Francis, J. E., Khurana, I. K., Martin, X., and Pereira, R. (2008). "The Role of Firm-Specific Incentives and Country Factors in Explaining Voluntary IAS Adoptions," *European Accounting Review*, 17: 331–60.
Frankel, R., McNichols, M., and Wilson, G. P. (1995). "Discretionary Disclosure and External Financing," *The Accounting Review*, 70: 135–50.

GARCÍA-MECA, E., and SÁNCHEZ-BALLESTA, J. P. (2010). "The Association of Board Independence and Ownership Concentration with Voluntary Disclosure," *European Accounting Review*, 19(3): 603–27.

GINTSCHEL, A., and MARKOV, S. (2004). "The Effectiveness of Regulation FD," *Journal of Accounting and Economics*, 37: 293–314.

GIVOLY, D., HAYN, C., and KATZ, S. (2010). "Does Public Ownership of Equity Improve Earnings Quality?" *The Accounting Review*, 85(1): 195–225.

Global Reporting Initiative (GRI) (2011). "Sustainability Reporting Guidelines," Version 3.1.

GLOSTEN, L. R., and MILGROMS, P. R. (1985). "Bid, Ask and Transaction Prices in a Specialist Market with Heterogeneously Informed Traders," *Journal of Financial Economics*, 14(1): 71–100.

GUO, R.-J., LEV, B., and ZHOU, N. (2004). "Competitive Costs of Disclosure by Biotech Firms," *Journal of Accounting Research*, 40(2): 319–55.

HAIL, L. (2002). "The Impact of Voluntary Corporate Disclosures on the Ex-Ante Cost of Capital for Swiss Firms," *European Accounting Review*, 11(4): 741–73.

HANIFFA, R. M., and COOKE, T. E. (2002). "Culture, Corporate Governance and Disclosure in Malaysian Corporations," *ABACUS*, 38(3): 317–49.

HEALY, P. M., and PALEPU, K. G. (2001). "Information Asymmetry, Corporate Disclosure, and the Capital Markets," *Journal of Accounting and Economics*, 31: 405–40.

HEFLIN, F., SUBRAMANYAM, K. R., and ZHANG, Y. (2003). "Regulation Fair Disclosure and the Information Environment," *The Accounting Review*, 78(1): 1–37.

HERMANN, D., and THOMAS, W. (2000). "An Analysis of Segment Disclosures under SFAS No. 131 and SFAS No. 14," *Accounting Horizons*, 14(3): 287–302.

HOPE, O.-K., and THOMAS, W. B. (2008). "Managerial Empire Building and Firm Disclosure," *Journal of Accounting Research*, 46(3): 591–626.

HUAFANG, X., and JIANGUO, Y. (2007). "Ownership Structure, Board Composition and Corporate Voluntary Disclosure," *Managerial Auditing Journal*, 22(6): 604–19.

HUGHES, J. S., LIU, J., and LIU, J. (2007). "Information Asymmetry, Diversification and the Cost of Capital," *The Accounting Review*, 82: 705–29.

JENNINGS, R. (1987). "Unsystematic Security Price Movements, Management Earnings Forecasts, and Revisions in Consensus Analyst Earnings Forecasts," *Journal of Accounting Research*, 25: 90–110.

JENSEN, M. C., and MECKLING, W. H. (1976). "Theory of the Firm: Managerial Behavior, Agency Costs and Ownership Structure," *Journal of Financial Economics*, 36: 225–57.

KATZ, S. (2009). "Earnings Quality and Ownership Structure," *The Accounting Review*, 84: 623–58.

LAMBERT, R., LEUZ, C., and VERRECCHIA, R. E. (2007). "Accounting Information, Disclosure, and the Cost of Capital," *Journal of Accounting Research*, 45: 385–420.

LANG, M., and LUNDHOLM, R. (1996). "Corporate Disclosure Policy and Analyst Behavior," *The Accounting Review*, 71(4): 467–92.

—— —— (2000). "Voluntary Disclosure and Equity Offerings," *Contemporary Accounting Research*, 17: 623–62.

LA PORTA, R., LOPEZ-DE-SILANES, F., SHLEIFER, A., and VISNHY, R. (2000). "Investor Protection and Corporate Governance," *Journal of Financial Economics*, 58: 3–27.

LEUZ, C., and VERRECCHIA, R. E. (2000). "The Economic Consequences of Increased Disclosure," *Journal of Accounting Research*, Supplement, 38: 91–124.

—— and WYSOCKI, P. (2008). "Economic Consequences of Financial Reporting and Disclosure Regulation," Working Paper, available at SSRN: <http://ssrn.com/abstract=1105398>.

Merton, R. C. (1987). "A Simple Model of Capital Market Equilibrium with Incomplete Information," *Journal of Finance*, 42: 483–510.

Nagar, V., Nanda, D. J., and Wysocki, P. (2003). "Discretionary Disclosure and Stock-Based Incentives," *Journal of Accounting and Economics*, 34: 283–309.

Nichols, D. C., Wahlen, J. M., and Wieland, M. (2009). "Publicly Traded versus Privately Held," *Review of Accounting Studies*, 14: 88–122.

Patelli, L., and Prencipe, A. (2007). "The Relationship between Voluntary Disclosure and Independent Directors in the Presence of a Dominant Shareholder," *European Accounting Review*, 16(1): 5–33.

Peek, E., Cuijpers, R., and Buijink, W. (2010). "Creditors' and Shareholders' Reporting Demands in Public Versus Private Firms," *Contemporary Accounting Research*, 27(1): 49–91.

Prencipe, A., Bar-Yosef, S., Mazzola, P., and Pozza, L. (2011). "Income Smoothing in Family-Controlled Companies," *Corporate Governance: An International Review*, 19(6): 529–46.

Shleifer, A., and Vishny, R. (1989). "Management Entrenchment," *Journal of Financial Economics*, 25: 123–39.

Van Caneghem, T., and Van Campenhout, G. (2012). "Quantity and Quality of Information and SME Financial Structure," *Small Business Economics*, 39(2): 341–58.

Van Overfelt, W., Deloof, M., and Vanstraelen, A. (2010). "The Quality of Unregulated Financial Reporting," *European Accounting Review*, 19: 7–34.

Van Tendeloo, B., and Vanstraelen, A. (2008). "Earnings Management and Audit Quality in Europe," *European Accounting Review*, 17: 447–69.

Verrecchia, R. (1983). "Discretionary Disclosure," *Journal of Accounting and Economics*, 5: 179–94.

Wagenhofer, A. (1990). "Voluntary Disclosure with a Strategic Opponent," *Journal of Accounting and Economics*, 12: 341–63.

Wang, K., Sewon, O., and Claiborne, M. C. (2008). "Determinants and Consequences of Voluntary Disclosure in an Emerging Market: Evidence from China," *Journal of International Accounting, Auditing and Taxation*, 17(1): 14–30.

Williamson, O. E. (1981). "The Modern Corporation: Origins, Evolution, Attributes," *Journal of Economic Literature*, 19(4): 1537–68.

CHAPTER 14

AUDITING AND CORPORATE GOVERNANCE

ANDREA MENNICKEN AND MICHAEL POWER

INTRODUCTION

THIS chapter discusses the roles and relevance of auditing in architectures of governance and management control. Auditing is one important element in a corporation's governance and reporting system, developing in constant interaction with other governance mechanisms (Gray and Manson, 2011; but see also Power, 1997; Robson et al., 2007). As Flint has highlighted in his classic treatise *Philosophy and Principles of Auditing*, "audit is a control mechanism to monitor conduct and performance, and to secure or enforce accountability" (Flint, 1988: 12). Yet, how audit and its relationship with other governance mechanisms play out in practice varies. Auditing as a mechanism "designed to monitor compliance with specified norms of what is acceptable behaviour" is "culturally, socially and politically dependent" (Flint, 1988: 13; but see also Power, 1997; Mennicken, 2008; Quick et al., 2008). It is a "social and institutional practice" (Hopwood and Miller, 1994; Porter et al., 2008) shaped by local and regional traditions, cultures, legal, political, and economic institutions. As Flint (1988: 13) puts it, "it is an evolving process, reacting with changing expectations about the performance or conduct of the individuals or organisations to which it is applied."

This chapter examines how internal and external auditing have come to be challenged and changed in different jurisdictions in the aftermath of high-profile company and audit failures, and the financial crisis of 2008–9. The list of cases is long, including JPMorgan Securities, Equitable Life, and Barings in the UK; Enron and WorldCom in the US; Parmalat in Italy; Yukos in Russia; Satyam in India; and Comroad in Germany. *External* audit refers to corporate financial audits conducted on the financial statements of an organization by an outside party—a registered public accounting firm or a qualified individual auditor. *Internal* audit is a control function established within the organization.

It can be seen as an extended "arm of management" aimed at ensuring the efficacy of internal control systems (Gray and Manson, 2011: 584–5). We show that despite an abundant history of corporate scandals and disappointments about the performance of auditing, internal and external auditing have come to assume an increasingly significant role in architectures of governance and management control across the globe. This significance has been achieved despite the fact that the very idea of good auditing or audit quality remains remarkably elusive. Indeed, definitions of auditing and its contribution to corporate governance are largely aspirational. They constitute idealized, normative projections of the hopes invested in the practice, rather than statements of its actual operational capability (Power, 1997).

Auditing has evolved from an activity aimed primarily at fraud detection and direct inspection of transactions, to a system of second-order "controls of controls," concerned with verifying systems of governance and management control. Yet, it is not only a series of technical procedures for gathering and evaluating evidence. It is also an *idea of governing* (Power, 1997). Auditing is not only one important element *in* corporate governance. It has advanced to become a governance paradigm in its own right, driving, and being driven by, the logic of *auditability* (Power, 1996, 1997). This logic emphasizes the construction of proper documentary appearances, and the production of auditable performance embodied in formalistic, externally verifiable systems of control. In following this logic, auditing may not only contribute to enhanced levels of accountability. It can also undermine accountability and ethical reasoning by promoting forms of ritualistic compliance and technical-procedural correctness, which in turn displace in-depth evaluation and scrutiny (see Power 1996, 1997; but also Gill, 2009).

We unfold this argument in five steps. In the next section we position auditing as a partial solution to the well-known agency problems which define corporate governance. This is followed by a discussion of the knowledge base of auditors and the growth of practice standards. We describe and analyze the expansion of audit services into a variety of different assurance and consulting services, the rise of business risk audit approaches, implications for the auditor–client relationship, and auditors' increased responsibilities with respect to the review of corporate governance following the collapse of Enron, and more recently, the financial crisis which began in 2008. Because the auditor is an economic agent in his/her own right, there are secondary agency problems which are addressed by a mixture of second-order governance and regulatory mechanisms focused on auditors and audit firms. The third section provides a brief overview of these mechanisms and examines ongoing attempts aimed to enhance the governance and independence of auditors and audit firms, as well as competition in the audit market. In the fourth section, we discuss the development of auditing as a governance paradigm in its own right. The fifth section concludes the chapter with a discussion of challenges ahead for auditing if it is to fulfill its role in corporate governance, and outlines some issues for future inquiry.

AUDITING IN CORPORATE GOVERNANCE

The US-American Center for Audit Quality, a body affiliated with the American Institute of Certified Public Accountants (AICPA), was set up in 2007 to "enhance investor confidence and public trust in the global capital markets by fostering high quality performance by public company auditors" (http://www.thecaq.org/about/index.htm, accessed 24 June 2011). It writes about external auditing and its roles in corporate governance:

> An independent financial statement audit is conducted by a registered public accounting firm. It includes examining, on a test basis, evidence supporting the amounts and disclosures in the company's financial statements, an assessment of the accounting principles used and significant estimates made by management, as well as evaluating the overall financial statement presentation to form an opinion on whether the financial statements taken as a whole are free from material misstatement. (Center for Audit Quality, 2011: 3)

Similarly, International Standards on Auditing (ISA), the most widely applied set of auditing rules, state that the purpose of auditing "is to enhance the degree of confidence of intended users in the financial statements" (ISA 200, International Federation of Accountants (IFAC), 2010: 72).

The demand for auditing, at least to a large extent, arises from the classic agency problem, much discussed elsewhere in this volume, where a principal, who could be an investor or a manager, entrusts a task or some assets to an agent, who could be management or employees (Jensen and Meckling, 1976; DeAngelo, 1981; Chow, 1982; Flint, 1988; Solomon, 2010). This structure generates inherent agency costs because the actions of agents may not be observable and knowable by principals (information asymmetry) and the agent's incentives may not be aligned with those of the principal (moral hazard). The agency problem defines the space of corporate governance understood as a range of mechanisms to incentivize and control agents (employees and management) and align their actions with the wishes of principals (investors). One such mechanism is the requirement for corporations to produce financial statements and related disclosures, in short a periodic flow of information about performance from the agent to principal (see Beuselinck et al., Chapter 13 in this volume). External auditing enters the picture as an independent check and opinion on the quality of the financial statements. In theory, this additional assurance by the auditors provides both a disincentive to managers to manipulate the accounting statements and also gives more confidence to providers of capital, thereby increasing the liquidity of capital markets. It is for this reason that auditors can be regarded as an important example of a "gatekeeper" (Coffee, 2006). Coffee (2006: 2) defines a gatekeeper as "some form of outside or independent watchdog or monitor, someone who screens out flaws or defects or who verifies compliance with standards or procedures." A gatekeeper, such as an auditor, contributes to corporate governance by providing "certification or verification services to investors, vouching for someone else who has a greater incentive than they to deceive" (p. 2).

While this general conception of the role of external auditing in corporate governance is easy to state, the history of its development is a complex and changing one, taking place in many different countries with different legal and economic frameworks. For example, in some countries, many enterprises are family-owned. Others are "insider" economies whereby providers of finance can obtain the assurance they need directly. In these cases, the agency problem is much less pronounced and the role of audit is historically less significant to governance than these other avenues of control by principals (see e.g. the cases of Belgium (Vanstraelen and Willekens, 2008) and Germany (Köhler et al., 2008)). Yet as capital markets grow and providers of finance become more remote, the need for external assurance as an element of corporate governance also grows. Indeed, for economies undergoing transition and developing financial markets there may be underdeveloped audit capability and a need to draw in, copy, and translate audit practices from more mature contexts (Fan and Wong, 2005; Mennicken, 2008, 2010; Sucher et al., 1998). For example, in a study of the relationship between auditing and legal environments in 39 different countries, Choi and Wong (2007) show that external auditors generally play a more important governance function in countries where legal institutions are weak than in countries where legal institutions are strong.

Auditing, in one form or another, can be traced back many centuries through commercial history (see e.g. Lee, 1988; Coffee, 2006; Matthews, 2006; Quick et al., 2008). However, it was the growth of corporate economies, first in the 19th century and then throughout the second half of the 20th century, which defined the context of modern corporate financial auditing. Over this period, auditing was established as a statutory requirement in many jurisdictions for most corporate entities. While accounting scholars and policymakers have addressed the conceptual foundations of financial reporting, such efforts have been less prominent in the field of auditing. There is nothing to match the conceptual framework programs of the American Financial Accounting Standards Board (FASB) and the International Accounting Standards Board (IASB). However, two conceptual efforts stand out. Mautz and Sharaf (1961) and Flint (1988) have developed a number of postulates and principles of auditing.

Mautz and Sharaf (1961) were the first to attempt to develop a theory of auditing, approaching the subject from a US-American perspective. Building on Mautz and Sharaf, Flint (1988), a leading Scottish academic, formulated seven audit postulates at a more general level, which conceptually underpin auditing. According to Flint, the primary condition for an audit is that there is a relationship of accountability or a situation of public accountability (Flint, 1988: 23–6), and this is enabled by independence and freedom from investigatory and reporting constraints (pp. 29–31). Flint also emphasized the investigatory and evidence based nature of the audit process and stated that if the subject matter of audit is "not susceptible to verification by evidence…an audit is not possible" (p. 31). Flint focuses on external auditing and places it explicitly in an accountability context, thus underscoring its importance for corporate governance. However, particularly in the last 20 years, internal auditing has also come to assume an increasingly important role for the assurance of corporate governance.

Although the internal auditor is an employee of the organization and not legally and contractually independent, his/her role has evolved to address an agency problem in a manner similar to that of the external auditor. An increased emphasis on the integrity of internal control systems and the reframing of financial auditing in terms of risk management, over the last 30 years, has given more prominence to internal auditing (Spira and Page, 2003; Carcello et al., 2005; IFAC, 2006; Power, 2007). Although not mandated, it has become a normalized feature of medium to large organizations (Financial Reporting Council (FRC), 2005; Power, 2007; Stiles, this volume). As corporations grew in size and complexity, they recognized the need to develop internal systems of control to safeguard assets and ensure compliance with management policies.

In the US, in 1992 the Committee of Sponsoring Organizations of the Treadway Commission produced a report specifically addressing the role of internal controls in securing improved corporate governance (COSO, 1992). In the UK, the provisions of the Cadbury Code, also published in 1992, were explicitly designed to improve internal control mechanisms, including internal audit (Cadbury Committee, 1992, para. 4.39). Until recently, internal audit has been viewed as a compliance-based monitoring function (Cadbury Committee, 1992, 4.39). This has changed as the internal auditor has come to be represented as an important advisory resource, adding value and improving the effectiveness of risk management, business controls, and governance (Bou-Raad, 2000; IIARF (Institute of Internal Auditors Research Foundation), 2007; Spira and Page, 2003).

In other words, the internal auditor's role is a mix of both supervisory and advisory functions and this can give rise to conflicts of interest (Norman et al., 2010; Spira and Page, 2003). In particular, after the Enron and WorldCom disasters concerns were expressed that internal auditors cannot objectively assess internal controls, financial disclosures, and risks when they report the results of this work to their supervisors, such as the CFO (Institute of Internal Auditors UK and Ireland, 2003; Norman et al. 2010). Furthermore, it can be difficult to adapt and combine the expertise of internal audit with that of risk management functions in practice (Crawford and Stein, 2002; Spira and Page, 2003). The scope of the internal and external auditors' work is often different; whereas external auditors are primarily concerned with the quality of financial statements, the internal auditor has a much wider remit covering controls over operations more generally. Despite these differences, the work of both auditors can overlap, leading to opportunities for cooperation, but also potential problems of coordination. Taken together both internal and external audit are part of the checks and balances which constitute corporate governance. They form part of an interdependent governance ecology, which is subject to many different forms of regulation: best-practice guidance, codes, and legal provisions (Center for Audit Quality, 2011). These have come to be challenged and changed over time. Of critical importance in the history of auditing specifically and corporate governance more generally have been corporate scandals and disasters. From the collapse of the City of Glasgow Bank in 1878 to Enron in 2001 and Lehman in 2008, corporate failure has inevitably been associated with audit failure leading to subsequent reform efforts by regulators and the professions to strengthen the audit. These reforms have taken many different forms, such as requiring more attention to fraud risk, being more skeptical and challenging and independent, or by reporting more frequently to regulatory bodies. It is to these and other pressures for change that we now turn.

Auditing Knowledge and Standards

As noted above, the role of financial auditing in corporate governance is subject to change. From the earliest days in the 19th century the presumed role of the auditor as revealed in practice texts was the prevention and detection of fraud (Dicksee, 1892; Chandler et al., 1993; Power, 1997). This ambition did not sit well with the practice of auditing, which had more to do with checking bookkeeping accuracy than the collection of substantive evidence about transactions (Chandler et al., 1993; Coffee, 2006: 109–11). Over time, as the corporate economy grew and capital markets developed, the objective of fraud detection became secondary and subservient to that of giving an opinion on the quality of the accounts, i.e. whether they presented a true and fair view or fairly represented the financial condition and performance of the entity. Yet while the objective of audit shifted away from the detection of minor employee fraud, public expectations were always reluctant to dissociate audit from fraud detection completely (Sikka et al., 1998). The continuing conflict over what the public expects from an audit (e.g. with regards to fraud detection) and what the auditing profession prefers the audit objectives to be, has come to be described in terms of an "audit expectations gap," which, according to Humphrey et al. "has shown considerable continuity and resilience against solution" (1992: 137; but see also Sikka et al., 1998).

The present position as prescribed by ISA 240 is that auditors have a duty to plan the audit in such a way that they have a reasonable expectation of detecting material misstatement, whether arising from fraud or error:

> An auditor conducting an audit in accordance with ISAs is responsible for obtaining reasonable assurance that the financial statements taken as a whole are free from material misstatement, whether caused by fraud or error. (IFAC, 2010: 158)

The standard further states:

> Owing to the inherent limitations of an audit, there is an unavoidable risk that some material misstatements of the financial statements may not be detected, even though the audit is properly planned and performed in accordance with the ISAs. (IFAC, 2010: 158)

It is emphasized that the primary responsibility for the prevention and detection of fraud rests with management and those charged with governance, i.e. the board of directors and not the auditor (IFAC, 2010: 157). In other words, fraud *prevention* as such is largely peripheral to the external audit, even though the public might prefer auditors to engage more explicitly in forensic work, particularly after the Enron and other financial scandals (Coffee, 2006: 132–42). Auditing standards were reformed in the wake of these events and auditors' duties to *detect and report* material fraud have become more clearly articulated as part of a risk based approach. Nevertheless, international auditing standards still do not make external auditors directly responsible for the detection of fraud.

Underlying the debate about audit objectives, and the auditor's role in fraud detection and corporate governance more generally, are shifting conceptions of the audit process itself. The operational objectives of financial auditing are to ensure that assets and revenues are not overstated, that liabilities and expenses are not understated, and that there is legal and regulatory compliance in the presentation of the accounts. Yet these generalities have been approached with different methods. Audit began as a 100 percent testing of transactions though, as noted above, the depth of the testing was questionable by modern standards. As transaction volumes grew and firms developed their own internal checks over account balances, external auditors found that they could justify a more selective basis for testing transactions and balances, a selectivity which eventually developed into formal statistical sampling (Power, 1992). Particularly in the 1970s and 1980s, increasing emphasis came to be placed on audit efficiency and cost-effectiveness in an attempt to keep auditing commercially viable in increasingly complex business environments (Higson, 1997). Audits increasingly adopted a systems-based approach, where the main focus was on an examination of accounting systems, with particular regard to information flows and the identification of internal controls (Higson, 1997: 200). If the auditor found that the internal controls were effective, the level of detailed substantive testing could be reduced. However, if the results of compliance testing revealed weaknesses in the controls, the auditor had no choice but to go back to substantive transactions testing. Further, auditors began to conduct reviews—analytical reviews—of the behavior of critical account totals, focusing on trends and deviations from plans and drawing more generally on an understanding of the business environment of the entity.

In the 1980s and 1990s, the audit process began to converge on a more explicitly risk-based approach (Higson, 1997; Spira and Page, 2003; Power, 1997, 2007; Knechel et al., 2007; Robson et al., 2007; Knechel 2007). The extent of detailed testing and other work carried out in an audit came to depend on the levels of identified *audit risk*, broken down into the components of inherent risk (the susceptibility of financial statements to be materially misstated irrespective of internal controls), control risk (the risk that material misstatement will not be prevented or detected by internal controls), and detection risk (the risk that auditors' substantive procedures will not detect material misstatement) (see e.g. IFAC, 2010; Gray and Manson, 2011). The audit risk model was, and still is, invoked by auditors to facilitate cost-effectiveness. It is also claimed to focus the audit on those financial statement areas perceived to have high inherent risk (e.g. because of the complexity of the transactions or the judgment involved) which is not sufficiently mitigated by internal controls. Examples of such high-risk financial statement areas are: accounting provisions, such as for bad debts; valuations, including impairment tests, of intangible assets, such as patents, or complex financial assets, such as financial instruments; and income recognition.

Two things stand out from these developments. First, the modern risk-based auditor must take account more than ever before of the wider business environment of the entity. Second and relatedly, the inherent and control risk of accounting systems will be a function of the risk management and control systems of the entity (Spira and Page, 2003;

Knechel, 2007; Power, 2007). In this way, financial auditing and organizational risk management necessarily overlap since the auditor has a great interest in the quality of a firm's risk management, particularly as it touches on the accounts.

These developments in the audit process have been reflected in an expansion of formal guidance for auditors in the form of auditing standards, at national and international level. To a large extent, auditing standards evolved in response to audit failures and criticisms of the audit profession by the public. In the UK, the first set of national auditing standards was issued by the Auditing Practices Committee of the profession in 1980 (Chandler, 1997). In the US, Congress gave the Security and Exchange Commission (SEC) the authority to set auditing standards for all SEC registrants in 1934 following the 1929 stock market crash (Francis, 2008). At the international level, the International Auditing Practices Committee of the International Federation of Accountants (IFAC) issued its first international auditing guideline in 1979 (Roussey, 1999). Today, the International Standards on Auditing (ISAs) comprise a body of 37 standards published in an 806-page handbook. Several further guidelines and detailed practice statements accompany it (IFAC, 2010). As Chandler (1997) points out, auditing standards do not only provide important guidance to auditors and are aimed at helping maintain acceptable levels of performance, they play also important legal and political roles (see also Mennicken, 2008). In court, auditing standards are used as a benchmark when establishing whether the auditor has exercised reasonable skill and care. Auditors have used the standards to defend and legitimize their practice, communicate professionalism, and limit responsibility, for example with respect to the responsibility to detect fraud (Chandler, 1997; Sikka et al., 1998; IFAC, 2010).

In addition to formal standards, the professional service firms have sought to develop their own proprietorial approaches to audit. For example, in the 1990s KPMG developed a "Strategic Systems Approach" which emphasized the links between business environment variables and financial statements, and considered client business risk as part of the audit process (Bell et al., 1997; Jeppesen, 1998). Similar approaches were developed within Arthur Andersen (*The Business Audit*) and Ernst & Young (the *Audit Innovation* project) (Knechel, 2007: 393). Attention came to be paid to a client's strategic positioning and its business risk, defined as the risk that a client will fail to meet its objectives. In the aftermath of the Enron and WorldCom scandals, business risk audit approaches were criticized. Further, auditors on the ground regarded the approach often as too radical and impractical (Curtis and Turley, 2007). Yet, a business review of some kind remains a very important dimension of audit practice and today, in the wake of the financial crisis, there is pressure for auditors to pay more attention to business models and to deepen their work on going concern. These issues were all part of the earlier much criticized KPMG experiment.

The audit process has developed and changed over time in response to crises, criticisms, and business complexity, and it has become formalized in standards. Yet despite these developments, "good" auditing remains difficult to observe by outsiders. Of course, good auditing can be defined as being in compliance with well-designed standards but the problem of audit quality is more than a series of technical processes. It has much to do with the behavior and motivation of auditors themselves. As we discuss next, the role of the auditor as an economic agent in his/her own right (Antle, 1982) further complicates the contribution of auditing to the mitigation of agency problems in corporate governance.

Governing Audit: Quality and Ethics

It is widely accepted that audit quality consists of two elements: the competence of the auditor to conduct an audit and the motivation of the auditor to report negatively on a company's financial statements should the need arise. Regarding competence, many studies have tended to take membership of a big audit firm as an observable proxy for relative quality (DeAngelo, 1981; Palmrose, 1988). Others have used years of experience to distinguish between the competence of senior and junior members of audit teams (see e.g. Abdolmohammadi and Wright, 1987). Although methodologically convenient, there is an element of circularity in these working assumptions since they assume the very thing in question: are auditors of large firms in some way more competent than their counterparts in smaller firms; are older auditors more competent than younger ones? However, the construction of proxies is necessary because the competence of the auditor is difficult, if not impossible, to observe in practice. It is also difficult to disentangle the quality of auditing from the quality of the auditee (Power, 1997: 27). Financial statements might be reliable because of good auditing *or* because of good internal company accounting policy and controls (Power, 1997).

Despite the practical and intellectual challenges of observing auditor competence, there is a considerable amount of regulation directed at ensuring and improving it (see e.g. Quick et al., 2008). Most jurisdictions require auditors to undergo extensive periods of training, involving a mixture of examinations and practice-based work. In addition there are regimes for continuing professional education. The quality of auditing has also become more highly regulated, with a mix of peer review and external inspection in many countries. The system of external quality control in Germany, for example, is one of "peer review with monitoring elements" (Köhler et al., 2008). Also in many other countries elements of peer review exist in combination with public accounting oversight boards and audit inspection units (see e.g. the Netherlands, USA, and UK) (Quick et al., 2008). The work of these bodies essentially involves a review of audit working papers and other documentation to determine the nature and extent of the work done, the correct application of auditing standards, and the reasonableness of the conclusions drawn. While this work has the potential to reveal important areas of weakness in the conduct of specific audits, it relies on records as traces which enable the indirect observation of audit quality.

The second component of audit quality—independence—has been debated as long as auditing has existed. As noted earlier, one of Flint's (1988: 29) postulates states that the "essential distinguishing characteristics of audit are the independence of its status and its freedom from investigatory and reporting constraints." Formally, independence can be taken to mean that there is a non-zero probability that an auditor will report negatively on the financial statements if necessary and this takes us to the heart of the auditor's incentives. The key issue is whether the auditor will risk losing both the valuable audit work and any related consultancy services by reporting negatively. This is important because of the growth of consulting services, particularly during the 1980s, and their significance to audit firms (Coffee, 2006; Jeppesen, 1998). During the 1980s and 1990s, we can observe a breaking down of the barriers between auditing and consulting. Jeppesen (1998: 531) even goes so far as to say that auditing was becoming what was previously known as consulting services. The relationship between auditing and consulting has been put into the spotlight after the Enron scandal, and the Sarbanes-Oxley Act of 2002 introduced severe restrictions on non-audit services.

There has always been a number of mechanisms to intervene in, and shape, the incentives of auditors. Regimes of professional ethics at the level of professional firms and institutes have tried to create the cultural conditions for independence as an objective attitude or "state of mind." In addition, the law of legal liability for negligent audit work exists to motivate auditors to do a good job. As highlighted above, the collapse of Enron in 2001 led to a range of regulatory reforms, not only in the US, aimed at increasing auditor independence and audit firm governance (Ali and Gregoriou, 2006). The Sarbanes-Oxley Act was intended to re-establish the audit function within audit firms as the primary service. To increase independence, the Act prohibited several non-audit services and introduced auditor rotation in the US (after five years for lead and concurring partners; after seven years for other audit partners). Companies, in both the US and UK, are required to disclose audit and non-audit fees paid to auditors. More generally, mechanisms of external and internal oversight have been strengthened (Ali and Gregoriou, 2006; Coffee, 2006; Quick et al., 2008).

Particularly noteworthy, in this context, is also the "intense focus on greater audit committee responsibility" (Beasley et al., 2009). In many countries, including the US and EU, listed companies are required to have an audit committee comprising independent directors to *oversee* the work of internal and external auditors. Audit committees are involved in the appointment and reappointment of external auditors. They are required to ensure that audit firms comply with legal and professional requirements in respect of auditor independence. They should assess the audit plan, discuss issues arising from the audit, and they should review and challenge the more judgmental areas of financial reporting and audit work (Gray and Manson, 2011: 715). If operating effectively, audit committees can play a significant role in the enhancement of audit quality, internal control processes, financial reporting and the reduction of corporate fraud. Yet, in the wake of Enron, WorldCom and other high-profile corporate collapses mentioned earlier, audit committees also became the subject of close scrutiny. Audit committees were criticized for their lack of independence (Beasley and Salterio, 2001; Carcello and Neal, 2000). Spira (1999) and Cohen et al. (2002) highlight the ceremonial components of audit committee meetings. In the US, the Sarbanes-Oxley Act includes several provisions aimed at increasing audit committee responsibility and effectiveness (e.g. Sections 301 and 407) (Rupley et al. 2011). In the UK, the Financial Reporting Council (FRC) set up an independent group chaired by Sir Robert Smith to clarify the role and responsibilities of audit committees (Smith Report, 2003) and to develop guidance (Financial Reporting Council, 2005a) which, subsequently, was integrated into the UK Corporate Governance Code (formerly Combined Code). These reforms are aimed at enhancing the expertise and independence of audit committee members, at improving audit committee authority (for example with respect to the audit committee's responsibility for external audit oversight, whistle blowing procedures and follow-up, access to internal and external auditors), and at enabling audit committee diligence.

Evidence of the impact of the reforms on the effectiveness of audit committees as a governance device is mixed. Beasley et al. (2009, p. 66) conducted interviews with 42 US audit committee members and find that, post-Sarbanes-Oxley, many of their interviewees "strive to provide effective monitoring of financial reporting and seek to avoid serving on ceremonial audit committees." Based on 30 interviews with external auditors, Cohen et al. (2010) also find that audit committees are perceived to be considerably more active and diligent. Turley and Zaman (2007) emphasize the importance of informal processes in establishing audit committee effectiveness (see also Gendron and Bedard, 2006). Based on an in-depth case study of an audit committee in a major UK company, they highlight that many of the factors contributing to effective governance cannot easily be codified in governance codes and audit committees' terms of reference. Notwithstanding the limitations of the reforms, audit committees have evolved as a central feature of corporate governance, particularly with respect to the governance of internal and external audit (Cohen et al., 2010).

More generally, during the twenty first century we observe a shift from auditor self-regulation to a regulatory set-up that aims to be more independent of the accountancy profession. To increase regulatory independence and oversight, not only audit committee regulations were tightened up. In the US, the Sarbanes-Oxley Act led to the creation of the Public Company Accounting Oversight Board (PCAOB), which replaced the AICPA as the private regulator of auditing. In the UK, audit monitoring was strengthened with the foundation of the Financial Reporting Council (FRC). Following the UK Government's post-Enron review of the regulation of the accountancy profession in 2003, a Professional Oversight Board (POB) was established under the FRC, which operates an independent Audit Inspection Unit (AIU). In order to enhance governance arrangements within audit firms, the FRC issued *The Audit Firm Governance Code* (Financial Reporting Council, 2010a). Inter alia, the Code recommends the appointment of independent non-executive directors to enhance the corporate governance of audit firms; the establishment of confidential whistle-blowing policies and procedures; and the publication of audited financial reports of audit firms including a management commentary. There has also been considerable regulatory activity at the regional level. The European Commission published a wide-ranging

Green Paper on Audit Policy (European Commission, 2010) which also highlighted the importance of audit firm governance, calling for heightened internal governance measures, increased public oversight and greater cooperation between the national audit oversight systems (for a critical review see Humphrey et al., 2011).

All these reforms place increased emphasis on independence. Yet, it is worth noting that particularly in recent years the problem of independence has changed its character and shifted its focus. In place of the post-Enron problem of non-audit services, the post-financial crisis debate has centered on a yet more fundamental issue, that of *auditor skepticism* (Auditing Practices Board (APB), 2010; EC, 2010; Financial Services Authority and Financial Reporting Council (FSA and FRC), 2010). The context for this shift is a view emerging from various enquiries that auditors have been too trusting of management representations and insufficiently challenging to the assumptions underlying client business models. The focus of the independence discussion has shifted away from economic incentives to a more fundamental debate about the auditor's *capacity to challenge*. Auditors are necessarily dependent on forming good working relationships with those they audit, and are dependent on receiving high quality auditable information from them. Given all these dependencies, it is argued that it is imperative for auditors to be more skeptical, an issue we return to in the concluding section.

The Market for Audit Services

In most jurisdictions the demand for audit is governed by statute: all enterprises of a particular size must have an external audit. This statutory requirement is normally justified by market failure arguments, namely the claim that without such a requirement there would be an undersupply of a service which is a "public good." However, Chow (1982), following Jensen and Meckling (1976), challenges these market failure arguments by investigating conditions under which agents (i.e. companies) themselves would have an incentive to be audited. In essence Chow argues that good firms will wish to signal their quality by volunteering to be audited, and will pay for this up to the point where the reduction in agency costs is matched by the audit fee. It is essential to Chow's argument, and to others who suggest radical deregulation of the demand for audit services, that auditing is a credible signaling device. However, as noted earlier, the audit might be a less than perfect signaling device because of the auditor's own incentives and the problem of observing good quality auditing (see also Francis, 2004). It remains debatable whether more or less regulation is needed if the market for audit services is to function effectively. In any case, recently a number of academic and regulatory papers have been published casting serious doubt on the effectiveness of the global audit market (see e.g. FRC, 2006; Sikka, 2009; EC, 2010).

The audit market has come to be criticized for its high degree of concentration. As Coffee (2006: 158) writes, the audit profession today is dominated by four firms—the "Big Four," which, in 2003, audited over 78 percent of all US public companies and 99 percent of all US public company revenues. In the UK, the Big Four audited in 2010 over 95 percent of all FTSE 250 companies and over 80 percent of all FTSE Small Caps (FRC, 2010b: 21). Similar statistics can be observed in other European countries (EC, 2010). The concentration statistics are accompanied by long periods of audit firm tenure and low switching rates. The US, UK, and EU regulators have articulated concerns that the audit market concentration may lead to a diminishing of audit quality (FRC, 2006; EC, 2010). In the UK, a parliamentary inquiry was conducted in 2010 that explicitly focused on the effectiveness of the audit market and risks connected to audit market concentration (House of Lords, 2011). Also the UK Office of Fair Trading (OFT) "has provisionally decided that there are competition problems in the audit market." (http://www.oft.gov.uk/news-and-updates/press/2011/59-11, accessed June 30, 2011). The EC Green Paper highlights that a failure of one of the Big Four firms could not only disrupt the availability of audited financial information but also damage investor trust and impact the stability of the financial system as a whole (EC, 2010). The paper further asks whether such "too big to fail" firms could potentially create the risk of moral hazard. To be sure, the links between auditor concentration and audit quality are far from clear-cut. Audit quality is difficult to observe and audit failure is often confused with corporate failure. However, the current regulatory debates highlight important risks which should not be overlooked when assessing the contribution of auditing to corporate governance.

Audit as an Expanding Governance Idea

Corporate governance has been described as the "accountant's friend" (Freedman, 1993). It has provided a platform for the expansion of audit services and the development of new audit and assurance practices (Jeppesen, 1998; Coffee, 2006; Greenwood and Suddaby, 2006; Robson et al., 2007). A number of developments are striking in this respect. First, new markets for internal audit services have been created and there has been a growth of outsourcing of internal auditing (Aldhizer et al., 2003). Second, new forms of reporting, such as sustainability accounting, have contributed to the expansion of audit and assurance services (O'Dwyer et al., 2011). Third, the auditee components of the audit risk model (control risk and inherent risk) have generated stand-alone markets for advice and assurance on internal control and risk management. Of particular importance in this respect is the Sarbanes-Oxley legislation, which requires senior officers to certify that controls over financial reporting are effective, thereby creating a very large market for controls advice, from which audit firms profit (Coffee, 2006; Power, 2007). Fourth, financial auditing not only provides assurance about the quality of financial statements and management reports within a statutory framework, but the same techniques and approach are also expandable to other "quality objects," such as education, health, or the management of security (Power, 1994; Elliot, 1995; Strathern, 2000). From this point of view, auditing is an idea or model of governance together with an assembly of expandable routines and procedures (Power, 1997).

The expandability of audit services described above is not simply a function of the economic interests of audit firms and their members. Auditing has come to be a model of governance in its own right, enabled by institutional changes, including changes in financial regulation, the rise of risk-based regulation, and New Public Management (Hood, 1995). Changes to the operation of the modern state, which some regard as being broadly neoliberal, i.e. operating at a distance via markets and regulatory structures (see e.g. Miller and Rose, 1990), have provided fertile ground for the expansion of audit as a governance model in its own right (Power, 1994, 1997; Strathern, 2000). The very idea of audit and its potential is critical in a world where governments increasingly delegate service provision to private bodies and agencies, and seek to retain central control via distant oversight. As more autonomous public and quasi-public entities are created, including regulatory bodies, there is growth of new entities requiring financial and non-financial audits (Power, 1994). From this point of view, auditing is not simply one aspect of corporate governance; it defines the entire style of oversight and regulation.

This is a style of formalized accountability based on checklists, documentary verification, and the utilization of the cognitive and economic resources of regulated entities to ensure compliance (Power, 1997). Audit has advanced to become a governance paradigm in its own right, driving, and being driven by, a logic of auditability, characterized by an increasingly precise codification of the operational dimensions of the audit task and a reliance on formal, externally verifiable processes and systems (Power, 1996, 1997). Audits require "audit trails" of controls, processes, transactions, or whatever provides an acceptable evidence base for the object of audit. Where these trails do not exist, they must be created. For example, the audit of the fair valuation of illiquid financial instruments involves verifying the reasonableness of models and assumptions which produce the valuation. During the financial crisis, auditors found themselves pushed to the limit to obtain sufficient, relevant, and reliable evidence to support such valuations. One way in which auditors, both internal and external, solve the problem of auditability is by auditing the process and the controls around such valuations.

To summarize, much of the earlier discussion has focused on the regulation of auditing. Yet, it is clear that corporate governance and the audit process go hand in hand. As governance expands, so too does the development of auditable performance measures and control systems (Power, 1996, 1997). However, such an increased emphasis on formalized auditability does not automatically enhance corporate governance. It can also undermine it by promoting forms of ritualistic compliance and technical-procedural correctness displacing ethical reasoning, in-depth evaluation and scrutiny (Gill, 2009). These side effects of an "auditized" form of corporate governance pose considerable challenges for the future.

Conclusions and Challenges Ahead

At the time of writing this chapter, the post-financial crisis debate about the role of auditors is still ongoing and the path of reform is uncertain. In the UK two parliamentary inquiries have focused on the role of the auditors, whether auditors have failed, and whether the audit model for large, systemically significant financial institutions is appropriate (House of Commons, 2009; House of Lords, 2011). The debate is also European in scope (EC, 2010). In all this discussion it is important to distinguish between two questions: first, did audit as it is currently constituted fail; and second, is audit as it is currently constituted in need of reform?

The first question leads to an analysis of the role of specific audits and auditors and whether it would have been reasonable to expect an audit focused on financial statements to discover and report weaknesses and risks in the funding structure of banks. The second question leads to a consideration of whether auditing as currently designed is really fit for purpose. From these discussions three reform trajectories can be distilled which are still under debate.

One issue to emerge from the crisis was a need to improve communication between regulators and auditors so that an effective conduit for concerns to be raised exists. In the UK, the FSA has issued a code of guidance in this respect (FSA and FRC, 2010). While this does not represent a move to make the financial auditor into an early warning system, it provides a mechanism for the escalation of issues which traditional audit reporting lacks.

In response to the widespread discussion about the auditor's role in evaluating risky business models, it is likely that the nature and extent of going concern review will be expanded. In the UK, the FRC is currently holding an inquiry into going concern and liquidity risk in order to determine whether the international auditing standard dealing with going concern (ISA 570) requires reform (the Sharman Inquiry, 2011). At the international level, questions have been raised about the extent to which it is practicable to obtain sufficient appropriate audit evidence on the going concern assumption. Here, it has been argued that the going concern review requirement has led to unreasonable expectations about the level of assurance the auditor can obtain in relation to going concern.

At a more fundamental level, there has been much debate about whether auditors were sufficiently skeptical (see also our discussion above). In the UK the APB has published a paper on this topic (APB, 2010), and the EU Green Paper states that auditors are important in "actively challenging...management from a user's perspective" and that it is critical that they exercise "professional scepticism" (EC, 2010: 7). However, it is difficult to see how skepticism can be regulated into existence; it is far more likely to be a function of personality, training, and audit firm culture (see also Humphrey et al., 2011). An underlying suggestion is that, because many audit firms have become more explicitly commercial over time (Hanlon, 1994) and have internalized elements of a sales culture, this is not an environment where skepticism is valued and can thrive. There is no doubt that skepticism is an essential ingredient of all the elements of corporate governance. A closely related issue is whether more might be disclosed about the audit process to reveal the challenge process, contentious discussions, and more on audit methodology. One proposal in the air is for audit committee reporting to include more information about what was discussed with auditors, in particular regarding judgmental and high risk elements.

As can be seen from the above, the three issues are not particularly radical, more a refinement of existing practice. This suggests some important features of audit reform debates. While critics would always like auditing to be "better," often meaning implicitly a forecasting or early warning practice, auditing is necessarily constrained by practicalities. Reporting can be enhanced and the process can be made more transparent, but little can be done to change the fact that the audit is essentially and necessarily a test basis over a limited period of time, focused on financial statements with very limited, if any, predictive ability. The audit that people may wish for when they are disappointed is not necessarily possible.

This chapter has examined how internal and external auditing have come to be challenged and changed in different jurisdictions in the aftermath of the financial crisis of 2008–9, and high-profile company and audit failures, such as Enron and WorldCom. These challenges are ongoing. We have shown that auditing constitutes an important element in a corporation's governance and reporting system, yet the roles of audit are also developing in constant interaction with other governance mechanisms. To recall Flint (1988, p. 13), "[auditing] is an evolving process, reacting with changing expectations about the performance or conduct of the individuals or organisations to which it is applied." Few research studies have drawn attention to the role of the audit process in shaping the practice of governance and management control, and to the dynamics of interaction between internal and external auditors, audit committees and finance directors (Cohen et al., 2002; Spira, 2002; Gendron and Bedard, 2006; Turley and Zaman, 2007; Beasley et al., 2009). The vast majority of research focuses on relations between externally verifiable auditor inputs and outputs. Not much attention has been paid to how auditing influences the production process of financial reports. What is the relation between formal and informal processes of auditing and audit oversight? What dynamics of interaction can we observe between auditors and audit committees, between auditors and audit inspection units?

Furthermore, it is important to develop a better understanding of auditing firms as organizations, and their governance structures and processes. How does an audit firm's organizational structures, its appraisal and mentoring arrangements, and hierarchies between junior and senior auditors impact on auditor independence and auditor skepticism? What is the impact of codified audit firm governance arrangements on auditors' shared ethos (Gill, 2009)?

To encourage debate about auditors' values and motivations, more research is needed examining the ethical demands and challenges that auditors face in their day-to-day practice. How do auditors determine whether or not their actions at work are right or wrong? How are responsibility and blame attributed or shifted (Hood, 2002)? What role does audit regulation play in this process? As Humphrey et al. (2011, p. 449) highlight, there is currently very little evidence on which to judge the quality of audit regulation. The effects of audit regulation, in particular with regards to recent reforms, and the interactions between auditors and regulatory agencies, need to be subjected to more in-depth investigation, not only to open up a hidden field for public scrutiny, but also to find out more about the conditions which frame the production of audit knowledge and governance.

Finally, perhaps the biggest challenge facing auditors and those who rely on them may not be independence or market concentration, but *auditability*. Fair value accounting and the more general financialization of organizations, involving the increased use of complex financial instruments with chains of contingent counterparties, place the audit process in a highly virtualized world defined by models rooted in financial economics. These settings challenge the capacity and meaning of audit evidence, because audit boils down to a view of the reasonableness of assumptions rather than the triangulation of independent sources of evidence. Auditing will have to adapt to these new challenges if it is to remain relevant. And, as Gill (2009) has highlighted, it will be important not only to develop auditors' technical financial expertise. Equally important is the ethical relationship to their practice and our understanding of it. To open up space for critically minded self-reflection and reform, it is vital that audit firm cultures and audit firm governance arrangements are regularly reviewed, including recruitment, training, and appraisal practices. Professional ethos cannot be legislated for directly, but attempts can be undertaken to re-emphasize the importance of ethical discourse and debate, with the aim of moving to a position where rules are trusted a little less and professional judgment is trusted a little more.

References

ABDOLMOHAMMADI, M., and WRIGHT, A. (1987). "An Examination of the Effects of Experience and Task Complexity on Audit Judgements," *The Accounting Review*, 62(1): 1–13.

ALDHIZER, G. R., CASHELL, J. D., and MARTIN, D. R. (2003). "Internal Audit Outsourcing," *The CPA Journal*, 73(8): 38.

ALI, P. U., and GREGORIOU, G. N. (eds.), (2006). *International Corporate Governance after Sarbanes-Oxley*. Hoboken, NJ: John Wiley & Sons.

ANTLE, R. (1982). "The Auditor as an Economic Agent," *Journal of Accounting Research*, 20(2): 503–27.

Auditing Practices Board (2010). *Auditor Scepticism: Raising the Bar*. London: APB.

BEASLEY, M. S., and SALTERIO, S. E. (2001). "The Relationship Between Board Characteristics and Voluntary Improvements in the Capability of Audit Committees to Monitor," *Contemporary Accounting Research*, 18(4): 539–70.

BEASLEY, M. S., CARCELLO, J. V., HERMANSON, D. R., and NEAL, T. L. (2009). "The Audit Comittee Oversight Process," *Contemporary Accounting Research*, 26(1): 65-22.

BELL, T. B., MARRS, F., SOLOMON, I., and THOMAS, H. (1997). "Auditing Organizations through a Strategic-Systems Lens," Montvale, NJ: KPMG.

BOU-RAAD, C. (2000). "Internal Auditors and a Value-Added Approach: The New Business Regime," *Managerial Auditing Journal*, 15(14): 182–7.

Cadbury Committee (1992). *Report of the Committee on the Financial Aspects of Corporate Governance*. London: Gee.

CARCELLO, J. V., and NEAL, T. L. (2000). "Audit Committee Composition and Auditor Reporting," *The Accounting Review*, 75(4): 453–67.

—— HERMANSON, D. R., and RAGHUNDANDAN, K. (2005). "Changes in Internal Auditing during the Time of the Major U.S. Accounting Scandals," *International Journal of Auditing*, 9: 117–27.

Center for Audit Quality (2011). "In-Depth Guide to Public Company Auditing," Washington, DC: Center for Audit Quality. Available at <http://www.thecaq.org/publications/In-Depth_GuidetoPublicCompanyAuditing.pdf>.

CHANDLER, R. A. (1997). "The Auditing Practices Board and Auditing Standards in the UK," in M. Sherer and S. Turley (eds.), *Current Issues in Auditing*. London: Sage, 165–80.

—— EDWARDS, J. R., and ANDERSON, M. (1993). "Changing Perceptions of the Role of the Company Auditor, 1840–1940," *Accounting and Business Research*, 23(92): 443–59.

CHOI, J.-H., and WONG, T. J. (2007). "Auditors' Governance Functions and Legal Environments," *Contemporary Accounting Research*, 24(1): 13–46.

CHOW, C. W. (1982). "The Demand for External Auditing," *The Accounting Review*, 57(2): 272–91.

COFFEE, J. C. (2006). *Gatekeepers*. Oxford: Oxford University Press.

COHEN, J., KRISHNAMOORTHY, G., and WRIGHT, A. (2002). "Corporate Governance and the Audit Process," *Contemporary Accounting Research*, 19(4): 573–94.

—— —— —— (2010). "Corporate Governance in the Post-Sarbanes-Oxley Era: Auditors' Experiences," *Contemporary Accounting Research*, 27(3): 751–86.

Committee of Sponsoring Organizations (COSO) (1992). *Internal Control*. New York: AICPA.

CRAWFORD, M., and STEIN, W. (2002). "Auditing Risk Management: Fine in Theory but who can do it in Practice?" *International Journal of Auditing*, 6: 119–131.

CURTIS, E., and TURLEY, S. (2007). "The Business Risk Audit: A Longitudinal Case Study of an Audit Engagement," *Accounting, Organizations and Society*, 32(4–5): 439–61.

DEANGELO, L. E. (1981). "Auditor Size and Audit Quality," *Journal of Accounting and Economics*, 3(3): 183–99.

DICKSEE, L. R. (1892). *Auditing: A Practical Manual for Auditors*. London: Gee.

ELLIOT, R. K. (1995). "The Future of Assurance Services," *Accounting Horizons*, 9(4): 118–27.

European Commission (2010). "Audit Policy," Green Paper. Brussels: EC.

FAN, J. H., and WONG, T. J. (2005). "Do External Auditors Perform a Corporate Governance Role in Emerging Markets?" *Journal of Accounting Research*, 43(1): 35–72.

Financial Reporting Council (2005a). *Guidance on Audit Committees (The Smith Guidance)*. London: FRC.

—— (2005b). *Internal Control*. London: FRC.

—— (2006). *Choice in the UK Audit Market*. Discussion Paper. London: FRC.

—— (2008). *The Audit Quality Framework*. London: FRC.

—— (2010a). *The Audit Firm Governance Code*. London: FRC.

—— (2010b). *Choice in the UK Audit Market*. London: FRC.

Financial Services Authority and Financial Reporting Council (2010). *Enhancing the Auditor's Contribution to Prudential Regulation*. London: FSA and FRC.

FLINT, D. (1988). *Philosophy and Principles of Auditing*. London: Macmillan Press.

FRANCIS, J. R. (2004). "What Do We Know about Audit Quality?" *The British Accounting Review*, 36(4): 345–68.

—— (2008). "Auditing in the United States," in R. Quick, S. Turley, and M. Willekens (eds.), *Auditing, Trust and Governance*. London: Routledge, 243–61.

FREEDMAN, J. (1993). "Accountants and Corporate Governance" *Political Quarterly*, 64(3): 285–97.

GENDRON, Y., and BEDARD, J. (2006). "On the Constitution of Audit Committee Effectiveness," *Accounting, Organizations and Society*, 31(3): 211–39.

GILL, M. (2009). *Accountants' Truth*. Oxford: Oxford University Press.
GRAY, I., and MANSON, S. (2011). *The Audit Process*, 5th edition. Andover: Cengage.
GREENWOOD, R., and SUDDABY, R. (2006). "Institutional Entrepreneurship in Mature Fields: The Big Five Accounting Firms," *Academy of Management Journal*, 49(1): 27–48.
HANLON, G. (1994). *The Commercialisation of Accountancy*. Basingstoke: Macmillan.
HIGSON, A. (1997). "Developments in Audit Approaches," in M. SHERER and S. TURLEY (eds.), *Current Issues in Auditing*. London: Sage, 198–215.
HOOD, C. (1995). "The "New Public Management" in the 1980s: Variations on a Theme," *Accounting, Organizations and Society*, 20(2–3): 93–109.
—— (2002). "The Risk Game and the Blame Game," *Government and Opposition*, 37(1): 15–37.
HOPWOOD, A. G., and MILLER, P. (eds.) (1994). *Accounting as Social and Institutional Practice*. Cambridge: Cambridge University Press.
House of Commons (2009). *Banking Crisis: Reforming Corporate Governance and Pay in the City*. London: House of Commons Treasury Committee.
House of Lords (2011). *Auditors: Market Concentration and their role. Volume 1: Report*. London: House of Lords Select Committee on Economic Affairs.
HUMPHREY, C., MOIZER, P., and TURLEY, S. (1992). "The Audit Expectations Gap: Plus ça change, plus c'est la même chose?," *Critical Perspectives on Accounting*, 3(2): 137–61.
—— KAUSAR, A., LOFT, A., and WOODS, M. (2011). "Regulating Audit beyond the Crisis," *European Accounting Review*, 20(3): 431–57.
Institute of Internal Auditors UK and Ireland (2003). *Independence and Objectivity: The New Challenge for Internal Auditors?* London: IIA UK and Ireland.
Institute of Internal Auditors Research Foundation (2007). *Internal Auditing: Assurance and Consulting Services*. Altamonte Springs, FL: IIA.
International Federation of Accountants (2006). *Internal Controls*. New York: IFAC.
—— (2010). *Handbook of International Quality Control, Auditing, Review, Other Assurance, and Related Services Pronouncements*. New York: IFAC.
JENSEN, M. C., and MECKLING, W. H. (1976). "Theory of the Firm: Managerial Behavior, Agency Costs and Ownership Structure," *Journal of Financial Economics*, 3(4): 305–60.
JEPPESEN, K. K. (1998). "Reinventing Auditing, Redefining Consulting and Independence," *European Accounting Review*, 7(3): 517–39.
KNECHEL, W. R. (2007). "The Business Risk Audit: Origins, Obstacles and Opportunities," *Accounting, Organizations and Society*, 32(4–5): 383–408.
KNECHEL, W. R., SALTERIO, S. E., and BALLOU, B. (2007). *Auditing: Assurance and Risk*, 3rd edition. Mason, MI: Thomson.
KÖHLER, A. G., MARTEN, K.-U., QUICK, R., and RUHNKE, K. (2008). "Audit Regulation in Germany," in R. Quick, S. Turley, and M. Willekens (eds.), *Auditing, Trust and Governance*. London: Routledge, 111–43.
LEE, T. A. (1988). *The Evolution of Audit. Thought and Practice*. New York: Garland.
MATTHEWS, D. (2006). *A History of Auditing*. London: Routledge.
MAUTZ, R. K., and SHARAF, H. A. (1961). *The Philosophy of Auditing*. Sarasota, FL: AAA.
MENNICKEN, A. (2008). "Connecting Worlds: The Translation of ISAs into Post-Soviet Audit Practice," *Accounting, Organizations and Society*, 33(4–5): 384–414.
—— (2010). "From Inspection to Auditing: Audit and Markets as Linked Ecologies," *Accounting, Organizations and Society*, 35(3): 334–59.
MILLER, P., and ROSE, N. (1990). "Governing Economic Life," *Economy and Society*, 19(1): 1–31.

NORMAN, C. S., ROSE, A. M., and ROSE, J. M. (2010). "Internal Audit Reporting Lines, Fraud Risk Decomposition, and Assessment of Fraud Risk," *Accounting, Organizations and Society*, 35(5): 546–57.

O'DWYER, B., OWEN, D., and UNERMAN, J. (2011). "Seeking Legitimacy for New Assurance Forms," *Accounting, Organizations and Society*, 36(1): 31–52.

PALMROSE, Z.-V. (1988). "An Analysis of Auditor Litigation and Audit Service Quality," *The Accounting Review*, 63(1): 55–73.

PORTER, B., SIMON, J., and HATHERLY, D. (2008). *Principles of External Auditing*, 3rd edition. Chichester: Wiley.

POWER, M. (1992). "From Common Sense to Expertise: The Pre-history of Audit Sampling," *Accounting, Organizations and Society*, 17(1): 37–62.

—— (1994). *The Audit Explosion*. London: Demos.

—— (1996). "Making Things Auditable," *Accounting, Organizations and Society*, 21(2–3): 289–315.

—— (1997). *The Audit Society: Rituals of Verification*. Oxford: Oxford University Press.

—— (2007). *Organized Uncertainty*. Oxford: Oxford University Press.

QUICK, R., TURLEY, S., and WILLEKENS, M. (eds.) (2008). *Auditing, Trust and Governance*. London: Routledge.

ROBSON, K., HUMPHREY, C., KHALIFA, R., and JONES, J. (2007). "Transforming Audit Technologies," *Accounting, Organizations and Society*, 32(4–5): 404–38.

ROUSSEY, R. S. (1999). "The Development of International Standards on Auditing," *CPA Journal*, 69(10): 14–20.

RUPLEY, K., ALMER, E., and PHILBRICK, D. (2011). "Audit Committee Effectiveness," *Research in Accounting Regulation*, 23: 138–44.

Sharman Inquiry (2011). *Going Concern and Liquidity*. London: FRC.

SIKKA, P. (2009). "Financial Crisis and the Silence of the Auditors," *Accounting, Organizations and Society*, 34 (6–7): 868–73.

—— PUXTY, A., WILLMOTT, H., and COOPER, C. (1998). "The Impossibility of Eliminating the Audit Expectations Gap," *Critical Perspectives on Accounting*, 9(3): 299–330.

Smith Report (2003). *Audit Committees*. London: Financial Reporting Council.

SOLOMON, J. (2010). *Corporate Governance and Accountability*, 3rd edition. Chichester: Wiley.

SPIRA, L. (1999). "Ceremonies of Governance: Perspectives on the Role of the Audit Committee," *Journal of Management and Governance*, 3(3): 231–60.

—— (2002). *The Audit Committee*. London: Kluwer Academic Publishers.

—— and PAGE, M. (2003). "Risk Management: The Reinvention of Internal Control and the Changing Role of Internal Audit," *Accounting, Auditing and Accountability Journal*, 16(4): 640–61.

STRATHERN, M. (ed.) (2000). *Auditing Cultures*. London: Routledge.

SUCHER, P., MOIZER, P., and ZELENKA, I. (1998). *The Evolution of Auditing in an Emerging Economy*. London: The Association of Chartered Certified Accountants.

TURLEY, S., and ZAMAN, M. (2007). "Audit Committee Effectiveness: Informal Processes and Behavioral Effects" *Accounting, Auditing and Accountability Journal*, 20(5): 765–88.

Turnbull Committee (1999). *Internal Control*. London: ICAEW.

VANSTRAELEN, A., and WILLEKENS, M. (2008). "Audit Regulation in Belgium," in R. Quick, S. Turley, and M. Willekens (eds.), *Auditing, Trust and Governance*. London: Routledge, 19–41.

CHAPTER 15

THE MARKET FOR CORPORATE CONTROL

CHARLIE WEIR

Introduction

The agency model proposes a number of corporate governance mechanisms that are designed to reduce the agency costs associated with the separation of ownership and control (Jensen and Meckling, 1976; Fama, 1980; Fama and Jensen, 1983). Their purpose is to align shareholder and manager interests. Governance mechanisms can be split into two categories, internal and external. Internal mechanisms include board structure variables such as duality and the proportion of non-executive directors, debt financing, and executive director shareholdings. The key external mechanism is the market for corporate control, which acts as a governance mechanism of last resort, Jensen (1986a). The probability of replacement following acquisition provides a direct incentive for top management to perform well (Martin and McConnell, 1991; Kennedy and Limmack, 1996).

The purpose of this chapter is to discuss the Manne (1965) argument that the market for corporate control can be seen as a response to the managerial discretion afforded in managerial models (Berle and Means, 1932). Manne's central argument is that managers are constrained by shareholders because they have the power to sell their shares if the shareholders believe that the incumbent management is not acting in their best interests. This occurs as a result of the failure of a company's internal mechanisms and so the market for corporate control may be regarded as an external disciplining mechanism of last resort (Jensen, 1986a). Ineffective internal mechanisms will manifest themselves in poor company performance and this will result in a takeover bid being made as other management teams attempt to gain control of the company. It is therefore important to understand the circumstances which may lead to this happening.

The structure of the chapter is as follows. We first discuss the terminology of mergers, takeovers, and acquisitions. There follows an analysis of the meaning of the term "market for corporate control." The next section examines the relationship between governance structures and the market for corporate control. One way to analyze the workings of the market for corporate control is to differentiate between hostile and non-hostile bids. We analyze the hostile–non-hostile distinction. The market for corporate control consists of a number of distinct subsections. One of these, public to private transactions, is discussed. This is followed by an overview of a number of issues that arise from the analysis of the market for corporate control. The issues to be covered deal with optimal boards, the meaning of disciplinary takeovers, private action, anti-takeover defenses, side payments, and competition policy issues.

Takeovers—Types and Motives

Terminology

Mergers, acquisitions, and takeovers are terms that relate to two or more firms combining to create either a new company or an enlarged existing company. Mergers tend to be associated with firms of similar size combining, whereas acquisitions and takeovers are more likely to be used when the buying firm is larger than the target. There is, however, no hard and fast rule for distinguishing between them and the terms are usually used interchangeably.

Merger Theories

Many theories have been advanced to explain why mergers occur. They are too numerous to discuss in detail in a chapter such as this one and so we will simply make reference to them. These theories include synergies (Weston, 1970); hubris (Roll, 1986); market power (Lang et al., 1989); free cash flows (Jensen, 1986b); managerial entrenchment (Shleifer and Vishny, 1989); valuation differences (Gort, 1969); growth (Marris, 1964); diversification (Mueller, 1969); and tax benefits (Gilson et al., 1988).

In addition to these individual theories, it has been noted that mergers also occur in waves and several theories have been put forward to explain why these merger waves occur. For example, Lambrecht (2004) proposes that mergers are likely to happen in periods of economic expansion. Maksimovic and Phillips (2001) show that mergers are more likely following positive demand shocks, resulting in pro-cyclical merger waves. Lambrecht and Myers (2006) argue that takeovers act as a mechanism that forces disinvestment in declining industries. Rhodes-Kropf et al. (2005) show that merger activity is correlated with high market valuations, causing overvalued bidders to make stock bids that are more likely to be accepted by targets.

The Market for Corporate Control

In addition to the theories outlined above, the market for corporate control is another attempt to provide a rationale for the takeover process. Manne (1965) argues that the market for corporate control can be seen as a response to the managerial discretion afforded in the managerial models that show the consequences of the separation of ownership and control (Berle and Means, 1932). Manne's argument is that managerial discretion is constrained by shareholders because they have the power to sell their shares if the shareholders believe that the incumbent management is not acting in their best interests. Therefore, at its most basic, the market for corporate control occurs when one set of managers competes with another set for the right to manage corporate resources (Jensen and Ruback, 1983).

The market is driven by competition between management teams, with shareholders being willing to sell their shares to the highest bidder, and it is this willingness that constrains managerial discretion. The fact that shareholders may agree to sell their shares sends a signal that they believe the company to be undervalued. The bidding company's actions do the same. If there is a general perception that the incumbent management has done badly, a successful bid will probably result in the management being replaced. The market for corporate control is therefore a disciplining mechanism of last resort which comes into operation when the internal governance mechanisms have failed to address the issue of poor management (Jensen, 1986a). The market for corporate control is associated with hostile bids as the managements of the target companies try to protect their jobs by rejecting the bid. However, it should be noted that the success of a hostile bid depends on many factors, including a firm's ownership structure and the rights of minority shareholders.

However, there are a number of potential impediments to the efficient working of the market. Grossman and Hart (1980) argue that, if ownership is widely held, tender or hostile bids will not succeed because of the free-rider problem. If ownership is atomistic, and each shareholder believes that his/her individual decision will have a marginal effect on the bid's success, then shareholders have an incentive not to sell. This is because they are expecting to retain their shareholding even after the bid has been successful and therefore will benefit from the subsequent increase in the share price that will accompany the successful bid. This belief is based on the expectation that other shareholders will have sold their shares. However, given that all shareholders think this way, the bid will fail because no one actually sells their shares. This outcome applies even to a value-increasing takeover.

There are a number of possible solutions to the free-rider problem, including diminishing the rights of minority shareholders (Grossman and Hart, 1980) and the presence of large shareholdings (Shleifer and Vishny, 1986). These enable wealth-enhancing takeovers to take place because the free-rider problem will no longer apply. The incumbent management, faced with being replaced after a successful takeover, therefore has an incentive to pursue actions consistent with value maximization. Thus the threat of a hostile bid is an effective mechanism because it ensures that management will not want their reputation to be damaged on the managerial labor market.

The market for corporate control makes a strong link between managerial performance and a company's share price. It is based on the proposition that the board, and its decisions, determine the share price. Good board decisions drive the share price up and bad ones drive it down. A relatively low share price therefore indicates a board that has not been pursuing shareholder interests. Hence it is argued that there is a strong positive correlation between managerial performance and the company's share price, with the quality of management decisions being the crucial factor. Other managers see a low share price, relative to the price associated with an efficient management, as an opportunity to manage the assets more effectively and therefore to generate greater capital gains. If successful, the market for corporate control should therefore result in resources being used to create increased value and therefore to benefit shareholders (Jensen, 1986a).

Corporate Governance Systems and Market for Corporate Control

Corporate governance involves external and internal mechanisms. The means by which shareholder interests are initially protected are the company's internal corporate governance structures. If a company's internal mechanisms fail, the market for corporate control acts as an external disciplining mechanism of last resort (Jensen, 1986a). Effective internal governance mechanisms indicate that appropriate decisions are being taken and the threat of takeover via the market for corporate control would not be an issue. Although dealt with in greater depth in other chapters of the book, it is worth outlining the main approaches to corporate governance, and therefore identifying what constitutes effective internal governance, and discussing their relationship with the market for corporate control.

There are a number of ways to define corporate governance systems. First, there is the Anglo-American system. The two main countries that this model applies to are the UK and US. Both countries have governance systems based on board independence and the primacy of shareholder interests.

The key UK report, Cadbury (1992), recommended that publicly quoted firms should adopt the specified internal governance structures contained within a code of best practice. The Code has been through various iterations and its current form is the UK Corporate Governance Code (2010). Although it is voluntary, firms are expected to comply with the governance structures recommended in the UK Corporate Governance Code. Further, the London Stock Exchange requires that all quoted companies include in their annual report a section which explains the extent to which they have complied with the Code, the "comply-or-explain" principle. Therefore transparency is a key requirement of UK corporate governance.

The main board-related structures relate to the balance of executive and non-executive directors and to the posts of CEO and chairman. The expectation is that boards will consist of a combination of executive and non-executive directors, with at least half (excluding the chairman) being independent non-executive directors. In the UK, combining the posts of CEO and chairman is regarded as undesirable.

Although similar to the UK approach, the US framework differs in certain respects. The US system involves mandatory disclosure and is based on a combination of state and federal laws, including the Sarbanes-Oxley Act (2002), and on the listing requirements of its various stock exchanges. There are also differences in board structure, for example, the US has a much higher non-executive director representation, 65 percent (Fich and Shivdasani, 2006), as opposed to 46 percent in the UK (Dahya and McConnell, 2003). The US system also gives an individual far greater decision-making power than does the UK's, with duality being much more common. For example, around 80 percent of listed US companies have the same person as CEO and chairman (Higgs, 2003), whereas the figure in the UK is around 6 percent (McKnight and Weir, 2009). However, both countries emphasize the importance of board independence, implying that inappropriate board structures will lead to poor performance which will in turn attract takeover bids. The "Anglo-American" system therefore identifies the market for corporate control as one of the central means by which shareholder interests are protected.

The second main governance approach is present in countries such as Japan, Germany, the Netherlands, and France. This system looks beyond shareholders and takes account of a wider range of stakeholders (Allen and Gale, 2000). A second key difference with the Anglo-American model relates to ownership structure. In countries such as Germany it is common for families to have significant shareholding, whereas in Japan there is significant ownership by banks (Yafeh, 2000). Importantly, the ownership structure in these countries is stable (Weinstein and Yafeh, 1998), which means that it is very difficult for a hostile takeover to succeed. This type of governance system does not experience an active market for corporate control.

Hostile—Friendly

The usual interpretation of the market for corporate control is that it is based on the premise that takeover bids are disciplinary and are therefore hostile. This perception means that the market for corporate control may therefore be regarded as a substitute for weak internal governance (Kini et al., 1995). Empirical studies tend to employ two main definitions of hostility. First, Shivdasani (1993) and Franks and Mayer (1996) define hostility in terms of the bid being rejected by the target's board. Second, a number of studies have looked at the replacement of senior management, and particularly that of the CEO, post-hostile acquisition (see e.g. Martin and McConnell, 1991; Franks and Mayer, 1996).

There are two main ways in which a bid may occur. First, it can be made direct to the shareholders by means of a tender offer; or second, negotiations can take place with the target's board. If an approach is made to the board, two outcomes are possible. First that the board recommends that shareholders should accept the bid and second, that the board recommends that it be rejected by shareholders. The board's reaction is therefore instrumental in determining whether the bid is classified as friendly (accepted by the board) or hostile (rejected by the board).

There are two main motivations behind a board's rejection of a bid. First, and contrary to shareholder interests, management fear for their jobs and therefore oppose the bid. This is more likely to apply when the target's performance has been poor. If this is the case, a successful bid will probably result in the replacement of the target company's management and their value on the managerial capital market will decline. As a consequence the takeover may be seen as disciplinary.

Second, the recommended rejection may be a negotiating tactic such that shareholders will benefit from a subsequent higher bid (Schwert, 2000). The initial rejection of a bid should therefore be regarded as the beginning of the negotiating process rather than providing a signal that the board is actually opposing the bid.

Important changes have occurred with respect to external and internal governance in the UK during the 1990s. First, there has been a decline in hostile takeover activity from a quarter of all acquisitions of UK listed companies in the mid-1980s (Franks and Mayer, 1996) to only 6.1 percent by the late 1990s (Weir and Laing, 2003), with a corresponding increase in friendly takeovers. The growth in the importance of non-hostile acquisitions is a phenomenon that has also been found in the US, where North (2001) reports 91.2 percent of takeovers were uncontested over the period 1990–7. This has also been noted to be a feature of acquisitions in Germany (Franks and Mayer, 2001). Second, as discussed above, there has been increased focus on the development of new "best practice" codes for enhancing internal corporate governance through, for example, the strengthening of corporate boards. The mechanisms identified in the Code should mitigate the agency problems associated with weak internal governance. Firms that do not exhibit these structures are likely to be poor performers and be subject to hostile takeover threat.

If the market for corporate control operates as presented above, ineffective corporate governance mechanisms should result in successful hostile bids being made (Fama, 1980). For example, using US data, Morck et al. (1988) and Shivdasani (1993) find governance differences between hostile targets and a control group of non-acquired firms. In the UK, studies by Weir (1997) and O'Sullivan and Wong (1999) also found governance differences. The UK evidence shows that hostile targets are more likely to have fewer non-executive directors, more likely to have duality, and to have lower board shareholdings. These findings lend support for the governance structures recommended in the UK corporate governance codes because hostile targets have structures consistent with ineffective internal governance systems.

The threat of takeover will only be an effective response to weak internal governance mechanisms if the target management is likely to lose their jobs and therefore experience a fall in their value on the executive labor market. A number of studies have found a significant turnover of senior management of the acquired firms following a hostile takeover (Martin and McConnell, 1991; Kennedy and Limmack, 1996; Franks and Mayer, 1996; Dahya and Powell, 1999; Kini et al., 2004). This suggests that the threat of hostile acquisition should be sufficient to provide management with the incentive to pursue shareholders' interests rather than risk losing their jobs and experiencing a resultant fall in their value on the managerial labor market. Hence, the threat of takeover provides incentives for incumbent management to improve performance.

In relation to governance characteristics, Weir (1997) found that governance mechanisms such as the percentage of non-executive directors and duality positively affected the probability of acquisition by means of a hostile bid. There is also evidence that the quality of non-executive directors significantly affects the likelihood of hostile acquisition (Shivdasani, 1993; O'Sullivan and Wong; 1999).

UK studies have also investigated the internal governance mechanisms of firms that were taken over after friendly bids. It was found that friendly targets were more likely to have duality, that is, the same individual acting as both chairman and chief executive, compared to a non-acquired control sample (O'Sullivan and Wong, 1998; Weir, 1997). In addition, Weir (1997) and Weir and Laing (2003) find that friendly targets have a higher proportion of non-executives on their boards.

Other studies have directly compared the characteristics of firms that were the subject of hostile bids with those subject to friendly bids. O'Sullivan and Wong (1998) found hostile targets had a greater incidence of duality and a higher proportion of non-executive directors than friendly targets. However, Dahya and Powell (1999) found no difference. The evidence dealing with hostile targets, relative to non-hostile targets or to non-acquired firms, is therefore mixed. The governance characteristics of hostile targets are not consistently associated with poor governance structures. The hostile–non-hostile distinction is further discussed in the next section.

In the UK there has been a significant adoption of the recommendations set out in the various governance codes (Dahya et al., 2002; Pope et al., 2003). Therefore the development of corporate governance codes will lead to a convergence of internal governance mechanisms, especially where adoption is high (Ezzamel and Watson, 2005). If internal governance mechanisms and the market for corporate control are substitute mechanisms, an improvement in internal governance standards should lead to a reduction in hostile takeover activity. This is what has happened with the increase in friendly takeovers and the adoption of recommended governance structures.

However, the results show that friendly takeover targets exhibit combinations of good governance, complying with the Code's recommended balance of non-executive directors (Weir and Laing, 2003), and poor governance–greater duality (O'Sullivan and Wong, 1998). The evidence therefore raises the question of the weight that can be applied to individual internal governance mechanisms. For example, is duality more important than the presence of a balance of executive and non-executive directors? The results suggest that the interpretation of the way the market for corporate control operates may have to change and that it is not always a substitute for poor internal governance.

The Market for Corporate Control—Public to Private Transactions

The market for corporate control is often presented as if it is a homogeneous concept. However, there are different types of takeover and it has been found that these groups have distinct characteristics (Weir and Wright, 2006). This section discusses the key characteristics of one of these types, public to private transactions (PTPs). This type of takeover has become much more common in the US and UK since the 1990s. PTPs have become an important part of takeover activity in the UK since the mid-1990s. Over the period 1991–7, 4.8 percent of publicly quoted acquisitions were PTPs and by 1998–2000 the figure was 23.7 percent (Weir and Wright, 2006). In addition, the value of assets taken private increased from £2.5 billion in 1998 to £9.3 billion in 2000. Public to private transactions are sometimes financed by debt and so have similarities with leveraged buyouts (LBOs). However, they are different types of acquisition and LBO are analyzed in Chapter 24.

In a PTP, the publicly owned equity of a company is acquired and the new company is taken private, creating a new independent entity. The new structure will usually have stronger governance and incentive mechanisms involving close monitoring by debt-holders, the participation of private equity firms, and significant equity stakes for executives of the new company. In some of these firms, incumbent management may take significant equity stakes, creating a management buyout (MBO), whilst in others equity may be largely held by new incoming management and the private equity financier, creating a management buy-in (MBI). When a transaction is funded primarily by debt, it is referred to a leveraged buyout (LBO). It is often taken to be the case that PTPs are LBOs and the two terms are sometimes used interchangeably. However, LBOs do not only apply to the purchase of quoted companies and not all PTPs are leveraged buyouts.

The emergence of PTPs extends not only traditional perspectives on the market for corporate control but also the nature of internal governance. On the one hand, firms subject to PTPs may have inferior internal governance mechanisms prior to going private. On the other, the involvement of private equity firms, with their specialist monitoring expertise and contractual mechanisms, represents a new external governance mechanism that involves taking these firms private and improving their internal governance.

Firms involved in PTP transactions have traditionally been argued to have characteristics associated with incentive misalignment and poor monitoring prior to the decision to go private. They will therefore have incurred higher agency costs than non-PTP targets (Jensen, 1986b). Firms going private are expected to be in mature, low-growth sectors with high free cash flow, with the PTP transaction enabling the return of some of the free cash flow to shareholders as a result of improved governance and incentive realignment post-buyout. Publicly quoted companies that are acquired and not going private are less likely to exhibit these characteristics, because if they did, there would have been pressure to take the firm private.

The US evidence regarding the extent of free cash flow in PTPs is, however, mixed. Lehn and Poulsen (1989) found that firms going private had higher free cash flows than firms that remained quoted. Other evidence suggests that free cash flow has no impact on the decision to go private (Opler and Titman, 1993; Halpern et al., 1999) and there is no evidence that other takeovers in general have high free cash flows (Morck, et al., 1988; Powell, 1997). Similarly, the US evidence on the growth of PTPs relative to other acquisitions is again mixed, with Lehn and Poulsen (1989) supporting this argument, while other studies using different measures find that firms going private did not have poorer growth prospects than firms remaining public (Opler and Titman, 1993; Halpern et al., 1999).

In relation to board structure governance mechanisms, there is no evidence that firms taken private had fewer non-executive directors, but they did have a greater incidence of duality (Weir et al., 2008). In addition there is no evidence that firms going private had excess free cash flows (Weir et al., 2005), but they did have lower growth prospects than firms remaining public (Weir et al., 2008). These results again point to the ambiguous relationship between key governance characteristics and takeovers.

Agency costs associated with high free cash flows and low growth prospects may induce the threat of a hostile, disciplinary takeover which substitutes for weak governance and poor incentive alignment (Jensen, 1986b; Lehn and Poulsen, 1989). The first wave of PTPs in the US was subjected to more takeover speculation in the financial press than firms that remained public (Lehn and Poulsen, 1989). In addition, Halpern et al. (1999) find that firms involved in PTPs were more likely to experience takeover speculation than traditional acquisitions of listed corporations. If PTPs did exhibit the characteristics of poor growth prospects, high free cash flows, poor stock market performance, and low board ownership, they would be susceptible to a disciplinary, outside bid. However, Weir et al. (2005) found that firms going private were more likely to experience press speculation than firms remaining public, but the result became insignificant when only hostile reports were included.

Issues

So far we have discussed the market for corporate control in relation to its operation within the framework of corporate governance. The key issues identified involve the hostile/non-hostile distinction, the empirical evidence about the relationship between targets and their internal governance structures, and the recognition that the market for corporate control is not a homogeneous concept. The discussion raises a number of issues about the working of the market for corporate control and these are discussed in this section. The issues relate to the optimal board structure hypothesis, the disciplinary nature of the takeover process, the bid process and the importance of private actions, anti-takeover provisions, the issue of side payments, and the relationship between the market for corporate control and the competition authorities.

Optimal Board Structures

An optimal board structure would be one that pursued policies consistent with shareholder interests. Therefore companies will adopt governance structures that are suitable for their particular situation. Demsetz and Villalonga (2001), Coles et al. (2008) and Boone et al. (2007) all argue that companies adopt a range of governance mechanisms, each of which is consistent with maximizing firm value, and that there is no single combination of governance mechanisms that is suitable for all circumstances. The traditional agency perspective, on the other hand, is that governance codes recommend "good governance" structures, as predicted by the agency model, and that the market for corporate control operates when these internal mechanisms fail. This results in a "one size fits all" approach to internal governance. The implicit assumption therefore is that governance structures that are different from the recommended structures represent a non-optimal outcome. In other words, adopting the Code's recommendations should reduce agency costs and improve performance.

The optimal structures model therefore assumes that the pre-Cadbury (1992) position represented a value-maximizing outcome for UK firms irrespective of the combination of governance mechanisms employed by them. The adoption of the Code, and its subsequent versions, has resulted in firms moving away from their existing governance structures. According to the optimal board structure model, this will result in one of two possible, contrasting, outcomes: first, it will enable firms to move to another value-maximizing governance structure or, second, it will cause firms to incur costs as they adopt the non-optimal structures recommended by the Code. If this is the case, as McConnell (2003) argues, it may not be helpful to make it difficult for firms not to adopt a prescribed set of board composition characteristics.

The model, therefore, questions the usefulness of moving toward governance systems that identify preferred mechanisms. Such a system may force a firm to move away from a value-maximizing structure and to adopt a non-optimal structure. Alternatively, there may be more than one optimal set of internal governance mechanisms and the adoption of the codes' recommendations may merely move the company to another optimal combination.

The optimal board structure model has implications for the workings of the market for corporate control. Given that hostile takeovers and strong internal governance mechanisms may be regarded as substitute control mechanisms, there is an expectation that acquired firms would have suboptimal board structures (Brickley and James, 1987). This could mean that, for example, hostile targets have few independent directors or that their monitoring committees lack independence. On the other hand, friendly bids that are accepted by the target directors are traditionally expected to have a non-disciplinary motive (Morck et al., 1988). However, the optimal structure theory would argue that factors other than differences in governance mechanisms account for takeover activity. These factors would fit in with any of those outlined in the first section. One problem with the model is that it assumes that any structure is optimal in any given set of circumstances and so it becomes difficult to test empirically because differences in governance structures are explained as being appropriate for the specific companies rather than indicating an ineffective structure.

Takeovers as a Disciplinary Mechanism

As discussed earlier, the market for corporate control acts as a court of last resort and the inference to be drawn is that it is associated with hostile takeovers. However, there is a growing recognition that hostile, and competing, public bids represent only a small part of the takeover process (Schwert, 2000; Moeller et al., 2004). Rather, many takeovers are either friendly (Weir and Laing, 2003) or involve private auctions and bargaining processes before the bid becomes public (Hansen, 2001; Boone and Mulherin 2007).

Schwert (2000) argues that the distinction between hostile and non-hostile acquisitions is likely to be a sign of bargaining strategy rather than entrenchment by the management. Further, he maintains that any initial rejection of an approach may simply indicate an attempt to get the bidder to enter into an auction process the purpose of which is to increase the value of the bid. In addition, Franks and Mayer (1996) suggest that an initial rejection of a bid may be due to a disagreement over terms rather than to the acquisition per se. When analyzing the characteristics of acquired firms, it is therefore important to recognize that classification by type of acquisition may cause problems.

This is important to our understanding of the workings of the market for corporate control. In relation to the classification of acquisitions, Schwert (2000) shows that defining a bid as friendly or hostile is not clear-cut. Further, he argues that the cost of opposing a bid is often prohibitive and so it is cheaper and easier to accept, rather than fight a bid, even though it is unwanted. Thus it may be that acquisitions that appear to be friendly, because they are not opposed, are in fact disciplinary in nature. This, therefore, raises the issue of the extreme case of significant misclassification of acquisitions as friendly when they were actually hostile. This is important because it makes it more difficult to explain why certain firms were selected for acquisition and the usual performance and governance hypotheses become difficult to test.

Further, the classification problem and the role of private negotiation mean that the quality of public information will be reduced. The result is that it becomes less straightforward to understand the workings of the market for corporate control.

In addition, recent studies have questioned the notion that hostile takeovers are more disciplinary than friendly takeovers (Franks and Mayer, 1996; Powell, 1997; Weir, 1997; Schwert, 2000; Kini et al., 2004). These studies find that hostile takeover targets do not underperform friendly targets or other control firms. This persists when takeovers are divides into those experiencing CEO turnover post-takeover and those which do not

(Dahya and Powell, 1999). These results therefore suggest that firms that are the subject of hostile takeovers are not characterized by poor financial performance and managerial self-interest, but that the rejection of the initial bid is part of a strategic bargaining ploy to maximize the price paid for the target. Thus bid hostility is a consequence of disagreement about the terms of the deal arising from valuation differences rather than a disciplinary mechanism.

A possible way round the hostile/non-hostile problem is to use takeover speculation as a proxy for hostile intent. For example, Lehn and Poulsen (1989) combined competing bids with press takeover speculation and Halpern et al. (1999) included any bids and rumors of interest. However, these takeover speculation measures refer to general speculation about the possibility of the companies being taken over. Some of the speculation may have been hostile and some may not. Therefore the relationship between takeover speculation and hostile bids and the part they play in the operation of the market for corporate control is unclear.

Further, as Nuttall (1999) argues, the ability to identify an acquisition as hostile or non-hostile depends, to a large extent, first, on whether or not the acquisition was reported in the financial press and, second, on whether any hostility was noted in that report. However, even if we accept a degree of misclassification, it does appear that friendly acquisitions are the most common type of takeover in the UK. The predominance of non-hostile takeovers therefore raises questions about the effectiveness of the market for corporate control as a court of last resort.

Private Actions and Irrevocable Commitments

The literature dealing with the market for corporate control tends to concentrate on information that is publicly available. This information generally consists of the reporting of a bid announcement and the subsequent recommendation to either accept or reject it. If the bid is a tender offer, it will be communicated directly to the shareholders; otherwise rumors of the bid, or the bid itself, may be reported in the financial press. The extent of the reporting may be influenced by the size of the company.

However, as discussed above, it has been recognized that rejection may merely be a means of negotiating a better offer (Schwert, 2000), and so using press coverage and takeover rumors represents only a partial solution to our understanding of the takeover process.

Publicly available information tells us nothing about the private negotiations that have taken place. Using US data, Boone and Mulherin (2007) identify a five-step takeover process consisting of an initiation event, contact with potential buyers, signing confidentiality agreements, private bidding, and finally public bidding. The process is similar to that which occurs in the UK. However there is no publicly available information about step four, private bidding. It is therefore not possible to use official documents to assess the extent of activity before a bid is announced. In addition, the private auction process implies an agreement between buyer and seller about the conduct of a bid. Unlike in the US, this is very uncommon in the UK (Freshfields Bruckhaus Deringer, 2002).

One way of investigating the private element of the market for corporate control is by means of irrevocable commitments. These are undertakings given by existing shareholders who agree to sell their shareholdings to the bidder before that bid is made public (Wright et al., 2007). By examining irrevocable commitments, it is therefore possible to gain important insights into the bid process because gaining these commitments involve private actions by the bidder before the bid is announced. This private activity is difficult to access and therefore makes the workings of the market for corporate control less transparent.

Irrevocable commitments are explicitly recognized in UK corporate law and takeover codes. The UK's City Code on Takeovers and Mergers includes both rules and restrictions relating to irrevocable commitments in terms of the number of shareholders that can be approached to obtain irrevocable commitments, the prohibition of favorable treatment for those offering irrevocable commitments without Takeover Panel consent, and the disclosure of irrevocable commitments.

Gaining irrevocable commitments therefore means that the bidder is sending a signal to other non-committed shareholders about the quality of the bid. The announcement of substantial irrevocable commitments may also make other potential bidders less likely to enter the contest with an alternative bid. If they do, a competing bid must be made within 21 days of the posting of the offer documents. It may, however, be difficult for an alternative buyer to complete due diligence within the required time. Private equity firms considering bidding are in particular likely to want to undertake due diligence (Graham, 2001; SJ Berwin, 2003). Existing shareholders may also have an incentive to give irrevocable commitments as they may be able to negotiate conditions that enable them to sell their shares to a new bidder offering a higher price (so-called "soft" commitments) (SJ Berwin, 2003). Wright et al. (2007) find significant levels of irrevocable commitments for UK public to private transactions. Therefore private activity is an important element of the market for corporate control and should be taken into account when analyzing how it operates. If the takeover process includes a significant amount of private activity, the way in which the market for corporate control is interpreted must be looked at again.

Anti-Takeover Defenses

The market for corporate control assumes that there are no distortions to the bidding process. If a team of management is identified as underperforming, a bid from an alternative team should be sufficient to replace the incumbent management. However, assuming there is no free-rider problem, there are ways in which the incumbent managers can insulate themselves from the pressures exerted by the market for corporate control. There are three main ways to achieve this: managerial resistance to a bid, pre-bid anti-takeover defenses, and post-bid defenses.

Studies have shown managerial opposition to a bid significantly increases the probability that the bid will be unsuccessful. O'Sullivan and Wong (1999) found that 45 percent of hostile targets successfully resisted a bid. Holl and Kyriazis (1996) reported that the probability of success for a resisted bid was 0.60 whereas for a friendly bid it was 0.95.

Anti-takeover defenses such as supermajorities, staggered board appointments, poison pills, and dual class shares are common pre-bid defenses in the US. These defenses make it more difficult for a bidder to mount a hostile bid because of the costs involved in overcoming the defenses. This creates an incentive to undertake a friendly approach to any proposed takeover.

Kini et al. (2004), who study a period in the US during which the incidence of hostile takeovers was lower, argue that the traditional concept of hostility no longer applies because the disciplinary role of the market for corporate control has been replaced by a combination of anti-takeover defenses and the growing importance of internal corporate governance mechanisms.

The use of anti-takeover mechanisms is much less common in the UK (Sudarsanam, 2003). As a result, anti-takeover defenses are linked to more effective management in areas such as better relations with institutional shareholders, better communication with analysts, and the improvement of earnings per share through continued improvements to operational efficiency. This suggests that, in the UK, there are fewer distortions to the working of the market for corporate control that in the US.

Sudarsanam (1995) finds that post-bid defenses such as friendly shareholders, white knights, and litigation increase the probability of successfully opposing a bid. In contrast, post-bid defenses such as the divestment of assets reduce the chances of a successful defense. Holl and Kriaziz (1997) show that most post-bid defenses increase the probability of successfully defending a bid, with recourse to the law being the most effective.

SIDE PAYMENTS

Manne (1965) was the first to set out the idea that the control of a corporation should be regarded as a means of controlling a valuable asset. One important aspect of the market, as initially discussed, is that he didn't regard the hostile/friendly distinction as important simply because managers can reject a bid. However, the argument that managers can block a bid by voting against it appears to be referring to companies in which managers have significant shareholdings, and does not to apply to the vast majority of quoted companies.

His second reason for not distinguishing between hostile and non-hostile bids is that of side payments. He makes the point that a friendly bid, one defined as not being opposed by the target management, will probably involve side payments to the target's management. The main side payment is likely to be the offer of a position in the bidding company's management structure. Without this, there will be no incentive to recommend acceptance. However, he also states that these payments will not be necessary the greater the management shareholding, presumably because of the financial gain made from the premium offered.

In spite of the ambiguity created by Manne's argument about the possibility of target managers being given jobs in return for not opposing a bid, empirical studies have looked at the turnover of top management post-merger and have also used the length of time before departure as a sign of a disciplinary outcome. However, even a relatively short contract could be sufficient to maintain a manager's value on the labor market because the departure is not perceived as a penalty for poor performance. The bidding company has to weigh up the costs of fighting a publicly hostile bid with those of employing a manager that supports the bid in return for a contract of employment. In such a case, the operation of the market for corporate control becomes less transparent and more difficult to interpret given the apparently friendly nature of the deal.

In spite of Manne's acceptance that non-hostile bids constitute part of the market for corporate control, most empirical work assumes that the hostile/friendly distinction is important when analyzing merger behavior.

There is also the problem that the legality of side payments is open to interpretation because directors have a duty to run a business in the interests of shareholders. How that is affected by side payments is open to question given the problems associated with the concept of legal side payments. How far side payments such as those suggested by Manne actually occur is an empirical question.

Competition Policy Issues

The original argument put forward by Manne (1965) is that the then prevailing attitude toward mergers was based on the view that horizontal mergers were undesirable because they reduced competition. However, the formulation of the market for corporate control took these undesirable economic consequences out of the picture by emphasizing the control of assets rather than the creation of market power and the potentially undesirable economic consequences that it might cause.

Manne (1965) recognizes the competition problems associated with horizontal mergers, but argues that information advantages work in favor of horizontal mergers and that the US antitrust laws have probably reduced the number of mergers that would have occurred under an unregulated market for corporate control.

This view has been influential in the US, EU, and UK where competition authorities investigate relatively small percentages of proposed bids that come within their remit. However, it does not recognize the potential problems faced by increasing concentration and the reduction in the number of competitors that has happened over time. Neither does it deal with the fact that many mergers fail. Therefore, the potential anti-competitive consequences of merger activity are ignored by the market for corporate control.

Conclusions

Many theories have been put forward to explain merger behavior and the choice of target firm. The initial idea of the market for corporate control offered the insight that managers compete for the control of resources. The empirical analysis of the market has used the hostile/non-hostile distinction as well as the post-acquisition turnover of top management as the main ways in which to analyze the market's workings. The original Manne paper did not make this distinction and proposed that side payments could encourage target managers to accept bids.

The workings of the market for corporate control have also been discussed in relation to corporate governance mechanisms. Empirical work into the relationship between the market for corporate control and governance assumes that the various governance mechanisms recommended in a number of codes represents optimal board structures. However, this ignores adjustment costs as companies move to adopt the recommended structures. It also fails to consider the possibility that there are a variety of efficient board structures, including those that do not comply with those of the codes.

The market for corporate control also ignores potential economic costs associated with reductions in efficiency and increased market power. The inherent conflict between actions consistent with shareholder interests and consumer interests are not directly addressed by the market.

There are a number of issues relating to the market for corporate control that could form the basis for future research. First, the increase in the importance of non-hostile bids suggests that the market for corporate control has become less important. This may be because the governance changes that have occurred in recent years have made the market for corporate control less meaningful. The relationship between the market for corporate control and friendly acquisitions may provide valuable insights into its effectiveness. Second, opposing a bid may show that the board is acting in the interests of the shareholders because the opposition is part of a bargaining strategy to increase the value of the bid. The reasoning behind a target management's initial response to a bid requires further study. Third, the relationship between innovations in the ways the takeover process operates, for example public to private transactions, and the market for corporate control may provide a better understanding of how the market operates.

References

Allen, F., and Gale, D. (2000). *Comparing Financial Systems*. Cambridge, MA: MIT Press.
Berle, A., and Means, G. (1932). *The Modern Corporation and Private Property*. New York: Harcourt, Brace & World.
Boone, A., and Mulherin, H. (2007). "How Are Firms Sold?" *Journal of Finance*, 62: 847–75.
—— Field, L., Karpoff, J., and Raheja, C. (2007). "The Determinants of Corporate Board Size and Composition: An Empirical Analysis," *Journal of Financial Economics*, 85: 66–101.

BRICKLEY, J., and JAMES, C. (1987). "The Takeover Market, Corporate Board Composition, and Ownership Structure," *Journal of Law and Economics*, 30(1): 161–81.

Cadbury Committee (1992). *Report of the Committee on the Financial Aspects of Corporate Governance*. London: Gee.

COLES, J. L., DANIEL, N. D., and NAVEEN, L. (2008). "Boards: Does One Size Fit All?" *Journal of Financial Economics*, 87: 329–56.

DAHYA, J., and MCCONNELL, J. (2003). "Outside Directors and Corporate Board Decisions," *Journal of Corporate Finance*, 11: 37–60.

—— and POWELL, R. (1999). "Top Management Changes Following Hostile and. Friendly Takeovers," *ACCA Research Report*, 61, London.

—— —— and TRAVLOS, N. (2002). "The Cadbury Committee, Corporate Governance and Top Management Turnover," *Journal of Finance*, 57: 461–83.

DEMSETZ, H. and VILLALONGA, B. (2001). "Ownership Structure and Corporate Performance," *Journal of Corporate Finance*, 7: 209–33.

EZZAMEL, M., and WATSON, R. (2005). "Board of Directors and the Role of Non-executive Directors in the Governance of Corporations," in K. Keasey, S. Thompson, and M. Wright (eds.), *Corporate Governance Accountability, Enterprise and International Comparisons*. Chichester: Wiley.

FAMA, E. (1980). "Agency Problems and the Theory of the Firm," *Journal of Political Economy*, 88: 134–45.

—— and JENSEN, M. (1983). "Separation of Ownership and Control," *Journal of Law and Economics*, 26: 301–49.

FICH, E., and SHIVDASANI, A. (2006). "Are Busy Boards Effective Monitors?" *Journal of Finance*, 61: 689–724.

FRANKS, J., and MAYER, C. (1996). "Hostile Take-Overs and the Correction of Managerial Failure," *Journal of Financial Economics*, 40: 163–81.

—— —— (2001). "Ownership and Control of German Corporations," *Review of Financial Studies*, 14: 943–77.

Freshfields Bruckhaus Deringer (2002). "Public Takeovers in the UK," London: Freshfields Bruckhaus Deringer.

GILSON, R., SCHOLES, M., and WOLFSON, M. (1988). "Taxation and the Dynamics of Corporate Control: The Uncertain Case for Tax-Motivated Acquisitions," in J. C. Coffe, L. Lowenstein, and S. Rose-Ackerman (eds.), *Knights, Raiders and Targets: The Impact of the Hostile Takeover*. New York: Oxford University Press.

GORT, M. (1969). "An Economic Disturbance Theory of Mergers," *Quarterly Journal of Economics*, 83: 624–42.

GRAHAM, C. (2001). "The Venture Capital Perspective: Why Do a Public to Private?" Presentation at IBC Conference on Public-to-private Takeovers, London, November 26.

GROSSMAN, S., and HART, O. (1980). "Takeover Bids, the Free-Rider Problem, and the Theory of the Corporation," *Bell Journal of Economics*, 11: 42–64.

HALPERN, P., KIESCHNICK, R., and ROTENBERG, W. (1999). "On the Heterogeneity of Leveraged Going Private Transactions," *The Review of Financial Studies*, 12: 281–309.

HANSEN, R. (2001). "Auctions of Companies," *Economic Inquiry*, 39: 30–43.

Higgs Report (2003). *Review of the Role and Effectiveness of Non-Executive Directors*. London: Department of Trade and Industry.

HOLL, P., and KYRIAZIS, D. (1996). "The Determinants of Outcome in UK Take-Over Bids," *International Journal of the Economics of Business*, 3: 165–84.

—— —— (1997). "Agency, Bid Resistance and the Market for Corporate Control," *Journal of Business Finance and Accounting*, 24: 1037–66.

JENSEN, M. C. (1986a). "The Take-Over Controversy: Analysis and Evidence," *Midland Corporate Finance Journal*, 4: 6–32.

—— (1986b). "Agency Costs of Free Cash Flow, Corporate Finance and Take-Overs," *American Economic Review*, 76: 323–39.

—— and MECKLING, W. (1976). "Theory of the Firm: Managerial Behaviour, Agency Costs and Ownership Structure," *Journal of Financial Economics*, 13: 305–60.

—— and RUBACK, R. (1983). "The Market for Corporate Control: The Scientific Evidence," *Journal of Financial Economics*, 11: 5–50.

KENNEDY, V. A., and LIMMACK, R. J. (1996). "Take-Over Activity, CEO Turnover, and the Market for Corporate Control," *Journal of Business Finance and Accounting*, 23: 267–85.

KINI, O., KRACAW, W., and MIAN, S. (1995). "Corporate Takeovers, Firm Performance and Board Composition," *Journal of Corporate Finance*, 1: 383–412.

—— —— —— (2004). "The Nature of Discipline in Corporate Takeovers," *Journal of Finance*, 59: 1511–52.

LAMBRECHT, B. (2004). "The Timing and Terms of Takeovers Motivated by Economies of Scale," *Journal of Financial Economics*, 72: 41–62.

——– and MYERS, S. (2006). "A Theory of Takeovers and Disinvestment," *Journal of Finance*, 62: 809–45.

LANG, L., STULZ, R., and WALKLING, R. (1989). "Managerial Performance, Tobin's Q, and the Gains from Successful Tender Offers," *Journal of Financial Economics*, 24: 137–54.

LEHN, K., and POULSEN, A. (1989). "Free Cash Flow and Stockholder Gains in Going Private Transactions," *The Journal of Finance*, 44: 771–87.

McCONNELL, J. (2003). "Outside Directors," *The Financial Review*, 38: 25–31.

McKNIGHT, P., and WEIR, C. (2009). "Agency Costs, Corporate Governance Mechanisms and Ownership Structure in Large Publicly Quoted Companies: A Panel Data Analysis," *Quarterly Review of Economics and Finance*, 49: 135–58.

MAKSIMOVIC, V., and PHILLIPS, G. (2001). "The Market for Corporate Assets: Who Engages in Mergers and Asset Sales and are there Efficiency Gains," *Journal of Finance*, 56: 2019–65.

MANNE, H. (1965). "Mergers and the Market for Corporate Control," *Journal of Political Economy*, 73: 110–20.

MARRIS, R. (1964). *The Economic Theory of Managerial Capitalism*. London: Macmillan.

MARTIN, K. J., and McCONNELL, J. J. (1991). "Corporate Performance, Corporate Take-Overs, and Management Turnover," *The Journal of Finance*, 46: 671–8.

MOELLER, S., SCHLINGEMANN, F., and STULZ, R. (2004). "Firm Size and the Gains from Acquisitions," *Journal of Financial Economics*, 73: 201–28.

MORCK, R., SHLEIFER, A., and VISHNY, R. W. (1988). "Characteristics of Targets of Hostile and Friendly Takeovers," in Auerbach, A. J. (ed.), *Corporate Takeovers: Causes and Consequences*. Chicago: University of Chicago Press.

MUELLER, D. C. (1969). "A Theory of Conglomerate Mergers," *Quarterly Journal of Economics*, 83: 643–59.

NORTH, D. S. (2001). "The Role of Managerial Incentives in Corporate Acquisitions: Evidence from the 1990s," *Journal of Corporate Finance*, 7: 125–49.

NUTTALL, R. (1999). "Take-Over Likelihood Models for UK Quoted Companies," Nuffield College Working Paper, Oxford University.

OPLER, T., and TITMAN, S. (1993). "The Determinants of Leveraged Buyout Activity: Free Cash Flow vs. Financial Distress Costs," *The Journal of Finance*, 48: 1985–99.

O'SULLIVAN, N., and WONG, P. (1998). "Internal versus External Control: An Analysis of Board Composition and Ownership in UK Takeovers," *Journal of Management and Governance*, 2: 17–35.

—— —— (1999). "Board Composition, Ownership Structure and Hostile Take-Overs: Some UK Evidence," *Accounting and Business Research*, 29: 139–55.

POPE, P., YOUNG, S., and PEASNELL, K. (2003). "Managerial Equity Ownership and the Demand for Outside Directors," *European Financial Management*, 9: 99–118.

POWELL, R. G. (1997). "Modelling Take-Over Likelihood," *Journal of Business Finance and Accounting*, 24: 1009–30.

RHODES-KROPF, M., ROBINSON, D., and VISWANATHAN, S. (2005). "Valuation Waves and Merger Activity: The Empirical Evidence," *Journal of Financial Economics*, 77: 561–603.

ROLL, R. (1986). "The Hubris Hypothesis of Corporate Takeovers," *Journal of Business*, 59: 197–216.

SCHWERT, G. (2000). "Hostility in Take-Overs: In the Eyes of the Beholders," *Journal of Finance*, 55: 2599–640.

SHIVDASANI, A. (1993). "Board Composition, Ownership Structure and Hostile Takeovers," *Journal of Accounting and Economics*, 16: 167–98.

SHLEIFER, A., and VISHNY, R. (1986). "Large Shareholders and Corporate Control," *Journal of Political Economy*, 94: 461–88.

—— —— (1989). "Management Entrenchment: The Case of Manager-Specific Investments," *Journal of Financial Economics*, 25: 123–39.

SJ BERWIN (2003). *Public-to Private: An Overview*. London: SJ Berwin.

SUDARSANAM, P. (1995). "The Role of Defensive Strategies and Ownership Structure of Target Firms: Evidence from UK Hostile Bids," *European Financial Management*, 1: 223–40.

—— (2003). *Creating Value from Mergers and Acquisitions: The Challenges*. Harlow: Pearson Education Limited.

UK Corporate Governance Code, The (2010). London: Financial Reporting Council.

WEINSTEIN, D., and YAFEH, Y. (1998). "On the Costs of a Bank Centred Banking System: Evidence from the Changing Main Bank Relations in Japan," *Journal of Finance*, 53: 635–72.

WEIR, C. (1997). "Corporate Governance, Performance and Take-Overs: An Empirical Analysis of UK Mergers," *Applied Economics*, 29: 1465–75.

—— and LAING, D. (2003). "Ownership Structure, Board Composition and the Market for Corporate Control in The UK: An Empirical Analysis," *Applied Economics*, 16: 1747–59.

—— and WRIGHT, M. (2006). "Governance and Takeovers: Are Public to Private Transactions Different from Traditional Acquisitions of Listed Corporations?" *Accounting and Business Research*, 36: 289–307.

—— LAING, D., and WRIGHT, M. (2005). "Incentive Effects, Monitoring Mechanisms and the Market for Corporate Control: An Analysis of the Factors Affecting Public to Private Transactions in the UK," *Journal of Business Finance and Accounting*, 32: 909–43.

—— —— and SCHOLES, L. (2008). "Public-to-Private Buy-Outs, Distress Costs and Private Equity," *Applied Financial Economics*, 18: 1–19.

WESTON, J. FRED (1970). "The Nature and Significance of Conglomerate Firms," *St. John's Law Review*, 44: 66–80.

WRIGHT, M., WEIR, C. M., and BURROWS, A. (2007). "Irrevocable Commitments, Going Private and Private Equity," *European Financial Management*, 13: 757–75.

YAFEH, Y. (2000). "Corporate Governance in Japan: Part Performance and Future Prospects," *Oxford Review of Economic Policy*, 16: 74–84.

PART III

THE CORPORATE GOVERNANCE LIFE CYCLE

CHAPTER 16

THE LIFE CYCLE OF CORPORATE GOVERNANCE

STEVE TOMS

INTRODUCTION

THE life cycle of corporate governance refers to the variation of purpose of governance functions in the different stages of an organization's development. It builds on the notion of the product life cycle (Abernathy and Utterback, 1978; Klepper, 1996), which identifies successive phases of development: typically introduction, growth, maturity, and decline. In these accounts the evolutionary pattern is determined by technological change, which in turn impacts on market entry and exit decisions, thereby determining the competitive dynamics of an industry. In each evolutionary phase, a firm faces a different set of strategic issues and its governance functions respond accordingly. For example, the dominating function of the board of directors in a business start-up and early growth phase will be to attract the resources the firm needs for expansion, whereas in the maturity phase monitoring on behalf of diversified passive shareholders will become a more dominant function.

By considering firms other than mature listed firms, the corporate governance life-cycle approach has the potential to broaden our understanding of its functions in important new contexts, including start-ups, initial public offerings, downsizing, exit and refocusing. In these situations the resource and strategy functions of governance (Zahra and Pearce, 1989) are likely to be more important. Taking a dynamic perspective, it also allows us to examine how the institutions of corporate governance for large, mature listed firms arise, for example by considering their interdependence with organizational learning (Zahra and Filatotchev, 2004) and how they might be undermined.

The notion of the corporate governance life cycle provides the opportunity to examine the interrelationships between business strategy, the firm's dynamics, financing patterns and performance, corporate entrepreneurship, and the varying purpose of governance arrangements. Governance research has shown that changes in ownership and board composition are important components of more general models of strategic change as firms modify their internal capabilities to adapt to environmental conditions (Goodstein and Boeker, 1991: 325). In this sense the corporate governance life cycle can be seen as an extension of the more general life cycle of the organization. As firms and industries move through their life-cycle phases, their financial characteristics alter in tandem: for example, the direction of cash flows, the mix of equity and debt finance, and financial performance measured in terms of key ratios such as dividend yield and price to earnings. To understand the relationship between strategy and governance through the life cycle it is also important to illustrate how it is mediated by these financial variables. In similar vein, corporate entrepreneurship has different tasks at each phase of the life cycle in terms of identifying and deploying resources.

The first section of this chapter explains the concept of the life cycle of corporate governance in more detail. The second section illustrates the financial life-cycle characteristics of the life cycle and shows how these mediate the governance and strategy relationship during the key phases. In the third section these relationships are drawn together in an integrative model. A fourth section uses a case study and empirical evidence to illustrate the workings of the model. The final section draws conclusions.

THE GOVERNANCE LIFE-CYCLE CONCEPT

The corporate governance life cycle is a relatively new and unexplored theme in the broader corporate governance literature. Filatotchev, Toms, and Wright (2006) argue that the corporate governance life cycle offers a useful extension of the usual agency theory-dominated explanations of managerial behavior. The agency perspective emphasizes the monitoring and control dimensions of governance, but corporate governance is also concerned with enabling more effective managerial entrepreneurship (Tricker, 1984; Keasey and Wright, 1993), particularly in small and medium-sized enterprises (SMEs) where ownership concentration among top management creates risk aversion and reluctance to make significant strategic change such as product and market diversification (Hill and Snell, 1988; Hoskisson et al., 2000; George et al., 2005). In addition to monitoring, therefore, the corporate governance life-cycle approach stresses other functions of corporate governance, with a focus on two in particular. First, the resource role, where governance functions such as outside directors or relationships with capital providers are used to secure access to additional resources, including expertise, network contacts, and further financial resources. The second function is the strategy role, in which governance provides a direct input into the development of the strategy of the business. In the life cycle of corporate governance these functions, including monitoring, vary in their relative importance (Zahra and Pearce, 1989; Filatotchev et al., 2006; Bonn and Pettigrew, 2009).

A further feature of the life-cycle approach is that it can combine theoretical perspectives such as the resource-based view and agency theory. Using these approaches in combination has been used to explain entrepreneurial behavior (Toms, 2006), strategic choice and organizational structure (Toms and Wright, 2002), network dynamics (Toms and Filatotchev, 2004) and the life cycle of corporate governance (Filatotchev et al., 2006).

An important advantage of the life-cycle approach is that it can overcome limitations in related literatures. For example in the strategy literature the emergence of the managerial corporation has formed the basis for the strategy and structure relationship, in which the former determines the latter (Chandler, 1962, 1977, 1990). However, the development of the managerial firm as a basis for competitive advantage (Lazonick, 1991) has been interpreted as prescriptive and linear, and in teleological fashion. In the UK in particular, the development of managerial corporations occurred for only a limited phase, circa 1950–80 and was subsequently replaced with more flexible and effective organizational forms (Toms and Wright, 2002, 2005). Moreover, the dominance of the managerial firm may also be a function of nationally specific aspects of competition policy, company law, and rules governing financial institutions (Fligstein, 1990). If managerial capitalism is conceived as a phase of development, rather than an end point, then the dynamics of business and the role of corporate governance can be more fruitfully analyzed and understood.

The Financial Life Cycle

One important life-cycle dimension that has not been fully integrated into discussions of the corporate governance life cycle is the financial life cycle. Bender and Ward (2002) illustrate how these relationships might be investigated further by showing the relationship between the product life cycle and financial variables such as cash flow, dividend, and investment policies. Figure 16.1 shows how the financial life cycle is related to the product life cycle in terms of the underlying cash flows generated by the product/market strategy, the distribution of cash flows, and the consequent valuation of the firm. These financial variables are measured in terms of net cash flow (after tax profit minus net investment),[1] dividend payout ratio (dividend paid divided by after-tax profit), financial leverage (long-term borrowing divided by total capital), and the price-earnings (P/E) ratio (market value divided by after-tax profit).

Clearly these variables are closely related to the evolution of the firm's resource base and a further important determinant of the governance life cycle is the corporate financial life cycle. A start-up firm, for example, will be characterized by negative cash flow and consequently low dividend pay-out, but, reflecting future growth prospects, a high price to earnings (P/E) ratio. These financial characteristics have a decisive influence on the structure and purpose of corporate governance arrangements. For example, in the

352 THE CORPORATE GOVERNANCE LIFE CYCLE

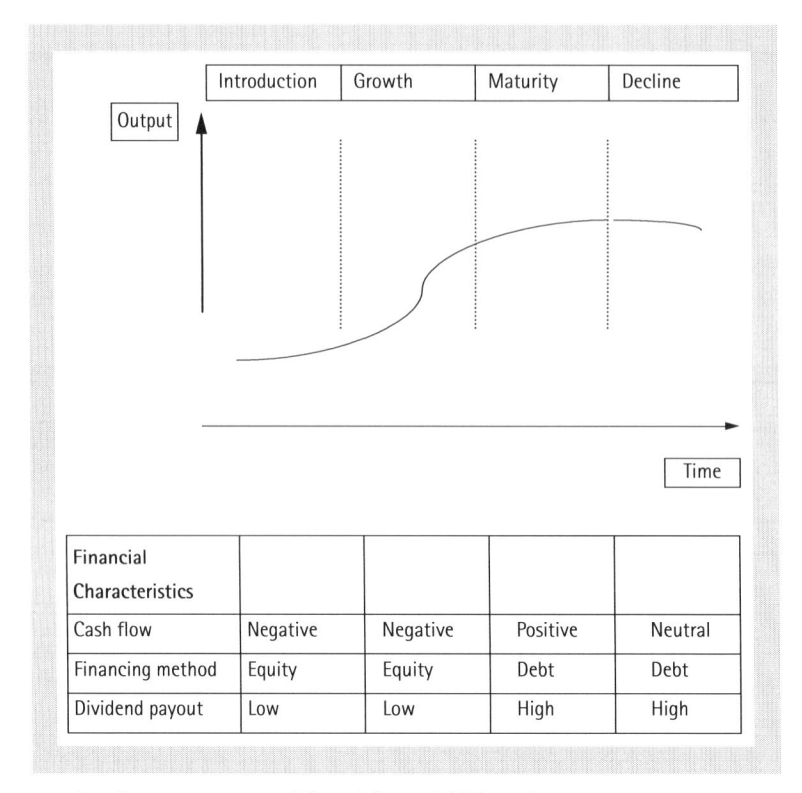

	Introduction	Growth	Maturity	Decline
Financial Characteristics				
Cash flow	Negative	Negative	Positive	Neutral
Financing method	Equity	Equity	Debt	Debt
Dividend payout	Low	Low	High	High

FIGURE 16.1. Product, entrepreneurial, and financial life cycles

start-up situation, loan finance will be risky and expensive and therefore equity finance preferred, which in turn will affect governance variables such as board composition.

Some of these relationships are helpfully illustrated by the literature on the relationship between financial structure and product markets. Hellman and Puri (2000) show that venture capital speeds up the introduction of innovation, thereby providing useful evidence of the interactions between investor involvement and product market strategy and financial performance. Jain and Kini (1995) find similar benefits for venture capital involvement, specifically at the initial public offering (IPO) stage. Other literature examines the impact of new product introductions on firm value (e.g. Chaney et al., 1991). For the most part these studies feature interactions between financial and strategic variables at some specific phase of the firm life cycle and do not offer a holistic conceptualization of their interactions across the full cycle.

However, the relationship between the financial and governance aspects of the life cycle has been neglected. There has been some research into the relationship between governance and financial performance variables (e.g. Zahra and Pearce, 1989). These studies have examined the relationship between board structure and financial performance. Others have looked at the relationship between managerial shareholding and corporate performance (Keasey et al., 1994; Short and Keasey, 1999; Davies et al., 2005).

None of these studies relates governance or performance directly to the life cycle. Finance researchers have examined specific aspects of the life cycle such as the IPO and involve governance variables to that extent. For example Berry, Reber, and Toms (2005) show that, in addition to the usual agency variables, the quality and experience of the board of directors has a positive impact on the proceeds realized. Meanwhile there is a wide-ranging literature that examines governance variables in a principal–agent framework to explain diversification through takeovers and mergers and refocusing through divestment and the associated gains and losses in value experienced by shareholder groups (for a recent review, see Haleblian et al., 2009; see also Chapter 15).

Corporate Entrepreneurship

A further closely related aspect of corporate governance affected by life-cycle dynamics is corporate entrepreneurship (CE). As Phan et al. (2009: 204) argue, there is a need to consider the time dimension and life-cycle characteristics of CE. Clearly certain characteristics of CE, such as creative destruction (Schumpeter, 1943) and price discovery (Kirzner, 1997), are likely to dominate at different stages of the product life cycle. Because these processes also involve the reordering of financial claims of different investor and stakeholder groups they are also strongly related to the governance and financial life cycles.

If Figure 16.1 is reconsidered, this time from the perspective of the entrepreneurial function, it can be seen how the role of entrepreneurship varies through the stages of the firm's development. In the introduction and growth phases, Austrian notions of entrepreneurship predominate. As new products and services are introduced and the potential for rapid growth created, there is a process of price discovery for values previously unknown and unknowable by the market and which can therefore only be priced with uncertainty (Knight, 1921). In the Austrian school, heterogeneity of beliefs about asset values creates entrepreneurial opportunity (Hayek, 1937; Kirzner, 1979, 1989, 1997; Casson, 1982), either for founders or immediate venture capital backers. These opportunities in introduction and growth phases are characterized by movement from disequilibrium to equilibrium through the process of price discovery.

As maturity is reached, entrepreneurship might be characterized as an ability to "optimise within constraints" (McCloskey and Sandberg, 1972), with managers engaging in intrapreneurial activities. In this "managerialist" view, entrepreneurs perform managerial tasks, competently or otherwise (Lazonick, 1991). In the mature phase, entrepreneurs may also appear as "rentiers," able to defend monopoly and privilege through effective lobbying (Green, 1988). As maturity switches to decline, entrepreneurship takes on a more Schumpeterian flavor in which acts of creative destruction are undertaken to remove constraints upon business activity (Schumpeter, 1943; Lazonick, 1991). The entrepreneur has also to defend the business against competitors, try to manage a declining cash flow, deal with unhappy creditors as the working capital gets stretched, and find new sources of funding. The role of the chairman has to be flexible to deal with the difficult internal and external tensions. An important necessary condition for such activities is access to external capital resources, a requirement that is accentuated where there are significant exit barriers associated with existing activities, and these features are often present in turnaround strategies which if successful might extend this phase of the life cycle (Filatotchev and Toms, 2006). Finally the decline phase might result in exit, and the subsequent development of new ventures may give rise to habitual, serial, or portfolio patterns of entrepreneurship.

An Integrated Model

Figure 16.2 provides a model to explain the dynamic interactions of the resource base and governance dimensions. It is adapted from the model in Filatotchev et al. (2006), with the addition of the financial and entrepreneurial variables discussed and a reconceptualization to explain the interaction of resource and governance evolutions. The model shows four quadrants arising from combinations of narrow and extensive resource bases and limited or transparent corporate governance arrangements. The firm's resource base, represented on the vertical axis, can be narrow or broad. Where the resource base is narrow, often for example where the firm is new or small, it acquires resources from outside the organization. These often possess external economy of scale characteristics, such as networks of external knowledge (Marshall, 1890; Kamien et al., 1992), and usually have a public good element such as local concentrations of experience and skilled labor. Where the firm's resource base is more extensive, its assets might typically comprise organization-specific idiosyncratic resources, including "tacit" knowledge (Penrose, 1959; Teece, 1980; Barney, 1997; Castanias and Helfat, 2001). They might include specialized production facilities, trade secrets, and engineering experience (Teece et al., 1997) and human capital assets (Teece, 1980). Such assets have the characteristic of being difficult to imitate, reflecting the heterogeneous nature of valuable assets in the resource-based view of the firm (Alvarez and Busenitz, 2001). The horizontal axis contrasts limited and high levels of accountability and transparency. Where accountability is limited, firms are typically not subject to public scrutiny through regulation or capital market-mandated practices and disclosures. The opposite is true for typically larger stock market-quoted firms which are subject to a great deal of monitoring and scrutiny.

As Figure 16.2 shows, combinations of resource diversity and accountability explain shifts between stages of organizational development. Movement from one quadrant to another requires a threshold to be crossed which is characterized by a transition in the resource base and ownership characteristics of the firm. Thresholds are crossed diagonally since changes in the resource base affect the firm's capital structure and therefore the processes of accountability to capital providers. The relative prominence of the three functions of corporate governance varies accordingly. Similarly, the financial characteristics of the firm vary by quadrant as a function of the interaction between the growth

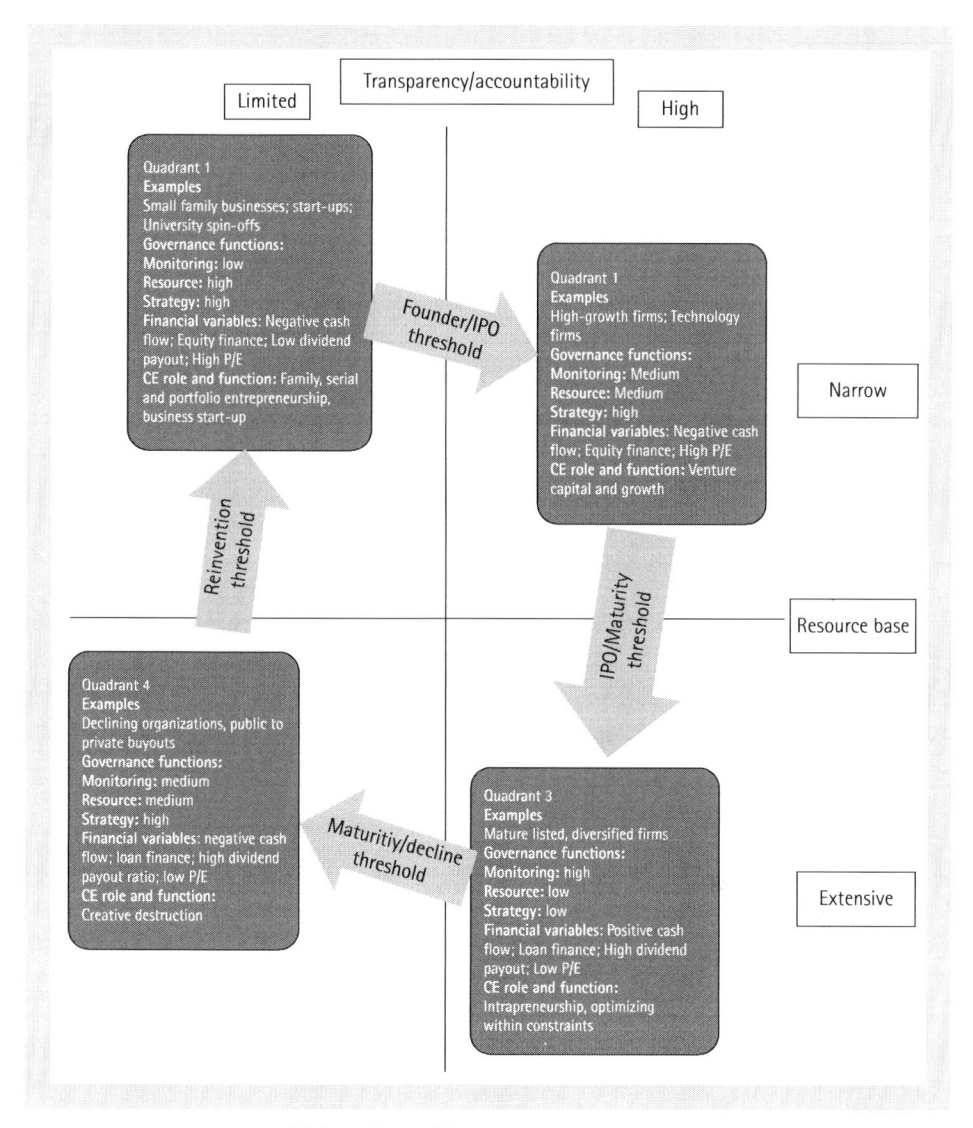

FIGURE 16.2. An integrated life-cycle model

Quadrant 1
Examples: Small family businesses; start-ups; University spin-offs
Governance functions:
Monitoring: low
Resource: high
Strategy: high
Financial variables: Negative cash flow; Equity finance; Low dividend payout; High P/E
CE role and function: Family, serial and portfolio entrepreneurship, business start-up

Quadrant 1 (2)
Examples: High-growth firms; Technology firms
Governance functions:
Monitoring: Medium
Resource: Medium
Strategy: high
Financial variables: Negative cash flow; Equity finance; High P/E
CE role and function: Venture capital and growth

Quadrant 4
Examples: Declining organizations, public to private buyouts
Governance functions:
Monitoring: medium
Resource: medium
Strategy: high
Financial variables: negative cash flow; loan finance; high dividend payout ratio; low P/E
CE role and function: Creative destruction

Quadrant 3
Examples: Mature listed, diversified firms
Governance functions:
Monitoring: high
Resource: low
Strategy: low
Financial variables: Positive cash flow; Loan finance; High dividend payout; Low P/E
CE role and function: Intrapreneurship, optimizing within constraints

Axes: Transparency/accountability (Limited / High); Resource base (Narrow / Extensive)
Thresholds: Founder/IPO threshold; IPO/Maturity threshold; Maturity/decline threshold; Reinvention threshold

---

rate implied by the product life cycle and the rational balancing of business and financial risk as a consequence. In high-growth phases when business risk is high, financial risk through additional leverage is to be avoided and equity finance preferred, and vice versa for mature and diverse organizations. To illustrate the joint dynamics of these processes, we consider each quadrant and each transition of the figure in turn.

In the first stage of the life cycle (quadrant 1), firms have narrow resource bases and are typically owned and controlled by founder-managers and/or family investors. At this stage the key entrepreneurial functions are performed by the founding group. As a result, the level of managerial accountability to external shareholders is low. So there is little need for the monitoring function of corporate governance, but the strategy and resource roles are of high importance. These roles are reflected in the financial variables, which show a strong need for cash to support early-stage operations and expansion, little opportunity for profit distribution to external stakeholders, reliance on internal equity resources, and the potential of high value related to the prospects of future growth.

The opportunity for growth and the financial imbalances for early stage firms explain the dynamic of the founder/IPO threshold (see Zahra et al., 2009, for a detailed discussion). Since the dominant requirement at this stage is access to new financial resources to fund rapid growth, the main function of CE is to engage with new capital providers and conforms most closely to the Austrian model of price discovery through knowledge acquisition. In this model, market processes follow from human action, so that entrepreneurial opportunities arise from abnormal profit opportunities associated with mispricing and price disequilibria (Mises, 1949; Kirzner, 1997). Such disequilibria are more likely for recently introduced products or services and for firms trading such products with limited histories of volatile profits, which have not been subject to public disclosure requirements. Resulting information asymmetries create pricing problems during the IPO share issue itself, where the process of price discovery is conducted by investment banks, venture capitalists, and syndicated firms. Assimilation of information to form estimates of the value of IPO businesses is the key function of the book-running investment bank, which can allocate capital according to the quality of investment analysis offered (Hanley, 1993).

From the IPO firm's point of view, the direction of change in Figure 16.2 is diagonal and to the right because the purpose of crossing the threshold is to widen the resource base as growth opportunities are exploited, whilst at the same time financing those opportunities through the increased involvement of external stakeholders. The slope of the line is determined by the extent to which the firm can fund substantial stages of early growth, thereby postponing the IPO until later stages, for example by securing funding from business angels and venture capitalists. In this event the slope will be steeper, as the resources generated will be disproportionate to any increase in external financial stakeholder scrutiny.[2] In the more general case represented in Figure 16.2, the slope is shallower, reflecting an early-stage IPO with a substantial tradeoff of accountability for resources, reflecting the wealth limits of early start-ups and other forms of capital rationing of high-risk projects as a hard constraint that can only be overcome by a stock market listing.

In quadrant 2, post-IPO firms have a new set of governance characteristics. The monitoring function is now more important, reflecting the involvement of outside stakeholders, and the resource function is less important as the firm has now accessed new tranches of capital as a result of crossing the IPO threshold. The strategy function of governance remains high and is now the most important attribute insofar as the firm has a further growth phase post the IPO. At this stage the board of directors, including non-executives, might contribute by direct involvement in formulating the mission and developing the strategy, including strategic investments. As a result of the IPO the firm will be able to make strategic investments in resources that allow the full exploitation of the growth phase of the product life cycle, for example production facilities, product development, and access to distribution networks. There will also typically be investment in managerial capacity as the firm is professionalized and the governance system developed. Access to stock market financial resources creates a requirement for greater transparency, in the form of compliance with legal disclosure rules and stock exchange regulations. These ongoing investments and consequent growth opportunities mean that net cash flow remains negative, and, notwithstanding stock market flotations and pressures, dividend payouts remain low, although investors benefit from correspondingly high P/E ratios. Newly raised equity remains the dominant source of finance, as the firm faces high business risk in the remaining portion of the growth phase.

As the firm further expands its resource base through product and market diversification, it crosses the IPO/maturity threshold and the downward shift in Figure 16.2 is limited when opportunities for profitable expansion are exhausted. The dominant CE characteristic in this phase is intrapreneurship, as professional managers optimize investments in a diversified portfolio of businesses through the operation of internal capital markets or parallel capital allocation mechanisms. In contrast to Schumpeterian entrepreneurship which removes constraints, the focus in this phase is optimization within constraints. The direction of transition is again diagonal, reflecting the continued acquisition of a resource base combined now with declining transparency and accountability. Such a decline occurs due to the progressive replacement of voice by exit as the shareholder base broadens, and block shareholders, including original owners and inside directors, tend to sell their holdings in an increasingly liquid market. The effect of declining outside shareholder scrutiny also arises from the increasing complexity of multi-product and process organizations, which can create opportunities for managerial rents (Toms, 2010), emphasizing the emerging divorce of ownership and control. As the firm exhausts its growth opportunities in the focal industry, it seeks further diversification into related and unrelated industries (Hitt et al., 2003), rendering a transparent system of governance less easily enforceable. The slope of the line is shallow or steep, reflecting the tradeoffs between the scale and complexity of additions to the resource base and the corresponding monitoring problems arising for outside shareholders.

The defining feature of quadrant 3 therefore is the dominance of the monitoring role of corporate governance. Static or slowly growing markets eliminate the need for further strategic investments, thereby reducing the value of the resource and strategy governance functions. Low investment requirements mean that cash flow is strongly positive and this can support increasing distributions of profits as dividends and low growth prospects reduce the P/E ratio. Low-growth sectors (for example, publishing) are dominated by firms with low P/E ratios, in contrast to high-growth sector such as semiconductors (Anderson and Brooks, 2006). Because business risk has diminished, either through the effects of consolidating market position or portfolio-style diversification, the firm can finance more of its activities through structured loans.

Misalignment of incentives leads to a managerial drive for ever-increasing expansion and diversification, producing performance deterioration and loss in shareholder value, leading firms to cross the maturity/decline threshold. Losses also arise as a direct function of declining markets. Although the inherited resource base is substantial, during this phase the governance system is insufficient in itself to prevent managerial opportunism or arrest organizational decline (Filatotchev and Toms, 2003). Crossing this threshold is clearly undesirable and it is at this stage that firms might attempt to develop turnaround strategies. Successful strategies depend on engaging outside stakeholders, particularly when decline threatens the capital value of their investments, and is a necessary precursor to internal reorganization and renewal. New outside investors can only be incentivized by the prospect of significant risk-adjusted profit opportunities which might typically arise from major asset realizations or redeployments. In some circumstances, sunk investments linked to the value of outsider investors' financial claims can prevent decisive action, so that governance itself may turn into a driver of further decline by imposing serious financial constraints that erode the organization's resource base (Toms and Filatotchev, 2004; Filatotchev and Toms, 2006). Because the engagement of outside stakeholders through the reordering of financial claims is necessary, it is likely that the firm will seek to reduce its dependence on outside passive stock market investors and look to the assistance of specialist capital providers and banks either via public to private transfers, management buyouts, or debt-to-equity swaps. Even in cases of orderly managed decline, dependence on outside shareholders will be reduced through share buy-backs and special dividends where the firm is starved of profitable inward investment opportunities. The dominant feature of CE in this phase is Schumpeterian creative destruction. The key agencies are the banks, which may be incentivized to recover debt through asset realization and hive downs, or other outside institutions, where asset disposal, refocusing, and refinancing create the profit opportunities. In these cases, the component transactions of deals such as leveraged buyouts might resemble asset stripping, particularly where there are significant differences between asset values in current use and realizable values for alternative development. The slope of the diagonal crossing the threshold depends on the fraction of resources destroyed through losses or disposed of through downsizing activities in relation to the re-concentration of financial claims amongst investors.

In quadrant 4, the strategy and resource functions of governance again become important, and the requirement for monitoring is reduced, as failing organizations are taken over by a narrower group of stakeholders. Firms might also be characterized by accumulated losses and debts. As a result, cash flow is negative, and outstanding debt may therefore be high notwithstanding asset disposals. Dividend payouts and price-to-earnings ratios are low. Capital restructuring, sometimes involving revaluation of ownership claims and replacement capital, is therefore often needed to rebalance the financial position.

Because quadrant 4 firms are failed turnarounds, the only remaining strategic option is to hive off the profitable aspects of an overdiversified business or to put the rescued assets to a new and profitable use. This represents the diagonal movement through the reinvention threshold into quadrant 1. Debt-to-equity substitution is also likely to be an important aspect of this threshold. Another feature is that CE combines the remaining aspects of Schumpeterian creative destruction with renewed elements of Austrian price discovery as the cycle is completed. This phase is best fulfilled by serial entrepreneurs or individuals practiced at relaunching businesses. Engagement of active governance functions in strategy formulation through the disposal of redundant assets and refocusing on a narrow resource base is the key governance function in these circumstances. Where this can be done successfully the resource function is less important since cash realizations of redundant assets, for example factory and property sites, can finance the acquisition of new and specialized assets to support the refocused business. Restructuring of a declining organization may therefore result in a reinvigoration of the life cycle as more direct and incentive-related governance mechanisms are introduced in the form of increased managerial equity, monitoring by private equity firms, and a commitment to service debt (Jensen, 1993; Thompson and Wright, 1995; Weir et al., 2005). As such, the organization may narrow the scope of its activities and move back toward the start of a new cycle by crossing the reinvention threshold back to quadrant 1. The slope of the diagonal is determined by the tradeoff between asset disposal and the extent to which new, if limited and non-public financial stakeholders need to be engaged to support the process.

Discussion and Examples

At the founder/IPO threshold the resource and strategy functions tend to dominate the agency perspective. Even so, at this stage agency problems can be critical as a result of the absence of market price history and associated valuation problems and conflicts of interest between underwriters and issuers (Loughran and Ritter, 2002). These agency costs are accentuated where the venture capital (VC) function is syndicated, and new governance arrangements need to develop as a result (Filatotchev et al., 2005). Competitive IPOs have been suggested as a possible solution. In this approach, book-building functions are segregated and the bidding period is limited, thereby restricting the possibility of collusive practices within investing syndicates. Using the example of the French *Pages Jaunes* IPO in 2004, Jenkinson and Jones (2009) show that such incremental market-based responses can mitigate conflicts of interest (see Zahra et al., 2009, for other examples).

Even if avoidable ownership dilution occurs at the IPO stage, it is not necessarily the reason for longer-run underperformance of post-IPO companies. Goergen and Renneboog (2005) show that agency problems do not typically impact on performance for UK and German companies in the post IPO period. Rather, performance is a function of the growth and risk characteristics of firms, which, with reference to Figure 16.2, can be interpreted as performance being a function of the decisions on deployment of financial resources acquired during the IPO. According to this evidence, the strategy function continues to dominate in the immediate IPO period and is not supplanted by the monitoring function in terms of relative importance until at least five years afterwards.

In mature firms, agency problems dominate, particularly in the form of managerial inspired empire building likely to result in the loss of value to shareholders. Haynes, Thompson, and Wright (2005) find that such risks can be mitigated through the use of options and that, indeed, managers are more likely to take downsizing decisions when incentivized by appropriate option packages. When mature firms face decline or crisis, for example as a result of over-extension through ill-conceived takeovers, reorganization of governance mechanisms is an important first stage (Filatotchev and Toms, 2006), ahead of any retrenchment and recovery plans (Robbins and Pearce, 1992). In 2005, following a botched takeover of Safeway, UK supermarket chain Morrisons faced a crisis of shareholder confidence. The company was in breach of the Combined Code on Corporate Governance and admitted that there was no formal training program for directors, that it had no non-executive directors on the board, that the nomination committee was made up only of the chairman and managing directors, and that it did not have a formal remuneration committee (William Morrison Supermarkets plc, 2004). These breaches were remedied by the appointment of new non-executive directors, who also became key agents in the subsequent turnaround. The key ingredient was the resource role, and in particular expertise, including the appointment of new investment bankers. The monitoring role was also crucial, particularly in restoring confidence in stock market investors, using the new governance structure to build communication channels with City institutions (Toms, 2011).

For declining organizations, refocusing strategies can be supported through re-concentrations in equity ownership. Examples might include public to private transactions. The effect of these concentrations is to improve monitoring but at the same time render that element of governance less problematic, although the dominant motive is the incentive effect associated with managerial wealth gains arising from concentrating shareholdings (Weir et al., 2005). Such wealth effects were accentuated in the original wave of leveraged buyout transactions in the 1980s in the US. There has been considerable debate about the effects of such transactions, with some UK evidence suggesting they are positive in terms of aggregate wealth effects, not so much characterized by hostility, and less dependent on debt finance than in the US (Wright et al., 1990; Wright et al., 1991; Weir et al., 2005; Cumming et al., 2007; Renneboog et al., 2007).

Conclusions

The chapter has reviewed the general literature on the corporate governance life cycle. It has identified specific aspects of other life cycles that integrate closely with the governance life cycle. These include the underlying product life cycle and the financial and corporate entrepreneurship life cycles. Considering all these aspects as an integrated model illustrates how corporate governance lies at the center of a number of processes impacting on the dynamic evolution of businesses. The resource, strategy, and monitoring functions of corporate governance are interrelated with the firm's financial characteristics and the dominant features and roles of corporate entrepreneurship.

Not only does considering the dynamic interrelationships of these factors enhance our understanding of corporate governance more broadly, it also allows the determinants of change through the use of thresholds to be more closely examined. Each threshold requires a re-ordering of resources which necessarily means a parallel re-ordering of financial claims and associated changes in control and governance.

Although the corporate governance life cycle is a relatively recent idea, the empirical processes described in this chapter have been persistent features of industrial organization and control. The examples used have been somewhat Anglo-centric, but the concept has obvious applicability to other jurisdictions and institutional settings, including public sector and public-private hybrid organizations. For these reasons, there is a large research agenda for governance life cycle theory. The dominance of the principal–agent approaches in the mature stock market-quoted corporation setting has been noted. By offering a more holistic approach, this literature can be widened so that empirical cases of successful resource governance combinations can be better documented through the full life cycle. Adopting an integrative and analytical approach, this chapter has highlighted the likely useful variables that can be examined and has illustrated how transitions in governance regimes might be modeled. Through such an integration of the resources of the firm, the structure of financial claims, the role of the corporate entrepreneur, and the major governance functions, the chapter has demonstrated the dynamic interrelationship between these vital components of corporate strategy.

Notes

1. Net investment is defined as additions to fixed assets plus depreciation minus proceeds from disposals plus change in working capital.
2. International and institutional variations may affect the slopes of the thresholds. For example IPOs tend to occur later in Germany than in the UK (Goergen and Renneboog, 2005), so the slope would be steeper for the UK, reflecting the earlier and more rapid financial resource acquisition.

References

Abernathy, W. J., and Utterback, J. M. (1978). "Patterns of Industrial Innovation," *Technology Review*, 80: 41–7.

Alvarez, S., and Busenitz, L. (2001). "A Resource Based View of Entrepreneurship," *Journal of Management*, 27: 755–75.

ANDERSON, K., and BROOKS, C. (2006). "Decomposing the Price-Earnings Ratio," *Journal of Asset Management*, 6(6): 456–69.

BARNEY, J. B. (1997). *Gaining and Sustaining Competitive Advantage*. New York: Addison-Wesley.

BENDER, R., and WARD, K. (2002). *Corporate Financial Strategy*, 2nd edition. Oxford: Butterworth-Heinemann.

BERRY, R. H., REBER, B., and TOMS, S. (2005). "Firm Resources and Quality Signalling: Evidence from UK Initial Public Offerings," *Applied Financial Economics*, 15: 575–86.

BONN, I., and PETTIGREW, A. (2009). "Towards a Dynamic Theory of Boards: An Organisational Life Cycle Approach," *Journal of Management and Organization*, 15(1): 2–16.

CASSON, M. (1982). *The Entrepreneur: An Economic Theory*. Oxford: Robertson.

CASTANIAS, R., and HELFAT, C. (2001). "The Managerial Rents Model: Theory and Empirical Analysis," *Journal of Management*, 27: 661–78.

CHANDLER, A. (1962). *Strategy and Structure: Chapters in the History of the Industrial Enterprise*. Cambridge, MA: Harvard University Press.

—— (1977). *The Visible Hand*. Cambridge, MA: Harvard University Press.

—— (1990). *Scale and Scope: The Dynamics of Industrial Capitalism*. Cambridge, MA: Belknap.

CHANEY, P. K., DEVINNEY, T. M., WINER, R. S. (1991). "The Impact of New Product Introductions on the Market Value of Firms," *Journal of Business*, 64(4): 573–610.

CUMMING, D., SIEGEL, D., and WRIGHT, M. (2007). "Private Equity, Leveraged Buy-Outs and Governance," *Journal of Corporate Finance*, 13(4): 439–60.

DAVIES, J. R., HILLIER, D., and McCOLGAN, P. (2005). "Ownership Structure, Managerial Behaviour and Corporate Value," *Journal of Corporate Finance*, 11: 645–60.

FILATOTCHEV, I., and TOMS, S. (2003). "Corporate Governance, Strategy and Survival in a Declining Industry: A Study of Lancashire Textile Companies," *Journal of Management Studies*, 40(4): 895–920.

—— —— (2006). "Corporate Governance and Financial Constraints on Strategic Turnarounds," *Journal of Management Studies*, 43(3): 407–33.

—— WRIGHT, M., and ARBERK, M. (2005). "Venture Capitalists, Syndication and Governance in Initial Public Offerings," in I. Filatotchev and M. Wright (eds.), *The Life Cycle of Corporate Governance*, Cheltenham: Edward Elgar.

—— TOMS, S., and WRIGHT, M. (2006). "The Firm's Strategic Dynamics and the CG Life Cycle," *International Journal of Managerial Finance*, 2(4): 256–79.

FLIGSTEIN, N. (1990). *The Transformation of Corporate Control*. Cambridge, MA: Harvard University Press.

GEORGE, G., WIKLUND, J., and ZAHRA, S. A. (2005). "Ownership and the Internationalization of the Small Firm," *Journal of Management*, 31(2): 210–33.

GOERGEN, M., and RENNEBOOG, L. (2005). "Insider Retention and Long Run Performance in German and UK IPOs," in I. Filatotchev and M. Wright (eds.), *The Life Cycle of Corporate Governance*. Cheltenham: Edward Elgar.

GOODSTEIN, J. G., and BOEKER, W. B. (1991). "Turbulence at the Top: A New Perspective on Governance Structure Changes and Strategic Change," *Academy of Management Journal*, 34(2): 306–30.

GREEN, E. (1988). "Rentiers versus Producers? The Political Economy of the Bimetallic Controversy, c.1880–98," *English Historical Review*, 103: 588–612.

HANLEY, K. W. (1993). "The Underpricing of Initial Public Offerings and the Partial Adjustment Phenomenon," *Journal of Financial Economics*, 34(2): 231–50.

HALEBLIAN, J., DEVERS, C. E., MCNAMARA, G., CARPENTER, M. A., and DAVISON, R. B. (2009). "Taking Stock of What We Know about Mergers and Acquisitions: A Review and Research Agenda," *Journal of Management*, 35(3): 469–502.

HAYEK, F. A. (1937). "Economics and Knowledge," *Economica*, 4(13): 33–54.

HAYNES, M., THOMPSON, S., and WRIGHT, M. (2005). "Divestment, Remuneration and Corporate Governance in Mature Firms," in I. Filatotchev and M. Wright (eds.), *The Life Cycle of Corporate Governance*, Cheltenham: Edward Elgar.

HELLMAN, T., and PURI, M. (2000). "The Interaction between Product Market and Financing Strategy: The Role of Venture Capital," *Review of Financial Studies*, 13(4): 959–84.

HILL, C. W. L., and SNELL, S. A. (1988). "External Control, Corporate Strategy and Firm Performance in Research Intensive Industries," *Strategic Management Journal*, 9(6): 577–90.

HITT, M. A., IRELAND, R. D., and HOSKISSON, R. E. (2003). *Strategic Management: Competitiveness and Globalization*. Minneapolis and New York: West Publishing Company.

HOSKISSON, R. E., HITT, M. A., JOHNSON, R. A., and GROSSMAN, W. (2000). "Conflicting Voices: The Effects of Institutional Ownership Heterogeneity and Internal Governance on Corporate Innovation Strategies," *Academy of Management Journal*, 45(4): 697–716.

JAIN, B. A., and KINI, O. (1995). "Venture Capitalist Participation and the Post-Issue Operating Performance of IPO Firms," *Managerial and Decision Economics*, 16(6): 593–606.

JENKINSON, T., and JONES, H. (2009). "Competitive IPOs," *European Financial Management*, 15(4): 733–56.

JENSEN, M. C. (1993). "The Modern Industrial Revolution, Exit and the Failure of Internal Control Systems," *Journal of Finance*, 48(3): 831–80.

KEASEY, K., and WRIGHT, M. (1993). "Corporate Governance: Issues and Concerns," *Accounting and Business Research*, 23: 301–13.

—— SHORT, H., and WATSON, R. (1994). "Directors' Ownership and the Performance of Small and Medium Sizes Firms in the UK," *Small Business Economics*, 6: 225–36.

KIRZNER, I. (1979). *Perception, Opportunity and Profit: Studies in the Theory of Entrepreneurship*. Chicago: University of Chicago Press.

—— (1989). *Discovery, Capitalism and Distributive Justice*. Oxford: Blackwell.

—— (1997). "Entrepreneurial Discovery and the Competitive Market Process: An Austrian Approach," *Journal of Economic Literature*, 35(1): 60–85.

KLEPPER, S. (1996). "Entry, Exit, Growth, and Innovation over the Product Life Cycle," *The American Economic Review*, 86(3): 562–83.

KNIGHT, F. H. (1921). *Risk, Uncertainty and Profit*. New York: Hart, Schaffner and Marx.

LAZONICK, W. (1991). *Business Organisation and the Myth of the Market Economy*. Cambridge: Cambridge University Press.

LOUGHRAN, T., and RITTER, J. R. (2002). "Why Don't Issuers Get Upset about Leaving Money on the Table in IPOs?" *The Review of Financial Studies*, 15(2): 413–33.

MARSHALL, A. (1890). *Principles of Economics*. London, Macmillan.

MCCLOSKEY, D., and SANDBERG, L. (1972). "From Damnation to Redemption: Judgements on the Late Victorian Entrepreneur," *Explorations in Economic History*, 9(2): 89–108.

MISES, L. VON (1949). *Human Action, a Treatise on Economics*. London: William Hodge and Company Limited.

PENROSE, E. (1959). *The Theory of the Growth of the Firm*. Oxford: Oxford University Press.

PHAN, P. H., WRIGHT, M., UCBASARAN, D., and TAN, W.-L. (2009). "Corporate Entrepreneurship: Current Research and Future Directions," *Journal of Business Venturing*, 24: 197–205.

Renneboog, L., Simons, T., and Wright, M. (2007). "Why do Public Firms Go Private in the UK?" *Journal of Corporate Finance*, 13(4): 591–628.

Robbins, K. D., and Pearce, J. A (1992). "Turnaround: Retrenchment and Recovery," *Strategic Management Journal*, 13: 287–309.

Schumpeter, J. A. (1943). *Capitalism, Socialism and Democracy*. New York: Harper.

Short, H., and Keasey, K. (1999). "Managerial Ownership and the Performance of Firms: Evidence from the UK," *Journal of Corporate Finance*, 5: 79–101.

Teece, D. (1980). "Economies of Scope and the Scope of the Enterprise," *Journal of Economic Behavior and Organization*, 1: 223–47.

—— Pisano, G., and Sheun, A. (1997). "Dynamic Capabilities and Strategic Management," *Strategic Management Journal*, 18: 509–33.

Thompson, S., and Wright, M. (1995). "Corporate Governance: The Role of Restructuring Transactions," *Economic Journal*, 105: 690–703.

Toms, S. (2006). "Accounting for Entrepreneurship: A Knowledge-Based View of the Firm," *Critical Perspectives on Accounting*, 17 (2–3): 336–57.

—— (2010). "Value, Profit and Risk: Accounting and the Resource-Based View of the Firm," *Accounting, Auditing and Accountability Journal*, 23(5): 647–70.

—— (2011). "Turnaround at William Morrison Supermarkets PLC, 2004–2007", Working Paper, University of York.

—— and Filatotchev, I. (2004). "Corporate Governance, Business Strategy and the Dynamics of Networks: A Theoretical Model and Application to the British Cotton Industry, 1830–1980," *Organization Studies*, 25(4): 629–51.

—— and Wright M. (2002). "Corporate Governance, Strategy and Structure in British Business History, 1950–2000," *Business History*, 44(3): 91–124.

—— —— (2005). "Corporate Governance, Strategy and Refocusing: US and British Comparatives, 1950–2000," *Business History*, 47(2): 267–95.

Tricker, R. (1984). *Corporate Governance*. Vermont: Gower.

Weir, C., Laing, D., and Wright, M. (2005). "Corporate Governance and the Public to Private Threshold," in I. Filatotchev and M. Wright (eds.), *The Life Cycle of Corporate Governance*, Cheltenham: Edward Elgar.

William Morrison Supermarkets plc (2004). "Annual Report and Financial Statements." Available at <http://www.morrisons.co.uk/Documents/AnnRet_FinState2004.pdf>.

Wright, M., Chiplin, B., Thompson, S., and Robbie, K. (1990). "Management Buy-Outs, Trade Unions and Employee Ownership," *Industrial Relations Journal*, 21(2): 137–46.

—— Thompson, S. Chiplin, B., and Robbie, K. (1991). *Buy-Ins and Buy-Outs: New Strategies in Corporate Management*. London: Graham and Trotman.

Zahra, S. A., and Filatotchev, I. (2004). "Governance of the Entrepreneurial Threshold Firm: A Knowledge Based Perspective," *Journal of Management Studies*, 41: 885–98.

—— and Pearce, J. A. (1989). "Boards of Directors and Corporate Financial Performance: A Review and Integrative Model," *Journal of Management*, 15: 291–334.

—— Gedajlovic, E., Neubaum, D. O., and Shulman, J. M. (2009). "A Typology of Social Entrepreneurs: Motives, Search Processes and Ethical Challenges," *Journal of Business Venturing*, 24(5): 519–32.

CHAPTER 17

CORPORATE GOVERNANCE IN HIGH-TECH FIRMS

FABIO BERTONI, MASSIMO G. COLOMBO,
AND ANNALISA CROCE

Introduction

THE growth of capitalist economies is significantly determined by their ability to foster innovation (Baumol, 2002), which, in turn, is essentially linked to high-tech investments (Mansfield, 1972; Nadiri, 1993; Berndt and Morrison, 1995). Economics and management scholars agree that many elements influence the innovation performance of high-tech firms, such as size, profitability, human and social capital, organizational structure and learning, access to financing, market structure and competitive pressures, appropriability regime, and intellectual property rights framework (e.g. Cohen and Levin, 1989; Cohen, 1995). It is only recently, however, that *corporate governance* has been included in this list. Several reasons may explain this prolonged exclusion. By its nature innovation is elusive and there is no universally accepted theoretical framework that encompasses all aspects involved in firms' innovation. Similarly, a precise definition of what should be considered high-tech or low-tech is also sometimes slippery (Von Tunzelmann and Acha, 2005). Corporate governance is also a blurred field of research and the notion of what constitutes corporate governance varies enormously from one author to the other. Most importantly, the traditional approach to corporate governance is relatively restrictive regarding which mechanisms fall within the domain of corporate governance and what objectives they pursue. Interestingly, the instruments and objectives of corporate governance according to its most traditional reading are those that are less relevant for high-tech companies (Belloc, 2012).

The narrow interpretation of corporate governance typically focuses on instruments, such as managerial accountability and board monitoring (Bitar and Somers, 2003). These instruments are used by financiers to assure themselves a return to their investment (Shleifer and Vishny, 1997). According to this perspective, corporate governance has a "value-protection" role: its objective is to avoid (or reduce) the misalignment of objectives between managers and shareholders (and other stakeholders), resulting for instance in underprovision of effort, extraction of private benefits, or even the misappropriation (tunneling) of firm's resources. In high-tech companies uncertainty is high, the time lag between investments and returns is long, and the real-option component of investment decisions makes it very hard to ascertain, even ex post, how effective these decisions have been. As we will show later in this chapter in more detail, these characteristics reduce dramatically the effectiveness of corporate governance as a means of value protection. This engenders substantial agency costs for external investors that, in turn, translate into a high cost of external capital for high-tech companies and under-investment in R&D (Carpenter and Petersen, 2002; Hall, 2002).

Recently, the narrow value-protection view of corporate governance has been complemented by a broader perspective according to which corporate governance includes a larger set of instruments and serves wider objectives. Proponents of this view have argued that corporate governance is not only aimed at protecting investors but contributes to creating value for the company (Filatotchev et al., 2006). Under this "value-creation" perspective, corporate governance instruments may constitute a very important source of valuable resources for companies. An emblematic example of this shift in perspective is the consideration of the role of the board of directors. In a value-protection perspective, the board is considered the ultimate instrument for monitoring managerial behavior. A board member is then evaluated in terms of her ability to keep the management accountable for its decisions. The value-creation view emphasizes the additional knowledge, reputation, social capital, and network of contacts that a company obtains through having particular individuals as board members. The two perspectives are likely to disagree about which members a company should wish to have on its board.

What is most interesting for the sake of this chapter is that the more innovative a company, the less effective are corporate governance mechanisms in terms of value protection. At the same time, however, these mechanisms become more and more important in terms of their value-creation potential. The relatively little attention that corporate governance has traditionally received as one of the ingredients that contribute to the success of high-tech companies can then be explained by the fact that the traditional view on corporate governance neglects exactly those aspects that make corporate governance useful for innovation in the first place.

The above discussion suggests that, in order to understand the role of corporate governance in high-tech companies, the broadest possible view should be taken. We will distinguish between three main dimensions of a firm's corporate governance system: ownership structure, internal governance mechanisms, and external governance mechanisms. Ownership structure is sometimes not included within the perimeter of corporate governance on its narrowest view, nor is it included among the internal mechanisms. However, in high-tech firms ownership structure plays a very different role than all other governance mechanisms and this suggests that we treat it separately. Internal and external governance mechanisms are distinguished on the basis of the degree of control that the company has over them: internal mechanisms are chosen by the company, while external mechanisms are exogenous. We will focus on three internal mechanisms that show distinct characteristics in high-tech companies: the board of directors, executive compensation, and capital structure. Among external mechanisms, we will focus on investor protection, the development of capital markets, and the market for corporate control.

The rest of the chapter is organized as follows. The next section will discuss issues regarding the ownership structure of high-tech companies. The following section discusses internal mechanisms of corporate governance. The section after that will deal with external instruments of corporate governance, and the final section will present some concluding remarks.

Ownership Structure

The standard theoretical framework used to understand the issue of ownership in a high-tech company is proposed by Aghion and Tirole (1994). The fundamental aspect of their model is that they distinguish the role played by different parties in the development of innovation. First, they distinguish between the producer and the user of innovation. The producer holds the intellectual capital needed to develop the innovation and obtains the necessary financial resources from the users. The exact nature of innovation is ill-defined ex ante and the parties cannot contract for delivery of a specific innovation. In this incomplete contracting framework, ownership determines who gets residual control rights over the innovation (Grossman and Hart, 1986). Ownership structure is determined so as to best protect the two parties' specific investments in the relationship. Property rights are given to the producer of innovation when it is more important to encourage its effort than to boost the users' investment. More interestingly, Aghion and Tirole (1994) extend the Grossman and Hart (1986) framework by introducing a third party into the model: investors. Like users, investors may provide finance to develop an innovation but, unlike them, they make no use of the innovation themselves. In other words, investors are pure financial actors. Aghion and Tirole (1994) show that it may be strictly optimal for users to give property rights to the producer and to demand co-financing by an investor. The presence of the purely financial player reduces the conflict of interests between producers and users, creating a socially preferable outcome.

What is essential for our purposes is that this theoretical framework shows that the ownership structure of a high-tech company should respond to the characteristics of the innovative process, and that parties that are endowed with (or set out to develop) a crucial resource to be combined with finance in order to achieve innovation should have a concentrated ownership position. Moreover, institutional investors may play a role in arbitrating conflicts among other owners. In summary: both ownership concentration and owners' identity are important in determining the innovation output. This gives rise to two streams of empirical literature that we briefly review in the next part of the section. The first subsection analyzes the link between ownership concentration and firm innovation. The second subsection studies the relationship between the identity of firm owners and innovation.

Ownership Concentration

Early studies on the link between ownership concentration and innovation have focused on large US companies and have generally found that the relationship is indeed as expected: the more a company is innovative, the more its ownership is concentrated. For instance, Hill and Snell (1988) find a positive correlation between ownership concentration and the level of corporate R&D spending per employee. They argue, along the lines of agency theory, that managers are more risk averse than investors (having their reputation at stake, besides the money invested in the company) and this results in lower R&D spending in the absence of financial blockholders. Francis and Smith (1995) is another classic study of the relationship between ownership concentration and innovation. The authors use patent awards as a measure of innovation and find that firms with more dispersed ownership have lower patenting activity. Interestingly, they also analyze the mode of innovation, and find that firms with dispersed ownership are more likely to grow by acquisition than by internal development of innovations.

It is important to highlight that shareholders with concentrated positions not only have their voice more easily heard by managers, but that it is also more difficult for them to exit from the investment (Hirschman, 1970). This tradeoff between liquidity and incentives (Aghion et al., 2004) becomes particularly important in high-tech firms. The difficulty of exiting may favor relational specific investments that characterize innovative companies (Mayer, 1997). This is consistent with evidence provided by Miozzo and Dewick (2002), who show that firm-specific investments are more easily financed when the ownership structure is difficult to "undo," as when blockholders and cross-holdings are present. This is also closely related to the idea that internal capital markets in business groups or conglomerates may reduce financial constraints for innovative projects (Stein, 1997).

However, the literature is not unanimous in supporting the view that ownership concentration always has a positive effect on innovation. In fact, while, as discussed above, ownership concentration increases the incentive for incumbent shareholders to exert effort and make relation-specific investments, it may reduce, in a dynamic framework, the incentives for small investors to participate in follow-on rounds of financing, thus increasing the cost of capital for the company. This is the basic argument, for instance, of Battaggion and Tajoli (2001), who argue that the large bargaining power of blockholders reduces their capabilities to make credible commitments to small outside investors. This argument is also in line with the literature on the horizontal agency costs that arise from opportunistic principals who, as controlling blockholders, may have conflicts of interest with minority shareholders (Claessens et al., 2000; Faccio and Lang, 2001). The horizontal agency costs of concentrated ownership may explain the results of Smith et al. (2004), who find that, among Danish firms, more significant innovative activity is observed when ownership is most dispersed. A similar result is found by Ortega-Argilés et al. (2005) for a sample of Spanish companies. The idea that beyond a certain limit ownership concentration is detrimental to innovation is also consistent with the findings of Li et al. (2010). The authors analyze a sample of Chinese companies and identify an inverse U-shaped relationship between ownership concentration and innovative activity.

The fact that, outside the US, the link between ownership concentration and innovation seems weaker may be explained by the fact that, on average, ownership is more dispersed in the US than elsewhere (La Porta et al., 1999). Therefore, what is a "high" level of concentration in a sample of US companies could actually be a "low" level of concentration elsewhere (see also the section on investor protection and capital market development later in the chapter). Cultural factors may also play a role. Lee and O'Neill (2003) compare the relationship between ownership structure, R&D investments, and goal alignment in the US and Japan. They observe that Japanese culture creates conditions that favor steward-like relations more than agency relations. In a stewardship setting, increasing ownership concentration does not affect the level of R&D investments since agents do not need explicit incentives to pursue what they perceive as the common good.

Finally, extreme care should be paid in taking the results that correlate ownership concentration and innovative output as indicative of a causal link. As shown by Cho (1998), ownership and value are endogenously determined and this also affects the relationship between ownership and innovation (that is in turn affected by firm value). Using simple an ordinary least squares (OLS) regression on a sample of large US companies, Cho (1998) finds a non-linear relationship between ownership concentration and R&D spending. However, when controlling for endogeneity, the relationship disappears. In other words, the mere fact that we observe a (non-linear) relationship between ownership concentration and innovation does not mean that, for a given company, an increase in ownership concentration would cause an increase in its innovative output.

The Identity of Owners

In the previous section we have shown that the highest level of innovation is observed in correspondence with an intermediate level of ownership concentration. Does it matter who holds these concentrated positions in the equity of high-tech firms? From a theoretical standpoint, we have already seen that, in a an incomplete contracting framework à la Grossman and Hart (1986), the identity of the owner matters and it is actually more important than the concentration of ownership itself. We will focus on four leading types of shareholders: managers, institutional investors, venture capitalists, and the government.

First, let us consider management ownership. As for most corporate governance mechanisms, the traditional theoretical approach to management ownership is agency theory. The management ownership structure can be seen as the outcome of the balancing between benefits and costs. The benefits of management ownership concentration derive from a reduction in agency costs: in the Jensen and Meckling (1976) framework, ownership provides "lazy managers" with an incentive to exert effort. Management ownership concentration can also limit the manager-specific entrenching investments (Shleifer and Vishny, 1989). The costs of internal ownership concentration derive from the lack of diversification in a manager's portfolio and, after a certain threshold, by the entrenchment of the management team (Morck et al., 1988). In high-tech companies, both benefits and costs of management ownership become more acute. Because of the innovative nature of their business, high-tech companies are characterized by high asymmetries in information, which make agency costs more problematic (Holmstrom, 1989). But they are also characterized by very uncertain returns, forcing managers with large stakes to bear a substantial burden of idiosyncratic risk (Hall and Woodward, 2008). So while information asymmetries increase the benefits of management ownership concentration, uncertainty increases its cost and it is hard to conclude which of the two effects will dominate.

Baysinger et al. (1991) examine R&D investments in US companies and distinguish between two types of owners: individual and institutional. They find that ownership concentration by large institutional investors favors corporate R&D spending. Their interpretation of this result builds upon the superior ability of large institutional investors to diversify their investments. In other words, to the extent to which the risk aversion of owner-managers is what holds back innovation, institutional investors are in a better position than individuals to solve the problem. Aghion et al. (2010) argue that institutional investors may also contribute to firms' innovative activity by reducing managers' risk aversion. Their theoretical model is built upon the classic model of career concerns by Holmstrom (1982): performance is perceived by the market as a signal of managerial quality. This motivates managers to exert effort, but, at the same time, increases their risk aversion. Large institutional owners, however, have the opportunity to observe how managers behave and, hence, will rely less on performance-related signals. Accordingly, managers of firms with institutional owners will be less inclined to under-invest in risky projects.

The literature also shows that institutional investors are not all the same. One of the reasons why institutional investors have a different impact on firm innovation is that they differ in terms of their investment objectives. This is clearly shown by Tribo et al. (2007), who find that bank ownership negatively influences R&D spending. Normally banks are not only shareholders but also creditors of the firms, making them more risk averse. Conversely, a substantial positive effect is associated with ownership by industrial corporations. Again, the explanation should be sought in the strategic objectives of this type of shareholder. The role played by strategic objectives is typically negative for banks (i.e. the risk exposure inherited from their credit position), but may be positive for non-financial corporations, which may use inter-corporate investments to open a window on promising new technologies (Dushnitsky and Lenox, 2005).

Differences among institutional investors may also translate into a different mode of innovation by high-tech firms. Hoskisson et al. (2002) compare two types of investors with a markedly different investment horizon: public pension funds and professional investment funds. While the objective of public pension funds is to achieve above-average long-term performance, professional investment funds are mostly interested in showing satisfying short-term performance, because of the short-term orientation on the part of fund managers. These different objectives are reflected in a preference for different types of innovative activity: professional investment fund managers prefer acquiring external innovation and public pension fund managers prefer internal innovation (that is on average riskier and takes longer to achieve commercialization).

A category of investors that has received specific attention from scholars for its impact on innovation is venture capital (VC). Venture capital is a financial intermediary specialized in investments in non-listed companies. Venture capital plays an important role in shaping the corporate governance of portfolio companies (see Chapter 23 in this *Handbook* for an in-depth analysis of this issue). Interestingly, venture capital can be considered as a provider of value-enhancing services that takes an equity share in the company more than as a mere provider of financing (Casamatta, 2003). Non-financial value-enhancing services include advice, professionalization, access to a vast network of contacts, and stock market orientation (e.g. Hellman and Puri, 2000; Hsu, 2004). The combination of financial and non-financial resources should improve the innovative performance of high-tech firms. The empirical literature is generally supportive of this claim. Kortum and Lerner (2000) test various specifications of a patent production function on US manufacturing industry-level data and find that venture capital is associated with a substantial increase in patenting. The evidence on the positive relation between venture capital financing and innovation is confirmed at country level (Popov and Roosenboom, 2009), industry level (Hirukawa and Ueda, 2011), and portfolio firm level (Hellman and Puri, 2000; Baum and Silverman, 2004; Bertoni et al., 2010). More recently, it has been shown that different types of venture capital investors produce a different impact on firm innovation performance, as a consequence of their different objectives (see e.g. Chemmanur et al. 2011)., Moreover, the combination of different types of venture capital investors may prove to be optimal thanks to the combination of their different resources and capabilities (Bertoni and Tykvová, 2012).

Finally, let us consider the role of the government as a shareholder in innovative firms. While the impact of state ownership on firm economic performance is a widely debated issue (e.g. Megginson and Netter, 2001), the link with innovation has been relatively neglected. Shleifer (1998) argues that only private ownership gives sufficient incentives to pursue innovation. However, Schmitz (2001) shows that private ownership could lead to excessive myopia and incentives to cut costs rather than invest in long-term projects. The empirical analysis of Munari et al. (2002) somehow combines these two perspectives. Their study shows that privatization processes are followed by a decrease in R&D investments. However, the aim of the privatized company ceases to be the generation of new knowledge for the general interest, and refocuses toward the creation of value for company's shareholders. As a consequence, privatization processes entail a shift toward more applied and business-oriented projects, and a complete reorganization of external collaborations.

Internal Governance Mechanisms

This section is devoted to the impact of internal governance mechanisms on high-tech companies. Specifically, we will focus on three of the most important mechanisms that play a specific role in high-tech companies: the board of directors, executive compensation, and capital structure. Following the discussion in the introduction to the chapter, for each mechanism we will contrast the prediction of the narrow view of corporate governance with a broader perspective of corporate governance as a means of value creation.

Board of Directors

In an agency framework, the board of directors is responsible for controlling, evaluating, and rewarding management performance (Eisenhardt, 1989). The board is an endogenously determined institution that seeks to ensure that shareholders' interests are pursued by managers (Hermalin and Weisbach, 2001). The most important characteristics of the board are its size and composition. Size refers to the number of directors, while composition refers to the distinction between inside board members (the executives of the firm on whose board they sit) and outside board members (who represent owners in board decisions). In high-tech companies, where technology is more complex and assets are less tangible, the monitoring role of the board is more complex and coordination costs are higher, with the result that the board of directors should be smaller and dominated by insiders (Raheja, 2005). This is consistent, for instance, with the findings by Yermack (1996), who shows that board size is negatively related to a firm's growth opportunities (measured by Tobin's Q).

The composition of the board may affect the nature of the innovative process. Hoskisson et al. (2002) show that the presence of outside board members tilts innovation toward acquisition rather than internal development. Compared to insiders, outside board members typically have more limited access to information on and knowledge of internal operations. Accordingly, they are at a comparative disadvantage when evaluating the performance of internal R&D and will favor acquisitions in extant technologies instead of performing internal R&D. Consistently with the view that inside board members have an advantage compared to outsiders in dealing with uncertainty, Baysinger et al. (1991) find that the percentage of inside board members on the company's board is positively related to R&D spending.

However, a different conclusion can be drawn if one considers that, as claimed by resource dependence scholars, the board is not only a monitoring mechanism but also a source of valuable additional resources for the company, including advising, legitimization, and networking (e.g. Daily and Schwenk, 1996; Westphal, 1999; Hillman et al., 2000). These functions, which make the appointment of outside board members especially beneficial, are particularly important for high-tech firms. In particular, their importance explains the prominent role of star scientists as board members. These individuals play an advising and signaling role (Lacetera, 2001; Catherine et al., 2004; Higgins et al., 2008), but may not excel at monitoring. Several studies suggest that star scientists represent a key factor in connecting high-tech firms with external key actors, because of their links with academia and their experience of cooperation (Gambardella, 1995; Zucker et al., 1995). Catherine et al. (2004) show that scientists on the board constitute a link with the academic world and with major industrial groups. Bjørnåli and Gulbrandsen (2010) also evidence the importance of social networks in the process of board formation in academic spinoffs. It is also important to acknowledge that the extent to which a company is able to benefit from the value-creating potential of the board is crucially determined by the firm's absorptive capacity: boards and absorptive capacity complement (and sometimes substitute for) each other in fueling corporate entrepreneurship (Zahra et al., 2009).

The effectiveness of the board of directors in monitoring and providing resources is affected by several contingencies. Hillman and Dalziel (2003) argue that board dependence (i.e. the degree to which insider and outsider board members with ties to the current CEO or organization dominate the board) and the type of compensation received by board members are two key moderating factors. Equity-linked pay has a positive impact on the incentives for board members to both monitor and provide resources. Board dependence, instead, has a negative effect on monitoring, but a positive effect on the provision of resources. In fact, while connections to the current CEO/organization may be a disincentive to monitor, they may be an incentive to provide resources to the firm: directors who are connected to the firm through family relationships or as stakeholders often have more of an incentive to provide advice and counsel, provide connections to other organizations, encourage communication flows, and act to improve the external image of the firm (Dalton et al., 1998; Westphal, 1999). This suggests that particular care should be taken in designing the composition of the board of directors in high-tech companies. Another crucial moderating factor is ownership structure, as is argued by Clarysse et al. (2007). They examine the complementarity of skills between the board of directors and the management team, and find that firms that have powerful external shareholders (e.g. venture capital-backed companies) are more likely to develop boards with complementary skills to those of the founding team. Conversely, firms where the founding team has autonomy in composing their own board tend to look for outside board members with similar human capital. Other studies focus on the relationship between the board of directors and the presence of external investors. Catherine et al. (2004) show that the human capital and the degree of involvement with the board of directors are central in firms invested by venture capital. In particular, the scientific visibility of academics involved in a start-up's board signals the firm's quality and, thus, increases the firm's scientific credibility and its ability to attract funding. Sapienza and Gupta (1994) show that, in venture-backed firms, equity stakes of both inside and outside board members are likely to be substantial. The role itself of the board of directors changes when strong shareholders, as venture capitalists, are present. In particular, venture capitalists' behavioral response in high uncertainty conditions is to increase their interaction with the CEOs of their portfolio companies. Broughman (2010) argues that the role of independent board members in a start-up firm invested by venture capitalists is also to "arbitrate" disputes between venture capital investors and entrepreneurs, as the presence of an unbiased third party can prevent opportunistic behavior that would occur if the firm were controlled by its entrepreneur or VC investor.

Executive Pay

In an agency relationship, high-powered incentives linking compensation to firm performance can be used to realign the agent's objectives with those of the firm (Holmstrom, 1989). However, with greater uncertainty, high-powered incentives become a less efficient mechanism to alleviate agency problems (Prendergast, 1999). As high-tech companies exhibit above-average uncertainty, we should expect them to use compensation packages for top managers with below-average pay-for-performance. There is substantial empirical evidence supporting these theoretical predictions. Beatty and Zajac (1994) show that executive compensation is seriously limited as a solution to agency problems due to the risk aversion of managers and that this problem is particularly acute in riskier firms. Wright et al. (2002) observe that while at low levels of pay-performance sensitivity, high-powered incentives may prompt risk-taking behaviors, risk-reducing strategies are adopted by managers exposed to higher levels of equity-based remuneration. To this extent, particular attention should be paid to the type of equity-linked incentive that is used. Smith and Stulz (1985) and Hirshleifer and Suh (1992) highlight that compensation in the form of stock options will lead managers to riskier behavior, whereas restricted stock will most likely lead to less risky choices.

Clearly, the fact that the equilibrium level of pay-performance sensitivity is lower in high-tech companies does by no means imply that incentives play no role. Cho (1992) finds that various measures of management stockholding are associated with a higher ratio of R&D expenditures to sales. Interestingly, Cho (1992) suggests a second channel through which straight equity incentives may influence risk taking: the larger is managerial stockholding, the higher will be its voting power and the ability of the manager to guarantee long-term employment. Lerner and Wulf (2006) find that executive's pay-performance sensitivity mitigates the tendency of executives to extract private benefits (e.g. funding of "pet" research projects).

An aspect of particular interest in high-tech companies is the structure of the remuneration system and, specifically, the extent to which pay should be linked to short-term or long-term performance. Lerner and Wulf (2006) suggest that long-term incentives should be preferred since decisions by R&D executives affect outcomes with a considerable time lag. They show that long-term incentives (e.g. stock options with a vesting period) are associated with better patent production (in terms of number, relevance, and originality). Wright et al. (2000) highlight that a major mistake in the design of executive compensation packages is to tie compensation to short-term financial performance. In fact, executive compensation based on short-term financial performance leads managers to focus on short-term activities, thus hampering R&D (Honoré et al., 2011).

Short-term incentives, however, may still play a role in high-tech companies. Using a resource-based view of the firm, Balkin et al. (2000) argue that it may be difficult to disentangle the short- and long-term implications of innovation so that both short- and long- term incentives must be given. The metric of the incentives will however be different: over the short term innovations should not be valued using financial performance, in line with the arguments illustrated above, but based on their technical merits. Long-term incentives may instead use market-based performance measures based on the assumption that successful innovation will be favorably reflected in firms' stock price. Consistently with this argument, Balkin et al. (2000) show that in high-tech firms CEO's short-term compensation is related to innovation over and above what could be expected on the basis of financial performance.

Manso (2011) highlights that standard pay-for-performance contracts used to induce effort or avoid tunneling are unlikely to foster innovation. Standard pay-for-performance schemes punish failures and may have an adverse effect on innovation, which inherently involves the exploration of new approaches that are likely to fail. Manso (2011) argues that the optimal incentive scheme to motivate innovation should exhibit tolerance for early failure and reward for long-term success. Commitment to a long-term compensation plan, job security, and timely feedback on performance are essential to motivate innovation. Conceptually, the most interesting aspect is that compensation depends not only on total performance, but also on the path of performance.

Finally, Wasserman (2006) highlights that, while agency theory might be the correct perspective to build an executive remuneration package in large companies, it could be misleading in small high-tech ventures. This is particularly true regarding the role of founders, whose behavior is psychologically more like that of stewards than agents. Wasserman (2006) suggests that stewardship theory helps explain why founders are willing to accept lower compensation than non-founders: founders are more intrinsically motivated and derive more non-monetary benefits from working in the companies they started.

Capital Structure

According to agency theory, debt makes misuse of resources more difficult, and puts a disciplinary pressure on managers (Jensen, 1986). In high-tech firms, this classic argument in favor of leverage is likely to be thrown out (Hall and Lerner, 2010). There are a number of reasons why debt is ill-suited for innovation (Hall, 2002; Gugler, 2003). In R&D-intensive industries, assets tend to be intangible and highly specific. This makes bankruptcy a very costly process in high-tech companies (Alderson and Betker, 1995 and 1996). More generally, asset specificity discourages the use of collateralized debt (Berger and Udell, 1998).

The empirical evidence confirms that limiting free cash-flow in high-tech firms is one of the least desirable methods of reducing agency costs. Baysinger and Hoskisson (1989) show a strong negative relationship between debt and R&D spending. Similar results are also found by Balakrishnan and Fox (1993). Chung et al. (1998) find that large debt in high-tech firms determines lower market valuation. In addition they find that, for high-tech companies, financial slack is favorably received by the stock market. Markman et al. (2001) and Hoskisson et al. (2002) find that debt not only tilts managers away from adopting strategies for innovation, but also leads to a short-term focus (see also Hall, 1990).

This notwithstanding, high-tech companies are sometimes engaged in operations involving a substantial increase in leverage. Buyouts are the most interesting example for their role in both leverage and governance (Cumming et al., 2007). These deals are normally conducted by private equity funds and involve companies in a later stage of development than venture capital investments. Even though private equity and venture capital investors share a similar limited-partnership structure, their role in the governance of portfolio firms is dramatically different due to the different phases in these firms' life cycle (Filatotchev et al., 2006). Most notably, while venture capital deals are normally associated with a decrease in firms' financial constraints, buyouts increase dramatically the leverage of portfolio companies, increasing the sensitivity of their investments to current cash flows (Bertoni et al., forthcoming). However, buyout targets are often under-leveraged and underperforming and face substantial restructuring after the deal (Tykvová and Borell, 2012). As a consequence, the net effect of increased leverage and improved productivity on a firm's investments is not obvious. Smith (1990) investigates changes in firm performance after a buyout and finds a sharp decline in ex post R&D expenditures. Similar results are found by Long and Ravenscraft (1993) and Hoskisson et al. (1994). More recent papers, however, suggest that buyouts are often followed by restructuring and productivity improvements, which may improve R&D and innovation performance. Zahra (1995) finds that, after a buyout, companies enhance their R&D unit's size and capabilities. Wright et al. (2001) argue that buyouts may create entrepreneurial opportunities, leading to increased R&D activity. Bruining and Wright (2002) show that buyouts are followed by an increase in new product development. Lerner et al. (2011) find that after a buyout patents are of better quality (a higher number of citations) and are more concentrated in the most important and prominent areas of companies' high-tech portfolios. This evidence suggests a refocusing of R&D activity on a firm's core technologies, rather than a reduction in innovative activity. Similarly, Le Nadant and Perdreau (2012) find that innovation expenditure is similar in buyout targets and in a matched sample of companies. Interestingly, the authors find that after a buyout the type of innovation activity changes, with less disruptive innovation and more incremental, market-oriented innovation (e.g. design). Ughetto (2010) finds that the post-buyout innovation output of acquired companies is better if the bidder is not an independent investor, is specialized in the buyout stage, is a European investor, and devotes a large amount of capital to the deal.

EXTERNAL GOVERNANCE MECHANISMS

Innovative activity is influenced by a large number of dimensions that characterize the environment in which firms operate (for a review, see Fagerberg et al., 2005). For the sake of concision, we will focus here only on those environmental characteristics that are most distinctively linked with corporate governance. First we will examine the role of investor protection and capital market development on high-tech companies. We will then analyze a typical external corporate governance mechanism that has very specific features with respect to high-tech companies: the market for corporate control.

Investor Protection and Capital Market Development

Investor protection is the most typical aspect highlighted by the "law and finance" literature to characterize the institutional context of countries (La Porta et al., 1998). Investor protection affects the ability of firms to pursue innovative activity in three ways. The first and most obvious way is that, other things being equal, better investor protection reduces problems linked with asymmetries in information. This translates into lower cost of capital, especially for high-tech firms subject to capital rationing (Mayer, 2002). Second, poor investor protection at country level often translates into poor corporate governance at company level. In principle, one could argue that investor protection at country level is irrelevant since companies can add clauses to their charter or securities that protect investors. Klapper and Love (2004) show that this is definitely not the case: firms in countries with poor investor protection actually have worse corporate governance practices than firms in countries with good investor protection. Moreover, evidence from companies in the former Soviet Union during the transition suggests that firms may lag behind in adopting corporate governance practices after significant regulatory changes (Estrin and Wright, 2002). Third, poor investor protection translates into higher ownership concentration, which, beyond a certain limit, may be detrimental to innovation (see also the Ownership Concentration section in this chapter). In fact, with more concentrated ownership and reduced shareholder diversification, the cost of capital increases proportionally with uncertainty (Himmelberg et al., 2002). As the uncertainty of innovative activities is typically very high, the effects on firms' innovation are disproportionately negative, other things equal.

On a broader perspective, the literature suggests that other institutional factors relating notably to capital markets influence innovation activity. In particular, Carlin and Mayer (2000) relate the specialization of a country in R&D-intensive industries to the availability of equity finance. An illustrative example is the comparison between Germany, which has a large banking system, a two-tier board structure, and a civil law code, and the US, which has a large stock market, a unitary board, and a common law system. The rankings of industries by the intensity of patent registrations for Germany are almost inversely related to those for the US. Indeed, the existence of well-functioning capital markets, both pre- and post-initial public offering (IPO), is particularly important for high-tech companies (Mayer, 2002). In countries where capital markets are less developed, the gap between the costs of financing innovative investments from internal and external sources are higher and, as a consequence, firms in high-technology industries have to rely more on internal funds (Hall and Lerner, 2010). Stock markets play a particularly important role (Lazonick, 2007): they decrease the cost of capital by enabling pre-IPO investors to monetize their stakes, reduce agency costs by facilitating the use of equity-based compensation, and make the threat of hostile takeovers more credible (albeit this last factor is not particularly applicable to high-tech firms, as we will discuss in the next section).

The type of innovation to which firms tend to devote effort also depends on national structures of governance. Hall and Soskice (2001) distinguish between market and non-market forms of business coordination. Market forms of coordination (such as those in Anglo-Saxon economies) are characterized by liquid capital markets and flexible labor markets. Non-market forms of coordination (prevalent in continental Europe and Japan) have institutional structures that facilitate the solution of incomplete contracting dilemmas. The two forms of coordination differ in the extent to which they are effective in supporting radical or incremental innovation, based on the different asset specificity inherent in these two types of innovation activity. Market forms of coordination should better support radical innovation, which requires low asset specificity. Non-market forms of coordination should facilitate the development of highly specific assets, which characterizes incremental innovation. Hall and Soskice (2001) support this view, again, by comparing Germany with the US. Similar evidence is also found in other countries or time periods (Lehrer et al., 1999; Goyer, 2001; Casper and Matraves, 2003).

The Market for Corporate Control

In an agency theory framework, takeover pressure is a means of correcting managerial failure and provide a disciplining device (Scharfstein, 1988). Nevertheless, the effect of takeover pressure on high-tech companies is uncertain and takeovers are found to negatively affect long-term-oriented innovation strategies. Takeover pressure effects on innovation are of two types, both of which are generally deemed to negatively affect innovation. First, the possibility of a hostile takeover implies that stakeholders may not agree to long-term implicit contracts with shareholders that are needed to promote their relationship-specific capital investments (Shleifer and Summers, 1988). The explanation is that, once the incumbent manager is removed after a takeover, the bidder can renege on the existing implicit contracts and expropriate rent from stakeholders. Second, under a market-myopia hypothesis, managers may be concerned that low short-term profits increase the chance that a takeover will occur. Thus, risk-averse managers will focus on projects with short-term payoffs at the expense of long-term investments such as those required for innovation (Stein, 1988). According to these arguments, Johnson and Rao

(1997) suggest that the use of anti-takeover amendments could enable managers to focus on long-term business strategies, thereby favoring innovation. Consistently with this, empirical evidence by Pugh et al. (1999) shows an increase in R&D expenditure following the introduction of an anti-takeover amendment.

More recently, Sapra et al. (2009) suggest that the link between innovation and takeover pressure might be U-shaped. When takeover pressure is very low, the expected takeover premium and the expected loss of control benefits are both insignificant. Therefore, the manager chooses innovative projects because they have a higher unconditional expected payoff. Conversely, when takeover pressure is very high, regardless of the degree of innovation, the expected loss in control benefits is very high. Because the expected takeover premium increases with the degree of innovation, it is again optimal to choose the more innovative project.

The market for corporate control also refers to acquisitions that represent a key aspect of an "open innovation" strategy. However, recent theoretical and empirical studies suggested a negative effect of acquisitions on innovation. Kapoor and Lim (2007) analyzed the post-acquisition patenting activity of inventors in semiconductor firms and found a significant decline in the patenting activity in the first year after the acquisition. This result is in accordance with findings by Ernst and Vitt (2000), who explain the decline in innovation activity after acquisition by the voluntary abandonment of inventors. However, the literature suggests that the effect of acquisitions on innovation is moderated by several factors. Puranam et al. (2006) show that post-acquisition innovation performance is lower if acquired firms are at an exploratory stage. Acquisitions may also be harmful for the innovative activity of the acquirer. Puranam and Srikanth (2007) report a decrease in the patenting activity of inexperienced acquirers after an acquisition.

Concluding Remarks

Corporate governance is a fundamental ingredient in innovation. As we have illustrated in this chapter, ownership concentration, owners' identity, the size and composition of the board of directors, the power and structure of managerial incentives, the capital structure, the degree of investor protection, and the market for corporate control all have a distinct impact on the innovative activity and performance of high-tech firms.

As a general remark, we have shown that the agency theory framework alone allows only a partial understanding of the complex impact of corporate governance on high-tech companies. In accordance with this view, in this chapter we have provided a selective overview of the link between corporate governance and innovation from a broader perspective. Corporate governance should be seen as a *value-creation* mechanism more than as a tool for value protection in high-tech companies. We have highlighted as much as possible this important conceptual distinction for each mechanism we have surveyed and, where relevant, its normative implications.

Clearly, this survey of the literature suffers from a series of limitations. First, works in the field of corporate governance that analyze directly or indirectly high-tech firms and their performance are countless. In this review, for the sake of synthesis, we have considered only those that are most directly linked to the topic. Second, we have deliberately decided to focus our attention only on those governance mechanisms that, in our view, have specific importance for high-tech companies. We have neglected other important mechanisms that, however important, do not present specific problems for high-tech companies (e.g. internal committees, external auditors, accounting rules, mandatory disclosure). Third, the linear nature of this review, in which each mechanism is singled out individually, might not give sufficient importance to the very relevant interaction among different mechanisms. Some of the most relevant interactions have been pointed out during the discussion, but it is very important to bring the attention of the reader to the fact that corporate governance is a "tangled" system and the role of a single component can be fully understood only in conjunction with all the others.

Finally, we would like to indicate some interesting avenues for future research. Generally speaking, and with the exclusion of a few seminal works, the broadening of the perspective on corporate governance is a relatively recent trend in the literature. Accordingly, a large number of theoretical and empirical contributions should be expected before we attain a complete understanding of how corporate governance may create value in high-tech firms. From a normative perspective, the prevalence of the value-creating components of corporate governance casts some doubt on the usefulness for high-tech companies of governance recommendations that instead focus mostly on accountability and monitoring (e.g. Cadbury, 1992).

An aspect that has been particularly overlooked by the literature is the relationship between corporate governance and organizational design in high-tech firms. O'Sullivan (2000) highlights that a theory of corporate governance in innovative companies should take into account the organizational and strategic dimensions of innovative resource allocation. We reckon that such a theoretical development has not yet been achieved. Interestingly, Colombo and Rossi (2012) identify several aspects of organizational design that favor innovation in high-tech start-ups and are closely related to corporate governance mechanisms (e.g. the role of the board of directors).

An aspect that deserves special attention is the link between corporate governance and the strategic organization of R&D (Cassiman and Valentini, 2009). First, it is well-known that radical innovation requires different strategy and structure than incremental innovation (Ettlie et al., 1984). The extent to which radical innovation also requires a specific corporate governance system has received relatively limited attention (see, for an exception, Baysinger et al., 1991). Similarly, the link between corporate entrepreneurship, which is intrinsically linked to the ability of companies to produce radical innovation (Lassen et al., 2006), and corporate governance deserves far more attention from scholars (Phan et al., 2009). Second, openness is another characteristic of innovation (Chesborough, 2003) whose role in shaping firm's corporate governance should be studied more closely. Conceptually, the open innovation paradigm alters the notion of a firm's boundaries and, as such, it challenges the scope of corporate governance which is, typically, local rather than systemic (i.e. is focused on the firm but neglects all other actors cooperating in an open innovation process). At the same time, open innovation strategies may emphasize the value-creation aspects of corporate governance and, in particular, its role in favoring network creation and access to external competences and resources. Third, the influence of corporate governance on the governance of knowledge requires further analysis. Krafft and Ravix (2008) indicate that corporate governance may be a fundamental ingredient of the knowledge creation process, and propose a new vision based on cooperation between managers and investors who collectively contribute to corporate development and coherence. New forms of knowledge diffusion within and between companies could also require the development of new models of corporate governance, fostering information flow and collaboration (Schneckenberg, 2009).

An issue that has gained increasing attention in the literature is how corporate governance changes along with the life cycle of the firm (Filatotchev and Wright, 2005). The value-protection and value-creation potential of corporate governance varies dramatically during the life cycle of high-tech companies, suggesting the need for a dynamic theory of corporate governance. This could be particularly important in high-tech firms that are characterized by critical junctures, marking significant changes in the resources and capabilities they need (Vohora et al., 2004). This raises some interesting issues. Corporate governance plays a crucial role in determining managerial inertia (Johnson et al., 1993). This suggests that corporate governance in high-tech firms should be designed to reduce managerial inertia in anticipation of critical junctures. Critical junctures could then also characterize corporate governance itself. The extent to which this conflicts with the path dependence that typically characterizes corporate governance (Bebchuk and Roe, 1999) is another interesting topic for future research.

In summary, important conceptual developments in our understanding of the role played by corporate governance in high-tech firms will be possible only once the theory of corporate governance is fully integrated with the organizational and strategic aspects that characterize firm's innovative activity.

References

Aghion, P., and Tirole, J. (1994). "The Management of Innovation," *Quarterly Journal of Economics*, 109(4): 1185–209.
—— Bolton, P., and Tirole, J. (2004). "Exit Options in Corporate Finance: Liquidity versus Incentives," *Review of Finance*, 8(3): 327–53.
—— Van Reenen, J., and Zingales, L. (2010). "Innovation and Institutional Ownership," Fondazione Eni Enrico Mattei Working Papers no. 488.
Alderson, M. J., and Betker, B. L. (1995). "Liquidation Costs and Capital Structure," *Journal of Financial Economics*, 39(1): 45–69.
—— —— (1996). "Liquidation Costs and Accounting Data," *Financial Management*, 25(2): 25–36.
Balakrishnan, S., and Fox, I. (1993). "Asset Specificity, Firm Heterogeneity and Capital Structure," *Strategic Management Journal*, 14(1): 3–16.

BALKIN, D. B., MARKMAN, G. D., and GOMEZ-MEJIA, L. R. (2000). "Is CEO Pay in High-Technology Firms Related to Innovation?" *The Academy of Management Journal*, 43(6): 1118–29.

BATTAGGION, M. R., and TAJOLI, L. (2001). "Ownership Structure, Innovation Process and Competitive Performance: The Case of Italy," KITeS Working Papers no. 120.

BAUM, J. A. C., and SILVERMAN, B. S. (2004). "'Picking Winners or Building Them?' Alliance, Intellectual, and Human Capital as Selection Criteria in Venture Financing and Performance of Biotechnology Start-Ups," *Journal of Business Venturing*, 19(3): 411–36.

BAUMOL, W. J. (2002). *The Free-Market Innovation Machine: Analyzing the Growth Miracle of Capitalism*. Princeton: Princeton University Press.

BAYSINGER, B. D., and HOSKISSON, R. E. (1989). "Diversification Strategy and R&D Intensity in Multiproduct Firms," *The Academy of Management Journal*, 32(2): 310–32.

—— KOSNIK, R. D., and TURK, T. A. (1991). "Effects of Board and Ownership Structure on Corporate R&D Strategy," *The Academy of Management Journal*, 34(1): 205–14.

BEATTY, R. P., and ZAJAC, E. J. (1994). "Managerial Incentives, Monitoring, and Risk Bearing: A Study of Executive Compensation, Ownership, and Board Structure in Initial Public Offerings," *Administrative Science Quarterly*, 39(2): 313–35.

BEBCHUK, A. L., and ROE, M. J. (1999). "A Theory of Path Dependence in Corporate Ownership and Governance," *Stanford Law Review*, 52(1): 127–70.

BELLOC, F. (2012). "Corporate Governance and Innovation: a Survey," *Journal of Economic Surveys* 26(5): 835–64.

BERGER, A. N., and UDELL, G. F. (1998). "The Economics of Small Business Finance: The Roles of Private Equity and Debt Markets in the Financial Growth Cycle," *Journal of Banking and Finance*, 22: 613–73.

BERNDT, E. R., and MORRISON, C. J. (1995). "High-Tech Capital Formation and Economic Performance in U.S. Manufacturing Industries: An Exploratory Analysis," *Journal of Econometrics*, 65(1): 9–43.

BERTONI, F., and TYKVOVÁ, T. (2012). "Which Form of Venture Capital is Best-Suited for Innovation?" ZEW Discussion Paper no. 12–018.

—— CROCE, A., and D'ADDA, D. (2010). "Venture Capital Investments and Patenting Activity of High-Tech Start-Ups: A Micro-Econometric Firm-Level Analysis," *Venture Capital: An International Journal of Entrepreneurial Finance*, 12(4): 307–26.

—— FERRER, M. A., and MARTÍ PELLÓN, J. (forthcoming). "The Different Role Played by Venture Capital and Private Equity Investors on the Investment Activity of their Portfolio Firms," *Small Business Economics*. Available at <http://www.springerlink.com/content/b781658172ku8m10/>.

BITAR, J., and SOMERS, W. J. (2003). "The Impact of Corporate Governance on Innovation: Strategy in Turbulent Environments," HEC Montreal Working Paper no. 05-01.

BJØRNÅLI, E. S., and GULBRANDSEN, M. (2010). "Exploring Board Formation and Evolution of Board Composition in Academic Spin-Offs," *The Journal of Technology Transfer*, 35(1): 92–112.

BROUGHMAN, B. J. (2010). "The Role of Independent Directors in Startup Firms," *The Utah Law Review*, 2010(3): 461–510.

BRUINING, H., and WRIGHT, M. (2002). "Entrepreneurial Orientation in Management Buy-Outs and the Contribution of Venture Capital," *Venture Capital: An International Journal of Entrepreneurial Finance*, 4(2):147–68.

CADBURY, A. (1992). *Report on the Committee of the Financial Aspects of Corporate Governance*. London: Gee Publishing.

CARLIN, W., and MAYER, C. (2000). "Finance, Investment and Growth," SSRN Working Paper no. 236104.

CARPENTER, R. E., and PETERSEN, B. C. (2002). "Capital Market Imperfections, High-Tech Investment, and New Equity Financing," *Economic Journal*, 112(477): 54–72.

CASAMATTA, C. (2003). "Financing and Advising: Optimal Financial Contracts with Venture Capitalists," *Journal of Finance*, 58(5): 2059–86.

CASPER, S., and MATRAVES, C. (2003). "Institutional Frameworks and Innovation in the German and UK Pharmaceutical Industry," *Research Policy*, 32(10): 1865–79.

CASSIMAN, B., and VALENTINI, G. (2009). "Strategic Organization of R&D: The Choice of Basicness and Openness," *Strategic Organization*, 7(1): 43–73.

CATHERINE, D., COROLLEUR, F., CARRÈRE, M., and MANGEMATIN, V. (2004). "Turning Scientific and Technological Human Capital into Economic Capital: The Experience of Biotech Start-Ups in France," *Research Policy*, 33(4): 631–42.

CHEMMANUR, T., LOUTSKINA, E., and TIAN, X. (2011). "Corporate Venture Capital, Value Creation, and Innovation," SSRN Working Paper no. 1364213.

CHESBOROUGH, H. W. (2003). *Open Innovation: The New Imperative for Creating and Profiting from Technology.* Cambridge, MA: Harvard Business School Press.

CHO, S. (1992). "Agency Costs, Management Stockholding, and Research and Development Expenditures," *Seoul Journal of Economics*, 5 (2): 127–52.

CHO, M. H. (1998). "Ownership Structure, Investment, and the Corporate Value: An Empirical Analysis," *Journal of Financial Economics*, 47(1): 103–21.

CHUNG, K. H., WRIGHT, P., and CHAROENWONG, C. (1998). "Investment Opportunities and Market Reaction to Capital Expenditure Decisions," *Journal of Banking & Finance*, 22(1):41–60.

CLAESSENS, S., DJANKOV, S., and LANG, L. (2000). "The Separation of Ownership and Control in East Asian Corporations," *Journal of Financial Economics*, 58(1–2): 81–112.

CLARYSSE, B., KNOCKAERT, M., and LOCKETT, A. (2007). "Outside Board Members in High Tech Start-ups," *Small Business Economics*, 29(3): 243–59.

COHEN, W. M. (1995). "Empirical Studies of Innovative Activities," in P. Stoneman (ed.), *Handbook of the Economics of Innovation and Technological Change.* Oxford: Oxford Blackwell.

—— and LEVIN, R. C. (1989). "Empirical Studies of Innovation and Market Structure," in R. Schmalensee and R. Willig (eds.), *Handbook of Industrial organisation*, vol. II. Amsterdam: North Holland, 1059–107.

COLOMBO, M. G., and ROSSI LAMASTRA, C. (2012). "The Organizational Design of High-Tech Start-Ups: State of the Art and Directions for Future Research," in A. Grandori (ed.), *Handbook of Economic Organization: Integrating Economic and Organization Theory.* Cheltenham: Edward Elgar Publishing.

CUMMING, D., SIEGEL, D. S., and WRIGHT, M. (2007). "Private Equity, Leveraged Buyouts and Governance," *Journal of Corporate Finance*, 13: 439–60.

DAILY, C. M., and SCHWENK, C. (1996). "Chief Executive Officers, Top Management Teams, and Boards of Directors: Congruent or Countervailing Forces?" *Journal of Management*, 22(2): 185–208.

DALTON, D., DAILY, C., ELLSTRAND, A., and JOHNSON, J. (1998). "Metaanalytic Review of Board Composition, Leadership Structure, and Financial Performance," *Strategic Management Journal*, 19: 269–90.

DUSHNITSKY, G., and LENOX, M. J. (2005). "When do Firms Undertake R&D by Investing in New Ventures?" *Strategic Management Journal*, 26: 947–65.

EISENHARDT, K. M. (1989). "Agency Theory: An Assessment and Review," *The Academy of Management Review*, 14(1): 57–74.

ERNST, H., and VITT, J. (2000). "The Influence of Corporate Acquisitions on the Behaviour of Key Inventors," *R&D Management*, 30: 105–20.

ESTRIN, S., and WRIGHT, M. (2002). "Corporate Governance in the Former Soviet Union: An Overview," *Journal of Comparative Economics*, 27(3): 398–421.

ETTLIE, J. E., BRIDGES, W. P., and O'KEEFE, R. D. (1984). "Organization Strategy and Structural Differences for the Radical versus Incremental Innovation," *Management Science*, 30(6): 682–95.

FACCIO, M., and LANG, L. (2001). "The Ultimate Ownership of Western European Corporations," *Journal of Financial Economics*, 65(3): 365–95.

FAGERBERG, J., MOWERY, D. C., and NELSON, R. R. (2005). *The Oxford Handbook of Innovation*. Oxford: Oxford University Press.

—— TOMS, S., and WRIGHT, M. (2006). "The Firm's Strategic Dynamics and Corporate Governance Life-Cycle," *International Journal of Managerial Finance*, 2(4): 256–79.

FILATOTCHEV, I., and WRIGHT, M. (2005). *The Life Cycle of Corporate Governance*. Cheltenham: Edward Elgar.

FRANCIS, J., and SMITH, A. (1995). "Agency Costs and Innovation: Some Empirical Evidence," *Journal of Accounting and Economics*, 19: 383–409.

GAMBARDELLA, A. (1995). *Science and Innovation: The US Pharmaceutical Industry During the 1980s*. Cambridge: Cambridge University Press.

GOYER, M. (2001). "Corporate Governance and the Innovation System in France 1985–2000," *Industry and Innovation*, 8(2): 135–58.

GROSSMAN, S. J., and HART, O. D. (1986). "The Costs and Benefits of Ownership: A Theory of Vertical and Lateral Integration," *Journal of Political Economy*, 94(4): 691–719.

GUGLER, K. (2003). "Corporate Governance, Dividend Payout Policy, and the Interrelation between Dividends, R&D, and Capital Investment," *Journal of Banking & Finance*, 27(7): 1297–321.

HALL, B. H. (1990). "The Impact of Corporate Restructuring on Industrial Research and Development," *Brookings Papers of Economic Activity: Microeconomics*, 85–135.

—— (2002). "The Financing of Research and Development," *Oxford Review of Economic Policy*, 18 (1): 35–51.

—— and LERNER, J. (2010). "The Financing of R&D and Innovation," in B. H. Hall and N. Rosenberg (eds.), *Handbook of the Economics of Innovation*. Amsterdam: Elsevier-North Holland.

—— and SOSKICE, D. (2001). *Varieties of Capitalism: The Institutional Foundations of Comparative Advantage*. Oxford: Oxford University Press.

HALL, R. E., and WOODWARD, S. E. (2008). "The Burden of the Nondiversifiable Risk on Entrepreneurship," NBER Working Paper no. 14219.

HELLMAN, T., and PURI, M. (2000). "The Interaction between Product Market and Financing Strategy: The Role of Venture Capital," *The Review of Financial Studies*, 13(4): 959–84.

HERMALIN, B. M., and WEISBACH, M. S. (2001). "Boards of Directors as an Endogenously Determined Institution: A Survey of the Economic Literature," NBER Working Paper no. 8161.

HIGGINS, M. J., STEPHAN, P. E., and THURSBY, J. G. (2008). "Conveying Quality and Value in Emerging Industries: Star Scientists and the Role of Learning in Biotechnology," NBER Working Paper no. 14602.

HILL, C. W., and SNELL, S. A. (1988). "External Control, Corporate Strategy, and Firm Performance in Research-Intensive Industries," *Strategic Management Journal*, 9(6): 577–90.

HILLMAN, A. J., and DALZIEL, T. (2003). "Boards of Directors and Firm Performance: Integrating Agency and Resource Dependence Perspectives," *The Academy of Management Review*, 28(3): 383–96.

—— CANNELLA, A. A., and PAETZOLD, R. L. (2000). "The Resource Dependence Role of Corporate Directors: Strategic Adaptation of Board Composition in Response to Environmental Change," *Journal of Management Studies*, 37(2): 235–56.

HIMMELBERG, C. P., HUBBARD, R. G., and LOVE, I. (2002). "Investment, Protection, Ownership, and the Cost of Capital," NBB Working Paper no. 25.

HIRSHLEIFER, D., and SUH, Y. (1992). "Risk, Managerial Effort, and Project Choice," *Journal of Financial Intermediation*, 2(3): 308–45.

HIRSCHMAN, A. O. (1970). *Exit, Voice, and Loyalty. Responses to Decline in Firms, Organizations, and States*. Cambridge, MA: Harvard University Press.

HIRUKAWA, M., and UEDA, M. (2011). "Venture Capital and Innovation: Which is First?" *Pacific Economic Review*, 16(4): 421–65.

HOLMSTROM, B. (1982). "Managerial Incentive Problems—A Dynamic Perspective," *Essays in Economics and Management in Honor of Lars Wahlbeck*. Stockholm: Swedish School of Economics.

—— (1989). "Agency Costs and Innovation," *Journal of Economic Behavior & Organization*, 12(3): 305–27.

HONORÉ, F., MUNARI, F., and VAN POTTELSBERGHE DE LA POTTERIE, B. (2011). "Corporate Governance Practices and Companies' R&D Orientation: Evidence from European Countries," Bruegel Working Paper 2011/1.

HOSKISSON, R. E., HITT, M. A., and IRELAND, D. (1994). "The Effects of Acquisition and Restructuring (Strategic Refocusing) Strategies on Innovation," in G. Von Krogh, A. Sinatra, and H. Singh (eds.), *The Management of Corporate Acquisitions: International Perspectives*. New York: Macmillan.

—— —— JOHNSON, R. A., and GROSSMAN, W. (2002). "Conflicting Voices: The Effects of Institutional Ownership Heterogeneity and Internal Governance on Corporate Innovation Strategies," *Academy of Management Journal*, 45(4): 697–716.

HSU, D. H. (2004). "What Do Entrepreneurs Pay for Venture Capital Affiliation?" *Journal of Finance*, 59: 1805–44.

JENSEN, M. C. (1986). "Agency Costs of Free Cash Flow, Corporate Finance, and Takeovers," *The American Economic Review*, 76(2): 323–9.

—— and MECKLING, W. H. (1976). "Theory of the Firm: Managerial Behavior, Agency Costs and Ownership Structure," *Journal of Financial Economics*, 3(4): 305–60.

JOHNSON, M. S., and RAO, R. P. (1997). "The Impact of Antitakeover Amendments on Corporate Financial Performance," *Financial Review*, 32(3): 659–90.

JOHNSON, R. A., HOSKISSON, R. E., and HITT, M. A. (1993). "Board of Director Involvement in Restructuring: The Effects of Board versus Managerial Controls and Characteristics," *Strategic Management Journal*, 14(S1): 33–50.

KAPOOR, R., and LIM, K. (2007). "The Impact of Acquisitions on the Productivity of Inventors at Semiconductor Firms: A Synthesis of Knowledge-Based and Incentive-Based Perspectives," *The Academy of Management Journal*, 50(5): 1133–55.

KLAPPER, L. F., and LOVE, I. (2004). "Corporate Governance, Investor Protection, and Performance in Emerging Markets," *Journal of Corporate Finance*, 10: 703–28.

Kortum, S., and Lerner, J. (2000). "Assessing the Contribution of Venture Capital to Innovation," *RAND Journal of Economics*, 31(4): 674–92.

Krafft, J., and Ravix, J. L. (2008). "Corporate Governance and the Governance of Knowledge: Rethinking the Relationship in Terms of Corporate Coherence," *Economics of Innovation and New Technology*, 17(1–2): 79–95.

Lacetera, N. (2001). "Corporate Governance and the Governance of Innovation: The Case of the Pharmaceutical Industry," *Journal of Management and Governance*, 5: 29–59.

La Porta, R., Lopez-de-Silanes, F., and Shleifer, A. (1999). "Corporate Ownership around the World," *Journal of Finance*, 54(2): 471–517.

—— —— —— and Vishny, R. W. (1998). "Law and Finance," *Journal of Political Economy*, 106(6): 1113–55.

Lassen, A. H., Gertsen, F., and Riis, J. O. (2006). "The Nexus of Corporate Entrepreneurship and Radical Innovation," *Creativity and Innovation Management*, 15(4): 359–72.

Lazonick, W. (2007). "The US Stock Market and the Governance of Innovative Enterprise," *Industrial and Corporate Change*, 16(6): 983–1035.

Lee, P. M., and O'Neill, H. M. (2003). "Ownership Structures and R&D Investments of U.S. and Japanese Firms: Agency and Stewardship Perspectives," *Academy of Management Journal*, 46: 212–25.

Lehrer, M., Tylecote, A., and Conesa, E. (1999). "Corporate Governance, Innovation Systems and Industrial Performance," *Industry and Innovation*, 6(1): 25–50.

Le Nadant, A. L., and Perdreau, F. (2012). "LBOs and Innovation: The French Case," CREM Working Paper no. 2012-09.

Lerner, J., and Wulf, J. (2006). "Innovation and Incentives: Evidence from Corporate R&D," NBER Working Paper no. 11944.

—— Sorensen, M., and Strömberg, P. (2011). "Private Equity and Long-Run Investment: The Case of Innovation," *Journal of Finance*, 66(2): 445–77.

Li, Y., Guo, H., Yi, Y., and Liu, Y. (2010). "Ownership Concentration and Product Innovation in Chinese Firms: The Mediating Role of Learning Orientation," *Management and Organization Review*, 6(1): 77–100.

Long, W. F., and Ravenscraft, D. J. (1993). "LBOs, Debt and R&D Intensity," *Strategic Management Journal*, 14: 119–35.

Mansfield, E. (1972). "Contribution of Research and Development to Economic Growth in the United States," *Science*, 175(4021): 477–86.

Manso, G. (2011). "Motivating Innovation," *Journal of Finance*, 66(5): 1823–60.

Markman, G. D., Balkin, D. B., and Schjoedt, L. (2001). "Governing the Innovation Process in Entrepreneurial Firms," *The Journal of High Technology Management Research*, 12(2): 273–93.

Mayer, C. (1997). "Corporate Governance, Competition and Performance," *Journal of Law and Society*, 24(1): 152–76.

—— (2002). "Financing the New Economy: Financial Institutions and Corporate Governance," *Information Economics and Policy*, 14: 311–26.

Megginson, W. L., and Netter, J. N. (2001). "From State to Market: A Survey of Empirical Studies on Privatization," *Journal of Economic Literature*, 39(2): 321–89.

Miozzo, M., and Dewick, P. (2002). "Building Competitive Advantage: Innovation and Corporate Governance in European Construction," *Research Policy*, 31: 989–1008.

Morck, R., Shleifer, A., and Vishny, R. W. (1988). "Management Ownership and Market Valuation: An Empirical Analysis," *Journal of Financial Economics*, 20: 293–315.

Munari, F., Roberts, E., and Sobrero, M. (2002). "Privatization Processes and the Redefinition of Corporate R&D Boundaries," *Research Policy*, 31(1): 31–53.

Nadiri, I. (1993). "Innovations and Technological Spillovers," NBER Working Paper no. 423.

O'Sullivan, M. (2000). "The Innovative Enterprise and Corporate Governance," *Cambridge Journal of Economics*, 24: 393–416.

Ortega-Argilés, R., Moreno, R., and Suriñach Caralt, J. (2005). "Ownership Structure and Innovation: Is There a Real Link?" *Annals of Regional Science*, 39: 637–62.

Phan, P. H., Wright, M., Ucbasaran, D., and Tan, W. L. (2009). "Corporate Entrepreneurship: Current Research and Future Directions," *Journal of Business Venturing*, 24: 197–205.

Popov, A. A., and Roosenboom, P. (2009). "Does Private Equity Investment Spur Innovation? Evidence from Europe," ECB Working Paper no. 1063.

Prendergast, C. (1999). "The Provision of Incentives in Firms," *Journal of Economic Literature*, 37(1): 7–63.

Pugh, W. N., Jahera, J. S., and Oswald, S. (1999). "Esops, Takeover Protection, and Corporate Decision Making," *Journal of Economics and Finance*, 48(5): 1985–99.

Puranam, P., and Srikanth, K. (2007). "What They Know vs. What They Do: How Acquirers Leverage Technology Acquisitions," *Strategic Management Journal*, 28: 805–25.

——Singh, H., and Zollo, M. (2006). "Organizing for Innovation: Managing the Coordination-Autonomy Dilemma in Technology Acquisitions," *The Academy of Management Journal*, 49(2): 263–80.

Raheja, C. G. (2005). "Determinants of Board Size and Composition: A Theory of Corporate Boards," *Journal of Financial and Quantitative Analysis*, 40(2): 283–306.

Sapienza, H. J., and Gupta, A. K. (1994). "Impact of Agency Risks and Task Uncertainty on Venture Capitalist-CEO Interaction," *The Academy of Management Journal*, 37(6): 1618–32.

Sapra, H., Subramanian, A., and Subramanian, K. (2009). "Corporate Governance and Innovation Theory and Evidence," Chicago Booth Working Paper no. 08-05.

Scharfstein, D. (1988). "The Disciplinary Role of Takeovers," *Review of Economic Studies*, 55(2): 185–99.

Schmitz, P. W. (2001). "Partial Privatization and Incomplete Contracts: The Proper Scope of Government Reconsidered," *FinanzArchiv*, 57(1): 394–411.

Schneckenberg, D. (2009). "Web 2.0 and the Shift in Corporate Governance from Control to Democracy," *Knowledge Management Research and Practice*, 7(3): 234–48.

Shleifer, A. (1998). "State Versus Private Ownership," NBER Working Paper no. 6665.

——and Summers, L. H. (1988). "Breach of Trust in Hostile Takeovers," in A. J. Auerbach (ed.), *Corporate Takeovers: Causes and Consequences*. Chicago: University of Chicago Press, 33–56.

——and Vishny, R. W. (1989). "Management Entrenchment: The Case of Manager-Specific Investments," *Journal of Financial Economics*, 25: 123–39.

—— —— (1997). "A Survey of Corporate Governance," *Journal of Finance*, 52(2): 737–83.

Smith, A. J. (1990). "Corporate Ownership Structure and Performance: The Case of Management Buyouts," *Journal of Financial Economics*, 27(1): 143–64.

Smith, C. W., and Stulz, R. M. (1985). "The Determinants of Firms' Hedging Policies," *Journal of Financial and Quantitative Analysis*, 20: 391–405.

Smith, V., Dilling-Hansen, M., Eriksson, T., and Madsen, E. S. (2004). "R&D and Productivity in Danish Firms: Some Empirical Evidence," *Applied Economics*, 36(16): 1797–806.

STEIN, J. C. (1988). "Takeover Threats and Managerial Myopia," *Journal of Political Economy*, 96(1): 61–80.

—— (1997). "Internal Capital Markets and the Competition for Corporate Resources," *Journal of Finance*, 52(1): 111–33.

TRIBO, J. A., BERRONE, P., and SURROCA, J. (2007). "Do the Type and Number of Blockholders Influence R&D Investments? New Evidence from Spain," *Corporate Governance: An International Review*, 15(5): 828–42.

TYKVOVÁ, T., and BORELL, M. (2012). "Do Private Equity Owners Increase Risk of Financial Distress and Bankruptcy?" *Journal of Corporate Finance*, 18(1): 138–50.

UGHETTO, E. (2010). "Assessing the Contribution to Innovation of Private Equity Investors: A Study on European Buyouts," *Research Policy*, 39(1): 126–40.

VOHORA, A., WRIGHT, M., and LOCKETT, A. (2004). "Critical Junctures in the Development of University High-Tech Spinout Companies," *Research Policy*, 33: 147–75.

VON TUNZELMANN, N., and ACHA, V. (2005). "Innovation in 'Low-Tech' Industries," in J. Fagerberg, D. C. Mowery, and R. R. Nelson (eds.), *The Oxford Handbook of Innovation*. Oxford: Oxford University Press.

WASSERMAN, N. (2006). "Stewards, Agents, and the Founder Discount: Executive Compensation in New Ventures," *The Academy of Management Journal*, 49(5): 960–76.

WESTPHAL, J. D. (1999). "Collaboration in the Boardroom: Behavioral and Performance Consequences of CEO-Board Social Ties," *The Academy of Management Journal*, 42(1): 7–24.

WRIGHT, M., HOSKISSON, R. E., and BUSENITZ, L. W., and DIAL, J. (2000). "Entrepreneurial Growth through Privatization: The Upside of Management Buyouts," *The Academy of Management Review*, 25(3): 591–601.

—— —— —— (2001). "Firm Rebirth: Buyouts as Facilitators of Strategic Growth and Entrepreneurship," *The Academy of Management Executive*, 15(1) 111–25.

WRIGHT, P., KROLL, M., KRUG, J. A., and PETTUS, M. (2002). "Influences of Top Management Team Incentives on Firm Risk Taking," *Strategic Management Journal*, 28(1): 81–9.

YERMACK, D. (1996). "Higher Market Valuation of Companies with a Small Board of Directors," *Journal of Financial Economics*, 40(2): 185–211.

ZAHRA, S. A. (1995). "Corporate Entrepreneurship and Financial Performance: The Case of Management Leveraged Buyouts," *Journal of Business Venturing*, 10(3): 225–47.

—— FILATOCHEV, I., and WRIGHT, M. (2009). "How Do Threshold Firms Sustain Corporate Entrepreneurship? The Role of Boards and Absorptive Capacity," *Journal of Business Venturing*, 24: 248–60.

ZUCKER, L. G., DARBY, M. R., BREWER, M. B., and PENG, Y. (1995). "Collaboration Structure and Information Dilemmas in Biotechnology: Organizational Boundaries as Trust Production," NBER Working Paper no. 5199.

CHAPTER 18

FAMILY BUSINESS AND CORPORATE GOVERNANCE

LORRAINE M. UHLANER

FAMILY business research is based on the assumption that family representation in the ownership, management, and governance (collectively referred to henceforth as *family involvement*) significantly influences a wide range of organizational processes and corporate policies, including corporate governance (Bammens et al., 2011). In the first decade of the 21st century, corporate governance was the most widely researched topic in family business (Debicki et al., 2009), providing a rich basis upon which to build future research on the topic. The primary aim of this chapter is to organize this literature into a research framework according to the primary types of research questions that have been addressed in the literature. Relevant theories, especially agency theory (Fama and Jensen, 1983), stewardship theory (Davis et al., 1997), the resource-based view (Wernerfelt, 1984), social capital theory (Nahapiet and Ghoshal, 1998; Adler and Kwon, 2002), and social identity theory (Ellemers, 2001; Uhlaner et al., 2007a) are incorporated into the discussion rather than presented separately. With the exception of papers that have become widely quoted and literature reviews, the inclusion of papers is biased toward empirical research (versus papers presenting untested frameworks) where available.

Several published reviews appeared at about the same time that this chapter was in preparation (Chrisman et al., 2010; Bammens et al., 2011; Gomez-Mejia et al., 2011; Lumpkin, Steier, and Wright, 2011; Wright and Kellermanns, 2011; Siebels and zu Knyphausen-Aufseβ, 2012) and provide a useful complement. For example, in their coverage of the 25 most influential articles in family business, Chrisman et al. (2010) heavily emphasize a number of agency theory-based articles related to corporate governance (i.e. Jensen and Meckling, 1976; Fama and Jensen, 1983; Morck et al., 1988; La Porta et al., 1999; Gomez-Mejia et al., 2001; Anderson and Reeb, 2003; Morck and Yeung, 2003; Schulze et al., 2003a, 2003b). Bammens et al. (2011) focus especially on the board of directors in family businesses. Given the availability of these reviews to the reader, coverage of agency theory is therefore downplayed somewhat in the current piece, in order to create space for other research directions. In addition, in their overviews of the family business research literature, Gomez-Mejia et al. (2011) and Wright and Kellermanns (2011) include sections on corporate governance.

The remainder of this chapter is organized as follows. For the benefit of students and scholars less familiar with the family business literature, the next section provides more background about the extent of family control and involvement worldwide and how family involvement has been defined. The same section also provides an overview of corporate governance definitions as used in the family business literature. The middle section presents an overview of extant research related to nine research questions on the topic of family business and corporate governance, as well as summaries of relevant findings and suggestions for future research. The concluding section highlights some of the more important findings and suggests some additional directions for future research not previously mentioned in the chapter.

Family Business and Corporate Governance: A Brief Introduction

Family Control and Involvement: A Worldwide Phenomenon

Family control, even among publicly held firms, is the rule rather than the exception, especially outside the United States and the United Kingdom (Shleifer and Vishny, 1997; La Porta et al., 1999). This fact is accentuated by the phenomenon referred to as *excess control rights*—that is, effective control exceeding cash-flow rights—created through various legal constructions including pyramids, holdings and dual share classes, and voting agreements, all of which are especially common among family-controlled publicly listed firms (Shyu and Lee, 2009; Villalonga and Amit, 2009). Although the earliest studies on family control were based on small country samples (e.g. La Porta et al., 1999), recent research focusing on larger samples continues to support this conclusion. For example, Gadhoum's (2006) study of a sample of 1,120 Canadian listed firms shows that families are the most prevalent form of controlling shareholders in Canada. In 56 percent of the companies studied, families hold an ownership stake of 10 percent; using a 20 percent cutoff in the same sample, 41 percent still have a family ownership stake.

Family ownership estimates for unlisted firms surpass those for listed firms. Even in the UK and the US the vast majority of firms—73 percent of UK businesses (Smyrnios and Walker, 2003), 80–90 percent of companies in the US (Astrachan and Shanker, 2003), and 80 percent of firms in the European Union[1] (European Commission, 2009) are considered family-owned firms. One should be aware, however, that such estimates often draw on definitions which ignore differences between individual owners and business-owning families (Nicholson, 2010). A study carried out by the Global Entrepreneurship Monitor (Reynolds et al., 2002) suggests that, if one were to exclude single-owner firms, the estimates would shrink considerably. In that study, based on large, random samples of adults (18–64 years of age) in each of ten countries, only about 37 percent of new firms (3–42 months) and 36 percent of established firms (older than 42 months) are owned by two or more family members. Of the remainder, 47 percent of new firms and 52 percent of established firms are owned and managed by one individual (Reynolds et al., 2002; Uhlaner and Berent, 2008).

Regardless of the exact numbers, family involvement in the world's businesses remains sizable, and equally important, represents practically all phases of the business life cycle and all corporate forms. Family firms include publicly listed companies as well as privately owned firms. They include start-ups, but also firms which are several hundred years old.[2] And they can be micro firms, employing just one or two employees, or major corporations with several thousand employees. They are also represented (though not always proportionately) in every sector and in every country of the world (Uhlaner and Berent, 2008). As a result of this variety, scholars must pay close attention to sampling characteristics in specific studies regarding family business before attempting to generalize about such findings. As noted by Nordqvist (2005), results and associated conclusions can differ significantly if a sample is made up of younger, single-owner firms or older, multigenerational, multi-owner firms, even though both samples may fit the same definition of family business.

Family Business Definitions

In the family business context, "family" usually refers to an extended family of cousins, siblings, parents, and children, related through either blood or marriage (Uhlaner, 2008), though this definition may vary somewhat by culture. Definitions and measurements of family involvement vary widely from single items to multidimensional sets of variables.[3] The simplest, but perhaps most problematic, measure is based on the proportion of the firm owned by a single family or individual. For private firms, a 50 percent cutoff is often used (e.g. Zahra, 2010), while a lower range (5–20%) is typically used as the cutoff for samples of listed firms (e.g. La Porta et al., 1999; Anderson and Reeb, 2003; Jaskiewicz and Klein, 2007). The first problem with such an indicator is that it combines individual and group ownership.

More recent research shows that the number of owners (especially comparing a sole owner to a business-owning family, i.e. two or more related members of the same family) can significantly moderate the particular relationships under study (e.g. Anderson and Reeb, 2004; Miller et al., 2007). Furthermore, especially in small and medium enterprises (SMEs), often the vast majority (80–90%) meet the criterion, creating variance problems in statistically based research (Uhlaner, 2005).

For these reasons, other family business researchers recommend a multidimensional approach, especially when engaging in quantitative research on privately held firms, although doing so does not always solve the problem of combined individual and group-owned firms. For instance, Westhead and Cowling (1998) use three criteria to define a family firm in their research: (1) one family has a clear majority of voting shares; (2) the family is represented in top management; and (3) the business is perceived as a family firm. But such a definition still fails to differentiate individual owners from business-owning families. To offset this problem, a multi-item scale by Uhlaner (2005) includes items measuring whether or not two or more members of the same family are owners and managers.

There are different ways to address the multidimensionality of the family business concept. One approach is to use a Guttman scale—a scaling technique which allows the combination of different family business aspects into one index (Uhlaner, 2005). A second approach is to split dimensions into different variables. Originally developed by Astrachan et al. (2002), the F-PEC scale (actually three separate variables standing for power, experience, and culture) has been further validated and modified (S. B. Klein et al., 2005; Holt et al., 2010).

To add to the confusion in family business definitions, researchers vary in their usage and assigned meanings for such terms as "family orientation," "familiness," "family influence," "family involvement," and "family essence." Chrisman et al. (2012), for example, use the term "family involvement" to refer to objective and structural measures, such as the number or proportion of owners, managers, or board members who are members of the same family (parallel to the power scale). In contrast, "family essence" refers to a broad range of attitudinal measures, such as family commitment, influence on strategy or culture, and intention to keep the firm within the family (Chrisman et al., 2012).

In summary, scholars do not agree on a single definition or measure of family business. However, in spite of its usage and continued popularity, scholars and students should be cautioned against use of the single indicator of majority ownership by an individual or family, to avoid confounding founder (or single owner) and family effects.

Corporate Governance as Defined in Family Business Research

Family business researchers vary in their definitions of corporate governance, often reflecting differences in the underlying theory and research questions chosen for study. For instance, in research based on agency theory, "corporate governance" typically refers to the protection and enhancement of the key stakeholder interests within the firm, especially—although not exclusively—the interests of the owners (Uhlaner, 2008). An alternative definition, and one perhaps more consistent with the resource-based and social capital views is proposed by Daily et al. (2003) as the "determination of the broad uses to which organizational resources will be deployed and the resolution of conflicts among the myriad participants in organizations" (2003: 371). "Corporate governance" can also refer to functions or processes of corporate governance (e.g. monitoring and enterprising), on the one hand, or to the structural entities inside or outside the organization that may contribute to governance (e.g. boards of directors, business-owning group, external auditors, and family governance practices).

The family business literature also makes use of the distinction made in the broader corporate governance literature between "contractual" and "relational" governance. "Contractual governance" refers to ways in which owners (or minority shareholders), as *principals*, can monitor management (or majority shareholders) as *agents* through formal, typically written agreements designed to hold management (or majority shareholders) accountable (Cadbury, 1992; Keasey and Wright, 1993; Mustakallio et al., 2002).[4] Examples of contractual governance include the monitoring function of the board of directors and performance-based incentives introduced to influence top management's (including the CEO) actions. Regardless of whether specific structures are examined, such research generally relies on agency theory explanations, and interprets governance as interest alignment (among owners, as well as between owners and management) that is achieved through incentives and strict financial discipline.

A second stream of research on family business and corporate governance focuses on "relational governance." In most interpretations, relational governance refers to informal social controls based on mutual trust, a shared vision, and a commitment to the success of the enterprise. Furthermore, such governance is embedded in social relationships among owners, and between owners and management (Huse, 1993; Mustakallio et al., 2002; Uhlaner Flören, et al., 2007). This stream not only centers on holding management accountable but also on the development of an enabling function—that is, guidance and support to management to ensure that shareholders can benefit from the upside potential in firms (Filatotchev and Wright, 2005; Uhlaner, Wright, et al., 2007). This second stream typically moves beyond agency theory as well as the monitoring and disciplinary focus to draw on such management theories as stewardship theory, stakeholder theory, the resource-based view, and social capital theory (e.g. Mustakallio et al., 2002; Uhlaner, Wright, et al., 2007).

A distinction is also made in the family business and corporate governance literature between business and family governance practices. Whereas "business governance practices" refer to structures and processes that protect or develop ownership and other stakeholder interests vis-à-vis the firm, "family governance practices" refer to the structures or mechanisms intended to facilitate the family's relationships with the business (Gersick et al., 1997; Aronoff and Ward, 2002; Neubauer and Lank, 1998; Mustakallio et al., 2002; Suáre and Santana-Martín, 2004; Berent-Braun and Uhlaner, 2012a). Depending on the study, family governance practices are either seen as a type of relational governance (e.g. Mustakallio et al., 2002) or as a precursor to relational governance (Berent-Braun and Uhlaner, 2012a). In the latter instance, such practices are believed to have the potential to enhance trust, associability, and other aspects of informal social control, but they do not guarantee such control (Berent-Braun and Uhlaner, 2012a).

An Overview of Research in Family Business and Governance

Figure 18.1 provides a quick representation of the typical research questions found in the extant family business and corporate governance literature and which are covered in this chapter. Based on this review of the literature, and as illustrated in Figure 18.1, research on the topic can be organized by nine distinct research questions. Some have been tested extensively, while others have been examined to a more limited degree. Each of these questions is described in a subsequent section of this chapter, where relevant underlying theories are incorporated as appropriate.[5]

The questions are as follows:

Research question 1: Do family-owned firms perform better than non-family firms solely because of their ownership form and related control rights?

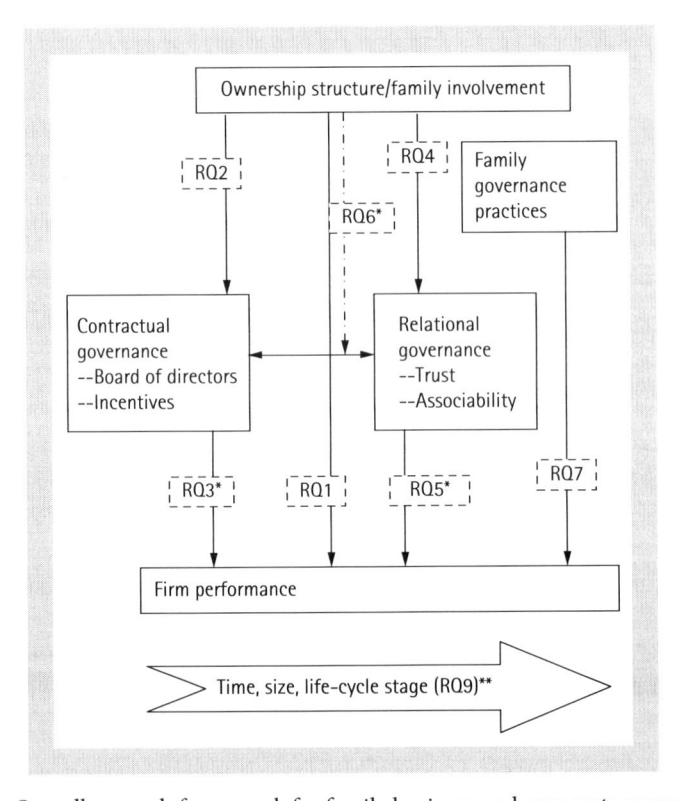

FIGURE 18.1. Overall research framework for family business and corporate governance

Notes: * This arrow actually reflects two related research questions: (a) whether this link exists amongst family firms only; (b) whether this link is moderated by family ownership or family involvement.
** This arrow represents proposed moderator variables for other relationships in the framework such as the passage of time, stage in the life cycle, or size of the firm.

Research question 2: Do family-owned firms have different types of contractual governance than non-family firms?

Research question 3: Does family ownership moderate the relationship between types of contractual governance and firm performance?; or alternatively

Research question 3a: Is there a positive or negative relationship between contractual governance and firm performance in family firms?

Research question 4: Does family ownership enhance relational governance, especially for firms with business-owning groups?

Research question 5: Does family ownership moderate the relationship between relational governance and firm performance?; or alternatively

Research question 5a: Is there a positive or negative relationship between relational governance and firm performance (or other intermediate outcomes) in family firms?

Research question 6: Does family ownership moderate the relationship between contractual governance and relational governance?; or alternatively

Research question 6a: Is there a positive or negative relationship between contractual and relational governance in family firms?

Research question 7: What are the effects of family governance practices on business and family performance?

Research question 8: Structural variables aside, what is the appropriate role of non-managing family owners in the governance of the firm?

Research question 9: Does the governance style most appropriate for a family firm change over time? Are certain styles more appropriate for different stages in the life cycle?

Note that in the three paired research questions (research questions 3, 5, and 6), differences are due in part to sampling choices. Some studies restrict their research to family firms (however defined), whereas other research purposely compares the proposed relationships for family vs non-family firms.

Research Question 1: Effects of Family Ownership on Performance

The predicted relationship between family ownership and firm performance is one of the most extensively researched topics in the field of family business (see arrow RQ1 in Figure 18.1). Arguments for the superiority of family-owned firms draw on both stewardship theory (Anderson and Reeb, 2003; Miller and Le Breton-Miller, 2006) and agency theory (see Bammens et al., 2011; Siebels and zu Knyphausen-Aufseβ, 2012).

Stewardship theory has been used to explain the positive relationship between family ownership and firm performance. Family owners, who are argued to have a stronger long-term commitment (Cliff and Jennings, 2005) and a higher proportion of personal investment than non-family owners, are likely to be better stewards in terms of looking after not only their own interests but also those of the firm as a whole (Anderson and Reeb, 2003). This is especially true for publicly listed firms. Carney (2005) takes this suggestion a step further, providing three rationales for a positive relationship between family ownership and performance: parsimony, personalism, and particularism. "Parsimony" refers to the idea that people are more prudent with their own wealth than that of others. "Personalism" refers to the idea that firms that concentrate authority are less subject to external constraints, which allows a family to project its own vision onto the business (Chua et al., 1999). Finally, "particularism"—Carney's term for psychological ownership—means that the family views the firm as "its business," even when the family holds only a minority stake. Other explanations for the expected positive effect of family ownership include its culture, resilience, tacit knowledge, and flexibility (Cliff and Jennings, 2005).

Agency theory has been used to predict both superior and inferior performance by family blockholders. The rationale for family involvement as a predictor of better financial performance is that families with a significant block of ownership will make sure that their companies are successful, since much of the family wealth resides in those companies. Agency theory is also used to argue that, as a result of owner–owner agency problems, family ownership may have precisely the opposite effect on performance. Majority blockholders may attempt to bypass minority shareholders and expropriate some of the wealth in the firm for their own use. Terms such as entrenchment, moral hazard, tunneling, and pyramidal structures are associated with the countervailing theory that dominant family coalitions (especially in firms with substantial non-family holdings) may be tempted to pull assets out of the firm in a way that will harm minority shareholders (Morck and Yeung, 2003). Another concern is that of altruism—parents, in particular, may be more generous or lenient toward their children and/or other family members who work within the firm than to non-family employees or even themselves (Schulze et al., 2002).

Family Ownership and Financial Performance in Publicly Listed Firms

The research on family ownership and performance can best be divided according to whether the sample used focuses on publicly listed or privately held firms. Empirical articles on family ownership and financial performance in publicly listed firms have arrived at conflicting conclusions. Anderson and Reeb (2003) have been frequently cited to support claims that family ownership has a positive effect on performance in publicly listed firms. In contrast, other studies (e.g P. Klein et al., 2005; Miller et al., 2007) have provided more equivocal evidence. For example, a large-scale literature review by Dyer (2006) and a subsequent meta-analysis by O'Boyle et al. (2012) conclude that family involvement has no significant main effect on firm performance. However, these authors and others identify several moderator variables that may help to explain the lack of main effects, including the "founder" effect (i.e. first vs later-generation ownership) (Wright and Kellermanns, 2011), number of owners (especially in first v. later generation), company size, and cross-country differences arising from cultural and formal institutional differences.

Several recent studies provide support for differentiating between a founder effect and a family effect. For instance, Villalonga and Amit's (2006) study of US data concludes that the performance premium originally observed and reported by Anderson and Reeb (2003) is due to founder-run firms—i.e. where at least one founder is CEO of the firm. Furthermore, they find a negative effect in second-generation firms. They also conclude that later-generation family firms trade at a discount compared with non-family firms when the former are run by a descendent of the founder. Sacristán-Navarro et al. (2011) reach a similar conclusion in their study of listed Spanish firms in that they report a positive founder effect, but a negative family effect. A study by Bertrand et al. (2008), which is based on 93 of the largest business families in Thailand, uses different methods but similarly highlights the dangers arising in the second generation. They find strong evidence of "tunneling"—the removal of assets from the core business—especially for firms owned by their founders' sons.

Somewhat in contrast to Villalonga and Amit's (2006) approach, Miller et al. (2007) retest Anderson and Reeb's (2003) conclusions by comparing the "family" effect to a "lone-founder" effect. Miller et al. (2007) create a dummy variable for those firms in which the CEOs do not have relatives in the business to distinguish them from firms with two or more active family owners and/or managers (regardless of generation). They test their hypotheses on two data sets, the first of which is identical to the sample used by Anderson and Reeb (2003), and the second of which includes a larger pool of smaller publicly listed firms. From analysis of the first data set, they conclude that when the lone-founder effect and the family effect are measured independently, the positive effects of financial performance can be attributed to the former. However, based on analyses from the second data set, they disconfirm the lone-founder effect. They conclude from their findings that it may be company size (smaller firms outperforming larger ones), and not family control or involvement, which explains the various results.

Cross-cultural differences in formal and informal institutions may also help to explain inconsistencies in results regarding family involvement and financial performance across different samples. One likely moderator of results in different countries is the degree of regulation, although this possibility has not yet been tested with meta-analysis techniques. Morck and Yeung (2003), for instance, suggest that the negative effect of family ownership evident outside the UK and the US, especially in several Asian countries, may be due to a lack of sufficient government regulation of dominant shareholders, in contrast to the Anglo-Saxon system. Peng and Jiang (2010), who compare several Asian economies, conclude that formal institutional factors help to explain differences in results across nations. In those countries with stronger rules of law (e.g. Singapore and Hong Kong), the family ownership effect appears to be more positive, suggesting that the expropriation of minority shareholders is held in check in such countries (Peng and Jiang, 2010). Peng and Jiang's (2010) index indicates that Taiwan is neither the highest nor the lowest ranked Asian country with respect to the rule of law, but their results may suggest, nevertheless, that the Taiwanese market reacts negatively to what it views as weaker protection of minority investors in such firms. In a separate study, and consistent with such investor skepticism, Wong et al. (2010) find that, among Taiwanese publicly listed firms, those firms with family-controlled boards and family CEOs receive a lower valuation on the market. Finally, Yoshikawa and Rasheed (2010) find that family control in Japan appears to be positively associated with dividend payouts.

With regard to other cross-country differences, a meta-analysis conducted by O'Boyle et al. (2012) shows significant moderator effects arising from individualism, with positive findings for family involvement and financial performance uncovered in more individualistic cultures. It would be interesting in future research to test whether, first of all, individualism and formal regulatory institutions are positively associated at the country level and, secondly, whether this helps to explain the moderating effects of individualism in past research.

The controversy about the relationship between family ownership and financial performance is far from settled. Moderator variables and alternative explanations will no doubt continue to form the basis for many future studies. Singal and Singal (2012), for instance, find in their sample of Indian listed firms that it may be concentrated ownership, and not family ownership, that matters. In any event, appropriate control variables are still being identified to provide a definitive answer to this research question.

Family Ownership and Intermediate Outcomes in Publicly Listed Firms

Research findings on the link between family control and intermediate outcomes related to governance appear to be more consistent than findings on the link between family control and financial performance, especially for listed firms (Bammens et al., 2011). For instance, Ho and Wong (2001), and Haniffa and Cooke (2002) find negative relationships between family dominance on the board and voluntary disclosure for firms listed in Hong Kong and Malaysia, respectively. In a sample of 105 initial public offerings (IPOs) in Germany, Ehrhardt and Nowak (2003) find evidence of expropriation of rents of minority shareholders in situations where the IPO includes the sale of non-voting shares to non-family shareholders. Executive entrenchment, which occurs when the CEO retains tenure much longer than his or her performance record would appear to justify, also seems to be more evident in family-owned and controlled firms. For instance, Gomez Mejia et al. (2001) find entrenchment to be a problem in Spanish newspapers, where family CEOs retain tenure seven years longer than non-family CEOs, on average. McConaughy (2000) and Cruz et al. (2010) arrive at comparable results.

Finally, other research confirms the relationship between family ownership and corporate social performance, especially for firms listed in the US (Dyer and Whetten, 2006; Berrone et al., 2010). For example, Berrone et al. (2010) confirm the importance of local embeddedness, or "local roots," as an independent predictor of environmental performance as well as a moderator of the effects of family ownership in the prediction of environmental performance. Their results are based on a sample of 194 large firms listed in the US.

Family Effects on the Performance of Unlisted Firms

In parallel with the explanations of the relationship between family involvement and the financial performance of listed firms, a number of rationales have been offered to explain the positive or negative effects of family involvement on financial performance in privately held firms. Some of the logics used for listed firms would seem to be less applicable in this context. For instance, Carney's principles of particularism, parsimony, and personalism do not necessarily differentiate between business-owning families and single owners. Whereas Carney argues that family-owned firms face less conflict, due to particularism, parsimony, and personalism, one could also argue that in the privately held firm, in comparison with individually owned firms, family-owned firms would logically be expected to face a greater likelihood of conflict, creating a negative influence on performance. Empirical research to date is equivocal. Though individual studies vary in their findings, a recent meta-analysis study concludes that for privately held firms, family involvement is not significantly related to financial performance (O'Boyle et al., 2012), consistent with previous conclusions drawn by Dyer (2006) in his literature review.

Conclusions and Directions for Future Research on Family Ownership and Performance

In summary, findings regarding the "family effect" remain inconclusive (see Dyer, 2006; O'Boyle et al., 2012), even though this issue is one of the most extensively tested in family business and corporate governance research. As noted by O'Boyle et al. (2012), future research on this topic may need to examine various moderator variables more closely. Some of the important moderating variables mentioned in this section include the number and generation of owners (especially the firm's status as a lone-founder firm or a family business), as well as potential cultural or formal institutional differences (especially governance regulations that protect minority shareholders). In addition, O'Boyle et al. (2012) finds support for some method-related moderator variables, including the year of publication (older articles tend to be more positive), the measurement of family involvement (self-reported measures are less significant), and whether the average family business is larger or smaller than the average non-family business in a particular sample (suggests size effects). For the generation variable, it may be important to check not only for possible linear effects but also for non-linear effects (i.e. whether second-generation firms appear to perform differently than first- or third- or later-generation firms). In future research, the overlap of ownership with management should also be more consistently controlled.

Family involvement may result in better predictions of certain intermediate governance-related outcomes, such as executive entrenchment and voluntary disclosure. However, such findings still need to be tested in different contexts to control for formal institutional differences across countries. Finally, in future research, sampling characteristics between family and non-family firms should be matched. Such characteristics include the stage in the life cycle and average company size.

For example, especially with regard to privately held firms, sampling needs to be sensitive to the degree to which young, first-generation firms are represented in order to allow for differentiation between family effects and lone-founder effects (Chrisman et al., 2004; Corbetta and Salvato, 2004). Furthermore, Sciascia and Mazzola (2008) provide some evidence to suggest that non-linear effects should be tested for family involvement, and that separate tests for family ownership and management should be undertaken. In their study of 620 privately held Italian SMEs, Sciascia and Mazzola (2008) control for several factors, including age and size, and they separately measure family involvement in ownership and management. They report a negative quadratic effect of family involvement in management (but not ownership) on firm performance.

Research question 2: Effects of Family Ownership on Contractual Governance

A second widely researched research question on family business and corporate governance addresses whether family-owned firms have different types of contractual governance than non-family-owned firms (see arrow RQ2 in Figure 18.1). The most commonly researched differences between family and non-family firms, especially for samples of listed firms, relate to the board of directors (see Bammens et al., 2011). These studies focus on board size, board composition (including the presence of independent directors, and whether the chairman of the board is related to or is the CEO), and types of committees established by the board (e.g. audit committee). In addition to board characteristics, researchers have also examined various aspects of CEO compensation packages, including overall levels and incentives.

Family Effects and Contractual Governance in Listed Firms

The most common rationale behind hypotheses relating family variables to the type of contractual governance, especially in listed firms, is probably the family's ostensible interest in maintaining decision-making control. For example, outsiders and other types of impartial monitoring devices are thought to be included in many boards primarily in response to pressures from non-family stakeholders (investors and banks) to safeguard non-family interests (Fiegener et al., 2000; Bammens et al., 2011). Consistent with this rationale, predictions are made that in family firms: (a) boards are smaller (and therefore more easily controlled) and have fewer independent directors; (b) that a member of the CEO's family or the CEO him/herself most likely serves as chairman, and (c) that audit committees and other such devices are more likely than in non-family firms.

Some of these hypotheses are supported by empirical research, while others are not. For instance, Anderson and Reeb (2004) find no difference in board size between family and non-family firms in their sample of US S&P 500 firms. However, they show that non-family firms have a significantly higher ratio of independent directors on their boards (61.2% versus 43.9% in family firms, on average) and a greater likelihood of CEO equity-based pay. Fiegener et al. (2000) find that firms with majority owner CEOs are more likely to have family members on their boards of directors, and Jaggi and Leung (2007) find that family firms are less likely to establish audit committees. However, Chau and Leung (2006) highlight a more complex relationship: as the proportion of family ownership increases from 5 to 25 percent, the likelihood that an audit committee will be established falls, while the reverse holds true when family ownership surpasses this range.

With respect to compensation levels, a somewhat counterintuitive pattern emerges. McConaughy (2000) presents the family control incentive alignment hypothesis, which suggests that given additional incentives derived from family membership, family CEOs are willing to receive lower compensation than non-family CEOs. In a study of 82 large, public firms in the US that are controlled by the founding family, McConaughy confirms this hypothesis. Family CEOs' willingness to receive less pay is also confirmed in other studies (see, for example, Gomez-Mejia et al., 2001, 2003; Combs et al., 2010).

As with the first research question, country and macro-level institutional differences may have significant moderating effects on outcomes. Oba et al. (2010) examine 151 family firms listed on the Istanbul Stock Exchange. They conclude that Turkish boards generally do not serve minority interests, and that non-executive directors are not well informed and do not play an important role in strategic decision-making. Furthermore, in these firms the control of the top management team (TMT) is not a priority. In short, the CEO sets the agenda and that agenda is not communicated in advance. Oba et al. (2010) further conclude that boards in Turkey mainly serve to provide legitimacy and that they do not offer an effective means of monitoring management and/or protecting (minority) shareholder interests.

Country and macro-level differences may also affect other relevant factors. For example, in a study of firms listed in Hong Kong, Jaggi and Leung (2007) find that family-controlled firms are less likely to establish an audit committee.

Family Effects and Contractual Governance in Privately Held Firms

Whereas the above studies focus on listed firms, a subset of the literature examines the effect of family ownership on contractual governance in privately held firms. Fiegener (2010), for instance, compares the presence of family members on the board of directors in three types of firms—family owned, owner managed, and outside owned. Fiegener (2010) finds that the first group has significantly greater family representation on the board. In their study of 112 large Spanish firms, Suáre and Santana-Martin (2004) note that first- and third-generation family firms are more similar to one another on a number of governance characteristics than they are to second-generation firms. Regardless of these generational differences, however, Suáre and Santana-Martin (2004) reaffirm what they call the "absolute dominance" of the leading family in the ownership, control, and management of Spanish family firms (p. 159). In sum, they find that the board serves a very limited function in regulating management.

Belgium may present a somewhat different case, as Belgian law requires limited liability companies to have at least three directors. In a study of 211 Belgian limited liability companies, Voordeckers et al. (2007) examine various predictors of board composition. They find that family firms nearing a generational change are more likely to have outside directors, and that both multigenerational and second-generation family firms are less likely to adopt an outside board. Family objectives, such as maintaining a family character within the firm, are negatively associated with the number of non-family directors. In contrast, firms with a profit-maximization objective are associated with the inclusion of more external directors. In addition, Voordeckers et al. find that mature firms are more likely than growing firms to have outside directors. Based on their rationale and findings, Voordeckers et al. (2007) conclude that resource dependence and the added-value perspective explain more of the variation in board composition than agency considerations. They also conclude that, at least in Belgium, the inclusion of outside directors is driven more by the advice and information needs of the firm (the potential value-added) than considerations of retaining family control.

In another study of Belgian SMEs, van den Berghe and Carchon (2002) find differences between family and non-family firms. In their study, boards of non-family firms tend to be larger and to include more outside professionals than boards of family firms. Non-family firms are also more likely to use formal criteria for board-member selection. Van den Berghe and Carchon further divide the family firms into person-backed family (PFB) firms (where one person owns more than 50% of shares) and family-backed (FFB) firms (where ownership is shared by a family). In comparing these two groups, they find that the number of owners (PFB versus FFB) provides a better explanation of differences in board characteristics (including size, types of members, and frequency of meetings) than generation of family ownership. FFBs tend to have larger boards but fewer independent members than PFBs, but FFB boards meet more than twice as often (five times a year vs twice a year, on average). In sum, the distinction between individually owned and business-family-owned groups is vital to obtaining a more accurate picture of contractual governance.

Summary and Directions for Future Research

Given the limited number of studies and the diversity of the countries in which such studies have been carried out, it is difficult to draw clear conclusions regarding the effect of family ownership on contractual governance. Nevertheless, research to date suggests that family ownership is likely to influence board characteristics and CEO compensation. Furthermore, as with the first research question, differentiating between firms with single owners and those with two or more family owners is of critical importance.

Although the emphasis to date has primarily been on quantitative studies and the independent variable of board composition, future research may use qualitative methods to explore differences in the ways that boards actually function and whether such differences can be attributed to family ownership. The study by Oba et al. (2010) provides one model for such research in that it examines not only board structure but also the types of roles assigned to (especially external) board members. The extensive literature review and factor analysis presented by van den Heuvel et al. (2006) on different potential roles of the board can also serve as a useful starting point for more in-depth research on boards in family firms, combining both quantitative and qualitative methods.

Research Question 3: Family Ownership Moderator Effects of Contractual Governance on Firm Performance–Relationships

The third research question examines whether specific aspects of family ownership or other family business characteristics moderate the relationship between types of contractual governance and firm performance. A related question asks whether there is a positive or negative relationship between contractual governance and firm performance in family firms (see arrow RQ3 in Figure 18.1). Once again, board structure—especially the presence of independent directors—is one of the most popular contractual governance variables examined in extant research.

Outside Directors, Other Contractual Governance Characteristics, and Financial Performance: The Moderating Effect of Family Ownership

Research findings to date indicate that the role of independent directors may vary between family firms and non-family firms. In their review of the general corporate governance literature, Daily et al. (2003) maintain that there is little evidence that independent directors aid performance (see also Dalton et al., 1999). Nonetheless, a closer look at the family business-related literature suggests that certain effects may be masked by the potential moderating effects of family ownership. An examination of such differences is important, as recommendations made for widely held firms and other non-family firms may, in fact, be detrimental for family-controlled firms (Lane et al., 2006).

Research regarding *outside* directors differentiates, when possible, between *independent* directors (those with no economic ties) (Anderson and Reeb, 2004; P. Klein et al., 2005; Arosa et al., 2010) and *affiliate* directors (those with some type of economic tie to the focal firm, either directly or by way of their employer). For example, Anderson and Reeb (2004) find that the presence of independent directors on the board of family firms has a positive effect on financial performance (as measured by Tobin's Q), whereas it has a negative effect for non-family firms. On the other hand, Anderson and Reeb (2004) report that the proportion of affiliate directors has a negative effect for family firms. These findings suggest not only that ownership may moderate the effects of board structure but that various types of outside directors may have different effects on the firm. One should note, however, that Anderson and Reeb's (2004) study does not distinguish between single owners and owning families nor does it distinguish between founders and later-generation owners. In another comparison of the effects of independent and affiliate directors, Arosa et al. (2010) study 369 non-listed Spanish SMEs. They conclude that affiliated directors (but not independent directors) have a positive effect on firm performance, but only during the first generation of ownership.

P. Klein et al. (2005) rely on a sample of 263 firms listed in Canada to provide evidence that "best-practice" recommendations for corporate governance do not always reflect empirical results. After adopting a stringent definition of board independence, these authors find no relationship between the presence of independent directors and financial performance in widely held firms. Furthermore, they find that independence has a negative effect on financial performance in family-controlled firms.

Finally, in an Asian sample of firms, Chen and Nowland (2010) identify interaction effects of ownership structure, concluding that the optimal proportion of outside directors (i.e. those listed as "independent" in annual reports) may be non-linear and vary depending on the ownership and control structures. However, they conclude that board monitoring does not always have a positive effect on performance, especially in family firms.

Family ownership may also have moderator effects on other governance variables. For example, Amran and Ahmad's (2009) study of firms listed in Malaysia shows that, whereas board size is negatively associated with firm value for non-family firms, it has no effect for family firms. Furthermore, family firms with separate leadership (the CEO and chairman are different people) perform better than those with dual leadership (the same person serves as CEO and chairman). This distinction makes no difference in non-family firms.

Outside Directors and Intermediate Outcomes: The Moderating Effect of Family Ownership

Other researchers examine the moderating effects of family ownership on the relationship between proportion of affiliate and/or independent directors and intermediate outcomes related to governance. For example, the accountancy literature examines various indicators for *earnings management* or manipulation. Jaggi and Leung (2007) find that the presence of family members on boards weakens the effectiveness of audit committees in controlling discretional accruals, a measure commonly used in accounting to indicate earnings manipulation or management. In a sample of Hong Kong firms, Jaggi et al. (2009) find that the presence of independent directors in non-family firms has a negative effect on earnings management. They conclude that, in family-controlled firms, independent directors are less likely to take on a monitoring role, especially if such a role may go against the wishes of the controlling family. In a different study, Chen and Jaggi (2000) find that a larger proportion of independent directors is associated with greater financial disclosure, but only in non-family firms.

CEO ownership, which is an aspect of family ownership, may also moderate the effect of overlap of the CEO with ownership. In this regard, Brunello et al. (2003) examine whether the CEO is also an owner. They find that an insider-dominated board reduces the likelihood that an underperforming CEO will be replaced, especially when the CEO is also an owner.

The prevalence of affiliate directors may have a positive influence depending on the dependent variable being predicted. For example, drawing their rationale from social capital theory, Jones et al. (2008) confirm that affiliate directors have a positive effect on diversification strategies, especially within family-controlled firms.

The studies mentioned thus far are based on samples of listed firms. Blumentritt (2006) compares the effects of boards of directors and advisory boards on planning in 133 privately held, family firms. The author finds that advisory boards play a more important role in the strategic process, especially with respect to strategy reviews, formal strategic processes, and the identification of a successor.

In another study linking board characteristics and strategic decision-making decisions, Mustakallio et al. (2002) find that, whereas active board involvement in the firm's strategy (referred to as board counsel) has a significant and positive effect on decision quality and commitment, monitoring of top management has no effect.

Summary and Directions for Future Research

Research to date, although incomplete, indicates that "best practices" for corporate governance do not always apply to family-controlled firms. Such results suggest the need to test for moderating effects of family-controlled firms before enforcing "best practices" across all types of firms. Moderating effects must not only be considered for such outcomes as financial performance but also for intermediate outcomes, such as financial disclosure, executive entrenchment, earnings manipulation, and diversification strategies. Furthermore, although quantitative models can be useful in drawing some conclusions, they provide an incomplete picture of actual decision-making processes within firms and how these processes are influenced by contractual governance practices. A better understanding of the decision-making process will improve the understanding of how and why family ownership may moderate relationships between governance practices and performance, and under which conditions.

Research Question 4: Family Ownership and Relational Governance

The fourth research question on the topic of family business and corporate governance examines the relationship between family ownership and relational governance (see arrow RQ4 in Figure 18.1). Daily and Dollinger (1992) suggest that family firms are more likely to use informal control systems than non-family firms (see also Chrisman et al., 2010). Chua et al. (1999) suggest that the intentions and vision of the dominant family coalition may be what distinguishes family from non-family firms.

Whereas much of the research for the first three research questions is based on a rationale drawn from agency theory (or its counterpart, stewardship theory), research assumptions regarding relational governance draw primarily on the social capital literature (Nahapiet and Ghoshal, 1998; Portes, 1998; Leana and van Buren, 1999; Adler and

Kwon, 2002; Mustakallio et al., 2002). For instance, Nahapiet and Ghoshal (1998) identify three types of social capital: structural, relational, and cognitive. Their model has been applied to describe the social capital of different social groups, including the board of directors (Hillman and Dalziel, 2003), family (Arregle et al., 2007; Pearson et al., 2008), and owners (Berent-Braun, 2010). The structural dimension of social capital reflects the type and density of social relationships among individuals in the group. The relational dimension refers to the "quality of relationships" among group members, such as trust, honesty, cooperative relations, and teamwork (Berent-Braun, 2010). The cognitive element is reflected in the extent of a shared vision among group members, such as their agreement about main goals, and their commitment to the group, rather than to individual interests.

Ensley and Pearson (2005) examine research question 4 by comparing top management teams (TMTs) composed of parent and child, other family combinations, or non-family members. They find that parental TMTs exhibit more positive group dynamics, as measured by cohesiveness and shared vision (aspects of relational and cognitive social capital, respectively), but other family TMTs exhibit weaker group dynamics than non-family firms.

In a sample of 233 privately held Dutch firms, and drawing from both social capital theory as well as social identity theory (Ellemers, 2001), Uhlaner, Wright, et al. (2007) find a positive relationship between family ownership and ownership commitment to the firm. Social identity theory, in particular, suggests that motivation of families toward collective goals may be due less to altruistic motives than to certain social needs. Indeed, consistent with that argument, Uhlaner, Wright, et al. (2007) find in their data set that the relationship between family ownership and ownership commitment is mediated by collective norms and goals. In a more recent study of 786 privately held Dutch firms, stratified by size and sector, Matser et al. (2011) find that family orientation predicts the quality of relationships (relational social capital) but not shared vision, somewhat consistent with the finding by Mustakallio et al. (2002) that family characteristics only indirectly predict shared vision (mediated in that case by social interaction). Further research is needed to clarify the effect of family involvement on relational governance, but initial research suggests that it may indeed enhance the relational aspects of social capital among group members.

Finally, LeBreton-Miller and Miller (2009) suggest that the extent of social embeddedness of the family in the firm may help to determine whether family ownership has a positive effect on relational governance. They propose a variety of ways in which embeddedness may be measured, including the percentage of total family ownership, the family's representation in management and on the board, the number of generations that the firm has been in the same family, and the number of different family factions, as well as the personal histories, values, and conflicts evident among family members.

Although the three aspects of relational governance provide one way of interpreting social capital, distinctions between bridging capital and bonding capital may also be useful (Salvato and Melin, 2008; Gedajlovic and Carney, 2010; Matser et al., 2011). Whereas bonding focuses on the relationships among group members, bridging focuses on its links with external parties (Adler and Kwon, 2002). Few empirical studies examine both bonding and bridging in the same data set. In an application to research on business-owning groups, Matser et al. (2011) find that, whereas family involvement has a positive effect on bonding (as measured by quality of relationship), it has a negative effect on bridging social capital.

Summary and Directions for Future Research

Only a limited number of empirical studies have tested the relationship between family ownership and relational governance. Research by Uhlaner, Flören, et al. (2007) reveals a positive relationship between family ownership and ownership commitment. The most recent research suggests that family involvement may enhance relational social capital, at least in privately held firms. Furthermore, the concept of social embeddedness, which was proposed by LeBreton-Miller and Miller (2009), may serve as an important moderator variable in the determination of the conditions under which family involvement may be associated with relational governance.

Future research should clarify the difference between family and ownership commitment, as different researchers vary in terms of the way in which they define and measure the commitment variable.

Research Question 5: Moderator Effects of Family Ownership on Relational Governance–Firm Performance Relationships

In parallel to research question 3, which explores contractual governance, the fifth research question addresses the relationship between relational governance and firm performance, with family ownership as a moderator (see arrow RQ5 in Figure 18.1). A related research question explores whether a relationship between relational governance and firm performance exists within family-owned firms.

One stream of research underpinning the relational governance literature examines the effect of conflict on performance. Ensley et al. (2007) contrast *cognitive* conflict, which is task oriented and focused on differences of opinion about how to achieve common objectives, and *affective* conflict, which reflects interpersonal disagreements. In both family firms and non-family firms, they find that cognitive conflict is positively related to growth, whereas growth and affective conflict are negatively related. In contrast, Kellermanns and Eddleston (2007) use a broader scale of performance and find that cognitive conflict has a negative effect on performance. However, this effect is moderated by ownership dispersion, as the effect is positive when dispersion is low, in other words when ownership is contained within a single generation. The differences between the two studies may be the result of different sampling frames. The data set in the Ensley et al. study is largely made up of younger, first-generation Inc 500 firms, while the Kellermanns and Eddleston study encompasses a wider range of owner dispersion.

Mustakallio et al. (2002) find that shared vision is positively associated with both the quality of and commitment to strategic decision-making in family firms. Berent-Braun et al. (2011) find that a shared vision of firm objectives among owners and the quality of relationships (i.e. trust and cooperation) among owners predict financial performance in privately held, family and non-family firms. Furthermore, family orientation is positively associated with the quality of relationships among owners but does not directly affect financial performance. However, in a model with all three variables (each representing an aspect of social capital), shared vision appears to have the most direct effect on financial performance, mediating the relationship between quality of relationships and financial performance (Berent-Braun et al., 2011).

Summary and Directions for Future Research

Less attention has been paid to the fifth research question than to some of those already covered. Future research examining both ownership and family social capital may shed more light on how relational governance may influence performance.

Research Question 6: Moderator Effects of Family Ownership on Contractual–Relational Governance Relationships

A sixth research question examines the relationship between contractual and relational governance, either in family firms or in situations where family orientation serves as a moderator variable (see arrow RQ6 in Figure 18.1). Trust has been examined as an especially important relational governance mechanism. Eddleston et al. (2010), for instance, suggest that trust is a governance mechanism that may reduce the amount of monitoring and incentives needed to resolve agency problems (see also Chrisman et al., 2007).

Puranam and Vanneste (2009) identify three arguments regarding potential relationships between contractual and relational governance (including trust). First, the two types of governance may have a positive association: contracts may increase the reliability of behaviors and thus rebuild trust (Sitken and Roth, 1993; Eddleston et al., 2010). Second, they may be negatively related: trust might reduce the amount of monitoring and incentives needed to resolve agency problems (Chrisman et al., 2007). Finally, contractual and relational governance may be independent of one another.

Jaskiewicz and Klein (2007) test these hypotheses in an empirical study of 548 family and non-family German firms with sales of more than EUR 1 million. They find that goal alignment (an aspect of relational governance) is associated with a number of board characteristics. In particular, goal alignment between owners and managers is associated with smaller boards, a smaller proportion of outside board members, and a larger proportion of affiliate board members. They find no relationship between goal alignment and the proportion of family-related board members. Thus, the relationships appear to depend on the types of variables chosen for study.

The limited amount of research to date makes it difficult to draw firm conclusions, but initial findings suggest that using family control or other family ownership variables as moderator variables in studies of the relationship between contractual and relational governance may shed further light on corporate governance research in general. In sum, this is a relatively unexplored area of corporate governance that offers opportunities for future research.

Research Question 7: Effects of Family Governance Practices on Business and Family Performance

The seventh question explored on the topic of family business and corporate governance relates to family governance practices (see arrow RQ7 in Figure 18.1). In the relational governance model, *family governance practices* (also referred to as family institutions) are the structures or mechanisms intended to facilitate the family's relationships with the business (Gersick et al., 1997; Neubauer and Lank, 1998; Aronoff and Ward, 2002; Mustakallio et al., 2002; Suáre and Santana-Martín, 2004). Although these practices are identified as an aspect of relational governance in some family business research (Mustakallio et al., 2002), they can also be viewed as a separate set of institutions specifically aimed at integrating the family and the firm. Regardless of how they are labeled, Mustakallio et al. (2002) point out that family governance practices can enhance cohesion and shared vision in the family, and simultaneously reduce the family's potentially harmful effects.

Family governance practices can be viewed as a means to enhance the entrepreneurship of the business-owning family (Berent-Braun and Uhlaner, 2012a), especially when the common purpose or vision is one of growing and maintaining family wealth. From a group dynamics perspective, therefore, family governance practices not only stimulate social interaction but also increase the likelihood that the business-owning family can form a shared vision, develop common norms, and agree upon rules to govern the behavior of family members with respect to the firm (Uhlaner, 2006). Thus, family governance practices can be seen as teambuilding tools that enhance the effectiveness of the business-owning family and the business it owns. In a study by Berent-Braun and Uhlaner (2012a), based on a sample of primarily older, larger, later-generation family firms, family governance practices are found to indirectly enhance financial performance. This relationship is mediated by the degree to which owners share a vision of maintaining and growing family wealth.

Summary and Directions for Future Research

To date, the majority of research on family governance practices has been qualitative. However, an empirical study by Mustakallio et al. (2002) confirms a positive relationship between such practices and positive social interaction among family members. In other words, in firms where family governance practices are evident, family members tend to maintain close social relationships and know each other on a personal level. More recent research confirms the relationship between family governance practices and financial performance, especially among large, late-generation firms. However, this relationship is mediated by a shared owner focus on building and maintaining shared wealth (Berent-Braun and Uhlaner, 2012a). Additional research, especially studies based on large, random samples and quantitative statistical methods, can be used to validate the current knowledge base regarding family governance practices (e.g. Gersick et al., 1997). A growing amount of literature points to the benefits of introducing such practices (Gray, 2007, 2010, 2011), and their use among family business consultants is becoming increasingly widespread. However, validation research remains limited and could provide a clearer picture of when such practices are most advantageous for family firms.

Research Question 8: The Role of Non-managing Family Owners in the of the Firm?

An eighth research question relates more specifically to non-managing owners and their role in firm governance, which is sometimes referred to as responsible ownership (Lambrecht and Uhlaner, 2005) (see arrow RQ8 in Figure 18.1). Literature on this topic identifies certain behaviors, such as active governance (monitoring), acquisition of resources (including patient capital and networking contacts), professionalism, and practices enabling the stimulation of strategy (Berent-Braun and Uhlaner, 2012b).

Although empirical research is fairly limited, initial findings in some samples suggest that monitoring by non-managing owners may create more interference than assistance in terms of improving financial performance (Berent-Braun and Uhlaner, 2012b). This finding is consistent with other research that has questioned the benefits of monitoring (Chen and Nowland, 2010). In contrast, owners that respect the boundaries of the firm, especially its hierarchy of authority and shareholder agreements, may create a more trusting atmosphere and, thereby, enhance the overall performance of the firm. Such findings appear to be less consistent with agency theory and perhaps more consistent with stewardship theory and social capital theory. However, future research will need to more closely examine the possible effects of ownership actions on decision-making and firm performance for business-owning families and, more generally, for business-owning groups.

Research Question 9: How Life Cycle Influences Appropriateness of Governance

A last research question (see arrow RQ9 in Figure 18.1) addresses the possibility that governance may need to change over time. Generations represent one way of capturing longitudinal changes in ownership. Gubitta and Gianecchini (2002) study a subsample of 34 SMEs with both boards of directors and executive boards in northeast Italy. They present an evolutionary model based on the concept of flexibility derived from a new theory of property rights. They propose that, as companies grow in size, governance may move toward greater openness (i.e. increasing proportions of non-family executives represented in the management or governing boards) and a clearer hierarchy of decision-making between the board of directors and top management. In a more quantitative study of the effect of generation as a moderator variable, Molly et al. (2012) find that next-generation companies grow more slowly because they are reluctant to take on as much debt as first-generation firms.

Case-study research by Lambrecht and Lievens (2008) suggests another interesting direction for future research on longitudinal issues. They find that "pruning" by certain family owners—the buying out of the majority of family owners in order to cut down or limit the total number of owners—can trigger important changes in governance, such as the installation of a more professional board of directors or a higher number of independent board members. In addition, business succession in general may trigger changes in governance (Lambrecht, 2005).

In summary, an examination of the governance changes taking place in tandem with changes in ownership and management may enhance our general understanding of the governance process. To this end, a limited amount of research to date has examined the effects of such life-cycle changes in the context of family firms.

Conclusions and Additional Directions for Future Research

The research presented in this chapter is organized in accordance with nine research questions. By far the largest amount of research to date has focused on "family effects" that predict financial performance. However, a broadening research agenda with respect to both contractual and relational governance provides scholars with numerous research opportunities. The field is likely to advance more rapidly as scholars develop a greater consensus regarding measurement and sampling issues.

The research accumulated thus far shows that conscientious researchers should avoid measuring family involvement exclusively with a single indicator of percentage ownership. Such an index potentially confounds the effects of founders with later generations, and single owners vs business-owning families.

Furthermore, given the pattern of research findings presented in this chapter, the importance of using some type of family business indicator as a moderator variable for a wide variety of corporate governance research questions should be obvious. This is particularly true for research into the relationship between contractual governance and financial performance and other outcomes. Best practices derived from research on US-based, widely held firms may be grossly misleading not only for non-US firms but also for family-controlled firms in the US (La Porta et al., 1999). Furthermore, a growing amount of literature suggests that it may not be the *direct* effect of family involvement variables per se, but their *indirect* effects (mediated by other variables, including contractual governance, relational governance, and family governance practices), that explain a firm's overall performance.

Additional Directions for Future Research

Although agency theory has provided the impetus for an entirely new field of research, researchers are increasingly calling for a re-evaluation of the theory's continued usefulness as the key driver of corporate governance research (Daily et al.,

2003; Lan and Heracleous, 2010). The family business field provides a rich range of examples for the possible application of other theories, largely from the field of management, including stewardship theory, the resource-based view, and social capital theory.

In addition to the many specific suggestions for research made throughout this chapter, opportunities for further research on family business and corporate governance appear especially ripe in the following areas:

Researchers can move beyond family involvement or related ownership structure indicators to examine the behaviors and roles of owners (both family and nonfamily) that may influence the strategic and operational decision-making processes of the firm.

Researchers may further explore the circumstances under which a business-owning family has the strongest (positive or negative) influence—e.g. in cases of greater social embeddedness (LeBreton-Miller and Miller, 2009); when family governance practices are used; in firms lacking a working board of directors; and in small firms or in business-owning families with more human capital (experience, education, specialized, or general knowledge).

Researchers may also wish to explore more fully how relational and contractual governance interact with one another in their impact on the family-owned firm. Are they substitutes or complements to one another? Are trust and shared vision (among family members, owners, board members, and executives within the firm) precursors to the effective functioning of the board and top management?

Researchers can also begin to examine how advisory boards interact with formal boards of directors in family-owned firms. Can they interfere with the proper functioning of boards of directors? How can they be set up to augment, rather than to replace or interfere with, the activities of boards of directors?

The challenge in this chapter has been to provide the reader with an overview of a rapidly growing topic of research in a relatively short space. Hopefully, the reader is convinced of the many rich opportunities open to further exploration.

Notes

1. According to the Expert Group of the European Commission on Family Business (often referred to as the "GEEF" definition), a "family business" must meet the following criteria: (1) the majority of ownership must (directly or indirectly) rest in the hands of a person and/or a natural family; and (2) at least one representative of the family or kin must be involved in the management or administration of the firm. For listed firms, GEEF modifies the first criterion to require only 25% ownership by one person or family (European Commission, 2009). See also <http://www.efb-geef.eu/>, accessed October 28, 2011.
2. See e.g. the Henokien website, <http://www.henokiens.com>, accessed October 28, 2011.
3. Readers seeking more detailed coverage of family business definitions may wish to refer to Flören (2002), Uhlaner (2005), or Nicholson (2010).

4. See Jensen and Meckling (1976) for a more complete description of agency theory. See also Daily et al. (2003) for a recent critique of agency theory and governance.
5. See e.g. Chrisman et al. (2010), Bammens et al. (2011) or Siebels and Knyphausen-Aufseβ (2012), for recent reviews of family business and corporate governance literature that are organized by theory.

REFERENCES

ADLER, P. S., and KWON, S. (2002). "Social Capital: Prospects for a New Concept," *Academy of Management Review*, 27: 17–40.

AMRAN, N. A., and AHMAD, A. C. (2009). "Family Business, Board Dynamics and Firm Value: Evidence from Malaysia," *Journal of Financial Reporting & Accounting*, 7(1): 53–74.

ANDERSON, R. C., and REEB, D. M. (2003). "Founding Family Ownership and Firm Performance: Evidence from the S&P 500," *Journal of Finance*, 58(3): 1301–28.

—— —— (2004). "Board Composition: Balancing Family Influence in S&P 500 Firms," *Administrative Science Quarterly*, 49: 209–37.

ARONOFF, C. E., and WARD, J. L. (2002). *Family Business Ownership: How to Be an Effective Shareholder*. Marietta, GA: Family Enterprise Publishers.

AROSA, B., ITTURRALDE, T., and MASEDA, A. (2010). "Outsiders on the Board of Directors and Firm Performance: Evidence from Spanish Non-listed Family Firms," *Journal of Family Business Strategy*, 1: 236–45.

ARREGLE, L.-J., HITT, M. A., SIRMON, D. G., and VÉRY, P. (2007). "The Development of Organizational Social Capital: Attributes of Family Firms," *Journal of Management Studies*, 44(1): 73–95.

ASTRACHAN, J. H., KLEIN, S. B., and SMYRNIOS, K. X. (2002). "The F-PEC Scale of Family Influence: A Proposal for Solving the Family Business Definition Problem," *Family Business Review*, 15: 45–58.

—— and SHANKER, M. C. (2003). "Family Businesses' Contribution to the U.S. Economy: A Closer Look," *Family Business Review*, 16(3): 211–19.

BAMMENS, Y., VOORDECKERS, W., and VAN GILS A. (2011). "Boards of Directors in Family Businesses: A Literature Review and Research Agenda," *International Journal of Management Reviews*, 13: 134–52.

BERENT-BRAUN, M. M. (2010). "Does Ownership Matter? Ownership Dynamics, Ownership Social Capital and Responsible Ownership in Private Firms." Doctoral dissertation, Nyenrode Business Universiteit, Breukelen, the Netherlands.

—— and UHLANER, L. M. (2012a). "Family Governance Practices and Teambuilding: Paradox of the Enterprising Family," *Small Business Economics*, 38(1): 103–19.

—— —— (2012b). "Responsible Ownership Behaviors and Financial Performance in Family Owned Businesses," *Journal of Small Business and Enterprise Development*, 19(1): 20–38.

—— —— and FLÖREN, R. (2011). "Ownership Social Capital and Firm Performance: Evidence from a Dutch Sample," 11th Annual IFERA World Family Business Research Conference, Palermo, Italy (June 28–July 1).

BERRONE, P., CRUZ, C., GOMEZ-MEJIA, L. R., and KINTANA, M. L. (2010). "Socioemotional Wealth and Corporate Responses to Institutional Pressures: Do Family-Controlled Firms Pollute Less?" *Administrative Science Quarterly*, 55(1): 82–113.

Bertrand, M., Johnson, S., Samphantharak, K., and Schoar, A. (2008). "Mixing Family with Business: A Study of Thai Business Groups and the Families behind Them," *Journal of Financial Economics*, 88: 466–98.

Blumentritt, T. (2006). "The Relationship between Boards and Planning in Family Businesses," *Family Business Review*, 19: 65–72.

Brunello, G., Graziano, C., and Parigi, B. (2003). "CEO Turnover in Insider-Dominated Boards: The Italian Case," *Journal of Banking and Finance*, 27: 1027–51.

Cadbury, A. (1992). *Report on the Committee of the Financial Aspects of Corporate Governance*. London: Gee Publishing.

Carney, M. (2005). "Corporate Governance and Competitive Advantage in Family-Controlled Firms," *Entrepreneurship Theory and Practice*, 29: 249–65.

Chau, G., and Leung, P. (2006). "The Impact of Board Composition and Family Ownership on Audit Committee Formation: Evidence from Hong Kong," *Journal of International Accounting, Auditing and Taxation*, 15: 1–15.

Chen, C. J., and Jaggi, B. (2000). "Association between Independent Non-executive Directors, Family Control and Financial Disclosures in Hong Kong," *Journal of Accounting and Public Policy*, 19: 285–310.

Chen, E. T., and Nowland, J. (2010). "Optimal Monitoring in Family-Owned Companies: Evidence from Asia," *Corporate Governance: An International Review*, 18(1): 3–17.

Chrisman, J. J., Chua, J. H., and Litz, R. A. (2004). "Comparing the Agency Costs of Family and Non-family Firms: Conceptual Issues and Exploratory Evidence," *Entrepreneurship: Theory and Practice*, 28: 335–54.

—— —— Kellermanns, F. W., and Chang, E. P. C. (2007). "Are Family Managers Agents or Stewards? An Exploratory Study in Privately Held Family Firms," *Journal of Business Research*, 60: 1030–38.

—— Kellermanns, F. W., Chan, K. C., and Liano, K. (2010). "Intellectual Foundations of Current Research in Family Business: An Identification and Review of 25 Influential Articles," *Family Business Review*, 23(1): 9–26.

—— —— Pearson, A. W., and Barnett, T. (2012). "Family Involvement, Family Influence, and Family-Centered Non-economic Goals in Small Firms," *Entrepreneurship: Theory and Practice*, 36(2): 267–93.

Chua, J. H., Chrisman, J. J., and Sharma, P. (1999). "Defining Family Business by Behavior," *Entrepreneurship: Theory and Practice*, 23(4): 19–39.

Cliff, J. E., and Jennings, P. D. (2005). "Commentary on the Multidimensional Degree of Family Influence Construct and the F-PEC Measurement Instrument," *Entrepreneurship & Regional Development*, 29: 341–48.

Combs, J., Penney, C., Crook, R., and Short, J. (2010). "The Impact of Family Representation on CEO Compensation," *Entrepreneurship Theory and Practice*, 36(6): 1125–44.

Corbetta, G., and Salvato, C. (2004). "Self-Serving or Self-Actualizing? Models of Man and Agency Costs in Different Types of Family Firms: A Commentary on 'Comparing the Agency Costs of Family and Non-Family Firms: Conceptual Issues and Exploratory Evidence,'" *Entrepreneurship Theory and Practice*, 28: 355–62.

Cruz, C., Gomez-Mejia, L. R., and Becerra, M. (2010). "Perceptions of Benevolence and the Design of Agency Contracts: CEO-TMT Relationships in Family Firms," *Academy of Management Journal*, 53(1): 69–89.

Daily, C. M., and Dollinger, M. J. (1992). "An Empirical Examination of Ownership Structure in Family and Professionally Managed Firms," *Family Business Review*, 5: 117–36.

—— Dalton, D. R., and Cannella, A. A. (2003). "Corporate Governance: Decades of Dialogue and Data," *Academy of Management Review*, 28: 371–82.

Dalton, D. R., Daily, C. M., Johnson, J. L., and Ellstrand, A. E. (1999). "Number of Directors and Financial Performance: A Meta-Analysis," *Academy of Management Journal*, 42(6): 674–86.

Davis, J. H., Schoorman, D. F., and Donaldson, L. (1997). "Toward a Stewardship Theory of Management," *Academy of Management Review*, 22: 20–47.

Debicki, B. J., Matherne, C. F., Kellermanns, F. W., and Chrisman, J. J. (2009). "Family Business Research in the New Millennium: An Overview of the Who, the Where, the What, and the Why," *Family Business Review*, 22: 151–66.

Dyer, Jr., W. G. (2006). "Examining the 'Family Effect' on Firm Performance," *Family Business Review*, 19: 253–73.

—— and Whetten, D. A. (2006). "Family Firms and Social Responsibility: Preliminary Evidence from the S&P 500," *Entrepreneurship: Theory and Practice*, 30(6): 785–802.

Eddleston, K. A., Chrisman, J. J., Steier, L. P., and Chua, J. H. (2010). "Governance and Trust in Family Firms: An Introduction," *Entrepreneurship: Theory and Practice*, 34(6): 1043–56.

Ehrhardt, O., and Nowak, E. (2003). "The Effect of IPOs on German Family-Owned Firms: Governance Changes, Ownership Structure and Performance," *Journal of Small Business Management*, 41(2): 222–32.

Ellemers, N. (2001). "Social Identity, Commitment, and Work Behavior," in M. A. Hogg and D. J. Terry (eds.), *Social Identity Process in Organizational Context*, Philadelphia, PA: Psychology Press, Taylor and Francis Group, 101–14.

Ensley, M. D., and Pearson, A. W. (2005). "An Exploratory Comparison of the Behavioral Dynamics of Top Management Teams in Family and Nonfamily New Ventures: Cohesion, Conflict, Potency, and Consensus," *Entrepreneurship: Theory and Practice*, 29(3): 267–84.

—— —— and Sardeshmukh, S. R. (2007). "The Negative Consequences of Pay Dispersion in Family and Non-Family Top Management Teams: An Exploratory Analysis of New Venture, High-Growth Firms," *Journal of Business Research*, 60: 1039–47.

European Commission (2009). "Final Report of the Expert Group. Overview of Family-Business-Relevant Issues: Research, Networks, Policy Measures, and Existing Studies. Enterprise and Industry Directorate-General," <http://ec.europa.eu/enterprise/policies/sme/promoting-entrepreneurship/family-business/family_business_expert_group_report_en.pdf> (accessed October 28, 2011).

Fama, E. F., and Jensen, M. C. (1983). "Separation of Ownership and Control," *Journal of Law and Economics*, 26: 301–25.

Fiegener, M. K. (2010). "Locus of Ownership and Family Involvement in Small Private Firms," *Journal of Management Studies*, 47 (2): 296–321.

——— Brown, B. M., Dreux, D. R., and Dennis, W. J. (2000). "The Adoption of Outside Boards by Small Private US Firms," *Entrepreneurship and Regional Development*, 12: 291–309.

Filatotchev, I., and Wright, M. (2005). *The Life Cycle of Corporate Governance*. Cheltenham: Edward Elgar.

Floren, R. H. (2002). *Crown Princes in the Clay: An Empirical Study on the Tackling of Succession Challenges in Dutch Family Firms*. Assen: Van Gorcum.

Gadhoum, Y. (2006). "Power of Ultimate Controlling Owners: A Survey of Canadian Landscape," *Journal of Management Governance*, 10: 179–204.

GEDAJLOVIC, E., and CARNEY, M. (2010). "Markets, Hierarchies, and Families: Toward a Transaction Cost Theory of the Family Firm," *Entrepreneurship: Theory and Practice*, 34(6): 1145–71.

GERSICK, K. E., DAVIS, J. A., MCCOLLOM-HAMPTON, M., and LANSBERG, I. (1997). *Generation to Generation: Life Cycles of the Family Business*. Boston, MA: Harvard Business School Press.

GOMEZ-MEJIA, L. R., NUNEZ-NICKEL, M., and GUTIERREZ, I. (2001). "The Role of Family Ties in Agency Contracts," *Academy of Management Journal*, 44: 81–95.

——LARRAZA-KINTANA, M., and MAKRI, M. (2003). "The Determinants of Executive Compensation in Family-Controlled Public Corporations." *Academy of Management Journal*, 46(2): 226–37.

——CRUZ, C., BERRONE, P., and DE CASTRO, J. (2011). "The Bind that Ties: Socioemotional Wealth Preservation in Family Firms," *The Academy of Management Annals*, 5(1): 653–707.

GRAY, L. (2007). "The Three Forms of Governance: A New Approach to Family Wealth Transfer and Asset Protection, Part I." *The Journal of Wealth Management*, 10(2): 10–19.

——(2010). *Generational Wealth Management: A Guide for Fostering Global Family Wealth*. London: Euromoney Institutional Investor, PLC.

——(2011). "The Three Forms of Governance: A New Approach to Family Wealth Transfer and Asset Protection, Part III," *The Journal of Wealth Management*, 14(1): 41–54.

GUBITTA, P., and GIANECCHINI, M. (2002). "Governance and Flexibility in Family-Owned SMEs," *Family Business Review*, 15 (4): 277–97.

HANIFFA, R. M., and COOKE, T. E. (2002). "Culture, Corporate Governance and Disclosure in Malaysian Corporations," *Abacus*, 38: 317–49.

HILLMAN, A. J., and DALZIEL, T. (2003). "Boards of Directors and Firm Performance: Integrating Agency and Resource Dependence Perspectives," *Academy of Management Review*, 28: 383–96.

HO, S. S., and WONG, K. S. (2001). "A Study of the Relationship between Corporate Governance Structures and the Extent of Voluntary Disclosure," *Journal of International Accounting, Auditing and Taxation*, 10: 139–56.

HOLT, D. T., RUTHERFORD, M. W., and KURATKO, D. F. (2010). "Advancing the Field of Family Business Research: Further Testing the Measurement Properties of the F-PEC," *Family Business Review*, 23(1): 76–88.

HUSE, M. (1993). "Relational Norms as a Supplement to Neo-Classical Understanding of Directorates: An Empirical Study of Boards of Directors," *Journal of Socio-Economics*, 22: 219–40.

JAGGI, B., and LEUNG, S. (2007). "Impact of Family Dominance on Monitoring of Earnings Management by Audit Committees: Evidence from Hong Kong," *Journal of International Accounting, Auditing and Taxation*, 16: 27–50.

————and GUL, F. (2009). "Family Control, Board Independence, and Earnings Management: Evidence Based on Hong Kong Firms," *Journal of Accounting and Public Policy*, 28: 281–300.

JASKIEWICZ, P., and KLEIN, S. (2007). "The Impact of Goal Alignment on Board Composition and Board Size in Family Businesses," *Journal of Business Research*, 60: 1080–9.

JENSEN, M. C., and MECKLING, W. H. (1976). "Theory of the Firm: Managerial Behavior, Agency Costs and Ownership Structure," *Journal of Financial Economics*, 3: 305–60.

JONES, C. D., MAKRI, M., and GOMEZ-MEJIA, L. R. (2008). "Affiliate Directors and Perceived Risk Bearing in Publicly Traded, Family-Controlled Firms: The Case of Diversification," *Entrepreneurship Theory and Practice*, 32: 1007–26.

KEASEY, K., and WRIGHT, M. (1993). "Issues in Corporate Accountability and Governance: An Editorial," *Accounting and Business Research*, 23(91A): 291–303.

KELLERMANNS, F. W., and EDDLESTON, K. A. (2007). "A Family Perspective on When Conflict Benefits Family Firm Performance," *Journal of Business Research*, 60: 1048–57.

KLEIN, S. B., ASTRACHAN, J. H., and SMYRNIOS, K. X. (2005). "The F-PEC Scale of Family Influence: Construction, Validation, and Further Implication for Theory," *Entrepreneurship: Theory and Practice*, 29: 321–39.

KLEIN, P., SHAPIRO, D., and YOUNG, J. (2005). "Corporate Governance, Family Ownership and Firm Value: The Canadian Evidence," *Corporate Governance: An International Review*, 13: 769–84.

LAMBRECHT, J. (2005). "Multigenerational Transition in Family Businesses: A New Explanatory Model," *Family Business Review*, 18(4): 267–82.

—— and LIEVENS, J. (2008). "Pruning the Family Tree: An Unexplored Path to Family Business Continuity and Family Harmony," *Family Business Review*, 21(4): 295–313.

—— and UHLANER, L. (2005). "Responsible Ownership of the Family Business: State-of-the-Art," position paper prepared for FBN-IFERA World Academic Research forum, EHSAL, Brussels, Belgium (September).

LAN, L. L., and HERACLEOUS, L. (2010). "Rethinking Agency Theory: The View from Law," *Academy of Management Review*, 35(2): 294–314.

LANE, S., ASTRACHAN, J., KEYT, A., and MCMILLAN, K. (2006). "Guidelines for Family Business Boards of Directors," *Family Business Review*, 19(2): 147–67.

LA PORTA, R., LOPEZ-DE-SILANES, F., and SHLEIFER, A. (1999). "Corporate Ownership around the World," *Journal of Finance*, 54: 471–517.

LEANA, C. R., and VAN BUREN III, H. J. (1999). "Organizational Social Capital and Employment Practices," *The Academy of Management Review*, 24(3): 538–55.

LEBRETON-MILLER, I., and MILLER, D. (2009). "Agency vs. Stewardship in Public Family Firms: A Social Embeddedness Reconciliation," *Entrepreneurship Theory and Practice*, 33: 1169–91.

LUMPKIN et al. (2011). "Strategic Entrepreneurship in Family Business," *Strategic Entrepreneurship Journal*, 5(4): 285–306.

MATSER, I., BERENT, M. M., UHLANER, L. M., and FLÖREN, R. (2011). "The Creation of Ownership Social Capital in Family Firms and Non-Family Firms: How Does Family Influence Shape the Development of Ownership Social Capital?," Seventh Workshop on Family Firms Management Research, Witten, Germany (May, 27–9).

MCCONAUGHY, D. (2000). "Family CEO vs. Non-family CEOs in the Family Controlled Firm: An Examination of the Level and Sensitivity of Pay to Performance," *Family Business Review*, 13(2): 121–31.

MILLER, D., and LE BRETON-MILLER, I. (2006). "Family Governance and Firm Performance: Agency, Stewardship and Capabilities," *Family Business Review*, 19: 73–87.

—— —— LESTER, R. H., and CANNELLA, JR., A. A. (2007). "Are Family Firms Really Superior Performers?" *Journal of Corporate Finance*, 13: 829–58.

MOLLY, V., LAVEREN, E., and JORISSEN, A. (2012). "Intergenerational Differences in Family Firms: Impact on Capital Structure and Growth Behavior," *Entrepreneurship Theory and Practice*, 36(4): 703–25.

—— Shleifer, A., and Vishny, R. (1988). "Management Ownership and Market Valuation: An Empirical Analysis," *Journal of Financial Economics*, 20(1–2): 293–315.

Morck, R., and Yeung, B. (2003). "Agency Problems in Large Family Business Groups," *Entrepreneurship Theory and Practice*, 27: 367–82.

Mustakallio, M. E., Autio, E., and Zahra, S. A. (2002). "Relational and Contractual Governance in Family Business: Effects on Strategic Decision Making," *Family Business Review*, 15(3): 205–22.

Nahapiet, J., and Ghoshal, S. (1998). "Social Capital, Intellectual Capital and the Organizational Advantage," *Academy of Management Review*, 23(2): 242–66.

Neubauer, F., and Lank, A. G. (1998). *The Family Business: It's Governance for Sustainability*. London: Macmillan.

Nicholson, L. A. (2010). "Jamaican Family-Owned Businesses: Homogeneous or Non-homogeneous," *Social and Economic Studies*, 59(3): 7–29.

Nordqvist, M. (2005). "Familiness in Top Management Teams: Commentary on Ensley and Pearson's 'An Exploratory Comparison of the Behavioral Dynamics of Top Management Teams in Family and Nonfamily New Ventures: Cohesion, Conflict, Potency, and Consensus,'" *Entrepreneurship: Theory and Practice*, 29: 285–91.

Oba, B., Ozsoy, Z., and Atakan, S. (2010). "Power in the Boardroom: A Study on Turkish Family-Owned and Listed Companies," *Corporate Governance*, 10: 603–16.

O'Boyle, Jr., E. H., Pollack, J. M., and Rutherford, M. W. (2012). "Exploring the Relation between Family Involvement and Firms' Financial Performance: A Meta-Analysis of Main and Moderator Effects," *Journal of Business Venturing*, 27(1): 1–18.

Pearson, A. W., Carr, J. C., and Shaw, J. C. (2008). "Toward a Theory of Familiness: A Social Capital Perspective," *Entrepreneurship Theory and Practice*, 32(6): 949–69.

Peng, M. W., and Jiang, Y. (2010). "Institutions behind Family Ownership and Control in Large Firms," *Journal of Management Studies*, 47: 253–73.

Portes, A. (1998). "Social Capital: Its Origins and Applications in Modern Sociology," *Annual Review of Sociology*, 24(1): 1–24.

Puranam, P., and Vanneste, B. S. (2009). "Trust and Governance: Untangling a Tangled Web," *Academy of Management Review*, 34: 11–31.

Reynolds, P. D., Bygrave, W. D., Autio, E., Cox, L. W., and Hay, M. (2002). *Global Entrepreneurship Monitor; 2002 Executive Report*. Kansas City, MO: Ewing Marion Kauffman Foundation.

Sacristán-Navarro, M., Gómez-Ansón, S., and Cabeza-Garcia, L. (2011). "Large Shareholders' Combinations in Family Firms: Prevalence and Performance Effects," *Journal of Family Business Strategy*, 2: 101–12.

Salvato, C., and Melin, L. (2008). "Creating Value across Generations in Family-Controlled Businesses: The Role of Family Social Capital," *Family Business Review*, 21: 259–76.

Schulze, W. S., Lubatkin, M. H., and Dino, R. N. (2002). "Altruism, Agency, and the Competitiveness of Family Firms," *Managerial and Decision Economics*, 23: 247–59.

—— —— —— (2003a). "Toward a Theory of Agency and Altruism in Family Firms," *Journal of Business Venturing*, 18: 473–90.

—— —— —— (2003b). "Exploring the Agency Consequences of Ownership Dispersion among the Directors of Private Family Firms," *Academy of Management Journal*, 46: 179–94.

Sciascia, S., and Mazzola, P. (2008). "Family Involvement in Ownership and Management: Exploring Nonlinear Effects on Performance," *Family Business Review*, 21: 331–46.

SHLEIFER, A., and VISHNY, R. W. (1997). "A Survey of Corporate Governance," *The Journal of Finance*, 52: 737–83.

SHYU, Y., and LEE, C. I. (2009). "Excess Control Rights and Debt Maturity Structure in Family-Controlled Firms," *Corporate Governance: An International Review*, 17(5): 611–28.

SIEBELS, J., and zu KNYPHAUSEN-AUFSEβ, D. (2012). "A Review of Theory in Family Business Research: The Implications for Corporate Governance," *International Journal of Management Reviews*, 14(3): 280–304.

SINGAL, M., and SINGAL, V. (2011). "Concentrated Ownership and Firm Performance: Does Family Control Matter?" *Strategic Entrepreneurship Journal*, 5(4): 373–96.

SITKEN, S. B., and ROTH, N. L. (1993). "Explaining the Limited Effectiveness of Legalistic 'Remedies' for Trust/Distrust," *Organization Science*, 4: 367–92.

SMYRNIOS, K. X., and WALKER, R. H. (2003). *Australian Family and Private Business Survey*. Australia: The Boyd Partners and RMIT.

SUÁRE, K. C., and SANTANA-MARTÍN, D. J. (2004). "Governance in Spanish Family Business," *International Journal of Entrepreneurial Behavior and Research*, 10: 141–63.

UHLANER, L. M. (2005). "The Use of the Guttman Scale in Development of a Family Orientation Index for Small-to-Medium-sized firms," *Family Business Review*, 43(1): 41–56.

—— (2006). "Business Family as Team: Underlying Force for Sustained Competitive Advantage," in P. Poutziouris, K. X. Smyrnios, and S. Klein (eds.), *Handbook of Research on Family Business*. Cheltenham: Edward Elgar, 125–44.

—— (2008). "The Role of Ownership in Governance: A Neglected Focus in Entrepreneurship and Management Research," Inaugural Lecture, Breukelen, The Netherlands: Nyenrode Business Universiteit.

—— and BERENT, M. M. (2008). "Entrepreneurship and Ownership in the Closely-Held Firm," in W. Burrggraaf, R. Flören, and J. Kunst (eds.), *The Entrepreneur and the Entrepreneurship Cycle*. Assen, The Netherlands: Van Gorcum, 327–41.

—— FLÖREN, R., and GEERLINGS, J. R. (2007). "Ownership Commitment, Family Ownership and Performance in the Privately-Held Firm," *Small Business Economics Journal*, 29(3): 275–93.

—— WRIGHT, M., and HUSE, M. (2007). "Private Firms and Corporate Governance: An Integrated Economic and Management Perspective," *Small Business Economics Journal*, 29(3): 225–41.

VAN DEN BERGHE, L. A., and CARCHON, S. (2002). "Corporate Governance Practices in Flemish Family Businesses," *Corporate Governance: An International Review*, 10: 225–45.

VAN DEN HEUVEL, J., VAN GILS, A., and VOORDECKERS, W. (2006). "Board Roles in Small and Medium-Sized Family Businesses: Performance and Importance," *Corporate Governance: An International Review*, 14: 467–85.

VILLALONGA, B., and AMIT, R. (2006). "How Do Family Ownership, Control and Management Affect Firm Value?" *Journal of Financial Economics*, 80: 385–417.

—— —— (2009). "How are U.S. Family Firms Controlled?" *The Review of Financial Studies*, 22(8): 3047–91.

VOORDECKERS, W., VAN GILS, A., and VAN DEN HEUVEL, J. (2007). "Board Composition in Small and Medium-Sized Family Firms," *Journal of Small Business Management*, 45: 137–56.

WERNERFELT, B. (1984). "A Resource-Based View of the Firm," *Strategic Management Journal*, 5: 171–80.

WESTHEAD, P., and COWLING, M. (1998). "Family Firm Research: The Need for a Methodological Rethink," *Entrepreneurship: Theory and Practice*, 23: 31–56.

WONG, Y., CHANG, S., and CHEN, L. (2010). "Does a Family-Controlled Firm Perform Better in Corporate Venturing?" *Corporate Governance: An International Review*, 18(3): 175–92.

WRIGHT, M., and KELLERMANNS, F. W. (2011). "Family Firms: A Research Agenda and Publication Guide," *Journal of Family Business Strategy*, 2(4): 187–98.

YOSHIKAWA, T., and RASHEED, A. A. (2010). "Family Control and Ownership Monitoring in Family-Controlled Firms in Japan," *Journal of Management Studies*, 47(2): 274–95.

ZAHRA, S. (2010). "Harvesting Family Firms' Organizational Social Capital: A Relational Perspective," *Journal of Management Studies*, 47(2): 345–66.

CHAPTER 19

CORPORATE GOVERNANCE IN IPOS

IGOR FILATOTCHEV AND DEBORAH ALLCOCK

INTRODUCTION

It is increasingly recognized in the management literature that the initial public offering (IPO) is an important stage in the life cycle of privately held and entrepreneurial firms. At this critical juncture, a firm has overcome the first challenges of its entrepreneurial phase and entered a growth stage. As Fama and French (2004: 229) emphasize, an IPO "is the point of entry that gives firms expanded access to equity capital, allowing them to emerge and grow." An IPO can provide an entrepreneurial firm with critical resources for its future expansion. It can also provide the entrepreneur with the first substantive access to cash from their investment of time and resources in the entrepreneurial effort.

Despite the growing awareness of the importance of IPOs among both academics and the investor community, the process by which a privately held firm transforms itself into a publicly traded company is still not well understood. While numerous studies have investigated the determinants of the going public decision (e.g. Booth and Smith, 1986; Jain and Kini, 1999) and post-issue performance (e.g. Beatty and Ritter, 1986; Michaely and Shaw, 1994; Espenlaub and Tonks, 1998; Brav, Geczy, and Gompers, 2000), there is relatively little research on the related but equally important issue of what factors influence the corporate governance mechanism of a firm at IPO stage, and how the specific characteristics of this mechanism such as board composition, executive incentives, and ownership interests of private equity investors may affect the IPO's performance.

Organizational theorists have increasingly drawn on agency theory (e.g. Beatty and Zajac, 1994; Brennan and Franks, 1997; Mikkelson et al., 1997) and upper echelon research (e.g. Hambrick and Mason, 1984; Higgins and Gulati, 1999; Certo, Daily, et al., 2001) to generate a body of conceptual and empirical research that is focused on corporate governance problems of IPOs. A major underlying assumption of this research is that of an information asymmetry between the IPO's team, underwriters, and public market investors that may create agency costs and lead to a substantial reduction in IPO performance (see Michaely and Shaw, 1994; and Certo, Covin, et al., 2001, for an extensive discussion). For example, underpricing of the stock at the IPO, the difference between the initial price at which a firm's stock is offered and the closing price of the stock on the first day of trading, is a major concern to the entrepreneurial firm and to the entrepreneur since it represents value the market ultimately sees in the stock but which the firm/entrepreneur did not obtain when the stock was first offered for sale (Ibbotson et al., 1988; Daily et al., 2003).[1]

This chapter is focused on complex interrelationships between corporate governance and performance of the IPO firm. Its first contribution is the exploration of agency conflicts, not as a unitary concept as has been done in prior research, but instead as two distinctive types of agency problems (adverse selection and moral hazard). It analyzes the effectiveness of firm-level signals associated with private equity ownership patterns with regard to each of these types of agency problems within entrepreneurial IPO firms. It brings in the debate about the development of executive pay schemes at this transitional time (particularly linked with the dilution of ownership and increase of agency problems). A third contribution is related to the discussion of the governance roles of venture capital syndicates since, as a rule, IPO firms have a number of private equity backers when they come to the stock market. Finally, it proposes further areas for research to improve knowledge of this particular change in strategy, organizational structure, and the dynamic development of the firm.

Information Asymmetries and the Roles of Corporate Governance in IPO Firms

Information asymmetries, or differences in information between the various parties to the listing process, including the IPO firm, banks-underwriters, entrepreneur, and external investors, has been the foundation of prior investigations of underpricing (Ritter and Welch, 2002). Bruton et al. (2009) show that information asymmetry leads to two distinctive types of agency problems—adverse selection and moral hazard. To illustrate adverse selection agency conflict a manager may not accurately reveal all he/she knows about a firm. As Ritter and Welch (2002: 1807) argue: "after all, small investors cannot take a tour of the firm and its secret inventions." Specifically, at IPO this may take the form of overly optimistic estimates of the firm's revenues by one of these parties. These overly optimistic estimates can increase the expected value of the firm and in turn increases the rewards from the IPO and are a type of adverse selection agency conflict. Moral hazard problems emerge when information asymmetries make it possible for managers to pursue self-serving objectives and not act at maximum efficiency and effectiveness for the firm. For example, founder-managers may hold significant equity stakes in the IPO firm, and there is the potential for these individuals to abuse public market investors (Bruton et al., 2010). An entrenched founder-CEO may also try to retain a leadership position even when his/her skills become inadequate to new challenges faced by the firm (Nelson, 2003). As a result of these information asymmetries, there are potential agency costs when a firm experiences an IPO since managers may not reveal actions within the firm or do not take certain actions that maximize the firm benefit (Sanders and Boivie, 2004).

At IPO investors recognize the potential impact of the agency costs associated with information asymmetries, and they will therefore anticipate potential agency costs and price-protect themselves, thus leading to an IPO discount. Prior research approximates this discount by a lower industry-adjusted offer price/book or price/sales ratios (e.g. Chahine and Filatotchev, 2008), while others associate it with greater underpricing, measured by the difference between the first-day-trading closing price and the offer price (e.g. Daily et al., 2003), suggesting that the aftermarket price provides a good proxy for an intrinsic value of the IPO firm. Some researchers, however, argue that the uncertainties and information asymmetries cannot be resolved on the first day of trading, and suggest using longer-term proxies for the stock market discount (Aggarwal and Rivoli, 1990; Loughran et al., 1994).

However, the IPO team may use corporate governance-related signals that allow potential investors to better understand the true value of the firm and reduce risks of agency problems, which in turn can improve the IPO firm's performance (Sanders and Boivie, 2004). Corporate governance studies in the IPO context have recognized a wide range of potential "good governance signals" that include board characteristics, executive incentives, and the governance roles of early stage investors. These governance factors play a dual role in addressing two types of agency conflicts in an IPO firm. First, they may convey important signals about the "quality" of IPO firm, and this may reduce the extent of adverse selection problems. For example, by attracting prestigious and experienced independent board members, an IPO firm can differentiate itself from other "poor quality" IPOs. At the same time, these independent directors may improve the extent and quality of monitoring, which imposes constraints on managerial discretion and reduces moral hazard-type agency conflicts. Likewise, venture capitalist may play important certification and monitoring roles that affect both types of agency conflicts. By carefully selecting their investment targets, they certify the quality of firms they bring to the stock market. In addition, venture capitalists (VCs) often retain their ownership after the flotation, and their objectives and post-issue monitoring incentives may be aligned with public market investors (Bruton et al., 2010).

A central premise of this research is that corporate governance factors may be important signals to investors with regard to the quality of a particular IPO firm, as well as the extent to which their interests are protected from insiders' opportunism during and after the flotation. As a result, corporate governance characteristics should have a significant impact on a wide range of IPO performance metrics, such as underpricing, longer-term performance, and survival. In the following sections, we look at different governance factors, such as board characteristics, early stage investors, and executive compensation in IPO firms, and how they may affect performance. Table 19.1 provides the main findings

Table 19.1. Content and findings of key papers focused on corporate governance in IPO firms

Research focus	Source	Sample	Key issues	Theoretical underpinning
Going public and post-issue performance	Brav, Geczy, and Gompers (2000)	USA. Sample of 4,622 IPOs, 1975–92	Underperformance of small issues with low market-to-book ratios	Agency/signaling theory
Going public and post-issue performance	Espenlaub and Tonks (1998)	UK. Sample of 428 IPOs, 1986–91	Partial support for IPO signaling hypothesis using underpricing of IPO issues	Agency/signaling theory
Going public and post-issue performance	Jain and Kini (1999)	USA. Sample of 877 IPOs, 1977–90	IPOs are tracked over a five-year period, with IPOs subdivided into survivors, non-survivors, and acquired firms. Survivors have significantly better operating performance, higher retained ownership, VC involvement, and prestigious underwriters	Agency/signaling theory
Going public and post-issue performance	Michaely and Shaw (1994)	USA. Two data sets 947 IPOs: IPO of Limited Partnerships (58) and standard IPOs, 1984–8	No support for signaling models. Research finds that lower levels of underpricing associated with higher dividends	Agency/signaling theory
Board composition and performance	Cohen and Dean (2005)	USA. Sample of 221 IPOs, January 1, 1998–December 31, 1999	Strength and attributes of top management team send positive signal to investors of future economic potential of the firm	Agency/signaling theory
Board composition, share ownership, and performance	Filatotchev and Bishop (2002)	UK. Sample of 251 IPOs, December 1, 1999–December 31, 2000	Endogeneity of board composition and share ownership. Both factors affect IPO underpricing	Agency/resource based view

Founders and boards	Certo, Daily, et al. (2001)	USA. Sample of 368 IPOs, 1990–8	Founder status on the board and founder management has a positive effect on levels of underpricing but is moderated by the proportion of insiders on the board	Agency/signaling theory
Founders and boards	Jain and Tabak (2008)	USA. Sample of 231 IPOs, 1997	Founder vs non-founder CEO firms. Find significant differences in the governance structures of founder and non-founder firms. Particular reference to ownership, board size, and venture capitalist involvement	Agency/signaling theory
Founders and boards	Nelson (2003)	USA. Sample of 157 IPOs, January 1–December 31, 1991	Founders are likely to exercise strong strategic leadership in firm governance in comparison with firms without founder CEOs and that this type of leadership may be valuable at the time of transition to public ownership	Agency/signaling theory
Executive remuneration	Beatty and Zajac (1994)	USA. Sample of 435 IPOs, 1984	Incentives used to lower agency costs are investigated within context of risk-averse executives	Agency theory
Executive remuneration	Allcock and Filatotchev (2010)	UK. Sample of 311 IPO companies, 1998–2002	Governance factors affect introduction of performance-related incentives at IPO. This is also affected by the risk-framing of the executives	Agency theory and prospect theory
Executive remuneration	Lowry and Murphy (2007)	USA. Sample of 874 IPOs, 1996–2000	No evidence that IPO options are related to IPO underpricing	Agency theory

(continued)

Table 19.1. Continued

Research focus	Source	Sample	Key issues	Theoretical underpinning
Governance and private equity firms	Barry et al. (1990)	USA. Sample of 433 VC-backed and 1233 non-VC-backed IPOs, 1978–87	The number of VCs invested in the issuing firm is negatively related to initial underpricing	Signaling theory
Venture capitalists and certification	Brav and Gompers (2003)	USA. Sample of 2,794 IPOs, 1988–96	Insiders of firms that are associated with greater potential for moral hazard lock up their shares for a longer period of time. Venture capitalist involvement seen in firms that have experienced larger excess returns	Agency/signaling theory
Venture capitalists and certification	Coakley and Hadass (2007)	UK. Sample of 590 IPOs, 1985–2003. Split as 316 VC-backed and 274 non-VC-backed	Support for venture capital certification in the early years, but a significantly negative relationship between operating performance and venture capitalist board representation during the bubble years (1998–2000)	Agency/signaling theory
Venture capitalists and certification	Jelic, Saadouni, and Wright (2005)	UK. Sample of 167 buyout IPOs, 1964–97	IPOs of MBOs backed by highly reputable venture capital firms provide better long-term investments as compared with those backed by less prestigious venture capitalist firms	Agency/signaling theory

Venture capitalists and certification	Loughran and Ritter (2004)	USA. Sample of 3,025 IPOs, 1990–8	Pre-IPO investors, in particular VCs, look to extract rents through deliberate underpricing, in exchange for preferential share allocation in further underpriced IPOs	Prospect theory
Venture capitalists and certification	Megginson and Weiss (1991)	USA. Matched sample of 320 non-VC-backed and 320 VC-backed, 1983–7	Matched by industry and offering size, they find that the initial underpricing of VC-backed IPOs is significantly lower than for non-VC-backed IPOs	Agency/signaling theory
Syndicated private equity	Bruton et al. (2010)	UK and France. Matched sample of 444 UK and French IPOs, 1996–2002	VC syndicates create principal–principal agency conflicts that negatively affect IPO performance. The extent of these conflicts and their remedies depend on national institutions	Agency and institutional theories
Syndicated private equity	Filatotchev, Wright, and Aberk (2006)	UK. Sample of 293 entrepreneurial IPOs, 1999–2002	Provide evidence that IPOs backed by syndicates of VCs are more likely to develop independent boards than are IPOs backed by single VCs	Agency theory

from the studies reviewed. Bearing in mind the large number of publications on this topic in economics, finance, and management, it is impossible to include all studies that have been published over last 30 years. Instead, we include some widely cited publications in this field, covering a range of country sample, periods of studies, and of some key studies that have explored the effects of governance factors on various performance indicators of IPO firms. As this table clearly shows, previous research on the governance in IPO firms has identified a wide range of governance mechanisms that may have both value-enhancing and value-destroying effects. This may explain the ambiguity of empirical findings that so far have failed to provide a consistent picture of the governance impacts in IPO firms.

Board Characteristics and Performance of IPO Firms

Boards of directors are a common feature of companies throughout the world, so it is easy to see that, for companies, the board of directors represents a prime strategic driver. Indeed, its duties range from the appointment of directors, self evaluation measures, collective responsibility, and reporting to external audiences. However, the board of directors has a particular role at the time of an initial public offering, starting with the decision to take the company public. In this process the board will have the challenge of selecting underwriters, approving offer terms, providing vital information for the prospectus document, and essentially overseeing the IPO process (and at the point of the IPO considerable information asymmetry will exist). More recently, the fiduciary duties of directors mean that the directors are subject to personal liability for statements made at this time.

Board Composition and Performance

Investors' perception of the board of directors is often gained via the prospectus document, and strong boards provide the investor with future governance signals (Certo, 2003). Investors may view the board from the perspective of managerial talent, board independence, and entrepreneurial founders.

Human capital theory shows that directors' expertise, experience, and specific knowledge can all add value to a company's successful performance (Hillman and Dalziel, 2003) and contribute to overall corporate governance (Carpenter and Westphal, 2001; Arthurs et al., 2008). Indeed D'Aveni (1990) argues that prestigious directors in terms of their human capital can be indicative of the overall quality of the firm (useful under the signaling hypothesis). Similarly, it is not just directors' experience that is examined here; studies have examined the age (Cohen and Dean, 2005) and educational levels (Lester et al., 2006) of directors. Arguably, age has a direct link to expertise, knowledge, and experience, translating into the ability to perform a job well (Tesluk and Jacobs, 1998).

There is also the notion of board characteristics as examined by the view of board independence. Board independence is often seen as the proportion of executives/non-executives, but can also be seen in terms of insiders and outsiders on the board (however, not all non-executives can be deemed independent). At the time of the IPO, the board may be in a development phase, and so strategic selection of non-executive directors to balance the existing executive directors' experience gaps is vital (Westphal, 1998; Shivdasani and Yermack, 1999;). As such, the requirements of balancing skills will often cause the IPO company to prefer directors who are involved with other boards (Beatty and Zajac, 1994). From a resource-based view of the firm (Pfeffer, 1972), broadening the board's experience at this particular point in the development life cycle is vital to future success. Similarly, the appointment of well-connected non-executives will provide bargaining power in discussions with underwriters and investors (Provan, 1980). They are also able to bring in further business contacts as the firm grows. A positive aspect of this practice is that, by gaining established non-executive directors on the board, certification of good governance practice is established, and thus at IPO this can (under signaling hypotheses) add additional value and differentiate a particular issue for future investors. However, the downside is that outside directors have the potential for high levels of "interlocks" (Zahra and Pearce, 1989; Dalton et al., 1999;), something the UK Corporate Governance Code (Financial Reporting Council, 2010) attempts to limit. Thus, in terms of good practice, listing authorities arguably prefer more independent boards and, in general, so do investors (Gompers, 1995).

Founders and Boards

Just as broader aspects of board characteristics can be considered, there is also the case of the entrepreneurial IPO that has the founders of the company on the board. Most founders who make decisions to float their companies are often considered by outside investors as "untested" from a board point of view when they take their firms public (Wat, 1983). However, in today's dynamic economy, we see the presence of founders within many company contexts (e.g. Steve Jobs at Apple, Bill Gates at Microsoft), and they are particularly relevant for younger, high-growth firms and technology firms (Eisenhardt and Schoonhoven, 1990). In the context of the initial public offering company, around one-third to one-half of flotations go public with founders at the helm, and receive handsome offer prices compared with non-founder valuations (Certo, Daily, et al., 2001b; Nelson, 2003). Thus, considering the role of the founder at the point of the flotation has value, particularly as founders have considerable power due to large ownership stakes (Jain and Tabak, 2008) and extensive skills.

As a founder member of the firm, their influence is seen in defining the firm's purpose, i.e. the mission statement which then translates through the company to organizational attributes such as structure (Kunze, 1990; Vesper, 1996). Some authors (Baron et al., 1999) argue that this is the founder "imprinting" his/her will on the firm, and this will then continue unless the founder exits the company (Mintzberg and Waters, 1982). Indeed Monks and Minow (2004) argue that this is a result of the extensive ownership that some founders have, enabling them to be revered in their company context, and greater ownership levels do indeed lead to founders commanding the CEO position (Nelson, 2003). Combined with the founder's position, this affords them extensive power, and it is not unusual to see founders in the dual role of CEO and chair (Beatty and Zajac, 1994; Finkelstein and D'Aveni, 1994; Daily and Dalton, 1997). There is also a further strengthening of founder power when a family is involved (particularly where parents and children are concerned) (Schulze et al., 2003).

The influence that the founder has through the structural aspects of the board does not, however, necessarily translate into performance. Several studies have begun to question whether firms managed by their founder perform differently from those managed by non-founders (Begley, 1995; Jayraman et al., 2000). However, the attribution of performance to founders has mixed support and is often entangled with other variables, namely ownership levels and board independence (Nelson, 2003; Villalonga and Amit, 2006; Adams et al., 2009).

The role of the founder is not infinite, though, and perhaps at the IPO, more than at any other time, it comes into question. Some question whether the founder is the best person managerially to lead a firm into the public-listing phase of its life cycle. Founders may not have the inclination to develop new skills to suit the challenges that come with a flotation (Jain and Tabak, 2008). Often changes in leadership are required (Greiner, 1972). The issue of a more independent board arises and, with it, the replacement of the founder with a professional successor just prior to the flotation process (Wasserman, 2003; Jain and Tabak, 2008).

Executive Remuneration in IPOs

For any private company undergoing an initial public offering, the process provides an opportunity to look at the key issues of executive pay and make some strategic decisions with regard to how executives are remunerated. Whilst other chapters look at executive remuneration in more detail, for the IPO, company executive pay is particularly tied to the life cycle of the firm and the professionalization aspects of the board of directors. First, the company must acknowledge the role that remuneration can play as a governance tool. Typically this comes from an agency perspective, relying on the objective of bridging the gap between owners and self-serving managers (Berle and Means, 1932; Jensen and Meckling, 1976; Fama, 1980). Second, managers must prepare themselves for the future reporting of their pay structures. From the flotation onwards, pay strategies and remuneration amounts will have to be transparent. Regardless of the wishes of the board of directors, following the IPO there will be the potential for public (and investor) scrutiny of executive pay via the annual report and accounts. The challenge for the IPO company thus is that the development of their scheme at the IPO needs to set the compensation philosophy for the immediate future of the company. It needs to address key issues about what the compensation mix should be (and how much should be provided), what incentives need to be addressed, what might be the role of share options schemes, and in particular how these might be structured with regard to performance measures, comparators, and targets.

The transfer of ownership into the public domain gives a unique opportunity for the company to consider its philosophy with regard to remuneration. It can be considered that this will serve the company throughout this life-cycle change and could provide grounding to strategically position pay for the board of directors. Furthermore, as the company seeks to grow, it will look to hire new people to the board, and thus compensation packages become an important asset in attracting and retaining talent.

COMPENSATION MIX

The compensation mix is related to discussions about and answers to questions such as: where do you want to position pay for your executives relative to your peers or industry? The professionalization of the board (Flamholtz, 1986; Daily and Dalton, 1992) and the need for the recruitment and retention of executive talent (Conyon, 2000; Daily and Dalton, 1992) makes these initial decisions particularly relevant. First, the mix generally comprises base salary, annual bonus, and long-term performance pay. To consider these aspects fully it is not unusual for the IPO company to begin the process at least six months before the IPO, and many of the details about rewards will be placed in the firm's IPO prospectus.

Base Salary and Annual Bonus

Little seems to be said about base salaries. However, the typical CEO in the US makes between $500,000 and $1 million per year in base salary (*Wall Street Journal*, 2010), with the figure for the UK being £131,000 (for companies with a turnover of up to £50m) (Institute of Directors, 2011). However, for an IPO company, base salary varies and perhaps can be better described in terms of market capital valuations at the point of the IPO. As with mature companies, there is a link to size of company, with average top directors gaining base salaries of £140,000 (for market capital of £30–50m) to £208,000 (for market capital of £101–250m) (Deloitte & Touche, 2005a). However, of greater impact (and perhaps a more cost-effective method) are the longer-term incentives provided at this point.

Long-Term Incentives

Since long-term incentives make up a large proportion of executive pay for both US and UK executives (Deloitte & Touche, 2005a, 2005b), it is vital that the IPO company remains in line with mature companies in terms of its pay structure. As with mature companies, the purpose of the long-term incentive is threefold: to align the interests of the executive managers with those of shareholders (Rosen, 1990; Tosi et al., 1997; Nohel and Todd, 2005), to strengthen the links between compensation and the long-term performance of the company (Jensen and Murphy, 1990; Hall, 1998; Conyon and Sadler, 2001; Buck et al., 2003; Kroll et al., 2007), and to reward/motivate the executive for/toward performance achievements (Tosi et al., 2000; Mackey, 2008; Liu and Stark, 2009).

After the report by Greenbury (1995), the variety of long-term incentives has increased. However, in general we can categorize them as taking one of two main forms. The executive share option (ESO) gives the recipient the right to purchase a number of shares at a specified price (usually the price when the option is granted: a point we will discuss later) for a specified period of time subject to performance criteria being met, whilst the long-term incentive plan (LTIP) awards a grant of shares (at zero cost) that vest (i.e. transfer ownership to the executive) upon the attainment of predetermined performance criteria. Both types of scheme have particular tax implications, but these are beyond the scope of this chapter, and both schemes provide a way of linking executive pay to performance (Fama and Jensen, 1983a, 1983b). The decisions with regard to performance benchmarks (which must be met in order for the shares to be bought or vested in the executive) can also be used to complement the company's strategy. For performance criteria, there are two general schools of thought, using either a market-based measure of performance such as shareholder return or shareholder wealth, or a more traditional accounting measure, i.e. earnings per share. When developing the particulars of the new scheme, the IPO company would be wise to look toward the particular practices of similar companies to provide adequate comparators to ensure ongoing competitive salaries.

Share Options Granted at the Point of the IPO Flotation

When it comes to paying executives, many IPO companies prefer equity rewards over cash compensation. They provide a good signal for agent alignment (Jensen and Meckling, 1976), with a potential upside of giving ownership in a company the executives are likely to lead. IPO options are also seen to encourage a higher propensity of risk taking (Beatty and Zajac, 1994; Wiseman and Gomez-Mejia, 1998), which in turn can lead to better performance (Hall and Leibman, 1998). However, more recently, there have also been discussions about the way particular reference is made to share options at the point of the IPO, given that the executives (in particular the CEO) are able to influence the timing of the IPO and thus the option grant (Yermack, 1997; Lie, 2005). This is more significant when the CEO is also the founder of the company (Certo et al., 2003). This is particularly relevant as the IPO share option will have an exercise price equal to the offer price for the IPO and high levels of underpricing for IPO issues have been seen for company floatations (Filatotchev and Bishop, 2002; Daily et al., 2003). With the option exercise price equal to the offer price, Lowry and Murphy (2007) argue that offer prices may be deliberately deflated so that executives maximize option gains due to underpricing (but their study shows no tangible link between options and underpricing). However, the picture is perhaps not just one of simple timing combined with CEO power and influence.

Other factors are deemed to come into play with regard to offer prices and underpricing of the IPO, for example, highly independent boards can counterbalance CEO power (Core et al., 1999) which would reduce underpricing (Filatotchev and Bishop, 2002). Furthermore, future investors might prefer companies with more independent boards (Gompers, 1995). There is also the impact that venture capitalist involvement might have on the choice of share options (Allcock and Filatotchev, 2010) and offer pricing levels (Fried et al., 1998). If venture capitalists are driving the timing of the IPO, then they may offer options at a low offer price in order to compensate the CEO for his support for the IPO timing.

For the executive, any underpricing at the point of the IPO represents money left on the table. Founder-CEOs who are granted stock options at the IPO may be seen as opportunistic managers (Zhang, 2006), using the options to generate gains that offset the wealth loss from underpricing due to their pre-IPO ownership. However, with large option awards, this might be counteracted because a low option price would provide the executive with high levels of future gains due to the increase of the share price immediately after the flotation. If shares continue to increase in value, the IPO option will ultimately increase the value and then significantly add to the level of the executives' compensation. The final caveat here would be that boards at IPO are undergoing a major transition and much of the rationale for grants relies on executives remaining within the company (usually for three years, i.e. a normal vesting period). Thus there may arguably be an alternative perspective for the IPO option, and rather than alignment, their potential for high gain can be a way of tying the executive to the board for a period of time. This may be viewed from a resource-based view of the firm perspective and might significantly attract investors as board stability could increase overall company performance.

The above demonstrates that planning remuneration for the IPO company, particularly as this takes part during the pre-IPO stage, can be difficult. There must be reference to developing schemes that balance cost efficiency and competition for talent in the sector, whilst ensuring that the scheme signals good governance for shareholder alignment. Perhaps with this in light, the following key points for the IPO company should be remembered. When initiating executive share option schemes, the board should plan and view schemes as complementary to core company strategy. This way they will link in with the life-cycle development of the firm. However, it is important to remember that the IPO process is a time of dynamic change. The board should thus keep challenging and refining compensation in line with the changes that are happening, remembering that plans will need to change as the market, company strategy, and maturity stages change. This also might be a time of change for the board of directors. With this in mind, existing board members will need to pay particular attention to compensation and reward when in negotiation to recruit and/or retain staff. In order to do this effectively and transparently, it is best if share option plans are kept simple.

THE GOVERNANCE ROLES OF PRIVATE EQUITY FIRMS

As entrepreneurial firms gradually "professionalize," they increasingly look outside for financial resources provided by various early stage investors. Venture capitalists serve an important role in the development of promising young ventures (Barry et al., 1990). VCs raise funds from passive investors and then invest those funds through staged financing in various portfolio firms (Gompers and Lerner, 1999). Although VCs often do not have detailed scientific knowledge about the specific technology in their portfolio firms, they are able to economize on their selection and monitoring costs by focusing their investments in certain industries. By specializing in these industries, they are able to develop a comparative advantage over other investors. Additionally, their involvement in corporate governance helps them to rapidly bring these ventures to a successful exit through an IPO and aids them in generating added value beyond the capital provided.

VENTURE CAPITALISTS AND "CERTIFICATION HYPOTHESIS"

Agency research and the related "certification" framework (e.g. Barry et al., 1990; Lerner, 1995; Black and Gilson, 1998) suggest that an entrepreneurial venture can signal its expected value by who has invested in the firm. Principal among early-stage investors are private equity investors who are the second most important group of shareholders, after founders, in an entrepreneurial venture (Lerner, 1998). This is because successful investors' time and ability to invest in numerous new ventures is limited so they will invest in those ventures they feel will be the most successful. Thus, private equity investors would be expected from an agency perspective to be involved with those ventures they feel are going to be successful. As a result, their presence can certify to public investors the value of the IPO firm.

Private equity investors, however, are not homogeneous and represent a diverse range of different types of investors, including VC firms, buyout firms, leveraged buyout (LBO) specialists, and "business angels." There are substantial differences in investment strategies and time horizons among these investors. For example, VCs, as a rule, specialize in investing in early-stage ventures such as entrepreneurial start-ups, whereas buyout firms and LBO experts focus on management buyouts and LBOs. VC firms are formed as partnerships, whereas "business angels" represent wealthy individuals investing on their own behalf. The vast majority of IPO-related papers focus on the "certification" role of VCs only, and we will return to this issue later. This research places an emphasis on the roles of VC investors in the price discovery process at the time of an IPO, arguing that they may reduce information asymmetry at the time of the issue, and their presence can have a value-enhancing effect (Lerner, 1995). Thus, the presence of VC investors can mitigate the adverse selection problem in an entrepreneurial venture.

Depending on their retained ownership, early-stage investors may also have an incentive to be involved in the decision-making process and to exert a significant influence on management before and after flotation. Since seed and development funding normally causes dilution of initial founders' holdings, it can create a misalignment of incentives in issuing firms. VC firms design their contracts to reduce this information asymmetry and maximize the disclosure of private knowledge by the entrepreneur-founder (Shane and Cable, 2002). The IPO is characterized by lock-up arrangements which make retained ownership by VCs relatively illiquid after the IPO. As a result, their retained concentrated ownership imposes a cost on them. Thus, their retained ownership signals their belief in the value of the firm to minority investors (Brav and Gompers, 2003). Second, concentrated private ownership leads to a reduction of coordination costs related to multiple types of private and public equity investors in the IPO firm and creates a Jensen-Meckling-type incentive alignment effect that jointly may mitigate the post-IPO risk of moral hazard (Jensen and Meckling, 1976). Therefore, VC investors' ownership concentration may be a particularly important governance parameter that enhances IPO firm performance and reduces the negative effects of the "IPO discount" arising from agency conflicts. Early prior US research suggests that VCs play a certification role at the time of IPOs. VCs act as third-party certifying agents, reducing initial underpricing (Jelic et al., 2005). Megginson and Weiss (1991) find lower initial returns for venture-backed IPOs.[2] Using a unique sample of private firms for which there is financial data available in the years before and after their IPO, Katz (2009) differentiates between those that have private equity sponsorship (PE-backed firms) and those that do not (non-PE-backed firms). The findings indicate that PE-backed firms generally have higher earnings quality than those that do not have PE sponsorship, engage less in earnings management, and report more conservatively both before and after the IPO. While more reputable VCs initially select better quality firms, more reputable VCs continue to be associated with superior long-run performance, even after controlling for VC selectivity. The authors find more reputable VCs exhibit more active post-IPO involvement in the corporate governance of their portfolio firms and this continued VC involvement positively influences post-IPO firm performance. In the UK, Levis (2008) examines the aftermarket performance of private equity-backed initial public offerings (IPOs), based on a hand-collected sample of private equity-backed and equivalent samples of venture capital-backed and other non-sponsored issues on the London Stock Exchange. The evidence suggests that private equity-backed IPOs exhibit superior performance compared with their counterparts throughout the 36-month period in the aftermarket; such performance is robust across different benchmarks and estimation procedures. However, Coakley and Hadass (2007) analyze the post-issue operating performance of 316 venture-backed and 274 non-venture UK IPOs for the period 1985–2003. Cross-section regression results indicate support for venture capital certification in the non-bubble years, but a significantly negative relationship between operating performance and venture capitalist board representation during the bubble years. Finally, Hochberg et al. (2007) find that better-networked VC firms experience significantly better fund performance, as measured by the proportion of investments that are successfully exited through an IPO or a sale to another company.

However, recent IPO literature suggests that potential conflicts of interest among pre-IPO investors may lead to higher underpricing. On the one hand, Gompers (1996) argues that less experienced VCs may grandstand, i.e. take firms public earlier than more established firms, in order to raise their profile in the market and attract capital in future rounds. On the other hand, Loughran and Ritter (2004) propose a "corruption hypothesis," where they argue that some pre-IPO investors (e.g. VCs) may look to extract rents through deliberate underpricing, in exchange for preferential share allocation in further underpriced IPOs. Within this framework, Francis and Hasan (2001) and Lee and Wahal (2004) show that, in recent years, US venture capital-backed IPOs experience larger first-day returns than comparable non-venture-backed IPOs. This suggests the existence of a potential conflict of interests between VC firms and the IPO firm. In addition, following Arthurs et al.'s (2008) conflicting voices argument, VCs have a dual identity as both principals and agents. These investors are often part of limited partnerships that place pressure on them to obtain fast results and to seek a timely realization of their investment. Hence VCs are relatively short-term investors who are likely to be seeking at IPO to realize their gains from their value-adding activities for the venture (Arthurs et al., 2008), as well as to establish their reputation in order to raise further funds. These results are in line with findings in Chahine and Filatotchev (2008), who show that bank-affiliated VCs lead to a poorer IPO performance in France.

Therefore, previous research on the governance role of private equity investors in IPO firms has identified both value-enhancing and value-destroying effects associated with this type of owner. On the one hand, private equity investors carefully select their portfolio companies and provide them with the financial and managerial support necessary to develop and grow a new venture. This leads to a strong "certification" effect that may reduce information asymmetries and associated adverse selection agency costs. On the other hand, a limited time horizon which is associated with lock-up arrangements and exit orientation may substantially undermine the monitoring capacity and incentives of private equity investors, leading to an increase in moral hazard costs.

Syndicated Private Equity Investments in IPO Firms

In a syndication, two or more venture capital firms come together to take an equity stake in an investment. The percentage of investments syndicated in the UK venture capital market rose in 1999 to 27 percent after having fallen for several years. This was followed by a sharp fall in 2000 and 2001 to about half this level as venture capital firms moved away from the high-tech sector following the collapse of the dot.com boom. By 2002, the more uncertain investment environment appears to have been associated with a further sharp increase, with 26.5 percent of investments being syndicated (Filatotchev et al., 2006). Private equity firms typically undertake repeat syndication over time with a network of partners (Bygrave, 1987, 1988).

Each syndicate usually contains lead and non-lead firms, with an individual venture capital firm playing both roles over time depending on the particular deal. Each syndicate is temporary in nature, with the financing structure constructed specifically for that transaction. This limited longevity of the syndicated investments may create moral hazard problems associated with the "principal–principal" relationship between syndicate members (Filatotchev et al., 2006).

Syndicated investments may be riskier than stand-alone ventures. A fully diversified portfolio is more difficult for private equity firms than for institutional investors who invest in listed stock because of the presence of large ex ante asymmetric information in investment decisions (Sahlman, 1990; Reid, 1998; Lockett and Wright, 2001). Syndication thus may be undertaken as a means of risk sharing through portfolio diversification as it permits private equity firms to invest in more portfolio companies than would otherwise be possible (Cumming, 2006).

Venture capital syndicates involve the sharing of decision-making among the syndicate members. The lower the level of cooperation among syndicate members, the greater the levels of relational risk and hence the associated agency costs. The origins of the agency costs in the syndicate may arise from the diverse objectives of members and the time-consuming nature of coordination. In VC deals with multiple rounds of financing, the lead investor may also have an informational advantage vis-à-vis other syndicate members who enter in later rounds (Admati and Pfleiderer, 1994).

This complex relationship between multiple principals is defined as a "principal–principal" agency problem (Filatotchev et al., 2006), as opposed to the principal–agent problem between investor and investee. These agency problems can in principle be addressed in a number of ways. Shared equity ownership in private equity firms syndicates may bring benefits in terms of higher levels of trust and knowledge acquisition (Beamish and Banks, 1987), as well as mutual forbearance and stability (Mjoen and Tallman, 1997; Yan and Gray, 2001), which provides an effective remedy to situations where the lead syndicate member has access to more information about the investee than the non-lead members.

However, lead venture capital firms may seek a larger equity stake in return for their greater effort in monitoring the investee and coordinating the syndicate (Wright and Lockett, 2003). The investment agreement between the syndicate members may be important in specifying rights of access to information, board membership rights, etc., for non-lead syndicate members, but may be limited by the problems associated with the complexity of contracting.

It is in the interests of the lead venture capital firm not to mislead syndicate partners in sharing information because of the potentially damaging impact on reputation and lack of willingness to reciprocate future deals (Wright and Lockett, 2003). Repeated interaction can lead to high levels of trust as syndicate members come to know how partners will behave (Lockett and Wright, 1999). As venture capital industries are typically small close-knit communities, this scope for building trust and reputations is enhanced (Black and Gilson, 1998).

Another possibility to reduce these "principal-principal" moral hazard problems is to use the IPO firm's governance system as a mechanism for "arbitrage" between the potentially diverse objectives of syndicate partners (Gompers, 1995; Filatotchev and Bishop, 2002;). Where skilled lead venture capital firms are less reliant on other syndicate members for specialist information (Admati and Pfleiderer, 1994) and are more likely than non-leads to exert hands-on influence over investees (Wright and Lockett, 2003), the development of an independent board may be important in ensuring that the syndicate functions effectively. Non-lead syndicate members may seek the appointment of an independent non-executive chair to perform the functions of an "arbiter." Non-executive board membership may be increased through the presence of non-lead syndicate members to enhance transparency in decision-making and thus c-operation (Wright and Lockett, 2003). Filatotchev et al. (2006) provide evidence that IPOs backed by syndicates of VCs are more likely to develop independent boards than are IPOs backed by single VCs.

In addition to the above arguments, a resource-based perspective suggests that syndication can bring specialized resources for the ex post management of investments. By syndicating deals, VC firms are able to increase the portfolio they can optimally manage through resource sharing (Kanniainen and Keuschnigg, 2003; Jääskeläinen et al., 2006). VC firms can access more information by syndicating with other reputable VC firms. However, in specialist areas, VC firms may seek to syndicate with industrial partners. These industrial partners may have more specialist knowledge than either the VC firm itself or other VCs. This knowledge can be important in evaluating the initial investment, in post-investment management, and in providing an eventual exit route.

As the investee develops, there may be a need to access further significant funds. The initial VC backer may have the specialist market-based skills, but need to access further funds to diversify the risk associated with scaling up the operation. As VC funds are typically small (Reid, 1998), they may seek to syndicate deals that are large relative to their fund size, which typically involve later-stage private equity funds (Lockett and Wright, 2001). VC syndicates may therefore also syndicate with private equity firms that specialize in later-stage ventures.

Again, these arguments emphasize the dual governance roles of private equity syndicates in IPO firms. By syndicating IPO deals, private equity investors may diversify their assets and undertake a substantial resource commitment to a portfolio firm. This may enhance the IPO firm's "value" and reduce agency costs associated with adverse selection problems, leading to a substantial improvement of performance. However, private equity syndicate may create their own set of agency problems associated with the the diverse interests of partners and partner opportunism. This would make post-issue monitoring less efficient and more problematic, leading to an increase in moral hazard agency costs.

Discussion and Future Research

Governance research is growing in importance and the governance role of boards, executive incentives, and ownership effects is a central feature of such research. Most studies on the effects of governance on performance have examined mature companies, and have used samples drawn from the common law environments of the US and, to a more limited degree, the UK. However, a growing appreciation is forming of the heterogeneity of governance mechanisms (Aguilera and Jackson, 2003) and of how the appropriate governance mechanisms may differ as the setting of the firm changes (Lynall et al., 2003; Filatotchev and Wright, 2005). To date, empirical work has not fully explored these conceptual developments, especially in the context of IPO firms.

For entrepreneurial firms, the IPO is both the sign of a high degree of success to date and an indication that the firm will have greater resources to pursue its strategic goals in the future. For entrepreneurs, who are often referred to as "paper millionaires" until the IPO stock market flotation, the IPO is the first opportunity to actually obtain cash from their entrepreneurial venture. The IPO is thus a highly significant event for the entrepreneurial firm, where "investors' discount" can steal part of the benefit that the entrepreneurial firm and the entrepreneur may seek from the IPO. This research extends our understanding of the role played by corporate governance in the IPO and informs future research on this important event in the life of an entrepreneurial firm.

However, whether governance mechanisms developed in mature companies are fully suitable for the "entrepreneurial nature" of the IPO process is still open to discussion among academics and practitioners. For example, the debate about just how the IPO company selects members of the board still remains open to interpretation. Should independent directors be advisors to an entrepreneur, monitors working on behalf of investors, or both? Whilst some researchers emphasize the importance of the resource-based view of the board in an IPO firm, there is limited qualitative data that enables this particular aspect of the firm's development to be investigated fully. Indicators point to selection being against both resources and peer-based knowledge of the executives rather than through nominations committees (as would be found in mature companies), and the covert world of executive search companies has certainly not been explored.

As for compensation, there are two particular issues that interact with the IPO company. First, the levels of survival have a major impact on the vesting and gains that can be made from any long-term incentives that may be awarded at the point of the IPO. The undertone is that executives gain vast rewards in this way, yet many firms disappear as a result of acquisition and mergers following their offering (and some even de-list). Some studies argue that failure rates within the first three years of flotation range from 6–42 percent (Schultz, 1993; Bradley et al., 2006; Kooli and Meknassi, 2007). This is particularly relevant as many option schemes follow a three-year vesting period, failure would mean that an option lapses, and any merger/acquisition would involve the restructuring of pay/incentives. Thus the incentive mantra of linking pay to equity to enhance IPO performance still has the potential for further investigation.

The research has strong implications for studies of the short-term IPO performance and venture capital, in line with Busenitz et al.'s (2005) arguments that there is a need for more refined and specific examinations of signaling theory. The key to such future research is employing finer-grained methods which allow richer insights to be drawn. As discussed earlier in the chapter, the inconclusive results seen in much of the prior research on the performance of VC-backed IPOs is likely in part due to the coarse methods that have been used. Greater specification of the sample and of the variables is required for the investigation of IPOs and signaling. The impacts of the variables are very distinct, and if these factors are blended in a coarse manner their organizational outcomes may be ambiguous. In addition, a growing body of research within corporate finance and organizational theory maintains that corporate governance factors should not be considered in isolation from each other, but instead they should be examined as "bundles" when determining their efficiency outcomes. For example, Sanders and Boivie (2004) argue that IPOs represent a number of interrelated governance signals which may complement or substitute for each other. Therefore, further theoretical refining of signaling theory is in order.

Our survey of IPO literature suggests that institutional factors, such as the depth and breadth of the private equity industry and corporate governance-related regulatory initiatives, may affect the IPO investment process in terms of both the extent of IPO performance and the role of different types of financier. There is growing recognition that governance and the operation of VC firms may depend on the institutional environment (Black and Gilson, 1998; Jeng and Wells, 2000; Chahine et al., 2012). Further research might usefully extend analysis of the role of risk financiers in other institutional contexts, such as countries associated with network-based corporate governance systems (La Porta et al., 1997). For example, it is clear that the extent of syndication is significantly greater in the US venture capital industry compared with that in Europe (Wright and Lockett, 2003). Future analysis may also shed light on the main drivers of syndicated investments as well as their organizational outcomes.

More generally, an increasing number of studies suggest that agency problems may be different in different national settings and imply that researchers should integrate the agency framework with institutional analysis to generate robust predictions (Chahine et al., 2012). Future research should expand on this concept further and seek to more explicitly examine the nature of agency conflicts and their implications in different institutional settings (Aguilera and Jackson, 2003). For example, in addition to French civil law contexts (e.g. Spain and Italy, Hoskisson et al., 2004), there are also German civil law and the distinctive Scandinavian legal environment (La Porta et al., 1998, 2000; Fiss and Zajac, 2004). Do these institutional environments have an impact similar to French civil law? Alternatively, investor protection in German civil law is less prevalent than in common law, but more so than in French civil law. Is the impact of German civil law somewhere between the other two legal environments?

It is important to look at specific corporate governance channels, such as board presence, contractual framework etc., which facilitate monitoring of IPO firms. Although a comprehensive analysis of this complex interplay of various governance factors goes beyond the scope of this chapter, Bruton et al. (2009) suggest that institutional differences significantly affect the roles played by different internal governance mechanisms. Researchers need to conduct a more fine-grained analysis to understand the aspects of the interplay of these variables on corporate governance.

Finally, an IPO is not the final stage in the corporate governance life cycle. In a dynamic perspective, corporate governance factors may be affected by strategic choices and outcomes, and the choice of the various governance options could be associated with changes in organizational strategy and firm performance. For example, board diversity may be driven by the organization's growing need to manage the important external elements of the environment that are related to changes in the organization's size and diversity (Provan, 1980). Therefore, the post-IPO evolution of the firm's governance system is a key research issue.

Notes

1. Researchers commonly focus on a one-day window (trading at the end of day one) when evaluating underpricing (Loughran and Ritter, 2004). A few studies have examined trading at the end of one month.
2. Megginson and Weiss (1991) compare VC-backed IPOs with non-VC-backed IPOs from 1983 to 1987. Matched by industry and offering size, they find that the initial underpricing of VC-backed IPOs is significantly lower than for non-VC-backed IPOs. Barry et al. (1990) analyze the monitoring role of VCs in IPOs from 1978 to 1987. They find that the number of VCs invested in the issuing firm is negatively related to initial underpricing.

References

Adams, R., Almeida, H., and Ferreira, D. (2009). "Understanding the Relationship between Founder-CEOs and Firm Performance," *Journal of Empirical Finance*, 16(1): 136–50.

Admati, A. R., and Pfleiderer, P. (1994). "Robust Financial Contracting and the Role of Venture Capitalists," *Journal of Finance*, 49: 371–402.

Aggarwal, R., and Rivoli, P. (1990). "Fads in the Initial Public Offering Market?" *Financial Management*, 19: 45–57.

AGUILERA, R. V., and JACKSON, G. (2003). "The Cross-National Diversity of Corporate Governance: Dimensions and Determinants," *Academy of Management Review*, 28: 447–65.

ALLCOCK, D., and FILATOTCHEV, I. (2010). "Executive Incentive Schemes in Initial Public Offerings: The Effects of Multiple Agency Conflicts and Corporate Governance," *Journal of Management*, 36(3): 663–86.

ARTHURS, J. D., HOSKISSON, R. E., BUSENITZ, L. W., and JOHNSON, R. A. (2008). "Managerial Agents Watching Other Agents: Multiple Agency Conflicts Regarding Underpricing in IPO Firms," *Academy of Management Journal*, 51: 277–94.

BARON, J., HANNAN, M., and BURTON, M. (1999). "Building the Iron Cage: Determinants of Managerial Intensity in the Early Years of Organizations," *American Sociological Review*, 63: 527–48.

BARRY, C. B., MUSCARELLA, C. J., PEAVEY, J. W., and VETSUYPENS, M. R. (1990). "The Role of Venture Capital in the Creation of Public Companies—Evidence from the Going-Public Process," *Journal of Financial Economics*, 27(2): 447–71.

BEAMISH, P., and BANKS, J. (1987). "Equity Joint Ventures and the Theory of the Multinational Enterprise," *Journal of International Business Studies*, 18(2): 1–16.

BEATTY, R. P., and RITTER, J. R. (1986). "Investment Banking, Reputation and the Underpricing of Initial Public Offerings," *Journal of Financial Economics*, 15(2): 213–32.

—— and ZAJAC, E. J. (1994). "Managerial Incentives, Monitoring and Risk Bearing: A Study of Executive Compensation, Ownership, and Board Structure in Initial Public Offerings," *Administrative Science Quarterly*, 39(2): 313–35.

BEGLEY, T. M. (1995). "Using Founder Status, Age of Firm, and Company Growth Rate as the Basis for Distinguishing Entrepreneurs from Managers of Smaller Businesses," *Journal of Business Venturing*, 10(3): 249–63.

BERLE, A., and MEANS, G. (1932). *The Modern Corporation and Private Property*. New York: Macmillan.

BLACK, B. S., and GILSON, R. J. (1998). "Venture Capital and the Structure of Capital Markets: Banks versus Stock Markets," *Journal of Financial Economics*, 47: 243–77.

BOOTH, J., and SMITH, R. (1986). "Capital Raising, Underwriting and the Certification Hypothesis," *Journal of Financial Economics*, 15(1–2): 261–81.

BRADLEY, D., COONEY, J., DOLVIN, S., and JORDAN, B. (2006). "Penny Stock IPOs," *Financial Management*, 39: 5–29.

BRAV, A., GECZY, C., and GOMPERS, P. A. (2000). "Is the Abnormal Return Following Equity Issuances Anomalous?" *Journal of Financial Economics*, 56(2): 209–49.

—— and GOMPERS, P. A. (2003). "The Role of Lockups in Initial Public Offerings," *Review of Financial Studies*, 16: 1–29.

BRENNAN, M. J., and FRANKS, J. (1997). "Underpricing, Ownership and Control in Initial Public Offerings of Equity Securities in the U.K," *Journal of Financial Economics*, 45(3): 391–413.

BRUTON, G. D., CHAHINE, S., and FILATOTCHEV, I. (2009). "Founders, Private Equity Investors and Underpricing in Entrepreneurial IPOs," *Entrepreneurship Theory and Practice*, 33(4): 909–28.

—— FILATOTCHEV, I., CHAHINE, S., and WRIGHT, M. (2010). "Governance, Ownership Structure and Performance of IPO Firms: The Impact of Different Types of Private Equity Investors and Institutional Environments," *Strategic Management Journal*, 31(5): 491–509.

BUCK, T., BRUCE, A., MAIN, B. G. M., and UDUENI, H. (2003). "Long Term Incentive Plans, Executive Pay and UK Company Performance," *Journal of Management Studies*, 40(7): 1703–21.

BUSENITZ, L., FIET, J. O., and MOESEL, D. M. (2005). "Signaling in Venture Capital—New Venture Team Funding: Does it Indicate Long Term Venture Outcomes?" *Entrepreneurship Theory and Practice*, 29(1): 1–12.

BYGRAVE, W. (1987). "Syndicated Investments by Venture Capital Firms: A Networking Perspective," *Journal of Business Venturing*, 2: 139–54.

—— (1988). "The Structure of Investment Networks in the Venture Capital Industry," *Journal of Business Venturing*, 3: 137–57.

CARPENTER, M. A., and WESTPHAL, J. D. (2001). "The Strategic Context of External Network Ties: Examining the Impact of Director Appointments on Board Involvement in Strategic Decision-Making," *Academy of Management Journal*, 44: 639–60.

CERTO, S. T. (2003). "Influencing Initial Public Offering Investors with Prestige: Signaling with Board Structures," *Academy of Management Review*, 28(3): 432–46.

—— COVIN, J. G., DAILY, C. M., and DALTON, D. R. (2001). "Wealth and the Effects of Founder Management among IPO-Stage New Ventures," *Strategic Management Journal*, 22(6–7): 641–58.

—— DAILY, C. M., and DALTON, D. (2001). "Signaling Firm Value through Board Structure: An Investigation of Initial Public Offerings," *Entrepreneurship Theory and Practice*, 26(2): 35–50.

—— —— CANNELLA, A. A., and DALTON, D. R. (2003). "Giving Money to Get Money: How CEO Stock Options and CEO Equity Enhance IPO Valuations," *The Academy of Management Journal*, 46(5): 643–64.

CHAHINE, S., ARTHURS, J., FILATOTCHEV, I., and HOSKISSON, R. (2012). "The Effects of Venture Capital Syndicate Diversity on Earnings Management and Performance of IPOs in the US and UK: An Institutional Perspective," *Journal of Corporate Finance*, 18(1): 179–92.

—— and FILATOTCHEV, I. (2008). "The Effects of Venture Capitalist Affiliation to Underwriters on Short- and Long-Term Performance in French IPOs," *Global Finance Journal*, 18(3): 351–72.

COAKLEY, J., HADASS, L., and WOOD, A. (2007). "Post-IPO Operating Performance, Venture Capital and the Bubble Years," *Journal of Business Finance and Accounting*, 34(9–10): 1423–46.

COHEN, B. D., and DEAN, T. J. (2005). "Information Asymmetry and Investor Valuation of IPOs: Top Management Team Legitimacy as a Capital Market Signal," *Strategic Management Journal*, 26: 683–90.

CONYON, M. J. (2000). *Directors pay in UK Plc's, A Guide To Executive Pay Determination*. London: Chartered Institute of Personnel and Development.

—— and SADLER, G. V. (2001). "Executive Pay, Tournaments and Corporate Performance in UK Firms," *International Journal of Management Reviews*, 3(2): 141.

CORE, J. E., HOLTHAUSEN, R. W., and LARCKER, D. F. (1999). "Corporate Governance, Chief Executive Officer Compensation, and Firm Performance," *Journal of Financial Economics*, 51(3): 371–406.

CUMMING, D. J. (2006). "The Determinants of Venture Capital Portfolio Size: Empirical Evidence," *The Journal of Business*, 79: 1083–126.

D'AVENI, R. A. (1990). "Top Managerial Prestige and Organizational Bankruptcy," *Organization Science*, 1: 121–42.

DAILY, C. M., and DALTON, D. R. (1992). "Financial Performance of Founder-Managed versus Professionally Managed Small Corporations," *Journal of Small Business Management*, 2: 25–34.

—— —— (1997). "CEO and Board Chair Roles Held Jointly or Separately: Much Ado About Nothing?" *Academy of Management Executive*, 11(3): 11–20.

—— CERTO, S. T., DALTON, D. R., and ROENGPITYA, R. (2003). "IPO Underpricing: A Meta-Analysis and Research Synthesis," *Entrepreneurship Theory and Practice*, 27(3): 271–95.

DALTON, D. R., DAILY, C. M., JOHNSON, J. L., and ELLSTAND, A. E. (1999). "Number of Directors and Financial Performance: A Meta-Analysis," *Academy of Management Journal*, 42(6): 674–86.

DELOITTE & TOUCHE (2005a). *On the Grid: The Importance of Executive Reward at Flotation*. London: Deloitte & Touche LLP.

—— (2005b). *Options Take a Hit but What Will Take their Place? The 2005 Deloitte Stock Compensation Survey*. London: Deloitte Development LLC.

EISENHARDT, K., and SCHOONHOVEN, C. (1990). "Organizational Growth: Linking Founding Team, Strategy, Environment, and Growth among U.S. Semiconductor Ventures, 1978–1988," *Administrative Science Quarterly*, 35: 504–29.

ESPENLAUB, S., and TONKS, I. (1998). "Post IPO Directors' Sales and Reissuing Activity: An Empirical Test of IPO Signalling Models," *Journal of Business, Finance and Accounting*, 25(9–10): 1037–79.

FAMA, E. F. (1980). "Agency Problems and the Theory of the Firm," *Journal of Political Economy*, 88(8): 288–307.

—— and FRENCH, K. R. (2004). "New Lists: Fundamentals and Survival Rates," *Journal of Financial Economics*, 73(2): 229–69.

—— and JENSEN, M. C. (1983a). "Agency Problems and Residual Claims," *Journal of Law and Economics*, 26(2): 327.

—— —— (1983b). "Separation of Ownership and Control," *Journal of Law and Economics*, 26: 301–25.

FILATOTCHEV, I., and BISHOP, K. (2002). "Board Composition, Share Ownership and 'Underpricing' of U.K. IPO Firms," *Strategic Management Journal*, 23(10): 941–55.

—— and WRIGHT, M. (2005). *The Life Cycle of Corporate Governance*. Cheltenham: Edward Elgar.

—— —— and ABERK, M. (2006). "Venture Capitalists, Syndication and Governance in Initial Public Offerings," *Small Business Economics*, 26(4): 337–50.

Financial Reporting Council. (2010). *The UK Corporate Governance Code*. London: Financial Reporting Council.

FINKELSTEIN, S., and D'AVENI, R. A. (1994). "CEO Duality as a Double-Edged Sword: How Boards of Directors Balance Entrenchment Avoidance and Unity of Command," *Academy of Management Journal*, 37(5): 1079.

FISS, P. C., and ZAJAC, E. J. (2004). "The Diffusion of Ideas over Contested Terrain: The (Non) Adoption of a Shareholder Value Orientation among German Firms," *Administrative Science Quarterly*, 49: 501–34.

FLAMHOLTZ, E. (1986). *Managing the Transition from an Entrepreneurship to a Professionally Managed Firm*. San Francisco: Jossey-Bass.

FRANCIS, B. B., and HASAN, I. (2001). "The Underpricing of Venture and Nonventure Capital IPOs: An Empirical Investigation," *Journal of Financial Services Research*, 19(2): 99–113.

FRIED, V. H., BRUTON, G. D., and HISRICH, R. D. (1998). "Strategy and the Board of Directors in Venture Capital-Backed Firms," *Journal of Business Venturing*, 13: 493–503.

GOMPERS, P. (1995). "Optimal Investment, Monitoring, and the Staging of Venture Capital," *Journal of Finance*, 50(5): 1461–89.

—— (1996). "Grandstanding in the Venture Capital Industry," *Journal of Financial Economics*, 42(1): 133–56.

—— and LERNER, J. (1999). *The Venture Capital Cycle*. New York: Wiley.

GREENBURY, S. R. (1995). *Director's Remuneration Report of a Study Group Chaired by Sir Richard Greenbury (Greenbury Report)*. London: Gee Publishing Ltd.

GREINER, L. (1972). "Evolution and Revolution as Organizations Grow," *Harvard Business Review*, 50: 37–46.

HALL, B. (1998). "The Pay to Performance Incentives of Executive Stock Options," NBER Working Paper.

—— and LEIBMAN, J. B. (1998). "Are CEOs Really Paid Like Bureaucrats?" *Quarterly Journal of Economics*, 113(3): 653–91.

HAMBRICK, D., and MASON, P. (1984). "Upper Echelons: The Organization as a Reflection of its Top Managers," *Academy of Management Review*, 9: 193–206.

HIGGINS, M., and GULATI, R. (1999). "Getting Off to a Start: The Effects Of Upper Echelon Affiliations On Prestige Of Investment Bank and IPO Success." Working Paper, Harvard Business School.

HILLMAN, A. J., and DALZIEL, T. (2003). "Boards of Directors and Firm Performance: Integrating Agency and Resource Dependence Perspectives," *Academy of Management Review*, 26(3): 383–96.

HOCHBERG, Y. V., LJUNGQVIST, A., and LU, Y. (2007). "Whom You Know Matters: Venture Capital Networks and Investment Performance," *The Journal of Finance*, 62(1): 251–301.

HOSKISSON, R. E., CANNELLA, A. A., TIHANYI, L., and FARACI, R. (2004). "Asset Restructuring and Business Group Affiliation in French Civil Law Countries," *Strategic Management Journal*, 25: 525–39.

IBBOTSON, R. J., SINDELAR, J., and RITTER, J. (1988). "Initial Public Offerings," *Journal of Applied Corporate Finance*, 1(2): 37–45.

Institute of Directors (2011). *Directors Pay Survey 2010*. London: IOD.

JÄÄSKELÄINEN, M., MAULA, M., and SEPPÄ, T. (2006). "Allocation of Attention to Portfolio Companies and the Performance of Venture Capital Firms," *Entrepreneurship Theory and Practice*, 30(2): 185–206.

JAIN, B. A., and KINI, O. (1999). "The Lifecycle of Initial Public Offering Firms," *Journal of Business, Finance and Accounting*, 26(9–10): 1281–317.

—— and TABAK, F. (2008). "Factors Influencing the Choice between Founder versus Non-founder Ceos for IPO Firms," *Journal of Business Venturing*, 23(1): 21–45.

JAYRAMAN, N., KHORANA, A., and NELLING, E. (2000). "CEO Founder Status and Firm Financial Performance," *Strategic Management Journal*, 21(12): 1215–24.

JELIC, R., SAADOUNI, B., and WRIGHT, M. (2005). "Performance of Private to Public MBOs: The Role of Venture Capital," *Journal of Business Finance and Accounting*, 32(3–4): 643–82.

JENG, L. A., and WELLS, P. C. (2000). "The Determinants of Venture Capital Funding: Evidence across Countries," *Journal of Corporate Finance*, 6(3): 241–89.

JENSEN, M. C., and MECKLING, W. H. (1976). "Theory of the Firm: Managerial Behavior, Agency Costs and Ownership Structure," *Journal of Financial Economics*, 3(4): 305–60.

Jensen, M. C., and Murphy, K. J. (1990). "Performance Pay and Top Management Incentives," *Journal of Political Economy*, 98(2): 225–64.

Kanniainen, V., and Keuschnigg, C. (2003). "The Optimal Portfolio of Start-Up Firms in Venture Capital Finance," *Journal of Corporate Finance*, 9(5): 521–34.

Katz, S. (2009). "Earnings Equality and Ownership Structure: The Role of Private Equity Sponsors," *Accounting Review*, 84(3): 623–58.

Kooli, M., and Meknassi, S. (2007). "The Survival Profile of U.S. IPO Issuers: 1985–2005," *Journal of Wealth Management*, 10: 105–19.

Kroll, M., Walters, B. A., and Le, S. A. (2007). "The Impact of Board Composition and Top Management Team Ownership Structure on Post IPO Performance in Young Entrepreneurial Firms," *Academy of Management Journal*, 50(5): 1198–216.

Kunze, R. (1990). *Nothing Ventured*. New York: Harper.

La Porta, R., Lopez-de-Silanes, F., Shleifer, A., and Vishny, R. (1997). "Legal Determinants of External Finance," *The Journal of Finance*, 52(3): 1131–50.

—— —— —— —— (1998). "Law and Finance," *Journal of Political Economy*, 106(6): 1113–55.

—— —— —— —— (2000). "Investor Protection and Corporate Governance," *Journal of Financial Economics*, 58(1–2): 3–27.

Lee, P. M., and Wahal, S. (2004). "Grandstanding, Certification and the Underpricing of Venture Capital Backed IPOs," *Journal of Financial Economics*, 73(2): 375–407.

Lerner, J. (1995). "Venture Capitalists and the Oversight of Private Firms," *Journal of Finance*, 50: 301–18.

—— (1998). "'Angel' Financing and Public Policy: An Overview," *Journal of Banking and Finance*, 22: 773–83.

Lester, R. H., Certo, S. T., Dalton, C. M., Dalton, D. R., and Cannella, A. A. (2006). "Initial Public Offering Investor Valuations: An Examination of Top Management Team Prestige and Environmental Uncertainty," *Journal of Small Business Management*, 44(1): 1–26.

Levis, M. (2008). *The London Markets and Private Equity Backed IPOs*. London: Cass Business School and BVCA.

Lie, E. (2005). "On The Timing of CEO Stock Option Awards," *Management Science*, 51(5): 802–12.

Liu, L. S., and Stark, A. W. (2009). "Relative Performance Evaluation in Board Cash Compensation: UK Empirical Evidence" *The British Accounting Review*, 41(1): 21–30.

Lockett, A., and Wright, M. (1999). "The Syndication of Private Equity: Evidence from the UK," *Venture Capital*, 1(4): 303–24.

—— —— (2001). "The Syndication of Venture Capital Investments," *Omega: The International Journal of Management Science*, 29: 375–90.

Loughran, T., and Ritter, J. (2004). "Why has IPO Underpricing Changed over Time?" *Financial Management*, 33: 5–37.

—— —— and Rydqvist, K. (1994). "Initial Public Offering: International Insights," *Pacific Basin Journal*, 2: 156–99.

Lowry, M. B., and Murphy, K. J. (2007). "Executive Stock Options and IPO Underpricing," *Journal of Financial Economics*, 85(1): 39–65.

Lynall, M. D., Golden, B. R., and Hillman, A. J. (2003). "Board Composition from Adolescence to Maturity: A Multitheoretic View," *Academy of Management Review*, 28(3): 416–31.

Mackey, A. (2008). "The Effect of CEOs on Firm Performance," *Strategic Management Journal*, 29: 1357–67.

MEGGINSON, W., and WEISS, K. (1991). "Venture Capitalist Certification in Initial Public Offerings," *Journal of Finance*, 46(3): 879–903.

MICHAELY, R., and SHAW, W. H. (1994). "The Pricing of Initial Public Offerings: The Test of Adverse-Selection and Signaling Theories," *Review of Financial Studies*, 7(2): 279–319.

MIKKELSON, W. H., PARTCH, M. M., and SHAH, K. (1997). "Ownership and Operating Performance of Companies that Go Public," *Journal of Financial Economics*, 44(3): 281–307.

MINTZBERG, H., and WATERS, J. (1982). "Tracking Strategy in an Entrepreneurial Firm," *Academy of Management Journal*, 25: 465–99.

MJOEN, H., and TALLMAN, S. (1997). "Control and Performance in International Joint Ventures," *Organization Science*, 8(3): 257–74.

MONKS, R. A. G., and MINOW, N. (2004). *Corporate Governance*. Malden, MA: Blackwells.

NELSON, T. (2003). "The Persistence of Founder Influence: Management, Ownership, and Performance Effects at Initial Public Offering," *Strategic Management Journal*, 24(8): 707–24.

NOHEL, T., and TODD, S. (2005). "Compensation for Managers with Career Concerns: The Role of Stock Options in Optimal Contracts," *Journal of Corporate Finance*, 11(1–2): 229–51.

PFEFFER, J. (1972). "Size and Composition of Corporate Boards of Directors: The Organization and its Environment," *Administrative Science Quarterly*, 17(2): 218–28.

PROVAN, K. (1980). "Board Power and Organizational Efficiency among Human Service Agencies," *Academy of Management Journal*, 23: 221–36.

REID, G. (1998). *Venture Capital Investment: An Agency Analysis of Practice*. London: Routledge.

RITTER, J. R., and WELCH, I. (2002). "A Review of IPO Activity, Pricing, and Allocations," *Journal of Finance*, 57(4): 1795–828.

ROSEN, S. (1990). "Contracts and the Markets for Executives," NBER Working Paper no. W3542.

SAHLMAN, W. A. (1990). "The Structure and Governance of Venture Capital Organizations," *Journal of Financial Economics*, 27(2): 473–521.

SANDERS, W. G., and BOIVIE, S. (2004). "Sorting Things Out: Valuation of New Firms in Uncertain Markets," *Strategic Management Journal*, 25(2): 167–86.

SCHULTZ, P. (1993). "Unit Initial Public Offerings," *Journal of Financial Economics*, 34: 199–229.

SCHULZE, W., LUBATKIN, M., and DINO, R. (2003). "Exploring the Agency Consequences of Ownership Dispersion among the Directors of Private Family Firms," *Academy of Management Journal*, 46: 217–29.

SHANE, S., and CABLE, D. (2002). "Network Ties, Reputation and the Financing of New Ventures," *Management Science*, 48(3): 364–81.

SHIVDASANI, A., and YERMACK, D. (1999). "CEO Involvement in the Selection of New Board Members: An Empirical Analysis," *Journal of Finance*, 54(5): 1829–53.

TESLUK, P. E., and JACOBS, R. R. (1998). "Toward an Integrated Model of Work Experience," *Personnel Psychology*, 51(2): 321–55.

TOSI, H. L., KATZ, J. P., and GOMEZ-MEJIA, L. R. (1997). "Disaggregating the Agency Contract: The Effects of Monitoring, Incentive Alignment, and Term in Office on Agent Decision Making," *Academy of Management Journal*, 40(3): 584–602.

—— WERNER, S., KATZ, J. P., and GOMEZ-MEJIA, L. R. (2000). "How Much Does Performance Matter? A Meta-Analysis of CEO Pay Studies." *Journal of Management*, 26(2): 301–39.

Vesper, K. (1996). *New Venture Experience*. Seattle, WA: Vector Books.

Villalonga, B., and Amit, R. (2006). "How Do Family Ownership, Control and Management Affect Firm Value?" *Journal of Financial Economics*, 80(2): 385–417.

Wall Street Journal (2010). "The Wall Street Journal Survey of CEO Compensation," *Wall Street Journal*, November 14.

Wasserman, N. (2003). "Founder CEO Succession and the Paradox of Entrepreneurial Success," *Organizational Science*, 14: 149–72.

Wat, L. (1983). *Strategies for Going Public*. New York: Deloitte, Haskins and Sells.

Westphal, J. D. (1998). "Board Games: How CEOs Adapt to Increases in Structural Board Independence from Management," *Administrative Science Quarterly*, 43(2): 511–37.

Wiseman, R., and Gomez-Mejia, L. R. (1998). "A Behavioral Agency Model of Risk Taking," *Academy of Management Review*, 23(1): 133–53.

Wright, M., and Lockett, A. (2003). "The Structure and Management of Alliances: Syndication in the Venture Capital Industry," *Journal of Management Studies*, 40(8): 2073–102.

Yan, A., and Gray, B. (2001). "Antecedents and Effects of Parent Control in International Joint Ventures," *Journal of Management Studies*, 38(3): 393–416.

Yermack, D. (1997). "Good Timing: CEO Stock Option Awards and Company News Announcements," *Journal of Finance*, 52(2): 449–79.

Zahra, S., and Pearce, J. (1989). "Boards of Directors and Corporate Financial Performance: A Review and Integrative Model," *Journal of Management*, 15(2): 291–72.

Zhang, G. (2006). "Market Valuation and Employee Stock Options," *Management Science*, 52(9): 1377–93.

CHAPTER 20

CORPORATE GOVERNANCE, MULTINATIONAL FIRMS, AND INTERNATIONALIZATION

NAI H. WU AND LASZLO TIHANYI

INTRODUCTION

CORPORATE governance scholars have provided helpful insights into the organizational and strategic implications of firm ownership and control, including diversification, CEO compensation, top management team composition, and research and development (Dalton et al., 2007). Although researchers have made great progress in understanding these areas, the field of international business has paid limited attention to the effects of corporate governance (Strange et al., 2009). According to Strange and Jackson (2008: 2):

> IB research focuses on the strategies of multinational enterprises (MNEs) for global expansion in diverse regions and countries. The emphasis here is on the corporate and business level strategies themselves, rather than the processes of strategic decision-making and hence corporate governance.

Multinational firms operate in multiple countries and control their subsidiaries through ownership and management. They are one of the most complex of modern business entities (Dunning and Lundan, 2008). According to the *World Investment Report* (UNCTAD, 2009), approximately 82,000 multinational firms own about 810,000 foreign affiliates, which in 2008 exported one-third of the total world exports. Moreover, multinational firms employed approximately 77 million in 2008, a 400 percent increase since 1982 and more than twice Germany's labor force. These figures are even more impressive if we consider the 100 largest multinational firms, which accounted for about 4 percent of the 2008 worldwide gross domestic product (GDP). Considering multinational firms' influence and complexity, it is somewhat surprising that researchers have under-explored their corporate governance (Aguilera and Jackson, 2010).

A study of corporate governance in multinational firms offers several benefits. First, these firms are more complex than domestic firms. Thus, their governance may have unique characteristics. By studying the differences, we can gain insights into how multinational firms manage their businesses across national boundaries. For example, how do multinational firms manage their subsidiaries? How do their top management team compositions differ from those of domestic firms? Second, international business scholars have studied important strategies such as internationalization, and prior literature has shown that corporate governance influences firm strategies, so we should investigate corporate governance as it affects internationalization. For example, do different investor types encourage internationalization or related strategies? In short, we seek to address how multinational firms differ in corporate governance from domestic firms and how these differences influence internationalization.

This chapter is structured as follows. First, we review literature on the governance of multinational firms and explore the differences between the governance of multinational firms and domestic firms. We identify three streams of research: coordination and control of foreign subsidiaries, headquarter governance, and knowledge flow within multinational firms. Second, we review the literature on governance's influence on the internationalization process and discuss the governance problems presented by the classic international business models, including the internationalization strategy, mode of entry, and managerial perceptions of the internationalization process.

Governance of Multinational Firms

Multinational firms may span the boundaries of several countries and operate in diverse institutional environments. To effectively leverage their technologies, operations, and product offerings in a global environment, many multinational firms have developed complex coordinating processes and control mechanisms. Two schools of thought in international business dominated the early studies on the governance of multinational firms. Stopford and Wells (1972) studied formal coordination mechanisms and found that multinational firms within similar industries pursued similar organizational structures. They concluded that multinational organizational structures would naturally follow their strategies. Based on Bower's (1970) work and advanced by scholars such as Prahalad, Doz, and Bartlett (e.g. Bartlett and Ghoshal, 1989; Doz and Prahalad, 1991), the second school of thought used the individual manager as their basic unit of analysis and emphasized global integration and local responsiveness. This paradigm, called the *process school* of international management, claimed to "put managerial relevance before theoretical elegance" (Doz and Prahalad, 1991: 161). The process school of thought significantly contributed to understanding multinational firms by shifting the focus to previously little studied factors and advocated a strong need for multidimensional approaches. Our literature review has identified three important literature streams that benefited from the early schools of thought on governance of multinational firms: coordination and control of foreign subsidiaries, headquarter governance, and knowledge flow within multinational firms. We discuss these three streams next.

Coordination and Control of Foreign Subsidiaries

The complexity of multinational organizations means that increasing internationalization presents important governance challenges. Local firms have relatively homogeneous labor markets and culturally familiar environments. When they expand abroad, however, they must manage diverse overseas subsidiaries, balance global efficiency, and respond to local customer preferences. The most critical for multinational firms, then, is coordinating and controlling foreign subsidiaries (Vora et al., 2007). One important question in this stream of research is how multinational firms should govern foreign subsidiaries. Birkinshaw and Morrison (1995) described three types of subsidiaries: local implementers, specialized contributors, and world mandates. Local implementers are subsidiaries established to respond to local demands; specialized contributors integrate strategies across borders; and world mandates are in the middle. Expanding that idea, Kim, Prescott, and Kim (2005) inferred that the headquarters of multinational firms are in a principal–agent relationship with subsidiaries and proposed that the corporate governance structure may vary among the three types of subsidiaries. They theorized that local implementers will have more agency problems, more outside directors, CEO duality, a larger board, and a more result-based executive compensation system, followed by subsidiaries that are world mandates and specialized contributors.

Another important question is how multinational firms can monitor and motivate subsidiaries to ensure that they perform well. In an earlier study, Edstrom and Galbraith (1977) showed that multinational firms create information networks by transferring managers across offices as a control strategy. Other studies have supported that position by studying headquarters' uses of expatriate top managers for control and monitoring (e.g. Boyacigiller, 1990). Research highlights two main mechanisms for controlling subsidiaries: formal control systems and executive compensation. Roth and Nigh (1992) found that formal control systems caused a positive association between effective headquarters–subsidiary relationships, personal integration, and coordination of primary activities. Alternatively, others have suggested that executive compensation enhances control of foreign subsidiaries (Hedlund and Rolander, 1990; Festing et al., 2007; Filatotchev and Wright, 2011). Based on a study of 100 subsidiaries from five countries, Roth and O'Donnell (1996) found higher incentive-based compensation when subsidiaries are responsible for products in terms of all the value-added activities in the global markets and when their senior managers are highly committed to the headquarters. However, compensation will be based more on corporate performance when subsidiary managers are less committed to the headquarters. They also found that incentive-based compensation is positively associated with cultural distance. In a subsequent study, O'Donnell (1999) found that compensation design is based more on corporate performance if subsidiaries follow a global strategy rather than a multidomestic strategy. These studies show that when subsidiaries have more autonomy, compensation will be more likely based on incentives.

Researchers have also called for investigation of subsidiaries' performance from the viewpoint of the relationship between headquarters and subsidiaries. O'Donnell's (1999) study indicated that treating a multinational firm as an interdependent network is more predictively accurate than treating it as a principal–agent relation. She found that when subsidiaries have more autonomy, the headquarters impose less monitoring. Other studies have also looked into how interdependence influences the performance of subsidiaries (Subramaniam and Watson, 2006) and the importance of social capital among different types of multinational firms (Kostova and Roth, 2003). Some scholars found that an alignment between the headquarters and subsidiaries can improve performance, such as coordinating marketing activities (Hewett et al., 2003). Finally, Vora et al. (2007) found that when managers in the subsidiaries identified with both the parent firm and their own unit, they were more likely to enjoy higher role fulfillment.

Governance in the Headquarters

Scholars have studied several governance mechanisms in multinational firms, such as executive compensation, board structure, and the composition of top management teams (Ghoshal and Nohria, 1989; Sanders and Carpenter, 1998). They have proposed that multinational firms could best use their resources and develop effective strategies with proper governance mechanisms in place. For example, how should multinational firms reward and motivate their executives and thereby minimize agency problems? Sanders and Carpenter (1998) have argued that, as firms' degree of internationalization increases (measured by foreign sales, foreign production, and geographic dispersion), their governance structure would be modified to mitigate agency problems and respond to complex information-processing demands. They showed that a multinational firm's degree of internationalization was positively associated with the CEO's long-term compensation and was positively related to the size of the top management team and the separation of the CEO and board chair. Sanders and Carpenter's (1998) findings suggest that, for firms to cope with the strains of internationalization (e.g. coordinating affiliates in different countries), they must change the structure of their corporate governance as well.

Furthermore, several other papers have addressed corporate governance in multinational firms from different perspectives. First, some researchers have concluded that multinational firms fail to effectively utilize talent management (Mellahi and Collings, 2010). Despite globalization and the potential benefits of having diverse top management teams, the upper echelon in most multinational firms remain homogeneous (Adler and Bartholomew, 1992), and fewer than a quarter of such managers have more than one-year experience of working overseas (Carpenter et al., 2001). However, research has shown that the combined international experience of the top management team and national diversity at the board level predicts the likelihood of having a non-national member on the top management team (Nielsen and Nielsen, 2010). Staples (2007) investigated the board composition of the world's largest multinational firms and found that about 55 percent have one non-national director out of four directors. Second, researchers are interested in how compensation influences the performance of multinational firms. Carpenter and Sanders (2004) found that total compensation and long-term incentives for top management teams were positively associated with subsequent performance, and the influence was even stronger when a multinational firm had a higher degree of internationalization. That study found that the pay gap between a CEO and the top management team negatively affected performance. Carpenter et al. (2001) found that highly international firms performed better when their CEOs had international experience and higher total compensation. Finally, researchers are also interested in how multinational firms influence the characteristics of their CEOs and their effect on firm performance. Roth (1995) found that, in highly international firms, CEOs had a stronger positive effect on firm performance when they had greater internal locus of control, international experience abroad, and cared more about how their decisions influenced others.

Knowledge Flow within the Multinational Firm

Because multinational firms involve headquarters and subsidiaries in different countries, the flow of knowledge among organizational units becomes increasingly difficult. However, some consider this obstacle to offer advantages. Indeed, some scholars have argued that multinational firms exist because they can leverage and transfer knowledge within their own units more efficiently (Kogut and Zander, 1993). Because imperfect markets cause information asymmetry, multinational firms can internalize knowledge within their units. Nevertheless, several scholars have shown that transferring knowledge can be costly (Zander and Kogut, 1995). Teece (1981) performed one of the first of these studies. He found that transferring technology costs amounted to approximately 2–60 percent of total project costs. Recognizing that knowledge transfer is costly, Kogut and Zander (1993) found that multinational firms could transfer knowledge less expensively to their wholly owned subsidiaries than to a third party if it was less codifiable and harder to teach.

Addressing knowledge flow within a multinational firm, Ghoshal and Bartlett (1990: 604) encouraged scholars to consider a multinational firm as "a network of exchange relationships among different organizational units." They proposed that multinational firms are indeed embedded in their interorganizational networks. Building on that work, Gupta and Govindarajan (1991) applied the concept of knowledge flows within multinational firms and found that, depending on a subsidiary's knowledge stock, motivation, transmission channels, and absorptive capabilities, knowledge could flow to other peer subsidiaries, to the headquarters, and vice versa. Other studies have also shown that knowledge flow within multinational firms depends on the subsidiary's strategic position and relative performance (Andersson et al., 2007; Driffield et al., 2010).

Multinational firms may also transfer knowledge through expatriates (Tan and Mahoney, 2006), who can enhance subsidiary performance through knowledge transfer (Wang et al., 2009). However, Fang et al. (2010) investigated Japanese multinational firms and found that expatriates could facilitate knowledge transfer in the short term but the effect diminished in the long term.

Though extensive work has been conducted on knowledge transference between headquarters and subsidiaries, researchers have not yet detailed the effect of corporate governance on knowledge flow within multinational firms (Kim et al., 2005). One notable exception is Fey and Furu's (2008) study on how incentive systems for top managers influence knowledge sharing within multinational firms. They studied foreign-owned subsidiaries in Finland and China and learned that when the bonus pay for the top managers in the subsidiary was tied to the performance of the entire multinational firm, knowledge was more readily shared throughout the multinational firm. In addition, when the subsidiary's top managers shared the entire corporation's vision, they were more likely to share knowledge.

The Internationalization Process

When firms decide to expand beyond their national boundaries, their managers must make many new strategic decisions. However, relatively limited research has considered the influence of corporate governance on internationalization processes. We first review two classic models on internationalization. We then discuss the role of corporate governance in internationalization strategies and mode of entry. Finally, we conclude with the managerial perception of the internationalization process.

Classic Models

Two models can help explain the implications of internationalization for corporate governance: Vernon's (1966) product life-cycle model and Johanson and Vahlne's (1977) internationalization process model. Both models are longitudinal and represent the stages that firms go through in the process of internationalization. Vernon's product life-cycle model suggests that the first stage is introducing a new product in the domestic market; the second stage is increasing production by exporting to other countries; the third stage is looking for ways to be cost-efficient when customer demand is saturated (maturity); and the final stage is declining demand. Vernon's product life-cycle model makes a major contribution in that it captures the change of production locations (Melin, 1992). For example, when a firm first invents a new product, it is important to maintain a shorter distance between the production facilities and decision-makers at the headquarters. As a product matures, it becomes standardized, so production facilities can relocate to lower-cost countries. Some have criticized Vernon's model. For example, Buckley and Casson (1976) pointed out that the model failed to address issues such as non-standardized products that are produced abroad and the increasing number of products that have relatively short life cycles.

The second model is Johanson and Vahlne's (1977) internationalization process model, which is based on their study of Swedish multinational firms at the University of Uppsala. They observe that firms tend to take small steps toward internationalization. For instance, they start by using overseas agents. When sales increase, they establish a sales subsidiary. As customer demand increases, they eventually produce the product in the host country. In essence, their model focuses on sequential and small steps in acquiring, integrating, and applying knowledge in the foreign market. In their later work, they further included that a multinational firm's management gains knowledge from working with partners abroad. Thus, the central ideas of the internationalization process model are knowledge, decision, and psychic distance (Aharoni et al., 2011). A major contribution of this model is the notion that firms will expand to new countries that appear to pose fewer risks. Some scholars have also criticized the internationalization process model for excluding other strategic choices (e.g. some firms do not follow those sequential steps) and for limiting its description to the early stages of internationalization (Melin, 1992).

Internationalization Strategy

Although the product life-cycle model and the internationalization process model considered temporal effects, both models assumed that globalizing firms follow rather homogeneous processes. As multinational firms become increasingly complex, researchers are exploring different antecedents in internationalization strategies (Hitt et al., 2006). Since corporate governance has been shown to influence firm strategy and outcome, more studies are examining the relations of corporate governance and internationalization strategies.

Research on corporate governance as an antecedent of internationalization can be divided into three broad areas: top management teams and managerial compensation, ownership heterogeneity, and boards of directors. First, top management teams play important roles in deciding to go abroad. One study showed that internationalization strategy may be positively associated with several factors, such as the top management team's international experience, lower average age, shorter tenure with the firm, and amount of elite and higher education (Tihanyi et al., 2000). One recent study found a positive influence on internationalization of contingent managerial compensation, stock options, and bonuses (Tihanyi et al., 2009).

Second, a corporate governance literature review reveals that ownership heterogeneity influences competitive strategies (David et al., 2001; Douma et al., 2006; Burns et al., 2010). For example, some scholars recently found that foreign investors are more likely to be involved in corporate governance activities when they share a common culture and language with the people in the acquired foreign firm (Kang and Kim, 2010). Another study by Benito et al. (2011) investigated why multinational firms locate their divisional headquarters abroad. They found that state ownership and ownership concentration were negatively related to locating headquarters in a host country. Tihanyi et al. (2003) found that internationalization strategy was positively associated with institutional owners that were pension or professional investment funds; outside board members strengthened the relationship for professional investment funds, whereas inside board members strengthened the relationship for pension funds. Bhaumik et al. (2009) investigated the ownership structure of firms in an emerging market. They found that family owners and concentrated ownership discouraged overseas investments, whereas foreign investors encouraged them. Finally, scholars have found that family owners influence the choice of foreign direct investment locations (Strange et al., 2009) and that domestic owners valued growth while foreign owners valued diversification (David et al., 2010). Third, researchers have investigated the effect of boards of directors on internationalization strategy (Filatotchev et al., 2001). Some scholars found that board size and independent directors positively related to foreign direct investment (FDI) in Taiwan (Lien et al., 2005). On the other hand, Lu et al. (2009) found that ownership concentration, outside directors, and CEO shareholding positively influenced export propensity. Finally, Connelly et al. (2011) identified that board interlocks influenced a firm's decision to expand into China. Ties to other boards that have successfully expanded to China were positively associated with the subsequent decision to follow the lead. Ties to those that tried unsuccessfully or avoided expanding to China were associated with avoiding expanding international strategy to China.

Mode of Entry

Although mode of entry is at the core of many international business studies, researchers have not investigated the topic of mode of entry from the corporate governance perspective. Most early works in mode of entry have tended to focus on transaction costs, assuming that firms and their managers are rational and efficient (Hennart, 1989). Based in economics, these studies have largely overlooked non-market factors. Other scholars pointed out that institutions matter and investigated entry mode choices using factors that earlier models of economics excluded, including cultural distance and other institutional characteristics (Kogut and Singh, 1988; Hennart and Larimo, 1998).

Recent studies further indicated that information asymmetry and risks influenced the mode of entry (Filatotchev et al., 2007). There are different levels of risk associated with a multinational firm's decision to enter a market by means of strategic alliances, joint ventures, or greenfield investments. Thus, firms must choose whether they want to assume risks associated with certain entry choices. In addition, owners and managers have different utility functions and risk preferences. As Buckley and Strange (2011) have suggested, managers may differ from owners because they assess risks and rewards differently. Rhoades and Rechner (2001) attempted to consider the influence of corporate governance and entry mode choices. They discovered that, in some years, outside directors, owner control, and board diversity were positively associated with higher-risk entry mode. They also found that the presence of blockholders was positively associated with higher-risk entry mode. In a related study, Filatotchev et al. (2007) investigated multinational firms from newly industrialized economies and found that family and institutional ownership affected multinational firms' equity stakes in their overseas affiliates. Greater family or domestic financial institutional ownership was negatively associated with the level of ownership of foreign affiliates. However, foreign financial institutional ownership was positively associated with the level of ownership of foreign affiliates. They also found that higher ownership in foreign affiliates was positively associated with similar backgrounds in multinational firms (e.g. economic, cultural, and historical links).

Managerial Perception of the Internationalization Process

Aharoni (1966: 15) defined the foreign investment decision process as "the continuous dynamic social process of mutual influences among various members of an organization, constrained by the organization's strategy, its resources, and the limited capacity, goal, and needs of its members, throughout which choices emerge." The concept of bounded rationality largely influenced his work (Simon, 1947; March and Simon, 1958) in which he identified five elements of the decision process: time, social system, risk propensity, decision-maker's perception of uncertainty and constraints, and interactions among managers and the organization.

Prahalad and Doz (1987) extended the work on decision processes by focusing on the relationship between a multinational firm's headquarters and subsidiaries. They suggested that multinational firms made decisions based on managers' cognitive varieties. Researchers have also applied agency theory to understand managerial perceptions. For example, when CEOs and top management teams own company shares, they may be less willing to take risks and more likely to align their goals with other owners. These agent-owners may choose to invest more conservatively. At least one study has shown that top management teams with managerial ownership are less likely to internationalize (George et al., 2005).

OPPORTUNITIES FOR CONTRIBUTIONS

We have reviewed literature on the governance of multinational firms and the internationalization process. As mentioned previously, an abundance of opportunities remain for contributions in each area. We discuss some of these opportunities below.

The Governance of Multinational Firms

First, in the stream of *coordination and control of foreign subsidiaries,* researchers have used agency theory to explain the relationship between headquarters and subsidiaries (Filatotchev and Wright, 2011). However, some have concluded that using agency theory to explain corporate governance generates mixed results (Dalton et al., 2007). We suggest that researchers consider different theoretical perspectives. For example, resource dependence theorists argue that organizations depend on their external environments for resources because they lack self-sufficiency (Pfeffer and Salancik, 1978). Since subsidiaries depend on the headquarters for resources, resource dependence theory may explain how coordination and control are established and then more accurately predict subsidiary performance.

Second, in the stream of *governance in the headquarters*, researchers have been interested in how governance is different for domestic and multinational firms. In this stream, researchers have generally agreed that, as a multinational firm increases its internationalization, its governance changes to cope with the increasing complexity of its structure. However, this may be a co-evolving process, so it is hard to tell whether the internationalization influences the governance structure or the governance structure influences the internationalization. For example, Sanders and Carpenters (1998) found that a firm's degree of internationalization is positively related to CEO's long-term compensation. Others may argue that the CEO's long-term compensation influences the degree of internationalization. Such examples make this stream an interesting area for further research. One suggestion would be to survey top management teams and investigate whether internationalization influences corporate governance or vice versa.

Finally, researchers have used the social network perspective to investigate *knowledge flow within the multinational firm* in determining how expatriates facilitate knowledge transfer. However, we know little about how other corporate governance mechanisms may influence knowledge flows. For example, family firms are more likely to have family members in top management and as heads of regional offices, which may facilitate knowledge flow between headquarters and subsidiaries. Thus, research that investigates how knowledge flows within a family-owned multinational firm could make a valuable contribution in this area.

The Internationalization Process

Internationalization strategy has been perhaps the most researched area in the subject of corporate governance in multinational firms (see Hitt et al., 2006, for a review). Researchers have investigated how top management teams, compensation, ownership, and boards of directors influence internationalization strategy. While extensive research has been conducted in this area, we suggest that scholars apply more recent theories. For example, multiple agency theory (Arthurs et al., 2008) has gained increasing attention in recent years. Scholars may investigate the influence of multiple owners and managers and their unique interactions in internationalization strategy.

Although the field of international business has well-researched *mode of entry*, it is only recently that researchers started to investigate the corporate governance influence. One promising area would be to determine how different ownership types influence mode of entry decisions. For example, do public pension fund owners prefer joint ventures over greenfield investments? Do compositions of top management teams and boards of directors influence the choices? This little studied area offers many valuable research opportunities.

Finally, investigating *managerial perception of the internationalization process* is another promising area for future research. As Lawrence (1997) suggested, however, scholars should look inside managerial processes rather than at demographic proxies, perhaps through surveys and psychometric measures. Scholars might also seize this excellent opportunity to incorporate a meso paradigm into their research. They may investigate internationalization processes through firm and individual manager analysis levels.

Other Opportunities

Although we have reviewed literature on the governance of multinational firms and the internationalization process, we have not discussed the heterogeneity of multinational firms and their institutional contexts. Because multinational firms are different, do their corporate governance structures differ as well? Furthermore, if their corporate governance differs, will their internationalization processes differ? In addition, most research has been conducted on multinational firms from advanced countries, so we know too little about firms from developing countries. Different institutional contexts mean that multinational firms from developing countries are likely to have different corporate governance than firms from advanced countries. For example, researchers have recently started to investigate foreign investors in emerging markets (Gorg et al., 2010; Kim et al., 2010). What is the role of governance in this context? Will different types of owners, such as pension funds and mutual funds, influence investment decisions differently? In addition, research in social networks may stress interconnectedness. For example, do core and peripheral firms differ in terms of their corporate governance structure and propensity toward internationalization?

Conclusion and Future Directions

Research on corporate governance can provide unique insights into the operation and strategies of multinational firms. As we illustrate in this chapter, studying the governance of multinational firms can advance the fields of both corporate governance and international business.

Integrating corporate governance and international business research is challenging, however, considering the limitations of theoretical frameworks and conflicting research results in a single-country setting (Daily et al., 2003; Strange et al., 2009). Multinational firms span boundaries over several countries, so researchers must consider additional variations in informal and formal institutions. Some of these complex issues can be addressed by validating and expanding existing theories and by carefully considering contextual heterogeneity and organizational complexity. Researchers can also use international governance research to develop new theories. Existing theories may be unable to explain the phenomenon of corporate governance in multinational firms, so this opens a wealth of opportunity for scholars to build new conceptualizations and theoretical models (Kostova and Roth, 2003).

In short, scholars can still explore further a wide range of topics. Although studying corporate governance in multinational firms is challenging, this exciting area offers ample research opportunities.

References

Adler, N. J., and Bartholomew, S. (1992). "Managing Globally Competent People," *Executive*, 6(3): 52–65.

Aguilera, R. V., and Jackson, G. (2010). "Comparative and International Corporate Governance," *Academy of Management Annals*, 4: 485–556.

Aharoni, Y. (1966). "The Foreign Investment Decision Process," *International Executive*, 8(4): 13–14.

—— Tihanyi, L., and Connelly, B. L. (2011). "Managerial Decision-Making in International Business: A Forty-Five-Year Retrospective," *Journal of World Business*, 46(2): 135–42.

Andersson, U., Forsgren, M., and Holm, U. (2007). "Balancing Subsidiary Influence in the Federative MNC: A Business Network View," *Journal of International Business Studies*, 38(5): 802–18.

Arthurs, J. D., Hoskisson, R. E., Busenitz, L. W., and Johnson, R. A. (2008). "Managerial Agents Watching Other Agents: Multiple Agency Conflicts regarding Underpricing in IPO Firms," *Academy of Management Journal*, 51(2): 277–94.

Bartlett, C. A., and Ghoshal, S. (1989). *Managing across Borders: The Transnational Solution*. Boston: Harvard Business School Press.

Benito, G. R. G., Lunnan, R., and Tomassen, S. (2011). "Distant Encounters of the Third Kind: Multinational Companies Locating Divisional Headquarters Abroad," *Journal of Management Studies*, 48(2): 373–94.

Bhaumik, S. K., Driffield, N., and Pal, S. (2009). "Does Ownership Structure of Emerging-Market Firms Affect their Outward FDI: The Case of the Indian Automotive and Pharmaceutical Sectors," *Journal of International Business Studies*, 41(3): 437–50.

Birkinshaw, J. M., and Morrison, A. J. (1995). "Configurations of Strategy and Structure in Subsidiaries of Multinational Corporations," *Journal of International Business Studies*, 26(4): 729–53.

Bower, J. L. (1970). *Managing the Resource Allocation Process: A Study of Corporate Planning and Investment*. Boston, MA: Harvard University Press.

BOYACIGILLER, N. (1990). "The Role of Expatriates in the Management of Interdependence, Complexity and Risk in Multinational Corporations," *Journal of International Business Studies*, 21(3): 357–81.

BUCKLEY, P. J., and CASSON, M. (1976). *The Future of the Multinational Enterprise*. London: Macmillan.

—— and STRANGE, R. (2011). "The Governance of the Multinational Enterprise: Insights from Internalization Theory," *Journal of Management Studies*, 48(2): 460–70.

BURNS, N., KEDIA, S., and LIPSON, M. (2010). "Institutional Ownership and Monitoring: Evidence from Financial Misreporting," *Journal of Corporate Finance*, 16(4): 443–55.

CARPENTER, M. A., and SANDERS, W. G. (2004). "The Effects of Top Management Team Pay and Firm Internationalization on MNC Performance," *Journal of Management*, 30(4): 509–28.

—— —— and GREGERSEN, H. B. (2001). "Bundling Human Capital with Organizational Context: The Impact of International Assignment Experience on Multinational Firm Performance and CEO Pay," *Academy of Management Journal*, 44(3): 493–511.

CONNELLY, B. L., JOHNSON, J. L., TIHANYI, L., and ELLSTRAND, A. E. (2011). "More than Adopters: Competing Influences in the Interlocking Directorate," *Organization Science*, 22(3): 688–703.

DAILY, C. M., DALTON, D. R., and RAJAGOPALAN, N. (2003). "Governance through Ownership: Centuries of Practice, Decades of Research," *The Academy of Management Journal*, 46(2): 151–8.

DALTON, D. R., HITT, M. A., CERTO, S. T., and DALTON, C. M. (2007). "The Fundamental Agency Problem and its Mitigation: Independence, Equity, and the Market for Corporate Control," *Academy of Management Annals*, 1: 1–64.

DAVID, P., HITT, M. A., and GIMENO, J. (2001). "The Influence of Activism by Institutional Investors on R&D," *Academy of Management Journal*, 44(1): 144–57.

—— O'BRIEN, J. P., YOSHIKAWA, T., and DELIOS, A. (2010). "Do Shareholders or Stakeholders Appropriate the Rents from Corporate Diversification? The Influence of Ownership Structure," *Academy of Management Journal*, 53(3): 636–54.

DOUMA, S., GEORGE, R., and KABIR, R. (2006). "Foreign and Domestic Ownership, Business Groups, and Firm Performance: Evidence from a Large Emerging Market," *Strategic Management Journal*, 27(7): 637–57.

DOZ, Y. L., and PRAHALAD, C. K. (1991). "Managing DMNCs: A Search for a New Paradigm," *Strategic Management Journal*, 12(S1): 145–64.

DRIFFIELD, N., LOVE, J. H., and MENGHINELLO, S. (2010). "The Multinational Enterprise as a Source of International Knowledge Flows: Direct Evidence from Italy," *Journal of International Business Studies*, 41(2): 350–59.

DUNNING, J. H., and LUNDAN, S. M. (2008). *Multinational Enterprises and the Global Economy*. Northampton, MA: Edward Elgar.

EDSTRÖM, A. and GALBRAITH, J. R. (1977). "Transfer of Managers as a Coordination and Control Strategy in Multinational Organizations," *Administrative Science Quarterly*, 22(2): 248–63.

FANG, Y., JIANG, G. F., MAKINO, S., and BEAMISH, P. W. (2010). "Multinational Firm Knowledge, Use of Expatriates, and Foreign Subsidiary Performance," *Journal of Management Studies*, 47(1): 27–54.

FESTING, M., EIDEMS, J., and ROYER, S. (2007). "Strategic Issues and Local Constraints in Transnational Compensation Strategies: An Analysis of Cultural, Institutional and Political Influences," *European Management Journal*, 25(2): 118–31.

FEY, C. F. and FURU, P. (2008). "Top Management Incentive Compensation and Knowledge Sharing in Multinational Corporations," *Strategic Management Journal*, 29(12): 1301–23.

FILATOTCHEV, I., and WRIGHT, M. (2011). "Agency Perspectives on Corporate Governance of Multinational Enterprises," *Journal of Management Studies*, 48(2): 471–86.

—— DYOMINA, N., WRIGHT, M., and BUCK, T. (2001). "Effects of Post-privatization Governance and Strategies on Export Intensity in the Former Soviet Union," *Journal of International Business Studies*, 32(4): 853–71.

—— STRANGE, R., PIESSE, J., and YUNG-CHIH LIEN. (2007). "FDI by Firms from Newly Industrialized Economies In Emerging Markets: Corporate Governance, Entry Mode and Location," *Journal of International Business Studies*, 38(4): 556–72.

GEORGE, G., WIKLUND, J., and ZAHRA, S. A. (2005). "Ownership and the Internationalization of Small Firms," *Journal of Management*, 31(2): 210–33.

GHOSHAL, S., and BARTLETT, C. A. (1990). "The Multinational Corporation as an Interorganizational Network," *Academy of Management Review*, 15(4): 603–25.

—— and NOHRIA, N. (1989). "Internal Differentiation within Multinational Corporations," *Strategic Management Journal*, 10(4): 323–37.

GORG, H., MUHLEN, H., and NUNNENKAMP, P. (2010). "FDI Liberalization, Firm Heterogeneity and Foreign Ownership: German Firm Decisions in Reforming India." *Journal of Development Studies*, 46(8): 1367–84.

GUPTA, A. K., and GOVINDARAJAN, V. (1991). "Knowledge Flows and the Structure of Control within Multinational Corporations," *Academy of Management Review*, 16(4): 768–92.

HEDLUND, G., and ROLANDER, D. (eds.). (1990). "Action in Heterarchies: New Approaches to Managing the MNC," in C. A. Bartlett, Y. L. Doz, and G. Hedlund (eds). *Managing the Global Firm*. London and New York: Routledge.

HENNART, J. (1989). "Can The 'New Forms of Investment' Substitute for the 'Old Forms?' A Transaction Costs Perspective," *Journal of International Business Studies*, 20(2): 211–34.

—— and LARIMO, J. (1998). "The Impact of Culture on the Strategy of Multinational Enterprises: Does National Origin Affect Ownership Decisions?" *Journal of International Business Studies*, 29(3): 515–38.

HEWETT, K., ROTH, M. S., and ROTH, K. (2003). "Conditions Influencing Headquarters and Foreign Subsidiary Roles in Marketing Activities and their Effects on Performance," *Journal of International Business Studies*, 34(6): 567–85.

HITT, M. A., TIHANYI, L., MILLER, T., and CONNELLY, B. (2006). "International Diversification: Antecedents, Outcomes, and Moderators," *Journal of Management*, 32(6): 831–67.

JOHANSON, J., and VAHLNE, J. (1977). "The Internationalization Process of the Firm: A Model of Knowledge Development and Increasing Foreign Market Commitments," *Journal of International Business Studies*, 8(1): 25–34.

KANG, J. K., and KIM, J. M. (2010). "Do Foreign Investors Exhibit a Corporate Governance Disadvantage: An Information Asymmetry Perspective," *Journal of International Business Studies*, 41(8): 1415–38.

KIM, B., PRESCOTT, J. E., and KIM, S. M. (2005). "Differentiated Governance of Foreign Subsidiaries in Transnational Corporations: An Agency Theory Perspective," *Journal of International Management*, 11(1): 43–66.

KIM, I. J., EPPLER-KIM, J., KIM, W. S., and BYUN, S. J. (2010). "Foreign Investors and Corporate Governance in Korea," *Pacific-Basin Finance Journal*, 18(4): 390–402.

KOGUT, B., and SINGH, H. (1988). "The Effect of National Culture on the Choice of Entry Mode," *Journal of International Business Studies*, 19(3): 411–32.

—— and Zander, U. (1993). "Knowledge of the Firm and the Evolutionary Theory of the Multinational Corporation," *Journal of International Business Studies*, 24(4): 625–45.

Kostova, T., and Roth, K. (2003). "Social Capital in Multinational Corporations and a Micro-Macro Model of its Formation," *Academy of Management Review*, 28(2): 297–317.

Lawrence, B. S. (1997). "The Black Box of Organizational Demography," *Organization Science*, 8(1): 1–22.

Lien, Y., Piesse, J., Strange, R., and Filatotchev, I. (2005). "The Role of Corporate Governance in FDI Decisions: Evidence from Taiwan," *International Business Review*, 14(6): 739–63.

Lu, J., Xu, B., and Liu, X. (2009). "The Effects of Corporate Governance and Institutional Environments on Export Behavior in Emerging Economies," *Management International Review*, 49(4): 455–78.

March, J. G., and Simon, H. A. (1958). *Organizations*. New York: Wiley.

Melin, L. (1992). "Internationalization as a Strategy Process," *Strategic Management Journal*, 13: 99–118.

Mellahi, K. and Collings, D. G. (2010). "The Barriers to Effective Global Talent Management: The Example of Corporate Élites in Mnes," *Journal of World Business*, 45(2): 143–9.

Nielsen, S., and Nielsen, B. B. (2010). "Why Do Firms Employ Foreigners on their Top Management Team? An Exploration of Strategic Fit, Human Capital and Attraction-Selection-Attrition Perspectives," *International Journal of Cross Cultural Management*, 10: 195.

O'Donnell, S. (1999). "Compensation Design as a Tool for Implementing Foreign Subsidiary Strategy," *Management International Review*, 39(2): 149–65.

Pfeffer, J., and Salancik, G. R. (1978). *The External Control of Organizations: A Resource Dependence Perspective*. New York: Harper & Row.

Prahalad, C. K., and Doz, Y. L. (1987). *The Multinational Mission*. New York: Free Press.

Rhoades, D. L., and Rechner, P. L. (2001). "The Role of Ownership and Corporate Governance Factors in International Entry Mode Selection," *International Journal of Organizational Analysis*, 9(4): 309.

Roth, K. (1995). "Managing International Interdependence: CEO Characteristics in Resource-Based Framework," *Academy of Management Journal*, 38(1): 200–31.

—— and Nigh, D. (1992). "The Effectiveness of Headquarters-Subsidiary Relationships: The Role of Coordination, Control, and Conflict," *Journal of Business Research*, 25(4): 277–301.

—— and O'Donnell, S. (1996). "Foreign Subsidiary Compensation Strategy: An Agency Theory Perspective," *Academy of Management Journal*, 39(3): 678–703.

Sanders, W. M. G. and Carpenter, M. A. (1998). "Internationalization and Firm Governance: The Roles of CEO Compensation, Top Team Composition, and Board Structure," *Academy of Management Journal*, 41(2): 158–78.

Simon, H. A. (1947). *Administrative Behavior: A Story of Decision Processes in Business Organization*. London: Macmillan.

Staples, C. L. (2007). "Board Globalization in the World's Largest TNCs 1993–2005," *Corporate Governance: An International Review*, 15(2): 311–21.

Stopford, J. M., and Wells, L. T. (1972). *Managing the Multinational Enterprise; Organization of the Firm and Ownership of the Subsidiaries*. New York: Basic Books.

Strange, R., and Jackson, G. L. (2008). *Corporate Governance and International Business: Strategy, Performance and Institutional Change*. Basingstoke: Palgrave Macmillan.

STRANGE, R., FILATOTCHEV, I., BUCK, T., and WRIGHT, M. (2009). "Corporate Governance and International Business," *Management International Review*, 49(4): 395–407.

SUBRAMANIAM, M., and WATSON, S. (2006). "How Interdependence Affects Subsidiary Performance," *Journal of Business Research*, 59(8): 916–24.

TAN, D., and MAHONEY, J. T. (2006). "Why A Multinational Firm Chooses Expatriates: Integrating Resource-Based, Agency and Transaction Costs Perspectives," *Journal of Management Studies*, 43(3): 457–84.

TEECE, D. J. (1981). "The Market for Know-How and the Efficient International Transfer of Technology," *The Annals of the American Academy of Political and Social Science*, 458: 81–96.

TIHANYI, L., ELLSTRAND, A. E., DAILY, C. M., and DALTON, D. R. (2000). "Composition of the Top Management Team and Firm International Diversification," *Journal of Management*, 26(6): 1157.

—— JOHNSON, R. A., HOSKISSON, R. E., and HITT, M. A. (2003). "Institutional Ownership Differences and International Diversification: The Effects of Boards of Directors and Technological Opportunity," *Academy of Management Journal*, 46(2): 195–211.

—— HOSKISSON, R. E., JOHNSON, R. A., and WAN, W. P. (2009). "Technological Competence and International Diversification," *Management International Review*, 49(4): 409–31.

UNCTAD (2009). *World Investment Report*. New York and Geneva: United Nations.

VERNON, R. (1966). "International Investment and International Trade in the Product Cycle," *Quarterly Journal of Economics*, 80(2): 190–207.

VORA, D., KOSTOVA, T., and ROTH, K. (2007). "Roles of Subsidiary Managers in Multinational Corporations: The Effect of Dual Organizational Identification," *Management International Review*, 47(4): 595–620.

WANG, S., TONG, T. W., CHEN, G., and KIM, H. (2009). "Expatriate Utilization and Foreign Direct Investment Performance: The Mediating Role of Knowledge Transfer," *Journal of Management*, 35(5): 1181–206.

ZANDER, U., and KOGUT, B. (1995). "Knowledge and the Speed of the Transfer and Imitation of Organizational Capabilities: An Empirical Test," *Organization Science*, 6(1): 76–92.

CHAPTER 21

CORPORATE GOVERNANCE IN BUSINESS GROUPS

DAPHNE W. YIU, XING CHEN, AND YUEHUA XU

INTRODUCTION

BUSINESS group, defined as a collection of legally independent firms that are linked by multiple ties, including ownership, economic means (such as interfirm transactions), and/or social relations (family, kinship, friendship) through which they coordinate to achieve mutual objectives (Khanna and Rivkin, 2001; Yiu et al., 2007), is a prevalent organizational form and accounts for significant economic contributions in many countries. Business groups carry different labels in different countries, such as *qiye jituan* in China (Keister, 2000), *business houses* in India (Encarnation, 1989), *chaebol* in South Korea (Chang and Choi, 1988), *keiretsu* in Japan (Gerlach, 1992), *grupos economicos* in Latin America (Strachan, 1976), *oligarchs* in Russia (Perotti and Gelfer, 2001), *guanxi qiye* in Taiwan (Numazaki, 1996), and *family holdings* in Turkey (Granovetter, 1994).

To a very large extent, business groups in many countries, especially in the less developed countries, have emerged and are sustainable in order to fill an institutional void and to mitigate governance failures (Khanna and Palepu, 1997, 2000). Research has suggested that the internalization and recurrence of market transactions within the business group facilitate the richness, tacitness, and reliability of information flows, as well as resource and risk sharing, among group affiliates (Chang and Hong, 2000; Guillen, 2000). Also, business groups are superior to the external labor market and market for corporate control in dealing with problems of managerial labor, as the internal labor market has better information about managers' performance and reduces managers' employment risks (Collin, 1998). In addition, the multiple long-term relational ties among group affiliates effectively develop norms and trusts, which allow reliance on informal contract enforcement (Weidenbaum and Hughes, 1996; Granovetter, 2005). Combining these views, the formation of business groups can be seen as fraught with agency costs arising from deficiencies in legal and labor market institutions (Morck et al., 2005).

Despite these governance benefits, business groups also suffer from governance problems that are more complex than for individual firms. Business groups have been criticized as instruments for the concentrated or dominant owner to appropriate private benefits through tunneling (a tactic used by the core owner to transfer assets or profits from peripheral affiliates to the core firms in which they hold ownership shares) and pyramiding (an ownership structure in which the dominant owner controls voting rights with limited capital investments through a set of cascading parent–affiliate ownership relationships) (Claessens et al., 2000; Friedman et al., 2003). Therefore, from the perspective of some group affiliates, their interests are being appropriated. In addition, it is argued that group affiliates are being "taxed" for securing survivals of other affiliates, because it is common for the resourceful and profitable group affiliates to prop up the underperforming ones within the group (Morck and Nakamura, 1999; Ferris et al., 2003).

In this chapter, we will examine in greater details the prevailing governance mechanisms adopted in business groups. Given that group affiliates are connected in both vertical and horizontal ways, we propose that vertical governance mechanisms, including concentrated ownership, pyramidal ownership, and strategic control, are adopted by the core owner to govern its group affiliates; while horizontal governance mechanisms, including cross-shareholdings, interlocking directorates, and relational governance, are in place for group affiliates to mutually monitor each other. Besides, we will also discuss the salient governance issues faced by business groups. Three governance problems commonly found in business groups are highlighted, namely tunneling, cross-subsidization, and mutual entrenchment. However, business groups are not homogeneous. Studies suggest and find variations among different ownership types of business groups. Hence, we will examine variations of governance structures across business groups by differentiating different ownership types of business groups, including family-controlled, state-owned, and widely held business groups. This chapter will end by discussions and implications for future research on the topic of corporate governance in business groups.

DISTINCTIVE GOVERNANCE MECHANISMS IN BUSINESS GROUPS

The aim of corporate governance is to devise a set of governance mechanisms to ensure that managers do not make improper decisions which will harm their firms (Denis and McConnell, 2003). Conventional corporate governance mechanisms that have been studied include ownership concentration, board of directors, and managerial compensation (Jensen and Meckling, 1976; Shleifer and Vishny, 1986; Dalton et al., 1999). In the context of business groups, due to the various ties between the group parent and group affiliates, as well as among group affiliates, governance issues are more complex than those in other organizational forms.

According to Yiu et al. (2007), a business group can be viewed as "a loosely coupled system" (Weick, 1976; Orton and Weick, 1990) in which group affiliates are connected through vertical and horizontal linkages. Vertical linkages refer to the source of coupling or order primarily through ownership control of resources in a business group, while horizontal linkages refer to the horizontal connectedness among distinctive and differentiated group-affiliated firms. Vertical linkages in a business group can be regarded as a tool for the core owner elite to exert its control and governance over other group affiliates, while horizontal linkages are regarded as the horizontal connections between sister group affiliates that serve to facilitate coordination and resource sharing among group affiliates (Maman, 1999). With regard to business group corporate governance, based on the vertical and horizontal linkages that characterize business groups, we categorize the governance mechanisms in business groups into vertical and horizontal dimensions. Vertical governance mechanisms refer to the governance mechanisms imposed by the core owner elite on its group affiliates along the hierarchy, while horizontal governance mechanisms refer to the governance mechanisms adopted among the group affiliates to govern each other and guard against opportunistic behaviors within a business group. We will examine the distinctive vertical and horizontal governance mechanisms of business groups in more detail below.

Vertical Governance Mechanisms

It is common to find one entity that dominates or controls the majority of shares in business groups. Yiu and her colleagues (2007) used the term "core owner elite" to refer to an individual, or an entity, or a collection of individuals/organizations, which, having the same interest, controls the dominant share of a business group's parent company and/or core companies. Through such vertical control, the core owner elite can effectively prevent opportunistic behaviors of the group affiliates. We will examine below three vertical governance mechanisms through which the core owner elite exerts control over its group affiliates. These include concentrated ownership, pyramidal ownership, and strategic control.

Concentrated Ownership

Concentrated ownership refers to an ownership structure in which the majority of a firm's ownership is dominated or controlled by one or a few shareholders. Concentrated ownership is regarded as an internal corporate governance mechanism for attenuating agency problems, for it is based on the assumption that dominant shareholders have both the incentive and the ability to effectively monitor managers (Davis, 1991; Gedajlovic and Shapiro, 1998).

A business group is characterized by relatively concentrated ownership structure in which the core owner elite holds dominant ownership not only of the group parent but also of some of its group affiliates. A main reason for the adoption of a concentrated ownership structure in business groups and, in particular, in emerging economies, is that concentrated ownership can substitute for external formal institutions in protecting the property rights of investors. In economies where legal protections of investors are quite weak, individual shareholders have to rely heavily on themselves to enforce property rights. In a concentrated ownership structure, dominant shareholders with high cash-flow rights have the incentive to monitor managers and protect property rights (Claessens and Fan, 2002). In addition, with control rights concentrated in a small number of shareholders, it is easier to achieve concerted actions than when control rights are dispersed (Shleifer and Vishny, 1997), thereby ensuring the enforcement of property rights. Such an internal governance mechanism is especially important for business groups in emerging economies such as China. For example, on average about 55 percent of shares of a listed firm in China are concentrated in the hands of the three largest shareholders of the firm, and 67 percent of these listed firms are group affiliates (Ma et al., 2006). In Korea, the average ownership controlled by dominant shareholders is 29.2 percent for firms affiliated to chaebols (Joh, 2003).

Pyramidal Ownership

The second vertical governance mechanism in business groups is pyramidal ownership structure in which the group parent exercises control over an affiliate through a hierarchical ownership chain of other affiliates (La Porta et al., 1999). For example, a group parent controls 50 percent of Affiliate A, which in turn owns 50 percent of Affiliate B's ownership, and this chain enables the parent firm to control 25 percent of Affiliate B's ownership.

Pyramidal ownership structure is often used in business groups for three governance purposes. First, with such an ownership structure, group parents can control group affiliates and leverage a large amount of assets with only a small share of direct investment (Lu and Yao, 2006). As shown in the last example, the group parent can achieve control of Affiliate B with only 25 percent of its ultimate cash-flow stake. Second, pyramidal ownership can be used by group parents to share the risks of group affiliates with other shareholders. For example, family-owned business groups usually use pyramid structure to acquire or establish new firms so as to spread risk without diluting family control (Almeida and Wolfenzon, 2006). Consequently, in family-owned business groups, the deviation between control rights and cash-flow rights is relatively larger than in other types of business groups (Claessens et al., 2000). Such a phenomenon is quite common in developing countries (Faccio et al., 2001). For example, it is observed that in Indonesia, Japan, and Singapore in excess of two-thirds of firms are controlled by a single shareholder (Claessens et al., 2000), and in Brazil more than half of the firms with families as ultimate owners are placed under pyramidal ownership structures (Rabelo and Coutinho, 2001). Third, some group parents also use pyramidal ownership structure to improve the efficiency of group affiliates. For example, this structure enables state-owned business groups to decentralize the decision rights of group affiliates to other shareholders, while keeping state cash-flow rights (Fan et al., 2005). Besides being kept at arm's length from the group parents, group affiliates at the bottom of the pyramidal structure can have more discretion in their decision-making, which could help improve the efficiency of their decisions (Lu and Yao, 2006). As described by Fan et al. (2005), since the early 1990s, the Chinese government has set up some large business groups to manage state-owned enterprises, in the hope of improving the efficiency of these enterprises by relieving them of administrative functions and, therefore, about 75 percent of state-owned listed firms in China are controlled through more than two pyramidal layers.

Strategic Control

The third vertical governance mechanism business groups use to control their affiliates is strategic control. Strategic control is a governance mechanism used in the multidivisional firm that entails the use of long-term and strategically relevant criteria for the evaluation of business-level managers' actions and performance (Hoskisson and Hitt, 1988). Strategic control is characterized by the open relationship between group-level managers and affiliate-level managers, and the willingness of management to employ subjective information to evaluate the performance of affiliate-level managers (Gupta, 1987). Thus, strategic control emphasizes whether the business units act according to the overall strategic mission of the whole firm. In this way, it acts as a governance mechanism to reorient business units toward the long-term strategic objective of the firm.

Strategic control is of critical importance in a business group for at least two reasons. First, given the diversity of group affiliates in terms of ownership background and industry characteristics, strategic control plays an important role in aligning affiliates' incentives with the overall group's interests, which, in turn, facilitates the sharing of knowledge and resources among group affiliates, such as in the case of Korean business groups (Chang and Hong, 2000). Besides, business groups need to balance the potential conflicts between the responsiveness of group affiliates and central coordination for the benefits of the whole group. Under the strategic control system, group affiliates are evaluated based on the strategic desirability of their decisions before implementation as well as on the financial performance of the affiliates after the implementation of the decisions (Baysinger and Hoskisson, 1990). Such a system provides the economic basis for the willingness of group affiliates to sacrifice their own interests for the overall group interest. Second, the use of strategic control helps reorient group affiliates toward long-term benefits by risk sharing. Through the implementation of strategic control, group affiliates can be protected from short-term failure, as their performance will be evaluated on a longer-term basis since it takes time for strategic benefits to be realized (Hoskisson and Hitt, 1988). Thus, strategic control provides incentives for group affiliates to undertake more risky strategies such as market innovation, because the risk is shared within the group. In the case of Chinese business groups, it has been proposed that an emphasis on strategic controls is associated with higher levels of affiliate firm market innovation (White et al., 2008). Viewed in this way, strategic control can mitigate against group affiliates maximizing short-term individual firm benefits at the expense of long-term overall group benefits. It is through strategic control that business groups such as Korea's Daewoo Group and Samsung Group can mobilize funds and management talent from from group affiliates to pursue long-term strategic goals, such as starting new business ventures or investing heavily in in-house training programs which can benefit all the group affiliates (Khanna and Palepu, 1999).

Horizontal Governance Mechanisms

Business groups are characterized by strong connectedness among their group affiliates. Although group affiliates are legally independent entities, they are interdependent in resource sharing and exchange (Yiu et al., 2007). Due to the resource-interdependence relationships, group affiliates have strong incentives to monitor and control each other in order to curb the opportunistic behaviors of others. Distinctive horizontal governance mechanisms for group affiliates to cross-monitor and cross-control include cross-shareholding, interlocking directorates, and relational governance.

Cross-shareholding

Cross-shareholding is an ownership structure in which an individual firm holds ownership shares in one or more of its shareholders or in the firms that control any of its shareholders (La Porta et al., 1999). There are two types of cross-shareholding: direct cross-shareholding in which two firms directly hold each other's shares, and indirect cross-shareholding in which one firm controls the shares of another through a complex, pyramidal, or circular chain (Joh, 2003). While direct cross-shareholding may be quite common in business groups in many markets (e.g. Taiwan), group affiliates usually use indirect cross-shareholding structures, since direct cross-shareholding is illegal in some countries such as Korea (Joh, 2003).

Cross-shareholding is much more common among firms from the same business group than among those that are not from the same business group (Brookfield, 2010). There are several governance benefits resulting from cross-shareholding in a business group. First, cross-shareholding creates mutual commitment and interdependence among group affiliates by engaging them in the exchange of equity stakes and the reciprocity of voting rights (Berglöf and Perotti, 1994). In this way, group parents can employ the shareholdings of other firms for concerted voting (Aoki et al., 1994), and form a coalition to exercise control over group affiliates' decision-making (Berglöf and Perotti, 1994), which helps reduce environmental uncertainties such as hostile takeovers (Isobe et al., 2006). Second, the coalition formed also enables group affiliates to collectively monitor managers, thus ensuring that managers of group affiliates act to the benefit of the group overall (Kim et al., 2004). Third, cross-shareholding not only facilitates the exchange of resources and information among group affiliates, but also creates incentives for them to cross-monitor the free-riding behaviors of each other (Cheng and Kreinin, 1996; Lincoln, Gerlach and Ahmadjian, 1996; Chang, 2003). As such, opportunistic behavior by group affiliates can be mitigated. For example, Berglöf and Perotti (1994) found that the most distinctive characteristic of Japanese financial keiretsu is widespread cross-shareholdings among group affiliates, and this plays an important role in group affiliates' mutual monitoring and collective enforcement.

Interlocking Directorates

Interlocking directorate is a type of non-ownership control mechanism which occurs when a person affiliated to one firm serves on the board of directors of another (Mizruchi, 1996). Interlocking directorates serve to promote information diffusion (Davis and Powell, 1992), facilitate collusion between firms, increase firm legitimacy and reputation, and even advance directors' personal careers (Mizruchi, 1996).

Business groups are typically characterized by the extensive existence of interlocking directorates (Maman, 1999; Khanna and Rivkin, 2006), especially in club-form business groups such as Japanese bank-centered keiretsu. Interlocking directorates act as an effective governance mechanism in business groups, because interlocking directors can obtain insider information in other affiliated firms. Such information conduits facilitate coordination and information sharing among boards, thus enhancing mutual monitoring among group affiliates and mitigating potential opportunistic problems and expropriation for fear of retaliation (Mizruchi, 1996; Keister, 2000). For example, as described by Collin (1998), in either of the two famous business groups in Sweden, i.e. the Wallenberg group, and the Handelsbank group, interlocking directorates form a closely knit network, which links all the firms involved together; however, there are very few overlapping interlocking directors across these two business groups. Similar results can be found in business groups in economies like Israel, Hong Kong, and Taiwan (Maman, 1999; Wong, 1996; Brookfield, 2010).

Relational Governance

Relational governance refers to the governance of interfirm exchange which involves a high level of relationship-specific assets and interfirm trust (Zaheer and Venkatraman, 1995). In contrast to governance by formal contracts, relational governance, which enforces obligations, promises, and expectations through social norms and agreed processes (Poppo and Zenger, 2002), may minimize transaction costs and mitigate opportunistic behaviors (Dyer, 1996; Dyer and Singh, 1998).

Business groups are known for their group solidarity, which characterizes the long-term and stable relationships among group affiliates (Granovetter, 1994). To a very large extent, group solidarity is cultivated due to the close relationship between the formation of business groups and the traditions, social practices, and national cultural heritage of a society (Orrù et al., 1991; Whitley, 1991; Hamilton and Feenstra, 1995; Collin, 1998; Chung, 2001; Luo and Chung, 2005;). In addition to formal ties, group affiliates are bound by informal, social ties that are referred to as the mechanism which enables two or more entities within the same social system to work with each other, and social norms are the infrastructure of social ties governance (Yiu, et al., 2007). Social ties between two group affiliates can result from family ties or other particularistic ties existing between managers of the two firms (Luo and Chung, 2005). Such social ties of group affiliates provide the basis for the development of relational governance, which serves to govern the behaviors of group affiliates in three ways. First, group affiliates are tied together by the expectations of continuity and longevity that accompany relational governance (Poppo and Zenger, 2002). Such expectations facilitate the long-term orientation of group affiliates in their exchanges and mitigate their opportunistic behaviors. Second, due to the long-term, exclusive, and reciprocal nature of social relationships among group affiliates, information asymmetry can be minimized as group affiliates become more willing to disclose proprietary information to each other. In this way, business groups can benefit from increased monitoring efficiency, as in the case of the bank-centered keiretsu in Japan (Wan et al., 2008). Third, social ties help the formation of trust among group affiliates, which serve as the basis for better coordination, improved communication, and cooperation (Silva et al., 2006). For example, it is found that in Chinese business groups firms are more likely to choose exchange partners inside the business groups which they have formal or informal ties with in order to reduce uncertainty (Keister, 2001).

In conclusion, the distinctive vertical and horizontal governance mechanisms in business groups discussed above can help enhance group solidarity and sustainability by promoting information sharing, mutual trust, and interfirm cooperation among group affiliates.

Corporate Governance Problems in Business Groups

Despite the fact that the various vertical and horizontal governance mechanisms are effective in mitigating the opportunistic behaviors of group affiliates and attenuating principal–agent conflict in business groups, corporate governance problems arise in business groups in the form of principal–principal conflicts that refer to the expropriation of other shareholders' interests by the dominant shareholder (Young et al., 2008). In the context of business groups, principal–principal conflicts are typically reflected in tunneling by the controlling shareholders, a decrease in firm performance of group affiliates due to cross-subsidization, and increased opportunities for mutual entrenchment (Claessens et al., 2002; Chang, 2003; Morck and Yeung, 2003; Lu and Yao, 2006).

Tunneling

Tunneling refers to controlling shareholders' transferring profits and assets out of firms for their own benefits (Johnson et al., 2000). There are two forms of tunneling: a controlling shareholder could transfer resources from firms where it has few cash-flow rights to firms where it has more cash flow rights through self-dealing transactions (Johnson et al., 2000; Bertrand et al., 2002); or the controlling shareholder can increase its shareholdings in firms that are more profitable and promising, through means such as dilutive share issues or creeping acquisitions (Johnson et al., 2000).

Tunneling in business groups can be intensified by the distinctive ownership structures, including concentrated ownership, pyramidal ownership, and cross-shareholding mentioned above (Lu and Yao, 2006). Concentrated ownership is usually coupled with management control, which is quite common in business groups in some developed markets such as Hong Kong, as well as in most emerging markets (La Porta et al., 1999; Carney and Gedajlovic, 2002). With the coupling of ownership and control, group parents in the business groups can use insider information to decide whether and when to increase shareholdings of group affiliates, and transfer profits of some affiliates to others (Chang, 2003). Compared to the case of concentrated ownership, group parents have stronger incentives to expropriate minority shareholders in the structures of pyramid ownership and cross-shareholding, because of the discrepancy between cash-flow rights and control rights in these situations. Besides, tunneling is more prevalent in business groups that are located in countries where the legal protection for minority shareholders is quite weak (La Porta et al., 1998, 2000; Coffee, 2001). Therefore, it is easy to find tunneling in business groups in emerging economies such as India, Korea, and China (Chang, 2003; Bertrand et al., 2002; Fisman and Wang, 2010).

Tunneling in a business group represents serious agency problems and frictions between the controlling owner and minority shareholders (Baek et al., 2006), which in turn affect the solidarity and effective functioning of the business group. Besides, illicit expropriation may reduce the transparency of the whole group, clouding group values and complicating any inference about the health of the group (Bertrand et al., 2002).

Cross-Subsidization

Cross-subsidization occurs "when a multi-product firm prices one good below average cost and makes up for the losses through revenues collected from the sales of other goods that are priced above the average cost" (Viscusi et al., 1992: 313). To put it simply, it refers to the practice of charging very low prices for products of firm A from firm B during their transactions in order to subsidize firm B, and usually these two firms have close relationships, such as belonging to the same business group. Such pricing behaviors may be in conflict with the principle of profit maximization for individual affiliate firms but can maximize the overall benefits of the whole group (Posner, 1971).

As business groups usually aim to maximize the wealth of the whole groups, they may use their internal financial transactions to subsidize underperforming group affiliates or those that are of great strategic importance, such as some new ventures (Chang and Hong, 2000). For example, Lincoln and his colleagues (1996) find that the Japanese keiretsu enhance their overall group viability by asking the profitable affiliates to help the other financially troubled ones. In addition to the form of unilateral wealth transfer, cross-subsidization in business group can take other forms such as loan provisions, debt guarantees, equity investment, and internal business trade (Chang and Hong, 2000).

Although cross-subsidization may benefit those group affiliates that receive subsidies through internal business transactions, it does bring an extra financial burden to the source affiliates. As Lincoln and his colleagues (1996) argue, firms subsidizing their business partners may eventually pay for themselves after the successful turnaround of the latter in the long run. However, in the short run, the burden could be severe and may lead to poor performance. Ultimately, cross-subsidization reduces the incentives for the group affiliates to perform well in the long run.

Mutual Entrenchment

Entrenchment is defined as the extent to which managers are not subject to discipline from the full range of corporate governance mechanisms such as board monitoring or threat of takeover (Berger, Ofek, and Yermack, 1997). Commonly used entrenchment tactics include manager-specific investment, poison pills, staggered board terms, and greenmail (Shleifer and Vishny, 1989).

In business groups, mutual entrenchment occurs when managers from group affiliates form a coalition to collectively pursue their own interests (e.g. making themselves difficult to be replaced) at the costs of shareholders' interests (Berglöf and Perotti, 1994). While group horizontal mechanisms such as cross-shareholding, interlocking directorates, and relational governance may facilitate interdependence and cross-monitoring among group affiliates, they also create chances for the mutual entrenchment of group affiliates. Through mutual entrenchment, these managers enjoy more autonomy in decision-making and have more opportunities to work for their own benefit. For example, Kim et al. (2004) find that keiretsu members who are more powerful are less subject to mutual monitoring. They then tend to pursue more diversifying growth that may hurt the overall keiretsu performance and the interests of their stakeholders.

In addition, entrenchment problems are more common in family-owned business groups as a result of the divergence between control rights and cash-flow rights arising from the structures of pyramidal ownership and cross-shareholding (Morck and Yeung, 2003). Such entrenchment could deprive the rights of minority shareholders and undermine the value of the whole business group (Claessen and Fan, 2002).

Governance Variations across Different Business Groups

In this section, we will examine variations in governance structures and issues across different ownership types of business groups. We propose that the effectiveness of vertical and horizontal governance mechanisms in business groups is contingent on the ownership type of business groups (see Figure 21.1). This is consistent with Rediker and Seth's (1995) argument that the effectiveness of a particular governance mechanism is contingent upon other governance mechanisms that simultaneously operate in a firm. Various founding owners of business groups, who may be families, financial institutions, or governments, have different ways of exerting monitoring and control in business groups (Hoskisson et al., 2005). Business groups founded by different owners can be associated with different governance mechanisms and performance. Cuervo-Cazurra (2006) differentiates business groups into three ownership types: family-owned, state-owned, and widely held business groups. Widely held business groups refer to those business groups which do not have an ultimate individual or entity that owns the business groups. In widely held business groups, such as bank-centered business groups in Japan, Spain, and Germany, there is no ultimate controlling shareholder to control member firms. Although the core firm or main bank might have concentrated ownership over member firms, the core entity is widely held. In the following, we will follow this categorization and examine the governance performance of distinct vertical and horizontal governance mechanisms in these three types of business groups.

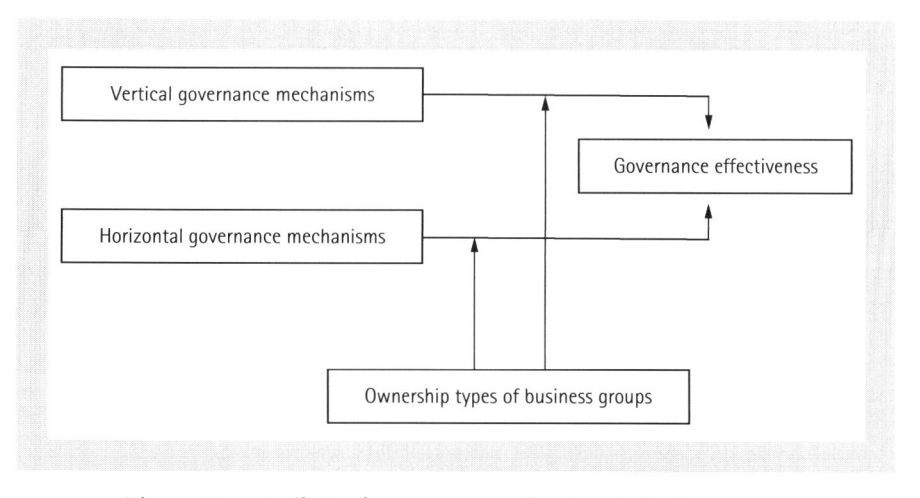

FIGURE 21.1. The contingent effects of governance mechanisms in business groups

Vertical Governance Mechanisms

Family-Controlled Business Groups

Family controlled business groups, characterized by complex pyramidal ownership structure, are particularly prevalent in Korea and Chile (Granovetter, 1995). With pyramidal ownership structures, families can employ limited investment to control large amounts of assets to maximize their own wealth. Almeida and Wolfenzon (2006) argue that a family tends to use existing firms to set up or acquire a new firm so as to share the risk with other existing shareholders. The less secured the strategic benefits, the more likely the new firm will be put under existing firms to form a pyramidal ownership structure.

With a longitudinal sample of chaebol-listed firms, evidence shows that family chaebols use well-established firms to acquire firms with low pledgeable income, while they choose to directly acquire firms with high pledgeable incomes (Almeida et al., 2011). However, such family-controlled pyramids may lead to worse agency problems as compared with independent firms (Joh, 2003; Morck et al., 2005). Compared with independent family-owned firms, family-controlled business groups are subject to more severe agency problems, because the vertical governance mechanisms increase the controlling shareholders' incentives to maximize their own interests through inappropriate resource allocation among member firms, which will harm the interests of external shareholders.

Kim et al. (2005) found that expropriation mainly occurs in firms with high internal ownerships. Korean chaebol and Chinese family business are associated with personal ownership (Whitley, 1991) and manager-owner alignment. Risk is concentrated in the hands of owner-managers, while the risk is borne by diverse shareholders with dispersed shareholding (Carney and Gedajlovic, 2002), so owner-managers tend to spread their concentrated risk by transferring resources out of the focal company. The capacity of insiders to misuse their rights depends on the concentration of economic rights. Much evidence shows that pyramidal ownership has a negative impact on firm performance only when managers have a high level of control rights (Lemmon and Lins, 2003). Baek et al. (2004) demonstrated that chaebol firms with concentrated ownership by controlling family shareholders experience greater drops in stock price during financial crisis. Therefore, concentrated ownership turns out to facilitate expropriation through pyramidal ownership in family-controlled business groups.

Strategic control is strong in family-controlled chaebol firms, since managers in affiliates are either family members or under strict control by the controlling shareholder. Strategic and financial decisions are made at group level rather than by board meetings of individual firms (Shin and Park, 1999). Such centralized control facilitates maximization by controlling shareholders of their own benefits at the expense of the interests of the affiliates' external shareholders. Therefore, given the dominance of the family owner, strategic control may become another mechanism by which the core family owner can expropriate the interests of its group affiliates.

State-Owned Business Groups

State-owned business groups often have pyramidal ownership structures to facilitate control and monitoring over member firms. A government usually has a large number of enterprises within its jurisdiction but lacks the incentives and capabilities to manage or monitor all state-owned enterprises. Thus, government ownership is associated with low monitoring intensity (Hoskisson et al., 2005).

State-owned business groups are prevalent in China. The Chinese government started to encourage formation of business group in the 1980s to facilitate economic development during industrial reform (Keister, 1998). Before the enterprise reforms in the 1980s, Chinese state-owned enterprises (SOEs) were subject to central planning. Managers of SOEs were under the complete control of the government, receiving quotas of raw materials, labor, and capital and handing over profits and losses to the state (Lin and Tan, 1999). Since enterprise reform has taken place, principal–agent conflict has been severe because the state delegated contractual and managerial rights to SOE managers (Peng, 2001). Peng argues that the 1980s reform increased the profit-maximization motives of SOEs and also triggered serious principal–agent problems such as state asset stripping and insider control. Since state-owned assets and equity stakes are prohibited from being freely traded, governments can only transfer their decision rights over a firm to a third party by creating pyramidal ownership layers to maintain the state assets (Fan et al., 2005). Although the Communist Party has the right to dismiss and appoint managers, they cannot completely eradicate managerial opportunistic behaviors (Seo et al., 2010).

In contrast to standalone SOEs that are directly owned and monitored by governments, state-owned business group affiliates are indirectly owned and monitored by their parent company. Such intermediate companies have stronger incentives and capabilities to monitor their affiliates than do governments. It is consistent with Ma et al.'s (2006) finding that state-owned group affiliates perform better than non-affiliated SOEs.

Widely Held Business Groups

In Japanese keiretsu, the main bank cannot hold more than a 5 percent shareholding of a member and each individual firm can only hold a small share of another member firm, but the financial institutions can actually have considerable shareholdings in member firms in the form of indirect stockholdings (Berglöf and Perotti, 1994). As an important shareholder and debtholder, the main bank has the incentives and capability to monitor member firms by tracing the financial status of each member firm. When a member firm has poor performance and is unable to meet its debt payments, the managers of the firm would lose managerial control. Evidence shows that bank ownership is positively related to firm performance at high ownership levels (Morck et al., 2000).

The concentrated ownership in widely held business groups also leads to strong strategic control. In a vertical keiretsu such as the Toyota business group, a manufacturing firm at the top monitors subcontractors and distributors at lower levels of the hierarchy (Lai, 1999). The lower-level member firms must comply with the overall strategic plan so that the whole system can operate efficiently and the core firm has an incentive to ensure that each member firm implements the plans and strategies expected of them. Gilson and Roe (1993) argue that vertical keiretsu business groups have slightly better performance than horizontal business groups, probably because of their strong top-down monitoring and control.

In conclusion, vertical governance mechanisms, reflecting the core entity's control over other group affiliates, are often associated with the inequality of power relationships in a business group. Asymmetries of power and dependence result in the uneven distribution of economic benefits and risks (Lai, 1999). When family control already aligns the interests of managers and those of the controlling shareholders, vertical governance mechanisms become a tool for the controlling shareholder to expropriate minority shareholders. However, with the presence of principal–agent conflicts between the controlling shareholder and managers in other types of business groups such as state-owned and widely held business groups, vertical governance mechanisms can effectively mitigate agency problems to some extent. However, vertical governance mechanisms may even intensify the conflicts between the controlling shareholders and external investors in family-controlled business groups.

Proposition 1: Vertical governance mechanisms of business groups are more effective in state-owned and widely held business groups than in family-controlled business groups.

Horizontal Governance Mechanisms

Family-Controlled Business Groups

Horizontal governance mechanisms in family-controlled business groups barely function effectively because the family member managers or directors cannot exert independent monitoring over one another. Baek and colleagues (2004) argue that cross-shareholding in the same chaebol prevents shareholders of affiliates from monitoring the respective managers effectively, because the controlling shareholders tend to make use of the cross-shareholding to secure control in order to maximize their own interests. Interlocking directors can hardly function effectively either, since family members are appointed on boards of affiliates to ensure family control. Besides, it is a kind of expropriation to appoint family members as top managers and to the board of directors, regardless of their capabilities and resources compared to outside professional managers (Faccio et al., 2001).

Relational governance may not provide advantages to family-controlled affiliates and state-owned group affiliates. Family ties among member firms allow the founding family to abuse their control rights, resulting in inefficient resource reallocation.

Internal transactions and exchanges become channels for families to transfer profits from one affiliate to another to maximize their own interests (Chang, 2003). In addition, the effectiveness of the horizontal governance mechanism is contingent on the coalition among managers and the board of directors in member firms. A horizontal governance structure can prevent opportunistic behavior among independent member firms that intend to maximize their own interests opportunistically. Such mechanisms hardly enhance governance performance of firms in family-owned business groups because all the affiliates act in the best interests of the ultimate shareholders.

State-Owned Business Groups

In state-owned business groups which are characterized mainly by vertical linkages (Yiu et al., 2007), horizontal governance mechanisms play a less important role than vertical governance mechanisms. Keister (2009) argues that interlocking directorates in Chinese state-owned business groups function mainly as a source of information exchange rather than monitoring. Lack of monitoring probably results from coalitions among government officers. A large amount of interlocking and cross-shareholdings within state-owned business groups allows many government officers sitting on boards of affiliates to reward themselves with high compensation (Su et al., 2008). Moreover, with a high level of interdependence, the managers of the member firms may form a coalition not only to entrench state-owned assets but also to expropriate external investors. Social ties among government officers in state-owned enterprises may intensify conflicts between controlling shareholders and external investors (Su et al., 2008). In state-owned business groups, extensive horizontal linkages can enhance the control of government officers who may neither maximize the benefit to external shareholders nor protect state-owned assets.

Widely Held Business Groups

The Japanese financial keiretsu is a typical widely held business group where member firms collaborate with each other as equals, based on mutual respect (Lincoln et al., 1996). Instead of shareholders, managers of banks or other firms exert monitoring over a member firm (Lincoln and Shimotani, 2010). Therefore, traditional principal–agent conflict resulting from the separation of management and control is the major concern. Cross-shareholdings facilitate productive exchange and reduce opportunism as long as partners do not expect anyone to systematically gain advantages over time (Gilson and Roe, 1993). Berglöf and Perotti (1994) propose the "collective enforcement mechanism" as a representation of the keiretsu's governance model. Mutual monitoring among managers of member firms reduces information asymmetry and creates reciprocal voting rights. Professional managers have the capabilities to differentiate managerial losses from market declines with their specific industry knowledge. Any manager acting opportunistically will be fired or demoted. Keiretsu is recognized as a substitute for external monitors to effectively control agency problems (Ferris et al., 1995).

In Japanese keiretsu, member firms collaborate based on mutual respect for each other's autonomy and mutual trust (Gilson and Roe, 1993). Social ties in a keiretsu network provide the infrastructure for keiretsu intervention in affiliates' affairs (Lincoln et al., 1996). Social ties among member firms can function as an effective relational governance tool to prevent managers' opportunistic behaviors. Nonetheless, Morck and Nakamura (1999) argue that keiretsu may become management entrenchment devices, for extensive cross-shareholdings prevent external investors from disciplining managers through takeovers. In this case, horizontal governance mechanisms result in collusive arrangements, such as extensive cross-subsidization and collective anti-takeover activities.

To conclude, horizontal governance mechanisms in business groups can deal with the agency problem more effectively among member firms without a common ultimate controller. Otherwise, the horizontal governance mechanism would be utilized by the controlling shareholder to maximize its own interests.

Proposition 2: Horizontal governance mechanisms are more effective in widely held business groups than in state-owned or family-controlled business groups.

Table 21.1 provides a summary of the variations of governance structures and effectiveness across family-controlled, state-owned, and widely held business groups.

Discussion and Conclusions

Business groups, as an organizational innovation, emerge and exist to realize the economies resulting from the inner workings of internal capital markets. However, from the governance perspective, it is the functioning of such internal capital markets that creates governance problems and increases agency costs. In widely held firms, the agency concern is that professional managers may fail in their fiduciary duty to act in the interests of the shareholders. In business groups, an additional agency concern is that the controlling firm in the group exploits the internal capital market for private gain at the expense of the interests of other group affiliates. Thus, although it is the intricacies among group affiliates that have contributed to the success and sustainability of business groups in many countries, such intricacies ironically have also led to a greater lack of transparency and monitoring, thus leading to higher agency costs and more complex corporate governance problems as compared with independent, standalone firms (Khanna and Palepu, 1998).

According to the propositions we have proposed, neither vertical nor horizontal governance mechanisms in business groups benefit family-controlled group affiliates. Since family control is already a strong governance mechanism to align the interests of managers and controlling shareholders, business group governance mechanisms can hardly

Table 21.1. Governance structures and governance outcomes of different types of business groups

Types of business groups	Salient governance structure	Benefits of the governance structure	Costs of the governance structure
Family-owned	*Vertical mechanism:* Concentrated ownership Pyramid ownership Strategic control *Horizontal mechanism:* Family ties	Eradicate traditional agency problems by guaranteeing controlling shareholders' control over target firms	Intensify principal–principal conflict by allowing owner elites to maximize their own interest at the cost of minority shareholders' interests through expropriation, tunneling, entrenchment, and so on
State-owned	*Vertical mechanism:* Concentrated ownership Pyramid ownership	Mitigate traditional agency problems by introducing intermediate monitors which are more effective than governments	Provide controlling shareholders with incentives and chances to expropriate external investors
Widely held	*Horizontal mechanism:* Main bank ties, cross-shareholdings	Mitigate traditional agency problems through mutual monitoring among managers of member firms and main bank monitoring	Give rise to management entrenchment to avoid external monitoring

make any further contribution to solve this agency issue. Instead, they become tools utilized by controlling families to maximize their own interests. Evidence shows that a large amount of family ownership and family relationships among top managers can make a firm less attractive to foreign investors (Luo and Chung, 2005; Luo et al., 2009). Such severe principal–principal agency problems result from lack of external monitoring. We suggest that effective external monitors should be introduced into family-owned business groups, such as outside board members, a significant level of foreign ownership, or ownership by institutions which have the incentives and capability to monitor the operation of family businesses. With a data set of 228 listed firms in Taiwan, Filatotchev and colleagues (2005) find that board independence from the founding family has a positive impact on firm performance.

Some researchers have even attributed the poor corporate governance systems in emerging markets to the agency problems found in business groups. In the case of Korean and Indian business groups, one finding is that the potential benefits of overcoming market imperfections decrease while the costs of agency problems increase in business groups as the economy continues to develop (Baek et al., 2004; Joh, 2003; Khanna and Palepu, 1998). In particular, empirical findings have consistently revealed that independent firms outperformed group-affiliated firms in normal times and they also suffer less loss than group-affiliated firm in crisis times. At the same time, the performance implications of group affiliates are highly heterogeneous (Carney et al., 2011). In addition, it is suspinfected that the weak corporate governance system in business groups is a major cause of the economic crises in emerging markets, as the weak group governance system allows poorly managed and underperforming affiliates to stay in the market while assets and non-performing loans continue to accumulate and weaken the financial sector of the country (Joh, 2003). Therefore, synthesizing the business group literature seems to suggest that the agency costs of business groups may outweigh the benefits of group affiliation.

In this chapter, we have highlighted various governance problems or issues that occur in business groups. However, we have yet to discover which agency problems are worse and which agency issues are more significant. Although business groups may be instruments by which the controlling core firm can expropriate the interests of other group affiliates, business groups on the whole remain stable and some underperforming group affiliates are able to survive even in economic downturns (Collin, 1998). Thus, future research could explore the potential tradeoffs among firm-level, group-level, and even societal-level governance.

Second, it seems that most of the governance problems originate from the ownership structure of business groups. Future research may explore the question of whether ownership restructuring can be a solution to mitigating agency problems arising from control–ownership disparity in business groups. For example, Chung and Luo (2008) found that the involvement of foreign firms can accelerate the divestitures of unrelated businesses in Taiwanese business groups. This, to a large extent, implies that getting foreign investment may bring with it a distinctive home-country corporate governance model in business groups.

Third, there are more and more studies calling for differentiating business groups across countries. Similarly, our chapter also proposes that governance structures and outcomes may vary across different ownership types of business groups. Future studies may take the insights of this chapter to further explore differences in governance mechanisms in different business groups. For example, governance mechanisms in family business groups are closely related to family norms, inheritance practices, and coordination among inner-circle executives (Chung and Luo, 2008). One way to blunt managerial incentives in family business groups is to internalize the costs of creative destruction (Morck and Yeung, 2003).

Whether business groups are paragons or parasites may be largely contingent on whether business groups are governed properly. However, business groups are highly variegated organizational forms and deeply embedded in societies. As such, theories from multiple sources and nuanced methodologies are necessary to unpack the complexity of corporate governance in business groups.

References

Almeida, H., and Wolfenzon, D. (2006). "A Theory of Pyramidal Ownership and Family Business Groups," *Journal of Finance*, 61(6): 2637–80.

—— Park, S. Y., Subrahmanyam, M. G., and Wolfenzon, D. (2011). "The Structure and Formation of Business Groups: Evidence from Korean Chaebols," *Journal of Financial Economics*, 99(2): 447–75.

Aoki, M., Patrick, H., and Sheard, P. (1994). "The Japanese Main Bank System: An Introductory Overview," in M. Aoki and H. Patrick (eds.), *The Japanese Main Bank System*. New York: Oxford University Press, 1–50.

Baek, J.-S., Kang, J.-K., and Park, K. S. (2004). "Corporate Governance and Firm Value: Evidence from the Korean Financial Crisis," *Journal of Financial Economics*, 71(2): 265.

—— —— and Lee, I. (2006). "Business Groups and Tunneling: Evidence from Private Securities offerings by Korean Chaebols," *Journal of Finance*, 61(5): 2415–49.

Baysinger, B., and Hoskisson, R. E. (1990). "The Composition of Boards of Directors and Strategic Control: Effects on Corporate Strategy," *Academy of Management Review*, 15(1): 72–87.

Berger, P. G., Ofek, E., and Yermack, D. L. (1997). "Managerial Entrenchment and Capital Structure Decisions," *The Journal of Finance*, (4): 1411–38.

Berglöf, E., and Perotti, E. (1994). "The Governance Structure of the Japanese Financial Keiretsu," *Journal of Financial Economics*, 36(2): 259–84.

Bertrand, M., Mehta, P., and Mullainathan, S. (2002). "Ferreting Out Tunneling: An Application to Indian Business Groups," *Quarterly Journal of Economics*, 117(1): 28.

Brookfield, J. (2010). "The Network Structure of Big Business in Taiwan," *Asia Pacific Journal of Management*, 27(2): 257–79.

Carney, M., and Gedajlovic, E. R. (2002). "The Coupling of Ownership and Control and the Allocation of Financial Resources: Evidence from Hong Kong," *Journal of Management Studies*, 39(1): 123–46.

—— —— Heugens, P. P. M. A. R., Essen, M. V., and Oosterhout, J. V. (2011). "Business Group Affiliation, Performance, Context, and Strategy: A Meta-Analysis," *Academy of Management Journal*, 54(3): 437–60.

Chang, S. J. (2003). "Ownership Structure, Expropriation, and Performance of Group-Affiliated Companies in Korea," *The Academy of Management Journal*, 46(2): 238–53.

—— and Choi, U. (1988). "Strategy, Structure and Performance of Korean Business Groups," *Journal of Industrial Economics*, 37: 141–58.

—— and Hong, J. (2000). "Economic Performance of the Group-Affiliated Companies in Korea: Resource Sharing and Internal Business Transactions," *Academy of Management Journal*, 43, 429–48.

Cheng, L. K., and Kreinin, M. E. (1996). "Supplier Preferences and Dumping: An Analysis of Japanese Corporate Groups," *Southern Economic Journal*, 63: 51–60.

Chung, C. N. (2001). "Markets, Culture and Institutions: The Emergence of Large Business Groups in Taiwan: 1950s–1970s," *Journal of Management Studies*, 38: 719–45.

—— and Luo, X. (2008). "Human Agents, Contexts, and Institutional Change: The Decline of Family in the Leadership of Business Groups," *Organization Science*, 19(1): 124–42.

Claessens, S., and Fan, J. P. H. (2002). "Corporate Governance in Asia: A Survey," *International Review of Finance*, 3(2): 71–103.

—— Djankov, S., Fan, J. P. H., and Lang, L. H. P. (2002). "Disentangling the Incentive and Entrenchment Effects of Large Shareholdings," *The Journal of Finance*, 57(6): 2741–71.

—— —— and Lang, L. H. P. (2000). "The Separation of Ownership and Control in East Asian Corporations," *Journal of Financial Economics*, 58: 81–112.

Coffee, J. (2001). "The Rise of Dispersed Ownership: Identifying the Precondition to the Separation of Ownership and Control," *Yale Law Journal*, 111: 1–82.

Collin, S.-O. (1998). "Why are these Islands of Conscious Power Found in the Ocean of Ownership? Institutional and Governance Hypotheses Explaining the Existence of Business Groups in Sweden," *Journal of Management Studies*, 35(6): 719–46.

Cuervo-Cazurra, A. (2006). "Business Groups and their Types," *Asia Pacific Journal of Management*, 23(4): 419–37.

Dalton, D., Daily, C., Johnson, J., and Ellstrand, A. (1999). "Number of Directors and Financial Performance: A Meta-Analysis," *Academy of Management Journal*, 42: 674–86.

Davis, G. F. (1991). "Agents without Principles? The Spread of the Poison Pill through the Intercorporate Network," *Administrative Science Quarterly*, 36(4): 583–613.

—— and Powell, W. W. (1992). "Organization-Environment Relations," in M. Dunnette (ed.), *Handbook of Industrial and Organizational Psychology*, 2nd edition. Palo Alto, CA: Consulting Psychologists Press, 315–75.

Denis, D. K., and McConnell, J. J. (2003). "International Corporate Governance," *Journal of Financial and Quantitative Analysis*, 38(1): 1–36.

Dyer, J. (1996). "Does Governance Matter? Keiretsu Alliances and Asset Specificity as Sources of Japanese Competitive Advantage," *Organization Science*, 7: 649–66.

—— and Singh, H. (1998). "The Relational View: Cooperative Strategy and Sources of Interorganizational Competitive Advantage," *Academy of Management Review*, 23: 660–79.

Encarnation, D. (1989). *Dislodging Multinationals: India's Comparative Perspective*. Ithaca, NY: Cornell University Press.

Faccio, M., Lang, L., and Young, L. (2001). "Dividends and Expropriation," *American Economic Review*, 91: 54–78.

Fan, J., Wong, T., and Zhang, T. (2005). "The Emergence of Corporate Pyramids in China," CEI Working Paper Series, 2006.

FERRIS, S. P., KUMAR, R., and SARIN, A. (1995). "The Role of Corporate Groupings in Controlling Agency Conflicts: The Case of Keiretsu," *Pacific-Basin Finance Journal*, 3(2–3): 319–35.

——— KIM, K. A., and KITSABUNNARAT, P. (2003). "The Costs (and Benefits?) of Diversified Business Groups: The Case of Korean Chaebols," *Journal of Banking & Finance*, 27: 251–73.

FILATOTCHEV, I., LIEN, Y.-C., and PIESSE, J. (2005). "Corporate Governance and Performance in Publicly Listed, Family-Controlled Firms: Evidence from Taiwan," *Asia Pacific Journal of Management*, 22(3): 257–83.

FISMAN, R., and WANG, Y. (2010). "Trading Favors within Chinese Business Groups," *American Economic Review: Papers and Proceedings*, 100: 429–33.

FRIEDMAN, E., JOHNSON, S., and MITTON, T. (2003). "Tunneling and Propping," *Journal of Comparative Economics*, 31(4): 732–50.

GEDAJLOVIC, E. R., and SHAPIRO, D. M. (1998). "Management and Ownership Effects: Evidence from Five Countries," *Strategic Management Journal*, 19(6): 533–53.

GERLACH, M. (1992). *Alliance Capitalism: The Social Organization of Japanese Business*. Los Angeles: University of California Press.

GILSON, R. J., and ROE, M. J. (1993). "Understanding the Japanese *Keiretsu*: Overlaps between Corporate Governance and Industrial Organization," *The Yale Law Journal*, 102(4): 871–906.

GRANOVETTER, M. (1994). "Business Groups," in N. J. Smelser and R. Swedberg (eds.), *Handbook of Economic Sociology*. Princeton, NJ: Princeton University Press.

——— (1995). "Cease Revisited: Business Groups in the Modern Economy," *Industrial and Corporate Change*, 4(1): 93–130.

——— (2005). "The Impact of Social Structure on Economic Outcomes," *Journal of Economic Perspectives*, 19: 33–50.

GUILLEN, M. F. (2000). "Business Groups in Emerging Economies: A Resource-Based View," *The Academy of Management Journal*, 43(3): 362–80.

GUPTA, A. K. (1987). "SBU Strategies, Corporate-SBU Relations, and SBU Ffectiveness in Strategy Implementation," *Academy of Management Journal*, 30(3): 477–500.

HAMILTON, G. G., and FEENSTRA, R. C. (1995). "Varieties of Hierarchies and Markets: An Introduction," *Industrial and Corporate Change*, 4: 51–91.

HOSKISSON, R. E., and HITT, M. A. (1988). "Strategic Control Systems and Relative R&D Investment in Large Multiproduct Firms," *Strategic Management Journal*, 9: 605–21.

——— JOHNSON, R. A., TIHANYI, L., and WHITE, R. E. (2005). "Diversified Business Groups and Corporate Refocusing in Emerging Economies," *Journal of Management*, 31(6): 941–65.

ISOBE, T., MAKINO, S., and GOERZEN, A. (2006). "Japanese Horizontal Keiretsu and the Performance Implications of Membership," *Asia Pacific Journal of Management*, 23(4): 453–66.

JENSEN, M., and MECKLING, W. (1976). "The Theory of the Firm: Managerial Behavior, Agency Costs, and Ownership Structure," *Journal of Financial Economics*, 3: 305–60.

JOH, S. W. (2003). "Corporate Governance and Firm Profitability: Evidence from Korea before the Economic Crisis," *Journal of Financial Economics*, 68(2): 287.

JOHNSON, S., LA PORTA, R., LOPEZ-DE-SILANES, F., and SHLEIFER, A. (2000). "Tunneling," *American Economic Review*, 90: 22–27.

KEISTER, L. A. (1998). "Engineering Growth: Business Group Structure and Firm Performance in China's Transition Economy," *American Journal of Sociology*, 104: 404–40.

KEISTER, L. A. (2000). *Chinese Business Groups: The Structure and Impact of Interfirm Relations during Economic Development.* New York: Oxford University Press.
—— (2001). "Exchange Structures in Transition: Lending and Trade Relations in Chinese Business Groups," *American Sociological Review,* 66(3): 336–60.
—— (2009). "Interfirm Relations in China: Group Structure and Firm Performance in Business Groups," *American Behavioral Scientist,* 52(12): 1709–30.
KHANNA, T. (2000). "Is Group Affiliation Profitable in Emerging Markets? An Analysis of Diversified Indian Business Groups," *Journal of Finance,* 55: 867–92.
—— (2006). "Interorganizational Ties and Business Group Boundaries: Evidence from an Emerging Economy," *Organization Science,* 17(3): 333–52.
—— and PALEPU, K. (1997). "Why Focused Strategies may be Wrong for Emerging Markets," *Harvard Business Review,* 75: 41–51.
—— —— (1998). "Corporate Scope and Institutional Context: An Empirical Analysis of Diversified Indian Business Groups," Working Paper, Harvard Business School, Boston.
—— —— (1999). "The Right Way to Restructure Conglomerates in Emerging Markets," *Harvard Business Review,* 77(4): 125–34.
—— and RIVKIN, J. W. (2001). "Estimating the Performance Effects of Business Groups in Emerging Markets," *Strategic Management Journal,* 22: 45–74.
KIM, H., HOSKISSON, R. E., and WAN, W. P. (2004). "Power Dependence, Diversification Strategy, and Performance in Keiretsu Member Firms," *Strategic Management Journal,* 25(7): 613–36.
—— JUNG, K., and KIM, I. J. (2005). "Internal Funds Allocation and the Ownership Structure: Evidence from Korean Business Groups," *Review of Quantitative Finance and Accounting,* 25(1): 33.
LA PORTA, R., LOPEZ-DE-SILANES, F., SHLEIFER, A., and VISHNY, R. (1998). "Law and Finance," *Journal of Political Economy,* 106: 1113–55.
—— —— —— (1999). "Corporate Ownership around the World," *Journal of Finance,* 65: 471–517.
—— —— —— VISHNY, R. (2000). "Investor Protection and Corporate Governance," *Journal of Financial Economics,* 58: 3–27.
LAI, G. M.-H. (1999). "Knowing Who You are Doing Business with in Japan: A Managerial View of Keiretsu and Keiretsu Business Groups," *Journal of World Business,* 34(4): 423–48.
LEMMON, M. L., and LINS, K. V. (2003). "Ownership Structure, Corporate Governance, and Firm Value: Evidence from the East Asian Financial Crisis," *The Journal of Finance,* 58(4): 1445–68.
LIN, J. Y., and TAN, G. (1999). "Policy Burdens, Accountability, and the Soft Budget Constraint," *The American Economic Review,* 89(2): 426–31.
LINCOLN, J. R., and SHIMOTANI, M. (2010). "Business Networks in Postwar Japan: Whether the Keiretsu. Corporate Governance of Business Groups," in A. M. Colpan, T. Hikino, and J. R. Lincoln (eds.), *The Oxford Handbook of Business Groups.* New York: Oxford University Express.
—— GERLACH, M., and AHMADJIAN, C. (1996). "Keiretsu Network and Corporate Performance in Japan," *American Journal of Sociology,* 61: 67–88.
LU, Y., and YAO. J. (2006). "Impact of State Ownership and Control Mechanisms on the Performance of Group Affiliated Companies in China," *Asia Pacific Journal of Management,* 23(4): 485–503.
LUO, X., and CHUNG, C. N. (2005). "Keeping it all in the Family: The Role of Particularistic Ties in Business Group Performance during Institutional Transition," *Administrative Science Quarterly,* 50: 404–39.

—— —— and SOBCZAK, M. (2009). "How Do Corporate Governance Model Differences Affect Foreign Direct Investment in Emerging Economies?" *Journal of International Business Studies*, 40(3): 444–67.

MA, X., YAO, X., and XI, Y. (2006). "Business Group Affiliation and Firm Performance in a Transition Economy: A Focus on Ownership Voids," *Asia Pacific Journal of Management*, 23(4): 467–83.

MAMAN, D. (1999). "Research Note: Interlocking Ties within Business Groups in Israel—A Longitudinal Analysis, 1974–1987," *Organization Studies*, 20(2): 323–39.

MIZRUCHI, M. S. (1996). "What Do Interlocks Do? An Analysis, Critique and Assessment of Research on Interlocking Directories," *Annual Review of Sociology*, 22: 271–99.

MORCK, R., and NAKAMURA, M. (1999). "Banks and Corporate Control in Japan," *The Journal of Finance*, 54(1): 319–39.

—— and YEUNG, B. (2003). "Agency Problems in Large Family Business Groups," *Entrepreneurship: Theory and Practice*, 27(4): 367–82.

—— NAKAMURA, I., and SHIVDASANI, A. (2000). "Bank, Ownership Structure and Firm Value in Japan," *Journal of Business*, 73(4): 539–67.

—— WOLFENZON, D., and YEUNG, B. (2005). "Corporate Governance, Economic Entrenchment, and Growth," *Journal of Economic Literature*, 43: 657–722.

NUMAZAKI (1986). "Networks of Taiwanese Big Business: A Preliminary Analysis," *Modern China*, 12(4): 487–534.

ORRÙ, M., BIGGARD, N. W., and HAMILTON, G. G. (1991). "Organizational Isomorphism in East Asia," in W. W. Powell and P. J. Dimaggio (eds.), *The New Institutionalism in Organizational Analysis*. Chicago, IL: University of Chicago Press.

ORTON, D. J., and WEICK, K. E. (1990). "Loosely Coupled Systems: A Reconceptualization," *Academy of Management Review*, 15: 203–23.

PENG, Y. (2001). "Chinese Villages and Townships as Industrial Corporations: Ownership, Governance, and Market Discipline," *The American Journal of Sociology*, 106(5): 1338–70.

PEROTTI, E., and GELFER, S. (2001). "Red Barons or Robber Barrons? Governance and Investment in Russian Financial-Industrial Groups," *European Management Journal*, 49: 1601–18.

POPPO, L., and ZENGER, T. (2002). "Do Formal Contracts and Relational Governance Function as Substitutes or Complements," *Strategic Management Journal*, 23: 707–25.

POSNER, R. (1971). "Taxation by Regulation," *Bell Journal of Economics*, 2: 22–50.

RABELO, F. M., and VASCONCELOS, F. C. (2002). "Corporate Governance in Brazil," *Journal of Business Ethics*, 37(3): 321–35.

REDIKER, K. J., and SETH, A. (1995). "Boards of Directors and Substitution Effects of Alternative Governance Mechanisms," *Strategic Management Journal*, 16(2): 85–99.

SEO, B.-K., LEE, K., and WANG, X. (2010). "Causes for Changing Performance of the Business Groups in a Transition Economy: Market-Level versus Firm-Level Factors in China," *Industrial and Corporate Change*, 19(6): 2041–72.

SHIN, H.-H., and PARK, Y. S. (1999). "Financing Constraints and Internal Capital Markets: Evidence from Korean Chaebols," *Journal of Corporate Finance*, 5(2): 169–91.

SHLEIFER, A., and VISHNY, R. (1986). "Large Shareholders and Corporate Control," *Journal of Political Economy*, 94(3): 461–88.

—— —— (1989). "Management Entrenchment: The Case of Manager-Specific Investments," *Journal of Financial Economics*, 25(1): 123–40.

—— —— (1997). "A Survey of Corporate Governance," *Journal of Finance*, 52(2): 737–83.

Silva, F., Majluf, N., and Paredes, R. D. (2006). "Family Ties, Interlocking Directors and Performance of Business Groups in Emerging Countries: The Case of Chile," *Journal of Business Research*, 59: 315–32.

Strachan, H. (1976). *Family and Other Business Groups in Economic Development*. New York: Praeger.

Su, Y., Xu, D., and Phan, P. H. (2008). "Principal–Principal Conflict in the Governance of the Chinese Public Corporation," *Management and Organization Review*, 4(1): 17–38.

Viscusi, W., Vernon, J., and Harrington, J. (1992). *Economics of Regulation and Anti-Trust*. Lexington, MA: Heath.

Wan, W. P., Yiu, D. W., Hoskisson, R. E., and Kim, H. (2008). "The Performance Implications of Relationship Banking during Macroeconomic Expansion and Contraction: A Study of Japanese Banks' Social Relationships and Overseas Expansion," *Journal of International Business Studies*, 39: 406–27.

Weick, K. E. (1976). "Educational Organizations as Loosely Coupled Systems," *Administrative Science Quarterly*, 21: 1–19.

Weidenbaum, M., and Hughes, S. (1996). *The Bamboo Network: How Expatriate Chinese Entrepreneurs are Creating a New Superpower in Asia*. New York: Free Press.

White, R. E., Hoskisson, R. E., Yiu, D. W., and Bruton, G. D. (2008). "Employment and Market Innovation in Chinese Business Group Affiliated Firms: The Role of Group Control Systems," *Management and Organization Review*, 4(2): 225–56.

Whitley, R. D. (1991). "The Social Construction of Business Systems in East Asia," *Organization Studies*, 12: 1–28.

Wong, G. (1996). "Business Groups in a Dynamic Environment: Hong Kong 1976–1986," in G. G. Hamilton (ed.), *Asian Business Networks*. Berlin: Walter De Gruyter, 87–113.

Yiu, D. W., Lu, Y., Bruton, G. D., and Hoskisson, R. E. (2007). "Business Groups: An Integrated Model to Focus Future Research," *Journal of Management Studies*, 44(8): 1551–79.

Young, M., Peng, M. W., Ahlstrom, D., Bruton, G. D., and Jiang, Y. (2008). "Corporate Governance in Emerging Economies: A Review of the Principal-Principal Perspective," *The Journal of Management Studies*, 45(1): 196.

Zaheer, A., and Venkatraman, N. (1995). "Relational Governance as an Interorganizational Strategy: An Empirical Test of the Role of Trust in Economic Exchange," *Strategic Management Journal*, 16(5): 373–92.

CHAPTER 22

GOVERNANCE IN FINANCIAL DISTRESS AND BANKRUPTCY

KENNETH M. AYOTTE, EDITH S. HOTCHKISS, AND KARIN S. THORBURN

INTRODUCTION

GOVERNANCE of a financially distressed firm is a complicated interplay of formal and informal control rights exercised by the firm's many stakeholders—its shareholders, managers, employees, and creditors, among others—subject to oversight and limits imposed by the law and courts. The relative influence of these groups shifts over time as a firm heads toward default. This leads to some striking stylized facts about distressed firms in the US:

- Management and board turnover are extremely high, by some estimates reaching 90 percent for firms exiting Chapter 11.
- Conflicts between the interests of equity holders and creditors (or even among creditors of differing priority) become exaggerated, potentially distorting investment incentives.
- Banks and other creditors gain influence on firm decisions, as control rights are triggered by default.
- Assets of the firm are redeployed by new owners who have purchased assets or have gained control of the firm via a restructuring.

In this chapter, we describe the framework that determines when and how control rights are exercised, and the empirical evidence that gives us a description of how the governance of the distressed firm evolves. In the US, which is the primary focus of our analysis, Chapter 11 is the endgame that influences the behavior of firms even prior to a default. As such, we first provide some brief background on the key provisions of Chapter 11 that are important to our understanding of the firm's governance. We then examine in turn the role of each of the firm's main constituencies who influence a potential restructuring.

Overview of the Legal Environment

From a governance perspective, one of the crucial features of a Chapter 11 filing is that the debtor remains in possession; in other words, the debtor's pre-bankruptcy managers can continue to manage the firm through the reorganization process. Allowing management to stay in control is thought to provide continuity and removes a disincentive to delay filing until the last minute.[1] The bankruptcy court can remove management in favor of a trustee, but such appointments are rare in practice and tend to occur only in cases of fraud or extreme mismanagement. Bankruptcy law does not, however, deprive the debtor's board of directors of the power to replace management, and managerial turnover in and around bankruptcy is commonplace.

The bankruptcy filing itself puts in place an "automatic stay" that limits creditor collection activities such as suing on debts and seizing collateral. Hence, the Bankruptcy Code provides substitute mechanisms to protect creditors that limit the debtor's control rights over firm assets. For example, courts must approve the terms of the debtor's post-bankruptcy credit facility (called debtor-in-possession, or DIP, financing). Courts must also approve sales of assets outside the ordinary course of business. Courts can limit the use of assets subject to a security interest as necessary to protect the creditor's interest in the collateral.

As is well-known, the traditional Chapter 11 reorganization requires a plan that determines the disposition of the firm's assets, places investors into classes, and allocates the proceeds of the assets across classes. Management has an exclusive right to propose a reorganization plan during the first 120 days of bankruptcy, and this exclusivity period can be extended by the court up to a maximum of 18 months. To confirm a plan consensually, a proponent must obtain a sufficient share of votes (2/3 in value and ½ in number) in each class of impaired claims and interests. As the plan is a negotiated outcome, it can be approved by the court even if it provides for distributions that violate the absolute priority of the claimants, i.e. junior claimants may receive some distribution even when more senior creditors have not been paid in full. Alternatively, the plan can be confirmed through a "cramdown," which requires convincing a judge that the absolute priority rule is satisfied with respect to impaired classes that do not approve the plan.

The Code provides that committees may be appointed to represent certain classes, increasing their voice and influence on the restructuring. The US Trustee's office, which oversees the administration of bankruptcy cases, typically appoints an unsecured creditors committee. This committee has the power to investigate the debtor's operations and finances, and to consult with the debtor on the plan of reorganization. Other committees must be approved by the court. For example, equity committees are much less frequently formed when it is clear to the court that equity has no remaining economic stake. Committee members, having access to non-public information regarding the development of the plan, are restricted from trading in the claims of the firm while serving in that role.

Overall, the process of developing the plan, distributing its details to the voting parties in a disclosure statement, soliciting votes, and obtaining court approval for the plan can lead to substantial cost and delay. The process has changed to some degree in recent years, however, as it has become increasingly common for firms to achieve a de facto reorganization by selling the firm's assets as a going concern to a new entity with a healthier capital structure. This can be done outside a plan of reorganization under Section 363 of the Bankruptcy Code. Because a creditor vote is not required in advance, the Section 363 sale provides a faster means of disposing of the firm's assets. Section 363(f), moreover, allows for assets to be sold free and clear of liens and other obligations, such as product liability claims, that might otherwise follow the assets to the buyer.

Given the many parties that exercise control rights in distress, we will proceed by analyzing theory and evidence regarding the influence of each of the major constituencies in turn. We begin by summarizing the relevant literature on shareholders, managers, and boards. We then discuss senior and junior creditors, respectively. Finally, we discuss the role of law, courts, and judges, and conclude with some brief suggestions for future research.

Shareholders, Managers, and Boards

The Role of Shareholders

As the firm becomes financially distressed, shareholders are increasingly "out of the money," raising two important governance concerns. First, to the extent that equity still has control rights, do equity holders (or management acting on their behalf) take actions to preserve their option-like value, perhaps at the expense of the ultimately recoverable firm value? Second, when does (or should) equity lose its control rights, and what role do equity holders have in a restructuring when that does occur?

Actions that benefit "out of the money" equity

A number of theoretical papers warn that the limited liability feature of equity provides incentives for excessive risk taking when the firm is distressed, particularly prior to a bankruptcy filing (these include Aghion et al., 1992; White, 1996; and Hart, 2000). Paying dividends to the equity holders of an already highly levered firm could also be viewed as symptomatic of this conflict (Hotchkiss et al., 2012).

Empirical evidence of this behavior has been elusive, and it may be the case that there are other factors which mitigate these incentives. For example, Eckbo and Thorburn (2003) suggest that the potential for managers to be rehired when a firm exits bankruptcy could limit incentives for risk shifting. They examine a sample of 170 bankruptcies in Sweden (between 1988 and 1991) where, unlike the US, the CEO loses control of the firm upon filing, a trustee is appointed, and the firm is auctioned. Income losses to CEOs of bankrupt firms are very large, indicating the personally costly nature of the filing. However, by investing conservatively, the CEO increases the probability that he/she will be rehired by the restructured firm. Other researchers have noted that restrictive loan or bond covenants could also limit risk-shifting behavior. Gormley and Matsa (2011) suggest that the agency problem between risk-averse managers and risk-seeking equity holders may explain the relative scarcity of risk seeking in distress. Consistent with this idea, they find evidence that managers whose firms are exposed to carcinogen liability are more likely to acquire cash-rich firms in unrelated industries to reduce bankruptcy risk.

The incentives of equity holders to increase risky investment should similarly provide incentives to delay default or filing, to the extent those events trigger a loss of equity's control rights. Within the asset-pricing literature, much of the existing theory of defaultable corporate debt focuses on equity holders' optimal default policy. Using a contingent-claims framework, Black and Cox (1976) and Geske (1977) value coupon-paying debt and solve for the equity holders' optimal default policy when asset sales are restricted. Fischer et al. (1989), Leland (1994), Leland and Toft (1996), Leland (1998), and Goldstein et al. (2001) examine default policy in the problem of optimal capital structure. In practice, since the optimal filing point is unobservable, we cannot readily determine whether filings are in fact delayed to the benefit of equity holders. In their empirical study of failures subsequent to highly leveraged transactions (HLTs), Andrade and Kaplan (1998) examine qualitative description of actions taken by 31 distressed firms, and find that 14 firms took actions that delayed the resolution of distress, and that the delay appears to have been costly for at least 9 firms. Adler et al. (2006) suggest that the firm will be in worse financial condition at the time of filing if it has delayed.

Once in bankruptcy, the change in legal environment may make it more difficult to increase risky investment on behalf of equity. As explained above, the incumbent management remains in control of the firm's operations in bankruptcy, but management is not free to act in the interests of shareholders alone. Most important actions require court approval and provide the opportunity for interested parties to object. Nevertheless, it may still be possible for management to take actions benefiting shareholders. For example, constituencies may disagree as to the best operating strategy for the firm, or whether certain asset sales, and the timing of these sales, are in the best interest of the overall bankruptcy estate.[2]

While direct evidence of risk shifting is sparse, continued investment in the existing assets of a failing company could be considered as risky investment, since immediate liquidation might provide a greater recovery value. An extreme illustration of the potential magnitude of creditor/shareholder conflicts in this setting is given by Weiss and Wruck (1998), who describe at length the 1989 bankruptcy of Eastern Airlines. Ex post, it is clear that creditor recoveries would have been substantially greater had Eastern been liquidated at the time of its Chapter 11 filing. However, under the supervision of the bankruptcy court, Eastern continued to fly and to generate large operating losses, ultimately ending in its liquidation 22 months later. Weiss and Wruck estimate that Eastern's value declined by over $2 billion while in bankruptcy, and that the company was insolvent well prior to the liquidation.

More generally, larger sample evidence on this type of behavior is difficult to produce. In their study of 31 distressed HLTs, Andrade and Kaplan (1998) find no evidence of risk shifting or asset substitution, which they define as large investments in unusually risky capital expenditures, projects, or acquisitions. Overall, it remains somewhat debatable whether management engages in riskier investment on behalf of equity holders, or whether they act more conservatively as the firm becomes distressed.

Equity control rights

Outside Chapter 11, shareholder control is subject to two limitations. The first stems from the shifting fiduciary obligations of the board of directors, since those fiduciary responsibilities expand to include the creditors of the company once the firm is near insolvency (Branch, 2000). The second limitation stems from the rights of creditors if the firm either violates covenants in its debt agreements or defaults on a contractual payment. We discuss each of these in turn below.

Shareholders can retain some influence over outcomes in distress through several mechanisms. First, shareholders retain their formal rights to replace the board and management inside and outside bankruptcy. Second, shareholders can represent their interests in bankruptcy through official committees, and they retain the rights to vote on a reorganization plan. The equity class must approve any consensual plan of reorganization, and cramdown is generally regarded as a more costly, time-consuming alternative because the firm must be valued to determine entitlements. The delay inherent in confirming a cramdown plan can give shareholders bargaining power.

Evidence for shareholder bargaining power can be found in the prevalence of deviations from priority toward equity, especially in the early days of the Bankruptcy Code. For example, Franks and Torous (1989), Eberhart et al. (1990), and Betker (1995) find that these deviations are common. Most recently, though, for a sample of 626 bankruptcy reorganizations between 1980 and 2005, Bharath et al. (2010) document a substantial decline in the frequency of deviations from the absolute priority rule (APR). Indeed, in 2000–5, absolute priority is violated in only 22 percent of their sample cases, in contrast to 75 percent of cases in the 1980s. They also find that deviations from priority in favor of equity are more likely when management has greater shareholdings, providing a greater incentive to act in equity's interest. Each of these empirical studies examines firms that were publicly registered companies prior to their bankruptcy; in private companies where management has a greater or even 100 percent stake, management has more incentive to act on behalf of equity interests. At the other extreme, even when management has no economic ties to equity, deviations from absolute priority may reflect the desire to reach a consensual plan outcome more quickly by paying equity holders their "nuisance" value.

The Role of Managers

Since management has the ability to stay in control even as a debtor in possession in Chapter 11, it is important to understand how their incentives, and therefore actions, are likely to be affected by financial distress. Early discussion of the merits of the Chapter 11 system included criticism that the process was too protective of incumbent management, allowing them to retain too much control and failing to punish managers for poor performance (Bradley and Rosenzweig, 1992).

The idea that bankruptcy provides a safe haven for management has been refuted in subsequent empirical research. Managers frequently lose their jobs in financial distress. Altman and Hotchkiss (2005: 222, table 10.1) summarize research showing that management turnover is extremely high; top management turnover by the time firms exit Chapter 11 ranges from 70 percent to 91 percent, depending on the sample studied. For out-of-court restructurings, turnover estimates range from 36 percent to 60 percent. Gilson (1989) is one of the earliest researchers to document management turnover conditional on financial distress. Studying 73 managers who depart from financially distressed firms between 1979 and 1984, he finds that none of the departing executives in his sample are employed by another exchange-listed firm in the subsequent three years. Gilson and Vetsuypens (1993) study 77 financially distressed public firms restructuring in 1981–7. They show that managers who remain on average take cuts to their compensation, and that CEO replacements from within the firm earn 35 percent less than their predecessor. This evidence suggests strongly the costly nature of distress for firms' managers.

More recently, Eckbo et al. (2012) quantify the personal cost to top managers of Chapter 11 firms. Their study covers CEOs of 342 US public companies filing for Chapter 11 between 1996 and 2007. More than half of incumbent CEOs regain full-time employment, the majority of whom become top executives at another firm. The change in compensation of those maintaining full-time executive employment is close to zero. The other half of CEOs who do not maintain full-time employment experience an income loss with a median present value of $4 million (discounted until retirement age). Overall, their estimates imply an ex ante expected median personal bankruptcy cost of $2.7 million (in constant 2009 dollars), or three times the typical annual compensation. To the extent that financial distress is a costly event, it will have a strong impact on managers' behavior prior to distress, providing incentives to choose lower leverage or less risky investments.

Given the complicated interplay of formal and informal control rights in bankruptcy, it remains an open empirical question: whose interests does management actually represent when a firm is distressed? There are reasons to expect management to be aligned with different constituencies depending on the circumstances of the case. When management has a large equity ownership stake prior to default, it has an incentive to preserve that value by pursuing equity's interests in a restructuring. On the other hand, management's loyalties may shift to the group that will control the company subsequent to the reorganization. For example, Gilson et al. (2000) argue that sometimes management will form a coalition with senior creditors when it is likely that this group will control the company subsequent to a restructuring. At the other end of the capital structure, new owners that contribute equity to an emerging firm may choose to keep the incumbent management in place (Gilson et al., 2000), similar to the behavior documented by Eckbo and Thorburn (2003).

The Role of the Board

In non-distressed settings, much of the discussion of the role of the board in our post-Sarbanes Oxley environment involves whether boards are effective monitors, and how best to populate the board with insider versus independent members. Much of that discussion becomes to some degree of secondary importance when the firm is distressed. Key questions involving the board become: where do their fiduciary duties lie if the firm is insolvent (and how is insolvency identified)? What happens when existing board members need to be replaced, and what interests do new board members typically represent?

The fiduciary duties of managers and directors to shareholders expand to the corporation, specifically including creditors, when the firm is in the "zone of insolvency."[3] Though the firm is generally insolvent upon filing a bankruptcy petition, there is an obvious measurement problem in determining the point in time prior to filing where insolvency occurs. Further, from the *Credit Lyonnais* case, the duty to creditors applies when the company is *near* insolvency, perhaps applying to the firm with serious operating problems.

Becker and Stromberg (2012) examine the impact of the Delaware court's ruling in the 1991 *Credit Lyonnais v Pathe Communications* case, which argued the fiduciary duties extend to creditors not when the firm is insolvent, but rather when it is in the "zone" of insolvency. They compare Delaware corporations to firms incorporated elsewhere before and after this ruling; in this way, they can show that the ruling increased the likelihood of equity issues, increased investment, and reduced firm risk for firms that were relatively closer to default. Thus, the ruling limited managers' incentives to take actions favoring equity over debt for firms near financial distress.

Determining at a given time whether a firm is at the point (or zone) of insolvency requires a valuation of the firm as a going concern, and therefore depends on the expected future performance of the company. Different constituencies may have different outlooks on the subsequent prospects of the firm, i.e. whether a decline is permanent or temporary (see Wruck, 1989: p. 423, figure 1). For example, Hotchkiss (1995) studies the cash-flow forecasts issued by management (in disclosure statements) for firms in Chapter 11, and shows that firms' incumbent management is on average overly optimistic in projecting future cash flows for a reorganized company.

The difficulties in determining in whose interest the board should be acting are exacerbated when the constituencies have conflicting interests. More senior claimants will tend to favor a liquidation of assets, particularly if it would lead to a full recovery of their claims at that point in time. Shareholders and possibly junior creditors, who potentially gain from a rebound in the value of the firm's assets, are more biased toward continuation of the firm's operations. Thus, if representing only shareholders, management and the board would be likely to support the actions described above which benefit shareholders, such as delayed filing, asset substitution, increased risk taking, or simply failure to liquidate poorly performing assets. When fiduciary duties expand to creditors, however, the board theoretically may support actions which help creditors but impair equity value. This conflict can be particularly problematic when management is also a large shareholder of the firm.

A significant number of incumbent board members resign when firms become distressed. Gilson (1990) is the first to study the composition of the board for distressed firms. Among 111 publicly traded firms that file for bankruptcy or restructure out of court between 1979 and 1985, only 46 percent of pre-distress directors remain post-restructuring. Attracting new board members can be difficult given the time and expertise required to work with the firm during the restructuring process. Liability concerns may be heightened. To the extent new board members represent different constituencies such as employees, lenders, or other investors, new members may represent conflicting interests. Investors may avoid membership on the board (or on bankruptcy committees) as it restricts their ability to continue trading claims in the firm. While it may make sense to have representatives of banks and other creditors on board once the fiduciary duties have shifted, populating the board while the firm is in the midst of a restructuring represents a challenge.

One source of new board members is investors who aim to have a longer-term stake in the restructured company, often gaining control of the restructured firm. This type of active "vulture" investor is studied by Hotchkiss and Mooradian (1997). While some distressed investors aim to passively gain from increases in value of the claims they hold, many become active in governance on the firm's board (while some ultimately gain control of the firm and/or assume management positions). They find that vultures join boards of 27 percent of the firms in their sample of 288 firms defaulting on public debt between 1980 and 1993, and retain these positions for at least one year post-restructuring for more than half of their sample.

Senior Secured Creditors

While equity holder value maximization is consistent with maximizing the total value of the non-distressed firm, senior creditors may prefer a less risky strategy that preserves the value of their claims. Thus, if senior lenders are in control, they may induce the firm to implement a suboptimal investment and financial policy. On the other hand, if the firm is deeply insolvent, senior creditors may in fact be the residual claimants, and as such promote firm value maximization. Chapter 11 determines the relative bargaining power of the different claimholders. Since voluntary out-of-court workouts are negotiated under the threat of bankruptcy filing, the outcome is substantially influenced by the allocation of control rights in Chapter 11. In this section, we survey studies of senior lender control over the firm in financial distress and bankruptcy.

Senior Lender Control in Financial Distress

As discussed above, managerial turnover rates increase when the firm performs poorly. Interestingly, a large fraction of these management changes are initiated by senior lenders. In Gilson's (1989) study of 381 public firms that experience large stock price declines in 1979–84, one-fifth of the management departures are initiated by bank lenders. While creditors do not own equity, they are able to force management changes by threatening shareholders with bankruptcy or to petition to the court to have a trustee appointed.

Bank lenders also try to align managerial incentives by tying the compensation of the firm's top executives to creditor wealth. Gilson and Vetsuypens (1993) report that over 10 percent of their sample firms enact plans that explicitly tie CEO compensation or wealth to the value of creditors' claims. This may or may not maximize the value of the firm. If banks are the residual claimants, such a compensation policy is consistent with firm value maximization. However, if a junior claim is the "fulcrum" security, it risks implementing a strategy that preserves the value of senior claims at the expense of junior creditors.[4]

Banks further influence the selection of directors in distressed firms. Gilson (1990) shows that banks affect the outcome of board elections and sometimes influence board membership directly, for example, by letting bank executives join the board while the firm is restructuring its debt. Such a strategy is not without problems, however. In particular, banks must balance a direct control over the firm with an increased risk of becoming a target of lender liability lawsuits.

Several studies emphasize the role of covenants as an important governance mechanism for bank lenders. In particular, these covenants become stricter after a distressed restructuring. Gilson (1990) reports that a large fraction of amended bank loan covenants grant banks veto power over the firm's dividend and payout policies, capital expenditures, divestitures, mergers, new financing, and senior management hiring and firing decisions. A similarly large percentage of restructurings enact more general restrictions on firms' investment and financing policies, often capping activities such as capital expenditures, asset dispositions, divestitures, payouts, and total borrowing. Following a default, creditors seem to acquire direct control over many corporate investment and payout policies.

When a financial covenant is violated (a technical default), creditors obtain the same contractual rights as in a payment default. This includes a right to immediate repayment of the principal and a termination of the loan commitment. Secured lenders typically use these rights to influence the firm's investment and financial policies while renegotiating the credit agreement.

Nini et al. (2012) examine 3,500 financial covenant violations by US non-financial public firms from 1997 to 2008. They document a decline in capital expenditures and acquisitions following a covenant violation. Moreover, violating firms decrease their leverage as well as payouts to shareholders. The amended credit agreements exhibit tighter terms, including reduced funding, shorter maturity, a higher frequency of collateral requirement and more restrictive financial covenants. There is also an increased likelihood of forced CEO turnover in the quarter that a firm violates its covenants. Importantly, the firm's operating performance and stock returns both improve following a technical default, suggesting that the increased creditor governance create value for shareholders.

Banks also play a role in the firm's decision to restructure out-of-court versus under Chapter 11. Gilson et al. (1990) examine this choice for 169 public companies that became severely financially distressed in 1978–87. They find that a distressed firm is more likely to recontract out of court when it has a larger fraction of bank debt in its capital structure, there are fewer lenders, and it has a relatively large fraction of intangible assets.

As the financially distressed firm is restructured, senior creditors frequently end up as major stockholders. While banks and other financial institutions typically are prohibited to own stock in non-financial firms, there are exceptions for equity obtained in a debt restructuring or bankruptcy reorganization plan.[5] Gilson (1990) documents that banks and insurance companies receive significant ownership—on average 37 percent of the common stock—in almost half of the restructured firms. Similarly, James (1995) finds that banks take equity in 31 percent of the restructured firms and receive on average 43 percent of the common stock. He studies a sample of 102 voluntary debt restructurings in 1981–90. The equity is awarded primarily in return for forgiveness of principal on the bank's loans (on average 41% of the loan amount). Banks continue to hold substantial amounts of common stock two years after the debt restructuring.

James (1995) further explores the role of banks in debt restructurings. He shows that, if the firm has public debt, banks rarely make concessions unless public debtholders also exchange their claims for equity (Asquith et al. (1994) make a similar point). In half of the restructurings where banks take equity, the firm has public debt outstanding. However, banks will not take equity without a restructuring of the public debt. The likelihood that the bank takes equity decreases with the proportion of public debt and increases with the firm's growth opportunities (market-to-book ratio). Firms in which banks take equity are more cash-flow constrained and have poorer operating performance prior to the restructuring. However, these firms have better cash-flow performance after the restructuring than firms with no bank ownership.

Not only is a restructuring of the public debt critical to the participation of banks, but bank concessions are also important for the success of the public debt exchange. Using a sample of 68 distressed debt exchange offers in the 1980s, James (1996) shows that exchange offers accompanied by bank concessions are associated with a greater reduction of the public debt outstanding and are more likely to succeed than restructurings where banks do not participate. He suggests that banks help reduce information asymmetries and thus holdout problems among the public debtholders.

Gilson (1997) examines leverage changes for 108 firms that file for Chapter 11 or restructure their debt out of court in 1979–89. He documents that leverage ratios remain relatively high after financially distressed firms recontract with their creditors and particularly high for firms that restructure in a workout. He suggests that transaction costs limit the extent to which creditors are willing to reduce their debt when distressed firms restructure out of court. Such transactions costs include various regulations that discourage lenders from writing down their principal and exchanging debt for equity, tax disadvantages, and holdout problems.[6] Consistently, he finds that debt reductions in out-of-court restructurings are lower the higher the number of long-term debt contracts and the higher the fraction of institutional debt. Asset sales are associated with debt reductions in workouts and even greater debt reductions in formal bankruptcy reorganizations, perhaps because Chapter 11 reduces the cost of selling assets as we discuss later. The new capital structure of firms restructuring their debt in Chapter 11 involves fewer long-term debt contracts, a higher debt ownership concentration, and greater flexibility in debt repayment.

Overall, the evidence indicates that senior creditors play an active role in corporate governance and the restructuring of distressed firms outside of bankruptcy.

Senior Lender Control Rights in Bankruptcy

Once a firm files for Chapter 11, pre-bankruptcy secured lenders can no longer enforce the rights triggered by loan covenant violations, due to bankruptcy's automatic stay. Nevertheless, banks and other secured lenders have become more adept in controlling a firm's activity before and during the bankruptcy. Pre-bankruptcy lines of credit can limit the borrower's access to cash to fund operations, putting the lender in control of the timing of a filing. Lenders can take a security interest in a debtor's entire asset base, leaving fewer free assets available for other potential lenders and, hence, limiting a borrower's liquidity. Once in bankruptcy, debtor-in-possession loans also increasingly dictate the outcomes of bankruptcy cases in direct and indirect ways. These important trends were first brought to light in the law literature (Baird and Rasmussen, 2002, 2006; Skeel 2003, 2004; Warren and Westbrook, 2003). The evidence in this early literature is largely anecdotal, documenting these trends through a small number of high-profile examples.

Ayotte and Morrison (2009) provide more comprehensive evidence of this creditor control trend. In particular, they document the pre- and post-petition financing activities of 153 large private and public US firms filing for Chapter 11 in 2001. In the sample of pre-petition credit facilities, 97 percent were secured by a lien on all, or nearly all, of the firm's assets. Interestingly, most of these credit facilities are originated in the year prior to bankruptcy filing. Through the security interest in the firm's assets, senior lenders effectively get control over the company's access to cash and thus the timing of its bankruptcy filing. Moreover, the firm cannot raise additional funds in bankruptcy without the permission of, or offering adequate protection to, the pre-petition secured lenders. As a result, these loans help senior lenders to obtain control rights inside and outside bankruptcy.

An important way for senior creditors to gain control over the bankrupt firm's day-to-day decisions is to provide additional financing in bankruptcy through a DIP loan. Dahiya et al. (2003) examine 538 firms that file for Chapter 11 in the period 1988–97. One-third of the firms in their sample obtain a DIP loan, a majority (58%) of which are provided by a pre-petition lender. There is an increasing trend in the use of DIP financing, with a higher fraction of firms obtaining DIP loans in the second half of the sample period. Larger firms, retail firms, and firms with more current assets are more likely to get DIP financing in bankruptcy.[7]

Ayotte and Morrison (2009) show that senior creditors exercise substantial control over the bankrupt firms through these DIP loan covenants. Three-quarters of the firms in their sample obtain post-petition financing either through a DIP facility (50%) or through a cash collateral order (26%), allowing the debtor to use cash in which a preexisting creditor has a security interest. Cash collateral motions frequently contain the same terms as those found in DIP loans.

Importantly, the vast majority of the post-petition financing contain detailed covenants restricting the firm's use of cash while operating in bankruptcy. Three-quarters of the loans impose specific line-item budgets on the firm, requiring the firm to submit detailed evidence of cash receipts and expenditures. A deviation from the budget of a specified margin (usually 5–15%) is considered a default. Other stringent covenants include limits on capital expenditures, operating profitability targets, and deadlines for submitting a plan of reorganization or selling assets. Ninety-two percent of the DIP loans in Ayotte and Morrison (2009) are secured by all of the firm's assets. This is imperative because if the bankrupt company violates any of the loan covenants, the DIP lender can cut off credit and force liquidation. Overall, senior secured lenders appear to exert significant control over the bankruptcy process through provisions attached to post-petition loans.

The control rights associated with new post-petition financing of bankrupt firms are also examined by McGlaun (2007). His sample is 90 US firms filing for Chapter 11 filings in 1997–2004. Similar to Ayotte and Morrison (2009), he documents that covenants give the lender control over the debtor's cash, and impose approval of line-item budgets, restrictions on the reorganization plans, and requirements to employ restructuring specialists. Consistent with the latter, Eckbo et al. (2012) find a higher forced CEO turnover rate when the firm's pre-petition lenders provide DIP financing to the bankrupt firm. McGlaun (2007) further shows that firms with a senior secured pre-petition lender are more likely to negotiate new financing in bankruptcy, providing the lender with continued control rights. It is possible that rights are more valuable to a senior secured lender that also serves as DIP lender, since the lender now is able to exercise control rights protecting the new DIP loan as well as the existing pre-petition loan.

Bharath et al. (2010) suggest that Chapter 11 has become more creditor friendly in recent years, in that deviations from absolute priority in favor of equity have declined. This is consistent with the conjecture by Skeel (2003), who argues that increasing creditor control through DIP financing, combined with bonuses to key executives that are explicitly tied to the reorganization process, deter deviations from APR.

The increased creditor control over the firm in Chapter 11 reorganization may affect managers' incentives to promptly file for bankruptcy. Adler et al. (2006) propose that debtors filing for Chapter 11 after 2001, when a change in the Uniform Commercial Code allowed creditors to take a security interest in the firm's bank accounts and thus gain greater control over the firm's liquidity, are in significantly worse financial condition than firms filing prior to 2000. Their sample is 443 large US firms filing for Chapter 11 between 1993 and 2004. They suggest that this is consistent with managers intentionally delaying bankruptcy filing in an attempt to entirely avoid the bankruptcy process, possibly with the support of secured creditors who primarily care about their own claim.

It appears that bank lenders also could play an important role when firms are auctioned. Eckbo and Thorburn (2009) examine mandatory auctions of distressed firms under the Swedish bankruptcy code. They find that the bank of the distressed firm often provides financing to a bidder in the auction. This increases liquidity and competition in the auction. However, consistent with a strategy to maximize expected recovery, the bank-financed bidder tends to bid more aggressively when the bank's claim is impaired, possibly resulting in an ex post inefficient allocation of the firm. Their evidence on firm post-bankruptcy operating performance, however, fails to support such allocation inefficiencies.

Woo (2011) argues that banks recently have been driven by financial regulations and regulatory policy to push their bankrupt borrowers to sell assets rather than reorganize under Chapter 11. Specifically, rules related to concentration risk and capital adequacy make it costly for banks to take new debt and equity claims in the restructured firm. For a sample of 285 US construction and development loans in 11/2007–12/2008, Woo finds that banks with a higher loan concentration as more likely to obtain relief from the automatic stay to pursue foreclosure. To the extent the assets are sold at fire-sale prices, this could lead to a suboptimal allocation of corporate assets.

Junior Creditors

Junior and senior creditors may have conflicting interests in bankruptcy. Since the distribution of claims under the reorganization plan is closely tied to the value of the firm, this conflict primarily involves the valuation of the firm. Junior unsecured claims are generally widely held and therefore often suffer from a coordination problem. However, these claims as well as senior debt claims are commonly acquired and consolidated by hedge funds and other distressed investors, who become major players in the restructuring of the distressed firm.

Hotchkiss and Mooradian (1997) were the first to systematically show that such vulture investors play an important role in the governance of distressed firms, finding evidence of vulture investor activity for 60 percent of the firms they study. These investors typically acquire more than one-third of the face value of the debt claims in which they invest, a position which gives them a blocking position in that class for voting on a bankruptcy plan. The vulture investors join the board of directors for 28 percent of the sample firms and become CEO or chairman for 9 percent of the firms. Moreover, the distressed investors gain a controlling position, defined as obtaining a majority of the voting stock in the restructured firm or holding the CEO or chairman position, in 16 percent of the firms, often through the purchase of bank loans. Importantly, Hotchkiss and Mooradian (1997) show that the improvement in the post-restructuring operating performance is greater when vulture investors gain control of the restructured firm or sit on the board, suggesting that these investors bring valuable governance to the target.

Much has happened with the trading of distressed claims since the 1980s. Jiang et al. (2012) examine vulture activity for a sample of 474 Chapter 11 cases from 1996 to 2007. Hedge fund presence has become a defining characteristic of the process, with hedge funds taking positions in 90 percent of the bankrupt sample firms. Hedge funds primarily invest in unsecured debt because it often is the fulcrum security, i.e. the debt class that gets converted into equity in the restructured firm. When hedge funds purchase junior debt claims, there is a higher likelihood of competing reorganization plans, CEO turnover, and adoption of key employee retention plans (KERP). Moreover, hedge fund presence increases the probability that the distressed firm successfully restructures, which is typically associated with higher total recovery rates and higher payoffs to junior creditors, often in the form of equity. The evidence is consistent with hedge funds bringing efficiency gains when they invest in distressed debt.

The role of hedge funds is also studied by Lim (2010) for a relatively recent sample of 184 financially distressed firms from the period 1998–2009. He finds that hedge funds invest in two-thirds of the sample firms and on average end up owning 35 percent of the equity in the reorganized firm. Interestingly, hedge funds tend to target the fulcrum security of economically healthier firms in order to participate in the reorganization of the distressed firm. Hedge funds' presence as creditors increases the likelihood of pre-packaged bankruptcy filing (where the reorganization plan is negotiated prior to filing) and debt-for-equity swaps. When hedge funds contribute new equity, the duration of the restructuring is reduced.

Ivashina et al. (2011) confirm the importance of active investors by examining detailed data on the capital structure for 136 firms filing for US Chapter 11 between 1998 and 2009. Using a unique dataset obtained from claims agents in Chapter 11 cases, they observe the evolution of ownership of these claims during the Chapter 11 case. They find that the trading of claims in bankruptcy leads to higher concentration of ownership, and in particular for debt claims that are eligible to vote on the reorganization plan. Active investors, such as hedge funds, are the largest net buyers and increase their ownership from 10 percent (at filing) to 15 percent of the bankrupt firm's claims at the time the votes are tabulated. This consolidation of claims is associated with a faster restructuring and a higher probability of a going-concern sale, but lower total recovery rates. Overall, vulture investors appear to fill an important governance role in the restructuring of distressed firms.

The valuation of the bankrupt firm plays an integral role in the distribution of value under the reorganization plan. Underestimating the firm's value increases the proportion of the value that goes to senior creditors, while overestimating the value allows junior creditors to get a free option on the reorganized firm. Gilson et al. (2000) study the relation between the market value of 63 firms emerging from Chapter 11 in 1979–93 and the value implied by cash-flow forecasts in their reorganization plans. They find that estimated firm values are systematically lower when a senior creditor gains control of the equity of the restructured firm and higher when creditors use junior debt to gain control. Estimated values are also lower when management receives stock or options in the restructured firm and when the distressed firm sells new equity to a third party under the reorganization plan, suggesting that valuations are used strategically in bankruptcy to promote desired outcomes.

Lemmon et al. (2009) examine the impact of labor unions on the restructuring of the distressed firm. For a sample of 505 firms filing for Chapter 11 in 1991–2004, they show that Chapter 11 is effective in reorganizing the capital structure of financially distressed firms, allowing them to emerge, while redeploying the assets of economically distressed firms into other uses. Among the firms that successfully reorganize, firms that are unionized reduce their workforce by 9 percent less than nonunionized firms, controlling for other factors. With an average employment reduction of 25 percent in their sample, this difference is meaningful, suggesting that labor unions maintain substantial bargaining power in Chapter 11 and influence the restructuring outcome.

LAW, COURTS, AND JUDGES

Though the various economic stakeholders analyzed above (shareholders, managers, and creditors) largely control the firm in distress, these control rights are limited in important ways by formal law and courts. The empirical evidence documented above suggests that the bankruptcy process has become faster and more creditor-controlled. Instead of the traditional reorganization—a restructuring of the claims of the going concern within its existing corporate shell—a majority of Chapter 11 cases are going-concern sales or piecemeal liquidation sales (Ayotte and Morrison, 2009). Some have suggested that, in this new environment, bankruptcy judges have become no more than de facto auctioneers (Buccola and Keller, 2010), while others have proclaimed these developments as the end of bankruptcy (Baird and Rasmussen, 2002).

Notwithstanding these important developments that would seem to de-emphasize the role of the law and courts, empirical research to date has found important differences in bankruptcy outcomes created by variation across jurisdictions, individual judges, and Bankruptcy Code chapters. Some research has also investigated the impact of important court decisions and statutory changes on firm and investor behavior.

The financial crisis brought about a new set of questions from a policy perspective involving the interaction of governance and financial distress. The Chapter 11 filing of Lehman Brothers in September 2008 raised important questions about the suitability of bankruptcy law for resolving distress in a systemically important financial firm. The Chrysler and General Motors cases have raised issues of government control and priority in "managed" bankruptcies, and exposed controversies regarding the "363 sale" as a substitute for traditional reorganization.

Venue and Chapter Choice

A debtor filing for bankruptcy in the US typically has a choice of several venues in which to file its bankruptcy petition, which include the district of the debtor's principal place of business, and the district that includes the company's state of incorporation.[8] This menu of options has led to patterns whereby one venue becomes the preferred "forum of choice" for debtors that seek to file outside their home district. In the 1980s, the Southern District of New York (SDNY) was the preferred forum of choice, but Delaware became the dominant forum in the 1990s. In the last decade, Delaware and SDNY have shared prominence. Scholars have tried to determine the reasons why companies choose certain venues and the consequences of these choices; i.e. whether venue choice produces a "race to the top" or a "race to the bottom."

The "race to the bottom" view is most associated with a series of papers by Lynn LoPucki and co-authors (Eisenberg and LoPucki, 1999; LoPucki and Kalin, 2001; LoPucki and Doherty, 2002; LoPucki, 2005). Under this view, courts compete for cases that offer more favorable outcomes to the constituencies that drive the venue decision—debtors, their managers, and their attorneys in particular—at the expense of overall value. The main evidence supporting this view is that Delaware and SDNY reorganizations were observed as more likely than reorganizations in other courts to refile for Chapter 11 a second time (informally known as a "Chapter 22"), and exhibit weaker financial performance following emergence. LoPucki (2005) argues that this evidence is consistent with an inefficient, laissez-faire approach to scrutinizing reorganization plans. In effect, this perspective leads to a normative argument for greater court control over plans of reorganization.

Much of the literature on venue choice disputes these conclusions on both theoretical and empirical grounds. Theoretically, the main criticism of these studies is the reliance on refiling rates as a measure of bankruptcy court effectiveness (Rasmussen and Thomas, 2001). For example, Kahl (2002) suggests that firms emerging from bankruptcy might be optimally kept on a "short leash" through higher leverage, so as to limit agency costs of inefficient continuation. This implies that higher refiling rates in a particular court can be consistent with a more efficient bankruptcy process.

Empirically, scholars have noted the potential selection biases that might lead firms with higher unobserved refiling propensities to file in Delaware or New York, leading to a mistaken inference that venue choice causes failure (Skeel, 2001). In addition, subsequent studies have found a countervailing advantage of speed in Delaware cases, and evidence that a Delaware filing is more likely when the company's home court has handled fewer Chapter 11 cases, suggesting a preference for experience (Ayotte and Skeel, 2004, 2006).

The vibrant debate on the costs and benefits of venue choice in the bankruptcy literature has cooled in the last decade, but the underlying issues remain important. Proposals to restrict venue choice in bankruptcy have reappeared in Congress recently. The creditor control trend, moreover, intensifies the importance of judicial decision-making early in the bankruptcy case. Anecdotally, courts differ in their practices with respect to approval of DIP loan terms, and motions to pay "critical vendors."[9] These decisions can be cast as a real option to keep the firm running (Baird, 2010): a denial of the motion may result in immediate liquidation, while approval keeps the liquidation/continuation option alive for another day. The extent to which these differences have affected venue choice and bankruptcy outcomes in the post-2000 period, to our knowledge, has not yet been addressed in empirical bankruptcy scholarship.

In addition to choosing venue, debtors (and sometimes creditors) choose the chapter under which the case is filed. There has been very little empirical literature examining differences across bankruptcy chapters, perhaps because of the very different circumstances under which Chapter 7, Chapter 11, and Chapter 13 filings might occur. Bris et al. (2006) take on these challenges and present evidence against the notion that Chapter 11 is a slower, more costly means of reallocating assets than Chapter 7. Controlling for non-random selection into a chapter, they find that asset value is preserved less in Chapter 7, and time spent in bankruptcy is not significantly shorter in Chapter 7 once self-selection into a chapter is taken into account.

Judges

Framing the bankruptcy judge's decision problem as a real option/optimal stopping problem has proven fruitful in the small business bankruptcy context as well. Morrison (2007) analyzes a sample of 95 Chapter 11 filings in the Northern District of Illinois in 1998. The study finds, contrary to received wisdom, that judges generally make quick shutdown decisions on non-viable firms by dismissing cases or converting them to Chapter 7. Over 70 percent of shutdowns occurred within six months of the bankruptcy petition. The time to shutdown, moreover, is positively correlated with proxies for uncertainty about going-concern value, consistent with judicial maximization of the real option.

As noted above in the venue choice literature, establishing causal effects of courts and judges has proven difficult. Chang and Schoar (2007) provide a notable exception, by exploiting random assignment of cases to judges within a judicial district. The random assignment allows for identification of differential tendencies across judges to approve "pro-debtor" and "pro-creditor" motions.[10] Chang and Schoar find significant effects of judicial bias on bankruptcy outcomes and post-bankruptcy performance. Surprisingly, they find that pro-debtor judges increase the probability of shutdown and weaken post-bankruptcy performance of reorganized firms.

The Rise of Section 363 and the Fire-Sale Problem

As noted above, while the substance of the Bankruptcy Code itself has changed little since its inception in 1978, corporate reorganization practice has changed dramatically. The rise of 363 sales as an alternative to a traditional reorganization, and the willingness of bankruptcy courts to approve them, has been the subject of criticism. LoPucki and Doherty (2007) analyze a sample of 363 sales and traditional reorganizations of the largest public companies in bankruptcy, and find that recovery rates in reorganization cases are substantially higher. They suggest that this is indication of a fire-sale bias in 363 sales, and conclude that permissive treatment of 363 sales is driven by the desire of courts to attract bankruptcy cases. LoPucki and Doherty (2007) do not address the endogeneity of the sale/reorganization decision, however, except through pre-bankruptcy controls for performance, such as return on assets.

The general notion that assets sold by financially distressed firms are sold at a discount relative to similar sales by healthy sellers is supported by the evidence in Pulvino (1998, 1999) on distressed and non-distressed sales of aircraft. In a different auction setting, Eckbo and Thorburn (2008) document a greater discount in piecemeal sales of assets in Swedish mandatory bankruptcy auctions when the firm's industry peers are financially distressed. However, they find no evidence of a fire-sale discount when the bankrupt firms are sold as going concerns.

The literature highlights several reasons why fire-sale problems may arise. Shleifer and Vishny (1992) suggest that industry insiders are liquidity constrained and therefore cannot participate in an auction, while industry outsiders are unable to operate the assets at their first-best use. LoPucki and Doherty (2007) find examples of buyers in 363 sales hiring pre-bankruptcy managers, and suggest this reflects a conflict of interest.[11] Ayotte and Skeel (2006) raise the concern that DIP lenders are sometimes asset purchasers in 363 sales.[12] Ayotte and Morrison (2009) find evidence that quick sales can be driven by secured creditor control, even when lenders are disconnected from buyers. They show that sales are most likely relative to reorganizations when secured creditors are over-secured. Over-secured creditors should have the strongest preference for an immediate sale over a longer reorganization: delay poses a downside risk if firm value declines, and little to no upside, since the creditor's recovery is capped at the value of its claim. Finally, as noted above, Woo (2011) provides theory and evidence that regulatory capital requirements based on portfolio concentration risk give secured lenders incentive to prefer liquidation over reorganization, even when the value of the secured creditor's claim is higher under reorganization.

The Auto Bankruptcies

The controversy over 363 sales reached new heights in the wake of the Chrysler and GM bankruptcies in 2009. Both companies used the 363 sale mechanism to reorganize their capital structures. The Chrysler 363 sale generated the most discussion in the academic literature due to the distribution of value: secured creditors received $2 billion in cash in exchange for their secured claims, for a recovery of only 29 cents on the dollar. Chrysler (unsecured) employee benefit claimants received debt and stock in the new Chrysler. In this sense, the outcome can be seen as a deviation from priority: some unsecured claims received value, while secured claims were not paid in full.

The legal literature following the case debated whether the Chrysler outcome was a severe departure from existing, and ideal, bankruptcy law practice. Under one view (Roe and Skeel, 2010), the Chrysler 363 sale dictated both the terms of the sale and the allocation of proceeds (sometimes called a *sub rosa* plan of reorganization). In these settings courts should, and often do, impose conditions on 363 sales that mimic creditor protections in a traditional reorganization. Morrison (2010), by contrast, argues that Chrysler is typical of modern bankruptcy practice in 363 sales, in which the DIP lender (in Chrysler, the government) controls the timing and terms of the sale. The decision to use taxpayer money to buy Chrysler and allocate a share to retirees can be seen as a question of bailout policy—one that is separate from the bankruptcy law question about whether the auction of Chrysler's assets yielded full value. In this regard, though, the most consistent criticism of the Chrysler bankruptcy in the literature is that the bankruptcy auction was not set up to yield the highest price for the assets. The bidding procedures approved by the court effectively prevented bids that would liquidate Chrysler (Adler, 2010; Baird, 2011).

Though the Chrysler case generated important questions about the proper use of 363 sales, the long-run impact of the case is probably limited. The Supreme Court vacated the Second Circuit's opinion authorizing the sale, which limits its impact on legal precedent. Empirical evidence on the short-run economic impact is mixed. Anginer and Warburton (2010) find that bond markets did not respond significantly to any news about the Chrysler bankruptcy, but bonds of unionized firms outperformed bonds of non-unionized firms in response to news about the bailout loans that preceded the bankruptcy. Blaylock et al. (2011), on the other hand, find that more unionized firms perform relatively worse on several Chrysler-related event days up to and including the date of the bankruptcy filing. But they do not find any relative differences in bond price reactions to any legal events after the filing.

Suggestions for Future Research

These recent bankruptcy developments provide many open avenues for future research. The most interesting questions, moreover, can benefit from theory and empirical evidence combined with detailed institutional and legal knowledge. For example, the increasing use of Chapter 11 as an auction mechanism presents interesting theoretical questions. When should courts approve of auctions in lieu of traditional reorganizations, given the prevalence of creditor control and the potential fire-sale problem?[13] What incentive effects are created by protections afforded to pre-arranged bidders in the auction, so-called "stalking horse" bidders? Empirically, how much variation is observed in auction procedures across cases, and what effects do these variations have on outcomes? Critical vendor payments, credit bidding, and claims trading are all important issues in bankruptcy that give rise to similar questions. Research on these questions can benefit from the expertise of both economists and legal scholars.

Notes

1. In a Chapter 7 liquidation, by contrast, management is automatically displaced in favor of a court-appointed trustee.
2. During its 1984 bankruptcy, StorageTek invested in a new technology for tape storage devices. The successful investment increased firm value enough to bring equity "in the money," and the pre-bankruptcy holders retained their stake when the firm emerged from bankruptcy as the dominant player in their market.

3. See *Credit Lyonnais v Pathe Communications*, available at <http://blogs.law.harvard.edu/corpgov/files/2007/06/20070202%20Credit%Lyonnais.pdf>.
4. The most senior class of claims which would be impaired if value were to be distributed according to absolute priority is referred to as the "fulcrum" security.
5. Commercial banks are prohibited from owning significant amounts of stock in non-financial firms under Section 16 of the Glass-Steagall Act, the Financial Services Modernization Act of 1999, the Bank holding Company Act, and the Federal Reserve Board's Regulation Y.
6. Such regulations restrict how much equity lenders can hold in non-financial firms and require banks to increase their risk-based regulatory capital when holding riskier assets such as stock.
7. See also Carapeto (1999), Chatterjee et al. (2004), and Dhillon et al. (2007) for evidence on DIP financing in Chapter 11.
8. A debtor can choose to file for bankruptcy in any of four locations: the district where the corporation is domiciled, the district where the debtor has its principal place of business, the district where its principal assets are located, or any district where an affiliate of the debtor has already filed for bankruptcy.
9. "Critical vendors" are typically unsecured trade creditors that demand payment on their pre-petition claims as a precondition for continuing to supply the debtor in bankruptcy. The practice of allowing these payments is controversial, because it elevates the priority of these "critical" vendors above other unsecured creditors. Denying these payments, however, may jeopardize the debtor's survival. The Seventh Circuit's disapproval of a bankruptcy judge's authorization of critical vendor payments in the Kmart bankruptcy may have affected the status of the Northern District of Illinois as a bankruptcy venue (Baird, 2010).
10. As Chang and Schoar acknowledge, the "pro-debtor/pro-creditor" categorization may not be clear-cut. For example, a lifting of the automatic stay might benefit a secured creditor at the expense of unsecured creditors. A sale of assets may benefit the debtor's management (who might be rehired by the purchaser in a going-concern sale) or it may be driven by secured creditor control over the debtor.
11. As noted above, Eckbo and Thorburn (2003) also find that a high fraction of incumbent managers are rehired by firms restructured through Swedish auction bankruptcy. Contrary to LoPucki and Doherty (2007), they suggest that these managers have firm-specific skills, which make them the best candidates to continue running the reorganized firms. Eckbo and Thorburn (2003) find no difference in the post-bankruptcy operating performance between firms rehiring old management and firms hiring new outside management, indicating that there are no systematic differences in their management skills.
12. One high-profile example is the TWA bankruptcy, in which American Airlines was the buyer and DIP financer.
13. For an alternative bankruptcy mechanism that is designed to resolve the fire-sale bias problem and induce the efficient sale/reorganization decision, see Casey (2011). For an analysis of optimal auctions when inside bidders have superior information to outside bidders, see Povel and Singh (2007).

References

Adler, B. E. (2010). "A Reassessment of Bankruptcy Reorganization after Chrysler and General Motors," *American Bankruptcy Institute Law Review*, 18: 305.

—— CAPKUN, V., and WEISS, L. A. (2006). "Destruction of Value in the New Era of Chapter 11," Working Paper, New York University.
AGHION, P., HART, O., and MOORE, J. (1992). "The Economics of Bankruptcy Reform," *Journal of Law, Economics and Organization*, 8: 523–46.
ALTMAN, E. I., and HOTCHKISS, E. S. (2005). *Corporate Financial Distress and Bankruptcy*. Hoboken, NJ: Wiley Finance.
ANDRADE, G., and KAPLAN, S. N. (1998). "How Costly is Financial (not Economic) Distress? Evidence from Highly Leveraged Transactions that Became Distressed," *Journal of Finance*, 53: 1443–93.
ANGINER, D., and WARBURTON, A. J. (2010). "The Chrysler Effect: The Impact of the Chrysler Bailout on Borrowing Costs," World Bank Policy Research Working Paper 5462.
ASQUITH, P., GERTNER, R., and SCHARFSTEIN, D. (1994). "Anatomy of Financial Distress: An Examination of Junk-Bond Issuers," *Quarterly Journal of Economics*, 109: 625–58.
AYOTTE, K. M., and MORRISON, E. R. (2009). "Creditor Control and Conflict in Chapter 11," *Journal of Legal Analysis*, 1(2): 511–51.
—— and SKEEL, D. (2004). "Why Do Distressed Firms Choose Delaware? An Empirical Analysis of Venue Choice in Bankruptcy," Working Paper, Northwestern University School of Law.
—— —— (2006). "An Efficiency-Based Explanation for Current Corporate Reorganization Practice," *University of Chicago Law Review*, 73: 425–68.
BAIRD, D. G. (2010). "Bankruptcy from Olympus," *University of Chicago Law Review*, 77: 959–75.
—— (2011). "Car Trouble," Working Paper, University of Chicago.
—— and RASMUSSEN, R. K. (2002). "The End of Bankruptcy," *Stanford Law Review*, 55: 751–89.
—— —— (2006). "Private Debt and the Missing Lever of Corporate Governance," *University of Pennsylvania Law Review*, 154: 1209–51.
BLAYLOCK, B., EDWARDS, A., and STANFIELD, J. (2011). "The Market-Wide Consequences of Government Intervention," Working Paper, University of New South Wales.
BECKER, B., and STROMBERG, P. (2012). "Fiduciary Duties and Equity-Debtholder Conflicts," Working Paper, Harvard Business School.
BETKER, B. L. (1995). "Management's Incentives, Equity's Bargaining Power, and Deviations from Absolute Priority in Chapter 11 Bankruptcies," *Journal of Business*, 68: 161.
BHARATH, S. T., PANCHAPEGESAN, V., and WERNER, I. M. (2010). "The Changing Nature of Chapter 11," Working Paper, Ohio State University.
BLACK, F., and COX, J. (1976). "Valuing Corporate Securities: Some Effects of Bond Indenture Provisions," *Journal of Finance*, 31: 351–67.
BRADLEY, M., and ROSENZWEIG, M. (1992). "The Untenable Case for Chapter 11," *Yale Law Journal*, 101: 1043.
BRANCH, B. (2000). "Fiduciary Duty: Shareholders versus Creditors," *Financial Practice and Education*, 10(2): 8–13.
BRIS, A., WELCH, I., and ZHU, N. (2006). "The Costs of Bankruptcy: Chapter 7 Liquidation versus Chapter 11 Reorganization," *The Journal of Finance*, 61(3): 1253–303.
BUCCOLA, V. S. J., and KELLER, A. C. (2010). "Credit Bidding and the Design of Bankruptcy Auctions," *George Mason Law Review*, 18: 99–124.
CARAPETO, M. (1999). "Does Debtor-in-Possession Financing Add Value?" Working Paper, London Business School.

Casey, A. (2011). "The Creditors' Bargain and Option-Preservation Priority in Chapter 11," *Chicago Law Review*, 78: 759–807.

Chang, T., and Schoar, A. (2007). "Judge Specific Differences in Chapter 11 and Firm Outcomes," Working Paper, MIT.

Chatterjee, S., Dhillon, U., and Ramirez, G. (2004). "Debtor-in-Possession Finance," *Journal of Banking and Finance*, 28: 3097–111.

Dahiya, S., John, K., Puri, M., and Ramirez, G. (2003). "Debtor-in-Possession Financing and Bankruptcy Resolution: Empirical Evidence," *Journal of Financial Economics*, 69: 259–80.

Dhillon, U. S., Noe, T., and Ramírez, G. G. (2007). "Debtor-in-Possession Financing and the Resolution of Uncertainty in Chapter 11 Reorganizations," *Journal of Financial Stability*, 3: 238–60.

Eberhart, A. C., Moore, W. T., and Roenfeldt, R. L. (1990). "Security Pricing and Deviations from the Absolute Priority Rule in Bankruptcy Proceedings," *Journal of Finance*, 45: 1457–69.

Eckbo, B. E., and Thorburn, K. S. (2003). "Control Benefits and CEO Discipline in Automatic Bankruptcy Auctions," *Journal of Financial Economics*, 69: 227–58.

—— —— (2008). "Automatic Bankruptcy Auctions and Fire-Sales," *Journal of Financial Economics*, 89: 404–22.

—— —— (2009). "Creditor Financing and Overbidding in Bankruptcy Auctions: Theory and Tests," *Journal of Corporate Finance*, 15: 10–29.

—— —— and Wang, W. (2012). "How Costly is Corporate Bankruptcy for Top Executives?" Working Paper, Dartmouth College.

Eisenberg, T., and LoPucki, L. M. (1999). "Shopping for Judges: An Empirical Analysis of Venue Choice in Large Chapter 11 Reorganization," *Cornell Law Review*, 84: 967–1003.

Fischer, E. O., Heinkel, R., and Zechner, J. (1989). "Dynamic Capital Structure Choice: Theory and Tests," *The Journal of Finance*, 44: 19–40.

Franks, J. R., and Torous, W. N. (1989). "An Empirical Investigation of U.S. Firms in Reorganization," *Journal of Finance*, 44: 747–69.

Geske, R. (1977). "The Valuation of Corporate Liabilities as Compound Options," *Journal of Financial and Quantitative Analysis*, 12: 541–52.

Gilson, S. (1989). "Management Turnover and Financial Distress," *Journal of Financial Economics*, 25: 241–62.

—— (1990). "Bankruptcy, Boards, Banks and Blockholders," *Journal of Financial Economics*, 27: 355–87.

—— (1997). "Transactions Costs and Capital Structure Choice: Evidence from Financially Distressed Firms," *Journal of Finance*, 52: 161–96.

—— John, K., and Lang, L. H. P. (1990). "Troubled Debt Restructurings," *Journal of Financial Economics*, 27: 315–53.

—— and Vetsuypens, M. (1993). "CEO Compensation in Financially Distressed Firms: An Empirical Analysis," *Journal of Finance*, 43: 425.

—— Hotchkiss, E., and Ruback, R. (2000). "Valuation of Bankrupt Firms," *Review of Financial Studies*, 13: 43–74.

Goldstein, R., Ju, N., and Leland, H. (2001). "An EBIT-Based Model of Dynamic Capital Structure," *Journal of Business*, 74: 483–512.

Gormley, T., and Matsa, D. (2011). "Growing Out of Trouble? Legal Liability and Corporate Responses to Adversity," *Review of Financial Studies*, 24: 2781–821.

HART, O. (2000). "Different Approaches to Bankruptcy," Harvard Institute of Economic Research Working Papers 1903, Institute of Economic Research, Harvard.

HOTCHKISS, EDITH S. (1995). "Postbankruptcy Performance and Management Turnover," *Journal of Finance*, 50: 3–21.

—— and MOORADIAN, R. M. (1997). "Vulture Investors and the Market for Control of Distressed Firms," *Journal of Financial Economics*, 32: 401–32.

—— SMITH, D. C., and STROMBERG, P. (2012). "Private Equity and the Resolution of Financial Distress," Working Paper, Boston College.

IVASHINA, V., IVERSON, B., and SMITH, D. C. (2011). "The Ownership and Trading of Debt Claims in Chapter 11 Restructurings," Working Paper, Harvard University.

JAMES, C. (1995). "When Do Banks Take Equity? An Analysis of Bank Loan Restructurings and the Role of Public Debt," *Review of Financial Studies*, 8: 1209.

—— (1996). "Bank Debt Restructuring and the Composition of Exchange Offers in Financial Distress," *Journal of Finance*, 51: 711–27.

JIANG, W., LI, K., and WANG, W. (2012). "Hedge Funds and Chapter 11," *Journal of Finance*, 67: 513–60.

KAHL, M. (2002). "Economic Distress, Financial Distress, and Dynamic Liquidation," *Journal of Finance*, 57: 135–68.

LELAND, H. E. (1994). "Corporate Debt Value, Bond Covenants, and Optimal Capital Structure," *Journal of Finance*, 49: 1213–52.

—— (1998). "Agency Costs, Risk Management, and Capital Structure," *Journal of Finance*, 53: 1213–42.

—— and TOFT, K. (1996). "Optimal Capital Structure, Endogenous Bankruptcy, and the Term Structure of Credit Spreads," *Journal of Finance*, 51: 987–1019.

LEMMON, M., MA, Y.-Y., and TASHJIAN, E. (2009). "Survival of the Fittest? Financial and Economic Distress and Restructuring Outcomes in Chapter 11," Working Paper, University of Utah.

LIM, J. (2010). "The Role of Activist Hedge Funds in Distressed Firms," Working Paper, Ohio State University.

LOPUCKI, L. M. (2005). *Courting Failure: How Competition for Big Cases is Corrupting the Bankruptcy Courts.* Ann Arbor: University of Michigan Press.

—— and DOHERTY, J. W. (2002). "Why are Delaware and New York Bankruptcy Reorganizations Failing?" *Vanderbilt Law Review*, 55: 1933–86.

—— —— (2007). "Bankruptcy Fire Sales," *Michigan Law Review*, 106: 1–60.

—— and KALIN, S. (2001). "The Failure of Public Company Bankruptcies in Delaware and New York: Empirical Evidence of a 'Race to the Bottom,'" *Vanderbilt Law Review*, 54: 231–82.

MCGLAUN, G. (2007). "Lender Control in Chapter 11: Empirical Evidence," Working Paper, University of Rochester.

MORRISON, E. (2007). "Bankruptcy Decision Making: An Empirical Study of Continuation Bias in Small Business Bankruptcies," *Journal of Law and Economics*, 50: 381.

—— (2010). "Chrysler, GM, and the Future of Chapter 11," Working Paper, Columbia Law School.

NINI, G., SMITH, D. C., and SUFI, A. (2012). "Creditor Control Rights, Corporate Governance, and Firm Value," *Review of Financial Studies*, 25: 1713–61.

POVEL, P., and SINGH, R. (2007). "Sale-Backs in Bankruptcy," *Journal of Law, Economics, and Organization*, 23: 710–30.

PULVINO, T. C. (1998). "Do Asset Fire Sales Exist? An Empirical Investigation of Commercial Aircraft Transactions," *Journal of Finance*, 53: 939–78.

—— (1999). "Effects of Bankruptcy Court Protection on Asset Sales," *Journal of Financial Economics*, 52: 151–86.

RASMUSSEN, R., and THOMAS, R. S. (2001). "Whither the Race: A Comment on the Effects of the Delawarization of Corporate Reorganizations," *Vanderbilt Law Review*, 54: 283–307.

ROE, M., and SKEEL, D. (2010). "Assessing the Chrysler Bankruptcy," *Michigan Law Review*, 108: 727–72.

SHLEIFER, A., and VISHNY, R. W. (1992). "Liquidation Values and Debt Capacity: A Market Equilibrium Approach," *Journal of Finance*, 47: 1343–66.

SKEEL, D. A. (2001). "What's So Bad About Delaware?" *Vanderbilt Law Review*, 54: 309–29.

—— (2003). "Creditors' Ball: The 'New' New Corporate Governance in Chapter 11," *University of Pennsylvania Law Review*, 152: 917–51.

—— (2004). "The Past, Present and Future of Debtor-in-Possession Financing," *Cardozo Law Review*, 25: 1905–34.

WARREN, E., and WESTBROOK, J. (2003). "Secured Party in Possession," *American Bankruptcy Institute Journal*, 22: 52–53.

WEISS, L. A., and WRUCK, K. H. (1998). "Information Problems, Conflicts of Interest, and Asset Stripping: Chapter 11's Failure in the Case of Eastern Airlines," *Journal of Financial Economics*, 48: 55.

WHITE, M. J. (1996). "The Costs of Corporate Bankruptcy: A US-European Comparison," in J. Bhandari and L. Weiss (eds.), *Corporate Bankruptcy: Economic and Legal Perspectives*. Cambridge: Cambridge University Press.

WOO, S. P. (2011). "Regulatory Bankruptcy: How Bank Regulation Causes Fire Sales," *Georgetown Law Journal*, 99: 1615–69.

WRUCK, K. H. (1989). "Equity Ownership Concentration and Firm Value: Evidence from Private Equity Financings," *Journal of Financial Economics*, 23: 3–28.

PART IV

TYPES OF INVESTORS

CHAPTER 23

VENTURE CAPITAL AND CORPORATE GOVERNANCE

DOUGLAS CUMMING AND SOFIA JOHAN

INTRODUCTION

VENTURE capitalists source their investment capital or funds from institutional investors such as pension funds, life insurance companies, banks, and endowments. High net-worth individuals and corporations are also potential sources of capital. Venture capital (VC) funds are then most commonly organized as limited partnerships with funds to be committed to the fund for 10–13 years, referred to also as lifespans. VC funds are typically in excess of $50 million in committed capital, and fund managers typically receive management fees of 1–3 percent of committed capital and 20 percent of carried interest, or share of the profits. VC funds do not invest in companies for the purpose of gaining interest on debt or dividends on equity; rather, VC funds invest in early-stage privately held companies with the view to exiting investments in three to seven years for the purpose of effecting a capital gain in an initial public offering (IPO) or acquisition exit.

VC relationships are governed by two main types of contracts (Cumming and Johan, 2006). First, there are contracts between institutional investors and fund managers to establish the terms of limited partnership. This contract is employed for the life of the fund. Limited partnership contracts are critical for institutional investors since it is their only means of governance over the activities of the fund manager and partners. That is, limited partners cannot get involved in the day-to-day activities of the fund, otherwise they risk losing their limited partner status. It is therefore crucial that the limited partnership contract determines the boundaries within which the parties operate for the life of the fund at the outset. One example of a specified boundary would be the types of investment made by the fund manager, i.e. the investment style. Fund managers have been known to style drift (Cumming et al., 2009), at the risk of breaching contractual covenants in the limited partnership agreement and as such leading to legal disputes and reputation costs. For this reason, Cumming et al. (2009) find that style drift is typically associated with better investment outcomes since fund managers do not wish to style drift unless outcomes are clearly going to be "sure bets" and lead to favorable outcomes.

Second, there are contracts between the VC fund itself and investee companies. These contracts are extremely detailed and set out the type of security and a long list of veto and control rights that the VC investor has over the investee. These contracts are very effective in allocating the cash-flow and control rights for the investor(s) and investee. Contracts govern the relationship in terms of providing incentives as well as decision rights for the future of the venture. Contracts are highly influential in shaping the actions of the parties and thereby the investment outcomes.

In this chapter, we review evidence on VC limited partnership agreements (in the first section) as well as VC contracts with investee companies (in the second section). We discuss international evidence in the spirit of Wright et al. (2005) and note salient differences in governance that therefore exist across countries. We also discuss non-contractual forms of VC governance over investee companies (in the third section). We provide concluding remarks in the final section of this chapter.

Contractual Corporate Governance I: Venture Capital Limited Partnerships

In this section we describe the types of restrictive covenants in private investment funds, and the rationale for such covenants, in the first subsection. In the second subsection we discuss evidence on limited partnership contracts.

Limited Partnership Restrictive Covenants

VC and private equity (PE) funds are financial intermediaries between institutional investors (such as banks, endowments, pension funds, life insurance companies, high net-worth private individuals) and private companies seeking funding. Institutional investors do not have the time and skills to carry out due diligence in selecting worthy entrepreneurial companies for financing, and carry out the monitoring and value-added advice to bring investments in small and medium-sized enterprises to fruition (the investment process in an investee company can take between two to seven years before an exit event such as an IPO, acquisition, or write-off). Institutional investors therefore commit capital to VC and PE funds so that specialized fund managers can manage the investment process in entrepreneurial companies.

The most common form of organization of VC and PE funds in the United States (US) has been a limited partnership structure that typically lasts for ten years, with an option to continue for an additional three years to ensure the investments have been brought to fruition and the fund can be wound up (Sahlman, 1990; Gompers and Lerner, 1996, 1999). Other countries around the world that allow limited partnership structures have likewise made use of such structures.[1] Countries that do not allow limited partnership structures have made use of corporate forms that closely resemble limited partnerships in the covenants governing the partnership.[2]

Limited partnerships and similar forms of organization involve an assignment of rights and responsibilities in the form of a very long-term contract over a period of ten or more years. The purpose of this contract is to mitigate the potential for agency problems associated with the VC fund managers' investing institutional investor capital in private entrepreneurial companies. The massive potential for agency problems in the reinvestment of capital (elaborated later in the chapter), and the long-term commitment by institutional investors in the limited partnership, make extremely important the assignment of rights and obligations in the contract in the form of restrictive covenants.[3] The characteristics of these restrictive covenants among funds in different countries around the world are the focus of this chapter.

We group the VC fund restrictive covenants into five categories, as follows. We formed four of the categories of covenants on the basis of Gompers and Lerner (1996). We have however made changes to those four categories to take into account new types of covenants more commonly used now and to include covenants relating to the limitation of the fund manager's liability. We have also made changes that reflect the structure of funds in non-US countries, where funds may be organized in various legal forms. The changes were made with advice provided by a VC practitioner, and we confirmed the appropriateness of the categorizations based on interviews with six fund managers at nine different funds in three different countries.

Category 1: Authority of Fund Manager Regarding Investment Decisions

The restrictions on investment decisions with a limited partnership agreement limit the agency problems associated with the investment of institutional investors' capital (Gompers and Lerner, 1996). This is important, since institutional investors cannot interfere with the day-to-day operations of the fund, otherwise they risk losing their limited liability status. These restrictions include, first, restrictions on the size of investment in any one portfolio company because otherwise a fund manager might lower his or her effort costs associated with diversifying the institutional investors' capital across a number of different entrepreneurial companies.[4] Second, there are restrictions on the ability of a fund manager to borrow money such as in the form of bank debt and reinvest that borrowed money alongside the institutional investors' capital. That type of behavior would increase the leverage of the fund and increase the risks faced by the institutional investors. Third, there are restrictions on co-investment by another fund managed by the fund manager, as well as restrictions on co-investment by the fund investors. Those restrictions limit the conflicts of interest in the allocation of opportunities to different institutional investors of the fund, as well as limiting the incentive for a fund manager to bail out the poorly performing investments of a companion fund operated by the same manager. Fourth, there are restrictions on the reinvestment of capital gains obtained from investments brought to fruition. Some fund managers might otherwise pursue a strategy of "fame not fortune" in terms of trying to get as many IPO successes as possible, at the risk of losing the profits from one investment by investing the profits in a new unproven venture. Fifth, there are restrictions on the overall ability and independence of the fund manager to make investment decisions. Finally, there are other less common covenants on other types of investment and divestment decisions (such as limits in terms of the timing of investment with drawdowns, and timing of exits).[5]

Category 2: Restrictions on Fund Managers' Investment Powers

The covenants in the class of restrictions on investment powers also limit the agency problems associated with the separation of ownership (i.e. by institutional investors) and control (i.e. by fund managers) in the investment process. The first restriction in this class involves the co-investment of the fund managers themselves. This is similar to co-investment by the fund's institutional investors and co-investment of prior funds (as described above in category 1), but instead involves the personal funds of the fund managers. This restriction limits the incentive problems associated with the allocation of attention by the fund managers to different entrepreneurial companies in the fund portfolio. If the fund manager were able to co-invest personal funds, there would be distorted incentives for fund managers to spend most of their time allocating effort to the companies in which they are personally invested, instead of trying to maximize the value of the overall portfolio (as would be expected by institutional investors). Second, there are covenants pertaining to the sale of fund interests by fund managers, since institutional investors' financial interest will be compromised by the addition of new institutional investors, and, more significantly, the loss of commitment of the fund manager who is usually also the general partner or most active fund shareholder. Third, key person provisions limit the addition of new investment principals as fund managers, since the contract is made with specific fund managers and the institutional investors want the management of their capital to be in the hands of specific people with whom they have contracted. Finally, there could be other types of restrictions on other actions of fund managers.

Category 3: Covenants Relating to the Types of Investment

Covenants pertaining to the types of investment ensure that the institutional investors' capital is invested in a way that is consistent with their desired risk/return profile. Restrictions include investments in other venture funds, follow-on investments in portfolio companies of other funds of the fund manager,[6] public securities, leveraged buyouts, foreign securities, and bridge financing. Without such restrictions, the fund manager could pursue investment strategies that would better suit the interests of the fund managers regardless of the interests of the institutional investors.

Category 4: Fund Operation

Covenants on fund operation are designed to oversee the administrative aspects of a fund, and include the sale of fund interests by fund investors,[7] restrictions against the fund manager on raising a new fund,[8] public disclosure of fund matters to investors, and provisions to allow fund investors to vote to remove the fund manager without cause (no-fault divorce clauses). The covenant restricting the sale of fund interest by fund investors (described here in category 4) is differentiated from the covenant restricting the sale of interest by fund manager (as specified in category 2) because the specific fund manager action of selling pertains to things fund managers cannot do, whereas category 4 pertains to administrative aspects of all investors. Recall that the fund manager is also the general partner or most active shareholder of a fund, unlike all other fund investors; hence, the different categorizations for seemingly related actions.

Category 5: Limitation of Liability of the Fund Manager

While categories 1–4 considered covenants constraining the activities of fund managers, this last category of covenants pertains to favorable awards of limited liability for fund managers. Fund manager liability can be limited in the event of disappointing returns from investments made, limited if the fund manager fails to invest committed capital within the agreed time, and/or limited if the fund manager is found to be mismanaging the fund.

EVIDENCE ON LIMITED PARTNERSHIP CONTRACTS

Cumming and Johan (2008) find evidence that the quality of law affects the use of covenants across countries. First, regarding the quality of the rule of law and related factors pertinent to the legality of a country, they observe a statistically significant positive relation between the quality of a country's laws and the number of covenants pertaining to fund operations (such as the sale of fund interests, restrictions on fundraising, and matters pertaining to public disclosure). An increase in the legality index from 20 to 21 (a typical improvement among developed nations) increases the probability of an extra covenant pertaining to fund operation by approximately 1 percent, whereas an increase from 10 to 11 (a typical improvement among emerging markets) increases the probability of an extra covenant pertaining to fund operation by approximately 2 percent. The data further indicate that civil law countries are approximately 6 percent more likely to have covenants pertaining to types of investment; however, the common/civil law differences were not notable for any other type of covenant.

Second, with respect to legally trained fund managers, an increase to one fund manager out of five with legal training increases the probability of additional covenants pertaining both to investment decisions (such as the size of any single investment and co-investment) and types of investment (in different asset classes) by approximately 10 percent. Taken together, therefore, while law and lawyers are both important, the presence of lawyers has a more economically significant impact on the use of covenants than the legal environment itself.

Third, it is noteworthy that a number of other factors indicate a significant influence on the probability of use of covenants. In particular, their analyses show an important relation between fund covenants and institutional factors such as offshore fund structures, as well as fund-specific variables such as fund size, industry market-to-book ratio, and the identity of the fund's investors. In particular, offshore funds have fewer covenants; larger funds have more covenants; funds that operate in industries with higher market-to-book ratios have more covenants; and funds with more experienced managers are more likely to be granted limited liability protections for fund managers. It is also noteworthy that, in times of stronger market conditions, institutional investors are more likely to grant limited liability protection to fund managers. There are other significant factors identified in the rich and detailed data introduced in Cumming and Johan (2008).

To complement the evidence on restrictive covenants, Cumming and Johan (2009) and Johan and Najar (2010) examine compensation arrangements in VC. In the US, VC funds typically have fixed management fees of around 1–3 percent of the committed capital of the fund (analogous to the case of mutual funds that often have management expense ratios of 1–2%), and carry interest or performance fees of typically 20 percent of the profits made (Gompers and Lerner, 1999; Metrick and Yasuda, 2009) (unlike the case of mutual funds). The fixed management fee enables fund operation overheads to be met prior to fund liquidity events. VC funds are typically organized as limited partnerships for a period of 10–13 years and invest in early-stage private companies that are considerably illiquid as liquidity events (such as an IPO or an acquisition) typically take two to seven years. Fixed management fees therefore should sufficiently meet foreseeable overheads arising from the investment and the divestment process to be carried out by the managers before any profits are earned. Performance fees on the other hand align the incentives of fund manager and their institutional investors.

Cumming and Johan (2009) also analyze fund clawback provisions against the fund manager for poor performance of the fund. Clawback provisions enable institutional investors to claw back any profits paid out to fund managers in the event subsequent investments result in losses exceeding the profits made. Clawbacks lower the risk faced by institutional investors in the event of poor performance; from the fund manager's perspective, a clawback is the exact opposite of an incentive performance fee. They compare and contrast the role of legality in "positive" performance incentive fees versus "negative" clawbacks (i.e. "carrots" versus "sticks" in compensation). Furthermore, they assess the probability that the fund structure enables share distributions to institutional investors, or whether the fund mandates cash-only distributions. Share distributions to a fund's investors shift the decision of when to liquidate an equity position in an entrepreneurial investee company from the fund manager to the funds' investors. The cash versus share distribution decision is important as it affects the timing of payment via the realization of capital gains among a fund's investors, and therefore affects institutional investor compensation, which it is interesting and useful to analyze in conjunction with fund manager compensation.

The data in Cumming and Johan (2009) indicate that legal conditions have by far the most statistically and economically significant effect on compensation: fixed fees are lower and performance fees are higher in countries with stronger legal conditions. For example, they show that a move from the Philippines to the US (one of the most extreme improvements in legal conditions in our data) gives rise to a reduction in fixed fees of approximately 1.5 percent, and an increase in performance fees of approximately 10 percent. A more modest improvement in legal conditions from the Philippines to South Africa, for example, gives rise to a reduction in fixed fees of approximately 0.9 percent and an increase in performance fees of 5.9 percent. These results are robust to controls for a variety of factors, including market conditions, institutional investor and fund manager characteristics, including education and experience, as well as fund factors such as stage and industry focus, among other control variables available in the detailed new international dataset. In fact, the legal environment is found to be the most robust, statistically significant, and economically significant factor in explaining the differences in fixed and performance fees among the funds in the international dataset introduced in Cumming and Johan (2009).

The data in Cumming and Johan (2009) further indicate that the legal environment is the most statistically and economically significant determinant of clawbacks among VC and PE funds. A reduction in the quality of legal conditions increases the probability of clawbacks: for example, clawbacks are approximately 26.8 percent more likely in the Philippines than South Africa, and approximately 44.9 percent more likely in the Philippines than the US.

Importantly, they notice the asymmetry in fund manager compensation in relation to legal conditions: on one hand, fund managers have higher fixed fees and lower performance fees in countries with weak legal conditions; on the other hand, fund managers in countries with weak legal conditions are more likely to face the downside risk of a clawback on their fees. This asymmetry is intuitive as risk-averse fund managers trade off a higher fixed fee for a lower performance fee when legal conditions are weak, whereas risk-aderse institutional investors are more likely to require downside protection in countries with poor laws via clawbacks against fund managers in the event of poor overall fund performance.

Finally, to complement the analysis of how fund managers are compensated, Cumming and Johan (2009) (see also Johan and Najar, 2010) further analyze the relation between legality and payment terms for a fund's institutional investors in terms of cash versus share distributions from realized investments in entrepreneurial companies. The data indicate a weak (not robust) relation between legality and cash distributions: cash-only distributions are more likely in countries with weak legal conditions. Much more significantly, however, they find that institutional investors mandate cash-only distributions (and do not allow for share distributions) for offshore funds. In fact, institutional investors are approximately 83.3 percent more likely to require cash-only distributions when the fund is established as an offshore fund. This finding is intuitive for two reasons. First, share distributions have tax advantages in that they allow the institutional investor to time the realization of capital gains (Gompers and Lerner, 1999, 1996). Offshore funds are by their very nature tax-lowering entities,[9] and hence the timing of realization of capital gains is a less pronounced concern among institutional investors of offshore funds. Second, aside from taxation, institutional investors in an offshore fund not only differ in terms of type of institution but are commonly from a diverse set of countries, and they typically face non-harmonized legal impediments to both acquiring and selling shares in entrepreneurial companies transferred to them from the fund manager. Hence, it is much more efficient for liquidity reasons to have cash-only distributions among offshore fund structures.

Contractual Corporate Governance II: Venture Capital Contracts with Investee Firms

In this section we describe types of clauses in VC contracts in the first subsection. Thereafter in the second subsection we review evidence on VC contracts with investee companies.

Types of Clauses in Venture Capital Contracts

VC contracts independently allocate cash-flow and control rights (Gompers, 1998; Kaplan and Stromberg, 2003; Isaksson et al., 2004; Parhankangas et al., 2005) through security design and various specific veto and control rights (summarized in Table 23.1). Common equity securities represent equity ownership in a corporation, providing voting rights, entitling the holder to a share of the company's success through dividends and/or capital appreciation. In the event of liquidation, common stockholders have rights to a company's assets only after debtholders and preferred stockholders have been satisfied. Preferred equity is capital stock that takes precedence over common equity in the event of bankruptcy, and provides that pre-specified dividends are paid before any dividends are paid to common equity. Preferred dividends are fixed and do not fluctuate. Preferred equity holders cannot force the company into bankruptcy in the event of non-payment of dividends, but must pay all preferred dividends in arrears prior to paying dividends to common equity holders. Convertible preferred equity is preferred equity that can be converted into a specified amount of common equity at the holder's option. Debt is an amount owed to a person or organization for funds borrowed.

Companies that fail to pay interest on debt can be forced into bankruptcy by debtholders. Convertible debt is debt that can be converted into a specified amount of common stock at the holder's option.

Control rights ensuing from the type of security held by the VC fund in the entrepreneurial company are proactive rights that enable the fund manager to bring about a change in the direction of the company. They give the fund manager, on behalf of the VC fund, the right to take a particular action as a residual right of control. Perhaps the most effective control right is the right to replace the CEO. VC fund managers typically retain the right to replace the founding entrepreneur as CEO even where they do not have a majority of the board or a majority of the voting rights. This right is either explicit or implicit by virtue of a combination of other rights (such as through a majority of board seats or holding other rights). There are of course other rights that VC fund managers incorporate into their contracts with entrepreneurs to regulate their relationship over the life of the investment. Drag-along rights enable the fund manager to force the entrepreneur to sell shares in the same way as the VC chooses (and tag along rights for syndicated partners; see Wright and Lockett, 2003). The holder of redemption shares has the right to make the entrepreneurial company redeem the shares as per the terms of the agreement. Typically, the terms specify the redemption price per share and the date at which the holder may seek redemption. Anti-dilution rights enable VCs to retain a majority holding of a company and give VCs more bargaining power over sequential financing rounds, albeit leading to a larger dilution of entrepreneurial control. The holder is entitled to proportional equity allocations that maintain a constant equity ownership percentage in the company. The holder of protection rights against new issues has the right to vote on this issue at the stakeholder level. The votes per share may be disproportionately allocated toward certain stakeholders such as the VC. Analogous to veto rights for changes in control, a co-sale right and a right of first refusal provide VCs with protection in the event the entrepreneur tries to sell the company in part or whole to a new owner, and hence can be used as threat points in negotiation. With a right of first refusal at sale, before the company can be sold, the holder of the right of first refusal at sale must be offered the same terms for sale of his or her own shares. The company cannot be sold to another party unless the holder turns down the terms that are offered. With a co-sale agreement, any stakeholder that wishes to sell his share of the company must also offer to the holder of a co-sale agreement the option to sell his or her shares on the same terms. Also, an IPO registration right can be used as a threat point in negotiation where the entrepreneurial company is not yet in a position to be a publicly listed company. The holder can compel the company to register shares held by the investor on a stock exchange. Often the holder of IPO registration rights also has piggyback registration rights, which enables the holder to compel the company that is already in the process of filing a registration statement to extend the registration statement to cover the holder's class of shares. Finally, information rights typically call for the company to supply timely financial statements and other items not generally available to other stakeholders.

Table 23.1. Specific terms used in VC contracts

Variable	Definition
Security	
Common Equity	Securities representing equity ownership in a corporation, providing voting rights, entitling the holder to a share of the company's success through dividends and/or capital appreciation. In the event of liquidation, common stockholders have rights to a company's assets only after debtholders and preferred stockholders have been satisfied.
Preferred Equity	Capital stock that takes precedence over common equity in the event of bankruptcy, and provides that pre-specified dividends are paid before any dividends are paid to common equity. Preferred dividends are fixed and do not fluctuate. Preferred equity holders cannot force the company into bankruptcy in the event of non-payment of dividends, but must pay all preferred dividends in arrears prior to paying dividends to common equity holders.
Debt	An amount owed to a person or organization for funds borrowed. Companies that fail to pay interest on debt can be forced into bankruptcy by debtholders.
Convertible Preferred Equity	Preferred equity that can be converted into a specified amount of common equity at the holder's option.
Convertible Debt	Debt that can be converted into a specified amount of common stock at the holder's option.
Veto Rights	
Asset Sales	The holder can prevent the board from raising the issue or resolution of asset sales at the shareholder level.
Asset Purchases	The holder can prevent the board from raising the issue or resolution of asset purchases at the shareholder level.
Changes in Control	The holder can prevent the board from raising the issue or resolution of changes in control of the company at the shareholder level.
Issuances of Equity	The holder can prevent the board from raising the issue or resolution of issuing new equity at the shareholder level.
Other Decisions	The holder can prevent the board from raising any particular issue or resolution at the shareholder level. For example, these issues include, but are not limited to, hiring key personnel, external consultants, legal and accounting advisors, releasing information to the public, or other decisions.
Control Rights	
Right to Replace CEO	The holder has the right to replace the founding entrepreneur as the CEO of the company. This right is either explicit or implicit by virtue of a combination of other rights (such as through a majority of board seats or holding other rights enumerated below).

Right of First Refusal at Sale	Before the company can be sold, the holder of the right of first refusal at sale must be offered the same terms for sale of his or her own shares. The company cannot be sold to another party unless the holder turns down the terms that are offered.
Co-Sale Agreement	Any stakeholder that wishes to sell his share of the company must also offer to the holder of a co-sale agreement the option to sell his or her shares on the same terms.
Drag-Along Rights	The holder can force the other stakeholders to sell their shares on the same terms as the share which is being sold by the holder.
Anti-Dilution Protection	The holder is entitled to proportional equity allocations that maintain a constant equity ownership percentage in the company.
Protection Rights against New Issues	The holder has the right to vote on this issue at the stakeholder level. The votes per share may be disproportionately allocated toward certain stakeholders such as the VC.
Redemption Rights	The holder of redemption shares has the right to make the entrepreneurial company redeem the shares as per the terms of the agreement. Typically, the terms specify the redemption price per share and the date on which the holder may seek redemption.
Information Rights	The holder has the right to obtain information above and beyond that usually provided to other stakeholders, if requested.
IPO Registration Rights	The holder can compel the company to register shares held by the investor on a stock exchange. Often the holder of IPO registration rights also has piggyback registration rights, which enables the holder to compel the company that is already in the process of filing a registration statement to extend the registration statement to cover the holder's class of shares.

Note: This table describes specific terms used in typical VC contracts. Contract terms are categorized into three areas: security design, veto rights, and control rights. Contract terms are independently negotiated and may or may not be used in conjunction with others.

Veto rights, in contrast, are passive rights that can be exercised by the fund manager on behalf of the VC fund to prevent certain actions being taken by the management or the board of directors of the investee company. Veto rights typically cover issues relating to asset sales, asset purchases, changes in control, and issuances of equity. Veto rights over asset sales enable the holder to prevent the board from raising the issue or resolution of asset sales at the shareholder level. A fund manager for example could veto the proposal of the purchase of a new physical asset to be tabled to the board of directors or shareholders if it for example feels an upgrade is more appropriate. This ensures that the fund manager will in effect influence the outcome of the capital expenditure decision to its satisfaction without being seen as impeding managerial/director/shareholder prerogative. Veto rights over asset purchases enable the holder to prevent the board from raising the issue or resolution of asset purchases at the shareholder level. Veto rights over changes in control enable the holder to prevent the board from raising the issue or resolution of changes in control of the company at the shareholder level. Veto rights over issuances of equity enable the holder to prevent the board from raising the issue or resolution of issuing new equity at the shareholder level. Veto rights over other decisions enable the holder to prevent the board from raising any particular issue or resolution at the shareholder level. For example, these issues include, but are not limited to, hiring key personnel, external consultants, legal and accounting advisors, releasing information to the public, and other decisions.

EMPIRICAL EVIDENCE ON VENTURE CAPITAL CONTRACTS WITH INVESTEE COMPANIES

Security Design

The outlier country with regard to VC security design is the US, as it is the only country in the world whereby the market has converged on one security: convertible preferred equity. Empirical evidence has clearly established that, while US VC fund managers finance US entrepreneurs with convertible preferred equity (Gompers, 1998; Kaplan and Stromberg, 2003), US VC fund managers finance entrepreneurial companies in other countries, such as Canada, with a variety of forms of finance. Cumming (2005a, 2005b) shows that the use of a variety of forms of finance by US VC fund managers for Canadian entrepreneurial companies is not attributable to the definition of VC by the stage of entrepreneurial company development, type of industry, staging, etc. Likewise, US VC fund managers use a variety of forms of finance and the same pattern of securities for investments that are not syndicated with Canadian VC fund managers. Cumming (2005a, 2005b) provides evidence of time-series changes in the pattern of security design for the 1991–2004 period. These patterns over time show security selection depends on the following four main factors (Cumming, 2005a, 2005b).

First, the characteristics of the transacting parties (both the entrepreneur and the VC fund) affect security design. Earlier-stage high-tech companies are less likely to use securities that mandate periodic payments back to the VC fund prior to exit. This is intuitive, as debt-like securities are inappropriate for companies with foreseeable negative cash flows in the initial stages of development. Seed-stage companies are more likely to be financed with either common equity or straight preferred equity, and less likely to be financed with straight debt, convertible debt, or mixes of debt and common equity. Life-science and other types of high-tech companies are more likely to be financed with convertible preferred equity. Corporate VC funds are less likely to use securities with upside potential, consistent with the evidence from corporate funds.

Second, market conditions affect contracts. Common equity securities without downside protection are less likely to be used after the crash of a bubble, consistent with Figures 23.1 and 23.2. Third, capital gains taxation affects contracts in a way consistent with the work of Gilson and Schizer (2003). In the US context, Gilson and Schizer (2003) have shown there exists a significant tax advantage associated with the use of convertible preferred equity. In brief, entrepreneurs receive incentive compensation in the form of stock options, and the use of convertible securities enables the VC funds' shares to be valued higher than the entrepreneurs' common shares, and hence the strike price of the entrepreneurs' stock options can be undervalued; as such, convertible preferred shares enable a unique high-powered form of entrepreneurial incentive compensation through the tax advantage. While this "tax practice" has evolved in the US and is not scrutinized by the Internal Revue Service (IRS), it is less clear as to whether Revenue Canada (the Canadian equivalent to the IRS) would permit this to operate in Canada (Sandler, 2001). Cumming (2005a, 2005b) nevertheless finds changes in taxation materially affected the security choice in ways that are consistent with Gilson and Schizer's theory.

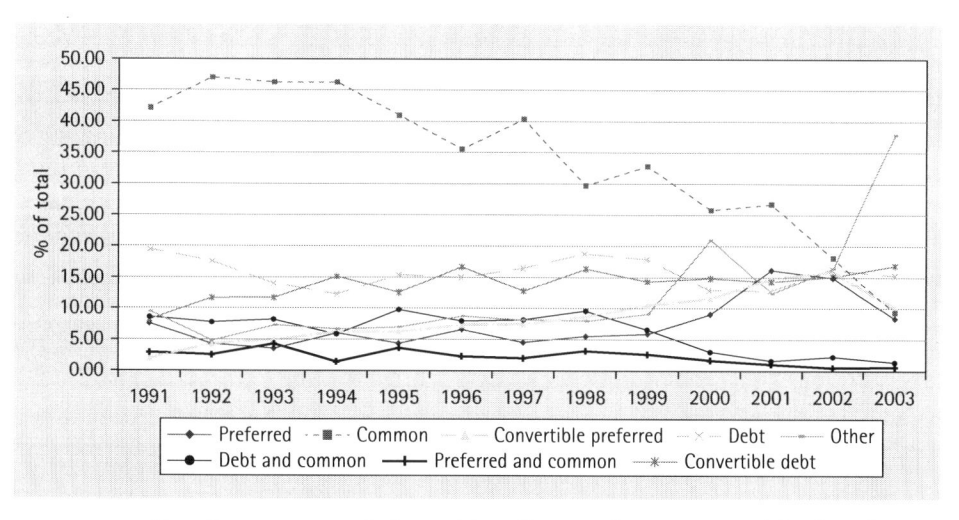

FIGURE 23.1. Canadian venture capital securities, all types of venture capital funds and entrepreneurial firms, 1991(Q1)–2003(Q3)

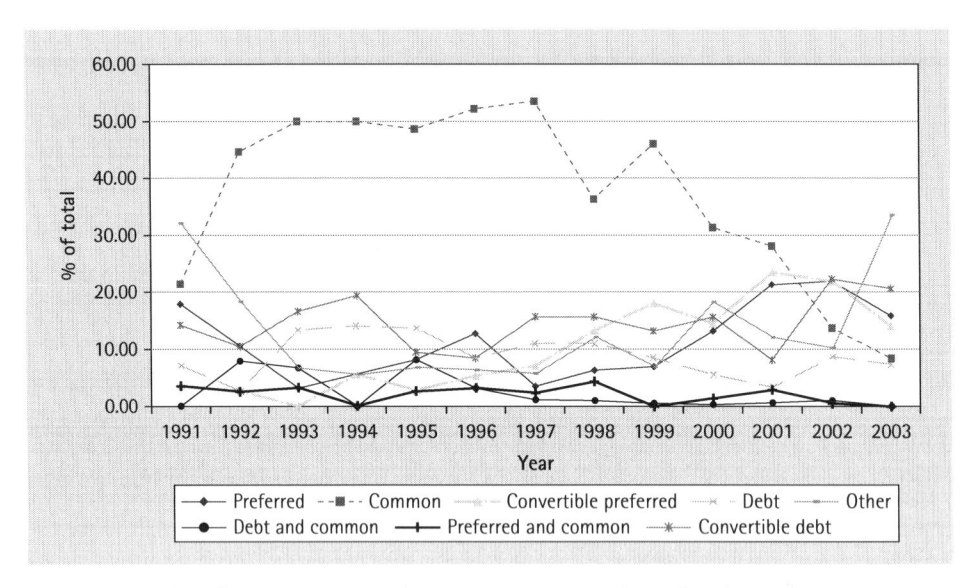

FIGURE 23.2. Canadian venture capital securities, private independent limited partner venture capitalists and start-up entrepreneurial firms only, 1991(Q1)–2003(Q3)

Fourth, there is some evidence of learning in that time trends point to changes in the intensity of different contracts over time, but this trend is not toward the use of convertible preferred equity (at least as at 2004). More favorable market conditions are associated with a more frequent use of securities with upside potential, and time trends show an increase in the frequency of use of convertible debt and a lower frequency of use of common equity.

Cumming (2005a, 2005b, 2006b) shows that both US and Canadian corporate VCs are more likely to employ securities without ownership interest (i.e. straight debt and/or straight preferred shares). On a broad level, therefore, one may generally infer that corporate VC funds on average select investments with less upside potential, which in turn limits returns. Prior evidence on corporate VC contracts in Europe is limited. Bascha and Walz (2007), Kaplan et al. (2007), and Schwienbacher (2008) have data from limited partnership VC funds in Europe, but do not have data on corporate VC funds. Cumming (2008) and Cumming and Johan (2008) have data on 78 captive (corporate) and 145 non-captive VC-backed companies from continental Europe. These data indicate that 46 percent (44%) of captive (non-captive) investments are made with common equity securities, 35 percent (31%) of captive (non-captive) investments are made with convertible securities, 10 percent (25%) of captive (non-captive) investments are made with mixes of debt, preferred and common equity securities, and 9 percent (0%) of captive (non-captive) investments are made with non-convertible preferred equity and debt securities.

In sum, US VC funds financing US entrepreneurs use convertible preferred equity most frequently, most probably as a result of the tax bias in favor of the use of convertible preferred shares for VC deals in the US. The data show that Canadian VC funds financing Canadian entrepreneurs, as well as US VC funds financing Canadian entrepreneurs, do use convertible preferred equity, although not prevalently, and instead employ many other financing instruments. As well, European VC funds use securities that resemble transactions carried out in Canada. This evidence is highly consistent with other evidence on VC contracts from Canada (Cumming, 2005a, 2005b), Europe (Bascha and Walz, 2007; Cumming, 2008; Schwienbacher, 2008; Hege et al., 2009), Taiwan (Songtao, 2001), and developing countries (Lerner and Schoar, 2005). It clearly shows VC funds use a variety of forms of finance and convertible preferred equity is not the most frequently used security by VC funds in any country in the world (i.e. where data have been collected) other than the US.

Covenants

Gompers (1998) and Kaplan and Stromberg (2003) examine specific details in US VC contracts based on hand-collected samples of 50 and 213 investments, respectively. More specifically, the Kaplan and Stromberg study comprises 213 investments in 119 US portfolio companies by 14 limited partnerships. Based on US-only datasets, both Gompers (1998) and Kaplan and Stromberg (2003) show that VC funds separately allocate cash-flow rights, voting rights, board rights, liquidation rights, and other control rights. They find that convertible preferred equity is used, and that cash-flow rights, voting rights, control rights, and future financings are often contingent on contingent on observable measures of financial and non-financial performance. As well, fund managers often include clauses to mitigate the potential hold-up between the entrepreneur and the VC fund investor. Kaplan and Stromberg show that VC fund managers retain control of the management of the investee company if the company performs poorly. If company performance improves then entrepreneurs regain control and also additional cash-flow rights. Fund managers relinquish control and liquidation rights as firm performance improves, but for the most part retain their cash-flow rights.

European evidence on VC contracts is provided by Cumming (2008) and Cumming and Johan (2008). The data indicate preplanned IPOs have a statistically significant greater proportion of common equity investments, while preplanned acquisitions have a statistically significant greater mean and median number of veto and control rights.

Multivariate tests in Cumming and Johan (2008) indicated preplanned acquisitions are associated with stronger VC fund veto and control rights, a greater probability that convertible securities will be used, and a lower probability that common equity will be used. An acquisition exit typically involves the ousting of the entrepreneur from the company, or at least a reduced scope of authority from their original position as CEO of the company they founded; either way, the permanent loss of control is typically distasteful to the entrepreneur (see Petty et al., 1999, for supportive case studies; see also Black and Gilson, 1998, for a supportive qualitative theory). As such, it is expected that VC fund managers preplanning acquisition exits would negotiate for stronger control rights in case it became necessary to force an entrepreneur to concede to an acquisition. They also hypothesized that it would be in the interest of both the VC fund and entrepreneur to allocate stronger control rights to the VC fund to maximize the value of the company upon an acquisition exit.

In testing the theories pertaining to preplanned exit and contracts with the use of a variety of control variables, it is noteworthy that Cumming and Johan (2008) found that VC funds take fewer control and veto rights and use common equity in countries of German legal origin, relative to countries of Socialist, Scandinavian, and French legal origin. Cumming and Johan (2008) also found that more experienced entrepreneurs are more likely to get financed with common equity and less likely to get financed with convertible preferred equity, while more experienced VC fund managers are more likely to use convertible preferred equity and less likely to use common equity. These results strongly support recent theoretical work on bilateral moral hazard and contracting in VC finance (Casamatta, 2003; Schmidt, 2003).

Other work, with a broader sample of 39 countries in the developing and developed world, has focused more specially on law quality in influencing VC contracts. Specifically, Cumming et al. (2010) provide evidence that cross-country differences in legality, including legal origin and accounting standards, have a significant impact on the governance structure of investments in the VC industry (see also Cumming and Walz, 2010): better laws facilitate faster deal screening and deal origination, a higher probability of syndication and a lower probability of potentially harmful co-investment, and facilitate investor board representation for the investor and the use of securities that do not require periodic cash flows prior to exit.

There is very little evidence relating contracts to actual outcomes of investee companies. One exception is Cumming (2008), who uses a new dataset to produce results that relate the characteristics of VC contracts to the means by which a VC fund exits. The VC fund IPO-and-acquisition transactions span the years 1996–2005 and 11 European countries (Austria, Belgium, the Czech Republic, Denmark, France, Germany, Italy, The Netherlands, Poland, Portugal, and Switzerland). The data include detailed and confidential information on 223 investments. Of these investments, there are 187 actual dispositions (32 IPOs, 74 acquisitions, 17 buybacks, and 64 write-offs) and 36 investments that had not exited by December 2005, the time of the study. In ascertaining the role of VC fund control rights in an IPO or acquisition, Cumming (2008) controls for a number of potentially relevant factors, including investor characteristics, entrepreneurial firm characteristics, transaction-specific characteristics, market sentiment, and institutional variables.

Cumming's (2008) results, which are robust and economically and statistically significant, indicate that strong VC fund control rights are associated with a higher probability of acquisitions and a lower probability of IPOs and write-offs. The data indicate that VC fund manager board control and the right to replace the founding entrepreneur as CEO is associated with a 30 percent greater likelihood of an acquisition. Also, the probability of an acquisition exit is higher if the VC fund uses other control rights. Cumming (2008) shows that a VC fund's use of common equity is associated with weak VC control rights, in contrast to convertible debt or convertible preferred equity. Cumming (2008) finds that this use of common equity is associated with a 12 percent greater likelihood of an IPO. Write-offs are approximately 30 percent less likely when VC funds use specific veto and control rights, including the right to replace the founding entrepreneur as CEO. Cumming's (2008) empirical specifications show that these results are robust to controls for endogeneity of contracts vis-à-vis exits. The unique data also enable Cumming (2008) to show, among a wide range of other robustness checks, robustness to the exclusion of cases in which the investor had a clear exit objective at the time of contract. Further research could examine the relation between contracts and exits in other contexts.

Contractual versus Non-contractual Forms of Governance

A common theme across the literatures in economics, finance, and law is the role of formal mechanisms (e.g. actual contracts that specify ownership and control, and the law that governs the enforcement of such contracts) versus informal mechanisms (e.g. trust, reputation, and management structures) in governing relationships. Contracts are by definition incomplete, as not all eventualities can be anticipated at the time of writing a contract (see e.g. Hart and Moore, 1999). We may therefore expect informal governance mechanisms will play a strong role in relationships that are formed by contract. For example, Kanniainen and Keuschnigg (2003, 2004) and Keuschnigg (2004) show an important role for formal and informal governance mechanisms in the context of portfolio size per manager of VC funds, which actively seek to add value to entrepreneurial companies not listed on stock exchanges (see also Keuschnigg, 2003, and Keuschnigg and Nielsen, 2001, 2003a, 2003b, 2004, for related analyses of taxation, agency costs, and entrepreneurship).

At issue therefore is the comparative importance of the more formal contracts and legal settings versus other informal non-contractual governance mechanisms for governing relationships. It is useful to assess legal systems in conjunction with contracts, as the law provides enforcement mechanisms for contracts as well as a basis for the interpretation of incomplete contracts (i.e. the law provides a set of default rules).

The VC setting is an interesting one in which to analyze the role of laws and contracts versus non-contractual mechanisms in business relationships. It is widely recognized that entrepreneurship is characterized by problems of information asymmetry, illiquidity, and non-diversification, and therefore high risk in terms of both idiosyncratic and market risk. An overriding issue is thus the role of the "expert" investor. In fact, one of the primary explanations for the existence of VC fund managers is the presence of pronounced problems of adverse selection and moral hazard in financing entrepreneurial firms (Sapienza, 1992; Amit et al., 1998; Zacharakis and Shepherd, 2001, 2005; Kanniainen and Keuschnigg, 2003, 2004; Mayer et al., 2005). Inherent in VC fund managers' ability use their expertise to provide valuable advice to the investee company is the ability to interfere in business or operational decision-making of start-ups. For example, as mentioned in an earlier section, VC fund managers often substitute the founder entrepreneur with a professional manager when they feel that the firm is best served by a manager with different skill sets to further develop the firm, regardless of the sweat equity put in by the founding entrepreneur. The VC setting is thus an interesting and important context in which to explore the management of investor–investee relations (or in this case, VC–entrepreneur/entrepreneurial firm relations), since the advice may be as important as the contributed capital, and conflict as detrimental as the absence of the contributed capital (Manigart et al., 2000, 2002a, 2002b, 2006).

In the investigation of the VC fund manager–entrepreneur relationship, Cumming and Johan (2007) consider "effort" put in by the VC fund manager, or the total number of hours per month spent with the entrepreneurial company by VC fund managers. They then differentiate this VC commitment to the entrepreneurial company along two effort dimensions, which we will further refer to as the provision of "advice" and addressing "conflict". They directly measure effort exertion on advice and conflict, based on the premise that providing advice is congruent while conflict is dissonant with respect to entrepreneurial interests. In particular, "advice" is the average of the VC fund manager's rankings, on a scale 1 (lowest) to 10 (highest), of the VC fund manager's contribution to the venture in the following advising fields: strategy, marketing, issues related to financing, R&D, product development, human resources, exit strategy advice, interpersonal support, help in networking, and any other. "Conflict" is the total number of issues for which the VC fund manager reported disagreement with the entrepreneur, including strategy, marketing, issues related to financing, R&D, product development, human resources, replacement of founder, and any other. Advice is equivalent to the provision of effort or expertise by the fund manager that constructively contributes to the value of the venture. On the other hand, conflict refers to a state of affairs that calls for the VC fund manager's effort to govern and interfere with the entrepreneur's activity. Note that advice and number of hours per month are correlated (the correlation coefficient is 0.39), but not perfectly so, since hours per month spent with the venture may also involve conflict, and VC fund managers may rank advice higher without spending more time advising the company.

Cumming and Johan (2007) develop a framework for distinguishing the role of contracts (specific details on VC cash-flow and control rights) from legal settings (the law of the country in which the entrepreneurial company resides) in providing formal governance mechanisms for VC fund manager–entrepreneur relationships. Cumming and Johan (2007) further consider and compare the role of formal governance mechanisms (contracts and legal systems) versus other informal non-contractual governance mechanisms (proxied by variables such as syndication and portfolio size per manager) and variables for project risk and success potential, among other things. Prior studies have not provided a unifying look at the role of actual VC contracts and legal settings versus other non-contractual governance mechanisms, risk, and success potential on VC fund manager–entrepreneur relationships in an international context.

Cumming and Johan's (2007) data support the view that formal contracts (both cash-flow and control rights) are important for facilitating VC fund manager advice, but not for mitigating VC fund manager–entrepreneur conflicts. The legal system is important for mitigating VC fund manager–entrepreneur conflicts, but not for facilitating VC fund manager advice. The data also indicate non-contractual governance mechanisms and project characteristics are as important as formal governance mechanisms both for facilitating VC fund manager advice and mitigating VC fund manager conflict.

In particular, Cumming and Johan (2007) show that the allocation of cash-flow and control rights and the different project and environment-related risk factors affect the three effort measures in different ways. Cash-flow and control rights seem to enhance advice but do not affect the likelihood of conflict. In particular, VC funds holding a convertible claim provide on average 10 percent more advice, large VC fund ownership percentages significantly increase the amount of VC fund manager hours spent with entrepreneurs, and VC fund managers with full veto control give roughly 30 percent more advice than VC fund managers who have no veto rights.

Also, the quality of a country's legal system matters for the propensity of conflicts between entrepreneurs and their investors. Cumming and Johan's (2007) data indicate that an approximately five-point increase in legality (which is roughly the difference in the legality index between Portugal and the Netherlands) gives rise on average to one less type of VC fund manager-entrepreneur dispute (such as in regard to strategic decisions, human resource policies of the firm, and the like).

Cumming and Johan (2007) also note that many non-legal and non-contractual features are also vitally important to both VC fund manager-advising activities as well as VC fund manager–entrepreneur conflicts. For instance, when VC fund managers consider a project to be 10 percent riskier, they provide on average 25 percent more advice. Moreover, VC fund managers spend on average eight to ten hours more with their early-stage ventures and provide them with roughly 10 percent more advice. They also have on average one or two more different types of disagreements with entrepreneurs at the early stages of development. They also find that if syndicate members provide one hour more every month, the VC fund manager will also spend up to an hour more with the entrepreneur. A related result in their paper is that VC fund managers give more advice to, and disagree less with, more experienced entrepreneurs. This implies that VC fund managers and entrepreneurs tend to have complementary skills or expertise, consistent with many theoretical models of VC financing (Cestone, 2001; Casamatta, 2003; Repullo and Suarez, 2004).

Cumming and Johan's evidence also indicates that VC funds that have more investments per number of managers tend to contribute less, as expected (Kanniainen and Keuschnigg, 2003, 2004; Keuschnigg, 2004; Cumming, 2006a). In their sample, VC funds with one extra entrepreneurial company per fund manager in their portfolio provided on average two to three hours less support per month, 20 percent less advice, and had 0.2 to 0.3 fewer disagreements with entrepreneurs. They also find a positive relationship between VC fund managers' involvement and successful exits, but the direction of causality in this context is highly ambiguous.

Overall, the data are consistent with the view that both formal contracts and legal systems are important to managing VC fund manager–entrepreneur relationships. But contracts and laws operate alongside other informal governance mechanisms such as syndication and portfolio size, as well as risk factors and success potential.

Conclusion

Financial contracting is critical to governance in VC. Financial contracts are material to the allocation of risks, incentives, and rewards for investors and investees alike. Financial contracts have a significant relationship with actual investment outcomes and success. We reviewed two main types of contracts in this chapter: contracts between VC funds and their institutional investors and, second, between VC funds and their investee companies. Limited partnership agreements define the covenants and compensation terms for VC investors. We reviewed evidence in this chapter that limited partnership contracts related to market conditions and fund manager characteristics, and how these contracts differ across countries.

Regarding contracts between VC funds and their investee companies, we examined in this chapter the cash-flow and control rights that are typically assigned in venture capital with investee companies, and when fund managers demand more contractual rights. We showed that different contractual rights assigned to different parties influence the effort provided by the investor(s). Also, we showed the ways different financial contracts are related to the success of VC investments.

By considering VC contracting in an international setting, one gains an understanding of why VC markets differ with respect to fund governance, investee company governance, and investee company performance.

By considering international datasets, and not data from just one country such as the US, we are able to gain a significant amount of insight into how VC funds operate in relation to their legal and institutional environment. It is the authors' hope that this chapter will not only provide an understanding of how VC funds operate through financial contracts, but also that it will inspire further empirical work in the field so that we may better understand the nature and evolution of VC markets in years to come.

Notes

1. For example, for funds in Europe, see <http://www.evca.com>.
2. Australia, for example, has only allowed limited partnerships since 2003; prior to that time funds were set up as trusts, but functionally these trusts involved rights and responsibilities that mimicked the limited partnership structure; see Cumming et al. (2005).
3. Agency costs may be mitigated but generally can never be eliminated. See, generally, Farmer and Winter (1986); see also e.g. Jensen (2001, 2004), Kaiser and Stouraitis (2001), Citron et al. (2003), Pawline and Renneboog (2005), and Peasnell et al. (2005) for specific contexts.

4. Note, however, in some cases funds are set up in a way that enables such restrictions to be waived upon approval of all the investors.
5. Waiver of these covenants may also be subject to approval of the Fund's Board of Advisors, which usually comprises institutional fund investors.
6. This is similar to the co-investment restriction in category 1, but where the category 1 restriction is against another fund managed by the fund manager investing in the fund, this restriction in category 3 is against the fund itself investing in another fund's (usually an earlier fund) portfolio company, also managed by the fund manager.
7. In category 2, we identified a similar covenant on sale of fund interests by fund managers.
8. This restriction on fundraising is typically either for a set period of time or a hurdle rate.
9. They are also referred to as tax pass-through entities. As a recent example, it has been recently reported that a private investment fund which made a US$1.2 billion profit from an investment in South Korea did not pay any taxes on the profit in that country as the transaction was conducted through an offshore fund set up in Labuan, Malaysia. Another fund reportedly made a US$1 billion tax-free profit in that same country. See "South Korean Tax Probe into Foreign Private Equity Funds," *Financial Times*, April 16–17, 2005: 2.

References

AMIT, R., BRANDER, J., and ZOTT, C. (1998). "Why Do Venture Capital Firms Exist? Theory and Canadian Evidence," *Journal of Business Venturing*, 13: 441–548.

BASCHA, A., and WALZ, U. (2007). "Financing Practices in the German Venture Capital industry: An Empirical Assessment," in G. N. Gregoriou, M. Kooli, and R. Kraeussl (eds.), *Venture Capital in Europe*. North Holland: Elsevier, ch. 15.

BLACK, B., and GILSON, R. (1998). "Venture Capital and the Structure of Capital Markets: Banks versus Stock Markets," *Journal of Financial Economics*, 47: 243–77.

CASAMATTA, C. (2003). "Financing and Advising: Optimal Financial Contracts with Venture Capitalists," *Journal of Finance*, 58: 2059–86.

CESTONE, G. (2001). "Venture Capital Meets Contract Theory: Risky Claims or Formal Control?" Working Paper, University of Toulouse and Institut d'Anàlisi Economica, Barcelona.

CITRON, D., WRIGHT, M., BALL, R., and RIPPINGTON, F. (2003). "Secured Creditor Recovery Rates from Management Buyouts in Distress," *European Financial Management*, 9: 141–62.

CUMMING, D. J. (2005a). "Agency Costs, institutions, Learning and Taxation in Venture Capital Contracting," *Journal of Business Venturing*, 20: 573–622.

—— (2005b). "Capital Structure in Venture Finance," *Journal of Corporate Finance*, 11: 550–85.

—— (2006a). "The Determinants of Venture Capital Portfolio Size: Empirical Evidence," *Journal of Business*, 79, 1083–126.

—— (2006b). "Adverse Selection and Capital Structure: Evidence from Venture Capital," *Entrepreneurship Theory and Practice*, 30: 155–84.

—— (2008). "Contracts and Exits in Venture Capital Finance," *Review of Financial Studies*, 21:1947–82.

—— FLEMING, G., and SCHWIENBACHER, A. (2005). "Liquidity Risk and Venture Finance," *Financial Management*, 34: 77–105.

—— —— —— (2009). "Style Drift in Private Equity," *Journal of Business Finance and Accounting*, 365(6): 645–78.

Cumming, D. J., and Johan, S. A. (2006). "Is it the Law or the Lawyers? Investment Covenants around the World," *European Financial Management*, 12: 553–74.
—— —— (2007). "Advice and Monitoring in Venture Capital Finance," *Financial Markets and Portfolio Management*, 21: 3–43.
—— —— (2008). "Preplanned Exit Strategies in Venture Capital," *European Economic Review*, 52: 1209–41.
—— —— (2009). *Venture Capital and Private Equity Contracting: An International Perspective*. Burlington, MA: Elsevier Science Academic Press.
—— and Walz, U. (2010). "Private Equity Returns and Disclosure around the World," *Journal of international Business Studies*, 414: 727–54.
—— Schmidt, D., and Walz, U. (2010). "Legality and Venture Capital Governance around the World," *Journal of Business Venturing*, 25: 54–72.
Farmer, R. E. A., and Winter, R. A. (1986). "The Role of Options in the Resolution of Agency Problems," *Journal of Finance*, 41: 1157–70.
Gilson, R. J., and Schizer, D. (2003). "Venture Capital Structure: A Tax Explanation for Convertible Preferred Stock," *Harvard Law Review*, 116: 875–916.
Gompers, P. A. (1998). "Ownership and Control in Entrepreneurial Firms: An Examination of Convertible Securities in Venture Capital investments," Harvard University Working Paper.
—— and Lerner, J. (1996). "The Use of Covenants: An Empirical Analysis of Venture Capital Partnership Agreements," *Journal of Law and Economics*, 39: 463–98.
—— —— (1999). *The Venture Capital Cycle*. Cambridge, MA: MIT Press.
Hart, O., and Moore, J. (1999). "Foundations of Incomplete Contracts," *Review of Economics Studies*, 66: 115–38.
Hege, U., Palomino, F., and Schwienbacher, A. (2009). "Venture Capital Performance: The Disparity between Europe and the United States," *Revue Finance*, 30: 1: 7–50.
Isaksson, A., Cornelius, B., Landström, H., and Junghagen, S. (2004). "Institutional Theory and Contracting in Venture Capital: The Swedish Experience," *Venture Capital: An International Journal of Entrepreneurial Finance*, 6: 47–71.
Jensen, M. (2001). "Value Maximization, Stakeholder Theory, and the Corporate Objective Function," *European Financial Management*, 7: 297–318.
—— (2004). "The Agency Costs of Overvalued Equity and the Current State of Corporate Finance," *European Financial Management*, 10: 549–66.
Johan, S., and Najar, D. (2010). "The Role of Law, Corruption and Culture in Investment Fund Manager Fees," *Journal of Business Ethics*, 95: 147–72.
Kaiser, K. N. J., and Stouraitis, A. (2001). "Agency Costs, and Strategic Considerations behind Sell-offs: The UK Evidence," *European Financial Management*, 7: 319–50.
Kanniainen, V., and Keuschnigg, C. (2003). "The Optimal Portfolio of Start-Up Firms in Venture Capital Finance," *Journal of Corporate Finance*, 9: 521–34.
—— —— (2004). "Start-Up Investment with Scarce Venture Capital Support," *Journal of Banking and Finance*, 28: 1935–59.
Kaplan, S., and Strömberg, P. (2003). "Financial Contracting Theory Meets the Real World: An Empirical Analysis of Venture Capital Contracts," *Review of Economic Studies*, 70: 281–315.
—— Frederic, M., and Strömberg, P. (2007). "How Do Legal Differences and Experience Affect Financial Contracts?" *Journal of Financial Intermediation*, 16: 273–311.
Keuschnigg, C. (2003). "Public Policy and Venture Capital Backed Innovation," Working Paper No. 2003-09, University of St Gallen.

—— (2004). "Taxation of a Venture Capitalist with a Portfolio of Firms," *Oxford Economic Papers*, 56: 285–306.

—— and NIELSEN, S. B. (2001). "Public Policy for Venture Capital," *International Tax and Public Finance*, 8: 557–72.

—— —— (2003a). "Tax Policy, Venture Capital and Entrepreneurship," *Journal of Public Economics*, 87: 175–203.

—— —— (2003b). "Progressive Taxation, Moral Hazard, and Entrepreneurship," *Journal of Public Economic Theory*, 6: 471–490.

—— —— (2004). "Start-Ups, Venture Capitalists, and the Capital Gains Tax," *Journal of Public Economics*, 88: 1011–42.

LERNER, J., and SCHOAR, A. (2005). "Does Legal Enforcement Affect Financial Transactions? The Contractual Channel in Private Equity," *Quarterly Journal of Economics*, 120: 223–46.

MANIGART, S., DEWAELE, K., WRIGHT, M., et al. (2000). "Venture Capital, Investment Appraisal, and Accounting Information: A Comparative Study of the US, UK, France, Belgium and Holland," *European Financial Management*, 6: 380–404.

—— —— —— et al. (2002a). "The Determinants of the Required Returns in Venture Capital investments: A Five-Country Study," *Journal of Business Venturing*, 17: 291–312.

—— —— —— et al. (2002b). "The Impact of Trust on Private Equity Contracts," Working Paper, Vlerick Leuven Gent Management School.

—— LOCKETT, A., MEULEMAN, M., et al. (2006). "Venture Capitalists' Decision to Syndicate," *Entrepreneurship Theory and Practice*, 30: 131–53.

MAYER, C., SCHOORS, K., and YAFEH, Y. (2005). "Sources of Funds and Investment Strategies of VC Funds: Evidence from Germany, Isreal, Japan and the UK," *Journal of Corporate Finance*, 11: 586–608.

METRICK, A., and YASUDA, A. (2009). "The Economics of Private Equity Funds," *Review of Financial Studies*, 236: 2303–41.

PARHANKANGAS, A., LANDSTRÖM, H., and SMITH, G. D. (2005). "Experience, Contractual Covenants and Venture Capitalists: Responses to Unmet Expectations," *Venture Capital: An International Journal of Entrepreneurial Finance*, 7: 297–318.

PAWLINE, G., and RENNEBOOG, L. (2005). "Is Investment-Cash Flow Sensitivity Caused by Agency Costs or Asymmetric information? Evidence from the UK," *European Financial Management*, 11: 483–514.

PEASNELL, K. V., POPE, P. F., and YOUNG, S. (2005). "Managerial Ownership and the Demand for Outside Directors," *European Financial Management*, 11: 231–50.

PETTY, J. W., MARTIN, J. D., and KENSINGER, J. W. (1999). *Harvesting Investments in Private Companies*. Morristown, NJ: Financial Services Research Foundation, inc.

REPULLO, R., and SUAREZ, J. (2004). "Venture Capital Finance: A Security Design Approach," *Review of Finance*, 8(1): 75–108.

SAHLMAN, W. A. (1990). "The Structure and Governance of Venture Capital Organizations," *Journal of Financial Economics*, 27: 473–521.

SANDLER, D. (2001). "The Tax Treatment of Employee Stock Options: Generous to a Fault," *Canadian Tax Journal*, 49: 259–302.

SAPIENZA, H. (1992). "When do Venture Capitalists Add Value?" *Journal of Business Venturing*, 7: 9–27.

SCHMIDT, K. M. (2003). "Convertible Securities and Venture Capital Finance," *Journal of Finance*, 58(3): 1139–66.

SCHWIENBACHER, A. (2008). "Venture Capital investment Practices in Europe and in the United States," *Financial Markets and Portfolio Management*, 22(3): 195–217.

SONGTAO, L. (2001). "Venture Capital Development in Taiwan," *Asia and Pacific Economics*, 3.

WRIGHT, M., and LOCKETT, A. (2003). "The Structure and Management of Alliances: Syndication in the Venture Capital Industry," *Journal of Management Studies*, 40(8): 2073–102.

—— PRUTHI, S., and LOCKETT, A. (2005). "International Venture Capital Research: From Cross-Country Comparisons to Crossing Borders," *International Journal of Management Reviews*, 7(3): 135–65.

ZACHARAKIS, A. L., and SHEPHERD, D. A. (2001). "The Nature of Information and Venture Capitalists' Overconfidence," *Journal of Business Venturing*, 16: 311–32.

—— —— (2005). "A Non-additive Decision-Aid for Venture Capitalists' Investment Decisions," *European Journal of Operational Research*, 162(3): 673–89.

CHAPTER 24

PRIVATE EQUITY, LEVERAGED BUYOUTS, AND CORPORATE GOVERNANCE

MIKE WRIGHT, DONALD S. SIEGEL, MIGUEL MEULEMAN, AND KEVIN AMESS

INTRODUCTION

LEVERAGED buyout transactions with private equity (PE) backing have become a significant phenomenon within the market for corporate control. Kaplan and Strömberg (2009) report 17,171 transactions from January 1970 to June 2007. Although Kaplan and Strömberg (2009) trace LBO transactions back to 1970, and buyout deals were identifiable decades earlier (Wright et al., 2000b), it is generally accepted that the LBO market became properly established in the US during the early 1980s. Later in the 1980s, an LBO market became established in the UK. The nominal value of LBO deals in the UK reached a peak in 2007 of £46.5 billion, which represented about 63 percent of total activity in the UK market for corporate control (CMBOR, 2010). PE-backed transactions represented about 48 percent of the total value of UK LBOs (CMBOR, 2010). An increasing number and value of transactions is being conducted around the world. Europe, for instance, saw a record level of transactions summing to €177.2 billion in 2007, €169.2 billion of which was PE backed (CMBOR, 2010).

The financial crisis of 2008 saw an end to the record levels of LBO activity outlined above. Indeed, the crisis brought with it some rare problems for LBO practitioners. First, it has become more difficult to gain access to credit during a period where financial institutions were taking stock of losses and were wary of taking risks in their lending. Second, it has become more challenging for PE firms to raise funds for their buyout activities during a time when investors err toward lower risk and more liquid investments.

Notwithstanding the problems outlined above, the LBO market, like that for mergers and acquisitions, has been through previous cycles (Toms and Wright, 2005). Therefore, we anticipate that LBOs and PE backing of such transactions will continue to be significant features of the market for corporate control.

Although the LBO governance structure is yet to eclipse the public corporation, as predicted by Jensen (1989), LBOs and PE are likely to be persistent features of the corporate restructuring landscape. There is now an extensive academic literature examining the LBO corporate governance structure. Nevertheless, among the wider public there is still a lack of understanding of LBO transactions, the LBO governance structure, and the role of PE firms. Furthermore, increased LBO activity has been accompanied by increased media, union, and political criticism. These criticisms typically reject the notion of LBOs and PE involvement improving corporate governance and providing incentives to improve strategic decision-making and operational performance. Rather, they suggest that LBOs create financial rewards for their investors by asset stripping, asset flipping (reselling assets within short periods of time), introducing restructuring that negatively impacts on employment and employee remuneration, and using (excessive) leverage to reduce tax charges.

Similar criticisms were also raised during the first wave of PE-backed buyouts in the 1980s (e.g. Jones and Hunt, 1991); however, there is probably greater attention in the second wave due to the LBO of household names, such as Alliance Boots, the AA, and Debenhams in the UK. Increased scrutiny of the industry has resulted in greater regulation (Walker, 2007; Commission of the European Communities, 2009). Yet, concerns remain, with successful buyouts that subsequently experienced trading difficulties receiving considerable media and union criticism many years after PE involvement has ceased (see e.g. the example of the Southern Cross Care Home group in the UK in June 2011).

In light of this controversy, we seek to enhance understanding of LBOs and private equity by providing a review of theory relating to private equity and of the evidence on its impact. Our review encompasses a wide range of articles in finance, economics, entrepreneurship, strategy, and human resource management (HRM). First we outline theoretical perspectives relating to why private equity governance may be expected to have positive or negative effects on financial, economic, and social performance. Second, we review the relevant empirical evidence.

Private Equity in Theory

The LBO and Private Equity Involvement

The principal investment vehicle for PE firms is the LBO. The key features of an LBO and its governance structure are as follows. First, the LBO transaction results in senior managers involved in the transaction holding a significant equity stake in the firm. Second, in order to facilitate the LBO transaction, debt is secured against the target firm's assets and future cash flows. Thus, the LBO transaction increases firm leverage. Finally, in about 50 percent of transactions in the UK, specialist PE firms raise cash to invest in and to facilitate the LBO transaction. In larger transactions, the PE firm is likely to be the majority equity holder. Post-buyout, the PE firm typically has board representation and takes an active involvement in strategic decisions and the monitoring of firm and management performance. See, for example, Jensen (1986), Thompson and Wright (1995), and Gilligan and Wright (2010).

The equity funding for the deal will normally be provided by a PE firm. In the US and UK, the fund is usually set up as a limited partnership with funding provided from pension funds, investment banks, insurance companies, wealthy individuals, and the fund's managers. In the short term, the PE firm generates cash from its involvement by charging management fees to its fund investors and by receiving dividends from the profits of firms it has invested in. However, in the medium term, the main source of return will be the exit value generated. Exit tends to take place on average about five years after the buyout (Wright, Burrows, et al., 2007). In addition, exit occurs in a variety of ways, for example, trade sale, flotation via an initial public offering (IPO) or re-IPO if the buyout took a publicly quoted firm private, a secondary buyout, a leveraged recapitalization, or bankruptcy.

The LBO Governance Structure: Aligning Incentives

It is well recognized in the corporate governance literature that agency problems arise when ownership and control are separate, with owners and managers optimizing different objective functions. Typically, owners are assumed to be maximizing firms' current profit stream, i.e. maximizing the value of the firm. Managers, however, are considered to be maximizing an objective function that includes: power, prestige, firm size, and the consumption of perquisites. In the presence of weak corporate governance mechanisms (e.g. a weak board of directors), managers can take actions seeking to maximize their utility, but, in doing so, do not maximize profits (Marris, 1964; Williamson, 1964; Jensen and Meckling, 1976; Jensen, 1986; Hart, 1995).

The corporate governance problem combined with "free cash flow" (FCF) is also problematic. FCF is the excess of that required to fund all projects with a positive net present value (Jensen, 1986). Jensen argues that, when managers and owners are optimizing different objective functions, there can be a conflict between managers and owners over how to use the FCF. Given that all profitable projects have been funded, Jensen (1986) argues that the FCF should be distributed between the firm's owners; however, this might not occur due to weak corporate governance. Indeed, the FCF could be used suboptimally in the pursuit of managerial objectives.

The LBO transaction implants a governance structure that attenuates managers' non-profit-maximizing behavior. The three key features of an LBO, outlined above, are important elements in aligning the objectives of owners and managers and are discussed in turn.

Management Equity Holdings

The significant ownership stake held by managers transforms them into owner-managers, which provides them with the financial incentives to pursue efficiency gains (Phan and Hill, 1995). Jensen and Meckling (1976) show that when an owner-manager owns 100 percent of a firm, if the manager decides to consume $1 of perquisites, he reduces the value of the firm by $1, and vice versa. So the owner-manager bears the total cost of not maximizing the value of the firm. When the owner-manager sells a proportion $(1 - \alpha)$ of the firm to outside equity holders, the owner-manager bears the cost $\alpha\$1$ for each dollar of perquisites consumed. The value of the firm is lower when the owner-manager's equity stake is diluted. It therefore follows that if the Jensen and Meckling (1976) analysis is reversed and the owner-manager's equity stake is significantly increased, as in the case of an LBO, the owner-manager has a greater financial incentive to reduce non-value-maximizing behavior.

PE firms recognize the importance of management equity holdings providing high-powered incentives. This is why PE firms, when structuring the post-buyout ownership of a firm, ensure that senior management are financially motivated (Gilligan and Wright, 2010).

Debt Bonding

The debt used to facilitate an LBO transaction results in a large-scale swap of debt for equity (Thompson and Wright, 1995). This debt acts as an important disciplinary device on managerial behavior. Debt has a fixed interest obligation, which means that managers are bonded to servicing debt using future cash flows. Failure to fulfill the fixed interest obligation of debt can lead to financial distress and ultimately bankruptcy. Jensen (1986) argues that debt is an important disciplinary device because FCF, which was used suboptimally in the pre-buyout firm, can be used to service debt in the post-buyout firm. Indeed, Thompson and Wright (1989) show that debt bonding in the context of an LBO is instrumental in reducing the consumption of managerial "perks," which raises the value of the firm. Furthermore, their analysis suggests that a purely debt-financed LBO addresses agency costs better than a deal using a combination of debt and outside equity.

Not only does debt serve as a monitor on managerial behavior, but it provides managers with the motivation to generate future cash flows in order to service the debt (Thompson et al., 1992). In addition, debt serves as a credible signal for the commitment of cash-generating behavior (Arzac, 1992). Therefore, it serves as a motivating factor in making the post-buyout firm more efficient (Jensen, 1986). Indeed, Wright et al. (1992) find a high incidence of tightening of working capital control by reducing debtor days and, to a slightly lesser extent, extending creditor days.

Monitoring by Private Equity Firms

Listed corporations have been criticized for having a weak board of directors due to a lack of financial incentives (Hart, 1995). This contrasts sharply with the board after an LBO. PE firms with significant, concentrated ownership have the financial incentive and mechanisms to monitor managers through board membership and detailed reporting requirements. Such arrangements go beyond those available to institutional investors in listed corporations. This involvement by PE firms may entail both close monitoring of financial progress against budgets, but also adding value through provision of strategic advice and contacts to enable new markets to be accessed. When portfolio firms underperform or enter distress, PE firms may engage in timely intervention that enables problems to be resolved through restructuring without the company going into formal insolvency (Demiroglu and James, 2009).

Entrepreneurship and Governance

Agency theory has been the dominant theoretical paradigm through which LBOs and PE firm involvement in governance have been understood. Using agency theory, LBOs are viewed as reducing the inefficiencies associated with weak corporate governance within the pre-buyout firm. More recently, PE firms have attracted theoretical attention from a strategic entrepreneurship perspective. From this perspective, PE firms not only provide finance and monitoring functions, but also provide complementary resources and capabilities to those that reside in the LBO target.

It is well recognized in the strategic management literature that, if firms are to have a competitive advantage, they need to have superior resources to their rivals (Peteraf, 1993). Whilst the resource-based view of the firm emphasizes "isolating mechanisms" and the difficulty in transferring resources and capabilities between firms in order to sustain competitive advantage (Barney, 1991; Peteraf, 1993), PE firms target firms for LBOs in order to fill resource and capability gaps in those firms. Such capabilities might be of an entrepreneurial nature and PE firms can learn from previous experience in order to create distinctive organizational capabilities. Evidence suggests that the scope for making these improvements may be greater in divisional buyouts than in buyouts involving family and in secondary buyouts (Meuleman et al., 2009).

The heterogeneity of buyout sources suggests there may be opportunities for upside value creation that are not simply due to better control and incentives, but which may require different cognitive skills (Wright, Hoskisson, et al., 2000). There may also be opportunities for buyouts where pre-ownership agency problems are not significant (Wright et al., 2001). A strategic entrepreneurship perspective complements an agency approach in helping explain value creation through the exploitation of entrepreneurial opportunities (Wright, Hoskisson, et al., 2000; Meuleman et al., 2009). A strategic entrepreneurship perspective is concerned with the coordination of entrepreneurial opportunities with the resources and capabilities needed to exploit those opportunities, which may include the superior governance abilities of private equity firms (Barney et al., 2001).

Heterogeneity of LBO Types

The classic agency theory of LBOs has generally been posited in the context of "public-to-private" transactions (henceforth, PTPs). Nevertheless, the agency perspective combined with an entrepreneurial perspective offer insights into the LBO of firms that are not publicly listed. Below we examine LBO types.

Public-to-private

PTPs may arise in response to the threat of hostile takeover. This has implications for the governance structures of firms since it implies that the threat is a substitute for ineffective boards. The threat of a hostile, disciplinary takeover substitutes for weak governance and poor incentive alignment (Jensen, 1986; Lehn and Poulsen, 1989).

Following the introduction of corporate governance regulations requiring significant non-executive director representation, as in the UK's Combined Code of Best Practice (1998, 2003), firms going private would have fewer non-executive directors and more duality than firms subject to traditional acquisitions by existing listed corporations. Evidence supports this contention (Weir et al., 2005a; Weir and Wright, 2006). UK PTPs have lower valuations than traditional acquisitions of listed corporations by other corporations, indicating managerial private information, and greater board ownership, suggesting that outside bidders have been deterred from bidding for the firms because of the potential difficulties involved in dealing with significant board ownership. In contrast, Australian PTP evidence indicates that insider ownership is not significantly higher in PTPs than for traditional acquisitions of listed corporations (Evans et al., 2005). Cornelli and Karakas (2008) find no significant change in board size from pre- to post-PTP. Board representation by PE firms changes according to PE firm style and anticipated challenges of the investment.

Adoption of the recommendations of the Combined Code (2003) in the UK has coincided with an increase in both friendly takeovers and PTPs. This suggests that the market for corporate control and internal governance mechanisms are complements rather than substitutes, as indicated by the higher board ownership and duality of CEO and Chair in UK PTPs, but not lower proportions of outside directors and pressure from the market for corporate control (Weir and Wright, 2006).

Irrevocable commitments by existing shareholders are used extensively in PTP transactions, reducing the costs associated with a failed bid (Wright, Weir, et al., 2007). The initial commitment ensures that, without any higher alternative bid, the agreement to sell the share becomes binding. PE firms can improve the chances of success in negotiating a buyout of a listed corporation by seeking irrevocable commitments from significant shareholders to accept the bidder's bid before the offer is made public. The announcement of substantial irrevocable commitments may make other potential bidders less likely to enter the contest with an alternative bid. Gaining these commitments by reputable PE firms sends a signal to other non-committed shareholders that the deal is an attractive one.

Managers of listed corporations with a significant equity stake may be able to resist hostile pressure for takeover by another corporation. These businesses may be attractive PTP candidates, however, as the private equity firms will likely seek to provide financial support for profitable entrepreneurial initiatives from management and also have the specialist expertise and contractual mechanisms to monitor and add value to them (Wright and Robbie, 1998). This might be attractive to managers unable to realize business opportunities if there are financial constraints.

Divisional LBOs

The strategic entrepreneurship perspective is easily extended to divisions of large, diversified organizations. Where the diversified corporation's existing governance structure truncates divisional managerial incentives and rewards, the opportunity for upside gains from a buyout may exist (Wright et al., 1991).

In multidivisional organizations, investment funds may not be allocated to divisions on the basis of rates of return but as a result of internal power dynamics (Wright and Thompson, 1987). Also, if a division is peripheral to the core activities of a parent company, managers might encounter investment restrictions from headquarters (Wright et al., 2001). These problems may be eased after the buyout as the PE provider becomes an "active investor" seeking profitable innovation and business development. A buyout creates entrepreneurial incentives and discretionary power for the new management team to decide what is best for the business (Wright, Hoskisson, et al., 2000, 2001; Meuleman et al., 2009).

Secondary LBOs

Secondary buyouts provide a means to continue the buyout organizational form, albeit with a different set of investors. In contrast to managers in divisions of larger corporations, increased managerial equity stakes and loosened controls by private equity firms, or the introduction of more skilled PE firms, may facilitate improved performance through pursuit of growth opportunities.

Family LBOs

In private and family firms there is typically no separation of ownership and control prior to the buyout (Howorth et al., 2004). Thus, there is less scope for improvements from improved control mechanisms (Chrisman et al., 2004). In family firms, owner-managers with substantial equity stakes have incentives to seek out profitable opportunities and, as peak-tier coordinators, have the flexibility to implement new opportunities they identify (Howorth et al., 2004). The prospects for gains arising from resolving any agency problems may be limited to those cases where ownership was dispersed before the buyout (Howorth et al., 2004).

LBO targets

When managers pursue growth strategies that are not consistent with value-maximizing behavior, this can lead to overdiversification. Overdiversified firms often underperform, particularly when the assets held within one firm are not complementary (Palich et al., 2000). Overdiversification and subsequent underperformance is a consequence of weak corporate governance. A distinguishing feature of LBOs financed by private equity is that PE firms choose LBO targets that have separable assets and businesses that can be sold (Seth and Easterwood, 1993). Consequently, private equity firms, by targeting overdiversified firms with assets that can be divested, are targeting firms with weak corporate governance.

Heterogeneity of Private Equity Firms

Although most attention focuses upon independent PE firms that raise limited life closed-end funds, PE firms have different investment time horizons and objectives. These include public sector PE firms, as well as captive PE firms that are part of banks and insurance corporations. Some PE firms associated with banks and insurance companies are semi-captive in the sense that they raise funds both from their parent and through limited life funds. Further, some PE firms are listed on stock markets. Among all these categories, PE firms vary in terms of the extent to which their business model involves more or less active monitoring or adding value to portfolio companies. PE firms are also heterogeneous, in terms of their experience, successful or otherwise, which may influence their ability to learn from prior deals in order to add more value in subsequent deals.

Variations in the types of equity and debt instruments available allow for different approaches to governance in deals. Some PE firms may make use of extensive performance-contingent remuneration contracts in relation to management's equity stakes, while others eschew such variable approaches. Leverage used may also take different forms, associated with different governance elements. For example, deals with standard secured repayment loans with accompanying covenants provide for both early warning signals of impending problems, while allowing for flexibility in the application of covenants (Citron et al., 1997, 2003). On the other hand, debt in the form of quoted bonds may have fewer covenants but allow for less flexible renegotiation if performance is below expectations.

THE IMPACTS OF PRIVATE EQUITY BUYOUTS

In this section we review the evidence in relation to stockholder returns on the announcement of a public-to-private buyout; the governance and other drivers of those returns; the extent and nature of the impact of private equity and buyouts on firm performance; transfers from other stakeholders; the longevity of effects; and the extent and nature of distress and failure in recession.

Impact on Stockholder Returns and Drivers of PTPs

There is substantial evidence of significant announcement effects of PTPs (see e.g. Renneboog et al., 2007). These significant increases in stock prices have been found in different institutional contexts, including the US, UK, continental Europe, and Australia (Cumming et al., 2007). However, the magnitude of announcement effects seems to be lower in Europe (Andres et al., 2007) and Asia (Lee, 2009) than in the US or UK (Renneboog et al., 2007). Explanations of PTP transactions in the US may not hold in Europe and Asia. First, there is heterogeneity between the three continents in terms of capital market development and regulation, legal and corporate governance frameworks, tax benefits, the use of debt in funding LBOs. Second, the ownership structure of listed corporations differs, with many continental European corporations, in contrast to the UK and the US, having dominant family shareholders (Geranio and Zanotti, 2012), which is also the case in several Asian countries including Japan (Wright et al., 2003). This also affects the functioning of the market for corporate control, which is less active. Third, although there has been some development of corporate governance codes, protection of minority shareholders is generally weaker in continental Europe and Asia. These differences suggest that PTPs in continental Europe and Asia may have different determinants, which impact on the wealth gains that are observed. We return to this point in the next section in the context of PE firms' rationales and actions in investing in PTPs.

Evidence suggests that, as in more traditional acquisitions, pre-buyout shareholders secure a higher price for their stock if outside acquirers compete for control with the proposed management buyout (MBO) (Easterwood et al., 1994). However, PE firms often make use of irrevocable commitments (Wright, Burrows, et al., 2007) to enhance their chances of success in negotiating a takeover of a listed corporation by persuading significant shareholders to accept their bid before it is made public.

Various studies of PTPs have examined the relative importance of different antecedents to the buyout and find, inter alia, that undervaluation is an important factor (Renneboog et al., 2007). However, in continental Europe, while undervaluation is important, deals promoted by family owners register higher abnormal returns (Geranio and Zanotti, 2012).

Evidence indicates that firms involved in PTP LBOs have significantly higher managerial share ownership than those involved in traditional acquisitions of listed corporations (Maupin, 1987; Halpern et al., 1999). In addition, firms going private had higher board and CEO ownership than firms remaining public (Weir et al., 2005a), but PE firms were more likely to be involved when board ownership was lower (Weir, Wright, et al., 2008).

Achleitner et al. (2010) also find that, since corporate control and ownership in continental Europe tend to be highly concentrated, the incentives of incumbent large shareholders to monitor management and the private benefits of control the latter may derive from the firm affect the likelihood of the firm being taken over by a private equity investor.

The evidence relating to FCF is, at best, mixed. With respect to the first wave of private equity buyouts, Lehn and Poulsen (1989) found that firms going private had higher FCFs than firms that remained quoted. However, other evidence suggests that FCF has no impact on the decision to go private (Opler and Titman, 1993; Halpern et al., 1999; Weir et al., 2005a).

Renneboog et al. (2007), considering the second private equity wave from the late 1990s, find that incentive realignment is one of the main sources of shareholder gains on the announcement of a PTP. They find no support for the FCF argument. In addition, Weir et al. (2005b) also find that an expected reduction of FCF does not determine the premiums.

Early US evidence suggests MBOs experienced significantly more takeover pressure prior to the MBO (Singh, 1990; Halpern et al., 1999). More recently, however, Weir et al. (2005b) and Renneboog et al. (2007) find that a defensive reaction against a takeover was not a significant explanation for UK PTPs.

There is some debate about the role of financial distress as an indicator of the attractiveness of a target corporation for PE firms, with Opler and Titman (1993) in the US arguing that PE firms are deterred from taking companies private that show signs of distress because firm failure is more likely following a buyout, due to the higher debt burden associated with the transaction.

Sudarsanam et al. (2011) challenge this view, suggesting that PE firms are not deterred by the risk of financial distress but consider it a value-creating opportunity due to their specialist governance skills. They find that UK PTPs have significantly higher default probability than non-acquired firms that remain public. Sudarsanam et al. (2011) also argue that better governance of the target pre-PTP is associated with lower bankruptcy risk where the PE investor inherits a strong governance structure, as manifested by the presence of independent boards. However, post-buyout, they find that those firms showing signs of distress before buyout are more likely to fail subsequently, raising questions about the ability of private equity governance structures to turn around troubled former stock market-listed corporations.

Impact on Performance

There is now a substantial body of empirical evidence on the performance effects of buyouts (recent comprehensive reviews are available in Cumming et al., 2007, and Kaplan and Strömberg, 2009).

A consistent feature of the post-buyout performance literature is that performance gains are reported by academic research, for example, early accounting data studies in the US by Kaplan (1989), Smith (1990), and Smart and Waldfogel (1994) and the later studies by Cressy et al. (2007) in the UK and in France by Boucly et al. (2011) and Gaspar (2009); and total factor productivity studies by Lichtenberg and Siegel (1990), Wright, Wilson, and Robbie (1996a), Amess (2002, 2003), Harris et al. (2005), and Davis et al.

(2009). In sum, a strong consensus has emerged, across different methodologies, measures, countries, and time periods, that leveraged buyouts, and especially management buyouts, enhance performance and have a salient effect on work practices.

More recent literature has also identified the differential effects of buyouts from different vendor sources. Desbrières and Schatt (2002) find that performance gains are especially strong for PTPs and divisional buyouts, but less so for buyouts of family firms and Meuleman et al. (2009) report that divisional buyouts have significantly greater growth than family or secondary buyouts, but not in terms of profitability. Jelic and Wright (2011) find significant improvements in output for PE-backed buyouts exiting by IPO but inconclusive results regarding profitability and efficiency. In the same study they find that the performance of secondary MBOs declines during the first buyout, but in the second buy-out performance stabilizes until year 3, after which profitability and efficiency fall while employment increases.

PTP buyouts in the first wave particularly seem to achieve performance improvements through strategies of cost and capital expenditure reductions and refocusing through divestment of unwanted parts (Liebeskind et al., 1992; Long and Ravenscraft, 1993; Seth and Easterwood, 1993; Smart and Waldfogel, 1994; Wiersema and Liebeskind, 1995; Weir, Jones, et al., 2008; Weir, Wright, et al., 2008). There is some evidence, however, that the gains in operating performance of PE-backed PTPs are less strong than in the first wave (Guo et al., 2011, in the US, and Weir, Jones, et al., 2008, in the UK).

Evidence from divisional and family firm buyouts indicates increases in corporate entrepreneurship, including new product development, better use of research and development, and increased patent citations (Bull, 1989; Green, 1992; Wright et al., 1992; Zahra, 1995; Lerner et al., 2008). Ughetto (2010) examines the number of patents granted by the EPO and the likelihood of filing at least one successful patent application in a sample of European buyouts, finding strong support that the innovation activity of portfolio firms is affected by the characteristics of firms and different types of lead investors, pursuing different objectives and differing in their risk propensity, expected returns, and investment policies.

Impact of Governance Mechanisms

Evidence for both the UK and US suggests that the most important governance characteristic is the management equity stake (Malone, 1989; Thompson et al., 1992; and Phan and Hill, 1995). However, contrary evidence from exited buyouts suggests that if management has a majority equity stake, this is related to negative performance (Nikoskelainen and Wright, 2007). Bruining et al. (2011) show that majority private equity-backed buyouts significantly increase entrepreneurial management practices, but increased debt negatively affects entrepreneurial management.

Active monitoring by PE investors and the characteristics of PE investors are important characteristics in driving firm performance (Cotter and Peck, 2001; Cornelli and Karakas, 2008; Guo et al., 2011). Acharya, Kehoe, et al. (2009) highlight the importance of high levels of PE firm interaction with executives during the initial 100-day value-creation plan, creating an active board, significant replacement of CEOs and CFOs either at the time of the deal or afterwards, and leveraging of external support. PE firms appear to have a greater role in changing management, compared to boards in listed corporations (Cornelli and Karakas, 2008; Acharya, Hahn, et al., 2009). Gong and Wu (2011) also find that over half of CEOs are changed within two years of LBO, especially in companies with high agency costs and if pre-LBO performance is low. Interestingly, they find that, in contrast to boards of directors in public companies, boards in post-LBO companies are likely to replace entrenched CEOs. Industry specialization of the PE firms also positively impacts on performance (Cressy et al., 2007; Gottschalg and Wright, 2008). In contrast, the impact of PE firm experience is mixed with evidence suggesting that it has a positive impact (Gottschalg and Wright, 2008) and evidence of no impact (Meuleman et al., 2009).

An additional source of value creation by PE firms in LBOs is that they enable their portfolio companies to borrow on more favorable terms because of the repeated interactions PE firms maintain with banks that finance their portfolio companies (Ivashina and Kovner, 2010). The cost of financing decreases because banks have acquired information about the PE firm from prior transactions, such as gaining confidence in a PE firm's due diligence process. There is also evidence that, during market peaks, deals done by bank-affiliated PE firms are financed on better terms when the parent bank leads the loan syndicate. The quality of the underlying deals seems to decrease when parent banks take the lead (Fang et al., 2011).

The ability of PE firms to become involved in monitoring may be affected by legislative changes. Cumming and Zambelli (2010) show, for a sample of buyouts in Italy, that following legislative changes PE investors become more involved in the management and governance of the target firm by increasing ownership stake, the use of convertible debt, adopting more control rights, especially the right to CEO appointment and the right to take a majority board position.

Impact on Employees

Union criticism of PE has typically focused on a small number of specific cases where at least some firms would have either closed or experienced job reduction without a buyout and where in some cases employment actually grew after buyout (Wood and Wright, 2010). At the same time, industry studies, while usually involving representative surveys, have typically not involved direct comparisons with other non-buyout private companies. This is, therefore, an area where there has been a crucial need for systematic academic evidence. Academic studies generally show an initial reduction in employment, followed by subsequent increases in employment (e.g. Smith, 1990, in the US, and Boucly et al., 2009, in France), although the impact on employment has been more positive in respect of MBOs than in management buy-ins (MBIs) (Amess and Wright, 2007).

However, much of the academic literature concerning the wage and employment consequences of LBOs has not distinguished between those buyouts with active PE involvement and those that do not have PE involvement. Davis et al. (2008) report US evidence of PE-backed buyouts having lower employment growth both pre- and post-buyout. They do report, however, that PE-backed firms engage in more greenfield job creation than other firms.

In contrast, Amess and Wright (2012) and Amess et al. (2008) find that PE-backed buyouts do not have significantly different levels of employment compared to control firms, although, specifically in the context of PTPs, Weir, Jones, et al. (2008) find reductions. In respect of wages, there does not appear to be a significantly different effect between buyouts and a control sample firms (Amess et al., 2008).

Goergen, O'Sullivan, and Wood (2011) extend recognition of the heterogeneity of acquiree types and their different employment effects to the case of investor-led buyouts (IBOs) of listed corporations. They find that IBOs are accompanied by falls in employment without there being a corresponding increase in productivity and profitability. These findings echo those in Weir, Jones, et al. (2008) who examine the full scope of public to private buyout transactions.

Comparative research on buyouts in the UK and the Netherlands shows that the positive effects of buyouts on employment practices are surprisingly greater in the less regulated UK context than in the Netherlands (Bruining et al., 2005; Bacon et al., 2008). A pan-European study of industrial relations (Bacon et al., 2008) indicates that private equity firms adapt their approaches to different social models and traditional national industrial relations differences persist. Bacon et al. (2010) further extend analysis of this sample and show that, with respect to the PE firms' country of origin, buyouts backed by Anglo-Saxon PE firms are as likely to introduce new high-performance work practices (HPWP), and are specifically more likely to extend performance-related pay schemes, as those backed by non-Anglo-Saxon PE firms. This study also suggests that the overall impact of PE on HPWP is affected more by length of the investment relationship than the countries where PE is going to or is coming from; PE investment results in the increased use of HPWP in buyouts the longer the anticipated time to exit.

Impact on Existing Shareholders

The concern relates to incumbent managers having a dual role in the buyout process. There is a conflict of interest between management's fiduciary duty to negotiate the highest possible price for the current owners whilst also being members of a buyout team that wants to pay the lowest possible price for the firm (Bruner and Paine, 1988). It seems reasonable to suggest that managers will only participate in an MBO if it is financially advantageous to do so. This could happen if a firm is currently undervalued, which could arise if managers are understating current earnings or managers possess inside information about future earnings. DeAngelo (1986) finds no evidence of earnings being understated and suggests this is because public stockholders scrutinize financial statements in order to prevent such manipulation. Moreover, management will employ an independent investment bank to evaluate the offer terms.

A strand of this literature has examined abandoned buyouts in order to ascertain whether management has exploited inside information. If managers propose a buyout only when they have inside information, the act of management making an offer will reveal the presence of inside information. This will have a positive effect on the target's stock price, which should persist whether the buyout is completed or not, since the presence of inside information has now been revealed. There is no evidence to support this argument, with positive stock price returns only occurring in completed buyouts (Smith, 1990; Lee, 1992).

However, pre-buyout shareholders get a higher price for their stock if outside acquirers compete for control with the proposed MBO (Easterwood et al., 1994). Moreover, this is the most successful method of obtaining a high valuation for stock compared to stockholder litigation or negotiation with the board. Although this appears to be supportive of the inside information argument, it is not unusual for a higher premium to be paid in a takeover where there is competition for control (Lowenstein, 1985).

More recent UK evidence relating to the second wave of buyouts in the 1990s/2000s finds that undervaluation contributes to shareholder gains and is a rationale for going private (Weir et al., 2005b; Renneboog et al., 2007). This evidence is only partly consistent with the early US evidence cited above; the undervaluation argument being more important in the UK, perhaps reflecting the significant numbers of PTPs completed where the founder had retained a significant equity stake.

Impact on Longevity

PE firms have been criticized for their short-term interest in investee firms because they seek to make a return for the investors in their funds. The implication, therefore, is that the governance structure involving active monitoring by PE firms is short to medium term in nature because of their time horizon. Systematic studies consistently cast doubt on the view that PE buyouts are short-term investments; rather their longevity is heterogeneous (Kaplan, 1991; Wright et al., 1993, 1994, 1995; Strömberg, 2008). Most studies of accounting performance gains focus on a period of up to three years, with gains appearing to be less strong over five years (Phan and Hill, 1995). Evidence from exits also shows that PE-backed MBOs in the UK tend to IPO earlier than their non-PE backed counterparts (Jelic et al., 2005; Von Drathen and Faleiro, 2008). Jelic (2011) finds for the UK that, although smaller PE backed deals take longer to exit, PE-backed MBOs tend to have higher exit rates but fewer liquidations. Jelic also finds that syndicated PE-backed MBOs exit sooner and deals backed by more reputable PE firms were more likely to exit by IPO.

A key problem with analyzing the consequences of PE firm exit and the termination of the LBO governance structure with active investors is that two competing arguments are observationally equivalent. First, if the theoretical prediction is that the involvement of PE firms is integral to improving investee firm performance, the exit of PE firms and the termination of the LBO governance structure will lead to a decline in firm performance. This will occur despite many firms retaining high leverage and a significant concentration of equity under management control after the buyout governance structure is terminated. This is because active monitoring by PE firms is a key ingredient in attenuating agency problems, which can re-emerge after PE firm exit.

Second, cost cutting in order to improve short-term performance will also mean that performance improvements are short term in nature and are not sustained after exit if PE firms select the time of exit to optimize investee firm value. Evidence indicates that post-IPO performance of LBOs exceeds that of other IPOs, but this does not persist into the longer term (Holthausen and Larcker, 1996; Bruton et al., 2002; Cao and Lerner, 2007).

Impact on Distress and Failure

Axelson et al. (2012) show that the share of debt in private equity buyout financing structures is primarily related to debt availability conditions and contributes to increasing the premia paid to acquire firms. The private equity market reached its apogee in the middle of 2007, with the availability of debt from a variety of domestic and foreign sources at lower interest rates than in the first private equity wave of the late 1980s. As the market neared its peak, the Financial Services Authority (2006) in the UK expressed concern that increased leverage would likely lead to higher failure rates. The 2008 global financial crisis has restricted the availability of debt, resulting in the total value of deals falling substantially, a situation that is likely to continue for some time (CMBOR, 2010).

The average share of debt in the financing structure of UK buyouts was not markedly out of line with that seen in the earlier peak period. Kaplan and Strömberg (2009) consider that the financial structures of US deals completed in the second wave are on average less fragile than those completed in the first wave due to high coverage ratios, looser covenants, and lower leverage. They thus expect default levels to be lower than following the first wave.

Earlier research does indicate that higher leverage is associated with a greater likelihood of failure in buyouts (Wright, Wilson, and Robbie, 1996). Further, evidence from the recession of the early 1990s demonstrated a sharp increase in failures (Wright, Kitamura, et al., 2000), particularly of management buy-ins that had been acquired at high prices in the boom years of the 1980s.

Recession is likely to see an increase in distress, resulting in pressure to restructure buyouts and for distressed debtholders to sell at more discounted prices. Absent pressures to exit, however, the number of sellers may be reduced as long as firms are able to service their debt. These conditions place major demands on the governance role of private equity firms in securing the viability of their portfolio firms, and will have major implications for private equity firms' fund performance and hence their ultimate survival.

The recessions of the early 1980s and 1990s were characterized by an increase in buyouts of distressed firms that have subsequently been restructured (Robbie et al., 1993). Traditional debt conditions appear to be significantly more difficult than in the recession of the early 1990s when, although they were heavily involved in restructuring portfolio companies and many providers left the market, banks were not facing such severe capital constraints (Wright, Kitamura, et al., 2000).

Studies relating to the first wave of private equity buyouts identified high leverage as a significant contributory factor to failure (Kaplan and Stein, 1993; Wright, Wilson, Robbie, and Ennew, 1996; Andrade and Kaplan, 1998).

Controlling for a range of risk factors, Wilson and Wright (2011) find, in a study involving the population of UK firms, that buyouts have a higher failure rate than the population of non-buyout companies, with the MBI subcategory having a higher failure rate than MBOs, which in turn have a higher failure rate than private equity-backed buyouts/buy-ins. Their findings indicate a default rate for UK private equity backed buyouts of 5.3 percent (5.8% for all buyouts), lower than Strömberg (2008), who found an 8 percent bankruptcy rate for the UK firms in his sample, but in line with Hotchkiss et al. (2011). A greater likelihood of failure is significantly associated with higher leverage for all firms. MBOs and private equity-backed buyouts only had a higher insolvency risk than the non-buyout population pre-2003, controlling for age, size, and sector; post-2003, when changes to the UK bankruptcy process were introduced, there is no significant difference. In contrast MBIs always have a higher propensity to insolvency.

Wilson et al. (2011) find that PE-backed buyouts show stronger economic performance before and during recession than comparable private and listed companies, with up to an 11 percent productivity differential. They also find that PE-backed buyouts experience stronger economic performance before and during recession than comparable private and listed companies, with up to 4.8 percent higher ROA. Hotchkiss et al. (2011) find, in their study of firms receiving leveraged loans, that 50 percent of defaults involve PE-backed firms. Consistent with Wilson and Wright (2011), they find that PE-backed firms are not more likely to default than other firms with similar leverage characteristics. PE-backed firms in distress are more likely to survive as an independent reorganized company.

PE investors appear to select companies which are less financially constrained than comparable companies, but higher mortality rates seem to be affected by backing by inexperienced private equity funds (Borell and Tykvova, 2011; Wilson and Wright, 2011). Demiroglu and James (2009) show that buyouts sponsored by high reputation PE firms are less likely to experience financial distress or bankruptcy ex post.

Timely restructuring through debt-for-equity swaps with banks and equity cures may enable distressed buyouts to continue if the underlying trading business was sound. While a debt-equity swap helps avoid the formal bankruptcy process, it can have a negative impact on growth strategies and future development, especially as often the PE firm's equity stake will be wiped out apart from a nominal signature stake (Wilson et al., 2010). As banks are typically ill-equipped to provide added strategic value, PE firms with a track record of deal doing and retaining a board seat can adopt a positive proactive approach to working with the banks, so that over time the business can recover value.

If PE firms take timely action when firms enter difficulties, it would be expected that significant value is preserved when buyouts enter distress or formal insolvency processes. US buyouts that defaulted on their loans in the 1980s generally had positive operating margins at the time of default and, from pre-buyout to distress resolution, experienced a marginally positive change in (market- or industry-adjusted) value (Andrade and Kaplan, 1998). In UK buyouts that defaulted, secured creditors recovered on average 62 percent of their investment (Citron and Wright, 2008) and this level was about double that obtained in comparable failed listed corporations (Wilson et al., 2010). In comparison with evidence from a more general population of small firms, MBOs experience fewer going-concern realizations in receivership (30%), make a lower average repayment to secured creditors and make fewer 100 percent repayments to these creditors. These results appear to contrast with expectations that the covenants accompanying high leverage in buyouts will signal distress sooner than in firms funded more by equity. However, that these MBOs entered formal insolvency procedures despite the presence of specialized lender monitoring suggests that these cases will have been the ones considered most difficult to reorganize. UK evidence on failed buyouts shows that coordination problems among multiple lenders do not create inefficiencies resulting in significantly lower secured creditor recovery rates (Citron and Wright, 2008). However, when there are multiple secured lenders, the senior secured lender gains at the expense of other secured creditors as the lender first registering the charge over assets obtains priority. Evidence on the returns to subordinated creditors in buyouts is generally lacking. However, Hotchkiss et al. (2011) do find that recovery rates for junior creditors are lower for PE-backed firms.

Conclusions

In this chapter, we reviewed theory and evidence on private equity-backed buyouts and governance. Our review has shown that the gains are not limited to cost cutting, but also include benefits from entrepreneurial growth strategies. Active monitoring by PE firms, especially by more experienced PE firms, contributes to these gains. Nevertheless, questions remain as to whether gains in second-wave PE buyouts will be as great as for those in the first wave. Relatedly, since secondary buyouts have become an important segment of the market, more analysis is needed about whether this deal type is able to generate further gains over time from the private equity governance structure.

Further research is needed to examine the extent, nature, and drivers of performance improvements in private equity buyouts completed post-2008 with substantially reduced debt levels. Debt availability seems unlikely to regain the levels seen in previous boom conditions. This makes it more difficult to generate returns on PE buyouts from the effects of leverage, though this in any case has been less important since the first wave of the 1980s. Increased emphasis is likely on the roles of management and PE executives to create value through gains in operating efficiencies and the exploitation of entrepreneurial opportunities.

There is some evidence of more active involvement by PE firm boards than is the case in listed corporations. However, it is debatable how widespread such expertise is across the PE sector. The ability to contribute to the development and subsequent overseeing of portfolio companies' strategy insightful active board participation will be an even more important differentiator of successful PE funds in the future. Many PE firms will need to recruit more executives who have the specialist industry, operational, and technical skills to create value in their portfolio companies. There will also be a need to pay careful attention to the selection of portfolio management with business skills who can identify and deliver development strategies. Further research will then be needed to examine the processes of involvement of these executives in generating value in PE-backed buyouts. This analysis will also need to add to understanding of differences in both the skills base of different types of PE firms and how they add value to portfolio firms.

To date, most recent research has focused on independent PE firms, but in some jurisdictions and market segments (especially the mid-market) dominant players are captive or semi-captive PE firms that are part of banks and insurance corporations.

Recent evidence has raised questions about whether private equity funds outperform the stock market. The need for major restructurings of portfolio companies and the writing of investments through debt-for-equity swaps in the financial recession since 2008 has also raised concerns about how PE firms interact with their limited partner investors to explain how they are dealing with problems in a fund and how this relates to how PE firms can persuade limited partners to invest in subsequent funds. Additional research on the governance relationship between limited partners and private equity firms would be highly useful. In addition to returns to limited partners, questions about the distribution of returns in PE-backed buyouts have led to suggestions that governance structures need to be put in place that allow for wider involvement by non-managerial employees. While there is extensive evidence on wider employee ownership and governance (see Chapter 28), further analysis is needed of the processes involved in introducing wider employee share ownership and involvement in PE equity-backed buyouts.

International or cross-border investment by private equity firms is long established, but has been little researched. Entering foreign markets poses major challenges for PE firms in terms of higher transactions costs in both identifying and monitoring investees, greater information asymmetries, and lower social capital (Meuleman et al., 2009). Future research needs to examine issues relating to how foreign PE firms approach governance of their portfolio companies to domestic counterparts and the extent to which syndication is adopted to help address governance problems. Further, we lack an understanding of how PE firms compete successfully in foreign markets.

References

Acharya, V., Hahn, M., and Kehoe, C. (2009). "Corporate Governance and Value Creation Evidence from Private Equity." Available at <http://ssrn.com/abstract=1324016>.

—— Kehoe, C., and Reyner, M. (2009). "Private Equity vs PLC Boards: A Comparison of Practices and Effectiveness," *Journal of Applied Corporate Finance*, 21(1): 45–56.

Achleitner, A., Betzer, A., Goergen, M., and Hinterramskogler, B. (2010). "Private Equity Acquisitions of Continental European Firms: The Impact of Ownership and Control on the Likelihood of Being Taken Private", *European Financial Management*, DOI: <10.1111/j.1468-036X.2010.00569.x>.

Amess, K. (2002). "Management Buyouts and Firm-Level Productivity: Evidence from a Panel of U.K. Manufacturing Firms," *Scottish Journal of Political Economy*, 49: 304–17.

—— (2003). "The Effects of Management Buyouts and on Firm-Level Technical Efficiency: Evidence from a Panel of U.K. Machinery and Equipment Manufacturers," *Journal of Industrial Economics*, 51: 35–44.

—— and Wright, M. (2007). "The Wage and Employment Effects of Leveraged Buyouts in the U.K," *International Journal of Economics and Business*, 14(2): 179–95.

—— —— (2012). "Barbarians at the Gate: Do LBOs and Private Equity Destroy Jobs?" Available at <http://ssrn.com/abstract=1034178>.

—— Girma, S., and Wright, M. (2008). "What are the Wage and Employment Consequences of Leveraged Buyouts, Private Equity and Acquisitions in the UK?" Nottingham University Business School Research Paper, No. 2008-01. Available at <http://papers.ssrn.com/Sol3/Papers.Cfm?Abstract_Id=1270581>.

Andrade, G., and Kaplan, S. (1998) "How Costly is Financial (Not Economic) Distress? Evidence from Highly Leveraged Transactions that Became Distressed," *Journal of Finance*, 53: 1443–93.

Andres, C., Betzer, A., and Weir, C. (2007). "Shareholder Wealth Gains through Better Corporate Governance—The Case of European LBO-Transactions", *Financial Markets and Portfolio Management*, 21: 403–24.

Arzac, E. R. (1992). "On the Capital Structure of Leveraged Buyouts," *Financial Management*, 21: 16–26.

Axelson, U., Jenkinson, T., Strömberg, P., and Weisbach, M. (2012). "Borrow Cheap, Buy High? The Determinants of Leverage and Pricing in Buyouts," Charles A. Dice Center Working Paper No. 2010-9; Fisher College of Business Working Paper No. 2010-03-009; ECGI Finance Working Paper No. 329/2012. Available at <http://ssrn.com/abstract=1596019> or <http://dx.doi.org/10.2139/ssrn.1596019>.

Bacon, N., Wright, M., Demina, N., Bruining, H. and Boselie, P. (2008). "HRM, Buyouts and Private Equity in the UK and the Netherlands," *Human Relations*, 61(10): 1399–433.

—— —— Scholes, L., and Meuleman, M. (2010). "Assessing the Impact of Private Equity on Industrial Relations in Europe," *Human Relations*, 63(9): 1343–70.

Barney, J. (1991). "Firm Resources and Sustainable Competitive Advantage," *Journal of Management*, 17(1): 99–120.

—— Wright, M., and Ketchen, D. (2001). "The Resource-Based View of the Firm: Ten Years after 1991," *Journal of Management*, 27(6): 625–41.

Borell, M., and Tykvova, T. (2011). "Do Private Equity Investors Trigger Financial Distress in their Portfolio Companies?" Paper Presented at Alternative Investment Funds Conference, New York, May.

Boucly, Q., Thesmar, D., and Sraer, D. (2009). "Leveraged Buyouts—Evidence from French Deals," in A. Gurung and J. Lerner (eds.), *The Global Economic Impact of Private Equity Report 2009: Globalization of Alternative Investments*, Working Papers Volume 2. Davos, Switzerland: World Economic Forum, 47–64.

Boucly, Q., Sraer, D., and Thesmar, D. (2011). "Growth LBOs," *Journal of Financial Economics*, 102: 432–53.

Bruining, H., Boselie, P., Wright, M., and Bacon, N. (2005). "The Impact of Business Ownership Change on Employee Relations: Buyouts in the U.K. and the Netherlands," *International Journal of Human Resource Management*, 16: 345–65.

—— Wervaal, E. and Wright, M. (2011). "How Does Private Equity Ownership Affect Entrepreneurial Management in Management Buyouts," Paper Presented at Private Equity and Venture Capital Conference, Ghent.

Bruner, R., and Paine, L. (1988). "Management Buyouts and Managerial Ethics," *California Management Review*, 30: 89–106.

Bruton, G., Keels, J. K., and Scifres, R. L. (2002). "Corporate Restructuring and Performance: An Agency Perspective on the Complete Buyout Cycle," *Journal of Business Research*, 55: 709–24.

Bull, I. (1989). "Management Performance in Leveraged Buyouts: An Empirical Analysis," *Journal of Business Venturing*, 3: 263–78.

Cao, J. X., and Lerner, J. (2007). "The Performance of Reverse Leveraged Buyouts," Swedish Institute for Financial Research Conference on the Economics of the Private Equity Market. Available at <http://ssrn.com/abstract=937801>.

Chrisman, J., Chua, J., and Litz, R. (2004). "Comparing the Agency Costs of Family and Non-family Firms: Conceptual Issues and Exploratory Evidence," *Entrepreneurship Theory and Practice*, 28(4): 335–54.

Citron, D., and Wright, M. (2008). "Bankruptcy Costs, Leverage & Multiple Secured Creditors: The Case of MBOs," *Accounting and Business Research*, 38(1): 71–90.

—— Robbie, K., and Wright, M. (1997). "Loan Covenants and Relationship Banking in MBOs," *Accounting and Business Research*, 27: 277–96.

—— Wright, M., Rippington, F., and Ball, R. (2003). "Secured Creditor Recovery Rates from Management Buyouts in Distress," *European Financial Management*, 9: 141–62.

CMBOR (2010). "Trends in Management Buy-Outs. Management Buy-Outs: Quarterly Review from the Centre for Management Buy-Out Research," spring. CMBOR, University Of Nottingham.

Combined Code (1998). *The Combined Code, Principles of Corporate Governance*. London: Gee.

—— (2003). *The Combined Code on Corporate Governance*. London: Financial Reporting Council.

Commission of the European Communities (2009). "Proposal for a Directive of the European Parliament and of the Council on Alternative Investment Fund Managers and Amending Directives 2004/39/EC and 2009/…/EC." Brussels, April 30.

Cornelli, F., and Karakas, O. (2008). "Private Equity and Corporate Governance: Do LBOs Have More Effective Boards?" in J. Lerner and A. Gurung (eds.), *The Global Impact of Private Equity Report 2008: Globalization of Alternative Investments*, Working Papers Volume 1. Davos, Switzerland: World Economic Forum, 65–84.

Cotter, J. F., and Peck, S. W. (2001). "The Structure of Debt and Active Equity Investors: The Case of the Buyout Specialist," *Journal of Financial Economics*, 59: 101–47.

Cressy, R., Malipiero, A., and Munari, F. (2007). "Playing to their Strengths? Evidence that Specialization in the Private Equity Industry Confers Competitive Advantage," *Journal of Corporate Finance*, 13: 647–69.

Cumming, D., and Zambelli, S. (2010). "Illegal Buyouts," *Journal of Banking and Finance*, 34: 441–56.

——Siegel, D. S., and Wright, M. (2007). "Private Equity, Leveraged Buyouts and Governance," *Journal of Corporate Finance*, 13: 439–60.

Davis, S., Lerner, J., Haltiwanger, J., Miranda, J., and Jarmin, R. (2009). "Private Equity, Jobs and Productivity," in A. Gurung and J. Lerner (eds.), *The Global Impact of Private Equity Report 2008: Globalization of Alternative Investments*, Working Papers Volume 1. Davos, Switzerland: World Economic Forum, 25–46.

DeAngelo, L. (1986). "Accounting Numbers as Market Valuation Substitutes: A Study of Management Buyouts of Public Stockholders," *Accounting Review*, 61: 400–20.

Demiroglu, C., and James, C. (2009). "Lender Control and the Role of Private Equity Group Reputation in Buyout Financing." Available at <http://ssrn.com/abstract=1106378>.

Desbrières, P., and Schatt, A. (2002). "The Impacts of LBOs on the Performance of Acquired Firms: The French Case," *Journal of Business Finance and Accounting*, 29: 695–729.

Easterwood, J. C., Singer, R. F., Seth, A., and Lang, D. F. (1994). "Controlling the Conflict of Interest in Management Buyouts," *Review of Economics and Statistics*, 76: 512–22.

Evans, J., Poa, M., and Rath, S. (2005). "The Financial and Governance Characteristics of Australian Companies Going Private," *International Journal of Business Studies*, 13: 1–24.

Fang, L. H., Ivashina, V., and Lerner, J. (2011). "Unstable Equity? Combining Banking with Private Equity Investing," Harvard Business School Finance Working Paper No. 10–106; AFA 2011 Denver Meetings Paper. Available at <http://ssrn.com/abstract=1571921>.

Financial Services Authority (2006). "Private Equity: A Discussion of Risk and Regulatory Engagement," Discussion Paper DP06/6. London: Financial Services Authority.

Gaspar, J. (2009). "The Performance of French LBO Firms: New Data and New Results," ESSEC Working Paper, Paris.

Geranio, M., and Zanotti, G. (2012). "Equity Markets Do Not Fit All: An Analysis of Public-to-Private Deals in Continental Europe," *European Financial Management*, 18(5): 867–95.

Gilligan, J., and Wright, M. (2010). *Private Equity Demystified*, 2nd Edition. London: ICAEW.

Goergen, M., O'Sullivan, N., and Wood, G. (2011). "Private Equity Takeovers and Employment in the UK: Some Empirical Evidence," *Corporate Governance: An International Review*, 19(3): 259–75.

Gong, J., and Wu, S. (2011). "CEO Turnover in Private Equity Sponsored Leveraged Buyouts," *Corporate Governance: An International Review*, 19(3): 195–209.

Gottschalg, O., and Wright, M. (2008). "Understanding the Buyers' Role in Private Equity Returns: The Influence of Skills, Strategy and Experience," Paper Presented at the Strategic Management Society Conference, Cologne.

Green, S. (1992). "The Impact of Ownership and Capital Structure on Managerial Motivation and Strategy in Management Buyouts: A Cultural Analysis," *Journal of Management Studies*, 29(4): 513–35.

Guo, S., Hotchkiss, E. and Song, W. (2011). "Do Buyouts (Still) Create Value?" *Journal of Finance*, 66(2): 479–517.

Halpern, P., Kieschnick, R. and Rotenberg, W. (1999). "On the Heterogeneity of Leveraged Going Private Transactions," *Review of Financial Studies*, 12: 281–309.

Harris, R., Siegel, D. S., and Wright, M. (2005). "Assessing the Impact of Management Buyouts on Economic Efficiency: Plant-Level Evidence from the United Kingdom," *Review of Economics and Statistics*, 87: 148–53.

HART, O. (1995). "Corporate Governance: Some Theory and Implications," *Economic Journal*, 105: 678–89.
HOLTHAUSEN, D., and LARCKER, D. (1996). "The Financial Performance of Reverse Leverage Buyouts", *Journal of Financial Economics*, 42: 293–332.
HOTCHKISS, E, SMITH, D., and STRÖMBERG, P. (2011). "Private Equity and the Resolution of Financial Distress," Paper presented at the NBER Conference on Systemic Financial Risk.
HOWORTH, C., WESTHEAD, P., and WRIGHT, M. (2004). "Buyouts, Information Asymmetry and the Family Management Dyad," *Journal of Business Venturing*, 19(4): 509–34.
IVASHINA, V., and KOVNER, A. (2010). "The Private Equity Advantage: Leveraged Buyout Firms and Relationship Banking," EFA 2008 Athens Meetings Paper. Available at <http://ssrn.com/abstract=1017857>.
JELIC, R. (2011). "Staying Power of UK Buy-Outs," *Journal of Business Finance and Accounting*, 38(7): 945–86.
—— and WRIGHT, M. (2011). "Exits, Performance, and Late Stage Private Equity: The Case of UK Management Buy-Outs," *European Financial Management*, 17(3): 560–93.
—— SAADOUNI, B., and WRIGHT, M. (2005). "Performance of Private to Public MBOs: The Role of Venture Capital," *Journal of Business Finance and Accounting*, 32: 643–82.
JENSEN, M. C. (1986). "Agency Costs of Free Cash Flow, Corporate Finance and Takeover," *American Economic Review Papers and Proceedings*, 76: 323–9.
—— (1989). "Eclipse of the Public Corporation," *Harvard Business Review*, 67(5): 61–74.
—— and MECKLING, W. H. (1976). "Theory of the Firm: Managerial Behavior, Agency Costs and Ownership Structure," *Journal of Financial Economics*, 3: 305–60.
JONES, T., and HUNT, R. (1991). "The Ethics of Leveraged Management Buyouts Revisited," *Journal of Business Ethics*, 10: 833–40.
KAPLAN, S. N. (1989). "The Effects of Management Buyouts on Operations and Value," *Journal of Financial Economics*, 24: 217–54.
—— (1991). "The Staying Power of Leveraged Buy-Outs," *Journal of Financial Economics*, 29: 287–313.
—— and STEIN, J. (1993). "The Evolution of Buy-Out Pricing in the 1980s," *Quarterly Journal of Economics*, 108: 313–57.
—— and STRÖMBERG, P. (2009). "Leveraged Buyouts and Private Equity," *Journal of Economic Perspectives*, 23(1): 121–46.
LEE, D. S. (1992). "Management Buyout Proposals and Inside Information," *Journal of Finance*, 47: 1061–80.
LEE, P. (2009). "Going Private Transactions: Announcement Effects on Stock Price and Characteristics of Acquired Firms in Malaysia," Available at <http://ssrn.com/abstract=1331295>.
LEHN, K., and POULSEN, A. (1989). "Free Cash Flow and Stockholder Gains in Going Private Transactions," *Journal of Finance*, 44: 771–88.
LERNER, J., STRÖMBERG, P., and SØRENSEN, M. (2008). "Private Equity and Long-Run Investment: The Case of Innovation," in J. Lerner and A. Gurung (eds.), *The Global Impact of Private Equity Report 2008: Globalization of Alternative Investments*, Working Papers Volume 1. Davos, Switzerland: World Economic Forum, 27–42.
LICHTENBERG, F. R., and SIEGEL, D. S. (1990). "The Effect of Leveraged Buyouts on Productivity and Related Aspects of Firm Behavior," *Journal of Financial Economics*, 27: 165–94.
LIEBESKIND, J., WIERSEMA, M., and HANSEN, G. (1992). "LBOs, Corporate Restructuring and the Incentive-Intensity Hypothesis," *Financial Management*, 21(1): 73–86.

LONG, W. F., and RAVENSCRAFT, D. (1993). "LBOs, Debt and R&D Intensity," *Strategic Management Journal*, 14: 119–35.

LOWENSTEIN, L. (1985). "Management Buyouts," *Columbia Law Review*, 85: 730–84.

MALONE, S. (1989). "Characteristics of Smaller Company Leveraged Buyouts," *Journal of Business Venturing*, 4: 345–59.

MARRIS, R. (1964). *The Economic Theory of Managerial Capitalism*. London: Macmillan.

MAUPIN, R. (1987). "Financial and Stock Market Variables as Predictors of Management Buyouts," *Strategic Management Journal*, 8: 319–27.

MEULEMAN, M., AMESS, K., WRIGHT, M., and SCHOLES, L. (2009). "Agency, Strategic Entrepreneurship and the Performance of Private Equity Backed Buyouts," *Entrepreneurship Theory and Practice*, 33: 213–39.

NIKOSKELAINEN, E., and WRIGHT, M. (2007). "The Impact of Corporate Governance Mechanisms on Value Increase in Leveraged Buyouts", *Journal of Corporate Finance*, 13(4): 511–37.

OPLER, T. C., and TITMAN, S. (1993). "The Determinants of Leveraged Buyout Activity: Free Cash Flow vs. Financial Distress Costs," *Journal of Finance*, 48(5): 1985–99.

PALICH, L. E., CARDINAL, L. B., and MILLER, C. C. (2000). "Curvilinearity in the Diversification-Performance Linkage: An Examination of Over Three Decades of Research," *Strategic Management Journal*, 21: 155–74.

PETERAF, M. (1993). "The Cornerstones Of Competitive Advantage: A Resource Based View," *Strategic Management Journal*, 14(3): 179–91.

PHAN, P., and HILL, C. (1995). "Organizational Restructuring and Economic Performance in Leveraged Buyouts: An Ex Post Study," *Academy of Management Journal*, 38: 704–39.

RENNEBOOG, L. D. R., SIMONS, T., and WRIGHT, M. (2007). "Why Do Public Firms Go Private in the UK?" *Journal of Corporate Finance*, 13(4): 591–628.

ROBBIE, K., WRIGHT, M., and ENNEW, C. (1993). "Management Buyouts from Receivership," *Omega*, 21(5): 519–30.

SETH, A., and EASTERWOOD, J. (1993). "Strategic Redirection in Large Management Buyouts: The Evidence from Post-Buyout Restructuring Activity," *Strategic Management Journal*, 14(4): 251–73.

SINGH, H. (1990). "Management Buyouts and Shareholder Value," *Strategic Management Journal*, 11: 111–29.

SMART, S. B., and WALDFOGEL, J. (1994). "Measuring the Effect of Restructuring on Corporate Performance: The Case of Management Buyouts," *Review of Economics and Statistics*, 76: 503–11.

SMITH, A. (1990). "Capital Ownership Structure and Performance: The Case of Management Buyouts," *Journal of Financial Economics*, 13: 143–65.

STRÖMBERG, P. (2008). "The New Demography of Private Equity," in J. Lerner and A. Gurung (eds.), *The Global Impact of Private Equity Report 2008: Globalization of Alternative Investments*, Working Papers Volume 1. Davos, Switzerland: World Economic Forum, 3–26.

SUDARSANAM, S., WRIGHT, M., and HUANG, J. (2011). "Target Bankruptcy Risk and its Impact on Going Private Performance and Exit," *Corporate Governance: An International Review*, 19(3): 240–58.

THOMPSON, S., and WRIGHT, M. (1989). "Bonding, Agency Costs and Management Buyouts: A Note," *Bulletin of Economic Research*, 41: 69–75.

Thompson, S., and Wright, M. (1995). "Corporate Governance: The Role of Restructuring Transactions," *Economic Journal*, 105: 690–703.

—— —— and Robbie, K. (1992) "Management Equity Ownership, Debt and Performance: Some Evidence from UK Management Buyouts," *Scottish Journal of Political Economy*, 39: 413–30.

Toms, S., and Wright, M. (2005). "Divergence and Convergence in Anglo-American Governance Systems: Divestment and Buy-Outs in the US and UK 1950–2000," *Business History*, 47: 267–95.

Ughetto, E. (2010). "Assessing the Contribution to Innovation of Private Equity Investors: A Study on European Buyouts," *Research Policy*, 39: 126–40.

Von Drathen, C., and Faleiro, F. (2008). "The Performance of Leveraged Buyout-Backed IPOs in the UK." Available at <http://ssrn.com/abstract=1117185>.

Walker, D. (2007). *Guidelines for Disclosure and Transparency in Private Equity*. London: BVCA.

Weir, C., and Wright, M. (2006). "Governance and Takeovers: Are Public to Private Transactions Different from Traditional Acquisitions of Listed Corporations?" *Accounting and Business Research*, 36(4): 289–308.

—— Laing, D., and Wright, M. (2005a). "Incentive Effects, Monitoring Mechanisms and the Threat from the Market for Corporate Control: An Analysis of the Factors Affecting Public to Private Transactions in the UK," *Journal of Business Finance and Accounting*, 32: 909–44.

—— —— —— (2005b). "Undervaluation, Private Information, Agency Costs and the Decision to Go Private," *Applied Financial Economics*, 15: 947–61.

—— Jones, P., and Wright, M. (2008). "Public to Private Transactions, Private Equity and Performance in the UK: An Empirical Analysis of the Impact of Going Private." Available at <http://ssrn.com/abstract=1138616>.

—— Wright, M., and Scholes, L. (2008). "Public to Private Buyouts, Distress Costs and Private Equity," *Applied Financial Economics*, 18: 801–19.

Wiersema, M., and Liebeskind, J. (1995). "The Effects of Leveraged Buyouts on Corporate Growth and Diversification in Large Firms," *Strategic Management Journal*, 16(6): 447–60.

Williamson, O. E. (1964). *The Economics of Discretionary Behavior: Managerial Objectives in a Theory of the Firm*. Englewood Cliffs, NJ: Prentice-Hall.

Wilson, N., and Wright, M. (2011). *Private Equity, Buyouts and Insolvency*. CMBOR, University of Nottingham.

—— —— and Cressy, R. (2010). *Private Equity and Distress*. London: British Venture Capital Association.

—— —— Siegel, D., and Scholes, L. (2011). "Private Equity Portfolio Company Performance through the Recession." Paper presented at Alternative Investment Funds Conference, New York, May.

Wood, G., and Wright, M. (2010). "Private Equity and Human Resource Management: An Emerging Agenda," *Human Relations*, 63(9): 1279–96.

—— Burrows, A., Ball, R., Scholes, L., Meuleman, M., and Amess, K. (2007a). *The Implications of Alternative Investment Vehicles for Corporate Governance: A Survey of Empirical Research*. Report Prepared for the Steering Group on Corporate Governance. Paris: OECD.

—— Hoskisson, R., and Busenitz, L. (2000). "Entrepreneurial Growth through Privatization: The Upside of Management Buyouts," *Academy of Management Review*, 25(3): 591–601.

—— —— and BUSENITZ, L. (2001). "Firm Rebirth: Buyouts as Facilitators of Strategic Growth and Entrepreneurship," *Academy of Management Executive*, 15(1): 111–25.

—— —— KITAMURA, M., (2003). "Management Buyouts and Restructuring Japanese Corporations," *Long Range Planning*, 36: 355–74.

—— KITAMURA, M., CHIPLIN, B., and ALBRIGHTON, M. (2000). "The Development of an Organizational Innovation: Management Buyouts in the UK, 1980–97," *Business History*, 42(4): 137–84.

—— KITAMURA, M., ROMANET, Y., THOMPSON, S., JOACHIMSSON, R., BRUINING, H., and HERST, A. (1993). "Harvesting and the Longevity of Management Buyouts and Buy-Ins: A Four Country Study," *Entrepreneurship Theory and Practice*, 18: 90–109.

—— —— THOMPSON, S., and STARKEY, K. (1994). "Longevity and the Life Cycle of MBOs," *Strategic Management Journal*, 15: 215–27.

—— —— —— and WONG, P. (1995). "Management Buyouts in the Short and Long Term," *Journal of Business Finance and Accounting*, 22: 461–82.

—— and ROBBIE, K. (1998). "Venture Capital and Private Equity: A Review and Synthesis", *Journal of Business, Finance & Accounting*, 25: 521–70.

—— and THOMPSON, S. (1987). "Divestment and the Control of Divisionalised Firms," *Accounting and Business Research*, 17: 259–68.

—— —— CHIPLIN, B., and ROBBIE, K. (1991). *Buy-Ins and Buyouts: New Strategies in Corporate Management*. London: Graham and Trotman.

—— —— and ROBBIE, K. (1992). "Venture Capital and Management-Led Leveraged Buyouts: A European Perspective," *Journal of Business Venturing*, 7: 47–71.

—— WEIR, C. M., and BURROWS, A. (2007). "Irrevocable Commitments, Going Private and Private Equity," *European Financial Management*, 13: 757–75.

—— WILSON, N., and ROBBIE, K. (1996). "The Longer Term Effects of Management-Led Buyouts," *Journal of Entrepreneurial and Small Business Finance*, 5: 213–34.

—— —— —— and ENNEW, C. (1996). "An Analysis of Failure in UK Buyouts and Buy-Ins," *Managerial and Decision Economics*, 17: 57–70.

ZAHRA, S. A. (1995). "Corporate Entrepreneurship and Financial Performance: The Case of Management Leveraged Buyouts," *Journal of Business Venturing*, 10: 225–47.

CHAPTER 25

HEDGE FUND ACTIVISM AND CORPORATE GOVERNANCE

NA DAI

Introduction

HEDGE funds have become critical players in both corporate governance and corporate control. The *Wall Street Journal* calls hedge funds the "new leader" on the list of activists haunting the corporate boardroom. A few eye-catching examples over the last few years include: hedge funds have pressured Time Warner to change its business strategy; threatened or commenced proxy contests at J. J. Heinz; made a bid to acquire Houston Exploration; pushed for a merger between Euronext and Deutsche Borse, pushed for changes in management and strategy at Nabi Biopharmaceuticals, and pushed for litigation against Calpine that led to the ouster of its top two executives, among many others.

At the same time, hedge funds are active players in distressed debt investing and the bankruptcy process. They provide financing to firms in bankruptcy, control the majority position of outstanding debt, sit on creditor and equity committees, form and negotiate reorganization plans, and adjust the management team and the board of directors. Hedge funds' increasing involvement in distressed firms is bringing dynamic changes to the bankruptcy process and has a profound impact on both the short-term and long-term performance of firms.

The growth in equity swaps and other privately negotiated equity derivatives, and related growth in the stock lending market, allow shareholders to readily separate voting rights from economic ownership of shares, at low cost, and on a large scale. Hedge funds activists utilize new vote-buying strategies such as empty voting and hidden ownership to greatly increase their flexibility and power in shareholder voting. Investors can have greater voting than economic ownership, a pattern that is termed "empty voting." Conversely, investors can have greater economic than voting ownership. In many cases, economic ownership can be quickly transformed to include voting ownership, resulting in "hidden ownership." This new trend brings changes to the traditional one-share-one-vote rule and plays an important role in hedge funds' increasing power over corporate governance.

There exist many different views regarding the role of hedge fund in corporate governance and corporate restructuring, as well as their use of new vote-buying strategies in their activities related to corporate governance and restructuring. The most fundamental question is whether hedge funds create or destroy value through their activism. Some view hedge fund activism as short term, which distracts management from long-term profitability. Some worry about the potential conflict between hedge fund shareholders and creditors, as well as other shareholders. Such conflicts would do damage to firm value. Others applaud the aggressive intervening in management by hedge fund activists and believe hedge funds are superior monitors to traditional institutional investors (such as mutual funds and pension funds) and play a positive and significant role in improving firm performance and value.

In this chapter, I review recent studies that document and examine the nature of hedge fund activism, how and why it differs from activism by traditional institutional investors as well as by private equity funds and venture capital funds, the tactics commonly applied by hedge fund activists, and its implications for firm performance and value. The ultimate goal is to give the reader a comprehensive review of what we know about hedge fund activism and its effect on corporate governance and ultimately firm value. The remaining chapter is organized as follows. I first discuss the differences between hedge funds and other institutional investors. I then review studies on hedge fund activism targeting underperforming firms in three respects: the type of firms hedge fund activists prefer, the usual tactics they adopt in their investment, and the performance implications. In the following section, I review studies on hedge fund activism targeting distressed firms. Similarly, I organize my review along the above-mentioned three dimensions. I go on to discuss the new vote-buying strategies and how hedge funds utilize these strategies to increase their influence on corporate governance and control. The final section discusses some limitations of the existing studies and potential topics for future research.

Differences between Hedge Funds and Other Institutional Investors

Shareholder activism is not something new. For the past 20 years, institutional investors, religious organizations, labor unions, individuals, and other groups have engaged in all forms of shareholder activism. For instance, public pension funds and other activist investors have engaged in shareholder activism using Rule 14a-8, which permits shareholder proposals on a variety of topics. Since the mid-1990s, institutions have actively engaged in private negotiations to get boards to make governance changes. However, as several literature surveys (Black, 1998; Gillan and Starks, 1998; and Karpoff, 2001) have shown, the results of shareholder activism by these traditional institutional investors have been rather disappointing. Most studies only find small changes to firms' corporate governance structures and fail to find evidence that traditional shareholder activism measurably improves stock prices or firm operating performance.

The disappointing results of traditional institutional investor activism are often blamed on the following factors: (i) regulatory and structural barriers, (ii) incentive problems, and (iii) potential conflicts of interest with funds' parent companies (Kahan and Rock, 2007; Brav et al., 2008a, 2008b). For example, traditional institutional investors are subject to restrictions on performance fees, shorting, borrowing, and investing in illiquid securities. They are constrained by law from taking overly concentrated positions in any one company or group of companies. Further, there is a lack of market mechanism for internalizing the benefits of activism, resulting in the "free riding" problem: investors who did not bear the costs of activism share the benefits of activism. This reduces the incentives for traditional institutional investors to actively monitor managers. In addition, many institutional investors face conflicts of interest. For instance, many mutual fund managers are affiliated with investment banks or insurance companies. Funds managers may be reluctant to alienate present or future clients of their parent company with their governance activities.

As pointed out by Kahan and Rock (2007) and Brav et al. (2008a, 2008b), hedge funds are potentially better positioned to act as informed monitors than are traditional institutional investors. Hedge funds privately organize investment vehicles that are administered by professional investment managers with performance-based compensation and significant investments in the fund. Hedge funds avoid the Investment Company Act of 1940 by having a relatively small number of sophisticated investors. The typical hedge fund is a partnership entity managed by a general partner; the investors are limited partners who are passive and have little or no say in the hedge fund's operation.

In contrast to traditional institutional investors, hedge funds are subject to less regulatory barriers. As a result, hedge funds have greater flexibility in trading than other institutions. For instance, hedge fund managers can take much larger relative positions than other institutions because they are not required by law to maintain diversified portfolios. Moreover, because hedge funds do not fall under the Investment Company Act regulation, they are permitted to trade on the margin and to engage in derivatives trading, strategies that are not available to other institutions such as mutual funds and pension funds.

Hedge fund managers also have greater incentives to generate positive abnormal returns because their compensation depends primarily on performance. A typical hedge fund charges its investors a fixed annual fee of 2 percent of its assets plus a 20 percent performance fee based on the fund's annual return. Although managers of mutual funds and pension funds can be awarded bonus compensation in part based on performance, they capture a much smaller percentage of positive returns because the Investment Company Act of 1940 limits the performance fees can be charged by these funds.

Finally, hedge fund managers potentially suffer fewer conflicts of interest than managers at other institutions. For example, unlike mutual funds that are affiliated to large financial institutions, hedge funds do not sell products to the firms whose shares they hold. Unlike pension funds, hedge funds are not subject to extensive state or local influence, or political control.

Many private equity or venture capital funds also have the above-mentioned characteristics. It is well documented that these funds play an important role in corporate governance and value creation. Hedge funds are distinguished from these funds in both investment structures and strategies. For instance, as Gilligan and Wright (2010) mentioned, hedge funds often use leverage within a fund and pursue a strategy primarily based on trading on the public market, which, on the other hand, is by no means the core skill of a private equity fund. Private equity investors typically target private firms or going private transactions, and acquire a larger percentage ownership stakes than hedge fund activists. They create value by addressing the principal–agent problem and re-align the interests of management and shareholders through active monitoring. Venture capital investors typically target private firms exclusively, with a view to selling the company, merging, or going public, and therefore they invest at much earlier stages than both private equity and activist hedge funds. Some venture capital funds also invest in public companies, typically through an investment vehicle called private investment in public equity (PIPE). Dai (2007) compares the roles of venture capital funds and hedge funds in PIPE investments and find that VCs are more likely to acquire concentrated ownership, request board seats, and keep their investment longer than hedge funds. She also shows that PIPEs invested by venture capital funds often have better stock performance in both the short and long runs than those invested by hedge funds.

In summary, unlike traditional institutional investors, hedge funds have the potential to influence corporate boards and managements due to key differences arising from their different organizational forms and the incentives that they face. On the other hand, in contrast to private equity funds and venture capital funds, hedge funds aim for abnormal returns primarily through trading strategies on the public market and have a relatively shorter investment horizon. Only a small proportion of hedge funds utilize activism strategy and these strategies could be very different from those utilized by other institutional investors.[1] Given the differences in incentives, organizational forms, and regulatory restrictions between hedge funds and other institutional investors as discussed above, it is expected that the targets, the methods, as well as the consequences of hedge fund activism would be different from activism by other investors. In the sections that follow, I explore and discuss how activist hedge funds influence corporate boards and management in underperforming firms, and distressed firms, respectively, with a focus on how they do it and the financial consequences of their activities.

Hedge Funds Activism Targeting Underperforming Firms

In this section, I start with two examples of hedge fund activism targeting underperforming firms, then discuss the targets hedge fund activists prefer, the tactics commonly used by hedge fund activists to influence corporate governance and control, and the outcomes of hedge fund activism. Finally, I discuss the differences in these three aspects between hedge fund activists and other activists.

Two Examples of Hedge Fund Activism

To give the reader a flavor of typical hedge fund activism, I start with two examples (one hostile and one not hostile) borrowed from Brav et al. (2008b).

Example 1: Hostile Approach

On November 17, 2005, Pirate Capital filed a Schedule 13D form with the SEC, indicating a 7.9 percent stake in James River Coal Co. On February 10, 2006, Pirate Capital sent a letter to James River Coal Co., stating that the hedge fund is concerned about the failure of the management and the resulted undervaluation of the firm's stocks. Pirate Capital requested that the James River's board consider strategic alternatives, including the potential sale of the Company and immediately redeem the shareholder rights plan effective no later than March 15, 2006. Pirate Capital further demanded that its representatives be placed on James River's board and that the company's board of directors repeal several anti-takeover by-laws. As a response, James River Coal's management first hired Morgan Stanley to explore alternatives and later on appointed three representatives from Pirate Capital to its board.

Example 2: Less Hostile Approach

On November 19, 2003, MLF Investments LLC filed a Schedule 13D indicating that it owned 5.8 percent of Alloy, Inc. In the Schedule 13D form, MLF investments proposed spinning off the Company's merchandise business into a separate publicly traded entity and indicated their intention to talk to management and the Board of Directors regarding this plan. Discussions had been initiated. After one year, Alloy appointed the founder of MLF Investments to its board. After several additional months of discussions, Alloy announced plans to spin off its merchandise business.

Characteristics of Hedge Fund Activism Target Firms

Like other institutional investors, activist hedge funds' investments are not random. Several studies show that certain types of firm are more likely to fall within activist hedge funds' screening radar. These firms typically have high agency costs due to the free cash-flow problem (Jensen, 1986). For instance, Brav et al. (2008b) find that hedge fund activists tend to target companies that are typically "value" firms, with low market value relative to book value, although they are profitable with sound operating cash flows and return on assets. Further, these firms often have lower payout, more excess cash, higher leverage, more takeover defenses, and pay their CEOs considerably more than their comparable peer companies before hedge funds' intervention. Similarly, Boyson and Mooradian (2010) document that targets of "intense" hedge fund activism have worse operating performance, larger cash positions, lower sales, smaller size, and higher expenses in the year prior to being targeted. These characteristics are generally associated with high agency cost due to the free cash-flow problem. In addition, Brav et al. (2008b) find that these firms often exhibit significantly higher institutional ownership and trading liquidity. The higher institutional ownership allows hedge funds to potentially work with other institutional investors. The trading liquidity allows hedge funds to accumulate a high stake quickly and at a relatively low cost.

Tactics of Hedge Fund Activism Targeting Underperforming Firms

Hedge fund activists take a variety of forms to influence the business strategy and management of corporations. Some are the same as the strategies utilized by other institutional investors, while others are less commonly used traditionally. As summarized in Kahan and Rock (2007) and Brav et al. (2008b), the typical tactics that activist hedge funds apply include the following:

- The hedge fund intends to communicate with the board/management on a regular basis with the goal of enhancing shareholder value.
- The hedge fund makes formal shareholder proposals, or publicly criticizes the company and demands change.
- The hedge fund launches a proxy contest in order to replace the board.
- The hedge fund seeks board representation without a proxy contest or confrontation with the existing management/board.
- The hedge fund threatens to wage a proxy fight in order to gain board representation, or to sue the company for breach of fiduciary duty, etc.
- The hedge fund sues the company.
- The hedge fund intends to take control of the company, for example, with a takeover bid.

It is noteworthy that hedge fund activism is strategic and ex ante, in contrast to the often incidental and ex post role of traditional institutional investors (Brav et al., 2008b). Concretely, hedge funds first determine whether a company would benefit from activism, then take a position and become active. As for traditional institutional investors, they typically have existing stakes in the companies and have been passive until something bad occurs.

Unlike private equity funds and venture capital funds, activist hedge funds do not typically seek control of target companies. Rather, they rely on cooperation from management or, in its absence, support from fellow shareholders to implement their value-improving agendas. It is also common for multiple hedge funds to coordinate by co-filing Schedule 13Ds or acting in tandem without being a formal block.

Opponents of hedge fund activism argue that hedge fund short-termism could cause managers not to make crucial long-term investments. However, in contrast to the claims of these critics, Brav et al. (2008b) provide empirical evidence that hedge funds activists are not short term in focus. They find the median holding period for completed deals is about one year, calculated as from the date a hedge fund files a Schedule 13D to the date when the fund no longer holds a significant stake in a target company.[2]

The Effect of Hedge Funds Activism Targeting Underperforming Firms

Regarding the role of hedge fund in corporate governance and firm value, the debate is unsettled. One view is that hedge funds destroy value by distracting managers from long-term projects. Further, there could be conflicts between hedge funds and other shareholders. Such conflicts of interest could cause value destruction. The other strand of opinion is that hedge fund benefits all shareholders by reducing agency cost and improving the efficiency of management. Although much anecdotal evidence expresses the former concerns, current empirical evidence largely supports the second view. For instance, Brav et al. (2008b) show that the market reacts favorably to hedge fund activism, consistent with the view that it creates value. In particular, the filing of a Schedule 13D revealing an activist fund's investment in a target firm results in large positive average abnormal returns, in the range of 7–8 percent, during the (−20, 20) announcement window. Importantly, this abnormal return is not reversed over time.

Furthermore, the gain from hedge funds activism is not only reflected in stock returns, but also in the target firm's operating performance. Brav et al. (2008b) show that hedge fund activism is associated with a reduction in excess cash and improved operating performance in the long run. Boyson and Mooradian (2007) find similar results using a different sample of hedge fund activism. Similarly, Clifford (2008) confirms that firms which are targeted by activist hedge funds earn larger excess stock returns and show improvements in profitability (return on assets (ROA)).

Brav et al. (2008b) further document that hedge fund activism is not kind to the CEOs of target firms. For instance, during the year after the announcement of activism, average CEO pay declines by about $1 million, and the CEO turnover rate increases by almost 10 percentage points, controlling for the normal turnover rates in the same industry, and for firms of similar size and stock valuation.

The above evidence suggests that hedge fund activism creates value by reducing agent cost through reducing excess cash and overpay to CEOs, increases payouts, and improves operating performance. However, Greenwood and Schor (2009) argue that the positive returns associated with hedge fund activism can largely be explained by the ability of activists to force target firms into a takeover. They show that firms targeted by activists are more likely than control firms to get acquired. Further, the announced returns and long-term abnormal returns are high for targets that are ultimately acquired, but not detectably different from zero for firms that remain independent.

Regardless of what is the real source of the value added (future studies could further clarify this), overall these empirical studies provide evidence of a strong positive link between hedge fund activism and later firm performance, which is rarely observed with other activists. Further, Boyson and Mooradian (2007) and Brav et al. (2008a) show that hedge fund activists are good at capturing the rents of their monitoring activities. Based on Boyson and Mooradian (2007), the risk-adjusted annual performance of activist hedge funds is about 7–11 percent higher than for non-activist hedge funds.

All the above empirical evidences are based on the US; it is questionable whether these findings apply to hedge fund activism in Europe and other territories as the regulation framework regarding hedge funds differs substantially across countries (Cumming and Dai, 2009, 2010a, 2010b). Work by Drerup (2010) analyzes the effect of hedge fund activism on German publicly listed companies. He finds that, although there is a short-term positive market reaction to hedge fund activist intention, in the long run there is a reversal of the initially positive effect. He fails to find improvements in firms' operating performance in the long run. His findings suggest that the successes of activist hedge funds observed in the US may not be transferable to the German capital market.

Differences Between Hedge Fund Activists and Other Activists

A recent study by Klein and Zur (2009) directly compares the targets, methods, and consequences of confrontational hedge fund activism and shareholder activism initiated by individuals, private equity funds, venture capital firms, and asset management groups for wealthy investors. Authors find similarities and disparities between hedge fund activists and other activists. The similarities include: for both groups, authors find a high success rate in achieving activists' original objective, a significantly positive market reaction around the 13D filing date, and a further significant increase in share price over the subsequent year. The disparities include: the types of companies each group targets and the activists' post-13D filing strategies. In particular, hedge fund activists target more profitable and financially healthier firms than other activists. Hedge funds appear to address the free cash-flow problem, and frequently demand that the target firm buy back its own shares, cut the CEO's salary, or initiate dividends, whereas other activists do not make such demands. Over the fiscal year following the initial Schedule 13D, hedge fund targets, on average, double their dividends, significantly increase their debt-to-assets ratio, and significantly decrease their cash and short-term investments. In contrast, other entrepreneurial activists appear to focus on redirecting the investment strategies of their targeted firms. They most frequently demand changes in the targets' operating strategies and their target firms often reduce their R&D and capital expenditures in the year following the 13D filling.

Hedge Funds Activism Targeting Distressed Firms

Hedge funds' participation in Chapter 11 bankruptcies has become commonplace more recently.

According to Jiang et al. (2012), over the period of 1996 to 2007, 94 percent of the bankruptcy cases have hedge fund involvement in some form. In the majority of cases, hedge fund presence in these firms is through investments in distressed debt, consistent with the increasing trend of activist distressed debt investing and the recent strengthening of creditors' rights in the bankruptcy process (Harner, 2008a, 2008b; Ayotte and Morrison, 2009). As many scholars observe, this trend is changing the dynamics of corporate restructurings in the US.

Hedge funds' participation in firms' bankruptcy process exhibits several features that are different from traditional creditors, such as banks and insurance companies. For instance, rather than striving to contain damages on their existing investments in distressed firms like traditional creditors, hedge funds strategically invest in distressed firms as profitable opportunities. Hedge funds typically initiate their investment on the debt side, but with the strategic goal of influencing the restructuring process. In many cases, they end up with a controlling stake in the company upon emergence. These features are illustrated by the following example.

An Example

On January 22, 2002, Kmart Corporation and 37 of its US subsidiaries filed for Chapter 11 protection in the US Bankruptcy Court for the Northern District of Illinois. ESL Investments, Inc. (ESL), the hedge fund established by Edward Lampert, shortly after Kmart's bankruptcy, began purchasing Kmart's prepetition debt.[3] Ultimately, ESL acquired approximately a total of approximately $1.6 billion in principal amount of debt (including bank loans, bonds, and trade debt). These investments resulted in ESL holding approximately 25 percent of Kmart's estimated total prepetition debt ($6 billion). ESL worked together with another hedge fund, Third Avenue, which owned $178 million in principal amount of debt. ESL and Third Avenue were Kmart's largest creditors and together controlled Kmart's restructuring process.

On September 11, 2002, ESL and Third Avenue were appointed to the Financial Institutions' Committee. As committee members, ESL and Third Avenue had access to Kmart's business plan, financial statements, and other information relating to Kmart's restructuring efforts. They also had a seat at the negotiating table. By the end of January 2003, Kmart's plan of reorganization terminated the current board of directors and gave ESL and Third Avenue the right to appoint four of the nine directors on the new, post-bankruptcy board. Edward Lampert ultimately was appointed as Kmart's chairman of the board.

Under Kmart's plan of reorganization, ESL and Third Avenue received approximately 50 percent of the company's new common stock. Kmart's common stock soared in value from $15 per share to $109 per share after the company's emergence from bankruptcy. ESL and Lampert continued to play an active role in Kmart's business and management after Kmart emerged from the bankruptcy. They streamlined Kmart's business operations and orchestrated its merger with Sears Roebuck & Co. in 2005.

Characteristics of Hedge Funds Investing in Distressed Firms

Recent empirical evidence (Lim, 2010; Jiang et al., 2012) shows that the selections of distressed firms by hedge funds as investment targets are non-random. Furthermore, hedge funds can invest in distressed firms from the debt side, the equity side, or both. Conditional on the claims that hedge funds have acquired, target firms exhibit very different characteristics. This makes intuitive sense as hedge funds strategically seek the type of distressed firms and investment vehicle that allow them to have a big impact in the bankruptcy and reorganization process.

As reported by Jiang et al. (2012), hedge funds, as creditors of the distressed firms, often prefer larger firms and firms with more cash and liquid assets. These features are typically associated with stronger capability of debt recovery. Further, hedge funds prefer firms with a lower ratio of secured debt to assets. A lower ratio of secured debt to assets indicates the senior debt is overcollateralized, which gives hedge funds, as the unsecured creditors, a more active role.

On the other hand, as equity investors of the distressed firms, hedge funds typically prefer firms with more cash holdings and higher returns on assets. Further, a hedge fund presence on the equity side is positively associated with institutional equity ownership before bankruptcy because hedge funds typically prefer to work with other institutional rather than individual investors when they intend to influence corporate policy and control. Finally, hedge funds' equity ownership is negatively associated with the number of claim classes, as more complex claim structure leads to less bargaining power by large shareholders.

Tactics of Hedge Fund Activism Targeting Distressed Firms

The activist strategies that hedge funds pursue in distressed firms often take the following forms, investing in debt claims, buying equity stakes, serving on the unsecured creditors or equity committees, and the pursuit of the "loan-to-own" strategy. Generally speaking, hedge funds can be involved in the debt side, the equity side, or both sides in the Chapter 11 process.

A hedge fund can be involved on the debt side through the following: (i) it is one of the largest unsecured creditors; (ii) it is on the unsecured creditors' committee; (iii) it is the recipient of debt claims during the bankruptcy process; or (iv) it is the provider of in-bankruptcy lines of credit (DIP financing). A hedge fund can be involved on the equity side if one of the following applies: (i) it is one of the largest shareholders; (ii) it files the Schedule 13Ds or discloses on the Form 13Fs an equity holding of greater than 2 percent; or (iii) it is on the equity committee.

Hedge funds make calculated choices in timing their involvement (before versus after the Chapter 11 filing) in the distressed firm, and in picking their entry point (e.g. acquiring debt versus equity) to the capital structure. Based on Jiang et al. (2012), overall, hedge funds' involvement on the equity side is smaller as compared to their presence on the debt side. In 79 percent of their sample, hedge funds are present on the debt side. Within the debt category, the most popular entry point for hedge funds is unsecured debt. In about half of cases, hedge funds are among the largest shareholders at a bankruptcy filing. In about 6 percent of cases, hedge funds serve on the equity committee. Conditional on having an equity committee, hedge funds have representation in more than half of cases. This evidence suggests that hedge funds often have strong incentives to represent shareholders by forming and joining the official equity committee.

An increasingly important strategy that hedge funds take in the Chapter 11 process is "loan-to-own," where a hedge fund enters the restructuring process as a major creditor with the intention of emerging from the process as a significant shareholder. Traditionally, the majority of providers of DIP financing were banks and financial institutions that had prior lending relationships with the borrower. In recent years (since 2003), hedge funds have become more involved in providing DIP financing to distressed firms. Often these DIP loans have trigger clauses that replace the DIP debt with preferred or common equity to avoid default, and that replace exit financing with debt-for-equity swaps. According to Jiang et al. (2012), in about one-third of bankruptcy cases, hedge funds use this "creditors-turn-shareholders" strategy.

Jiang et al. (2012) further document that hedge funds participating in bankruptcy do not have as short a horizon as their counterparts specialized in pure trading. These hedge funds benefit more from companies' emergence where the long-term prospects of the firm are important, especially when they pursue a loan-to-own strategy.

The Effect of Hedge Funds Activism Targeting Distressed Firms

On one hand, hedge fund investors in distressed firms offer new capital to the restructured company. These investors can create value by deleveraging the company's balance sheet either through direct equity investment or through a debt-for-equity exchange. They can also create value by improving the firm's business plan, adjusting the management team, and enforcing other various operational changes. They can create additional value by finding an appropriate bidder for the restructured firm.

On the other hand, the potential conflicts between the hedge fund creditors/shareholders and the management and other creditors/shareholders can be value destructive. For instance, some observers believe that the bankruptcy process could be delayed and becomes more costly due to the conflicts mentioned earlier.

Regarding whether hedge funds add value or destroy value when they invest in distressed firms, existing evidence is largely anecdotal, often in the opposite direction. Two recent comprehensive empirical studies by Jiang et al. (2012) and Lim (2010) show that, overall, the effect of hedge funds on the bankruptcy process is positive. I summarize their findings in four dimensions, including the probability of emergence, the probability of absolute priority rule (APR) violations, CEO turnover, and implementation of key employee retention plans, and the market reaction to the announcement of hedge funds' involvement in the distressed firms.

As shown in Jiang et al. (2012), when hedge funds are among the largest unsecured creditors or serve on the unsecured creditors' committee, the likelihood of firm emergence from Chapter 11 is significantly higher. In contrast, there is no significant relation between hedge fund presence on the equity side and firm emergence. However, when the stated goal of hedge funds equity investment in distressed firms is to influence the restructuring process, hedge fund presence as shareholders does increase the probability of successful emergence. Both Lim (2010) and Jiang et al. (2012) show that the duration of the reorganization process is significantly reduced when hedge funds participate as creditors.

Jiang et al. (2012) also report that there is higher CEO turnover in cases involving hedge funds and there is also increased implementation of key employee retention plans. Such a combination reflects hedge funds' desire to replace failed leaders while also ensuring continuity of management and operation after a firm emerges.

Jiang et al. (2012) further examine the impact of hedge fund participation on the probability of APR. An APR violation occurs when a reorganization plan distributes value to junior interests even though senior interests have not been paid in full. Jiang et al. (2012) find that a hedge fund presence on the unsecured creditors or equity committee is associated with more favorable distributions to that class of claims, and hedge funds' pursuance of a loan-to-own strategy is associated with more favorable distributions to both types of junior claims.

Both Lim (2010) and Jiang et al. (2012) find that the stock market responds positively to revealed hedge fund presence in the distressed firms, suggesting a positive effect of hedge fund creditors on the total value of the firm. Lim (2010) also shows evidence that distress-focused hedge funds have produced an annual compounded return of 8.6 percent over the 1998–2009 period, which is economically significant, compared to 3.2 percent generated by the stock market over the same period.

Hedge funds' active participation in bankruptcy firms not only has profound effects on the firm and the various stakeholders of the bankruptcy firm, but also has a nontrivial influence on the formation of an emerging bankruptcy process. For instance, traditionally, the existing board of directors and the management team of the firm play a critical role as the expertise of existing management is regarded necessary for the operation of the business and the implementation of a turnaround plan. This is, nevertheless, no longer the case when hedge funds are involved. There are cases in which hedge funds investors, together with the company's other stakeholders, including junior creditors, shareholders, labor unions, and major contract parties, negotiate the company's restructuring plan. Management for the most part listens and reacts to the restructuring proposals and at most tries to mediate disputes among the stakeholders. Management rarely controls the restructuring process or insists on a particular restructuring plan. In fact, when there is disagreement between management and controlling hedge fund investors, management is often replaced by a new team proposed by the controlling hedge fund investors, as we saw in the case of Kmart. This emerging phenomenon is called "management neutrality" or a "management neutral process" (Harner, 2008a, 2008b).

Hedge Funds Activism and New Vote Buying

Most US public companies have a one-share-one-vote structure. However, the growth in equity swaps and other privately negotiated equity derivatives, and related growth in the stock lending market, now allow shareholders to readily separate voting rights from economic ownership of shares, at low cost, and on a large scale. Hedge funds are prominent users of these decoupling techniques, which give them greater flexibility in increasing their negotiation power and control over material corporate decisions, including the two types of activism discussed earlier in the chapter. The increasing use of these decoupling techniques by hedge funds has had profound effects on shareholder voting and challenges current corporate governance rules.

There are a number of ways to separate votes from economic ownership according to Hu and Black (2006). One method relies on the stock lending market, which lets one investor "borrow" shares from another. Under standard share loan agreements, the borrower acquires voting rights but no economic ownership, while the lender has economic ownership without voting rights. A second approach involves holding shares but hedging the economic risk on the shares by holding a short equity swap position. In a typical equity swap, the person with the long equity side acquires the economic return on shares (but not voting rights) from the short side. Gains or losses are cash settled at the swap maturity date. The combined position (long shares, short equity swaps) conveys voting rights without net economic ownership. Conversely, a long equity swap position conveys economic ownership without voting rights. One can also hedge a long share position—thus ending up with voting rights but not economic ownership—through such derivatives-based strategies as buying puts or writing calls. Irrespective of such activities, the total votes held by all investors do not change. Investors can have greater voting than economic ownership, a pattern that is termed "empty voting." Conversely, investors can have greater economic than voting ownership. In many cases, economic ownership can be quickly transformed to include voting ownership, resulting in "hidden ownership."

Hedge funds have been using these new note-buying techniques in various scenarios (e.g. takeover bids, shareholder meeting, proxy contest, etc.) to increase their negotiation power. Some of the uses could be beneficial to all shareholders; others may cause conflicts of interest. As empty voting and hidden ownership so far have been largely undisclosed and unregulated, there is a lack of comprehensive empirical analysis on the economic effect of new vote buying. I use a few examples provided by Hu and Black (2006) to illustrate how hedge funds utilize these new vote-buying techniques to influence voting outcomes and how this challenges the existing corporate governance rules.

Perry Corp., a hedge fund, owned 7 million shares of King Pharmaceuticals. In late 2004, Mylan Laboratories agreed to buy King in a stock-for-stock merger. When the deal was announced, King's shares soared, but Mylan's shares dropped sharply. To help Mylan receive shareholder approval for the merger, Perry bought 9.9 percent of Mylan and became Mylan's largest shareholder. But because Perry hedged its market risk on the Mylan shares, Perry thus had 9.9 percent voting ownership but zero economic ownership of Mylan. In fact, including Perry's position in King, Perry's overall economic interest in Mylan was negative.

Thus, given Perry's long position in the target King, together with its voting power as the largest shareholder of the acquirer Mylan without economic ownership, Perry has the incentive and power to push through the merger deal. Furthermore, the more Mylan (over) paid for King, the more Perry would profit. However, it may not be so for other shareholders of Mylan. When hedge funds are the shareholders of the merger target and at the same time hold significant empty voting in the acquirer, there is a risk that the process of shareholder approval of merger is manipulated by these hedge funds and that the interests of other shareholders of the acquirer are hurt.

An alternate empty voting strategy is known as record date capture. This strategy involves borrowing shares in the stock loan market just before the record date of the shareholder meeting and returning the shares immediately afterwards. Under standard borrowing arrangements, the borrower has the voting right but no economic exposure to the company. A UK example illustrates how this works. In 2002, Laxey Partners, a hedge fund, held about 1 percent of the shares of British Land, a major UK property company. To support its proposal to dismember British Land at British Land's shareholder meeting, Laxey Partners borrowed 8 percent of British Land's shares and emerged (surprisingly) with over 9 percent of the votes. For outside investors, this strategy can be used to fight entrenched managers or insiders at relatively low cost.

Perry's stake in a New Zealand company, Rubicon Ltd., illustrates how investors can have hidden ownership. New Zealand shareholder disclosure rules, like Section 13D under US law, require disclosure by 5 percent of shareholders. In early 2001, Perry was a major holder of Rubicon Ltd. In June 2001, Perry reported that it was no longer a 5 percent holder. A year later, in July 2002, Perry suddenly disclosed that it held 16 percent of Rubicon just in time to vote at Rubicon's shareholder meeting. What had happened was that, in May 2001, Perry sold 31 million shares to Deutsche Bank and UBS Warburg and simultaneously acquired from them an equivalent long equity swap position. When Perry needed voting rights, it terminated the swaps and reacquired the shares from those derivatives dealers.

As shown in the above examples, these techniques of vote buying seriously challenge the traditional rule of one share, one vote. Standard measures of corporate ownership and control ignore these new vote-buying strategies and thus overstate economic ownership and understate the disparity between controllers' voting and economic ownership. It gives hedge funds activists greater flexibility and power in shareholder voting on material corporate decisions. In certain cases, this could be beneficial, for instance, when fighting against entrenched managers and insiders. In other cases, there could be serious concerns over possible manipulation and conflicts of interest between hedge fund shareholders and others.

Conclusion

In this chapter, I discuss the increasingly important role that hedge funds play in corporate governance from three dimensions, including hedge fund activism targeting underperforming firms, hedge funds' participation in the bankruptcy and reorganization process, and hedge funds' utilization of new vote-buying techniques to increase their voting power in corporate governance-related activities. The discussions are developed regarding the type of firms that are affected by hedge fund activism, how hedge funds realize their strategies, and the economic outcomes of such activism.

The current evidence generally supports the view that hedge fund activism creates value for firms. However, most existing evidence focus on short-run market reactions and at maximum one year of firm performance. It is not clear what the longer-run effect of hedge fund activism is. Similarly, it is not clear what the real source of the increased value is, whether reduced agency cost, the higher probability of being acquired, or better operating performance. Furthermore, most existing evidence is limited to the US. It remains questionable whether a similar link between hedge fund activism and firm value will be found under different regulatory frameworks. It is also noteworthy that hedge funds may play important roles in other aspects of corporate governance not disclosed or studied by the current literature and thus not discussed in this chapter. These unsettled issues warrant further studies in the future.

The existing studies document that, unlike private equity funds and venture capital funds, activist hedge funds do not typically seek control in target companies. Rather, they rely on cooperation from management and fellow shareholders to implement their activist strategies. It would be interesting to further explore the relationship (e.g. potential conflicts of interest or cooperation) between hedge funds and other parties, such as management and other shareholders when pursuing activist strategies.

It is quite common for multiple hedge funds to coordinate by co-filing Schedule 13Ds or acting in tandem without being a formal block. This is similar to but not exactly the syndication strategy commonly used by private equity and venture capital funds. Studies on how hedge funds work as a group and its economic implications would also have important merits.

Moreover, with continuous financial innovations and changing regulations, hedge funds may play a greater (or smaller) role in future corporate governance and adopt different investment strategies. Since the 2007 financial crisis, there have been proposals for changes in the regulatory framework regarding hedge funds all over the world. It is both academically and practically important to study how hedge funds would respond to the proposed increase in regulatory barriers and how this would affect activist hedge funds.

Notes

1. Although hedge fund activism attracts much attention, it is important to note that only a minority of hedge funds pursue shareholder activism. According to a recent estimate by JP Morgan, only 5 percent of hedge fund assets, or about $50 billion, are available for shareholder activism.
2. This measure underestimates the actual holding period as Schedule 13D is filed on a quarterly basis.
3. Prepetition debt is the debt that a company incurs before filing the bankruptcy protection.

References

Ayotte, K. M., and Morrison, E. R. (2009). "Creditor Control and Conflict in Chapter 11," *Journal of Legal Studies* 1: 511–51.

Black, B. S. (1998). "Shareholder Activism and Corporate Governance in the U.S.," in P. Newman (ed.), *The New Palgrave Dictionary of Economics and the Law*. Basingstoke: Palgrave Macmillan.

Boyson, N. M., and Mooradian, R. M. (2007). "Hedge Funds as Shareholder Activists from 1994–2005," Working Paper, Northeastern University.

—— —— (2010). "Intense Hedge Funds Activists," Working Paper, Northeastern University.

Brav, A., Jiang, W., Portnoy, F., and Thomas, R. S. (2008a). "The Returns to Hedge Fund Activism," *Financial Analysts Journal*, 64: 45–61.

—— —— —— —— (2008b). "Hedge Fund Activism, Corporate Governance, and Firm Performance," *Journal of Finance*, 63: 1729–75.

Clifford, C. (2008). "Value Creation or Destruction? Hedge Funds as Shareholder Activists," *Journal of Corporate Finance*, 14: 323–36.

Cumming, D., and Dai, N. (2009). "Capital Flows and Hedge Fund Regulation," *Journal of Empirical Legal Studies*, 6: 848–73.

—— —— (2010a). "A Law and Finance Analysis of Hedge Funds," *Financial Management*, 39: 997–1026.

—— —— (2010b). "Hedge Fund Regulation and Misreported Returns," *European Financial Management*, 16: 829–67.

Dai, N. (2007). "Does Investor Identity Matter? An Empirical Examination of Investments by Venture Capital Funds and Hedge Funds in Pipes," *Journal of Corporate Finance*, 13: 538–63.

Drerup, T. (2010). "The Effects of Hedge Fund Activism in Germany," Working Paper, Bonn Graduate School of Economics.

Gillan, S. L., and Starks, L. T. (1998). "A Survey of Shareholder Activism: Motivation and Empirical Evidence," *Contemporary Finance Digest*, 2:10–34.

Gilligan, J., and Wright, M. (2010). "Private Equity Demystified: An Explanatory Guide," 2nd edition. Available at <http://ssrn.com/abstract=1598585>.

GREENWOOD, R., and SCHOR, M. (2009). "Investor Activism and Takeovers," *Journal of Financial Economics*, 92: 362–75.

HARNER, M. (2008a). "The Corporate Governance and Public Policy Implications of Activist Distressed Debt Investing," *Fordham Law Review*, 77: 101–71.

——(2008b). "Trends in Distressed Debt Investing: An Empirical Study of Investors' Objectives," *American Bankruptcy Institute Law Review*, 16: 69–110.

HU, H. T. C., and BLACK, B. (2006). "Empty Voting and Hidden (Morphable) Ownership: Taxonomy, Implications, and Reforms," *Business Lawyer*, 61: 1011–70.

JENSEN, M. C. (1986). "Agency Costs of Free Cash Flow, Corporate Finance, and Takeovers," *American Economic Review*, 76: 323–9.

JIANG, W., LI, K., and WANG, W. (2012). "Hedge Funds and Chapter 11," *Journal of Finance*, 67: 513–59.

KAHAN, M., and ROCK, E. (2007). "Hedge Funds in Corporate Governance and Corporate Control," *University of Pennsylvania Law Review*, 155: 1021–93.

KARPOFF, J. M. (2001). "The Impact of Shareholder Activism on Target Companies: A Survey of Empirical Findings," Working Paper, University of Washington.

KLEIN, A., and ZUR, E. (2009). "Entrepreneurial Shareholder Activism: Hedge Funds and Other Private Investors," *Journal of Finance*, 64: 187–228.

LIM, J. (2010). "The Role of Activist Hedge Funds in Distressed Firms," Working Paper, Ohio State University.

CHAPTER 26

THE FINANCIAL ROLE OF SOVEREIGN WEALTH FUNDS

VELJKO FOTAK, JIE GAO, AND
WILLIAM L. MEGGINSON

Introduction

The role of governments in the economic sector has been evolving over the past decades. In the economically developed world, since the first privatization waves affecting British firms, government ownership of productive assets has been subject to alternating trends. But despite three waves of privatizations sweeping OECD countries (Megginson, 2011; Plimmer, 2011), the long-term trend has been of fairly stable government ownership, and governments nowadays still account for a large portion of productive asset ownership. As Borisova et al. (2012) discuss, contrary to common perceptions, over the past 30 years governments have acquired assets as fast as they have been privatizing: since 1980, the authors identify worldwide government divestments to an aggregate value of US$1.3 trillion and government investments of approximately US$1.2 trillion. But since 2000, they report US$725 billion in divestments and US$969 billion in investments and the trend is even more apparent after the recent financial crisis: since May 2007, governments have sold US$157 billion of assets, but purchased US$470 billion.[1] Historically, government participation in the economy has been more substantial in developing economies—and that holds true even today.

Yet, the last decade has seen a novel trend in the increasing participation of governments in the ownership of *publicly traded* corporations. In ongoing research (Bortolotti et al., 2011), we have identified over 3,500 government investments that took place between 1980 and 2010, worth over US$1 trillion, just in listed-firm equity, by state-owned investment companies, stabilization funds, commercial and development banks, pension funds, and state-owned enterprises. Given the difficulty of obtaining data on state-owned investment vehicles, especially in less developed economies, we believe our data shines light only on the tip of the iceberg, yet, it allows us a glimpse of the magnitude of government's presence in publicly traded markets.

While the government-created champion is becoming less common in OECD countries, both local and foreign governments are increasingly becoming shareholders of publicly traded firms. This trend is exemplified by the emergence of sovereign wealth funds (SWFs). SWFs are a new and extremely important category of state-owned investor that has attracted significant attention from policy-makers, academics, and investors alike since they were assigned this vivid moniker by Andrew Rozanov some years ago (Rozanov, 2005). Several characteristics of SWF investing and organization make these funds especially interesting to financial economists, beginning with the facts that they are quite large, with assets under management conservatively estimated at over US$2 trillion in 2010, and are expected to grow to US$7 trillion or more by 2015 (Jen and Andreopoulos, 2008; Kern, 2009).

While they are very heterogeneous financial institutions, differing in goals, strategy, and organizational structure, some broad generalizations can be made. The "prototypical" SWF originates in a country rich in natural resources that wishes to diversify its economy through investments in equity. We argue in this chapter that SWFs are the result of a process of evolution of state ownership which is largely shaped by governance and agency-related issues.

Governments face fundamental governance challenges that differentiate their ownership from that of the private sector. The traditional government ownership model is direct—a state-owned enterprise that often benefits from privileged access to government contracts and financing through state-owned banks. Yet, as a large financial literature has shown, direct government ownership has often been associated with poor governance. Empirical evidence is indirect, yet strong, often based on observed improvements in operational efficiency post-privatization (for a literature review, see Megginson and Netter, 2001). The underlying reasons are many: government employees often lack incentives to increase productivity, as the link between compensation and performance is weaker than in the private sector, while employees enjoy relatively stronger job protection; monitoring and oversight of managers is often weaker than in the private sector, since there are no direct shareholders with an economic incentive to monitor; access to privileged funding channels tends to isolate state-owned firms from the kind of discipline that stock markets impose on public firms. The result is often a governance gap, which frequently is value-destroying.

Yet, when governments have attempted stronger oversight of state-owned firms to remedy these governance issues, a second set of problems has emerged—the imposition of political costs. Government intervention in firm governance often means allowing politicians the power to influence the use and allocation of state-owned assets to impose goals often not consistent with long-term value maximization. Political interference in day-to-day management has led to the prioritization of employment goals and to distortion of market forces in the name of favoring socially important industries (such as defense) at the expense of pure value-maximization, leading to poor long-term performance.

In other words, governments are stuck between a rock and a hard place—a "hands-off" approach leads to a governance gap, while intervention inevitably allows politicians to allocate resources suboptimally in the name of the "social good." In this framework, SWFs and the associated investments in publicly traded equities can be seen as the emergence of a "third way" for governments. Publicly traded firms often benefit from the discipline and oversight imposed by investors and governments, when acquiring stakes, indirectly benefit from the monitoring exercised by other shareholders. SWF themselves often buy large stakes in publicly traded firms, enough to allow for the acquisition of seats on the board of directors of investment targets and to exercise active governance, yet they are, typically, insulated from direct interference by the government and politicians.

Yet, results are very mixed. SWFs face special challenges when investing in foreign companies, especially those headquartered in western economies. As foreign, state-owned investment funds, any posture that SWFs take, other than being purely passive investors, might generate political pressure or a regulatory backlash from recipient-country governments. Even when SWFs do take majority stakes, which Monitor Group and Fondazione Eni Enrico Mattei (FEEM) (2008) show occurs almost exclusively when SWFs invest in domestic companies, the funds rarely seem to challenge incumbent managers in a manner that resembles the behavior of other state-owned investors. Woidtke (2002) documents similar behavior by public-sector pension funds in the United States. While, in this chapter, we discuss how China was at least partially successful in using its domestic SWF, Central Huijin, to reorganize its banking industry, academic research finds that SWFs are often reluctant to engage in governance activism, especially when the investment target is foreign.

A second set of challenges lies in protecting the SWF itself from domestic political interference. In this, well-developed internal governance systems are paramount, yet a cursory analysis indicates that not all countries have been equally successful in insulating their SWFs from domestic political forces.

Sovereign Wealth Funds: Data and Descriptive Analysis[2]

Defining a "Sovereign Wealth Fund"

There is no consensus on the exact definition of a "sovereign wealth fund". Hence, we focus on some defining characteristics that seem common to those investment vehicles labeled with such a moniker. While SWFs are an extremely heterogeneous group, most evolved from funds set up by governments whose revenue streams were highly dependent on the value of a single underlying commodity and thus wished to diversify investments, with the goal of stabilizing revenues over time. Accordingly, a large proportion of SWFs have been established in countries that are rich in natural resources, with oil-related SWFs being the most common and, by virtue of their size, the most important. This category includes the funds established by Arab Gulf countries, the ex-Soviet republics, Brunei, and Norway. The other important group of SWFs includes those financed out of accumulated foreign currency reserves resulting from persistent and large net exports; this second group includes the funds based in Singapore, Korea, China, and other East Asian exporters. Because definitions vary and because few funds have disclosed key organizational details, extremely heterogeneous investment vehicles are grouped within the SWF category, even though there are substantial differences. State-owned funds differ in terms of organizational structure (separately incorporated holding companies versus pure state ministries), investment objectives (preservation of wealth versus wealth diversification and growth), compensation policies and status of fund managers (incentivized professionals versus fixed-wage bureaucrats), and degree of financial transparency (Norway's Government Pension Fund-Global (GPFG) versus almost all others).

Most definitions of "sovereign wealth fund" agree on them being state-owned investment funds (rather than operating companies) that make long-term domestic and international investments in search of financial returns. In addition, most definitions exclude funds directly under the control and management of central banks or finance ministries, such as currency stabilization funds, funds allocated to specific development projects, or funds aimed at the development of specific economic sectors, as these often have very different priorities and asset allocation strategies. Some definitions are much broader than this, such as the one proposed by Truman (2008), who defines a sovereign wealth fund as "a separate pool of government-owned or government-controlled financial assets that includes some international assets." On the other hand, Balding (2008) adopts an even more expansive definition encompassing government-run pension funds, development banks, and other investment vehicles, which yields a truly impressive total value of "sovereign wealth." Adding all investments in publicly traded firms we identify, worth over US$1 trillion (Bortolotti et al., 2011), to state purchases of government and corporate bonds, plus other SWF holdings and foreign exchange reserves of roughly US$8 trillion, we estimate that the total value of state-owned financial assets may already exceed US$15 trillion.

In this chapter, we apply the SWF definition presented in Bortolotti et al. (2010), which is itself based on the selection criteria presented in Monitor Group and FEEM (2009). This defines a SWF as: (1) an investment fund rather than an operating company; (2) that is wholly owned by a sovereign government, but organized separately from the central bank or finance ministry to protect it from excessive political influence; (3) that makes international and domestic investments in a variety of risky assets; (4) that is charged with seeking a commercial return; and (5) which is a wealth fund rather than a pension fund, meaning that the fund is not financed with contributions from pensioners and does not have a stream of liabilities committed to individual citizens.

While this sounds clear-cut, some ambiguities remain. Several funds headquartered in the United Arab Emirates are defined as SWFs, even though they are organized at the emirate rather than federal level, on the grounds that the emirates are the true decision-making administrative units. We also include in our list Norway's GPFG, as the Norwegian government itself considers this a SWF and, most importantly because, despite its official name, it is financed through oil revenues rather than through contributions by pensioners. These criteria yield a sample of 33 sovereign wealth funds from 23 countries, which operate through over 150 subsidiaries and investment vehicles. Table 26.1 presents our list of sovereign wealth funds, estimates of their size as of November 2011,

Table 26.1. Global sovereign wealth funds, 2010

Country	Fund name	AUM $US bn	Launch year	Source of funds
Norway	Government Pension Fund–Global	523.0	1990	Commodity (Oil)
China	China Investment Corporation	409.6	2007	Trade Surplus
UAE–Abu Dhabi	Abu Dhabi Investment Authority	342.0	1976	Commodity (Oil)
Kuwait	Kuwait Investment Authority	296.0	1953	Commodity (Oil)
Singapore	Government of Singapore Investment Corporation	220.0	1981	Trade Surplus
Singapore	Temasek Holdings	153.2	1974	Government-Linked Companies
Qatar	Qatar Investment Authority	100.0	2003	Commodity (Oil & Gas)
Russia	National Wealth Fund	91.2	2008	Commodity (Oil)
Australia	Australian Future Fund	71.3	2006	Commodity (Various)
Libya	Libyan Investment Authority	64.9	2006	Commodity (Oil)
UAE–Abu Dhabi	International Petroleum Investment Company	49.7	1984	Commodity (Oil)
Kazakhstan	Kazakhstan National Fund	50.9	2000	Commodity (Oil)
Brunei	Brunei Investment Agency	39.3	1983	Commodity (Oil)
Republic of Korea	Korea Investment Corporation	37.6	2005	Trade Surplus
Malaysia	Khazanah Nasional Berhad	36.5	1993	Government-Linked Companies
Azerbaijan	State Oil Fund of Azerbaijan	32.2	1999	Commodity (Oil)
UAE–Abu Dhabi	Mubadala Development Company	27.6	2002	Commodity (Oil)
UAE–Dubai	Investment Corporation of Dubai	19.6	2006	Government-Linked Companies
Oman	State General Reserve Fund	15.0	1980	Commodity (Oil & Gas)
Bahrain	Mumtalakat Holding Company	13.7	2006	Government-Linked Companies

(continued)

Table 26.1. Continued

Country	Fund name	AUM $US bn	Launch year	Source of funds
UAE/Dubai	Istithmar World	11.5	2003	Government-Linked Companies
UAE–Abu Dhabi	Abu Dhabi Investment Council	10.0	2007	Commodity (Oil)
UAE–Federal	Emirates Investment Authority	10.0	2007	Commodity (Oil)
East Timor	Timor-Leste Petroleum Fund	8.9	2005	Commodity (Oil & Gas)
UAE–Ras Khaimah	Ras Al Khaimah (RAK) Investment Authority	2.0	2005	Commodity (Oil)
Vietnam	State Capital Investment Corporation	0.6	2005	Trade Surplus
Kiribati	Revenue Equalization Reserve Fund	0.4	1956	Commodity (Phosphates)
São Tomé & Principe	National Oil Account	0.009	2004	Commodity (Oil)
Oman	Oman Investment Fund	N/A	2006	Commodity (Oil & Gas)
UAE–Dubai	DIFC Investments (Company) LLC	N/A	2006	Government-Linked Companies
Angola	Fundo Soberano Angolano	N/A	2009	Commodity (Oil)
Equatorial Guinea	Fund for Future Generations	N/A	N/A	Commodity (Oil)
Gabon	Fund for Future Generations	N/A	1998	Commodity (Oil)
	Total Oil & Gas Related	$1,662.7		
	Total Other	$974.0		
	TOTAL	$2,636.7		

their inception dates, the principal source of their funding, and their disclosed investment allocations regarding asset classes and geographic regions. This table is based on a more comprehensive description of SWF organization, investment strategy, and mission presented in Barbary (2010). Table 26.1 shows total assets for all SWFs of US$2.64 trillion, with oil and gas-financed SWFs managing aggregated total assets of US$1.66 trillion and non-oil SWFs managing assets worth US$974 billion. Mehropouya et al. (2009) present a similar total asset value of US$2.6 trillion held by SWFs in September 2009.[3]

Sovereign Wealth Fund Investment Patterns

While no fully comprehensive database tracking SWF investments exists, we use the dataset presented by Bortolotti et al. (2010) to gain some insight into investment patterns by SWFs, specifically focusing on investments into publicly traded firms, keeping in mind that aggregate values are lower-bound estimates. Panel A of Table 26.2 details SWF investments in publicly traded firms by year from May 1985 through November 2009, for a total of 802 deals with an aggregate value of US$182 billion. We note that very few investments were made in any single year prior to 2001 and that 2003 was the first year during which the total value of investments exceeded US$1 billion. The total number and aggregate value of SWF investments have since surged—reaching a peak of 340 investments worth US$61.3 billion during 2008. While the number of investments drops very sharply during 2009, to 50 deals, the aggregate value only drops by about half, to US$29.3 billion. Clearly, SWFs invested strongly during the recent global financial crisis, in part because that was when political opposition to their investment was lowest, in part because that was when funds were most needed to overcome binding financial constraints.

Panel B of Table 26.2 describes the number and aggregate value of investments made by individual SWFs. All the deals by the main fund and its various subsidiaries are aggregated to obtain the main fund's totals. While Norway's GPFG makes by far the largest number of investments in listed stocks, these are on average quite small (US$12 million) and the total value is a relatively small US$4.76 billion.[4] The second most active SWF by number of transactions, Temasek Holdings, totals only one-third as many investments as Norway's GPFG (132 versus 403), but the aggregate value of these deals is nine times as large, US$42.4 billion, the largest of any SWF. Singapore's Government Investment Corporation is the third most active investor both in number and value (79 investments, worth US$22.6 billion), while the China Investment Corporation ranks only seventh in terms of the number of investments (18), but second in aggregate value (US$38.9 billion). Other active investors include Khazanah Nasional Berhad (32 transactions, worth US$3.2 billion), Qatar Investment Authority (31 deals, worth US$15.3 billion), Kuwait Investment Authority (19 investments, worth US$13.2 billion), and Abu Dhabi Investment Authority (18 transactions, worth US$8.5 billion).

Panel C of Table 26.2, which details the industrial allocation of SWF investments, shows that the SWFs investing in publicly traded firms favor investments in the financial industry over all others. The 137 investments in banking (78) and financial service (59) firms account for only one-sixth (16.6%) of all deals by number, but their aggregate value (US$118.6 billion) accounts for almost two-thirds (65.3%) of the value of all acquisitions. This preference for financial investments is, however, a fairly recent phenomenon; sovereign funds allocated less than one-fifth of their investment funds to financial firms as recently as 2006, and allocated even smaller fractions to financial companies over the previous years. Other industries attracting significant SWF investment are real estate development and services and real estate investment trusts (REITs) (7.9% of deals, 4.0% of value), oil and gas producers (4.1% of deals, 3.8% of value), chemicals (3.0% of deals, 3.2% of value), and general industrials (1.2% of deals, 3.2% of value).

Panel D of Table 26.2 details the geographic distribution of SWF investments by target country. The United States is the most popular target nation for SWFs, in terms of both number and total value of investments, accounting for 53.1 percent of the number (426 of 802) and 32.1 percent of the total value (US$58.3 billion of US$181.6 billion) of SWF investments being channeled to US-headquartered publicly listed companies. This

Table 26.2. Characteristics of the sample of SWF investments in publicly traded firms

Panel A. Annual distribution of SWF investments in listed firm stocks

Year	Number of investments	Total value, $US million	Average value, $US million
1985	1	24	24
1987	1	—	—
1988	3	1,952	1,952
1990	1	24	24
1991	2	112	58
1992	2	65	33
1993	3	713	357
1994	9	373	41
1996	4	75	24.9
1997	2	100	100
1998	1	—	—
1999	4	116	39
2000	7	360	72
2001	13	850	95
2002	17	978	109
2003	20	5,641	313
2004	32	2,621	175
2005	42	4,337	181
2006	49	11,492	328
2007	198	61,162	336
2008	340	61,306	191
2009	50	29,306	733
1985–2009	802	181,606	266

Panel B. Investments by individual sovereign wealth funds

Fund name	Country	Number of investments	Total value $US millions	Average value, $US millions
Government Pension Fund–Global	Norway	403	4,762	12
Temasek Holdings	Singapore	132	42,375	441
Government Investment Corporation (GIC)	Singapore	79	22,571	364
Khazanah Nasional Berhad	Malaysia	32	3,240	154
Qatar Investment Authority (QIA)	Qatar	31	15,297	1,177
Kuwait Investment Authority (KIA)	Kuwait	19	13,235	1,018
China Investment Corporation (CIC)	China	18	38,933	2,781
Abu Dhabi Investment Authority (ADIA)	UAE–Abu Dhabi	18	8,518	710
Libyan Investment Authority	Libya	17	1,519	127
Istithmar World	UAE–Dubai	16	2,788	232
Mubadala Development Company PJSC	UAE–Abu Dhabi	11	2,618	436
International Petroleum Investment Company	UAE–Abu Dhabi	10	14,651	1,628
Dubai International Financial Center	UAE–Dubai	6	2,386	477
Investment Corporation of Dubai	UAE–Dubai	4	6,430	1,607
Brunei Investment Agency	Brunei	2	112	112
Oman Investment Fund	Oman	2	2	2
Korea Investment Corporation	Korea	1	2,000	2,000
Mumtalakat Holding Company	Bahrain	1	170	170

Panel C. Industrial distribution of SWF investments in listed firm stocks

Industry	Number of investments	Total value, $US mn	Average value, US$ mn
Banking	77	55,243	1,228
Real estate development and services	46	49,782	1,158
Financial services	59	43,322	850
Oil and gas producers	33	6,918	239
General industrials	10	5,850	585
Chemicals	24	5,807	264
Technology hardware and equipment	29	4,434	153
Construction and materials	17	3,740	249
Automobiles and parts	22	3,048	160
Electricity	20	2,609	137
Mining	10	2,424	269
General retailers	22	2,376	113
Industrial transportation	30	2,025	78
Real estate investment trusts (REIT)	20	1,791	90
Fixed line telecommunications	19	1,753	117
Unclassified	11	25,308	48
Others (23 industries)	376	11,275	35

Panel D. Geographic distribution of SWF investments in listed firm stocks

Industry	Number of investments	Total value, $US mn	Average value, US$ mn
United States	426	58,336	140
China	43	32,049	916
Singapore	39	10,936	377
Malaysia	38	2,195	100
India	34	1,386	53
United Kingdom	28	20,883	906
Canada	19	5,517	307
Indonesia	16	3,758	470
Italy	15	1,092	135
Thailand	10	2,458	351
France	10	2,376	396
Australia	9	1,026	128
Qatar	7	1,085	362

Sweden	6	5,238	1,310
United Arab Emirates	6	2,810	937
Switzerland	5	12,839	3,210
OECD countries	560	120,207	232
Non-OECD countries	242	61,399	372
BRIC countries	85	34,166	502
Foreign (cross-border) investments	723	141,252	224
Domestic (home country) investments	79	40,351	761

Note: This table characterizes the sample of 802 sovereign wealth fund investments in listed companies between 1985 and November 2009. Panel A describes the number, total value, and average size of investments each year from 1985 through 2009. Panel B describes the funds for which investments are recorded and the total number, total value, and average value (both in US$ millions) made by each fund. Panel C describes the industrial distribution of SWF investments in listed companies, and Panel D describes the geographic distribution of these investments.

includes investments by Norway's GPFG, for which we have data only for US-listed investments, which possibly biases our aggregate analysis, yet the United States remains the most popular SWF target even after excluding the 320 investments worth US$4.0 billion made by GPFG in US-headquartered firms. China is the second most popular target country in terms of both total number and aggregate value of investments, though the majority of the 43 deals worth US$32.0 billion are domestic investments by the China Investment Corporation or its subsidiaries, including the US$20 billion, December 2007 purchase of an equity stake in China Development Bank, the largest single investment in our database (Dickie, 2008). Singapore ranks third in number (39) but only sixth in value (US$10.9 billion), again with the majority of investments being domestic, whereas the United Kingdom ranks third in value (US$20.9 billion) but only sixth in number (28). The majority of SWF investments, by count (560, or 69.8%) and value (US$120.2 billion, or 66.2%), is targeted at OECD-headquartered companies, and cross-border investments represent 90.2 percent of the number and 77.8 percent of the total value of all SWF investments in publicly traded firms.

Finally, when analyzing how SWFs acquire stakes in listed companies, we find that a large majority of the investments that all SWFs (except Norway's) make in publicly traded companies are privately negotiated, primary share offerings rather than open-market share purchases. In contrast, all of Norway's investments are open-market purchases, usually of stakes in listed firms, but that fund is unique in this respect. Excluding Norway, we have data related to the method of investment for 129 transactions, and 91 of these (70.5%) are direct purchases and thus represent capital infusions for target firms, while only 38 (29.5%) are open-market share purchases. In terms of deal size, capital infusions are even more dominant, accounting for 88.2 percent of the US$92.1 billion worth of deals for which we can identify investment method. This method of acquiring equity stakes sets SWFs (and private equity investors, who have a fundamentally different investment objective) apart from other institutional investors; pension funds, hedge funds, mutual funds, and other types of internationally active institutional investors generally tend to acquire stock through open-market purchases rather than by direct sales and thus do not inject capital in investment targets.

SOVEREIGN WEALTH FUNDS AND GOVERNANCE

As discussed at the beginning of this chapter, SWFs are a manifestation of changing trends in government ownership. While overall government ownership in developing economies has been fairly stable over time, there has been a well-defined shift from full and direct ownership to shareholding of publicly traded firms; we interpret this shift as being largely motivated by government's desire to use public markets to minimize the agency costs imposed by its own presence as a shareholder. In other words, the scrutiny and monitoring by public investors is likely to mitigate the adverse impact of government's own poor monitoring, poor managerial oversight, and induced moral hazard and, even more, to minimize political influence on day-to-day company management. This partial ownership of public firms can arise from partial share privatizations—that is, from a government sale of ownership of a previously state-owned firm—or by government investment in domestic or foreign publicly traded firms—as is often the case with SWFs. This growing trend makes understanding the governance challenges associated with partial government ownership increasingly relevant and urgent. We attempt to derive some general lessons from the SWF experience, noting that the challenge, as with everything related to SWF lies in finding general principles among a large set of extremely heterogeneous funds.

SWFs invest large sums and often become prominent shareholders in target companies, so there is reason to believe that they might be capable of exercising a value-increasing impact on the corporate governance of target firms. Shleifer and Vishny (1986) hypothesize that large shareholders, or "blockholders," have both the proper incentives to monitor portfolio firm managers and the capability to intervene decisively to punish or replace executives performing poorly. Empirical research (Brav et al., 2008; Ferreira and Matos, 2008; Klein and Zur, 2009; Cronqvist and Fahlenbrach, 2009; Ferreira et al., 2010; and Dai, Chapter 25 in this volume) shows that at least one class of large institutional investors, hedge funds, is generally successful at improving governance of portfolio firms.

Yet, governments as blockholders face additional challenges that are different—and often more acute—than those affecting private blockholders. With the usual disclaimers regarding heterogeneity, we recognize that initial forays into public markets by governments tend to be associated with passive ownership. But the lack of direct intervention and monitoring of management creates a governance gap that leads to shareholder value destruction. On the other side, previous experience indicates that allowing politicians to interfere with the management of government investments can have equally deleterious consequences for shareholders. We have so far argued that SWFs offer a solution to the governance of state investments, allowing for monitoring of management while insulating them from direct political interference. But how successful have SWFs been in this dual role? In reality, results have been, at best, mixed.

First of all, SWFs have often failed to exercise proper monitoring. This seems particularly true in the case of foreign investments, as SWFs investing abroad often commit to a passive strategy, presumably in order to minimize political opposition to their investments. The China Investment Corporation, in its 2009 annual report, states clearly its commitment to a passive stance. Similarly, the Abu Dhabi Investment Authority sent a letter to western financial regulators, stating it would not use its investments as a foreign policy tool. Consistent with their stated intentions, academic research largely finds that SWFs are passive investors. Mehropouya et al. (2009) analyze SWF voting records, shareholder initiatives, and board of directors' presence, finding no evidence of active involvement in governance. Kotter and Lel (2011) find low CEO turnover rates associated with SWF investments. Analysis of patterns of engagement and voting records indicated that, when SWFs do vote, they do so overwhelmingly in favor of management-endorsed positions. SWFs very rarely introduce shareholder resolutions—with the notable exception of the Norwegian GPFG. Yet, even this fund has a policy of initiating resolutions only in relation to blatant violations of so-called environmental, social, and governance standards—in other words, activism justified by a moral stand reflecting social responsibility, rather than wealth maximization. SWFs rarely hold seats on the board of their portfolio companies.

But SWFs are not necessarily passive only ex post. SWFs often design their investments so as to avoid a political backlash—and are careful not to upset regulators or public opinion in foreign markets. Rose (2008) indicates that SWFs avoid acquiring large, controlling stakes in the United States. This trend is particularly strong in investments in the financial sector, as SWFs are careful to avoid becoming "bank holding companies" because of the additional oversight by the Federal Reserve that label would entail.

On the other side, SWFs have also had mixed success in insulating their internal management from political interference. Some, such as the Norwegian GPFG, have very clear internal governance structures and are operating independently—in Norway's case, the SWF is managed largely by Norges Bank, which reports periodically to the government. But other SWF experiments have failed disastrously, lacking proper protection from political interference and falling prey to political short-termism, as in the case of the Venezuelan government raiding its own SWF.

Further, SWFs are often accused of acting as stalking horses for the governments that own them, and of trying to impose non-value-maximizing objectives on target firms. These objectives could be purely political, such as forcing the firm to trade with a home-country state-owned enterprise or refraining from doing business with or in a country hostile to the fund's government (i.e. Israel or Taiwan). Similarly, the objectives could be strategic, such as pushing investment targets to take actions that are suboptimal from a wealth-maximization perspective but which further the goals of the state, like favoring the development of specific sectors or reducing unemployment through targeted investment. Alternatively, SWFs could simply use their large stake to tunnel wealth out of the target company, harming the firm's other shareholders, as documented by Johnson et al. (2000), Atanasov et al. (2010), and Jiang et al. (2010).

The ultimate empirical test lies in the impact on the value of the firm. While it is often hard to isolate the impact of changes in governance, an analysis of changing valuation of SWF investment targets allows at least a glimpse of their net impact. Yet, existing empirical research on SWFs offers conflicting evidence about whether and how SWFs create value by investing in publicly traded companies. All of the studies that examine such SWF investments using event-study techniques (Karolyi and Liao, 2009; Bortolotti et al., 2010; Dewenter et al., 2010; Kotter and Lel, 2011; Knill et al., 2012) find significantly positive announcement period returns of between 0.88 percent and 2.25 percent, suggesting that the market welcomes SWF as investors. However, the studies that examine long-term excess returns (Bernstein et al., 2009; Dewenter et al., 2010; Bortolotti et al., 2010; Kotter and Lel, 2011; Knill et al., 2012) generally document statistically significant negative median returns over six-month or one-year holding periods after SWF investment announcements, and statistically non-significant negative median excess returns over longer holding periods. Bortolotti et al. (2010) focus particularly on the impact of SWFs on investment targets through the governance channel. In long-term analysis, they find that SWF holdings tend to underperform similar firms—where "similar" is defined in terms of industry, size, risk profile, and country of origin. Consistent with the idea that governments navigate a perilous channel between a passive approach, liable to lead to a monitoring gap, and an active stance, carrying the dangers of political interference, their empirical analysis indicates that shareholder value destruction is particularly acute for two categories of funds: funds that act as passive investors and active funds suffering from strong internal political interference.

Yet, it would be misleading to portray SWFs as homogeneous in their approach and, ultimately, in their performance, which possibly explains why not all academic research agrees on the stance of SWFs being passive. Hence, we cite the dissenting voices: Fernandes (2009) claims to document dramatic improvements in target firm profitability and valuation after SWF investments; Dewenter et al. (2010) offer evidence indicating that SWFs are actually actively involved with the management of their investment targets.

Sovereign Wealth Funds and Governance: China's Case

In this section, we focus our sights on the Chinese experience. Central Huijin, an early Chinese SWF, was established at the end of 2003 as a wholly state-owned company, authorized by the State Council to exercise rights and obligations as an investor in major state-owned financial enterprises. The purpose of Central Huijin was not purely commercial, in the sense that it was not simply a return-seeking investor. Rather, Central Huijin's main mandate was to promote Chinese financial institution reform, mainly in the area of governance, especially of the "Big Four" state-owned banks.

A second SWF, the China Investment Corporation (CIC), was established on September 29, 2007 by the Chinese government as a semi-independent, quasi-governmental investment firm designed to invest a portion of the nation's foreign exchange reserves. Under the direct management of the State Council, the purpose of CIC was, and is, to improve the rate of return on China's foreign exchange reserves and soak up some of the country's excess liquidity (Martin, 2008). Since CIC's inception, Central Huijin has been incorporated as a subsidiary and, as such, it has continued to play a key role in Chinese financial institution reform. Our focus here is on Central Huijin's mandate and performance, rather than on its parent.

As we shall discuss, the Chinese financial system suffered from deep-seated governance problems, typical of those associated with government ownership. Yet, the Chinese government faced great hurdles in revitalizing its financial sector. Initial attempts at prompting reform through direct government intervention led to the imposition of political goals and priorities, with disastrous consequences for the profitability of the state-directed banking sector. The solution eventually implemented was to seek the involvement of external, often foreign, investors and to transfer control of key banking companies to a domestic SWF, capable of active monitoring but, at least partially, insulated from political interference. While it is still early to judge the ultimate level of success of this process, initial results have been very promising.

Chinese Bank Reform

Until the late 1970s, the Chinese financial system was essentially structured as a monobank system, with the People's Bank of China (PBOC) acting simultaneously as both a central bank and a commercial bank. The economy was still largely centralized, with the government controlling and planning almost all business activities. The government had control over the overall capital allocation processes, but also production plans, labor markets, and product markets. State-owned enterprises (SOEs) were still responsible for most economic activity, yet, their objectives focused on fulfilling the government's economic plans and serving social objectives such as achieving a high employment rate, often at the expense of wealth-maximization objectives. Chinese banks mainly served SOEs and bank loans were allocated not on the basis of purely economic considerations, rather according to political priorities. As a result, the financial sector suffered from low levels of efficiency and from a large proportion of nonperforming loans.

In 1978, the Chinese government began to implement banking reforms focused on adjusting the structure and operations of its domestic banking system. A two-tiered banking system emerged and various banking functions were separated from the People's Bank of China as it began to truly act as central bank. Four specialized state-owned banks, the "Big Four," each focused on a different market segment, emerged: the

Bank of China (BOC) focused on foreign exchange business, the Agriculture Bank of China (ABC) focused on agriculture finance, the emphasis of the Construction Bank of China (CBC) was on large infrastructure project finance, and the Industrial and Commercial Bank of China (ICBC) served city savings and lending businesses. Despite the separation of functions, the performance of the banking system remained poor, mainly due to the unchanged government influence on the fund allocation process. As it became increasingly clear that political lending was leading to deterioration in asset quality in all banks, the government decided to establish financing vehicles purely dedicated to such political, or social, lending, in order to allow other banks to pursue purely commercial goals. Hence, three specialized "policy" banks were established, the China Development Bank (CDB), the Export–Import Bank of China (Chexim), and the Agricultural Development Bank of China (ADBC).

By the end of the 1990s, it became obvious that, despite initial attempts at encouraging banks to follow economic, rather than political, priorities, government intervention and influence were still very strong. Political lending was still pervasive, and led to very high proportions of nonperforming loans (NPLs). In fact, most state-owned banks were technically insolvent. As the Asian Financial Crisis developed, the Chinese government advocated a series of additional reforms of state-owned banks in order to ensure financial safety. In 1998, the Ministry of Finance recapitalized the Big Four by issuing US$32.6 billion of 30-year special government bonds and using the proceeds to enhance the banks' capital-adequacy ratios. One year later, the government established four asset management companies, aiming to take over the bad assets of the Big Four and the China Development Bank. Accordingly, most nonperforming loans were transferred at face value to the asset management companies, further strengthening the banks' balance sheets. Other measures were undertaken as well, mostly aimed at improving the governance of banks. These included the strengthening of internal management, the elimination of credit ceilings, and the imposition of managerial performance assessment linked to assets quality and loan portfolio performance.

After the turn of the century, despite the many reforms made, the combined assets of the Big Four accounted for 70 percent of the Chinese banking system and their performance remained the top concern and priority in the national economy. Problems generated by nonperforming loans and deteriorating asset quality still threatened to impede economic development. Banks still confronted many problems, especially capital constraints. Bridging the funding gap was a constant challenge and the capital supplemented by the Ministry of Finance was only temporarily sufficient. Despite multiple recapitalizations, banks were quickly becoming, once more, undercapitalized. The culprit, as before, was the high proportion of nonperforming loans, which analysts attributed largely to political interference with the lending process. Perversely, every round of government-led recapitalization led to a banking system even more closely tied to the political class. The attempts to actively manage the operations of the largest banks led to ever-increasing political interference, rather than the hoped-for improvements in governance. Clearly, governance reforms in the banking sector had not been fully successful. In order for the banking sector to survive and become self-sustaining, the government had to induce governance reforms, while at the same time protecting the banking sector from the deleterious consequences of political interference and oversight. The Chinese government was stuck between a rock and a hard place: a hands-off approach involving simple recapitalization of the banking sector had provided only temporary relief, while every attempt to reform governance had strengthened political influence, reinforcing the problems associated with political involvement: namely, funds being used to further political, rather than economic, priorities, leading to high ratios of nonperforming loans. As internal reforms were not successful, the envisioned solution was to further deepen governance reform by involving non-politicized institutions: first, by transferring control of the process to a state-owned, yet (in theory, at least) independently managed institution, Central Huijin, and, second, by attracting foreign investors.

This new process of reform involved four steps. In the restructuring phase, the major goal was, once more, to reduce exposure to nonperforming assets. By May 2004, most of

Table 26.3. Companies held by Central Huijin Investment Ltd. as of Dec. 31, 2011

Name	Core business	Date of investment by Central Huijin	Stake owned by Central Huijin
China Development Bank	Commercial Banking	12/31/07	48.63%
Industrial and Commercial Bank of China	Commercial Banking	04/22/05	35.43%
Agricultural Bank of China	Commercial Banking	10/29/08	40.12%
Bank of China	Commercial Banking	12/30/03	67.60%
China Construction Bank	Commercial Banking	12/30/03	57.13%
China Everbright Bank	Commercial Banking	11/30/07	48.37%
China Reinsurance (group) Corporation	Insurance	04/11/07	84.91%
China Jianyin Investment	Investment Banking	09/09/04	100.00%
China Galaxy Financial Holding Company Ltd.	Investment Banking	07/14/05	78.57%
Shenyin & Wanguo Securities Co. Ltd.	Securities	09/21/05	37.23%
Guotai Junan Securities	Securities	10/14/05	21.28%
New China Life Insurance Co. Ltd.	Insurance	11/23/09	31.26%
China International Capital Co. Ltd.	Securities	08/24/10	43.35%
China Securities Co. Ltd.	Securities	11/02/05	40.00%
China Investment Securities Co. Ltd.	Securities	09/28/05	100.00%
USB Securities Co. Ltd.	Securities	11/23/11	14.01%
China Everbright Industry Group Ltd.	Investment Banking	11/30/07	100.00%
Jianton Zhongxin Asset Management Co. Ltd.	Assets Management	n/a	70.00%

Note: China Construction Bank (CCB) used to be written as Construction Bank of China (CBC).
Source: <http://www.huijin-inv.cn>.

the bad assets had been stripped off and transferred to external asset management companies. The second step of the process was partial transfer of control to a newly established vehicle, Central Huijin Investment Ltd., which, despite being government-owned, was managed by an independent team. Central Huijin assumed stakes in a number of companies, including six large commercial banks, four investment banks, and one reinsurance firm, as detailed in Table 26.3.

Between 2003 and 2005, Central Huijin used foreign reserves to infuse US$22.5 billion into BOC, US$22.5 billion into CBC, US$15 billion into ICBC, and, later, US$19 billion into ABC. Central Huijin became a controlling shareholder in each of the Big Four, with the goal of addressing the ever-present governance issues. During the shareholding system reform of state-owned banks, in order to ensure the safety of injected funds,

Table 26.4 Investments by international strategic investors

Chinese bank	Acquisition year	International Strategic Investors	Shareholding %
China Everbright Bank	1996	Asia Development Bank	1.90%
Nanjing City Commercial Bank	2001	International Finance Corporation	15.00%
Bank of Shanghai	2002	HSBC, International Finance Corporation	15.00%
China Minsheng Bank	2003	Asia Financial Holdings PTE Ltd., Temasek, International Finance Corporation	5.77%
Shanghai Pudong Development Bank	2003	Citigroup Incorporation	4.62%
Bank of Communications	2004	HSBC	19.90%
Industrial Bank Co. Ltd.	2004	Heng Seng Bank, Government of Singapore Investment Corporation, International Finance Corporation	24.98%
Jinan City Commercial Bank	2004	Commonwealth Bank of Australia	11.00%
Shenzhen Development Bank Co. Ltd.	2004	Newbridge Asia AVI III. LP	17.89%
Bank of Beijing Co. Ltd.	2005	ING Bank NV, International Finance Corporation	24.90%
Hangzhou City Commercial Bank	2005	Commonwealth Bank of Australia	19.90%
Bank of China	2005	Royal Bank of Scotland, Merrill Lynch, Li Ka-shing, Temasek, UBS, ADB	16.80%
China Construction Bank	2005	Bank of America, Temasek	14.10%
Industrial & Commercial Bank of China	2006	Goldman Sachs, Allianz, American Express	10.00%

Sources: Website, annual report, and other published information for each bank.

Central Huijin took a significant number of board seats, usually exceeding a third of all positions. This system allowed Central Huijin to exercise veto power in all significant affairs. These recapitalization and governance reforms were seen as significant steps toward attracting external investors and leading to the public listing of the Big Four.

The third step was to attract international strategic investors. From 1996 to 2005, 14 banks were partially sold to foreign investors, including five city commercial banks, six domestic joint-equity banks, and three of the Big Four, as shown in Table 26.4. Investment by foreign investors boosted market confidence in Chinese banks and it was hoped that the new shareholders would improve governance standards.

The fourth step was to encourage banks to conduct initial public offerings. The first listings of this privatization wave were all on the Hong Kong Stock Exchange. In June 2005, the Bank of Communications went public, raising more than US$2 billion. In October 2005, CBC raised US$8 billion. In June 2006, BOC raised US$11.2 billion on the Hong Kong Stock Exchange and US$2.5 billion on the Shanghai Stock Exchange. In October 2006, ICBC raised about US$16 billion on the Hong Kong Stock Exchange and US$5.9 billion on the Shanghai Stock Exchange, making it the world's biggest IPO at the time. IPOs by state-owned banks provided new financing, but also increased transparency and led to monitoring by shareholders, which in turn led to improvements in corporate governance and operational efficiency. The nonperforming loan ratios and capital adequacy ratios of state-owned banks have since risen significantly, to levels most analysts today consider sustainable.

Was Central Huijin Successful?

In some ways, the challenges facing China in the reorganization of its banking sector were exemplary of the governance problems associated with state ownership. The government, noting inefficiencies in its banking sector, attempted internal governance reforms, just to run into the issue of excessive political interference. The solution was to involve external shareholders—and, amongst those, a politically insulated SWF—and, ultimately, to attract market-imposed discipline through public listing.

Yet, for Central Huijin, the challenges were—and still are—severe. Its task was not economic in nature—in the sense that it did not act as a purely profit-seeking investor. Rather, Central Huijin was used to introduce reforms within the state banking sector, ahead of recapitalization and in preparation for public listing of some of the largest banks. For the moment, those goals appear to have been successfully achieved, yet the future depends, in part, on Central Huijin's success in avoiding excessive political interference.

Another issue with Central Huijin's operation is not related to governance. One of the problems highlighted by analysts is that Central Huijin raised capital in the domestic interbank market through bond issues, with the objective of recapitalizing the three largest state-owned banks, one policy bank, and one insurance company. But more than 80 percent of Central Huijin's first bond issue was bought by state-owned banks, thus raising questions about whether any new funds had really been injected. Overall, rather than building new reserves, recent bond sales may have increased risk in the banking system. In a sense, banks were providing funding to themselves but no fresh cash flowed in. The rating agency Moody's criticized the whole process, noting that recapitalizing banks with bond proceeds purchased by the same banks effectively increases the leverage of the entire banking system. Moody's expressed doubts about the sustainability of this practice, noting that problems are likely to arise if leverage continues to increase while economic growth slows.

Moving forward, Central Huijin is growing beyond its initial mandate and focus. As a financial investor, Central Huijin imitates Singapore's Temasek model in supporting the reform of state-owned financial institutions through equity investment, and gradually developing into a large financial holding company. In August, 2010, Central Huijin injected funds into the Export-Import Bank of China and China Export and Credit Insurance Company, significantly expanding its previous mandate. This trend is likely to continue—but it is to be seen whether the Chinese government will utilize its domestic SWF as an agent for initiating governance reforms in other, non-financial, sectors.

Lessons from Sovereign Wealth Funds for State Ownership and Governance

As discussed at the start of this chapter, governments are likely to retain ownership of productive assets—in emerging markets and the better developed OECD economies. Yet, state ownership, traditionally associated with full ownership of state champions and control of state-owned conglomerates, is increasingly taking new forms—often with participation in publicly traded firms. Sovereign wealth funds are a new form of investment vehicle largely employed to further government ownership of publicly traded firms and, while emerging as a remedy for governance problems associated with government ownership, have carried their own, at times novel, set of governance challenges.

The Chinese experience exemplifies the governance problems associated with state ownership, and the ultimate solution—the involvement of a SWF tasked with investing in publicly traded firms—is exemplary of a learning process that is taking place.

What emerges is a life cycle marking the evolution of state investments. State ownership initially takes the form of full control of state-owned enterprises or conglomerates. But the experience of such an approach has been disappointing—in the absence of market-imposed discipline and lacking internal monitoring mechanisms, government-appointed managers have acted just as agency theory predicts: they have engaged in empire building, made little effort to see their firms prosper, and extracted as many private benefits as possible. The end result, as could easily have been predicted, is general underperformance by the state-owned sector, by now widely documented in financial literature.

The second stage of this cycle is the realization that the ultimate owner—in this case, the government—cannot be purely passive. Hence, we have seen the emergence of higher levels of direct government involvement, in the hope of steering management toward more efficient uses of state resources. Yet, with government-imposed discipline came government involvement, in the form of political pressures, aimed at employing resources toward such political goals as employment maximization. Once again, the end result, predictably enough, was underperformance by state-owned enterprises, at least from a purely economic point of view.

The natural end points of such life cycles are distinct. On the one hand, the increasingly obvious inefficiencies associated with government ownership have led to governments reducing their presence in the economic system: in western economies, for example, the government has progressively attempted to reduce its footprint in the economy, namely through a process of privatization. Yet, even in OECD countries, the process has only been partial and the government has still retained a large direct role in the productive process. The other path leads to governments simply changing their preferred style of involvement—from direct control of state-owned firms to increasingly partaking in private equity markets, often through SWFs. Within this framework, we interpret SWFs as one of the tools employed to reduce the governance problems associated with government ownership through market-imposed discipline.

Yet, the success of SWFs has been mixed. SWFs, in practice, have floated between the same-old Scylla and Charybdis: on one side, a monitoring gap, on the other, political interference. In some cases, their approach has been too passive—and their quiet investments have become blank checks for managers, leading to agency waste. In other cases, their insulation from political pressures has only been theoretical—exemplary are the plundering of their own SWFs by the Russian and Venezuelan governments and the political pressures on Middle East and North African (MENA) SWFs, forced to invest domestically in times of distress.

Yet, it is not all bleak. Success stories are few, yet they do exist and provide models for others to emulate. In environments with strong and well-developed financial markets, the model to follow is that of Norway's SWF, which has prospered thanks to a strong internal governance structure that has delegated fund management to private and politically insulated entities. Its investments are mostly foreign and its goals purely financial. Such an approach is optimal for countries with developed markets—but, in countries with emerging, still developing financial markets, China's approach with Central Huijin is exemplary of how a SWF can be used to mitigate the governance problems typically associated with state ownership, by introducing the initial governance reforms necessary to attract outside, foreign investors into public markets.

So far, most academic research has focused on the impact of SWFs on the firms and markets which are recipients of their investments (e.g. Fernandes 2009; Bortolotti et al., 2010; Dewenter et al., 2010). Largely, academics have accepted the idea that SWFs are stable, long-term investors, capable of stabilizing markets by providing both a solid capital base and access to additional financing channels. Yet, the recent financial crisis (over the years 2007–9) has indicated that this view of SWFs as "long-term, stable" investors impervious to economic cycles is possibly flawed. Many SWFs, under political pressures, have retreated domestically, some more so than others. A reallocation of assets by such large investors could, contrary to expectations and to previous predictions of added stability, amplify market volatility, especially in the markets where SWFs tend mostly to invest (developed economies, especially the USA and Western Europe). At the same time, SWF investments during a crisis could provide support to home markets. The impact of SWFs on market stability during a financial crisis, in both foreign and domestic markets, has not yet been addressed by formal empirical research. Given the "perfect storm" that the recent financial crisis has created, such a study is overdue. Even in broader terms, it is specifically the domestic role of SWFs that has so far been ignored by academia. Western researchers have prioritized questions from their own biased perspective—how do SWFs affect western, developed markets?—largely, the markets and firms in which the funds invest. Yet, surprisingly little empirical research has been conducted on the impact of SWFs in the home market, to answer the fundamental question: are SWFs a good idea in the first place?

Notes

1. Borisova et al. (2012) base their analysis largely on the SDC Platinum database which is, as far as we know, one of the most comprehensive sources regarding mergers and acquisitions and, by extension, on state investments. Yet, the reader should keep in mind that state operations are rarely transparent and that no data source will ever offer truly comprehensive information. The numbers presented here—and, similarly, elsewhere in this chapter, are to be interpreted as lower-bound estimates.
2. The content presented in this section is partially based on a discussion of SWF investment patterns presented in a working paper by Bortolotti et al. (2010).
3. Given that observers lack consensus on the exact definition of "sovereign wealth funds," it shouldn't be a surprise that estimates of their aggregate size vary dramatically as well. The Sovereign Wealth Fund Institute, which seems to employ a more inclusive definition of SWFs and tracks over 50 funds, estimated their total size as US$3.809 trillion as of December 2009 (<http://www.swfinstitute.org/funds.php>). On the other hand, Greene (2009) cites studies showing that SWF assets under management shrank to around US$3.0 trillion by late 2008 and that SWFs have no more than US$1.0 trillion invested in global equities. Mehropouya et al. (2009) also estimate that SWFs have less than US$1 trillion invested in international stocks. Contributing to the confusion is the fact that assets owned by individual SWFs are often hard to track. It has been reported, for example, that some of the earlier estimates of current SWF size were overstated. For example, a *Wall Street Journal* article from May 20, 2009 (Davis, 2009) reports that, while earlier estimates of ADIA's size put their assets under management at US$875 billion, current estimates put the figure at US$282 billion. While part of the decline is due to lower oil prices and investment losses, most of the discrepancy is simply the result of the very limited public fact base on ADIA's portfolio. To the surprise of many, ADIA actually published a 36-page "Review of Fund Operations" on March 15, 2010, and this report disclosed much information about investment strategy and allocations (across

asset classes and geographic regions). The report did not, however, disclose the most important unknown data item, total assets under management.

4. Because the database tracks Norway's investments largely by relying on SEC disclosures in Forms 13F, almost all of Norway's observations in the database involve investments in US-listed stocks after the third quarter of 2006 (which is the first quarter for which such disclosures by Norway are available), and four-fifths of these deals are made in the stocks of companies headquartered in the United States.

REFERENCES

ATANASOV, V., BLACK, B. S., CICCOTELLO C. S., and GYOSHEV, S. B. (2010). "How Does Law Affect Finance? An Examination of Equity Tunneling in Bulgaria," *Journal of Financial Economics*, 96: 155–73.

BALDING, C. (2008). "A Portfolio Analysis of Sovereign Wealth Funds," Working Paper, University of California, Irvine.

BARBARY, V. (2010). "The Asset Allocation of Sovereign Wealth Funds," in William Miracky and Bernardo Bortolotti (eds.), *2009 Sovereign Wealth Fund Annual Report*. Boston and Milan: Monitor Group and Fondazione Eni Enrico Mattei.

BERNSTEIN, S., LERNER, J., and SCHOAR, A. (2009). "The Investment Strategies of Sovereign Wealth Funds," Working Paper, Harvard University.

BORISOVA, G., FOTAK, V., HOLLAND, K., and MEGGINSON, W. L. (2012). "Government Ownership and the Cost of Debt: Evidence from Government Investments in Publicly Traded Firms," Working Paper, Iowa State University and University of Oklahoma.

BORTOLOTTI, B., FOTAK, V., and MEGGINSON, W. L. (2010). "Sovereign Wealth Fund Investment Patterns and Performance," Working Paper, Sovereign Investment Lab, Paolo Baffi Centre for Central Banking and Financial Regulation.

—— —— HOLLAND, K., and MEGGINSON, W. L. (2011). "The Color of Sovereign Investors' Money," Working Paper, Fondazione Eni Enrico Mattei.

BRAV, A., JIANG, W., PARTNOY, F., and THOMAS, R. S. (2008). "Hedge Fund Activism, Corporate Governance, and Firm Performance," *Journal of Finance*, 63: 1729–75.

CRONQVIST, H., and FAHLENBRACH, R. (2009). "Large Shareholders and Corporate Policies," *Review of Financial Studies*, 22: 3941–76.

DEWENTER, K. L., HAN, X., and MALATESTA, P. H. (2010). "Firm Value and Sovereign Wealth Fund Investments," *Journal of Financial Economics*, 98: 256–78.

DAVIS, B. (2009). "Wealth Funds aren't as Big as Assumed," *Wall Street Journal*, May 20.

DICKIE, M. (2008). "Injection of USD 20bn Aids CDB Transition," *Financial Times* (online), <http://www.ft.com>, accessed January 2, 2008.

FERNANDES, N. G. (2009). "Sovereign Wealth Funds: Investment Choices and Implications around the World," Working Paper, IMD International.

FERREIRA, M. A., and MATOS, P. (2008). "The Color of Investors' Money: The Role of Institutional Investors around the World," *Journal of Financial Economics*, 88: 499–533.

—— MASSA, M., and MATOS, P. (2010). "Shareholders at the Gate? Institutional Investors and the Cross-Border Mergers and Acquisitions," *Review of Financial Studies*, 23(2): 601–44.

GREENE, S. (2009). "SWFs Prove Not to Be so Big, Bad or Secretive," *Financial Times* (online), <http://www.ft.com>, accessed October 11, 2009.

Jen, S., and Andreopoulos, S. (2008). "SWFs: Growth Tempered—USD 10 Trillion by 2015," Report, Morgan Stanley Views.

Jiang, G., Lee, C. M., and Yue, H. (2010). "Tunneling through Intercorporate Loans: The China Experience," *Journal of Financial Economics*, 98: 1–20.

Johnson, S., Laporta, R., Lopez-De-Silanes, F., and Shleifer, A. (2000). "Tunnelling," *American Economic Review*, 90: 22–7.

Karolyi, A., and Liao, R. (2009). "What is Different about Government Controlled Acquirers in Cross-Border Acquisitions?" Working Paper, Cornell University.

Kern, S. (2009). "Sovereign Wealth Funds: State Investments during the Financial Crisis," Report, Deutsche Bank Research.

Klein, A., and Zur, E. (2009). "Entrepreneurial Shareholder Activism: Hedge Funds and Other Private Investors," *Journal of Finance*, 64: 182–229.

Knill, A., Lee, B., and Mauck, N. (2012). "Sovereign Wealth Fund Investment and the Return-to-Risk Performance of Target Firms," *Journal of Financial Intermediation*, 21(2): 315–40.

Kotter, J., and Lel, U. (2011). "Friends or Foes? The Stock Price Impact of Sovereign Wealth Fund Investments and the Price of Keeping Secrets," *Journal of Financial Economics*, 101: 360–81.

Martin, M. (2008). "CRS Report for Congress: China's Sovereign Wealth Fund," Report, Congressional Research Office.

Megginson, W. L. (2011). "Privatization Trends and Major Deals in 2010," in *The Privatization Barometer Report 2010*, 12. Privatization Barometer.

—— and Netter, J. M. (2001). "From State to Market: A Survey of Empirical Studies on Privatization," *Journal of Economic Literature*, 39: 321–89.

Mehropouya, A., Huang, C., and Barnett, T. (2009). "An Analysis of Proxy Voting and Engagement Policies and Practices of Sovereign Wealth Funds," Report, Riskmetrics Group.

Monitor Group and Fondazione Eni Enrico Mattei (FEEM) (2008). "Assessing the Risks: The Behavior of Sovereign Wealth Funds in the Global Economy," Report, Monitor Group.

—— (2009). "Weathering the Storm: Sovereign Wealth Funds in the Global Economic Crisis of 2008," Report, Monitor Group.

Plimmer, G. (2011). "Privatization Fever Takes Grip," *Financial Times*, June 26.

Rose, P. (2008). "Sovereign Wealth Funds: Active or Passive Investors?" *Yale Law Journal Pocket Part*, 118: 104.

Rozanov, A. (2005). "Who Holds the Wealth of Nations," *Central Banking Journal*, 15(4): 52–7.

Shleifer, A. and Vishny, R. W. (1986). "Large Shareholders and Corporate Control," *Journal of Political Economy*, 94: 461–88.

Truman, E. M. (2008). "A Blueprint for Sovereign Wealth Fund Best Practices," Policy Brief, Peterson Institute for International Economics, Washington, DC.

Woidtke, T. (2002). "Agents Watching Agents? Evidence from Pension Fund Ownership and Firm Value," *Journal of Financial Economics*, 63: 99–131.

PART V

CORPORATE GOVERNANCE, STRATEGY, AND STAKEHOLDERS

CHAPTER 27

CORPORATE GOVERNANCE AND NONPROFITS

Facing up to Hybridization and Homogenization

JENNY HARROW AND SUSAN D. PHILLIPS

INTRODUCTION

THE notion of the "nonprofit sector" provides a blanket descriptor for a fragmented, shifting amalgam of organizational forms, operating for social value purposes, mainly beyond the organizing frames, but not the regulatory frames of business and government. Such forms range from service-providing charities that are supported mainly by private donations and government contracts to endowed, in-perpetuity foundations that fund the work of charities and other nonprofit organizations. They include social enterprises operating (or aspiring to operate) within the conventions of the market, advocacy organizations intent on changing public policy, and mutually focused and member-led bodies, all operating in local, national, and global spheres. Salamon (1999: 10) identifies six nonprofit organizational characteristics (organized, private, self-governing, voluntary, public benefit in nature, not distributing surplus or profits). However, other scholars note the interchangeability and looser meanings of terminology, regarding what are described, variously, as "nonprofits," "civil society organizations," "not-for-profit organizations," "voluntary organizations." "third sector organizations," "the charitable sector," and "the independent sector" (Hasenfeld and Gidron, 2005; Horton Smith et al., 2006). For this chapter, "nonprofits" is used in its widest possible meaning, differentiating organizations from those in the public and business spheres, to the extent to which their primary goals are independently (i.e. not public) and non-business (i.e. not profit) directed. A common operating characteristic of nonprofits is however their organizational boundary spanning as a means to secure resources: nonprofits with major public services contracts become de facto public bodies, whilst those partnering with business for such contracts contribute to for-profit performance

(Rathgeb Smith, 2010). Thus, organizational hybridity is a marked sectoral feature, with governance implications that may be far from clear.

The governance literatures for this sector differentiate between internal and external governance issues, although due to the complexity of relationships that boundary spanning entails, both emphasize responsiveness to the interests of multiple stakeholders (Renz, 2009; Cornforth and Chambers, 2010). The diversity of stakeholders includes those who are in effect "shareholder" proxies, as well as members and broader constituencies who expect to be involved as participants in democratic processes of decisions-making or as moral adjudicators and champions in competitive social-problem-solving arenas (Rehli and Jäger, 2011). This literature contains broad acceptance of nonprofits' need to review and improve their governance, in line with corporate governance developments in for-profits. It also contains arguments that nonprofits represent a governance special case, either collectively or in subsectors, so that bespoke governance models are required. Yet corporate governance, with its assessment of decision-making systems and decision-makers' performance that concerns fundamentally the exercise of power, is important to nonprofits, both as they support, promote, and engage with the public interest and as they interact with business in offering blended value from social and financial propositions.

This chapter takes as its starting point, therefore, the case that corporate governance perspectives have critical relevance for nonprofits, particularly where these develop frameworks for public accountability regarding boards' and organizations' mission effectiveness, performance, probity, and ownership, regardless of whether these are seen as overly business-led models. Indeed, Hopt and Von Hippel (2010) contend that the rise of nonprofits as welfare providers "resembles the rise of the modern corporation in the first and second half of the nineteenth century," when "the need to set up rules for them quickly became obvious" (Hopt and Von Hippel, 2010: xxxviii). From this standpoint, corporate governance overlays on this sector are less efforts to impose firm-style behaviors on nonprofits (as, for example, wariness about the gains from mergers among nonprofits; Prüfer, 2011) and more reflections of the relative importance of hitherto less prominent organizational actors.

Unsurprisingly, as nonprofits face concurrent rising public demand and receding state capability, Cadbury's original advocacy of adherence to corporate governance principles as a matter of "striking the right balance" between behavior required from them and "retaining the essential spirit of enterprise" sounds as applicable to nonprofits as to business (Cadbury Review, 1992: 1.5). This is especially so, as pressures to reframe (or rebrand) more conventional nonprofits into what is described loosely as "social enterprise" are coming from public policy sources (see e.g. Coburn and Rijsdijk, 2010). Particular governance challenges for social enterprises, such as the role of boards of directors in gaining access to knowledge that enhances entrepreneurship (Zahra et al., 2009), are being uncovered by research (see also Spear et al., 2009). Although specific governance issues differ by the degree of embeddedness in the market, and also by organizational size and life stage, debates over the suitability of corporate governance practices, and broadly how to apply them so as to improve governance, are now pervasive across the nonprofit sector. The attention to and shape of the corporate governance debates is strongly reinforced by the expanded presence of both governments and nonprofit sectors in regulating—or self- and co-regulating—"good" governance which is demanding more detailed and consistent definition(s) of what constitutes good governance for nonprofits.

The chapter begins by identifying the range of conceptual frameworks used to depict nonprofit governance practice and predict its directions, and considering key criticisms of sectoral governance. Whilst these lenses are more kaleidoscope than solitary vision, two central issues about the nature of corporate governance are prevalent: (1) what counts as nonprofit ownership? and (2) how can nonprofit governance respond to a rapidly changing environment? These questions and their implications for strategy and accountability, particularly of nonprofit boards, are the focus of the second section. The chapter then broadens out to consider the variety of public regulatory and self-regulatory contexts within which nonprofits' governance occurs, and concludes with reflections on governance research and practice directions.

Theoretical Developments in Nonprofit Governance

The theoretical lenses through which most scholarship on nonprofit governance has developed are mostly focused on what boards do. Arguably, a greater onus of responsibility for defining an organization and its work rests on boards in the nonprofit than in the for-profit sector. Nonprofit directors are often the founders, fundraisers, strategists, builders of coalitions, sources of democracy and representation of members and users, and in very small organizations, the substitutes for staff. In part because nonprofit directors (normally) serve in a volunteer capacity, they are often looked to as defining the spirit of the organization in a way that ripples through its entire culture, and they hold liability for its shortcomings and wrongdoings. Building on this central preoccupation with the action of boards, Kreutzer (2009) identifies six quite distinct theoretical approaches to nonprofit governance, as summarized in Table 27.1.

The assurance of compliance, against an inclination to self-interest—the key element in agency theory—continues to underpin the case for extending compliance for nonprofits' financial accountability, notably in the US concerning the implications of the Sarbanes-Oxley legislation (e.g. Greenlee et al., 2007; Mead, 2007). Yet Boozang (2007: 1), also in a US context, argues that "early results of governance reform suggest that corporate compliance supersedes preservation and pursuit of mission in many of today's nonprofit board rooms," and that "a disproportionate focus on legal and financial accountability, with the attendant pressure to appoint directors qualified for performance of compliance activities, can divert attention from the more important

Table 27.1. Explanatory theoretical lenses for nonprofit governance, following Kreutzer (2009)

Explanatory theory	Nonprofit board's main role	Sources
Agency theory	Ensuring managerial compliance	Fama and Jensen, 1983
Stewardship theory	Improving organizational performance while partnering with management	Donaldson, 1990
Resource dependency theory	Boundary spanning; maintaining relations with external stakeholders, to sustain resources flow	Pfeffer and Salancik, 1978
Democratic perspective	Represent the interests of one or more of the constituencies the organization serves	Cornforth, 2003
Stakeholder theory	Political role in negotiating/resolving conflicting interests between many stakeholders	Freeman, 1984; Cornforth, 2003
Managerial hegemony theory	Largely symbolic; voluntary role and limited time means that power is ceded to senior managers	Mace, 1971; Cornforth, 2003

question of what kind of board will serve as the best steward of the entity's resources as it pursues its mission and serves its constituencies."

What is evident in the application of these theoretical perspectives is not only their range, but the tendency by theorists to borrow from and blend differing frameworks into more nuanced explanations of board behavior. For example, Lambright (2009) finds evidence to support both stewardship and agency theories in monitoring activities in seven cases of early childhood support programs. Mersland (2011: 327), guided by stakeholder and agency theories, explores historical parallels in savings banks to present corporate governance lessons for nonprofit micro-finance institutions, and argues that a "broader and more stakeholder-based understanding of corporate governance is necessary." Kreutzer and Jacobs (2011: 613) posit a "lack of consensus" on how best to understand nonprofit governance, and juxtapose agency and stewardship theory in a case "informed by a paradox perspective to give more adequate conceptualization."

Cornforth's (2004a, 2004b) earlier and continuing usage of paradox thinking to better understand the multiple perspectives on board governance is, however, already established: the central paradox revolves around the board's need to control and yet simultaneously support managerial action. This challenge is further complicated by the comparatively long tenure of nonprofit CEOs (Crutchfield and McLeod Grant, 2010; Santora and Sarros, 2001), enabling them to be gatekeepers of information when dealing with the board. Indeed, consideration of managerial hegemony as driving board practice in governance roles becomes an expression of agency theory, but in another guise, as managerial and director roles are reversed. Harrow (2011a) also draws on this use of paradox thinking, in her exploration of philanthropy governance in local contexts, as "place-based philanthropy" becomes prominent. She argues that, whilst institutional isomorphism may represent a barrier to variations in governance to reflect local philanthropy's needs and aims, it may also be a means of making local as well as national and international-level philanthropy increasingly legitimate and attractive to donors. Moreover, donors will also have an interest in governance structures, including those which safeguard their gifts or investments (Wood and Hagerman, 2010); and some major donors may monitor board decision-making in ways similar to those of large shareholders of for-profit boards.

Yet stakeholder theory, in contrast to business governance models, is increasingly used to examine the drawing into the nonprofit governance circle of those who are among the least powerful of a nonprofit's interested parties. Changing governance structures, first to accommodate, and then to enhance stakeholders' contributions at the margins of organizations, are advocated where the intent concerns organizational capacity building as well as improving governance per se (Freiwirth and Letona, 2006). Whilst nonprofit organizations generally are highly familiar with stakeholder constraints (Bryson, 2004; Cordery and Baskerville, 2005), philanthropic foundations are often far less so. The Bertelsmann Foundation-funded study on stakeholder interactions in philanthropy, "Who Comes to the Table?" (Backer et al., 2005), argued for a protective, proactive approach to stakeholder recognition in foundation governance. Their contention is that "especially in uncertain times, foundations can benefit from interacting openly with their key stakeholders" (Backer et al., 2005: 5). This study defines a stakeholder expansively (almost intuitively), as "someone who belongs at the table to debate how decisions are made about the allocation of resources and actions... either because they have some socially legitimated right to be there or because they influence or are influenced by the outcomes of those decisions, or both" (p. 5).

For Backer et al., stakeholder-led governance changes are represented as more than giving space for new conversations, but are also pragmatically led, since when "foundations cut their giving because their investment portfolios are diminished, emotional reactions among grantees and communities abound" (p. 5). Such a rationale (preceding the most recent world economic downturn) appears to argue that the shocks of rejection by foundations are more easily assuaged (or managed to a final and better outcome) by stakeholder interactions and associations within governance levels. This remains for the present untested on a wide scale, whilst research on grant-makers' and grant-seekers' perceptions of grant refusal from foundations found no evidence of rejected organizations being prompted to seek governance roles, nor of foundations bringing applicants more closely into the decision-making process (Harrow et al., 2011). Similarly, Sharp and Brock (2011) model how risk-mitigating behaviors can facilitate strategic processes in nonprofits "by promoting the harmonious interaction of internal and external stakeholders" (Sharp and Brock, 2011). Such approaches are tempered, however, by Speckbacher's advancement of stakeholder theory in governance using transaction costs economics (Speckbacher, 2008). Here he argues that "the core problem of governance (in nonprofits) is how to enhance valuable specific contributions of the relevant stakeholders while keeping the costs of bargaining between stakeholders and the costs of collective decision making low" (Speckbacher, 2008: 295).

Further theoretical blending marries stakeholder and resource dependency thinking; for example, Young (2011) in a US context demonstrates the contribution of governance to improving resource generation through stakeholder groups and the development of a regime of "economic stakeholder governance." Stakeholder and stewardship theories are brought together, with the addition of "institutional theory as a further lens for explaining the governance dynamic in social enterprises" by Mason et al. (2007). Verbruggen et al. (2011) link together theories of resource dependence and coercive isomorphism to explain nonprofits' compliance with financial reporting standards, using Belgian nonprofit examples. Callen et al. (2010), however, use a different theoretical pairing, agency and resource dependency perspectives, to study relations between stability of the environment, board structure, and board performance. From a sample of US nonprofits, they find that board mechanisms related to monitoring are more likely to be effective for stable organizations, whereas board mechanisms related to boundary spanning are more effective for less stable organizations. Thus they find that "the two theories are complementary and address different aspects of nonprofit performance" (Callen et al., 2010: 101). Unsurprisingly, these authors are drawn to Miller-Millesen's (2003) contention that in the complex and heterogeneous world of nonprofits, no one theory can describe all the tasks of a nonprofit board. Two key concerns that are common to all six of these theories and their various intersections pertain to understanding the nature and role of "owners" and stakeholders and the challenges of being strategic and responsive to a changing environment without compromising accountabilities.

GOVERNANCE IN NONPROFITS: OWNERSHIP AND ACCOUNTABILITY DEBATES

Accountability is the "flipside" of governance. Whereas governance entails the processes by which organizations set direction and make their important decisions, deciding in the process who is involved and how, ensuring a challenge function has been exercised, and developing and overseeing appropriate control systems, accountability involves the rendering of accounts and acceptance of responsibility for this direction, its implementation and its consequences, including responsibility to fix things that went wrong. Accountability has both a vertical dimension, flowing from the top of an organization through subordinate levels, members, and users, and a horizontal one, encompassing the mutual accountability between an organization and its partners or co-producers of policy and services (see Considine, 2002; Friedman and Phillips, 2004).

As Graham et al. (2003: 1) note, since such processes are in themselves hard to observe, attention is paid to governance *systems*, that is to "the agreements, procedures, conventions and policies that define who gets power, how decisions are taken and how accountability is rendered." "How accountability is rendered" is necessarily accompanied by questions of "for what?" and "to whom?" Valentinov (2011: 32) considers that "in all parts of the world, nonprofit organizations are under increasing pressure to demonstrate their congruence with the public interest," notwithstanding that their operations have been "traditionally associated with public virtues."

That public trust, or the trust of numerous publics, needs to be both earned and continually demonstrated by nonprofits is then a central feature in a range of national regulatory frameworks. In the UK, for example, with its multiple regulatory bodies (for Scotland, Northern Ireland, and England and Wales), the "public benefit" test for charity registration has been a source of contention as well as opportunity, and is currently under review (Cabinet Office, 2011). However, Morgan (2010) emphasizes that such a test applies only to charities, omitting all those nonprofits outside this organizational form. Populist expectations of nonprofits' behavior and challenges to trust, articulated by the media, also impinge in different socio-political contexts on governance decisions. For example, in the UK again, recommendations by an "independent group of experts" on disclosure and internal management of charities' expenses (National Council for Voluntary Organisations, 2010) appeared to imply a sector "catch-up," if not laggardly recognition of an area which so often presents the "face" of for-profit corporate governance: "when the MPs' expenses scandal led to wider debate... it was inevitable that the matter would be raised for charities" (National Council for Voluntary Organisations, 2010: 3).

From this standpoint, the inference may be drawn that, in many instances, members of the "general public," whether or not they are members, users, or donors, consider that particular nonprofits are in effect "theirs," if only through familiarity produced by sustained charity advertising. This points to the importance of understanding the nature of organizational identities (Young, 2001) in relation to governance arrangements. That widespread identification with an organization can produce ties that "bind and blind," and resulting governance dilemmas, is attested by Yip et al. (2010) in reporting on leadership issues in faith-based organizations.

Since accountability and ownership are importantly intertwined, who then "owns" nonprofits? Connelly et al. (2010: 1561) argue that firm ownership is an increasingly influential form of corporate governance, cautioning that governance researchers pay little academic attention to understanding owners from a behavioral standpoint. Such a call for an increasingly nuanced view of the role of ownership in firms' governance has equal importance for nonprofits. Representation of "owners" or users on governing boards is a longstanding issue among membership organizations that are heavily invested in a collective identity or social movement. For example, an international trend over the past two decades has been the transformation of organizations working on behalf of persons with disabilities into organizations directed and "owned" by persons with disabilities. More recently, issues of ownership have become prevalent in what is known as "venture philanthropy," which subsumes or retitles (or relegitimizes) grant-making as "mission-related investment," as well as the notion of "social investment" and its embedded association with the growing if ambiguous field of social entrepreneurship (Nicholls, 2010a). Certainly studies of outright nonprofit governance failure, and resulting organizational scandal, invariably place an overweening and misplaced sense of ownership (whether naïve or venal) at their heart, from plausible, dominant, and fraudulent CEOs to the creation of nonprofit institutions specifically to reap personal rewards (Tropman and Shaefer, 2004; Chen et al., 2009; Carman, 2011.) Since governance systems are rarely static and abrupt shifts may occur with leadership change, a sense of ownership may often be suspended or in flux. This is particularly so in the non-profit sector because succession planning seems recognized minimally as a key governance task (Froelich et al., 2011), in line with less evident focus on career planning (Harrow and Mole, 2005.)

Scale is also central to current debates on ownership and accountability given that nonprofits operate in different arenas, from the grassroots to the global, in increasingly complex and hybrid ways. Cornforth (2010) argues that, in nonprofit governance research, the extensive attention given to the working of boards of unitary organizations has led to an ignoring of wider governance systems and the more complex multi-level and multifaceted governance structures that many organizations have evolved as they take on a transnational scale of activity.

Whilst in theory governance and accountability occur at the top of organizations (the vertical dimension), in reality they appear crucially at the point where an organization interacts with its owners (the horizontal dimension). In service-oriented nonprofit organizations working with members and citizens, this occurs further down the organizational chain, at the point of that service (Halachmi, 2007); in the co-production of services or policy, this may occur within a collaboration or coalition. The exercise of horizontal accountability implies that conflict among competing owners of nonprofits, prompted by ownership disagreements, whether or not legitimate, may occur at a critical point of service. Examples would include a board-proposed closure of a service which users value, or where external funders seek to narrow a widely available nonprofit program (Smith, 2008, uses the example of a youth nonprofit's openness to working with all adolescents in its neighborhood, as contrasted with a funder's preference for the "neediest" youth). Implicitly, the question of nonprofit investor activism begins to arise, particularly in times of austerity and in nonprofit–business partnerships, as a factor in governance processes (Seitanidi, 2007). Table 27.2 identifies these many direct and "proxy" owners and the varying governance challenges they may present, citing relevant literature.

Table 27.2 also suggests degrees of opportunity for obfuscating governance questions in nonprofits when such a wide range of horizontal and vertical governance players are implicated, and for giving rhetorical significance but limited attention in practice to the complex oversight issues that may thus arise. This potential for obfuscation is further enhanced by the fact that, in ownership terms, the table is not fully complete. It omits, for example, the concept of "community governance," whereby it could be argued that "everyone"—but only in particular communities, often geographically located—owns some nonprofits. Though most associated with research on localism and

Table 27.2. Ownership issues in nonprofit governance, selected literatures

Potential owner type or would-be owner role	Key issues include	Examples of relevant literature
Charity founders	Prominent influence on board, directly or indirectly; "founder's syndrome"	Block and Rosenberg, 2002; Block, 2004
	"Directed philanthropy," e.g. requiring use of business models	Phillips, 2007
	Family philanthropy, members on boards	Pharoah et al., 2011
Boards	Longstanding, "non-revolving" membership; loyalty prized more than expertise	Steane and Christie, 2001
	Unevenly distributed expertise, especially financial	Harrow and Palmer, 2003
	Governance interpreted as leadership	Chait et al., 2005
	Stewardship and performance	Ostrower, 2007
	Processes affected by contextual/historical factors	Cornforth, 2011
	Complexities of shared leadership	Ferkins et al., 2009
	Allegiance to fellow directors and "groupthink"	Leslie, 2010
	Failure to curb CEO compensation	Carman 2011
Major donors Individuals, other nonprofits, Corporates	Leverage in decision-making, organization directions; growing or high expectations of reporting	Jones, 2007; Zainon et al., 2011; van Iwaarden et al., 2009
	Competition for influence	Young, 2011
Government as major donors or contractors or creator of the organization	Seeking and setting accounting/reporting standards	Hyndman and Macmahon, 2011
	Challenges to representational characteristics of nonprofits	Guo, 2007
	Government-owned/organized nonprofits where democracy less than fully functioning	Mulligan, 2007
Government as partners/collaborators	Identifying or redirecting funding priorities	Harrow and Jung, 2011
	Developing hybridity	Cornforth and Spear, 2010; Anheier, 2011
CEOs, other professional staffs	Faithfulness in implementing decisions	Burke, 2008
	Taking decisions at service level	Halachmi, 2007
	Varying quality of relationships	Iecovich and Bar-Mor, 2007
	Charismatic leadership	Hernandez and Leslie, 2001
	CEO competence crowds out board influence	Hough, 2009
	Fraud and its detection	Chen et al., 2009
Organizational members (of a network, federation, or associated group)	Relative influence of multiple groups	Cornforth and Robson, 2010
	Roles of affiliated outsiders	Kreutzer, 2009; Hayden, 2007
Individual members, acting individually or collectively (mutuals, cooperatives)	Inner circles, delegated governance	von Schnurbein, 2009; Cornforth, 2004
	Trust among members critical for common-pool resources governance	Leviten-Reid and Fairbairn, 2011

(continued)

Table 27.2. Continued

Potential owner type or would-be owner role	Key issues include	Examples of relevant literature
Organization beneficiaries/users	Lack of knowledge, lack of salience in crises Democratic opportunities when public services run by nonprofits Professionals/beneficiaries interactions Downward accountabilities in rights-based NGOs	van Iwaarden et al., 2009 LeRoux, 2009 Wellens and Jegers, 2011 O'Dwyer and Unerman, 2010

local government (see e.g. Somerville, 2005, examining the persistence of oligarchies at local levels and countervailing power building), the widest possible operation of "community governance" is demonstrated by Freiwirth and Letona (2006). Their case study explores a US Latino nonprofit's move to a "system-wide governance" model, whereby governance responsibilities were shared across the organization, and the lived experiences of community members served were the organization's drivers, "in contrast to the prevailing trend of professionalizing nonprofit boards" (Freiwirth and Letona, 2006: 26). Nevertheless, such levels of community governance engagement are not easy to maintain. For example, in her study of the added value of trust and foundations' support for health and social welfare nonprofits in Japan, Lawman (2008: 30) reports the findings of the Okayama Community Chest's 2007 ten-year review: that their "social relations with the people" had "thinned" in spite of the organization's efforts to stem this through citizens' taking on planning and decision allocation roles beyond volunteering.

A complicating factor is that ownership issues are underpinned by the cultural climates and mores within particular nonprofits which affect the tenor, direction, and language used in ownership debates. Thus Lew and Wójcik (2010), seeking to lay the groundwork for a transnational study of "foundation (i.e. philanthropic) governance" as "mirroring that of corporate governance," suggest that "while philanthropic culture and governance exist, they bear the features of national business cultures and governance" (Lew and Wójcik, 2010: 152). Nevertheless, "inferring from the critiques in the literature concerning the lack of performance metrics in philanthropy," Lew and Wójcik (2010: 158) note that they would not expect "many foundations to make extensive usage of performance metrics compared to the corporate sector," a view likely to be refuted by scholar-practitioners (Emerson, 2003; Bugg-Levine and Emerson, 2011). The effect of owner-influenced culture is also evident in Beamon and Balcik's (2008) study of performance metrics in humanitarian relief. They show that NGOs, dependent on attracting resources, focus unduly on measures of inputs (e.g. donations, funding, hours spent) as this is what their donors, funders, and volunteers want to know, whereas the decentralized nature of the delivery of humanitarian relief means that they should concentrate to a much greater extent on metrics related to the operational logistics of supply chains, as would commercial suppliers which do not feel the same pressures of ownership. Again, the "service" level and the environment in which that service (or other activity) occurs is a key focus for nonprofit governance questions. It is illustrative of why the issue of managing an appropriate fit of governance and environment is a second enduring theme in contemporary and especially comparative nonprofit governance debates (see e.g. Kuan et al., 2011).

Standardization versus Adaptation: The Issue of Environmental Fit

Pressures to identify and promote adherence to "best" practices—a core set of governance processes and systems that apply, with minor modifications, to all organizations—run deep in the nonprofit sector as a means to encouraging self-improvement. The "best-practice" movement has been buttressed by reviews by panels of experts (PAGVS, 1999; Panel on the Nonprofit Sector, 2007; National Council for Voluntary Organisations, 2010), a substantial and growing governance consulting industry, "associational entrepreneurs" (Sidel, 2005) such as nonprofit associations and self-declared third party watchdogs, and by state regulators which have begun to identify standards or "hallmarks" (Morris, 2011; Phillips, 2012) of good governance. An alternative perspective advocates the primacy of contextual factors in shaping how boards and governance systems are structured and how they work (Cornforth, 2003). In particular, contingency theory (Bradshaw, 2006; Bradshaw et al., 2007; Bradshaw, 2009; Ostrower and Stone, 2010) argues for the importance of environmental factors and the need for nonprofits to be responsive to these. The implication is that there is no one best form of corporate governance, but also that various forms of governance are not all equally good; while promoting responsiveness, contingency theory does not allow for an "anything goes" approach (Bradshaw, 2009: 61).

Drawing on the literatures that stress the importance of an organization's fit within its environment and on the recognition that "what works in one setting or at one period of time may not work in another and that efficiency is related to the ongoing alignment of various contingencies" (Bradshaw, 2009: 62), Bradshaw is committed to enabling nonprofit boards to reflect on their choices of governance configurations, with understanding of how relevant contingency factors affect these choices. As shown in Table 27.3, by taking into account the environment-organization fit, Bradshaw and colleagues (2007) identify four core types of governance models, each with distinctive advantages and disadvantages depending on the fit.

Leading from this work, Bradshaw and colleagues moved on to what appears the ultimate contingency-led governance model, that is, a hybrid model capable of recognizing

Table 27.3. Nonprofit, governance models, reflecting contrasting environmental features, drawn from Bradshaw (2007: 9–13)

Environmental context	Governance model	Expressed governance features include
Unitary organization, in conditions of stability	"Policy governance model"	Board focuses on vision, mission, and strategy; CEO on operational leadership; "familiar and comfortable framework" for many nonprofits
Pluralistic organization, in conditions of stability	"Constituency representation model"	Broad base of participation on the (larger) board, reflecting constituents' clear role in policy and planning; CEO empowered by board but vulnerable to changes there
Unitary organization, in conditions of innovation	"Entrepreneurial model"	Board with CEO concentrate on effectiveness and efficiency measures, pushing organization to success in its core "business"; adaptive, market share valued
Pluralistic organization, in conditions of innovation	"Emergent cellular model"	Distributed groups work together and independently; small core board, flexible, drawing on others as needed; combination of independence and interdependence

and responding to the inbuilt tensions as well as opportunities within the four conceptualized models, set out in Table 27.3. Presenting this as the "Vector Model" (from mathematics, where the vector is indicated symbolically by an arrow), and relating this to a leading Canadian health nonprofit with whom they were working, Bradshaw et al. (2007: 14) suggest that four vectors were each pulling away from a central hybrid model, drawn as a circle within a quadrant of the models: the resulting shape of the (governance) circle in the middle being dependent on the amount of force pulling at each corner (Bradshaw et al., 2007). They make a strong case that the dominance of any one model of governance for the nonprofit sector as advocated by some leading consultants, notably Carver (1997), in the governance "industry" is not healthy for the field. Instead, they see "plurality and diversity as a strength" (Bradshaw et al., 2007: 18; see Murray, 2007). Intriguingly, in their case study of the health nonprofit, the primary funder ultimately decided "that the hybrid model was not one they were comfortable with and the Board returned to a more traditional Advisory Board" (Bradshaw et al., 2007). However, the case for and use made of contingency theory does not in any way release nonprofits (both leaders and followers) from their own responsibilities for reflecting on and choosing particular governance paths, and for changing these as external change occurs.

The use of contingency theory is also central to the US-located work of Ostrower and Stone (2010) to "move governance research forward." Working on a single contingency-based framework, which links internal organizational and external conditions to board attributes, thence to board roles and organization effectiveness, they draw on findings from the Urban Institute's National Survey of Nonprofit Governance (Ostrower, 2007), undertaken in 2005 with responses from over 5,000 US nonprofits, "the largest sample in the (nonprofit) governance literature to date" (Ostrower and Stone, 2010: 905). Examining the wide range of variables impacting on board governance, they apply their framework to studying boards' adoption of accountability practices, specifically in relation to variations in adoption of Sarbanes-Oxley-related practices. Recognizing the normative pressures on nonprofit boards "to assess the adequacy and public acceptability of their policies in relationship to standards set by the Act" (Ostrower and Stone, 2010: 914), they find considerable heterogeneity among nonprofits with respect to adoption of most practices; "for instance, half have a conflict of interest policy but half do not" (Ostrower and Stone, 2010). Moreover, the study found "an intriguing link between diversity and accountability (with) the percentage of racial and ethnic minorities on the board positively associated with the adoption of most Sarbanes-Oxley-related policies" (Ostrower and Stone, 2010: 918). Further critical questions for governance studies generally include the question of whether and how board members with corporate (i.e. business) ties serve "as conduits for other business practices" (p. 919), as well as the recurring challenges around board size and diversity as governance change levers (see e.g. Hartaska and Nadolnyak, 2012).

The depth and breadth of this study and its findings underscore the complexity of variables affecting board governance behaviors and practices; and for Ostrower and Stone (2010: 920) the argument is further made that "advancement on board research will…depend on working inductively from research findings to theory." The study size is especially critical, given the extent to which governance studies for this sector offer small and often single case examples (albeit illustrative of the sector's organizational singulatory) and push-back against any assertion that an all-purpose and all-embracing governance framework is feasible, let alone desirable for its work. (See e.g. Burke, 2008, concerning fidelity to financial decisions and board–CEO communications, or Miller, 2008, examining how an "aged care organisation board" can develop "an evaluation process that maintains their cultural identity and yet conforms to sound governance principles".)

Harrow and Wilding (2010) reflect on the prominence of small-scale, snapshot-style work as a general characteristic of management research in this sector, noting its rationale of uniqueness, thereby denying replicability and comparison. However, it may be that in the field of governance, academics are treading especially warily, given the voluntary nature of board membership and thus the extent to which they judge much of the sector's governance structures to be somewhat fragile, given its reliance on that volunteerism. Hough et al. (2005), for example, address in detail the range of social trends impacting negatively on board member availability, including, paradoxically, the heightened social and legal expectations of those members; and they identify possible "fresh approaches to governance," including the appointment of "inside directors" (those who are management or other staff) (Hough et al., 2005, 15.) Ironically, the completion of the Urban Institute's groundbreaking study was reliant on survey completion by CEOs, whose interpretations and responses may or may not reflect the perspectives of their boards and chairs.

Across the range of theoretical examinations and explanations of nonprofit governance directions and mechanisms, the factor of the formal governmental regulatory regime under which (or despite which) various groups of nonprofits operate, looms very large. DeMarzo et al. (2005: 688) deem that "regulating is core government business," and where self-regulation of any industry is successful, Newman and Bach see this as occurring "within the shadow of the state" (2001). It is therefore to the regulatory aspects of nonprofit governance that this chapter now turns.

Regulation: The Complexities of Regulating for and by Private Governance

Regulation has become a complex set of governmental and quasi-governmental activities, seeking to direct and promote, if not control and command, certain practices and behaviors to protect the public. The case for a "regulatory society" rather than a "regulatory state" is made by Black (2002: 1), who argues that "regulation is 'decentred', defused throughout society," not state "centred." Black emphasizes that "command and control" regulation has a myriad sources of failure (Black, 2002: 2) and observes that decentered approaches involving multiple actors other than the state are being harnessed in the design of hybrid regulatory mechanisms to enable the state to "best act to further public policy objectives" (Black, 2002). In construing regulation as a co-produced, multiple-directional process, a decentering analysis of regulation then assumes a complexity of interactions among a variety of actors (Hutter, 2006). In this "post-regulatory state" (Scott, 2004), government approaches to regulation for the nonprofit sector are in flux, with evidence of reduced, co-produced, and expanded regulation, as well as self-regulation trends or efforts (Gugerty et al., 2010). Harrow (2006), in addressing the kinds of regulatory space in which voluntary organizations find themselves, explores the extent to which their increased involvement in the delivery of public services makes growing state regulation inevitable, particularly regulation conducted within compliance-dominant frameworks that have been set up, as Parker (2000) argues, to "solve a problem." Increasingly, this "problem" is about the regulation of their corporate governance.

State regulation of this sector grew out of, and some would argue is still stuck in, a model of "charity" (Phillips, 2010) derived from the 1601 Statute of Elizabeth I and not adequately modernized. Although a number of countries, including the UK, have in recent years legislated a modern approach to defining public benefit, the regulatory regime remains bifurcated into an elaborate system of registration, rules, and reporting for charities (and other officially recognized public benefit organizations), which has a heavy emphasis on transparency and financial controls in the interest of safeguarding the charitable gift, and a minimalist system for other nonprofits. The thrust of the rules governing charities has been to ensure they spend "substantially all" of their tax receipted revenues on their charitable purposes, thereby placing strict limits on administrative and fundraising costs, but also on political and business activities.

The growing hybridity of the nonprofit sector has created significant challenges for existing regulation, including how to reconcile limitations on business activities with social enterprise and mission-related investing for which the social purpose is achieved through the business model, the need for new legal forms of incorporation that accommodate both social and business purposes, and how to regulate on a scale suitable to global operations, the internet fundraising and transnational advocacy activities of many nonprofits. As Hopt and Von Hippel (2010; see also Dunn, 2011) emphasize, national and continental laws have not kept up with the economic as well as social importance of the nonprofit sector, although incremental reform is advancing in some jurisdictions. For example, in a seminal paper, Nicholls (2010b) explores the regulatory context and climate in which the British community interest companies (CICs, a vehicle for social enterprise) are developing. Drawing on content from a sample of 80 CIC annual reports, he demonstrates how the CIC Regulator acts as a mediator of disclosure information across multiple user constituencies. In the US, not so much boundary-blurring as boundary-melting is occurring, with interesting regulatory and governance implications, as a small number of states are creating new legal structures to enable profitable corporations to operate with stated social purpose without fear of litigation; a leading example is California's Corporate Flexibility Act, which came into effect in January 2012, enabling "flexible purpose corporations" and "benefit corporations" (Hernand et al., 2011).

A second development is that the preoccupation with accountability and financial controls, reinforced by the sense of public ownership of nonprofits as well as some spillover effects from for-profit governance scandals, has increased the appetite of many government regulators for increased oversight of the corporate governance of nonprofits. In countering the view that the US Internal Revenue Service (IRS) should stick to the tax code and "get out of the governance business," the Commissioner of Tax Exempt and Government Entities was emphatic that "we are in this discussion to stay" (Williams, 2010). Justifying the need for greater oversight of good governance as a means of promoting tax compliance and as part of its system of risk regulation, the IRS now requires reporting on several aspects of governance and management practices on its revised 990 annual return. In addition, the IRS collaborates with *Guidestar*, an independent watchdog of nonprofits, to make the tax return information widely available on the popular *Guidestar* website. It also provides greater direction to nonprofits to better articulate and demonstrate good governance (for example, its determination letters may encourage nonprofits to incorporate such principles into their organizing documents) and it provides IRS examination agents with training on good corporate governance so they can better identify good practices in their assessments of nonprofits. Similarly, the Charity Commission of England and Wales issued a set of "hallmarks" of effective charities in 2008 that specifies the legal requirements related to governance and provides soft law guidance as to what it considers the practices of good corporate governance. More recently, and in the context of major budget reductions over the next four years, the Charity Commission (2011a) reports at the outset of its "new strategy" that "the public expects us to be a robust regulator—that message emerged clearly from the focus groups we held."

The regulatory society is thus also in play and, indeed, many governments are promoting self-regulation as the first principle, backed by state regulation as needed or co-mingled and co-produced as joint regulatory regimes. Self-regulation is variously motivated. It is sometimes seen to be a "buyoff" outcome to ensure little change where further government regulation is unwanted and organizations seek to protect their self-interest, in effect, "... permitting the wolf to guard the sheep" (Newman and Bach, 2001: 6). Alternatively, it is viewed as the "better regulation option," whereby costs are transferred to the regulated industry (as the Charity Commission for England and Wales' 2012–15 Strategic Plan aims to do with its priority of developing the "self-reliance of the sector"; Charity Commission, 2011b). Or, it may represent a "coming of age" in an industry where the regulatees are acknowledged as trustworthy and effectively able to self-monitor in the best interests of their users/customers/clients.

For nonprofits as well as for-profits, a degree of co-production of regulation offers crucial advantages, for example, in self-regulation of fundraising where adherence to conduct codes may offer competitive advantage as well as boosting public confidence. This sector has long had a variety of voluntary codes of conduct, often operated by associational entrepreneurs, which have varied greatly in their success in changing behavior or enhancing trust in nonprofits (Gugerty and Prakash, 2010). The new features of self-regulation are that these voluntary codes are morphing into full-blown systems of third party accreditation, complete with monitoring and compliance mechanisms, and are extending beyond certification related to fundraising, as in the Netherlands (Bekkers, 2003), to comprehensive coverage of nonprofit governance and management. With its "Standards Program" (involving 89 standards covering fundraising, financial accountability, staff management, volunteer involvement, and corporate governance) currently in the pilot phase, Canada has gone the farthest in developing this sort of nonprofit-led certification involving extensive self- and peer-review processes and spot checks of compliance (Phillips, 2012). Whilst aimed at creating "a community of practice" for continuing improvement, the self-regulation scheme is also intended to forestall stricter government regulation following the announcement by the regulator that it would be more closely examining a charity's governance systems as part of its own auditing processes.

Whether the expanded state oversight of corporate governance and these sector-run certification systems will operate as separate, dual systems or whether they will evolve into integrated regimes of co-regulation is still an open question. The future may resemble what Harrow and Douthwaite (2006) refer to as a "New Auspices" approach, suggesting a muddle rather than coordinated co-production of regulation, with regulators falling out and claiming others' spheres of influence, and continuing public uncertainties as to who—if anyone—regulates and for whom. As charity regulation becomes "everybody's business" under these new auspices, it becomes fragmented and variable in impact and intent. Under such a model, assertions over what is or might be "good governance" for nonprofits may also become increasingly qualified and, very appropriately, open to debate, disagreement, and contradiction. A hint of this possibility is the recent resurgence in the UK of the case for payment of charity board members, animated, in part, to avoid such service in a nonprofit context being dismissed to a "governance little league" (Harrow, 2011b).

Equally uncertain is the impact on nonprofit governance. Will the self-assessment and detailed reporting on corporate governance encourage nonprofits to adaptively fit their processes and structures to their environment, as contingency theory encourages? Or, will it simply impel standardization and, despite protestations, a "one-size-for-all" model? What is clear is that greater regulation *of* corporate governance and greater regulation *by* private governance is on the agenda for the foreseeable future.

Conclusions

Nonprofit governance, as a means of strategically identifying and managing change and of building and making effective use of stakeholder relationships, faces increasing directional dilemmas. One path leads toward greater hybridity. New business models and organizational forms are creating different ways of blending social purpose and financial sustainability, while traditional government grants and contracts are shrinking. After several decades of learning how to compete effectively in pursuit of project and contract funding, a renewed emphasis on "relational governance" (Phillips and Smith, 2011) is promoting closer collaboration, not only with other nonprofits but with governments and business. Place-based philanthropy is encouraging strategic alliances among stakeholders at the local level, requiring them to put aside their organizational turf. The imperative for corporate governance that accompanies such diversification is innovation. Strategically adaptive nonprofits would be expected to do exactly as contingency theory advocates: assess and act on their situations to develop bespoke models of governance, leading to a greater variety of governance approaches. Further, the theories of nonprofit governance—which already represent a kaleidoscope of lenses rather than any single theoretical perspective or any empirically driven "model"—should be able to provide adequate support for such experimentation whilst themselves innovating and adapting.

Another direction presents pressures for standardization and homogenization. For example, a substantial number of public "owners" and business leaders (and increasingly foundations and other funders) no longer see a myriad of community organizations providing similar services or pursuing related causes as responsive to community needs and as building social capital, but merely as inefficient. Thus, the pressures for nonprofit mergers so as to create economies of scale, although talked about for a decade, have accelerated. Critically, the notion that any nonprofit is "too good to fail" has faded. Both funders and the general public owners are demanding that nonprofits demonstrate their impact in measurable and transparent ways, and a variety of independent watchdogs have sprung up to assess their effectiveness in doing so. A large and growing industry of "good governance" consultants promote "best" practices, compelling nonprofits to conform rather than experiment in pursuit of standards of excellence. Government regulators have made it clear that, in the interests of accountability, they are, indeed, in the governance discussion to stay, and that this will increasingly involve the identification and audit of nonprofit corporate governance systems. An interesting question is whether the regulators' interpretation of what constitutes good governance will consistently coincide with the standards developed and certified by the nonprofit sector. The implication of this standard-driven process is likely to be a convergence in governance models, and perhaps of theoretical perspectives, as emphasis on adaptation to situational differences and stakeholder relationships gives way to publicly accounting for accepted good practice.

Whilst the nonprofit sector has always defended its distinctiveness and resisted standardization, the public and stakeholders may be less willing than in the past to accept mediocre governance. Alternatively, they may be glad to have volunteers willing to serve on nonprofit boards even if they do not exercise their challenge function all that well. Facing up to directional dilemmas in approaches to nonprofit governance may also include a recognition that some of the talk around governance innovation can be too beguiling and that in some nonprofit settings bespoke models of governance may be just too forgiving.

The future of nonprofit governance is, of course, not likely to be a simple choice and subsequent channelization of either greater diversification *or* greater standardization. Given the new and multiple pressures, the contributions of empirical research and theorizing on nonprofit governance are more important and timely than ever, assessing both the nature and consequences of these unfolding developments. The range of research opportunities is expansive but several priorities stand out in our view. Whilst this chapter has made a case for the centrality of stakeholder relationships, empirical research on the nature and impact of these relationships is actually quite spotty. For a sector that prides itself on its diversity, evidence in many developed countries suggests that nonprofit boards remain surprisingly white, middle class, and middle-aged. A better understanding of the reasons that representation and meaningful engagement of minority communities has been lacking, and of how to create and make good use of board (and organizational) diversity, is still needed. Similarly, as increased scrutiny of and reflection on "women on boards" debates takes hold in for-profit research, questions of women's underrepresentation on nonprofit boards, important though they are, need to be extended toward deepening understanding also of those boards' dynamics, especially where the respective nonprofit chief executive posts are also held by women.

Moreover, most of the extant research on stakeholder engagement has focused on service-providing nonprofits. Thus we still know very little about the governance of foundations, which are inherently more private in terms of the "ownership" of their money, but perhaps also of their decision-making, in spite of the broader significance of their work. In times of austerity, are investor-owners and funders exerting a stronger presence in governance, with what consequences? A second theme of this chapter has been the tension between best-practice models and those stressing responsiveness to environmental contingencies. As nonprofits become more hybrid, questions of the effectiveness of governance models for differing blends of private and public, and of social and business purposes need to be understood. Increasingly, the imperative is not to simply adapt to a changing environment but to lead social innovation—to inspire, affect, and manage change—and governance research is only beginning to tackle the implications of social innovation and of balancing innovation with risk management and accountability.

Finally, future research needs to be more creative not only in what it examines, but also in how it does so, particularly in moving beyond examination of single cases to embrace more systematic studies and comparative (across subsectors, locales, and jurisdictions) approaches. In spite of this sector's argument for its "exceptionalism" and a certain wariness of admonishments to become more "business-like," research could also usefully explore comparisons and lessons from—and for—the for-profit sector. Wherever the paths of future research lead, they could all be more effective in mobilizing new knowledge to actually making corporate governance, and performance measurement, more effective in the rapidly changing relationships and regulatory environments of the nonprofit sector.

REFERENCES

ANHEIER, H. K. (2011). "Governance and Leadership in Hybrid Organisations, Comparative and Interdisciplinary Perspectives," Background Paper for International Symposium, December 5–6, Centre for Social Investment, Heidelberg University.

BACKER, T. E., SMITH, R., and BARBELL, I. (2005). "Who Comes to the Table? Stakeholder Interactions in Philanthropy," in D. Eilinghof (ed.), *Rethinking Foundation Effectiveness: Lessons from an International Network of Foundation Experts*. Gütersloh: Bertelsmann Stiftung, 111–27.

BEAMON, B. M., and BALCIK, B. (2008). "Performance Measurement in Humanitarian Relief Chains," *International Journal of Public Sector Management*, 21(1): 4–25.

BEKKERS, R. (2003). "Trust, Accreditation and Philanthropy in the Netherlands," *Nonprofit and Voluntary Sector Quarterly*, 32(4): 596–615.

BLACK, J. (2002). "Critical Reflections on Regulation," Centre for Analysis of Risk and Regulation Discussion Paper Series, Paper 4, London School of Economics and Political Science.

BLOCK, S. R. (2004). *Why Nonprofits Fail: Overcoming Founder's Syndrome, Fundphobia and Other Obstacles to Success*. San Francisco, CA: Jossey-Bass.

—— and ROSENBERG, S. (2002). "Toward an Understanding of Founder's Syndrome: An Assessment of Power and Privilege among Founders of Nonprofit Organizations," *Nonprofit Management and Leadership*, 12(4): 353–68.

BOOZANG, K. (2007). "Does an Independent Board Improve Nonprofit Corporate Governance?" Seton Hall Public Law Research Paper No. 1002421, <http://works.bepress.com/cgi/viewcontent.cgi?article=1000&context=kathleen_boozang>.

BRADSHAW, P. (2006). "A Contingency View of How Boards Can Best Contribute to the Efficient Management of Nonprofit Organizations," York-Mannheim Symposium, September 13–14. Toronto, Canada: York University. Available at <http://scholar.googleusercontent.com/scholar?q=cache:X10l_-NrrOUJ:scholar.google.com/+typologies+of+nonprofit+governance,+Bradshaw&hl=en&as_sdt=0,5>.

——(2009). "A Contingency Approach to Nonprofit Governance," *Nonprofit Management and Leadership*, 20(1): 61–81.

Bradshaw, P., Hayday, B., and Armstrong, R. (2007). "Nonprofit Governance Models: Problems and Prospects," *The Innovation Journal*, 12(3): 1–22. Available at <http://www.innovation.cc/scholarly-style/bradshaw5final.pdf>.

Bryson, J. (2004). "What to Do when Stakeholders Matter? Stakeholder Identification and Analysis Techniques," *Public Management Review*, 6(1): 21–54.

Bugg-Levine, A., and Emerson, J. (2011). "Impact Investing: Transforming How We Make Money While Making a Difference," *Innovations*, 6(3): 9–18.

Burke, T. H. (2008). "Nonprofit Service Organizations: Fidelity with Strategic Plans for Financial Survival—Critical Roles for Chief Executive Officers," *Journal of Human Behavior in the Social Environment*, 18(2): 204–23.

Cabinet Office (2011). "Review of the Charities Act, 2006: Terms of Reference," November 8. Available at <http://www.cabinetoffice.gov.uk/resource-library/review-charities-act-2006-%E2%80%93-terms-reference>.

Cadbury Review (1992). *Report of the Committee on the Financial Aspects of Corporate Governance*. London: Gee. Available at <http://www.jbs.cam.ac.uk/cadbury/report/index.html>.

Callen, J. L., Klein, A., and Tinkelman, D. (2010). "The Contextual Impact of Nonprofit Board Composition and Structure on Organizational Performance: Agency and Resource Dependency Perspectives," *Voluntas: International Journal of Voluntary and Nonprofit Organizations*, 21(1): 101–25.

Carman, J. C. (2011). "What You Don't Know Can Hurt Your Community: Lessons from a Local United Way," *Nonprofit Management and Leadership*, 21(4): 443–8.

Carver, J. (1997). *Boards that Make a Difference: A New Design for Leadership in Nonprofit and Public Organizations*, 2nd edition. San Francisco, CA: Jossey-Bass.

Chait, R. P., Ryan, W. P., and Taylor, B. E. (2005). *Governance as Leadership: Reframing the Work of Nonprofit Boards*. Hoboken, NJ: Boardsource and Wiley.

Charity Commission (2011a). "Charity Commission News No. 36," Autumn. Available at <http://www.charitycommission.gov.uk/about_us/About_the_Commission/ccnews36.aspx>.

——(2011b). *Strategic Plan 2012–2015*, December. Available at <http://www.charity-commission.gov.uk/about_us/about_the_commission/strategic_plan_2012.aspx?>.

Chen, Q., Salterio, S., and Murphy, P. (2009). "Fraud in Canadian Nonprofit Organisations as Seen through the Eyes of Canadian Newspapers," *The Philanthropist*, 22: 24–39. Available at <http://journals.sfu.ca/philanthropist/index.php/phil/article/viewFile/511/517>.

Coburn, J., and Rijsdijk, R. (2010). "Evaluating the Success Factors for Establishing a Thriving Social Enterprise in Scotland," The Scottish Government, Voluntary Issues Research Findings 3/2010. Available at <http://www.scotland.gov.uk/Publications/2010/11/23094433/0>.

Connelly, B. L., Hoskisson, R. E., Tihanyi, L., and Certo, S. T. (2010). "Ownership as a Form of Corporate Governance," *Journal of Management Studies,* Special Issue, Offshoring and Outsourcing, 47(8): 1561–89.

Considine, M. (2002). "The End of the Line? Accountable Governance in the Age of Networks, Partnerships and Joined-Up Services," *Governance*, 15(1): 21–40.

Cordery, J., and Baskerville, R. F. (2005). "Hegemony, Stakeholder Salience and the Construction of Accountability in the Charity Sector," Centre for Governance and Taxation Research, Working Paper No. 25. Wellington, New Zealand: Victoria University. Available at <http://papers.ssrn.com/sol3/papers.cfm?abstract_id=1199503>.

CORNFORTH, C. (2003). *The Governance of Public and Non-Profit Organizations.* London: Routledge.

—— (2004a). "The Governance of Co-operatives and Mutual Associations: A Paradox Perspective," *Annals of Public and Co-operative Economics,* 75(1): 11–32.

—— (2004b). "The Governance of Social Enterprises: A Paradox Perspective," *Économie et solidarités,* 35(1–2): 81–99.

—— (2010). "Challenges and Future Directions in Nonprofit Governance Research," Tenth EURAM Conference, Rome, Italy, May 19–23. Available at <http://oro.open.ac.uk/23548/1/Euram-Challenges_and_Future_Directions_for_Third_Sector_Governance_Research.pdf>.

—— (2011). "Nonprofit Governance Research: Limitations of the Focus on Boards and New Directions for Research," *Nonprofit and Voluntary Sector Quarterly,* online, November 17 DOI: <10.1177/0899764011427959>.

—— and CHAMBERS, N. (2010). "The Role of Corporate Governance and Boards in Organisational Performance," in K. Walsh, G. Harvey, and P. Jas (eds.), *Connecting Knowledge and Performance in Public Services: From Knowing to Doing.* Cambridge: Cambridge University Press, 99–127.

—— and ROBSON, P. (2010). "Governance Issues in Voluntary Organisations with Local-National Structures," Voluntary Sector Studies Network Conference, May 2010, Sheffield Hallam University, UK. Available at <http://www.vssn.org.uk/events/day-conferences/item/229>.

—— and SPEAR, R. (2010). "The Governance of Hybrid Organizations," in D. Billis (ed.), *Hybrid Organizations and the Third Sector: Challenges for Practice, Theory and Policy.* Basingstoke, UK: Palgrave, 70–89.

CRUTCHFIELD, L., and MCLEOD GRANT, H. (2010). "Share Leadership," in J. L. Perry (ed.), *The Jossey-Bass Reader on Nonprofit and Public Leadership.* San Francisco, CA: Jossey-Bass, 124–49.

DEMARZO, P. M., FISHMAN, M., and HAGERTY, K. M. (2005). "Self Regulation and Government Oversight," *Review of Economic Studies,* 72(3): 687–706.

DONALDSON, L. (1990). "The Ethereal Hand: Organizational Economics and Management Theory," *Academy of Management Review,* 25(3): 369–81.

DUNN, A. (2011). "Gatekeeper Governance: The European Union and Civil Society Organizations," in S. D. Phillips and S. R. Smith (eds.), *Governance and Regulation in the Third Sector: International Perspectives.* London: Routledge, 164–97.

EMERSON, J. (2003). "The Blended Value Proposition: Integrating Social and Financial Returns," *California Management Review,* 45(4): 35–51.

FAMA, E. F., and JENSEN, M. (1983). "Separation of Ownership and Control," *Journal of Law and Economics,* 26(2): 301–25.

FERKINS, L., SHILBURY, D., and MACDONALD, G. (2009). "Board Involvement in Strategy: Advancing the Governance of Sports Organizations," *Journal of Sport Management,* 23(3): 247–77.

FREEMAN, R. E. (1984). *Strategic Management: A Stakeholder Approach.* Boston, MA: Pitman.

FREIWIRTH, J., and LETONA, M. E. (2006). "System-Wide Governance for Community Empowerment," *The Nonprofit Quarterly,* 13(4): 24–7.

FRIEDMAN, A., and PHILLIPS, M. (2004). "Balancing Strategy and Accountability: A Model for the Governance of Professional Associations," *Nonprofit Management and Leadership,* 15(2): 187–204.

Friewirth, J., and Letona, M. E. (2006). "System-Wide Governance for Community Empowerment," *The Nonprofit Quarterly*, 13(4): 24–7. Available at <http://nonprofitsa.com/resources/System-Wide+Governance+Model.pdf>.

Froelich, K., McGee, G., and Rathge, R. (2011). "Succession Planning in Nonprofit Organisations," *Nonprofit Management and Leadership*, 22(1): 3–20.

Graham, J., Amos, B., and Plumptre, T. (2003). "Principles for Good Governance in the Twenty First Century," Policy Brief No. 15. Ottawa, Canada: Institute on Governance. Available at <http://iog.ca/en/publications/iog-policy-brief-no-15-principles-good-governance-21st-century>.

Greenlee, J., Fischer, M., Gordon, T., and Keating, E. (2007). "An Investigation of Fraud in Nonprofit Organizations: Occurrences and Deterrents," *Nonprofit and Voluntary Sector Quarterly*, 36(4): 676–94.

Gugerty, M. K., and Prakash, A. (eds.) (2010). *Voluntary Regulation of NGOs and Nonprofits: An Accountability Club Framework*. Cambridge: Cambridge University Press.

—— Sidel, M., and Bies, A. L. (2010). "Introduction to Minisymposiim: Nonprofit and Self Regulation in Comparative Perspective, Themes and Debates," *Nonprofit and Voluntary Sector Quarterly*, 39(6): 1027–38.

Guo, C. (2007). "When Government Becomes the Principal Philanthropist: The Effect of Public Funding on Patterns of Nonprofit Governance," *Public Administration Review*, 67(3): 456–71.

Halachmi, A. (2007). "Where the Rubber Meets the Road: Governance and Accountability Issues in Civil-Society-Based Organizations," *The Public Sector Innovation Journal*, 1(3): 2–13.

Harrow, J. (2006). "Chasing Shadows? Perspectives on Self-Regulation in UK Charity Fundraising," *Public Policy and Administration*, 2(3): 86–104.

—— (2011a). "Governance and Isomorphism in Local Philanthropy," *Public Management Review*, 13(1): 1–20.

—— (2011b). "Going For Gold?" *Charity Finance*, December, 44.

—— and Douthwaite, S. (2006). "Fundraising Regulation: For Who and by Whom?" in J. Mordaunt and R. Paton (eds.), *Thoughtful Fundraising: Concepts, Issues and Perspectives*. London: Routledge.

—— and Jung, T. (2011). "Philanthropy is Dead: Long Live Philanthropy," *Public Management Review*, 13(8): 1047–56.

—— and Mole, V. (2005). "'I Want to Move Once I Have Got Things Straight': Voluntary Sector Chief Executives' Career Accounts," *Nonprofit Management and Leadership*, 16(1): 79–100.

—— and Palmer, P. (2003). "The Financial Role of Charity Boards," in C. Cornforth (ed.), *The Governance of Public and Nonprofit Organisations: What Do Boards Do?* London: Routledge, 97–114.

—— and Wilding, K. (2010). "Working with the Voluntary Sector: Some Reflections on Management Research in and for the Voluntary and Community Sector," in C. Cassell and B. Lee (eds.), *Challenges and Controversies in Management Research*. London: Routledge, 292–313.

—— Fitzmaurice, J., McKenzie, T., and Bogdanova, M. (2011). "The Art of Refusal: The Experiences of Grant Makers and Grant Seekers," London: Cass Business School and the Charities Aid Foundation. Available at <http://www.cass.city.ac.uk/__data/assets/pdf_file/0014/107006/Art_Refusal_Main_2011-FINAL.pdf>.

HARTASKA, V., and NADOLNYAK, D. (2012). "Board Size and Diversity as Governance Mechanisms in Community Development Loan Funds in the USA," *Applied Economics*, 44(3): 4313–29.

HASENFELD, Y., and GIDRON, B. (2005). "Understanding Multi-purpose Hybrid Voluntary Organisations: The Contribution of Theories on Civil Society, Social Movements and Non-profit Organisations," *Journal of Civil Society*, 1(2): 97–112.

HAYDEN, E. W. (2007). "Governance Failures Also Occur in the Nonprofit World," *International Journal of Business Governance and Ethics*, 2(1–2): 16–118.

HERNAND, D., MCDOWALL, S., and RICHARD, C. (2011). "Two New Corporate Forms to Advance Social Benefit in California," *Business Ethics, the Magazine of Corporate Responsibility*, November 21. Available at <http://business-ethics.com/>.

HERNANDEZ, C., and LESLIE, D. R. (2001). "Charismatic Leadership," *Nonprofit Management and Leadership*, 11(4): 493–97.

HOPT, K. J., and VON HIPPEL, T. (2010). *Comparative Corporate Governance of Non-Profit Organizations*. Cambridge: Cambridge University Press.

HORTON SMITH, D., STEBBINS, R. A., and DOVER, M. A. (eds.) (2006). *A Dictionary of Nonprofit Terms and Concepts*. Bloomington, IN: Indiana University Press.

HOUGH, A. (2009). "How Nonprofit Boards Monitor, Judge and Influence Organisational Performance," Ph.D. thesis, Queensland University of Technology, Australia. Available at <http://eprints.qut.edu.au/36376/>.

—— MCGREGOR-LOWNDES, M., and RYAN, C. (2005). "The Training Grounds of Democracy? Social Trends and Nonprofit Governance," Centre of Philanthropy and Nonprofit Studies and School of Accountancy, Working Paper CPNS 31. Queensland University of Technology, Brisbane, Australia. Available at <http://eprints.qut.edu.au/4453/1/4453.pdf>.

HUTTER, B. M. (2006). "The Role of Non-State Actors in Regulation," Centre for Analysis of Risk and Regulation Discussion Paper Series, Paper 37, London School of Economics and Political Science.

HYNDMAN, N., and MACMAHON, G. (2011). "The Hand of Government in Shaping Accounting and Reporting in the UK Charity Sector," *Public Money and Management*, 31(3): 167–74.

IECOVICH, E., and BAR-MOR, H. (2007). "Relations between Chairpersons and CEOs in Nonprofit Organisations," *Administration in Social Work*, 31(4): 21–40.

JONES, B. (2007). "Citizens, Partners or Patrons? Corporate Power and Patronage Capitalism," *Journal of Civil Society*, 3(2): 159–77.

KREUTZER, K. (2009). "Nonprofit Governance during Organizational Transition in Voluntary Associations," *Nonprofit Management and Leadership*, 20(1): 117–33.

—— and JACOBS, C. (2011). "Balancing Control and Coaching in CSO Governance: A Paradox Perspective on Board Behavior," *Voluntas: International Journal of Voluntary and Nonprofit Organizations*, 22(4): 613–38.

KUAN, Y.-Y., CHAN, K.-T., and WANG, S.-T. (2011). "The Governance of Social Enterprise in Taiwan and Hong Kong: A Comparison," *Journal of Asian Public Policy*, 4(2): 149–70.

LAMBRIGHT, K. (2009). "Agency Theory and Beyond: Contracted Providers' Motivations to Properly Use Service Monitoring Tools," *Journal of Public Administration Research and Theory*, 19(2): 207–27.

LAWMAN, S. (2008). "A Preliminary Investigation of the Added Value of Trust and Foundation Funding to the Health and Social Welfare Nonprofit Sector in Japan," MSc Grantmaking Management Dissertation, Cyril Kleinwort Learning Resource Centre, Cass Business

School, City University. Available at <http://www.cass.city.ac.uk/library/electronic/index.html>.

Leslie, M. J. (2010). "The Wisdom of Crowds? Groupthink and Nonprofit Governance," Yeshiva University, Cardozo School of Law. Available at <http://works.bepress.com/Paternalistic_or_Participatory Governance,cgi/viewcontent.cgi?article=1001&context=melanie_leslie>.

LeRoux, K. (2009). "Paternalistic or Participatory Governance/Examining Opportunities for Client Participation in Nonprofit Social Service Organisations," *Public Administration Review*, 69(3): 504–17.

Leviten-Reid, C., and Fairbairn, B. (2011). "Multi-Stakeholder Governance in Co-Operative Organizations: Toward a New Framework for Research," *Canadian Journal of Nonprofit and Social Economy Research*, 2(2): 25–36.

Lew, S., and Wójcik, D. (2010). "The Variegated Cultures of Philanthropy: National and Corporate Impacts on Private Foundation Governance," *Competition and Change*, 14(3–4): 152–75.

Mace, M. (1971). *Directors: Myth and Reality*. Cambridge, MA: Harvard University Press.

Mason, C., Kirbride, J., and Bryde, D. (2007). "From Stakeholders to Institutions: The Changing Face of Social Enterprise Governance Theory," *Management Decision*, 45(2): 284–301.

Mead, J. (2007). "Confidence in the Nonprofit Sector through Sarbanes-Oxley-Style Reforms," *Michigan Law Review*, 106(5): 881–900.

Mersland, R. (2011). "The Governance of Non-profit Micro Finance Institutions: Lessons from History," *Journal of Management and Governance*, 15(3): 327–48.

Miller, P. (2008). "Corporate Governance in Aged Care: How to Evaluate Board Performance," *The International Journal of Health & Ageing Management*, 2(1): 1–11.

Miller-Millesen, J. (2003). "Understanding the Behavior of Nonprofit Boards of Directors: A Theory-Based Approach," *Nonprofit and Voluntary Sector Quarterly*, 32(4): 521–47.

Morgan, G. G. (2010). "The Use of Charitable Status as the Basis for Regulation of Nonprofit Accounting," *Voluntary Sector Review*, 1(2): 209–32.

Morris, D. (2011). "The Case of England and Wales: Striking the Right Balance of 'Hard' Law versus 'Soft' Law," in S. D. Phillips and S. R. Smith (eds.), *Governance and Regulation in the Third Sector: International Perspectives*. London: Routledge, 37–68.

Mulligan, M. (2007). "On the Trail of Malaysia's Weirdest Animal: The GONGO," *The Round Table, Commonwealth Quarterly*, 96(391): 429–34.

Murray, V. (2007). "Dr. Carver's Odyssey," *Nonprofit Management and Leadership*, 18(1): 101–107.

National Council for Voluntary Organisations (2010). "Report of the Independent Expert Group on Expenses," National Council for Voluntary Organisations, London February. Available at <http://www.ncvo-vol.org.uk/sites/default/files/ExpensesReportfinal.pdf>.

Newman, A., and Bach, D. (2001). "In the Shadow of the State: Self Regulation Trajectories in a Digital Age," Annual Convention of the American Political Science Association, August 30–September 2, San Francisco, CA.

Nicholls, A. (2010a) "The Institutionalisation of Social Investment: The Interplay of Investment Logics and Investor Rationalities," *The Journal of Social Entrepreneurship*, 1(1): 70–100.

—— (2010b). "Institutionalizing Social Entrepreneurship in Regulatory Space: Reporting and Disclosure by Community Interest Companies," *Accounting, Organizations and Society*, 35(4): 394–415.

O'Dwyer, B., and Unerman, J. (2010). "Enhancing the Role of Accountability in Promoting the Rights of Beneficiaries in Development NGOs," *Accounting and Business Research*, 40(5): 451–71.

Ostrower, F. (2007). "Nonprofit Governance in the United States, Findings on Performance and Accountability from the First National Representative Study," Urban Institute, Washington, DC. Available at <http://www.urban.org/UploadedPDF/411479_Nonprofit_Governance.pdf>.

—— and Stone, M. M. (2010). "Moving Governance Research Forward: A Contingency-Based Framework and Data Application," *Nonprofit and Voluntary Sector Quarterly*, 39(5): 901–24.

PAGVS (Panel on Accountability and Governance) (1999). "Building on Strength: Governance and Accountability in Canada's Voluntary Sector," Voluntary Sector Roundtable, Ottawa, Canada.

Panel on the Nonprofit Sector (2007). "Report on Good Governance and Ethical Practice," Independent Sector, Washington, DC. Available at <http://www.nonprofitpanel.org/press/Principles/20071018.html>.

Parker, C. (2000). "Reinventing Regulation within the Corporation: Compliance-Oriented Regulatory Innovation," *Administration and Society*, 32(5): 529–65.

Pfeffer, J., and Salancik, G. R. (1978). *The External Control of Organization: A Resource Dependency Perspective*. New York: HarperCollins.

Pharoah, C., with Keidan, C. and Gordon, J. (2011). "Family Foundation Giving Trends 2011," London: Alliance Publishing Trust. Available at <http://www.cgap.org.uk/uploads/reports/FFGT_2011.pdf>.

Phillips, K. A. (2007). "The Application of Business Models to Medical Research: Interviews with Two Founders of Directed-Philanthropy Foundations," *Health Affairs*, 26(4): 1181–5.

Phillips, S. D. (2010). "Canada: Civil Society under Neglect," *The Philanthropist*, 23(1): 63–73. Available at <http://www.lephilanthrope.ca/index.php/phil/article/viewFile/819/663>.

—— (2012). "Canadian Leapfrog: From Regulating Charitable Fundraising to Co-Regulating Good Governance," *Voluntas: International Journal of Nonprofit and Voluntary Organizations*, 23(3): 808–28.

—— and Smith, S. R. (2011). "Between Governance and Regulation, Evolving Government–Third Sector Relationships," in S. D. Phillips and S. R. Smith (eds.), *Governance and Regulation in the Third Sector: International Perspectives*. London: Routledge, 1–36.

Prüfer, J. (2011). "Competition and Mergers among Nonprofits," *Journal of Competition Law and Economics*, 7(1): 69–92.

Rehli, F., and Jäger, U. P. (2011). "The Governance of International Nongovernmental Organizations: How Funding and Volunteer Involvement Affect Board Nomination Modes and Stakeholder Representation in International Nongovernmental Organizations," *Voluntas: International Journal of Voluntary and Nonprofit Organisations*, 22(4): 587–612.

Renz, P. (2009). "Project Governance: Implementing Corporate Governance and Business Ethics in Nonprofit Organizations," *Journal of Management and Governance*, 13(4): 355–63.

Salamon, L. M. (1999). *America's Nonprofit Sector: A Primer*, revised edition. New York: The Foundation Center.

Santora, J. C., and Sarros, J. C. (2001). "CEO Tenure in Nonprofit Community-Based Organizations: A Multiple Case Study," *Career Development International*, 6(1): 56–60.

Scott, C. (2004). "Regulation in the Age of Governance: The Rise of the Post-Regulatory State," in J. Jordana and D. Levi-Faur (eds.), *The Politics of Regulation: Institutional Reforms for the Age of Governance*. Cheltenham: Edward Elgar, 145–74.

Seitanidi, M. M. (2007). "Intangible Economy: How Can Investors Deliver Change in Businesses? Lessons from Nonprofit—Business Partnerships," *Management Decision*, 45(5): 853–65.

Sharp, Z., and Brock, D. M. (2011). "Implementation through Risk Mitigation: Strategic Processes in the Nonprofit Organization," *Administration and Society*, 43(6), online, September 7. DOI: <10.1177/0095399711418325>.

Sidel, M. (2005). "The Guardians Guarding Themselves: Comparative Perspectives on Nonprofit Self-Regulation," *Chicago-Kent Law Review*, 80: 803–35.

Smith, S. R. (2008). "The Challenge of Strengthening Nonprofits and Civil Society," *Public Administration Review*, 68, Supplement S1: S132–45.

—— (2010). "Nonprofits and Public Administration: Reconciling Performance Management and Citizen Engagement," *American Review of Public Administration*, 40(2): 129–52.

Somerville, P. (2005). "Community Governance and Democracy," *Policy and Politics*, 33(1): 117–44.

Spear, R. G., Cornforth, C. J., and Aiken, M. (2009). "The Governance Challenges of Social Enterprises: Evidence for a UK Empirical Study," *Annals of Public and Cooperative Economics*, 80(2): 247–73.

Speckbacher, G. (2008). "Nonprofit versus Corporate Governance: An Economic Approach," *Nonprofit Management and Leadership*, 18(3): 295–320.

Steane, P. D., and Christie, M. (2001). "Nonprofit Boards in Australia: A Distinctive Governance Approach," *Corporate Governance*, 9(1): 48–56.

Tropman, J., and Shaefer, H. L. (2004). "Flameout at the Top—Executive Calamity in the Nonprofit Sector," *Administration in Social Work*, 28(3–4): 161–82.

Valentinov, V. (2011). "Accountability and the Public Interest in the Nonprofit Sector: A Conceptual Framework," *Financial Accountability and Management*, 27(1): 32–42.

van Iwaarden, J., van der Wiele, T., Williams, R., and Moxham, C. (2009). "Charities: How Important is Performance to Donors?" *International Journal of Quality and Reliability Management*, 26(1): 5–22.

Verbruggen, S., Christiaens, J., and Milis, K. (2011). "Can Resource Dependence and Coercive Isomorphism Explain Nonprofit Organizations' Compliance with Reporting Standards?" *Nonprofit and Voluntary Sector Quarterly*, 40(1): 5–32.

von Schnurbein, G. (2009). "Patterns of Governance Structures among Trade Associations and Unions," *Nonprofit Management and Leadership*, 20(1): 97–115.

Wellens, L., and Jegers, M. (2011). "Beneficiaries' Participation in Nonprofit Organisation: A Theory Based Approach," *Public Money and Management*, 31(3): 175–82.

Williams, G. (2010). "IRS Continues its Focus on Governance Matters," Government and Politics Watch, *The Chronicle of Philanthropy*, April 22. Available at <http://philanthropy.com/blogs/government-and-politics/irs-continues-its-focus-on-governance-matters-official-says/23358>.

Wood, D., and Hagerman, L. (2010). "Mission Investing and the Philanthropic Toolbox," *Policy and Society*, 29(3): 257–68.

Yip, J., Twohill, E., Ernst, C., and Munusamy, V. P. (2010). "Leadership in Faith-Based Nonprofits: The Power of Identity to Bind and Blind," *Nonprofit Management and Leadership*, 20(4): 461–72.

Young, D. R. (2001). "Organizational Identity in Nonprofit Organizations: Strategic and Structural Implications," *Nonprofit Management and Leadership*, 12(2): 139–57.

—— (2011). "The Prospective Role of Economic Stakeholders in the Governance of Nonprofit Organizations," *Voluntas: International Journal of Voluntary and Nonprofit Organizations*, 22(4): 566–86.

Zahra, S. A., Filatotchev, I., and Wright, M. (2009). "How do Threshold Firms Sustain Corporate Entrepreneurship? The Role of Boards and Absorptive Capacity," *Journal of Business Venturing*, 24(3): 248–60.

Zainon, S., Atan, R., Bee Wah, Y., and Theng Nam, R. Y. (2011). "Institutional Donors' Expectation of Information from the Non-Profit Organizations (NPO) Reporting: A Pilot Survey," *International NGO Journal*, 6(8): 170–80.

CHAPTER 28

CORPORATE GOVERNANCE AND LABOR

ANDREW PENDLETON AND HOWARD GOSPEL

Introduction

Corporate governance has steadily moved up the political agenda in recent years in response to company collapses, steeply rising executive pay, and the recent economic and financial crisis. Discussions about corporate governance have mainly focused on the role of managers and shareholders, but there has also been a growing awareness that labor can both be affected by corporate governance and play an important role within it. At the same time, there has been a rapidly growing body of academic literature that has highlighted linkages between labor and corporate governance. It has become clear that labor is an important actor in corporate governance even though direct involvement in formal governance processes may be minimal in many circumstances.

Corporate governance is viewed as the processes influencing key decisions about how wealth is created, resources allocated, and returns distributed in business organizations. It is essentially about power relationships between various key actors such as owners, managers, and labor. It is concerned with who controls the firm, in whose interests the firm is governed, and the various ways in which control is exercised (Gospel and Pendleton, 2003: 560). In common with several other writers, we believe that contests for control of key decisions can lead to coalitions or alliances between actors in governance. For instance, managers may ally with shareholders to the detriment of labor or may form alliances with labor for mutual protection against shareholders. These alliances may form in the context of particular issues such as takeovers (Jackson, 2005; Pagano and Volpin, 2005) or can be seen as systemic features of national governance systems (Gourevitch and Shinn, 2005).

This chapter considers the role of labor in governance, and the impact of governance regimes and arrangements upon labor. It is in four sections. The first provides an overview of theories and perspectives on the role of labor in corporate governance. The second then considers broad empirical models of governance in different parts of the world as they relate to labor. The third section examines in more detail how labor can be involved in corporate governance, drawing attention to ways in which labor can be involved in governance. Finally, the fourth section considers how labor is affected by corporate governance, by outlining a set of relationships and considering outcomes in the area of employment, work, and industrial relations.

THE ROLE OF LABOR IN CORPORATE GOVERNANCE: THEORY AND PERSPECTIVES

There are two sets of literatures pertaining to labor and corporate governance. One is the corporate governance literature, much of which dates from the last 30 years or so, and the other is a much older literature on industrial relations and the role of labor in societal transformation. Within the corporate governance field there are two, opposing perspectives. First, there is the "shareholder value" perspective, based on "principal–agent" theory, which has had considerable sway since the 1980s but which has older origins. Second, there are "stakeholder" models, which have been articulated in opposition to the "shareholder value" perspectives. Differences in the role and importance of labor are a key distinguishing feature between the two perspectives. There are also considerable differences in prescriptions for the role of labor in governance between various strands of writing on governance in the industrial relations and labor literatures.

As discussed in other chapters in this *Handbook*, the "shareholder value" perspective has probably been the most influential model of the governance of large, publicly listed corporations, in particular in the US and UK. It is based on principal–agent theory, with the central governance issue being the control of managerial behavior by owners and shareholders. According to this view, principals (owners, shareholders) establish governance systems to ensure that agents (managers) run the organization in the best interests of the owners. A fundamental argument is that owners and shareholders bear risk from investing in the firm, and in return for risk-bearing they should possess control rights. The challenge is that owners and managers (who are, of course, employees, albeit very powerful ones) may have different interests. Whilst the owners seek a return on their investment, managers may have objectives which conflict with this, such as high salaries, a "quiet life," and harmonious relations with other employees. Corporate governance is therefore concerned with protecting investors and has a number of goals—the prevention of fraud, wealth creation, and the distribution of returns. This perspective is espoused by many owners and managers and has been the conventional wisdom in analyses of corporate governance in economics and finance, as well as in the corporate world in countries such as the US and UK (Jensen and Meckling, 1976; Shleifer and Vishny, 1997).

Labor has little or no role in this conception of corporate governance. Governance is essentially about how owners and shareholders control managers so that the latter do not pursue their own interests at the expense of shareholders. Intellectual support for this perspective has been provided by the argument that labor does not bear risk. Hansmann and Kraakmann (2000) have argued that the employment contract is relatively complete and well-specified so that workers bear little or no un-contracted risk. Hence governance rights for workers cannot be justified. A further set of arguments has been that employee participation in governance is inefficient because workers lack appropriate managerial expertise and have divergent and conflicting interests. Involvement in governance is also likely to dilute managerial control (Jensen and Meckling, 1979).

The "stakeholder" perspective, by contrast, views organizations, including private sector firms, as public entities rather than just the private property of owners. These entities have a variety of stakeholders, including insiders such as owners, managers, and employees, and outsiders such as lenders, suppliers, and customers. The purpose of the firm is to serve the interests of all stakeholders not just to deliver financial returns to shareholders. As a result, corporate governance is about checks and balances so that the company pursues a balanced approach to all of its stakeholders. The role of managers is to act as stewards, balancing out the interest of the different parties for the long-term good of the enterprise (Freeman, 1984; Donaldson and Preston, 1995)

The implication of this perspective is that labor should have a central role in corporate governance because it is an especially important stakeholder in the firm. Support for this claim is provided by Blair (1995). She argues that, in developing firm-specific human capital, workers make "relation-specific" investments in their employer, thereby incurring opportunity costs and bearing risk. For this reason, she argues, workers should have governance rights commensurate with those held by financial investors (Blair, 1995). Underlying this view is the belief that, contrary to Hansmann and Kraakman, the labor contract is incomplete and employees bear risks of adverse changes in wages and conditions and possible job loss.

The "shareholder value" and "stakeholder" views can be seen as diametrically opposed in their view as to the role of labor in governance. However, "enlightened shareholder value" may provide a middle way between the two perspectives, and recent reforms of corporate law in the UK have drawn in part on this. The 2006 Companies Act (Section 172) requires directors to promote the success of the company in the interests of the shareholders, while also taking into account a wider view of interests, including those of employees (see Pendleton and Deakin, 2007). This enlightened shareholder value view accepts shareholder primacy, but suggests that it makes sense for owners and managers to take account of the interests of other stakeholders. An enlightened organization will pursue policies that accept labor has legitimate interests, because a well-motivated workforce will be good for profits. Providing workers with a voice in governance assists in exchanging production-relevant information, motivates workers, and enables managers to respond to employee concerns and grievances before they have serious adverse effects.

Turning to industrial relations literatures, there is no single perspective on the role of labor in corporate governance. Instead, over many years and in different countries, there have been several important standpoints which we outline along a perspective from radical/left-wing, through rather more moderate and conservative, to right-wing theories. These have been expressed by important political movements, and in some cases have influenced the formal design of governance systems.

On the political left, syndicalist theorists saw an oppositional and revolutionary role for labor in capitalist corporate governance. Essentially, labor should oppose owners and managers, encroach on the power of capital, and ultimately take control over ownership and management (Cole, 1917; Sorel, 1999). However, outside of a few periods in certain countries, such as France at the beginning of the 20th century, such ideas had little impact. On the Marxist left, the belief was similarly that, under capitalism, workers could not properly participate in the running of the capitalist firm. Trade unions had a role to play in challenging management and contributing to the ultimate political transformation of society. It was only under socialism that workers could really govern the firm, albeit subject in the Leninist version to the direction of the Communist Party. Of course, such ideas had an enormous effect in Soviet Russia after the Revolution and in other countries after the Second World War. Such ideas still have vestiges in China, though very much transmuted now that China has evolved into a form of state-directed capitalism (Huang, 2008; Hurst, 2009).

Moving along the political spectrum, an influential industrial relations perspective in the UK and USA stressed that labor, in the form of trade unions, had a key role to play in representing worker interests but should not become directly involved in the governance of the private sector firm. Unions might press for nationalization of private firms and for some rights on the boards of such enterprises. But the best way for labor to be involved in governance was via a system of pluralism and opposition, based on trade unions and collective bargaining. Unions would remain a "permanent opposition" untainted by the complexities and ambiguities of direct involvement in management and governance (Clegg, 1960). The power of unions would provide checks and balances on owners and managers (Webb and Webb, 1897; Perlman, 1928). Such an approach had an appeal to many workers and indeed to some managers and owners, but it also had its limitations. First, in most countries, collective bargaining never covered the whole of the working population. Second, collective bargaining tended to take place at either establishment or industry level and seldom at the level of the firm (where many corporate governance processes take place).

In some countries in Western Europe, especially after the two world wars, parts of the labor movement were more prepared to look for an active role in governance. In Germany, for example, statutory works councils with rights to information and consultation in certain areas were established. Employees were also given seats on company boards, sometimes in parity with owner directors, but more usually in a minority. This very much fitted with continental Social Democratic and Christian Democrat views of the enterprise as a public and pluralistic entity. This has provided employees with a voice in corporate decision-making (Daubler, 1989; Bosch, 1997; Lower, 2010).

Moving to the right of the political and economic spectrum, there has been a persistent body of thought on the role of labor in the governance of the enterprise. Here the intellectual origins are very diverse, but tend to stress the following: the loss of a sense of community under industrialism; a unitarist belief that employers (and the state) know the best interests of employees; a need to move away from contract and back toward status, especially national or ethnic status, as the basis for organizing labor relations; and an emphasis on harmony and community at enterprise and national levels. Such ideas have been associated with nationalist and racist ideologies and with certain fundamentalist religious beliefs. At one extreme, they were to be found in fascist and military regimes in Italy, Germany, and Japan during the interwar years (Guerin, 1936; Hazama, 1997). In the post-war period, variants on these were to be found in countries such as Spain, Portugal, and Argentina, and can still be found in some militarist and nationalist regimes.

Finally, there have been many human resource management perspectives which have dealt with employee direct participation and indirect involvement in corporate governance. The literature here recognizes a large number of employee "voice" mechanisms at different levels, from indirect participation on company boards and via works councils and trade unions, to more direct forms via committees and "town hall" meetings. Some of this literature has also focused on employee share ownership and financial participation in the firm. However, much of the human resource literature has been concerned with direct task participation at work and in problem solving as part of high performance work systems via quality and production committees. As such, the interest in involvement in higher-level aspects of corporate governance is limited (Boxall and Purcell, 2010; Lower, 2010).

NATIONAL MODELS OF CORPORATE GOVERNANCE AND LABOR

Another set of literatures, mainly located in political economy, has focused on systems of corporate governance, which in turn are located in broader "national business systems" or "varieties of capitalism." As with the various perspectives on governance discussed above, variations in the role of labor, alongside the structure of ownership, is a key difference between the various governance systems.

One body of literature has distinguished between "market-outsider" and "relational-insider" governance systems (Franks and Mayer, 1997; Gospel and Pendleton, 2003). In market-outsider systems, large companies are typically listed on stock markets, and are owned by institutional investors such as pension funds and insurance companies. These owners have highly diversified portfolios of stocks, with each holding being only a small fraction of the ownership of the investee company. With these arrangements, direct involvement in governance is costly, with the gains of monitoring shared between all other owners. As a result, governance is exercised by "exit" rather than "voice": it is believed to be more efficient for investors to discipline managers by buying and selling shares rather than taking a direct voice in the governance of firms. The combination of this mode of governance and the relative liquidity of this structure of ownership means that the market for corporate control tends to be well-developed in these types of regime. The need to maintain stock price to protect the firm (and management) from takeovers or to facilitate takeovers is said to provide strong market-based discipline on managers. Since governance is marketized in this way, it is believed that there is little or no need for insiders such as employees to be involved in governance. The US and UK are usually said to exemplify systems of this type.

Relational-insider systems have been characterized by concentrated ownership by block holders, substantial involvement in company financing by banks, and interlocking ownership between industrial firms. In contrast to market-outsider countries, family ownership of the largest firms remains very important. In some countries of this type, there are fewer listed firms, and stock markets are typically smaller and with lower turnover of shares. This means that the market for corporate control is much less active and hostile takeovers are rare. Governance takes a very different form to that found in market-outsider systems. Because owners typically have a large ownership stake, it is efficient to play a direct role in governance as "insiders." Governance is exercised by voice rather than exit. In turn, this has implications for employees who can also play a role as part of this insider governance. Germany and Japan are typically seen as exemplars of this kind of system.

These differences between regime types have been encapsulated in the recent "varieties of capitalism" literature (Hall and Soskice, 2001). This literature distinguishes between "liberal market" and "coordinated market" economies. In the former, coordination between economic actors is achieved through market mechanisms and corporate governance is exercised on the basis of the external market for corporate control. Employees have predominantly market relationships with the firm (i.e. there is a strong reliance on external rather than internal labor markets). Hence there is little or no role for employees in corporate governance. By contrast, in coordinated market economies, where ownership is typically more concentrated, the firm's operations are substantially coordinated through cooperative relationships between actors. This implies that labor should have a voice in the governance of the firm, and these systems tend to be characterized by forms of board representation and works councils. In some instances, employee participation may take the form of legally based involvement of employee representatives in company boards, as in German codetermination, whilst in others employee voice is achieved via managerial representation and cultural ideas of the community enterprise, as in Japan (Inagami and Whittaker, 2005).

The "varieties of capitalism" approach has been very influential over the last ten years, as it provides a systematic approach to comparing some of the largest national economies and to explaining the systemic differences between them. However, this approach has also been extensively criticized recently for a variety of reasons (Hancke et al., 2007). "Varieties" focuses on a small number of countries and omits consideration of governance arrangements and labor systems in large parts of the world such as Asia and South America. Within Europe, it tends to ignore southern European countries, where labor's role in politics has arguably influenced the development of governance systems in alternative ways to those portrayed for countries like Germany. The central role of the state in governance in some countries tends not to be captured in the varieties perspective. The varieties of capitalism perspective also arguably downplays differences within varieties of capitalism, both between countries grouped within varieties and within the countries themselves.

At the same time as the "varieties of capitalism" literature emerged, there has been considerable interest in the evolution of corporate governance systems. In some accounts labor plays a central role in the development of systems, but in others labor tends to be absent. A good case of the latter is the influential "law and finance" view associated with La Porta et al. (1998). This emphasizes legal traditions and differences between "common-law" countries, such as the US and UK, providing greater protection to minority investors than European "civil law" countries, but says little about how labor may influence the development of legal traditions. Similarly, others have stressed the early development and continuity of efficient stock markets as an explanation for the nature of governance systems in countries like the UK (Franks et al., 2009; Foreman-Peck and Hannah, 2012).

However, others have emphasized factors which touch very much on labor. For instance, in the US, it has been argued that popular movements (including labor) against the power of finance capital in the early 20th century led to legal prohibition of corporate ownership by banks and discouraged concentrated ownership. It is suggested that this contributed to the spread of dispersed ownership in the US and hence the marketized system of corporate governance. In other countries, by contrast, where labor has been more strongly organized as a class political interest, stakeholder models of the firm have tended to emerge, as in Germany and other parts of continental Europe (Roe, 2003). It has also been argued that strong labor rights in corporate governance have tended to discourage dispersed ownership because minority investors fear expropriation by strong labor (Roe, 1996; Pistor, 1999). In this reckoning, the pattern of labor representation helps to determine ownership structure and governance rather than vice versa.

Another set of arguments has suggested that "workers' capital" has influenced the development of ownership and governance systems. In those countries where pension provision has been funded by worker and company contributions to pension schemes (rather than through taxation), large pools of capital have been generated and then invested mainly in the listed company sector by institutional investors such as pension funds and insurance funds. This capital has driven the expansion of stock markets, encouraged dispersed ownership (because these funds typically diversify over a large number of companies), and encouraged an emphasis on financial returns (Jackson and Vitols, 2001). In this way, and perhaps paradoxically, "workers' capital" can be said to have contributed to the development of governance systems which are sometimes viewed as operating against labor's interests.

Employee Involvement in the Processes of Governance

Three main actors may be discerned in corporate governance: investors and owners, managers, and labor (Gourevitch and Shinn, 2005; Jackson, 2005: Pagano and Volpin, 2005). All have an interest in the governance of the firm, even though their direct involvement will vary considerably. As suggested above, mainstream corporate governance analysis tends to focus on two of these actors: investors and managers. Nevertheless, even in countries where labor is generally excluded from governance in the sense of formal decision rights, there can be considerable involvement, albeit often indirectly. We now discuss the various ways labor can be involved in governance.

Employee Board-Level Representation

Labor may be represented on the company board, and thus may have a potentially strong influence on management decision-making. The representation of employees on company boards is legally mandated in a sizeable number of European countries. In fact, 18 of the 27 EU member states have some legal provision of workers to be represented on supervisory boards or boards of directors in certain circumstances (Conchon and Waddington, 2011). In Germany, for instance, legislation on codetermination from the 1950s to 1970s provides for 50 percent employee representation in firms with 2,000 or more employees and one-third representation in public companies with 500–2,000 employees. Approximately 5 million German employees work in companies with board-level representation (Commission on Codetermination, 1998). There is now also provision for European companies to incorporate as a European Company (SE), which includes board representation on German lines, though few companies have done so (Conchon and Waddington, 2011). There are no legal requirements to have employee directors in the major liberal or outsider market economies, though a very small numbers of firms do have workers on the board. These have included major firms in the steel industry in the US.

A key question concerns the effects of board representation on the practice of governance, management decision-making, and company policies. Advocates of board-level representation argue that companies will benefit from greater information flows and worker consent, whilst workers will gain from greater understanding and access to the key decision-making forum in the company (Commission on Codetermination, 1998). Critics claim that board-level representation will "dilute" the pursuit of profit, thereby promoting managerial confusion and economic inefficiency (Jensen and Meckling, 1979). However, the evidence suggests that labor's influence may be limited for a combination of reasons. These include lack of expertise on the part of labor representatives and a degree of exclusion by other board members, arising from anxieties about conflicts of interest amongst labor representatives. Worker directors tend to be most involved and effective in labor management and industrial relations decisions (Batstone et al., 1983; Hammer et al., 1991). Research evidence from the US and UK indicates that worker directors need to be closely linked to unions to be effective, though the downside is that this can reduce their legitimacy with other directors. Recent German evidence similarly indicates that board representation requires the support of works councils and trade unions for it to be effective (Muller Jentsch, 2003; Vitols, 2004; Frick and Lehman, 2005). However, some research suggests that involvement of union representatives or outsiders removes any positive economic effects of codetermination (Fauver and Fuerst, 2006).

Ownership and Shareholder Involvement

Even where labor has little or no formal role in the institutions of governance, such as company boards, involvement may be observed in other ways. For instance, employees may have some involvement in shareholder bodies, which may in turn be involved directly or indirectly in governance of companies. One example is employee involvement in the management of pension funds. In most liberal market economies, a substantial proportion of private sector employees (and some public sector employees) contribute to employer-provided pension funds. There is considerable scope for employee participation in the management of these funds. In the UK, up to one-third of fund trustees are nominated by members, whilst American industry-wide schemes are jointly managed by employers and unions. In determining the investment policies of these funds, labor representatives may influence governance (and indirectly labor management) in investee companies. For example, ethical investment policies may prohibit investment in companies perceived to have poor labor standards (e.g. child labor).

Recently, some trade unions in countries with extensive funded pension arrangements (such as the US and UK) have attempted to coordinate the activities of union representatives on pension funds so that "workers" capital can be mobilized more effectively at shareholders' meetings (Williamson, 2003). In the US, union-mounted campaigns are the fastest-growing variant of this form of shareholder activism and around 40 percent of shareholder resolutions come from "union funds," with a key focus being executive pay (Gillen and Starks, 2007). However, in practice, the impact of this representation is highly constrained by fiduciary responsibilities, ambiguous interests, and lack of expertise. US evidence suggests that this form of shareholder activism can be effective if the focus is "mainstream" corporate governance issues, such as board composition, for their activism (Schwab and Thomas, 1998). Nevertheless, attempts to increase "shareholder value" for the benefit of workers in pension funds do highlight the potentially contradictory role of "workers capital."

Employees may also secure involvement in corporate governance via direct ownership of company shares. Employee share ownership schemes are widespread among large, listed companies in most liberal market economies and becoming more common in other countries (Kaarsemaker et al., 2010). In principle, employee share ownership provides employee owners with governance rights, and this might be expected to give employees a role in corporate governance. This is most clearly seen in France, where employee shareholders have the right to representation on the company board when they own more than 3 percent of the company's equity between them. However, in most countries, liberal market economies especially, the role and influence of employee shareholders in governance is typically limited to non-existent.

Several factors constrain the effectiveness of share schemes as an instrument of employee voice in governance. One, whilst share schemes facilitate the acquisition of company stock, employees do not always convert their participation into actual shareholdings. This is the case in option-based plans. Two, in most employee share schemes, managements do not view employee shareholding as a vehicle for employee participation in governance. Instead, share schemes are seen primarily as an employee benefit. This view seems to be widely shared by participating employees themselves. Three, the proportion of the company owned by employees is usually relatively small. It is rare for employees to own more than about 5 percent. Even where the employee stake is substantial, coordinating employee shareholders to present a substantial bloc in governance is problematic. In most companies, there are no institutions to bring employee shareholders together. The exceptions are employee shareholder associations in some European companies. However, the presence and activities of these seem to be highly dependent on management efforts to support the representation of employee shareholders.

Other Forms of Labor Involvement in Corporate Governance

Employees may gain some involvement in governance via information sharing by employers. The disclosure of information by managers to employees is mandated by law in some countries. This applies in particular in Germany, the Netherlands, France, and other continental European countries. It is also more widely mandated in the EU in specific governance circumstances, such as where there are transfers of undertakings, mergers and acquisitions (M&As), collective lay-offs, and where joint councils have been established. However, such legal rights are often minimal, restricted to information which is operational rather than strategic, and often backward-looking. It is often no better than the basic information formally provided to all shareholders (Gospel and Willman, 2005).

In terms of empirical research on information provision, there have been a number of studies of information provision within different countries. These suggest that *de jure* rights to information matter and make for higher de facto levels of information provision, as in continental Europe. We also know that, over and above the law, information is likely to be provided to employees where managements pursue more sophisticated human resource policies, where there is some financial distress, and where there is a trade union or works councils. The evidence suggests some positive effects of information sharing on organizational climate and performance (Kleiner and Bouillon, 1988; Morishima, 1989, 1991; Peccei et al., 2010).

A further indirect means by which labor participates in governance is where unions attempt to build relationships with major investors with a view to influencing the governance policies and practices of the latter. In countries such as the US and UK this tends to be uncommon probably because most unions lack resources (expertise and time) to initiate such relationships (they are unlikely to be initiated by investors). However, where unions organize in single industries dominated by a small number of firms, or where there is a small number of major investors, resource constraints are less onerous, and there are instances of unions attempting to engage with major investors. In the US, some unions have attempted to build relationships with private equity fund managers with a view to influencing the labor management practices of investee companies (Beeferman, 2009). Alternatively, labor may form alliances with managements to protect themselves against investors. It has been argued that, where managers have small levels of ownership but considerable de facto control, they will seek alliances with labor to prevent takeovers that might lead to the replacement of the management team (Pagano and Volpin, 2005).

The Impact of Corporate Governance on Labor

A recent body of literature on labor and corporate governance has argued that corporate governance can have powerful effects on labor and employment (Gospel and Pendleton, 2003, 2005; Black et al., 2007). There are several ways in which governance impacts upon employees and labor, primarily via its impact upon management decision-making. These are: (1) the allocation of resources and returns by company managements in response to governance pressures and constraints; (2) the time frame of management decision-making; (3) the nature of company business strategies and practices (Gospel and Pendleton, 2003). We examine each in turn, with reference to variations between national governance regimes.

First, the allocation of resources and returns by company managements increasingly favors shareholders rather than workers in liberal market economies such as the US and UK. This both reflects and reinforces processes of corporate governance from which labor is generally absent. In recent years investors in these countries have emphasized the importance of shareholder value and the notion that management's primary duty is to maximize returns for shareholders (Lazonick and O'Sullivan, 2000: 16–17). The support for shareholder interests in these economies arises from a variety of sources, such as the absence of formal governance rights for labor, the presumptions of corporate and securities law, key governance mechanisms such as incentive pay, and active markets for corporate control. These factors have combined together to generate strong ideological support for "shareholder value" amongst managers and policy-makers (Fligstein, 2001), though the capacity of managers to self-serve in these countries should not be underestimated.

In other countries, especially those that can be described as coordinated market economies such as Germany and Japan, managers' duties and responsibilities are seen to be to a broader group of stakeholders, as outlined earlier. This arises partly from formal governance rights for labor in some countries in Europe and partly from a strong ideological commitment to the rights and interests of employees, as exemplified by the case of Japan. However, it is clear that there have been changes toward Anglo-Saxon patterns of governance in many countries. Banks have reduced their shareholdings, cross-ownership between companies has been reduced, and equity markets have been liberalized. These changes have encouraged managers in some companies to adopt Anglo-Saxon practices, and there has been a shift, the extent of which has been hotly debated in the literature, toward greater emphasis on shareholder returns (Vitols, 2004; Jacoby, 2005).

The rise of alternative investment funds such as private equity and hedge funds has reinforced the imperative for managers to serve owners' interests, though in differing ways (Gospel et al., 2010). These funds have been most prevalent in liberal market economies such as the US and UK, but they have also been active in other countries such as Sweden, Germany, and France. Private equity is notable for transferring ownership and control from dispersed shareholders to concentrated private ownership (in the case of buyouts of public companies) and more generally for instigating tight control and monitoring of investee companies. The reliance on debt for buyouts places tight constraints on "free cash flow" post-transaction, thereby limiting managers' capacity to allocate rents and resources to other stakeholders such as labor.

The impact of hedge funds is felt primarily in listed, public companies. Activist hedge funds secure returns by active interventions in governance to force managers to redirect resources in favor of shareholders. Typically, these funds acquire substantial minority shareholdings in target firms and then put pressure on top managers to change business strategy, to appoint new shareholder representatives to the board, to increase dividend payments to shareholders, and to instigate share buybacks. Most hedge funds, however, operate directional trading strategies, of which the most well-known is "short-selling." This can have powerful effects by accentuating falls in company share price, forcing companies to change strategy. It can also encourage companies to mount share buy-backs and special dividends to "shake-out" short-sellers. Share buy-backs and special dividends reallocate resources from the company, and potentially other stakeholders such as labor, to shareholders.

A second way in which governance impacts on labor is through its effects on managerial time frames. In governance systems where ownership is dispersed amongst highly diversified institutional investors, the structure of incentives is said to encourage short-termism by companies and their managers. For instance, pension fund managers compete for business on the basis of short-term returns, and it is common for pension funds to regularly change their fund managers (Myners, 2001). This encourages churn in fund manager portfolios. This also feeds into the market for corporate control. The potential for changes in ownership and control, facilitated by equity markets with large "free float," encourages managers to manage for short-term results. This has been accentuated in recent years with the rise of hedge funds operating "directional" or "momentum" investment strategies. Once share sales reach a certain level, this can cause funds to dump shares onto the market, often triggered almost instantaneously by automated electronic trading. Companies now have to devote considerable attention to keeping short-term traders at bay, and this can require rapid management action to respond to market sentiment. A recent example from the UK is that of the supermarket chain Tesco. In January 2012 the company's share price fell an unprecedented 16 percent in one day in response to poor seasonal trading results. Tesco management announced significant changes to strategy (including an expansion of employment) before the day was out. By contrast, in countries where share ownership is more concentrated, and equity markets are less liquid, share-based governance pressures on management tend to be weaker (though direct governance pressures from major owners can of course be substantial).

A third way in which governance impacts on labor is through its effects on company business strategies, as has been argued in a series of influential critiques of liberal market economies (Hutton, 1996; Porter, 1997) and by the "varieties of capitalism" literature (Soskice, 1999; Hall and Soskice, 2001). Here it has been claimed that the governance system in liberal market economies such as the US and UK encourages companies to prioritize financial returns from company activities and to seek higher financial returns from investments. These are reinforced by pressures for short-termism as outlined above. As a result, many companies in these countries are said to invest in research and development (R&D) and human resource development at lower levels than their counterparts in countries with different governance regimes (Porter, 1997). Of particular importance is a reluctance to make long-term investments in human capital development (Soskice, 1999). As a result, companies in these regimes find it difficult to develop high value-added, complex products. The number of manufacturing industries which are viewed as internationally competitive is considerably lower than in countries with alternative governance regimes (Soskice, 1999). The preference for business strategies which do not rely on the long-term development of complex products then impacts on labor management within the firm and in the approach to labor, skills development, and employment more generally within the regime.

The combined effects of these three mechanisms—the allocation of returns, time frames, and business strategies—have had significant effects on labor and employment. These pressures, emanating from the system of governance, impel managers to act in certain ways in the management of labor. These labor effects can be observed at company and country level. In describing these effects, we are not proposing a simple model of causation with governance always leading to certain labor effects. This is partly because the role (or absence) of labor in governance will influence what subsequently happens to labor. More importantly, there are likely to be multiple feedback loops between governance, management, and labor, with various dimensions of activity reinforcing others. For this reason, many authors prefer to speak of "complementarities." The notion of complementarity highlights the importance of both governance and labor management systems. First, the fact that the two "go together" tends to limit the potential for "deviant" combinations. For instance, where corporate governance prioritizes short-term financial returns for shareholders, it can be difficult for companies to make long-term promises to employees. Second, alternative combinations can be equally economically successful, though the criteria for success may well be different. Long-term governance and employment relationships can generate competitive advantage, as can combinations of short-term governance and employment (Jackson, 2005).

Taking into account these considerations, we now consider the labor and employment characteristics that are typically associated with corporate governance regimes. Where available, we also draw on evidence from within particular regimes. This highlights how variations in the governance relationship between managers and owners can have differential impacts on labor.

Employment

In regimes where labor has a small role in governance, and where the governance system functions to prioritize owner interests, short-term time frames, and the type of business strategies described above, there are likely to be effects on employment duration. Most obviously, the capacity of managements to offer long-term employment commitments to employees may be highly constrained. On top of this, the importance of the market for corporate control as a governance mechanism in this type of regime is likely to subject labor in target firms to employment shocks. The unwillingness of companies to commit to employees is likely to be reciprocated by a corresponding reluctance on the part of employees to develop commitments to the firm. On the basis of this it is likely that average employment will be shorter in this type of governance regime.

The evidence so far is consistent with this claim. Hall and Gingerich (2009) find a strong relationship between a corporate governance index (comprising shareholder power, dispersion of control, and size of stock markets) and a labor coordination index of which labor turnover is a key dimension. Black et al. (2007) find that job tenure in OECD countries is negatively related to equity market activity (value of share trading plus new issues normalized against stock market size). They also find that job tenure is negatively associated with the level of M&A activity (M&As per million of population). Jackson (2005) finds significant negative correlations between ownership dispersion (and M&As) and long-term employment. Using company-level information, he finds significant correlations between dispersed ownership and reductions in employment. More complex analysis using fuzzy sets methodology suggests that the labor effects of corporate governance regimes are concentrated at the extreme ends of the spectrum. Strongly market-oriented corporate governance may preclude strongly relational regimes of employment (2005: 304), though governance alone may not be sufficient to explain employment patterns.

A specific instance of the impact of corporate governance on employment is that of M&As. It has been argued that restructurings of this type disrupt implicit contracts between firms and employees, thereby facilitating a shift of wealth from labor to capital (Shleifer and Summers, 1988). This may take the form of employment cuts or wage reductions. Most of the evidence here is from the US and the predicted effects are largely, though not always, confirmed (Lehto and Bockerman, 2008). In Lichtenberg and Siegel (1990), for example, growth in white-collar employment and payroll costs in firms subject to ownership change is lower than in firms not changing owners. In the UK, Conyon et al. (2001) find that M&As, especially hostile takeovers, tend to be followed by substantial falls in employment and output. Kuvandikov et al. (2013), however, show that reductions in employment are found after one year in just over half of M&A transactions, with an average reduction of nearly 15 percent. However, in the remainder there is employment growth.

An interesting angle on the relationship between corporate governance, takeovers, and employment change concerns the role of managerial ownership. Kuvandikov et al. find that M&A transactions where managers have larger equity stakes (in the acquiring firm) are followed by larger employment growth. Although they could reflect managerial entrenchment, selection effects are also likely to be important: managers with large ownership stakes are more likely to undertake M&As with good growth prospects. An alternative perspective to the "implicit contracts" view suggests that the opportunities and pressures on managers after takeovers may enhance matches between workers and firms, with benefits for both. Takeovers may lead to employment reductions, but those leaving will primarily be those that are ill-matched to the company. This leads to higher average worker quality in the restructured plant (from which workers will benefit), whilst departing workers experience higher earnings growth in their new, better-matched, employment (Siegel and Simons, 2010).

Recently, the employment implications of ownership change have attracted considerable attention because of the activities of private equity investors. Concern has been widely expressed that public-to-private transactions and other large private-equity-backed buyouts have led to job losses and reductions in union voice (Clark, 2009), though other accounts have pointed to a more complex set of effects (Wright et al., 2009). The largest study yet conducted (of 3,200 target firms in the US) has found that employment is reduced at target establishments by about 3 percent over two years. However, target firms create more new jobs at new establishments and divest and acquire establishments more rapidly than control firms. The overall picture is that net employment reduction overall is under 1 percent, but gross job creation and destruction exceeds that of the controls by 13 percent (Davis et al., 2011). A large-scale study of the effects of management buyouts in UK manufacturing establishments in the late 1990s found substantial falls in employment and output in all sectors, and rises in productivity in most (Harris et al., 2005). However, there is also evidence from Europe of little or no employment change after buyouts (Gospel et al., 2010). Much seems to depend on methodological issues, and also the nature of the transaction (see Wright et al., 2009). It also depends on the nature of the industrial relations system, which acts as a moderating variable (Bacon et al., 2010).

Rewards

Corporate governance influences reward systems. As shown elsewhere in this book, pay incentives for top managers are an important tool of corporate governance. In governance systems characterized by separation of ownership and control, there is likely to be greater use of incentive systems to align managerial interests with those of shareholders (Shleifer and Vishny, 1997). These incentives typically include cash bonuses, stock options, stock awards, and other long-term incentive plans. These incentives may have a variety of behavioral effects besides apparently aligning managerial and shareholder interests. It has been shown, for example, that option awards may encourage excessively risky behavior, a shortening of time horizons, a decline in R&D expenditure, and even accounting misreporting and fraud (DeFusco et al., 1991; Ericksen et al., 2006). All of these may have potentially adverse effects on labor.

Steeply rising executive pay has become a major focus of shareholder activism in both the US and UK. It is not surprising that trade unions are becoming increasingly active on the topic of executive pay, partly on equity grounds, partly because of fears about perverse incentives. In Germany, employee board representatives will often sit on the company board remuneration committee and play a role in fixing criteria for pay and actual levels of pay. Recently in the UK, it has been suggested that employees might be represented on remuneration committees (Department for Business, 2011). It is possible that greater employee involvement and participation in AGMs, on boards, and in works councils would constrain somewhat the growth in executive pay; though, to date, there is little firm evidence on this issue. It is noticeable, however, that in those European countries with extensive codetermination arrangements, executive pay has risen more slowly than in the liberal market economies.

Greater pay dispersion may be expected in firms operating in highly marketized equity systems. One, active markets for managerial talent and purported attempts to align executive pay with company performance may produce very high rewards for those at the top of the firm. By contrast, pressures for high returns from shareholders may constrain employee incomes at lower levels of the firm. Two, where internal labor markets are being undermined by equity market pressures, integrated and transparent company-wide grading systems that compress pay differentials between top executives and workers may be fragmented. Evidence in support of these contentions is provided by Sjoberg (2009): increases in earnings inequality have been more pronounced over the period 1979–2000 in countries where the size, activity, and efficiency of the stock market have increased the most.

Recent evidence also indicates that the relationship between owners and managers within regimes influences the level of workers' pay and rewards. Where managers have greater discretion and protection from shareholders, workers' pay tends to be higher. Managers may use their protection from shareholders to benefit from harmonious relationships with employees. Using Swedish data, Cronqvist et al. (2009) find that CEOs with stronger control relative to shareholders tend to pay their workers higher wages. Bertrand and Mullainathan (1999, 2003) show that protection from takeovers is associated with higher levels of employee pay. They investigate this by comparing wages in US states with strong anti-takeover legislation against those with weaker protection against takeovers. After the passage of anti-takeover legislation, production workers' wages rise by about 1 percent and white-collar wages by about 4 percent compared with companies in states without this legislation. They suggest that managerial desire for a "quiet life" is probably the best explanation for these results.

As noted earlier, employee share ownership plans are especially prevalent in liberal market economies. There are several explanations for this. One, more developed equity markets in these countries facilitate the use of share-based rewards. Two, they may be used to counter the potentially negative effects on employee commitment and human capital development of weaker guarantees of long-term employment (Blair, 1995; Black et al., 2007). They can signal to employees that managers will not opportunistically expropriate all the gains from firm-specific human capital investments (Pendleton and Robinson, 2011).

Skill Development and Work Organization

It has been argued by some that governance systems that rely heavily on market rather than relational characteristics may inhibit long-term investments in human capital and have less internal flexibility in the use of a wide set of skills and the deployment of labor over a broad set of tasks, at least in established industries (Soskice, 1999; Hall and Soskice, 2001). It is argued that the discouragement of long job tenures, and the encouragement provided for certain types of business strategy, are likely to inhibit investments by companies in firm-specific human capital. For their part, employees will be reluctant to invest in firm-specific skills when there is little payoff in long-term "career" employment and there is a threat that payoffs from training may be expropriated by the employer to the benefit of shareholders. In these circumstances, firms may rely instead on ostensibly cheaper external labor markets for the supply of employees with the requisite skills or firms may deskill work to make it easier to source external skills. By contrast, where firms are less exposed to short-term pressures from owners and equity markets, investments in skills and flexible modes of work organizations are facilitated.

There is some evidence which is consistent with these arguments. Various studies have shown that countries such as Germany and Japan have placed more emphasis on investment in human capital over many years (Thelen, 2004; Aoki, 2010). Black et al. (2007) found that countries with less marketized finance and insider governance were more likely to invest in deep initial skills training of young entrants of an apprenticeship nature. This is the kind of skills training which provides deep competence and knowledge and provides a platform for later upgrade training. By contrast, countries with more marketized finance and outsider governance were more likely to invest in continuing training of adults on the basis of immediate production needs. Similarly, Ryan et al. (2010) investigate whether listed companies with dispersed ownership invest less in training than do other firms. They develop a framework, involving three factors, high agency costs between shareholders and managers of listed firms with dispersed ownership; the use of performance-related pay to reward top managers; and accounting conventions which shape performance measures by requiring that spending on intangible assets be expensed not amortized. Managers then have the incentive and ability to restrict spending on training in order to increase their remuneration. Their evidence for initial training programs of companies in engineering and retailing in Britain, Germany, and Switzerland is consistent with ownership effects.

Related to investment in skills are arguments about work organization. In countries or firms where governance pressures discourage investment in firmspecific human capital, firms may choose to organize work on lines where jobs are narrow and where work can be subcontracted. In these circumstances, there may also be reduced functional labor flexibility In such situations, firms may also rely more on a larger cadre of managers to coordinate the labor force and to substitute for the lower levels of skills. In turn, this may have consequences for the international division of labor. Thus, these factors may make certain countries more likely to engage in flexible quality production in more traditional sectors, such as metalworking in Germany (Soskice, 1999).

Industrial Relations

Corporate governance may be associated with institutions and patterns of industrial relations. By this we mean arrangements for employee voice and representation. Thus, where governance is characterized by a strong emphasis on returns to shareholders and short time frames, collective bargaining with unions may be discouraged. In such systems, where collective bargaining does take place, employers may well prefer for it to be decentralized to the level of the establishment and away from company level, where major corporate governance-type decisions are taken.

The evidence to support these arguments suggests that the relationships are highly complex. It is difficult to prove these propositions because union membership and the coverage of collective bargaining has been in decline for some years in many countries, and this is due to a range of factors besides corporate governance. Nevertheless, the available evidence is supportive of these complementarities between corporate governance and industrial relations. It is striking that collective bargaining, where it exists, tends to be decentralized in corporate governance regimes characterized by the ideology and practice of "shareholder value," such as the US and UK. The association between levels of wage bargaining and governance regime is shown by Hall and Gingerich (2009): there appears to be a strong relationship between the decentralization of wage fixing and shareholder power, dispersion of control, and size of stock markets. Similarly, Black et al. (2007) find a significant negative association between bargaining centralization and the volume of equity market activity.

On the level of pay bargaining, there is a related argument. Over the last three or four decades, as suggested above, pay fixing via collective bargaining has increasingly moved to the level of the individual establishment. This is so that pay can be aligned to productivity movements and local cost of living, while keeping it away from company-level considerations. This is certainly the case in the US and UK (Katz, 1993). By contrast, in other countries, elements of pay fixing remain strong at the industry level. Examples which might be cited here are Germany, with its system of industry *Tarif* bargaining and

Japan, with the annual *Shunto* wage system. In the Scandinavian countries, industry-level bargaining is also more widespread. Various factors may contribute to these arrangements, but one is the existence of a more cooperative and coordinated form of capitalism in these countries which fits with insider governance. However, in recent years, pressures in these countries toward a more Anglo-Saxon form of shareholder value may be putting pressure on such arrangements.

Finally, in corporate governance and industrial relations, there is evidence on the case of private equity and hedge fund interventions. It might be expected that such forms of ownership and governance would be inimical to labor involvement in governance. There has been some evidence to this effect and it would seem that interventions by such investment funds rarely involve prior information and consultation with employees and their representatives. However, the evidence seems to suggest that for the most part such interventions tend not to lead to the exclusion of existing trade unions and forms of employment participation. Indeed, there is some evidence that these interventions actually stimulate employee collective action, while at the same time such owners tend to adjust to national industrial relations patterns (Bacon et al., 2010; Gospel et al., 2010).

Conclusions

This chapter has considered the relationships between labor and corporate governance. Governance has been viewed broadly as being about control of the corporation rather than just a set of mechanisms used by shareholders to control managers. On this basis labor has been seen as a key factor in governance, even when it has a limited direct role in the formal institutions of governance. Attention has been drawn to the potential relationships and linkages between labor, owners, and managers, and it has been noted that workers and their representatives may form alliances or coalitions of interests with either managers or investors (Jackson, 2005), though the latter is fairly rare in most regimes for most of the time.

Although the "conventional wisdom" of corporate governance in liberal market economies such as the US and UK see little role for direct involvement of labor in formal corporate governance, there are bodies of thought (stakeholder theory, for instance) which provide normative support for involvement. There are also governance systems elsewhere in Europe that incorporate labor into governance institutions. But even in liberal market economies, where there is little ideological support for labor involvement in governance, there are various ways in which labor can influence the governance of the company. Whilst it is difficult to quantify, the involvement, and possible influence, of labor appears to be increasing in liberal market regimes. However, there are substantial obstacles, in part ideological, to a greater role in governance, and it is unlikely that there will be substantial enhancements of labor's governance role without legal changes (such as European legislation).

The chapter has also considered how labor is affected by corporate governance regimes. It has been noted that patterns of employment, work organization, and industrial relations are associated with types of governance regime. At the same time, changes can be observed in governance regimes, and there is some evidence that these may impact upon labor, though the consensus seems to be that effects are muted so far. Within regimes, it is possible to discern differences in labor "outcomes" according to the relative power of managers and owners. Where managers have more discretion, labor appears to fare better. This is based on observations mainly within liberal market economies. Our knowledge of labor and governance will be advanced further by more research into variations in governance in different types of organizations and within other economies.

References

Amable, B. (2004). *The Diversity of Modern Capitalism*. Oxford: Oxford University Press.

Aoki, M. (2010). *Corporations in Evolving Diversity*, Oxford: Oxford University Press.

Bacon, N., Wright, M., Scholes, L., and Meuleman, M. (2010). "Assessing the Impact of Private Equity on Industrial Relations in Europe," *Human Relations*, 63(9): 1343–70.

Batstone, E., Ferner, A., and Terry, M. (1983). *Unions on the Board: An Experiment in Industrial Democracy*. Oxford: Blackwell.

Beeferman, L. (2009). "Private Equity and American Labor: Multiple, Pragmatic Responses Mirroring Labor's Strengths and Weaknesses," *Journal of Industrial Relations*, 51(4): 543–56.

Bertrand, M., and Mullainathan, S. (1999). "Is There Discretion in Wage Setting? A Test Using Takeover Legislation," *Rand Journal of Economics*, 30(3): 535–54.

—— —— (2003). "Enjoying the Quiet Life? Corporate Governance and Managerial Preferences," *Quarterly Journal of Economics*, 111(5): 1043–75.

Black, B., Gospel, H., and Pendleton, A. (2007). "Finance, Governance, and the Employment Relationship," *Industrial Relations*, 46(3): 643–50.

Blair, M. (1995). *Ownership and Control: Rethinking Corporate Governance for the Twenty First Century*. Washington, DC: Brookings Institution.

Bosch, A. (1997). *Vom Interessenkonflikt zur Kultur der Rationalitat*. Munich: Rainer Hampp.

Boxall, P., and Purcell, J. (2010). "An HRM Perspective on Employee Participation," in A. Wilkinson, P. Gollan, M. Marchington, and D. Lewin (eds.), *The Oxford Handbook of Participation in Organizations*. Oxford: Oxford University Press.

Clark, I. (2009). "Private Equity in The UK: Job Regulation and Trade Unions," *Journal of Industrial Relations*, 51(4): 489–500.

Clegg, H. A. (1960). *A New Approach to Industrial Democracy*. Oxford: Blackwell.

Cole, G. D. H. (1917). *Self-Government in Industry*. London: Bell and Sons.

Commission on Codetermination (1998). *The German Model of Codetermination and Cooperative Governance*. Gutersloh: Bertelsmann Foundation Publishers.

Conchon, A., and Waddington, J. (2011). "Board-Level Employee Representation in Europe," in S. Vitols and N. Kluge, *The Sustainable Company: A New Approach to Corporate Governance*. Brussels: European Trades Union Institute.

Conyon, M., Girma, S., Thompson, S., and Wright, P. (2001). "The Impact of Mergers and Acquisitions on Company Employment in the United Kingdom," *European Economic Review*, 46: 31–49.

CRONQVIST, H., HEYMAN, F., NILSSON, M., SVALERYD, H., and VLACHOS, J. (2009). "Do Entrenched Managers Pay Their Workers More?" *Journal of Finance*, 64(1): 309–39.

DAUBLER, W. (1989). *Das Grundrecht auf Mitbestimmung*. Frankfurt: Europaische Verlagsanstalt.

DAVIS, S., HALTIWANGER, J., JARMIN, R., LERNER, J., and MIRANDA, J. (2011). "Private Equity and Employment," Working Paper, Harvard Business School.

Department for Business, Innovation, and Skills (2011). *Executive Remuneration*. London: Stationary Office.

DEFUSCO, R., ZORN, T., and JOHNSON, R. (1991). "The Association between Executive Stock Option Plan Changes and Managerial Decision-Making," *Financial Management*, 20: 36–43.

DONALDSON, T., and PRESTON, L. (1995). "The Stakeholder Theory of the Corporation: Concepts, Evidence, and Implications," *Academy of Management Review*, 20: 65–91.

ERICKSEN, M., HANLON, M., and MAYDEW, E. (2006). "Is There a Link between Executive Compensation and Accounting Fraud?" *Journal of Accounting Research*, 44(1): 113–43.

FAUVER, L., and FUERST, M. (2006). "Does Corporate Governance Include Employee Representation? Evidence from German Corporate Boards," *Journal of Financial Economics*, 82: 673–710.

FILATOTCHEV, I., JACKSON, G., GOSPEL, H., and ALLCOCK, D. (2007). *Identifying the Key Drivers of "Good" Corporate Governance and the Appropriateness of Policy Responses*. London: DTI.

FLIGSTEIN, N. (2001). *The Architecture of Markets*. Princeton: Princeton University Press.

FOREMAN-PECK, J., and HANNAH, L. (2012). "Extreme Divorce: The Managerial Revolution in UK Companies Before 1914," *Economic History Review*, forthcoming.

FRANKS, J., and MAYER, C. (1997). "Corporate Ownership and Control in the U.K., Germany, and the U.S.," in D. Chew (ed.), *Studies in International Corporate Finance and Governance Systems*. New York: Oxford University Press.

—— —— and ROSSI, S. (2009). "Ownership: Evolution and Regulation," *Review of Financial Studies*, 22(10): 4009–56.

FREEMAN, R. (1984). *Strategic Management: A Stakeholder Approach*. Boston MA: Pitman.

FRICK, B., and LEHMANN, E. (2005). "Corporate Governance in Germany: Ownership, Codetermination, and Firm Performance in a Stakeholder Economy," in H. Gospel and A. Pendleton (eds.), *Corporate Governance and Labour Management*. Oxford: Oxford University Press.

GILLEN, S., and STARKS, L. (2007). "The Evolution of Shareholder Activism in the United States," *Journal of Applied Corporate Finance*, 19(1): 55–73.

GOSPEL, H., and PENDLETON, A. (2003). "Finance, Corporate Governance, and the Management of Labour: A Conceptual and Comparative Analysis," *British Journal of Industrial Relations*, 41: 557–82.

—— —— (eds.) (2005). *Corporate Governance and Labour Management*. Oxford: Oxford University Press.

—— and WILLMAN, P. (2005). "Statutory Information Disclosure for Consultation and Bargaining: A German, French, British Comparison," in J. Storey (ed.), *Adding Value through Information and Consultation*. London: Palgrave.

—— —— VITOLS, S., and WILKE, P. (2010). *The Impact of Investment Funds on Restructuring Practices and Employment Levels*. Dublin: European Foundation for the Improvement of Living and Working Conditions.

GOUREVITCH, P., and SHINN, J. (2005). *Political Power and Corporate Control: The New Global Politics of Corporate Governance*. Princeton: Princeton University Press.

GUERIN, D. (1936). *Fascism and Big Business*. New York: Macmillan (1983 edition).

HALL, P., and GINGERICH, D. (2009). "Varieties of Capitalism and Institutional Complementarities in the Macro-Economy: An Empirical Analysis," in R. Hancke (ed.), *Debating Varieties of Capitalism*. Oxford: Oxford University Press.

—— and SOSKICE, D. (eds.) (2001). *Varieties of Capitalism: The Institutional Foundations of Comparative Advantage*. Oxford: Oxford University Press.

HAMMER, T., CURRALL, S., and STERN, R. (1991). "Worker Representation on Corporate Boards of Directors: A Competing Roles Model," *Industrial and Labor Relations Review*, 44: 661–80.

HANCKE, R., RHODES, M., and THATCHER, M. (2007). *Beyond Varieties of Capitalism: Conflict, Contradictions, and Complementarities in the European Economy*. Oxford: Oxford University Press.

HANSMANN, H., and KRAAKMAN, R. (2000). "The End of History for Corporate Law," Yale University, Law and Economics Working Paper 235.

HARRIS, R., SIEGEL, D., and WRIGHT, M. (2005). "Assessing the Impact of Management Buyouts on Economic Efficiency: Plant-Level Evidence from the United Kingdom," *Review of Economics and Statistics*, 87: 148–53.

HAZAMA, H. (1997). *The History of Labour Management in Japan*. London: Macmillan.

HUANG, Y. (2008). *Capitalism with Chinese Characteristics*. New York: Cambridge University Press.

HURST, W. (2009). *The Chinese Workers after Socialism*. Cambridge: Cambridge University Press.

HUTTON, W. (1996). *The State We're In*. London: Vintage.

INAGAMI, T., and WHITTAKER, D. H. (2005). *The New Community Firm: Employment, Governance and Management Reform in Japan*. Cambridge: Cambridge University Press.

JACKSON, G. (2005). "Towards a Comparative Perspective on Corporate Governance and Labour Management: Enterprise Coalitions and National Trajectories," in H. Gospel and A. Pendleton (eds.), *Corporate Governance and Labour Management*. Oxford: Oxford University Press.

—— and VITOLS, S. (2001). "Between Financial Commitment, Market Liquidity and Corporate Governance: Occupational Pensions in Britain, Germany, Japan and the USA," in B. Ebbinghaus and P. Manow (eds.), *Comparing Welfare Capitalism: Social Policy and Political Economy in Europe, Japan, and the USA*. London: Routledge.

—— HOPNER, M., and KURDELBUSCH, A. (2005). "Corporate Governance and Employees in Germany," in H. Gospel and A. Pendleton (eds.), *Corporate Governance and Labour Management*. Oxford: Oxford University Press.

JACOBY, S. (2005). *The Embedded Corporation: Corporate Governance and Employment Relations in Japan and the United States*. Princeton: Princeton University Press.

JENSEN, M., and MECKLING, W. (1976). "Theory of the Firm: Managerial Behavior, Agency Costs and Ownership Structure," *Journal of Financial Economics*, 3: 305–60.

—— —— (1979). "Rights and Production Functions: An Application to Labor-Managed Firms and Codetermination," *Journal of Business*, 52: 469–506.

KAARSEMAKER, E., PENDLETON, A., and POUTSMA, E. (2010). "Employee Share Ownership," in A. Wilkinson, P. Gollan, M. Marchington, and D. Lewin (eds.), *The Oxford Handbook of Participation in Organizations*. Oxford: Oxford University Press.

Katz, H. (1993). "The Decentralisation of Collective Bargaining: A Literature Review and Comparative Analysis," *Industrial and Labour Relations Review*, 47(1): 3–22.

Kleiner, M., and Bouillon, M. (1988). "Providing Business Information to Production Workers: Correlates of Compensation and Profitability," *Industrial and Labor Relations Review*, 41: 605–17.

Kuvandikov, A., Pendleton, A., and Higgins, D. (2013). "Employment Change after Takeovers: The Role of Executive Ownership," *British Journal of Industrial Relations*, forthcoming.

La Porta, R., Lopez-de-Silanes, F., Schleifer, A., and Vishny, R. (1998). "Law and Finance," *Journal of Political Economy*, 106: 1113–55.

Lazonick, W., and O'Sullivan, M. (2000). "Maximising Shareholder Value: A New Ideology for Corporate Governance," *Economy and Society*, 29: 13–35.

Lehto, E., and Bockerman, P. (2008). "Analysing the Employment Effects of Mergers and Acquisitions," *Journal of Economic Behavior and Organization*, 68: 112–24.

Lichtenberg, F., and Siegel, D. (1990). "The Effects of Ownership Changes on the Employment and Wages of Central Office and Other Personnel," *Journal of Law and Economics*, 33: 383–408.

Lower, M. (2010). *Employee Participation in Governance*. Cambridge: Cambridge University Press.

Morishima, M. (1989). "Information Sharing and Firm Performance in Japan," *Industrial Relations*, 30: 37–61.

—— (1991). "Information Sharing and Collective Bargaining in Japan: Effects on Wage Negotiations," *Industrial and Labor Relations Review*, 44: 469–85.

Muller Jentsch, W. (2003). "Reassessing Co-Determination," in W. Muller Jentsch and H. Weitbrecht (eds.), *The Changing Contours of German Industrial Relations*. Munich: Rainer Hampp Verlag.

Myners, P. (2001). *Institutional Investment in the UK: A Review*. London: HM Treasury.

Pagano, M., and Volpin, P. (2005). "Managers, Workers, and Corporate Control," *Journal of Finance*, 60: 841–68.

Peccei, R., Bewley, B., Gospel, H., and Willman, P. (2010). "Who's Been Doing All the Talking and Does It Matter? Determinants and Outcomes of Information Disclosure to Employees," *Human Relations*, 63(3): 1–20.

Pendleton, A., and Deakin, S. (2007). "Corporate Governance and Workplace Employment Relations: The Potential of WERS 2004," *Industrial Relations Journal*, 38(4): 338–55.

—— and Robinson, A. (2011). "Employee Share Ownership and Human Capital Development: Complementarity in Theory and Practice," *Economic and Industrial Democracy*, 32(3): 439–57.

Perlman, S. (1928). *A Theory of the Labor Movement*. New York: Macmillan.

Pistor, K. (1999). "Codetermination: A Socio-political Model with Governance Externalities," in M. Blair and M. Roe (eds.), *Employees and Corporate Governance*. Washington, DC: Brookings Institution.

Porter, M. (1997). "Capital Choices: Changing the Way America Invests in Industry," in D. Chew (ed.), *Studies in International Corporate Finance and Governance Systems*. New York: Oxford University Press.

Roe, M. (1996). *Strong Managers, Weak Owners: The Political Roots of American Corporate Finance*. Princeton: Princeton University Press.

—— (2003). *Political Determinants of Corporate Governance: Political Context, Corporate Impact*. Oxford: Oxford University Press.

Ryan, P., Wagner, K., Teube, S., and Backes-Gellner, U. (2010). "Corporate Ownership and Initial Training in Britain, Germany and Switzerland," SKOPE Research Paper No. 99, December.

Schwab, S., and Thomas, R. (1998). "Re-aligning Corporate Governance: Shareholder Activism by Labor Unions," *Michigan Law Review*, 96(4): 1018–94.

Shleifer, A., and Summers, L. (1988). "Breaches of Trust in Hostile Takeovers," in A. Auerbach (ed.), *Corporate Takeovers: Causes and Consequences*. Chicago: University of Chicago Press.

——— and Vishny, R. (1997). "A Survey of Corporate Governance," *Journal of Finance*, 52: 737–83.

Siegel, D., and Simons, K. (2010). "Assessing the Effects of Mergers and Acquisitions on Firm Performance, Plant Productivity, and Workers: New Evidence from Matched Employer-Employee Data," *Strategic Management Journal*, 31: 903–16.

Sjoberg, O. (2009) "Corporate Governance and Earnings Inequality in the OECD Countries 1979–2000," *European Sociological Review*, 25(5): 519–33.

Sorel, G. (1999). *Reflections on Violence*. Cambridge: Cambridge University Press.

Soskice, D. (1999). "Divergent Production Regimes: Coordinated and Uncoordinated Market Economies in the 1980s and 1990s," in H. Kitschelt, P. Lange, G. Marks, and J. Stephens (eds.), *Continuity and Change in Contemporary Capitalism*. Cambridge: Cambridge University Press.

Thelen, K. (2004). *How Institutions Evolve: The Political Economy of Skills in Germany, Britain, the United States and Japan*. New York: Cambridge University Press.

Vitols, S. (2004). "Continuity and Change: Making Sense of the German Model," *Competition and Change*, 8(4): 331–8.

Webb, S., and Webb, B. (1897). *Industrial Democracy*. London: Longmans.

Whitley, R. (1999). *Divergent Capitalisms: The Social Structuring and Change of Business Systems*. Oxford: Oxford University Press.

Williamson, J. (2003). "A Trade Union Congress Perspective on the Company Law Review and Corporate Governance Reform," *British Journal of Industrial Relations*, 41(3): 511–30.

Wright, M., Bacon, N., and Amess, K. (2009). "The Impact of Private Equity and Buyouts on Employment, Remuneration, and Other HRM Practices," *Journal of Industrial Relations*, 51(4): 501–16.

CHAPTER 29

CORPORATE GOVERNANCE AND PRINCIPAL–PRINCIPAL CONFLICTS

MIKE W. PENG AND STEVE SAUERWALD

INTRODUCTION

PRINCIPAL–principal (PP) conflicts refer to the conflicts between two classes of principals—controlling shareholders and minority shareholders (Dharwadkar et al., 2000; Young et al., 2008). While principal–agent (PA) conflicts are especially relevant in firms characterized by a separation of ownership and control, PP conflicts are important in firms with concentrated ownership and control with a controlling shareholder (Young et al., 2008; Globerman et al., 2011).

Why do corporations in many parts of the world have a controlling shareholder (La Porta et al., 1999)? An institution-based view of corporate governance suggests that institutions—defined as the "rules of the game" (North, 1990)—are the driving forces behind concentrated firm ownership (Peng et al., 2009; Peng and Jiang, 2010). According to this view, weak formal institutions such as laws and regulations for investor protection result in high ownership concentration (La Porta et al., 1998, 1999). Concentrated firm ownership in combination with weak investor protection is a *root cause* of PP conflicts (Dharwadkar et al., 2000; Young et al., 2008). PP conflicts are often found in emerging and transition economies characterized by concentrated firm ownership and weak institutional support. In developed economies, on the other hand, the predominant corporate governance problems are PA conflicts—defined as conflicts of interest between shareholders (principals) and managers (agents) (Jensen and Meckling, 1976). The PP model brings institutions into the foreground and complements agency theory that has focused on PA conflicts with more attention to institutional conditions (Young et al., 2008).

The argument that institutions matter is hardly novel or controversial, but the debate on *how* institutions matter is far from being solved (Peng et al., 2008). Institutions play a

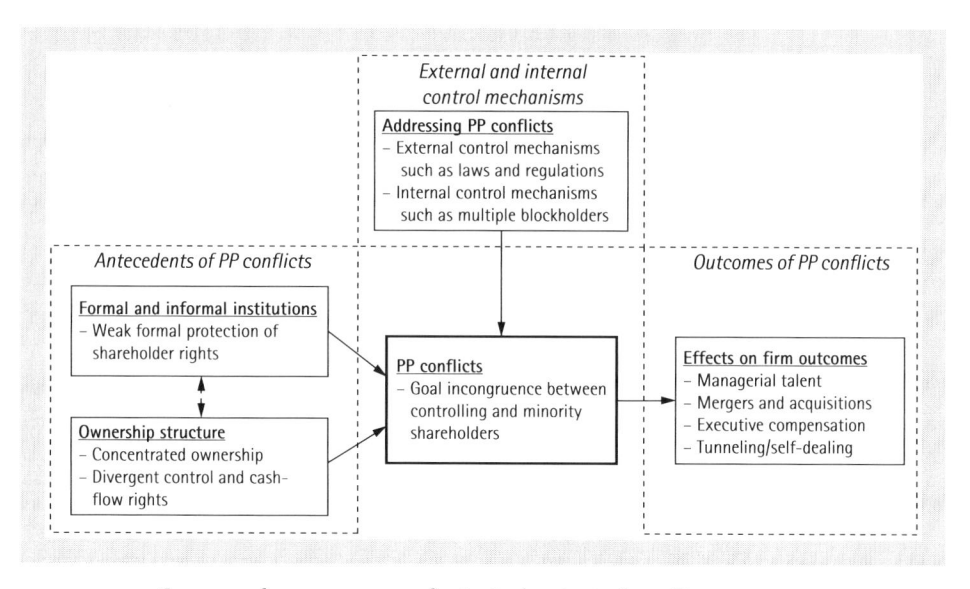

FIGURE 29.1. Causes and consequences of principal–principal conflicts

Source: Adapted from Young et al. (2008: 204).

major role in PP conflicts by directly affecting the incentives of the controlling shareholder to extract private benefits of control—defined as the tangible and intangible benefits from firm control that are not shared with other shareholders (Dyck and Zingales, 2004; Young et al., 2008). Private benefits of control are experienced by minority shareholders as expropriation (Shleifer and Vishny, 1997) and affect firm performance as well as economic development (Morck et al., 2005). Institutions are typically considered external control mechanisms that complement and substitute for internal control mechanisms such as board of directors (Walsh and Seward, 1990; Dharwadkar et al., 2000). The better the external control mechanisms provided by the institutional framework, the less willing or able controlling shareholders are to extract benefits at the expense of other shareholders (Dyck and Zingales, 2004).

Following a call to study how institutions matter (Peng et al., 2008; Young et al., 2008; Peng et al., 2009; Peng and Jiang, 2010; Jiang and Peng, 2011a), this chapter addresses PP conflicts by focusing on three questions. (1) What are the antecedents of PP conflicts? (2) What are the consequences of PP conflicts? (3) How can PP conflicts be addressed? Figure 29.1 illustrates the flow of our arguments.

Principal–Principal Conflicts

Agency theory assumes that shareholders as principals of the firm share common objectives such as shareholder value maximization. Managers as agents of principals are assumed to be potentially opportunistic actors that may take advantage of dispersed shareholders and extract firm value for their own benefit (Eisenhardt, 1989; Shleifer and

Vishny, 1997). Accordingly, the resulting PA conflicts are addressed by *internal* governance mechanisms such as board of directors and *external* governance mechanisms such as an active takeover market. As a result, different institutional arrangements and ownership structures are not explicitly considered and often assumed away (Lubatkin et al., 2007; Young et al., 2008). The PP model, on the other hand, emphasizes the importance of the institutional environment by referring to institutional conditions as important antecedents of PP conflicts. As such, the PP model acknowledges that many institutional environments do not lend themselves to efficient enforcement of arm's-lengths agency contracts (Peng, 2003; Zhou and Peng, 2010). Consequently, the controlling party cannot effectively transfer firm control to professional managers and therefore must maintain control (Young et al., 2008). This leads to situations in which the classic agency model assumption of separation of ownership and control becomes irrelevant. The controlling shareholder not only owns but also controls the firm, thus shifting the research focus to conflicts of interest between controlling shareholders and minority shareholders.

A related stream of research addresses the multiple governance roles of agents, a perspective known as multiple agency model (Arthurs et al., 2008; Bruton et al., 2010; Filatotchev et al., 2011). The multiple agency model applies to situations in which some agents are connected to more than one principal. For instance, venture capitalists (VCs) on the board of a firm that underwent an initial public offering (IPO) are agents to at least two principal groups: (1) the shareholders of the new public corporation and (2) the investors in the VC fund. These complex interdependencies may result in conflicting choices concerning which principal's interests to serve (Arthurs et al., 2008). Similarly to the PP model, the multiple agency model assumes that different principal groups influence organizational decision-making and have potentially conflicting interests (Hoskisson et al., 2002; Arthurs et al., 2008). The PP model and multiple agency model also differ in some ways. On the one hand, the PP model applies to situations in which a controlling shareholder has both the ability and incentives to influence organizational outcomes (Young et al., 2008). Hence, principals are either directly involved in organizational decision-making or entrust a close associate with this task. On the other hand, the multiple agency model applies to situations in which agents are supposed to protect the interests of different principals (Arthurs et al., 2008). Principals in this model may not be able to effectively monitor their agents' actions. In our earlier example, the VC fund and IPO firm shareholders may be too dispersed to effectively monitor their agents on the board of directors.

ANTECEDENTS OF PP CONFLICTS

PP conflicts are most likely to emerge from a combination of (1) concentrated firm ownership and control and (2) poor institutional protection of minority shareholder rights (Young et al., 2008; Peng and Jiang, 2010). Concentrated firm ownership is an important internal governance mechanism, whereas institutions are an important external governance mechanism (Walsh and Seward, 1990; Gedajlovic and Shapiro,

1998). The combination of external and internal governance mechanisms determines the effectiveness of a given corporate governance system (Gedajlovic and Shapiro, 1998; Young et al., 2008). For two reasons, concentrated firm ownership is a central construct in the PP model because it is both a root cause and a possible answer to PP conflicts (Young et al., 2008).

First, concentrated ownership accompanied by weak external institutions is a direct cause of PP conflicts. Agency theory assumes that managers are in quasi-control of the firm—a condition that requires dispersed firm ownership. In many emerging economies, however, ownership and control are concentrated in a controlling shareholder. As such, controlling shareholders are able to use their voting power to decide who sits on the board of directors and who is appointed to the top management team. The resulting internal organizational structure puts the controlling shareholder in a position of ultimate control (Jiang and Peng, 2011b). This powerful internal position provides the opportunities to take advantage of minority shareholders, thus increasing the potential for PP conflicts if the institutional environment does not effectively protect (minority) shareholder rights.

Second, concentrated ownership is also a strategic response by the controlling shareholder to potential PP conflicts when facing weak external corporate governance mechanisms, thus making it an important internal governance mechanism (La Porta et al., 1998; Young et al., 2008; Peng and Jiang, 2010). The economic consequences of concentrated ownership are controversial and depend on external constraints such as laws and regulations (La Porta et al., 1998) and internal constraints such as dividend rights that are tightly coupled to control rights (La Porta et al., 1998: 1126; Dyck and Zingales, 2004). The institutional framework can help to create more effective internal constraints by, for instance, imposing regulations that align voting and dividend rights (La Porta et al., 1998). External governance mechanisms, however, do not work perfectly (Jiang and Peng, 2011b). Internal constraints therefore may substitute for external constraints (Gedajlovic and Shapiro, 1998; Gedajlovic et al., 2004). From this point of view, weak institutional protection of shareholder rights is an important reason for the controlling shareholder to remain in control. Hence, controlling shareholders will only diversify their portfolio if they can be assured of sufficient investor protection because otherwise the threat of another party buying up a controlling stake in the firm and extracting private benefits of control is too high.

Interestingly, in countries with strong investor protection, concentrated firm ownership is considered to have positive effects on firm value and performance (Fama and Jensen, 1983). Concentrated ownership structures in these countries—typically found in developed economies such as the United States—give the controlling party enough incentives to monitor firm performance, while external governance mechanisms prevent expropriation of minority shareholders, thus emphasizing the importance of institutions for the protection of investor rights. Sampling firms from eight Asian countries, Jiang and Peng (2011a) report supportive evidence. In Hong Kong, which is characterized by a high level of investor protection, concentrated ownership is *beneficial* to firm performance. But in Indonesia, which is characterized by a low level of investor protection, concentrated ownership is *detrimental* to firm performance (Jiang and Peng, 2011a).

Consequences of Principal–Principal Conflicts

PP conflicts manifest themselves at multiple levels of analysis. At the country level, for example, PP conflicts negatively affect capital market developments and standards of living (Morck et al., 2005). At the firm level, PP conflicts directly affect firm performance. As we have shown earlier, PP conflicts emerge from differences in principals' goals and objectives that are not countered by appropriate internal or external control mechanisms (Wright et al., 2005; Young et al., 2008). Different interests among shareholders allow the controlling party to extract private benefits at the expense of minority shareholders. This form of expropriation can be accomplished though legal or illegal means. However, the distinction is not always clear-cut and often a "gray area" (La Porta et al., 2000; Young et al., 2008). Tangible private benefits of control result from real firm resources that are divided unevenly between controlling and minority shareholders. Intangible private benefits of control, on the other hand, involve no transfer of real firm resources.

In this section, we highlight the consequences of PP conflicts in four areas: (1) managerial talent; (2) mergers and acquisitions; (3) executive compensation; and (4) tunneling/self-dealing. The firm-level consequences following from each of these areas can directly affect organizational performance and/or increase operating costs (Filatotchev et al., 2001; Bae et al., 2002; Dalziel et al., 2011).

Managerial Talent

Controlling shareholders—and especially family owners—value intangible private benefits such as the ability to run a major business empire (Gomez-Mejia et al., 2003; Morck et al., 2005). Although the intangible value derived from running a business itself does not extract real assets from the firm, organizational consequences that may impact firm performance are nonetheless likely to occur. In the case of family businesses, successive generations are likely to regress to the mean in terms of managerial talent (Gilson, 2006). Hence, placing unqualified family members or close relatives in control and overlooking better qualified outside professional managers reduces the competitiveness of the firm and harms stock performance (Faccio et al., 2001).

The degree to which intangible benefits affect the ownership structure of corporations depends on the institutional environment (Gilson, 2006). This institution-based perspective helps us to explain why we can find concentrated firm ownership in countries with strong shareholder protection. The functionally good protection of shareholder rights in many countries characterized by concentrated ownership (e.g. Sweden) should give controlling shareholders a strong economic incentive to diversify their portfolio. However, the intangible benefits of being one of the leading business families in a small economy such as Sweden seem to provide high intangible private benefits that motivate the controlling owners to stay in control (Gilson, 2006: 1666). It seems likely that the limited managerial talent pool puts these firms at a disadvantage, thus creating PP conflicts because minority shareholders cannot access the intangible benefits of running the business empire while at the same time bearing lower firm performance and financial returns.

Mergers and Acquisitions

Mergers and acquisitions (M&As) are a major strategic decision with different performance consequences for acquiring and acquired firms (Hitt et al., 2005). Recent corporate governance research has identified PP conflicts in M&A deals in both emerging and developed economies. Chen and Young (2010) examine the effects of concentrated government ownership on the stock market consequences of cross-border M&As undertaken by Chinese state-owned firms. They find that the government as a controlling shareholder has political motives to push through deals that are not in the best interest of minority shareholders, thus destroying value for minority shareholders. Political motivations and a lack of effective corporate governance drive many mergers with concentrated state ownership in emerging economies (Chen and Young, 2010). Other studies in the same national context support the position that government ownership creates PP conflicts (Su et al., 2008).

PP conflicts during M&As are not restricted to emerging economies such as China. Interestingly, PP conflicts also affect M&As in developed countries with formally strong investor protection (Goranova et al., 2010). According to agency theory, negative returns to the acquiring firm are attributed to weak governance mechanisms because managers are pursuing their self-interest. The PP model, on the other hand, highlights divergent interests among shareholders. Goranova et al. (2010) show that merger activity with well-diversified institutional investors on both sides of M&A deals results in PP conflicts. Shareholders who hold ownership positions in the acquiring and acquired firms are willing to take a loss in one transaction when their wealth at the aggregate level is increased. Managers of the acquiring firm may still pursue their self-interest (e.g. empire building), but shareholders with overlapping ownership positions are silent about this issue because they still come out positive. Hence, controlling shareholders with a stake in both the acquiring and acquired firms may benefit, while minority shareholders lose out, thus creating PP conflicts from looking the other way and failing to monitor firm management effectively. Controlling shareholders on both sides of the M&A deal may undertake a related party transaction—defined as a transaction between two parties that established a relationship prior to the M&A deal. Although in many countries related party transactions are not illegal per se, they entail extensive disclosure and approval requirements in many countries.

Executive Compensation

The effect of concentrated ownership on executive compensation is another field of potential PP conflicts. Excessive executive compensation is a tangible private benefit of control that transfers real firm resources to top executives of the firm. The quality of internal and external governance mechanisms plays an important role in setting executive compensation (Sun et al., 2010). Su et al. (2010) investigate the effects of ownership concentration on executive compensation in China—a national context prone to PP conflicts. They find a U-shaped relationship between ownership concentration and executive compensation in private Chinese firms. This suggests that low levels of ownership concentration allow managers to set high compensation levels, thus resulting in PA conflicts (Core et al., 1999). High ownership concentration, on the other hand, allows owner-managers to set high compensation levels, thus resulting in PP conflicts that put minority shareholders at a disadvantage (Su et al., 2010).

Other studies have found that ownership structure directly influences the CEO pay–performance link. Sun et al. (2010) highlight how ownership structure and owner identity affects executive compensation. Their study highlights the prevalence of conflicts of interest between different ownership categories, thus creating PP conflicts. For instance, Firth et al. (2006) show that state agencies as majority shareholders in Chinese firms often fail to link pay to performance, thus failing to maximize shareholder value that would benefit all shareholders—including minority shareholders. Linking pay to performance targets seems especially important in state-owned enterprises (SOEs) in emerging economies (Adithipyangkul et al., 2011).

The identity of the controlling shareholder also affects executive compensation. Concentrated family ownership, for example, influences PP conflicts both positively and negatively. Gomez-Mejia et al. (2003) report that family CEOs earn less than non-family CEOs in firms with concentrated family ownership. They reason that family CEOs value intangible benefits from running a business firm. This stewardship orientation of owner-managers has positive effects for the firm as a whole—assuming the family managers are competent.

These positive effects are conditioned on several aspects. First, the family itself can be a source of PP conflicts when they appoint owner-managers who are not qualified to run the business enterprise (Faccio et al., 2001; Gilson, 2006). Stewardship behavior and good intentions cannot compensate for lack of managerial talent. Second, the presence of other family members as large shareholders in the firm can result in mutual monitoring (Combs et al., 2010). Firms with a controlling owner often lack an effective board and other monitoring devices (Young et al., 2008) so that strategic control by other family members becomes important. Combs et al. (2010) find that family CEOs monitored by multiple family members receive less compensation than CEOs of non-family firms, whereas lone-family-member CEOs typically receive more cash compensation than CEOs of non-family firms. This suggests that, in the absence of mutual monitoring among family owners (an internal governance mechanism), family CEOs extract more firm value, thus potentially creating PP conflicts.

Tunneling and Self-Dealing

Tunneling refers to inter-company transfers that favor the company in which the controlling shareholder has a larger equity stake (Johnson et al., 2000; Liu and Magnan, 2011). In the US context, tunneling is typically referred to as self-dealing and must adhere to the highest standard of legal scrutiny (Gilson, 2006). The transfer of resources that benefit the controlling shareholder puts minority shareholders at a disadvantage and is especially severe in times of crisis (Jiang and Peng, 2011b; Johnson et al., 2000). As a result, in the absence of effective minority shareholder protection, corporate valuation suffers (La Porta et al., 2002).

Institutional constraints such as anti-self-dealing regulations not only affect firm performance and valuation, but also country-level equity market developments (Djankov et al., 2008). At the firm level, formal protection through public and private control mechanisms of self-dealing is important to curb opportunistic behavior of controlling shareholders. Private control of self-dealing highlights disclosure requirements and shareholder approval, thus decreasing the risk of expropriation and cost of capital (Liu and Magnan, 2011). In countries with stronger private control of self-dealing regulation, firm value is generally higher. However, the more control and cash-flow rights diverge, the less effective the anti-self-dealing regulations are. These dynamics potentially create PP conflicts (Liu and Magnan, 2011).

Addressing Principal–Principal Conflicts

The previous sections have outlined causes and consequences of PP conflicts. In this section we propose two ways to address PP conflicts by focusing on the effects of external and internal governance mechanisms. Investor protection laws and regulations may act as external governance mechanisms to protect minority shareholders (La Porta et al., 1998; Jiang and Peng, 2011a). Additionally, multiple blockholders may act as internal governance mechanisms that help to address PP conflicts (Jiang and Peng, 2011b).

External Governance Mechanisms

Controlling shareholders are typically considered a *root cause* of PP conflicts (Faccio et al., 2001; Young et al., 2008). This finding is conditioned on external governance mechanisms such as protection by laws and regulations (Peng and Jiang, 2010; Jiang and Peng, 2011a). The incentives for the controlling shareholder to extract private benefits of control are tightly coupled with the corporate governance system in place (Gedajlovic and Shapiro, 1998; Gedajlovic et al., 2004;). Institutions can directly affect organizational structure by prescribing a certain organizational form or by providing necessary support for effective internal control structures. For instance, formal institutions may prescribe one-share-one-vote ownership structures and so effectively reduce the ability of the controlling shareholder to expropriate minority shareholders (La Porta et al., 1998; Faccio et al., 2001), thus directly affecting organizational structure. Additionally, the institutional environment is also important in supporting complex internal structures such as an effective board of directors that protects investor rights (Aguilera and Jackson, 2003).

Strong external governance mechanisms (e.g. effective laws and regulations) coupled with effective internal control mechanisms (e.g. low divergence of control and cash flow rights) are consistent with the notion of low private benefits of control and respect for minority shareholder rights. Hence, the level of shareholder protection embedded in the legal and regulatory institutions affects the scale and scope of private benefits of control (Dyck and Zingales, 2004; Jiang and Peng, 2011b). Serious PP conflicts emerge when external and internal governance mechanisms are weak, thus providing the controlling shareholders with ample opportunities to expropriate minority shareholders. The incentives for minority shareholder expropriation may always exist, but these incentives may be particularly high in times of crisis (Jiang and Peng, 2011b).

Given the widely known economic benefits of improving external governance mechanisms (La Porta et al., 1997), one may ask the question why effective external governance mechanisms are not implemented in countries that currently lack effective investor protection. In many countries with currently weak external governance mechanisms, controlling owners often have little interest in improving investor protection laws—a situation known as economic entrenchment (Morck et al., 2005). These controlling owners, often very wealthy families, use their powerful position to influence not only their own private firm, but also public policy. Hence, effective external governance mechanisms may not develop if large parts of a country's economic sector are controlled by an elite of corporate owners who want to preserve the status quo (Morck et al., 2005).

Internal Governance Mechanisms

Although external governance mechanisms such as laws and regulations are important, they do not work perfectly and often must be supplemented by internal mechanisms. An important internal governance constraint is the presence of multiple blockholders rather than just one controlling shareholder and numerous small shareholders (Faccio et al., 2001; Jiang and Peng, 2011b). Multiple blockholders are in a position to form coalitions to take actions against the controlling shareholder (Jiang and Peng, 2011b), thus effectively providing internal safeguards. Firth et al. (2006) provide supporting evidence for this claim by showing that private blockholders in Chinese firms link CEO pay to shareholder wealth or increases in profitability, thus better aligning management and shareholder interests.

The most effective internal mechanism to credibly protect shareholder rights seems to be low divergence of voting rights from cash-flow rights. This intuitive argument directly relates to the incentives of the controlling shareholder to expropriate minority shareholders. For instance, the typical controlling shareholder in Europe owns 34.6 percent of shares versus 15.7 percent in Asia, suggesting that controlling shareholders in European firms have fewer incentives to expropriate minority shareholders than controlling shareholders in Asian firms (Faccio et al., 2001: 59).

In systems characterized by weak external but strong internal constraints (e.g. low divergence between control and cash-flow rights), controlling shareholders have a "great incentive to increase firm value" because "one does not steal his own money" (Peng and Jiang, 2010: 255). It is especially in these contexts that firms with a controlling shareholder can build a reputation for respecting minority shareholder rights. For instance, firms can list their shares on a stock exchange with higher formal minority shareholder protection or build a reputation for good firm governance over time (Young et al., 2008). It should be noted, however, that these mechanisms are imperfect and often abandoned in times of crisis (Jiang and Peng, 2011b). More credible signals constitute "groups of firms whose businesses do not lend themselves to intragroup supply transactions" (Gilson, 2006: 1658).

The lack of effective internal governance mechanisms can have several reasons. One often cited reason is managerial entrenchment (Morck et al., 1988; Gompers et al., 2003). Managerial entrenchment generally refers to organizational arrangements that effectively protect company insiders from the market for corporate control or other shareholder interventions (Gompers et al., 2003) and is often caused by large equity holdings by company insiders (Morck et al., 1988). Company insiders with a controlling stake have the necessary means to stay in control even if performance does not meet expectations. Hence, managers with large equity holdings enjoy the private benefits of continued employment while outside shareholders suffer lower shareholder wealth.

Future Research Directions

While PP conflicts have received some attention in the management literature, clearly more work needs to be done (Young et al., 2008). In this section, we highlight three key areas that offer promising research opportunities. First, recent corporate governance scholarship calls for more attention to the institutional environment (Aguilera and

Jackson, 2003; Aguilera et al., 2008). Some studies in the tradition of the institution-based view of corporate governance show how *formal* institutions such as laws and regulations affect PP conflicts and minority shareholder expropriation (Jiang and Peng, 2011a). Future studies may turn their attention to how *informal* institutions such as social norms affect PP conflicts (Coffee, 2001).

Second, future research may also deepen our understanding of how the identity of the controlling shareholder affects PP conflicts. A natural starting point in this endeavor is family ownership and control as the dominant ownership form in many parts of the world. Two family firm issues warrant closer attention: (1) making the transition from family to professional management; and (2) informal inheritance rules.

The transition of family firms to non-family or professionalized firms is a critical period in the life of family firms (Gedajlovic et al., 2004; Zahra and Filatotchev, 2004). From a PP perspective, outside investors may benefit from professional managers since managerial talent in the family is limited. However, several factors seem to impede the transition to professional firms in many parts of the world. Most prominent among these factors are institutional conditions (e.g. lack of formal institutions to establish arm's-length contracts with professional managers) and cultural values (e.g. trust toward outsiders). Future studies may investigate how governance mechanisms can support professional outside management even if formal institutions are weak (Young et al., 2008) and trust toward outsiders is lacking (Zhang and Ma, 2009).

Future research may also pay attention to the informal rules that influence succession in family firms cross-nationally. The two primary ways to handle family firm successions around the world are *coparcenary*—defined as an inheritance system that divides the business equally among successors—and *primogeniture*—defined as inheritance by one (often male) successor (Chau, 1991). We have a relatively underdeveloped understanding of how these informal rules affect PP conflicts. For instance, succession according to the coparcenary principle in (overseas) Chinese firms has been identified as a major source of intrafamily rivalry that increases the chances of break-up or diversification of the family firm (Chau, 1991; Fukuyama, 1995). More studies are needed to gain a better understanding of how governance arrangements can protect minority shareholders during the turbulent succession period.

Finally, research may also pay closer attention to potential collaboration among large shareholders (i.e. blockholders). Mutual monitoring associated with multiple blockholders prevents the controlling shareholder from diverting firm resources for private use (Young et al., 2008). This argument assumes that shareholders act independently. Some evidence, however, suggests that shareholders form coalitions to influence firm outcomes (Zwiebel, 1995; Bennedsen and Wolfenzon, 2000). Future research may investigate (1) the antecedents that lead to the formation of shareholder coalitions as well as (2) the effects that these shareholder coalitions have on PP conflicts.

Conclusion

This chapter contributes to the corporate governance literature by going beyond the usual "institutions matter" proposition and tackling the harder but also more interesting question of how institutions matter (Peng et al., 2009, 2008). Specifically, we have argued that weak institutions and concentrated firm ownership are a root cause of PP conflicts and shown how PP conflicts affect organizational outcomes in four management areas: (1) managerial talent; (2) mergers and acquisitions; (3) executive compensation; and (4) tunneling/self-dealing.

So why should researchers and practitioners turn their attention to the emerging view of PP conflicts? PP conflicts can help managers, investors, and policymakers to create better governance structures. Agency theory's assumption that principals pursue a common goal—often defined as shareholder value maximization—leaves out findings showing that divergent principal interests can affect monitoring effectiveness and firm performance (Young et al., 2008). For policymakers, the PP perspective holds important implications during times of institutional transition (Peng, 2003). Corporate governance solutions for emerging and transition economies need to pay more attention to the institutional environment than the agency model can provide (Lubatkin et al., 2007; Globerman et al., 2011). Adopting policies designed for developed economies may be less effective and even counterproductive when this call is ignored (Young et al., 2008). For instance, abolishing concentrated firm ownership without reforming the institutional conditions, including effective law enforcement, is prone to create a "governance vacuum" that supports unchecked managerial opportunism (Filatotchev et al., 2003; Young et al., 2008). Therefore, the creation of effective institutions becomes a priority for policymakers in countries facing institutional transitions.

An institution-based view of corporate governance has emerged in the literature. The PP model is one of the frameworks used to understand how institutions influence the relative payoffs of powerful firm insiders such as controlling shareholders and affiliated managers. Compared with the traditional PA model, the PP model is relatively new in the corporate governance literature, but the phenomena of PP conflicts are certainly not new. In conclusion, if research is to keep up with practice, it seems imperative that corporate governance researchers pay more attention to PP conflicts in the 21st century.

References

Adithipyangkul, P., Alon, I., and Zhang, T. (2011). "Executive Perks: Compensation and Corporate Performance in China," *Asia Pacific Journal of Management*, 28(2): 401–25.

Aguilera, R. V., Filatotchev, I., Gospel, H., and Jackson, G. (2008). "An Organizational Approach to Comparative Corporate Governance: Costs, Contingencies, and Complementarities," *Organization Science*, 19(3): 475–92.

Aguilera, R. V., and Jackson, G. (2003). "The Cross-National Diversity of Corporate Governance: Dimensions and Determinants," *Academy of Management Review*, 28(3): 447–65.

Arthurs, J. D., Hoskisson, R. E., Busenitz, L. W., and Johnson, R. A. (2008). "Managerial Agents Watching Other Agents: Multiple Agency Conflicts Regarding Underpricing in IPO Firms," *Academy of Management Journal*, 51(2): 277–94.

Bae, K.-H., Kang, J.-K., and Kim, J.-M. (2002). "Tunneling or Value Added? Evidence from Mergers by Korean Business Groups," *Journal of Finance*, 57(6): 2695–740.

Bennedsen, M., and Wolfenzon, D. (2000). "The Balance of Power in Closely Held Corporations," *Journal of Financial Economics*, 58(1–2): 113–39.

Bruton, G. D., Filatotchev, I., Chahine, S., and Wright, M. (2010). "Governance, Ownership Structure, and Performance of IPO Firms: The Impact of Different Types of Private Equity Investors and Institutional Environments," *Strategic Management Journal*, 31(5): 491–509.

Chau, T. T. (1991). "Approaches to Succession in East Asian Business Organizations," *Family Business Review*, 4(2): 161–79.

Chen, Y. Y., and Young, M. N. (2010). "Cross-Border Mergers and Acquisitions by Chinese Listed Companies: A Principal–Principal Perspective," *Asia Pacific Journal of Management*, 27(3): 523–39.

Coffee, J. C. (2001). "Do Norms Matter? A Cross-Country Evaluation," *University of Pennsylvania Law Review*, 149(6): 2151–77.

Combs, J. G., Penney, C. R., Crook, T. R., and Short, J. C. (2010). "The Impact of Family Representation on CEO Compensation," *Entrepreneurship Theory and Practice*, 34(6): 1125–44.

Core, J. E., Holthausen, R. W., and Larcker, D. F. (1999). "Corporate Governance, Chief Executive Officer Compensation, and Firm Performance," *Journal of Financial Economics*, 51(3): 371–406.

Dalziel, T., White, R. E., and Arthurs, J. D. (2011). "Principal Costs in Initial Public Offerings," *Journal of Management Studies*, 48(6): 1346–64.

Dharwadkar, R., George, G., and Brandes, P. (2000). "Privatization in Emerging Economies: An Agency Theory Perspective," *Academy of Management Review*, 25(3): 650–69.

Djankov, S., La Porta, R., Lopez-de-Silanes, F., and Shleifer, A. (2008). "The Law and Economics of Self-Dealing," *Journal of Financial Economics*, 88(3): 430–65.

Dyck, A., and Zingales, L. (2004). "Private Benefits of Control: An International Comparison," *Journal of Finance*, 59(2): 537–600.

Eisenhardt, K. M. (1989). "Agency Theory: An Assessment and Review," *Academy of Management Review*, 14(1): 57–74.

Faccio, M., Lang, L. H. P., and Young, L. (2001). "Dividends and Expropriation," *American Economic Review*, 91(1): 54–78.

Fama, E. F., and Jensen, M. C. (1983). "Separation of Ownership and Control," *Journal of Law and Economics*, 26(2): 301–25.

Filatotchev, I., Kapelyushnikov, R., Dyomina, N., and Aukutsionek, S. (2001). "The Effects of Ownership Concentration on Investment and Performance in Privatized Firms in Russia," *Managerial and Decision Economics*, 22(6): 299–313.

—— Wright, M., Uhlenbruck, K., Tihanyi, L., and Hoskisson, R. E. (2003). "Governance, Organizational Capabilities, and Restructuring in Transition Economies," *Journal of World Business*, 38(4): 331–47.

—— Zhang, X., and Piesse, J. (2011). "Multiple Agency Perspective, Family Control, and Private Information Abuse in an Emerging Economy," *Asia Pacific Journal of Management*, 28(1): 69–93.

Firth, M., Fung, P. M. Y., and Rui, O. M. (2006). "Corporate Performance and CEO Compensation in China," *Journal of Corporate Finance*, 12(4): 693–714.

Fukuyama, F. (1995). *Trust: The Social Virtues and the Creation of Prosperity*. New York: Free Press.

Gedajlovic, E., and Shapiro, D. M. (1998). "Management and Ownership Effects: Evidence from Five Countries," *Strategic Management Journal*, 19(6): 533–53.

——, Lubatkin, M. H., and Schulze, W. S. (2004). "Crossing the Threshold from Founder Management to Professional Management: A Governance Perspective," *Journal of Management Studies*, 41(5): 899–912.

Gilson, R. J. (2006). "Controlling Shareholders and Corporate Governance: Complicating the Comparative Taxonomy," *Harvard Law Review*, 119(6): 1641–79.

Globerman, S., Peng, M. W., and Shapiro, D. (2011). "Corporate Governance and Asian Companies," *Asia Pacific Journal of Management*, 28(1): 1–14.

Gomez-Mejia, L. R., Larraza-Kintana, M., and Makri, M. (2003). "The Determinants of Executive Compensation in Family-Controlled Public Corporations," *Academy of Management Journal*, 46(2): 226–37.

Gompers, P., Ishii, J., and Metrick, A. (2003). "Corporate Governance and Equity Prices," *Quarterly Journal of Economics*, 118(1): 107–55.

Goranova, M., Dharwadkar, R., and Brandes, P. (2010). "Owners on Both Sides of the Deal: Mergers and Acquisitions and Overlapping Institutional Ownership," *Strategic Management Journal*, 31(10): 1114–35.

Hitt, M. A., Ireland, R. D., and Harrison, J. S. (2005). "Mergers and Acquisitions: A Value Creating or Value Destroying Strategy?" in M. A. Hitt, R. E. Freeman, and J. S. Harrison (eds.), *The Blackwell Handbook of Strategic Management*. Oxford: Blackwell, 384–408.

Hoskisson, R. E., Hitt, M. A., Johnson, R. A., and Grossman, W. (2002). "Conflicting Voices: The Effects of Institutional Ownership Heterogeneity and Internal Governance on Corporate Innovation Strategies," *Academy of Management Journal*, 45(4): 697–716.

Jensen, M. C., and Meckling, W. H. (1976). "Theory of the Firm: Managerial Behavior, Agency Costs and Ownership Structure," *Journal of Financial Economics*, 3(4): 305–60.

Jiang, Y., and Peng, M. W. (2011a). "Are Family Ownership and Control in Large Firms Good, Bad, or Irrelevant?" *Asia Pacific Journal of Management*, 28(1): 15–39.

—— —— (2011b). "Principal-Principal Conflicts during Crisis," *Asia Pacific Journal of Management*, 28(4): 683–95.

Johnson, S., La Porta, R., Lopez-de-Silanes, F., and Shleifer, A. (2000). "Tunneling," *American Economic Review*, 90(2): 22–7.

La Porta, R., Lopez-de-Silanes, F., and Shleifer, A. and Vishny, R. W. (1997). "Legal Determinants of External Finance," *Journal of Finance*, 52(3): 1131–50.

—— —— —— (1999). "Corporate Ownership around the World," *Journal of Finance*, 54(2): 471–517.

—— —— —— (1998). "Law and Finance," *Journal of Political Economy*, 106(6): 1113–55.

—— —— —— (2000). "Investor Protection and Corporate Governance," *Journal of Financial Economics*, 58(1–2): 3–27.

—— —— —— (2002). "Investor Protection and Corporate Valuation," *Journal of Finance*, 57(3): 1147–70.

Liu, M., and Magnan, M. (2011). "Self-Dealing Regulations, Ownership Wedge, and Corporate Valuation: International Evidence," *Corporate Governance: An International Review*, 19(2): 99–115.

Lubatkin, M., Lane, P. J., Collin, S., and Véry, P. (2007). "An Embeddedness Framing of Governance and Opportunism: Towards a Cross-nationally Accommodating Theory of Agency," *Journal of Organizational Behavior*, 28(1): 43–58.

Morck, R., Shleifer, A., and Vishny, R. W. (1988). "Management Ownership and Market Valuation: An Empirical Analysis," *Journal of Financial Economics*, 20: 293–315.

—— Wolfenzon, D., and Yeung, B. (2005). "Corporate Governance, Economic Entrenchment, and Growth," *Journal of Economic Literature*, 43(3): 655–720.

North, D. C. (1990). *Institutions, Institutional Change and Economic Performance*. Cambridge: Cambridge University Press.

Peng, M. W. (2003). "Institutional Transitions and Strategic Choices," *Academy of Management Review*, 28(2): 275–96.

—— and Jiang, Y. (2010). "Institutions behind Family Ownership and Control in Large Firms," *Journal of Management Studies*, 47(2): 253–73.

—— Wang, D. Y. L., and Jiang, Y. (2008). "An Institution-Based View of International Business Strategy: A Focus on Emerging Economies," *Journal of International Business Studies*, 39(5): 920–36.

—— Sun, S. L., Pinkham, B., and Chen, H. (2009). "The Institution-Based View as a Third Leg for a Strategy Tripod," *Academy of Management Perspectives*, 23(3): 63–81.

Shleifer, A., and Vishny, R. W. (1997). "A Survey of Corporate Governance," *Journal of Finance*, 52(2): 737–84.

Su, Y., Xu, D., and Phan, P. H. (2008). "Principal–Principal Conflict in the Governance of the Chinese Public Corporation," *Management and Organization Review*, 4(1): 17–38.

Su, Z., Li, Y., and Li, L. (2010). "Ownership Concentration and Executive Compensation in Emerging Economies: Evidence from China," *Corporate Governance*, 10(3): 223–33.

Sun, S. L., Zhao, X., and Yang, H. (2010). "Executive Compensation in Asia: A Critical Review and Outlook," *Asia Pacific Journal of Management*, 27(4): 775–802.

Walsh, J. P., and Seward, J. K. (1990). "On the Efficiency of Internal and External Corporate Control Mechanisms," *Academy of Management Review*, 15(3): 421–58.

Wright, M., Filatotchev, I., Hoskisson, R. E., and Peng, M. W. (2005). "Strategy Research in Emerging Economies: Challenging the Conventional Wisdom," *Journal of Management Studies*, 42(1): 1–33.

Young, M. N., Peng, M. W., Ahlstrom, D., Bruton, G. D., and Jiang, Y. (2008). "Corporate Governance in Emerging Economies: A Review of the Principal–Principal Perspective," *Journal of Management Studies*, 45(1): 196–220.

Zahra, S. A., and Filatotchev, I. (2004). "Governance of the Entrepreneurial Threshold Firm: A Knowledge-Based Perspective," *Journal of Management Studies*, 41(5): 885–97.

Zhang, J., and Ma, H. (2009). "Adoption of Professional Management in Chinese Family Business: A Multilevel Analysis of Impetuses and Impediments," *Asia Pacific Journal of Management*, 26(1): 119–39.

Zhou, J. Q., and Peng, M. W. (2010). "Relational Exchanges versus Arm's-Length Transactions during Institutional Transitions," *Asia Pacific Journal of Management*, 27(3): 355–70.

Zwiebel, J. (1995). "Block Investment and Partial Benefits of Corporate Control," *Review of Economic Studies*, 62(2): 161–85.

CHAPTER 30

MULTIPLE AGENCY THEORY

An Emerging Perspective on Corporate Governance

ROBERT E. HOSKISSON,
JONATHAN D. ARTHURS,
ROBERT E. WHITE, AND
CHELSEA WYATT

INTRODUCTION

AGENCY theory is a powerful model that serves as the basis for much of the corporate governance literature. But, like all models in the social sciences, agency theory presents a simplified version of reality. At its most rudimentary level, agency models consist of one agent and one principal with a contracting relationship tying them together (Jensen and Meckling, 1976). In this model, neither agent nor principal maintains other contracting relationships. Indeed, each has a singular identity as principal or agent, with the loyalty of the agent due completely to the principal, and any efforts or resources the principal wishes to expend devoted completely to the agent. However, beyond the fact that each has a singular identity, in this model principal and agent have no outside relationships. The only connection that exists is with the contracting partner. Neither principal nor agent has outside affiliations that might influence his or her behavior. Finally, this simple agency model does not have a strong sense of temporality. While there is some possibility of change in the contract (i.e. if the agent is let go for poor performance), the general sense is that the contracting period is indefinite, with both principal and agent largely acting as if they expect to be in the relationship for the long term.

Naturally, reality does not correspond well to the simplest agency models with their emphasis on singular identities, a lack of outside relationships, and a weak sense of temporality. Take, for instance, the notion of a single unified principal, or owner. Over the past several decades there has been a move toward increased complexity in the ownership structure of public corporations with the rise of institutional investors. Currently, over 70 percent of the ownership in large US firms is managed by institutional shareholders (Gillan and Starks, 2007). This same trend toward institutional ownership is progressing throughout the world (Goyer and Jung, 2011). As a result, we have a new class of "agent-owners"—principals in the traditional agency sense of the term—who collect investment capital from "ultimate principals" and then act on their behalf to invest that capital (see Figure 30.1). This pattern is also followed by private equity firms, hedge funds, venture capitalists, and other institutions, all of whom serve simultaneously as principal to the firms in which they hold ownership and yet as agent to those individuals and entities who have invested with them. Our chapter aims to extend agency theory by reflecting the increased variety of interests between managerial agents, agent-owners, ultimate principals, and other contracting parties that play important roles in the new governance landscape.

Our extension of agency theory identifies an increasing number of interests which often conflict with one another. No longer is there potential divergence of interest merely between principal and interest, but among a web of interrelated parties. As noted in Arthurs et al. (2008: 277): "Traditional agency theory examines conflicts of interest between a principal and agent; *multiple agency theory* examines conflicts of interests among more than one agent group when at least one of those agents is connected to a different principal." Instead of addressing a one-to-one relationship, multiple agency theory examines a many-to-many relationship to explain outcomes. Such settings create both a potential for "conflicting voices" among the various principal groups (Hoskisson et al., 2002), and also a situation in which each agent may face conflicting choices concerning which principals' interests will be served.

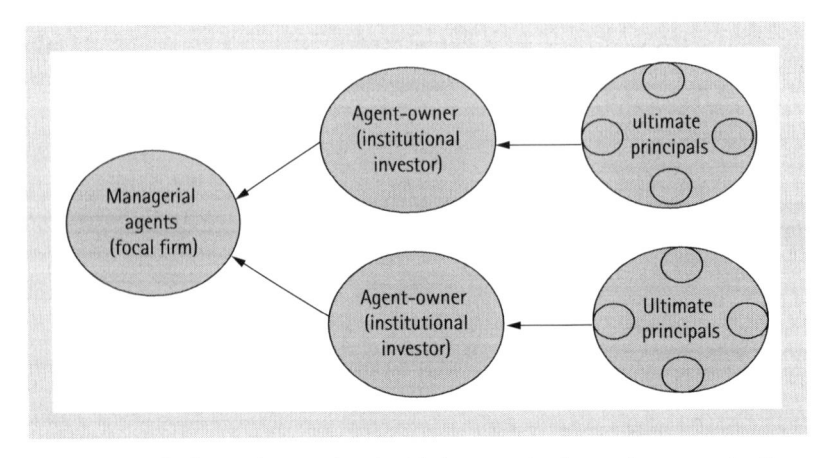

FIGURE 30.1. Layered relationships and embedded agency in the modern organization

Our work builds on the research of others who have elaborated very effectively on the basic agency model. For example, principal–principal agency theory focuses on conflicts among firm principals and appropriation of one principal by another. This can occur, for instance, when family owners dominate minority owners in emerging economies, where investment rights and minority shareholders are not well protected (Chang, 2003). However, multiple agency theory goes beyond this basic conflict between principals, which is already established in the literature. The aspiration of this chapter ultimately is to develop a more general application of multiple agency theory where a number of settings are represented. The multiple agency framework has already been introduced into initial public offerings (IPOs) by the work of Arthurs and colleagues (2008). In addition to informing this context more fully with multiple agency theory, we also propose that the theory might be useful in research addressing mergers and acquisitions, joint ventures, leveraged buyouts, and bankruptcy situations.

The particular arguments set forward in this chapter will seek to make clear that multiple agency theory may be useful in understanding events where significant changes in a firm's capital providers are taking place. These changes usually highlight the different interests of the managerial agents and the agent-owners involved. Ultimately, it is hoped that this perspective will also incorporate multiple agent interests in broader contexts (such as those noted above) as well as dynamics and processes that are not part of traditional agency theory, which is generally static in nature.

Conflict between Owner-Agents

Perhaps the best starting point is to examine the work of Jensen and Meckling (1976). Most of the work using traditional agency theory in the corporate governance literature has examined the conflict between managerial agents and diffused principals. There are numerous examples in the literature of this type of principal–agent conflict which the seminal work of Jensen and Meckling originally described. However, there is a growing body of literature which addresses the issue of ownership heterogeneity and how different owner groups can conflict regarding issues of firm strategy.

A significant amount of the work on owner heterogeneity has been done in the area of internal innovation. Kochhar and David (1996) found that pressure-resistant agent-owners, or agent-owners who are independent of possible pressure from customer groups (e.g. pension funds), are positively related to expenditures on firm innovation. Similarly, from the accounting literature, Bushee (1998) found that transient owners (those that hold onto their stock for a relatively short time frame) are likely to cut R&D expenditures. As such, they suggest that firms with these types of owners have shorter investment time horizons. Alternatively, those firms that have active owners, usually pension fund owners, have higher relative R&D than other firms. Hoskisson et al. (2002) suggest that pension funds had a stronger preference for internal innovation than did mutual funds. Finally, Zahra (1996) found that ownership by long-term investors was positively related to corporate entrepreneurship. In total, these studies are indicative of potential conflict between various agent-owners with different preferences toward innovation and toward the expenditures necessary to pursue that innovation.

In addition to work in the area of innovation, there is a body of research tying the time horizon of certain owners with investments in corporate social responsibility. For example, Johnson and Greening (1999) found that pension fund holders were more likely than mutual fund holders to be associated with firms that invested in corporate social responsibility. This was echoed in later work by Cox et al. (2004) which produced similar results. Neubaum and Zahra (2006) found that not only did corporate social responsibility increase with long-term investors, but the relationship grows stronger as the activism of these long-term investors increases. Activism suggests that they are more involved in the content of corporate strategy, such as R&D expenditures, commitment to innovation, and corporate social responsibility (for further discussion of the relationships between corporate governance and corporate social responsibility see Chapter 32 of this volume). All of these strategies take time to implement because of the effort required to build the needed internal culture and external reputation. Pension funds, which are generally a more patient type of capital, are often more amenable to this approach.

The literature has also examined other ways in which firm strategies are impacted by the composition of the firm's ownership. For example, Connelly, Tihanyi, et al. (2010) found that transient owners are likely to constrain executive decision-making to tactical (versus strategic) moves that are likely to enhance short-term quarterly earnings reports. On the other hand, longer-term owners are more likely to allow strategic moves. Woidtke (2002) found that substantial pension fund ownership in firms is positively related to firm growth, while international expansion is found to be related to pension fund ownership by Tihanyi et al. (2003). Tihanyi and colleagues (2003) also found that there is alignment between pension fund holders and inside directors who tend to be more long term in their orientation. Interestingly, Bushee and Noe (2000) found that short-term investors such as retail mutual fund holders who hold a firm's stock for less than a year prefer frequent disclosure. Such a high volume of disclosure exacerbates stock price volatility. Finally, Bushee (2001) found that short-term institutional investors prefer to examine short-term earnings and are often associated with mispricing of equity ownership. The upshot of this research is that differences of opinion among owners can lead to significant conflict regarding firm strategy. Because substantial ownership heterogeneity exists in many firms (Bennett et al., 2003), we should not be surprised to find such conflicts playing out on a regular basis.

Given the ubiquity of conflict in various settings, we will show how multiple agency insights extend insights from traditional agency theory. In the following section we discuss how multiple agency theory builds upon traditional agency theory. We begin by discussing the elements creating agency conflicts. We then show how dual identities, transcending relationships, and investment time horizon differences can create goal conflict in a multiple agency setting. Given the importance of the specific context in explaining the nature of multiple agency conflicts, we will extend multiple agency theory to a variety of situations, including IPOs, mergers and acquisitions, joint ventures, leveraged buyouts, and bankruptcies.

Multiple Agency Theory—Sources of Conflict

In a traditional agency situation, a principal who employs an agent faces potential agency conflicts owing to the information asymmetry between the two and due to potentially conflicting goals (Eisenhardt, 1989). The traditional agency problem is often illustrated with the CEO who engages in opportunism by doing things such as purchasing excessive perquisites (Jensen and Meckling, 1976) or seeking unprofitable growth through acquisitions and overdiversifying the organization. These things tend to reduce the CEO's employment risk owing to the smoothing of cash flows (Amihud and Lev, 1981). However, the costs of these opportunistic acts are borne by the principals. To overcome this problem, principals utilize monitoring and incentives to reduce information asymmetry and help align the goals of the agent with those of the principal. While monitoring and incentives can be costly, they are established in the hopes of ameliorating more expensive agency problems a priori.

Although multiple agency theory and traditional agency theory share the same assumptions concerning human nature and the potential for agent self-interest-seeking behavior (Williamson, 1996), three elements distinguish the two theories. These three elements indicate the sources of conflict arising in any specific multiple agency context. First, at least one of the parties in the focal situation faces a dual identity (Pratt and Foreman, 2000). One way this could occur is through a principal also serving as agent to principals beyond the focal situation. For example, in the IPO setting, venture capitalists typically serve as principals to the firms they invest in, but they are also agents to the investors in their venture capital fund. Dual identity could also exist when an agent in the focal situation serves as agent to other principals beyond the focal relationship. For example, the underwriter in an IPO deal is the agent to the issuing firm, but is also an agent to institutional investors who purchase shares. This dual identity creates an implicit tension for the actor and can generate conflicting interests. Second, when some actors in the focal situation maintain a relationship which transcends that situation, incentives for favoring the transcending or ongoing relationship create potential goal incongruence among the actors in the focal situation. This may occur, for example, between venture capitalists and underwriters. These two parties have an incentive to maintain a longer-term relationship which transcends (and can undermine) the focal IPO deal. Third, when the relationship among some actors transcends the focal situation, these types of relationships can lead to differing investment horizons which can not only interfere with appropriate incentives, but also undercut current responsibilities. Here again, the venture capitalists in an IPO deal face an implicit undermining of their oversight as principals because of their relationship with the underwriter and their short investment horizon in the IPO firm.

Having provided an overview of how multiple agency theory differs from traditional agency theory, we will elaborate on these issues and inform these differences with specific examples from various contexts. We will provide a brief description of each context and then discuss when sources of multiple agency conflict may arise in each particular setting. While some settings exhibit all three forms of potential conflict, others do not. We begin with the IPO context.

MULTIPLE AGENCY THEORY IN THE INITIAL PUBLIC OFFERING CONTEXT

While the IPO has been researched extensively in finance (Jenkinson and Ljungqvist, 2002) and entrepreneurship (Daily, Certo, et al., 2003), it is becoming an increasingly important topic of research in strategic management and other fields (Certo et al., 2001; Bruton et al., 2010). The IPO is an important event in the life of a new venture as it transitions from being a privately held company to a publicly traded firm. Most IPO companies have enjoyed a modicum of early success, and the IPO allows them to raise significantly more capital for such things as new technology and product development, paying down previous debt, expansion of the asset base, and so forth (Leone et al., 2007). In a typical IPO, the new venture hires an investment banker (underwriter) to float the shares of stock. The underwriter sells the shares to a group of institutional investors at the offer price and then any leftover shares are offered on the open market on the first day of trading (Pollock et al., 2004). Most IPOs experience significant underpricing, which is typically calculated as the difference between the offer price of the stock on the first day of trading and its higher closing price. This underpricing represents money "left on the table" by the IPO firm and reduces the total amount of capital raised by the new venture (Loughran and Ritter, 2002).

Information asymmetry is a common element in most of the theories used to explain the existence of IPO underpricing (Rock, 1986). While information asymmetry would seem to justify underpricing, the nature of the deal network tends to undermine pure information asymmetry for potential buyers as a logical reason for underpricing (Pollock et al., 2004). More specifically, the various actors in the process each have potentially conflicting goals based on their dual identities, the relationships they maintain beyond the IPO process, and their investment horizons.

Sources of Multiple Agency Conflict in the Initial Public Offering Context

From a multiple agency perspective, the main actors in the IPO process typically include the board members of the IPO firm (particularly insiders who are employed by the firm), venture capitalists who have provided funding for the venture and who also occupy positions on the board of directors, the investment banker who is underwriting the shares, and institutional investors such as pension funds or mutual funds who agree to buy shares from the investment banker at a pre-specified offer price.

Although the investment banker (underwriter) is the agent (to the issuing firm) in the IPO deal, each of the other actors maintains its own agency beyond the focal situation. For example, the insiders on the board of directors are agents within the firm to current and future shareholders. Venture capitalists (VCs) are agents to those institutions and wealthy individuals who have invested in the VCs' funds. The investment banker maintains an agency to the institutional investors who are purchasing the shares of the IPO firm. The dual identity of each of these parties creates tension for each actor to decide which identity will supersede, particularly if the identities can have conflicting goals.

In the case of the insiders on the board, their agency beyond the focal IPO deal makes them better principals and monitors of the underwriter. Recent research has confirmed their efficacy in this role (Arthurs et al., 2008). Since they have an employment with the focal firm, they have an incentive to ensure that it raises as much money from the offering as possible. This employment naturally leads to a transcending relationship with current and future shareholders of the IPO firm and is also associated with a longer investment horizon. So, in each case, the insiders' identities lead to unified internal goal congruence, their transcending relationships do not conflict with their goal in the IPO process (to raise as much capital as possible), and their investment horizon also supports this goal in the IPO process.

While insiders' identities, transcending relationships, and investment horizon are associated with uniform goal congruence, the same cannot be said for VCs. Although VCs are principals to the underwriter in the IPO process, their agency to their fund shareholders can potentially lead to goal conflict. More specifically, because VC funds maintain a short lifespan (typically five to ten years) (Sahlman, 1990), they face pressures to show returns quickly. This situation might not normally induce goal conflict if each of the new ventures in which VCs have invested is successful. But because VCs are compensated based on the amount of capital under investment (charging their fund investors a management fee), they have a strong incentive to avoid writing off bad investments until they can show higher returns with some of the other investments (Kunze, 1990). The problem here is that VCs have a strong incentive to obtain close ties with reputable underwriters so that they can take new ventures through the IPO as soon as possible (Gompers, 1996). These ties (transcending relations) become valuable to both the VC and the underwriter since they represent future deals and income associated with those deals. These ties build trust between the two parties and communicate to the underwriter that the ventures the VC brings for IPO are of high quality. Like the dual identity of VCs, this transcending relationship with underwriters works against the best interests of the firm. Additionally, VCs' investment horizon becomes much shorter at the time of the IPO (Dalziel et al., 2011). In sum, these issues contribute to an undermining of the VCs' motivation to provide strong oversight and monitoring as a principal in the IPO process and lead to a lack of goal unity and subsequent multiple agency conflict.

Underwriters are agents in the focal IPO process, and they also maintain an agency with the institutional investors to whom they market and sell the shares (Pollock et al., 2004). Unfortunately for the IPO firm, underwriters have a clear incentive to favor their agency with institutional investors because, in pleasing these serial investors in IPO offerings, underwriters reduce the effort it takes to sell future shares. This preference for favoring institutional investors comes at the expense of the IPO firm. Indeed, Pollock (2003) found, that as underwriter deal network embeddedness increased, underpricing increased as well. The problem here is that the underwriter rarely will maintain a future relationship with the IPO firm. Although a seasoned equity offering deal (offering additional shares of the firm for sale in the future) is possible, it is unlikely (Jenkinson and Ljungqvist, 2002). Additionally, since the underwriter by nature maintains a short investment horizon, the lack of any future relationship with the IPO firm makes it difficult to maintain goal congruence. In sum, underwriters, as agents to the new venture, may lack goal congruence from a traditional agency perspective. However, their multiple agency (i.e. their agency to their institutional investors) creates even more severe goal incongruence between the underwriter and the new venture.

Multiple Agency Theory in the Mergers and Acquisitions Context

Mergers and acquisitions are an important part of the global economy (Thomson Reuters, 2011). While the IPO is viewed as a positive event in the life of a venture, the same is not always true for mergers and acquisitions (M&A). A merger occurs when one company absorbs another. An acquisition differs from a merger in that one company purchases the voting stock of a target firm and eventually tenders an offer to the target shareholders. Because an acquisition often bypasses the target's board of directors or management, it can be seen as "hostile" and can result in proxy contests in an attempt to get control of the target's board of directors (Ross et al., 1996). Tender offers can also result in two-tier offers wherein the acquiring firm tenders an offer at a significant premium to those who will sell immediately. Later, after acquiring a controlling interest, the acquiring firm may offer a reduced price to remaining shareholders (Sundaramurthy and Rechner, 1997).

While agency theory has been used extensively to explain the motivation and outcomes for M&A activity, multiple agency theory has applicability to the context in several different ways. Because the M&A process can be quite complex, the use of investment bankers by the acquiring firm (and even the target firm) is not unusual (Hayward, 2003). This use of professionals creates problems because monitoring on the part of principals becomes much more difficult when the agent is a professional (Sharma, 1997). Additionally, investment bankers often have internally conflicting interests as it relates to the M&A deal because these investment banks have both a corporate finance arm whose revenue is driven by generating client M&A deals as well as a security analyst arm which provides independent advice to investors about securities (Morley, 1988). Hayward and Boeker (1998) find that analysts in an investment bank whose corporate finance arm is involved in the deal tend to make positive pronouncements about the deal even when other analyst groups (outside the investment bank) hold a negative view of the deal. This implicit conflict of interest has led to pressure from regulators to create a wall of separation between investment banking deal-making and analyst research (Galanti, 2006).

Sources of Multiple Agency Conflict in the Mergers and Acquisitions Context

While the multiple agency conflict in the IPO setting is easily apparent, the same is not always true in an M&A setting. In the IPO setting, the underwriter's institutional investors benefit at the expense of the IPO firm. However, in the M&A setting, one party does not always benefit at the expense of another. Moreover, the multiple agency conflict is much more nuanced and therefore muted. We believe there are at least four situations in this context where multiple agency conflict can arise.

The first situation where a multiple agency conflict can occur is in a "merger of equals." Over the past 20 years, there have been several noteworthy deals that have been termed mergers of equals, including Travelers Group and Citicorp, GlaxoWellcome and SmithKline Beecham, and Viacom and CBS (Wulf, 2004). In this situation, both companies cease to exist independently, and existing stock in each company is surrendered for new stock in the merged company. What distinguishes a merger of equals from a regular merger (or acquisition) is that the target CEO and board are given shared power in the new organization as part of the merger agreement. Although this can be seen as a way to enhance post-merger integration, there are some troubling aspects of mergers of equals which point to a multiple agency problem. The actors who may be influenced by multiple agency conflict in this situation include the target company CEO, the target company board of directors, and the offering company CEO. The CEO of the target firm maintains an agency with the target firm, but his or her interests may become aligned with the offering firm given the CEO's future agency with that organization. While a CEO would normally want to bargain for higher valuation of his or her targeted company, the CEO who is able to maintain employment in the merged organization would have little incentive to try to squeeze more value from the offering firm (particularly if there were potential hostile takeover threats which would lead to a loss of employment if the merger of equals fell through). Wulf (2004) found that CEOs in mergers of equals freely traded higher valuation for power in the merged organization. Additionally, board members from the target companies in mergers of equals tended to maintain a higher proportion of the board seats in the merged company relative to a control sample of mergers. In this instance, the target CEO and the target board of directors tend to find that their interests more forcefully align with the acquiring firm. Not only do they have a future agency with shareholders from the acquiring firm, but their relationship with the acquiring firm transcends the focal merger and their investment horizon is longer (compared to those CEOs and board members whose employment ceases in a regular merger).

The acquiring CEO is benefited by a merger of equals for two reasons. First, the merger of equals typically results in positive returns at the announcement of the merger, but the target company's stock does not go up as much. As a result, the value of the merger is not typically captured as fully by the target company shareholders as would occur in a regular merger. Second, the acquiring CEO's compensation is likely to increase regardless of how well the merger performs in the future (Haleblian et al., 2009). Thus, in the short term, the acquiring CEO's reputation is often enhanced by the valuation effects and this may give the CEO additional power to pursue future mergers and personal gain through empire building (Amihud and Lev, 1981).

The second situation where a multiple agency conflict can occur in the M&A context is one to which we alluded earlier. When an organization becomes an acquisition target, certain governance provisions—such as fair price provisions (Sundaramurthy and Rechner, 1997)—become very salient. When a fair price provision has been adopted by the board of directors, it mandates that all shareholders should receive the same price for their shares of stock should a tender offer be made. Without a fair price provision, the acquirer can tender a share offer to those shareholders who are willing to sell immediately at the tendered price. If shareholders in the targeted firm maintain their solidarity, they can resist the initial terms in order to obtain a higher offer (after ongoing haggling). When the acquisition process is drawn out, there may be additional suitors who join the acquisition fray, extending a competing offer, and so there is a strong incentive on the part of an acquirer not to let the negotiations get drawn out (Turk, 1992). The problem here is that the situation creates a sort of prisoner's dilemma for target firm shareholders. If some decide to hold out for a better offer, other shareholders can sell out, thereby giving the acquirer sufficient control to enact controlling interest. Afterward, the acquirer can complete the acquisition but offer those other shareholders a lower price for their shares of stock. So a key question here is which shareholders would want to sell out quickly. Research tends to indicate that institutional investment managers might be willing to jump at an early tender offer for a quick gain. For example, since institutional investors typically maintain large blocks of shares in any company, they provide strong oversight and have a strong incentive to monitor managerial actions that individual shareholders may lack; they will also have information quickly and will be first to act on the information. Furthermore, Sundaramurthy and Rechner (1997) found that organizations with higher institutional holdings are less likely to adopt a fair price provision, implying that institutional investors are the ones who would adopt a short-term investment horizon if the firm were targeted for acquisition. More recent research would tend to point to mutual fund managers (as opposed to pension fund managers) as ones who would maintain a short investment horizon (Hoskisson et al., 2002). Since mutual fund managers are pressured by their investors to show returns each year, they have an incentive to focus on short-term returns. While this pattern of investing results in an emphasis on acquiring innovation rather than developing it internally over a long period of time (for example), we believe it also impacts how much value is ultimately captured by target shareholders in an acquisition. In short, the multiple agency conflict where mutual fund managers have a shorter investment horizon may reduce the total value that targeted shareholders will ultimately obtain.

The third situation where a multiple agency conflict may arise concerns the aligning of interests among investment bankers in the M&A deal process. Kesner et al. (1994) identify the potential agency problem in M&A deals between the investment bankers and their clients who are acquiring another firm. Since investment bankers are paid as a percentage of the size of the deal and because they are largely compensated only when the deal closes (McGlaughlin, 1990), they have an incentive to see the acquiring firm pay a higher premium for the target firm. This is true not only for the investment bankers who represent the acquiring firm but also for the investment bankers representing the target firm. For the target firm, it will not have an agency problem with its representative investment bank; their goals are aligned because they both want to see the highest valuation possible since both will benefit from this. However, the acquiring firm wants to pay less for the acquisition. So, in any M&A deal, the interests of the target firm, its investment bankers, and the acquiring firm's investment bankers all align and are contrary to the interests of the acquiring firm. Indeed, Porrini (2006) finds that acquisition premiums are higher when acquirers use investment bankers than when they do not.

Multiple agency conflict may also arise in the M&A context when investment banks repeatedly work on opposite sides of deals. In other words, when an investment bank represents an acquiring firm and another investment bank represents a target firm, they begin to develop a relationship over the focal deal. Given the relatively small size of the investment banking industry and its geographic clustering, there is a distinct opportunity for investment banking firms to develop longer-term relationships among themselves. Given that their interests already align in any single deal, a longer-term relationship would create multiple agency conflict. Because they would have an agency in multiple future deals, they could begin to work together to minimize haggling in any single deal and to maximize the premiums while simultaneously reducing the amount of time it takes to complete any single deal. We have not seen any empirical work examining this potential situation. However, certain outcomes would occur if this is indeed occurring. For example, we should expect to see higher premiums paid the more that investment banks have worked together (on prior deals). Additionally, we should expect to see the time to complete a deal decrease as investment banks have worked together more. Whether this multiple agency conflict exists and whether reputational effects can mitigate this conflict remain to be seen. In sum, dual identities, transcending relationships, and differing investment time horizons can create significant problems in the context of mergers and acquisitions. We now consider joint venture situations.

Multiple Agency Theory in the Joint Venture Context

The joint venture is a special form of strategic alliance wherein two or more organizations contribute equity to form a new entity (Hennart, 1988). Strategic alliances and joint ventures remain popular organizational forms in the US and abroad (Ernst and Halevy,

2004; Meschi, 2005). The benefit of a joint venture is that it is a hybrid form between the extremes of the market and hierarchy and so it retains greater flexibility for joint venture partners, while still providing governance devices to minimize contracting hazards (Kogut, 1988). More specifically, equity ownership by the parent organizations provides a bond to ensure that each parent is jointly tied to the outcomes of the relationship (Williamson, 1996). This allows for the joint venture parties to share knowledge and resources and risk in a manner that would be less likely in a looser organizational form (Luo, 2007).

While a joint venture seems to provide several benefits in creating a relationship that allows for efficient contracting between or among parties, the failure rate for joint ventures is quite high, potentially up to 70 percent (Bleeke and Ernst, 1991; Johnson et al., 2002). Failure is often caused by partner incompatibility, management problems, poor HR practices (Schuler and Tarique, 2005), changing parent strategy, and even opportunism—particularly when environmental uncertainty is higher, as often occurs in an international setting (Reuer and Ariño, 2002; Ariño and Reuer, 2004; Luo, 2007).

Sources of Multiple Agency Conflict in the Joint Venture Context

While several causes for joint venture failure have been identified, multiple agency theory seems particularly salient in this context (Child and Rodrigues, 2003). In the joint venture, the parent firms represent principals to the joint venture. Managers who are employed in the joint venture are agents to the joint venture but also agents in their respective parent organizations. As such, the managers face issues of dual identity (Pratt and Foreman, 2000). This problem of dual identity and the concomitant problems that it creates is also evident in multinational corporations (MNCs), where a local senior executive identifies with a local staff but must also represent the non-local organization headquarters among the local staff (Zhang et al., 2006). Ring and Van de Ven (1994) make an interesting point about all interorganizational relationships in that the individuals representing their organization may develop trust in their personal relationships, but may be unable to do so when acting as an agent for their respective organization. So this dual identity can lead to problems for the agent in deciding whether to favor the parent organization or the local organization.

Because joint ventures tend to have a relatively short life cycle (Kogut, 1991), and because they can have a relatively high rate of entry and exit among partner firms (Meschi, 2005), the investment horizon of partners in the joint venture may differ. So the joint venture context produces two elements or sources of conflict that are associated with potential multiple agency conflict—dual identities among actors and potentially differing investment time horizons. The third element that underlies potential multiple agency conflict is the existence of transcending relationships among some of the actors in the context.

From a multiple agency perspective, we think that the third source of conflict is the most interesting and least researched to date. There has been recent research on alliances and networks which has examined past and concurrent relationships and how they affect alliance activity, but none that we know of examining transcending relationships among two or more actors if a relationship they collectively held with a different actor ceases. For example, Greve et al. (2010) found that higher relational embeddedness in the form of prior alliance ties was associated with lower withdrawal rates from an alliance. On the other hand, contrary to their expectations, they found that higher structural embeddedness, defined as third-party ties among actors, increased withdrawal rates from an alliance. So, on the one hand, trust (as evidenced by stronger previous ties) reduces withdrawal rates from an alliance. However, third-party ties present an interesting competitor tie that may motivate a conflict of interest (or possibly a co-alignment of interests among a subgroup of actors) and lead to withdrawal from a focal alliance. It would be interesting to examine from a multiple agency perspective whether withdrawal from one joint venture or alliance by two parties was associated with a new, separate joint venture between the two parties. Also, it would be interesting to examine how prior rivalries affect joint ventures and alliances; perhaps partners would more likely ally with their rival's former partners than direct rivals to the focal firm.

In addition to this recent research on alliances, Lavie et al. (2007) found that, when a firm in one alliance was also involved in competing multipartner alliances, it enjoyed greater benefits such as higher productivity and market success. This is an intriguing finding in light of multiple agency theory, because the focal partner with the transcending relationship (among other alliance partners outside the focal alliance) has an incentive to favor either the focal alliance or the other (non-focal) alliance. We think this situation could provide an interesting extension to examining how technology and technological capabilities evolve among the different parties. For example, if the focal alliance firm began to favor one alliance at the expense of another, we should expect to see one alliance developing new technology or new products faster than the other. As such, multiple agency theory may present extensions to alliance competitive dynamics as well.

Multiple Agency Theory in the Leveraged Buyout Context

Private equity or leveraged buyout (PE-LBO) firms are a relatively new form of financial institution which generally makes acquisitions by substituting public equity for private debt. Acharya et al. (2007) suggest PE-LBO firms emerged in the late 1970s and early 1980s, growing rapidly until 1990. After a contraction in the economy, they again grew rapidly and much larger through 2007 (see Chapter 24 of this volume for further discussion). The latter period of private equity grew dramatically primarily because obtaining capital from the debt market was relatively cheap. Interestingly, research suggests that, net of fees, these firms produce results that are slightly less than the S&P 500 (Kaplan and Schoar, 2005). Management fees of PE-LBO firms for those investing in funds to pursue private equity investments cost 2 percent of the uncommitted capital (about 4%

of average invested capital) and 20 percent of the profits. Additionally, compensation for the top managers of PE-LBO firms is very high relative to publicly listed companies.

To illustrate how PE-LBO firms traditionally operate, the first step is to solicit and accept investment funds from banks, pension funds, sovereign wealth funds, hedge funds, endowments, and wealthy individuals. These individual PE-LBO firms, or syndicates of such firms acting together, use primarily borrowed money to buy publicly traded companies and then take them private. As such, these companies are taken off publicly traded stock exchanges for a period of time, one to four years on average. Typically, these PE-LBO firms increase the debt of the acquired company by five to eight times its prior debt level as a listed company. The new debt, borrowed primarily from banks, is securitized and then resold to hedge funds, pension funds, mutual funds, insurance companies, and other investors. This puts banks into the non-traditional role of reselling long-term debt and making most of their money from short-term fees and commissions rather than from holding the loans as long-term assets. Much of the acquired PE-LBO portfolio firm's new debt can be conceptualized as being used to pay dividends to the PE-LBO firms themselves. Once restructured, the acquired company is often resold in the public equity market. Many times PE-LBO firms combine acquired firms to build economies of scale or scope. Once the firm goes public again, the newly publicly traded firm has to repay the new, much larger, and more expensive debt principal and interest, or roll over and refinance the new debt to even newer debt (Guerrera and Politi, 2006).

Sources of Multiple Agency Conflict in the Leveraged Buyout Context

This arrangement leads to a number of potential conflicts. First, managers of the companies going private are able to take large amounts of money with them because of change-of-control provisions and the immediate vesting of options and restricted stock. This opportunity, in actuality, may make the managers of publicly traded firms more short-term oriented because it triggers increased short-term payouts for them if they go private. It also may make bankers more short-term oriented in that they focus less on the long-term ability of the firm to pay back its debts, since much of the risk for these has been moved off the banks' balance sheets. Such financial institutions may now earn more money from short-term commissions and fees for advising, arranging the financing, and trading the new types of highly leveraged financial transactions and financially engineered deals than they could from returns on long-term bank debt or bonds. In regard to multiple agency theory, managers associated with going-private deals have dual identities (to their former shareholders and to the new PE firm), and in the transition they become more short-term oriented. Likewise, bankers may become less focused on the PE portfolio firm's viability (due to fees and debt securitization) and more focused on the relationship with the PE firm itself from which it derives significant fees.

Another conflict exists between the PE-LBO firm and bondholders. Because the debt of acquired PE-LBO companies increases five to eight times in order to pay dividends (to PE-LBO firms) and help restructure the acquired companies, the debt owned by older bondholders is considered more risky, and the price often falls by about 15 percent. When the old bondholders made their investment, they did not perceive the significant additional borrowing that would take place (Cass, 2007). Thus, the new principal of the firm makes it more difficult for prior contracts with capital providers to be fulfilled.

Besides old debtholders, a leveraged buyout may also not be in the interest of long-term shareholders because current managers have an incentive to sell the firm owing to often increased salaries and bonuses associated with such a transaction, where staying on not only as managers but also as manager-investors leads to increased potential wealth. Under the new ownership arrangement, so much money is taken out of the system to pay fees and dividends to the new owners that managers will often not have enough capital to make long-term investments. As PE-LBO deals foster restructuring, this also puts downward pressure on worker wages and benefits. Job growth and decline appear to be directly related to the difficulty of paying back the highly leveraged amounts of debt (Ulrich and Brockbank, 2005). Again, the PE investment makes it difficult to fulfill the dual identity of firm managers who are becoming agents to the PE firms and also historical agents to firm employees who desire to retain their wages and employment.

MULTIPLE AGENCY THEORY IN THE BANKRUPTCY CONTEXT

While not as often studied as other governance events such as IPOs or acquisitions, bankruptcy presents an intriguing case for those interested in studying agency conflicts (Daily, Dalton, et al., 2003). The typical firm declaring bankruptcy has experienced a sharp reversal of fortune after earlier successes, leading to a situation of cash-flow inadequacy in which the firm is unable to pay its bills as they become due. As firms enter bankruptcy, they face a momentous change in purpose: once bankrupt, the firm must be managed primarily for the good of its creditors, rather than its shareholders (D'Aveni, 1990; Cieri et al., 1994). This can be quite difficult for managers who are accustomed to managing the firm primarily for the benefit of shareholders and whose equity holdings and stock options continue to tie their financial interests closely to the interests of shareholders (White et al., 2011). In the midst of this, managers are frequently turning over, old sets of shareholders are being exchanged for new ones, and a variety of actors possess incentives which do not bode well for the future health of the bankrupt firm.

In the US,[1] bankruptcy does not necessarily signify the end of a firm. Most large corporate debtors file for bankruptcy under Chapter 11 of US Code Title 11. So-called "Chapter 11" filings are designed to allow firms to reorganize their debts and then exit bankruptcy as a newly viable enterprise. Filing under Chapter 11 provides firms with three significant privileges. First, firms are protected from the immediate collection efforts of their creditors. This allows them to keep assets pledged as collateral and to shelter much-needed cash in hand. Second, firms are able to continue operating while in bankruptcy. This provides them with the ability to maintain many customers, continue business development efforts, and work toward necessary changes in their business processes. Finally, firms in Chapter 11 are able, with the approval of the court, to renegotiate or renege on certain contracts in an effort to streamline their cost structure so that they can be more competitive in the future. In some locations (e.g. Sweden), management is automatically replaced when a firm files for bankruptcy protection (Thorburn, 2000). However, in the US, bankruptcy court judges typically allow firm executives to continue to manage the firm through the period of insolvency.

During bankruptcy, which can vary from a few months to several years, firms negotiate with creditors and other business partners to restructure their debts in such a way that the firm may once again have a viable business model. As part of this, top managers draw up a bankruptcy reorganization plan that is submitted to the bankruptcy judge. Firm creditors and residual claimants are divided into seniority classes (e.g. secured bondholders, other secured creditors, unsecured creditors, preferred shareholders, common shareholders). Creditors whose rights are affected by the reorganization plan then have the opportunity to vote by class on the plan. On the basis of an affirmative vote, the judge can confirm the plan and allow the firm to exit bankruptcy.

Key to US bankruptcy law is a provision that creditors must generally be paid off completely before shareholders are able to retain any value in the firm. Since bankrupt firms typically do not have the needed assets to satisfy all of their debts, Chapter 11 reorganizations usually result in pre-bankruptcy shareholders losing their firm equity holdings. All old shares of stock are canceled, and new stock is issued to creditors whose debts could not be completely paid by the firm. This reapportioning of firm assets and equity creates a unique level of potential conflict among the different classes of creditors and the pre-bankruptcy shareholders. In effect, it creates a complex and high stakes endgame scenario which pits the various firm claimants against each other for control of the firm, post-bankruptcy. In such a setting, issues related to multiple agency theory are seen in clear contrast.

Sources of Multiple Agency Conflict in the Bankruptcy Setting

When examining bankruptcy from the multiple agency perspective, we must pay careful attention to the key actors in the bankruptcy process. These include the firm's senior executives, specialized bankruptcy lawyers, and firm creditors. Other important participants in the bankruptcy process who won't be fully considered here include the bankruptcy judge and the firm's shareholders.

Throughout this chapter, we have highlighted the fact that dual identities, transcending relationships, and differences in investment horizons tend to engender multiple agency problems in many governance contexts. We find the same to be true in the situation of bankruptcy. As noted above, under US bankruptcy law, firm executives owe their fiduciary obligations primarily to firm creditors but must act under a governance structure that can still incentivize them to seek the best interests of shareholders. Facing this dual identity situation—one identity new and foreign (yet legally mandated) versus another that has been long ingrained in their attitudes and behaviors—leads to difficult conflicts for the managers. Take, for instance, the issue of the firm's reorganization plan. As noted earlier, this plan specifies which firm claimants will receive what type of payment and which other claimants will be left empty-handed. When assembling the reorganization plan, both the potential transcendence of employment relationships beyond bankruptcy and looming time horizon issues will weigh on managerial decisions. If firm executives do not expect to be retained by the new owners of the firm post-bankruptcy, they may do their best to favor influential owners or investors who may be able to help shepherd them into a position in another firm. On the other hand, if they anticipate the possibility of remaining with the firm post-bankruptcy, they will be strongly incentivized to ingratiate themselves with the class of current creditors who will become the firm's new owners upon exit of the firm from bankruptcy (LoPucki and Whitford, 1993). Thus, dual identities, transcending relationships, and differences in investment time horizons may strongly influence the behavior of firm managers in bankruptcy situations.

A second group that plays an important role in the bankruptcy process is the specialized lawyers that aid firms in navigating the bankruptcy process. Because these experts are familiar with court procedure and legal regulations and norms, their assistance is invaluable to the firm. However, they are expensive to maintain. In some cases, professional services fees related to bankruptcy can dissipate a significant proportion of the value of a firm. And while the lawyers that provide these services have a vital role as agents to the firm, their service is compromised by the outside relationships that they maintain with each other. In studying the relations between these bankruptcy lawyers, LoPucki and Whitford (1990: 156) observed the following:

> The [lawyers] who negotiated reorganization plans were not only representatives of the parties in interest, but also members of professions, of independent firms, and of the bankruptcy community... [T]he lawyers in the cases we studied had an incentive to be concerned not only with the welfare of their clients but also with their relationships to each other.

When lawyers broke industry norms by advocating too aggressively for their clients, their reputations suffered, and they might find it more difficult to obtain business in the future (LoPucki and Whitford, 1990). Thus, the dual identity of the lawyers (as agents to the firm but also as members of a professional community) and their transcending relationships with others in the legal field compromised their ability to fully advocate on behalf of the bankrupt firm. This type of thinking was driven by an eye toward maintaining a strong flow of legal clients over a time horizon that extended well past the anticipated end of the relationship with the firm they were hired to serve. Like the firm's managers, the legal specialists serving the firm during bankruptcy are likely compromised by multiple agency conflicts.

Finally, firm creditors are key resource providers for the firm. These creditors include firms providing "debtor-in-possession financing," allowing firms to access the capital needed to continue operations while in bankruptcy, banks providing lines of credit, and corporate bondholders. While conventional creditors, such as banks, would prefer to have cash in hand rather than shares of stock in a firm emerging from bankruptcy, other entities that sometimes act as creditors—such as hedge funds and private equity funds—may see the bankruptcy process as an inexpensive way of gaining control over the firm. Employing what's known as a "loan to own" strategy, such funds either loan the bankrupt firm money directly or they buy up deeply discounted firm debt. Then, when it appears the struggling company may not be able to fulfill all its debt obligations, the private equity fund pushes the firm into bankruptcy. Because creditors often receive equity in the restructured firm in exchange for cancellation of firm debt, this strategy can enable these entities to gain controlling ownership of the firm at a sizeable discount.

Such transactions are viewed by many participants, particularly other creditors, as not showing good faith, but they are structured in such a way that they typically do not run afoul of legal requirements (Robertson and Cicarella, 2008). Cases such as this are clearly not motivated by any sense of duty to the struggling firm. Rather, hedge fund and private equity fund managers seeking to lead firms into bankruptcy are focused on maximizing returns for their fund investors. The identity most salient to hedge and private equity funds in these situations is not that of capital provider but of investment manager. Whereas the managers of the soon-to-be bankrupt firm hope for longer-term capital access, the hedge and private equity funds (much as the VC firms during IPO) seek to move as quickly as possible toward exit. Thus, dual identity, transcending relationships, and differences in investment horizons can conspire together to turn the capital provider from friend to foe.

Discussion

Traditional agency models investigate one-to-one relationships between principal and agent (Arthurs et al., 2008). In these models, singular identities of actors as principal to one agent or agent to one principal, a lack of outside business or social relationships, and a weak sense of temporality can sometimes limit theorizing. In contrast, multiple agency theory loosens these key restrictions. First, multiple agency theory examines the dual identities of contracting parties. Some principals have multiple agents, some agents serve multiple principals, and some entities are principal and agent simultaneously. Second, many contracting parties have transcending relationships—outside their focal principal–agent relationship—that significantly influence their behavior as principal or agent. Finally, when the relationship among some actors transcends the focal situation, these relationships can lead to differing investment time horizons which can interfere with appropriate incentives.

To explore multiple agency theory more fully, in this chapter we've applied the theory to a variety of important corporate governance contexts. As the sections above illustrate, there are increasing opportunities for conflict in agency settings, not only between traditional principals and agents but also among agent-owners representing ultimate principals and other influential business partners and governance participants. Interestingly, multiple agency theory may even suggest role reversals vis-à-vis traditional agency theory expectations (e.g. managerial agents working to protect shareholders' wealth from short-term owner-agents). Below we elaborate more fully on the theoretical ramifications and contributions of multiple agency theory in each of the settings highlighted earlier: IPOs, mergers and acquisitions, joint ventures, leveraged buyouts, and bankruptcy.

Ramifications for Multiple Agency Conflicts

The Initial Public Offering Context

Earlier, we showed how multiple agency conflict can lead to higher underpricing in the IPO process. An important point to make regarding multiple agency conflict in this setting is that viewing the situation from a traditional agency perspective would provide not only inconsistent pronouncements but would also underestimate the potential agency problem. For example, from a traditional agency perspective, one would assume that VCs, as experienced principals, would provide superior monitoring of the underwriter and that insiders (who are often seen as the "source" of an agency problem) may lack the motivation to provide sufficient oversight. As it turns out, the opposite appears to be the case in that insiders have unified goals based on their agency (and concomitant employment) and longer investment horizon, whereas VCs' motivation to monitor is undermined by their outside agency, transcending relationship with the underwriter, and shorter investment horizon. Research shows that insiders on the board of IPO firms serve to improve governance and reduce underpricing, and thus increase money available for the new venture IPO firm (Arthurs et al., 2008). Additional research using a multiple agency approach shows, however, that, if VCs stay on as principal after the IPO, they can counter the trend of founder-centric firms who tend to avoid contingent compensation (Allcock and Filatotchev, 2010).

The agency problem between the underwriter and the issuing firm faces severe goal incongruence problems which are not easily overcome. Specifically, the underwriter's agency beyond the focal IPO creates an additional motivation to please its other principals (institutional investors) at the expense of the IPO firm. In this situation, it seems unlikely that typical agency mechanisms will be very effectual. In other words, the IPO firm must increase the level of monitoring and use of incentives and bonding to overcome the stronger incentives the underwriter has to favor its other principals. One solution to the underpricing problem is to make sure that firms do not just take the price offered by investment banks and leave too much money on the table. Insiders on the board need to take their governance role seriously. Another potential multiple agency context is found in mergers and acquisitions.

The Mergers and Acquisitions Context

While the multiple agency conflict in the M&A context is more nuanced, the ramifications are that some parties can work together in ways to take advantage of other parties in the process. For example, in the case of mergers of equals, shareholders of target firms are left with lower premiums for their shares of stock, while the target CEO and board of directors maintain (at least partial) post-merger employment. There seems to be little recourse for these shareholders except to exit their investment. After all, it would seem that the board of directors is being subverted in the process. It would be interesting to identify whether the relational and reputational capital of board members can have an impact on the likelihood that a merger of equals occurs. Those board members who maintain multiple directorships would have less incentive to agree to a merger of equals (to preserve their board membership) if this meant lower valuation of the target firm. In the case of fair price provisions, shareholders would be wise to act quickly and sell out (accepting the original tender offer) if their company does not have a fair price provision. This is the dominant choice (defection) in a prisoner's dilemma game and fits appropriately in this context as well. Finally, it remains to be seen whether multiple agency conflict arises with investment bankers working increasingly together. If this truly occurs, then acquiring firms would have an incentive to identify an investment bank with no previous ties to the target firm's investment banks.

The Joint Venture Context

Unlike the M&A setting, the multiple agency conflict in the joint venture setting is straightforward. When a joint venture is only between two firms, the conflict arises out of the competing interests of the joint venture managers as well as competing interests between the two organizations putting up the capital. While issues of identity and loyalty to the joint venture are important and may influence how managers approach their relations with other managers in the joint venture, we find it unlikely that managers would actually favor the joint venture over their respective parent organization. Unless the managers' employment was attached to the life of the joint venture, they would have no transcending relationship with the joint venture unless it were ultimately spun off or sold off to another organization. As such, their employment with their parent firm should provide an incentive for them to favor their parent organization. However, in an international setting, joint ventures are often funded with capital from local exchanges and may create diffusion of power around the world and make change difficult to accomplish. This has certainly been the case for Philips Electronics. Because of its decentralized structure with many joint ventures, management has found it difficult to restructure the firm to become more centralized (Bartlett, 2009).

Child and Rodrigues (2003) argue that, since partners in a joint venture contribute complementary tangible and intangible assets, they (in effect) become agents to one another. When a joint venture or strategic alliance includes more than two parties, additional sources of multiple agency conflict may arise. For example, two members in the joint venture can work together to take advantage of a third party. In this situation, it seems important for joint venture members to maintain additional safeguards beyond ownership in the joint venture. For example, it may be possible to create licensing agreements concerning any technology that is developed in the joint venture so that the rights to ownership create legal encumbrances for any technology that is developed in the future. In this way, each member of the joint venture could create a tool to prevent side dealing at the expense of any other joint venture member. This would also create incentives to maintain the joint venture because two parties establishing a transcending relationship would have less ability to profit together (without the third party also profiting).

The Leveraged Buyout Context

The ramifications of multiple agency conflicts have had important consequences for all parties involved in the private equity-LBO setting. One such implication is herd behavior when conditions are right for LBOs; this has led to periods of boom and bust not only for PE-LBO firms but also for the M&A market more generally. Because private equity firms invest for relatively short periods of time and banks gain short-term fees for facilitating buyouts, it appears that firm managers might be pushed toward short-term-oriented behaviors that result in underinvestment and losses to longer-term shareholders. This would suggest, for instance, that private equity deals would lead to lower R&D expenditures in the long term. There is research to suggest that this concern is, in fact, valid (Long and Ravenscraft, 1993). However, there are other perspectives that suggest that being released from the control system of a large firm hierarchy can release the separate private buyout firm to be much more entrepreneurial (Wright et al., 2000). This may also be true if better incentives are applied (Phan and Hill, 1995) and a new entrepreneurial mindset is developed (Wright et al., 2001; Moschieri, 2011). There may also be evidence that leveraged buyouts lead to lower wages and net loss in employment gains, although there is some argument with respect to this question (Sorkin, 2008).

The Bankruptcy Context

Over the past several decades, scholars have turned to traditional agency theory to provide insights into the bankruptcy process. Some have investigated the root cause of bankruptcy, suggesting that the act of bankruptcy may be reflective of conflicts between top executives of the firm and outside parties (Daily and Dalton, 1994) or that bankruptcy represents "the legal resolution of severe shareholder-creditor conflicts" (D'Aveni, 1989: 1120). Others have drawn inferences from the outcome of bankruptcy back to the quality of managers (Daily, Dalton, et al., 2003). While these agency theory propositions are insightful, it's clear that they fail to fully capture the complexity inherent in a process in which there are "perplexing layers of agency" (LoPucki and Whitford, 1990: 154), with multiple parties maintaining multiple relationships. While traditional agency theory does recognize that agents have their own priorities and preferences that can conflict with those of the principal, it does not make strong allowance for the possibility of outside loyalties, or dual identities, of agents that interfere with their ability to serve the principal. In the case of bankruptcy, we have seen how these transcending relationships can impact the ability of key players to fulfill their prescribed roles, particularly when differences in time horizon are present.

A second insight of multiple agency theory into the bankruptcy situation is an enhanced understanding of the difficulty of agents in meeting the simultaneous demands of multiple principals, particularly when these demands are sharply at odds, as they are during bankruptcy. While creditors and shareholders have largely overlapping interests during the normal course of business (both want higher earnings, the continued health and existence of the organization, etc.), during the endgame process of bankruptcy when their share of the assets of the firm is being measured out and ownership interests in the new firm are being set, the interests of the two groups sharply conflict (Asher et al., 2005). For instance, shareholders—who are typically underwater at the point of bankruptcy—have an interest in pushing managers to take extremely risky actions in the hope that a long-shot investment pays off big and the firm becomes solvent once more, allowing them to retain some value in their equity holdings (LoPucki, 2004). On the other hand, creditors want the firm to be extremely conservative in its decision-making while in bankruptcy so that the resource base of the firm (which could be used to pay their claims) is not squandered. As managers, it is very difficult to satisfy both of these groups simultaneously. Perhaps this is why the court is often involved to referee bankruptcy settings.

In the subsections that follow, we briefly address two other important issues—cooperation among agent-owners and the managerial processes associated with multiple agency theory—before offering concluding remarks.

Cooperation among Agent-Owners

We have focused the majority of this chapter on conflicts occurring between parties to the agency relationship. However, multiple agency theorizing may also elucidate increasing opportunities for *cooperation* between subsets of principals and agents. Research examining these complementarities might provide additional contributions to this line of research. For example, Hoskisson et al. (2009) suggest there might be complementarity between monitoring and bonding over time rather than a concurrent substitution effect in governance (Deutsch et al., 2011). Allcock and Filatotchev (2010) also demonstrate the possibility of complementarities in their examination of incentive effects among IPO firms.

Another area of study pertaining to cooperation among institutional investors is in formal organizations that institutional investors have used to manage issues pertaining to poor portfolio firm performance, such as executive compensation and shareholder rights issues. The Council of Institutional Investors is one such organization. Research, for example, by Ward et al. (2009), has shown the impact of such third-party advocacy. They found that institutional investors responded to negative third-party signals by reducing their holdings in a group of 93 firms placed on the Focus List of the Council of Institutional Investors. However, the negative repercussions were lessened if the firm signaled that it had a strong set of outside directors and demonstrated responsiveness, for instance, by increasing CEO incentives associated with performance.

As noted previously, another area where complementarities might be found is within a single agent-owner where the institutional investor can receive an advantage by owning both sides of a transaction, for instance, in acquisitions or joint ventures. If a single institutional investor owns both the acquiring and target firm in a potential acquisition, they may be able to manage the transaction in a way that will create value (Goranova et al., 2010). For instance, often the acquiring firm's stock price is reduced upon announcement, whereas the target firm usually increases in value due to the premium that must be paid in an acquisition. As such, if you are able to forecast which firms are more likely to pursue an acquisition in a particular industry, you may be able to sell short or use a put option to take advantage of such a potential transaction. Alternatively, you could go long on the stock by using a call option on the potential target firm to take advantage of the future rise in price. In this way, the single institutional investor can take advantage of potential transactions in the short term.

Managerial Processes to Deal with Multiple Agent-Owners

In order to manage the potentially complex interests of multiple agent-owners, managerial processes will necessarily be more complex as well. For example, if there is potential for conflicting requests by agent-owners, top-level managers will have to find ways to deal with these conflicting interests. There is some work in finance regarding getting the appropriate numbers of blockholders relative to managerial effectiveness to jointly optimize governance and managerial efforts (Edmans and Manso, 2011). This will likely raise, for example, the visibility of the investor relations department, which is often the first contact with large investors for publicly traded firms (cf. Bushee, 2004). Recent research by Westphal and Bednar (2008) suggests that managers of firms are able to participate in discussions with institutional investors in a way that reduces the need to make changes being sought by some agent-owners. Westphal and Bednar find that, through ingratiation, executive officers of large publicly traded firms are able to lessen the impact of intense activism. Similarly, Westphal and Graebner (2010: 15) find that negative reports by financial analysts encourage firms to "increase externally visible dimensions of board independence without actually increasing board control [over] management" and additionally spur firms to pursue impression management strategies to improve the nature of analyst coverage. As such, it is likely that conflicts among agent-owners would increase the intensity with which firms seek to manage their relationships with owners. This may be accomplished, for example, by a focus on attracting the right investors through advertising and communication or more actively seeking to partner with certain types of owners (White, 2010).

Other Future Research Areas

In addition to the research ideas we have already highlighted in this chapter, we would like to conclude with a few additional thoughts on areas where multiple agency theory could be advanced or where it could offer significant theoretical contributions to the literature. Most importantly, development of formal theories in this area will be of significant importance. In this chapter we have suggested that dual identities, transcending outside relationships, and investment time horizon differences play important roles in the development of multiple agency conflicts. How do these factors determine the extent of such conflicts? Are their effects independent and additive, or are they perhaps multiplicative?

Additionally, the multiple agency perspective can allow us to examine agent-owners coming from different institutional contexts, such as diffused agent-owners coming from developed countries versus dominant agent-owners (for example, family owners) in emerging markets (Filatotchev et al., 2011). Outside board members, usually lumped together as independent outsiders focusing on more intensive monitoring for shareholders, might be seen as agents representing different interests, such as representatives of specific institutional blockholders (Deutsch et al., 2011), labor groups (e.g. in Germany boards often have labor or government representatives), or top professionals that have their own individual motives. As such, multiple agency theory as a perspective should allow us to examine more aspects of corporate governance than the traditional narrow incentive and monitoring notions of traditional agency theory.

Because multiple agency theory can house many important corporate strategy and governance concerns (as illustrated by the broad set of issues covered in this chapter), middle-range models focused on particular phenomenological settings may be especially pertinent to the literature. The work of Arthurs and colleagues (2008) in the IPO context gives an example of how this type of research could move forward profitably.

Besides the contexts explored directly in our chapter (IPOs, mergers and acquisitions, joint ventures, leveraged buyouts, and bankruptcies), other settings that might be useful to cover would include family ownership in both developed and emerging economies (e.g. Breton-Miller et al., 2011), government ownership, and so-called sovereign wealth funds (Connelly, Hoskisson, et al., 2010). Despite our call for middle-range models, we emphasize that an overarching theoretical approach which would help bind the use of the perspective in particular empirical settings is also essential.

Finally, the breadth of the multiple agency perspective should allow us to cover less-addressed issues of principal opportunism (White and Hoskisson, 2012; Shleifer and Summers, 1988). While traditional agency theory has focused on agents as the opportunistic partners in contracting relationships, multiple agency theory makes clear that principals can likewise engage in guileful actions that are detrimental to the contracting relationship. This insight brings into question many of the hidden assumptions of traditional agency theory. For instance, traditional agency theory often presupposes that actions taken by managers to entrench their positions in the organization are likely to be associated with opportunistic behavior. However, if we admit the possibility that managers may need to defend the firm against opportunistic actions by principals (Dalziel et al., 2011), then such managerial efforts to hold and retain power may well be beneficial to the firm and its future performance rather than detrimental.

It is our hope that additional work in the emerging multiple agency perspective will open up new frontiers in our understanding of corporate governance. We look forward to gaining a greater understanding of the web of relationships that influence the incentives and actions of owners, managerial agents, and other important contracting parties.

Note

1. In this section, we focus on bankruptcy in the United States. While bankruptcy procedures vary somewhat in other locations, many of the multiple agency issues we highlight are emblematic of the types of problems to be found in other nations.

References

Acharya, V. V., Franks, J., and Servaes, H. (2007). "Private Equity: Boom or Bust?" *Journal of Applied Corporate Finance*, 19(4): 44–53.

Allcock, D., and Filatotchev, I. (2010). "Executive Incentive Schemes in Initial Public Offerings: The Effects of Multiple-Agency Conflicts and Corporate Governance," *Journal of Management*, 36: 663–86.

Amihud, Y., and Lev, B. (1981). "Risk Reduction as a Managerial Motive for Conglomerate Mergers," *Bell Journal of Economics*, 12: 605–17.

Ariño, A., and Reuer, J. J. (2004). "Designing and Renegotiating Strategic Alliance Contracts," *Academy of Management Executive*, 18(3): 37–48.

Arthurs, J. D., Hoskisson, R. E., Busenitz, L. W., and Johnson, R. A. (2008). "Managerial Agents Watching Other Agents: Multiple Agency Conflicts Regarding Underpricing in IPO Firms," *Academy of Management Journal*, 51: 277–94.

Asher, C. C., Mahoney, J. M., and Mahoney, J. T. (2005). "Towards a Property Rights Foundation for a Stakeholder Theory of the Firm," *Journal of Management and Governance*, 9: 5–32.

Bartlett, C. A. (2009). *Philips versus Matsushita: The Competitive Battle Continues*. Boston: Harvard Business School Press.

Bennett, J. A., Sias, R. W., and Starks, L. T. (2003). "Greener Pastures and the Impact of Dynamic Institutional Preferences," *The Review of Financial Studies*, 16: 1203–38.

Bleeke, J., and Ernst, D. (1991). "The Way to Win in Cross-Border Alliances," *Harvard Business Review*, 69(6): 127–35.

Breton-Miller, I. L., Miller, D., and Lester, R. H. (2011). "Stewardship or Agency? A Social Embeddedness Reconciliation of Conduct and Performance in Public Family Businesses," *Organization Science*, 22: 704–21.

Bruton, G. D., Filatotchev, I., Chahine, S., and Wright, M. (2010). "Governance, Ownership Structure, and Performance of IPO Firms: The Impact of Different Types of Private Equity Investors and Institutional Environments," *Strategic Management Journal*, 31: 491–509.

Bushee, B. J. (1998). "The Influence of Institutional Investors on Myopic R&D Investment," *Accounting Review*, 73: 305–33.

—— (2001). "Do Institutional Investors Prefer Near-Term Earnings over Long-Run Value?" *Contemporary Accounting Research*, 18: 207–46.

—— (2004). "Identifying and Attracting the 'Right' Investors: Evidence on the Behavior of Institutional Investors," *Journal of Applied Corporate Finance*, 16(4): 28–35.

—— and Noe, C. F. (2000). "Corporate Disclosure Practices, Institutional Investors, and Stock Return Volatility," *Journal of Accounting Research*, 38, Supplement: 171–202.

Cass, D. (2007). "Borrowing without Limits," *The Wall Street Journal*, March 19, C12.

Certo, S. T., Covin, J. G., Daily, C. M., and Dalton, D. R. (2001). "Wealth and the Effects of Founder Management among IPO-Stage New Ventures," *Strategic Management Journal*, 22: 641–58.

Chang, S. J. (2003). "Ownership Structure, Expropriation, and Performance of Group-Affiliated Companies in Korea," *Academy of Management Journal*, 46: 238–53.

Child, J., and Rodrigues, S. B. (2003). "Corporate Governance and New Organizational Forms: Issues of Double and Multiple Agency," *Journal of Management and Governance*, 7: 337–60.

Cieri, R. M., Sullivan, P. F., and Lennox, H. (1994). "The Fiduciary Duty of Directors of Financially Troubled Companies," *Journal of Bankruptcy Law and Practice*, 3: 405–22.

Connelly, B. L., Hoskisson, R. E., Tihanyi, L., and Certo, S. T. (2010). "Ownership as a Form of Corporate Governance," *Journal of Management Studies*, 47: 1561–89.

—— Tihanyi, L., Certo, S. T., and Hitt, M. A. (2010). "Marching to the Beat of Different Drummers: The Influence of Institutional Owners on Competitive Actions," *Academy of Management Journal*, 53: 723–42.

Cox, P., Brammer, S., and Millington, A. (2004). "An Empirical Examination of Institutional Investor Preferences for Corporate Social Performance," *Journal of Business Ethics*, 52: 27–43.

Daily, C. M., and Dalton, D. R. (1994). "Bankruptcy and Corporate Governance: The Impact of Board Composition and Structure," *Academy of Management Journal*, 37: 1603–17.

——Certo, S. T., Dalton, D. R., and Roengpitya, R. (2003). "IPO Underpricing: A Meta-analysis and Research Synthesis," *Entrepreneurship Theory and Practice*, 27: 271–95.

—— —— and Cannella, A. A. (2003). "Corporate Governance: Decades of Dialogue and Data," *Academy of Management Review*, 28: 371–82.

Dalziel, T., White, R. E., and Arthurs, J. D. (2011). "Principal Costs in Initial Public Offerings," *Journal of Management Studies*, 48: 1346–64.

Daveni, R. A. (1989). "Dependability and Organizational Bankruptcy: An Application of Agency and Prospect Theory," *Management Science*, 35: 1120–38.

—— (1990). "Top Managerial Prestige and Organizational Bankruptcy," *Organization Science*, 1: 121–42.

Deutsch, Y., Keil, T., and Laamanen, T. (2011). "A Dual Agency View of Board Compensation: The Joint Effects of Outside Director and CEO Stock Options on Firm Risk," *Strategic Management Journal*, 32: 212–27.

Edmans, A., and Manso, G. (2011). "Governance through Trading and Intervention: A Theory of Multiple Blockholders," *Review of Financial Studies*, 24: 2395–428.

Eisenhardt, K. (1989). "Agency Theory: An Assessment and Review," *Academy of Management Review*, 14: 57–74.

Ernst, D., and Halevy, T. (2004). "Not by M&A Alone," *McKinsey Quarterly*, 2004(1): 68–9.

Filatotchev, I., Zhang, X., and Piesse, J. (2011). "Multiple Agency Perspective, Family Control, and Private Information Abuse in an Emerging Economy," *Asia Pacific Journal of Management*, 28: 69–93.

Galanti, S. (2006). "Which Side Are You On? How Institutional Positions Affect Financial Analysts' Incentives," *Journal of Economic Issues*, 40: 387–94.

Gillan, S. L., and Starks, L. T. (2007). "The Evolution of Shareholder Activism in the United States," *Journal of Applied Corporate Finance*, 19(1): 55–73.

Gompers, P. A. (1996). "Grandstanding in the Venture Capital Industry," *Journal of Financial Economics*, 42: 133–56.

Goranova, M., Dharwadkar, R., and Brandes, P. (2010). "Owners on Both Sides of the Deal: Mergers and Acquisitions and Overlapping Institutional Ownership," *Strategic Management Journal*, 31: 1114–35.

Goyer, M., and Jung, D. K. (2011). "Diversity of Institutional Investors and Foreign Blockholdings in France: The Evolution of an Institutionally Hybrid Economy," *Corporate Governance: An International Review*, 19: 562–84.

Greve, H., Baum, J. C., Mitsuhashi, H., and Rowley, T. J. (2010). "Built to Last but Falling Apart: Cohesion, Friction, and Withdrawal from Interfirm Alliances," *Academy of Management Journal*, 53: 302–22.

Guerrera, F., and Politi, J. (2006). "Flipping is a Flop for Investors, Study Says," *Financial Times*, September 20: 13.

Haleblian, J., Devers, C. E., McNamara, G., Carpenter, M. A., and Davison, R. B. (2009). "Taking Stock of What We Know about Mergers and Acquisitions: A Review and Research Agenda," *Journal of Management*, 35: 469–502.

Hayward, M. L. A. (2003). "Professional Influence: The Effects of Investment Banks on Clients' Acquisition and Performance," *Strategic Management Journal*, 24: 783–801.

—— and Boeker, W. (1998). "Power and Conflicts of Interest in Professional Firms: Evidence from Investment Banking," *Administrative Science Quarterly*, 43: 1–22.

Hennart, J.-F. (1988). "A Transaction Costs Theory of Equity Joint Ventures," *Strategic Management Journal*, 9: 361–74.

HOSKISSON, R. E., HITT, M. A., JOHNSON, R. A., and GROSSMAN, W. (2002). "Conflicting Voices: The Effects of Ownership Heterogeneity and Internal Governance on Corporate Strategy," *Academy of Management Journal*, 45: 697–716.

—— CASTLETON, M. W., and WITHERS, M. C. (2009). "Complementarity in Monitoring and Bonding: More Intense Monitoring Leads to Higher Executive Compensation," *Academy of Management Perspectives*, 23(2): 57–74.

JENKINSON, T., and LJUNGQVIST, A. P. (2002). *Going Public: The Theory and Evidence on How Companies Raise Equity Finance*, 2nd edition. New York: Oxford University Press.

JENSEN, M. C., and MECKLING, W. H. (1976). "Theory of the Firm: Managerial Behavior, Agency Costs and Ownership Structure," *Journal of Financial Economics*, 3: 305–60.

JOHNSON, R. A., and GREENING, D. W. (1999). "The Effects of Corporate Governance and Institutional Ownership Types on Corporate Social Performance," *Academy of Management Journal*, 42: 564–76.

JOHNSON, J. P., KORSGAARD, M. A., and SAPIENZA, H. J. (2002). "Perceived Fairness, Decision Control, and Commitment in International Joint Venture Management Teams," *Strategic Management Journal*, 23: 1141–60.

KAPLAN, S. N., and SCHOAR, A. (2005). "Private Equity Returns: Persistence and Capital Flows," *Journal of Finance*, 60: 1791–823.

KESNER, I. F., SHAPIRO, D. L., and SHARMA, A. (1994). "Brokering Mergers: An Agency Theory Perspective on the Role of Representatives," *Academy of Management Journal*, 37: 703–21.

KOCHHAR, R., and DAVID, P. (1996). "Institutional Investors and Firm Innovation: A Test of Competing Hypotheses," *Strategic Management Journal*, 17: 73–84.

KOGUT, B. (1988). "Joint Ventures: Theoretical and Empirical Perspectives," *Strategic Management Journal*, 9: 319–32.

—— (1991). "Joint Ventures and the Option to Expand and Acquire," *Management Science*, 37: 19–33.

KUNZE, R. J. (1990). *Nothing Ventured: The Perils and Payoffs of the Great American Venture Capital Game*. New York: HarperCollins.

LAVIE, D., LECHNER, C., and SINGH, H. (2007). "The Performance Implications of Timing of Entry and Involvement in Multipartner Alliances," *Academy of Management Journal*, 50: 578–604.

LEONE, A. J., ROCK, S., and WILLENBORG, M. (2007). "Disclosure of Intended Use of Proceeds and Underpricing in Initial Public Offerings," *Journal of Accounting Research*, 45: 111–53.

LONG, W. F., and RAVENSCRAFT, D. J. (1993). "LBOs, Debt and R&D Intensity," *Strategic Management Journal*, 14: 119–35.

LOPUCKI, L. M. (2004). "The Myth of the Residual Owner: An Empirical Study," *Washington University Law Quarterly*, 82: 1341–74.

—— and WHITFORD, W. C. (1990). "Bargaining over Equity's Share in the Bankruptcy Reorganization of Large, Publicly Held Companies," *University of Pennsylvania Law Review*, 139: 125–96.

—— —— (1993). "Corporate Governance in the Bankruptcy Reorganization of Large, Publicly Held Companies," *University of Pennsylvania Law Review*, 141: 669–800.

LOUGHRAN, T., and RITTER, J. R. (2002). "Why Don't Issuers Get Upset about Leaving Money on the Table in IPOs?" *Review of Financial Studies*, 15: 413–43.

LUO, Y. (2007). "Are Joint Venture Partners More Opportunistic in a More Volatile Environment?" *Strategic Management Journal*, 28: 39–60.

McGlaughlin, R. M. (1990). "Investment-Banking Contracts in Tender Offers," *Journal of Financial Economics*, 28: 209–32.

Meschi, P.-X. (2005). "Stock Market Valuation of Joint Venture Sell-Offs," *Journal of International Business Studies*, 36: 688–700.

Morley, A. (1988). "Overview of Financial Analysis," in S. N. Levine (ed.), *The Financial Analyst's Handbook*. Homewood, IL: Irwin, 3–33.

Moschieri, C. (2011). "The Implementation and Structuring of Divestitures: The Unit's Perspective," *Strategic Management Journal*, 32: 368–401.

Neubaum, D. O., and Zahra, S. A. (2006). "Institutional Ownership and Corporate Social Performance: The Moderating Effects of Investment Horizon, Activism and Coordination," *Journal of Management*, 32: 108–31.

Phan, P., and Hill, C. (1995). "Organizational Restructuring and Economic Performance in Leveraged Buyouts: An Ex Post Study," *Academy of Management Journal*, 38: 704–39.

Pollock, T. G. (2003). "The Benefits and Costs of Underwriters' Social Capital in the US Initial Public Offerings Market," *Strategic Organization*, 2: 357–88.

—— Porac, J. F., and Wade, J. B. (2004). "Constructing Deal Networks: Brokers as Network 'Architects' in the U.S. IPO Market and Other Examples," *Academy of Management Review*, 29: 50–72.

Porrini, P. (2006). "Are Investment Bankers Good for Acquisition Premiums?" *Journal of Business Research*, 59: 90–9.

Pratt, M. G., and Foreman, P. O. (2000). "Classifying Managerial Responses to Multiple Identities," *Academy of Management Review*, 25: 18–42.

Reuer, J. J., and Ariño, A. (2002). "Contractual Renegotiations in Strategic Alliances," *Journal of Management*, 28: 47–68.

Ring, P. S., and Van de Ven, A. H. (1994). "Developmental Processes of Cooperative Interorganizational Relationships," *Academy of Management Review*, 19: 90–118.

Robertson, J. R., and Cicarella, J. (2008). "Developments in the World of Loan to Own," ABI Committee News, 6/2. Available at <http://www.abiworld.org/committees/newsletters/UTC/vol6num2/devel.html>.

Rock, K. (1986). "Why New Issues are Underpriced," *Journal of Financial Economics*, 15: 187–212.

Ross, S. A., Westerfield, R. W., and Jaffe, J. (1996). *Corporate Finance*, 4th edition. Chicago: Irwin.

Sahlman, W. A. (1990). "The Structure and Governance of Venture-Capital Organizations," *Journal of Financial Economics*, 27: 473–521.

Schuler, R., and Tarique, I. (2005). "International Joint Venture System Complexity and Human Resource Management," in I. Bjorkman and G. Stahl (eds.), *Handbook of Research in IHRM*. Cheltenham: Edward Elgar, 385–404.

Sharma, A. (1997). "Professional as Agent: Knowledge Asymmetry in Agency Exchange," *Academy of Management Review*, 22: 758–98.

Shleifer, A., and Summers, L. H. (1988). "Breach of Trust in Hostile Takeovers," in A. J. Auerbach (ed.), *Corporate Takeovers: Causes and Consequences*. Chicago: University of Chicago Press, 65–88.

Sorkin, A. R. (2008). "Private Equity Buyouts Get Split Review of Job Losses," *International Herald Tribune*, January 26: 13.

Sundaramurthy, C., and Rechner, P. L. (1997). "Conflicting Shareholder Interests," *Business and Society*, 36: 73–87.

THOMSON REUTERS (2011). "M&A Back to 2008 Levels," January 12. Available at <http://thomsonreuters.com/content/news_ideas/articles/financial/379492>.

THORBURN, K. S. (2000). "Bankruptcy Auctions: Costs, Debt Recovery, and Firm Survival," *Journal of Financial Economics*, 58: 337–68.

TIHANYI, L., JOHNSON, R. A., HOSKISSON, R. E., and HITT, M. A. (2003). "Institutional Ownership Differences and International Diversification: The Effects of Boards of Directors and Technological Opportunity," *Academy of Management Journal*, 46: 195–211.

TURK, T. A. (1992). "Takeover Resistance, Information Leakage, and Target Firm Value," *Journal of Management*, 18: 502–22.

ULRICH, D., and BROCKBANK, W. (2005). *The HR Value Proposition*. Boston: Harvard Business School Press.

WARD, A. J., BROWN, J. A., and GRAFFIN, S. D. (2009). "Under the Spotlight: Institutional Investors and Firm Responses to the Council of Institutional Investors' Annual Focus List," *Strategic Organization*, 7: 107–35.

WESTPHAL, J. D., and BEDNAR, M. K. (2008). "The Pacification of Institutional Investors," *Administrative Science Quarterly*, 53: 29–72.

—— and GRAEBNER, M. E. (2010). "A Matter of Appearances: How Corporate Leaders Manage the Impressions of Financial Analysts about the Conduct of their Boards," *Academy of Management Journal*, 53: 15–44.

WHITE, R. E. (2010). "Shall We Dance? The Role of Agents in Managing the Principal-Agent Relationship," in L. A. Toombs (ed.), *Proceedings of the Seventieth Annual Meeting of the Academy of Management* (CD), ISSN 1543–8643.

—— and HOSKISSON, R. E. (2012). "Owner Opportunism and its Effects on Corporate Governance," Iowa State University Working Paper.

—— ARTHURS, J. D., HOSKISSON, R. E., and DALZIEL, T. (2011). "Can Governance Mechanisms Interfere with the Fulfillment of Corporate Elites' Fiduciary Duties? The Case of Chapter 11 Bankruptcy," Iowa State University Working Paper.

WILLIAMSON, O. E. (1996). *Mechanisms of Governance*. New York: Oxford University Press.

WOIDTKE, T. (2002). "Agents Watching Agents? Evidence from Pension Fund Ownership and Firm Value," *Journal of Financial Economics*, 63: 99–131.

WRIGHT, M., HOSKISSON, R. E., and BUSENITZ, L. W. (2001). "Firm Rebirth: Buyouts as Facilitators of Strategic Growth and Entrepreneurship," *Academy of Management Executive*, 15(1): 111–25.

—— —— —— and DIAL, J. (2000). "Entrepreneurial Growth through Privatization: The Upside of Management Buyouts," *Academy of Management Review*, 25: 591–601.

WULF, J. (2004). "Do CEOs in Mergers Trade Power for Premium? Evidence from Mergers of Equals," *Journal of Law, Economics, and Organization*, 20: 60–101.

ZAHRA, S. A. (1996). "Governance, Ownership and Corporate Entrepreneurship: The Moderating Impact of Industry Technological Opportunities," *Academy of Management Journal*, 39: 1713–35.

ZHANG, Y., GEORGE, J. M., and CHAN, T.-S. (2006). "The Paradox of Dueling Identities: The Case of Local Senior Executives in MNC Subsidiaries," *Journal of Management*, 32: 400–25.

CHAPTER 31

AN AGE OF CORPORATE GOVERNANCE FAILURE?

Financialization and its Limits

GEOFFREY WOOD AND MIKE WRIGHT

INTRODUCTION

THE 2008 financial crisis has raised fundamental questions as to the extent to which large-scale corporate governance failures have undermined the basis of the global economy. Although its emergence predated the crisis, the growing body of literature on "financialization" has argued that a feature of contemporary liberal market economies, which has gradually seeped into other national contexts, is that there has been a fundamental change in the way in which firms are governed and the interests of owners and other stakeholders are served. Financialization can be defined as "a pattern of accumulation in which profits accrue primarily through financial channels, rather than through trade and commodity production" (Krippner, 2005: 174). In other words, financialization concerns the process "whereby financial markets, financial institutions, and financial elites gain greater influence over economic policy and economic outcomes" (Palley, 2008). This process also involves fundamental changes in corporate governance (Epstein, 2006a); financialization is concerned with the intensification of pressures on managers to prioritize what are ostensibly "owner" interests in the light of changes in investor composition and behavior (Adler et al., 2008). The literature on financialization suggests that the decline of the managerial revolution and its replacement by a supposedly shareholder-dominant paradigm has, in fact, been little of the sort; rather, both ordinary investors and traditional managers have been emasculated through the rise of financial intermediaries. This has given birth to excessive speculation and the diversion of resources away from the productive areas of the economy. Moreover, not only have "normal" shareholders and managers lost out through this process, but also stakeholders generally: employees have had to contend with worsening terms and conditions of service, whilst customers and other stakeholders are treated in a similarly cavalier fashion.

This chapter reviews and critiques the literature on financialization. We begin our critique with a caveat. The literature on financialization is relatively diverse, so diverse that it can be argued that any review is a futile task: work on financialization brings accounts from regulation perspectives, aspects of the varieties of capitalism (VOC) theory, various types of cultural economics (including postmodern perspectives), and Chandlerian approaches. However, what is common to the academic literature on financialization is that it focuses on the growing power of finance, and the increased impact of financial engineering (Blackburn, 2006: 107). At the heart of this concept lie some fundamental assumptions regarding the global political economy: that finance capital has assumed a particular historic significance that is somehow different from the past.

There have been numerous attempts to bring together, consolidate, and compare and contrast the different approaches to financialization from a starting point that finance is the "leading actor" in present-day capitalism, "works through processes that are powerful, variously understood, variably articulated...and often undisclosed" (Froud et al., 2007: 343). In other words, the financial sector is taken to be the central player in the contemporary governance of firms, serving specific insider interests at the expense of all others. Attempts to bring together the diverse body of the literature on financialization would include an influential (2000) issue of the journal, *Economy and Society* (Williams, 2000), and three edited books (Epstein, 2006b; Froud et al., 2006b; Erturk et al., 2008). Whilst financial institutions and actors "may not be coherent wholes," at the same time, the financial sector has gained predominance over other areas of the economy (Froud et al., 2007: 343).

A key concern with the recent literature on financialization has been with the use of narrative by firms and industries to justify or explain practices, in such a manner that, in key instances, it deliberately obscures specific happenings and realities (see Froud et al., 2006a, 2007; Adler et al., 2008). Similarly, Greenfield and Williams (2004: 417) argue that governments and the popular media have played an active role in sustaining the system, actively promoting the individualization of risk, self-reliance, opposition to state handouts, encouraging self-financing of housing, health, and pensions, a point that has been more fully developed in other accounts (e.g. Froud et al., 2006a). In other words, the large-scale corporate governance failure that is financialization is sustained across the cultural sphere.

Dealing with the Crisis of Fordism

One of the more influential strands of contemporary institutionalist thinking is regulation theory. Regulation theory concerns itself with seeking to explain the underlying institutional conditions for growth and prosperity (Jessop, 2001). It points to the tendency for periods of strong economic performance in particular times and places to be superseded by periods of mediocre growth and recession and vice versa. It suggests that periods of growth are made possible by a supportive institutional framework, encompassing both employment relations, relations with stakeholders, government, and wider society. Hence, for example, compromises between key social interest groupings and associations made possible the long boom of the golden age that preceded the recession of the early 1970s (Jessop, 2001). Regulation theory is concerned with both a particular accumulation regime and a broader mode of regulation, that is, an "assembly of institutions designed to stabilize a specific growth process" (Grahl and Teague, 2000: 162; Mellahi and Wood, 2002).

In practice, the abiding concern of regulationist thinking has been to understand the conditions and circumstances under which growth may (or may have) resumed following the economic crisis of the early 1970s. What concerned this point of view was how work was organized, and which sectors do well at specific times, rather than changes in defining features of corporate governance. Central to a mode of regulation was a dominant production paradigm, with other societal features such as corporate governance following on. Boyer (2000: 112) notes that, since the early 1970s, there have been numerous alternative experiments and potential growth regimes: these included an ICT-driven era, a service sector-driven growth pattern, and more, recently, a finance-driven one. What the latter would suggest is that, rather than the conventional model of the firm creating value through the combination of capital and labor, the main area of growth within the economy has become sectoral, with financial services draining resources away from more productive areas of economic activity.

Initially, the literature suggested that a stable basis for accumulation could be found through the wider adoption of more flexible production paradigms, as had developed in collaborative market economies such as Germany and Japan, in the 1980s, building on earlier institutional traditions and preceding industrial strengths (Dore, 2000). The reversal of fortunes of such economies in the 1990s, and the apparent resurgence of deregulated liberal markets, reopened this debate. Liberal markets undertook far-reaching deregulation of product and labor markets which, proponents argued, enabled liberal market economies to be particularly innovative (Hirst and Zeitlin, 2001: 506). Manufacturing had been eclipsed by a service sector, geared to servicing an increasingly diverse and pluralist society (p. 506). Meanwhile, the greater empowerment of employees eroded existing class solidarities (p. 506). However, new employment opportunities in the service sector were often demonstrably inferior to those offered in traditional manufacturing work, orientated to low-cost low-value-added production paradigms (Walsh and Deery, 1999).

Despite unevenness in the recovery of liberal markets, their continued performance despite occasional shocks into the close of the 1990s reopened the question as to whether a new mode of regulation had emerged, defined not so much by a dominant production paradigm, but rather by a dominant form of corporate governance. Already in the 1980s, it had been argued that liberal markets had transformed into "post-Fordist" economies, centering on personal services and high-technology industry, characterized by innovative forms of work organization and employee empowerment (Hirst and Zeitlin, 2001: 506). Given considerable evidence to the contrary (p. 506), post-Fordist viewpoints were slowly superseded by an alternative approach: rather than post-Fordism, it was argued that liberal markets were increasingly characterized by a dominance of finance, redefining the governance of the firm. In a particularly influential 2000 edition of *Economy and Society*, the possibility of a new era of "financialization" was mooted, drawing on both regulationist thinking and empirical evidence (cf. Williams, 2000). Whilst it was acknowledged that changes in western economies were localized and limited, financialization had the effect of reorienting the firm toward satisfying professional fund managers, rather than real owners or stakeholders (Williams, 2000: 6).

Tickell (2001) argues that active restructuring of institutions has made a new economic trajectory possible: financialization could, if certain prerequisites are met, represent a new growth regime to replace Fordism (Boyer, 2000). The system was no longer defined by work relations, but rather by corporate governance features.

However, despite the emergence of a number of apparently new systemic features, as early as 2000, Boyer (2000: 134) cautioned that a finance growth regime requires complementarity between household behavior (shareholding, purchasing financial products), employment relations (insecure and flexible), profits, and firm governance, changes which, in practice, it may be difficult to secure: hence, there was insufficient evidence to conclude that a coherent new model had yet emerged (p. 140). In other words, Boyer (2000) never argued that financialization was a present state, but rather that certain preconditions had to be fulfilled before it could be considered to be a proper mode of regulation.

Aglietta and Riberioux (2005) explore the legal origins of the shareholder value revolution, and the extent to which managers are encouraged to collude with financial institutions in promoting shareholder value as a leading principle, which, in turn, may encourage the prioritization of speculation over production. This suggests that a shareholder value-orientated paradigm may not actually suit many categories of investor, such as those with longer time horizons, and/or who are committed to a specific firm or industry, either because of personal ties or owing to linkages with other stakeholder groupings. They argue that shareholder value has thus become a defining principle of corporate governance: however, this remained primarily a liberal market phenomenon, and there are strong barriers against its dissemination worldwide (Aglietta and Riberioux, 2005). Hence, financialization has yet to either coalesce into a sustainable mode of regulation, or attain the ubiquity of the Fordist paradigm (Aglietta and Riberioux, 2005). These caveats have not deterred later writers from reiterating the possibility that financialization represents a potential new wealth-based growth regime (Froud et al., 2004: 888). Redistribution of resources from employees to shareholders results in increasing share prices, in turn fueling consumption by savers, in addition to new opportunities for consumption through more readily available credit (in contrast to the Keynesian era where wage increases did this) (Boyer, 2000; Stockhammer, 2004: 721).

Changing Relations between Stakeholders and Sectors

Financialization describes both transformations in the financial sector, and its relations to other sectors (Stockhammer, 2004). In practical terms, much of the writing on financialization sees it as a process characterized by a shift in power toward institutional investors at the expense of other stakeholders: in other words, a corporate governance system characterized by altered priorities, making for both a reallocation of resources and changes in the relative performance of different areas of economic activity. Lazonick and O'Sullivan (2000: 33) argued that a central feature of this shift was a guiding logic of downsizing and distribution: returns were generated through the liquidation of corporate assets at the expense of sustainability. Whilst this may reallocate funds to more productive areas, it may also leave new enterprises dependent on fickle, demanding, and short-term sources of capital (p. 33).

Financialization was characterized by the dominance of financial calculations in organizational structuring (Marchington et al., 2005), encouraging downsizing and the liquidation of physical assets. Froud et al. (2000: 104) argue that financialization represents not only a focus on short-term returns, with attention being concentrated in only one specific direction, at the expense of others. Despite the spread of financialization being constrained by structural barriers, it is likely to spread in part because of the rise of value-orientated investors (p. 88). Froud et al. (2000) argue that, in practice, universal pressures in one direction may be at the cost of failures elsewhere; for example, pressure toward downsizing and distribution may make it difficult to develop human capital (p. 108), with knock-on effects across an economy (Froud et al., 2000: 88). In other words, if a spreading phenomenon, financialization was also likely to privilege certain interests—most notably those of fund managers—at the expense of others—employees and other stakeholders.

However, the spread of financialization has been uneven. Hence, *a first critique of the financialization literature* is that it fails to take account of different sectoral and, indeed, spatial dynamics. In other words, critics of the financialization assume that financialization is detrimental for some (employees, manufacturing, frontline services) and beneficial for others (fund managers, consultants) (Froud et al., 2007). This would suggest a zero-sum relationship where owner and stakeholder rights are mutually exclusive (see Djankov et al., 2003). In other words, if owner rights are improved, worker rights must necessarily suffer. In practice, whilst downsizing, and the short-term prioritization of shareholder value, has proved inimical to key areas of incrementally innovative manufacturing (e.g. traditional manufacturing), it has also proved rather more conducive to innovative new areas of industry and frontline services (Thelen, 2001). In the US, the state has played a central role in promoting specific sectors, not only in terms of the enormous military industrial, security, and penal complexes, but also through effectively cross-subsidizing a sizable component of research and development (R&D) in the biotechnology and IT sectors.

Further, from a spatial perspective in the UK this led to a boom in the south-east, where the financial services industry is centered, but severe recession in the traditionally heavily industrialized regions of the north. In turn, this has led to state-driven regeneration efforts that are very different in both nature and effects from what would normally be associated with institutional reform in a finance-driven economy (Hudson, 2006).

Rethinking Financialization

A Cultural Economy of Financialization: Narrative and Financialization

As noted earlier, regulationist accounts initially focused on the extent to which financialization could represent a new growth regime to replace earlier Fordism (Langley, 2004: 542). In contrast, later approaches have pointed to the incoherence and developing nature of financialization, although it has continued to be treated as an umbrella term to denote a specific and developing pattern of economic activity that has assumed a dominant role in specific national varieties of capitalism (p. 542). Indeed, Froud et al. (2000: 106) argued that financialization was not a coherent or complete project, but rather an emerging one that has overshadowed alternative paradigms. This, in turn, led to a focus on the cultural dimensions of financialization: how extra-firm institutions have helped promote financialization both in terms of neoliberal economic reforms and at an ideological level, and why this has happened. This might represent a logical extension of existing regulationist thinking, pointing to the role of institutions in stabilizing a particularly growth regime. However, this argument has been developed in a manner that is rather more distant from the orthodox regulationist tradition. For example, Froud et al. (2004: 889) argue that the new economy bubble represented ways of thinking about economies rather than economies themselves. Business and its allies in government and the media "spin a narrative": in other words, propaganda as a cover for business misdealings and failure, rather than institutions as supporters of firm-level effectiveness (cf. Froud et al., 2006a). This would include the bidding up of share prices through rhetoric (Leaver, 2007; cf. Froud et al., 2006a). Enron has been cited as a prime example: a success story, inflated by the business press, academics, and politicians, who drove attention away from current failings (p. 890). Erturk et al. (2004: 698–9) argue that financialization created new dangers associated with the passing on of risk and debt. Securitization rendered debt liquid, leading to huge chains of debt and the risk that value could be counted more than once.

Again, Langley (2004: 542) argues that financialization represents speculative accumulation through the dictates of finance and the associated prevalence of financial capital. Through the supportive role of government and media, speculative accumulation became the defining feature of contemporary capitalism (Langley, 2004). In short, it has been argued that financialization represents a system that works in a way that enriched a small group of insiders at the expense of others: a period of speculative excess. Mackenzie (2000) argues that: "Markets, despite their thing-like character, their global reach and their huge volumes, remain social constructs and the feedback loops that constitute them are intricate, knotted...." Hence, what is important is not just objective material issues, but the relationship to subjective interpretations, reflecting dominant agendas and discourses.

This focus on the role of governments is further developed by Froud et al. (2004), who argue that scandals such as Enron highlight not just the failure of governance mechanisms, but the corruption of government. In other words, government does not just play a role in legitimizing the system (a narrow emphasis on share prices led to a growing narrative on innovation), but actively facilitates corruption (Froud et al., 2004). Froud et al. (2004: 886) argue that whilst Enron was a "criminal fraud," it also highlighted broader themes and mechanisms that are of a broader relevance to understanding the system as a whole. Enron presented itself as a company to investors, who uncritically bought its rhetoric. As such, financialization is not just about changing patterns of investor behavior, but a privileging of the capacity of firms to convince individuals and markets about the possibility of generating real value, and hence bidding up share prices, rather than real performance (Froud et al., 2004).

Whilst doubtless correct in highlighting specific instances of corruption that permeate the system (many more have emerged during the financial crisis from 2008), these arguments lead to fairly universalistic conclusions, based on a limited number of examples, and do not take account of regulatory counter-movements. Indeed, a *second critique of the financialization literature* is that it does not take account of the fact that the bulk of organizations continue to function on orthodox lines: producing and selling goods and services to customers, generating real value through the process of production, as has been the case since the inception of capitalism. In the United States, the Enron scandal led to regulatory changes (notably Sarbanes-Oxley). Whilst this has not ended dubious accounting practices, it has highlighted the extent to which checks and balances may be introduced into the system, in the interests of most firms.

This is not to dispute the fact that corruption made possible through both institutional arrangement and actions cannot have system-challenging implications. For example, fraudulent behavior within leading investment banks, and the widespread repackaging of risky mortgages as secure debt, contributed to the 2008 financial crisis. However, the latter represented the product of many causes, both direct and indirect, ranging from fundamental changes in primary commodities prices, to the flooding of western markets by cheap Chinese goods. Whilst it would be incorrect to dismiss systemic corruption as an aberration, it is only one of many factors impacting on the behavior of firms and corporate governance.

The financialization-as-corruption school of thought does embody some basic truths: persistent governance scandals represent not just regulatory oversights, but the political clout of key players. Indeed, Wood and Frynas (2006) argue that even manifestly corrupt systems may be functional if they are effective in servicing elite interests. However, in advanced, highly diversified economies, corruption and malpractice are likely to be leavened by more orthodox practices. This is not to dispute that a fair degree of what Galbraith referred to as "bezzling" may take place in the financial services industry (cf. Blackburn, 2006: 54), and, indeed, will also manifest itself in other areas of what remains fairly diverse economy.

It is more debatable whether there is a self-sustaining monoculture of corruption within the financial services industry: the sector is itself sufficiently diverse with complex and mixed outcomes to suggest that it is not functioning as a coherent whole in the interests of insiders. Indeed, specific instances of corruption may prove dysfunctional even to insiders (Blackburn, 2006), the Enron scandal being a case in point. Moreover, contemporary US evidence points to the extent to which different manifestations of corruption may undermine, rather than support, each other (Mann, 2003).

Financialization and Postmodernism

If a first strand of the literature explored financialization as a potential new growth regime, and the second, as a process associated with the large-scale corruption of governance, state, and markets, a third strand—developing cultural economy approaches—has focused on the power and knowledge dimensions of corporate governance, drawing heavily on postmodern theory. Leaver (2007) argues that there is considerably more to financialization than an emphasis on downsizing and distribution. As suggested earlier, rhetoric can boost share prices, encouraging flows of investment and "irrational exuberance," bidding up share prices beyond material reality (Froud et al., 2006a). Hence, the situation can be termed "postmodern," in that the boundaries of reality become deliberately blurred, with what is immaterial assuming disproportionate importance relative to what is real (Baudrillard, 1990).

Drawing on and developing both this viewpoint and the earlier "financialization as corruption thesis," later writers have focused on providing a critique of agency theories of corporate governance on the grounds that they privilege certain interests at the expense of others (cf. Erturk et al., 2004, 2006). However, this critique disputes the extent to which managers may not necessarily be aligned to owner interests (Erturk et al., 2004: 686) and argues that a more serious issue is the shift in the balance of power away from employees and ordinary investors to financial intermediaries (Erturk et al., 2006).

Hence, Erturk et al. (2004: 677) argue that the present system enriched only certain agents, a relatively small number of political and financial elites. Governance is thus seen to be really about access to key knowledge, power, and control (Erturk et al., 2004: 683). Martin (2002) argues that, although direct or indirect share ownership has become widely spread (owing to middle-class savings and pensions), this ownership has not translated into power or, indeed, knowledge (Martin, 2002). Hence, wealth may be spread across society, without it being "socialized" (Martin, 2002). Drawing on Foucault, Langley (2004) argues that wider society is linked to financial markets in a new grid of power and knowledge relations, which in turn will invariably be contested and redefined as were previous ones.

Intermediaries skim off rewards, whilst shareholders are often relegated to the role of "passive surfers" (Erturk et al., 2006). This makes financialized capitalism very different from rentier capitalism (Erturk et al., 2006). This is not to suggest that Erturk et al. (2004) are in the mainstream postmodern camp, given their cautions against epochalism. However, the tools and concepts—of differing conceptualizations and boundaries of reality, power and knowledge, rhetoric and reality—draw heavily on the postmodern tradition. Whilst the development of the cultural economy approach to financialization represents a synthetic project, the links to, and ready use of, aspects of postmodern theory, most notably a focus on the realm of ideas and knowledge, rather than simply material conditions, bring with them both strengths and serious weaknesses.

On the one hand, a postmodern viewpoint recognizes that power is about not only physical wealth, but differentials in access to power and knowledge (Foucault, 1988). A major supplier of capital to institutional investors—middle-class savers—appears to have few rights vis-à-vis fund managers as to how it is spent. Young and Scott (2004) argue that studies that have focused on the agency problem often ignore the issue of holders of private pensions and buyers of investment products, who entrust their savings to institutional investors on the basis of long-term reliability, rather than as high-risk investments to gain short-term value. These authors argue that real investors in business need to take a very long-term view for optimal returns. In contrast, analysts of institutional investors, appraised on short-term returns, have an opposite agenda (Young and Scott, 2004), which forces firm managers to be financially orientated. It is also suggested that a focus on mergers, takeovers, divestments, financial planning distracts attention from sustainable operations (Young and Scott, 2004). This situation reflects, in the end, imbalances in power and knowledge.

A limitation of postmodern approaches is that they tend to assume that something is somehow different or new about the postmodern era. Yet, as Kelly (1998: 118) notes, since its inception, capitalism has been characterized by periods where owners are relatively strong, and other periods where they are forced into greater compromises with competing social interests: this represents both a cause and effect of broader changes in the macroeconomic cycle. Hence, a *third critique of the more postmodern-inspired strands of the literature (and a number of earlier accounts in the political economy tradition) on financialization is that it assumes that the process is somehow different or special when compared to previous eras*. In the end, the only differences are in the extent to which institutional arrangements can help secure growth and stability. Whilst some writers (e.g. Erturk et al., 2004) incorporate elements of anti-epochalism in their arguments, a further critique can be delivered on cultural economic strands of the financialization literature: the eclectic deployment of theoretical constructs, with little attempt to ground such deployment in terms of specific theoretical traditions (or to fully explore the implications of their usage), even if the aim is explicitly synthetic. This may make for an approach that is quintessentially postmodern: plastic, malleable, and open to reinterpretation as befits either the writer or reader at a particular time and place.

Financialization—Political Economy Perspectives

Within the broad political economy tradition, Foster (2007) argues that financialization represented a response to extended crisis, which, whilst containing a strongly speculative element, was one of the few functional responses open. Financialization constituted a fundamental shift from the preceding "golden age," and represented "an ongoing process transcending particular financial bubbles" (Foster, 2007). In contrast, Arrighi (2005: 85) argues that financialization is nothing new, but rather a recurrent strategy that has been employed in response to the over-accumulation of capital at different times in history, most notably in the 1920s, and at the present day. In other words, the domination of financially based areas of economic activity periodically reemerges in response to crises that, in turn, after a period of expansion, face crises of their own, and the redefinition of economic relations.

Dumenil and Levy (2004: 132) note that two distinct levels of capital ownership have emerged: those who own large amounts of property and have close relations with "their" financial institutions, and smaller savers, whose role is "passive and subordinate." What distinguishes their account from postmodern accounts is that the basis of this divide is viewed in terms not of confusion, rhetoric, and imbalances between power and knowledge, but of real differences in the material resources available (Piketty and Saez, 2003; Dumenil and Levy, 2004). As Piketty and Saez (2003: 35–6) note, those in the former category, at the top of the income distribution, are the "working rich," senior managers within financial institutions, and associated firms. Hence, in the tradition of Hobson and Lenin, they see financialization as reflecting the rise of a *rentier* class (Krippner, 2005: 181).

Unlike, Piketty and Saez (2003), and Dumenil and Levy (2004), Erturk et al. (2006), do not see financialization as a process whereby some active owners of capital "skim off" value at the expense of "passive ones." Rather, financialization is, in part, about a divide between smaller holders of capital and larger ones. Proponents cite a succession of speculative bubbles and the deterioration in wages and conditions of service of those in the lowest job bands in the United States and the United Kingdom in support of this argument (Wright and Dwyer, 2006). However, this viewpoint also has shortfalls.

Worsening economic conditions have focused attention on the potentially dysfunctional dimensions of the present order. Harvey (2004: 145) argues that contemporary capitalism is about accumulation of wealth not just by production, but also by dispossession, by the reallocation of resources to elites by political power and influence. This would initially be through the bilking of middle-class savers, but more ambitiously by the reallocation of resources on a global basis. He argues that, in response to crises, financialization's need for further infusion of resources has led to a "spatial fix," with imperialist policies by the United States facilitating "accumulation by dispossession" (Harvey, 2004; cf. Arrighi, 2005). In other words, financialization's failings have encouraged a turn to coercive means, to war (Harvey, 2004; Arrighi, 2005: 85). Arrighi (2005) argues that imperial adventures by the US have proven very costly and open ended. More importantly, these adventures have primarily benefited a small pool of insider corporations, many of which are relatively small and which have little to do with the financial services industry (private military companies such as Blackwater, logistics providers, etc.) (Mann, 2003). Hence, the links between specific patterns of investor behavior, speculation in financial markets, and military adventures are tenuous.

FINANCIALIZATION AS AN INCOMPLETE EXPERIMENT

A fourth critique of the financialization literature is that it is overly functionalist: it assumes that institutions and firms operate together on a coherent basis, to secure growth, and/or to bilk workers and middle-class savers, and/or to further concentrate power and knowledge in the interest of insiders. Even if the system is diverse and ever changing, the financialization literature assumes that it *works* for groupings of insiders. No matter how diverse and changing these groupings are, the outcomes are similar (Froud et al., 2007). Finally, it should be noted that, in the case of US, the financial assets of households have not—despite periodic fluctuations—increased since the 1970s (Dumenil and Levy, 2004: 121–3): middle-class savings do not constitute an expanding pool of capital to be looted. Yet, writers within the mainstream financialization tradition suggest it is a coherent phenomenon, undergoing successive developmental phases or mutations (cf. Erturk et al., 2004: 688).

In contrast, the recent literature on complementarity has argued that institutions often work together in a manner that copes with systemic failings and weaknesses, as well as building on strengths: the results may be a seemingly more unstable system with many obvious contradictions, but one that is well equipped to further modify itself in the light of events, and to withstand crises even of an allegedly terminal nature.

The recent literature on financialization has taken on board the work of writers such as Deeg and Crouch on the mixed (both building on systemic strengths and weaknesses) nature of complementarity, of the contingency and recombativity of institutional arrangements, and the incomplete nature of any new set of arrangements (Froud et al., 2007: 342). This represents a fundamental departure from earlier epochal accounts (Martin, 2002; Froud et al., 2007: 342). Froud et al. (2007: 342) argue that the role of banks as financial intermediaries has changed, with new actors such as private equity assuming greater prominence. However, whilst acknowledging the world is a more complex place, Froud et al. (2007: 345) cling to the assumption of "simple outcomes": however, mixed and incoherent, the outcome of financialization has been to direct resources to a few, with detrimental effects for many.

Boyer (2006) argues that conflicts of interests may lie at the heart of systemic fluidity and change. More powerful actors may seek to innovate to secure their position, whilst new actors may emerge, forcing further changes (Boyer, 2006). Practices may cross sectors, as firms may adopt new innovations in seeking to maintain their current position (for example, organizations downsizing to discourage hostile takeovers). The actual process of change may involve hybridization, innovation, or an alteration of existing hierarchies. Any existing set of institutional relations is always transitory, opening up the possibilities for future contestations and change: the development of national economies is a non-linear process, characterized by both incrementalism and rupture (Boyer, 2006). Hence, a contemporary regulationist approach would query the coherence and sustainability of a finance-driven growth regime that continuously mutates in response to crises. If, as has been charged, the neoliberal age is one of persistent and recurrent speculative bubbles and "crises" (Brenner, 2002), most recently in credit markets, another distinguishing feature has been its remarkable ability to weather them, reflecting the space open to experimentation and innovation, and the relative strength of a hybrid model.

In sum, we are suggesting that the existing literature on financialization suggests a coherence and uniformity of purpose. It is likely that one encounters more than one set of investor preferences, more than one set of expectations, and more than one set of outcomes, contingent on sector and locale, the nature of the investment, variations in markets and technologies, and the relative countervailing power of different stakeholders: financial services are a very diverse sector, with even areas such as private equity incorporating many different areas of activity. This, of course, does not assume that issues emerging in one sector may not spill over to another, or that other sectors may undergo further changes, to compensate for a wider institutional environment that is not fully conducive to local needs. Again, some local systems may be more separable from the wider context than others, allowing more room for experimentation and innovation (Boyer, 2006).

Conclusion

An obvious rejoinder to this critique would be that it fails to take account of the diversity of debates about corporate governance and financialization (any review is necessarily incomplete), and the fact that many of the points in the literature are subsequently qualified. We recognize that the literature in this area is both diverse and still evolving. It may be seen as a twisting and turning phenomenon, combining spin with economic trends (Erturk et al., 2004: 688) or as a process whereby accumulation mainly takes place via financial channels (Krippner, 2005: 199). However, it should be noted that a distinguishing feature of the broad literature on financialization has been the making of very bold (if sometimes contradictory) claims regarding the operation of contemporary capitalism. Central to the financialization literature is an attempt to develop a trans-sectoral understanding of the firm, based on structural changes in the economy and financial markets (Krippner, 2005: 201).

In engaging critically with what has been written in the area, it is inevitable that specific claims and arguments made at specific times are critically interrogated. We would argue that it is helpful neither for future debates, nor, indeed, for the credibility of the body of literature that deploys the concept and underlying assumptions of financialization, for its proponents to retreat into a kind of postmodernism where all claims made and concepts advanced are plastic and open to redefinition in response to critiques and awkward social facts. Moreover, it is worth re-noting that the theoretical diversity of the literature on financialization is not just a reflection of the interest of many different scholars from different backgrounds in the rise of financial services. Rather, it reflects an apparent tendency in sections of this literature to employ and discard the rhetoric and constructs of a range of different theoretical traditions to approach issues and to justify arguments as and when they arise, without a systematic attempt to develop a rigorous synthesis or an alternative theoretical paradigm.

A further caveat is required. We would share the view of Kelly (1998) that the post-1970 period has seen a general strengthening of employer and owner interests at the expense of other stakeholders. The financialization literature correctly points to the key importance of this development. However, there is nothing particularly new or postmodern about the latter, which, in fact, is a cyclical (and spatially variable) phenomenon (Kelly, 1998).

We would also take issue with the view that financial-services-centered growth can be likened to the Fordist growth regime that characterized the "golden age" or a pathological and inevitably doomed mutation. Whilst the 2008 banking crisis has highlighted many of the regulatory shortcomings of financial markets (Blackburn, 2008), it has also underscored the intricacy of the financial services sector. In the end, the greatest weakness of the literature on financialization is the tendency of most accounts to draw very general conclusions from very limited empirical bases: general statistics, secondary accounts, newspaper reports, popular websites, etc., and/or a hodge-podge of theory (cf. Williams, 2000; Froud et al., 2004; Langley, 2004; Froud and Williams, 2007; Blackburn, 2008). Where primary empirical evidence is indeed marshaled, it appears limited and partial, with a great deal of vagueness surrounding the specific combination of research methods and therefore the underlying rationale (Folkman et al., 2007: 567). We do find it alarming that a large number of insiders in the financial services sector appear to have been unable to grasp the implications of using some of the very complicated financial instruments that have emerged over the past decade: however, we remain equally convinced that writers in the financialization tradition need to do a lot more to engage with the technical side of finance, and/or amass more detailed primary evidence as to the specific outcomes at firm level (even if purely descriptive). It is relatively easy to critique superficially a diverse sector that has yielded mixed performance outcomes: it is another thing to actually *understand* in detail what is really going on, and to systematically define and distinguish better practices from worse, what has worked from what has not, what is demonstrably sustainable (the 2008 crisis notwithstanding) from what is not. Whilst the inability to marshal systematic evidence may, in part, be the product of the apparent secretiveness of areas of the financial services industry, when combined with the previously mentioned use of theory that is too often ad hoc and eclectic, it makes for arguments that are less than convincing.

We would disagree with Froud et al. (2007) that financialization is about simple outcomes. Socio-economic change is a process of continual evolution (with uncertainty regarding ultimate direction), and one that embodies continuities going back to preceding eras (Streeck, 2005: 580). Institutions are not likely to be perfectly aligned with or follow what is done at firm level (cf. Chandler, 1977). At the same time, this diversity may make for different strengths and weaknesses from those encountered in Chandlerian managerial capitalism. Hence, much of the literature on financialization seems to be at some variance with the evidence.

References

ADLER, P., FORBES, L., and WILLMOTT, H. (2008). "Critical Management Studies: Premises, Practices and Prospects," Draft review for the Annals of the Academy of Management, Cardiff University.

AGLIETTA, M., and RIBERIOUX, A. (2005). *Corporate Governance Adrift: A Critique of Shareholder Value*. Cheltenham: Edward Elgar.

ARRIGHI, G. (2005). "Hegemony Unravelling," *New Left Review*, 33: 83–116.

BAUDRILLARD, J. (1990). *Revenge of the Crystal*. London: Pluto.

BLACKBURN, R. (2006). "Finance and the Fourth Dimension," *New Left Review*, 39: 39–70.

—— (2008). "Financialization and the Sub-Prime Crisis," *New Left Review*, 50: 63–106.

BOYER, R. (2000). "Is a Financialization Led Growth Regime a Viable Alternative to Fordism", *Economy and Society*, 29(1): 111–45.

—— (2006). "How do Institutions Cohere and Change," in G. Wood and P. James (eds.), *Institutions, Production and Working Life*. Oxford: Oxford University Press.

BRENNER, R. (2002). *The Boom and the Bubble*. London: Verso.

CHANDLER, A. D. (1977). *The Visible Hand: Managerial Revolution in American Business*. Cambridge, MA: Belknap Press.

DJANKOV, S., GLAESER, E., LA PORTA, R., LOPEZ-DE-SILANES, F., and SHLEIFER, A. (2003). "The New Comparative Economics," *Journal of Comparative Economics*, 31: 595–619.

DORE, R. (2000). *Stock Market Capitalism: Welfare Capitalism*. Cambridge: Cambridge University Press.

DUMENIL, G., and LEVY, D. (2004). "Neoliberal Income Trends," *New Left Review*, 30: 105–33.

EPSTEIN, G. (2006a). "Introduction: Financialization and the World Economy," in G. Epstein (ed.), *Financialization and the World Economy*. Cheltenham: Edward Elgar.

—— (2006b). *Financialization and World Economy*. Cheltenham: Edward Elgar.

ERTURK, I., FROUD, J., JOHAL, S., and WILLIAMS, C. (2004). "Corporate Governance and Disappointment," *Review of International Political Economy*, 11(4): 677–713.

—— —— —— LEAVER, A., and WILLIAMS, K. (2006). "Against Agency: A Positional Critique," *Economy and Society*, 36(1): 51–77.

—— —— —— —— and WILLIAMS, K. (eds.) (2008). *Financialization at Work: Key Texts and Commentary*. London: Routledge.

FOLKMAN, P., FROUD, J., JOHAL, S., and WILLIAMS, K. (2007). "Working for Themselves: Financial Intermediaries and Present Day Capitalism," *Business History*, 49(4): 552–72.

FOSTER, J. (2007). "The Financialization of Capitalism," *Monthly Review*, 58: 11.

FOUCAULT, M. (1988). "On Power," in L. Kritzman (ed.), *Foucault: Politics, Philosophy, Culture*. New York: Routledge.

FROUD, J., and WILLIAMS, K. (2007). "Private Equity and the Culture of Value Extraction," *New Political Economy*, 12(3): 405–20.

—— HASLAM, C., JOHAL, S., and WILLIAMS, K. (2000). "Shareholder Value and Financialization," *Economy and Society*, 29(1): 80–110.

—— JOHAL, S., PAPAZIAN, V., and WILLIAMS, K. (2004). "The Temptation of Houston: A Case Study of Financialization," *Critical Perspectives on Accounting*, 15: 885–909.

—— —— LEAVER, A., and WILLIAMS, K. (2006a). "Introduction," in J. Froud, S. Johal, A. Leaver, and K. Williams (eds.), *Financialization and Strategy: Narrative and Numbers*. London: Routledge.

—— —— —— —— (eds.) (2006b). *Financialization and Strategy: Narrative and Numbers*. London: Routledge.

—— —— —— —— (2007). Memorandum submitted to Treasury Select Committee Inquiry into Private Equity. Centre for Research on Socio-Cultural Change, University of Manchester.

GRAHL, J., and TEAGUE, P. (2000). "The Regulation School, the Employment Relationship and Financialization," *Economy and Society*, 29(1): 160–78.

GREENFIELD, P., and WILLIAMS, C. (2004). "Financialization, Finance Rationality, and the Role of the Media in Australia," *Media, Culture and Society*, 29(3): 415–33.

HARVEY, D. (2004). *The New Imperialism*. Oxford: Oxford University Press.

HIRST, P., and ZEITLIN, J. (2001). "Flexible Specialization and Post Fordism," in B. Jessop (ed.), *Regulation Theory and the Crisis of Capitalism—Volume 4: Country Studies*. Cheltenham, UK: Edward Elgar.

HUDSON, R. (2006). "The Production of Institutional Complementarity," in G. Wood and P. James (eds.), *Institutions, Production and Working Life*. Oxford: Oxford University Press.

JESSOP, B. (2001). "Series Preface," in B. Jessop (ed.), *Regulation Theory and the Crisis of Capitalism—Volume 4: Country Studies*. Cheltenham, UK: Edward Elgar.

KELLY, J. (1998). *Mobilization, Collectivism and Long Waves*. London: Routledge.

KRIPPNER, G. (2005). "The Financialization of the American Economy," *Socio-Economic Review*, 3(2): 173–208.

LANGLEY, P. (2004). "In the Eye of the Perfect Storm: The Final Salary Pensions Crises and the Financialization of Anglo-American Capitalism," *New Political Economy*, 9(4): 539–58.

LAZONICK, W., and O'SULLIVAN, M. (2000). "Maximizing Shareholder Value: A New Ideology for Corporate Governance," *Economy and Society*, 29(1): 13–35.

LEAVER, A. (2007). "Financialization and Capitalism's Resourceful Remaking," *Soundings*, 22. Available at <http://www.lwbooks.co.uk/journals/soundings/debates/left_futures12.html>.

MACKENZIE, D. (2000). "Fear in the Markets," *London Review of Books*, April. Available at <http://www.lrb.co.uk/v22/n08/mack01_.html>.

MANN, M. (2003). *Incoherent Empire*. London: Verso.

MARCHINGTON, M., GRIMSHAW, D., RUBERY, J., and WILLMOTT, H. (eds.) (2005). *Fragmenting Work*. Oxford: Oxford University Press.

MARTIN, R. (2002). *The Financialization of Daily Life*. Philadelphia: Philadelphia University Press.

MELLAHI, K., and WOOD, G. (2002). "Desperately Seeking Stability: The Remaking of the Saudi Arabian Labour Market," *Competition and Change*, 6(4): 345–62.

PALLEY, T. (2008). "Financialization: What it is and Why it Really Matters," Levy Economics Institute Working Paper No. 525. Available at <http://papers.ssrn.com/sol3/papers.cfm?abstract_id=1077923>.

PIKETTY, T., and SAEZ, E. (2003). "Income Inequality in the United States: 1913–1998," *Quarterly Journal of Economics*, 118(1): 1–39.

STOCKHAMMER, E. (2004). "Financialisation and the Slowdown in Accumulation," *Cambridge Journal of Economics*, 28: 719–41.

STREECK, R. (2005). "Rejoinder: On Terminology, Functionalism, (Historical) Institutionalism and Liberalization," *Socio-Economic Review*, 3(3): 577–87.

THELEN, K. (2001). "Varieties of Labor Policies in Developed Democracies," in P. A. Hall and D. Soskice (eds.), *Varieties of Capitalism*. Oxford: Oxford University Press, 71–104.

TICKELL, A. (2001). "Prosperity and Equality: Observations on Bluestone and Harris," *Antipode*, 33(1): 101–20.

WALSH, J., and DEERY, S. (1999). "Understanding the Peripheral Workforce: Evidence from the Service Sector," *Human Resource Management Journal*, 9(2): 50–63.

WILLIAMS, K. (2000). "From Shareholder Value to Present Day Capitalism," *Economy and Society*, 29(1): 1–12.

WOOD, G., and FRYNAS, G. (2006). "The Institutional Basis of Economic Failure: Anatomy of the Segmented Business System," *Socio-Economic Review*, 4(2): 239–77.

WRIGHT, E. O., and DWYER, R. (2006). "The Patterns of Job Expansion in the USA," in G. Wood and P. James (eds.), *Institutions, Production and Working Life*. Oxford: Oxford University Press.

YOUNG, D., and SCOTT, P. (2004). *Having their Cake...* London: Kogan Page.

CHAPTER 32

CORPORATE GOVERNANCE AND CORPORATE SOCIAL RESPONSIBILITY

STEPHEN J. BRAMMER AND STEPHEN PAVELIN

Introduction

CORPORATE governance (henceforth, CG) and corporate social responsibility (henceforth, CSR) share common roots. Corporate governance scholarship has noted that significant legal, organizational, and technological innovations in the late 19th and early 20th centuries led to the emergence of larger and more widely owned companies in which the traditional influence of owners was eroded (Berle and Means, 1932; Morck and Steier, 2005; Hilt, 2008). These trends necessitated the creation of a system whereby owners were able to exert greater control over managers (Jensen and Meckling, 1976; Shleifer and Vishny, 1997). At the same time, the greater scale and propensity for risk taking associated with the emerging corporate form, and the shift in residual responsibility implied by limited liability, heightened the interdependence between commercial activities and social well-being (Avi-Yonah, 2005; Carroll, 2007; Ireland, 2010). While most extant corporate governance research has been strongly shareholder-centric in orientation, contemporary debates in corporate governance explicitly address the need to balance the needs of multiple stakeholders systematically within an overarching system of governance. For example, the Organisation for Economic Co-operation and Development's (OECD's) basic principles of corporate governance encompass the needs both to protect shareholder rights and interests and to "skilfully consider and balance the interests of all stakeholders including employees, customers, partners, and the local community" (Jamali et al., 2008: 445).

Concern regarding the failure of large companies to adequately address their social responsibilities lies at the heart of the recent upsurge in interest in corporate governance within academia, business practice, public policy, and wider society. Accounting scandals, egregiously high executive pay, and persistently low demographic diversity among corporate boards, all raise questions regarding how systems, structures, and processes of governance relate to social outcomes. At a macroeconomic level, some commentators have suggested that corporate governance failure contributed to the recent global financial crisis and subsequent recession. For example, the OECD concluded that the "financial crisis can be to an important extent attributed to failures and weaknesses in corporate governance arrangements" (Kirkpatrick, 2008: 2).

These, and other, perceived failings of corporate governance and their consequent social fallout have stimulated additional regulation of corporate governance. An objective of this legislation is to provide greater transparency and accountability in the governance landscape. Most notably, the introduction of the Sarbanes-Oxley Act (2002) in the United States, and the related developments in stock exchange listing rules, brought within a mandatory framework many aspects of corporate governance that had previously been the subject of only voluntary recommendations (Gillan, 2006; Coates, 2007). Alongside these developments in (both formal and soft) law, voluntary codes of good corporate governance have proliferated throughout the world (Aguilera and Cuervo-Cazurra, 2009) and provide increasingly specific guidance regarding a range of structures and processes that is expected to facilitate improved board function and practice in ways that reduce the likelihood of adverse events.

In light of these observations, it is surprising that greater attention has not yet been paid to the examination of the relationships between corporate governance and corporate social responsibility, and that these fields of study have not been better integrated to provide for a more complete picture of their joint contribution to our understanding of the place of business in society. A notable exception is Buchholtz et al.'s (2008) review of corporate governance and corporate social responsibility that appears in the *Oxford Handbook of Corporate Social Responsibility*. In addition to reviewing developments in the legislative arena, Buchholtz et al. (2008) emphasize four central issues at the heart of debates on the relationship between CSR and CG: defining the purpose of the contemporary firm (Does the firm exist only for shareholders?), evaluating the nature of the professional (senior) manager (Are managers really opportunistic and self-serving?), questioning the relevance of a range of features of boards of directors for CSR (Does board composition and structure matter for CSR?), and evaluating the processes whereby individuals obtain board positions (Are selection and appointment processes sufficiently open and how effectively can the voice of shareholders be heard?). These are important foundational questions and echoes of them can be heard in some of our analysis. At the same time, other questions, particularly in relation to the state of empirical evidence regarding CSR and CG, deserve greater attention. Hence, reflecting the rapid pace of change in the governance landscape, in this chapter we more systematically explore the state of extant knowledge regarding the relationship between corporate governance and corporate social responsibility. We pay particular attention to developments in the literature since the beginning of 2007—a period not covered by Buchholtz et al. (2008)—and attempt to provide a more detailed and complete analysis of the empirical evidence relating to the link between CSR and CG.

The remainder of the chapter is organized as follows: First, we examine the definitional landscape and examine the overlaps, differences, and prospects for convergence between CSR and CG. Next, we turn our attention to examining research that examines links between features of firms' boards of directors and CSR before reviewing literature investigating the relationship between aspects of company ownership and CSR. A final section concludes.

CG AND CSR: CONCEPTS, CONTENT, AND CONTEXT

In this section, we provide an initial exploration of the relationship between corporate governance and corporate social responsibility through an analysis of definitions and conceptualizations of both concepts. In so doing, we provide a backdrop to the subsequent, more detailed examination of empirical evidence regarding the relationships between the two fields.

CG and CSR: Where are the Shared Interests?

Corporate governance and corporate social responsibility are similar, in terms of business practice and as lines of scholarly inquiry. First, both CG and CSR are pragmatic fields of study that sprang to prominence in light of the need to address perceptions that large corporations, and those who manage them, are not sufficiently accountable to particular stakeholder groups—owners in the case of CG, and the wider society in the case of CSR. Consistent with this, the precise concerns of each field vary somewhat over time and between countries as the specific problems created by any such lack of accountability become manifest. For example, while CG in the US and UK has tended to address the problems associated with exerting control over management in an environment characterized by highly dispersed shareholdings, CG in other regions, notably Germany and Japan, has tended to emphasize the importance of protecting minority shareholder rights in a context characterized by large, and potentially dominant, family shareholdings. Similarly, the most prominent features of CSR have changed over time and across countries, reflecting cultural change and the salience of particular issues and challenges.

Second, both CG and CSR are multi-level phenomena that encompass themes and issues in relation to individual actors, teams and groups, organizations, national and supra-national institutions and wider socio-economic systems. In the case of CSR, Aguilera et al. (2007) highlight that CSR activity within firms, and the corresponding positive overall social change, stems from pressure from "multiple actors (e.g., employees, consumers, management, institutional investors, governments, nongovernmental organizations [NGOs], and supranational governmental entities) that push organizations to act in a socially responsible or irresponsible manner" (Aguilera et al., 2007: 837). Moreover, Aguilera et al. show that these pressures exerted upon firms by actors at different levels, along with their associated motivations and interdependencies, shape the overall propensity for social change to occur. Similarly, corporate governance has long been understood to be a multi-level phenomenon encompassing actors, structures, processes, and practices internal to organizations (such as executive management, boards of directors, roles and responsibilities), relating to relationships between organizations and stakeholders (patterns of firm ownership, involvement of broader stakeholders through works councils), and features of the wider economic and regulatory climate within which companies operate (laws, codes of conduct, nature of markets for corporate control) (Kirkbride and Letza, 2003). Moreover, research has shown that there are strong interdependencies between these levels of corporate governance such that a number of *models* of corporate governance have emerged across the world, each of which is characterized by a coherent and complementary set of structures, rules, and responsibilities that seek to promote effective business performance in light of local contextual features (Aguilera and Jackson, 2003). These alternative models of corporate governance "allocate power within the firm differently. The most widely accepted, stylized dichotomy of power allocation is between the so-called shareholder-oriented models, characterized by seeking to maximize shareholder value (e.g. USA) versus stakeholder-oriented models, characterized by fulfilling the interests of the diverse stakeholders in the firm (e.g. Continental Europe and Asia)" (Aguilera, 2005: 41).

In both fields, important recent developments have recognized that CG and CSR are embedded within broader economic and social institutions. This has led to the development of a body of research that sees variation in CG and CSR practices as shaped by significant differences in underlying institutions. Research on comparative capitalism has convincingly argued that nation states exhibit varied configurations of mutually reinforcing formal and informal institutions which shape patterns of social and economic activity (Whitley, 1999; Hall and Soskice, 2001; Jackson and Deeg, 2008). These configurations of institutions are often deeply historically embedded and encompass a wide range of arenas, including labor markets (patterns of unionization, training, education), financial systems (prevalence of banks, importance of stock markets, laws on investor protection), and legal systems. Distinct institutional contexts also shape the pressures firms face to engage in CSR (Logsdon and Wood, 2005; Matten and Crane, 2005). Campbell (2007) argues that companies are more likely to behave in socially responsible ways when they belong to trade or employee associations and when they are engaged in institutionalized dialogue with unions, employees, and other stakeholders.

Matten and Moon (2008) provide another perspective on national differences in CSR. Their framework stresses the implicit-explicit dimension of CSR practices. Explicit CSR is used to describe CSR manifest in the form of corporate activities, mainly voluntary policies and strategies, motivated by perceived expectations of different stakeholders of the company. Implicit CSR consists of values, norms, and rules, usually codified and mandatory, emerging from the society itself and its expectations of the role of the corporation. They see the most prominent forms of engagement with CSR as being critically shaped by the nature of the wider business systems within which companies operate. In national business systems that favor the explicit element of CSR, it is relatively common that corporations report their CSR initiatives extensively and in the language of CSR. On the other hand, corporations within business systems with strong implicit elements of CSR—often, the requirements for which are codified in laws and regulations—less commonly report such CSR-related activities—perhaps because compliance is not regarded as noteworthy.

A final parallel between research on CSR and CG reflects the fact that a significant amount of empirical research investigates which features of each are systematically related to improved corporate financial performance (henceforth, CFP), with very mixed results. In the case of CSR, a number of recent reviews of the literature and meta-analyses (Margolis and Walsh, 2003; Orlitzky et al., 2003; Margolis et al., 2007; Beurden and Gossling, 2008) suggest that CSR is associated with moderate improvements in CFP. At the same time, studies have continued to identify contingencies within the CSR-CFP relationship and to highlight a wide range of methodological caveats relating to the operationalization and measurement of both CSR and CFP, and the direction of causality present in any significant relationship between the two. In a similar vein, a substantial body of literature examines the association between elements of corporate governance and CFP (Shleifer and Vishny, 1997; Bebchuk et al., 2009; Love, 2011). Numerous studies demonstrate that better corporate governance is associated with improved CFP, although findings are mixed and most recent literature demonstrates that such effects are driven by the importance of a small number of specific provisions, generally reflecting the absence of managerial entrenchment (Bebchuk et al., 2009). At the same time, a growing literature highlights methodological flaws in prior research, including sampling issues, the importance of outliers, and omitted variables (Core et al., 2006).

These characterizations of the fields help to identify two key, related bases for shared interests between CG and CSR, which relate to: a common theoretical focus upon the nature and appropriate breadth of responsibilities pertaining to managerial decision-making; and the empirical investigation of relationships between governance characteristics and a firm's social performance. The former alludes to discussions of concepts of appropriate governance, which assess imperatives for decision-making to adequately represent, and reflect the interests, demands, and expectations of, one or more relevant constituencies that might otherwise be overlooked by more narrowly drawn, private interests. Within CG, the most commonly followed line of enquiry focuses upon the principal–agent problem in the shareholder–manager relationship, wherein owners seek to avoid managers furthering their own ends to the detriment of corporate performance and, therefore, return on share ownership. In that case, the narrowly drawn private interest favors the maximization of managerial utility (which may include excessive spending on managerial perks or a dash for revenue growth at the expense of profits), and shareholders are the key, potentially overlooked constituency.

While the imperative that governance reflects shareholder interests is a central issue for CG research, the purview of the field extends to the accommodation of a broader range of interests and constituencies, such as customer groups, employees, local communities, and the natural environment. These broader, more inclusive discussions of CG question whether it is appropriate for governance over corporate decision-making to build in mechanisms that promote a regard for the demands and welfare of interested parties that lie outside the potentially closed world of the shareholder–manager relationship. Such discussions can lead toward concepts of CG that equate good governance with infrastructures that facilitate effective stakeholder management that systematically identifies the demands and expectations of stakeholders and promotes their reflection in corporate strategy.

Such themes within CG research are similarly motivated in discussions within CSR research of the nature and extent of corporations' responsibilities, as defined with reference to a firm's stakeholder environment—for example, to protect stakeholders from harm arising from the firm's operations, and/or to address social and environmental issues to reflect stakeholders' concerns. Such conceptions of CSR are grounded in the reflection of interests that lie beyond the narrowly drawn private interests of corporate performance to potentially include not only the promotion of beneficial impacts from firms' business activities, but also the furtherance of social and/or environmental objectives that—perhaps due to significant economic power or distinctive technological capabilities—firms may be distinctively well-placed to address.

In addition to the similarities between these two lines of enquiry, it is worth noting the potential for the two to work synergistically together. While CSR research has extensively considered conceptions of corporate responsibility and comprehensively described and evaluated the theoretical underpinnings of various approaches, it has offered little insight into how CSR can be facilitated in practice, through the adoption of specifically appropriate governance structures. In contrast, the related CG stream has less comprehensively discussed the theoretical groundings of a broad conception of corporate responsibilities, but has developed informative lessons for the practical tailoring of governance structures to facilitate managerial decision-making that is more representative of those stakeholder interests that might otherwise be overlooked. Thus, at the interface of these two research streams resides the useful prospect of the matching of relatively detailed, theoretically grounded conceptions of responsible governance, with informative lessons for how such conceptions might be effectively realized through the appropriate tailoring of governance structures.

As noted above, a second key basis for shared interests between CG and CSR is empirical, and arises from the potential for relationships between governance characteristics and a firm's social performance. Thus, the second basis for shared interests follows from the first: the first promises a theoretical underpinning of responsible governance, which identifies how governance characteristics can best ensure that corporate strategy is effectively informed by stakeholder interests beyond the shareholder–manager relationship; and the second empirically investigates the manner in which CSR actions and impacts are affected by the governance structures that firms employ. Therefore, these two points of interface between CG and CSR work usefully in tandem—just as theory and evidence should—where theory provides hypothesized relationships between CG and CSR, which are tested, and results feed back into further theory development and refinement, and so on in a virtuous loop.

CG and CSR: Prospects for Convergence?

A recurrent theme in studies of CSR and CG is the prospect for a closer, possibly convergent, relationship between the two concepts (Gill, 2008; Jamali et al., 2008; Kang and Moon, 2012). As Gill (2008: 463) puts it, "where there were once two separate sets of mechanisms, one dealing with 'hard core' corporate decision-making and the other with 'soft,' people-friendly business strategies, scholars now point to a more hybridized, synthesized body of laws and norms regulating corporate practices" (Gill, 2008). There are a number of trends that underpin the closer relationship between CG and CSR articulated in recent research. First, active regulation and legislation in relation to a range of issues have introduced an increasingly mandatory imperative in relation to aspects of CSR. For example, in the United States "the Securities and Exchange Commission (SEC), the Occupational Safety and Health Administration (OSHA), and the Environmental Protection Agency (EPA) have played an increasingly large role in making CSR more binding [by] granting business licenses and permissions conditioned upon integrity and disclosure performance, [introducing] whistle-blower protections, government-sponsored auditing schemes and tax incentives, and using a company's implementation of a compliance program as a basis for sentencing guidelines used to determine corporate criminal liability" (Gill, 2008: 470).

Second, business is increasingly playing a central role in more collaborative processes through which both formal regulation and legislation and informal standards and norms are emerging in relation to a range of social and environmental issues (Fransen, 2012; Conzelmann, 2012). For example, Fransen (2012) examines the processes of competition between business-led and multi-stakeholder initiatives within the case of initiatives in European retailing, exposing the political strategies and tactics employed by business-led initiatives in their attempts to build and maintain legitimacy in the eyes of societal stakeholders. Hence, the boundaries between formal hierarchical governmental regulation and alternative forms of regulation are often blurred in practice as companies play an important role in shaping the governance of social and environmental issues.

BOARDS OF DIRECTORS AND CSR

Having reflected on the relationships between CSR and CG at a conceptual level, we turn our attention to exploring how aspects of boards of directors relate to elements of CSR. A summary of prominent recent contributions to this literature is provided in Table 32.1. Boards of directors—their membership, structure, and the distribution of decision-making authority therein—have attracted considerable attention within CSR scholarship. Research has shown that boards of directors have become more actively and directly engaged with CSR (Kassinis and Vafeas, 2002; Kakabadse, 2007; Spitzeck, 2009). Such engagement provides for the prospect that the characteristics of boards affect how firms engage with CSR. Indeed, there are a variety of reasons for expecting this to be the case. Agency-theoretic thinking has informed a considerable volume of research that has sought to investigate the extent to which engagement with CSR stems from self-serving behavior on the part of managers seeking to enhance their prestige or to establish or reinforce entrenched positions (Ibrahim and Angelidis, 1995; Dahyaa and McConnell, 2004). Within such a worldview, significant emphasis is placed upon the monitoring role of boards and so on both the balance between inside and outside directors on a firm's board—i.e. board composition—and the desirability of separating the board roles of chair and chief executive.

Alternative theoretical perspectives have highlighted the importance of the members of boards of directors as providers of information, expertise, and resources and have stressed the importance of bringing a diverse range of perspectives onto boards to create the conditions where good decisions are made and where firms have access to the necessary resources to succeed (Fama and Jensen, 1983; Adams and Ferreira, 2007; Masulis and Mobbs, 2009). Still other authors have emphasized the board as a strategic signaling device whereby the membership and structure of boards signal firms' strategic intent to external constituencies (Pfeffer and Salancik, 1978).

Empirical evidence that has sought to disentangle the various mechanisms through which boards influence CSR has provided extremely mixed findings. Regarding research that emphasizes the monitoring role of boards, both positive and negative findings have been found in relation to the link between board composition and engagement with CSR (Wang and Coffey, 1992; Coffey and Wang, 1998; Johnson and Greening, 1999; Kassinis and Vafeas, 2002). To some extent, the diversity in findings seen in prior literature is related to the particular elements of CSR that studies have examined, something that the most recent studies have been keen to clarify by focusing on one aspect of CSR in detail, or disaggregating CSR into a range of elements in order to facilitate a comparative analysis. For example, Post et al. (2011) restrict their attention to environmental performance and find that firms with a higher percentage of independent directors have better environmental performance, particularly in the sense that they have more environmental strengths. Similarly, de Villiers et al. (2011) identify a positive relationship between board independence and environmental performance. Walls et al. (2012) find that board characteristics play a particularly important role in relation to negative aspects of firms' environmental performance, showing that firms have more environmental concerns when their boards are more independent, larger, and less diverse. In contrast, Mallin and Michelon's (2011) analysis encompasses multiple dimensions of CSR in their analysis and show that board independence relates differently to these distinct elements. Specifically, they show that, controlling for a range of other features of firms' boards, the percentage of independent directors is only significantly related to performance in relation to human rights, where they identify a strong positive relationship.

Table 32.1. Recent evidence relating to board characteristics and CSR

Authors	Year published	Measure of board characteristics	Measure of CSR	Key findings
Surroca & Tribo	2008	Sustainable Investment Research International Company (SIRI) PRO database that examines the existence of anti-takeover devices, limitation of shareholders' voting rights, existence of multiple classes of stock with different voting rights, managers' stake and tenure. In addition, dummy variables are constructed to reflect the presence or absence of key board committees—e.g. remuneration, audit, nomination.	Data are drawn from SIRI and are used to create a corporate social performance index defined as the weighted sum of non-shareholders' stakeholder scores (the scores of community, customers, employees, environment, and vendors and contractors).	Firms with more entrenched managers have significantly higher CSP ratings. This effect is strongest in firms with independent control committees, and separation between the CEO and the chairman of the board.
Harjoto & Jo	2011	The study uses numerous measures of firm governance characteristics, mostly drawn from the Investor Responsibility Research Center's (IRRC's) database. These measures include the Gompers' index of corporate governance, and an index of managerial entrenchment.	A binary variable derived from Kinder, Lydenberg, and Domini's (KLD's) Socrates database that classifies a firm as socially responsible if it has engaged in positive CSR activities in a given period.	Firms with a higher proportion of outside independent directors, a higher proportion of institutional investors, and more analysts following them are more likely to be socially responsible.
Mallin & Michelon	2011	Data on board composition are collected from the firms' annual reports and proxy statements. Board composition is measured by the proportion of independent directors, board competence is captured through the proportion of community influentials (politicians, military officers, and members or directors of social/non-profit organizations), board diversity is measured by the proportion of women sitting on the board, and CEO duality by a dummy variable, as is the presence of a director or committee that oversees social responsibility issues.	Data on corporate social responsibility are collected from the KLD's Socrates database. Separate measures are extracted for measures for performance in the following domains: community performance, employee relations performance, environmental performance, human rights performance, and product quality performance ratings. In addition, an overall aggregate measure is calculated as an average of the constituent ratings.	Better social performance is associated with independent boards, boards with a higher percentage of community influentials, more diverse boards, separation of the roles of CEO and chairman, independent directors holding more directorships in other companies.

(continued)

Table 32.1. Continued

Authors	Year published	Measure of board characteristics	Measure of CSR	Key findings
Post, Rahman, & Rubow	2011	Annual reports and Dun & Bradstreet were used to compile the list of directors for sample companies. The insider/outsider status of directors was obtained through the Company Insight Center of Business Week Online. Data were collected regarding directors' gender, age, and education (i.e. degree attained and place of education) using Dun & Bradstreet, Reuters, and Lexus Nexus Academic. Corporate websites were examined for any information the reference materials could not supply.	CSR is measured using an analysis of disclosures as reported in firms' annual reports, corporate environmental reports, corporate websites, and government websites. Additionally, data from the proprietary KLD STATS database, issued by Kinder, Lydenberg, Domini, Inc. (KLD) were used. Three specific metrics were used: (1) KLD strengths, the sum of the KLD ratings in the environmental strengths areas; (2) KLD concerns, the sum of the KLD ratings in the environmental concerns areas; and (3) Total KLD, the sum of environmental strengths from which the sum of environmental concerns were subtracted.	A higher proportion of outside board directors is associated with more favorable ECSR and higher KLD strengths scores. Firms with boards composed of three or more female directors received higher KLD strengths scores. And, boards whose directors average closer to 56 years in age and those with a higher proportion of Western European directors are more likely to implement environmental governance structures or processes.
de Villiers, Naiker, & Staden	2011	Data on boards of directors are obtained from the Corporate Library's Board Analyst database. From this database indicators of numerous board features are extracted, including director independence, CEO-chair duality, directors appointed after CEO, CEO-director ownership, insider-director ownership, and outsider-director ownership, board size, multiple directorships, active CEOs, law experts, and board tenure.	The environment element of the KLD ratings are used. The focus is on the tendency to have environmental strengths, and these are summed to provide an indicator of environmental performance.	Environmental performance is better in firms with higher concentration of independent directors, lower concentration of directors appointed after the CEP, large boards, a larger representation of active CEOs on the boards, more legal experts on the board.

| Wong, Ormiston, & Tetlock | 2012 | Data on the key board characteristics—integrative complexity and decentralization—were obtained via evaluations of qualitative information from the business and industry press that discussed a TMT's management philosophy and/or how decisions are made within the TMT and wider organization. Having read articles, assessors were asked to follow a card-sorting technique that allowed the creation of scales. | CSR data come from Kinder, Lydenberg, Domini, and Company (KLD), and take the form of an aggregated score, for which total concerns on all seven stakeholder service category indicators were subtracted from total strengths on all seven stakeholder service category indicators. | Results indicated that integrative complexity is positively related to KLD strengths, and that decentralization is negatively related to KLD concerns. Additionally, decentralization moderates the relationship between integrative complexity and KLD concerns: firms with low-integrative-complexity TMTs realize higher levels of corporate social performance from greater decentralization of decision-making than do firms with high-integrative-complexity TMTs. |

An alternative approach to resolving the mixed evidence on board composition and CSR involves specifying contingencies in the relationship that help to qualify the equivocal findings. Arora and Dharwadkar (2011) show that the availability of free financial resources, in the form of abundant cash, significantly moderates the relationship between board composition and CSR, such that greater board independence is associated with improved social performance only on the condition that spare financial resources are available.

Empirical research related to evaluating the effects of boards on strategic decisions (through the information, breadth of perspectives, and resources board members possess) has also been highly equivocal. Most prominent among this line of enquiry are studies that examine the importance for engagement with CSR of the balance between male and female directors on boards. A considerable amount of early literature identified a positive relationship between CSR and female representation on boards. For example, Wang and Coffey (1992) found that the proportion of female board members was positively, but statistically insignificantly, associated with firms' charitable contributions, while Williams (2003) found that firms with a higher proportion of women serving on their boards engaged in charitable giving to a greater extent than other firms. More recently, Bear et al. (2010) identified a strongly positive relationship between Kinder, Lydenberg, and Domini (KLD) strength ratings for corporate social responsibility and the number of women on firm's boards.

Recent research on board characteristics and CSR has sought both to better specify the processes by which boards relate to CSR, and to measure more effectively important elements of boards of directors. Hence, for example, investigations of the role of board diversity have sought to incorporate more sophisticated measures of diversity that encompass directors' educational background, professional experience, and wider roles held in society. Following Hillman et al. (2000), Bear et al. (2010) construct a diversity index that captures the degree to which a board is balanced across four categories of directors—insiders (current or retired members of management), business experts (executives or officers of other public corporations), support specialists (lawyers, bankers, consultants, accountants, etc.), and community influentials (current and former academics, physicians, government officials, leaders of NGOs and community organizations)—but find it is unrelated to firms' engagement with CSR. In contrast, de Villiers et al. (2011) find a positive relationship between firms' environmental performance and the number of legal experts present on their boards of directors.

In a particularly notable recent contribution, Wong et al. (2011), argue that the degree to which firms decentralize decision-making in relation to CSR and the extent to which top management teams have the "capacity and willingness to tolerate different points of view, and [are able to] generate linkages between points of view, to confront trade-offs, and to appreciate interactive patterns of causation" (Wong et al., 2011: 1208) are likely to play an important role in shaping engagement with CSR. They find strong support for their hypotheses, albeit within a relatively small sample of companies.

Recently, firms have begun to integrate CSR into the formal functions of their boards by allocating dedicated responsibility for CSR to a specific director and instituting board-level CSR committees. The impacts of these on CSR are as yet unclear. However, the limited evidence that is currently available offers some thought-provoking findings. Walls et al. (2012) find that the presence of environmental board committees is positively associated with both environmental strengths and environmental concerns, concluding that "environmental committees seem to have a dual purpose: while they can support firms' environmental strengths by providing expertise and resources via board members, they can also help a firm to mitigate environmental problems such as litigation by placing emphasis on environmental issues at the board level" (Walls et al., 2012: 18).

Company Ownership and CSR

The ownership structure of firms has typically been understood to encapsulate significant information regarding a firm's governance and to have important potential effects on the engagement of companies with CSR (Coffey and Fryxell, 1991; Jamali et al., 2008). Ownership characteristics, like board characteristics, are multi-faceted and thus influence firms' CSR activities through a number of mechanisms. Ownership structure, as reflected in the number and relative size of a firm's shareholders, has typically been interpreted as providing an insight into the existence of agency problems whereby the absence of substantial shareholders permits managers to pursue self-aggrandizing pro-social activities at the expense of shareholders. Alternatively, some authors, for example Anderson et al. (2003), have argued that, where very significant, especially majority, shareholders exist, such owners are typically motivated by a desire to protect the long-run prosperity and survival of the company and to maintaining their own reputation, which is closely associated with that of the firm. Such large shareholders, unable to sell their substantial shareholdings without eroding their value, might thus be motivated to promote CSR because of its capacity to enhance firm reputation and survival. The scale of ownership in a firm also affects the forms of influence that are available to shareholders. Beyond ownership structure per se, a considerable amount of research has argued that the particular identities of owners are likely to play a role in shaping attitudes to CSR. Institutional investors dominate ownership in most large companies and are highly heterogeneous in their investment approach and consequently in their preferences regarding CSR. The preferences of financial institutions are largely driven by the products and services they provide and thus by their needs for performance over particular time horizons and liquidity (Bushee, 1998; Ryan and Schneider, 2002). The attitudes and preferences of other owners of firms' stock (for example, employees, families, private individuals, and governments) regarding CSR is also highly heterogeneous, reflecting their varied goals, scale, and access to information.

Empirical research has addressed a number of themes relating to how the structure and identity of firms' ownership influence the pattern of engagement with CSR. Table 32.2 highlights the key features of some notable recent contributions. Possibly reflecting the ambiguous preferences of shareholders regarding CSR activities and investments,

Table 32.2. Recent evidence relating to firm ownership characteristics and CSR

Authors	Year published	Measure(s) of ownership characteristics	Measure(s) of CSR	Key findings
Mahoney & Roberts	2007	The institutional ownership data was taken from the year-end Standard and Poor's Stock Guides, from which two measures were created: (1) as the number of institutions that held shares in each company and (2) as the percentage of each company's outstanding shares owned by institutions.	Data on CSR were drawn from the Canadian Social Investment Database (CSID). The CSID ratings of Canadian firms are similar to those found in the KLD for US companies and provide across eight dimensions of social performance—community, diversity, employee relations, environment, international, product, business practices, and other. An aggregated "net strengths" measure is included, as are net strengths disaggregated by area.	Firms with better social performance have significantly larger numbers of institutional investors, and the proportion of firms owned by institutions is significantly higher for firms with better social performance in respect of international elements.
Barnea & Rubin	2010	The degree of insiders' ownership is captured by summing the percentage of common stock held by all officers and directors of the company plus beneficial owners who own more than 5 percent of the subject company's stock. Institutional ownership is captured by the percentage of common stock held by all investment institutions (pension funds etc).	Binary indicators based on the Kinder, Lydenberg and Domini ratings. Firms are classified as being socially responsible or socially irresponsible on the basis of their inclusion into the KLD's Broad Market Social Index.	Greater insider ownership is associated significantly with a reduced probability of being classified as socially responsible. In contrast, there is no relationship between institutional ownership and social responsibility. A subsidiary analysis demonstrates no relationship between Gompers' governance index and the likelihood a firm is socially responsible.

Berrone, Cruz, Gomez-Mejia, & Larraza-Kintana	2010	Proxy statements from the Securities and Exchange Commission were used to extract ownership and governance information. Firms were classified as family firms if family members owned or controlled at least 5 percent of the voting stock. Dichotomous variables that reflect whether the CEO is a member of the controlling family, and whether the same individual was both CEO and board chair, were created. The percentage of stock owned by the CEO, and the level of the CEO's stock options as a percentage of outstanding stock, were also included to reflect aspects of CEO ownership.	The study focuses on environmental performance as disclosed in the Toxic Release Inventory (TRI) program of the Environmental Protection Agency (EPA). Environmental performance is captured by aggregating a firm's total toxic releases, each weighted by the Human Toxicity Potential (HTP) factor to account for the differential toxicity of particular releases.	Family-owned companies have better environmental performance than other companies. Non-family firms with higher CEO ownership have poorer environmental performance.
Cox & Gaya-Wicks	2011	Data on corporate ownership are drawn from BARRA, an investment software and research company. Using this data, the proportion of a firm's stock owned by the following institutional investors was calculated: mutual funds, life insurance funds, externally managed pension plans, inhouse-managed public sector pension plans, and inhouse-managed private sector pension plans.	Corporate responsibility is measured using data drawn from Factiva, a Dow Jones & Reuters product and The Ethical Investment Research Service (EIRIS). These sources are used to construct firm performance in four domains: health and safety, equal opportunities, environment, and non-financial news.	The demand for ownership of stock is positively influenced by corporate responsibility for "dedicated"—long-term—investors, but significantly less so for "transient"—short-term investors.
Dam & Scholtens	2012	Data on ownership percentages is extracted from Amadeus, a database that contains accounting information for a large number of European firms. The percentage of ownership of firms in each of six groups—state, self or employee ownership, bank ownership, private/individual ownership, financial company ownership, and firm ownership.	Data on social performance are drawn from the Ethical Investment Research Service (EIRIS). An original set of 20 indicators are reduced to three—performance in the domains of "stakeholders," "ethics," and "environment"—by factor analysis.	There is no relationship between the extent of ownership by banks, financial investors, and other firms, but a significantly negative association between the extent of ownership by the state, self-ownership/employees, and blockholders and CSR.

(continued)

Table 32.2. Continued

Authors	Year published	Measure(s) of ownership characteristics	Measure(s) of CSR	Key findings
Oh, Chang, & Martynov	2011	Ownership data are drawn from the Korea Listed Companies Association's Directory of Corporate Management and KISVALUE, a Korean electronic database similar to COMPUSTAT in the US. Ownership structure was classified into institutional ownership, managerial ownership, and foreign ownership, and institutional ownership was further broken down into four groups of institutional owners: (1) public pension funds; (2) insurance firms; (3) securities firms; and (4) investment and commercial banks.	Firms' CSR is evaluated using data from the Korea Economic Justice Institute (KEJI). Firms are rated in seven major sub-domains, including environment, community, corporate governance, corporate integrity, customer satisfaction, with product quality & safety, employee relations, and long-term orientation.	Higher CSR ratings are associated with firms with higher percentages of ownership by institutions—especially pension funds—with higher percentage ownership by foreign investors, and with lower rates of internal ownership by management.
Walls, Berrone, & Phan	2012	A range of ownership, board, and management variables were drawn from RiskMetrics, ExecuComp, and Thompson/Reuters. These include measures of ownership concentration and institutional ownership, CEO duality, board diversity, board independence, activist pressure from shareholders, and the presence of an environmental committee at board level.	Data on environmental performance was drawn from Kinder, Lydenberg, and Domini's (KLD) dataset. The KLD rates firms on a number of strengths and concerns, and summed values of the items of strengths and concerns are constructed.	Firms with more concentrated ownership have fewer environmental strengths, firms with board-level environment committees had both more strengths and more concerns. Firms with smaller, less independent, and more diverse boards had improved environmental performance.

the evidence pertaining to the degree of ownership concentration is very mixed. Prado-Lorenzo et al. (2009) show that the presence of a dominant shareholder is associated with improved CSR, as reflected in a higher prevalence of reporting on social and environmental impacts using the Global Reporting Initiative standards. In contrast, Walls et al. (2012) find that firms with more concentrated ownership, as reflected in the percentage of shares held by a firm's top five institutional investors, had significantly fewer environmental strengths, concluding that such firms "have less freedom to pursue above and beyond compliance environmental activities, possibly because they may be seen to incur unnecessary costs" (Walls et al., 2012).

Regarding the evidence in respect of the preferences and influence of institutional investors on CSR, a number of recent studies have added substantially to the body of knowledge in this area. Early studies provided conflicting evidence. For example, Graves and Waddock (1994) found no relationship between institutional ownership and corporate social responsibility (CSR), while other researchers (Johnson and Greening, 1999) identified a strong, positive relationship. Subsequently, both Cox et al. (2004) and Neubaum and Zahra (2006) found that long-term institutional investment is positively related to CSR. The most recent evidence remains equivocal regarding the overall relationship between ownership by particular institutional investor types and engagement with CSR. So, for example, Barnea and Rubin (2010) and Dam and Scholtens (2012) both find no overall relationship between institutional ownership and CSR, while Oh et al. (2011) and Cox and Gaya Wicks (2011) both find positive associations between the extent of firm ownership by long-term institutions, especially pension funds, and CSR.

While the overall picture in respect of the role of institutional investors in shaping engagement with CSR remains mixed, recent studies have helped to bring additional nuance to our understanding of when and how owners exhibit strong preferences regarding firms' CSR performance. For example, Dam and Scholtens (2012) explore the relationships between institutional ownership and specific subdimensions of CSR, and show that

> different investor types are related in a different manner to particular dimensions of CSR. We conclude that in many cases ownership does matter for CSR. More specifically, firm ownership by corporations, individuals, and employees generally is to be associated with relatively poor CSR performance of firms. State ownership in particular is associated with poor stakeholder relations of the firm in which it owns shares. Employee ownership relates to below average ethical and environmental performance. Corporate ownership negatively loads on all three measures of CSR: environment, ethics, and stakeholders. (Dam and Scholtens, 2012)

Walls et al. (2012) also adopt the approach of examining distinct elements of a firm's CSR, in their case firm environmental performance, in unpicking the potential role of ownership. They note that

> only shareholder activism and concentration have a direct impact on environmental performance. When environmental performance is poor, firms can expect investor activism to be rife, possibly because poor environmental performance can be detrimental to firms in the form of violations, fines, remediation costs, and exposure to risk. (Walls et al., 2012)

Arora and Dharwadkar (2011) explore the role of meeting performance expectations in shaping the influences of institutional investors on CSR, testing the argument that the discretion that managers have to make investments in CSR (which relates directly to the extent to which performance objectives have been met and the availability of slack resources) drives involvement with CSR. Consistent with this view, they find that the impact of CG on the tendency for firms to invest in "positive" projects is stronger when firms have little slack and when firms have underperformed relative to expectations, while the relationship between governance and investments that reduce negative impacts is stronger when slack resources are abundant and when firms have outperformed expectations.

While financial institutions have attracted considerable attention in relation to the impact of their ownership and activism on engagement with CSR, the recognition that many firms retain substantial blocks of family ownership has prompted several studies to explore the potential influence of family ownership on firms' CSR. Dyer and Whetten (2006) provide the first robust analysis of the relationship between family ownership and engagement with CSR within the context of S&P 500 companies over a ten-year period. Their analysis shows that while family and non-family companies exhibit very similar types of "positive" engagement with CSR, family firms have significantly fewer areas of negative social and environmental impact than their non-family counterparts. Thus, overall, family firms have better social performance than non-family firms. Dyer and Whetten suggest that their findings are "likely due, in part, to the fact that families see their images and reputations as inextricably connected to the firms they own, and therefore will be unwilling to damage those reputations through irresponsible actions on the part of their firms" (2006: 797).

Consistent with work on financial institutions, more recent work has attempted to examine the influence of family ownership on distinct dimensions of CSR. Berrone et al. (2010) explore the influence of family ownership on multiple dimensions of CSR, and find that the impact of family ownership on CSR varies considerably across dimensions of CSR. Specifically, greater family ownership is negatively associated with performance in respect of community-related aspects of CSR, but is positively associated with performance in respect of diversity-, employee-, environment-, and product-related aspects of CSR, with the most substantial effect of family ownership on CSR performance relating to product-related aspects of CSR. They conclude that firms with substantial family ownership "prioritize stakeholder demands in a manner that differs from that of other firms; for family firms, the customers of their products are more important and the local community is less important, compared with other types of firms" (Berrone et al., 2010).

While the majority of the research that examines the relationship between ownership in companies and their pattern of engagement with CSR does not directly observe how owners influence CSR practices, the growing body of research concerned with shareholder activism provides a more direct insight into the preferences and pressures associated with owners that seek to further particular social and environmental goals. Shareholder activism, or "relationship investing," focuses on a range of practices that shareholders in companies can embark upon in an attempt to shape their conduct introducing proposals under Rule 14a-8, the Securities and Exchange Commission's (SEC) proxy proposal rule, embarking upon direct negotiations or dialogue with management and public targeting of a corporation, typically using media campaigns (Logsdon and Van Buren, 2008; Rehbein et al., 2012). Religious investors were at the forefront of early shareholder activism and submitted a wide range of shareholder resolutions on social and environmental issues (Proffitt and Spicer, 2006). More recently more "mainstream" institutional investors, NGOs, and trade unions have become engaged in shareholder activism and numerous shareholder proposals are made each year in relation to a wide range of issues, including climate change, anti-discrimination policies, and social reporting (Proffitt and Spicer, 2006; Gillan and Starks, 2007; Slater, 2007; Sjöström, 2008). Research has demonstrated that activists tend to target larger, more profitable companies with poorer social performance (Rehbein et al., 2004), and the most recent empirical research has shown that the tendency for activists to target firms on social issues is greater in countries with higher levels of income inequality (Judge et al., 2010).

Faced with activist pressure, companies have a range of responses open to them, including petitioning to the SEC for exclusion of proposal, agreeing to the activist's demands prior to the annual meeting, in which case the activist typically withdraws the proposal, electing to engage in dialogue with activists to see whether a negotiated outcome can be reached, and choosing to put the proposal to a vote at the shareholder meeting (Logsdon and Van Buren, 2008; Rehbein et al., 2012). The evidence indicates that votes occur in about half of the cases of shareholder activism, and that proposals are withdrawn in about a third of the cases (Tkac, 2006), providing some support for the idea that activism leads to material change in firms' social and environmental impacts.

More systematic evaluations of the potential impacts of activism on behavior provide more mixed evidence. David et al. (2007), show that subsequent social performance is lower for firms that face shareholder resolutions in prior years than for firms not facing activism, concluding that "activism may merely engender diversion of resources away from CSP into political activities used by managers to resist external pressures and retain discretion" (David et al., 2007: 97). In contrast, Lee and Lounsbury (2011) provide some concrete evidence of the impacts of shareholder proposals on firms' environmental performance. Their evidence shows that firms targeted by activists had significantly improved subsequent pollution management practices. Additionally, this effect was more pronounced among firms that can potentially incur higher disruption costs, among larger firms, and for those in industries that are closer to end-user consumers.

Discussion and Conclusion

In this chapter, we have reviewed research on the interface between corporate governance and corporate social responsibility, emphasizing findings from the most recent empirical studies. Not surprisingly, given the breadth and scope of these two concepts, the research we have discussed is highly heterogeneous in character and encompasses varied phenomena, several distinct levels of analysis, and diverse contexts. Notwithstanding this heterogeneity, it is possible to identify clusters of research that share common concerns. One prominent strand of research has sought to better understand CG, CSR, and the relationship between the two in conceptual terms. This research has noted the parallel rise in popular salience of each concept and the evolving, perhaps converging, emphasis of each field against a backdrop of changing social expectations of business. Perhaps paradoxically, conceptual research on the character, scope, and contextual embeddedness of CG and CSR has only recently led to a new area of research on how features of the governance of specific companies relate to their engagement with social and environmental issues. Empirical research has tended to focus on a relatively narrow range of indicators of corporate governance, for example, board diversity, as proxied by the prevalence of women on boards, the balance between independent and insider directors on boards, and overall levels of institutional shareholdings and on crude measures of engagement with CSR. Hence, empirical research on the relationship between CSR and CG is a triumph of technology and opportunity over the search for real meaning and understanding.

Despite the recent progress that has been made in understanding the relationship between CSR and CG, much remains to be done. An important area of future research concerns the need for a more integrated and coherent conceptual treatment of the relationship between CG and CSR. In our view, the pragmatic orientation of most extant research has contributed to a somewhat confusing literature characterized by widespread interest and substantial activity, but relatively little overarching theoretical development. We believe it is important that the straw-men assumptions (regarding investor and manager preferences, organizational objectives, the nature of CG and CSR, etc.) that have characterized the bulk of the research undertaken to date are questioned and more concretely specified in future research. Some recent research reflects and addresses these concerns, but we still need a more effective integration of theoretical and empirical work on the nexus between CG and CSR.

References

Adams, R. B., and Ferreira, D. (2007). "A Theory of Friendly Boards," *Journal of Finance*, 62(1): 217–50.

Aguilera, R. V. (2005). "Corporate Governance and Director Accountability: An Institutional Comparative Perspective," *British Journal of Management*, 16: 1–15.

—— and Cuervo-Cazurra, A. (2009). "Codes of Good Governance," *Corporate Governance: An International Review*, 17: 376–87.

—— and Jackson, G. (2003). "The Cross-national Diversity of Corporate Governance: Dimensions and Determinants," *Academy of Management Review*, 28: 447–65.

—— Rupp, D. E., Williams, C. A., and Ganapathi, J. (2007). "Putting the S Back in Corporate Social Responsibility: A Multilevel Theory of Social Change in Organizations," *Academy of Management Review*, 32(3): 836–63.

ANDERSON, R. C., MANSI, S. A. and REEB, D. M. (2003). "Founding Family Ownership and the Agency Cost of Debt," *Journal of Financial Economics*, 68: 263–85.

ARORA, P., and DHARWADKAR, R. (2011). "Corporate Governance and Corporate Social Responsibility (CSR): The Moderating Roles of Attainment Discrepancy and Organization Slack," *Corporate Governance: An International Review*, 19(2): 136–52.

AVI-YONAH, R. (2005). "The Cyclical Transformations of the Corporate Form: A Historical Perspective on Corporate Social Responsibility," *Delaware Journal of Corporate Law*, 30: 767–818.

BARNEA, A. and RUBIN, A. (2010). "Corporate Social Responsibility as a Conflict between Shareholders," *Journal of Business Ethics*, 97: 71–86.

BEAR, S., RAHMAN, N., and POST, C. (2010). "The Impact of Board Diversity and Gender Composition on Corporate Social Responsibility and Firm Reputation," *Journal of Business Ethics*, 97(2): 207–22.

BEBCHUK, L., COHEN, A., and FERRELL, A. (2009). "What Matters in Corporate Governance?" *Review of Financial Studies*, 22: 783–827.

BERLE, A., and MEANS, G. (1932). *The Modern Corporation and Private Property*. New York: Macmillan.

BERRONE, P., CRUZ, C., GOMEZ-MEJIA, L. R., and LARRAZA-KINTANA, M. (2010). "Socioemotional Wealth and Corporate Responses to Institutional Pressures: Do Family Controlled Firms Pollute Less?" *Administrative Science Quarterly*, 55(1): 82–113.

BEURDEN, P., and GOSSLING, T. (2008). "The Worth of Values—A Literature Review on the Relation between Corporate Social and Financial Performance," *Journal of Business Ethics*, 82(2): 407–24.

BUCHHOLTZ, A. K., BROWN, J., and SHABANA, K. (2008). "Corporate Governance and Corporate Social Responsibility," in A. Crane, A. McWilliams, D. Matten, J. Moon, and D. S. Siegel (eds.), *The Oxford Handbook of Social Responsibility*. New York: Oxford University Press.

BUSHEE, B. (1998). "The Influence of Institutional Investors on Myopic R&D Investment Behavior," *The Accounting Review*, 73: 305–33.

CAMPBELL, J. L. (2007). "Why Would Corporations Behave in Socially Responsible Ways? An Institutional Theory of Corporate Social Responsibility," *Academy of Management Review*, 32: 946–67.

CARROLL, A. B. (2007). "A History of Corporate Social Responsibility: Concepts and Practices," in A. Crane et al. (eds.), *The Oxford Handbook of Corporate Social Responsibility*. New York: Oxford University Press, 19–46.

COATES, J. C., IV (2007). "The Goals and Promise of the Sarbanes–Oxley Act," *Journal of Economic Perspectives*, 21: 91–116.

COFFEY, B., and FRYXELL, G. E. (1991). "Institutional Ownership of Stock and Dimensions of Corporate Social Performance: An Empirical Examination," *Journal of Business Ethics*, 10: 437–44.

—— and WANG, J. (1998). "Board Diversity and Managerial Control as Predictors of Corporate Social Performance," *Journal of Business Ethics*, 17: 1595–603.

CONZELMANN, T. (2012). "A Procedural Approach to the Design of Voluntary Clubs: Negotiating the Responsible Care Global Charter," *Socio-Economic Review*, 10: 193–214.

CORE, J. E., GUAY, W. E. and RUSTICUS, T. O. (2006). "Does Weak Governance Cause Weak Stock Returns? An Examination of Firm Operating Performance and Investors' Expectations," *Journal of Finance*, 61: 655–87.

Cox, P., and Gaya Wicks, P. (2011). "Institutional Interest in Corporate Responsibility: Portfolio Evidence and Ethical Explanation," *Journal of Business Ethics*, 103(1): 143–65.

—— Brammer, S., and Millington, A. (2004). "An Empirical Examination of Institutional Investor Preferences for Corporate Social Performance," *Journal of Business Ethics*, 52: 27–43.

Dahyaa, J., and McConnell, J. J. (2004). "Outside Directors and Corporate Board Decisions," *Journal of Corporate Finance*, 11(1–2): 37–60.

Dam, L. and Scholtens, B. (2012). "Does Ownership Type Matter for Corporate Social Responsibility?" *Corporate Governance: An International Review*, 20: 233–52.

David, P., Bloom, M., and Hillman, A. (2007). "Investor Activism, Managerial Responsiveness, and Corporate Social Performance," *Strategic Management Journal*, 28: 91–100.

de Villiers, C., Naiker, V., and Staden, C. J. (2011). "The Effect of Board Characteristics on Firm Environmental Performance," *Journal of Management*, 37: 1636–63.

Dyer, W. G., and Whetten, D. A. (2006). "Family Firms and Social Responsibility: Preliminary Evidence from the S&P 500," *Entrepreneurship Theory and Practice*, 30(6): 785–802.

Fama, E., and Jensen, M. (1983). "Separation of Ownership and Control," *The Journal of Law and Economics*, 26(2): 301.

Fransen, L. (2012). "Multi-stakeholder Governance and Voluntary Program Interactions: Legitimation Politics in the Institutional Design of Corporate Social Responsibility," *Socio-Economic Review*, 10: 163–91.

Gill, A. (2008). "Corporate Governance as Social Responsibility: A Research Agenda," *Berkeley Journal of International Law*, 26: 452–78.

Gillan, S. L. (2006). "Recent Developments in Corporate Governance: An Overview," *Journal of Corporate Finance*, 12(3): 381–402.

—— and Starks, L. (2007). "The Evolution of Shareholder Activism in the United States," *Journal of Applied Corporate Finance*, 19: 55–73.

Graves, S. B., and Waddock, S. A. (1994). "Institutional Owners and Social Performance," *Academy of Management Journal*, 37(4), 1034–46.

Hall, P. A., and Soskice, D. (2001). "An Introduction to Varieties of Capitalism," in P. A. Hall and D. Soskice (eds.), *Varieties of Capitalism: The Institutional Foundations of Comparative Advantage*. Oxford: Oxford University Press, 1–70.

Harjoto, M., and Jo, H. (2011). "Corporate Governance and CSR Nexus," *Journal of Business Ethics*, 100(1): 45–67.

Hillman, A. J., Cannella, J., and Paetzold, A. A. (2000). "The Resource Dependence Role of Corporate Directors: Strategic Adaptation of Board Composition in Response to Environmental Change," *Journal of Management Studies*, 37 (2): 235–55.

Hilt, E. (2008). "When Did Ownership Separate from Control? Corporate Governance in the Early Nineteenth Century," *Journal of Economic History*, 68(3): 645–85.

Ibrahim, N. A., and Angelidis, J. P. (1995). "The Corporate Social Responsiveness Orientation of Board Members: Are There Differences between Inside and Outside Directors?" *Journal of Business Ethics*, 14: 405–10.

Ireland, P. (2010). "Limited Liability, Shareholder Rights and the Problem of Corporate Irresponsibility," *Cambridge Journal of Economics*, 34(5): 837–56.

Jackson, G., and Deeg, R. (2008). "From Comparing Capitalisms to the Politics of Institutional Change," *Review of International Political Economy*, 15(4): 680–709.

Jamali, D., Safieddine, A. M., and Rabbath, M. (2008). "Corporate Governance and Corporate Social Responsibility: Synergies and Interrelationships," *Corporate Governance: An International Review*, 16: 443–59.

Jensen, M. C., and Meckling, W. (1976). "Theory of the Firm: Managerial Behavior, Agency Costs and Capital Structure," *Journal of Financial Economics*, 3: 305–60.

Johnson, R. and Greening, D. (1999). "The Effects of Corporate Governance and Institutional Ownership on Corporate Social Performance," *Academy of Management Journal*, 42: 564–80.

Judge, W., Gaur, A., and Muller-Kahle, M. (2010). "Antecedents of Shareholder Activism in Target Firms: Evidence from a Multi-Country Study," *Corporate Governance: An International Review*, 18(4): 258–73.

Kakabadse, A. (2007). "Being Responsible: Boards are Re-examining the Bottom Line." *Leadership in Action*, 27(1): 3–6.

Kang, N., and Moon, J. (2012). "Institutional Complementarity between Corporate Governance and Corporate Social Responsibility: A Comparative Institutional Analysis of Three Capitalisms," *Socio-Economic Review*, 10: 85–108.

Kassinis, G., and Vafeas, N. (2002). "Corporate Boards and Outside Stakeholders as Determinants of Environmental Litigations," *Strategic Management Journal*, 23: 399–415.

Kirkbride, J., and Letza, S. (2003). "Establishing the Boundaries of Regulation in Corporate Governance: Is the UK Moving Toward a Process of Collaboration?" *Business and Society Review*, 108: 463–85.

Kirkpatrick, G. (2008). "The Corporate Governance Lessons from the Financial Crisis," Report, OECD, Paris, France.

Lee, M. D. P., and Lounsbury, M. (2011). "Domesticating Radical Rant and Rage: An Exploration of the Consequences of Environmental Shareholder Resolutions on Corporate Environmental Performance," *Business & Society*, 50: 155–88.

Logsdon, J. and Van Buren, H. (2008). "Justice and Large Corporations: What Do Activist Shareholder Want?" *Business & Society*, 47: 523–48.

—— and Wood, D. J. (2005). "Global Business Citizenship and Voluntary Codes of Ethical Conduct," *Journal of Business Ethics*, 59(1): 55–67.

Love, I. (2011). "Corporate Governance and Performance around the World: What We Know and What We Don't," *The World Bank Research Observer*, 26: 42–70.

Mahoney, L. S., and Roberts, R. W. (2007). "Corporate Social Performance, Financial Performance and Institutional Ownership in Canadian Firms," *Accounting Forum*, 31: 233–53.

Mallin, C. A., and Michelon, G. (2011). "Board Reputation Attributes and Corporate Social Performance: An Empirical Investigation of the US Best Corporate Citizens," *Accounting and Business Research*, 41(2): 119–44.

Margolis, J., and Walsh, J. P. (2003). "Misery Loves Companies: Rethinking Social Initiatives by Business," *Administrative Science Quarterly*, 48: 268–305.

—— Elfenbein, H., and Walsh, J. (2007). "Does it Pay to be Good? A Meta-Analysis and Redirection of Research on the Relationship between Corporate Social and Financial Performance," Mimeo, Ross School of Business, University of Michigan.

Masulis, R. W., and Mobbs, H. S. (2009). "Are All Inside Directors the Same? Do They Entrench CEOs or Facilitate More Informed Board Decisions?" Finance Working Paper 241/2009, ECGI.

Matten, D. A., and Crane, A. (2005). "Corporate Citizenship: Towards an Extended Theoretical Conceptualization," *Academy of Management Review*, 30: 166–80.

—— and Moon, J. (2008). "Implicit and Explicit CSR: A Conceptual Framework for a Comparative Understanding of Corporate Social Responsibility," *Academy of Management Review*, 33: 404–24.

MORCK, R. K., and STEIER, L. (2005). "The Global History of Corporate Governance: An Introduction," in R. K. Morck (ed.), *A History of Corporate Governance around the World: Family Business Groups to Professional Managers*. Chicago: University of Chicago Press, 1–64.

NEUBAUM, D. O., and ZAHRA, S. A. (2006). "Institutional Ownership and Corporate Social Performance: The Moderating Effects of Investment Horizon, Activism, and Coordination," *Journal of Management*, 32: 108–31.

OH, W. Y., CHANG, Y. K., and MARTYNOV, A. (2011). "The Effect of Ownership Structure on Corporate Social Responsibility: Empirical Evidence from Korea," *Journal of Business Ethics*, 104(2): 283–97.

ORLITZKY, M., SCHMIDT, F. L., and RYNES, S. L. (2003). "Corporate Social and Financial Performance: A Meta-Analysis," *Organization Studies*, 24: 403–41.

PFEFFER, J., and SALANCIK, G. R. (1978). *The External Control of Organizations—A Resource Dependence Perspective*. New York: Harper & Row.

POST, C., RAHMAN, N., and RUBOW, E. (2011). "Green Governance: Board of Directors' Composition and Environmental Corporate Social Responsibility," *Business & Society*, 50(1): 189–223.

PRADO-LORENZO, J. M., GALLEGO-ALVAREZ, I., and GARCIA-SANCHEZ, M. (2009). "Stakeholder Engagement and Corporate Social Responsibility Reporting: The Ownership Structure Effect," *Corporate Social Responsibility and Environmental Management*, 16(2): 94–107.

PROFFITT, W. T., and SPICER, A. (2006). "Shaping the Shareholder Activism Agenda: Institutional Investors and Global Issues," *Strategic Organization*, 4(2): 165–90.

REHBEIN, K., WADDOCK, S. A., and GRAVES, S. B. (2004). "Understanding Shareholder Activism: Which Corporations are Targeted?" *Business & Society*, 4: 239–67.

—— LOGSDON, J. M., and VAN BUREN, H. J. (2012). "Corporate Responses to Shareholder Activists: Considering the Dialogue Alternative," *Journal of Business Ethics*. DOI: <10.1007/s10551-012-1237-2>.

RYAN, L. V., and SCHNEIDER, M. (2002). "The Antecedents of Institutional Investor Activism," *Academy of Management Review*, 27: 554–73.

SHLEIFER, A., and VISHNY, R. (1997). "A Survey of Corporate Governance," *Journal of Finance*, 52: 737–83.

SJÖSTRÖM, E. (2008). "Shareholder Activism for Corporate Social Responsibility: What Do We Know?" *Sustainable Development*, 3: 141–54.

SLATER, D. (2007). "Resolved: Public Corporations Shall Take Us Seriously," *New York Times Magazine*, August 12.

SPITZECK, H. (2009). "The Development of Governance Structures for Corporate Responsibility," *Corporate Governance*, 9(4): 495–505.

SURROCA, J., and TRIBO, J. (2008). "Managerial Entrenchment and Corporate Social Performance," *Journal of Business Finance and Accounting*, 35: 748–89.

TKAC, P. (2006). "One Proxy at a Time: Pursuing Social Change through Shareholder Proposals," *Economic Review—Federal Reserve Bank of Atlanta*, 91(3): 1.

WALLS, J. L., BERRONE, P., and PHAN, P. H. (2012). "Corporate Governance and Environmental Performance: Is There Really a Link?" *Strategic Management Journal*, 33: 885–913.

WANG, J., and COFFEY, B. S. (1992). "Board Composition and Corporate Philanthropy," *Journal of Business Ethics*, 11: 771–8.

WHITLEY, R. (1999). *Divergent Capitalisms: The Social Structuring and Change of Business Systems*. Oxford: Oxford University Press.

WILLIAMS, R. J. (2003). "Women on Corporate Boards of Directors and their Influence on Corporate Philanthropy," *Journal of Business Ethics*, 42(1): 1–10.

WONG, E. M., ORMISTON, M. E., and TETLOCK, P. E. (2011). "The Effects of Top Management Team Integrative Complexity and Decentralized Decision Making on Corporate Social Performance," *Academy of Management Journal*, 54(6): 1207–28.

Index

AA (Automobile Association) 540
Aaronovitch, S. 204–5
Abbott, L. J. 179, 180, 182, 184
ABC (Agricultural Bank of China) 596, 538
Abdolmohammadi, M. 316
ABF (Associated British Foods) 261
ABI (Association of British Insurers) 37
abnormal returns 128, 547
  hedge funds aim for 567
  long-term 570
  positive 566, 570
absorptive capacity 373, 453
Abu Dhabi Investment Authority 593, 602 n.(3)
academic journals 1
access to capital 137
accountability 11, 164, 380, 623, 625, 720
  board 4, 167, 192
  declining 357
  diversity and 619
  early-stage IPO with substantial tradeoffof 356
  electoral 24, 25
  enhanced levels of 309
  executive lack of 57
  financial 622
  financial, extending compliance for 609
  formalized 321
  horizontal 614
  implications for 609
  limited and high levels of 354
  managerial 46, 47, 49, 59, 99, 356, 366, 393
  ownership and 612–17
  public 311, 608
Accountancy Age 286 n.(9)
accounting 6, 234, 246, 301, 675
  assessment of principles 310
  conventions which shape performance measures 650

direct/indirect costs of reports 294
disclosure of information 300
dubious practices 709
early data studies in US 548
fair value 15, 324
management generally adept at exploiting rules 277
manipulation of numbers 38
misreporting 649
performance measures 274
quality in private firms 301
regulation of 303 n.(2)
  see also AICPA; GAAP; IFAC
accounting standards 28, 109, 301
  cross-country differences in 530
  regulating 57
  see also FASB; IASB
Acemoglu, D. 75, 92 n.(11)
Acharya, V. 549–50, 685
acquisitions, *see* M&As; takeovers
Actelion Ltd 259
adaptation 617–20
ADBC (Agricultural Development Bank of China) 596
added-value 402, 429, 434, 436, 451, 545, 616
  high, difficult to develop 646
Adler, B. E. 492, 500, 507
Adler, N. J. 452
Adler, P. S. 389, 406, 407
adverse selection 293, 422, 531
  agency costs associated with 436, 439
  investors can mitigate 435
  reducing the extent of 423
Aeon Co 258
affiliate directors 403, 404
  positive effect on diversification strategies 405
affiliation rights strategy 103, 112–13, 119

INDEX

AFL-CIO (American Federation of Labor and Congress of Industrial Organizations) 83
agency cost theory 51, 55
agency costs 25–6, 32–3, 38, 69, 70, 79, 422, 437, 531
  accentuated 359
  adverse selection 436, 439
  associated with high free cash flows and low growth prospects 336
  debt-financed LBO addresses 542
  deficiencies in legal and labor market institutions 466
  high 650
  higher 335
  horizontal 368
  information asymmetries increase 290
  inherent 310
  mitigated 534 n.(3)
  more problematic 370
  potential 423
  reduction in 300, 319, 328, 337, 370, 377, 378, 439
  substantial, for external investors 366
  two types faced by minority shareholders 35
agency problems 55, 101, 102, 272
  basic 98
  central 273
  classic 310
  corporate constituents 99
  critical 359
  domination of 360
  executive compensation seriously limited as solution to 374
  increase of 422
  key ingredient in attenuating 553
  less efficient mechanism to alleviate 374
  local implementers have more 451
  major types of 123
  may be different in different national settings 440
  mechanism that may reduce the amount of monitoring and incentives needed to resolve 408
  mitigation of 316, 333, 452
  much less pronounced 311
  new and sometimes unexpected 12
  owner-owner 396
  potential 112, 119, 301, 683
  principal-principal 437, 482
  private equity syndicates may create their own 439
  reducing risks of 423
  risk-averse managers and risk-seeking equity holders 492
  secondary 309
  severe 103, 185, 482
  studies focused on 711
  substantial 103
  two distinctive types of 422
  well-known, partial solution to 309
  see also principal-agent problems
agency theory 12, 17, 18, 55, 135, 151, 165, 172, 179, 207, 247, 255, 273, 351, 368, 369, 375, 378, 379, 392, 393, 395, 406, 410, 412, 541, 543, 663, 726
  applied to understand managerial perceptions 457
  classic 180, 544
  coverage downplayed 389–90
  evidence to support in monitoring 610
  explicit test of 185
  limited evidence to support 163
  more complete description of 413 n.(4)
  multiple 458–9, 660, 673–702
  organizational theorists have increasingly drawn on 421
  principal-principal 675
  significant weakness of 258
  used to predict superior and inferior performance by family blockholders 396
Agenda 2010 (Germany) 90
agent-owners 674
  conflict between 675–8
  cooperation among 694–5
  multiple, managerial processes to deal with 695–6
  potential conflicts and ramifications caused by 12
  short-term 691
Aggarwal, R. K. 231, 233, 238, 302, 423
aggregate demand 275
aggregations 67, 81, 84–8, 360

Aghion, P. 367, 368, 370, 491
Aglietta, M. 706
Agrawal, A. 205, 248, 280
agriculture 75
Aguilera, R. V. 2, 17, 24, 26, 30, 31, 32, 36, 37, 38, 163, 171, 439, 441, 449, 666, 667–8, 720, 721–2
Aharoni, Y. 455, 457
Ahmad, A. C. 404
Ahrens, T. 142, 164
AICPA (US Institute of Certified Public Accountants) 310–11, 318
  see also PCAOB
AIFM (EU Alternative Investment Fund Management) Directive 14–15, 296
AIG (American International Group) 13
AIMR (US Association for Investment Management and Research) 298
airline industry 238
Akerlof, G. 285 n.(5)
Alesina, A. 92 n.(7/13)
Alexander, A. 206
Ali, A. 303 n.(1)
ALI (American Law Institute) 36, 49, 52, 55
  Tentative Draft No. 1 (1982) 50, 51
alignment approach 247, 248
alignment of interest 248, 299
Allcock, D. 7, 433, 691, 695
Alliance Boots 540
allocation of capital, see capital allocation
allocation of resources, see resource allocation
Alloy, Inc. 568
Almeida, H. 468, 476
Altman, E. I. 494
Alves, C. 38
American Assembly (think-tank) 49, 54
American Bar Association 49, 80
American Civil War (1861–5) 80
American Express 53
American federalism 85–7
Amess, Kevin 10
Amess, K. 550, 551
Amihud, Y. 293
Amit, R. 390, 397, 430
Amran, N. A. 404
analysts 84, 87, 231, 262, 290–1, 298, 303 n.(1)

absolute price impact of information disseminated by 297
better communication with 341
economics-oriented 91
negative reports by 696
analytics 141
Andersen, see Arthur Andersen
Anderson, R. C. 389, 391, 396, 397, 400, 403–4, 731
Andrade, G. 492–3, 554, 555
Andres, C. 547
Andrews, K. R. 50
angels 259, 356, 435
Anginer, D. 507
Anglo-centrism 361
anti-takeover mechanisms 6, 53, 108, 340–1, 379
  effects of provisions 230
  strong laws/legislation 83, 86, 649–50
antitrust 204, 342
anti-dilution rights 523
APB (UK Auditing Practices Board) 319, 322
Apple 429
appointment rights strategy 103–4, 110–11
APR (absolute priority rule) 493, 500
  violations 575
Arab Gulf countries 583
  see also Abu Dhabi; Kuwait; Qatar; UAE
arbitrage 254
Argentina 638
Armour, J. 90
Arora, P. 730, 736
Arrighi, G. 712
Arthur Andersen 137, 295, 315
Arthurs, J. D. 12, 428, 436, 458–9, 660, 674, 675, 679, 690, 691, 696
Ashton, Richard 210, 211
Asian countries 404, 547, 640, 667, 722
  negative effect of family ownership 397
  see also Brunei; East Asia; Indonesia; Malaysia; Philippines; Singapore; Taiwan
Asian Financial Crisis (1997) 58, 596
Asian stock exchanges 298
asset flipping 540
asset management companies 597
asset specificity 378
asset-stripping 13, 14, 358, 540
  state 477

asset substitution 493, 495
asset-turnover ratio 275
asset values 300
    heterogeneity of beliefs about 353
Astrachan, J. H. 392
Atanasov, V. 594
AT&T 202
auctions 338, 340, 491, 503, 507, 508 n.(11)
    mandatory 500-1, 506
    optimal 503 n.(13)
audit committees 177, 178, 179-82, 228, 400
    ceremonial interpretations/functions of
        184, 185
    chair of 109, 149
    family firms less likely to establish 401
    family members on boards weakens
        effectiveness of 404
    importance of informal processes
        related to 185
    influence on internal control
        activities 183-4
    investor perceptions regarding 183
    listed companies required to have 318
    overlapping of compensation committee
        and 190
    role of 303 n.(2)
auditing 4, 181-2, 137, 190, 308-27
    analyzed as powerful model of
        governance 6
    confidence in 295
    government-sponsored schemes 725
    high quality 301
    internal 6, 181, 185, 191
    nonprofit systems 624
    plethora of regulations 273
    see also external audit; internal auditing;
        ISA; US-American Center
Auditing Practices Committee (UK) 315
Australia 534 n.(2), 544, 547
    CEO cash compensation 236
Austria 353, 356, 530
    see also Schumpeter
auto bankruptcies 506-7
Avon Rubber 144
Axelson, U. 553
Ayotte, K. M. 8, 499, 500, 503, 504,
    506, 572

Babenko, I. 234
Bach, D. 620, 622
Backer, T. E. 611
Bacon, N. 551
Baek, H. Y. 298, 299
Baek, J.-S. 476, 482
bailout loans 507
Bainbridge, S. M. 50, 51, 246
Balakrishnan, S. 376
Balcik, B. 616
Balding, C. 584
Balkin, D. B. 375
Ball, R. 301
Bammens, Y. 389, 395, 398, 400, 413 n.(5)
Banesto 58
Bank Holding Company Act (US
    1956/2012) 81, 508 n.(5)
bank lenders:
    important governance mechanism
        for 497
    management departures are initiated
        by 497
    role when firms are auctioned 500
Bank of America 201
Bank of Communications (China) 599
Bank of England 138, 201
banking collapse (2008) 141
banking crisis (1933) 71
bankruptcy 12, 33, 47, 124, 269, 495-8, 502,
    508 nn.(8-13), 541
    better governance of target pre-PTP
        associated with lower risk 548
    bringing dynamic changes to the
        process 564
    debt-equity swap helps avoid 554
    failure to fulfill debt obligation can lead
        to 543
    formal and informal control rights in
        9, 494
    hedge fund participation in 578
    made very costly 375
    managerial turnover in and around 489,
        490, 494
    multiple agency theory in 675, 687-90,
        693-4, 697 n.
    national 113
    senior lender control rights 499-501

typical firm declaring 687
see also auto bankruptcies; US Bankruptcy Code; *also under following entries prefixed* "bankruptcy"
bankruptcy courts 490, 492, 505, 688
  measure of effectiveness 504
  see also US Bankruptcy Court
bankruptcy law 113, 490, 503, 506, 507, 688, 689
  creditors' rights 272
  new wave of reforms 122
  reorganized legislation 121
bankruptcy reorganization 490, 491, 493–5, 498–507, 508 nn.(11/13), 689
  hedge fund participation in 572, 573, 578, 575
  legislation 121
Banks, T. L. & F. Z. 228
banks 67–8, 139, 204, 254, 489
  Chinese reform 595–9
  DIP financing 574
  director networks in 205
  distressed firm 501
  driven by financial regulations and regulatory policy 501
  Europe 82
  forgiveness of principal on loans 498
  incentivized to recover debt 358
  information acquired about PE firm from prior transactions 550
  interlocks between firms and 207
  international mega-banks 201
  joint-equity 598
  law that reduced the power of 34
  loan concentration 501
  nation-spanning, with significant stock ownership 81
  normally more risk averse 370
  private information flows between firms and 294
  recapitalizations 597, 598, 599
  reorganization of 583, 599
  reports of 301
  roles of 498, 713
  significant ownership by 332
  softinformation between borrower and 294

state-owned 582, 595–6, 598, 599
stock market capitalism vs 71
substantial involvement in company financing 639
see also central banks; commercial banks; development banks; investment banks
Barbary, V. 587
Barings Bank 137, 308
Barnard, C. 145
Barnard, J. W. 279, 281
Barnea, A. 208, 735
Baron, J. 429
Barry, C. B. 292, 434
Barth, M. 300
Bartholomew, S. 452
Bartlett, C. A. 450, 453
Baruch, F. 204, 205
Bascha, A. 528, 529
Bass brothers 53
Battaggion, M. R. 368
Baudrillard, J. 710
Baysinger, B. 208, 259, 370, 372, 376, 380, 469
BB Biotech AG 259
BCCI (Bank of Credit and Commerce International) 309
Beamon, B. M. 616
Bear, S. 730
Beasley, M. S. 178, 181, 182, 184
Beattie, V. 183
Beatty, R. P. 374, 421, 429, 430, 432
Bebchuk, L. A. 37, 72, 92 n.(3), 93 n.(19), 98, 101, 223, 293, 723
Becht, M. 57, 99, 100, 102
Becker, B. 495
Bédard, J. 177, 178, 179, 180, 181, 184, 192
Bednar, M. K. 168, 170, 246, 260, 262, 263, 696
Beekes, W. 142
Beesley, M. 202
Belgium 311, 401, 530, 612
Bender, R. 187, 351
Benito, G. R. G. 456
Benito, M. 186
Benson, L. 78
Berent, M. M. 391
Berent-Braun, M. M. 393, 408, 410
Berger, P. G. 233, 474
Bergh, D. D. 247

Berglöf, E. 58, 170, 171, 174, 177, 179
Berle, A. 6, 25, 51, 52, 92 n., 99, 328, 330, 430, 719
Berlin Wall (1989) 136
Berrone, P. 235, 398, 736
Berry, R. H. 353
Bertelsmann Foundation 611
Bertoni, Fabio 7, 376
Bertrand and Mullainathan 649
best practice 11, 31, 36, 57, 138, 179, 187, 312, 331, 404, 405, 411, 617, 623, 624
   new 333
   regulation and codes of 203
Betker, B. L. 493
Beuselinck, Christof 6, 310
Beyer, A. 291, 293, 297
"bezzling" 710
Bharath, S. T. 493, 500
Bhaumik, S. K. 456
bid-ask spread 293
Biddle, Nicholas 80
Big Four auditing firms 319
biotechnology industry 259, 294, 707
Birkinshaw, J. M. 451
Bishop, K. 433, 438
Bjørnåli, E. S. 373
Black, B. 647, 650, 651
Black, B. S. 52, 53, 54, 434, 438, 440, 529, 565, 576, 577
Black, F. 492
Black, J. 620
BlackBerry pinging 140
Blackburn, R. 710, 715
Blackwater 713
Blair, M. 636, 650
Blair, Tony 89
Blankespoor, E. 303
Blaylock, B. 507
blockholders 252–3, 259, 262, 357, 695
   additional challenges 592
   concentrated ownership by 639
   controlling, opportunistic principals as 368
   family 396
   incumbent 101
   individual 252
   institutional 696
   large, bargaining power of 368
   legally constrained 26
   monitoring of 108
   multiple 667, 668
   ownership by 298
   preferences of 261
   strong 119, 123
   see also large blockholders
blue-chips 204
Blumentritt, T. 405
BM&FBovespa 38
board committees 37, 177–99, 224–5
   CSR 731
   environmental 731
   primary 4
   see also audit committees; nomination committees; remuneration committees
board composition 104, 350, 352, 400, 421, 720, 726
   particular care should be taken in designing 373
   performance and 428–9
   resolving mixed evidence on CSR and 730
   various predictors of 402
   world's largest multinational firms 453
board independence 223–4, 299, 332, 428–9, 430
   adopting a stringent definition of 404
   externally visible dimensions of 696
   positive relationship between environmental performance and 726
board-investor relationships 139
board members 248, 260, 281, 374
   ability to keep management accountable for its decisions 366
   affiliate 409
   allies as 263
   employment ceases in regular merger 681
   exclusion of labor representatives by 641–2
   family-related 409
   female 730
   independent 270, 279, 280, 285
   inside, advantage in dealing with uncertainty 372
   legal responsibilities 285
   loyalty biases 285

multiple directorships 692
need to pay attention to compensation and reward 434
non-executive 438
non-family firms more likely to use formal criteria for selection 402
outside 372–3, 409, 456, 696
part-time 270
responsible for appointment of CEO 286 n.(12)
type of compensation received by 373
ways of eliminating 261
women 189
board performance 4, 147, 168, 169, 170, 189, 428–9
board power 5, 164, 166
 qualitative studies on exercise of 4
 relationship to organizational effectiveness 165
board size 164, 212, 400–1, 544
 negatively associated with firm value for non-family firms 404
 negatively related to firm's growth opportunities 372
 positively related to FDI 456
board structures 720
 one- and two-tier 108–9, 149
 optimal 337–8
BoardEx 144
boards of directors 32, 135–62, 200, 248, 269, 332, 367, 372–4, 410–11, 459, 466, 568
 acquiescent 271
 adjusting 564
 adoption of accountability practices 619
 behavior and effectiveness 163–76
 broad-based view of responsibilities 16
 central preoccupation with the action of 609
 CEO relations with 164
 changes in 7
 characteristics and performance of IPOs 428
 coalition among managers and 479
 companies traded on NYSE 189
 complementarity of skills between management team and 373
 conduct of 145–7

confronting self-serving managerial initiatives 271
CSR and 725–31
decision processes 279–82
dependence of 373
differences in structure 332
effectiveness of 262, 279–83
employee representation 104, 109, 639, 641–2
family businesses 389
family members on 401
female representation on 730
FFB 402
fiduciary obligations 493
founders and 429–30
functioning of 38, 50
good/bad decisions and share price 331
hedge funds have the potential to influence 567
independent 433, 548
insider-dominated 405
issues facing 142
legal responsibilities of 273
loyalty biases 279–83
mandatory minority shareholder representation 111
merger target 681
monitoring 169, 185–6, 225
monitoring function of 393
number of legal experts present on 730
optimal structures 337–8
power struggle between CEO and 205
professionalization of 431
quality and experience of 353
racial and ethnic minorities on 619
roles of 4, 145–9, 165, 373, 495–6, 608
shareholder right to nominate candidates 48
staggered 37, 223, 474
strong 225
structure of 452
subgroups of 190
target 692
time of change for 434
turnover extremely high 489
two-tier structure 377
unitary organizations 614

boards of directors (*cont.*)
　urging to remove underperforming chief
　　executives 53
　value-creating potential of 373
　values of 258
　vulture investors join 501
　weak 541
　women on 624, 730
　see also interlocking directorates; *also
　　entries above prefixed* "board"
BOC (Bank of China) 596, 598, 599
Boeker, W. 680
Boivie, S. 440
Boix, C. 75
Bolton, P. 108
bond markets 507
bonding mechanisms 247, 248, 252, 259
bonuses 214, 227, 232, 234, 237, 247, 286 n.(8),
　　455, 566
　annual 282, 431
　bid to maximize the value of 239
　cash 283, 649
　compensation structure that focuses
　　on 237
　increased 687
　linked to reported corporate profits 276
　multi-million dollar 13
　risk adjustment factor in determining 284
　taxed 13
　top managers 454
book-building functions 359
Boone, A. 337, 338, 339
Boot, A. 294
Booth, J. 421
bootstrapping hypothesis 128
Boozang, K. 609
Borisova, G. 581, 602 n.(1)
Bortolotti, B. 581, 584, 587, 594, 601, 602 n.(2)
Boss, David S. 5
Boston Associates 201
Botosan, Christine A. 303 n.(1)
Boucly, Q. 548, 550
bounded rationality 457
Bower, J. L. 450
Boyacigiller, N. 451
Boyd, B. K. 164, 172, 229, 231, 234, 235
Boyer, R. 705, 706, 713, 714

Boyson, N. M. 569, 570–1
BP Amoco 201
BP oil spill (Gulf of Mexico 2010) 12–13, 15
Bradshaw, P. 617–18
Brammer, Stephen J. 12
Brandeis, Louis D. 200, 290
Brandes, P. 5, 227, 240, 248
Brav, A. 421, 435, 566, 568, 569, 570–1, 592
Brazil 89
Brazilian Stock Exchange 38
BRC (NYSE Blue Ribbon Committee
　　1999) 180, 181
breakthrough rule 110, 112
Bremer Vulkan 58
Brennan, M. J. 421
Brickley, J. A. 254
Bris, A. 505
Britain, *see* United Kingdom
British Land 577
British Midland metal industries 202
Brock, D. M. 611
Broughman (2010) 374
Brown, A. D. 137
Brown, P. 142
Brown, R. 214
Brown, S. J. 292
Bruining, H. 376, 549
Brunei 583
Brunello, G. 404
Brussels Stock Exchange 296
Bruton, G. D. 422, 423, 441, 660, 678
Buchholtz, A. K. 720
Buckley, P. J. 455, 456–7
Buffett, Warren 229
Bulgaria 116
Burke, T. H. 619
Burris, V. 205
Burt, R. 205
Busenitz, L. 440
Bushee, B. J. 246, 254, 260, 261, 292, 297, 304,
　　675, 676, 695, 731
Bushman, R. M. 231, 292, 296, 299
business coordination 378
business elites 83
　core owner 467, 468
　interests of 74–6
　masses vs 69

business groups 253, 465–88
　family-controlled; *see* family business
　internal capital markets in 368
　large 8
　see also group affiliates
business risk 270, 272, 274, 278
　corporate equity insufficient to absorb 273
　diminished 357
　excessive 276
　high 5, 275, 276, 355
　ignoring of 277
Business Roundtable 49, 50, 80, 83
Business Sector Advisory Group on Corporate Governance 58
Butler, H. 208
buybacks 530, 645
buyouts 645
　large private-equity-backed 648
　see also IBOs; LBOs; MBOs; PTPs
Byrd, J. W. 237
Byrne, D. 191

Cadbury Report (FRC 1992) 1, 26, 36, 38, 57, 137, 138, 142, 177, 180, 282, 287 n.(14), 291, 295, 303 n.(2), 331, 380, 393, 608
Cadman, B. 225, 232, 235, 236
Cai, J. I. E. 230
Calcagno, R. 99
Callen, J. L. 612
Calpers (California Public Employees Retirement System) 53, 54, 59
Calpine 564
Cambridge hi-tech cluster 206
Camm, G. 149, 151
Canada 404
　CEO compensation 236
　leading health nonprofit 618
　most prevalent form of controlling shareholders 390
　public corporations 184
　securities regulations 234
　venture capital 526, 527, 528, 529
Cannella, A. A. 135, 142, 151
capital adequacy 501, 599
capital allocation 356
capital allocation accurate 292
　efficient 292, 296
　inefficient 100
　parallel mechanisms 357
　scarce 296
capital controls 26
capital expenditures 526
　decline following covenant violation 497
　reductions in 549, 571
　unusually risky 493
capital gains 515, 517–18
　realization of 521, 522
　taxation 527
capital market development 88, 313, 367
　investor protection and 369, 377–8
　PP conflicts negatively affect 662
capital markets 38, 311
　controlling shareholders vs 72
　demand for information in 302
　effectiveness of 3
　financial politics and 65–96
　global 310–11
　institutional factors influence innovation activity 377
　internal 357, 368
　investor confidence in 297, 310–11
　liberalization of 58
　liquidity of 310, 378
　managerial 333
　managers vs 72
　mutual funds dominant in 37
　political economy of 3
　public trust in 310–11
　social democracy vs 69–70
　strong 66, 67, 82
　transparent and truthful information important for proper functioning of 291
　weak 66, 87–8
　well-functioning 378
　worldwide 291
capital rationing 377
capital structure 367, 375–6, 491, 494, 498, 499
　optimal 492
　reorganizing 502–3, 506
capitalism:
　bank-oriented 82, 92 n.(16)
　characterized 711
　contemporary 712

capitalism (*cont.*)
    cooperative and coordinated form of 652
    financialized 711
    interactions between politics and 66
    managerial 12, 716
    political institutions must support 3
    political problem of 91
    present-day, finance is "leading actor" in 704
    rentier 711
    state-directed 637
    stock market 71
    see also politics of capitalism; varieties of capitalism
Carapeto, M. 508 n.(7)
Carcello, J. V. 179, 183, 312
Carchon, S. 402
career concerns 370
Carlin, W. 377
Carney, M. 396, 399, 407, 473, 476, 482
Carpenter, M. A. 208, 230, 428, 452, 453, 458
Carpenter, V. L. 178
Carrington, P. 208
Carroll, T. M. 55
Carter, Jimmy 48
Carter, M. E. 234, 235
Carver, J. 618
Casey, A. 503 n.(13)
cash flow 112, 233, 293, 350
    better performance 498
    control rights and 468, 473, 474, 516, 522, 529, 532–4, 665
    declining 353
    distribution of 351
    forecasts issued by management in disclosure 495
    free 329, 335–6, 376, 541, 542, 548, 569, 571, 645
    future 541, 542
    keeping state rights 469
    negative 351, 357, 358
    strongly positive 357
Casson, M. 455
Catherine, D. 373
causality 207, 208, 216–17, 369, 723
    negative 77
Cawdron, Peter 203

CBS 681
CCB (China Construction Bank) 596
CDB (China Development Bank) 591, 596
CE (corporate entrepreneurship) 350, 353–4, 357, 359
    dominant features and roles of 358, 361
    increases in 549
    ownership by long-term investors positively related to 675–6
Central and Eastern Europe 88, 102, 116
    redrawing state boundaries 136
central banks 80, 595
Central Huijin 583, 594–5, 597–8, 599–600, 601
centrality measures 209, 213, 215
    direct 211, 213, 214
    indirect 211, 214
CEO-board relations 164
CEO pay/compensation 1, 54, 185, 186, 449, 568–9, 667
    average decline 570
    base salary 237, 431
    based in large part on stock prices 233
    benchmarks for 235
    board interlocks and 207
    cash 236, 237, 238
    compensation committees bend GAAP to preserve 233
    effects of remuneration committee on earnings 187
    equity-based 401
    family 401, 402
    firm performance and 238–9
    firm size cited as important predictor of 232
    high 229, 236
    increased 216, 223, 230, 236, 282
    large and inefficient 216
    long-term 452, 458
    more contingent on performance 239
    ownership concentration can lower 227
    ratios to lower-level employees 237
    salary cut 571
    short-term 375
    variation in 236
CEO tenure 229–30, 398
    comparatively long 610
    family/non-family 398

CEO turnover 338, 497, 500, 502, 575
  low 593
CEOs (chief executive officers) 5, 148, 165, 169, 181, 188
  appointment of 286 n.(12), 550
  appointment of friends as outside directors 207
  assessing the performance of 189
  award-winning 230
  bankrupt firm, income losses to 491
  better connected 208
  board members responsible for appointment of
  chairmen and 109, 145, 146, 332, 400, 404, 430
  characteristics 232
  connections may be a disincentive to monitor 373
  dominant 614
  duality of 37, 170, 172, 186, 451, 544
  family 233, 401, 664, 665
  founder 397, 423, 430, 433
  fraudulent 614
  hedge fund activism not kind to 570
  impression management used by 260
  incentives for 393
  incumbent regaining full-time employment 494
  ingratiation tactics to achieve board membership 260
  less willing to take risks 457
  loss of control of the firm upon filing for bankruptcy 491
  loyalty to 280–1
  major corporation 49
  majority owner 401
  multinational firms influence characteristics of 453
  network used to extend power of 210
  overlap with ownership 405
  plausible 614
  poorly performing 239
  portfolio company 374
  power counterbalanced 433
  power struggle between board and 205
  powerful 189, 205, 207, 238
  probability of rehiring by restructured firm 491–2
  productivity differences 230
  reduced scope of authority from original position 529
  retirement income 232
  right to replace founding entrepreneur as 531
  shareholding by 456
  significant replacement of 550
  strong preference for particular candidates 190
  stronger control relative to shareholders 649
  talent among 236
  target 681, 692
  top 230
  typical US base salary 431
  underperforming 53, 405
  unstudied reasons for supporting M&As 230
  venture capitalists' interaction with 374
  vulture 501
  see also entries above prefixed "CEO"
ceremonial function/role 178, 184, 185, 192
certification hypothesis 434–6
Certo, S. T. 421, 422, 428, 429, 432, 678
CFOs (chief finance officers) 181
  significant replacement of 550
Chadha, S. 280
chaebols 465, 468, 476, 478
Chahine, S. 423, 436, 440
chairmen CEOs and 109, 145, 146, 332, 400, 404, 430, 544
  desirability of separating roles of chief executive and 726
  subcommittee 149–51
  vulture 501
Chambers of Commerce 80, 83
Chandler, A. D. 12, 351, 704, 716
Chandler, R. A. 313, 315
Chaney, P. K. 352
Chang, T. 505, 508 n.(10)
charities 607, 613, 620, 621, 622
  effective 621
Charity Commission of England and Wales 621
  Strategic Plan (2012–15) 622

Chatterjee, S. 508 n.(7)
Chau, G. 401
checks and balances 636, 637, 709
Cheffins, Brian R. 2, 2, 37, 47, 51, 57, 59
Chemmanur, T. 371
Chen, C. J. 404
Chen, E. T. 404, 410
Chen, M. A. 238
Chen, S. 298, 299
Chen Xing 8
Chen, Y. Y. 663
Cheng, Q. 237, 238
Cheng, S. 230, 232, 233
Chevron Texaco 201
Chexim (Export-Import Bank of China) 596, 600
Chhaochharia, V. 224–7
Child, J. 684, 693
child labor 642
Chile 139, 476
China 10, 88, 258, 369, 594–600, 637
   business groups 253, 465, 470, 472, 473, 476, 477, 479
   cross-border M&As 663
   decision to expand into 456
   effects of ownership concentration on executive compensation 664
   firms controlled through pyramidal layers 469
   flooding of western markets 709
   foreign-owned subsidiaries in 454
   private blockholders 667
   shares concentrated in the hands of three largest shareholders 468
   see also ABC; ADBC; BOC; CCB; CDB; Central Huijin; Chexim; CIC; ICBC; PBOC; Shanghai
Cho, M. H. 369, 374
Choi, J.-H. 311
Chow, C. W. 319
Chrisman, J. J. 389, 392, 400, 405, 408, 413 n.(5), 545
Chrysler 503, 506–7
Chua, J. H. 396, 405
Chung, C. N. 472, 482, 483
Chung, K. H. 376

CIC (China Investment Corporation) 587, 591, 593
   Regulator 621
CII (US Council of Institutional Investors) 53, 217 n.
   Focus List 695
Citicorp 681
Citigroup 201
Citron, D. 534 n.(3), 546, 555
City of Glasgow Bank 312
City of London 37, 138, 139
   building communication channels with institutions 360
   significant effect on 137
   see also London Stock Exchange
civil law 29, 377, 519, 640
Clapman, P. C. 47
Clarysse, B. 373
class 30, 78
   see also middle class
class conflict 30
clawbacks 520, 521
Clay, Henry 80
Clayton Act (US 1914) 200, 201–2, 204
Clifford, C. 570
Clinton presidency 90
Coakley, J. 436
coalitions 66, 76, 87
   banker-labor 82
   capital-market-affecting 82
   dominant 84
   implicit 81
   managerial-labor 83
   middle-poor 85
   more complex 75
   multiple possible 83
   national 85, 90
   politically dominant 75
   redistributive 84, 85
   sectoral 30
   shifting 82–4
   transparency 30
Coase, R. 97
Coburn, J. 608
Cochran, P. L. 55, 207
codetermination 29–30, 32, 81, 100, 104, 639, 641
   removal of positive economic effects 642

Coffee, J. C. 54, 92 n.(6), 310, 311, 313, 317, 319, 320
Coffey, B. S. 730, 731
cognitive conflict 169, 170, 171
Cohen, A. 98, 101
Cohen, J. 182, 184, 191
Coles, J. L. 337
collateral 375, 497, 688
  cash 500
  right to pull 113
  seizing 490
collective bargaining 637, 651
  pay fixing via 651
collective enforcement mechanism 479
Collin, S.-O. 465, 472, 482
Collins, D. W. 223, 227, 235
collusion 471, 480, 796
  director networks and 204–5
Colombo, M. G. 7, 380
Columbia University 49
Colville, I. D. 147, 154
Combined Code of Corporate Practice (UK) 137, 148, 189, 282, 283, 360, 544
  see also Corporate Governance Code
commercial banks 508 n.(5), 581, 595
  city 598
  large 597
commercialization 371
Commissioner of Tax Exempt and Government Entities (US) 621
committed capital 515, 519, 520
Committee on Corporate Governance, *see* Hampel Report
committees:
  anti-fraud 109
  bankruptcy 496
  creditor 564
  equity 490
  equity 564
  shareholder 493
  unsecured creditor 490, 575
  see also board committees; subcommittees
common law 28–9, 377, 519, 640
communist-bloc countries (former) 116, 120, 121, 125
communist parties 88, 477, 637
Companies Act (UK 2006) 138, 636

Company Law 273
comparative advantage 284, 434, 647
comparative disadvantage 372
compensation 9, 234, 440
  basis for setting 5
  benchmarks for 235
  cash 230, 232, 233, 236, 238, 432
  contentious issue of 13
  depends primarily on performance 566
  entrepreneurial incentive 527
  equity-based 54, 214, 239, 378
  extra 206
  high 479
  incentive-based 451
  indexing 238
  influence on performance of multinational firms 453
  institutional investor 521
  link is weaker between performance and 582
  linking to firm performance 374
  long-term 230
  more aligned with shareholder interests after M&As 232
  more likely based on incentives 452
  non-equity 223
  performance-based 566
  relating cash flow measures to 233
  role of debt in 234
  stock option 223, 235
  type received by board members 373
  variability of 231
  VC arrangements 520
  visible incentive 70
  weighted 230
  see also executive compensation; managerial compensation; *also under following entries prefixed* "compensation"
compensation committees 48, 237, 240, 282
  CEO labor markets and 235
  composition of 185, 186
  GAAP bent to preserve CEO compensation 233
  managerial capture of 185
  overlapping of audit committee and 190
  presence of significant shareholders on 185

compensation mix 431–2
compensation packages:
    major mistake in design of 374–5
    typical 282
    various aspects of 400
competition policy 342, 351
competitive advantage 253, 543
    managerial firm as basis for 351
competitive strategies 247
competitiveness 359, 455, 685, 688
    international 646
    reduced 294, 662
complementarities 18, 646, 694, 713
    institutional 30
compliance 36, 37–8, 138, 310, 312, 315, 321, 357, 622, 725
    legal and regulatory 314
    nonprofits 609, 612
    ritualistic 309, 321
    standard of 14
    testing 314
comply-or-explain principle 26, 36, 37, 38, 110, 138, 322
computer software 141
conflicts of interest 99, 108, 368, 570, 577, 619, 636
    anxieties amongst labor representatives 641–2
    avoiding 138
    incremental market-based responses can mitigate 359
    many institutional investors face 566
    outsiders with 188
    potential 247, 566, 578, 660
    shareholders and managers 658
conglomerates 58, 159 n.(4)
    internal capital markets in 368
    state-owned, full control of 600
Connelly, B. L. 5, 247, 248, 252, 253, 262, 456, 613, 676, 697
consequences 78, 238–9, 273
    contextually bounded 26–7, 32
    deleterious 593
    disastrous 595
    distributional, important 30
    inevitable 277
    intended 5

performance 663
positive 5
potentially undesirable 342
PP conflicts 662
separation of ownership and control 6, 330
unintended 32, 239–40
wage and employment, LBOs 551
Considine, M. 612
contingency theory 617, 618, 623
contractual governance 393, 395, 400, 403, 405, 407, 516–19, 522–6
    and family effects in privately-held firms 401–2
    non-contractual vs 531–4
    relationship between relational and 408, 409, 411, 412
control mechanisms:
    external 659, 662
    internal 659, 662, 666
    public and private 665
    see also control rights; family control; internal control; market for corporate control; ownership and control; private benefits of control; strategic control
control of controls 309
control rights 293, 490, 516, 531
    adopting more 550
    allocation of 496, 530
    cash-flow rights and 468, 473, 474, 516, 522, 529, 532, 533, 534, 665
    concentrated 468
    dispersed 468
    equity 491, 492, 493
    family ties allow founding family to abuse 479
    formal and informal 9, 489, 494
    high level of 476
    limited 503
    most effective 523
    senior lender 499–501
    various ways in which exercised 634
controlling shareholders 11, 34–5, 290, 294, 475, 476, 598, 658, 669
    aligning the interests of 478, 480
    capital markets vs 72
    coalitions to take actions against 667

conflicts between managers and 478, 479, 660
family 390, 476
government as 663
identity of 664, 668
incentives of 659, 667
independence of directors from 111–12
intangible private benefits 662
maximizing own interests 480
opportunistic behavior of 665
ownership and control concentrated in 661
private benefits of control 293, 659
strong economic incentive to diversify 663
tunneling by 472–3
typically considered root cause of PP conflicts 666
Conyon, M. J. 180, 185, 186, 216, 237, 648
Cooke, T. E. 299, 303 n.(1), 398
Coombe, John 210
coordinated market economies, see Germany; Japan
coordination costs 372
coordination problems 108, 501
 multiple lenders 555
 small shareholders 99
coparcenary principle 668
Core, J. 208
Cornelli, F. 544, 549–50
Cornforth, C. 608, 610, 614, 617
corporate control market, see market for corporate control
Corporate Director's Guidebook 49
Corporate Flexibility Act (California 2012) 621
corporate governance:
 auditing and 308–27
 boards and 135–62
 business groups 465–88
 comparative 23–45
 corporate control market and 331–4
 corporate social responsibility and 1, 12, 719–44
 database of 102
 director networks 206–9
 disclosure and 6, 298–300
 emerging perspective on 673–702

evolution of regimes 100–2
executive compensation and 222–45
failures 5, 703–18
family business and 389–420
financial distress and bankruptcy 489–512
financial leverage and 269–89
financial reporting, disclosure and 290–308
hard and soft law in 35–8
hedge fund activism and 564–80
high-tech firms 365–88
history of 2–3, 46–64
important dimension of 5
insider model in liberal market economies 30
institutional shareholders "find" 52–4
international index 97–131
internationalization 56–8, 449–64
IPOs 421–48
labor and 11, 634–57
life-cycle of 6–9, 349–64, 366
multinational firms and 449–64
multiple agency theory and 673–702
national institutions and 17–18
new financial landscape 12–15
nonprofits and 11, 607–33
ownership interests, incentives and conflicts 246–68
PP conflicts and 11, 658–72
private equity, leveraged buyouts and 539–63
reduced confidence in quality of 1
reform of 50–2
regulation of 2–3, 23–45, 99–110, 234–5
risk management and 15–17
strategy and stakeholders 10–12
venture capital and 515–38
 see also contractual governance; governance mechanisms; international governance; relational governance
Corporate Governance Code (UK) 203
corporate strategy 233–4
corporatism 76, 84, 87
 see also Germany; Japan; Netherlands
CORPRO (panel of lawyers) 51

corruption 253, 436
  large-scale 710
  made possible 709
  systemic 709
cost of capital 100, 295, 304 n.(4)
  bidder's concerns about 128
  decreased 378
  directly influenced 293
  higher 300
  increasing 368, 377
  lower 377
  reduced 293
courts 8, 50, 53, 73, 113
  commercial 70
  last resort 338
  effectiveness of 114
covenants 520, 529–31
  flexibility in application of 546
  less common 518
  looser 553
  restrictive 492, 497, 500, 516–17, 519
  risk of breaching 515
  stringent 500
  violated 493, 497, 499, 500
Cox, J. 492
Cox, P. 676, 735
Craighead, J. A. 236, 237
cramdown plan 490, 493
creative destruction 353, 358, 359
credit facilities 499
Credit Lyonnais v Pathe Communications (Delaware 1991) 495, 507 n.(2)
credit markets 714
creditor control 504, 506
  prevalence of 507
creditor rights protection 120–2, 301
  regulatory provisions aimed at 113
creditors 270, 273, 492, 493, 496, 542
  agency problems between shareholders and 98
  attempt by owners to defraud 286 n.(7)
  conflicts between interests of equity holders and 489
  debt-financing risks to 272
  duty to 495
  junior 491, 495, 501–3, 555, 576
  key resource providers for the firm. 690
  major 574
  outside 272
  oversecured 506
  potential conflict between hedge fund shareholders and 565
  secured 506, 508 n.(10), 555
  secured 688
  senior 9, 490, 491, 494, 496–501
  strengthening of rights in bankruptcy 572
  subordinated 555
  substitute mechanisms to protect 490
  unsecured 508 n.(9), 573–4, 575, 688
creditors-turn-shareholders strategy 574, 575
Crespi, R. 99
Cressy, R. 548, 550
critical vendors 504, 507, 508 n.(9)
Croatia 116
Croce, Annalisa 7
Cronqvist, H. 649
Crosby, James 210
cross-country differences 398, 530
cross-cultural differences 397
cross-ownership 263
cross-section regression 436
cross-shareholding 368, 466, 470–1, 473, 474, 478, 479, 480
  regulatory restrictions on 104
cross-subsidization 8, 466, 473–4
  decrease in performance by group affiliates due to 472
  extensive 480
  R&D 707
Crouch, C. 713
Cruz, C. 398
CSR (corporate social responsibility) 1, 2, 12, 59, 676, 719–44
  issuance of standalone reports 303
Cuervo-Cazurra, A. 31, 36, 163, 171, 475, 720
Cullinan, C. P. 190
cultural distance 456
  incentive-based compensation positively associated with 451
cultural factors 369, 391, 392, 396, 398, 451
  national heritage 472
  potential differences 399
  shared 455, 457

Cumming, D. 9, 519, 520, 521, 526, 527, 528, 529, 530–1, 532, 533, 534 n.(2), 547, 548, 550, 571
Cuomo, F. 171
Curtis, E. 315
Cuyvers, L. 208

Daewoo Group 470
Dahiya, S. 499
Dahl, R. 78
Dahya, J. 332, 334, 339
Dai, Na 10, 567, 571, 592
Daily, C. M. 372, 392, 403, 405, 411, 413 n.(4), 422, 423, 430, 431, 433, 460, 678, 687, 694
Daily, D. M. 135, 142, 151, 186, 224
Dalton, C. R. 135, 142, 151
Dalton, D. R. 247, 248, 255, 403, 429, 430, 431, 449, 458, 466, 694
Dalziel, T. 373, 406, 428
Dam, L. 735
Danish firms, *see* Denmark
Datta, S. 233, 238
D'Aveni, R. A. 206, 428, 430, 687, 694
David, P. 227, 247, 675, 737
Davies Report (UK 2012) 189
Davila, A. 238, 301
Davila, F. 230
Davis, B. 602 n.(3)
Davis, G. 206, 207
Davis, G. F. 471
Davis, S. 548, 551
Dawson, Jo 210
DBIS (UK Department of Business, Innovation and Skills) 159 n.(5)
De Villiers, C. 726, 730
Deakin, S. 636
Deal Decade (1980s) 52
Deb, Palash 5
Debenhams 540
Debicki, B. J. 389
debt:
    actions favoring equity over 495
    arrangements designed to hide 284
    asset sales associated with reductions 498–9
    may be incentivized to recover 358
    collateralized 375
    commitment to service 359
    convertible 523, 527, 528, 531, 550
    deceptive financial reporting methods that hide 271
    defaultable 492
    distressed 502, 564, 572
    excessive 271
    innovation and 375, 376
    leverage opportunities of 269
    liquid 708
    long-term, reselling 686
    misuse of resources made more difficult by 375
    mitigating incentives and attractiveness of 270
    outstanding 564
    overreliance for corporate investment initiatives 269
    prepetition 572
    PTP transactions sometimes financed by 335
    public 498
    reliance on, for buyouts 645
    rendered liquid through securitization 708
    restricted availability of 553
    restructuring 497
    role in compensation 234
    secured 540–1, 573, 709
    senior 573
    strong negative relationship between R&D spending and 376
    unrecoverable 272
    unsecured 502
    use in funding LBOs 547
    voluntary restructurings 498
    see also DIP; *also under following entries prefixed* "debt"
debt-to-assets ratio 571
debt bonding 542, 546
debt-equity swaps 358, 359, 554, 574
debt-financing 272, 277, 278, 283, 284, 286 n.(9), 328, 542
    excessive 274
    less dependence on 360
    leverage from using 274
    mix of equity and 350

debt-financing (*cont.*)
　risk arising from the use of 278
　risky business investments with 270
debt guarantees 474
debt-oriented codes 113
debtor-in-possession financing 690
Dechow, P. 234
decision-making process 166–7, 405, 608, 641, 660
　autonomy in 474
　board 279–82, 611
　clearer hierarchy between board and top management 411
　constrained 676
　decentralized in relation to CSR 730
　discretion in 469
　early-stage investors' incentive to be involved in 435
　employees provided with voice in 637
　group affiliates, control over 470
　imperatives for 723
　operational 412, 532
　perception of uncertainty and constraints 457
　transparency in 438
　see also strategic decision-making
decision rights 103, 108, 111, 117, 118, 119, 124, 477, 516
　formal 641
　state-owned business groups decentralize 469
Dedman, E. 38
Deeg, R. 713, 722
default policy 492
Delaware 51, 85–7, 495, 503–4
DeLong, J. B. 73
Deloof, Marc 6
demand 455, 608
　declining 454
　saturated 454
　uncertainty of 275–6
demand shocks 329
DeMarzo, P. M. 620
Demb, A. 166–7
Demiroglu, C. 543, 554
Democrat states (US) 14
demographic variables 169, 188, 189, 191

Demsetz, H. 246, 252, 337
Denis, D. K. 54, 56
Denmark 368, 530
Dent, G. W. 52
dependent variables 405
depreciation policies 277
depression (1930s) 295
deregulation 23, 26, 136
derivatives 566, 578
　privately negotiated 564, 576
　see also equity swaps
Desbrières, P. 549
Deutsche Bank 201, 578
Deutsche Börse 564
Deutsch, Y. 164
development banks 581, 584, 591
Devers, C. E. 238
Devos, E. 207
Dewenter, K. L. 594, 601
Dewick, P. 368
Dhaliwal, D. 303
Dharwadkar, R. 227, 730, 736
Dhillon, U. 508 n.(7)
Dikolli, S. S. 227
DIP (debtor-in-possession) financing 490, 499–500, 504, 506, 508 nn.(7/12)
　majority providers of 574
director networks 4, 200–21
　see also multiple directorships
directors:
　Act that requires to promote success of the company 636
　advancing personal careers 471
　changes in roles, relationships and conduct 145–51
　external 402
　fiduciary duties of 428
　FTSE (100) 136
　incentives of 285 n.(5)
　inside 357, 429
　mutual exchange of 211
　non-national 453
　outside 182, 207, 208, 402, 403, 404–5, 429, 451, 456, 457
　owner 637
　pay ratcheted up 2458
　responsibilities to shareholders 271

restrictions imposed on length of contracts 103
selection process 47, 103, 188, 189, 191
shared 206, 210
top, base salaries 431
worker 642
see also affiliate directors; boards of directors; finance directors; independent directors; NEDs; SIDs
disclosure 25, 48, 70, 100, 109, 273, 519, 602 n.(3)
  accounting 277
  audit process 322–3
  benefits of 292–4
  biased 294
  cash-flow forecasts issued by management 495
  closely-held companies and 300–2
  compensation 234
  costs of 291, 294
  demands for 290, 291, 295
  enforcing strict requirements 103
  extensive 664
  family firm 299, 404, 405
  frequent 676
  geographic earnings 298
  help to improve levels of 14
  interim 179
  irrevocable commitments 340
  mandatory 292, 296, 297, 332
  mediator of information across multiple user constituencies 621
  ownership 31, 33
  private knowledge 435
  risk 16
  selective 297, 303 n.(1)
  strong powers to ensure 296
  transparent and perceptive 291
  voting and cash flow rights 112
  see also voluntary disclosure
disclosure regulation 6, 15
  more strict 117
  national 291
  need for 295–8
discretionary accruals 404
Disraeli, Benjamin 269, 285 n.(1)
distressed firms 8

hedge funds and 501, 564, 565, 567, 570
  activism targeting 571–6
  characteristics of 573
  restructuring 9
  role of 502
  see also financial distress
distributional differences 78
Dittmann, I. 236
diversification 230, 233, 235, 238, 329, 353, 358, 449
  intrafamily rivalry increases the chances of 688
  lack of, in manager's portfolio 370
  market 350, 357
  portfolio-style 357
  positive effect on strategies 405
  product 350, 357
  see also overdiversification
divestment 247
  refocusing through 353
dividends 351, 491, 541, 687
  double 571
  payouts remain low 357
  pre-specified 522
  special 358, 645
divisional buyouts 543, 545, 549
Djankov, S. 97, 100, 129 n.(2), 253, 707
Dobbin, F. 54
Dodd-Frank Act (US 2010) 1, 29, 37, 229
Doherty, J. W. 504, 505, 506, 508 n.(11)
Dollinger, C. M. 405
Dooley, P. 204, 205
dot.com boom/collapse 59, 137, 141
Douglas, W. O. 69
Douthwaite. S. 622
Dow, J. 233
downsizing 349, 358, 360, 714
  pressure toward 707
Doz, Y. L. 450, 457
Drerup, T. 571
Duddy, Terry 210, 211
due diligence 340, 516
Dumenil, G. 712, 713
dummy variable approach 209, 397
Dunn, A. 621
Durisin, B. 55, 142, 164
Duru, A. 233
Dutch matters, *see* Netherlands

Dwyer, R. 712
Dyer, W. G. 396, 398, 399, 736

early childhood support programs 610
earnings-based metrics 270
East Asia 87
　funds based in 584
　see also China; Hong Kong; Japan; Korea; Taiwan
East India Company 46
Easterbrook, F. H. 51, 52, 55
Easterly, W. 77, 92 n.(13)
Eastern Airlines 492
Eastern Europe, see Central and Eastern Europe
Easterwood, J. C. 546, 547, 549, 552
Eberhart, A. C. 493
EBIT (earnings before interest and tax) 274, 275, 276, 277, 286 n.(11)
Eckbo, B. E. 491, 494, 500, 506, 508 n.(11)
Ecoles Polytechniques 204
econometric techniques 217
economic growth:
　law and 97
　long-term 101
　lower 100
economic rationality 67
economics 246, 248, 540
　see also transaction costs
economies of scale 273
　external characteristics 354
economists 54–6
Economist, The 54, 57
Eddleston, K. A. 407, 408
Edström, A. 451
Ehrhardt, O. 398
Eichengreen, B. 90, 93 n.(23)
Eisenberg, Melvin 49
Eisenberg, T. 504
electronic equipment 140
Elenkov, D. 231
elites 710
　financial 703
　reallocation of resources to 712
　see also business elites
Ellemers, N. 389, 406

Elson, A. 51
emerging economies 253, 664
　concentrated ownership 468
　family owners dominate minority owners in 675
　PP conflicts in M&A deals 663
　PP conflicts often found in 658
　tunneling in business groups 473
employees 252
　direct participation 638
　disclosure of information by managers to 643
　government 582
　impact of buyout on 550–1
　implications for 639
　implicit coalition between managers and 81
　interests of 636
　involvement in governance processes 641–4
　key, retention plans 575
　long-term promises to 647
　mechanisms to incentivize and control 310
　negative impact on remuneration 540
　non-family 396
　number of 232
　predominantly market relationships with firm 639
　specialized 273
　voice in corporate decision-making 637
employment 273
　average reduction in distressed firms 503
　characteristics typically associated with corporate governance regimes 647
　continued 667
　expansion of 646
　increased 549
　internal labor market reduces managers' risks 465
　long-term 647, 650
　net loss in gains 693
　positive effects of buyouts on practices 551
　positive impact on 550
　post-merger 692
　pressures having significant effects on 646
　prioritization of goals 582

restructuring that negatively impacts on 540
short-term 647
showing how governance can affect 11
white-collar 648
see also labor
employment contracts 636
empty voting 564, 577
ENA *(Ecole Nationale d'Administration)* 204
endogeneity 208, 216, 369, 372, 531
endowments 254, 686
Eng, L. L. 298, 299
Engelberg, J. 207–8, 214
Engerman, S. L. 75, 77, 92 n.(11)
England 77, 116, 117, 118, 121, 124, 125
and Wales 613
Enriques, L. 27, 28, 34, 35
Enron 38, 59, 137, 171, 246, 273, 281, 291, 295, 308, 309, 312, 315, 317, 318, 709, 710
cited as success story 798
Ensley, M. D. 406, 407, 408
entrepreneurship 7, 9, 254, 351, 356, 422, 540, 608, 678
associational 616, 622
Austrian notions of 353
buyouts may create opportunities 376
disputes between venture capital investors and 374
financial support for profitable initiatives 545
governance and 543–4
habitual 354
IPOs and 421
key functions 355
managerial 350, 549
new mindset 693
portfolio 354
role of boards in gaining access to knowledge that enhances 608
Schumpeterian 357
serial 354, 359
social 614
strategic 543–4
venture capital and 516–18, 521–34
see also CE
environmental fit 617–20

EPA (US Environmental Protection Agency) 725
EPO (European Patent Office) 549
EPS (earnings per share) 278, 286 n.(8)
improvement of 341
equal treatment principle 31, 33, 110, 112, 119
Equitable Life 137
equity finance 355
equity swaps:
growth in 564, 576
long 578
short 576
typical 576
see also debt-equity swaps
Ernst, H. 379
Ernst & Young 315
Erturk, I. 704, 708, 710, 711, 712, 713, 714
ESL Investments Inc. 572
ESMA (European Securities and Markets Authority) 159 n.(5), 291
European Securities and Markets Authority
ESO (executive share option) 432
Espenlaub, S. 421
ESRC (Economic and Social Research Council) 4, 135, 154, 158 n.(1)
estimation risk 292
Estrin, S. 377
ethics:
accountability and 309
audit quality and 316–19
professional 317
fractionalization 77
ethnicity 78
EU (European Union) 14–15, 26, 36, 261
accession countries 116, 117, 119, 121, 124
competition authorities 342
Corporate Governance Code 141
family ownership estimates for unlisted firms 390
listed companies required to have audit committee 317
regulatory reforms 32, 33
Transparency Directive (2007) 295
Euronext 303 n.(3), 564
Europe 722
banks in 82
corporate VC contracts 528

Europe (cont.)
  geography over the centuries 88–9
  hedge fund activism 571
  labor in 79, 82
  LBO transactions 539
  low prominence of shareholder value in social democracies 30
  most listed firms are closely-held 110
  non-market forms of coordination prevalent in 378
  regulatory provisions in all countries 98
  retailing initiatives 725
  significant increases in stock prices 547
  stakeholder-based regime 114
  understaffing of stock market regulatory agencies 29
  venture capital funds 534 n.(1)
  see also Central and Eastern Europe; Western Europe
European Commission 38, 296, 318
  Expert Group on Family Business 412 n.(1)
  Green Paper on Audit Policy (2010) 319, 322
European Corporate Governance Institute 36
European Parliament 14
Eurozone crisis 141
ExecuComp firms 225, 231, 232, 236
executive compensation/pay/remuneration 11, 16, 36, 37, 53, 56, 57, 59, 222–45, 247, 282–3, 367, 375, 451, 452, 664–5
  concerns and anger regarding 13
  development of schemes 422
  ever-increasing 149
  high 79, 720
  institutional investor pressure on decision-makers 5
  IPOs 430–1
  level and structure of 5
  long-term incentives 431–2
  major mistake in the design of packages 374–5
  performance, leverage and earnings-based 274–9
  seriously limited as solution to problems 374
  steeply rising 649
  subject to greater scrutiny 13
  trade unions on the topic of 649
  tying to creditor wealth 497
  see also CEO pay/compensation
executive entrenchment 398, 399, 405
executive ethics 238
executive search companies 439
executives:
  C-level 248
  dysfunctional "corporate autocracy" oriented around 48
  escalation in salaries 229
  fiduciary obligations 689
  increasing proportions of non-family 410–11
  making strategic decisions 246–7
  maximizing option gains due to underpricing 433
  need for recruitment and retention of talent 431
  performance of 191, 592
  powerful 51
  protecting shareholders from self-interested whims of 142
  senior 49, 282
  separating non-executives and 109
  strong preference for particular candidates 190
  tendency to extract private benefits 374
  top 47, 57, 564, 649
  vast rewards 440
  see also CEOs
exit orientation 436
expectations 73, 83, 178, 330, 332, 337, 723
  audit 313
  CEO-chairman 146
  demands and 724
  downward spiral in 270
  overly optimistic 270
  performance 16, 736
  populist 613
  public 313
  social 738
  TMT 145
  unrealistic 270
  unreasonable 322

expropriation 476, 482
  accomplished though legal or illegal means 662
  external investors 479
  illicit 473
  minority shareholders 99, 122, 397, 398, 473, 478, 659, 661, 666, 667, 668
external audit 6, 183, 179, 180, 181, 185, 191, 308, 310–11, 313, 319
  appointment and reappointment of external auditors 317
  listed companies required to have books audited by 109
  oversight of 183, 318
  relationship between internal and 183
  scope of 312
external governance mechanisms 6, 7, 11, 366–7, 377–9
  key 328
  new 335
  strong 666
externalities 297
Exxon Mobil 201
Ezzamel, M. 185, 186, 235, 272, 280, 282, 285, 334

Faccio, M. 99, 662, 664, 666–7
Facebook 303
Fagerberg, J. 377
Fama, E. F. 51, 55, 99, 177, 247, 273, 328, 333, 389, 421, 430, 432, 661, 726
family business 8, 163, 252–3, 261, 311, 389–420, 430, 468, 476, 478–9
  disclosure in 299
family buyouts 543, 545, 549
family control 398, 480
  aligns interests of managers and controlling shareholders 478
  incentive alignment hypothesis 401
  publicly listed firms 390, 391, 395
  spreading risk without diluting 468
Fang, Y. 454
Farber, D. B. 237
Farmer, R. E. A. 534 n.(3)

FASB (US Financial Accounting Standards Board) 222, 234, 286 n.(9), 291, 297, 303 n.(3), 311
fascist regimes 638
fault-line theory 170
FDI (foreign direct investment) 456
FDIC (Federal Deposit Insurance Corporation) 202
Federal Register 47
Federal Reserve 80, 593
  Regulation Y 508 n.(5)
feedback loops 646
FEEM (Monitor Group and Fondazione Eni Enrico Mattei) 583, 584
Fennema, M. 205
Fernandes, N. G. 594, 601
Fernández-Rodríguez, E. 38
Feroz, E. H. 178
Ferruzzi 58
Festing, M. 451
Fey, C. F. 454
FFB (family-backed) firms 402
Fich, E. 208
fiduciary duty 28, 428, 493, 495–6, 551, 642, 689
  breach of 569
Fiegener, M. K. 400, 401
Filatotchev, I. 6, 7, 8, 39 n., 142, 164, 349, 350, 354, 358, 359, 360, 366, 376, 381, 393, 423, 433, 436, 437, 438, 439, 451, 456, 457, 458, 482, 660, 662, 668, 669, 691, 695, 696
finance directors 148, 180
  relationship between CEO and 145
financial choices 234
financial crisis (2007–9) 1, 5, 9, 12–13, 15, 59, 308, 309, 321, 539, 553, 579 n.(1), 709, 715, 720
financial distress 493, 495, 502
  failure to fulfill debt obligation can lead to 543
  impact of buyout on 553–5
  interaction of governance and 503
  managers frequently lose their jobs in 8, 494
  PE firms not deterred by risk of 548
  senior lender control in 496–9
  severe 498

financial institutions 139, 201, 206, 272, 704,
    712, 736
  centralized 67, 71
  connections through common
    directors 203
  considerable shareholdings via indirect
    stockholdings 477
  DIP financing 574
  interlocks via 205
  large, systemically significant 322
  managers encouraged to collude
    with 706
  preferences of 731
  rules governing 351
  voting power 34
  wary of taking risks in lending 539
Financial Institutions' Committee 572
financial instruments:
  complex 324
  illiquid, audit of fair valuation of 321
  intrinsic risk characteristics of 291
  very complicated 715
financial intermediaries 12, 273, 711
financial life-cycle 351-3
financial metrics 223
financial performance 7, 10, 164, 165, 170, 182,
    186, 352, 405, 409
  affiliates 469
  family effects that predict 411
  family ownership in publicly listed
    firms 396-8
  innovations over short term should not be
    valued using 375
  measured in terms of key ratios 350
  monitoring by non-managing owners may
    create interference in improving 410
  negative effect in family-controlled
    firms 404
  observable measures of 529
  poor 253, 339
  privately-held, family and non-family
    firms 408
  short-term 374-5
  weaker following emergence 504
  widely-held firms 404
financial politics 65-96
financial reporting 5, 171, 281, 286 n.(9)

audit committees ineffective in
  controlling 184
confidence in 295
deceptive 271, 278
disclosure and corporate
  governance 290-308
firms make choices about 234
frequency of 110
incentive to monitor management and 179
integrity of 181
major impact in global companies 137
manipulation of 280
new forms of 320
nonprofits' compliance with standards 612
optimal outcome in the market for 301
financial reporting (cont.)
  oversight of quality 182-3
  plethora of regulations 273
  standardized obligations 291
  strategies and choices 274
  uncovering and resolving potential
    problems in 180
financial returns:
  encouraged emphasis on 640
  lower 663
financial risk 274
  assessing 284
  corporate equity insufficient to
    absorb 273
  differences in 278
  hidden 5
  high 5
  increasing 277-8
  lower 170
Financial Services Modernization Act (US
    1999) 508 n.(5)
Financial Stability Board (UK) 138
Financial Times 57
financialization 12, 703-18
Finkelstein, S. 163, 164, 223, 229, 231, 235, 430
Finland 119, 454
fire-sale problem 501, 505-6, 508 n.(13)
firm characteristics 232-3
firm size 232
  increasing 273
first-past-the-post systems 84
Firth, M. 664, 667

Fischel, D. R. 51, 52
Fischer, E. O. 492
Fischer, H. M. 223
Fiss, P. C. 248, 441
fixed costs 276, 277
flexibility 396, 545, 546, 564, 684
  evolutionary model based on 410
  internal 650
Fligstein, N. 207
Flint, D. 308, 310, 311, 316
Flören, R. H. 413 n.(3)
Florida 139
Folkman, P. 715
Forbes, D. P. 169, 170
Forbes, W. 285, 287 n.(15)
Ford administration 48
Ford Motors 202
Fordism 704–6, 708, 715
foreclosure 501
foreign exchange reserves 583, 584, 595, 598
foreign subsidiaries 39
  autonomy of 452
  coordination and control of 8, 450, 451–2, 458
  dependence on headquarters 458
  interdependence influences performance of 452
  performance 453, 454
  relationship between MNE headquarters and 457
  sales 455
  strategic position 453
Fortune 500 firms 248
Fortune 1000 companies 165, 170, 189
Foster, G. 301
Foster, J. 712
Fotak, Veljko 10
Foucault, M. 710, 711
foundations 254, 616, 623
  governance of 624
  shocks of rejection by 611
founder effect 396–7, 400, 411
Fox, I. 376
Fox, J. 53
F-PEC scale 392
France 31, 35, 89, 332, 359, 548, 550, 637, 645
  civil law 441

  communist party 88
  conglomerates 58
  director networks 203–4
  employee shareholders 643
  legal origins 116, 118, 119, 120, 121, 124, 125, 530
  state activism 30
  VC investments 436, 530
  women board members 189
Francis, B. B. 436
Francis, J. R. 315, 319, 368
Frankel, R. 294
Franks, J. 73, 93 n.(23), 99, 108, 280, 332, 333, 334, 338, 421, 493
Fransen, L. 725
fraud 109, 239, 272, 286 n.(7), 295, 614, 649
  detection of 309, 313, 314
  leading investment banks 709
  prevention of 313
  reporting 291
  widespread 303 n.(2)
FRC (UK Financial Reporting Council) 36, 57, 137, 138, 149, 151, 181, 203, 284, 312, 319, 322, 324 n.(10)
  Audit Firm Governance Code (2010) 318
  Audit Inspection Unit 318
  Guidelines for Board Effectiveness (2011) 146
  Professional Oversight Board 318
  see also Cadbury Report
Fredrickson, J. W. 230, 233
free-rider problem 6, 72, 273, 285, 330, 340, 471, 566
Freiwirth, J. 616
Fremeth, A. R. 1
French, K. R. 421
Fried, J. M. 223
Friedman, A. 612
Frost, P. 151
Froud, J. 704, 706, 707, 708, 709, 710, 713, 715, 716
Frynas, G. 709–10
Fryxell, G. E. 731
FSA (UK Financial Services Authority) 137–8, 319, 322, 553
  tightening regulation of banks 139

FTSE (Financial Times-Stock Exchange)
    companies 4, 14, 135–62, 203, 217 n.
    women directors 189
fulcrum security 502, 508 n.(4)
functional approach 98
fund managers 14, 254, 522, 523, 529–34, 535
    nn.(6–7), 645, 711
    affiliated 566
    alternative investment 296
    authority regarding investment
        decisions 517–18
    churn encouraged in portfolios 645
    common for pension funds to regularly
        change 645
    compensation policies and status of 584
    contracts between institutional investors
        and 515
    covenants relating to limitation of
        liability 517
    fees 515, 520, 521, 541
    financialization effect of reorienting the
        firm toward satisfying 706
    incentives to generate positive abnormal
        returns 566
    limitation of liability 519
    passive rights that can be exercised by 526
    public pension 371
    reluctant to alienate clients 566
    restrictions on investment powers 518
    risk of breaching contractual covenants 515
    short-term orientation of 371
    unions attempt to build relationships
        with 644
fundamentalist religious beliefs 638
fundraising 609, 620
    internet 621
    standards covering 622
Furu, P. 454
fuzzy sets methodology 647

GAAP (generally accepted accounting
    principles) 178, 228, 233, 297
Gabaix, X. 232–3, 236
Gadhoum, Y. 390
Galbraith, J. K. 710
Galbraith, J. R. 451

Gao Jie 10
García-Meca, E. 299
Garratt, B. 148
Gaspar, J. 548
gatekeepers 310
Gates, Bill 429
Gaved, M. 138–9
Gaya Wicks, P. 735
GDP (gross domestic product) 449
Geczy, C. 421
Gedajlovic, E. 407, 467, 473, 476, 660, 661,
    666, 668
GEEF (European Commission Expert Group
    on Family Business) 412 n.(1)
Geletkanycz, M. A. 235
Gely, R. 86
Gendron, Y. 177, 178, 181, 184, 192
geopolitics 88–9
Georgeson Annual Corporate Governance
    Review (2010) 228–9
Germany 31, 38, 56, 57, 58, 84, 89, 311, 332,
    640, 643, 645, 705
    abolition of deviations from one share-one
        vote standard 32
    agency problems do not typically impact
        on performance for 359
    bank-centered business groups 475
    board representation 642, 649, 696
    boards of directors 32
    civil law 441
    codetermination 29–30, 32, 81, 639, 641
    costly post-unification economic
        adjustments 57
    director networks 203, 204
    effect of hedge fund activism on publicly
        listed companies 571
    elimination of unequal voting rights 35
    emphasis on investment in human
        capital 650
    employee representation on the board
        104, 649
    external quality control 316
    family and non-family firms 408
    fascist and military regimes 638
    feature of acquisitions in 333
    insider governance 639
    IPOs 361 n.(2), 398

legal origins 116, 117, 118, 120, 121, 124, 125, 530
legal reforms designed to promote shareholder value 32
protecting minority shareholder rights 721
rankings of industries by intensity of patent registrations 377–8
regulatory reforms of proxy voting 33–4
statutory works councils 637
training programs 651
uncontested takeovers 333
VC investments 530
works councils 642
see also Comroad; Schröder
Gersick, K. E. 393, 409, 410
Geske, R. 492
Ghoshal, S. 389, 406, 450, 452, 453
Gianecchini, M. 410
Gill, A. 725
Gill, M. 309, 321, 323
Gillan, S. L. 565, 674, 720, 737
Gillies, J. 136
Gilligan, J. 541, 542, 567
Gilson, R. J. 29, 32, 33, 38, 51, 56, 329, 434, 438, 440, 478, 479, 480, 527, 529, 662, 663, 664, 665, 667
Gilson, S. 494, 496, 497, 498, 502
Gingerich, D. 647, 651
Gini coefficients 77, 78
Glass-Lewis 259, 260
Glass-Steagall Act (US 1933) 71, 81, 508 n.(5)
GlaxoWellcome 681
Global Entrepreneurship Monitor 390–1
Global Reporting Initiative standards 735
globalization 26, 31, 452
GM (General Motors) 53, 229, 503, 506
goal alignment 369, 408–9, 457
Goergen, M. 34, 98, 99, 101, 102, 109, 111, 112, 280, 359, 361 n.(2), 551
Goertz, Gary 38
going concerns 322, 324 n.(11)
Golden, B. R. 164
Goldstein, R. 492
Gomez-Mejia, L. R. 233, 235, 238, 252, 253, 389, 390, 398, 401, 432, 662, 664
Gompers, P. A. 246, 255, 421, 429, 433, 434, 435, 436, 438, 516, 517, 522, 526, 529, 679

Goncharov, I. 38
Gong, G. 223
Gong, J. 550
Google 140, 142
  CEO of 262
Goranova, M. 227, 663
Gordon, J. N. 53, 54
Gormley, T. 492
Gort, M. 329
Gospel, H. 11, 634, 638, 643, 644, 645, 648, 652
Gottschalg, O. 550
Gourevitch, P. A. 34, 83
governance mechanisms 3–4, 177, 343, 369, 380, 421, 428, 452, 458
  attitude of management toward 192
  board structure 336
  companies adopt a range of 337
  distinctive 8, 466–70
  formal 8, 531, 532, 533
  heterogeneity of 439
  horizontal 8, 466, 467, 470–2, 475, 478–80
  impact of buyout on 549–50
  incentive-related 359
  ineffective 333
  informal 8, 531, 532, 533
  interventionist and inefficient 253
  last resort 328
  non-contractual 531, 532, 533
  prevailing 466
  processes and 163–76
  relational 408
  reorganization of 360
  vertical 8, 466, 467, 468, 475, 476–8, 479
  weak 541
  see also external governance mechanisms; internal governance mechanisms
government intervention 582, 595, 596
government/state ownership 252, 253, 263
  business groups 8, 466, 477, 479
  developing economies 592
  fairly stable 581
  impact of 298–9, 371, 456
  investment companies/funds 581, 583, 584
  lessons from SWFs for governance and 600–2 see also SOEs
Govindarajan, V. 453

Goyer, Michel 2, 30, 31, 38, 674
GPFG (Norwegian Government Pension Fund-Global) 584, 587, 591, 593
Graebner, M. E. 171, 260, 696
Graham, J. 612–13
Grandes Ecoles 203
Granovetter, M. 208, 214, 465, 472, 476
graph theory 209–14
Graves, S. B. 735
Gray, I. 314, 317
Greckhamer, T. 236
Green, Mark 48
green management practices 1
Greenbury, Sir Richard 57
Greene, S. 602 n.(3)
Greenfield, P. 704
greenfield investments 456, 459
　job creation 551
Greening, D. W. 676, 735
Greenlee, J. 609
greenmail 262, 474
Greenough, W. C. 47, 50
Greenwood, R. 570
Gresham's Law 281
Greve, H. 685
Grinstein, Y. 224–7
Grossman, S. J. 99, 330, 367
group affiliates 8, 473
　control over 467, 468, 470, 478
　cross-subsidization may benefit 474
　decentralizing the decision rights of 469
　exchange of resources and information among 471
　family-controlled 480
　improving the efficiency of 469
　indirect cross-shareholding structures 470
　interdependence and cross-monitoring among 474
　long-term and stable relationships among 472
　multiple long-term relational ties among 465
　mutual commitment and interdependence among 470
　mutual monitoring 466, 471
　performance implications of 482
　resourceful and profitable 466
　sharing of knowledge and resource among 469
　state-owned 477, 478
　strategic control can mitigate against 470
　strong connectedness among 470
　ties among 467, 472
　underperforming 466, 474, 482
　widespread cross-shareholdings among 471
　see also horizontal linkages; vertical linkages
groupthink 151, 168, 279
growth 329, 354–5, 359
　future prospects 351, 356
　low prospects 336, 357
　opportunities for 498
　opportunity for 356, 357
　phases of 349, 353, 356, 357
　poorer prospects 336
　rapid 353, 356
　see also economic growth
Grundfest, J. 72
grupos economicos 465
guanxi qiye 465
Gubitta, P. 410
Guedj, I. 208
Guidelines Monitoring Group 14
Guidestar 621
Gulati, R. 421
Gulbrandsen, M. 373
Guo, R.-J. 294, 301
Guo, S. 549
Gupta, A. K. 373, 453
GUS plc 210
Gutierrez, L. 208
Guttman scale 392

Haber, S. H. 75
Hadass, L. 436
Hail, L. 303 n.(1)
Haleblian, J. 353
Hall, B. H. 375, 376, 378
Hall, B. J. 238–9
Hall, P. 647, 651
Hall, P. A. 93 n.(21), 722
Hallock, K. 207

Halpern, P. 336, 339
Hambrick, D. C. 135, 142, 143, 163, 421
Hampel Report (UK 1998) 57, 287 n.(14)
Handelsbank group 471
Haniffa, R. M. 299, 303 n.(1), 398
Hansmann, H. 102–3, 636
Harford, J. 225
Harianto, I. 207
Harris, D. 232
Harris, R. 548
Harrow, Jenny 11, 610–11, 610, 614, 619, 620, 622
Hart, O. 36, 99, 330, 367, 491, 531, 543
Hartaska, V. 619
Harvey, D. 712
Hasan, I. 436
Haunschild, P. 206–7
Haynes, M. 360
Hayward, M. L. A. 680
HBOS (Halifax-Bank of Scotland) 209
He, L. 185
hedge funds 9, 10, 137, 139, 230, 255, 258, 262, 296, 501–2, 564–80, 581, 592, 652, 686, 690
  alleged impact on asset-stripping and short-termism 13
  claims commonly acquired and consolidated by 501
  directional or momentum strategy 645–6
  directional trading strategies 645–6
  impact felt primarily in listed, public companies 645
  potential to influence boards 567
  role in distressed firms 502
  short-term initiatives 259
Hedlund, G. 451
Hegarty, W. H. 253
Heinz (J.J.) 564
Heinze, T. 203
Helfat, C. 232
Hellman, T. 352, 371
Henderson, A. D. 230, 233
Hendry, C. 186–7
Henokiens 413 n.(2)
herd-like behavior 149, 270, 281
Hessen, R. 52
Higgins, M. 421

Higgs Review (UK 2003) 137, 148, 179, 180, 190, 191, 203, 287 n.(14)
high-tech firms 7, 365–88
Higson, A. 314
Hill, C. W. 368
Hill, S. 167
Hillegeist, S. 235
Hillman, A. J. 372, 373, 406, 428
Hillman, A. J. 730
Himmelberg, C. P. 248
Hippel, T. von 608, 621
Hirano, Hidekazu 258
Hirshleifer, D. 374
Hirst, P. 705, 706
Hitt, M. A. 458, 469
HLTs (highly leveraged transactions) 492–3
Ho, S. S. 398
Hobson, J. 712
Hochberg, Y. 208, 436
Hoff, K. 75
Hogg, Sir Christopher 138
holding companies 600
Holl, P. 341
Hollinger 281
Holmstrom, B. 54, 370, 374
Home Retail Group plc 210
Hong Kong 397, 398, 401, 404, 661
  business groups 471, 473
Hong Kong Stock Exchange 299, 599
Hope, O.-K. 298
Hopt, K. J. 608, 621
Hopwood, A. G. 308
horizon problem 232
horizontal linkages 467
  extensive 479
Hornby, Andy 203, 209–10
Hoskisson, R. E. 5, 12, 246, 253, 254, 259, 350, 370–1, 372, 376, 441, 469, 475, 477, 660, 674, 675, 682, 695, 697
hostile takeovers 6, 86, 332–4, 337, 648
  disruptions of 79–80
  downsizing to discourage 714
  friendly vs 33
  managers seek laws that impede or bar 72
  non-hostile and 329, 338, 339, 341, 342
  opposed 83
  poison pill to deter 53

hostile takeovers (cont.)
  successfully resisted 341
  threat of 108, 330–1, 336, 378
Hotchkiss, E. S. 8, 491, 494, 495, 496, 501, 554, 555
Hough, A. 619
Houston Exploration 564
HPWP (high-performance work practices) 551
HRM (human resource management) 540, 638
Hsu, D. H. 371
Hu, H. T. C. 576, 577
Huafang, X. 298, 299
hubris 329
Hudson's Bay Company 46
Hughes, Penny 211
human capital 707
  firm-specific 650, 651
  long-term investments in 650
human resource development 646
  see also HRM
Humphrey, C. 313
Hunt, R. 540
Huntington, S. P. 76
Huse, M. 136
Hutton, A. 234
Hutton, W. 646
Hwang, B. 214
hybridization 714
  facing up to 607–33

IASB (International Accounting Standards Board) 286 n.(9), 291, 303 n.(3), 311
IBM 53
IBOs (investor-led buyouts) 551
ICAEW (Institute of Chartered Accountants of England and Wales) 137
Icahn, Carl 263
ICBC (Industrial and Commercial Bank of China) 596, 598, 599
Iceland 119
identity of owners 369–71
IFAC (International Federation of Accountants) 11, 313, 314, 315, 324 n.(11)
  International Auditing Practices Committee 315

IFRS (International Financial Reporting Standards 8) 297
illiquidity 321, 435, 520, 531, 566
imperfect markets 453
Inc.500 first-generation firms 408
incentives 179, 223, 227, 246–68, 285 n.(5), 370, 371, 373, 436, 451, 492, 567, 592, 660
  additional risk 232
  agent-principal 310
  aligned 225, 520, 541
  assessment of 271
  auditor 317
  bank 477
  compensation more likely based on 452
  controlling shareholder 659, 667
  cross-monitoring free-riding behaviors 471
  derived from family membership 401
  direct, for top management 328
  disclosure that will reduce competitive position 294
  economic 582, 663
  effect associated with managerial wealth gains 360
  entrepreneurial 545
  equity 185
  equity-linked 374
  excessive risk-taking 491
  executive 421
  explicit, agents do not need 369
  financial 542, 543
  government employees lack 582
  high-powered 374
  highly leveraged 274
  incumbent large shareholders 547
  insufficiently strong 271
  investment 489
  leverage 494
  long-term 178, 282, 374, 375, 431–2, 440, 453, 649
  micro-level 291
  misalignment of 358, 435
  misleading outside investors 272
  mitigating 270
  non-disclosure 298
  optimal 375
  ownership 236, 252, 273

pay for top managers 648
performance-based 393
possibility to reduce 284
reduced 474
short-term 375
small investors in follow-on rounds of financing 368
straight equity 374
strategic control provides for group affiliates 469
strong 272, 574, 663, 692
stronger mechanisms 335
sufficient to pursue innovation 371
systems for top managers influence knowledge sharing 454
tax 725
threat of takeover provides 334
tradeoff between liquidity and 368
see also managerial incentives
independent directors 31, 48, 111–12, 271, 400–1, 439
may improve extent and quality of monitoring 423
part-time 274
positively related to FDI 456
presence in non-family firms 404
role may vary between family and non-family firms 403
see also SIDs
India 90
business houses 465, 473, 482
see also Satyam
individualism 398
Indjejikian, R. J. 230, 231
Indonesia 468, 661–2
industrial relations 551, 642, 648, 651–2, 653
external flexibility in 30
literatures 637
showing how governance can affect 11
industrial revolution 77
inequality 77–9
income 737
information advantages 342
information asymmetries 290, 299, 310, 356, 421–8
assumption that disclosures would only be able to solve 300

imperfect markets cause 453
increased benefits of management ownership concentration 370
IPO underpricing and 678
news which directly mitigates 296–7
reducing 292, 300, 303, 435
information flows 641
fostering 381
private, between firms and banks 294
information risk 292
inheritance 668
innovation 365, 714
CEO's short-term compensation is related to 375
costs of financing investments 378
debt and 375, 376
development of 367
effect of acquisitions on 379
external 371
fundamental ingredient in 379
growing narrative on 709
incremental 376, 378
influences on 377
internal 675
long-term-oriented strategies 378
market-oriented 376
motivating 375
negative effect of acquisitions on 379
openness a characteristic of 380–1
organizational design aspects that favor 380
ownership concentration and 367–8, 369, 377
pay-for-performance schemes may have an adverse effect on 375
preference for different types of 371
presence of outside board members tilts toward acquisition 372
private ownership gives sufficient incentives to pursue 371
radical 378, 380
risk-aversion of owner-managers holds back 370
short- and long-term implications of 375
social 624
successful 375
takeover pressure on 378, 379
venture capital financing and 371

776   INDEX

innovation performance:
　high-tech 365
　performance post-acquisition 379
inside information 300
　access to 302
　revelation to the public 292
　specific stakeholders may require 300
　whether management has exploited 552
insider control 477
insider economies 311
insider equity 248
insider trading:
　large blockholders 112
　pernicious dealings 73
　regulation 98
　sanctions 70
　well-connected directors likely to trade on information 216
insiders 30, 223, 248, 636
　access to private information 300
　adventures that benefited a small pool of corporations 712–13
　board should be smaller and dominated by 372
　controlling 72
　4enriched at the expense of others 709
　equity owned by 247
　monitors on 33
　opportunistic 423
　private benefits of control 293
　unmonitored 26
　unprecedented conduct by 28
　see also relational-insider systems
insolvency 492, 493, 495, 596
　deep 496
　formal 543, 555
　MBIs have higher propensity to 554
instant messaging 140
Institute of Directors (UK) 283
institutional governance 5, 234–5
institutional investors 38, 54, 56, 58, 186, 285, 516, 518, 522, 534, 543, 638, 640, 678, 679–80, 681, 682, 691, 696
　advisory bodies provide corporate governance solutions to 259
　analysts of 711
　characteristics of 37

　contracts between fund managers and 515
　cooperation among 695
　CSR and 731, 735
　desires take high priority 247
　encouraging greater engagement by 284
　family preferences overshadowing those of 261
　growth in stakes held by 52
　hedge funds and other 255, 565–7, 568, 569, 592
　highly diversified 645
　individual blockholders differ from 252
　internationally active 592
　large 297, 370
　limited partnership contracts critical for 515
　long-term 262, 517
　mainstream 737
　major supplier of capital to 711
　most important activist in US 59
　pacification of 263
　percentage of shares held by firm's top five 735
　pressure on executive remuneration decision-makers 5
　pressure on managers to make changes in R&D 247
　pressure-resistant 254
　prevalence of 261
　risk-averse 521
　savings entrusted on basis of long-term reliability 711
　share distributions to 520
　shareholder value-oriented 37
　shift in power toward 707
　substantial and active owners 246
　types of 254
　see also banks; hedge funds; insurance companies; CII; mutual funds; pension funds
institutional theory 181, 612
　central concern of 178
institutionally hybrid market economies, see France; Spain
institutions 662–3
　aggregation 67

building communication channels with 360
capitalist 91
economic 3, 722
endogenously determined 372
external 468
formal 397, 468, 658
government 73–4
inequality-perpetuating 77
informal 397
investor protection 66
labor market 466
major role in PP conflicts 658–9
micro-finance 610
nonprofit 610, 614
oppressive 78
preferences and 65–96
pressure-indeterminate 254
pressure-resistant 254
property rights 70
religious 254
social 722
state-owned 597
transient 292
weak 658
see also financial institutions; legal institutions; national institutions; political institutions; regulatory institutions
instrumental variables 217
insurance companies 37, 81, 201, 254, 541, 572, 599, 600, 638
 major life 81
 mutual fund managers affiliated with 566
integrated model 354–9, 361
intellectual property rights 365
interbank market 599
interest alignment:
 executive 248
 governance interpreted as 393
interlocking directorates 466, 470, 471, 474, 478, 479
internal auditing 311–12
 outsourcing of 320
internal control 183–4
internal governance mechanisms 5, 7, 11, 228–9, 328, 330, 366–7, 372–6, 468, 544, 666–7

convergence of 334
effective 331
growing importance of 341
inferior 335
optimal set of 337
roles played by 441
strong 337
weak 333
international division of labor 651
international governance 39
international management 450
internationalization 56–8
 managerial perception of 8
 multinational firms and 449–64
 process model 454, 455
intranet sites 140
investment banks 68, 73, 139, 541, 678, 681, 683, 692
 book-running, key function of 356
 leading, fraudulent behavior within 709
 mutual fund managers affiliated with 566
investment boom 269
Investment Company Act (US 1940) 566
investment decisions:
 authority of fund manager regarding 517–18
 real-option component of 366
investment managers 566
investor confidence:
 improvements to restore 303 n.(2)
 international 296
 public trust in capital markets 310–11
investor protection 77, 90, 367, 441, 662
 and capital market development 369, 377–8
 countries that currently lack 666
 countries with high rights 299
 degree of 379
 formally strong 663
 high level of 661
 institutions of 661
 laws and regulations for 658, 665, 722
 poor 377
 weak(er) 76, 658
investor relations departments 263

investors 9–10, 513–604
  angel 259
  arrangements to mislead 284
  benefit from high P/E ratios 3547
  cooperation between managers
    and 381
  discipline and oversight imposed by 583
  distressed 496, 501
  early-stage 270, 405, 434
  external 373, 422, 479, 598
  financial 600
  foreign 597, 598–9, 601
  induced to discount value of non-
    disclosing firm 292
  information acquisition costs 303
  informed 292
  international 598
  large 601
  legal protections quite weak 468
  long-term 675–6
  major 644
  managers might have incentives to
    mislead 294
  minority 25, 27, 28, 31, 32, 435, 640
  outside 84, 272, 358
  passive 434, 583
  practice in reporting to 14
  pressure-sensitive 227
  protecting the property rights of 468
  religious 737
  risk-averse 276, 368
  sophisticated 566
  state-owned 582, 583
  strategic 598
  transient 260
  uninformed 292
  update expectations of managers'
    behavior 300
  vulture 9, 496, 501, 502
  weaker legal protection for 18
  wealthy 571
  see also hedge funds; institutional investors;
    outside investors; private equity;
    shareholders; small investors; venture
    capital
inward investment opportunities 358
iPads 140

IPOs (initial public offerings) 7, 294, 349, 352,
    353, 357, 360, 361 n.(2), 378, 398, 430–2,
    434–5, 437–48, 541
  competitive 359
  deployment of financial resources acquired
    during 359
  early-stage 356
  effecting capital gain in 515
  entrepreneurial 422, 429
  founder-CEOs granted stock options at 433
  growing awareness of the importance of 421
  holder of registration rights 523
  information asymmetries and roles of
    corporate governance in 422–8
  multiple agency theory in 675, 678–80,
    691–2
  output for PE-backed buyouts exiting
    by 549
  post-IPO performance of LBOs exceeds
    other 553
  preplanned 529
  probability of 530
  trying to get as many successes as
    possible 518
  underpricing of stock at 422
  venture capital-backed 436
irrevocable commitments 340
IRS (US Internal Revue Service) 527, 621
ISA (International Standards on
  Auditing) 310, 313, 315, 322, 324 n.(11)
Ishii, Joy L. 215
Iskandar-Datta, M. 233
Israel 471, 593
ISS (Institutional Shareholder Services) 53,
  229, 239, 259–60
Istanbul Stock Exchange 401
IT (information technology) 303, 707
Italy 30, 35, 109, 116, 410, 441
  buyouts 550
  communist party 88
  director networks 204
  fascist regime 638
  large manufacturing firms 169
  privately-held SMEs 400
  VC investments 530
  women board members 189
  see also Parmalat

Ittner, C. D. 223, 237–8
Ivashina, V. 502, 550
Iversen, T. 84–5
Iyengar, R. J. 233

Jackson, Andrew 80
Jackson, G. 24, 30, 439, 441, 449, 666, 668, 722
Jackson, H. E. 92 n.(14)
Jacobs, C. 610
Jacobs Engineering 229
Jaggi, B. 401, 404
Jain, B. A. 352, 421, 429, 430
James, C. 498, 543, 554
James River Coal Co. 568
Japan 56, 58, 73, 84, 88, 258, 547, 645, 705
    annual Shunto wage system 652
    bank-centered business groups 475
    bubble economy and stagnation 296
    emphasis on investment in human capital 650
    family control 398
    firms controlled by single shareholder 468
    health and social welfare nonprofits 616
    insider governance 639
    military regime 638
    multinational firms 454
    nation-spanning banks with significant stock ownership 81
    non-market forms of coordination prevalent in 378
    ownership structure, R&D investments and goal alignment 369
    prolonged and pronounced recession 57
    protecting minority shareholder rights 721
    significant ownership by banks 332
    social norms and informal arrangements 30
    understaffing of stock market regulatory agencies 29
    see also JFSA; keiretsu; Toyota
Jaskiewicz, P. 391, 408
Jelic, R. 549, 552
Jenkinson, T. 359
Jensen, M. C. 25, 51, 55, 81, 92 n.(2), 99, 177, 233, 247, 255, 273, 293, 310, 319, 328, 329, 330, 331, 335, 336, 359, 370, 375, 389, 413 n.(4), 430, 432, 435, 466, 534 n.(3), 540, 541, 542, 544, 568, 635, 636, 641, 658, 661, 673, 675, 677, 719, 726
Jeppesen, K. K. 315, 317, 320
JFSA (Japanese Financial Services Agency) 296
Jiang, W. 501, 572, 573, 574, 575, 594
Jiang, Y. 397, 658, 659, 660, 661, 662, 665, 666, 667, 668
Jianguo, Y. 298, 299
Jobs, Steve 429
jobs:
    creation and destruction 648
    discouragement of long tenures 650
    losses 648
    see also employment
Johan, S. A. 519, 520, 521, 528, 529, 530, 532, 533
Johanson, J. 454, 455
Johnson, J. P. 684
Johnson, M. F. 237
Johnson, M. S. 378–9
Johnson, R. 735
Johnson, R. A. 676
Johnson, S. 75, 594
Johnston, D. 234–5
Johnston, J. 185, 186, 287 n.(15)
joint ventures 12, 263, 456
    decentralized structure with 693
    equity 39
    multiple agency theory in 683–5, 692–3
Jones, C. D. 405
Jones, H. 359
Jones, T. 540
Joseph, J. 47, 48, 54, 55, 56
JP Morgan Chase 201, 579 n.(1)
judges 8, 28, 49, 505–7, 688
    bankruptcy, de facto auctioneers 503
Jung, D. K. 674
jurisprudence 28

Kabbach de Castro, Luiz Ricardo 2
Kabir, R. 216
Kaczmarek, Szymon 154
Kahan, M. 52, 53, 54, 93 n.(19), 255, 258, 259, 566, 569

Kahl, M. 504
Kaiser, K. N. J. 534 n.(3)
Kalin, S. 504
Kamar, E. 93 n.(19)
Kanniainen, V. 531–2, 533
Kaplan, S. 1, 54, 229, 492–3, 528, 529, 539, 548, 552, 553, 554, 555
Kapoor, R. 379
Karakas, O. 544, 549–50
Karmel, R. S. 51
Karpoff, J. M. 565
Katz, S. 435
Keasey, K. 280, 286 n.(7), 350, 352, 393
Keenan, J. 146
keiretsu 465, 471, 472, 474, 477, 479
    social ties in 480
    vertical 478
Keister, L. A. 479
Kellermanns, F. W. 389, 390, 396, 407, 408
Kelly, J. 711, 715
KERPs (key employee retention plans) 502
Kesner, I. 206, 683
Keuschnigg, C. 531–2, 533
Keynesian era 706
Khan, R. 227
Khanna, P. 168
Khanna, T. 208 465, 470, 471, 480, 482
Khazanah Nasional Berhad 587
Kiel, G. C. 208
Kim, B. 451
Kim, H. 471, 474, 476
Kim, S. 214
Kim, S. M. 451
Kimono, Satomi 154
King Pharmaceuticals 577
Kini, O. 332, 334, 338, 341, 352, 421
Kirchmaier, T. 206, 208, 214
Kirkpatrick, G. 720
Kirzner, I. 353, 356
Klapper, L. F. 377
Klasa, S. 225
KLD (Kinder, Lydenberg, Domini) strength ratings 730
Klein, A. 179, 571, 592
Klein, S. 391, 392, 396, 403, 404, 408
Kmart Corporation 572, 576
Knechel, W. R. 315

Knoeber, C. 205, 248
knowledge acquisition 356
knowledge flow:
    addressing within a multinational firm 453
    multinational firms 8, 451, 453–4
knowledge transfer 206
    can be costly 453
    expatriates and 454, 458
Knyphausen-Aufseß, D. zu 389, 395, 413 n.(5)
Kochhar, R. 227, 675
Kodak 53
Koenig, T. 205
Kogut, B. 34, 453, 456
Köhler, A. G. 311, 316
Kollo, M. 206, 208, 214
Kontrag Law 29, 33–4
Korea 84, 88, 482, 535 n.(9)
    business groups 469
    tunneling in 473
    direct cross-shareholding illegal in 470
    dominant shareholders 468
    funds based in 584
    see also chaebols; Daewoo; Samsung
Kortum, S. 371
Kostova, T. 452, 460
Kotter, J. 593, 594
Kovner, A. 550
KPMG Strategic Systems Approach 315
Kraakman, R. 102–3, 636
Krafft, J. 381
Kreutzer, K. 609, 610
Kripke, H. 48, 52
Krippner, G. 703, 712, 714
Kroll, M. 231, 233, 432
Kuhnen, C. 207, 208
Kulp, S. L. 227
Kuvandikov, A. 648
Kuwait Investment Authority 587
Kwon, S. 389, 406, 407
Kyriazis, D. 341

La Porta, R. 97, 97–8, 100, 113, 114, 123, 129 n.(2), 253, 369, 377, 389, 390, 391, 411, 440, 441, 468, 470, 473, 640, 658, 661, 662, 665, 666

labor 11, 69–70, 79, 91, 634–57, 696
　creating value through the combination of capital and 705
　dominant stockholders and 83–4
　interests often in conflict with shareholders 109
　managerial, dealing with problems of 465
　national institutions 85
　representation of interests 104
　severe shortage 77
　skilled 87, 354
　unskilled 78
labor markets 87, 90, 466, 595
　CEO 229–30, 232, 235, 237
　executive 334
　external 465, 639
　flexible 378
　internal 465
　managerial 284, 331, 342
　rigid 30
　supposed pressures 282
labor unions 9, 69, 83, 565, 576
　bargaining power 503
　impact on restructuring of distressed firm 502
　institutionalized dialogue with 722
　private equity fund managers and 644
　representatives on pension funds 642
　see also trade unions
Labour Party (UK) 89
Labuan 535 n.(9)
Laing, D. 338
Lambert, R. 293
Lambrecht, B. 329
Lambrecht, J. 410, 411
Lambright, K. 610
Lampert, Edward 572
Landier, A. 232–3, 236
Lang, J. 205
Lang, L. 329
Lang, M. 294, 303 n.(1)
Langevoort, D. 71
Langley, A. 144
Langley, P. 708–9, 710–11, 715
language 455
Larcker, D. F. 208, 223

large blockholders 34, 69, 98, 119, 290
　director independent of 110
　insider trading or self-dealing by 112
　less power concentration in the hands of 111
　market allowed to monitor 112
　monitoring and control activities of 273
　potential opportunistic behavior by 111
　protecting minority shareholders from expropriation 122
Larraza-Kintana, M. 233
Latin America 465
Latino nonprofits 616
Laux, V. 223
Lavie, D. 685
law 8, 28, 51, 73, 80, 86, 98, 246, 248, 441
　anti-takeover, strong 83, 86, 649–50
　antitrust 342
　Asian countries with stronger rules of 397
　company 351
　economic growth and 97
　enforcement mechanisms for contracts 531
　enhancing transparency 29
　formal 720
　hard 26, 27, 35–8, 39, 74, 102
　implications for reforms 101
　investor protection 665, 722
　literature on 499
　minimum federal standards 48
　reorganization 113
　scholarly work to clarify and modernize 49
　significant changes in 116
　soft 26, 27, 35–8, 39, 102, 720
　see also bankruptcy law; civil law; common law; legal environment
Lawman, S. 616
Lawrence, B. S. 459
Lawrence, T. B. 178
Laxey Partners 577
lay-offs 9
Lazonick, W. 351, 353, 378
LBOs (leveraged buyouts) 6, 12, 255, 376, 434
　enhancing understanding of 10
　funding of 9
　multiple agency theory in 685–7, 693

LBOs (leveraged buyouts) (cont.)
  original wave of 360
  prevented 14
  private equity and 539–63, 685–7, 693
  PTP similarities with 335
  see also divisional buyouts; family buyouts; secondary buyouts
Le Nadant, A. L. 376
Lease, R. C. 254
Leaver, A. 708, 710
Leblanc, R. 136
LeBreton-Miller, I. 406, 407, 412
Lee, C. L. 188
Lee, H. Y. 179, 183
Lee, M. D. P. 737
Lee, P. 547
Lee, P. M. 369, 436
Leech, D. 185
left-wing theories 637
legal environment 441, 490–1, 520, 521
  change in 492
legal institutions 3
  agency costs arising from deficiencies 466
  hard-edged, government-facilitated 73
  weak/strong 311
legal origins 18, 114, 116–21, 124, 125
  cross-country differences 530
legal rights 643
legal systems:
  assessing in conjunction with contracts 531
  evolution of 100–2
  global convergence of 124
  improved 125–6
  indices that characterize effectiveness of 98
  superiority of 101
legislative reforms 116
Lehman Brothers 139, 503
Lehn, K. 336, 339, 548
Lel, U. 593, 594
Leland, H. E. 492
Lele, P. 90
Lemmon, M. 502–3
Leninist socialism 637
Lenin, V. I. 712
Lennox, C. S. 183
Lerner, J. 371, 374, 375, 376, 378, 434, 435, 516, 517, 522

Letona, M. E. 616
Leung, P. 401
Leung, S. 401, 404
Leuz, C. 294, 297, 300
Levant Company 46
leverage 207, 234, 355, 491, 494, 599
  classic argument in favor of 375
  excessive 540
  financial 5, 269–89
  firms emerging from bankruptcy 504
  hedge funds often use 567
  operational 275–6, 277, 284
  portfolio companies 376
  violating firms decrease 497
  see also HLTs; LBOs
Levine, R. 92 n.(13), 100
Levis, M. 435–6
Levitas, E. 227
Levy, D. 712, 713
Lew, S. 616
Li, H. 223
Li, K. A. I. 225
Li, Y. 369
liberal market economies 639, 643
  influential critiques of 646
  institutional investors 31
  see also United Kingdom; United States
liberalization 23, 26
  capital market 58
Lichtenberg, F. R. 548
Liebman, J. B. 238–9
Lievens, J. 411
life-cycle concept 6–9, 349–64, 366
Lim, J. 502, 574
Lim, K. 379
limited liability 99, 269, 402, 491
  generates moral hazard 270
  overturning of protection of 272
  owners benefit from 272
  shift in residual responsibility implied by 719
limited partnership contracts 9, 515, 534 n.(2), 541, 556, 566
  evidence on 519–22
  restrictive covenants 516–17
Lincoln, J. R. 474, 479, 480
Lions Gate Entertainment 263

liquidation 107, 113, 492, 507, 522, 552, 707
  escaping 121
  forced 500
  piecemeal sales 503
liquidation rights 529
liquidity 23, 69, 84, 87, 293, 295, 310, 357, 520, 522, 539, 569, 573, 708, 731
  borrower, limiting 499
  capital market 378
  excess 575
  gaining greater control over 500
  less 646
  relative 639
  tradeoff between incentives and 368
liquidity risk 322
litigation 341, 564
  fear of 621
Liu, Y. 208
Livingston, J. A. 47
loan-to-own strategies 573, 574, 575, 690
lobbying 353
local government 616
lock-up arrangements 436
Lockett, A. 437, 438, 440, 523
Lockhart, D. 205
London Stock Exchange 57, 137, 261, 331–2, 435
Long, W. F. 376
Long-Term Capital Management 137
looting 285 n.(5)
Lopez-de-Silanes, F. 97, 97–8, 113, 114, 123, 129 n.(2)
LoPucki, L. M. 504, 505, 506, 508 n.(11), 689, 694
Lorsch, J. W. 165, 170, 189
Loughran, T. 423, 436, 441 n.(1), 678
Lounsbury, M. 178, 737
Love, I. 377
Lowry, M. B. 433
low-tech 365
LTIP (long-term incentive plan) 432
Lu, J. 456
Lumpkin, G. T. 389
Lundholm, R. 294, 303 n.(1)
Luo, X. 472, 482, 483
Luxembourg 104
Lynch, L. J. 234

Ma, X. 477
Maag, Rudolph 259
M&As (mergers and acquisitions) 11, 12, 82, 108, 215, 225, 233, 254, 333, 572, 643, 663–4
  CEOs have unstudied reasons for supporting 230
  compensation more aligned with shareholder interests after 232
  creeping 473
  cross-border 126, 663
  decline following covenant violation 497
  diversification through 353
  effect on innovation 379
  equals 692
  European directive on 112
  firms more likely to engage in 207
  friendly 206
  harmful for innovative activity of acquirer 379
  horizontal 342
  job tenure negatively associated with level of activity 647
  likely to happen in periods of economic expansion 329
  many firms disappear as a result of 440
  may be influenced by director networks 217
  multiple agency theory in 680–3, 692
  negative effect on innovation 379
  presence of outside board members tilts innovation toward 372
  probability of 530
  replacement following 328
  stock-for-stock 577
  value-reducing 103
Macey, Jonathan 51, 52, 71
MacIver, E. 165, 170, 189
Mackenzie, D. 709
Maclean, M. 142
Madrid Stock Exchange 299
Magnan, M. L. 234
Mahoney, P. 74, 92 n.(6)
Main, B. G. M. 178, 181, 185, 186, 191, 287 n.(15)
Mak, Y. T. 298, 299
Makri, M. 233

Maksimovic, V. 329
Malaysia 398, 404, 535 n.(9)
Malaysia Stock Exchange 299
Mallin, C. A. 726
Malmendier, U. 230
managed corporations 47
management entrenchment devices 480
management equity holdings 542
management forecasts 303 n.(1)
management neutrality 576
manager-owner alignment 476
managerial compensation 109, 206, 207, 281, 466
   linked to earnings-based performance measures 271
managerial corporation:
   characterized by executive dominance 56
   emergence of 351
managerial discretion 273, 330
managerial entrenchment 648, 667
   absence of 723
managerial incentives 5, 273, 285 n.(5), 300, 497
   appropriate risks 227
   divisional 545
   misleading investors 294
   motivating to take on excessive debt 271
   supplying higher quality financial information 296
managerial performance 271, 275, 278, 284, 331, 334, 465, 596
   controlling, evaluating and rewarding 372
managerial talent 11, 55, 662–3
managerial turnover 207, 298, 431
   in and around bankruptcy 490, 494
   rates increase when firm performs poorly 496
managers 80, 262, 290
   affiliate-level 469
   autonomy in decision-making 474
   behavior prior to distress 9
   burden of idiosyncratic risk 370
   capital markets vs 72
   checks and balances on 637
   coalition among board of directors and 479
   coalition enables group affiliates to collectively monitor 471
   coalition forming to expropriate external investors 479
   conflict between owners and 541
   conflicts between controlling shareholders and 478
   conflicts of interest between shareholders and 658
   constraints on autonomy 30
   cooperation between investors and 381
   debt puts disciplinary pressure on 375
   decisions inconsistent with shareholder interests 270
   disclosure of information to employees 643
   diversion by 25
   dominant shareholders have incentive and ability to effectively monitor 467
   downsizing decisions 360
   dual identity issues 684
   encouraged to collude with financial institutions 706
   entrenched 248, 329, 480
   exposed to extreme moral hazard 272
   family 397
   family control aligns interests of 478
   goal alignment between owners and 408–9
   group-level 469
   hedge fund 230
   implicit coalition between employees and 81
   incentive to sell the firm 687
   incumbent removed after takeover 378
   intensification of pressures on 703
   interactions among 457, 458
   labor should oppose 637
   lack of diversification in portfolio 370
   lazy 370
   learning how to respond to hedge fund owners 255
   loss of jobs in financial distress 8
   lower information asymmetry between family members and 299
   maximizing an objective function 541
   monitoring of 5, 32, 79
   more risk-averse than investors 368
   mutual monitoring among 479

negligence of 113
nonprofit-maximizing behavior 541
opportunistic 113, 433
opportunistic 720
opportunities and pressures after takeovers 648
outside owners' motivation to check up on 247
owners able to exert greater control over 719
populism and 82–3
protection from shareholders 649
pursuing self-interest 663
risk-averse 368, 370, 374, 492
role of 493–4, 636
self-aggrandizing pro-social activities 731
self-serving 430, 720, 726
senior 5, 270, 274, 285, 451
short-term decisions to avoid earnings drop 260
significant ownership stake held by 542
subsidiary 451
takeover target 342
taxed bonuses 13
transferring across offices as control strategy 451
unconstrained agendas for continuance, size and risk avoidance 81
unduly rewarded for taking hidden financial risks 271
managers ways of eliminating 261
see also fund managers; managers and shareholders; owner-managers; top managers; *also headings above prefixed* "managerial"
managers and shareholders 99, 273, 372
agency problem/conflicts between 103, 292
best interests 330
comparative advantage 284
constraint 6, 328
divergence of interests 34
misalignment of objectives between 366
mandatory bid rule 31, 33
mandatory rules 26, 50
Mangena, M. 179
Mangham, I. L. 145, 153, 159 n.(6)
Manigart, Sophie 6

manipulation 38, 280, 284
  possible 578
Manjon, M. 102
Manne, H. 6, 328, 330, 341, 342, 343
Manning, B. 51
Manso, G. 375
Manson, S. 314, 317
March, J. G. 457
Marconi 137
Marcus, Alfie 1
market capitalization 236
  FTSE 100 top ten largest 139
market entry/exit 297, 489, 529, 530, 531, 541
  difficulty of exiting 368
  mode of entry 450, 454, 456–7
  technological change impacts on decisions 349
market failures 253
market for corporate control 230, 328–46, 367, 378–9, 645
  external 639
  functioning affected 547
  governance mechanism 647
  importance of 647
  obstacles to operation of 6
  primary external governance role 6
  rules governing 31
  see also ownership and control; private benefits of control
market governance 229–30, 231–2
market-myopia hypothesis 378
market-outsider systems 638, 639, 647
market power 329, 342
  increased 343
market-to-book ratios 498, 521
Markman, G. D. 376
Markowitz, L. 207
Marris, R. 329
Martin, K. J. 332, 334
Martin, R. 710, 713
Martynova, Marina 3, 101, 126, 128, 129 n.(2)
Marxist socialism 637
Mason, C. 612
Mason, P. A. 135, 421
Matolcsy, Z. P. 236
Matsa, D. 492
Matser, I. 406, 407

Matsunaga, S. 225
Matten, D. A. 722
Maug, E. 236
Mautz, R. K. 311
Maxwell, Robert 137
Maxwell Communications 171
Mayer, C. 32, 73, 280, 332, 333, 334, 338, 377, 378
Mazzola, P. 400
MBIs (management buy-ins) 335, 550
  higher propensity to insolvency 554
MBOs (management buyouts) 335, 358, 550, 551, 554, 555
  outside acquirers compete for control 547
  PE-backed 552
McCahery, J. 114
McCloskey, D. 353
McConaughy, D. 398, 401
McConnell, J. J. 56, 332, 334, 337
McGlaun, G. 500
McKinsey & Co. 58
McLiesh, C. 129 n.(2)
McNulty, T. 4, 142, 167, 166, 170, 172, 190
Mead, J. 609
Means, G. 6, 25, 51, 52, 92 n., 99, 328, 330, 430, 719
Meckling, W. 25, 51, 55, 92 n.(2), 177, 233, 273, 293, 310, 319, 328, 370, 389, 413 n.(4), 430, 432, 435, 466, 541, 542, 635, 636, 641, 658, 673, 675, 677, 719
Meeusen, W. 208
Megginson, W. L. 10, 371, 435, 441 n.(2), 581, 582
Mehropouya, A. 587, 593, 602 n.(3)
Melias 206
MENA (Middle East and North African) SWFs 601
Mendelson, H. 293
Mendes, V. 38
Mennicken, Andrea 6, 308, 311, 315
mergers and acquisitions, see M&As
Mersland, R. 610
Metallgesellschaft 58
Metrick, A. 246
Metzenbaum, Howard 48, 50
Meuleman, M. 9–10, 549
MHR Fund Manager 263

Michaely, R. 421, 422
Michelon, G. 726
Microsoft 429
middle class 85
  decisive 82, 84–5
  savings and pensions 710, 712, 713
Middle East 258, 601
  see also Abu Dhabi; Israel; Kuwait; Qatar; Turkey; UAE
Mikkelson, W. H. 421
Milan Stock Exchange 299
Milgram, S. 281
Milhaupt, C. 28
military adventures 713
military regimes 638
Miller, D. 391, 396, 397, 406, 407, 412
Miller, G. 71, 93 n.(20)
Miller, P. 308, 321, 619
Miller-Millesen, J. 612
Milliken, F. J. 169, 170
Minhat, M. 216
Minichilli, A. 169–70
minority shareholder protection 660, 668, 675, 721
  laws aimed at 98
  legal reforms 58
  progressively higher levels 38
  regulatory reforms aimed at 33
  weak 473
minority shareholder rights 28, 29, 31, 34, 35, 118–20
  diminishing 330
  entrenchment and 479
  protection of 660, 721
  respect for 666, 667
minority shareholders 3, 11, 25, 110–13, 658
  agency costs faced by 35
  agency problems between majority and 98, 103
  cannot access intangible benefits 663
  conflicts of interest between controlling shareholders and 660
  disadvantaged 664, 665
  expropriating 99, 122, 397, 398, 473, 478, 659, 661, 666, 667, 668
  external governance mechanisms to protect 661, 665

extracting private benefits at the expense of 662
mechanism to defend the interests of 32
opportunistic principals may have conflicts of interest with 368
potential opportunistic behavior toward 99
preferences of 29
purchase of enough stock to risk takeover 262
rationally choosing to free-ride on analysis of information intermediaries 273
Minow, N. 429–30
Mintzberg, H. 429
Miozzo, M. 368
Mirror Group 137
misallocation of capital 100
Miwa, Y. 73
Mizruchi, M. 205, 207
MLF Investments 568
moderator effects 398, 404
moderator variables 398, 408, 409, 411
  important 407
  method-related 399
Mofsky, J. S. 50, 51
Mole, V. 614
Molly, V. 410
monitoring 25, 32, 33, 49, 79, 109, 170, 227, 248, 259, 290, 350, 380, 393, 451, 622
  active 546, 549, 552, 553, 555, 567, 595
  audit 318
  blockholder 108
  board 169, 185–6, 225, 372, 404, 474
  CEOs who lack 234
  compliance-based 312
  difficult 680
  diligent 271
  directors continually balance promoting legitimacy with 178
  effectiveness of board in 373
  family owner 299
  function of board of directors 393
  gains of 638–9
  geographical or product segments 298
  government 592
  headquarters impose less 452
  important mechanisms of corporate governance 26

independent directors may improve extent and quality of 423
intensive 696
lack of 271, 479, 480
larger quoted firms subject to a great deal of 354
less vigilant 231
little need for 356
management 101, 179, 592, 593
managerial discretion 273
market, in the form of stock liquidity 232
mutual 474, 479, 665, 668
non-managing owners 410
peer review with 316
poor 592
private equity firm 335, 359, 543
problems for outside shareholders 357
research that has questioned the benefits of 410
senior manager 5
shareholder 38, 599
stewardship and agency theories in 610
substantially undermined 436
see also Guidelines Monitoring Group
Monks, R. A. G. 53, 429–30
monopolies 276
  local 71
  natural 253
  rentiers defend privilege and 353
Monsanto 229
Mooney, A. C. 163
Moon, J. 722
Mooradian, R. M. 496, 501, 569, 570–1
Moore, J. 531
moral hazard 310, 396, 422–3, 531
  bilateral 530
  extreme 272
  generous pay schemes that encourage 271
  increase in costs 436, 439
  induced 592
  limited liability generates 270
  manifestations of 284
  principal-principal problems 437, 438
  risk of 320, 435
Morck, R. 46, 92 n.(4), 281, 333, 336, 337, 389, 466, 472, 474, 476, 477, 480, 483, 659, 662, 666, 667, 719

Morgan, G. G. 613
Morgan Stanley 568
Mori Trust 258
Morrison, A. J. 451
Morrison, E. R. 499, 500, 503, 505, 506, 572
Morrison (William) Supermarkets plc 360
mortgage interest rates 137
Mueller, D. C. 85, 329
Mulherin, H. 338, 339
Mullainathan, S. 238
multinational firms 461–4
   board composition of world's largest 453
   coordination and control of foreign subsidiaries 8, 450, 451–2, 458
   divisional headquarters located abroad 456
   foreign affiliates 449
   governance of 450–4, 458, 459, 460
   how compensation influences performance of 453
   importance of social capital among different3 types of 452
   knowledge flow within 8, 451, 453–4
   newly industrialized economies 457
   relationship between headquarters and subsidiaries 457
   segment information 297
   small steps toward internationalization 455
   strategies for global expansion 449
multiple directorships 206, 208, 209
   board members who maintain 692
   discouraged 202, 203
multivariate tests 529
Mumbai 139
Munari, F. 371
Murphy, K. J. 59, 229, 235, 247, 432, 433
Murray, V. 618
Murrell, P. 253
Mustakallio, M. 393, 405, 406, 408, 409–10
mutual entrenchment 8, 466, 474
   increased opportunities for 472
mutual funds 37, 54, 254, 262, 565, 592, 675, 679, 682, 686
   managers awarded bonus compensation 566
   retail holders 676
Myers, S. 329

Myint, Y. 206, 208
Mylan Laboratories 577
myopia 371

Nabi Biopharmaceuticals 564
Nader, Ralph 48–9
Nadir, Asil 137
Nadolnyak, D. 619
Nagar, V. 298, 303 n.(1)
Nahapiet, J. 389, 406
Najar, D. 520, 521
Nakamura, M. 466, 480
NAPF (UK National Association of Pension Funds) 37
Narayanan, M. P. 236, 239
NASD (US National Association of Securities Dealers) 235
Natarajan, R. 233
National Association of Corporate Directors (US) 228
National Association of Manufacturers 83
National Bank Act (US 1863–4) 80–1
national business systems 26, 638
national institutions 17–18
   labor 85
national security 88–9
nationalist ideologies 638
natural monopolies 253
Navigation Mixte 58
Neal, T. L. 179, 183
NEDs (non-executive directors) 13, 109, 110, 138, 139, 144, 148, 171, 185, 190, 333, 336, 356
   appointment of 360
   balance of 332, 334
   challenges faced in decision-making processes 166–7
   conduct vis-à-vis executives 163, 168, 172, 186, 192
   effectiveness of 137, 191
   high effort norms 170
   new 360
   noteworthy implications for executive and 139
   part-time 282

percentage of 334
proportion of 328, 334
quality of 334
role of 137
separating executives and 109
shrinking of the talent pool for 179
see also director networks
Neeman, Z. 72
net investment 351, 361 n.(1)
Netherlands 84, 111, 118, 332, 622, 643
   audit inspection units 316
   buyouts 551
   chairs and chief executives 169
   privately-held firms 406
   self-regulation initiative 38
   shareholder election power 104
   VC investments 530
   women board members 189
Netter, J. 371, 582
network dynamics 351
Neubauer, F. F. 166-7
Neubaum, D. O. 676, 735
New Deal (US 1930s) 87
New England textile mills 201
new product development 549
New Public Management 321
new vote buying 564, 565, 576-8
New York 503, 504
   Twin Towers attack (2001) 136
   see also NYSE
New York Times 49
New Zealand 577
Newman, A. 620, 622
NGOs (nongovernmental organizations) 616, 721-2, 730, 737
Nicholls, A. 614, 621
Nicholson, G. J. 208
Nicholson, L. A. 413 n.(3)
Nichols, D. C. 301
Nielsen, S. B. 531
Nigh, D. 451
Nikoskelainen, E. 549
Nini, G. 497
Nixon administration 48
Noe, C. F. 292, 304, 676
Nohria, N. 452

nomination committees 4, 177, 181, 187-90, 228
non-bank trusts 254
non-elites' interests 76
non-linear effects 369, 399, 400, 404, 714
nonperforming loan ratios 599
nonprofit organizations 11, 607-33
   boards of 163
Norburn, D. 137
Nordqvist, M. 391
normative associations 235
North, D. 74
North, D. S. 333
Northern District of Illinois 505, 508 n.(9), 572
Northern Ireland 613
Northern Rock plc 139
Norway 169-70, 189, 583, 601, 602 n.(4)
   employee representation on the board 104
   women board members 189
   see also GPFG
Nowak, E. 398
Nowland, J. 404, 410
NPLs (nonperforming loans) 596
NPV (net present value):
   negative 276, 277
   positive 277
Nuttall, R. 339
Nwaeze, E. T. 233
NYSE (New York Stock Exchange) 1, 38, 49, 50, 189, 246, 303 n.(3)
   board committees required to have independent directors 223
   corporate governance guidelines 188
   Listed Company Manual (2009) 228
   listing requirements 47
   nomination committee proposal 187
   Principles of Corporate Governance (2010) 37
   reporting policies of listed firms 296

Oba, B. 401, 402-3
objective functions 541
O'Boyle, E. H. 396, 398, 399
Obstfeld, D. 143

790　INDEX

Ocasio, W. 47, 48, 54, 55, 56
O'Donnell, S. 451, 452
OECD (Organization for Economic Co-operation and Development) 58, 582, 591, 600, 601, 720
  basic principles of corporate governance 719
  job tenure negatively related to equity market activity 647
  waves of privatizations 581
Ofek, E. 227, 233, 474
offshore funds 520, 522, 535 n.(9)
OFT (UK Office of Fair Trading) 320
Ogden, S. 186, 187, 282
Ogus, A. 36
Oh, W. Y. 735
oil companies 201
Okayama Community Chest 616
oligarchy 75, 76, 84, 465
  persistence at local levels 616
oligopolies 71
OLS (ordinary least squares) regression 369
Olson, M. 24, 75
one-share-one-vote principle 564, 576
  adherence to 110
  ban on deviating from 111
O'Neill, H. M. 369
O'Neill, Tip 85
Ong, C. H. 169, 208
openness 380–1, 410–11
Opler, T. C. 548
opportunistic behavior:
  controlling shareholders 665
  curbing 665
  insider 423
  managerial 433, 477, 480, 684, 720
  mitigating 103
  owner-manager incentives to engage in 273
  partner 439
  potential 99, 111
  preventing 374, 479
  self-seeking 180
opportunity costs 636
optimal default policy 492
optimization:
  private 66
  rational 66
  systemic 79
organizational forms 467, 567, 613, 623
  blanket descriptor for 607
  buyout 545
  flexible and effective 351
  highly variegated 483
  prevalent 465
organizational theory 440
Ortega-Argilés, R. 368–9
Ortiz-Molina, H. 233
OSHA (US Occupational Safety and Health Administration) 725
Ostrower, F. 617. 618–19
O'Sullivan, M. 380
O'Sullivan, N. 333, 334, 341, 551
OTC (over-the-counter) markets 159 n.(5)
out-of-the money options 239
out-of-the-money equity 491–3
outside investors 429
  small 368
  strong incentives to mislead 272
outsiders 223, 232, 248, 290, 315
  equity owned by 247
  firms trying to signal above average quality to 292
  independent 696
  inside board members have advantage compared to 372
  insiders providing untruthful information to 291
  trust toward 668
  voluntary disclosure not always valuable to 293–4
  see also market-outsider systems
overcapacity 277
overdiversification 546
overseas Chinese firms 668
owner-managers 273, 476, 370, 542, 545, 664
ownership 138, 302
  accountability and 612–17
  agency costs arising from separation between control and 300
  attracting 261–2
  bank 477
  blockholder 298
  board 16, 544, 547

capturing longitudinal changes in 410
CEO 227, 405, 547
changes impacting on FTSE boards and governance 138–9
checks and balances on 637
conflict among 255–60, 263, 675–8
consequences of separation of control and 6
CSR and 731–7
diffused 26, 32, 34, 35
dilution of 422
disclosure of 31, 33
economic 564, 576, 577, 578
employee 252, 642–3
employee 735
equity 573
extensive, founders 429–30
family 7, 26, 252–3, 261, 396–405, 457, 482, 547, 662, 664, 736
foreign 298
governance systems characterized by separation of control and 648–9
heterogeneity of 455, 675, 676
hidden 564, 577
identity of 369–71
inside 247–52, 544
institutional 225–7, 259, 260, 292, 370, 456, 457, 569
interlocking, between industrial firms 639
joint 263
labor should ultimately take control over 637
limited 248
managerial 298, 370
nature and distribution of 5
not translated into power or knowledge 710
notable impact on the concept of 141
organizational and strategic implications of control and 449
outside 252–5
parent-affiliate relationships 466
patterns of 722
personal 476
psychological 396
responsible 410
revaluation of 358

shareholder involvement and 642–3
significant stake held by managers 542
transfer into public domain 431
transient 261, 676
transparency of 110
voting 564, 577
see also agent-owners; government/state ownership; pyramidal ownership; *alsounder following entries prefixed* "ownership"
ownership alignment 248
ownership and control:
  concentrated in controlling shareholder 661
  emerging divorce of 357
  potential for changes in 645
  private equity notable for transferring 645
  resources in business group 467
  separation of 51, 83, 270, 273, 328, 330, 518, 545, 649
  separation of 658, 660
  standard measures of 578
ownership concentration 8, 18, 32–3, 81, 99, 101, 237, 379, 466, 467, 473, 475, 476, 478, 645, 646, 660
  beneficial to firm performance 661
  blockholder 639
  countries with strong shareholder protection 663
  detrimental to firm performance 662
  discouraged 640
  driving forces behind 658
  effect on executive compensation 664
  encouraged 34
  evidence pertaining to degree of 735
  government 663
  high(er) 377, 658, 664
  higher debt 499
  horizontal agency costs of 368
  innovation and 367–8, 369, 377
  institutional 225–7
  internal 370
  labor power associated with 70
  main reason for adoption of 468
  management 369–70
  negatively related to locating headquarters in host country 456

ownership concentration (*cont.*)
　positive effect on innovation 368
　presupposed 35
　retained 435
　R&D spending and 369
　significant 543
　top management 350
　total CEO compensation and 227
　VC investor 435
ownership dispersion 99, 120, 368, 369, 407
　investment in training 650
　negative correlations between long-term employment and 647
　spread of 640
　wider range of 408
ownership management 262-3
ownership structure 247, 332, 366, 367-8, 373, 662, 731
　around the world 114
　CEO pay directly influenced by 664
　concentrated 99
　difficult to "undo" 368
　dispersed 237
　dominant family shareholders 547
　emerging market firms 456
　evolving 263
　interaction effects of 404
　management 369
　origin and 299
　related indicators 412
　relatively concentrated 468
　R&D investments, goal alignment and 369
　see also pyramidal ownership structure
Oxford Handbook of Corporate Social Responsibility 720

Pagano, M. 84, 92 n.(16)
Page, Larry 262
Page, M. 312, 314
Pages Jaunes (French IPO) 359
Palepu, K. 465, 470, 480, 482
Parco 258
Paris Stock Exchange 204
Park, C. W. 183
parliamentary systems 84-5
Parmalat 291, 308

parsimony 396, 399
particularism 396, 399
patents 368, 374, 377
　increased citations 549
　post-acquisition activity of inventors in semiconductor firms 379
path dependence 77
Pavelin, Stephen 12
Pawline, G. 534 n.(3)
pay-for-performance 375
　below-average 374
　long-term 431
　equilibrium level of 374
　low levels of 374
pay-performance sensitivity 214, 225, 227, 229, 233, 239
pay mix/structure 237
　see also remuneration
Payne, G. T. 170
payoff distribution 292
PBOC (People's Bank of China) 595
PCAOB (US Public Company Accounting Oversight Board) 295, 318
P/E (price-earnings) ratio 351, 357, 358
Peace, John 210, 211
Pearce, J. A. 165, 167, 168, 349, 350, 352, 429
Pearson, A. W. 406
Peasnell, K. V. 534 n.(3)
Peck, S. I. 185, 237
peer review 316
Penalva, A. 230
Pendleton, A. 11, 634, 638, 636, 644
Peng, M. W. 11, 397, 658, 659, 660, 661, 662, 665, 666, 667, 668
Peng, Y. 477
Penn Central 47
Pennsylvania Chamber of Business and Industry 83
pension funds 50, 82, 258, 261, 262, 541, 565, 566, 581, 592, 638, 640, 679, 682, 686
　attempts to increase shareholder value for benefit of workers in 642
　common to regularly change fund managers 645
　CSR and 676, 735
　employee involvement in management of 642

employer-provided 642
government-run 584
inside board members strengthened the relationship for 456
long-term orientation of 37
managers awarded bonus compensation 566
preference for internal innovation 675
public 565, 583
substantial ownership 676
union representatives on 642
see also NAPF; public pension funds
PepsiCo 202
Perdreau, F. 376
performance 5, 54, 206, 398
  above-average 371
  accounting 274, 552
  affiliated directors have a positive effect on 404
  after buyout 376
  aftermarket 435, 436
  agency problems do not typically impact on 359
  annual 571
  attainment of predetermined criteria 432
  bank ownership positively related to 477
  board monitoring does not always have a positive effect on 404
  bonus tied to 454
  buyout effects on 548–9
  cash-flow 498
  CEO 189, 214, 233, 239
  changes during economic downturns/expansion 236
  compensation and 374, 375, 451, 453, 566, 582
  concentrated ownership detrimental to 662
  contractual governance and 395
  corporate governance effects on 2
  differences in links between pay and 234
  director networks affect 208
  disclosures about 290
  diversification-producing deterioration 358
  earnings-based measures 271
  economic 10, 705
  environmental 2, 398, 726, 730, 735, 737
  ethical 735
  evaluating internal R&D 372
  evaluation of business-level managers' actions and 469
  executive 191, 592
  failure to link pay to 664
  family ownership and 396
  financial statement manipulations that flatter 284
  flattering 271
  helping maintain acceptable levels of 315
  high quality 310–11
  impact of PE and buyouts on 546–7, 548–9
  implications of group affiliates 482
  individual 231
  inferior 396
  interpreting 139
  IPO 421, 422, 423, 435, 436
  little evidence that independent directors aid 403
  loan portfolio 596
  long-term 371, 374, 375, 564, 582
  managerial shareholding and 352
  mixed outcomes 715
  negatively affected 453
  operating 540, 566, 569, 570, 571, 578
  ownership concentrated beneficial to 661
  past 216–17
  perceived by the market as a signal of managerial quality 370
  periodic flow of information about 310
  poor 299, 333, 342, 474, 477, 494, 520, 582, 735, 737
  post-acquisition innovation 379
  post-bankruptcy operating 501
  post-issue 421
  PP conflicts directly affect 662
  pyramidal ownership has negative impact on 476
  relational governance and 395
  relationship between pay awards and 282
  relative evaluation of 231
  risk-adjusted 571
  short-term 371, 374, 553, 564
  social 2, 10, 398, 723, 737
  state ownership impact on 371
  stock 567
  subsidiaries 452

performance (cont.)
  superior 277, 396, 436
  TMT 145
  unlisted firms, family effects on 399
  see also board performance; financial performance; HPWP; innovation performance; managerial performance; pay-for-performance; performance metrics
performance metrics 223, 237–8, 279, 350, 431, 625, 650
  accounting-based 271, 274, 432
  choice of 277
  earnings-based 271
  earnings-related 283
  IPO 423
  lack of, in philanthropy 616
  market-based 375, 432
  ROA-related 284
  shareholder 283
performance-related pay 650
Perkins, S. 186–7
Perotti, E. C. 82, 89, 92 nn.(7/17), 470, 471, 474, 477, 479
Perrow, C. 258
Perry, T. 248
Perry Corp. 577–8
personalism 396, 399
Persson, T. 84
Pettigrew, A. M. 136, 141, 142, 164, 165, 166, 167, 170, 172, 190
Petty, J. W. 529
PFB (person-backed family) firms 402
Phan, P. H. 353
philanthropy 610–11, 616
  place-based 623
  venture 613–14
Philippines 521
Philips Electronics 693
Phillips, G. 329
Phillips, M. 612
Phillips, Susan D. 11
photocopiers 140
piggyback registration rights 523
Pigou, A. 100
Pike, R. 179
Piketty, T. 712

PIPE (private investment in public equity) 567
Pirate Capital 568
Pistor, K. 28
pluralistic ignorance 168, 170, 171
poison pills 474
Poland 530
police-control mechanism 24
political change 89–90
political institutions 3
  capital markets' dependence on 67
  must support capitalism 3
  preference aggregation and 84–8
political interference 582, 583, 601
  dangers of 594
  ever-increasing 596
  excessive 599
  insulating from 593, 595
  protecting the banking sector from deleterious consequences of 597
political stability 73, 74, 76–7
politics of capitalism 91, 92
Pollock, T. G. 223, 678, 679, 680
Polly Peck International 137
Pombo, C. 208
populism 71, 72, 80–1, 86
  managers and 82–3
  power vs 69
Porrini, P. 683
Porter, B. 308
Porter, M. 646
Porter, S. L. 237
portfolio companies 437
  buyouts increase dramatically leverage of 376
  private equity investors carefully select 436
  shaping the corporate governance of 371
  VC interaction with CEOs of 374
Portugal 38, 530
Portugal 638
positive feedback mechanisms 269, 270
postmodernism 710–11, 715
Poulsen, A. 336, 339, 548
Pound, J. 47, 53
Povel, P. 503 n.(13)
Powell, R. 334, 339

Powell, W. W. 471
Power, M. 6, 308, 309, 312, 314, 315, 316, 320, 321
PP (principal-principal) conflicts 11, 472, 658–72
  agency problems 437, 482
Prado-Lorenzo, J. M. 735
Prahalad, C. K. 450, 457
pre-emption rights 108
preference aggregation:
  and combinatorics 81
  political institutions and 84–8
preferences 5, 29, 31, 262
  blockholder 261
  disclosure 298
  financial institutions 731
  geographic 258
  institutions and 65–96, 261
  managerial 72
  meeting 24, 25
  shareholder 284, 731–5
  widely shared, deeply-held 3
preferred equity 522
  convertible 526, 527, 528, 529, 530, 531
Prendergast, C. 374
Prescott, J. E. 451
presidential systems 84–5
price competition 275
price discovery 353, 356, 359
price disequilibria 356
primogeniture 668
principal-agent problems 23, 24, 102, 177, 310, 353, 362, 478, 635
  approaches to resolve 102–3
  conflict 658, 660, 690, 723
  importance of 25
  PE investors create value by addressing 567
  serious 477
  traditional 479
  see also PP conflicts
Prinz, E. 203
prisoner's dilemma 692
private actions 329, 336, 339–40
private benefits of control 293, 659
  corporate rules affect 72
  experienced by minority shareholders as expropriation 659
  extraction of 32–3, 37, 366, 661, 666
  incentives of controlling shareholders to capture 35
  intangible 662
  low 666
  tangible 662, 664
  variations in size of 30–1
private equity 9–10, 15, 68, 254–5, 296, 422, 435–6, 516, 569, 571, 578, 591, 645, 652, 674, 690, 713, 714
  alleged impact on asset-stripping and short-termism 13
  characteristics 567
  contractual mechanisms 335
  deals normally conducted by 376
  disclosure of information 300, 301
  due diligence 340
  governance roles of firms 434
  government increasingly partaking in 601
  greater transparency to 14
  heterogeneity of firms 546
  investors carefully select portfolio companies 436
  large buyouts 648
  LBOs and 539–63, 685–7, 693
  monitoring by firms 335, 359, 543
  notable for transferring ownership and control 645
  ownership interests of investors 421
  reporting quality 302
  role and managerial implications 14
  syndicated investments in IPOs 437–9
  syndication strategy commonly used by 579
  unions attempt to build relationships with 644
privatization 23, 26, 601
  followed by decrease in R&D investments 372
  partial share 592
  waves of 581, 599
product life-cycle model 454–5
product markets 231, 352, 595
  entering or exiting 297
  regulated 296

productivity:
  government employees lack incentives to increase 582
  higher 685
  rises in 648
professional investment funds 254, 370–1, 456
  tolerance for loss 258
profit maximization 402, 474, 477, 541
profitability 276
  collapse in 277
  disastrous consequences for 595
  efficiency and 549
  improvements in 570, 594
  increases in 667
  long-term 248, 565
  maximizing 18
  targets 500
property 253, 577
  distribution of 77, 78
property rights 70, 93 n.(17), 367, 410
  basic 76
  broad-based 75, 78
  ensuring the enforcement of 468
  protecting 468
  see also intellectual property rights
proportional representation 84, 84–5
propping 8
proprietary information 292
Protection of Shareholders' Rights Act (US 1980) 48, 50
proxy contests/fights 564, 569, 577
Prudential 201
psychological factors 280–1
PTPs (public-to-private) buyouts 6, 335, 360, 544–5, 547–8, 551, 648
  extent of free cash flow in 336
  irrevocable commitments for 340
Public Company Accounting Oversight Board 235
public information:
  lower demands for 300
  quality of 301, 338
public pension funds 53, 54, 58, 254, 370, 459
  objective of 371
Pugh, W. N. 379
Pugliese, A. 164, 166

Pulvino, T. C. 506
Puranam, P. 379, 408
Puri, M. 352, 371
Putin, Vladimir V. 75
Puzone, F. 55, 142, 164
Pye, Annie J. 4, 136, 139, 141, 144, 145, 147, 149, 151, 152, 153, 159 n.(6), 164, 167
pyramidal ownership structure 8, 263, 290, 390, 396, 466, 467, 468–9, 470, 473
  divergence between control rights and cash-flow rights arising from 474
  family-controlled 476
  separation of ownership and control rights via 293
  state-owned business groups often have 477

Qatar Investment Authority 590
Quick, R. 308, 311, 317
quota approaches 189

race 78
Rachesky, Mark 263
racist ideologies 638
R&D (research & development) 233, 370, 449, 646
  bank ownership negatively influences spending 370
  better use of 549
  corporate governance and the strategic organization of 380
  cross-subsidizing a sizable component of 707
  decline in expenditure 649
  hampering 375
  higher relative 675
  increase in expenditure following introduction of anti-takeover amendment 379
  institutional investors may pressure managers to make changes in 247
  intensive 375, 377
  internal, evaluating performance of 372
  lower spending in the absence of financial blockholders 368

management stockholding associated with
higher ratio of expenditures to sales 374
ownership structure, goal alignment
and 369
positive correlation between ownership
concentration and level of spending per
employee 368
privatization processes followed by
decrease in investments 372
sharp decline in ex post expenditures 376
strong negative relationship between debt
and spending on 376
target firms often reduce 571
under-investment in 366
railroad companies 201, 204
Rajan, M. V. 223
Rajan, R. 74, 93 n.(23), 272
Rajgopal, S. 237
Raman, K. 233
Ramseyer, M. 73
Rao, R. P. 378–9
Raposo, C. C. 233
Rasheed, A. A. 398
Ratcliff, R. 207
Ravenscraft, D. J. 376
Ravix, J. L. 381
RD/Shell 201
Reagan, Ronald 48, 50, 89
real estate 296
Reber, B. 353
recapitalizations 597, 598, 599
  leveraged 541
  multiple 596
recession 57, 137, 547, 553, 705, 720
Rechner, P. L. 457, 680, 682
Rediker, K. J. 475
redistribution 69, 84, 85, 90, 91, 99, 100
  codetermination 104
Reeb, D. M. 389, 391, 396, 397, 400,
    403–4
refocusing 349, 353, 359, 360
Reg FD (US Regulation Fair Disclosure
    2000) 297
regulation 2–3, 13–15, 23–45, 203, 205, 234–5,
    540, 609, 706
  accounting 303 n.(2)
  anti-self-dealing 665

change impacting on FTSE boards and
    governance 137–8
charity 622
creditor rights protection 113, 120–2
director networks 201
disclosure 295, 296, 297
evolution around the world 114–22
financial 9, 273, 501
for and by private governance 620–3
formal governmental and alternative
    forms 725
functional approach 98
government, lack of 397
hedge fund 571, 579
investor protection 665
majority-minority shareholders'
    relationship 110–13
management-shareholder relations
    103–10
provisions addressing 110–13
risk-based 321, 621
robust 51
role of 99–102
strong, information provision 291
see also disclosure regulation; FSA;
    self-regulation; SEC
regulation theory 704–5
regulatory institutions 23
  characterized by understaffing and
    underdeveloped budgets 28
  design and implementation of 30
  differences in 29
  national and transnational bodies 292
reinsurance companies 597
reinvention threshold 359
relational governance 8, 393, 395, 404, 407,
    466, 470, 471–2, 474, 478
  effect of family involvement on 406
  effective 480
  family ownership and 405
  relationship between contractual and 408,
    409, 411, 412
relational-insider systems 638, 639, 647
religious organizations 565
remuneration 4
  equity-based 374
  excessive 103

remuneration (*cont.*)
  extensive performance-contingent contracts 546
  restructuring that negatively impacts on 540
  see also compensation; remuneration committees
remuneration committees 5, 149, 185–7, 228, 279, 283, 360
  chair of 181
  employees represented on 649
  legitimacy aim for 178
  most listed companies have introduced 109
  professionalism of 180
  see also compensation committees
remuneration consultant networks 215
Renneboog, Luc 3, 4, 98, 99, 101, 102, 109, 114, 126, 128, 202–3, 214, 215, 216, 280, 359, 360, 361 n.(2), 534 n.(3), 547, 548, 552
rentier class 712
reorganization 113
  banking sector 583, 599
  external collaborations 371
  governance mechanisms 360
  internal, necessary precursor to 358
  see also bankruptcy reorganization
replacement capital 358
Republic of Ireland 114
Republican states (US) 14
reputation 368, 471, 531, 731
  building 436, 438
  costs to 515
  potentially damaging impact on 438
resilience 396
resource allocation 611, 644
  inappropriate 476
  limiting capacity to 645
  reallocation to elites 712
resource-based view 351, 375, 389, 393, 412, 429, 433, 438, 543
  board in IPO firm 439
  heterogeneous nature of valuable assets in 354
resource dependence 402, 458, 612
  coercive isomorphism and 612
returns 27
  allocation of 646

  higher 573
  long-term excess 594
  negative 663
  risk-adjusted 56
  short-term 645, 646
  time lag between investments and 366
  very uncertain 370
  see also abnormal returns; financial returns; ROA
Revenue Canada 527
rewards 278, 282, 545, 648–50
  cash 233
  equity 432
  executive 227
  family, socio-emotional 253
  financial 540
  highly leveraged 279
  intermediaries skim off 711
  long-term success 375
  personal 614
  share-based 650
  showing how governance can affect 11
  undue 5, 271
  vast 440
Rhoades, D. L. 457
Rhodes-Kropf, M. 329
Riberioux, A. 706
Richardson, R. 205–6
right-wing theories 637
Rijsdijk, R. 608
Ring, P. S. 684
risk-aversion 276
  CEO 236
  institutional investor 521
  manager 368, 370, 374, 492
  shareholder 275
  top management 350
risk management 315, 320
  governance and 15–17
  improving the effectiveness of 312
risk profile 248
  truncated downside 272
risk-reducing strategies 374
risk-taking
  debt-financed 270, 272, 274, 283
  egregious 270, 278
  excessive 491

high-powered incentives may prompt 374
remuneration schemes that encourage 280
straight equity incentives may
    influence 374
Ritter, J. R. 421, 422, 436, 441 n.(1), 678
Rivkin, J. W. 471
Rivoli, P. 423
ROA (return on assets) 274, 275, 276, 277,
    278, 284, 286 n.(11)
Robbie, K. 544, 554
Roberts, J. 167, 168, 171, 172, 190, 191
Robinson, J. A. 75
Robson, K. 308, 314, 320
Rock, E. B. 52, 53, 54, 73, 255, 258, 259, 566, 569
Rodrigues, S. B. 684, 693
Rodrik, D. 75
Roe, Mark J. 3, 28, 29, 30, 31, 32, 33, 35, 37, 56,
    70, 71, 72, 75, 76, 80, 83, 87, 88, 89, 92
    nn.(3/14/15), 93 nn.(20/21/23), 101, 272,
    478, 479, 480, 506
ROE (return on equity) 274–5, 277–8, 286
    nn.(8/11)
Rolander, D. 451
Roll, R. 329
Romania 116
Romer, P. 285 n.(5)
Romney, Mitt 14
Roosevelt, T. 295
Rose, N. 321
Rosenberg, H. 53
Rossi, S. 73
Rossi Lamastra, C. 380
Roth, K. 451, 452, 453, 460
Rothschild (N. M.) & Sons 201
Royal Bank of Canada 201
Rozanov, Andrew 582
Ruback, R. 330
Rubicon Ltd. 577–8
Rubin, A. 735
Rubin, R. D. 50, 51
Ruigrok, W. 189
Russia 75, 258
    oligarchs 465
    plundering of own SWFs 601
    see also Soviet Union; Yukos
Ryan, L. V. 164
Ryan, P. 650

Sacristán-Navarro, M. 397
Sadler, G. V. 237
Saez, E. 712
Safeway 360
Sainsbury 206
Salamin, A. 234
Salamon, L. M. 607
salaries 254
    base 237, 431
    cut 571
    escalation in 229
    increased 687
Samsung Group 470
Samwick, A. A. 231, 233, 238
Sánchez-Ballesta, J. P. 299
Sandberg, L. 353
Sanders, W. G. 230, 440, 452,
    453, 458
Sandino, T. 235
Santana-Martín, D. J. 401, 409
Santos, R. 208
S&P (Standard & Poor's) 500 indexes 189,
    190, 225, 234, 299
    board size 400–1
    family ownership and engagement with
        CSR 736
S&P-MIB (Milano Italia Borsa) 40
    index 204
Sapienza, H. J. 373
Sapra, H. 379
Sarbanes-Oxley Act (US 2002) 1, 26, 29, 37,
    137, 184, 228, 236, 246, 291, 295,
    303 n.(2), 317–18, 320, 332, 609, 619,
    709, 720
Satyam India 308
Sauerwald, Steve 11
scandals 168, 187, 303 n.(2)
    abundant history of 309
    accounting 719–20
    British MPs' expenses 613
    for-profit governance 621
    key 137
    major 295
    organizational 614
    see also Arthur Andersen; Barings; BCCI;
        Enron; Hollinger; Lehman; Maxwell;
        WorldCom

Scandinavia 118, 120, 121, 124, 530
　industry-level bargaining 652
　legal environment 441
　shareholder protection 116
　see also Denmark; Finland; Iceland; Norway; Sweden
Schattsneider, E. E. 78
Schatt, A. 549
Schedule 13Ds, *see* SEC
Schijf, H. 205
Schizer. D. 527
Schmitz, P. W. 371
Schneider, A. A. 178
Schoar, A. 505, 508 n.(10)
Scholtens, B. 735
Schor, M. 570
Schröder, Gerhard 90
Schulze, W. S. 389, 396, 430
Schumpeter, J. A. 357, 353, 358, 359
Schwartz, D. J. 47, 52
Schwenk, C. 372
Schwert, G. 338, 339
Schwienbacher, A. 92 n.(17), 528, 529
Sciascia, S. 400
scientific credibility 373
Scotland 613
Scott, P. 711
Scott, W. R. 178
SDNY (Southern District of New York) 503, 504
SE (The European Company: Societas Europaea) 641
Sears Roebuck & Co. 572
SEC (US Securities and Exchange Commission) 47, 48, 50, 54, 69, 177, 182, 188, 202, 252, 291, 295, 297, 315, 602, 725
　Rule 14a-8 proposals 737
　Schedule 13Ds 568, 569, 570, 571, 574, 579
　State Boards of Accountancy 235
Second Bank of the United States 80, 87
secondary buyouts 541, 543, 545, 549
Securities Act (US 1933) 290, 295, 303 n.(2)
security design 526–9
Sedatole, K. L. 227
self-dealing 11, 662, 665
　large blockholders 112
self-financing 704

self-interest 142, 247, 248, 677
　managerial 339, 663
self-regulation 11, 14, 25, 26, 38, 609, 620, 622
　justified in terms of public interest 36
　long tradition of 37
self-serving behavior 720, 726
Seligman J. 47, 48, 49, 50
Senior Supervisors Group (US 2011)
　report 16
separation pay, *see* severance arrangements
SERPs (Senior Executive Retirement Programs) 232
Seth, A. 475, 546, 549
severance arrangements 223, 230, 237
　excessive 207
Seyhun, H. N. 239
SFAS (Statement of Financial Accounting Standards 131) 297
Shad, John 50
Shakman, M. L. 51
Shanghai Stock Exchange 599
Shapiro, D. M. 467, 660, 661, 666
Sharaf, H. A. 311
share buy-backs 358
share capital 275
share options 432–4
　role schemes 431
　see also stock options
share traders 141
shareholder activism 36, 59, 736–7
　institutional 54
shareholder interests:
　aligning managerial and 270, 282, 649
　compensation more aligned with 232
　furtherance of 285
　goals not in 25
　long-term 101
　managerial decisions inconsistent with 270
　managers have strong incentives to act contrary to 283
　strategies not consistent with 5
shareholder power 81, 373, 651
　selecting or removing directors 103
shareholder value 25, 28, 29, 33, 34, 37, 86, 706
　agency costs contribute to destruction of 35
　ambiguous consequences for 32

Anglo-Saxon form of 652
attempts to increase for benefit of
    workers 642
debt-finance does not actually create 284
destruction 570, 592, 594
enlightened 636
focus on 101
fundamental strategies to unlock 31
goal of enhancing 569
ideology of 644, 651
importance of 644
loss in 358
low prominence in European social
    democracies 30
maximizing 255, 722
opposition to 635
preservation and promotion of 56
salience of social norms around 17
short-term prioritization of 707
shareholders:
  advisory bodies strive to enable and
      empower 259–60
  agency problems 98, 103
  ambiguous preferences of 731–5
  atomistic 108
  bargaining power 493
  board members risk losing the support
      of 248
  cohesive counter-coalition in the
      boardroom 81
  collaboration among 11
  concerns of 58
  conflicts between hedge funds and 570
  conflicts of interest between managers
      and 658
  control of managerial behavior by 635
  creditors threatening with bankruptcy 497
  crisis of confidence 360
  deleterious consequences for 593
  directors tend to downplay responsibilities
      to 271
  dispersed 645, 721
  divergent interests among 663
  dominant 397, 467, 468, 472, 547, 735
  entitlement to vote on pay 229
  exposed to financial risks 277–8
  external 373, 476, 479
  friendly 262, 341
  gains and losses in value experienced
      by 353
  impact of buyout on 551–2
  income belonging to 275
  increased benefit to 331
  influence over outcomes in distress 403
  institutional 52–4, 341, 674; see also ISS
  interests of 636
  labor interests often in conflict with 109
  laws aimed at protecting 98
  legal empowerment of 35
  limited liability of 99
  long-term 687, 693
  major structural constraint faced by 273
  majority 3, 98, 103, 108, 110–13, 664, 731
  misalignment of objectives between
      managers and 366
  monitoring by 38, 599
  non-employee 239
  non-family 299
  outside 357
  ownership and involvement 642–3
  payoff functions to 272
  preferred 688
  pre-buyout 547
  protection of 114–20, 142
  public and private bank 301
  relegated to the role of "passive surfers" 711
  representing the needs of 262–3
  response to possible takeover attempt 262
  re-aligning the interests of management
      and 567
  risk-averse 275
  risk-neutral 276–7
  role of 491–3
  short-changed without robust
      regulation 51
  significant 185, 544, 547, 574, 731
  small, coordination problem among 99
  unfriendly action 262
  voting reform efforts 72
  see also blockholders; controlling
      shareholders; managers and
      shareholders; minority shareholders;
      also entries above prefixed "shareholder"
Sharp, Z. 611

Shaw, G. 206
Shaw, W. H. 421, 422
Shevlin, T. 237
Shimotani, M. 479
Shinn, J. 34, 83
Shivakumar, L. 301
Shivdasani, A. 188, 208, 332, 333, 334, 429
Shleifer, A. 56, 97, 97–8, 99, 113, 114, 123, 129 n.(2), 298, 329, 366, 370, 371, 378, 390, 466, 468, 474, 506, 592, 635, 647, 649, 659–60, 697, 719, 723
Short, H. 352
short-selling 262, 645
short-termism 13
   agent-owners 691
   governance and employment 647
   managerial 260, 299, 371
   performance 371, 374–5, 553, 564
   political 593
   pressures for 646, 650
side payments 341–2
SIDs (senior independent directors) 148, 153
Siebels, J. 389, 395, 413 n.(5)
Siegel, D. S. 1, 9–10, 548
Siegel, J. 76
signaling hypotheses 429, 440
Sikka, P. 313, 315, 319
Simon, H. A. 457
Singapore 169, 397, 468, 591
   funds based in 584
Singapore Government Investment Corporation 587
Singapore Stock Exchange 299
Singapore Temasek model 600
Singh, H. 207, 456
Singh, R. 503 n.(13)
Skeel, D. A. 500, 504, 506
skills development 646, 650–1
   showing how governance can affect 11
Skocpol, T. 69
Sloan, R. 234
Small, M. L. 49
small investors 368, 422
Smart, S. B. 548, 549
SMEs (small- and medium-sized enterprises) 144, 163, 350, 391, 402, 410
   privately-held 400

SmithKline Beecham 681
Smith, A. 231, 368, 546, 550, 552
Smith, A. J. 292, 296, 299, 376
Smith, C. W. 254, 374
Smith, R. 421
Smith, S. R. 614
Smith, V. 368
Smith Committee (UK 2003) 180, 181, 185, 187
Smith Review (UK 2003) 137
Snell, S. A. 368
social capital 389, 392, 393, 405, 410, 412
   importance among different types of multinationals 452
   relational 406, 407
social democracy 81
   capital markets vs 69–70
social distancing 168, 171
social enterprises 608, 612, 621
social fractionalization 77
social identity theory 389, 406
social media 303
   see also Facebook; Twitter
social networks 373
social responsibility 593
   see also CSR
social welfare 253
   maximization of 100
socialism 637
Socialist legal origin 530
SOEs (state-owned enterprises) 581, 595, 593, 663
   full control of 600
   linking pay to performance targets 664
   stronger oversight of 582
   underperformance by 600
Sokoloff, K. L. 75, 77
Sombart, W. 78
Somerville, P. 616
Sommer, A. A. 47
Sonin, K. 75
Soskice, D. 84–5, 93 n.(21), 378, 722
South Africa 521
South America 640
Southern Cross Care Home group 540
sovereign funds 229
Soviet Union 377, 637

countering 88
former republics 583
Spain 30, 38, 58, 118, 189, 369, 441, 638
    bank-centered business groups 475
    director networks 204
    large firms 401
    newspapers, family CEO tenure 398
Spear, R. G. 608
Speckbacher, G. 611–12
speculative bubbles 712
    persistent and recurrent 714
Spencer Stuart Board Index (2010) 189
Spiller, P. 86
Spira, L. 178, 181, 184, 187, 192, 312, 314
Srikanth, K. 379
St James's Place plc 209
stabilization funds 581, 584
Stablein, R. 151
stakeholder theory 393, 610, 611, 636, 652
    stewardship and 612
standardization 26, 623, 624
    adaptation vs 617–20
standards of living 662
Staples, C. L. 453
Starks, L. T. 565, 674, 737
start-ups 349, 351–2, 391
    aspects that favor innovation in 380
    early, wealth limits of 356
    entrepreneurial 435
    operational decision-making of 532
    role of independent board members in 374
    scientific visibility of academics involved in board 373
state ownership, see government/state ownership
Stathopoulos, K. 208, 214
Statute of Elizabeth I (England 1601) 620
statutory rules 36
Stearns, L. 207
Steier, L. 389, 719
Stein, J. 554
Stern, I. 168, 260
Stewardship Code (UK 2010) 137–8, 284
stewardship theory 369, 375, 389, 393, 395, 406, 410, 412
    evidence to support in monitoring 610
    stakeholder and 612

Stiglitz, J. E. 75
Stiles, Philip 4, 164, 166, 167, 170, 190, 312
stock exchanges 686
    listing requirements 332
    regulations 102
    see also Brussels; Hong Kong; Istanbul; London; Madrid; Milan; NYSE; Paris; Shanghai; Singapore
stock market crashes:
    Asia (1997) 58
    US (1929) 295, 315
stock markets 71, 82–3, 273, 663
    de-listing in 74
    diffuse 69
    early development and continuity of 640
    enforcement 74
    entry through IPO 7
    expansion of 640
    financial slack favorably received by 376
    flotations and pressures 357
    hard constraint that can only be overcome by listing 356
    large 377
    liquid 69, 84, 87
    longer-term proxies for discount 423
    nascent 73
    size of 647
    typically smaller 639
    understaffing of regulatory agencies 29
stock options 54, 186, 234, 235, 236, 238, 247, 248, 455, 649
    compensation in the form of 374
    fraud among firms with CEOs that received 239
    repricing 223, 239
    timing of awards 239
stock price synchronicity 208
Stocken, Oliver 210, 211
Stokman, F. 206
Stolin, D. 99
Stone, M. M. 617. 618–19
Stopford, J. M. 450
StorageTek 507 n.(2)
Stoughton, N. M. 227
Stouraitis, A. 534 n.(3)
Stout, S. 207
Strange, R. 449, 456–7, 460

804　INDEX

strategic alliances 263, 693
　decision to enter a market by means of 456
strategic control 8, 254, 466, 467, 469–70
　strong 476, 478
strategic decision-making 246–7, 401, 412, 430, 449, 454, 476
　aligning incentives with 225
　board characteristics and 405
　boards as groups 4, 168–71
　incentives to improve 540
　quality of and commitment to 408
strategic investments 357
strategic objectives 370
strategy 248, 351, 450, 540, 621
　activist 567, 578
　business 646, 650
　changes in 564
　competitive 247, 455
　control 451
　creditors-turn-shareholders 574, 575
　cross-border 451
　decision rights 103, 108, 111, 117, 118, 119, 124
　directional trading 645–6
　implications for 609
　internationalization 230, 455–6, 458–9
　investment 571, 646
　loan-to-own 573, 574, 575, 690
　momentum 645–6
　multidomestic 451
　new vote-buying 564, 565, 578
　operating 571
　passive 593
　political 724
　practices enabling the stimulation of 410
　significant changes to 646
　syndication 579
　trading on the public market 567
Streeck, R. 716
Strömberg, P. 495, 529, 539, 548, 552, 553, 554
structural variables 410
Stulz, R. M. 374
style drift 516–17
Suáre, K. C. 401, 409
subcommittees 49
　chairmen of 48, 149–51
suboptimal contracts 237
Subrahmanyam, A. 208

subsidiaries 572, 591, 595
　see also foreign subsidiaries
subsidies, see cross-subsidization
subsistence 76
Sudarsanam, P. 341, 548
Suddaby, R. 178
Suez (French conglomerate) 58
Suh, Y. 374
Summers, L. H. 378, 647, 697
Sundaramurthy, C. 680, 682
Sundaram, R. K. 233
sunk investments 358
supermarket retail techniques 206
Sutcliffe, K. M. 143
Sweden 83, 236, 471, 645, 649
　bankruptcies 491, 500–1, 506, 508 n.(11), 688
　concentrated ownership 663
　multinational firms 455
SWFs (sovereign wealth funds) 253, 686, 697
　financial role of 10, 581–604
　largest 258
　substantive control of major corporations 258
Switzerland 189, 259, 530, 651
SWX (Swiss Stock Exchange) 189
syndicalist theorists 637
syndicates 356, 579
　PE investments in IPOs 437–9
　VC 359, 422, 440, 523, 526, 530, 532–4
synergies 329

Tabak, F. 429, 430
Tabellini, G. 84
tacit knowledge 354, 396
Taiwan 88, 397–8, 456, 465, 471, 482, 529, 593
　direct cross-shareholding in business groups 470
Tajoli, L. 368
Takeover Panel (UK) 340
takeovers 53, 280, 480, 569
　botched 360
　circumvented 262
　corporations become blockholders before engaging in 253
　defenses 206
　defensive reaction against 548

disciplinary mechanism 338–9
diversification through 353
firm considering 216
friendly 333, 334, 337, 338, 339, 341, 342, 343, 544
full 126
ill-conceived, over-extension through 360
innovation and 379
mechanism that forces disinvestment in declining industries 329
more defenses 568
partial 127–8
pressure prior to MBO 548
probability of being the target in 207
protection against 33, 649
regulatory reforms in EU 32, 33
shareholder response to possible attempt 262
suitability as target 215
techniques to engineer bids 52
threat of 110, 334, 474
types and motives 329
unwelcome bids 52
wealth-enhancing 330
see also anti-takeover mechanisms; hostile takeovers
talent management 452
Talmor, E. 227
Tate, G. 230
taxation issues 531
  advantage 527
  authorities 300, 301
  benefits 329
  bias 528
  excessive leverage to reduce charges 540
  implications 432
  incentives 725
  pass-through entities 535 n.(9)
  return information 621
Taylor, B. 190
technical default 497
technological change:
  evolutionary pattern is determined by 349
  impacting on FTSE boards and governance 140–1
Teece, D. J. 453
tenure 223, 229–30, 232, 248, 398, 455

negatively related to equity market activity 647 see also CEO tenure
Tesco 206, 646
Tetlock, P. E. 152, 153
Texaco 53
textile industry 201
Thadden, E.-L. von 82, 89, 108
Thatcher, Margaret 136
Thevaranjan, A. 233
Third Avenue (hedge fund) 572
Thomas, C. 208
Thomas, W. B. 298
Thompson, S. 359, 360, 541, 542, 545
Thomsen, S. 142, 164
ThomsonReuters database 144
Thorburn, K. S. 8, 491, 494, 500, 506, 508 n.(11)
Thorne, L. 234
Tiebout, C. 86
Tihanyi, L. 5, 8, 253, 455, 456, 676
time horizons 246, 258, 731
  differing 676, 683, 684, 689, 690, 694, 696
  longer 706
  looming issues 689
  shortening of 649
Time Warner 202, 564
Times, The 57
Tirole, J. 367
Titman, S. 548
TMTs (top management teams) 135, 137, 142, 146, 248, 280
  capacity and willingness to tolerate different points of view 730
  comparing 406
  compositions of 459
  diverse, potential benefits of having 452
  expectations and conduct 145
  family 401, 406
  less willing to take risks 457
  likelihood of having a non-national member on 453
  MNE, composition of 449, 452
  total compensation and long-term incentives for 453
Tobin's Q 372, 403
Toms, S. 7, 350, 351, 353, 358, 354, 357, 360, 540
Tonks, I. 421

top managers 1, 207, 208, 260
  clearer hierarchy of decision-making between board and 411
  compensation packages for 374
  expatriate 451
  family ownership and family relationships among 482
  incentives for 328, 393, 454, 648
  ownership concentration 350
  pay incentives for 648
  risk-aversion 350
  turnover 494
  see also TMTs
Torous, W. N. 493
Tosi, H. L. 236
total factor productivity 548
tournament theory 207, 238
Toyota 478
trade unions 638, 642, 643, 652, 737
  active on executive pay 649
  power of 637
trading strategies 292
transaction costs 293, 611
transition economies 658
transparency 11, 30, 109–10, 123, 152, 332, 620, 649, 720
  complete 185
  declining 357
  dramatic changes in overall standards 117
  enhancing 29, 103, 291, 438
  financial 28, 584
  heavy emphasis on 620
  help to improve levels of 14
  increased 599
  lack of 100, 291, 480
  less 340, 342
  less easily enforceable 357
  limited and high levels of 354
  more 322
  reduced 473
  state operations 602 n.(1)
  strong powers to ensure 296
  tightened rules 295
Travelers Group 681
Tribo, J. A. 370
Tricker, B. 142
Truman, E. M. 584

trust 531, 616, 668
  building 436, 438
  challenges to 613
  cooperation and 408
  interfirm 471
  mutual 480
  rebuilding 408
trusteeship strategy 103, 108–9, 119
  independence of directors from controlling shareholders 111–12
Tuggle, C. S. 170
Tuna, I. 234
tunneling 8, 11, 252, 366, 396, 466, 472, 473, 665
  avoidance of 375
  strong evidence of 397
Turkey 401, 465
Turley, S. 178, 181, 183, 185, 192, 315
turnover-performance sensitivity 207
  see also CEO turnover; managerial turnover
Twitter 303

UAE (United Arab Emirates) 258, 584
UBS Warburg 578
Ughetto, E. 376, 549
Uhlaner, L. M. 389, 391, 392, 393, 406, 408, 409, 410, 413 n.(3)
UK Corporate Governance Code (2010) 36, 137, 138, 147, 150, 203, 331–2, 333, 334, 337, 429
UK City Code on Takeovers and Mergers 340
uncertainty 423, 716
  above-average 374
  cost of capital increases proportionally with 377
  decision-maker's perception of 457
  demand 275–6
  environmental 470, 684
  going concern 324 n.(11)
  high 366, 374
  innovative activities 377
  inside board members have advantage in dealing with 37
  management ownership concentration 370

news which directly mitigates 297
  proprietary information introduces 292
  reducing 472
  values which can only be priced
    with 353
underperformance 466, 474, 482, 546
  hedge fund activism targeting 565, 567–71
  state-owned enterprises 600
  SWF holdings 594
underpricing 423
  deliberate 436
  evaluating 441 n.(1)
  executives maximize option gains due
    to 433
  high(er) 433, 436
  initial 435, 441 n.(2)
  investigations of 422
undervaluation 568
Uniform Commercial Code 500
unintended consequences negative 5
United Kingdom 26, 28–9, 30, 56, 58, 73, 88,
    93 n.(23), 171, 179, 181, 186, 721
  accounting standards 57
  administration procedure 113, 121
  agency problems do not typically impact
    on performance for 359
  audit 137, 317, 318, 319
  "bidding up" of compensation 235, 283
  board committee members 228
  boom in south-east and recession in the
    north 708
  buyouts 539, 551
  charities 613, 622
  competition authorities 342
  corporate governance practices 37, 137
  director networks 202–3, 204
  disclosure of audit and non-audit fees paid
    to auditors 317
  equity held by overseas investors 139
  executive pay levels 282
  external and internal governance
    changes 333
  family ownership estimates for unlisted
    firms 390
  hostile takeovers 648
  housing market collapse 137
  information quality 301

IPOs 361 n.(2), 436
  irrevocable commitments for PTP
    transactions 340
  largest family firm 261
  legal system 101
  lowest job bands 712
  major focus of shareholder activism 649
  managerial corporations 351
  MBOs 648
  non-executive director representation 332
  powerful insurers 81
  privatizations 581
  PTPs 544, 548
  publicly quoted shareholdings controlled
    by financial institutions 139
  receivership 121
  reforms of corporate law 636
  regulation 28–9, 141, 203
  self-regulation 37
  shareholder-based system 114
  significant increases in stock prices 547
  supermarket retailers 206, 360
  syndicated venture capital market 437
  takeovers 335, 360
  training programs in engineering and
    retailing 651
  typical CEO base salary 431
  unemployment 158 n.(2)
  see also ABI; APB; Barings; BCCI;
    Cadbury; City of London; Companies
    Act; England; FRC; FSA; FTSE; Hampel;
    NAPF; OFT; Southern Cross; Northern
    Ireland; Scotland; Stewardship Code;
    UK Corporate Governance Code
United States 46, 57–8, 66, 71, 72, 77, 78, 85,
    88–9, 97, 185, 186, 377–8, 397, 721
  accounting principles among state
    governments 178
  antitrust laws 342
  audit 317, 319
  bankruptcy 697 n.
  boundary-melting 621
  CEO compensation 236, 431
  corporate restructurings 572
  director networks 201–2, 204
  disclosure of audit and non-audit fees paid
    to auditors 317

808　INDEX

United States (*cont.*)
　dissimilarities between UK corporate governance and 37
　early accounting data studies in US 548
　family ownership 411;
　　and corporate social performance 398
　family ownership: estimates for unlisted firms 390
　financial distress and bankruptcy 489–512
　imperialist policies 712
　institutional complementarities 30
　labor 83
　lack of national banking system 81
　large firms managed by institutional shareholders 674
　legal restrictions 205
　legal system 101
　leveraged buyout transactions 360
　limited partnership structure 516
　lowest job bands 712
　major conduit for capital in 82
　major focus of shareholder activism 649
　managed corporations 47
　managers 79–80, 83
　mandatory disclosure 332
　manufacturing industry-level data 371
　market for corporate control 341
　most important institutional investor activist in 59
　most popular SWF target 591
　nonprofits 612, 616
　non-executive director representation 332
　non-hostile acquisitions 333
　ownership issues 51, 368, 369
　popular movements against finance capital 640
　populism 80–1
　private equity and its managerial implications 14
　property rights institutions 70
　PTPs 336
　R&D investments 370
　regulation 28–9, 98, 203, 295
　senior executive pay awards 282
　shareholder-based system 114
　shareholder voting reform efforts 72
　significant increases in stock prices 547
　state role in promoting specific sectors 707
　steel industry 641
　supermarket retail techniques 206
　SWFs 593, 601
　takeovers 335, 336
　venture capital 436, 440, 520, 526, 529
　wages 649
　widespread fraud 303 n.(2)
　see also AFL-CIO; ALI; AIMR; Calpers; Carter; Chrysler; Clayton Act; Clinton; Delaware; Dodd-Frank; Enron; FDIC; Federal Reserve; GM; Glass-Steagall; IRS; ISS; Jackson (A.); Lehman; New York; Nixon; NYSE; PCAOB; OSHA; Reagan; Roosevelt; Sarbanes-Oxley; SEC; Second Bank; Senior Supervisors Group; WorldCom; also under entries prefixed American; US
university endowment funds 254
University of Uppsala 455
unlisted firms:
　family effects on performance of 399
　family ownership estimates for 390
Unruh, Jesse 53
Urban Institute (National Survey of Nonprofit Governance) 618–19
US-American Center for Audit Quality 310, 312
US Bankruptcy Code 493
　Chapter 11 filings 8, 9, 113, 490, 492–6, 498, 499–505, 507, 508 n.(7), 571, 572, 573, 574, 575, 687–8
　(Section 363) 491, 503, 505–6, 507
US Bankruptcy Court 572
US Department of Labor 53
US Government Accountability Office 235
US House of Representatives 180
　Staff Report to Antitrust Committee 200
US Supreme Court 51, 86–7, 200, 290, 507
Useem, M. 52, 54
utility maximization 541

Vahlne, J. 454, 455
Valentinov, V. 613
valuation 321, 398, 665
　differences 329, 339

lower 376, 692
market capital 431
non-founder 429
value creation 103, 279, 372, 373, 379, 380, 381
  hedge fund activism and 570, 575, 578
  opportunity for 548
  PE firms 548, 550
  upside 543
value-enhancing effects 371, 428, 435, 436
value maximization 239, 337, 496, 497, 518, 530, 541, 542, 659
  growth strategies not consistent with 546
  long-term 582
  pure 582
value protection 366, 379
Van de Ven, A. H. 684
Van den Berghe, L. A. 402
Van den Heuvel, J. 402
Van Ees, H. 169
Vanneste, B. S. 408
Vanstraelen, A. 311
variable costs 276
varieties of capitalism 76, 84, 87, 638, 639, 646
  differences within 640
Veasey, E. Norman 51
Venezuela 601
Venkatachalam, M. 237
venture capital 7, 9, 10, 254–5, 294, 296, 302, 356, 359, 437, 373–4, 376, 440, 515–38, 569, 571, 578, 678
  benefits for involvement 352
  certification hypothesis and 434–6
  characteristics 567
  firms come together to take an equity stake 437
  immediate backers 353
  impact on choice of share options 433
  innovation and 352, 371
  lead firms 438
  roles of 301, 422, 423, 434
  syndication strategy commonly used by 579
  see also private equity
venue and chapter choice 503–5
Verbruggen, S. 612
Verhoeven, P. 142
Vernon, R. 454–5

Verrecchia, R. E. 292, 300
vertical linkages 467, 479
veto rights 523, 526, 530, 533
Vetsuypens, M. 494, 497
Viacom 681
Vijh, A. M. 230
Villalonga, B. 246, 337, 390, 397, 430
Viscusi, W. 473
Vishny, R. W. 56, 99, 97, 97–8, 113, 114, 123, 298, 329, 366, 370, 390, 466, 468, 474, 506, 592, 635, 649, 659–60, 719, 723
Vitt, J. 379
Volpin, P. 34, 35, 84, 92 n.(16)
voluntary disclosure 6, 290–1, 292, 293, 298, 303, 399
  board independence and 299
  difficcult to quantify empirically 303 n.(1)
  extent relatively low 299
  impacts on 302
  increased 298
  positive effects of 300
  public availability of 297
  questions about perceived credibility of 294
volunteerism 609, 616, 619, 621, 624
Voordeckers, W. 402
Vora, D. 451, 452
voting caps 108, 110, 111, 119
voting rights 522, 523, 529
  differential 293
  dominant owner controls 466
  low divergence from cash-flow rights 677
  one share-one vote principle 31
  reciprocity of 470, 479
  separating from economic ownership of shares 564
  unequal 34–5

Waddock, S. A. 735
Wade, J. B. 207, 223, 230
wage-fixing 651
Wagenhofer, A. 294
wages:
  deterioration in 712
  lower 693
  white-collar 649

Wahal, S. 436
Waldfogel, J. 548, 549
Walker, G. 34
Walker Guidelines (UK 2007) 14
Walker Review (UK 2009) 1, 139, 150
Wall Street Journal 564, 602 n.(3)
Wallenberg group 471
Walls, J. L. 726, 731, 735
Walsh, J. 1
Walz, U. 528, 529
Wan, D. 169
Wang, J. 730
Warburton, A. J. 507
Ward, K. 351
Warfield, T. D. 239
Warner, J. B. 55
Wartick, S. L. 55
Washington 85–7
Wasserman, N. 232, 375, 430
watchdogs:
  independent 621
  third-party 617
Waters, J. 429
Watson, R. 5, 185, 186, 187, 235, 272, 280, 282, 285, 286 n.(7), 287 n.(15), 334
weak capital 87–8
wealth:
  accumulation of 712
  aggregate effects 360
  business groups aim to maximize 474
  CEO, related to power of ownership incentives 236
  creditor 497
  disparities of income and 78
  distribution of 77
  facilitating a shift from labor to capital 647
  gains that offset loss from underpricing 433
  individual 679, 686
  managerial gains 360
  negative outcomes 285 n.(5)
  potential 687
  redistribution of 99, 100
  shareholder 667
  socio-emotional 253
  spread across society 710
  substantial growth in 137
  transfers to corporations 284
  unilateral transfer 474
wealth-maximization 593, 595
  see also SWFs
Weick, K. E. 135, 141, 143, 151
Weinberger, Caspar 48
Weingast, B. 74
Weir, C. 6, 334, 335, 336, 338, 359, 360, 544, 548
Weiss, E. J. 50
Weiss, K. 435
Weiss, L. A. 492
Welbourne, T. M. 252
Welch, I. 422
Wells, H. 46
Wells, L. T. 450
Werder, A. V. 142
Werner, S. 247
West, R. R. 51
Western Europe 66, 69, 72, 82, 84, 87, 88, 90
  SWFs 601
  see also under individual country names
Westinghouse 53
Weston, J. Fred 329
Weston family 261
Westphal, J. D. 136, 139, 167, 168, 170, 171, 178, 188, 189, 191, 205, 208, 223–4, 246, 260, 262, 280, 372, 373, 428, 429, 696
Whetten, D. A. 398, 736
whistle-blower protections 725
White, L. J. 208
White, M. J. 491
White, R. E. 12, 697
white knights 262, 263, 341
Whitford, W. C. 689, 694
Whittington, R. 39
widely-held business groups 8, 466, 475, 477–8, 479–80
Wilcox, J. C. 52, 53, 54
Wilding, K. 619
Willekens, M. 311
Williams, C. 37, 704
Williams, H. 50
Williams, K. 706, 715
Williams, R. J. 730
Williamson, O. E. 55, 92 n.(12), 298
Willman, P. 643
Wilson, N. 554, 555

Winter, R. A. 534 n.(3)
Wiseman, R. 432
Woidtke, T. 583
Wójcik, D. 616
Wolfenzon, D. 468, 476
Wolfson, N. 51
Wong, E. M. 730
Wong, K. S. 398
Wong, P. 333, 334, 341
Wong, T. J. 311
Woo, S. P. 501, 506
Wood, G. 12, 550, 551, 709–10
work organization:
    showing how governance can affect 11
    skill development and 650–1
works councils 638, 639, 643, 649
    board representation requires the support of 642
    statutory 637
World Investment Report (UNCTAD 2009) 449
WorldCom 59, 137, 281, 308, 315
Wright, A. 316
Wright, E. O. 712
Wright, M. 6, 8, 9–10, 12, 335, 340, 350, 351, 359, 360, 374–5, 376, 377, 381, 389, 390, 393, 396, 437, 438, 439, 440, 451, 458, 516, 523, 539, 540, 541, 542, 543, 544, 545, 547, 548, 549, 550, 551, 552, 553, 554, 555, 567, 648
Wright, P. 231, 232, 374–5, 376
Wright Patman, J. W. 81
write-offs 530
Wruck, K. H. 492
Wu, Nai H. 8
Wu, S. 550
Wulf, J. 374
Wyatt, Chelsea 12
Wysocki, P. 294, 297

Xerox 202
Xu Yuehua 8
Xuan Yuhai 215
Xue, Y. 233

Yang, S. S. M. 233
Yermack, D. L. 188, 227, 233, 239–40, 280, 372, 429, 432, 474
Yeung, B. 389, 396, 397, 472, 474, 483
Yin, J. Q. 233
Yip, J. 613
Yiu, Daphne W. 8, 467, 470, 472, 479
Yoshikawa, T. 398
Young, D. 711
Young, D. R. 612, 613
Young, M. N. 663
Yukos 308

Zábojník, J. 229
Zahra, S. A. 165, 167, 168, 349, 349, 350, 352, 356, 359, 376, 391, 429, 608, 668, 675–6, 735
Zajac, E. J. 136, 139, 142, 164, 178, 189, 191, 205, 206, 260, 374, 421, 429, 430, 432, 441
Zalecki, P. H. 54
Zaman, M. 178, 181, 183, 185, 192
Zambelli, S. 550
Zamora, V. 237
Zander, U. 453
Zattoni, A. 169, 171
Zeitlin, J. 705, 706
Zenner, M. 248
Zhang, X. 238
Zhao Yang 3, 4, 202–3, 214, 215, 216
Zheng Xiaochuan 190
Zingales, L. 74, 93 n.(23), 272
Zona, F. 169
Zorn, D. 54
Zur, E. 571, 592